Mastering Java 2

Mastering™ Java™ 2

John Zukowski

SYBEX®

San Francisco • Paris • Düsseldorf • Soest

Associate Publisher: Amy Romanoff
Contracts and Licensing Manager: Kristine Plachy
Acquisitions & Developmental Editor: Maureen Adams
Editors: Lisa Duran, Kim Wimpsett
Technical Editor: Matthew Fiedler
Book Designer: Kris Warrenburg
Graphic Illustrator: Tony Jonick
Electronic Publishing Specialist: Maureen Forys, Happenstance Type-O-Rama
Production Coordinators: Charles Mathews, Susan Berge
Indexer: Ted Laux
Companion CD: Ginger Warner
Cover Designer: Design Site
Cover Illustrator/Photographer: David Gaz

Screen reproductions produced with Collage Complete.

Collage Complete is a trademark of Inner Media Inc.

SYBEX is a registered trademark of SYBEX Inc.

Mastering is a trademark of SYBEX Inc.

TRADEMARKS: SYBEX has attempted throughout this book to distinguish proprietary trademarks from descriptive terms by following the capitalization style used by the manufacturer.

Netscape Communications, the Netscape Communications logo, Netscape, and Netscape Navigator are trademarks of Netscape Communications Corporation.

Netscape Communications Corporation has not authorized, sponsored, endorsed, or approved this publication and is not responsible for its content. Netscape and the Netscape Communications Corporate Logos are trademarks and trade names of Netscape Communications Corporation. All other product names and/or logos are trademarks of their respective owners.

The author and publisher have made their best efforts to prepare this book, and the content is based upon final release software whenever possible. Portions of the manuscript may be based upon pre-release versions supplied by software manufacturer(s). The author and the publisher make no representation or warranties of any kind with regard to the completeness or accuracy of the contents herein and accept no liability of any kind including but not limited to performance, merchantability, fitness for any particular purpose, or any losses or damages of any kind caused or alleged to be caused directly or indirectly from this book.

Photographs and illustrations used in this book have been downloaded from publicly accessible file archives and are used in this book for news reportage purposes only to demonstrate the variety of graphics resources available via electronic access. Text and images available over the Internet may be subject to copyright and other rights owned by third parties. Online availability of text and images does not imply that they may be reused without the permission of rights holders, although the Copyright Act does permit certain unauthorized reuse as fair use under 17 U.S.C. Section 107.

Library of Congress Card Number: 97-80470
ISBN: 0-7821-2180-2

Manufactured in the United States of America

10 9 8 7 6 5 4 3

In memory of Sir Dudley Fuzzybuns McDuff

ACKNOWLEDGMENTS

The development of *Mastering Java 1.2* was a long and arduous process that required support from many to transform these chapters into a cohesive, in-depth exploration of Java technology.

At Sybex, many people processed the less-than-perfect raw manuscript. Foremost were the editors, Maureen Adams, Kim Wimpsett, and Lisa Duran; and the technical editor, Matthew Fiedler. And let's not forget Sybex's Tony Jonick, Patrick Dintino, and Inbar Berman, who transformed Stone Age sketches into the quality illustrations and diagrams you see in the book; Electronic Publishing Specialist Maureen Forys, who meticulously laid out every page of this big book; Production Coordinators Charles Mathews and Susan Berge, who worked to ensure that these pages were error free; and finally the CD-ROM Producers Molly Sharp and Ginger Warner, who created the high-quality CD that accompanies this book.

As always, I am grateful to my wife, Lisa, for her patience during this writing process. A special thanks to our new Old English sheepdog puppy, Jaeger, who has been especially fun trying to train while writing. May he one day like his crate. Also, I would like to thank my parents, who bought me my first computer, a Commodore Vic 20, way back when.

—John Zukowski

CONTENTS AT A GLANCE

TABLE OF CONTENTS

INTRODUCTION

Welcome to *Mastering Java 1.2, First Edition,* the book that provides comprehensive coverage of the latest version of the Java platform. This book takes you through introductory, intermediate, and advanced topics to lead you on your way to becoming a proficient Java programmer.

A Road Map

Is this book for you? Although this book was designed with a logical sequence in mind, most readers will not pick it up and read it from cover to cover. Depending on your particular background, the following should help you figure out how to make this book suit your individual needs.

For Non-C/C++ Programmers

If you are new to Java and the C/C++ style of programming, you will probably need to go through the whole book. Some concepts will be similar to those of other languages, but in order to get a grasp on how Java does things, you should work through each of the examples yourself. You might want to take a break of a few hours or days between sections to make sure you understand the material you have read.

For C/C++ Programmers

Due to the similarities between C/C++ and Java, C/C++ programmers can probably breeze through several chapters of this book. C programmers can skim through most of Chapters 4 and 6; C++ programmers can additionally skim Chapter 3, the sections in Chapter 5 on classes, and Chapter 7 if you have dealt with exception handling. While these chapters are worth reviewing, they do not demand the attention that the completely new material in the remainder of the book requires.

For Java Programmers

If you have played with Java on your own and decided it was time to get a book to help you out, most of Part I will probably be review. Skim through it to see if there is anything you might have missed in your prior travels, paying special attention to Chapters 7 and 8, which cover exception handling and multithreading, respectively. If Java 1.1 is new to you, be sure to look through the description of inner classes in Chapter 5. If Java 1.2 is new to you, be sure to examine the thread local variable section in Chapter 8.

For Everyone

Once you have your bearings, use the table of contents to find the areas that interest you most. Chapters 10 and 11 together describe animation and graphics programming within Java. Chapters 12, 13, 14, and 15 go together; they deal with building and using Java forms. (Some people might find reading Chapter 13 before reading Chapter 12 more helpful.) If you are particularly interested in network programming (the subject of Chapter 20), you need to have a grasp of I/O first (covered in Chapter 19), since networking builds upon input and output streams. It helps if you know about networking for the servlet chapter (Chapter 23) and if you know about serialization (from Chapter 19) for the RMI chapter (Chapter 25). You can read the other chapters in almost any order.

The examples given in each chapter clarify the concepts explained, and reviewing the code provides a better understanding of the topic. All the source code is on the enclosed CD, so you do not need to type in the examples yourself.

Features and Structure of This Book

The goal of this book is simple: to make you productive with Java as quickly as possible. This book contains a great deal of information; use the table of contents in the front and/or the extensive index in the back to locate the information you need. Here are brief descriptions of what is in the book and where you can find it.

Part I: Foundations of Java

The first part of the book introduces you to Java—the history, the language, and the programming concepts. Chapter 1 starts off with a lesson on what Java is and where Java came from. Chapter 2 gets you started using the Java development environment. In Chapter 3, you learn about object-oriented programming basics. Chapter 4 describes the Java language grammar. In Chapter 5, you start to build up your understanding of Java by learning about classes, interfaces, and packages. Chapter 6 explains how Java deals with arrays and flow control. In Chapter 7, you learn about Java's exception-handling mechanisms. Finally, in Chapter 8, you learn how to create multithreaded programs in Java.

Part II: Applying Standard Java Classes

The next part of the book examines the Java libraries (or *packages* in Java-speak). Chapter 9 provides a brief overview of the different Java packages and their parts. Chapter 10 describes the basic animation capabilities of Java, while Chapter 11 describes the more advanced 2D capabilities. Chapter 12 describes the windowing package and how you can position objects on the screen. In Chapter 13, you learn about some of the different objects a user interacts with. Chapter 14 explains how to deal with those interactions through events. In Chapter 15, you discover some of the more advanced objects users can interact with. Chapter 16 explores the mechanisms available to transfer information between applications. Chapter 17 describes the data structure support classes within Java for dealing with collections. In Chapter 18, techniques from the previous several chapters are put together for more advanced programming. Chapter 19 introduces you to I/O programming through Java streams. Finally, Chapter 20 teaches you how to make your programs Internet savvy.

Part III: Advanced Topics

The third part of the book is designed for those who want to learn more about Java. Read these chapters if you are interested in taking your Java programs to the next level.

Chapter 21 introduces Java Database Connectivity (JDBC) for access to SQL databases. Chapter 22 discusses the JavaBeans API and how it stretches your software development budget. In Chapter 23, you learn about the Java Web Server and extending your Web server through servlets. Chapter 24 describes how Java's security mechanisms can protect sensitive operations. In Chapter 25, Remote Method Invocation (RMI) for distributed computing within a homogeneous Java environment is explained. Finally, Chapter 26 takes a look at Java and CORBA for distributed computing within a heterogeneous computing environment.

Online

At the book's Web site `http://www.sybex.com/cgi-bin/rd_bookpg.pl?2180back.html`, you will find bonus material. This site provides links to other Web sites where you can download demo copies of third-party tools. In addition, the glossary provides you with definitions of terms related to Java programming. Sun also provides a Deprecated API list at `http://java.sun.com/products/jdk/1.2/docs/api/deprecated-list.html`, which contains a list of classes and methods deprecated in the Java 1.2 libraries. When Java 1.1 was released, Sun decided that old method names were not good enough. Numerous methods were renamed, mostly to follow various design patterns. With Java 1.2, even more became deprecated. The Deprecated API list provides a mapping of old names to new. Although you can continue to use the old names for now, the compiler generates a warning if you do.

What Is on the CD?

The CD contains all the source code from the examples in the book, along with the appropriate HTML applet loaders. See the readme file on the CD for details.

Conventions

This book uses various conventions to help you find the information you need quickly. Tips, Notes, and Warnings, shown here, are placed throughout the book to help you locate important highlights quickly.

TIP This is a tip. Tips contain helpful hints and information to make you more productive with Java faster.

NOTE

This is a note. Notes contain extra information related to the discussion at hand.

WARNING

This is a warning. Warnings contain information that flags potential trouble spots.

In addition, the book takes advantage of various font styles. **Bold** font in text indicates something that the user types (in a text field, for instance). A `monospaced` program font is used for program code.

The program code itself follows the standard conventions for capitalization used by the Java API. For example, in class names, each word is capitalized, and in function names, each word but the first one is capitalized. The code formatting follows standard programming conventions: a left brace is placed at the end of a line (or the start of the next line), the right brace is on its own line, and indentation is used to highlight the grouping of code.

Technical Support

When you need help, there are several sources available for technical support. Some of your options are described here.

FAQs

There is a plethora of Java-related Frequently Asked Question lists (FAQs) available online. The following are some FAQ sites:

URL	Description
`http://java.sun.com/sfaq/`	Maintained by Sun. It answers numerous security-related Java questions.
`http://sunsite.unc.edu/javafaq/javafaq.html`	This answers questions for people new to Java development.
`http://java.miningco.com/msub3.htm`	An index that lists some other FAQs.
`http://www.best.com/~pvdl/javafaq.html`	Intended for people who already have some programming experience, though maybe not in Java.

Product Support

Depending on the tools you are using, it may be prudent to go through the technical support channels available for a particular product. This could involve toll-free or 1-900 support (live or prerecorded), the World Wide Web, or online newsgroups, among other options.

Check the documentation provided with the tool or Web-based source you are using to see what support is available. If you are using the Java Development Kit (JDK) from Sun, the first place to look is the Bug Parade at the Java Developer Connection (JDC) `http://developer.java.sun.com/developer/bugParade/` to see if the problem you have encountered is a product bug. (If you are not already a member of the JDC, you will be prompted to create a free account, prior to accessing the Bug Parade.) Symantec's Visual Café for Java users should start at `http://cafe.symantec.com`, while JBuilder support is available at `http://www.inprise.com/jbuilder`. Most other products maintain similar sites.

Newsgroups

When the Java hype was just beginning, there were no newsgroups, and Sun was running a handful of mailing lists to keep everyone informed and provide a question-and-answer medium. The Sun mail server quickly got bogged down due to popularity (and cross-mailing list postings), and the newsgroup `comp.lang.java` was born (along with `alt.www.hotjava`). Over time, `comp.lang.java` became so popular (thousands of messages per week) that the signal-to-noise ratio nearly made the group useless. After much debate, the single group split into eight and later reorganized again. The current set of groups under `comp.lang.java.*` is as follows:

```
comp.lang.java.advocacy
comp.lang.java.announce (moderated)
comp.lang.java.beans
comp.lang.java.corba
comp.lang.java.databases
comp.lang.java.gui
comp.lang.java.help
comp.lang.java.machine
```

```
comp.lang.java.programmer
comp.lang.java.security
comp.lang.java.softwaretools
```

Somewhere in one of those groups is either the answer to your question or someone who will read your question and be able to answer it. If the question has already been asked and answered, you can search the archives at DejaNews (a Usenet search utility), `http://www.dejanews.com`. For a list of around 100 Java-related newsgroups, go to `http://java.miningco.com/msub6.htm`. For those who are inclined not to read the news, MageLang maintains a moderated mailing list (`http://www.MageLang.com/mailing_list.html`) that is monitored by some of the members of the early development team.

User Groups

Another good source of information is area user groups. Focus tends to vary widely, but it is a great place to network with other people in the field. And there is usually someone in the group who can answer your question. To find a group in your area, look at Sun's user group list at `http://java.sun.com/aboutJava/jug/usergroups.html` or the Focus on Java list I maintain at `http://java.miningco.com/msubjugs.htm`. Most groups maintain a mailing list of some sort where you can send technical questions.

Books and Periodicals

Sybex offers many books at all levels of expertise. For more advanced questions, the *Java 1.2 Developer's Handbook* (Sybex, 1999) may hold the answers. Or if you encounter a problem that is not Java related, another Sybex offering may provide the solution. For the latest catalog, write to:

Sybex Inc.
1151 Marina Village Parkway
Alameda, CA 94501
Tel: (800) 227-2346
Fax: (510) 523-2373

You can also visit the Sybex Web page at `http://www.sybex.com`, where you will find a searchable catalog and updates to this book.

On the Java side, there are also some magazines you might want to read. *Java-World* is an online publication at `http://www.javaworld.com`. *Java Report* is a print publication with information available from `http://www.javareport.com/`. Also, *Java Pro* is a combined print/online publication at `http://www.java-pro.com/`. There are others, and more are popping up all the time.

Now that you've seen what's in store for you inside *Mastering Java 2*, move onward and enjoy it.

NOTE   Due to a version number upgrade by Sun Microsystems, all references to Java 1.2 should be Java 2.

PART 1

Foundations of Java

CHAPTER
ONE

Introducing Java

- Java and its history

- Java and the World Wide Web

- The Java architecture

Java is a technology that makes it easy to build *distributed applications*, which are programs executed by multiple computers across a network. The state of the art in network programming, Java has expanded the Internet's role from an arena for communications to a network on which full-fledged applications run. Its breakthrough technology allows businesses to deploy full-scale transaction services that deliver real-time, interactive information over the Internet.

Java also simplifies the construction of *software agents*, which are programs that move across a network and perform functions on remote computers on the user's behalf. With and without the help of Java, users may send software agents from their PCs out onto the Internet to locate specific information or make time-critical transactions anywhere in the world.

Before Java, the Internet was used primarily for sharing information. Though the Internet was created in the 1960s, it only started to realize its business potential in the 1990s, thanks to the World Wide Web. The Web is a technology that treats Internet resources as linked documents, and it has revolutionized the way people access information. The Web has enabled Internet users to access Internet services without learning cryptic commands. Through the Web, businesses easily create online corporate images, provide product information, and even sell merchandise directly through PCs. Java technology takes this a step further by making it possible to serve fully interactive applications via the Web. The reasons so much attention has been paid to Java are summarized in the following list of what Java allows developers to do:

- Write robust and reliable programs

- Build applications on almost any platform and run those applications on any other supported platforms without recompiling the code

- Distribute applications over an untrusted network in a trusted fashion

In particular, Java programs can be embedded into Web documents, turning static pages into applications that run on the user's computer. No longer is online documentation limited to articles, like a printed book. With Java, the documentation can include simulations, working models, and even specialized tools. This means Java has the potential to change the function of the Internet, much as the Web has changed the way people access the Internet. In other words, not only will the network provide information, it will also serve as an operating system.

In this chapter, you will learn about the history and evolution of Java, see how Java is enhancing the Web, and begin to understand how the Java programming language enables developers to build robust Internet applications.

A Brief History of Java

In 1990, Sun Microsystems began a project called *Green* to develop software for consumer electronics. Sun is best known for its popular Unix workstations but has also engineered several popular software packages, including the Solaris operating system and the Network File System (NFS). James Gosling, a veteran of classic network software design, was assigned to the new Green project.

Gosling began writing software in C++ for embedding into such items as toasters, VCRs, and Personal Digital Assistants (PDAs). The embedded software makes appliances more intelligent, typically by adding digital displays or by using artificial intelligence to better control the mechanisms. However, it soon became apparent to Gosling that C++ was the wrong tool for the job. C++ is flexible enough to control embedded systems, but it is susceptible to bugs that can crash the system. In particular, C++ uses direct references to system resources and requires the programmer to keep track of how these resources are managed, which is a significant burden on programmers. This burden of resource management is a barrier to writing reliable, portable software, and it is a serious problem for consumer electronics. After all, computer users have come to expect their software to have some bugs, but few expect their toasters to crash.

Java's Predecessor: Oak

Gosling's solution to the problems of C++ was a new language called *Oak*. Oak preserved the familiar syntax of C++ but omitted the potentially dangerous features like explicit resource references, pointer arithmetic, and operator overloading. Oak incorporated memory management directly into the language, freeing the programmer to concentrate on the tasks to be performed by the program. To be successful as an embedded systems programming language, Oak needed to be able to respond to real-world events within microseconds. It also needed to be portable; that is, it had to be able to run on a number of different microprocessor chips and environments. This hardware independence would allow a toaster manufacturer to change the chip used to run the toaster without changing the software. The manufacturer could also use some of the same code that ran the toaster to run a similar appliance, such as a toaster oven. This would cut down on development and hardware costs, as well as increase reliability.

As Oak matured, the World Wide Web was growing dramatically, and the development team at Sun realized Oak was perfectly suited to Internet programming. Thus, in 1994, they completed work on a product known as *WebRunner*, an early Web browser written in Oak. WebRunner was later renamed *HotJava*, and it demonstrated the power of Oak as an Internet development tool. HotJava is well known in the industry, and the HotJava project is still active, with new versions under development.

Finally, in 1995, Oak was renamed *Java* (for marketing and legal reasons) and introduced at SunWorld '95. Since then, Java's rise in popularity has been meteoric. Even before the first release of the Java compiler in January 1996, the development community considered Java a standard for Internet development.

NOTE   Perhaps the most common question about Java's history is about the origin of the name. The answer is that the name *Java* survived the trademark search.

Java's Arrival on the Market

In the first six months of 1996, a number of leading software and hardware companies licensed the Java technology from Sun, including Adobe, Asymetrix, Borland, IBM, Macromedia, Metrowerks, Microsoft, Novell, Oracle, Spyglass, and Symantec. These companies, and other Java licensees, have been incorporating Java into their desktop products, operating systems, and development tools ever since.

Also in 1996, substantial new additions to the Java language were introduced. Sponsored by many of the aforementioned companies, new Application Program Interfaces (APIs)—libraries of functions that application developers can use to construct software—now provide advanced graphics, multimedia, networking, and security enhancements to the Java environment. The new JavaOS will bring Java to special low-end markets such as PDAs and special network computers. Also, the advent of Java 1.2, released at the end of the summer of 1998, has significantly improved Java's portability, security, and functionality. And more improvements are on the horizon, with new companies signing on every day.

Several integrated development environments are also now available for Java developers from Sun, Symantec, Metrowerks, Borland, and IBM. Many major companies, like Lotus, are creating desktop application suites in Java, allowing them functionality across the Internet. Even the giant Microsoft is making its applications Internet-aware and Java-compatible. (Of course, companies like Microsoft have their own agendas and are trying to lock Java into their proprietary operating systems and application architectures. This has caused a whole slew of lawsuits between Sun and Microsoft, which could take years to iron out.) It is clear the momentum of this technology is so great that few doubt Java's ability to transform the computer industry as we know it.

Java and the Web

Today, the most likely place you'll find Java is on the World Wide Web. The Web acts as a convenient transport mechanism for Java programs, and the Web's ubiquity has popularized Java as an Internet development tool.

An Introduction to the Web

This section is a brief introduction to the World Wide Web. If you are already familiar with the Web, you may want to skip this introduction and go on to the next section.

The World Wide Web is a huge collection of interconnected hypertext documents on the Internet. A *hypertext* document is a document that contains *hot links* (or *links*) to other documents. Hypertext links are usually visible as highlighted words in the text, but they can also be graphics. Clicking on links with a mouse activates them.

The Internet has many thousands of hypertext authors, each of them free to connect their documents to anyone else's. It follows then that the Web has no beginning and no end, although groups of associated pages are usually structured hierarchically. Since organization of the Web is not enforced, finding your way around can be difficult. Fortunately, Web directories and search engines, such as Yahoo!, Excite, and Infoseek, have alleviated much of the navigation problem by allowing users to search by keyword, name, or subject. The lack of regulation has gone a long way toward broadening the user base and enriching the content. As things stand, anyone who learns to write hypertext documents can make information available over the Internet.

The Web is based on two standards: the Hypertext Transfer Protocol (HTTP) and the Hypertext Markup Language (HTML). HTTP describes the way hypertext documents are fetched over the Internet, and HTML specifies the layout and linking commands present in the hypertext documents.

NOTE   For the purposes of this book, a *protocol* is a set of rules that are followed by computers. By following these rules, the computers provide a specific communication service to each other as part of an Internet conversation. The most popular application protocols on the Internet are HTTP, File Transfer Protocol (FTP), and Simple Mail Transfer Protocol (SMTP). Each protocol defines commands sent to a server from a program requesting services and defines the way the server may respond.

Resources on the Web are specified with a Uniform Resource Locator (URL). A URL specifies the protocol used to fetch a document as well as its location. For example, the URL for a page about the history of Sybex publishing is `http://www.sybex.com:80/about/history.html`. The URL can be divided into five pieces:

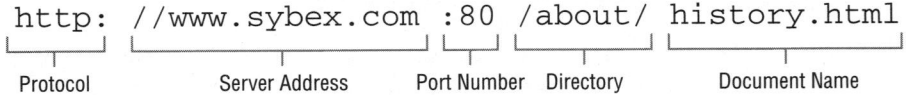

http:	//www.sybex.com	:80	/about/	history.html
Protocol	Server Address	Port Number	Directory	Document Name

The `http:` prefix indicates the document should be fetched via HTTP. The `//www.sybex.com` specifies the machine running the Web server. The `:80` refers to the port number; each protocol server on a machine is typically assigned its own port number.

NOTE   The default port number for HTTP is 80, and Web server administrators rarely change it. For this reason, the port number is rarely specified in HTTP URLs.

The file itself is `history.html`, and it is located in the directory `/about`.

The HTTP protocol is implemented in software on the server and on the user's machine (also known as the *client machine* or simply the *client*). The server software is called a *Web server* or *HTTP server*, and the client software is called a *Web browser*.

To open an HTML document, the Web browser sends an HTTP command to the server requesting the document by its URL. The Web server responds by sending the HTML document to the client. The client then displays the document on the user's screen. If the HTML document contains graphics, the Web browser makes additional requests for the graphics files to be sent and then displays the graphics with the text. Figure 1.1 illustrates this process.

FIGURE 1.1:

How Web documents are fetched with HTTP

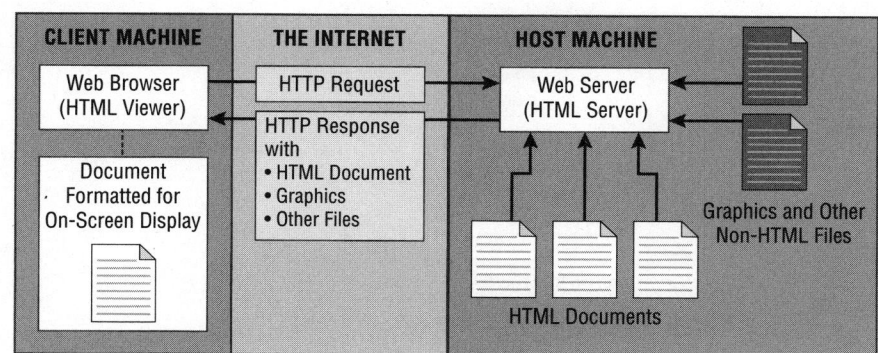

Thus, Web documents are essentially static objects. When the HTML document reaches the browser, it is in its final form.

NOTE   The latest protocol versions permit an HTML document to be refreshed after reaching the client. These extensions are called *server-push*, *client-pull*, and *dynamic HTML*, and they are written into documents or scripts on the server. These enhancements force the HTML document downloaded from the server to be refreshed dynamically.

Some servers generate HTML upon request using Common Gateway Interface (CGI) programs. With the ability of CGI and HTML to create fill-in-the-blank forms, you can create form-based applications on the Web. One notable application like this was created by Federal Express for package tracking. Figure 1.2 shows an example of this application. Users can track their FedEx packages over the Internet at `http://www.fedex.com/us/tracking/`.

Note that CGI is not suited for real-time display of information. Although CGI programs generate HTML upon request, the document returned to the browser is still a static document.

FIGURE 1.2:

The FedEx tracking form. The user selects a destination, fills in a tracking number and ship date, and then clicks a button to send the data to the server. This type of form is usually handled by CGI scripts on the server.

©1995-1998 Federal Express Corporation. All Rights Reserved.

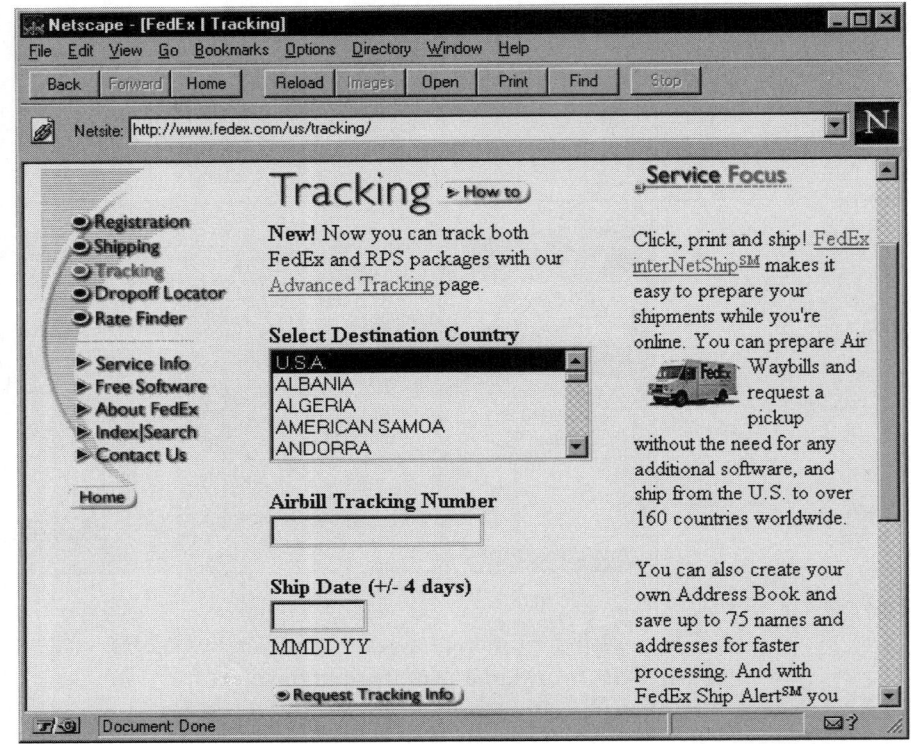

CGI programs are widespread and have generally been successful, but they are prone to performance problems. When the Web server runs a CGI program to create an HTML document on the fly, it usually creates a new operating system process for that program on the Web server machine. Creating new processes is time-consuming and inefficient. Nonetheless, CGI is used on the Internet simply because it is compatible with almost every Web browser.

Another option for doing even more dynamic serving is Sun's Servlet API. This API allows client-side programs, similar to Web-based applets, to provide dynamic content or to interface with applets on the client. For more information on servlets, see Chapter 23.

Extending Web Browser Capability

Much of the power of the World Wide Web stems from its platform independence; that is, it presents information in a way that can be viewed on almost every type of machine and operating system. It doesn't matter whether you use a PC, Macintosh, or Unix workstation—the Web is architecture-neutral, which is why so many people have access to it.

Unfortunately, being so widely accepted also has its drawbacks. It is difficult to extend the Web protocols without leaving many Web users behind. For instance, Web content developers are constantly trying to extend the capability of the Web by integrating new types of media, like 3-D worlds and animation, but these developers then face the prospect of excluding people without those viewing capabilities, which limits their audience.

The existing Web standards permit seamless integration of graphics with text. Other forms of media, such as sound, video, and animation, are accessible via the Web, but they are not smoothly connected with normal Web content. For example, it is easy to create a link to a sound file in an HTML document; the Web browser will either play the sound or download it to a file when the user clicks on the link. However, there is no browser-independent way to create background music for a document or give audio feedback when a button is pressed. This is just one of the many creative limitations that have frustrated Web developers over the past few years.

Until now, the solution to this extensibility problem has been to create a proprietary protocol, and then try to sell the solution to as many users on as many platforms as possible. This is a hard sell and has had limited success. As a result, Web pages tend to cater to the lowest common denominator; therefore, the content has not reached its full potential in many instances.

A good example of this is Adobe's Portable Document Format (PDF). This is a cross-platform solution for creating robust documents and distributing them on the Internet. PDF provides support for documents far richer than simple HTML, allowing groups like the Internal Revenue Service to ship tax forms across the Web. Adobe provides the viewer for free but tries to make money on the tools that create PDF documents. PDF's main limitation is that you need to download a special program from Adobe to view the files.

Java as a Universal Protocol

Java has begun to address the protocol problem by using Java applets. An *applet* is a Java program that appears embedded in a Web document, just as graphics are. The Java applet runs when a Java-enabled Web browser, such as Netscape

Navigator, loads it. The running applet then draws itself in the user's browser window according to the programmer's instructions.

Let's say you want to create a stock market ticker applet for a Web page (a stock market ticker is a horizontally scrolling summary of stock prices and stock price changes). The stock quotes must be sent to the user's Web browser in real time so users can get up-to-the-minute information. Since a continuous stream of stock quotes is needed, HTTP is not a good protocol for this application (HTTP is really a kind of file transfer protocol, not a continuous data stream protocol). Therefore, you need to design a new protocol, say the Simple Stock Quote Protocol (SSQP).

Imagine a conversation between the client and the server:

Client:	GET NASDAQ
Server:	OK
Server:	AAA 104 3/8 – 1 1/2 ICP 80 1/4 + 1/4 …

(Client displays data continuously as long as user requires.)

Client:	STOP

This conversation is the blueprint for the SSQP. The server responds to the GET commands by acknowledging the request and then sending back a continuous stream of data. The STOP command terminates the conversation.

You can implement the SSQP server in whichever language is best for the job. This could be C, Java, or a nonportable language because you know it will run on your server machine. In Java, you can easily write a stock ticker applet that implements the client side of the conversation and displays the returned data. When executed by the browser, the applet connects to the server using the SSQP and displays a stock ticker with live data. Thus, without any manual intervention from the user, a stock ticker appears in the browser window.

Figure 1.3 shows a Web page using a Java applet to display the latest sports scores. You'll notice the applet integrates seamlessly with the rest of the page. The browser's functionality has been extended automatically and transparently. In this way, Java acts like a protocol for adding new protocols. It would be impractical for Web browser manufacturers to build in every new protocol that comes along. Instead, browsers can be equipped with Java and learn new protocols on demand.

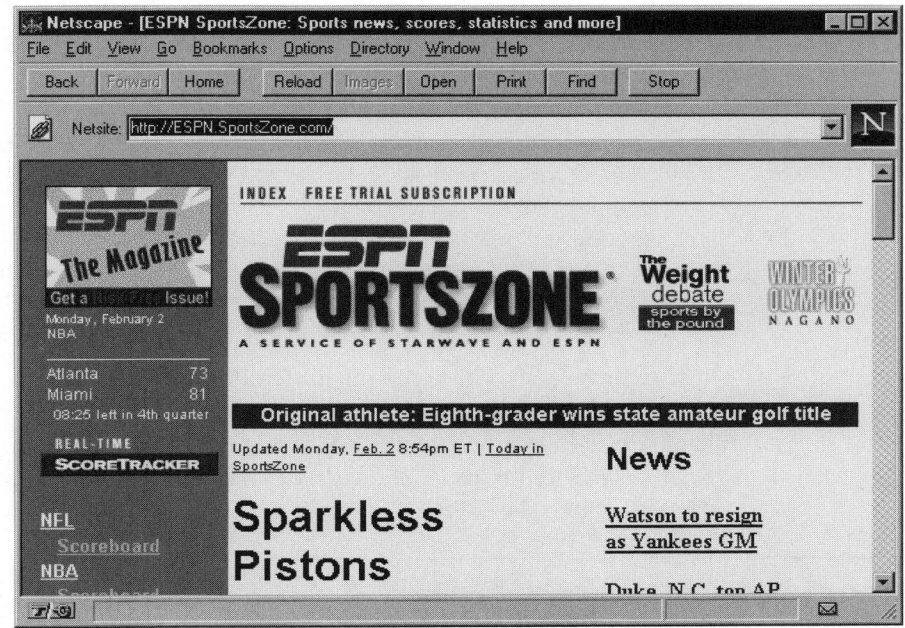

The image in the top left is a Java applet that displays up-to-the-minute sports scores. The underlined text are hypertext links.

The Java Architecture

Java's strength comes from its unique architecture. The designers of Java needed a language that was, above all, simple for the programmer to use. Yet in order to create reliable network applications, Java needed to be able to run securely over a network and, at the same time, work on a wide range of platforms. Java fulfills all of these goals and more. The next few sections describe how Java works and what the features are that make Java a powerful network application development tool.

How Java Works

As with many other programming languages, Java uses a compiler to convert human-readable source code into executable programs. Traditional compilers produce code that can be executed by specific hardware; for example, a Windows 95 C++ compiler creates executable programs that work with Intel *x*86–compatible processors. In contrast, the Java compiler generates architecture-independent *bytecodes*. The bytecodes can be executed by only a Java Virtual Machine (VM), which is an idealized Java architecture, usually implemented in software rather than hardware.

NOTE   The VM has also been implemented as a hardware chip by Sun Microsystems, and several other electronics companies have announced plans to manufacture Java processors. These processors are expected to have significant performance advantages over VMs written in software. They will also make it easier for Java to be embedded into consumer electronics products such as toasters and TV sets.

The compilation process is illustrated in Figure 1.4. Java bytecode files are called *class files* because they contain a single Java class. Classes will be described in detail in Chapter 3. For now, just think of a class as representing a group of related routines or an extended datatype. The vast majority of Java programs will be composed of more than one class file.

FIGURE 1.4:

Java compilers produce Java bytecodes, not traditional executable files.

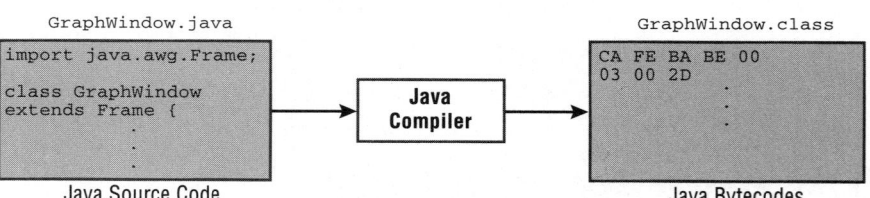

To execute Java bytecodes, the VM uses a *class loader* to fetch the bytecodes from a disk or a network. Each class file is fed to a *bytecode verifier* that ensures the class is formatted correctly and will not corrupt memory when it is executed. The bytecode verification phase adds to the time it takes to load a class, but it actually allows the program to run faster because the class verification is performed only once, not continuously as the program runs.

The execution unit of the VM carries out the instructions specified in the bytecodes. The simplest execution unit is an *interpreter*, which is a program that reads the bytecodes, interprets their meaning, and then performs the associated function. Interpreters are generally much slower than native code compilers because they continuously need to look up the meaning of each bytecode during execution.

Fortunately, there is an elegant alternative to interpreting code, called *Just-in-Time* (JIT) compilation.

The JIT compiler converts the bytecodes to native code instructions on the user's machine immediately before execution. Traditional native code compilers run on the developer's machine, are used by programmers, and produce nonportable executables. JIT compilers run on the user's machine and are transparent to the user; the resulting native code instructions do not need to be ported because they are already at their destination. Figure 1.5 illustrates how JIT compilers work. In the example, both a Macintosh and a Windows PC receive identical bytecodes, and each client performs a local JIT compilation.

FIGURE 1.5:

The JIT compiler in the client system improves performance by compiling bytecodes to platform-specific instructions just before execution. The resulting machine-level instructions are executed directly.

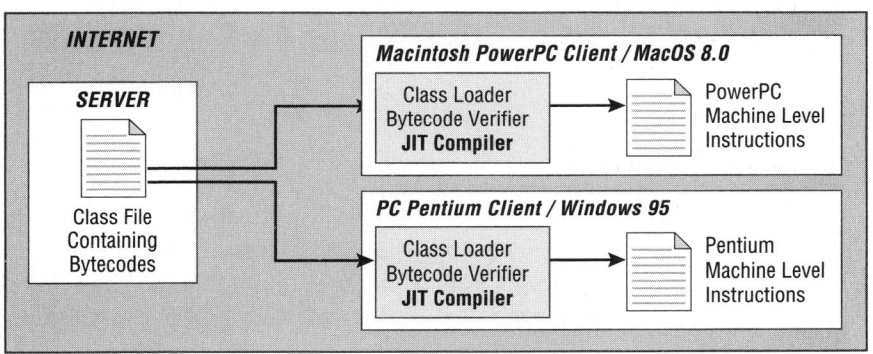

Java-Enabled Browsers

A Java-enabled Web browser contains its own VM. Web documents with embedded Java applets must specify the location of the main applet class file. The Web browser then starts up the VM and passes the location of the applet class file to the class loader. Each class file knows the names of any additional class files that it requires. These additional class files may come from the network or from the client machine. This may require the class loader to make a number of additional class-loading operations before the applet starts. Note that supplemental classes are fetched only if they are actually going to be used or if they are necessary for the verification process of the applet.

After loading the class file, execution begins, and the applet is asked to draw itself in the browser window. Figure 1.6 shows the Java VM fetching classes.

FIGURE 1.6:

The Java Virtual Machine fetches classes from a disk or from the network and then verifies that the bytecodes are safe to be executed.

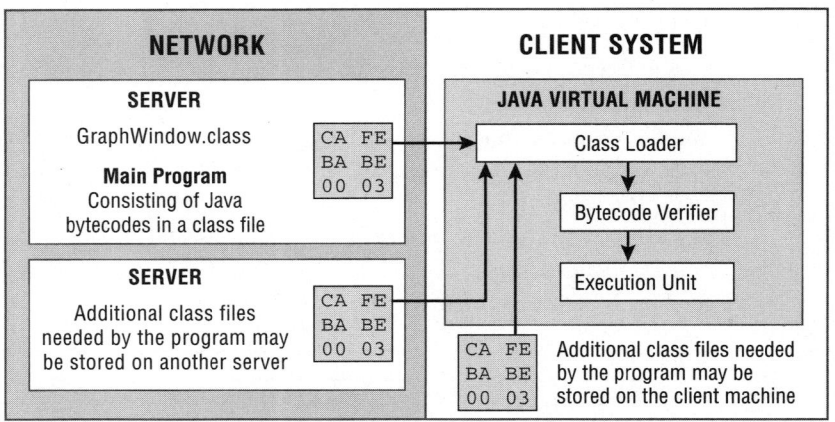

Java Features

In this section, we will look briefly at the major characteristics that make Java such a powerful development tool. These include its security features, the Core API, open standards, and memory management. Also covered are Java's distributed and dynamic, object-oriented, and multithreaded characteristics.

Security Features

Security is probably the main problem facing Internet developers. Users are typically afraid of two things: confidential information being compromised and their computer systems being corrupted or destroyed by hackers. Java's built-in security addresses both of these concerns.

Java's security model has three primary components: the class loader, bytecode verifier, and SecurityManager. You have already learned the bytecode verifier ensures that the Java programs have been compiled correctly, that they will obey the VM's access restrictions, and that the bytecodes will not access "private" data when they shouldn't. Without these defenses, the other security constraints within the VM could be bypassed, and there would be no limit to what the applet could do to the system.

The class loader provides the next layer of security. When the class loader retrieves classes from the network, it keeps classes from different Web spaces separate from each other and from local classes. Through this separation, the class loader prevents a class loaded off the network from pretending to be one of the standard built-in classes or from interfering with the operation of classes loaded from other servers.

The SecurityManager implements a security policy for the VM. The security policy determines which activities the VM is allowed to perform and under what circumstances. A key example is file input/output (I/O); for example, saving or loading documents in disk files. Java has the capability to read and write files, but requests to perform such an I/O pass through the SecurityManager first. This allows the SecurityManager to determine if the Java program is trusted to access the disk files without doing malicious damage to the file system.

The SecurityManager is generally written to err on the side of caution. In the most popular Java-enabled browser, Netscape Navigator, the security policy does not even permit file access from untrusted applets. However, the SecurityManager is itself written in Java (it is a Java class file) so that it can be overridden if required. Of course, safeguards prevent hostile Java programs from writing their own security policy! These safeguards prevent alternate SecurityManagers from being added to the system while the Web browser is running.

On a private network, file access or arbitrary network access may be necessary to address business requirements. For example, when implementing a client/server database application on a private network, it may be necessary for a Java applet to establish connections with multiple servers. The standard SecurityManager prohibits this because it is a security risk on a public network. The application developers may therefore change the SecurityManager source code and recompile it into the Web browser for each PC on the network. This customizes the security policy for the private network. Custom SecurityManagers are more difficult to write if the private network has any gateways to public networks such as the Internet. Great care must be taken when overriding the SecurityManager, or hostile applets from the public network may take advantage of the relaxed internal security policy. Java 1.2 extends the security mechanism with a permission-based security policy. This does away with the need to *extend* a security manager simplifying the process.

With the advent of Java 1.1, developers have been able to add another layer of security to their applets. An addition to the Core API is an extensive Security API that allows Java classes to be *signed*. A *digital signature* is used in the same way your normal signature is used every time you write a check—it ensures the check really came from you and not from an impostor. Digital signatures allow developers to sign the code they write, using a nearly unbreakable public-key encryption system. Users can then use this signature to decide if they trust the program being loaded.

The program can be given limited access to local disk, memory, or network resources based on the level of trust. The encryption itself is rather complicated, but the entire process happens transparently to both the user and the developer, making it even easier to deliver secure content over the Web.

To summarize, Java's built-in security measures ensure Java programs will operate within the rules of the VM and prevent untrustworthy programs from accessing system resources that might contain proprietary information or jeopardize the integrity of the client. Java also allows developers or institutions to sign the programs they create, allowing users to grant limited access to "trusted" applets or applications.

The Core API

Java's Core API (formerly known as the JavaApplet API) provides a common set of functions on all certified Java platforms.

The API is divided into *packages*, which are groups of classes that perform related functions. One of these packages includes some core language functionality, such as text handling and error processing; it is almost impossible to write a Java program without using this library. The other packages contain utilities, networking, I/O, graphical user interface tools, and Web browser interaction. Packages that deal with security, database access, reusable software components, collections, drag-and-drop, accessibility, and reference objects are also available, and new ones are in development all the time.

Open Standards

Today, Java VMs are available for more than a dozen different hardware and operating system combinations. The most exciting aspect of Java's cross-platform capability is that Java class files do not need to be compiled for each platform in advance. The same compiled Java program will work on the PC, Macintosh, and every other platform that runs a Java VM. A Java application you write on your system today should run on every supported platform, even those that don't exist yet.

Another key to being a successful cross-platform development tool is having a common core set of functions on every platform. The Core API is the same for all implementations of Java, and it is sophisticated enough that native code does not need to be written for desktop applications.

Of course, the real world is slightly more complicated. Java is a relatively new language, and most implementations of the Java VM and Core API have minor problems conforming to the Java specifications, especially with respect to the user interface. To combat this problem, Sun has an exhaustive test suite that all Java-compatible systems must pass to claim compatibility with the Java APIs. This, along with a porting and tuning center operated with Netscape and IBM, should help eliminate any differences between implementations of the Java VM. In addition to being a de facto standard, Java should now move into the international standards arena because of the approval of Sun as the Publicly Available Specification (PAS) submitter for Java by the members of ISO/IEC JTC-1 (International Organization for Standardization/International Electrotechnical Commission Joint Technical Committee 1).

> **NOTE**
>
> If interested in the standardization process, be sure to read ISO/IEC guidelines at `http://www.iso.ch/dire/jtc1/pas.html` and directives at `http://www.iso.ch/dire/jtc1/suppl.html`. These documents describe the process Sun must follow toward international standardization of Java. For Sun's perspective on the whole effort, read the documents available at `http://java.sun.com/aboutJava/standardization/`.

In addition to common desktop operating systems, you can expect to see Java VMs implemented on-chip for embedded systems and smart cards. Sun has created a CPU chip, picoJava I, that provides direct execution of Java bytecodes on such devices as personal appliances, smart phones, and network computers. Also, Sun has announced plans for two additional Java processors, known as microJava and UltraJava. Working with numerous partners, Java is on its way toward fulfilling the original goals of the Green project and is now showing up in telephones, television set–top boxes, and hand-held devices.

Distributed and Dynamic

In the Windows operating system, parts of programs can be placed into dynamic link libraries (DLLs) so they can be shared and loaded dynamically; that is, when the program is running. The operating system does the final stage of linking at execution time. Using shared DLLs saves memory and improves the modularity of the software. Under Unix, this same type of dynamic linking is accomplished via shared libraries.

Java takes dynamic libraries a step further. The VM class loader fetches class files from the network, as well as from the disk, providing location transparency, making Java applications distributed as well as dynamic. These features allow a

Java-enabled browser to adapt automatically to protocols available at a new Web site.

Java has the potential to change the software distribution model used by the industry. Instead of buying software on disk or CD-ROM, people could "rent" just the pieces (Java classes) of the applications they need directly over the Internet, much like "renting" online time. The software would be the latest version because it came directly from the manufacturer. However, today two major obstacles make this scenario all but impossible:

- The time it takes to download a real-world application is prohibitive for most users. For downloaded software to compete with today's disk-based applications, users will likely need connections that are 100 times faster than today's standard 28.8kbps modems.

- No prevailing standard for making secure software rental payments exists. Without such a standard, it would be as if each software vendor had its own form of currency, requiring you to make a special arrangement with each vendor before renting the software.

There is also a third obstacle worth mentioning, although it has been overcome. Using trusted Java programs, local file access is permitted, allowing one to save work locally. The original Java security model did not permit this capability.

Although these problems are not insurmountable, it will be some time before the network infrastructure can support this kind of distribution model. One positive first step toward this goal is the Java Enterprise APIs, which include support for electronic commerce and added security, as well as support for other industry standards pioneered by Netscape and Visa, among others. Also, with the advent of distribution methods, such as Marimba's Castanet product, you should start to see commercial Java applications delivered over the Internet in the very near future.

Object-Oriented

Object-oriented programming (OOP) is a way to write software that is reusable, extensible, and maintainable. Java is an object-oriented language; that is, it has facilities for OOP incorporated into the language. The Core API is actually a collection of prefabricated OOP components, known to object-oriented programmers as a *class library*. Class libraries give programmers a big head start when it comes to developing new projects. A detailed explanation of object-oriented technology is presented in Chapter 3.

Multithreaded

A single-threaded application has one thread of execution running at all times, and such programs can do only one task at a time. If a single-threaded program needs to perform a task that will take several minutes—for example, downloading—its user interface will usually become unresponsive while the task is in progress.

A multithreaded application can have several threads of execution running independently and simultaneously. These threads may communicate and cooperate and will appear to be a single program to the user. Multithreading is commonly used to perform the following functions:

Maintaining user interface responsiveness   If your application needs to perform a time-consuming task, you can use multiple threads to prevent your user interface from becoming unresponsive while the task is in progress. If your program will be downloading information from the Internet (which is very likely), you can create a separate thread for the download routine. This will keep your user interface running at nearly full speed while the download is in progress.

Waiting for a wake-up call   The best way to have a routine wait for a specified time is to place the routine in a sleeping thread. The alternative—continuously watching the time-of-day clock—is very processor-intensive. For instance, if you wanted an applet to download new data from a server every 60 seconds, you could place the download routine in a thread that sleeps for a minute between transfers.

Simple multitasking   Multithreading allows you to run multiple instances of a process quite easily. The downloading routine just mentioned can be extended so that the program can transfer multiple files simultaneously and still keep the user interface well behaved. All you need to do is create another thread for each file to download.

Building multiuser applications   Multithreading is often used when building server applications. Server applications wait for requests to arrive and then establish conversations with the requester. It is much easier to write a routine that handles a single conversation and spawns multiple copies of that routine than it is to write a piece of code that handles multiple conversations at once.

Multiprocessing   Many operating systems support machines with multiple processors. Most of these systems are unable to break a single thread of execution into multiple pieces for execution on different processors. By breaking an application into different threads, it is possible to make the best use of processing power.

Every item in this list applies to Internet and embedded-systems applications. Java implements multithreading through a part of its class library, but Java also has language constructs to make programs thread-safe. A *thread-safe* program guarantees that the different threads will not accidentally harm one another. Java's `synchronized` keyword can be used to prevent two threads from entering the same critical block of code at the same time. This is vital because some program steps need to be made together as one atomic group.

Memory Management and Garbage Collection

Memory management is the bane of all C and C++ programs. During the course of a program's execution, memory will be required for temporary operations, such as sorting lists or displaying images. In C and C++, it is the programmer's responsibility to allocate the required memory and free that memory after the task has been completed. If the memory allocations do not match memory deallocations perfectly, the program will either crash immediately or consume system resources until exhausted. In either case, the result is abnormal termination of the program, often bringing down the operating system with it.

Java overcomes this problem by using *garbage collection*. Temporary memory is automatically reclaimed after it is no longer referenced by any active part of the program. This frees the developer from much of the housekeeping that would otherwise be required.

Historically, the problem with garbage collection has been performance. The garbage collector must scan memory for objects that can be eliminated and then sweep the removable objects from memory. Taking out the trash too often is inefficient, but checking too infrequently causes the system to pause while large amounts of garbage are collected. To improve performance, Java's garbage collector runs in its own low-priority thread, providing a good balance of efficiency and real-time responsiveness.

Memory management reinforces the security of the VM. In C and C++, the programmer can access any part of the system available to an application. This can be done by using *pointers*, which are variables that reference specific memory locations. Java does not use pointers in the strict sense of the word. Java's "pointers" are actually references to VM resources, and no arithmetic is permitted with such variables; this prevents programmers from accessing system resources outside the VM. Although this eliminates some of the most advanced programming "tricks" of C++, it greatly simplifies the lives of developers and users alike. And because the Core API provides many important data structures built into the language, arbitrary pointers lose much of their usefulness anyway.

Using Java with Other Tools

Java is a unique development tool and is already a highly successful product. As an Internet development tool, Java joins several other Internet development tools vying for market acceptance. Recognizing that Java is here to stay, vendors are making their products interoperable with Java.

The following is a brief survey of Java-related Internet technologies, including native code, JavaScript, Netscape plug-ins, ActiveX, JDBC, and JavaBeans.

Native Code

Native code refers to code that is native to a specific processor. On Windows 95, native code refers to code compatible with Intel x86 processors. Java can call native code quite easily, although such calls are not subject to the VM's security measures; this is why most Web browsers do not permit Java applets to make native calls. In Java 1.2, however, native calls are subject to at least a minimal amount of security checking.

Native code access means that Java can call upon millions of lines of existing code and can be used as a development tool for stand-alone, platform-specific applications.

NOTE   The means to access native code differs between Microsoft and Netscape Web browsers. This is one of the reasons for Sun's lawsuit against Microsoft. Because Microsoft's environment doesn't support the Java standard means, Sun claims Microsoft's implementation is not Java. Until the problems are resolved, using native code with Java programs can be tricky.

JavaScript

JavaScript is a separate programming language loosely related to Java. JavaScript can be coded directly in an HTML document, which makes the JavaScript source code part of the document itself. JavaScript is less powerful than Java, but it gives the programmer a bit more control over the browser, and it is used primarily to create dialog boxes and animation on Web pages.

JavaScript does have a limited ability to call Java applet routines and alter Java applet variables. However, the Core Java API has no mechanisms for calling JavaScript code or changing JavaScript variables. Netscape does offer a Java/JavaScript connectivity package when working within their browser.

Netscape Plug-Ins

Netscape Communications has created a standard interface to its Navigator browser product line. Products adhering to the specification are called Netscape *plug-ins*. Netscape provides a Software Development Kit (SDK) so that third parties can implement plug-ins for new types of media, and it allows the new media to integrate seamlessly with the browser. Currently available plug-ins support a number of multimedia formats, as well as spreadsheets, AutoCAD drawings, and live news feeds.

Plug-ins are written with native code; that is, they are platform-specific. The SDK itself changes only slightly from platform to platform, but the implementation details may be totally different between platforms. If you want to use a plug-in, you will need to download it for your specific platform before being able to utilize the new media. The advantage of this approach is that after downloading a plug-in to your hard disk, the new media will appear in your browser with no delay. With the advent of JavaBeans (see Chapter 22), components like Netscape plug-ins and Java applets will be able to integrate seamlessly into the browser and other environments.

ActiveX

ActiveX is Microsoft's answer to the Netscape plug-in. ActiveX (formerly known as OCXs, now part of WindowsDNA or Windows Distributed interNet Applications Architecture) uses controls based on the Component Object Model (COM). COM is used throughout Microsoft's desktop applications for communication and automation. Integrating a Web browser with ActiveX extends the Microsoft desktop across the Internet.

Like Netscape plug-ins, ActiveX controls are native code modules, and Microsoft intends to support ActiveX on other platforms, not just Microsoft Windows. Unlike plug-ins, ActiveX controls are designed to be downloaded as needed. A digital signature guarantees the ActiveX control has not been tampered with. Interestingly, Ncompass Labs has created a Netscape plug-in that runs ActiveX controls. Also, Software AG's EntireX product offers access to ActiveX and DCOM (Distributed COM) for the UNIX and mainframe community.

Java interfaces and COM interfaces are semantically similar, and Microsoft has designed a VM that allows ActiveX and Java to communicate automatically. Sun also provides a bridge to unite Java with ActiveX through JavaBeans. These bridges make Java an excellent development tool for creating components that can be used in Windows-based development tools and applications like Word, Excel, Visual C++, Visual Basic, and Delphi. Microsoft has also proposed its own Windows-platform VM that will run both ActiveX and Java. Although this will make writing Java programs for the Windows platform much easier, it will limit Java's usefulness to platforms that support ActiveX and have a Microsoft Virtual Machine; this will give Microsoft major control over Java.

JDBC

Java Database Connectivity (JDBC) is an API for linking Java programs to databases. JDBC is quite similar to Microsoft's Open Database Connectivity (ODBC) standard. JDBC-compliant database applications are not tied to a specific database vendor. As with ODBC, a vendor-specific driver is used to link JDBC applications to the actual database.

Suppose you write an employee database application using JDBC. There is no need to decide which vendor's database management system (for example, Oracle, Sybase, or Informix) you want to use when you write the code because your program will work with any database that has a JDBC driver.

Also, a JDBC-ODBC bridge was released by Sun in 1996. This bridge gives JDBC the ability to interface with the large number of existing ODBC drivers. Many other vendors have released bridges of their own. JDBC is likely to be critical to industry acceptance of Java as a corporate client/server development tool. For more information about JDBC, see Chapter 21.

JavaBeans

More than just another coffee metaphor in Java's vocabulary, JavaBeans is a powerful API for creating reusable software components. With Java "Beans," Java objects can be easily wired together by nonprogrammers, with the help of bean connection tools like JBuilder. Look for more information about JavaBeans in Chapter 22.

New Features in Java 1.1

Java 1.1 has been out since early 1997. If you are moving to Java 1.2 from Java 1.0, several features will appear new and different. Here is a summary of the new features of Java 1.1:

Internationalization   New classes and methods have been added to make writing programs for international users even easier. This includes support for non-English characters and text sorting, as well as a variety of time and date standards.

Security   Several enhancements, including digital signing, have been incorporated into a new and improved `SecurityManager`. Also, security for native method calls has been enhanced.

Performance enhancements   A new AWT event model and complete rewrite of the native code for AWT has boosted GUI performance dramatically. Also, much of the compiler and interpreter code has been rewritten.

Network and I/O enhancements   New classes provide extra network functionality, as well as greater customization. New `Reader` and `Writer` classes provide high-performance, internationalized, buffered input and output.

Object reflection   A special API for getting privileged information about a specific object has been added. This is especially useful for debuggers and other VM-enhancement programs.

The JDBC and JavaBeans capabilities previously mentioned are also new to Java 1.1.

New Features in Java 1.2

Java 1.2 adds even more enhancements, some improving capabilities added in Java 1.1, with others completely new. The following summarizes the features new to Java 1.2:

Enhancements to security, JavaBeans, reflection, and performance
Numerous Java packages received enhancements in Java 1.2. The security architecture incorporates policy-based access control to enhance permission-management. JavaBeans adds drag-and-drop support, while reflection includes the ability to bypass security, specifically when using object reflection. Also, the performance of various pieces of the Java libraries was improved, for instance, faster memory allocation, reduced memory usage for loaded classes, and Just-in-Time compilers.

Java Foundation Classes   The Java Foundation Classes (JFC) encompass a broad range of enhancements. There is now support for assistive technologies with an Accessibility API, a Java 2-D API for enhanced graphics and imaging, and Swing for a new set of GUI components, in addition to the AWT components.

Collections   The Collections API makes working with groups of objects much easier. Prior to Java 1.2, you basically used the earlier `Vector` and `Hashtable` classes, as well as the `Enumeration` interface. Here, you can work with things like balanced trees, circular linked lists, and simplified array sorting.

In addition to these changes, a whole host of changes to methods, classes, and packages have provided extra functionality. These changes are documented throughout this book.

Summary

This chapter introduced you to the history of Java, its effect on the World Wide Web, and the underlying Java architecture. Now that you have a feeling for Java's background and where it fits into Internet development efforts, the next chapter moves into the specifics of developing with Java.

Applets, Applications, and the Java Development Kit

- The difference between Java applets and applications

- The Java Development Kit (JDK)

- Java application creation with the JDK

- Java applet creation with the JDK

- The Java Runtime Environment (JRE)

- New features in JDK 1.2

Java programs come in three flavors: *applets*, *servlets*, and *applications*. Simply speaking, a Java applet is a program that appears embedded in a Web document; a servlet is a special Java program that runs inside a Web server. A Java application is the term applied to all other kinds of Java programs, such as those found on network servers and consumer electronics. Much of this chapter will be devoted to the differences between applets and applications, along with the ways these differences affect the Java software development path. Servlets are discussed in Chapter 23.

The Java Development Kit (JDK) from Sun's Java Software division contains the basic tools and libraries necessary for creating and executing Java applets and applications. It also contains a number of useful utilities for debugging and documenting Java source code and for interfacing C to Java code. You will learn how to download, install, and apply the JDK to the construction of both applets and applications. Along the way, you will receive a primer on HTML for applets and get your first taste of Java source code. You'll also learn about the Java Runtime Environment (JRE), which is what you deliver with your Java applications so others can run your programs.

Java Applets versus Java Applications

Traditionally, the word *applet* has come to mean any small application. In Java, an applet is any Java program that is launched from a Web document; that is, from an HTML file. Java applications, on the other hand, are programs that run from a command line, independent of a Web browser. The size or complexity of a Java applet has no limit. In fact, Java applets are in some ways more powerful than Java applications. However, with the Internet, where communication speed is limited and download times are long, most Java applets are small by necessity.

The technical differences between applets and applications stem from the context in which they run. A Java application runs in the simplest possible environment—its only input from the outside world is a list of command-line parameters. On the other hand, a Java applet receives a lot of information from the Web browser. It needs to know when it is initialized, when and where to draw itself in the browser window, and when it is activated or deactivated. As a consequence of these two very different execution environments, applets and applications have different minimum requirements.

The decision to write a program as an applet versus an application depends on the context of the program and its delivery mechanism. Because Java applets are always presented in the context of a Web browser's graphical user interface (GUI), Java applications are preferred over applets when graphical displays are unnecessary. For example, an HTTP server written in Java needs no graphical display; it requires only file and network access.

The convenience of Web protocols for applet distribution makes applets the preferred program type for Internet applications, although applications can easily be used to perform many of the same tasks. With Java, writing Internet-based software, either as applets or applications, is extremely easy. Non-networked systems and systems with small amounts of memory are much more likely to be written as Java applications than as Java applets.

Table 2.1 summarizes the differences between these two flavors of Java programs.

TABLE 2.1:   Differences between Java Applets and Applications

	Java Applet	**Java Application**
Uses graphics	Inherently graphical	Optional
Memory requirements	Java application requirements plus Web browser requirements	Minimal Java application requirements
Distribution	Linked via HTML and transported via HTTP	Loaded from the file system or by a custom class loading process
Environmental input	Browser client location and size; parameters embedded in the host HTML document	Command-line parameters
Method expected by the Virtual Machine (VM)	`init`—initialization method `start`—startup method `stop`—pause/deactivate method `destroy`—termination method `paint`—drawing method	`main`—startup method
Typical applications	Public-access order-entry systems for the Web, online multimedia presentations, Web page animation	Network server, multimedia kiosks, developer tools, appliance and consumer electronics control and navigation

You should consider one other major factor when deciding applet or application. If you are using features of newer Java versions, you need to wait until browsers support the capabilities. With an application, you can provide the Java Runtime Environment (the JRE is discussed later in this chapter). However, within an applet, you can only use the capabilities a browser offers. In an Internet environment, you can expect users to still be using older browser versions, which do not support either Java 1.1 or Java 1.2. In a corporate intranet environment, where there tends to be more control over software versions, you can know what versions are available and develop accordingly. Also, you may want to consider using Sun's Java Plug-in product which can automatically update the Java version of browsers when a new version becomes available.

Using the Java Development Kit (JDK)

The JDK was the original Java development environment for many of today's Java professionals. Although many programmers have moved on to third-party alternatives, the JDK is still considered to be the reference implementation of Java. If you can build and test an application with the JDK, it should run on any third-party implementations, such as those in Web browsers, development tools, or device-specific VMs. In fact, Sun has a whole suite of tests to ensure that third-party Java environments conform to the JDK version.

TIP   The latest version of the JDK is available from Sun's Web site at `http://java.sun`
`.com/products/jdk/1.2/`. You can download it for free (excluding connection charges). For more information, see "Downloading and Installing the JDK," coming up shortly.

The JDK can create and display graphical applications, but the JDK itself has a somewhat primitive command-line interface. For instance, you run the JDK programs by typing commands into a command-shell window (in Windows, a DOS box; on Unix systems, a normal command shell). Do not be discouraged by the apparent complexity of the JDK commands; they are all quite easy to use after a bit of practice.

The JDK consists of a library of standard classes and a collection of utilities for building, testing, and documenting Java programs. As explained in Chapter 1, the Core Java API is the library of prefabricated classes. You need these classes to access the core functionality of the Java language.

The Core API includes some important language constructs (including `String` datatypes and exceptions), as well as graphics, network, and file I/O capabilities. It is generally safe to assume that the Core API is common to all platforms running Java. The EmbeddedJava and PersonalJava APIs specify well-defined subsets for specific environments. For instance, a Java VM in a toaster or other household appliance is unlikely to support the graphics part of the API, but it will almost certainly implement `String` datatypes and other Core API language classes. A Web browser running on a desktop computer will likely implement the complete Core API (and also many of the optional Extension APIs, which are additional libraries discussed later in this book).

TIP

For additional information on the upcoming EmbeddedJava API for small-footprint embedded systems, see `http://www.java.sun.com/products/embeddedjava/`. For information on the PersonalJava specification for networkable consumer appliances, see `http://www.java.sun.com/products/personaljava/`.

JDK Utilities

Version 1.2 of the JDK includes the following utilities:

javac   The Java *compiler*. Converts Java source code into bytecodes.

java   The Java *interpreter*. Executes Java application bytecodes directly from class files.

appletviewer   A Java interpreter that executes Java applet classes hosted by HTML files.

javadoc   Creates HTML documentation based on Java source code and the comments it contains.

jdb   The Java *debugger*. Allows you to step through the program one line at a time, set breakpoints, and examine variables.

javah   Generates C header files that can be used to make C routines that can call Java methods, or make C routines that can be called by Java programs.

javap   The Java *disassembler*. Displays the accessible functions and data in a compiled class file. It also displays the meaning of the bytecodes.

rmic   Creates class files that support Remote Method Invocation (RMI). See Chapter 25 for information about RMI.

rmiregistry   Registry used to gain access to RMI objects on a specific machine.

rmid   Activation system daemon for RMI object registration and activation.

serialver   Serialization utility. Permits versioning of persistent objects. See Chapter 19 for information about serialization.

native2ascii   Special program used to convert between standard Latin-1 Unicode characters and other international encoding schemes.

jar   Java Archive (JAR) file generator. JAR files allow multiple Java classes and resources to be distributed in one compressed file.

keytool   Used for security key generation and management.

jarsigner   Implements digital signing of JAR and class files. Allows applets to be certified by trusted authorities.

policytool   Allows user-installation-level security policy configuration.

tnameserv   The Java IDL transient name server.

The way these tools are applied to build and run Java applications is illustrated in Figure 2.1. When building applets, the flowchart looks slightly different, as you can see in Figure 2.2.

After the descriptions of how to download and install the JDK, you will see how Figure 2.1 applies to a sample Java application. Then you will see how to follow Figure 2.2 for building applets.

FIGURE 2.1:

How Java applications are built using the JDK

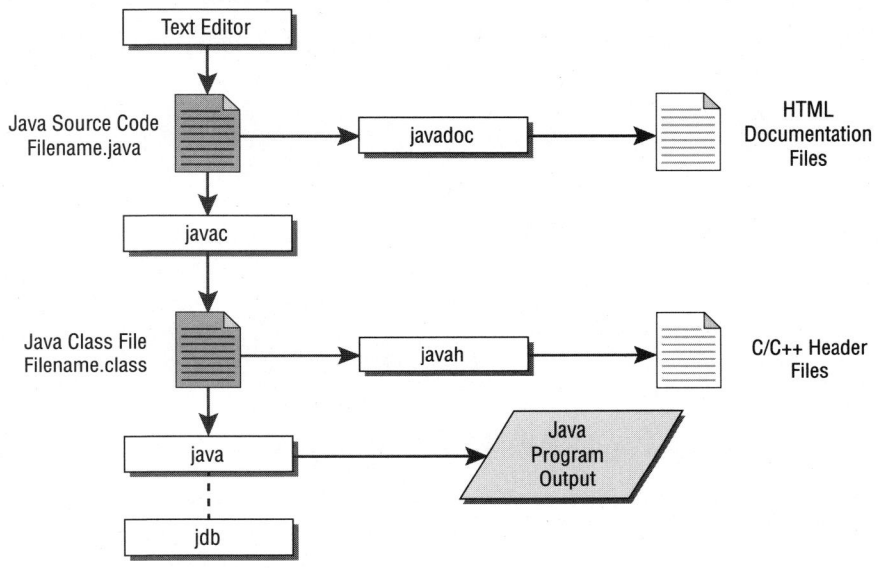

FIGURE 2.2:

How Java applets are built using the JDK

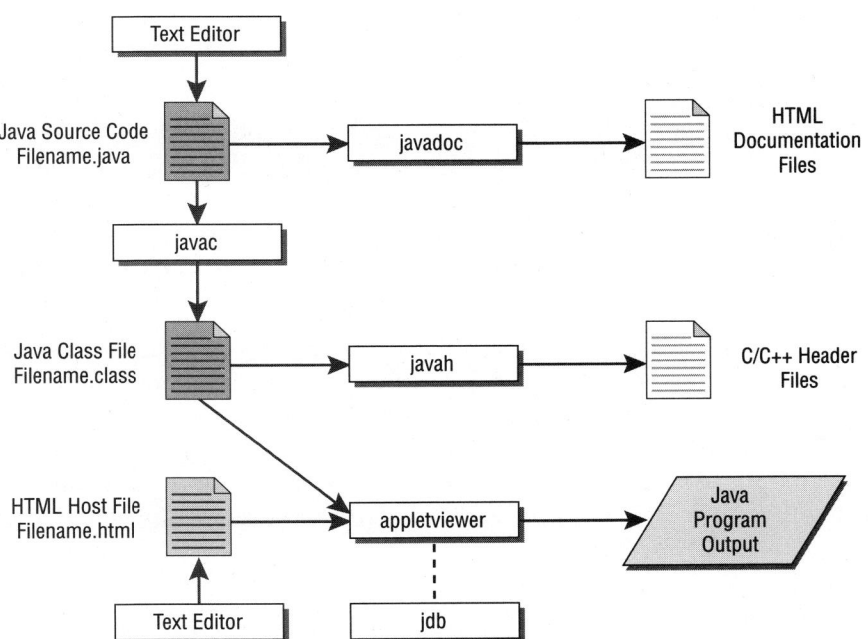

Downloading and Installing the JDK

To help get you started with Java, the following sections summarize the steps you need to install the JDK on your machine. You need to install it before you can follow any of the exercises presented in this book.

Downloading the JDK

The latest version (1.2) of the JDK can be downloaded from Sun's Java Web site at `http://java.sun.com/products/jdk/1.2/`. The JDK is a self-extracting, compressed, executable file. Version 1.2 is available from Sun for the following platforms:

- Solaris 2.4/2.5 for both SPARC and *x*86 architectures
- Windows 95, Windows 98, and Windows NT 4 for *x*86 architectures

---

NOTE   If you want to develop with Java on another platform, you have to get the JDK from another source. Sun maintains a list of third-party JDK ports at `http://java.sun.com/cgi-bin/java-ports.cgi`. While some of these efforts have successfully ported Java 1.0 and 1.1, Java 1.2 ports may not be immediately available on every one.

The first step in downloading the JDK is to locate the correct binary files at Sun's Java Web site or from the appropriate site if you are using a platform other than those supported by Sun. The complete JDK is distributed as a single file, and the download may take 90 minutes with a 33.6kbps modem, or about half as long with a single-channel ISDN connection, assuming that the server is not busy. It may help to try downloading the file early in the morning or late in the evening when the server is not as busy.

Sun also has a separate distribution file for the JDK documentation. This includes release notes, help files, and documentation for all of the classes and tools distributed with the JDK. It is strongly recommended that you download this as well. It is about 9MB (megabytes) compressed and is well worth the download time. The GZIP compressed version is smallest and is readable by WinZip on Windows platforms. You can also access this documentation online on Sun's Java Web page.

Installing the JDK

The JDK installation process is fairly straightforward but generally takes a little manual setup to finish off. To give you a head start, Table 2.2 summarizes the installation procedure for JDK 1.2 for each platform supported by Sun.

TABLE 2.2: JDK Installation Instructions for Windows and Solaris Platforms

Installation Procedures	Windows 95/98 & Windows NT	Sun Solaris*
Downloaded file type	Self-extracting executable (`.exe`)	Packed archive (`.sh`)
Where to install the JDK	Usually installed in `c:\jdk1.2`, by the self-extracting executable	Usually installed in `jdk1.2`, by the self-extracting executable
If you have already installed a previous version of the JDK	Should install in different directory by default so both versions are available. Otherwise, save any files you have changed or created in the original Java directory tree in a separate directory, and then delete the original installation	Should install in different directory by default so both versions are available. Otherwise, save any files you have changed or created in the original Java directory tree in a separate directory, and then delete the original installation
Decompression procedure	Run the executable to decompress and install	Use **sh** to decompress and run the install script
Additional setup	Add the `jdk1.2\bin` directory to your path	Add the `jdk1.2/bin` directory to your path
If you have already installed a previous version of the JDK[**]	If your **CLASSPATH** environment variable refers to `classes.zip`, remove the entry.	If your **CLASSPATH** environment variable refers to `classes.zip`, remove the entry.

* Versions 2.51 and 2.6 for Solaris/SPARC and Solaris/x86.

** If you do not have a **CLASSPATH** environment variable set, it is not necessary to set one.

Building Applications with the JDK

Now that you have installed the JDK, it's time to take it for a test drive. To smooth the ride, this section describes how to create a small Java application, applying each JDK utility to the code. You will see the same code compiled, executed, disassembled, documented, and interfaced to the C language.

Java Application Source Code

Java source code can be written with a simple text editor. In Unix, vi or emacs will do; in Windows, you can use Notepad or EDIT. Many programmers have a preferred text editor or use the editor shipped with third-party integrated development environments (IDEs).

NOTE   For your convenience, the source code examples are included on the CD-ROM accompanying this book.

The first example is a little Java program that you can use to play with the JDK:

```
public class TestDrive {
  public static void main (String args[]) {
    System.out.println ("JDK Test Drive");
  }
}
```

This is a rework of the classic HelloWorld program; it simply prints the words "JDK Test Drive." It is the simplest Java program you can write, but to the uninitiated, it may still look rather cryptic. For the purposes of this chapter, there is no need to understand it all perfectly; don't worry too much about what each keyword means.

The code defines a Java class called TestDrive, which contains a single method called main().When the Java interpreter tries to execute the TestDrive class, it will look for a method called main(). The public, static, and void keywords will be explained in detail in later chapters; for now, you just need to know that they are required for the main() method to behave correctly.

In fact, every Java application must define a function called main as:

```
public static void main (String args[])
```

The VM will execute this function to run the program. Here, args is an array of String (text) variables. When you run the program, the array will be filled with the values of any arguments it was given on the command line.

If you know how to program in C, the `main()` function will look familiar. The C equivalent:

```
int main (int argc, char *argv[0])
```

includes `argc`, an integer variable that tells you how many arguments are in the array. In Java, this is unnecessary because arrays know how many elements they contain. Another difference between Java and C is that in C, the first element in the `argv` array, `argv[0]`, contains the name of the program itself. In Java, `args[0]` is the first parameter on the command line.

Type the Java source code for the `TestDrive` class into your text editor and save it under the name `TestDrive.java`.

NOTE   The name of the Java source file is not arbitrary; it must be the same as the name of the public class defined in the `.java` file. Consequently, only one public class can be defined in each source file, although additional nonpublic classes can be defined in each file. If no public class is defined in the Java source file, the name of the file can be anything you want.

You are now ready to compile your first Java program.

Using *javac*

The `javac` compiler converts Java source code into Java bytecodes, which can then be executed by `java` (the Java interpreter), the `appletviewer`, or any other Java VM, such as within Netscape Communicator.

You can compile your `TestDrive` program by entering the following at the shell prompt:

```
javac TestDrive.java
```

If the Java code is acceptable to the compiler, the file `TestDrive.class` will be created (no messages will be displayed).

If you are curious and would like to see the details of the compilation, you can use the `verbose` option. The `verbose` option is rarely used, but it is instructive to see it at least once. The `verbose` option will cause the `javac` compiler to tell you which other Java classes the compiler needs to create the compiled class file and how long it took to do the compilation. When you enter:

```
javac -verbose TestDrive.java
```

it produces something like this (your times and locations may vary):

```
[parsed TestDrive.java in 1032 ms]
[loaded c:\jdk1.2beta4\jre\lib\rt.jar(java/lang/Object.class) in 171 ms]
[checking class TestDrive]
[loaded c:\jdk1.2beta4\jre\lib\rt.jar(java/lang/String.class) in 91 ms]
[loaded c:\jdk1.2beta4\jre\lib\rt.jar(java/io/Serializable.class) in 0 ms]
[loaded c:\jdk1.2beta4\jre\lib\rt.jar(java/lang/Comparable.class) in 10 ms]
[loaded c:\jdk1.2beta4\jre\lib\rt.jar(java/lang/System.class) in 10 ms]
[loaded c:\jdk1.2beta4\jre\lib\rt.jar(java/io/PrintStream.class) in 0 ms]
[loaded c:\jdk1.2beta4\jre\lib\rt.jar(java/io/FilterOutputStream.class) in 0 ms]
[loaded c:\jdk1.2beta4\jre\lib\rt.jar(java/io/OutputStream.class) in 10 ms]
[loaded c:\jdk1.2beta4\jre\lib\rt.jar(java/io/IOException.class) in 0 ms]
[loaded c:\jdk1.2beta4\jre\lib\rt.jar(java/lang/Exception.class) in 0 ms]
[loaded c:\jdk1.2beta4\jre\lib\rt.jar(java/lang/Throwable.class) in 10 ms]
[wrote TestDrive.class]
[done in 5057 ms]
```

Behind the scenes, the compiler must check that the TestDrive program is consistent with any other classes it uses. String, System, PrintStream, Filter-OutputStream, OutputStream, and Serializable are included in Java's standard class libraries, the Core API. All of these classes are essential to print a string to the standard output.

TIP

In version 1.2 of the JDK, there are about 2,500 classes in the standard class library, the Core API, and about 2,000 supplementary classes provided as a tools and debugging class library. The Core API contains a wealth of ready-to-use functionality and will save you a great deal of development time. These classes are stored in a Java archive (jar) file in the jdk1.2/jre/lib directory. Do not remove the rt.jar file because the Java compiler and VM access the library classes from this file directly. If you want to see the source code for the library classes, this is included in the src.jar file, included with the installation.

After running `javac` to compile `TestDrive.java`, the file `TestDrive.class` contains bytecodes that can be executed by any Java VM on any platform. The class file format is an open standard, and a detailed specification for it is available at Sun's Web site. If you use a binary file viewer to analyze the file, you will notice that there is text as well as binary data in the file. The names of classes and methods used by the class file must be stored in the bytecodes in order to access those classes and methods on the destination system.

Using *java*

After compiling `TestDrive`, you can run the program with the Java interpreter by entering the following command:

```
java TestDrive
```

The output will be the words "JDK Test Drive," as shown in Figure 2.3.

FIGURE 2.3:

A sample Windows 95 command-line session that compiles `TestDrive.java` and executes `TestDrive.class`

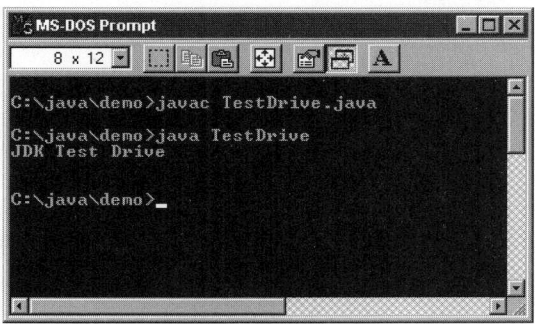

The interpreter has many command-line options—most of which are functions likely to be used only by advanced Java programmers. Nevertheless, it is worth your while to look at a useful, relatively simple feature built into the interpreter: a *profiler*. A profiler is used to analyze how much time a program spends in each part of the code. You can use this information to determine which parts of a program to optimize. If you use the `prof` option of the interpreter, with the command:

```
java -prof TestDrive
```

a file called `java.prof` will be created. This file shows how many times each method is called and how many milliseconds are spent executing each one. An excerpt of the profile for `TestDrive.class` is shown here:

```
count callee caller time
341 java/lang/String.charAt(I)C
java/util/Properties.loadConvert(Ljava/lang/String;)Ljava/lang/String; 10
341 java/lang/StringBuffer.append(C)Ljava/lang/StringBuffer;
java/util/Properties.loadConvert(Ljava/lang/String;)Ljava/lang/String; 0
317 java/lang/String.indexOf(II)I java/lang/String.indexOf(I)I 0
287 java/lang/String.charAt(I)C
java/io/Win32FileSystem.normalize(Ljava/lang/String;)Ljava/lang/String; 0
278 java/lang/String.charAt(I)C
java/util/Properties.load(Ljava/io/InputStream;)V 0
...
handles_used: 740, handles_free: 26214, heap-used: 117176, heap-free: 721680
sig   count  bytes   indx
[C     147 26340      5
[B       4 10400      8
*** tab[253] p=4b19f80 cb=1609fe8 cnt=1 ac=0 al=0
 Lsun/misc/Launcher; 1 4
*** tab[244] p=4b19ef0 cb=160b7a0 cnt=1 ac=0 al=0
 Ljava/util/zip/Inflater; 1 28
*** tab[235] p=4b19e60 cb=1609f58 cnt=2 ac=0 al=0
 Ljava/io/PrintStream; 2 48
*** tab[232] p=4b19e30 cb=1609f40 cnt=3 ac=0 al=0
 Ljava/io/FileInputStream; 3 12
...
```

The first section of the file shows which methods are called in order of decreasing frequency. The next section shows how much memory is used, providing handles and heap information. The third section lists the variable types created and how many bytes are necessary to store them. This output stores plenty of other information; most of it is too complicated to go into here.

As you learn more about Java, you will be able to put this information to good use. It is particularly helpful for deciding how to optimize your software. Programs often follow an 80/20 rule: 80 percent of the execution time is spent in 20 percent of the code. The profiler points out which methods are using up the most time so you can optimize the most time-consuming parts of the code.

Using *javadoc*

By adding a few comments to your Java source code, you make it possible for javadoc to automatically generate HTML documentation for your code. Add the following few comments to your `TestDrive.java` file:

```
/** TestDrive – A test file for demonstration of the JDK. */
public class TestDrive {
  /** This method is called first by the Java interpreter.
    * It prints a message to the console. */
  //  javadoc will ignore this comment
  public static void main(String argv[]) {
    /* javadoc will also ignore this comment */
    System.out.println("JDK Test Drive");
  }
}
```

C and C++ programmers will immediately notice the similarities between Java and C syntax. The curly braces ({ }) group code together into blocks. As in C, line indentation is unnecessary, but it helps make the code more readable.

Java also uses the same kind of comments as C++, but a comment beginning with multiple asterisks has a special meaning for javadoc. It signifies the start of a *documentation comment* block, which is a comment block that will be used by javadoc to create documentation. Given our newly commented `TestDrive.java`, javadoc will produce the files `AllNames.html`, `tree.html`, `packages.html`, and `TestDrive.html`, all of which can easily be viewed using a standard Web browser, as shown in Figure 2.4. To run javadoc, simply enter the following command:

```
javadoc TestDrive.java
```

Using *javah*

In order for Java to be applied to platform-specific or performance-critical problems, Java needs the ability to call native code written in C or other languages. Embedded applications are prime examples of where a Java program would need to access platform-specific information, such as LED displays, relays, and sensors. Similarly, until the Java3D API becomes available, rendering complex 3-D graphics in real time is an application that demands the raw speed of C. Because Java was originally based on an embedded systems language, Java has built-in support for calling native routines.

FIGURE 2.4:

Viewing source code documentation in HTML format produced by javadoc

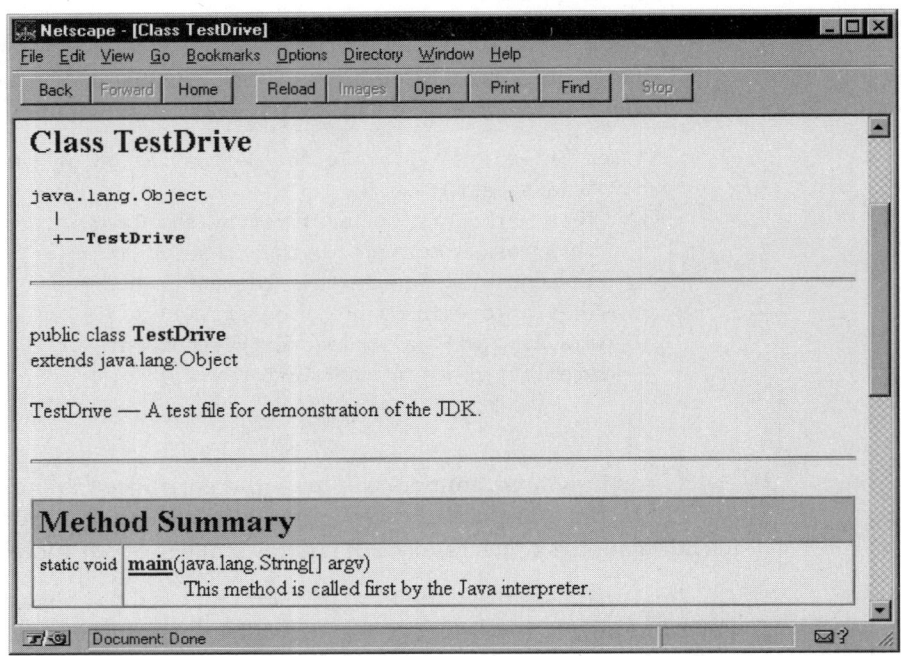

To help you write C code that interfaces with Java, the JDK includes javah, a utility that, given a class file, generates the C header files needed by C programs to access the class's data.

Using *jdb*

The Java debugger, jdb, monitors and controls the execution of a Java program so that bugs can be found. With jdb, a running program can be stopped at any point so that the variables and internal operation of the program can be examined.

NOTE   Many programmers prefer third-party debuggers, like the ones included with Symantec's Visual Café and Borland's JBuilder development environments. They have all of the features of jdb and allow you to set breakpoints directly in the code and view the program internals with separate windows for variables, threads, and function calls.

Although jdb may seem difficult to use, it can still be a useful tool. It is worthwhile to take a few moments to learn how to use some of the more basic features of jdb. Once you get started, learning more advanced techniques is much easier. Also, Unix C programmers who are used to using tools such as dbx and gdb will probably find jdb very easy to use.

Here is the procedure to use jdb on TestDrive.class, performing only a few basic functions:

1. Load the TestDrive class into jdb, and set a breakpoint. When the debugger hits a breakpoint in the code, it stops executing the program and allows the user to inspect the state of the program. Tell the debugger to stop when it reaches the main() method.

2. Take a look at the source code for TestDrive. The debugger lists the code and also shows where it is about to execute a new instruction (it uses a => to indicate its current position). If there were many lines of code, you could also have jdb step through the code one line at a time.

3. Clear the breakpoint and allow jdb to finish executing the program.

Here's the output of the jdb session just described:

```
C:\internet\MasteringJava\ch02>jdb TestDrive
Initializing jdb...
0xa50198:class(TestDrive)
> stop in TestDrive.main
Breakpoint set in TestDrive.main
> run
run TestDrive
running ...
main[1]
Breakpoint hit: TestDrive.main (TestDrive:8)
main[1] list
4              * It prints a message to the console. */
5             // javadoc will ignore this comment
6             public static void main (String argv[]) {
7                 /* javadoc will ignore this comment */
8       =>        System.out.println("JDK Test Drive");
9             }
10          }
main[1] clear TestDrive.main
```

```
Breakpoint cleared at TestDrive.main
main[1] cont
main[1] JDK Test Drive

Current thread "main" died. Execution continuing...
>
TestDrive exited
```

Note that this debugger can connect to a VM that is running in another process, even on a remote machine. This could be especially useful when debugging VMs running on remote servers, appliances, or consumer electronics. To learn more about jdb, type **?** at the prompt.

Using *javap*

It is possible to examine the bytecodes of a compiled class file and identify its accessible variables and functions. The javap utility creates a report that shows not only what functions and variables are available, but what the code actually does, albeit at a very low level. If you run javap with no command-line arguments:

```
javap TestDrive
```

the output shows from which file the class was compiled and the accessible functions and variables, like this:

```
Compiled from TestDrive.java
public class TestDrive extends java.lang.Object
    /* ACC_SUPER bit set */
{
    public TestDrive();
    public static void main(java.lang.String []);
}
```

In this case, we have no "public" variables, so only the main() and TestDrive() methods are displayed. The TestDrive() function is a *default constructor*, a special function that is automatically created by the compiler if you do not write one. You will learn more about default constructors in the next chapter.

If you use javap with the -c option to display the meaning of the bytecodes in the file:

```
javap -c TestDrive
```

the output shows each step that will be taken by the VM to execute the methods of the class:

```
Compiled from TestDrive.java
public class TestDrive extends java.lang.Object{
    public TestDrive();
    public static void main(java.lang.String[]);
}

Method TestDrive()
   0 aload_0
   1 invokespecial #6 <Method java.lang.Object()>
   4 return

Method void main(java.lang.String[])
   0 getstatic #7 <Field java.io.PrintStream out>
   3 ldc #1 <String "JDK Test Drive">
   5 invokevirtual #8 <Method void println(java.lang.String)>
   8 return
```

This is much more complicated than the original TestDrive.java file, but it shows each step that the VM will take when executing the program. As you can see, javap is a tool for advanced Java programmers.

Building Applets with the JDK

So far, you have seen the process by which you build Java applications using the JDK. In this section, you will learn about creating Java applets and the HTML documents in which you host them.

This section presents a sample Java applet called FilledBox.java, whose only function is to display a filled rectangle in an HTML document. The HTML document can control the color of the rectangle by passing a parameter to the applet, which illustrates the relationship of HTML to Java applets.

Before going any further, you may find it helpful to take a minute to understand the following short lesson in HTML. After a brief introduction to HTML, you will be up and running with Java applets in no time. If you're already familiar with HTML, feel free to skip this section.

HTML for Java Applets

HTML files are text files with special character sequences that specify the document-formatting characteristics. The special character sequences are called *tags*, and they consist of symbols placed between left and right angle brackets, as shown in the following excerpt:

```
Here is some normal text. <I>Here is some italic text.</I>
```

The <I> start tag sets the italic formatting, and the </I> end tag unsets it. A Web browser or HTML viewer interprets the HTML file and produces the corresponding output. This excerpt of HTML produces the following output:

```
Here is some normal text. Here is some italic text.
```

Most HTML tags use the *<tag>* and *</tag>* sequences to set and unset their relevant properties. For example, <B> turns on bold, and </B> turns it off. Other tags, such as the paragraph tag, may not require an end tag.

A complete HTML file has both formatting and structure tags:

```
<HTML>
 <HEAD>
  <TITLE>Sample HTML Document</TITLE>
 </HEAD>
 <BODY>
  <H1>HTML Demo</H1>
  This document is a sample of HTML.
 </BODY>
</HTML>
```

The <HTML> tag indicates that the file is an HTML document. The <HEAD> tag marks the start of an invisible header section normally used for recording the title and author of the document. Some programs will only look at the header section of a document. The phrase between the <TITLE> and </TITLE> tags is the name of this document. The body section of the document, marked by the <BODY> tag, contains all the displayed information; in this case, a level-one heading (signified by <H1> and </H1>) and a line of normal text. The output generated by this HTML file is shown in Figure 2.5.

FIGURE 2.5:

A sample HTML file
displayed in Netscape
Navigator

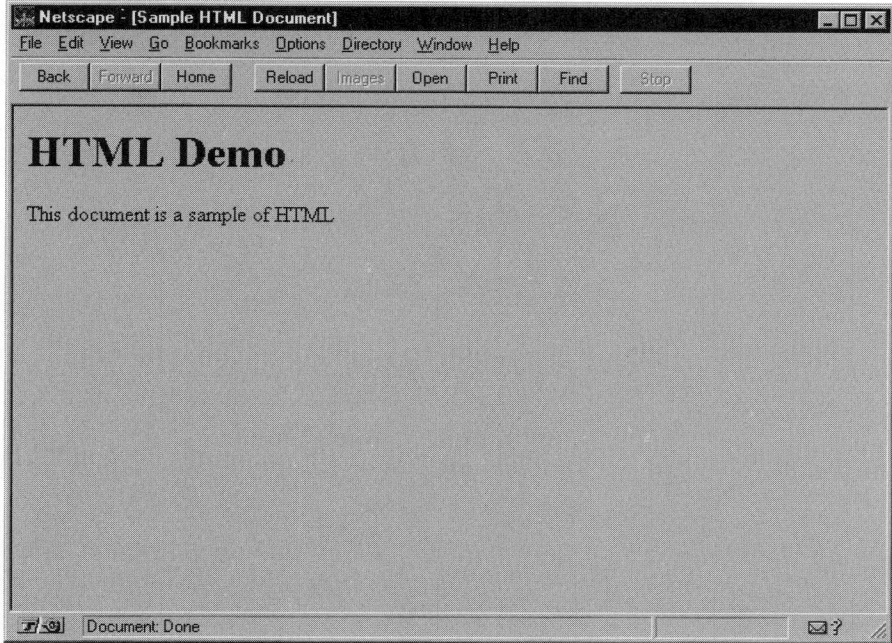

To include an image in an HTML file, use the <IMG> tag and specify the name
and location of the image you want to load. You can use the full URL of the
image; a simpler relative reference can be used if the graphic is located on the
same server as the HTML file itself:

```
<HTML>
 <HEAD>
  <TITLE>Sample HTML Document</TITLE>
 </HEAD>
 <BODY>
  <IMG SRC="sybex.gif">
  <H1>HTML Demo</H1>
  This document is a sample of HTML.
 </BODY>
</HTML>
```

The resulting display is shown in Figure 2.6.

FIGURE 2.6:

An HTML document with an embedded image

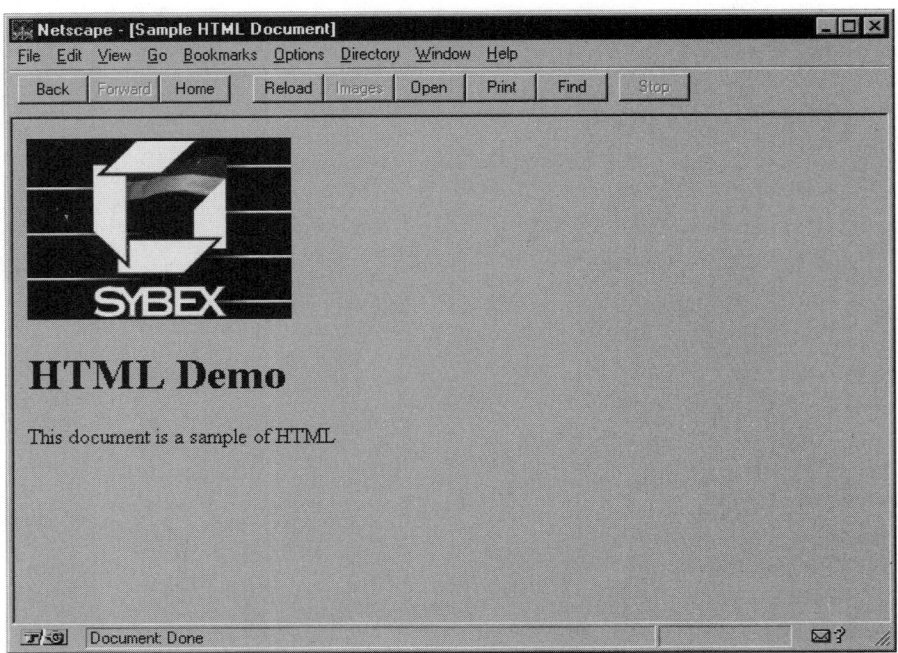

> **NOTE**
>
> Web browsers can display image files in GIF and JPEG. GIF means Graphics Interchange Format, and JPEG stands for Joint Photographic Experts Group, the group that created it. Most browsers also support animated and transparent GIF images (also known as GIF89a format). All of these formats are supported by the Core API. In the future, other graphics formats will be supported via Extension APIs.

If you want to connect this page to another document via a hypertext link, you must insert an *anchor* tag (<A>). Everything between the anchor tag and the end anchor tag will be highlighted, so the user knows that the highlighted text or graphics can be clicked on. The following will build a hypertext link to Sun's Java home page in the sample document:

```
<HTML>
<HEAD>
<TITLE>Sample HTML Document</TITLE>
```

```
</HEAD>
<BODY>
 <IMG SRC="sybex.gif">
 <H1>HTML Demo</H1>
 This document is a sample of HTML.
 <P>
 You can get the Java Development Kit from the
 <A HREF="http://java.sun.com">Sun's Java Home Page</A>.
 </BODY>
</HTML>
```

The paragraph tag (<P>) makes the text easier to read. A Web browser ignores excess spaces and new lines when displaying a document, so if you need to break a line or begin a new paragraph, you must insert <BR> or <P> tags as necessary. Now the HTML document has text, graphics, and a link, as shown in Figure 2.7.

FIGURE 2.7:

A sample HTML document including text, an image, and a hypertext link

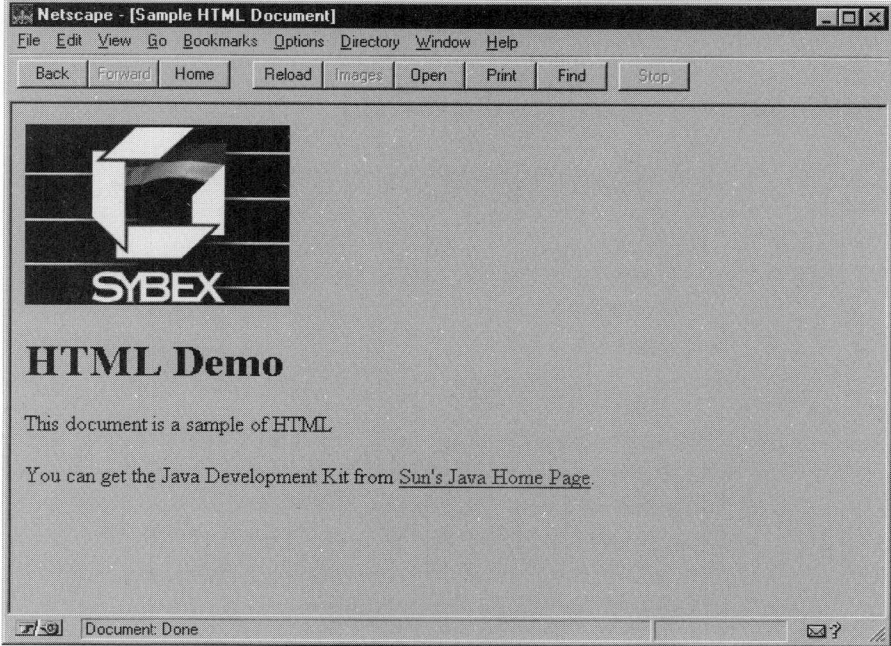

Adding a Java applet to an HTML document is quite straightforward. There is an <APPLET> tag that specifies the location of the class file and the display area allocated to the applet. Suppose you want to add a Clock applet that will display the current time in hours, minutes, and seconds. A compiled Clock applet, called Clock.class, is included on the CD-ROM accompanying this book. Here is a simple example of an <APPLET> tag that loads the Clock applet:

```
<APPLET CODE="Clock.class" WIDTH=200 HEIGHT=60> </APPLET>
```

When a browser encounters these tags, it will start the VM and ask it to load Clock.class. It also tells the VM that the applet may draw in a region that is 200 × 60 pixels. The location of the <APPLET> tag in the document determines the coordinate of the top left of the applet's display area. Add the line to load the Clock applet to the HTML file:

```
<HTML>
 <HEAD>
  <TITLE>Sample HTML Document</TITLE>
 </HEAD>
 <BODY>
  <IMG SRC="sybex.gif">
  <H1>HTML Demo</H1>
  This document is a sample of HTML.
  <P>
  You can get the Java Development Kit from
  <A HREF="http://java.sun.com">Sun's Java Home Page</A>.
  <P>
  <APPLET CODE="Clock.class" WIDTH=200 HEIGHT=60> </APPLET>
 </BODY>
</HTML>
```

The output should look like the document in Figure 2.8.

As you can see, embedding applets into Web pages is simple. Java is able to create plug-in components that can be used by novices as well as experts. For this component strategy to work, the HTML author must be able to customize the properties and behavior of the applet via HTML. The Java programmer decides which parameters will have meaning for the applet, and the HTML author uses <PARAM> tags to pass initial parameters to the applet.

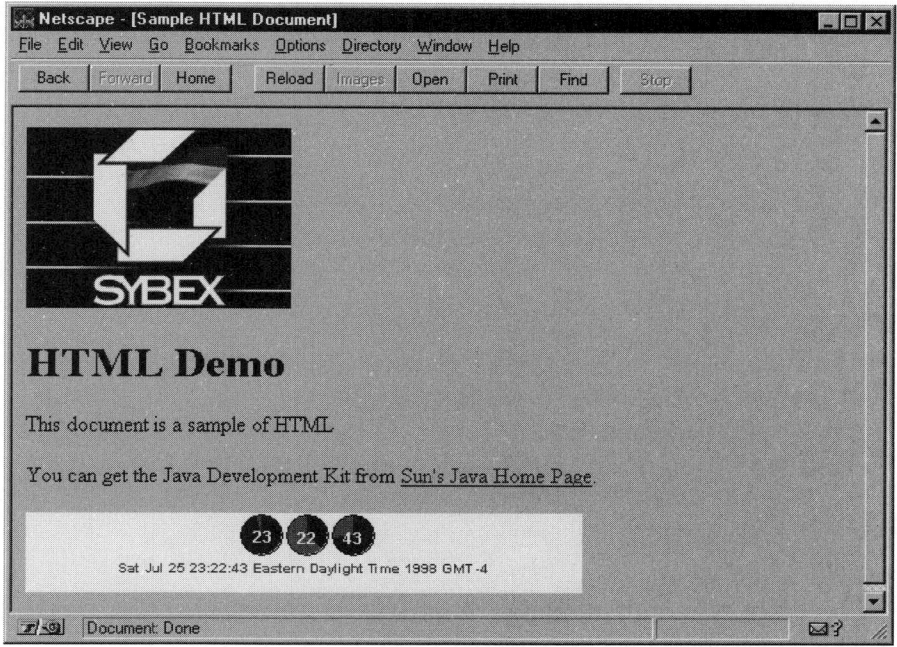

The Clock applet needs no parameters; telling the time is a universal function. On the other hand, the sample FilledBox applet needs to know what color to make the box. You can write the FilledBox applet to expect a parameter called color in the HTML using the <PARAM> tag:

```
<APPLET CODE="FilledBox.class" WIDTH=50 HEIGHT=50>
<PARAM NAME=color VALUE="blue">
</APPLET>
```

The <PARAM> tag accepts two arguments: NAME and VALUE. The NAME argument is used to specify the name of the parameter, and the VALUE argument defines its value. As far as Java is concerned, all parameters are String objects, although they can be converted to any other Java datatype quite easily. The output of the FilledBox applet is shown in Figure 2.9. Notice that only the applet is displayed.

FIGURE 2.9:

The appletviewer running
the FilledBox applet from
`FilledBox.html`

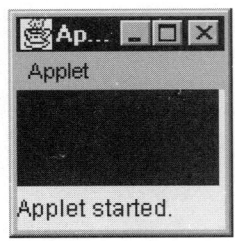

If the Web browser includes a Java VM, it will display the applet and ignore everything but the <PARAM> tags, which lie between <APPLET> and </APPLET>. Web browsers that are not Java-enabled, or have Java disabled, will ignore the <APPLET> and <PARAM> tags and display any valid HTML between the <APPLET> and </APPLET> tags. This allows you to provide an alternative for non–Java-enabled browsers, which is important because some users cannot (or choose not to) run Java applets. If you want your Web page to be accessible to everyone, you need to make it readable by non-Java platforms.

Web Browser Applet Processing

A Java-enabled Web browser follows a specific series of steps when it encounters an <APPLET> tag in an HTML document:

1. The browser reserves space in the document for displaying the applet. The WIDTH and HEIGHT parameters of the <APPLET> tag determine the amount of space used by the applet.

2. The browser reads the parameters from the <PARAM> tags.

3. The VM starts and is asked to load and initialize the applet. The applet has access to the names and values in the <PARAM> tags.

4. The VM creates a running copy of the applet based on the class file.

5. The browser calls the applet's `init` method so the applet will initialize itself.

6. The VM calls the `start` method of the applet when it is ready for the applet to start processing. It also calls `paint` to draw the applet in the browser window.

7. Whenever the applet needs to be redrawn (for example, when the user scrolls the applet into view), the browser calls the applet's `paint` method.

8. The browser calls the `stop` method when the user moves on to another HTML document.

9. The browser calls the `destroy` method when it clears the applet out of memory.

Java Applet Source Code

Java applet source code is written in the same way as Java application source code—with a text editor. The difference is that Java applets do not have a `main` method. Instead, they have several other methods that are called by the VM when requested by the browser. Here is the source code for the simple `FilledBox` applet:

```java
import java.awt.*;
import java.applet.Applet;
/** FilledBox displays a filled, colored box in the browser window
*/
public class FilledBox extends Applet {
  // This variable stores the color specified in the HTML document
  Color boxColor;
  /** Get the box color from the host HTML file
   */
  public void init() {
    String s;
    s = getParameter("color");
    // The default color is gray
    boxColor = Color.gray;

    // We expect a parameter called color, which will have
    // the value red, white, or blue. If the parameter
    // is missing, s will be null
    if (s != null) {
      if (s.equals("red")) boxColor = Color.red;
      if (s.equals("white")) boxColor = Color.white;
      if (s.equals("blue")) boxColor = Color.blue;
    }
  }

  /** Paint the box in region assigned to the applet.
   *  Use the color specified in the HTML document
   */
```

```
public void paint(Graphics g) {
  g.setColor (boxColor);
  g.fillRect (0, 0, size().width, size().height);
}
}
```

It's a little more complicated than the Java application example, but that is because it does more. You will recall that a main method is required by all Java applications; it is conspicuously absent in this applet. In fact, Java applets do not have any required methods at all. However, there are five methods that the VM may call when requested by the Web browser (or appletviewer):

public void init()   Initializes the applet. Called only once.

public void start()   Called when the browser is ready to start executing the initialized applet. Can be called multiple times if user keeps leaving and returning to the Web page. Also called when browser deiconified.

public void stop()   Called when the browser wishes to stop executing the applet. Called whenever the user leaves the Web page. Also called when browser iconified.

public void destroy()   Called when the browser clears the applet out of memory.

public void paint(Graphics g)   Called whenever the browser needs to redraw the applet.

If the applet does not implement any of these methods, the applet will have no functionality for the specific method not implemented. In the example, init and paint are implemented. The init function obtains the desired box color from a parameter in the host document (applet parameters were explained previously in "HTML for Java Applets"). The paint method draws the filled box in the browser window.

Save this Java applet source as FilledBox.java.

Using *javac*

The javac compiler works the same on applets as it does on Java applications:

```
javac FilledBox.java
```

Here are a few tips that may help you get started. First, applet classes must always be declared `public` or they will not get compiled. Also, remember that Java is case-sensitive; `filledbox.java` is *not* the same as `FilledBox.java` and will not be compiled.

If the Java code is acceptable to the compiler, the only message you will see is about a deprecated API:

```
Note: FilledBox.java uses a deprecated API. Recompile with
"-deprecation" for details.
1 warning.
```

For now, ignore the warning. As long as there were no error messages, the file `FilledBox.class` will be created. If there were error messages, you need to go back and fix your code. There are many different types of error messages that the compiler may generate when given a source file. The simplest to fix are syntax errors, such as a missing semicolon or closing brace. Other messages will highlight incorrect use of variable types, invalid expressions, or violation access restrictions. Getting your source code to compile is only the first part of the debugging process; error-free compilation does not guarantee that your program will do what you want. But don't worry about debugging just yet; this example is simple enough that it should run without any problems.

> **NOTE**
>
> Between Java 1.0 and Java 1.1, several method names were renamed. Until everyone upgrades their browsers to support the Java 1.1 version, it still may be necessary to use 1.0 methods. If you happen to be using a 1.1-compliant browser, you can change the `size()` calls to `getSize()` to remove the warning message.

Before you can run your applet, you must create an HTML document to host it.

Creating an HTML File

Now that you know a little about HTML, it is easy to create a simple HTML file to host your applet:

```
<HTML>
 <HEAD>
  <TITLE>Sample HTML Document With Filled Box</TITLE>
 </HEAD>
 <BODY>
  <H1>FilledBox Demo</H1>
```

```
<P>
<APPLET CODE="FilledBox.class" WIDTH=50 HEIGHT=50>
<PARAM NAME=color VALUE="blue">
</APPLET>
</BODY>
</HTML>
```

You can create this file by simply typing it into a text editor. Save the file as FilledBox.html. HTML files can be named anything you like, although it is common practice to name them after the applets they host.

WARNING   If you name the .html file after the applet and then run javadoc on the source code, the .html file will be overwritten.

Using *appletviewer*

The appletviewer utility is used to display the applet as it would be seen by the browser without displaying any of the HTML document itself. In the case of FilledBox.html, appletviewer will display a filled box in its own window:

```
appletviewer FilledBox.html
```

Refer back to Figure 2.9 to see the output. For comparison, you can open the file FilledBox.html using a Java-enabled Web browser. Figure 2.10 shows this output as it would be seen by Netscape Navigator. Both the applet and the text are displayed.

If there is more than one applet in a page, appletviewer will open a separate window for each applet; a Web browser will show them in their respective locations within the same Web page. One rather nice feature of appletviewer is that it can load classes from across the network, not just from files. Just give appletviewer the URL of the HTML document containing one or more applets, and it will load the applets as if they were on your local disk. Note, however, that the SecurityManager for the appletviewer may expose your system to greater risks from network-loaded applets than would a Web browser like Netscape Navigator.

FIGURE 2.10:

Netscape Navigator
displaying the file
FilledBox.html

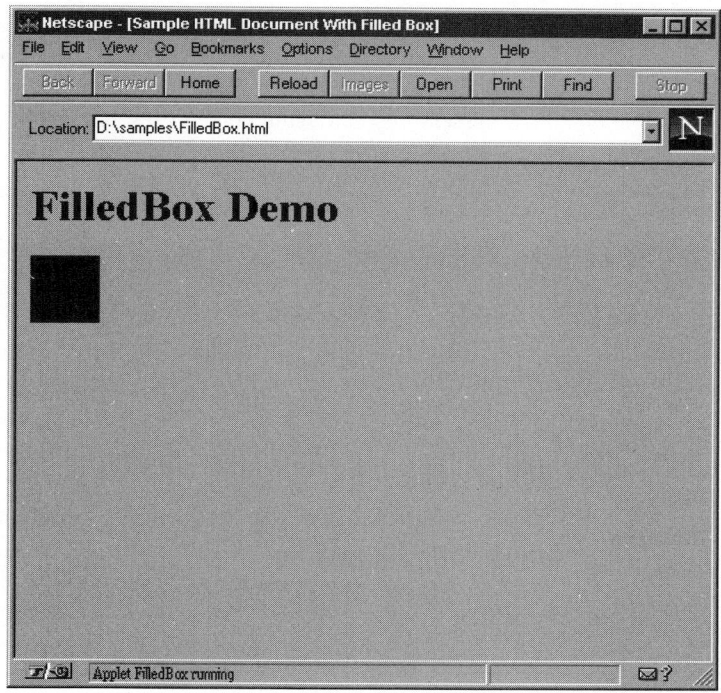

appletviewer makes it possible to distribute and run Java applets without the aid of a Web browser, so the choice between writing applets versus applications becomes less critical. Most applets are easy to convert into applications and vice versa. The key to this convertibility is to avoid placing a lot of code directly in the main, init, start, stop, and destroy methods, and use calls to generic methods instead.

Using *javadoc* and *javah*

The javadoc and javah utilities work on applet source code, too. The command lines are just like the application command lines:

```
javadoc FilledBox.java
```

and

```
javah FilledBox.class
```

> **TIP**
>
> Because we commented this example code well, `javadoc` will produce useful results. This will make maintenance of the code easier, as the comments explain what all of the code does. Although this is not critical for a simple applet like this, it is a valuable lesson to remember as you go on to more complicated applets.

Delivering Applications with the Java Runtime Environment (JRE)

The Java Runtime Environment (JRE) is something first introduced with Java 1.1. If you want to distribute a Java application, you need to provide users with a Java platform to run the program. The JRE is just such a program; it provides a Java VM for users to execute your application. You can either package the JRE with your application or let them download it separately. Either way, they should only need to install the JRE once for all the Java applications they want to run. By distributing the JRE, you are assured that the user of your application has a compatible Java VM.

> **TIP**
>
> You can also download it free from Sun's Java Web site. For software development, the JRE is not necessary; however, it is required for application distribution.

What's New in JDK 1.2

If you're already familiar with writing programs with JDK 1.1, there really aren't any changes with creating general applets and applications with Java 1.2. However, if you happen to be transitioning from a Java 1.0 environment, you may have noticed some changes introduced with the 1.1 release. Here we present a brief list of these changes, most of which will be dealt with in detail in later chapters. This list consists of changes that affect the JDK tools; it is not meant to be a comprehensive list of the new features of Java 1.2:

(appletviewer) <APPLET> tag changes   The tag used to load Java applets has been modified. You can now specify resources and other objects to be loaded along with the applet.

(javac) @deprecated tag   The `javac` compiler will now warn you if you use methods that were supported in previous releases of the JDK but are not the preferred ones in the current release. For a complete list of deprecated methods, see `http://java.sun.com/products/jdk/1.2/docs/api/deprecated-list.html`.

(jar) Java archives   Java classes and resources, such as images and sounds, can now be bundled into compressed archives called JAR files. This facilitates digital signing and reduces download time.

(javah) New native method interface   The interface for calling native methods has been reworked and standardized across all platforms.

The code signing tools changed between Java 1.1 and 1.2. In Java 1.1, `javakey` managed everything, now there are three tools:

(keytool) Java key generator   The program used to generate keys to digitally sign classes.

(jarsigner) Java archive signer   The program used to digitally sign class and JAR files so that they can be authenticated.

(policytool) Security policy manager   Application to assist in configuring the security policy for a user or installation.

Two brand new tools introduced with Java 1.2 are specific to some very advanced concepts. The Interface Definition Language (IDL) support tools will be discussed in Chapter 26, while the RMI support tool will be discussed in Chapter 25.

(tnameserv) IDL Transient Name Server   The name server needs to be started before CORBA COS (Common Object Services) naming services can be used.

(rmid) RMI activation system daemon   The daemon needs to be started before using activatable RMI objects.

The 1.2 JDK also includes a Just-in-Time (JIT) bytecode compiler to increase performance. It is enabled by default. To disable, either set the `JAVA_COMPILER` environment variable to NONE or run the program by setting the `java.compiler` system property to NONE.

```
java -Djava.compiler=NONE MyAppClass
appletviewer -J-Djava.compiler=NONE myapplet.html
```

Summary

This chapter explained the differences between Java applets and Java applications. Although their initialization processes and context differ, you will find that the practical aspects of Java programming do not change. Indeed, it is usually easy to convert an applet into an application and vice versa (as long as the applet does not require services built into a browser).

After downloading and installing the JDK, and following the examples presented in this chapter, you should have no problem running the demos and examples provided with the JDK and the CD-ROM. Several third-party compilers and development environments (such as Symantec's Visual Café, Borland's JBuilder, and IBM's VisualAge for Java) are also available, if you prefer an integrated development environment over the command-line tools of the JDK.

Working with Java Objects

- Object-oriented programming (OOP) data structures and classes

- Simplifying code with polymorphism

- Defining constructors for classes

- Using finalizers for cleanup before garbage collection

The object-oriented programming (OOP) paradigm has swept through the software industry over the last decade, bringing with it advances in programmer productivity, software reuse, and maintainability. OOP is now considered "best practice" in the development business. A fully object-oriented language, Java requires a thorough understanding of object-orientation to be effective. To that end, this chapter begins with an introduction to OOP.

An Introduction to OOP

At its core, OOP is simply a way of thinking about problems and their solutions. Instead of tackling programs in a top-down, linear fashion (as with traditional programming languages such as Pascal or C), OOP attempts to break a problem into its component parts. The solution focuses on these independent *objects* and their relationships to other objects. This approach is better suited to most tasks because most problems are complex and multifaceted and do not conform easily to a linear approach.

Classes of objects closely resemble structures and record types in non-OOP languages, so this section starts by reviewing simple data structures and by looking at the software development problems inherent in structures. To maintain continuity with the sample code presented in this chapter, as well as to provide an illustrative example of OOP, these concepts will be applied to the design of an air traffic control system.

> **NOTE**   Although C++ is an OOP language, it also supports non–object-oriented techniques. Because C++ and Java syntax are so similar, the examples of non–object-oriented code are in C++.

Data Structures

In almost all programming languages, data is stored in variables that have a specific *datatype*; for example, integer datatypes hold whole numbers, character datatypes hold individual alphanumeric characters, and string datatypes hold groups of alphanumeric characters. Many languages also allow you to create your own datatypes by grouping several simple datatypes together. In C++, these "compound" datatypes are *structures*; in Pascal, they are *record types*. Here is a sample structure written in C++ that represents an aircraft's flight segment:

```
struct Flight {
  int    altitude;
  int    heading;
  int    speed;
  float  latitude;
  float  longitude;
}
```

The Flight structure is a new datatype made up of built-in C/C++ types, namely integers and floating-point numbers. The components of a structure (the integers and floating-point numbers, in this example) are *members*. The Flight structure could also contain members for the destination of the flight, the type of aircraft, and other pieces of information, but the members listed here are sufficient for these examples.

The structure itself stores no information; it is only a pattern for creating new Flight variables. To declare a new Flight variable called incomingFlight, you would use the following code:

```
struct Flight incomingFlight;
```

You access the members of incomingFlight by using the name of the Flight variable followed by a period and the name of the member:

```
incomingFlight.altitude = 3000;
if (incomingFlight.heading < 180) { … }
```

In Pascal or Visual Basic, you would use similar code to create the Flight structure and to access member variables.

In non-OOP (structure-specific programming, referred to here as *structure-oriented code*), the code that accesses the Flight variables is separate and specific to the datatype. For example, a C++ routine that represents a turn of an aircraft might be declared as follows:

```
void turnFlight (Flight &aFlight, int angle) {
  aFlight.heading = (aFlight.heading + angle) % 360;
  // make sure angle is in the range 0-359 degrees
  if (aFlight.heading < 0)
    aFlight.heading = aFlight.heading + 360;
}
```

The turnFlight routine expects to be given variables that are Flight and int datatypes, respectively. Turning an incoming flight 90 degrees to the right is now achieved with this code:

```
turnFlight (incomingFlight, 90);
```

You could write similar routines to descend the aircraft and display it on a computer screen. Figure 3.1 shows a schematic representation of this code and data structure.

FIGURE 3.1:

A schematic view of the Flight data structure and the code that references it

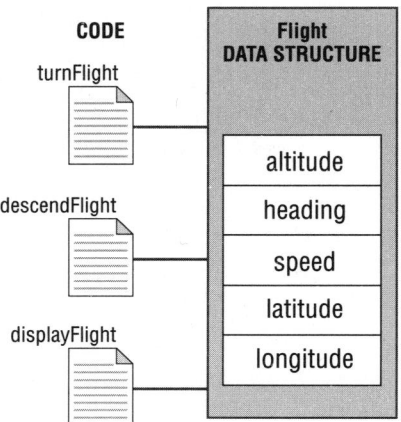

The next step is to model commercial flights. You create a new structure called CommercialFlight that includes everything that the Flight structure included, plus the flight number and number of passengers:

```
struct CommercialFlight {
    // extra members in CommercialFlight
    int     flightNumber;
    int     passengers;
    // members in Flight
    int     altitude;
    int     heading;
    int     speed;
    float   latitude;
    float   longitude;
}
```

Again, to create a CommercialFlight variable called incomingCommercialFlight, you could simply type:

```
struct CommercialFlight incomingCommercialFlight;
```

However, the routines written for generic flights will not work with Commercial-Flight variables because CommercialFlight variables have no relationship to Flight variables. For example, the compiler will not allow you to use the turnFlight routine with a CommercialFlight variable. Therefore, the following call is illegal:

```
turnFlight (incomingCommercialFlight, 90);
```

Figure 3.2 shows a schematic representation of the CommercialFlight datatype and its functions.

FIGURE 3.2:

The Flight and CommercialFlight data structures and associated routines

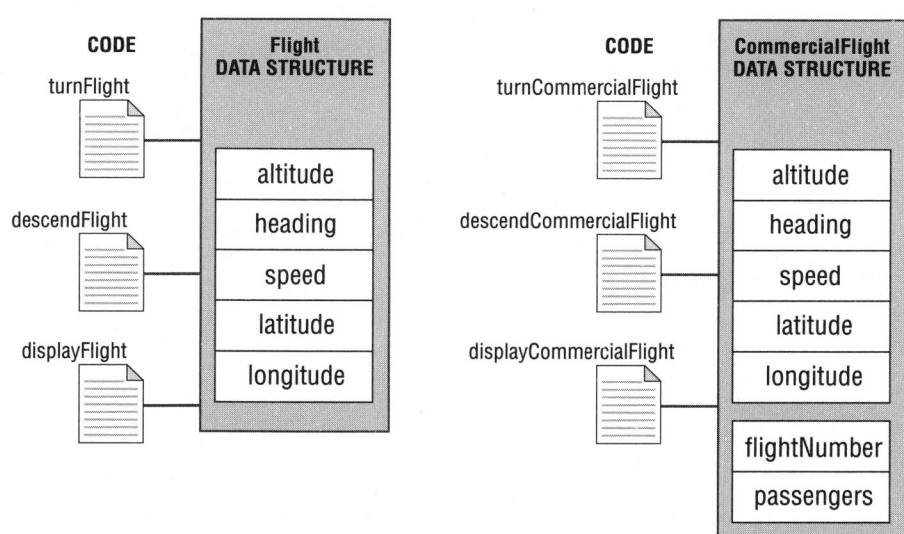

Although you can use tricks to circumvent the datatype problem, they make the code harder to read, more complex, and less reliable. The only safe alternative is to create a new routine for commercial flights called turnCommercialFlight:

```
void turnCommercialFlight (CommercialFlight &aFlight,
                           int angle) {
```

```
aFlight.heading = (aFlight.heading + angle) % 360;
// make sure angle is in the range 0-359 degrees
if (aFlight.heading < 0)
   aFlight.heading = aFlight.heading + 360;
}
```

However, this kind of code duplication presents a maintenance problem. If changes need to be made for 10 different structures, 10 different routines need to be modified. Not only is this hard work, but it is also an opportunity to introduce additional defects into the code.

Maintenance is only one of several problems with non-OOP structures. Traditional structures are also difficult to use more than once. Structures and their associated routines can quickly become entangled, making it difficult for someone to extract the required code for reuse in a new program. In effect, these entanglements force programmers to look at every detail of the original code in order to use it as part of a new piece of program. To avoid this, developers must exercise a lot of discipline to keep the interface of a structure and its routines—in other words, the parts that need to be used by future applications—separate from the details of their implementation.

Finally, structure-oriented code has some inherent safety flaws. In the previous examples, routines were created to turn aircraft by any angle. These routines guaranteed that the angle would always be between 0 and 359 degrees, inclusive. However, with structures, nothing stops a programmer who is unfamiliar with the design from bypassing the turnFlight routine and entering the following code:

```
// right turn 90 degrees
incomingFlight.heading = incomingFlight.heading + 90;
```

Although the code may be essentially correct, it may lead to headings greater than 359 degrees. This, in turn, may break some other part of the code that assumes all angles will be in the range 0–359 degrees. This lack of data protection also contributes to the fragility of source code.

NOTE From this point forward, Java source code, not C++ source code, is used. But note that in many cases, the two may appear similar.

From Structures to Classes: Encapsulation

In OOP, the routines for a structure and the structure itself are combined, or *encapsulated*, into a single entity called a *class*. Here is the Java source code for a Flight class, an object-oriented version of the Flight structure:

```
class Flight {
    int     altitude;
    int     heading;
    int     speed;
    float   latitude;
    float   longitude;
    // change the flight's heading by angle degrees
    void turnFlight (int angle) {
      heading = (heading + angle) % 360;
      // make sure angle is in the range 0-359 degrees
      if (heading < 0)
        heading = heading + 360;
    }
    // print information about the flight
    void printFlight() {
      System.out.println (altitude + "/" + heading + "/" + speed);
    }
}
```

The turnFlight routine is now a *member function* of the class; that is, the routine is part of the structure itself. You will notice that the code for the function is actually a little cleaner because you no longer need to refer to the heading as a member of a dummy variable—the variable aFlight has been eliminated altogether. The routine now also includes a member function, printFlight, that prints some flight information on the console.

NOTE   Member functions are more properly referred to as *methods*, although other terms are often used.

Just as with the structure definition, this class definition is a pattern, or template, for variables to be created with the Flight class datatype. Variables with the Flight class datatype are called Flight *objects* (hence the name object-oriented programming). An object is a storage variable that is created based on a class. Objects are said to be an *instance* of a class. Classes define the variables and routines that are members of all objects of that class. This may sound confusing if you've never worked with objects before, but a look at how the sample `Flight` class is applied will help you get a feel for using objects.

The next step is to create a `Flight` object variable based on the `Flight` class (this process is often referred to as *instantiation*). An *object variable* is a reference to an object; creating a reference to an object and creating the object itself are two separate steps. To create the object variable, use:

```
Flight incomingFlight;
```

The `Flight` variable can have two possible kinds of values: `null` or a `Flight` object. The default value of the previous `incomingFlight` is `null`; it is simply a name and does not yet refer to any object. To create an object referenced by `incomingFlight`, use the `new` operator:

```
incomingFlight = new Flight();
```

Now `incomingFlight` refers to a new `Flight` object, and you can access its member variables:

```
incomingFlight.altitude = 2500;
if (incomingFlight.heading < 180) { … }
```

Methods are called in an analogous way:

```
incomingFlight.turnFlight (90);
```

To understand how this works, imagine that `incomingFlight` points to an object that understands how to turn itself, and that you are sending a message to the object, asking it to turn right by 90 degrees. In fact, in OOP systems, all objects interact by sending messages to each other. The object-oriented equivalent of Figure 3.1 now looks like Figure 3.3.

Encapsulation also allows you to use *data hiding*, which is a way to prevent direct access to the variables in an object. This can force other objects to use methods to alter or read data in member variables, rather than accessing them directly. This is a key strength of encapsulation: It separates the interface to the class from its implementation, so you do not need to know the implementation details of the class to safely reuse the code. You can modify the `Flight` class to hide the `heading` member variable by using the `private` keyword:

```
class Flight {
    int    altitude;
```

FIGURE 3.3:

The Flight data structure and associated routines as an encapsulated class

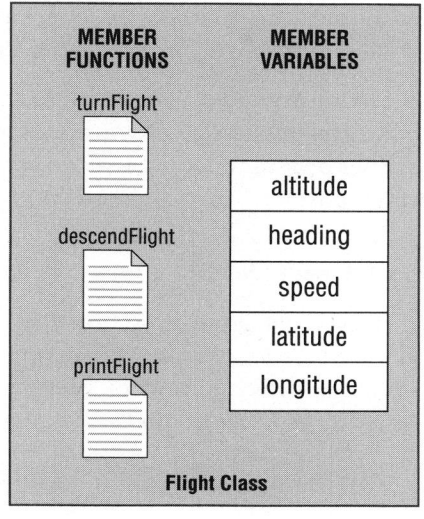

```
private int    heading;
int    speed;
float  latitude;
float  longitude;
void turnFlight (int angle) {
  heading = (heading + angle) % 360;
  // make sure angle is in the range 0-359 degrees
  if (heading < 0)
    heading = heading + 360;
}
void setHeading (int angle) {
  heading = angle % 360;
  // make sure angle is in the range 0-359 degrees
  if (heading < 0)
    heading = heading + 360;
}
int getHeading() {
  return heading;
}
void printFlight() {
  System.out.println (altitude + "/" + heading + "/" + speed);
}
}
```

Now that the `heading` variable is private and hidden to code outside the class, two additional functions are needed: `setHeading`, in order to set the heading, and `getHeading`, to obtain the current heading.

It is generally good practice to hide as many variables as possible. This separates the implementation of your class from its interface, making it more difficult for another programmer to break your code by bypassing the safety measures in your methods.

Class Inheritance

Using classes instead of structures also solves the problem of code duplication. Recall that for extended structures, such as `CommercialFlight`, you need to create a new copy of each function that acts on the original structure (`Flight`). With classes, you can inherit both the data members and methods when creating a new class:

```
class CommercialFlight extends Flight {
  // extra members in CommercialFlight
  int    flightNumber;
  int    passengers;
}
```

The `CommercialFlight` class, a *subclass* of `Flight`, automatically inherits all the data members and methods of the `Flight` class, so you can write:

```
CommercialFlight incomingCommercialFlight;
incomingCommercialFlight = new CommercialFlight();
incomingCommercialFlight.altitude = 2500;
incomingCommercialFlight.setHeading (45);
incomingCommercialFlight.flightNumber = 101;
incomingCommercialFlight.passengers = 24;
```

As you can see, inheritance makes life much easier. It also makes code more maintainable because the code to alter the heading of both a `Flight` and a `Commercial-Flight` is all in one place, namely in the definition of the parent or *base class*. Figure 3.4 shows a schematic for the relationship of class and subclass.

In many cases, you will want a subclass to override one or more methods of a parent class. Continuing with the example, you may want a commercial flight to print in a special way on the console, displaying the flight number in addition

FIGURE 3.4:

The CommercialFlight class inherits member variables and functions from Flight and then adds its own member variables.

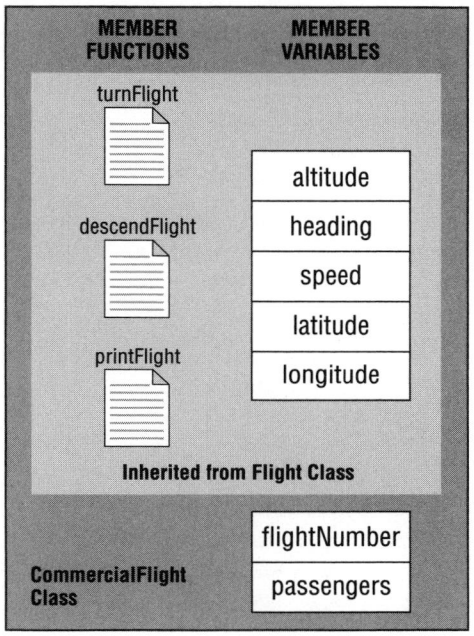

to other information. You can easily override the printFlight routine of the Flight class by reimplementing it in the CommercialFlight class:

```
class Flight {
  int    altitude;
  private int    heading;
  int    speed;
  float  latitude;
  float  longitude;
  void turnFlight (int angle) {
    heading = (heading + angle) % 360;
    // make sure angle is in the range 0-359 degrees
    if (heading < 0)
      heading = heading + 360;
  }
  void setHeading (int angle) {
    heading = angle % 360;
    // make sure angle is in the range 0-359 degrees
    if (heading < 0)
```

```
          heading = heading + 360;
    }
    int getHeading() {
      return heading;
    }
    // print the flight's altitude, heading and speed on the console
    void printFlight() {
      System.out.println (altitude + " ft / " + heading
                                   + " degrees / " + speed + " knots");
    }
}
class CommercialFlight extends Flight {
    // extra members in CommercialFlight
    int flightNumber;
    int passengers;
    // reimplement the printFlight routine to
    // override the previous definition
    void printFlight() {
      System.out.print ("Flight " + flightNumber + " ");
      super.printFlight();
    }
}
```

Notice that the new `printFlight` method calls `super.printFlight()`. The `super` keyword refers to the *superclass* of `CommercialFlight` (in this case, the `Flight` class) and so `super.printFlight()` is a call to the original `printFlight` function as defined in the `Flight` class. You will often see the `super` keyword used when overriding methods because the overriding function usually implements supplementary processing—it does all its parent class did and more.

If you call a `Flight` object's `printFlight` function:

```
incomingFlight.printFlight();
```

you will get output like the following:

```
 2500 ft / 270 degrees / 240 knots
```

If you call a commercial flight's `printFlight` routine:

```
incomingCommercialFlight.printFlight();
```

the output might look like the following:

```
 Flight 101 3000 ft / 185 degrees / 350 knots
```

Figure 3.5 shows how the CommercialFlight class reimplements the printFlight function.

FIGURE 3.5:

The CommercialFlight class inherits member variables and functions from Flight, adds its own member variables, and overrides the printFlight function.

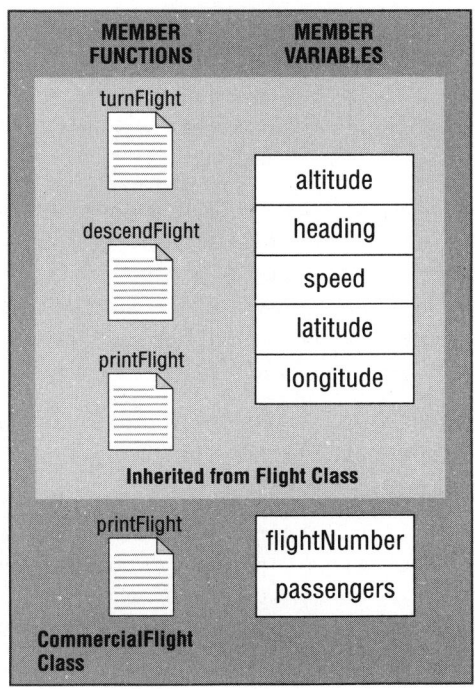

It is sometimes advantageous to use inheritance even when the base class is so generic that it cannot be implemented. You can do this using the concept of abstract classes.

Abstract Classes

This section describes how to incorporate air traffic control facilities into the example by including classes for flight control towers (for aircraft flying, landing, and taking off) and ground control towers (for taxiing aircraft). To begin, you create ControlFacility as a parent class, and then create FlightControlTower and GroundControlTower as subclasses. Then create a method called getClearance, which is called to see if a facility will clear a flight for landing, taking off, taxiing, and so on. However, you cannot create a generic ControlFacility object because you cannot implement getClearance without knowing whether you control space on the ground or in the air. On the other hand, you still want to insist that every subclass of ControlFacility implements the getClearance method.

The solution to this dilemma is provided by Java's ability to define *abstract classes*. The code for the ControlFacility class illustrates how abstract classes work:

```
abstract class ControlFacility {
  abstract boolean getClearance (FlightAction request);
}
```

In this piece of code, you declare your new class and the getClearance method function that returns a boolean (true or false) value. The function will accept an object of a class named FlightAction (which is not defined here; it is just part of the illustration). However, the function is defined as abstract, and it has no implementation. Any class that has such abstract functions is said to be an *abstract class*, and no objects of such classes can ever be created.

The FlightControlTower and GroundControlTower subclasses must implement the getClearance function so you can create objects that represent such facilities:

```
class FlightControlTower extends ControlFacility {
  boolean getClearance (FlightAction request) {
    // implementation of the getClearance function for
    // flight control towers
    .
    .
    .
  }
}
class GroundControlTower extends ControlFacility {
  boolean getClearance (FlightAction request) {
    // implementation of the getClearance function for
    // ground control towers
    .
    .
    .
  }
}
```

Since both these subclasses—FlightControlTower and GroundControlTower— implement the abstract functions defined in the parent class, they are not abstract classes and can both be instantiated. In addition to formalizing the interface, abstract classes give the programmer other advantages, which are discussed in the next section.

Polymorphism

Polymorphic functions are functions that do not care which variable types are passed to them. The PRINT statement in BASIC and the writeln statement in Pascal are examples of polymorphic routines because you can pass any type of variable to them and they always act appropriately. Standard BASIC does not need a PRINTINTEGER or PRINTSTRING statement because PRINT is smart enough to take care of any datatype. However, the PRINT statement has this ability specially coded into the BASIC interpreter, and its ability does not extend to user-defined structures. BASIC also has no provision for creating user-defined polymorphic routines.

Java makes it possible for programmers to simplify their code with polymorphism in three ways:

Inheritance Allowing subclasses to automatically inherit methods from their parent classes. Also, any method that accepts a particular class as an argument will also accept any subclass of that class as an argument.

Overloading Implementing identically named methods that take different arguments within the same class.

Interfacing Implementing identically named methods that take identical arguments in different classes.

Let's look at these three cases in turn.

Inheritance

Inheritance is the simplest kind of polymorphism, as well as one you have already encountered. In the air traffic control example, you can ask any Flight object or Flight-subclassed object to turn left by calling the method turnFlight (-90). This means that instead of requiring a multitude of function names like turnFlight, turnCommercialFlight, or turnMilitaryFlight (for a MilitaryFlight class), you can use turnFlight consistently:

```
incomingFlight.turnFlight (-90);
incomingCommercialFlight.turnFlight (-90);
incomingMilitaryFlight.turnFlight (-90);
```

Better still, you can easily write code that works with the Flight class and all subclasses of the Flight. For example, you can create a new class called Airport that has a method called aircraftInbound; in turn, this adds a flight to the list of inbound flights:

```
class Airport {
  String airportName;
  Flight inboundFlights[], outboundFlights[];
  void aircraftInbound (Flight aFlight) {
    //implementation of aircraftInbound function
    .
    .
    .
  }
}
```

An Airport object will now accept any Flight object or object that is a subclass of Flight. For example, you could type:

```
Airport cityAirport;
cityAirport = new Airport();
cityAirport.airportName = "City National Airport";
cityAirport.aircraftInbound (incomingFlight);
cityAirport.aircraftInbound (incomingCommercialFlight);
cityAirport.aircraftInbound (incomingMilitaryFlight);
```

Polymorphism by inheritance also allows you to take full advantage of abstract classes. Inheriting from a generic abstract class allows you to group together classes that share common functions but not common implementation. Having created the abstract class ControlFacility in the previous section, you can now write code that refers to ControlFacility objects and works with all subclasses of ControlFacility, even though ControlFacility objects themselves can never be created.

Overloading

Another way to add polymorphic functions is known as *function overloading*. In Java, C++, and other languages that support function overloading, it is possible to define the same function twice while using different parameters for each definition. For example, in the previous listing, the aircraftInbound function does the same thing no matter which subclass of Flight is passed to it. Suppose you want to add inbound aircraft to the Airport class's list of the inbound flights with different priorities according to the type of flight. By overloading the `aircraftInbound` function, you can customize its behavior for each kind of `Flight` object:

```
class Airport {
  String airportName;
  Flight inboundFlights[], outboundFlights[];
  // aircraftInbound function accepting Flight objects
  void aircraftInbound (Flight aFlight) {
    // implementation of aircraftInbound function for
    // generic flights
    .
    .
    .
  }
  // aircraftInbound function accepting CommercialFlight objects
  void aircraftInbound (CommercialFlight aFlight) {
    // implementation of aircraftInbound function for commercial
    // flights
    .
    .
    .
  }
  // aircraftInbound function accepting MilitaryFlight objects
  void aircraftInbound (MilitaryFlight aFlight) {
    // implementation of aircraftInbound function for
    // military flights
    .
    .
    .
  }
}
```

NOTE Note that the method signature for polymorphic methods does not include the return type. You cannot have two methods with the same name and parameter list that have different return types.

Just as before, you call the function identically, no matter which type of `Flight` object is passed to the function:

```
Airport cityAirport;
cityAirport = new Airport();
```

```
cityAirport.aircraftInbound (incomingFlight);
cityAirport.aircraftInbound (incomingCommercialFlight);
cityAirport.aircraftInbound (incomingMilitaryFlight);
```

Polymorphism can be achieved by implementing the same methods in different classes, a technique called *interfacing*.

NOTE   Overloading is not a feature of object-oriented languages per se although it is most commonly implemented in object-oriented languages.

Interfacing

Suppose you need to create a report that lists both airports and all their incoming and outgoing flights. You can do this by writing a `printOnReport` function for both the `Airport` and `Flight` classes:

```
class Airport {
   String airportName;
   Flight inboundFlights[], outboundFlights[];
   // printOnReport function prints an Airport entry on the report
   void printOnReport() {
      System.out.println ("Airport: " + airportName);
   }
}
class Flight {
   int     altitude;
   private int     heading;
   int     speed;
   float   latitude;
   float   longitude;
   // print the flight's altitude, heading, and speed on the console
   void printOnReport() {
      System.out.println("Flight: " + altitude + " ft / " + heading
                                  + " degrees / " + speed + " knots");
   }
}
```

You can call these new functions in the following way:

```
incomingFlight.printOnReport();
cityAirport.printOnReport();
```

Informally speaking, these classes now have a common interface as far as print-ing reports is concerned. Java allows you to formalize the interface so that you can guarantee that a class will support all the functions (there may be more than one) that make up an interface. By using formal interfaces, you can write a function that will accept an argument of any class that implements a particular interface.

Let's define a formal interface for the report printing example. Java's `interface` keyword is used just like the `class` keyword:

```
interface ReportPrintable {
  void printOnReport();
}
```

Note that `ReportPrintable` is not a class and cannot be instantiated; essen-tially, the methods declared in an interface are abstract. To tell the compiler that the `Airport` and `Flight` classes implement the `ReportPrintable` interface, add an `implements` clause to the class declarations:

```
class Airport implements ReportPrintable {
    .
    .
    .
}
class Flight implements ReportPrintable {
    .
    .
    .
}
```

Next, you can create a `ReportGenerator` class that creates a report from any object that implements the `ReportPrintable` interface:

```
class ReportGenerator {
    void addToReport (ReportPrintable anObject) {
        anObject.printOnReport();
    }
}
```

The `addToReport` function of `ReportGenerator` will accept *any* class that implements the `ReportPrintable` interface.

As you can see, polymorphism greatly simplifies writing code, especially when modeling complex, real-world situations. The programmer does not need to remem-ber as many function names, and the source code becomes much more readable.

Constructors and Finalizers

You can define two special kinds of methods:

> **Constructors**   Methods that return new instances of the class. If you do not write a constructor, you can use a default constructor to create instances of the class.

> **Finalizers**   Functions that are called just before an object is garbage-collected.

The following sections describe these special methods, as well as garbage collection.

Constructors

Going back to the `Airport` class, you will recall that you created and initialized the code as follows:

```
Airport cityAirport;
cityAirport = new Airport();
cityAirport.airportName = "City National Airport";
```

After the first line, `cityAirport` has been defined as an object variable. After the second line, an object is created, and `cityAirport` refers to the object. The third line initializes the name of the `Airport` object. The function `Airport()` is the *default constructor* for the `Airport` class.

The default constructor is inherited from `Airport`'s parent class, `Object`, and it is automatically added to the class by the Java compiler. The `Object`'s constructor allocates storage for any member variables that are declared as one of Java's built-in datatypes. In this case, none of the `Airport`'s member variables are allocated because neither the `String` variable nor the `Flight` datatypes are built-in (the built-in datatypes will be discussed in the next chapter). For example, the `airportName` member object variable is `null` until you allocate space for the corresponding `String` or assign an object to it.

To simplify the object creation process, and to protect yourself from uninitialized object variables, you can create your own constructor for the `Airport` class:

```
class Airport {
    String airportName;
```

```
Flight[] inboundFlights, outboundFlights;
// a new constructor that takes no arguments
Airport() {
   super();
   airportName = "Unknown";
}
   .
   .
   .
```
}

A constructor is defined in the same way as an ordinary method, but it must have the same name as the class and have no return datatype. In this example, the constructor calls super(), which is a reference to the constructor in the parent class, Object. Writing the call to super() is optional because the compiler will implicitly call the parent class's constructor if you do not call it. You can call the new constructor exactly as you called it earlier:

```
Airport cityAirport = new Airport();
cityAirport.airportName = "City National Airport";
```

Now, after calling the new constructor, cityAirport.airportName will default to "Unknown." However, because you will always change the airport name, you can save a step by writing another constructor that creates the Airport object and sets the airportName to the caller's choice, as follows:

```
class Airport {
  String airportName;
  Flight inboundFlights[], outboundFlights[];
  // a new constructor that takes no arguments
  Airport() {
    super();
    airportName = "Unknown";
  }
  // a new constructor that takes the new airport's name as
  // an argument
  Airport (String newName) {
    super();
    airportName = newName;
  }
    .
    .
    .
```
}

This is an example of overloading: The two constructors have the same name but accept different parameters. Now you can write the following:

```
Airport cityAirport = new Airport ("City National Airport");
```

Constructors can call other constructors. You can rewrite the `Airport()` constructor so that it calls the `Airport (String newName)` constructor by using the `this` keyword:

```
// a new constructor that takes no arguments
Airport() {
    this ("Unknown");
}
```

The keyword `this` followed by parentheses (and arguments, if any) refers to a constructor for this class. In this case, the compiler knows you are referring to the `Airport (String newName)` constructor because it is the only constructor that takes a `String` as an argument. Since the different constructors of a class typically perform common tasks, you will find the ability to call other constructors very useful.

Garbage Collection

What happens when an object is no longer needed by the system? The following code and Figures 3.6 and 3.7 illustrate what "no longer needed" means:

```
cityAirport = new Airport ("City National Airport");
cityAirport = new Airport ("Potter's Field");
```

FIGURE 3.6:

The object variable `cityAirport` initially references the object representing City National Airport.

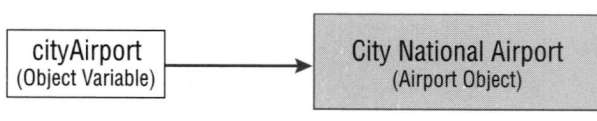

FIGURE 3.7:

The object variable then references a new object representing Potter's Field. Since there are no references to the first object, it will be automatically discarded by the garbage collector.

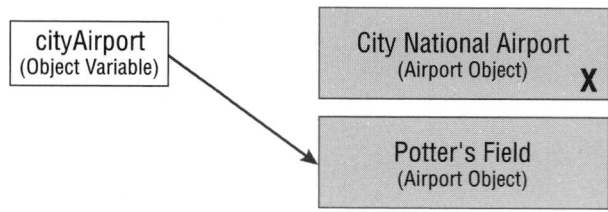

Two objects are created in this code, but only one object variable is here. After the first statement, `cityAirport` points to the object representing City National Airport. After the second statement, `cityAirport` points to the other object representing Potter's Field, and nothing points to the first object. Just as you would expect, the original object is lost from the system. Java automatically reclaims memory used by an object when no object variables refer to that object, a process known as *garbage collection*. Consider the following assignments and the corresponding Figures 3.8 and 3.9:

```
localAirport = new Airport ("City National Airport");
cityAirport = localAirport;
cityAirport = new Airport ("Potter's Field");
```

In this instance, the object representing City National Airport is not garbage-collected because `localAirport` still refers to it.

FIGURE 3.8:

The object variables `localAirport` and `cityAirport` initially reference the new object representing City National Airport.

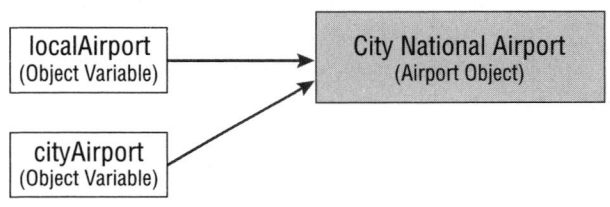

FIGURE 3.9:

Next the object variable `cityAirport` is used to refer to the new object representing Potter's Field. Since there is still a reference to the first object (`localAirport`), the original object will not be discarded by the system.

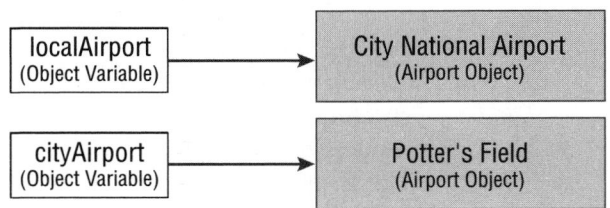

Finalizers

A few situations exist in which a class needs to clean itself up before garbage collection. It can do this by implementing a finalizer method. Finalizers are called just before a class is garbage-collected. *Finalizers* are typically used to close open files or connections, or to ensure that related tasks are completed before the object is forgotten.

To create a finalizer, simply define a method called `finalize`:

```
protected void finalize() throws Throwable {
  System.out.println ("This object is about to be garbage collected");
  super.finalize();
}
```

The protected keyword will be explained in the next chapter (it limits the classes that may call the finalizer function). The `throws Throwable` clause will be explained in Chapter 7, "Exception Handling." (It describes what to do when the unexpected happens.) The `super.finalize()` call ensures that the `finalize()` method of your superclass will be called, finalizing its part of the object.

Finalizers are rather tricky to write because it is impossible to determine exactly when an object will be garbage-collected; it could be within microseconds or, if the program is terminated, may never occur. This means that a finalizer should rely as little as possible on the existence of other objects because there is no guarantee that the other objects were not garbage-collected first. It is also possible for an object to avert its own garbage collection by creating a new reference to itself in the finalizer. Therefore, if your class must perform some shutdown or cleanup operation before being garbage-collected, you should write a non-finalizer method to take care of the operation and call that method explicitly before discarding the object.

For example, suppose you write a class called `ComLink` that handles network communications and a method called `close` that closes the network channel. You know you need to close the network channel before discarding any `ComLink` objects, so the simplest solution might appear to be calling `close` from `ComLink`'s `finalize` method. However, it is possible that `close` will not be called for an extended period of time, or perhaps not at all. This could cause the system to exhaust available network channels because channels have not been freed in a timely manner by discarded `ComLink` objects. The only reliable solution in such cases is to make sure you call the `close` function explicitly, before any objects are discarded.

Summary

OOP languages support encapsulation, inheritance, and polymorphism. Encapsulation separates the interface from the implementation by hiding data within the object and making that data accessible via methods. Subclasses inherit the methods and variables of their parent classes, making it easy to reuse the functionality in the parent class. Polymorphism allows you to create generic, reusable code that will work with a wide range of different class datatypes. Because Java supports all these features, Java code is reusable and reliable.

The Java Core API contains about 2500 prefabricated classes you can use to do everything from graphics to network programming to database access. You can use Java's object-oriented features to inherit functionality from the class library as you write your own programs. In fact, most interface-related classes will inherit much of their capability from the class library.

The next chapter provides a detailed discussion of the Java language datatypes, keywords, and expressions, as well as the finer points of data hiding.

Datatypes, Modifiers, and Expressions

- Java syntax

- Basic datatypes

- Inner classes

- Datatypes and method modifiers

Java's program structure and syntax is quite similar to that of C++. The first part of this chapter describes basic Java syntax and Java keywords. You will learn a standard way to choose variable, class, and function names, and how to enter data values into your code.

Java datatypes come in three varieties: basic built-in (or *primitive*) datatypes, system classes that have been defined in Java's Core API, and user-defined classes. The built-in datatypes hold atomic units of information, such as individual characters, numbers, or `true`/`false` values. The built-in datatypes themselves are not classes so they do not have member methods. The API includes a language package (`java.lang`), which has class equivalents of the basic datatypes and other commonly used datatypes, such as the `String` class for storing strings of characters and the `Thread` class for multithreading.

In the previous chapter, you learned how to create your own user-defined classes. In this chapter, you will learn how to define your own classes with more advanced data hiding.

Using Java Syntax

A language *syntax*, or *grammar*, defines how and when words can be used, as well as the punctuation required. Java's syntax specifies the way the following are written:

Comments   Remarks added by the programmer for documentation purposes.

Statements   A single "line" of the program.

Code blocks   A set of statements grouped together as a unit.

File structure   The components of a Java source file and the order in which they are defined.

Keywords   Predefined words in the Java language (not to be used as identifiers).

Identifiers   The names you give to classes, variables, and methods. Identifiers have restrictions on length and leading characters. There are also some optional, yet widely used, conventions for identifiers.

Literals   Constant values that are written differently, depending on the datatype; for example, to distinguish the characters "123" from the number 123.

Expressions   A combination of terms that evaluate to a single data value.

Operators   Operators perform addition, subtraction, multiplication, and other operations.

Each of these concepts is described in the following sections.

Comments

You can add comments to Java source code in the same two ways as you add them in C++. The first type of comment begins with /* and ends with */ and allows you to add comments that extend across several lines of text:

```
a = b + c;
/* Here is a comment which
   extends across two lines */
```

Generally, you cannot *nest* comments (that is, place comments within comments):

```
a = b + c;
/* Here is a comment which /* a comment within a comment */
   extends across two lines */
```

In this example, the first comment ends at the first */, leaving the second line of text without a starting comment marker. This results in a compile-time error.

As mentioned in Chapter 2, multiple-line comments have special meaning for the javadoc utility when the first character inside the comment is an asterisk; that is, when the comment begins with /** (/* is not a javadoc comment; the slash must be followed by two or more asterisks):

```
a = b + c;
/** This comment has special meaning for the javadoc utility.
    It will be part of documentation automatically generated
    by the javadoc program. */
```

The second type of comment extends from the comment marker // to the end of the line of text:

```
a = b + c; // this comment extends to end of this line of text
```

These comments can be embedded within comments that begin with /* and end with */.

Statements

A *statement* is a single "line" of Java code. There is not a one-to-one correspondence between lines of code and lines of text in a Java source file. Java uses the semicolon to indicate the end of a line of code. This line:

```
a = b + c + d + e + f + g;
```

is the same as this one:

```
a = b + c + d +
    e + f
+ g;
```

The spaces between terms in a statement can consist of any number of *whitespace* characters. Whitespace characters are spaces, tabs, linefeeds, and carriage returns.

NOTE   On Unix and Macintosh systems, a carriage return character (ASCII code 13) usually terminates each line of text. In Windows, lines of text are usually delimited by carriage return and linefeed characters (CR/LF or ASCII code 13 followed by ASCII code 10). Java compilers see all these characters as whitespace, and they do not care how lines of text are terminated. For more information about ASCII, see "The Character Datatype," later in this chapter.

Code Blocks

You can group statements together into blocks so that a single statement can easily control the execution of many other statements. Java code blocks are delimited with braces ({ and }). You have already seen code blocks used to group the statements belonging to a class, as well as code blocks nested within other blocks, as in this example from Chapter 3:

```
public class Flight {
    int   altitude;
    int   heading;
    int   speed;
    float latitude;
```

```
  float longitude;
  // change the flight's heading by angle degrees
  void turnFlight(int angle) {
    heading = (heading + angle) % 360;
    // make sure angle is in the range 0-359 degrees
    if (heading < 0)
      heading = heading + 360;
  }
}
```

The amount of whitespace between braces and statements is arbitrary, but conventionally a left brace is placed at the end of a line (or the start of the next line), the right brace is placed on its own line, and indentation is used to highlight the grouping of code. Of course, code style is a matter of individual choice, and every programmer has his or her own method of formatting code. Ultimately, it does not matter which style you choose, as long as you are consistent throughout your source code files.

Source File Structure

Java source files may contain only three types of statements that are not contained within code blocks:

package   Defines the package to which the classes in the file will belong.

import   Establishes a shorthand for referring to existing classes (such as those in the API) by class name only, without specifying the full package name.

class   Defines your top-level classes.

The package and import statements are both optional. A *package* is a group of related classes. Classes in the same package have freer access to each other's member variables and methods, and they need to be stored in a predefined location on the server or on the client machine. In addition, classes that are immediately contained within a package are said to be *top-level classes*. This distinguishes them from *inner classes*, which are defined within other classes. (See Chapter 5 for more information about Java packages.)

Note that the statements in a source file must appear in the order listed (package, import, then class).

Here is a sample Java source file with all three types of components:

```
package com.sybex.examples;
import java.awt.Panel;
import java.awt.Color;
class ColorPanel extends Panel {
  ColorPanel      .
    .
    .
}
```

This code fragment defines a new class called `ColorPanel` that belongs to a package called `com.sybex.examples`. Another program referring to this class would refer to the class as `com.sybex.examples.ColorPanel`.

The import statements make it easier to refer to classes in an existing package called `java.awt`. The `java.awt` package is the AWT (Abstract Window Toolkit) package, part of the Core API. The first import statement allows you to refer to class `java.awt.Panel` from the package `java.awt` as simply `Panel`. Similarly, the second import statement allows you to refer to the `Color` class in the same package by its class name, `Color`, rather than the package and class name, `java.awt.Color`.

The last statement in the file is a class definition. It is a compound statement; that is, it is a statement containing a block of other statements. Additional class definitions may follow this one.

Keywords

A *keyword* is a word that has a special meaning for the Java compiler, such as a datatype name or a program construct name. The complete list of Java keywords is shown in Table 4.1.

TABLE 4.1: Java Keywords

abstract	else	long	switch
boolean	extends	native	synchronized
break	final	new	this
byte	finally	null	throw
case	float	package	throws
catch	for	private	transient

Continued on next page

TABLE 4.1 CONTINUED: Java Keywords

char	goto*	protected	try
class	if	public	void
const*	implements	return	volatile
continue	import	short	while
default	instanceof	static	widefp
do	int	strictfp	
double	interface	super	

* Reserved but currently not used by the language.

Identifiers

An *identifier* is a name you give to a variable, class, or method. You can choose identifiers to be anything you want, as long as the identifier begins with a letter, consists of letters, numbers, '_', and '$', and is not spelled the same as a keyword.

You may have noticed a pattern in the way the identifiers in this book are capitalized. The capitalization follows the identifier conventions used in the Java Core API, and it is recommended that you follow the same convention to keep your code readable. Familiarity with these conventions will also make it easier to read the sample code provided. Table 4.2 lists these identifier conventions. Although their use is recommended, the compiler will not complain if you do not follow these conventions.

TABLE 4.2: Conventions for Naming Identifiers

Type of Identifier	Convention	Examples
Class names	Capitalize each word within the identifier	Flight, CommercialFlight
Function names	Capitalize every word within the identifier except the first	printFlight, turnFlight
Variable names	Capitalize every word within the identifier except the first	altitude, flightNumber
Constant variable names	Capitalize every letter; underscores between words	MAX_INBOUND_FLIGHTS

Identifiers are not restricted to ASCII characters. If your editor supports it, you can have Unicode characters in variable names. Also, there is no limit to the number of characters in an identifier. If you have two variables that differ at the 512th position (or beyond), the compiler will detect this, and treat them as separate. Of course, most humans reading your code probably won't be that accurate, so be careful.

Literals

Whereas an identifier is a symbol for a value, a *literal* is an actual value such as 35, or "Hello". Table 4.3 summarizes the formats for literals for each datatype. As you can see, a datatype may have more than one format for a literal.

By default, integer literals are of type int, but you can override this by adding the letter L to the end of the number to make it of type long. Similarly, a floating-point literal represents a double-precision number unless the F suffix is used to mark it as float.

TABLE 4.3: Formats for Literals of Each Datatype

Datatype	Literal
int	Decimal digits (not starting with 0) 0x followed by hexadecimal digits, e.g., 0xFF 0 followed by octal digits, e.g., 0726
long	Same as for int datatype but followed by the character l or L, e.g., 1234L, 0x12FABL, 043543212L, 1234l
float	Digits with a decimal point and/or exponent, followed by the character f or F, e.g., 1.234f, 1.234E+5F (1.234×10^5 = 123400), .1234F
double	Same as for float datatype but without the f or F suffix and with an optional d or D suffix, e.g., 1.234D, 1.234, 1.234E-5 (1.234×10^{-5} = 0.00001234), .1234
boolean	true or false
char	Unicode (or ASCII) character within single quotation marks, e.g., 'a' or 'B' (if your editor supports input of Unicode characters, these can go right into the single quotation marks), a predefined escape sequence within single quotation marks, e.g., '\t', '\012', '\u000A' (see Table 4.4)
String	A sequence of characters or escape sequences within double quotation marks, e.g., "Hello World\n"

For the char datatype, you can use predefined escape sequences (see Table 4.4).

TABLE 4.4: Character Escape Sequences

Escape Sequence Type	Escape Sequence	Character Represented
Special	\b	Backspace
	\t	Horizontal tab
	\n	Linefeed
	\f	Form feed
	\r	Carriage return
	\"	Double quotation mark (")
	\'	Single quotation mark (')
	\\	Backslash
Octal	\DDD	Character with ASCII code DDD octal, where DDD is a sequence of three octal digits (0-7), e.g., \071 is ASCII character 71 octal, 57 decimal
Unicode	\uHHHH	Character with Unicode value HHHH hex, where HHHH is a sequence of four hexadecimal digits (0-9, A-F, a-f), e.g., \u0041 is Unicode character 41 hex, 65 decimal

Expressions and Operators

Expressions are combinations of variables, keywords, or symbols that evaluate to a value of some type. The value may be a number, string, or any other class or datatype. You might think of an expression as something that could be written on the right side of an assignment statement.

The simplest expressions are merely variables or literals, as in 15, a, or "Hello". These expressions may be found on the right side of an assignment statement such as the following one, which assigns the string "Hello" to the variable s:

```
s = "Hello";
```

As in C or C++, an assignment has a value of its own; namely, the value of the assignment is the value of the right side of the assignment itself:

```
b = a = 15;
```

In this example, the value 15 is assigned to a, and the value of the assignment "a = 15" is itself 15, so 15 is also assigned to b.

Method Calls

Another type of expression is the *method call*. As you have seen, methods can evaluate to a datatype, so they can appear on the right side of an assignment:

```
a = incomingFlight.getHeading();
b = weatherStation.getCelsius (fahrenheit);
```

The generic structure of a method or variable reference is:

```
object.membervariable
object.method (arguments)
```

or in the case of static methods and variables (see "Storage and Lifetime Modifiers," later in this chapter):

```
class.membervariable
class.method (arguments)
```

Object Allocation

Object allocation is just a special kind of function call. You can use the new keyword to call the constructor for the class you are instantiating:

```
new classname (arguments)
```

Here are three different examples:

```
Flight f;
f = new Flight();
Airport f;
f = new Airport ("City National Airport");
Airport f = new Airport ("City National Airport");
```

If you do not provide a constructor for your class, a default constructor that accepts no arguments is created. However, if you provide only a constructor that requires arguments/parameters, there will not be a constructor that accepts no parameters. Note that a class cannot be instantiated if the class is abstract.

The *this* and *super* Reserved Words

Two special reserved words can also be used to form expressions. If you want to refer to the current instance of the class in which the code is written, you can use the this keyword. The super keyword refers to the superclass of the class in which the code is written. Note that static methods may not use these keywords because they do not have an instantiated object to which to refer.

Using the `this` keyword, you can have an object print itself on the console when you call its `print()` method, by adding the following code to any class:

```java
public void print() {
   System.out.println (this);
}
```

If, for example, you added this code to the `Flight` class, you could write:

```java
Flight incomingFlight = new Flight();
incomingFlight.setHeading (140);
incomingFlight.print ();
```

In the `print()` method, `this` points to `incomingFlight`, so the last line of this listing is equivalent to:

```java
System.out.println(incomingFlight);
```

As shown in Chapter 3, you can also use `this` when referring to a constructor from within another constructor. In this case, the reference appears as a method call:

```java
public Flight (int heading) {
   setHeading(heading);
}
public Flight (int heading, int newAltitude) {
   this(heading);
   altitude = newAltitude;
}
```

The call to `this(heading)` in the second constructor calls the first constructor.

The `super` keyword is used to refer to the methods or member variables of the superclass. If a subclass defines a member variable with the same name as its parent's member variable, you can use the `super` keyword to reference the parent's variable from the subclass. `super` is also used to refer to the methods of the parent class:

```java
class Parent {
   String name;
   void print () {
      System.out.println("Parent " + name);
   }
   .
   .
   .
}
class Child extends Parent {
```

```
String name;
String childName() {
  return name;
}
String parentName() {
  // return the name of the parent
  return super.name;
}
void print() {
  System.out.println ("Child " + name + " is child of");
  super.print();
}
  .
  .
  .
}
```

Operator Expressions

The other types of expressions involve combinations of variables, literals, function calls, and operators. An *operator* is a symbol that transforms a variable or combines it in some way with another variable or literal. The multiplication operator, *, combines two numbers to form a third number:

```
a = b * c;
```

The expressions on which an operator acts are called *operands*. The multiplication operator is an example of a *binary operator*—it takes two operands and creates a new result.

Other operators act on a single variable to produce another value:

```
a = - b;
```

Here, the negation operator (−) transforms a single variable b into another quantity that is then assigned to a. An operator that creates output from a single operand is called a *unary operator*. Another type of unary operator automatically assigns a new value to the operand; the auto-increment (++) and auto-decrement (−−) operators add and subtract one from the operand, respectively:

```
a = 10;
a++; // add one to a (a is now 11)
a--; // subtract one from a (a is now 10)
```

Operator Precedence

When you use several operators in a single expression, it is important to know in which order the operators will be applied. If you use addition and multiplication as shown here:

```
a = 4 + 5 * 6;
```

do you get 34 or 54? The answer depends on *operator precedence* (that is, the order in which the operators will be applied). As with standard math, multiplication (*) has higher precedence than addition (+), so the multiplication is done first, and the answer is 34. If you want to do the addition before the multiplication, use parentheses to group parts of the calculation together:

```
a = (4 + 5) * 6; // the number 54 will be assigned to a
```

Java will evaluate expressions in parentheses as a single unit before proceeding with the rest of the calculation. You can take advantage of parentheses to program defensively. Use parentheses to group parts of the calculation together whenever possible, even when they are not needed:

```
a = 4 + (5 * 6);
```

This is unambiguous and helps you—and the reader of your programs—know what is going on. It also means you won't need to remember the precedence of the operators.

If two operators have the same precedence, the computations will be performed in a well-defined order: from left to right or right to left. This property of an operator is known as the operator's *associativity*. The multiplication operator is left associative, so when evaluating the product 2 * 3 * 4, the leftmost product will be evaluated first to get 6 * 4, before finally performing the last product and arriving at the result of 24.

Arithmetic Operators

Java's *arithmetic operators* are summarized in Table 4.5. These operators accept integer or floating-point operands and produce integer or floating-point results. The auto-increment and auto-decrement operators are included as arithmetic operators.

TABLE 4.5: Arithmetic Operators

Operator	Purpose	Precedence (1 = highest)	Associativity
++, --	Auto-increment, auto-decrement	1	Right
+, -	Unary plus, unary minus	1	Right
*	Multiplication	2	Left
/	Division	2	Left
%	Remainder (modulo division)	2	Left
+, -	Addition, subtraction	3	Left

The remainder operator (%) returns the remainder of dividing the first operand by the second, so 24 % 10 is the remainder left over after dividing 24 by 10, namely 4. This operator also works with floating-point operands.

Relational Operators

Relational operators compare two quantities to determine if they are equal or if one is greater than the other. The operator that tests for equality is the == operator. If the operands are built-in types (arithmetic, character, or boolean), the equality operator returns the boolean value true if the operands have the same value or false if they do not. If the operands are object variables, the equality operator returns true if the object variables refer to the same object (or are both null). If the object variables refer to different objects, or if one refers to an object and the other is null, the equality operator returns false.

When the operands are built-in types, the equality operator works as you would expect:

```
boolean a, b;
a = (2 == 2);   // a will be true
b = (2 == 3);   // b will be false
```

In contrast, if two objects are compared for equality, two equivalent objects are equal only if they are the same physical object in memory:

```
boolean a, b;
Flight f1, f2;
// f1 and f2 will be two separate Flight objects
```

```
// with the same default values
f1 = new Flight();
f2 = new Flight();
a = (f1 == f2); // a will be false because f1 and f2 refer
                // to different instances, even though they
                // contain exactly the same data
f1 = f2;
b = (f1 == f2); // b will be true because f1 and f2 now refer
                // to the identical instance
```

TIP

Because you often need to check to see if the *contents* of two objects are equal, most objects implement the `equals()` method, which allows you to check the equality of objects in the same way that you would with primitives.

The inequality operator (!=) does the exact opposite of the equality operator. It returns `true` when the operands are not equal.

Numeric operands can be compared with each other using the greater than (>), less than (<), greater than or equal (>=), and less than or equal (<=) operators:

```
boolean a, b, c, d;
a = (1 > 2);   // a is false
b = (1 < 2);   // b is true
c = (1 <= 2);  // c is true
d = (1 >= 0);  // d is true
```

TIP

Similar to the `equals()` method, some objects implement the `compareTo()` method to ensure ordering. This allows you to check the natural ordering of objects, as well as primitives.

Java has kept C's and C++'s conditional operator (?:) that takes three operands (it is a *ternary operator*). The first operand is `boolean`, and the two other operands may be of any type. If the `boolean` operand is `true`, the result is the second operand; if it is `false`, the result is the third operand:

```
boolean b;
int c;
b = true;
c = (b ? 1 : 2); // 1 will be assigned to c because b is true
b = false;
c = (b ? 1 : 2); // 2 will be assigned to c because b is false.
```

WARNING   Be wary of this particular conditional operation. Although it is useful, it can make your code less readable.

These comparison operators are usually used in conjunction with conditional statements (these are covered in Chapter 6). Table 4.6 summarizes the relational operators.

TABLE 4.6: Relational Operators

Operator	Purpose	Precedence	Associativity
>, <, >=, <=	Tests relative magnitude	5	Left
==	Tests equality	6	Left
!=	Tests inequality	6	Left
?:	Conditional—returns one of two operands based on a third	13	Left

Boolean Operators

Boolean operators act on `boolean` operands and return a `boolean` result. They implement the standard `boolean` algebraic operations: AND, OR, NOT, and XOR (eXclusive OR).

The AND operator returns `true` if both operands are `true`. The OR operator returns `true` if either operand is `true`, or both. Java has two versions of each of these operators. The first version (& for AND; | for OR) forces evaluation of both operands. The second version (&& for AND; | | for OR) will not evaluate the second operand if it can determine the result after evaluating the first. Here is an example to illustrate the difference between these two versions of the OR operation:

```
boolean b;
// to compute the following, the VM will evaluate both expressions
// and, therefore, will perform both multiplication operations
b = ( 100 > ( 5 * 6 ) )  | ( 100 > (8 * 8));  // b will be true
// to compute the following, the VM will evaluate only the
```

```
// expression the left, and, therefore, will perform only
// one multiplication (7 * 9)
b = ( 100 > ( 7 * 9 ) )  || ( 100 > (4 * 5));  // b will be true
```

The two AND operators work analogously.

On occasion, you want the Virtual Machine to evaluate both sides, whether the result of the AND/OR operation can be deduced by evaluating only one operand. In other situations, you do not want the VM to continue because it will result in needless comparisons or exceptions, if you are assuming previous conditions succeeded.

The XOR operator returns `true` if the operands are not the same—one operand is `true`, and the other is `false` (`true ^ false == true`). The NOT operator is a unary operator that returns the opposite of its operand (`!false == true`).

Table 4.7 summarizes the boolean operators.

TABLE 4.7: Boolean Operators

Operator	Purpose	Precedence	Associativity
!	NOT	1	Right
&	Boolean AND	7	Left
^	XOR	8	Left
|	Boolean OR	9	Left
&&	Conditional AND	10	Left
||	Conditional OR	11	Left

Bitwise Operators

The integral types (`byte`, `short`, `int`, and `long`) are represented in the computer's memory as a sequence of *bits* (binary digits). Just like decimal numbers, binary numbers have their most significant digits to the left. In decimal, the most significant digit in the number 325 is the 3 because it represents 300, and the least significant digit is the 5. Written as a binary number, 325 is 101000101. The leftmost digit represents 100000000 binary (256 decimal) and is the most significant digit.

Java's integers are signed numbers, so Java must use the leftmost bit of storage to represent the sign of the integer. For Java's integer datatypes, the high bit is used to represent the sign of the number, as shown in Figure 4.1. If the high bit is 1, the number is negative.

FIGURE 4.1:

Java's integral datatypes use the high bit to indicate the sign of the number. If the high bit is 1, the number is negative.

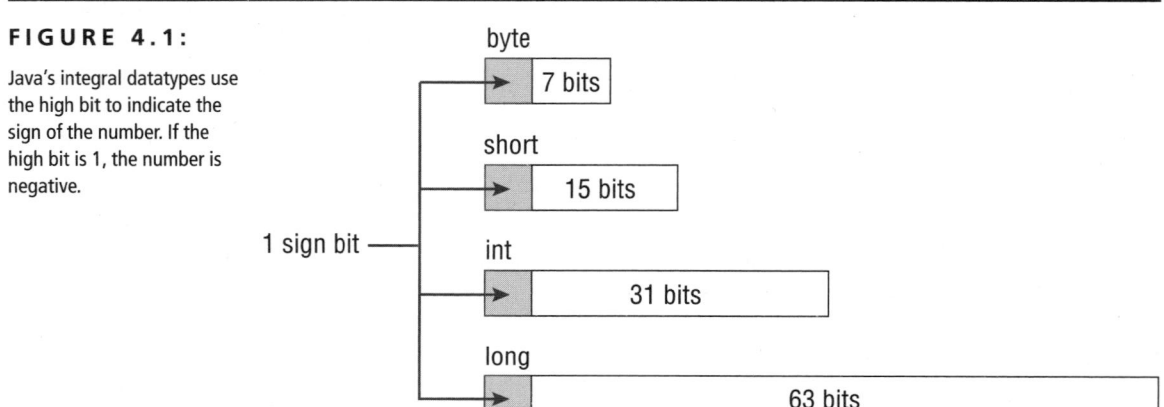

Java uses the same operators as the C language to manipulate the bits of integers. Because all of Java's integral datatypes are signed, Java supplements the C operators with an additional operator. Bit-manipulation operators are referred to as *bitwise* operators. The bitwise operators perform the same sorts of functions as the `boolean` operators, as well as bit shift operators.

The bitwise AND operator applies the AND operation to the corresponding bits of each operand. The bitwise OR, XOR, and NOT operators work in a similar fashion. The bitwise operators are illustrated in Figure 4.2.

The shift operators move all the bits in an integral type to the left or the right, as shown in Figure 4.3. The shift operators are binary operators. The second operand is an integer that determines the number of bits to shift. The standard C shift operators act slightly differently in Java. In Java, all numbers are signed, and the sign bit is preserved through all shifts. Although this sign bit is shifted, it is also copied so that the resulting number will have the same sign as the original. Java adds the >>> operator, which shifts all bits to the right as if the integer were unsigned.

FIGURE 4.2:

Boolean bitwise operators

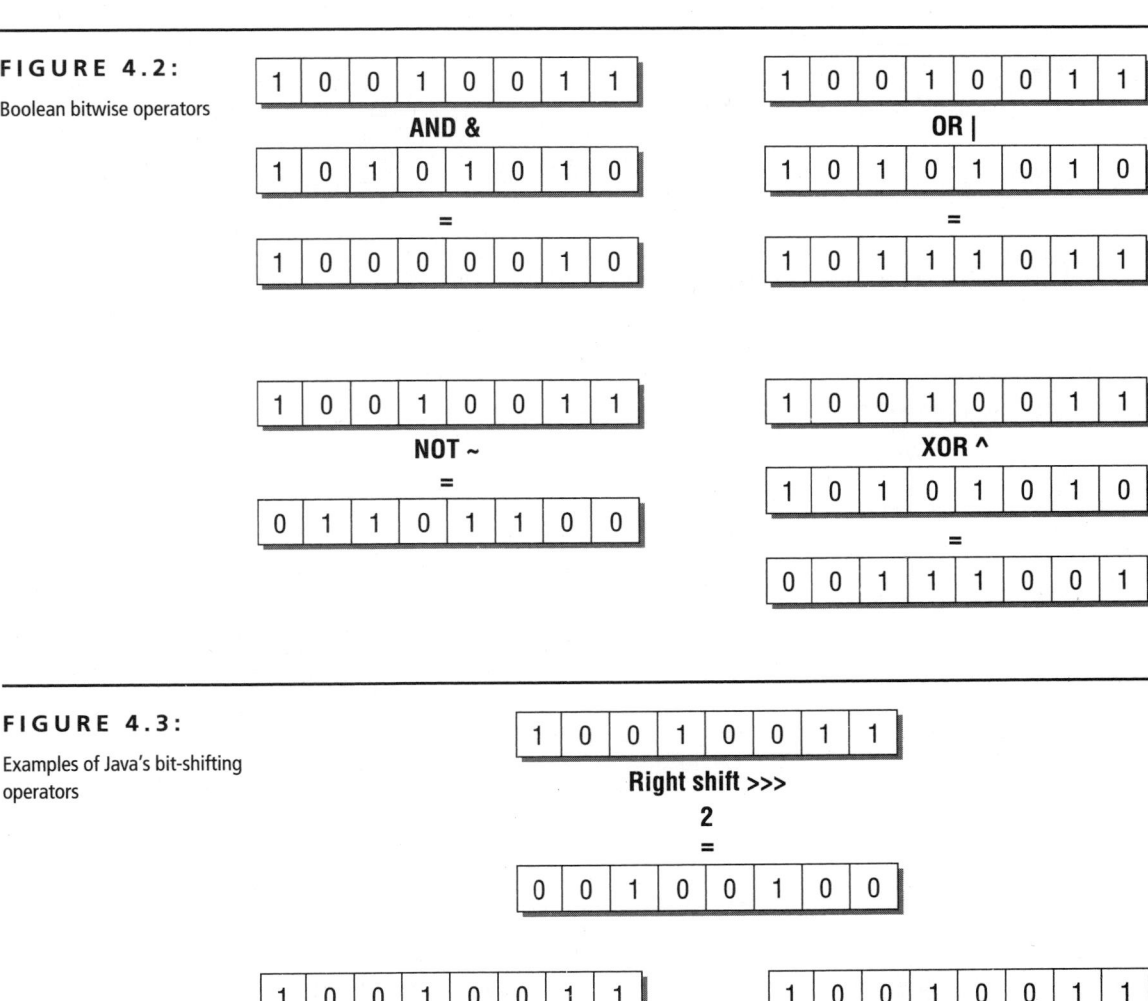

FIGURE 4.3:

Examples of Java's bit-shifting operators

NOTE   For simplicity, Figure 4.3 uses signed 8-bit bytes. However, you should be aware that Java's shift operators work with `int` and `long` datatypes only. If you shift a negative short to the right using the `>>` operator, you may end up with a larger number than you started with. This is because the left operand is *cast* (converted) into an `int` before being shifted.

Table 4.8 summarizes the bitwise operators.

TABLE 4.8: Bitwise Operators

Operator	Purpose	Precedence	Associativity
~	NOT (bitwise complement)	1	Right
<<, >>	Left shift, Right shift	4	Left
>>>	Right shift as if unsigned	4	Left
&	Bitwise AND	7	Left
^	Bitwise XOR	8	Left
|	Bitwise OR	9	Left

String Operators

The concatenation operator (+) is the only operator that applies to strings in particular. It glues two strings together to form a third:

```
String s;
s = "Hello" + " " + "World"; // "Hello World" is assigned to s
```

If only one operand is a string, the other operand is converted to a string automatically:

```
String s;
s = "5 * 6 =" + (5 * 6); // "5 * 6 = 30" is assigned to s
```

If the operand that is not a string is an object, Java uses the `toString()` method to obtain a string equivalent of the object. The `toString()` method is inherited by all classes because it is implemented by the `Object` class. The default behavior of `toString()` is to return the name of the class of the object along with an @ and the *hashcode* of the object. The hashcode is a unique number calculated by the hashCode() method. All objects can call this method since it is defined in class Object. The following code illustrates the implicit use of toString():

```
String s;
SomeObject m;
s = "m is " + m; // "m is a SomeObject@1393870" assigned to s
```

The concatenation operator, like the addition operator, has a precedence of 3 and is left-associative.

Assignment Operators

As mentioned earlier, the assignment operator assigns the second operand to the first and returns the second operand as a result.

Other assignment operators serve as shorthand for combined operation and assignment. If you wanted to add 5 to a number, you could write:

```
int i;
i = i + 5;
```

You could also use the assignment operator +=:

```
int i;
i += 5; // this is the same as i = i + 5
```

Assignment operators exist for most of the operators already mentioned (see Table 4.9).

T A B L E 4 . 9 : Assignment Operators

Operator	Purpose	Precedence	Associativity
=	Assignment	13	Right
*=	Assignment with operation	13	Right
/=	Assignment with operation	13	Right
%=	Assignment with operation	13	Right
+=	Assignment with operation	13	Right
-=	Assignment with operation	13	Right

Continued on next page

TABLE 4.9 CONTINUED: Assignment Operators

Operator	Purpose	Precedence	Associativity
>>=	Assignment with operation	13	Right
<<=	Assignment with operation	13	Right
>>>=	Assignment with operation	13	Right
^=	Assignment with operation	13	Right
|=	Assignment with operation	13	Right
&=	Assignment with operation	13	Right

Special Operators

The *cast* operator converts from one datatype into another. A cast is written, within parentheses, as the name of the type into which you are casting the operand:

```
int i;
long l;
l = 1 << 40; // l is a very large number
l--;
i = (int) l; // l is being cast into an integer
```

If you are assigning a value of lower precision to a variable of higher precision, no cast is necessary. For example, no cast is needed to assign an `int` to a `long`, or a `float` to a `double`.

WARNING   C/C++ programmers need to be careful here. In C, typecasting is automatic for related datatypes. Java, however, requires that you explicitly specify any cast that might alter the contents (or *precision*) of a variable. Java objects can also be cast into any superclass of the same object.

Typecast operators have a precedence of 1 and are right-associative.

The `instanceof` operator is used to test the class of an object:

```
boolean b;
Flight f;
```

```
CommercialFlight cf; //CommercialFlight is a subclass of
                     //Flight
f = new Flight();
cf = new CommercialFlight();
b = f instanceof Flight;   // b will be true
b = f instanceof String;   // b will be false
b = cf instanceof Flight; // b will be true because cf is a
                          //subclass of Flight
```

The instanceof operator has a precedence of 5 and is left-associative.

TIP

Here's an easy way to remember associativity: Only unary, assignment, and conditional operators are right-associative; all others are left-associative.

Java's Built-In Datatypes

Java's built-in datatypes are understood by the compiler itself, without reference to any libraries or the Core API. These types can be classified into numeric, boolean, and character datatypes.

Before using any variable, it must first be declared. A variable declaration specifies the datatype, the variable name, and, optionally, the default value for the variable. The following sections describe variable declarations, each of the basic datatypes, and class declarations.

Variable Declarations

A general variable declaration looks like the following:

```
datatype identifier [ = defaultvalue ] {, identifier [ = defaultvalue ] }  ;
```

Identifiers are just symbols; in this case, they are the names of the variables being defined. To define integer variables i, j, and k, and initialize them to 1, 2, and 3, respectively, you can enter:

```
int i;
int j;
int k;
```

```
i = 1;
j = 2;
k = 3;
```

or in an abbreviated form:

```
int i = 1, j = 2, k = 3;
```

You can place variable declarations anywhere in your code, as long as they precede the first use of the variable. However, it is common practice to place the declarations at the top of each block of code. This makes your code easier to read, especially for programmers who are used to languages that require you to declare your variables at the beginning of functions. Later in this chapter, you will see how to limit access to a variable in its declaration.

The Numeric Datatypes

Java has six numeric datatypes that differ in the size and precision of the numbers they can hold. The basic numeric datatypes are listed in Table 4.10.

TABLE 4.10: Java's Built-in Numeric Datatypes

Type	Description	Size	Minimum Value	Maximum Value
byte	Tiny signed integer	8 bits	-128	127
short	Short signed integer	16 bits	-32768	32767
int	Signed integer	32 bits	-2147483648	2147483647
long	Long signed integer	64 bits	-9223372036854775808	9223372036854775807
float	Floating-point number	32 bits	Positive: $1.40239846 \times 10^{-45}$ Negative: $-3.40282347 \times 10^{38}$	Positive: $-3.40282347 \times 10^{38}$
double	Double precision floating-point	64 bits	Positive: $4.94065645841246544 \times 10^{-324}$ Negative: $-1.79769313486231570 \times 10^{308}$	Positive: $1.79769313486231570 \times 10^{308}$

Generally, when choosing a datatype for a variable, you will want to use the smallest datatype that holds the largest number you will work with, either now or in the foreseeable future. This saves memory yet provides room for expansion, should your code require modifications. For example, suppose a company carries 6,000 items in its catalog, and you need to choose a datatype to represent each item's number. You might select a short integer to save space, but if the company catalog grows to more than 32,767 items, the company will need to rewrite the software. Choosing a standard integer datatype will give your code greater longevity.

Choosing the right floating-point datatype is a little trickier because the decision depends on both the size and precision of the numbers with which you will be working. For example, if you are converting Celsius to Fahrenheit, you probably need only four digits of precision and a range of temperatures between ±150 degrees, so you should use a float. Scientific applications, which involve a large number of computations—for example, orbital trajectories—require higher precision to reduce rounding errors, even if the results themselves will not exceed single-precision magnitudes.

A feature added with Java 1.1 is a pair of special object classes, called `BigDecimal` and `BigInteger`, which can be used to create arbitrary precision numbers apart from those available to primitive datatypes. This can be useful if you need more precision or a larger range than `double` can offer.

The Java VM initializes every numeric instance or class variable to zero before it is used—only local variables are not automatically initialized. This is in contrast to most other programming languages where uninitialized variables contain random values. This issue generally does not arise because the use of uninitialized variables is detected and prevented by most Java compilers.

Not-a-Number and Infinity

Java's floating-point datatypes have special values for "Not-a-Number," positive infinity, and negative infinity. Not-a-Number, or NaN, is the result of an invalid mathematical operation, such as dividing zero by zero or multiplying an infinity by zero. Positive infinity is the result of dividing a positive number by zero. Negative infinity is the result of dividing a finite negative number by zero. This is only true of high-precision IEEE-standard datatypes (like float and double); integer division by zero is not allowed.

The Boolean Datatype

Boolean variables hold `true` or `false` values. Many older languages treated integers as boolean variables, regarding zero as `false` and nonzero as `true`. However, like Pascal, Java has its own `boolean` datatype, separate from any numeric datatype. Although it requires a slightly more verbose programming style, it is considerably safer than using integers as boolean types because integers will never accidentally be treated as boolean variables. Uninitialized boolean variables are initialized to `false`.

The Character Datatype

The character datatype, `char`, holds a single character. Each character is a number or character code that refers to a *character set*, an indexed list of symbols. For example, in the ASCII (American Standard Code for Information Interchange, pronounced "as-key") character set, the character code 65 corresponds to the letter *A*, and the character code 33 refers to the digit 1.

Most PC character sets use an extended form of the ASCII character set with 256 character codes so each character can be stored in a byte. The first 127 characters of such character sets are standard across character sets (except for the currency symbol); the last 128 characters vary from set to set and are used for special characters, such as foreign alphabetic characters or currency symbols.

Java's creators designed Java with expandability and internationalization in mind. The Java `char` datatype is 16-bits wide and holds a Unicode symbol rather than an ASCII character. The initial value of a char variable is `'\u0000'`.

NOTE   Unicode is an extended version of the ASCII character set, designed for handling multiple languages. Fortunately, Unicode corresponds to a standard extended ASCII character set (ISO-LATIN-1) for the first 127 characters. It is possible to write Java programs and not know you are using Unicode. Unicode also gives Java the ability to use other encoding schemes than the simple ISO-LATIN-1, including character codes for non-Latin–based languages like Japanese, Chinese, and Hebrew. For more information about Unicode, refer to this Web page: `http://www.unicode.org/`.

The *String* Datatype

A string is a sequence of characters. The `String` datatype is actually a class of the Core API (`java.lang.String`), rather than a built-in type, but it is used so frequently that it is appropriate to cover here. The `String` class has special status in

Java, because the compiler recognizes `String` constants; the compiler recognizes characters within double quotation marks as `String` literals.

Strings can contain as many characters as you want; no maximum string length is specified in the Java language specification. However, most implementations will probably limit you to about two billion characters, which is plenty for almost any application.

Strings are immutable in Java; that is, you cannot change the contents of a string, although you can redefine a `String` object variable. For instance, the string message is initially defined as

```
String message = "Hello World";
```

There is no way to change the contents of the object pointed to by a message by, say, passing it to another method:

```
changeString(s); // impossible to change object pointed to by s
```

However, you can make the string variable message refer to a new string object:

```
message = message + "!!";
```

This is a rather subtle point, and the key to understanding it is to keep the concept of an object variable and the object itself distinct. There is an additional string-handling class in the API called `StringBuffer`. A `StringBuffer` is like the `String` datatype, but it has methods for modifying the contents of the `StringBuffer`. When the Java compiler encounters the code in the preceding example, it rewrites it as follows:

```
message = new StringBuffer(message).append("!!").toString();
```

The compiler converts the original message into a `StringBuffer`, appends the exclamation points to the `StringBuffer`, and then converts the `StringBuffer` back into a `String`.

Class Declarations

As explained in Chapter 3, a class declaration begins with the keyword `class`, then specifies the name of the class, the name of the superclass (if different from `Object`), and any interfaces supported by the class:

```
class classname extends parentclassname implements interfacename {
    member-variable-declarations
    member-function-declarations
```

```
    class-initializer
    instance-initializer
}
```

Member variable declarations are just like other variable declarations, but they may have modifier keywords that alter their visibility outside the class:

```
modifier(s) datatype-specifier identifier = initial-value;
```

(Modifiers are described in the next section.)

Sample member functions were shown in Chapter 3. Their general structure is:

```
modifier(s) datatype-specifier identifier (argument-list) {
    code-block
}
```

The *datatype-specifier* can be any datatype or the keyword void, which means no datatype. Functions can be declared to return void, meaning that they return no value. The *argument-list* specifies the parameters that will be accepted by the function:

```
datatype identifier, datatype identifier, datatype identifier
```

Finally, the *code-block* consists of one or more statements (refer to earlier sample code for examples).

The *class-initializer* contains code that will be executed once when the class is loaded by the VM. The structure of the class initializer is as follows:

```
static { code-block }
```

An example of the use of the class initializer appears later in this chapter, in the "The static Modifier" section.

The *instance-initializer* contains code that will be executed when an instance of the class is created. Normally, you would place this code in the constructor for the object. The structure of the instance initializer is as follows:

```
{ code-block }
```

Scope Rules

In early programming languages such as COBOL, all variables were considered global variables. A *global variable* is a variable accessible from any part of a program, and, consequently, global variables must have unique names. Since all variables in COBOL were global, every variable in a COBOL program needed to be unique. This led to the practice of using a single variable for different purposes in different parts of the program.

Keeping track of global variables is a difficult task and makes such programs prone to bugs. In particular, a change in one small part of the code can adversely affect a completely different part of the program.

The solution to the problem of global variables is to use *local* variables, which are variables with limited life spans that relate to only a single part of the code. You can use two local variables with identical names as long as they are in different parts of the program. The rules that dictate which parts of the program can see which variables are called *scope rules*.

Variables defined within a member function are local to that member function, so you can use the same variable name in several member functions, as shown in this example:

```
class MyClass {
  int i; // member variable
  int first() {
    int j; // local variable
    // both i and j are accessible from this point
    return 1;
  }
  int second() {
    int j; // local variable
    // both i and j are accessible from this point
    return 2;
  }
}
```

The variable j defined in the function first() is created when it is declared as the function is called, and it is destroyed when the function exits. The same is true for the local variable j in the function second(). With multithreading, it is possible for the interpreter to be in both functions simultaneously, but this causes no conflict because the two local variables are completely independent of each other. Another way to think of these local variables is to imagine that the compiler renames them uniquely (for example, j1 and j2).

Java's Inner Classes

A feature added with Java 1.1 is support for inner classes. *Inner classes* are classes defined within other classes, much in the way other types of variables are defined within those classes. These inner classes have the same scope and access as other variables and methods defined within the same class. Here is an example:

```java
public class PrivateAirport extends Airport {
  String owner;
  PrivateAirport (String str) {
    owner = str;
  }
  class PrivateFlight extends Flight {
    String flightOwner;
    PrivateFlight() {
      flightOwner = owner;
    }
  }
  Flight getFlight() {
    return new PrivateFlight();
  }
}
```

This example uses the classes presented in Chapter 3, which define classes for `Airport` and `Flight` objects. In this example, a top-level class, called `Private-Airport`, represents an airport owned by some individual. This `Airport` can create `Flight` objects that cannot be created by any other class because no other class knows the name of the owner of the `Airport`. However, other objects can ask the `Airport` to create a new `Flight` object for them, which in this case is `PrivateFlight`, an inner class. Other objects do not have access to the name of the owner of `Flight` because they do not know about the `PrivateFlight` class. Nevertheless, a `PrivateFlight` object can use this information internally.

Java's Datatype and Method Modifiers

A *modifier* is a keyword that affects either the lifetime or the accessibility of a class, a variable, or a member function. Table 4.11 shows the applicability of each modifier to classes, functions, member variables, and local variables.

TABLE 4.11: Applicability of Modifiers to Classes, Member Functions, Member Variables, and Local Variables

Modifier	Classes	Member Functions	Member Variables	Local Variables
abstract	✓	✓	—	—
static	✓	✓	✓	—
public	✓	✓	✓	—
protected	✓	✓	✓	—
private	—	✓	✓	—
synchronized	—	✓	—	—
native	—	✓	—	—
transient	—	—	✓	—
volatile	—	—	✓	—
final	✓	✓	✓	✓

Storage and Lifetime Modifiers

The following sections describe the storage and lifetime modifiers: abstract, static, synchronized, native, volatile, transient, and final.

The *abstract* Modifier

When applied to a class, the abstract modifier indicates that the class has not been fully implemented and that it should not be instantiated. If applied to a member function declaration, the abstract modifier means that the function will be implemented in a subclass. Since the function has no implementation, the class cannot be instantiated and must be declared as abstract. Interfaces are abstract by default.

The *static* Modifier

Ordinarily, each instance of a class has its own copy of any member variables. However, it is possible to designate a member variable as belonging to the class itself, independent of any objects of that class. Such member variables are called *static* members and are declared with the `static` modifier keyword. Static member variables are often used when tracking global information about the instances of a class. The following class tracks the number of instances of itself using a static member variable called `instanceCount`:

```
public class MyClass {
    public static int instanceCount;
    public MyClass() {
        // each time this constructor is called,
        // increment the instance counter
        instanceCount++;
    }
    static {
        instanceCount = 0;
    }
}
```

Notice that a static initializer is used to initialize the static variable.

Methods can also be declared as `static`. For example, a static method called `resetCounter()` can reset the `instanceCounter` variable for `MyClass`:

```
public class MyClass {
    public static int instanceCount;
    public MyClass() {
        // each time this constructor is called,
        // increment the instance counter
        instanceCount++;
    }
    public static void resetCounter() {
        instanceCount = 0;
    }
    static {
        instanceCount = 0;
    }
}
```

The `resetCounter()` method can be called via the class `MyClass` or via an instance of `MyClass`:

```
MyClass m, n;
m = new MyClass(); // instanceCount will equal 1 after this constructor call
n = new MyClass(); // instanceCount will equal 2 after this constructor call
System.out.println(MyClass.instanceCount + " instances have been created");
```

```
m.resetCounter();        // reset the counter
MyClass.resetCounter(); // another way to reset the counter
```

The `System` class that is in the `java.lang` package of the API defines all its public methods and variables as `static`. All variables and functions are accessed via the class directly, not via an instance of the `System` class. In fact, the constructor for the `System` class is `private` so you cannot create a new `System` object with the usual code:

```
System MySystem = new System(); // this is illegal
```

Instead, all variables and functions of the `System` class are accessed via the class itself. Recall from previous examples that you can print information on the console with the following code:

```
System.out.println("Hello World");
```

The member variable `out` is a static member variable of type `PrintStream`. It is defined in the API as:

```
public final static PrintStream out;
```

Because the `System` class defines its functions as `static`, you can call the function `currentTimeMillis()` to get the current time, with the following expression:

```
long timeNow = System.currentTimeMillis();
```

`currentTimeMillis()` is defined in the `System` class as:

```
public static native long currentTimeMillis()
```

Use totally static classes (classes in which all members are static) when you want to model a unique entity. Use static member variables when you want only a single unique copy of a variable, such as when you want to track the number of times that instances have been created.

If you use the `static` keyword when you declare an inner class or interface, this makes the inner class a nested top-level class. Other classes outside of the containing class can access the nested class with a hierarchical name, assuming its accessibility modifiers, like `public` or `protected`, permit it. For example, the following class defines the nested interface `AirportLounge` within `WetAirport`:

```
public class WetAirport extends PrivateAirport {
    static public interface AirportLounge {
        public void orderDrink(String drink);
    }
    Lounge lounge = new Lounge();
```

```
WetAirport (String str) {
  super(str);
}
class Lounge implements AirportLounge {
  public void orderDrink(String drink) {
    System.out.println ("Please pay $10 for a " + drink);
  }
}
public AirportLounge getLounge() {
  return lounge;
}
}
```

Now, a class outside `Airport` would access the nested interface as `WetAirport`
`.AirportLounge`:

```
WetAirport.AirportLounge lounge;
WetAirport wet = new WetAirport ("George");
lounge = wet.getLounge();
lounge.orderDrink("Molson");
```

The *synchronized* Modifier

A *synchronized* member function allows only one thread to execute the function at
a time. This prevents two threads of execution from undoing each other's work.
(For details about threads, see Chapter 8.)

For example, suppose you have two threads, called threads A and B, responsible for updating a bank balance. Suppose also that the account has $100 in it.
Now, simultaneously, thread A tries to deposit $50 in the account, while thread B
tries to deposit $75. Both threads proceed to query the account balance. They both
find it at $100. Each of them, independently, adds its deposit to the old sum and
sets the new balance accordingly. If thread A finishes last, the account contains
$150. If thread B finishes last, the account balance is $175. Of course, neither of
these new figures is correct! The account should have $225 in it (100 + 50 + 75).
The problem is that both threads tried to execute the same code (querying and
changing the balance) at the same time. This is exactly the scenario that the synchronized keyword can prevent.

Synchronized methods are not `static` by default, but they may be declared as
`static`.

The synchronized modifier does not apply to classes or member variables.

The *native* Modifier

Native methods are implemented in other languages, such as C, so they have no code block. Many of the classes in the Core API are native because they need to access operating system–specific routines, such as those for drawing graphics on the screen. Here is an excerpt from the API's Math class:

```
/**
 * Returns the trigonometric sine of an angle.
 * @param a an assigned angle that is measured in radians
 */

public static native double sin(double a);
```

This declaration calls a function in a native code library that calculates the sine of the angle a. On an Intel *x*86 platform, the native code would call the sine function in the *x*86 processor's floating-point unit or coprocessor. On other platforms, the native code function may do the computation with software instead. This function also happens to be declared with the public and static modifiers also.

The native modifier applies to functions only.

The *volatile* Modifier

A *volatile* variable is one whose value may change independent of the Java program itself. Typically, *volatile* variables represent input from the outside world, such as a variable that denotes the time of day. They are also used to flag variables that could be changed by other threads of execution. The volatile keyword will prevent the compiler from attempting to track changes to the variable. The variable will always be assumed by the compiler to have a (potentially) new value each time it is accessed by Java code. Use of this modifier is rare but necessary, as Just-in-Time (JIT) compilers are now common in most Java Virtual Machines.

The *transient* Modifier

One of the changes introduced with Java 1.1 is adding meaning to the transient modifier. Java 1.0 supported the modifier, but it had no purpose. It is used in conjunction with serialization to provide for persistent objects. These objects can be saved to disk and restored on another machine or on the same machine. For more information about serialization, see Chapter 19. The transient modifier means not to save the variable.

The *final* Modifier

Most languages have a way to declare a variable as *constant* (that is, unchangeable), which is true of Java as well. The `final` keyword indicates that a local variable or member variable cannot be altered. The main use of `final` variables is as symbolic constants. You can refer to a constant by name and define that name in a single location in your code. If you later need to change the number in your code, you need only make the change at the point your final variable is defined.

Note that if you declare a variable as `final`, you must also initialize it at the same time:

```
final int MAX_PAGES = 23;
```

(The use of all caps for final variables is in accordance with the naming conventions used here, listed in Table 4.2.)

> **NOTE**   For instance variables, you can initialize final instance variables in every constructor. More about this in Chapter 5.

Member functions and classes can also be declared as final. A final member function cannot be overridden, and a final class cannot be subclassed.

When anything is declared final, the compiler/optimizer can make many assumptions that can dramatically increase performance.

Accessibility Modifiers

Java has other modifiers used to change the accessibility of classes and their members to other classes. By default, a class, its member functions, and its variables are known only to other classes in the same package. For simple applets, this means that a class is accessible only to other classes in the same directory.

The effects of the modifiers are listed here and shown in Figure 4.4. In the figure, there are two bars for each type of member modifier. The first bar represents the ability of a subclass to inherit a member variable or function. The second bar denotes the accessibility of a member.

FIGURE 4.4:

The accessibility of classes and their member functions and variables depends on the modifier used when the class or member was declared.

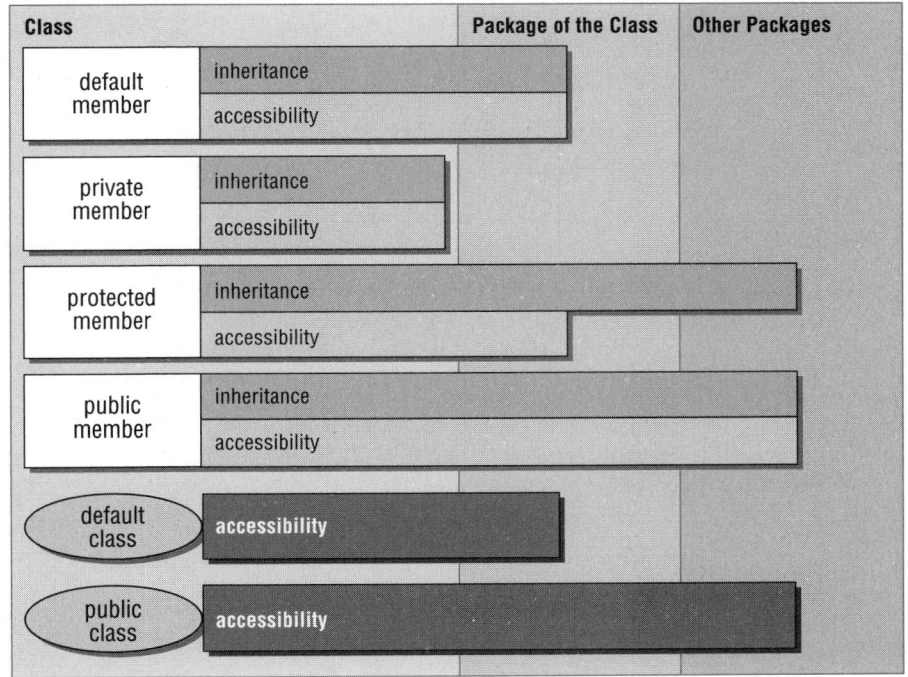

For example, the figure shows that member functions or variables declared as `protected` have the following characteristics:

- Will be inherited by subclasses, whether the subclasses are in the same package or not. This allows a subclass to access these members in instances of the subclass only.

- Can be accessed by any class within the same package, otherwise not at all visible.

A public class can be accessed by any other class. When a VM is asked to execute a new applet, the class for the applet must be public. However, any other classes required by the applet need not be public, as long as they are accessible.

Methods and member variables of `public` classes that are themselves declared as `public` can be accessed by code from other classes. Public members can also be accessed by JavaScript, VBScript, and ActiveX controls operating outside the VM. If members of a nonpublic (default) class are declared as `public`, those members will be accessible to all other classes within the same package. As a guideline, avoid defining methods and variables as `public` unless it is necessary.

If no modifier is specified, the default accessibility for the class, variable, or method is assumed.

NOTE   Default is not actually a modifier; that is, there is no keyword for default accessibility. Don't be misled by the `default` keyword that is used in `switch` statements (see Chapter 6); it is not a modifier. Some people call the default behavior "friendly," but that is not a modifier either (although there is a `friend` modifier in C++).

The following sections describe the accessibility modifiers: `private` and `protected`.

private

The `private` modifier restricts access to members of a class so that no other classes can call member functions or directly access member variables.

protected

A `protected` member is similar to default access but gives preferred access for subclasses in other packages. Member functions are sometimes created within a class for utility purposes (that is, to be used only within the class itself and not for general consumption). Declaring utility functions as `protected` allows them to be used not only by the class itself but by its subclasses as well.

Suppose you create a class called `Chicken`, which knows how to cross the road. The public member function `crossRoad()` has two steps: (1) check for oncoming traffic and (2) walk across the road. These steps would be written as two utility member functions called `checkTraffic()` and `walkAcrossRoad()`. The utility functions should not be public because you wouldn't want a programmer who is simply using the class to call `walkAcrossRoad()` without first calling `checkTraffic()`; this could have adverse consequences for `Chicken`. However, if you make the utility functions `private`, you will not be able to reuse these functions yourself when you write the subclass `SmarterChicken`. Ideally, the `SmarterChicken` class can override the crossRoad() function to check for a traffic light, then call check-Traffic() and walkAcrossRoad() as required. By declaring the utility functions as protected, they will be available to programmers such as yourself who will be creating subclasses of Chicken, and who should, therefore, understand the dangers inherent in crossing roads.

> **WARNING** Earlier versions of Java had an accessibility modifier of private protected. A private protected member was similar to a protected member but inaccessible by any non-subclass, whether in the same package or not. However, Java no longer supports this modifier.

Summary

The datatypes, modifiers, and expressions described in this chapter make up the essential building blocks of the Java language. Although some of the information in this chapter is reference material, you should now have a basic understanding of how to define your own datatypes for best use of storage space, ease of use, and interaction with other classes.

The next chapter describes interfaces and packages and will help you understand the finer points of class design. It also explains how to use existing Java packages.

CHAPTER
FIVE

Java Classes, Interfaces, and Packages

- Casting between datatypes

- Keywords for member and constructor references

- Java's object memory model

- Interfaces for multiple inheritance and callback functions

- Java's packages of classes and interfaces

This chapter introduces some important elements in Java programming. In particular, you will learn about *casting*, or explicitly converting a value from one datatype to another. In addition, you will learn about using `this` and `super` to refer to the otherwise hidden data members, hidden method members, and constructors of a class and its superclass.

This chapter also covers the object memory model (showing you how the memory of an object is handled) and interfaces, Java's solution for multiple inheritance and callback functions. Finally, this chapter introduces packages for grouping classes and interfaces to achieve better organization and minimize naming conflicts.

Casting for Converting Datatypes

The general form of a casting operation is:

```
(datatype) expression
```

where the datatype can be either a reference type or a primitive type. As a unary operator, casting has the highest operator precedence of the unary operators like `++` and `--`. For example, the following expression uses casting to make sure floating-point division, rather than integer division, is performed:

```
(float) 5 / 2
```

Since `(float)` has higher operator precedence than the division operator (`/`), the integer 5 will be converted into a floating number before the division. When one of the operands of a division is a floating number, the other operand will be converted into a floating number, and the division will be performed as a floating-number operation. If the expression is changed into:

```
(float) 3 + 5 / 2
```

an integer division followed by a floating-point addition will be performed because the division operator has higher operator precedence than the addition operator.

Rule number one in casting is that you cannot cast a primitive type to a reference type, nor can you cast the other way around. The compiler will check for all violations of casting rules. However, when dealing with object references, the correctness of casting can be checked in some cases only at run time. If a casting violation is detected at run time, the exception `ClassCastException` will be thrown. (You will learn more about exception handling in Chapter 7.) The next sections cover the rules for casting between primitive types and reference types in more detail.

Casting between Primitive Types

As explained in Chapter 4, the primitive datatypes can be divided into the boolean type and the numeric types. The boolean type cannot be cast from or to any other datatype.

Casting from any numeric type—byte, char, short, int, long, float, or double—to any other numeric type is allowed. Casting from one numeric type to another may cause loss of information, however. Casting from a wider type (like int) to a narrower one (like byte) will cause the higher-order bits to be discarded. For a signed number, the sign of the number may be changed after the conversion. For example, the result of (byte) 256 is 0, and the result of (byte) 255 is -1, because the byte type can hold only numbers ranging from -128 to 127.

If you are casting in a way that does not present the possibility of information loss, such as from byte to int or from int to float, the casting is automatic; you do not need to manually cast. If the possibility of information loss exists, you must cast yourself.

Assignment of a primitive value to a variable of a primitive type is allowed only if the assignment will not cause any loss of information. Otherwise, explicit casting is needed. The same rule applies to arguments of method calls. Automatic widening of the data will be performed if the value of the argument is of a numeric type narrower than the argument type prescribed for the method. For example, in the second statement of the following program fragment, a variable of float type is passed into method sqrt(), which requires an argument of double type. The value of the variable f will be converted into double type before the method (remember, a *method* is the same thing as a *member function*) is called.

```
float f = 4;
double d = Math.sqrt(f);
int  i = 1;
byte b = i;
```

Also, the last statement is not a legitimate one because conversion of an int type to a byte type could lose information. The compiler will produce an error message similar to this one:

```
CastTest.java:6: Incompatible type for declaration. Explicit
cast needed to convert int to byte.
     byte b = i;
         ^
```

To make it pass compiler checking, the statement must be changed as follows:

```
byte b = (byte) i;
```

Casting between Reference Types

The first rule of casting between reference types is that one of the class types involved must be the same class as, or a subclass of, the other class type. Assignment to different class type is allowed only if a value of the class type is assigned to a variable of its superclass type. Assignment to a variable of the subclass type needs explicit casting. For example, the second statement of the following program fragment is not a legitimate one because class String is a subclass of class Object:

```
Object o = new Object();
String s = o;
```

The compiler will issue an error message similar to this one:

```
CastTest.java:12: Incompatible type for declaration. Explicit
cast needed to convert java.lang.Object to java.lang.String.
    String s = o;
          ^
```

An explicit casting is necessary:

```
String s = (String) o;
```

If the casting turns out to be illegal at run time, a ClassCastException will be thrown. This can happen because explicit casting can fool the compiler to allow an object to access the data or method members of its subclass. The attempt at run time to make such a method or data reference will fail, and an exception will be thrown. For example, adding either one of the following two statements to the previous program fragment will incur a runtime exception, because both s and o refer to an object of Object type at run time, and the method length() is defined in class String:

```
int i = s.length();
int j = ((String)o).length();
```

If the exception is not handled, the execution will be terminated, and an error message similar to the following will be displayed:

```
java.lang.ClassCastException: java.lang.Object
        at CastTest.main(CastTest.java:12)
```

Using *this* and *super* for Member and Constructor References

The use of this and super keywords is twofold:

- To override the scope rules so that the otherwise hidden data and method members of a class and its superclass can be referred to

- To act as method names representing the constructor methods of the current class and its superclass

Both of these uses are discussed in the following sections.

this and *super* for Member References

Local variables in a method can share the same names as instance variables or class variables. Subclasses can define their own instance variables to shadow those defined in the superclasses. Subclasses can also define methods to override the methods defined in their superclasses. Two special reference variables are available inside any instance method to allow for access to the shadowed variables or overridden methods of that instance:

this   Used to refer to the object the method is called upon

super   Used to access the methods or data members defined in the superclass

For example, the constructor of a Point2D class to hold the x- and y-coordinates of a two-dimensional point can be defined as follows:

```
public class Point2D {
  int x, y;
  Point2D() {
    x = 0;
    y = 0;
  }
  Point2D (int x, int y) {
    this.x = x;
    this.y = y;
  }
```

```
    double length() {
      return Math.sqrt (x * x + y * y);
    }
  }
```

Here, `this.x` on the left side of the assignment statement refers to the instance variable x, whereas the x on the right side refers to the argument variable. The `sqrt()` method is defined in class `Math` of package `java.lang` to calculate the square root of the input argument.

You may define a subclass of the `Point2D` class with the same set of instance variables:

```
  public class MyPoint extends Point2D {
    int x, y;
    MyPoint (int x, int y) {
      this.x = super.x = x;
      this.y = super.y = y;
    }
    double length() {
      return Math.sqrt (x * x + y * y);
    }
    double distance() {
      return Math.abs (this.length() - super.length());
    }
  }
```

Here, `this.x` refers to the instance variable x defined in class `MyPoint`, and `super.x` refers to the instance variable x defined in class `Point2D`. The `abs()` method is defined in class `Math` of package `java.lang` to calculate the absolute value of its argument. The `this.length()` and `super.length()` methods are defined in classes `MyPoint` and `Point2D`, respectively.

NOTE It is necessary to override the `length()` method defined in class `Point2D` because the one defined in class `Point2D` can access only data members defined in class `Point2D`, not those defined in its subclass, `MyPoint`.

---

this and *super* for Constructor References

In constructors, there is an implied first statement; the superclass constructor with no parameters is automatically called. If you do not like this default behavior, you can override it by using a different `this()` or `super()` method call in the first statement to refer to other constructors of the object and its superclass, respectively. For example, to make the constructor of the `Point2D` class defined earlier more polymorphic, another constructor can be added with only the x-coordinate as the argument:

```
Point2D (int x) {
   this (x, 0);
}
```

Here, the y-coordinate is set to a default value of zero when not specified. Or you can replace the no argument constructor to set the coordinates to default values, as follows:

```
Point2D() {
   this (0, 0);
}
```

Also, the constructor of class `MyPoint` can be rewritten as follows:

```
MyPoint (int x, int y) {
   super(x, y);
   this.x = x;
   this.y = y;
}
```

Here, `super` refers to the constructor with two integer arguments defined in class `Point2D`.

Accessing Superclass Members from Outside the Class Definition

Data references are resolved at compile time. If a data member is defined in both a class and its superclass, the data member referred to is decided syntactically by the class type the object is declared to be. Therefore, you can cast an object to its superclass so that you can access the otherwise hidden data member. For example, assume three variables are declared as follows:

```
Point2D p  = new Point2D(11,0);
MyPoint mp = new MyPoint(4,5);
Point2D q  = mp;
```

`p.x`, `mp.x`, and `q.x` refer to the data member defined in classes `Point2D`, `MyPoint`, and `Point2D`, respectively. On the other hand, `((Point2D)mp).x` and ((MyPoint)q).x refer to the data member defined in classes Point2D and MyPoint, respectively.

Method references are resolved at run time. The class type an object belongs to when it is first created will determine which method will be called. Casting the object to its superclass, or assigning the object to a variable declared as its superclass type, will not change where the called method is from. For example, both mp.length() and q.length() refer to the length() method defined in class MyPoint, whereas p.length() refers to the method defined in class Point2D. The following code is added to the definition of classes Point2D and MyPoint to demonstrate this example:

```java
import java.io.PrintWriter;
public class PointTest {
  public static void main(String args[]) {
    PrintWriter out = new PrintWriter(System.out, true);
    MyPoint mp = new MyPoint(4,3);
    Point2D p  = new Point2D(11);
    Point2D q  = mp;
    mp.x = 5; mp.y = 12;
    out.println("\n\tData Member Access Test:\n");
    out.println("mp = (" + mp.x + ", " + mp.y + ")");
    out.println(" p = (" +  p.x + ", " +  p.y + ")");
    out.println(" q = (" +  q.x + ", " +  q.y + ")");
    out.println("\n\tCasting Test:\n");
    out.println("(Point2D)mp = (" + ((Point2D)mp).x + ", " +
      ((Point2D)mp).y + ")");
    out.println("(MyPoint)q  = (" + ((MyPoint)q).x + ", " +
      ((MyPoint)q).y + ")");
    out.println("\n\tMethod Member Access Test:\n");
    out.println("mp.length()   = " + mp.length());
    out.println(" p.length()   = " +  p.length());
    out.println(" q.length()   = " +  q.length());
    out.println("mp.distance() = " + mp.distance());
    out.println("\n\tCasting Test:\n");
    out.println("((Point2D)mp).length()   = " + ((Point2D)mp).length());
    out.println("((Point2D)q).length()    = " + ((Point2D)q).length());
    out.println("((MyPoint)q).distance() = " +
((MyPoint)q).distance());
  }
}
```

NOTE   `PrintWriter` is a class contained in the `java.io` package, which is concerned with output. See Chapter 19 for details.

The class definition for classes `Point2D` and `MyPoint` is restated as follows:

```
public class Point2D {
  int x, y;
  Point2D() {
    this (0, 0);
  }
  Point2D (int x) {
    this(x, 0);
  }
  Point2D (int x, int y) {
    this.x = x;
    this.y = y;
  }
  double length() {
    return Math.sqrt(x * x + y * y);
  }
}

public class MyPoint extends Point2D {
  int x, y;
  MyPoint (int x, int y) {
    super (x, y);
    this.x = x;
    this.y = y;
  }
  double length() {
    return Math.sqrt (x * x + y * y);
  }
  double distance() {
    return Math.abs (length() - super.length());
  }
}
```

The output of this program is shown here:

```
C:\MasteringJava\Ch05>java PointTest

      Data Member Access Test:
```

```
mp = (5, 12)
 p = (11, 0)
 q = (4, 3)

        Casting Test:

(Point2D)mp = (4, 3)
(MyPoint) q = (5, 12)

        Method Member Access Test:

mp.length() = 13.0
 p.length() = 11.0
 q.length() = 13.0
mp.distance() = 8.0

        Casting Test:

((Point2D) mp).length() = 13.0
((Point2D)  q).length() = 13.0
((MyPoint)q).distance() = 8.0
```

The Object Memory Model

The dynamically changing part of program memory can be divided into two areas:

- A stack memory area, which is used to store the local variables declared in methods or blocks. The stack memory will always grow in one direction and shrink in the opposite direction. The memory grows as the declaration of local variables (including argument variables in method calls) is encountered. These variables are popped out of the stack upon exit from the enclosing methods or blocks.

- A heap memory area, which is used to store the memory for objects. References to the objects can be put in the stack area, but the space for data members of the objects must reside in the heap area. A heap is a huge table of memory cells. Small blocks of memory cells are reserved or allocated from time to time when the new statement creates new objects. And whenever a block of memory cells is no longer referred to by any existing variables, these unused cells can be freed, or garbage-collected.

The term *heap* is also used to mean a complete binary tree where each node is at least as large as the values at its children, as in heap sort. These two usages of heap represent two totally different concepts and happen to have the same name for historical reasons.

To demonstrate memory-type usage, assume that you have two methods defined as follows, where class `Point2D` is defined to hold the x- and y-coordinates of a two-dimensional point (as in the earlier example of `this` and `super`):

```
void m1() {
    int a1 = 1;
    Point2D p1;              // checkpoint #1
    p1 = new Point2D (2,3);  // checkpoint #2
    m2 (a1, p1);
    a1 = 8;                  // checkpoint #5
}
void m2 (int a2, Point p2) {
    int a3 = 4;
    Point2D p3;              // checkpoint #3
    p3 = new Point2D (5,6);
    a2 = 7;                  // checkpoint #4
}
```

When method `m1()` is called, and its local variable declaration is executed—that is, when checkpoint #1 is reached—the two local variables, `a1` and `p1`, will be put on the stack memory area with values 1 and `null`, respectively. The memory model at this point is shown in Figure 5.1.

FIGURE 5.1:

The memory model after checkpoint #1

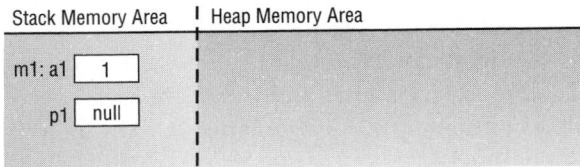

A new object of `Point2D` type is then created at checkpoint #2. The newly created object is put in the heap area, and a reference to the object is stored in local variable `p1` on the stack. The memory model at this point is shown in Figure 5.2.

FIGURE 5.2:

The memory model after checkpoint #2

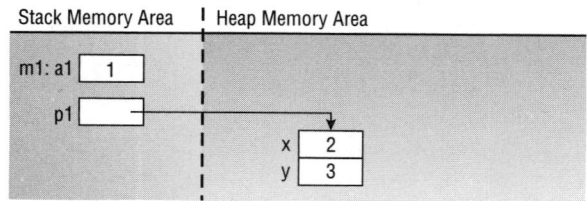

Next, method m2() is called with two arguments. Java basically calls by values for arguments of primitive datatypes; that is, in a method call, the arguments are passed by their values if they are of primitive datatypes. If the arguments are objects, the values are references to the objects, and the effect is call-by-reference. Therefore, the argument variable p2 refers to the same object as the local variable p1 of method m1(). At checkpoint #3, where the local variables a3 and p3 are declared, the memory model after the declaration looks like Figure 5.3.

FIGURE 5.3:

The memory model after checkpoint #3

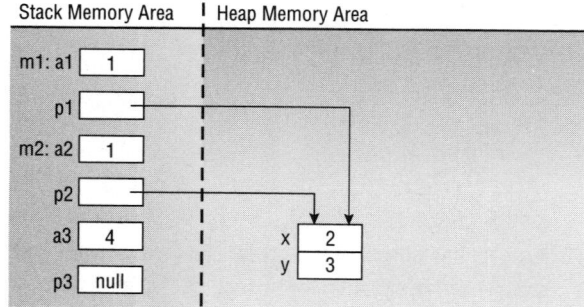

Next, a new object is created by a new statement and assigned to local variable p3. Again, the newly created object is put in the heap area. Then the argument variable a2 is assigned a new value. Since it is call-by-value, the value of the local variable a1 of method m1() is not affected. The memory model at this point is shown in Figure 5.4.

Finally, method m2() is exited, and the memory for the local and argument variables is popped out of the stack area. This leaves the object memory originally allocated for the local variable p3 hanging freely in the heap area with no reference to the block of memory cells. This free-hanging object will be reclaimed later by the garbage collector when needed. At checkpoint #5, an assignment statement is executed; the memory model after the execution is shown in Figure 5.5.

FIGURE 5.4:

The memory model after checkpoint #4

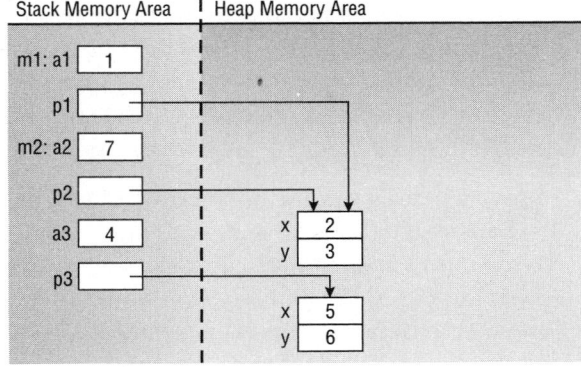

FIGURE 5.5:

The memory model after checkpoint #5

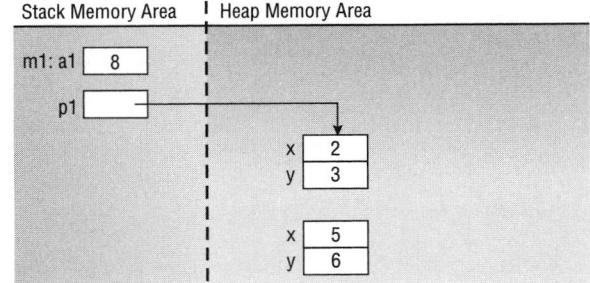

Using Java Interfaces

In Java, a class can have only one immediate superclass. Multiple inheritance, where a class has more than one superclass (as used by C++), is not allowed in Java. Problems may arise when each superclass offers an implementation of the same method and the subclass delays the decision on which implementation of a method to execute until run time.

In Java, the class where the method is defined must be present at compile time so that the compiler can check the signature of the method to make sure the method call is legitimate. All the classes that could possibly be called for the aforementioned method need to share a common superclass so that the method can be defined in the superclass and overridden by the individual subclasses. If you want to force every subclass to have its own implementation of the method, the method can be defined as an abstract one. Chances are you will want to move the method definition higher and higher up the inheritance hierarchy so that more and more classes can override the same method. And—guess what—you will find yourself pondering how you can add a few new methods to the Object class, the root of all classes, so that these methods can be implemented in many otherwise unrelated classes.

Java's interfaces come to the rescue here. An *interface* is a collection of constants and abstract methods. A class can implement an interface by adding the interface to the class's implements clause and overriding the abstract methods defined in the interface. A variable can be declared as an interface type, and all the constants and methods declared in the interface can be accessed from this variable. All objects whose class types implement the interface can then be assigned to this variable. Therefore, to solve the problem of how to decide which method implementation to execute at run time, you can define an interface with the method for sharing among classes. All these classes will declare to implement the interface and create their own implementation of the method. Instances of these classes can then be assigned to a variable of the interface type. Reference to this commonly implemented method from the interface variable will then be resolved at run time.

Defining an Interface

Defining an interface is just like defining a class, except the class keyword is replaced with the interface keyword, and only constants and abstract methods are allowed in an interface. Every interface is by default abstract. All the methods declared in an interface are by default abstract and public, so you do not need to explicitly put the abstract or public modifiers before them. Similarly, all the data members declared in an interface are by default public constants, and you do not need to explicitly insert the final, static, or public modifiers before them. For example, the java.lang package has a Runnable interface defined as follows:

```
public interface Runnable {
  void run();
}
```

Interfaces can form hierarchies just like classes. An interface uses the extends clause to inherit the methods and constants defined in the superinterface. An interface can never extend a normal class, however.

Additionally, the major difference between extending classes and extending interfaces is that you can allow for multiple inheritance in an interface by putting a list of interfaces, separated by commas, in the `extends` clause. For example, the following program fragment shows that the declaration of an interface, `Operable`, inherits two other interfaces, `Openable` and `Closeable`:

```
interface Operable extends Openable, Closeable {
    . . .
}
```

The *implements* Clause

A class declares all of the interfaces it is implementing in its `implements` clause of the class declaration. The `implements` clause consists of the keyword `implements` followed by a list of interfaces separated by commas, and it must be put after the `extends` clause (if there is one).

A class can implement more than one interface. A class implementing an interface will need to override all the methods declared in the interface and all its superinterfaces. Otherwise, the class must be declared as an abstract one. For example, the following class definition fragment implements the `Runnable` interface declared earlier:

```
class MyClass extends MySuperClass implements Runnable {
    . . .
    public void run() {
        . . .
    }
}
```

Since all the methods defined in an interface are inherently public, the overriding methods implemented in the class need to be declared public, too. In Java, methods cannot be overridden to be more private. If you try to declare an overriding method without the `public` modifier, the compiler will issue an error message similar to this one:

```
InterfaceTest.java:51: class InterfaceTest must override void method()
with a public method in order to implement interface MyInterface
public class InterfaceTest implements MyInterface
                 ^
```

If you forget to override one of the methods in an interface and do not declare your class to be abstract, the compiler will issue an error message as follows:

```
OneError.java:1: class OneError must be declared abstract. It does not
define void run() from interface java.lang.Runnable.
public class OneError implements Runnable {
               ^
```

Using an Interface to Implement Callback Functions

A *callback function* in C or C++ is a pointer to a function or to a function object. A service requester then provides the function reference for a server to execute when some previously specified event happens. Callback functions are frequently used in event handling, where event handlers are registered as callback functions to be called when events happen.

In Java, references to methods cannot be passed around. Instead, an object is passed to the server, and the method defined for the object is called from the server. If the clients are instantiated from otherwise unrelated classes, an interface needs to be created to define the method for the server to call. Moreover, all the classes whose instances are requesting a service from the server class must implement the interface. A client can then pass itself as an argument to the server so that the server can execute the method defined in the client class.

In the next example, a message server is created to call the method, `print-Message()`, to be implemented by the client, in regular intervals. The length of the interval and the number of times the method is called is provided by the client when the server instance is created. The server will create a new thread running concurrently with the client when the constructor is called (see Chapter 8 for details on threads). The client repeatedly increments a counter after some computation until the counter reaches some preset value. The program listing is as follows:

```
import java.io.PrintWriter;
public class CallbackTest {
  public static void main(String args[]) {
    LoopingClient client = new LoopingClient();
    new MessageServer (5, 100, client); // create a new server
    client.run();                       // run the client
  }
}
class LoopingClient implements MessagePrintable {
  int counter = 0;
  PrintWriter out = new PrintWriter (System.out, true);
```

```java
    void run() {
      while (counter++ < 2000000) {
        int dummy = counter * counter / (counter + 1);
      }
    }
    public void printMessage() {
      out.println("The counter value is now: " + counter);
    }
}
class MessageServer extends Thread {
  int times;
  int interval;
  MessagePrintable object;
  MessageServer (int times, int interval, MessagePrintable object) {
    this.times    = times;
    this.interval = interval;
    this.object   = object;
    this.setPriority (Thread.NORM_PRIORITY + 2); // let server get
                                                 // higher priority
    this.start();             // start running the new thread
  }
  public void run() {
    // repeat sleep-printMessage several times
    for (int i = 0; i < times; i++) {
      try { // try-catch is for exception handling
        sleep (interval);
      } catch (InterruptedException e) {}
      object.printMessage();
    }
  }
}
interface MessagePrintable {
  void printMessage();
}
```

The try-catch statement is for exception handling (the topic of Chapter 7). An example of the output of the above program is as follows; your output may vary:

```
C:\MasteringJava\Ch05>java CallbackTest
The counter value is now: 29750
The counter value is now: 57739
The counter value is now: 87719
The counter value is now: 122998
The counter value is now: 149327
```

Using Java Packages

A *package* is a collection of related classes and interfaces. As the first noncomment statement of a file, you can use a `package` statement to specify to which package the classes and interfaces defined in the program file belong. You can then use `import` statements to specify the packages whose classes are going to be referred to in the rest of the program.

A package is a grouping mechanism with two main purposes:

- Reducing the potential for name conflicts
- Controlling the visibility of classes, interfaces, and the methods, as well as the data defined within them

Resolving Class Names

Classes can share the same name only if they belong to different packages. When a class is referred to in a program, the compiler will check all the imported packages to find out where the class is defined.

If there is only one imported package in which the named class is defined, the definition of the class in that package will be used. If more than one imported package contains the definition of the named class, you must use the package name as a prefixing qualifier so that no ambiguity occurs when regarding the referred class. You use a period as the separator between the class name and the package name. For example, you may define a `Point` class to hold the x-, y-, and z-coordinates of a three-dimensional point in a user-defined `threeD` package, and another `Point` class to hold the x- and y-coordinates of a two-dimensional point in a `twoD` package. If both the `threeD` and `twoD` packages are imported to the program, you will need to use `threeD.Point` and `twoD.Point` to refer to the `Point` class of three- and two-dimensional points, respectively.

Packages can be nested to form a nice hierarchy. This nesting capability helps further in grouping classes, just as the hierarchy of directories helps you organize your files. To refer to a class of a nested package, you can use a fully qualified name with all the containing package names prefixing the class name. For example, to refer to the `Point` class of the `awt` package under the `java` package, use the fully qualified class name, `java.awt.Point`. However, if `java.awt` is imported and the class name will not conflict with the class names of other imported packages, you can use `Point` without any qualifier to refer to the class.

All classes and interfaces in a package are accessible to all other classes and interfaces in that package. All the data and method members of a class can be accessed from any method of any class under the same package, except when the data and method members are declared `private`.

Packages and Directories

Every package must be mapped to a subdirectory of the same name in the file system. Nested packages will be reflected as a hierarchy of directories in the file system. For example, the class files of package `java.awt.image` must be stored under the directory `java/awt/image` in a Unix file system and `java\awt\image` in a Windows file system.

You can put package directories anywhere in the file system as long as the users have read access to them. In addition, you can place whole directory structures of class files within .zip or .jar files. In order to tell the Java compiler where to locate the packages, you must set the CLASSPATH environment variable. With Java 1.2, you do not have to tell the Java compiler or run time where to find the system classes. (With prior versions you did.) You only need to tell it where you've placed the extra packages you need to use with your program. The list of directories is separated by semicolons on Windows systems and by colons on Unix systems. With Windows, for example, a command line similar to the following might be placed in your `autoexec.bat` file:

```
SET CLASSPATH=.;c:\jaz\myclasses.jar
```

And with Unix, the following command line might be used under C-shell:

```
setenv CLASSPATH .:/users/jaz/myclasses.jar
```

When a class reference like `util.MyClass` is encountered, the directory list is searched from start to end, and the MyClass class of the first directory containing `util\MyClass.class` (or `util/MyClass.class` on Unix) will be used. The Java Virtual Machine also checks inside CLASSPATH entries ending with `.jar` or `.zip`. Therefore, if you define your CLASSPATH variable as above and there is an entry of `.\util\MyClass.class` and another in `myclasses.jar`, the local directory will be used instead of the one in the archive file.

TIP   You should try to avoid having the fully qualified package name conflict with the names of other publicly available packages. Other users running your program with the **CLASSPATH** environment variable set differently may get different behavior or may not be able to run your program at all.

All of the Java built-in classes (that is, the Java Core API) are under the `java` package. Twelve subpackages are defined under the `java` package, as listed in Table 5.1. These packages are discussed in later chapters.

TABLE 5.1:   Subpackages under the `java` Package

Package	Description
java.applet	Applet creation, including an audio clip interface
java.awt	Graphic user interface components and drawing capabilities
java.beans	Classes for JavaBeans support
java.io	Input/output streams and files
java.lang	Essential classes, like `String`, `Object`, and `Thread`
java.math	Classes for extended precision arithmetic
java.net	Networking-related classes
java.rmi	Classes for remote method invocation (RMI)
java.security	Classes for security-related operations, such as digital signatures, data encryption, key management, and access control
java.sql	Classes for sending SQL statements to relational databases
java.text	Classes related to text handling for internationalization
java.util	Utility classes for special data structures, like `Properties`, `Iterator`, and `Calendar`

The *package* Statement

The general form of a `package` statement is:

```
package name;
```

where *name* is either a single package name or a list of package names separated by commas. For example, the following two statements are both legitimate `package` statements:

```
package myPackage;
package java.awt.image;
```

Only one `package` statement is allowed in a program file, and it must be the first noncomment statement in the file. If the `package` statement is omitted from the program file, the classes generated will be put under an unnamed default package that is always imported.

NOTE   The recommended standard for naming packages is to start with your domain name reversed. For instance, the CORBA support packages come from `omg.org`, so the package is named `org.omg.CORBA`.

The *import* Statement

The `import` statement allows classes and interfaces defined in packages to be referred to solely by the class names instead of the fully qualified names. There are two forms of `import` statements:

```
import packageName.ClassName
import packageName.
```

where `packageName` is a single package name or a list of nested package names separated by periods.

In the first form, only the specified class of the named package is imported. In the second form, all the classes and interfaces in the named package are directly accessible by simple names. You must put `import` statements at the beginning of a program file. The only noncomment statement allowed before an `import` statement is a `package` statement. In the following program fragment, class `Vector` of the `java.util` package is imported, as are all the classes and interfaces of the `java.awt` package, but not those defined in the subpackage `java.awt.image`. Therefore, `Vector` can be directly referred to by a simple name, as are the classes (like `Label` and `Button`) defined in the `java.awt` package. However, neither the `java.io` package nor the `PrintStream` class defined in the package is imported, and `PrintStream` must be referred to by its fully qualified name:

```
import java.util.Vector;
import java.awt.*;
class ImportTest {
    Vector v;                      // in java.util package
    Label  label;                  // in java.awt package
    Button button;                 // in java.awt package
    java.io.PrintStream out;       // fully qualified class name
                                   // required
}
```

TIP   Having a class or package imported does not mean the class or classes inside the package will necessarily be loaded at run time. The `import` statement is used only to give the Java compiler hints on resolving class names. The classes or packages mentioned in the `import` statements might never be referred to in the program body.

Summary

Casting is used to convert a value from one datatype to another type. It can only be done between two primitive types or reference types. If an assignment statement causes loss of information or extension of the datatype, an explicit casting operation is necessary.

The `this` and `super` keywords can be used as method names referring to the constructors in the current class and the superclass, respectively. They also can be used to refer to the current object and members in the superclass, respectively.

An interface is a collection of constants and abstract methods. Interfaces are Java's solution to multiple inheritance and callback functions. A class implements an interface by adding the interface to the `implements` clause and overriding the abstract methods defined in the interface and its superinterfaces.

A package is a collection of classes and interfaces. Packages can be nested to form a tree-like hierarchy. A package is reflected as a directory of the same name in the file system. A class defines the package it belongs to with a `package` statement. Also, `import` statements allow classes and interfaces defined in packages to be referred to by their simple names.

This chapter provided information about objects and classes that, together with the information presented in previous chapters, is the key to creating Java programs in an object-oriented way. Combine this with arrays, flow-control statements, exceptions, and threading (the topics of the following chapters), and you have the core of the Java language.

Arrays and Flow-Control Statements

- Arrays in Java

- Conditional statements

- Loop statements

- Flow-breaking statements

Up until this point, you have seen examples of programs that use variables of a single object type or primitive datatype only. In addition, the line of execution in these programs is sequential, from the first line to the last one, with occasional excursions to execute linearly the code segments in methods. The tasks that can be accomplished using these language constructs are limited, and inevitably you will need to execute portions of the code repeatedly or selectively, as well as handle a group of similar objects as a whole. In this chapter, you will learn to manipulate groups of objects and to use conditional, loop, and flow-breaking statements. Together, these program constructs will allow you to perform tasks that are much more complicated.

Using Arrays

This section describes basic array operations, including accessing array elements and declaring, creating, and copying arrays. But first, you should understand just what an array is.

What Is an Array?

An *array* is a group of variables of the same type referable by a common name. The type can be either a primitive datatype like `int` or an object type like `String`. For example, you can define an array of integers to hold the daily high temperature in a month as:

```
int dailyHigh[];
```

On the other hand, using the `Point` class defined in the `java.awt` package, you can define an array to hold a list of two-dimensional points as:

```
Point points[];
```

An array is an object; that is, it is handled by reference. When you pass an array to a method, only the reference to the array is passed, rather than the whole array of elements. Declaring an array variable creates only a placeholder for the reference to the array, not the memory holding the array of elements per se. Also, the actual memory used by the array elements is dynamically allocated either by a new statement or an array initializer. The memory referenced by the array variable will be automatically garbage-collected when no longer referenced. Every array object has a public instance variable `length` to hold the size of the array.

The following example gives you a close look at the memory model of an array. First, a class to hold a point in two-dimensional graphics is defined as follows:

```
class Point {
  int    x;
  int    y;
  Point (int x, int y) {  // constructor
    this.x = x;
    this.y = y;
  }
}
```

After declaring the array to hold a list of points, the memory model looks like Figure 6.1.

FIGURE 6.1:

The memory model after adding an array declaration: `Point points[];`

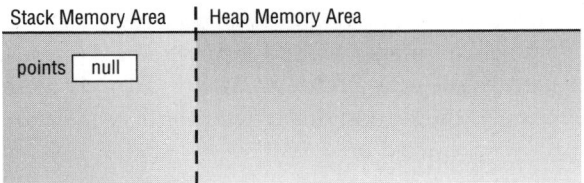

You can then use the following **new** statement to allocate memory space for holding two references to the `Point` object:

```
points = new Point[2];
```

After the allocation, you can access the size of the array as `points.length`. The memory model is shown in Figure 6.2.

FIGURE 6.2:

The memory model after allocating space for array elements: `points = new Points [2];`

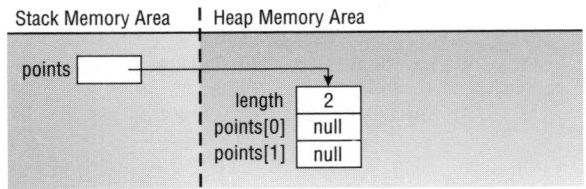

The first element of the array can be filled by:

```
points[0] = new Point(1,2);
```

Figure 6.3 shows the memory model after adding the above statement.

FIGURE 6.3:

The memory model after the first element of the array is assigned: `points [0] = new point (1,2);`

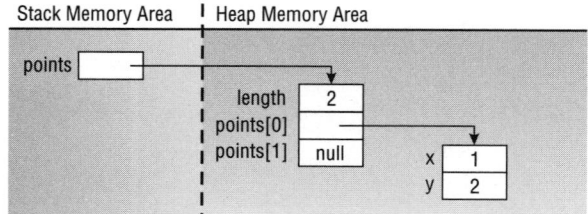

Accessing Array Elements

Java follows normal C-style indexing for accessing an array element; that is, you attach an integer-valued expression between square brackets after the name of the array. The array index starts with zero. Therefore, to get the daily high temperature of the second day of the month, you can use the following code fragment:

```
dailyHigh[1]
```

All subscript accesses will be checked to make sure they are within the legal range: greater than or equal to zero and less than the array length. If the value is out of bounds, the exception `ArrayIndexOutOfBoundsException` is thrown. See Chapter 7 for details on what exceptions are and how to handle them.

Declaring and Creating an Array

Square brackets are used to declare an array type. There are two formats for declaring an array:

- Put the brackets after the datatype.

- Put the brackets after the array name.

For example:

```
int[] a;
```

is equivalent to:

```
int a[];
```

The author of this book prefers the latter format, but either format is acceptable. The one difference between the two forms exists when multiple array variables are declared on the same line:

```
int[] a, b[];
```

declares a one-dimensional array and a two-dimensional array. While:

```
int a, b[];
```

declares one `int` variable and a one-dimensional array.

A `new` statement is used to allocate the space needed for either holding the actual values of the array elements (if the elements are of primitive datatype) or holding the references to array elements (if they are of object type). For example, to create an array to hold the daily high temperature for the month of January, you can use the following statement:

```
int dailyHigh[] = new int[31];
```

To create an array to hold the coordinates of the three vertices of a triangle, you can declare an array as:

```
Point[] triangle = new Point[3];
```

An array created by a `new` statement will have the elements automatically initialized to the default value of the element types. For example, elements of `int` or `double` type will be initialized to 0s, and elements of an object type will be set to `null`.

An array initializer may be used to create an array with preset values. A list of comma-separated expressions that will each be evaluated to the array's element type is enclosed in curly braces. For example, to initialize an array to hold the number of days in each month of a leap year, you can declare the array as:

```
int monthDays[] = {31, 29, 31, 30, 31, 30, 31, 31, 30, 31, 30, 31};
```

After declaring an array variable, you can use an array initializer on the right side of a normal assignment statement. The format is slightly different, but the result is the same.

```
int monthDays[];
monthDays = new int[] {31, 29, 31, 30, 31, 30, 31, 31, 30, 31, 30, 31};
```

Copying an Array

Because an array is an object, assigning the value of an array variable to another array variable will copy only the reference to that array. For example, you can assign the value of the `points` array described in previous examples to the new array variable `points2` as:

```
Point points2[] = points;
```

The memory model for these two variables is shown in Figure 6.4.

FIGURE 6.4:

The memory model after assignment: `Point points2[] = points;`

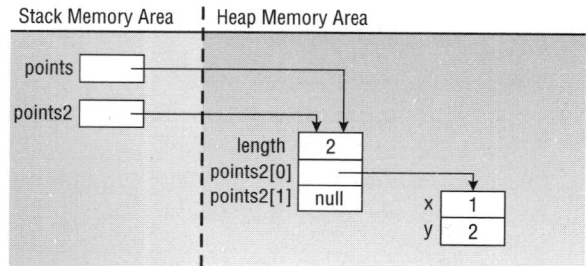

To actually copy the values or a portion of the values stored in an array into another array, the `arraycopy()` method of the `System` class under the `java.lang` package can be used. The synopsis of that method is:

```
void arraycopy (Object sourceArray,
                int sourceStartPosition,
                Object destinationArray,
                int destinationStartPosition,
                int numberOfElementsToBeCopied);
```

For example, to copy all the values in `points` into `points2`, you can use:

```
System.arraycopy(points, 0, points2, 0, points.length);
```

Be aware that the memory space for the destination array must be allocated before calling the `arraycopy()` method. For the above example, `points2` may first need to be created as:

```
points2 = new Point[points.length];
```

Figure 6.5 shows the memory model after copying the array.

FIGURE 6.5:

The memory model after array copy: System.arraycopy (points, 0,points2, 0, points.length);

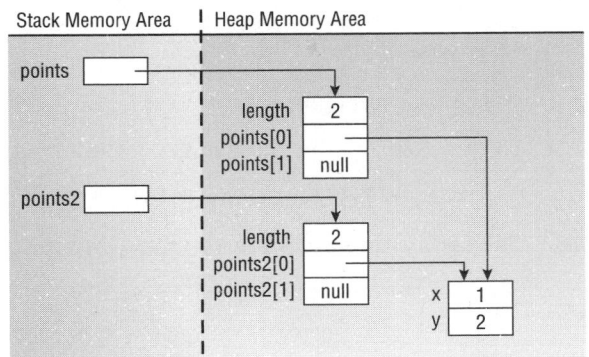

For an array of objects, the values stored in an array are references to the objects. To duplicate an array with its component object elements, you can use the clone() method of the Object class (the root of all objects) in conjunction with the array-copy() method. Only classes implementing the Cloneable interface may be cloned. They include the Vector, HashMap, and BitSet classes defined in the java.util package. See Part Two for more details about these classes.

For example, if val is already declared and created as an array of Vector, the following code fragment can be used to duplicate val as va2:

```
Vector va2[] = new Vector[val.length];
System.arraycopy (val, 0, va2, 0, val.length);
for (int i = 0; i < val.length; i++)
  va2[i] = (Vector) val[i].clone();
```

The System.arraycopy() method copies the array of vector reference variables. Then, the for loop creates a new copy of each vector that is in the array. If there is no clone() or similar method available, you will need to explicitly create a new copy of each element in the array. For example, the following code segment can be added to the earlier example so that points2 is a full duplicate of points:

```
points2[0] = new Point(points[0].x, points[0].y);
```

Multidimensional Arrays

A multidimensional array is implemented as an array of arrays. You can create a nonrectangular multidimensional array by having elements of an array refer to arrays of different sizes. To initialize a multidimensional array, nested curly braces are used. For example, to initialize a two-dimensional array of which the first element has two sub-elements and the second one has three sub-elements, you can declare it as:

```
int a[][] = {{1,2}, {3,4,5}};
```

To create a three-by-three matrix of integers, you can say:

```
int matrix[][] = new int[3][3];
```

The earlier statement for declaring and initializing a can be rewritten as:

```
int a0[]  = {1,2}, a1[] = {3,4,5};
int a[][] = {a0, a1};
```

Or even lengthier, as:

```
int a0[]  = {1,2};
int a1[]  = {3,4,5};
int a[][] = new int[2][];
a[0] = a0;
a[1] = a1;
```

The memory model for this example is shown in Figure 6.6.

FIGURE 6.6:

The memory model for a multidimensional array:
```
int a[][] = {{1,2},
{3,4,5}};
```

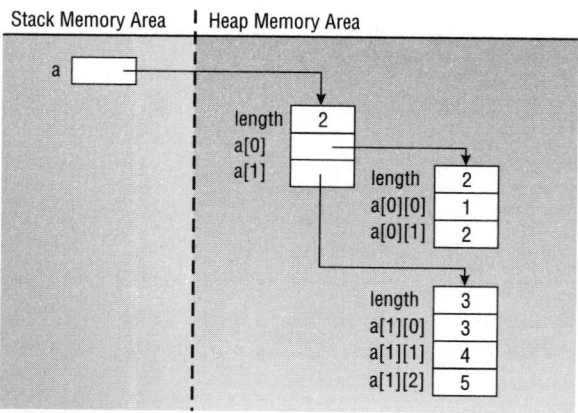

You should be careful when you are declaring a list of multidimensional arrays with different dimensionalities. In the following code fragment, b is declared as a one-dimensional array, and c as a two-dimensional array:

```
int[] b, c[];
```

The previous statement can be legitimately rewritten as:

```
int b[], c[][];
```

TIP　This can be a little bit confusing to C and C++ programmers. It might help if you treat the set of square brackets after the datatype as a modifier to the datatype rather than to the array name(s).

Using Flow-Control Statements

Java's flow-control statements are basically modeled after those of C and C++:

- if and switch statements are used for selective execution of code segments.

- for, while, and do statements are used for repeated execution of code segments.

- break, continue, and return statements are used for breaking the flow.

Two major differences exist in Java, however. First, the conditional expressions used in if, for, while, or do statements must be valid boolean expressions that will be evaluated to values of either true or false. In Java, the values 0 or null cannot be a substitute for false. Neither can nonzero or non-null values be used in place of true. Furthermore, you cannot explicitly cast an int type into a boolean type. The other difference is that there is no goto statement in Java; labeled break and continue statements are provided as better solutions where the use of goto statements may be justified.

Conditional Statements

Conditional statements allow for the selective execution of portions of the program according to the value of some expressions. Java supports two types of conditional statements: if and switch statements. In addition, the tertiary ?: operators can sometimes be used as alternatives to if-else statements.

if Statements

The general form of an if statement is:

```
if (conditionalExpression)
   ifStatement
else
   elseStatement
```

An if statement will first test its conditional expression. If it is evaluated to true, the statement or block of statements immediately after the conditional expression will be executed. Otherwise, the statement or block of statements after else will be executed. The else part is optional. For example, the following code fragment will test if a character is a digit, a whitespace, or another type of character, and set the appropriate boolean variable to true:

```
char ch = 'a';
boolean isDigit = false, isSpace = false, isOther = false;
if (Character.isDigit(ch))
   isDigit = true;
else if (Character.isWhitespace(ch))
   isSpace = true;
else
   isOther = true;
```

isDigit() and isWhitespace() are class methods of the Character class defined in the java.lang package; they are used to determine if the character argument passed in belongs to a certain character type.

As another example, the following code fragment will assign a character grade according to the score in a 100-point system:

```
int score = 65;
char grade;
if (score >= 90)
   grade = 'A';
else if (score >= 80)
   grade = 'B';
else if (score >= 70)
   grade = 'C';
else if (score >= 60)
   grade = 'D';
else
   grade = 'F';
```

Using nested ?: operators, the above example can be succinctly rewritten as:

```
int score = 65;
char grade = (score >= 90) ? 'A' :
             (score >= 80) ? 'B' :
             (score >= 70) ? 'C' :
             (score >= 60) ? 'D' : 'F';
```

TIP

Although `if (score = 70)` is valid in C and C++, it will result in a compilation error in Java, because `score = 70` is an assignment operation evaluated to an integer value of 70, not a conditional expression that will be evaluated to a boolean value of `true` or `false`.

---

switch Statements

The general form of a `switch` statement is:

```
switch (expression) {
  case value1:
    codeSegment1
  case value2:
    codeSegment2
    . . .
  case valueN:
    codeSegmentN
  default:
    defaultCodeSegment
}
```

A `switch` statement is used for multiple-way selection that will branch to different code segments based on the value of a variable or an expression. The optional default label is used to specify the code segment to be executed when the value of the variable or expression cannot match any of the `case` values. If there is no `break` statement as the last statement in the code segment for a certain `case`, the execution will continue on into the code segment for the next `case` clause without checking the `case` value. `break` statements are discussed later in this chapter.

TIP

It is a common programming error to forget to have a `break` statement as the last statement of a code segment for a `case` clause of a `switch` statement.

The expression used in a `switch` statement must be an integral expression or one whose evaluated result can be implicitly cast into an `int` type without losing information. Datatypes that can be cast into an `int` type without losing information include `byte`, `char`, and `short`. For datatypes like `long`, `float`, and `double`, explicit casting is required. The `case` values must be constant expressions that can be evaluated to or later implicitly cast to a constant value of `int` type at compile time.

Similar to the earlier example of `if` statements, the following code fragment will set the appropriate boolean variable according to the character type of the character variable `ch`. This `switch` statement will recognize only digits and whitespaces defined in ASCII; the `if` statement shown earlier can handle digits and whitespaces defined in other languages or code sets covered by Unicode. Here's the code:

```
switch (ch) {
  case '0': case '1': case '2': case '3': case '4':
  case '5': case '6': case '7': case '8': case '9':
    isDigit = true;
    break;
  case ' ':
  case '\t':
  case '\n':
    isSpace = true;
    break;
  default:
    isOther = true;
}
```

If the `break` statement after `isDigit = true` is missing, both `isSpace` and `isDigit` will be set to `true` for characters of `digit` type.

Loop Statements

Loop statements allow for the repeated execution of blocks of statements. There are three types of loop statements: `for`, `while`, and `do` loops. `for` and `while` loops test the loop condition at the top of the loop, before the loop body is executed. `do` loops check the condition at the bottom of the loop, after the loop body is executed.

for Statements

The general form of a `for` statement is:

```
for (initializationStatement; conditionalExpression;
    incrementStatement)
  loopBody
```

To execute a `for` statement, the initialization statement is first executed. The conditional expression is then evaluated. If it is evaluated to `true`, the loop body is executed, followed by the `increment` statement. The evaluation of the conditional expression and the execution of the loop body and the increment statement are repeated until the conditional expression evaluates to `false`. Multiple initialization or increment statements are allowed if separated by commas.

As in C++, local loop variables can be declared in the initialization section of a `for` loop. The scope of the loop variables is just the loop itself. These loop variables follow the general rules for declaring variables inside a block delimited by curly braces: They cannot have the same names as any variables declared in an outer scope, and they cannot be referred to outside the loop.

For example, the following code fragment can be used to prepare a two-dimensional array for holding a full year's daily high temperatures, grouped by months:

```
int monthDays[] = {31, 28, 31, 30, 31, 30, 31, 31, 30, 31, 30, 31};
int dailyHigh[][] = new int[monthDays.length][];
for (int i = 0; i < monthDays.length; i++) {
  dailyHigh[i] = new int[monthDays[i]];
}
```

Moreover, the following method can be defined to return the highest temperature in a year:

```
int getYearlyHigh (int dailyHigh[][]) {
  int yearlyHigh = Integer.MIN_VALUE;
  for (int i = 0; i < monthDays.length; i++)
    for (int j = 0; j < dailyHigh[i].length; j++)
      if (yearlyHigh < dailyHigh[i][j])
        yearlyHigh = dailyHigh[i][j];
  return yearlyHigh;
}
```

`MIN_VALUE` is a class variable (a constant, in fact) of the `Integer` class under the `java.lang` package defined as the smallest possible value of type `int`.

while Statements

The general form of a `while` statement is:

```
while (conditionalExpression)
    loopBody
```

To execute a `while` statement, the conditional expression will first be evaluated. If it is evaluated to `true`, the loop body is executed. Otherwise, program control passes to the line after the loop body. The testing of the conditional expression and the execution of the loop body is repeated until the conditional expression is evaluated to `false`. For example, the following code fragment will calculate the sum of the numbers from 1 through 100:

```
int i = 1, sum = 0;
while (i <= 100)
    sum += i++;
```

do Statements

The general form of a do statement is:

```
do
    loopBody
while (conditionalExpression);
```

The only difference between a do statement and a `while` statement is in the order of execution. In a do statement, the loop body will be executed before the conditional expression is evaluated. Therefore, the loop body will be executed at least once in a do statement; the loop body in a `while` statement may never be executed. For example, the following code fragment will repeatedly prompt the user until the user enters "exit":

```
String buffer;
BufferedReader myIn =
    new BufferedReader(new InputStreamReader(System.in));
PrintWriter out = new PrintWriter(System.out);
do {
    out.print("Enter a command: ");
    out.flush();
    buffer = myIn.readLine();
} while (! buffer.equals("exit"));
```

`BufferedReader` is a class defined in the `java.io` package with methods allowing you to read text lines from an underlying character-input stream, which, in the previous example, is the byte stream of standard input, `System.in`, translated into a character stream by the `InputStreamReader` class.

Flow-Breaking Statements

Java supports three types of flow-breaking statements:

- `break` statements are used to exit from `switch` statements, loop statements, and labeled blocks.

- `continue` statements are used to jump to the end of the loop body just past the last line of the statement.

- `return` statements are used to exit from a method or a constructor.

Statements and blocks of statements delimited by curly braces can be labeled and later referred to by the enclosed `break` statements. However, only labels of enclosing loop statements can be referred to by `continue` statements.

break Statements

The general form of a `break` statement is:

```
break label;
```

where the label is optional. Without a label, the `break` statement will transfer the program control to the statement just after the innermost enclosing loop or `switch` statement. With a label, it will transfer the program control to the statement just after the enclosing statement or block of statements carrying the same label. For example, the following code fragment will print the third day in a year with a daily high of above 70 degrees:

```
PrintWriter out = new PrintWriter(System.out);
outerLoop:
  for (int i = 0, count = 0; i < dailyHigh.length; i++)
    for (int j = 0; j < dailyHigh[i].length; j++)
      if ((dailyHigh[i][j] > 70) & (++count == 3)) {
        out.println("The date is: month = " + (i + 1) +
          ", day = " + (j + 1));
        break outerLoop;
      }
// break outerLoop, if executed, will reach here
```

continue Statements

The general form of a `continue` statement is:

```
continue label;
```

where the label is optional. Without a label, it behaves exactly the same as in C and C++. The program control is transferred to the point right after the last statement in the enclosing loop body. In `while` and `do` statements, the conditional expressions will now be retested. In `for` loops, the increment statements will be executed next. With a label, the program control will be transferred to the end of the enclosing loop body with the same label, instead of the innermost one.

For example, the following code segment defines a method to return the offset position of the first occurrence of one string, `str2`, in the other string, `str1`:

```
int indexOf (String str1, String str2) {
  int len1 = str1.length();
  int len2 = str2.length();
  char str2FirstChar = str2.charAt(0);
advanceOneCharAtStr1:
  for (int i = 0; i + len2 <= len1; i++)
    if (str1.charAt(i) == str2FirstChar) {
      for (int j = 1; j < len2; j++)
        if (str1.charAt(i + j) != str2.charAt(j))
          continue advanceOneCharAtStr1;
        return i;
    }
  return -1;
}
```

return Statements

The general form of a `return` statement is:

```
return expression;
```

A `return` statement is used to return control to the caller from within a method or constructor. If the method is defined to return a value, the expression must be evaluated to the return type of that method. Otherwise, only an unlabeled `return` statement can be used.

An Example: The Daily High

This section presents an example that demonstrates the use of one- and two-dimensional arrays and various flow-control statements. Three arrays are used in the example:

- monthDays, a one-dimensional array of int type to hold the number of days in each month

- monthNames, a one-dimensional array of String type to hold the names of the months

- dailyHigh, a two-dimensional array of int type to hold a full year's daily high temperatures, grouped by months

The program first initializes the dailyHigh array with random numbers between 10 and 100. random() is a class method defined in the Math class of the package java.lang. This method will return a random number between 0 and 1 of double type. The program then prints a year's daily high grouped by months. It continues on to print the third day in the year with a daily high above 76 degrees. At last, it reports the number of months with monthly highs less than or equal to 96 degrees. The entire program is listed here:

```
import java.io.PrintWriter;
public class DailyHigh {
  static int monthDays[] = {31,28,31,30,31,30,31,31,30,31,30,31};
  static String monthNames[] =
    {"Jan", "Feb", "Mar", "Apr", "May", "Jun",
     "Jul", "Aug", "Sep", "Oct", "Nov", "Dec"};
  int dailyHigh[][];
  PrintWriter out;
  // constructor
  DailyHigh (PrintWriter out) {
    dailyHigh = new int[12][];
    this.out = out;
    for (int i = 0; i < 12; i++)
      dailyHigh[i] = new int[monthDays[i]];
  }
  // fill in the 2-D array with random temperatures between 10 and 100
  void init() {
    for (int i = 0; i < 12; i++)
```

```java
        for (int j = 0; j < monthDays[i]; j++)
            dailyHigh[i][j] = (int) (Math.random() * 90.0 + 10.0);
    }
    // print the dailyHigh array
    void print() {
      out.println("\nDaily High:\n");
      for (int i = 0; i < 12; i++) {
        out.print(monthNames[i] + ":");
        for (int j = 0; j < monthDays[i]; j++) {
          if ((j != 0) && (j % 7 == 0))
            out.print(j % 14 == 0 ? "\n      " : "   ");
          out.print(" " + dailyHigh[i][j]);
        }
        out.println();
      }
    }
    // the number of months with monthly high less than or equal to
    // certain number; a demonstration of usage of labeled continue
    int monthlyHighNotMoreThan (int reference) {
      int count = 0;
  outerLoop:
      for (int i = 0; i < dailyHigh.length; i++) {
        for (int j = 0; j < dailyHigh[i].length; j++)
          if (dailyHigh[i][j] > reference)
            continue outerLoop;
        count++;
      }
      return count;
    }
    public static void main (String args[]) {
      PrintWriter out = new PrintWriter (System.out, true);
      DailyHigh t = new DailyHigh(out);
      t.init();
      t.print();
      // find the third day in the year with daily high above 76
      // a demonstration of use of labeled break
  out:
      {
        out.print("\nThe third day with daily high above 76 is: ");
        for (int i = 0, count = 0; i < t.dailyHigh.length; i++)
          for (int j = 0; j < monthDays[i]; j++)
            if ((t.dailyHigh[i][j] > 76) && (++count == 3)) {
```

```
                out.println(monthNames[i] + " " + (j + 1));
                break out;
            }
        // reach here only when the 3rd date cannot be found
        out.println("no such date");
    }
    int reference = 96;
    out.println("The number of months with monthly high <= " +
            reference + " is " +
            t.monthlyHighNotMoreThan (reference));

    }
}
```

Here is an output of the program (your output may be different due to the random numbers):

```
C:\MasteringJava\Ch06>java DailyHigh
Daily High:
Jan: 81 16 30 35 60 37 38    25 11 59 72 68 23 86
     94 72 85 24 59 95 32    46 37 30 54 29 28 72
     89 56 36
Feb: 90 24 14 44 92 21 66    64 37 71 40 52 40 68
     33 99 10 37 28 26 69    19 74 48 53 63 59 95
Mar: 26 95 64 61 17 62 20    16 68 52 26 62 71 81
     25 25 87 24 26 40 25    45 93 77 77 65 65 48
     14 21 10
Apr: 84 71 74 84 62 55 42    62 84 36 76 70 46 21
     56 10 53 27 58 67 59    76 92 14 18 28 23 36
     70 34
May: 49 22 63 18 34 46 85    65 86 16 38 85 62 58
     35 79 62 28 26 12 82    14 61 80 28 17 98 88
     10 74 62
Jun: 38 21 91 78 81 57 53    99 92 15 59 58 89 56
     17 13 19 33 73 98 43    96 45 83 12 83 58 60
     14 78
Jul: 88 38 36 32 14 54 42    20 53 13 24 37 74 47
     47 43 88 88 27 77 45    61 38 20 70 54 24 43
     51 95 46
Aug: 97 37 67 69 77 59 86    49 70 69 83 87 36 62
     56 82 23 40 46 35 70    82 96 21 81 61 32 47
     72 15 23
Sep: 14 16 85 22 87 24 51    27 97 35 90 78 97 38
     41 16 10 10 74 14 56    96 14 16 57 59 51 13
     51 27
```

```
Oct:  80 28 94 55 64 67 29    58 97 96 64 26 82 85
      86 80 55 32 19 58 20    50 94 84 92 61 33 84
      59 26 46
Nov:  51 54 61 52 26 38 85    21 66 66 59 43 81 16
      86 51 95 23 72 13 42    94 43 88 26 43 92 91
      13 40
Dec:  81 27 24 95 75 41 18    76 37 46 42 93 61 68
      86 96 86 88 93 67 32    61 83 58 72 38 19 24
      73 90 90
The third day with daily high above 76 is: Jan 15
The number of months with monthly high <= 96 is 6
```

Summary

This chapter introduced the use of Java arrays and control statements. An array is a group of variables of the same type that can be referred to by a common name. An array is an object. Declaring an array variable creates only a placeholder for the reference to the array. You need to use either a new statement or an array initializer to allocate the space for the array. A multidimensional array is implemented as an array of arrays and therefore can be nonrectangular.

Java's flow-control statements are similar to those in C and C++: if and switch statements are used for selective execution of code segments; for, while, and do statements are used for repeated execution of code segments; and break, continue, and return statements are used for breaking the flow. Java has no goto statement, but labeled break and continue statements are usually good solutions in places where you would want to use a goto statement.

Arrays allow you to handle similar data objects as groups. Flow-control statements allow you to selectively and/or repeatedly execute program fragments. Together with exception handling for handling abnormal conditions and multithreading for concurrent execution of programs, they allow you to manage complicated program control for your applications.

CHAPTER

SEVEN

7

Exception Handling

- Exception-handling basics

- The hierarchy of exception classes

- Constructs for exception handling

- Customized exception classes

As programs become more complicated, making them robust is a much more difficult task. Traditional programming languages like C rely on the heavy use of `if` statements to detect abnormal conditions, `goto` statements to branch to the error handlers, and cryptic `return` codes for propagating the abnormal conditions back to the calling methods. Thus, normal program flow gets buried in the web of exception detection and handling statements, or robustness is sacrificed for the sake of clarity.

Using an exception-handling mechanism similar to that of C++, Java provides an elegant way to build programs that are both robust and clear. In this chapter, you will learn to use this cleaner mechanism to handle errors and unusual conditions.

Overview of Exception Handling

An *exception* is an abnormal condition that disrupts normal program flow. There are many cases where abnormal conditions happen during program execution, such as the following:

- The file you try to open may not exist.

- The class file you want to load may be missing or in the wrong format.

- The other end of your network connection may be nonexistent.

- The network connection may be disrupted for some mysterious reason.

- An operand is not in the legal range prescribed for operations or methods. For example, an array element index cannot exceed the size of the array, and a divisor in a division operation cannot be zero.

If these abnormal conditions are not prevented or at least handled properly, either the program will be aborted abruptly or the incorrect results or status will be carried on, causing more and more abnormal conditions. Imagine a program that reads from an unopened file and does computations based on those input values!

The Basic Model

Java follows the basic C++ syntax for exception handling. First, you `try` to execute a block of statements. If an abnormal condition occurs, something will `throw` an exception that you can catch with a handler. In addition, finally, there may be a block of statements you always want executed—no matter whether an exception occurred and no matter whether the exception is handled if it does occur.

Throwing an exception is friendlier than terminating the program because it provides the programmer with the option of writing a handler to deal with the abnormal condition. For example, the following program fragment causes the program to sleep for 10 seconds (10,000 milliseconds) by calling the sleep() class method defined in class Thread of the java.lang package. If sleep is interrupted before the time expires, a message is printed and the execution continues with the statement following this try-catch construct:

```
PrintWriter out = new PrintWriter(System.out, true);
try {
  Thread.sleep(10000);
} catch (InterruptedException e) {
  out.println("Sleeping interrupted.");
}
// reaches here after try-block finished or exception handled
```

The next program, which copies the contents of one file to another, demonstrates exception handling in a more practical setting. The program first takes filenames from the command-line arguments. Then, it opens the files and copies data in 512-byte block increments. The number of bytes copied is tracked, and the byte count is reported once the operation is completed. The program fragment to carry out these operations is as follows:

```
int     byteCount = 0;
byte buffer[] = new byte[512];
String inputFile  = null;
String outputFile = null;
PrintWriter out = new PrintWriter(System.out, true);
FileInputStream  fin;
FileOutputStream fout;
inputFile  = args[0];
outputFile = args[1];
fin  = new FileInputStream(inputFile);
fout = new FileOutputStream(outputFile);
int bytesInOneRead;
while ((bytesInOneRead = fin.read(buffer)) != -1) {
  fout.write(buffer, 0, bytesInOneRead);
  byteCount += bytesInOneRead;
}
out.println(byteCount + " written");
```

The FileInputStream and FileOutputStream classes are defined in the java.io package. Their constructors allow you to open files by name, and their methods let you read data from or write data into a single byte or a byte array.

But what if the user does not provide the input and output filenames? Or what if the user provides a nonexistent input file? In Java, these abnormal conditions are system-defined exceptions that will be thrown by the system as they occur. Accessing an array with an index larger than or equal to the array size will cause an ArrayIndexOutOfBoundsException to be thrown. The constructor of the FileInputStream class will throw a FileNotFoundException exception if the file cannot be located. The constructor for FileOutputStream and the read() and write() methods will throw an IOException exception for an I/O error.

Furthermore, exception handlers can be located together. A catch clause is necessary for each exception handler to identify the abnormal condition to which the handler is attending. Three handlers need to be added to the previous program to attend to the abnormal conditions mentioned previously:

- One handler will print the usage of the program when the user does not provide both the input and output filenames.

- The next handler will notify the user when the input file does not exist.

- Another handler will print an error message when other I/O exceptions occur.

The program to print the number of bytes copied is moved to the finally clause so that it will always be executed—even if some abnormal condition disrupts the normal program flow. Here is the full program:

```
import java.io.*;
public class MyCopy {
  public static void main (String args[]) {
    int    byteCount = 0;
    byte buffer[] = new byte[512];
    String inputFile  = null;
    String outputFile = null;
    PrintWriter out = new PrintWriter(System.out, true);
    FileInputStream  fin;
    FileOutputStream fout;
    try {
      inputFile  = args[0];
      outputFile = args[1];
```

```
        fin  = new FileInputStream(inputFile);
        fout = new FileOutputStream(outputFile);
        int bytesInOneRead;
        while ((bytesInOneRead = fin.read(buffer)) != -1) {
          fout.write(buffer, 0, bytesInOneRead);
          byteCount += bytesInOneRead;
        }
      } catch (ArrayIndexOutOfBoundsException e) {
        out.println("Usage: java MyCopy [inputFile] [outputFile]");
      } catch (FileNotFoundException e) {
        out.println("Cannot open input file: " + inputFile);
      } catch (IOException e) {
        out.println("I/O exception occurs!");
      } finally {
        if (byteCount > 0)
          out.println(byteCount + " bytes written");
      }
    }
  }
```

Here is a sample output of the previous program run under different conditions:

```
C:\MasteringJava\Ch07>java MyCopy
Usage: java MyCopy [inputFile] [outputFile]
C:\MasteringJava\Ch07>java MyCopy MyCopy.java temp.java
1095 bytes written
C:\MasteringJava\Ch07>java MyCopy NoSuchFile.java temp.java
Cannot open input file: NoSuchFile.java
```

Why Use Exception Handling?

You should use exception handling for several reasons. One is that error-handling code is separated from normal program flow to increase the readability and maintainability of the program.

Imagine how you would rewrite the example from the previous section in C if exception handling was not available. You would need an if statement after every I/O operation to make sure they were completed successfully. You would also need to use an if statement to check whether the user provided enough filenames. To handle these abnormal conditions, you would either add more code in place or use goto statements to branch to the code fragment that handles common failures. Add a few more I/O calls, and even you, the author of the program, will not be able to easily recognize what the program was originally intended to accomplish. With Java, there is no need to test if an exception condition happens. Adding more handlers requires adding more `catch` clauses, but the original program flow is unaffected.

Another reason to use exception handling is so you can easily say where the exception will be handled. Exceptions propagate up the call stack at run time—first up the enclosing `try` blocks and then back to the calling method—until an exception handler catches them. For example, the previous example can be rewritten as a method with input and output filenames as the arguments. The synopsis of this new method is as follows:

```
int copyFile(String inputFile, String outputFile)
```

The caller of this method may want to handle the abnormal condition itself. For example, an application with a GUI may want to display a dialog box prompting the user for another filename when the input file does not exist. In this case, the error handler for an I/O exception is removed from the method and a `throws` clause is added to the method declaration. The caller can then have its own error-handling routines for these abnormal conditions. Here is the modified method definition:

```
int copyFile(String inputFile, String outputFile) throws IOException {
   int bytesInOneRead, byteCount = 0;
   byte buffer[] = new byte[512];
   FileInputStream  fin = new FileInputStream(inputFile);
   FileOutputStream fout= new FileOutputStream(outputFile);
   while ((bytesInOneRead = fin.read(buffer)) != -1) {
      fout.write(buffer, 0, bytesInOneRead);
      byteCount += bytesInOneRead;
   }
   return byteCount;
}
```

Here is a code fragment to call this method and handle the abnormal conditions itself:

```
int byteCount = 0;
String inputFile = null;
String outputFile = null;
PrintWriter out = new PrintWriter(System.out, true);
try {
   inputFile  = args[0];
   outputFile = args[1];
```

```
        byteCount = copyFile(inputFile, outputFile);
    } catch (ArrayIndexOutOfBoundsException e) {
        out.println("Usage: java MyCopy [inputFile] [outputFile]");
    } catch (FileNotFoundException e) {
        out.println("Cannot open input file: " + inputFile);
    } catch (IOException e) {
        out.println("I/O exception occurs!");
    } finally {
        if (byteCount > 0)
            out.println(byteCount + " bytes written");
    }
```

Exceptions are objects with hierarchical relationships. You can create a single exception handler to catch all exceptions from a class and its subclasses, or you can create a series of exception handlers, each handling exceptions from individual subclasses. The MyCopy example demonstrates another option. The second catch clause deals with FileNotFoundException, and the next one catches any other IOException. FileNotFoundException is a subclass of IOException so you can check for both subclass and superclass exceptions.

Hierarchy of Exception Classes

Just like nearly everything else in Java, exceptions are either objects or class instances. Exception classes form their own class hierarchy. The root class of all the exception classes is the Throwable class, which is an immediate subclass of the Object class. Methods are defined in the Throwable class to retrieve the error message associated with the exception and to print the stack trace showing where the exception occurs (see the next section for more details).

Class Throwable has two immediate subclasses: class Error and class Exception. Subclasses of class Exception have the suffix Exception. Subclasses of class Error have the suffix Error (and then there is ThreadDeath, a subclass of Error). The subclasses of Error are basically used for signaling abnormal system conditions. For example, an OutOfMemoryError signals that the Java Virtual Machine has run out of memory and that the garbage collector is unable to claim any more free memory. A StackOverflowError signals a stack overflow in the interpreter. These Error exceptions are, in general, unrecoverable and should not be handled.

The subclasses of the Exception class are, in general, recoverable. For example, an EOFException signals that a file you have opened has no more data for reading. A FileNotFoundException signals that a file you want to open does not exist in the file system. You can choose to handle the exceptions by using a `try-catch` block to enclose the statements whose exceptional conditions will be handled.

Figure 7.1 illustrates the hierarchical relationships among some of the more common errors and exceptions. Many more exceptions exist, but they are not important at this point. They will be explained as we come to them throughout this book.

FIGURE 7.1:

Hierarchy of common exceptions

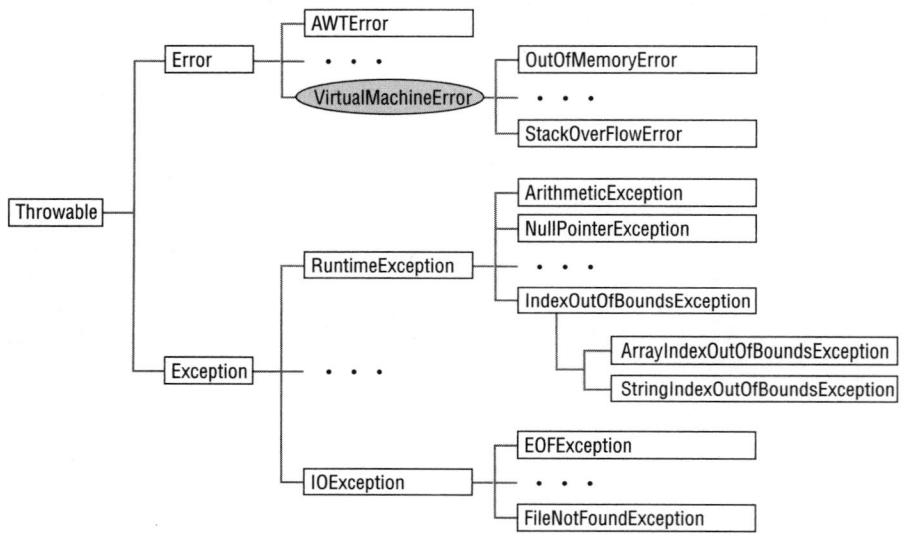

The following example loops through four pathological cases in which the system throws four types of `RuntimeException`:

ArithmeticException   For exceptional arithmetic conditions like integer division by zero

NullPointerException   For accessing a field or invoking a method of a null object

ArrayIndexOutOfBoundsException   For accessing an array element by providing an index value less than zero or greater than or equal to the array size

StringIndexOutOfBoundsException   For accessing a character of a `String` or `StringBuffer` with an index less than zero or greater than or equal to the length of the string

Here is the test program:

```java
import java.io.*;
public class ExceptionTest {
  public static void main(String args[]) {
    PrintWriter out = new PrintWriter(System.out, true);
    for (int i = 0; i < 4; i++) {
      int k;
      try {
        switch (i) {
          case 0:     // divided by zero
            int zero = 0;
            k = 911 / zero;
            break;
          case 1:     // null pointer
            int b[] = null;
            k = b[0];
            break;
          case 2:     // array index out of bound
            int c[] = new int[2];
            k = c[9];
            break;
          case 3:     // string index out of bound
            char ch = "abc".charAt(99);
            break;
        }
      } catch (Exception e) {
        out.println("\nTest case #" + i + "\n");
        out.println(e);
      }
    }
  }
}
```

The output of the previous test program is shown here:

```
C:\MasteringJava\Ch07>java ExceptionTest
Test case #0
java.lang.ArithmeticException: / by zero
Test case #1
java.lang.NullPointerException:
Test case #2
java.lang.ArrayIndexOutOfBoundsException: 9
Test case #3
java.lang.StringIndexOutOfBoundsException: String index out of range: 99
```

Exception-Handling Constructs

The general form of an exception-handling construct (the `try` statement) is:

```
try {
    normalProgramBody
} catch (ExceptionClass1 exceptionVariable1) {
    exceptionHandlerProgramBody1
} catch (ExceptionClass2 exceptionVariable2) {
    exceptionHandlerProgramBody2
. . .
} finally {
    exitProgramBody
}
```

TIP   Early versions of the JDK (before 1.0.2) did not require curly braces in the body of a `try-catch-finally` construct if the program body consisted of only a single statement. However, curly braces are always required in JDK versions 1.0.2 and newer.

The `try` keyword is used to specify a block of statements whose exceptions will be handled by the succeeding `catch` clauses. There can be any number of `catch` clauses. When an exception condition occurs, the body of the first exception handler whose exception class type is the same class as or is a superclass of the thrown exception will be executed.

Since exception matching is done sequentially, an exception handler may never be reached if its `catch` clause is after the `catch` clause for its superclass exception handler. For example, in an earlier example, the handler for `FileNotFoundException` needed to be placed before the handler for `IOException`, the immediate superclass of `FileNotFoundException`. The compiler checks to ensure all exception handlers are reachable. If you exchange the order of the handlers for `FileNotFound-Exception` and `IOException`, the compiler will issue the following error message:

```
MyCopy.java:16: catch not reached.
    } catch (FileNotFoundException e) {
      ^
1 error
```

The exit program block after the `finally` keyword will be executed before the program control is transferred outside the programming construct. This will eventually happen when the execution of the program body or the exception handler is finished, a flow-breaking statement (a break, continue, or return statement) is encountered, or an exception is thrown with no handler inside the construct capable of catching it.

The catch clause is optional, as is the finally clause. However, at least one of the catch or finally clauses must exist in a try-catch-finally construct. The exit program body comes in handy for freeing resources like file handles allocated in the normal program body.

The following example demonstrates the effects of break and continue statements on a finally clause. Inside the nested for loop, labeled and unlabeled break and continue statements are executed, and the flow is traced:

```java
import java.io.*;
public class FinallyTest {
  public static void main(String args[]) {
    PrintWriter out = new PrintWriter(System.out, true);
outerLoop:
    for (int i = 0; i < 3; i++)
      for (int j = 0; j < 3; j++)
        try {
          out.println("try before if: i=" + i + ", j=" + j);
          if ((i == 0) && (j == 1))
            continue;
          else if ((i == 0) && (j == 2))
            continue outerLoop;
          else if ((i == 1) && (j == 0))
            break;
          else if ((i == 2) && (j == 1))
            break outerLoop;
          out.println("try after  if: i=" + i + ", j=" + j);
        } finally {
          out.println("finally:       i=" + i + ", j=" + j + "\n");
        }
  }
}
```

The output of the program is shown next. You can see that the finally clause is always executed once the try block is entered:

```
C:\MasteringJava\Ch07>java FinallyTest
try before if: i=0, j=0
try after  if: i=0, j=0
finally:       i=0, j=0
```

```
try before if: i=0, j=1
finally:       i=0, j=1

try before if: i=0, j=2
finally:       i=0, j=2

try before if: i=1, j=0
finally:       i=1, j=0

try before if: i=2, j=0
try after  if: i=2, j=0
finally:       i=2, j=0

try before if: i=2, j=1
finally:       i=2, j=1
```

If the exception is not caught in the current `try-catch-finally` construct, it will be propagated up the program stack. The same exception-matching process will be repeated for all the enclosing `try-catch-finally` constructs, from the innermost construct to the outermost one, until a matching exception handler can be found. If no match can be found in the current method, the same process will be repeated for all the `try-catch-finally` constructs of the calling method, again from the innermost construct to the outermost one, until a match is found.

As the system tries to find a handler for the exception, from innermost to outermost, it executes the `finally` clauses of the `try-catch-finally` construct, from the innermost to the outermost. When the program runs out of `try-catch-finally` constructs and does not find a matching exception handler, it will print the message associated with the exception and a stack trace showing where the exception occurred; then it will terminate.

Here is a sample output of a program with an uncaught exception:

```
java.lang.ArithmeticException: / by zero
        at NoHandler.inner(NoHandler.java:6)
        at NoHandler.outer(NoHandler.java:11)
        at NoHandler.main(NoHandler.java:15)
```

Even if an exception is caught, the handler can rethrow the exception or throw another exception, and the exception-matching process will continue. The next example generates three different exceptions in the `for` loop of the `method()` method. The first exception, `ArithmeticException`, is caught in the inner `try-catch-finally` construct because of an exact match in exception type. The second exception, `ArrayIndexOutOfBoundsException`, is caught in the inner `try-catch-finally` construct because it is a subclass of `IndexOutOfBoundsException`, but then it is rethrown and caught by the outer `try-catch-finally` construct. The last exception, `StringIndexOutOfBoundsException`, is caught in the inner `try-catch-finally` construct because it is also a subclass of `IndexOutOfBoundsException`. It is then rethrown, but no handler in the outer `try-catch-finally` construct can catch it. It is thus propagated to the calling method and caught because it is a subclass of `RuntimeException`.

Here's the example:

```java
import java.io.*;
public class NestedException {
  static PrintWriter out = new PrintWriter(System.out, true);
  public static void method() {
    for (int i = 0; i < 3; i++) {
      int k;
      try {
        out.println("\nOuter try block; Test Case #" + i);
        try {
          out.println("Inner try block");
          switch (i) {
            case 0:     // divided by zero
              int zero = 0;
              k = 911 / zero;
              break;
            case 1:     // array index out of bound
              int c[] = new int[2];
              k = c[9];
              break;
            case 2:     // string index out of bound
              char ch = "abc".charAt(99);
              break;
          }
        } catch (ArithmeticException e) {
          out.println("Inner ArithmeticException>" + e);
        } catch (IndexOutOfBoundsException e) {
          out.println("Inner IndexOutOfBoundsException>" + e);
          throw e;
        } finally {
          out.println("Inner finally block");
        }
      } catch (ArrayIndexOutOfBoundsException e) {
```

```
      out.println("Outer ArrayIndexOutOfBound>" + e);
    }
    finally {
        out.println("Outer finally block");
    }
  }
}
public static void main(String args[]) {
  try {
    method();
  } catch (RuntimeException e) {
    out.println("main() RuntimeException>" + e);
  } finally {
    out.println("\nmain() finally block");
  }
}
}
```

Here is the output of the program:

```
C:\MasteringJava\Ch07>java NestedException

Outer try block; Test Case #0
Inner try block
Inner ArithmeticException>java.lang.ArithmeticException: / by zero
Inner finally block
Outer finally block

Outer try block; Test Case #1
Inner try block
Inner
IndexOutOfBoundsException>java.lang.ArrayIndexOutOfBoundsException:
Inner finally block
Outer ArrayIndexOutOfBound>java.lang.ArrayIndexOutOfBoundsException:
Outer finally block

Outer try block; Test Case #2
Inner try block
Inner
IndexOutOfBoundsException>java.lang.StringIndexOutOfBoundsException:
String index out of range: 99
Inner finally block
Outer finally block
```

```
main() RuntimeException>java.lang.StringIndexOutOfBoundsException:
String index out of range: 99

main() finally block
```

Methods Available to Exceptions

All errors and exceptions are subclasses of class `Throwable` and thus can access the methods defined in it. Of them, the following are the most commonly used:

getMessage()   To obtain the error message associated with the exception or error

printStackTrace()   To print a stack trace showing where the exception occurs

toString()   To show the exception name along with the message returned by `getMessage()`

Most exception classes have two constructors: one with a `String` argument to set the error message that can later be fetched through the `getMessage()` method; the other with no argument. In the second case, the `getMessage()` method will return `null`. The same error message will be embedded in the return of the `toString()` method or be a part of the stack trace output by the `printStackTrace()` method. An example of output or return from these methods is listed here:

```
*** example of return from getMessage() ***
/ by zero
*** example of return from toString() ***
java.lang.ArithmeticException: / by zero
*** example of output by printStackTrace() ***
java.lang.ArithmeticException: / by zero
        at NoHandler.inner(NoHandler.java:6)
        at NoHandler.outer(NoHandler.java:11)
        at NoHandler.main(NoHandler.java:16)
```

The *throw* Statement

A `throw` statement causes an exception to be thrown. The synopsis of a `throw` statement is:

```
throw expression;
```

where the expression must be evaluated to an instance of class `Throwable` or its many subclasses.

In the most common usage, a new statement is used to create an instance in the expression. For example, the following statement will throw an IOException with "cannot find the directory" as the error message:

```
throw new IOException("cannot find the directory");
```

The *throws* Clause

A method that throws an exception within it must catch that exception or have that exception declared in its throws clause unless the exception is a subclass of either the Error class or the RuntimeException class. When multiple exceptions are to be put in one throws clause, use commas to separate them. For example, the following program segment declares a method that propagates out IOException and InterruptedException:

```
int readModel(String filename) throws IOException, InterruptedException
```

There are four reasons why exceptions that are subclasses of the Error or RuntimeException class need not be declared or handled in a method:

- If you need to catch or declare a throws clause for every such exception that might occur in the method, the program will look very cumbersome.

- It is difficult to check at compile time whether such exceptions will occur. For example, every reference to an object potentially can throw a NullPointer-Exception. It is a formidable task for a compiler to make sure that every object referred to will be non-null at run time, especially when the object is passed in as an argument of the method.

- Most of the errors can occur beyond the programmer's control. It does not make much sense to ask the programmer to be responsible for handling these errors.

- Most of the runtime exceptions tend to be the result of programmer error. Correct code will not generate them.

The compiler relies on the declaration of throws clauses to determine if an exception may occur in an expression, a statement, or a method. The exceptions that may occur in a method are the union of all the exceptions that can be generated by the throw statements within the method and all the exceptions contained in the throws clauses of the methods that might be called within the method. The compiler issues an error message for any method that does not declare all (non-error/non-runtime) exceptions in its `throws` clause. A sample output for such an error message is shown here:

```
DontCompile.java:8: Exception java.io.FileNotFoundException must be
caught, or it must be declared in the throws clause of this method.
        FileInputStream fin = new
FileInputStream("BasicException.java");
                    ^
```

Creating Your Own Exception Classes

When writing a method, there are two ways to report abnormal conditions to the calling method: Use a predefined error code as the return value or throw an exception.

If an exception is thrown, the calling method is automatically handed the convenience and power of the whole exception-handling mechanism to respond to the abnormal conditions. It will also be possible for the compiler to check if these abnormal conditions are dealt with properly since these abnormal conditions are declared in the `throws` clause of the method.

When throwing an exception, you can create an instance from an exception class already defined in the language or from one you define on your own. It may be difficult to find a predefined exception that is designed for your particular situation. By using an exception already prescribed for other conditions, you may complicate the exception handler's task. The reason is that the exception handler may need to differentiate your abnormal condition from ones the exception class is originally prescribed for, if they can both occur in the method.

The common practice in creating a customized exception class is to subclass the `Exception` class. This ensures the compiler checks if it is dealt with properly. However, if you are writing system- or hardware-related utilities, you may be justified in creating subclasses from either `Error` or `RuntimeException` classes. You should not subclass `Error` or `RuntimeException` just so you do not need to create `throws` clauses for your methods. That defeats the whole purpose of using exceptions.

Because exception classes are class objects, they can have data members and methods defined within them. As an example, `InterruptedIOException`, defined in the `java.io` package, has a public instance variable, `bytesTransferred`, to hold the number of bytes read or written before the operation is interrupted. You may choose to create customized exception classes in a hierarchy so that the handler has the option of handling the superclass as a whole, handling the subclasses individually, or handling both classes simultaneously.

An Example: Age Exceptions

The example presented in this section demonstrates how to create a hierarchy of user-defined exception classes for abnormal conditions and how to write a program using these user-defined exceptions for abnormal condition handling. In the first part of the example, you construct a hierarchy of exception classes to report age-related anomalies, as shown in Figure 7.2.

FIGURE 7.2:

The class hierarchy for the `AgeException` class

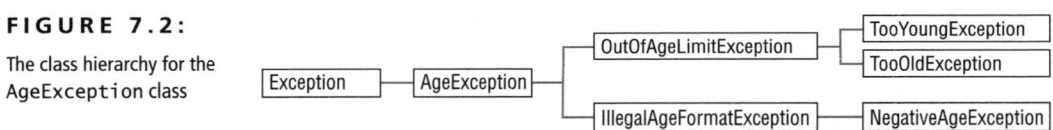

The root of this hierarchy is the `AgeException` class. It has a data member, `age`, to hold the age causing the occurrence of the exception. It has two subclasses: `OutOfAgeLimitException` for cases where the age given is too young or too old to perform a certain activity and `IllegalAgeFormatException` for cases where the age given is out of the legal age range or in the wrong format. The former class has a data member, `ageLimit`, to hold the limit being violated. The program for defining these classes is listed here:

```
class AgeException extends Exception {
  int age;
  AgeException(String message) {
    super(message);
  }
  AgeException() {
    super();
  }
}
class OutOfAgeLimitException extends AgeException {
  int ageLimit;
  OutOfAgeLimitException(int ageLimit, String message) {
```

```
      super(message);
      this.ageLimit = ageLimit;
    }
    OutOfAgeLimitException(String message) {
      super(message);
    }
  }
  class TooYoungException extends OutOfAgeLimitException {
    TooYoungException(int age, int ageLimit, String message) {
      super(ageLimit, "You are too young to " + message + ".");
      this.age = age;
    }
    TooYoungException() {
      super("too young");
    }
  }
  class TooOldException extends OutOfAgeLimitException {
    TooOldException(int age, int ageLimit, String message) {
      super(ageLimit, "You are too old to " + message + ".");
      this.age = age;
    }
    TooOldException() {
      super("too old");
    }
  }
  class IllegalAgeFormatException extends AgeException {
    IllegalAgeFormatException(String message) {
      super(message);
    }
    IllegalAgeFormatException() {
      super("Illegal age format");
    }
  }
  class NegativeAgeException extends IllegalAgeFormatException {
    NegativeAgeException(String message) {
      super(message);
    }
    NegativeAgeException(int age) {
      super("Age must be nonnegative.");
      this.age = age;
    }
  }
```

TIP   As with all Java classes, the only classes that need to go into separate files are public Java classes. Therefore, all these exception classes could go into one file, separate files, or placed in the same file as the **AgeExceptionTest** program below.

The second part of the example is a program to use the previous exception hierarchy. The program will loop through different ages to see if a person of the age specified can ride a roller coaster. The method rideRollerCoasterAtAge() will throw TooYoungException, TooOldException, or NegativeAgeException if it finds an age that is too young, too old, or negative, respectively. The program listing is as follows:

```java
import java.io.*;
public class AgeExceptionTest {
  static PrintWriter out = new PrintWriter(System.out, true);
  static void rideRollerCoasterAtAge(int age)
      throws NegativeAgeException, OutOfAgeLimitException {
    out.println("Trying to ride a roller coaster at age " +
      age + "...");
    if (age < 0)
      throw new NegativeAgeException(age);
    else if (age < 5)
      throw new TooYoungException(age, 5,
        "ride a roller coaster");
    else if (age > 45)
      throw new TooOldException(age, 45,
        "ride a roller coaster");
    out.println("Riding the roller coaster....");
  }
  public static void main(String args[]) {
    int ages[] = {-3, 2, 10, 35, 65};
    for (int i = 0; i < ages.length; i++)
      try {
        rideRollerCoasterAtAge(ages[i]);
        out.println("Wow! What an experience!");
      } catch (OutOfAgeLimitException e) {
        out.println(e.getMessage());
        if (ages[i] < e.ageLimit)
          out.println((e.ageLimit - ages[i]) +
            " more years and you'll be able to try it.");
```

```
        else
          out.println((ages[i] - e.ageLimit) +
            " years ago riding it was like a piece of cake.");
      } catch (NegativeAgeException e) {
        out.println(e.getMessage());
      } finally {
        out.println();
      }
    }
  }
```

The output of the sample program is listed here:

```
C:\MasteringJava\Ch07>java AgeExceptionTest
Trying to ride a roller coaster at age -3...
Age must be nonnegative.

Trying to ride a roller coaster at age 2...
You are too young to ride a roller coaster.
3 more years and you'll be able to try it.

Trying to ride a roller coaster at age 10...
Riding the roller coaster....
Wow! What an experience!

Trying to ride a roller coaster at age 35...
Riding the roller coaster....
Wow! What an experience!

Trying to ride a roller coaster at age 65...
You are too old to ride a roller coaster.
20 years ago riding it was like a piece of cake.
```

Summary

Java provides a clean and robust mechanism for handling abnormal conditions. First, you try to execute a block of statements. If an abnormal condition occurs, the system throws an exception, and you can catch the exception. And, finally, there can be a code fragment you always want to execute, whether or not an exception happens and is handled.

Exceptions are objects, and exception classes form their own class hierarchy. The root of all error and exception classes is the `Throwable` class. You can create your own exception classes as subclasses of the `Exception` class. The whole exception-handling mechanism is then at your disposal. You can even create a hierarchy of exception classes so that the handler has more flexibility in handling the exceptions.

A method that may cause an exception to be thrown must catch that exception or have that exception defined in its `throws` clause, unless the exception is a subclass of either the `Error` or `RuntimeException` class. Checking of this rule is done at compile time.

It is always unpleasant for a user to encounter errors in your application. How you deal with these errors will make a difference to the user and will be an important factor in your application's success. The clean and robust exception-handling capability provided with Java makes writing a friendly program an easier task.

CHAPTER

EIGHT

8

Threads and Multithreading

- Thread creation and execution

- Methods for controlling threads

- Thread synchronization

- Communications between threads

- Thread priorities and scheduling

Up until now, all of our sample programs have been single-threaded; that is, they have had only one line of execution. If the program execution is blocked while waiting for the completion of some I/O operation, no other portion of the program can proceed. However, users of today's modern operating systems are accustomed to starting multiple programs and watching them work concurrently, even if there is only a single CPU available to run all the applications. Multithreading allows multiple tasks to execute concurrently within a single program.

The advantage of multithreading is twofold. First, programs with multiple threads will, in general, better utilize system resources, including the CPU, because another line of execution can grab the CPU when one line of execution is blocked. Second, multiple threads solve numerous problems better. For example, how would you write a single-threaded program to show animation, play music, display documents, and download files from the network at the same time?

Java was designed from the beginning with multithreading in mind. Not only does the language itself have multithreading support built in, allowing for easy creation of robust, multithreaded applications, but also the virtual machine relies on multithreading to concurrently provide multiple services—like garbage collection—to the application. In this chapter, you will learn to use multiple threads in your Java programs.

Overview of Multithreading

A thread is a single flow of control within a program. It is sometimes called the *execution context* because each thread must have its own resources—like the program counter and the execution stack—as the context for execution. However, all threads in a program still share many resources, such as memory space and opened files. Therefore, a thread may also be called a *lightweight process*. It is a single flow of control like a process (or a running program), but it is easier to create and destroy than a process because less resource management is involved.

TIP   The terms *parallel* and *concurrent* occur frequently in computer literature, and the difference between them can be confusing. When two threads run in parallel, they are both being executed at the same time on different CPUs. However, two concurrent threads are both in progress, or trying to get some CPU time for execution at the same time, but are not necessarily being executed simultaneously on different CPUs.

A program may spend a big portion of its execution time just waiting. For example, it may wait for some resource to become accessible in an I/O operation, or it may wait for some time-out to occur to start drawing the next scene of an animation sequence. To improve CPU utilization, all the tasks with potentially long waits can run as separate threads. Once a task starts waiting for something to happen, the Java run time can choose another runnable task for execution.

The first example demonstrates the difference between a single-threaded program and its multithreaded counterpart. In the first program, a `run()` method in the `NoThreadPseudoIO` class is created to simulate a 10-second I/O operation. The main program will first perform the simulated I/O operation, then start another task. The method `showElapsedTime()` is defined to print the elapsed time in seconds since the program started, together with a user-supplied message. The `current-TimeMillis()` method of the `System` class in the `java.lang` package will return a `long` integer for the time difference, measured in milliseconds, between the current time and 00:00:00 GMT on January 1, 1970. The single-threaded program is listed here:

```java
import java.io.*;
public class WithoutThread {
  static PrintWriter out = new PrintWriter (System.out, true);
  public static void main (String args[]) {
    //  first task: some pseudo-I/O operation
    NoThreadPseudoIO pseudo = new NoThreadPseudoIO();
    pseudo.run();
    //  second task: some random task
    showElapsedTime ("Another task starts");
  }
  static long baseTime = System.currentTimeMillis();
  // show the time elapsed since the program started
  static void showElapsedTime (String message) {
    long elapsedTime = System.currentTimeMillis() - baseTime;
    out.println (message + " at " +
      (elapsedTime / 1000.0) + " seconds");
  }
}
// pseudo-I/O operation run in caller's thread
class NoThreadPseudoIO {
  int data = -1;
  NoThreadPseudoIO() {   // constructor
    WithoutThread.showElapsedTime ("NoThreadPseudoIO created");
  }
  public void run() {
```

```
WithoutThread.showElapsedTime ("NoThreadPseudoIO starts");
try {
   Thread.sleep (10000);   // 10 seconds
   data = 999;             // the data is ready
   WithoutThread.showElapsedTime ("NoThreadPseudoIO finishes");
} catch (InterruptedException e) {}
}
}
```

Even if the second task does not refer to any data generated or modified by the pseudo-I/O operation, the task cannot start until the I/O operation is finished. For most real I/O operations, the CPU will be sitting idle most of the time waiting for a response from the peripheral device, which is really a waste of precious CPU cycles. A sample output of this program is shown here:

```
C:\MasteringJava\Ch08>java WithoutThread
NoThreadPseudoIO created at 1.642 seconds
NoThreadPseudoIO starts at 2.113 seconds
NoThreadPseudoIO finishes at 10.044 seconds
Another task starts at 10.044 seconds
```

The multithreaded second program declares the class for the pseudo-I/O operation as a subclass of the Thread class:

```
class ThreadedPseudoIO extends Thread {
```

After the thread is created, it uses the start() method of the Thread class to start the I/O operation:

```
ThreadedPseudoIO pseudo = new ThreadedPseudoIO();
pseudo.start();
```

The thread's start() method in turn calls the run() method of the subclass.

TIP

Up through JDK version 1.0.2, there is a bug in the code for running multiple threads under Windows 95 and NT: Programs that start multiple threads will not automatically exit. The workaround is to either have the last running thread call the System.exit() method or have a thread monitor other threads by calling the join() methods of the monitored threads. exit() is a class method defined in the System class of the java.lang package for terminating Java run time. For security reasons, an applet is not allowed to call exit(). Forcibly calling exit() from an applet will cause a SecurityException to be thrown. The workaround is not necessary for other platforms or with Java 1.1 or 1.2.

A full listing of this multithreaded program is as follows:

```java
import java.io.*;
public class WithThread {
  static PrintWriter out = new PrintWriter(System.out, true);
  public static void main (String args[]) {
    //  first task: some pseudo-I/O operation
    ThreadedPseudoIO pseudo = new ThreadedPseudoIO();
    pseudo.start();
    //  second task: some random task
    showElapsedTime ("Another task starts");
  }
  static long baseTime = System.currentTimeMillis();
  // show the time elapsed since the program started
  static void showElapsedTime (String message) {
    long elapsedTime = System.currentTimeMillis() - baseTime;
    out.println (message + " at " +
      (elapsedTime / 1000.0) + " seconds");
  }
}
//  pseudo-I/O operation run in a separate thread
class ThreadedPseudoIO extends Thread {
  int data = -1;
  ThreadedPseudoIO() {    // constructor
    WithThread.showElapsedTime ("ThreadedPseudoIO created");
  }
  public void run() {
    WithThread.showElapsedTime ("ThreadedPseudoIO starts");
    try {
      Thread.sleep (10000);   // 10 seconds
      data = 999;             // data ready
      WithThread.showElapsedTime ("ThreadedPseudoIO finishes");
    } catch (InterruptedException e) {}
  }
}
```

Here is the output of the multithreaded program. You will notice that the second task starts even before the pseudo-I/O operation starts; this is natural when you have only one CPU running two threads. The run() method of the newly created thread will not be executed until the currently running thread relinquishes program control.

```
C:\MasteringJava\Ch08>java WithThread
ThreadedPseudoIO created at 0.11 seconds
Another task starts at 0.25 seconds
ThreadedPseudoIO starts at 0.27 seconds
ThreadedPseudoIO finishes at 10.025 seconds
```

Thread Basics

The following sections introduce the basics of working with threads, including how to create and run threads, control thread executions, and get information about threads and thread groups. You will also learn about the life cycle of a thread and thread groups.

Creating and Running a Thread

When you have a task you want to run concurrently with other tasks, there are two ways to do this: create a new class as a subclass of the Thread class or declare a class implementing the Runnable interface.

Using a Subclass of the *Thread* Class

When you create a subclass of the Thread class, this subclass should define its own run() method to override the run() method of the Thread class. This run() method is where the task is performed.

Just as the main() method is the first user-defined method the Java run time calls to start an application, the run() method is the first user-defined method the Java run time calls to start a thread. An instance of this subclass is then created by a **new** statement, followed by a call to the thread's start() method to have the run() method executed. This is exactly what was done with the ThreadedPseudoIO class in the previous example.

Implementing the Runnable Interface

The Runnable interface requires only one method to be implemented—the run() method. You first create an instance of this class with a **new** statement, followed by the creation of a Thread instance with another **new** statement, and finally a call to this thread instance's start() method to start performing the task defined in the run() method. A class instance with the run() method defined within it must be passed in as an argument in creating the Thread instance, so that when the start() method of this Thread instance is called, Java run time knows which run() method to execute.

This alternative way of creating a thread comes in handy when the class defining the run() method needs to be a subclass of another class. The class can inherit all the data and methods of the superclass, and the Thread instance just created can be used for thread control.

The previous multithreaded example can be reimplemented using the Runnable interface by first changing the class definition to implement the Runnable interface, instead of subclassing the Thread class:

```
class RunnablePseudoIO implements Runnable {
```

Then, an instance of the class is created and passed to a newly created Thread instance, followed by a call to the start() method to start the execution of the run() method as follows:

```
RunnablePseudoIO pseudo = new RunnablePseudoIO();
Thread thread = new Thread (pseudo);
thread.start();
```

A full listing of the program is included here:

```
import java.io.*;
public class RunnableThread {
  static PrintWriter out = new PrintWriter (System.out, true);
  public static void main (String args[]) {
    //  first task: some pseudo-I/O operation
    RunnablePseudoIO pseudo = new RunnablePseudoIO();
    Thread thread = new Thread (pseudo);
    thread.start();
    //  second task: some random task
    showElapsedTime ("Another task starts");
  }
  static long baseTime = System.currentTimeMillis();
  // show the time elapsed since the program started
  static void showElapsedTime (String message) {
    long elapsedTime = System.currentTimeMillis() - baseTime;
    out.println (message + " at " +
      (elapsedTime / 1000.0) + " seconds");
  }
}
//  pseudo I/O operation run in a separate thread
class RunnablePseudoIO implements Runnable {
  int data = -1;
  RunnablePseudoIO() {   // constructor
    RunnableThread.showElapsedTime("RunnablePseudoIO created");
  }
  public void run() {
    RunnableThread.showElapsedTime("RunnablePseudoIO starts");
    try {
```

```
        Thread.sleep (10000);   // 10 seconds
        data = 999;             // data ready
        RunnableThread.showElapsedTime ("RunnablePseudoIO finishes");
      } catch (InterruptedException e) {}
   }
}
```

The output of the program is similar to that of the earlier program:

```
C:\MasteringJava\Ch08>java RunnableThread
RunnablePseudoIO created at 0.01 seconds
Another task starts at 0.11 seconds
RunnablePseudoIO starts at 0.11 seconds
RunnablePseudoIO finishes at 10.145 seconds
```

The Thread-Control Methods

Many methods defined in the Thread class control the running of a thread. Java 1.2 deprecated several of them to prevent data inconsistencies or deadlocks. If you are just starting with Java 1.2, avoid the deprecated methods and use the equivalent behavior described later in the chapter. However, if you are transitioning from Java 1.0 or 1.1, you will need to modify your code to avoid the deprecated methods if you used them. Here are some of the ones that were most commonly used:

start()   Used to start the execution of the thread body defined in the run() method. Program control will be immediately returned to the caller, and a new thread will be scheduled to execute the run() method concurrently with the caller's thread.

stop()   Deprecated. Used to stop the execution of the thread no matter what the thread is doing. The thread is then considered dead, the internal states of the thread are cleared, and the resources allocated are reclaimed. Using this method has the potential to leave data in an inconsistent state and should be avoided.

suspend()   Deprecated. Used to temporarily stop the execution of the thread. All the states and resources of the thread are retained. The thread can later be restarted by another thread calling the resume() method. Using this method has a strong potential for deadlocks and should be avoided. You should use the Object.wait() method described later instead.

resume()   Deprecated. Used to resume the execution of a suspended thread. The suspended thread will be scheduled to run. If it has a higher priority than the running thread, the running thread will be preempted; otherwise, the just-resumed thread will wait in the queue for its turn to run. Using this method has a strong potential for deadlocks and should be avoided. You should use the `Object.notify()` method described later instead.

`sleep(long sleepTimeInMilliseconds)`   A class method that causes the Java run time to put the caller thread to sleep for a minimum of the specified time period. The exception, `InterruptedException`, may be thrown while a thread is sleeping or any time if you `interrupt()` it. Either a `try-catch` statement needs to be defined to handle this exception or the enclosing method needs to have this exception in the `throws` clause.

`join()`   Used for the caller's thread to wait for this thread to die—for example, by coming to the end of the `run()` method.

`yield()`   A class method that temporarily stops the caller's thread and puts it at the end of the queue to wait for another turn to be executed. It is used to make sure other threads of the same priority have the chance to run.

TIP

All the class methods defined in the `Thread` class, such as `sleep()` and `yield()`, will act on the caller's thread. That is, it is the caller's thread that will sleep for a while or yield to others. The reason is that a class method can never access an instance's data or method members unless the instance is passed in as an argument, created inside the method, or stored in a class variable visible to the method.

The following example shows how some of the above methods are used. The main thread creates two threads, then waits for the first thread to finish by calling the first thread's `join()` method. The first thread calls the `sleep()` method to be asleep for 10 seconds. Meanwhile, the second thread calls its own `wait()` method to suspend itself until the main thread calls its `notify()` method. After the first thread comes to an end, the main thread will resume its execution, wake up the second thread by calling the second thread's `resume()` method, and wait until the second thread also comes to an end by calling the second thread's `join()` method. The program is as follows:

```
import java.io.*;
public class MethodTest {
   static PrintWriter out = new PrintWriter (System.out, true);
   public static void main (String args[]) {
```

```
      FirstThread  first  = new FirstThread();
      SecondThread second = new SecondThread();
      first.start();
      second.start();
      try {
        out.println ("Waiting for first thread to finish...");
        first.join();
        out.println ("It's a long wait!");
        out.println ("Waking up second thread...");
        synchronized (second) {
          second.notify();
        }
        out.println ("Waiting for second thread to finish...");
        second.join();
      } catch (InterruptedException e) {
      }
      out.println("I'm ready to finish too.");
    }
  }
class FirstThread extends Thread {
  public void run() {
    try {
      MethodTest.out.println ("  First thread starts running.");
      sleep (10000);
      MethodTest.out.println ("  First thread finishes running.");
    } catch (InterruptedException e) {
    }
  }
}
class SecondThread extends Thread {
  public synchronized void run() {
    try {
      MethodTest.out.println ("  Second thread starts running.");
      MethodTest.out.println ("  Second thread suspends itself.");
      wait();
      MethodTest.out.println ("  Second thread runs again and
finishes.");
    } catch (InterruptedException e) {
    }
  }
}
```

The output of this program is shown here:

```
C:\MasteringJava\Ch08>java MethodTest
Waiting for first thread to finish...
   First thread starts running.
   Second thread starts running.
   Second thread suspends itself.
   First thread finishes running.
It's a long wait!
Waking up second thread...
Waiting for second thread to finish...
   Second thread runs again and finishes.
I'm ready to finish too.
```

NOTE   If you are not familiar with the synchronized keyword, it will be explained shortly in the "Advanced Multithreading" section.

The Thread Life Cycle

Every thread, after creation and before destruction, will always be in one of four states: newly created, runnable, blocked, or dead. These states are illustrated in Figure 8.1 and described in the following sections.

FIGURE 8.1:

The thread life cycle

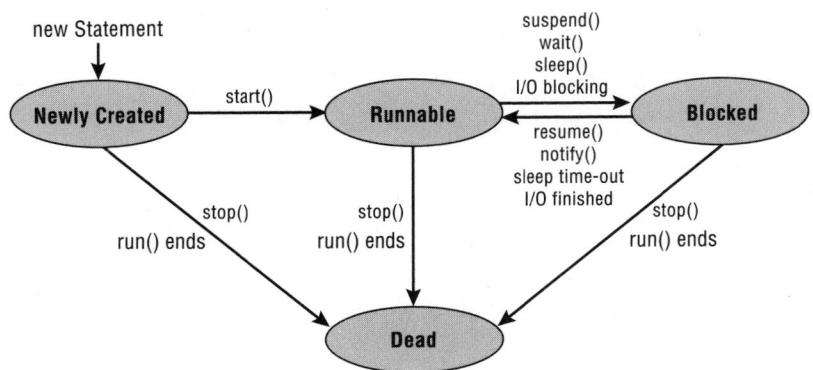

Newly Created Threads

A thread enters the newly created state immediately after creation; that is, it enters the state right after the thread-creating new statement is executed. In this state, the local data members are allocated and initialized, but execution of the run() method will not begin until its start() method is called. After the start() method is called, the thread will be put into the runnable state.

Runnable Threads

When a thread is in the runnable state, the execution context exists and the thread can be scheduled to run at any time; that is, the thread is not waiting for any event to happen.

For the sake of explanation, this state can be subdivided into two substates: the running and queued states. When a thread is in the running state, it is assigned CPU cycles and is actually running. When a thread is in the queued state, it is waiting in the queue and competing for its turn to spend CPU cycles. The transition between these two substates is controlled by the virtual machine scheduler. However, a thread can call the yield() method to voluntarily move itself to the queued state from the running state.

Blocked Threads

The blocked state is entered when one of the following events occurs:

- The thread itself or another thread calls the suspend() method.
- The thread calls an object's wait() method.
- The thread itself calls the sleep() method.
- The thread is waiting for some I/O operation to complete.
- The thread will join() with another thread.

A thread in a blocked state will not be scheduled for running. It will go back to the runnable state, competing for CPU cycles, when the counter-event for the blocking event occurs:

- If the thread is suspended, another thread calls its resume() method.
- If the thread is blocked by calling an object's wait() method, the object's notify() or notifyAll() method is called.

- If the thread is put to sleep, the specified sleeping time elapses.
- If the thread is blocked on I/O, the specified I/O operation completes.

Keep in mind you should never call suspend() or resume(), even before Java 1.2. Java 1.2 strongly discourages their usage by deprecating the methods.

Dead Threads

The dead state is entered when a thread finishes its execution or is stopped by another thread calling its stop() method.

To avoid the use of stop(), the proper way to exit out of a while (true) loop is to maintain a state variable that is used as the while loop condition check. So, instead of run() looking like the following and using stop() to halt the thread:

```
public void run () {
  while (true) {
    ...
  }
}
```

you would change the test case to be some boolean condition. Then, when you want the thread to stop, instead of calling stop(), you change the state of the boolean. This causes the thread to stop on the next pass and ensures that the thread doesn't leave data in an inconsistent state.

```
public void run () {
  while (aBooleanVariable) {
    ...
  }
}
```

Under the JDK 1.1 and earlier implementations of the Java virtual machine, stop() will be ignored if a thread is created but not yet started.

To find out whether a thread is alive—that is, currently runnable or blocked— use the thread's isAlive() method. It will return true if the thread is alive. If a thread is alive, it does not mean it is running, just that it can.

Thread Groups

Every thread instance is a member of exactly one thread group. A thread group can have both threads and other thread groups as its members. In fact, every thread group, except the system thread group, is a member of some other thread group. All the threads and thread groups in an application form a tree, with the system thread group as the root.

When a Java application is started, the Java virtual machine creates the main thread group as a member of the system thread group. A main thread is created in this main thread group to run the main() method of the application. By default, all new user-created threads and thread groups will become the members of this main thread group unless another thread group is passed as the first argument of the new statement's constructor method. A new thread group is created by instantiating the ThreadGroup class. For example, the following statements create a thread group named MyThreadGroup as a member of the default main thread group, and then create a thread named MyThread as a member of the newly created thread group:

```
ThreadGroup group = new ThreadGroup ("MyThreadGroup");
Thread thread = new Thread (group, "MyThread");
```

Three methods are defined in the ThreadGroup class to manipulate all the threads in the Thread class group and its subthread groups at once: stop(), suspend(), and resume(). As with Thread, the stop(), suspend(), and resume() methods are now deprecated and should be avoided. (Basically, the methods had a use that didn't work properly, so Sun deprecated them.) Proper use of condition variables should diminish the dependency on these methods.

Getting Information about Threads and Thread Groups

Many methods are defined in Thread and ThreadGroup for getting information about threads and thread groups.

Thread Information

The following are some of the most commonly used methods for getting information about threads:

currentThread()   Returns the caller's thread

getName()   Returns the current name of the thread

getThreadGroup()   Returns the parent thread group of the thread

getPriority()   Returns the current priority of the thread

isAlive()   Returns true if the thread is started but not dead yet

isDaemon()   Returns true if the thread is a daemon thread

Thread Group Information

The following are some of the most commonly used methods for getting information about thread groups:

getName()   Returns the name of the thread group.

getParent()   Returns the parent thread group of the thread group.

getMaxPriority()   Returns the current maximum priority of the thread group.

activeCount()   Returns the number of active threads in the thread group.

activeGroupCount()   Returns the number of active thread groups in the thread group.

enumerate(Thread list[], boolean recursive)   Adds all the active threads in this thread group into the list array. If recursive is true, all the threads in the subthread groups will be copied over as well. This method will return the number of threads copied. The activeCount() method is often used to size the list when the space of this thread array is to be allocated.

Thread priorities and daemon threads will be discussed in later sections.

A Program to Get and Print Thread Information

This section presents an example that uses the methods described in the previous sections to show information about all the threads and thread groups in an application. The program creates a thread group named MyThreadGroup and creates four threads in the thread group. It then continues on to print all the information by calling the printAllThreadInfo() method.

The printAllThreadInfo() method first locates the root thread group of all the running threads and thread groups. It then prints the information about the

underlying threads and thread groups recursively from the root. The output is
indented to show the depth of individual threads or thread groups in the tree.
The full program is as follows:

```java
import java.io.*;
public class ThreadInfo {
  static PrintWriter out = new PrintWriter (System.out, true);
  public static void main (String args[]) {
    Thread[] threads = new Thread[4];
    ThreadGroup group = new ThreadGroup ("MyThreadGroup");
    if (args.length > 0) {
      Thread thread = Thread.currentThread();
      thread.setName (args[0]);
    }
    for (int i = 0; i < 4; i++)
      threads[i] = new Thread (group, "MyThread#" + i);
    ThreadInfo.printAllThreadInfo();
  }
  // list information about all the threads and thread groups
  // in the application
  public static void printAllThreadInfo() {
    ThreadGroup parent, root;
    // find the root of all running threads
    root = parent = Thread.currentThread().getThreadGroup();
    while ((parent = parent.getParent()) != null)
      root = parent;
    // print information recursively from the root
    out.println();
    printThreadGroupInfo ("", root);
  }
  // print information about a thread group
  public static void printThreadGroupInfo
      (String indent, ThreadGroup group) {
    final int SAFETY = 5;
    if (group == null)
      return;
    out.println (indent +
      "THREAD GROUP: " + group.getName() +
      "; Max Priority: " + group.getMaxPriority() +
      (group.isDaemon() ? " [Daemon]" : ""));
    // print information about component threads
```

```
      int numThreads = group.activeCount();
      Thread threads[]  = new Thread[numThreads+SAFETY];
      numThreads = group.enumerate (threads, false);
      for (int i = 0; i < numThreads; i++)
        printThreadInfo(indent + "    ", threads[i]);
      // print information about component thread groups
      int numGroups  = group.activeGroupCount();
      ThreadGroup groups[] = new ThreadGroup[numGroups+SAFETY];
      numGroups = group.enumerate (groups, false);
      for (int i = 0; i < numGroups; i++)
        printThreadGroupInfo (indent + "    ", groups[i]);
    }
    // print information about a single thread
    public static void printThreadInfo
        (String indent, Thread thread) {
      if (thread == null)
        return;
      out.println (indent +
        "THREAD: " + thread.getName() +
        "; Priority: " + thread.getPriority() +
        (thread.isDaemon() ? " [Daemon]" : "") +
        (thread.isAlive() ? " [Alive]" : " [NotAlive]") +
        ((Thread.currentThread() == thread) ? " <== current" : ""));
    }
  }
```

NOTE   Since the number of threads running may change between the `activeGroup-Count()` call and the `enumerate()` call, a safety margin is added in case the count increases. The "Advanced Multithreading" section later in this chapter discusses ways to solve this problem.

The output of the previous program run under Windows NT is as follows:

```
C:\MasteringJava\Ch08>java ThreadInfo
THREAD GROUP: system; Max Priority: 10
   THREAD: Signal dispatcher; Priority 10 [Daemon] [Alive]
   THREAD: Reference handler; Priority 10 [Daemon] [Alive]
   THREAD: Finalizer; Priority: 8 [Daemon] [Alive]
   THREAD GROUP: main; Max Priority: 10
      THREAD: main; Priority: 5 [Alive] <== current
      THREAD GROUP: MyThreadGroup; Max Priority: 10
```

The same program run under Solaris 2.5 produces similar output, as follows:

```
harpoon:/users/me/java/examples/ch8> java ThreadInfo
THREAD GROUP: system; Max Priority: 10
    THREAD: Clock; Priority: 12 [Daemon] [Alive]
    THREAD: Idle thread; Priority: 0 [Daemon] [Alive]
    THREAD: Async Garbage Collector; Priority: 1 [Daemon] [Alive]
    THREAD: Reference handler; Priority: 10 [Daemon] [Alive]
    THREAD: Finalizer; Priority: 8 [Daemon] [Alive]
    THREAD: SoftReference sweeper; Priority: 9 [Daemon] [Alive]
    THREAD GROUP: main; Max Priority: 10
        THREAD: main; Priority: 5 [Alive] <== current
        THREAD GROUP: MyThreadGroup; Max Priority: 10
```

Your output may differ slightly, depending on how the vendor of your Java implementation manages system-threading resources.

Advanced Multithreading

The following sections introduce some advanced multithreading topics: thread synchronization, inter-thread communications, thread priorities and scheduling, and daemon threads.

Thread Synchronization

Synchronization is the way to avoid data corruption caused by simultaneous access to the same data. Because all the threads in a program share the same memory space, it is possible for two threads to access the same variable or run the same method of the same object at the same time. Problems may occur when multiple threads are accessing the same data concurrently. Threads may race each other, and one thread may overwrite the data just written by another thread. Or one thread may work on another thread's intermediate result and break the consistency of the data. Some mechanism is needed to block one thread's access to the critical data, if the data is being worked on by another thread.

For example, suppose that you have a program to handle a user's bank account. There are three subtasks in making a deposit for the user:

- Get the current balance from some remote server, which may take as long as five seconds.

- Add the newly deposited amount into the just-acquired balance.

- Send the new balance back to the same remote server, which again may take as long as five seconds to complete.

If two depositing threads, each making a $1,000 deposit, are started at roughly the same time on a current balance of $1,000, the final balance of these two deposits may reflect the result of only one deposit. A possible scenario is depicted in Table 8.1.

TABLE 8.1: Two Depositing Threads Running Concurrently

Time	Thread #1	Thread #2	Balance in Remote Server
a	Getting balance		$1,000
b	Waiting…	Getting balance	$1,000
c	Get balance = $1,000	Waiting…	$1,000
d	Compute new balance = $2,000	Waiting…	$1,000
e	Setting new balance	Waiting…	$1,000
f	Waiting…	Get balance = $1,000	$1,000
g	Waiting…	Compute new balance = $2,000	$1,000
h	Waiting…	Setting new balance	$1,000
i	New balance set	Waiting…	$2,000
j		New balance set	$2,000

The balance stored in the remote server increases by only one deposit amount!

The following sample program simulates the scenario in Table 8.1. An Account class is defined with three methods: getBalance() to fetch the current balance from some pseudo-server, with a simulated five-second delay; setBalance() to write back the new balance to the same pseudo-server, with (again) a simulated five-second delay; and deposit() to use the other two methods to complete a deposit transaction. A DepositThread class is declared to start the deposit operation on the account passed in. The main program creates an account instance and then starts two threads to make a deposit of $1,000 each to that account. The full program listing is as follows:

```java
import java.io.*;
public class Deposit {
  static int balance = 1000; // simulate balance kept remotely
  public static void main (String args[]) {
    PrintWriter out = new PrintWriter (System.out, true);
    Account account = new Account (out);
    DepositThread first, second;
    first  = new DepositThread (account, 1000, "#1");
    second = new DepositThread (account, 1000, "\t\t\t\t#2");
    // start the transactions
    first.start();
    second.start();
    // wait for both transactions to finish
    try {
      first.join();
      second.join();
    } catch (InterruptedException e) {}
    // print the final balance
    out.println ("*** Final balance is " + balance);
  }
}
class Account {
  PrintWriter out;
  Account (PrintWriter out) {
    this.out = out;
  }
  void deposit (int amount, String name) {
    int balance;
    out.println (name + " trying to deposit " + amount);
    out.println (name + " getting balance...");
    balance = getBalance();
    out.println (name + " balance got is " + balance);
    balance += amount;
    out.println (name + " setting balance...");
    setBalance (balance);
    out.println (name + " new balance set to " + Deposit.balance);
  }
```

```
int getBalance() {
  try {    // simulate the delay in getting balance remotely
    Thread.sleep (5000);
  } catch (InterruptedException e) {}
  return Deposit.balance;
}
void setBalance (int balance) {
  try {    // simulate the delay in setting new balance remotely
    Thread.sleep (5000);
  } catch (InterruptedException e) {}
  Deposit.balance = balance;
}
}
class DepositThread extends Thread {
  Account account;
  int    depositAmount;
  String  message;
  DepositThread (Account account, int amount, String message) {
    this.message  = message;
    this.account  = account;
    this.depositAmount = amount;
  }
  public void run() {
    account.deposit (depositAmount, message);
  }
}
```

An example of the output of the above program is as follows:

```
C:\MasteringJava\Ch08>java Deposit
#1 trying to deposit 1000
#1 getting balance...

                                    #2 trying to deposit 1000
                                    #2 getting balance...

#1 balance got is 1000
#1 setting balance...

                                    #2 balance got is 1000
                                    #2 setting balance...

#1 new balance set to 2000

                                    #2 new balance set to 2000

*** Final balance is 2000
```

Java's Monitor Model for Synchronization

Java uses the idea of monitors to synchronize access to data. A *monitor* is like a guarded place where all the protected resources have the same locks. Only a single key fits all the locks inside a monitor, and a thread must get the key to enter the monitor and access these protected resources. If many threads want to enter the monitor simultaneously, only one thread is handed the key; the others must wait outside until the key-holding thread finishes its use of the resources and hands the key back to the Java virtual machine.

Once a thread gets a monitor's key, the thread can access any of the resources controlled by that monitor countless times, as long as the thread still owns the key. However, if this key-holding thread wants to access the resources controlled by another monitor, the thread must get that particular monitor's key. At any time, a thread can hold many monitors' keys. Different threads can hold keys for different monitors at the same time. Deadlock may occur if threads are waiting for each other's key to proceed.

In Java, the resources protected by monitors are program fragments in the form of methods or blocks of statements enclosed in curly braces. If some data can be accessed only through methods or blocks protected by the same monitor, access to the data is indirectly synchronized. You use the keyword `synchronized` to indicate that the following method or block of statements is to be synchronized by a monitor. When a block of statements is to be synchronized, an object instance enclosed in parentheses immediately following the `synchronized` keyword is required so the Java virtual machine knows which monitor to check.

You can think of a monitor as a guarded parking lot, where all the synchronized methods or blocks are just like cars you can drive (or execute, if you are a thread). All the cars share the same key. You need to get this unique key to enter the parking lot and drive any of the cars until you hand back the key. At that time, one of the persons waiting to get in will get the key and be able to drive the car(s) of their choice. This concept is illustrated in Figure 8.2.

For example, the `deposit()` method in the previous example can be synchronized to allow only one thread to run at a time. The only change needed is a `synchronized` keyword before the method definition, as follows:

```
synchronized void deposit(int amount, String name) {
```

FIGURE 8.2:

Threads need a unique key to access resources protected by a Java monitor.

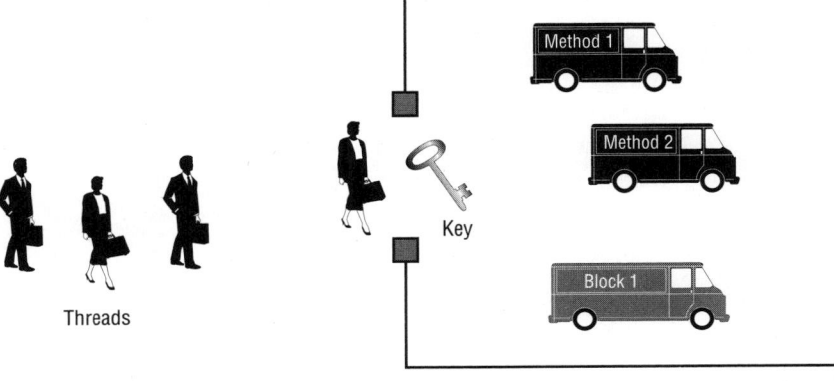

A sample output of the modified program is as follows:

```
#1 trying to deposit 1000
#1 getting balance...
#1 balance got is 1000
#1 setting balance...
#1 new balance set to 2000
                                   #2 trying to deposit 1000
                                   #2 getting balance...
                                   #2 balance got is 2000
                                   #2 setting balance...
                                   #2 new balance set to 3000
*** Final balance is 3000
```

Alternatively, a block of statements in the deposit() method can be synchronized on the called object, as follows:

```
void deposit (int amount, String name) {
  int balance;
  out.println (name + " trying to deposit " + amount);
  synchronized (this) {
    out.println (name + " getting balance...");
    balance = getBalance();
    out.println (name + " gets balance = " + balance);
    balance += amount;
    out.println (name + " setting balance...");
```

```
    setBalance (balance);
  }
  out.println (name + " set new balance = " + balance);
}
```

The output of this program is almost the same as the previous one, except the first message from the second thread will be interleaved in the messages from the first thread, because the first `println()` method is not inside the synchronized block. Here is an example of the output:

```
#1 trying to deposit 1000
#1 getting balance...
                                        #2 trying to deposit 1000

#1 balance got is 1000
#1 setting balance...
#1 new balance set to 2000
                                        #2 getting balance...
                                        #2 balance got is 2000
                                        #2 setting balance...
                                        #2 new balance set to 3000

*** Final balance is 3000
```

One unique key will be issued to every object containing any synchronized instance method or being referred by any synchronized block. For synchronized class methods, the key is issued to the class because the method may be called before any class instances exist. This means that every object and every class can have a monitor if there are any synchronized methods or blocks of statements associated with it. Furthermore, a class monitor's key is different from any of the keys of its class instance monitors.

Differences in Synchronization Techniques

The next example demonstrates the difference between a synchronized method and a synchronized block, and the difference between class-based synchronization and object-based synchronization. Class SyncToken contains three methods, all synchronized differently and all calling the `ticker()` method to print out three ticks in random intervals. Class SyncTestRunner is a thread class that will choose different methods of class SyncToken to run based on the ID given. The `main()` method of the SyncTest class will generate 10 threads running the tickers with different synchronization schemes so the comparison can be made. The program listing is as follows:

```
import java.io.*;
public class SyncTest {
```

```java
    public static void main (String args[]) {
      SyncToken token = new SyncToken();
      SyncTestRunner runners[] = new SyncTestRunner[10];
      for (int i = 0; i < 10; i++) {
        runners[i] = new SyncTestRunner (token, i);
        runners[i].start();
      }
    }
  }
  class SyncTestRunner extends Thread {
    SyncToken token;
    int       id;
    SyncTestRunner (SyncToken token, int id) {
      this.token = token;
      this.id   = id;
    }
    public void run() {
      switch (id % 3) {
        case 0:
          SyncToken.classTicker ("\t\t\tClass #" + id, token);
          break;
        case 1:
          token.methodTicker ("Method #" + id);
          break;
        case 2:
          token.blockTicker ("Block  #" + id);
          break;
      }
    }
  }
  class SyncToken {
    PrintWriter out = new PrintWriter (System.out, true);
    //  the ticker method: give three ticks in random interval
    void ticker (String message) {
      for (int i = 0; i < 3; i++) {
        try {
          Thread.sleep ((int) (800 * Math.random()));
        } catch (InterruptedException e) {
        }
        out.println(message + ", tick #" + i);
      }
    }
```

```
// class-based synchronization
static synchronized void classTicker (String message, SyncToken token) {
  token.ticker(message);
}
// object-based synchronization: synchronized block
void blockTicker (String message) {
  synchronized(this) {
    ticker (message);
  }
}
// object-based synchronization: synchronized method
synchronized void methodTicker (String message) {
  ticker (message);
}
}
```

The output of this program is as follows:

```
                        Class  #0, tick #0
Method #1, tick #0
                        Class  #0, tick #1
Method #1, tick #1
Method #1, tick #2
Block  #2, tick #0
                        Class  #0, tick #2
                        Class  #3, tick #0
Block  #2, tick #1
                        Class  #3, tick #1
                        Class  #3, tick #2
Block  #2, tick #2
Method #4, tick #0
Method #4, tick #1
Method #4, tick #2
                        Class  #6, tick #0
Block  #5, tick #0
                        Class  #6, tick #1
Block  #5, tick #1
Block  #5, tick #2
                        Class  #6, tick #2
Method #7, tick #0
Method #7, tick #1
                        Class  #9, tick #0
```

```
Method #7, tick #2
                    Class #9, tick #1
                    Class #9, tick #2
Block  #8, tick #0
Block  #8, tick #1
Block  #8, tick #2
```

You can see that object-based synchronized methods and synchronized blocks share the same monitor key if they are for the same object. Also, class-based synchronization and object-based synchronization do use different keys because their output interleaves each other.

Synchronization is an expensive operation, and the use of it should be kept to a minimum, especially for frequently executed methods or blocks of statements. However, synchronization can help reduce the interference among different threads. Good use of it will definitely improve the stability and robustness of the program.

Inter-thread Communications

Inter-thread communications allow threads to talk to or wait for each other. You can have threads communicate with each other through shared data or by using thread-control methods to have threads wait for each other.

Threads Sharing Data

All the threads in the same program share the same memory space. If the reference to an object is visible to different threads by the syntactic rules of scopes, or explicitly passed to different threads, these threads share access to the data members of that object. As explained in the previous section, synchronization is sometimes necessary to enforce exclusive access to the data to avoid racing conditions and data corruption.

Threads Waiting for Other Threads

By using thread-control methods, you can have threads communicate by waiting for each other. For example, the join() method can be used for the caller thread to wait for the completion of the called thread. Also, a thread can suspend itself and wait at a rendezvous point using the suspend() method; another thread can wake it up through the waiting thread's resume() method, and both threads can run concurrently thereafter.

Deadlock may occur when a thread holding the key to a monitor is suspended or waiting for another thread's completion. If the other thread it is waiting for needs to get into the same monitor, both threads will be waiting forever. This is why the `suspend()` and `resume()` methods are now deprecated and should not be used. The `wait()`, `notify()`, and `notifyAll()` methods defined in class `Object` of the `java.lang` package can be used to solve this problem.

The `wait()` method will make the calling thread wait until either a time-out occurs or another thread calls the same object's `notify()` or `notifyAll()` method. The synopsis of the `wait()` method is:

```
wait()
```

or

```
wait (long timeoutPeriodInMilliseconds)
```

The former will wait until the thread is notified. The latter will wait until either the specified time-out expires or the thread is notified, whichever comes first.

When a thread calls the `wait()` method, the key it is holding will be released for another waiting thread to enter the monitor. The `notify()` method will wake up only one waiting thread, if any. The `notifyAll()` method will wake up all the threads that have been waiting in the monitor. After being notified, the thread will try to reenter the monitor by requesting the key again and may need to wait for another thread to release the key.

Note that these methods can be called only within a monitor, or `synchronized` block. The thread calling an object's `notify()` or `notifyAll()` method needs to own the key to that object's monitor; otherwise, `IllegalMonitorStateException`, a type of `RuntimeException`, will be thrown.

The next example demonstrates the use of the `wait()` and `notify()` methods to solve the classical producer and consumer problem. In this problem, the producer will generate data for the consumer to consume. However, if the producer produces data faster than the consumer can consume, the newly created data may be over-written before it is consumed. On the other hand, if the consumer consumes faster than the producer can produce, the consumer may keep using already processed data. Synchronization alone will not solve the problem because it only guarantees exclusive access to the data, not availability.

The first implementation uses a monitor, an instance of the `NoWaitMonitor` class, to control the access to the data, `token`. The producer and consumer will `set` and get, respectively, the token value in random intervals, with the maximum interval length regulated by the speed argument passed to their constructors. The main program accepts up to two command-line arguments for setting the producing and consuming speed, creates an instance of the monitor, creates a producer and a consumer, and watches them run for 10 seconds. The program is listed as follows:

```java
import java.io.*;
public class NoWaitPandC {
  static int produceSpeed = 200;
  static int consumeSpeed = 200;
  public static void main (String args[]) {
    if (args.length > 0)
      produceSpeed = Integer.parseInt (args[0]);
    if (args.length > 1)
      consumeSpeed = Integer.parseInt (args[1]);
    NoWaitMonitor monitor = new NoWaitMonitor();
    new NoWaitProducer (monitor, produceSpeed);
    new NoWaitConsumer (monitor, consumeSpeed);
    try {
      Thread.sleep (1000);
    } catch (InterruptedException e) {
    }
    System.exit(0);
  }
}
class NoWaitMonitor {
  int token = -1;
  PrintWriter out = new PrintWriter (System.out, true);
  // get token value
  synchronized int get () {
    out.println ("Got: " + token);
    return token;
  }
  // put token value
  synchronized void set (int value) {
    token = value;
    out.println ("Set: " + token);
  }
}
class NoWaitProducer implements Runnable {
  NoWaitMonitor monitor;
  int   speed;
```

```
    NoWaitProducer (NoWaitMonitor monitor, int speed) {
      this.monitor = monitor;
      this.speed = speed;
      new Thread (this, "Producer").start();
    }
    public void run() {
      int i = 0;
      while (true) {
        monitor.set (i++);
        try {
          Thread.sleep ((int) (Math.random() * speed));
        } catch (InterruptedException e) {
        }
      }
    }
  }
  class NoWaitConsumer implements Runnable {
    NoWaitMonitor monitor;
    int   speed;
    NoWaitConsumer (NoWaitMonitor monitor, int speed) {
      this.monitor = monitor;
      this.speed = speed;
      new Thread (this, "Consumer").start();
    }
    public void run() {
        while (true) {
          monitor.get();
          try {
            Thread.sleep((int) (Math.random() * speed));
          } catch (InterruptedException e) {}
        }
    }
  }
```

Here is an example of the output of the program where the producer outpaces the consumer:

```
C:\MasteringJava\Ch08>java NoWaitPandC 100 400
Set: 0
Got: 0
Set: 1
Set: 2
Set: 3
```

```
Set: 4
Got: 4
Set: 5
Set: 6
Set: 7
Set: 8
Set: 9
Set: 10
Got: 10
Set: 11
Set: 12
```

You can see there is a lot of data generated (shown as Set) but overwritten before it is processed (shown as Got).

Here is an example of the program's output where the consumer is faster than the producer:

```
C:\MasteringJava\Ch08>java NoWaitPandC 400 100
Set: 0
Got: 0
Got: 0
Got: 0
Got: 0
Got: 0
Got: 0
Set: 1
Set: 2
Got: 2
Set: 3
Got: 3
Got: 3
Got: 3
Got: 3
Got: 3
Set: 4
Got: 4
Got: 4
Got: 4
Got: 4
Got: 4
```

This time, some of the data is processed multiple times.

The second implementation of the sample program uses the wait() and notify() methods to make sure all data is created and used exactly once. The program is the same as the previous one, except for the implementation of the monitor. A boolean variable, valueSet, is added to indicate whether the data is ready for consumption or already used. The get() method will first test if the data is ready for consumption. If not, the calling thread will wait until some other thread sets the data and notifies the current thread. The boolean variable is then set to indicate that the data is consumed. Any thread waiting to produce new data will then be notified to start the production. If there is no thread waiting to produce, the notify() method will be ignored. The get() method is shown here:

```
synchronized int get() {
  if (! valueSet)
    try {
      wait();
    } catch (InterruptedException e) {
    }
  valueSet = false;
  out.println ("Got: " + token);
  notify();
  return token;
}
```

Symmetrically, the set() method will first test whether the data is already used. If not, the calling thread will wait until some other thread uses the data and notifies the current thread. The boolean variable is then set to indicate that the data is ready for consumption. Any thread waiting to consume the data will then be notified to start the consumption. If there is no thread waiting, the notify() method will be ignored. The set() method is shown here:

```
synchronized void set (int value) {
  if (valueSet)
    try {
      wait();
    } catch (InterruptedException e) {
    }
  valueSet = true;
  token = value;
  out.println ("Set: " + token);
  notify();
}
```

The full program listing is shown here:

```
import java.io.*;
public class PandC {
  static int produceSpeed = 200;
  static int consumeSpeed = 200;
  public static void main (String args[]) {
    if (args.length > 0)
      produceSpeed = Integer.parseInt (args[0]);
    if (args.length > 1)
      consumeSpeed = Integer.parseInt (args[1]);
    Monitor monitor = new Monitor();
    new Producer(monitor, produceSpeed);
    new Consumer(monitor, consumeSpeed);
    try {
      Thread.sleep(1000);
    } catch (InterruptedException e) {
    }
    System.exit(0);
  }
}
class Monitor {
  PrintWriter out = new PrintWriter (System.out, true);
  int token;
  boolean valueSet = false;
  // get token value
  synchronized int get () {
    if (! valueSet)
      try {
        wait();
      } catch (InterruptedException e) {
      }
    valueSet = false;
    out.println ("Got: " + token);
    notify();
    return token;
  }
  // set token value
  synchronized void set (int value) {
    if (valueSet)
      try {
        wait();
      } catch (InterruptedException e) {
      }
```

```java
      valueSet = true;
      token = value;
      out.println ("Set: " + token);
      notify();
    }
  }
class Producer implements Runnable {
  Monitor monitor;
  int speed;
  Producer (Monitor monitor, int speed) {
    this.monitor = monitor;
    this.speed = speed;
    new Thread (this, "Producer").start();
  }
  public void run() {
    int i = 0;
    while (true) {
      monitor.set (i++);
      try {
        Thread.sleep ((int) (Math.random() * speed));
      } catch (InterruptedException e) {
      }
    }
  }
}
class Consumer implements Runnable {
  Monitor monitor;
  int speed;
  Consumer (Monitor monitor, int speed) {
    this.monitor = monitor;
    this.speed = speed;
    new Thread (this, "Consumer").start();
  }
  public void run() {
    while (true) {
      monitor.get();
      try {
        Thread.sleep ((int) (Math.random() * speed));
      } catch (InterruptedException e) {
      }
    }
  }
}
```

Here is an example of the output of this program:

```
C:\MasteringJava\Ch08>java PandC 400 100
Set: 0
Got: 0
Set: 1
Got: 1
Set: 2
Got: 2
Set: 3
Got: 3
Set: 4
Got: 4
```

This time, every piece of data generated is consumed exactly once.

Priorities and Scheduling

Priorities are the way to make sure important or time-critical threads are executed frequently or immediately. *Scheduling* is the means to make sure priorities and fairness are enforced.

If you have only one CPU, all of the runnable threads must take turns executing. Scheduling is the activity of determining the execution order of multiple threads.

Thread Priority Values

Every thread in Java is assigned a priority value. When more than one thread is competing for CPU time, the thread with the highest priority value is given preference. Thread priority values that can be assigned to user-created threads are simple integers ranging between Thread.MIN_PRIORITY and Thread.MAX_PRIORITY. User applications are normally run with the priority value of Thread.NORM_PRIORITY. Through JDK 1.2, the following constants of the Thread class—MIN_PRIORITY, MAX_PRIORITY, and NORM_PRIORITY—have the values of 1, 10, and 5, respectively. Every thread group has a maximum priority value assigned. This is a cap to the priority values of member threads and thread groups when they are created or want to change their priority values.

When a thread is created, it will inherit the priority value of the creating thread if the priority value doesn't exceed the limit imposed by its parent thread group. The setPriority() method of Thread class can be used to set the priority value of a thread. If the value to be set is outside the legal range, an `IllegalArgument-Exception` will be thrown. If the value is larger than the maximum priority value of its parent thread group, the maximum priority value will be used.

The `setMaxPriority()` method of class `ThreadGroup` can be used to set the maximum priority value of a thread group. For security reasons (so that a user-created thread will not monopolize the CPU), a Web browser may not allow an applet to change its priority.

Preemptive Scheduling and Time-Slicing

Java's scheduling is *preemptive*; that is, if a thread with a higher priority than the currently running thread becomes runnable, the higher priority thread should be executed immediately, pushing the currently running thread back to the queue to wait for its next turn. A thread can voluntarily pass the CPU execution privilege to waiting threads of the same priority by calling the `yield()` method.

In some implementations, thread execution is *time-sliced*; that is, threads with equal priority values will have equal opportunities to run in a round-robin manner. Even threads with lower priorities will still get a small portion of the execution time slots, roughly proportional to their priority values. Therefore, no threads will be starving in the long run.

Other implementations do not have time-slicing. A thread will relinquish its control only when it finishes its execution, is preempted by a higher-priority thread, or is blocked by I/O operations or the `sleep()`, `wait()`, or `suspend()` method calls. For computation-intensive threads, it is a good idea to occasionally call the `yield()` method to give other threads a chance to run. It may improve the overall interactive responsiveness of graphical user interfaces.

TIP   Up to JDK 1.1, the Java virtual machine for Windows 95 and NT is time-sliced; the Java virtual machine for Solaris 2 is not time-sliced. However, in Java 1.2, a time-sliced variety is available for Solaris. It does require several patches to be installed and, because of this, is not enabled by default. See the **README** file that comes with the JDK for the list of patches to install for Solaris 2.5.1 and Solaris-x86. Once the patches are installed, to change thread scheduling from non–time-sliced to time-sliced, set the environment variable THREADS_FLAG to `native` for time-sliced, or set it to **green** (or leave it unset) for the default behavior. You can also specify runtime options of `-native` or `-green` to the command-line tools, like `java` and `javac`.

Scheduling Threads with Different Priorities

The next example demonstrates the effect of scheduling on threads with different priorities. The main program will accept an optional command-line argument to indicate whether the threads created will yield to each other regularly.

The main program starts four threads with priority values of 1, 2, 4, and 4, respectively. Each thread will increment its counter 600,001 times and optionally yield to threads with equal priority on every three-thousandth increment. Because the main thread has a higher priority value, 5, than these computation-intensive threads, the main thread may grab the CPU every 0.3 second to print the counter values of these four computing threads. The program is listed as follows:

```java
import java.io.*;
public class PriorityTest {
  static int    NUM_THREADS = 4;
  static boolean yield = true;
  static int counter[] = new int[NUM_THREADS];
  public static void main (String args[]) {
    PrintWriter out = new PrintWriter (System.out, true);
    int numIntervals = 10;
    if (args.length > 0)
      yield = false;
    out.println ("Using yield()? " + (yield ? "YES" : "NO"));
    for (int i = 0; i < NUM_THREADS; i++)
      (new PrTestThread ((i > 1) ? 4 : (i + 1), i)).start();
    ThreadInfo.printAllThreadInfo();
    out.println();
    //   repeatedly print out the counter values
    int step = 0;
    while (true) {
      boolean allDone = true;
      try {
        Thread.sleep (300);
      } catch (InterruptedException e) {
      }
      out.print ("Step " + (step++) + ": COUNTERS:");
      for (int j = 0; j < NUM_THREADS; j++) {
        out.print (" " + counter[j]);
        if (counter[j] < 2000000)
          allDone = false;
      }
```

```
        out.println();
        if (allDone)
          break;
      }
      System.exit(0);
    }
  }
  class PrTestThread extends Thread {
    int  id;
    PrTestThread (int priority, int id) {
      super ("PrTestThread#" + id);
      this.id = id;
      setPriority(priority);
    }
    public void run() {
      for (int i = 0; i <= 2000000; i++) {
        if (((i % 3000) == 0) && PriorityTest.yield)
          yield();
        PriorityTest.counter[id] = i;
      }
    }
  }
```

Here is an example of the output when the program is run on a time-sliced system (Windows 95/NT or Solaris with native threads), with the computing threads frequently yielding to each other:

```
C:\MasteringJava\Ch08>java PriorityTest
Using yield()? YES
THREAD GROUP: system; Max Priority: 10
    THREAD: Signal dispatcher; Priority: 10 [Daemon] [Alive]
    THREAD: Reference handler; Priority: 10 [Daemon] [Alive]
    THREAD: Finalizer; Priority: 8 [Daemon] [Alive]
    THREAD GROUP: main; Max Priority: 10
        THREAD: main; Priority: 5 [Alive] <== current
        THREAD: PrTestThread#0; Priority: 1 [Alive]
        THREAD: PrTestThread#1; Priority: 2 [Alive]
        THREAD: PrTestThread#0; Priority: 4 [Alive]
        THREAD: PrTestThread#1; Priority: 4 [Alive]

Step 0: COUNTERS: 2999 0 530999 533999
Step 1: COUNTERS: 5999 2999 1073999 1085999
Step 2: COUNTERS: 8999 5999 1607999 1637999
Step 3: COUNTERS: 149999 149999 2000000 2000000
```

```
Step 4: COUNTERS: 704999 701999 2000000 2000000
Step 5: COUNTERS: 1249866 1259999 2000000 2000000
Step 6: COUNTERS: 1796999 1817999 2000000 2000000
Step 7: COUNTERS: 2000000 2000000 2000000 2000000
```

From the output, you can see some surprising results. The two threads with the highest priority tend to hog most of the CPU time. However, since the priority 1 thread is so close to priority 2, there is a closer splitting of CPU time.

Here is an example of the output when the same program is run on a Java virtual machine, with no time-slicing and, again, the threads yielding to each other regularly.

```
harpoon:/users/me/java/examples/ch8> java PriorityTest
Using yield()? YES
THREAD GROUP: system; Max Priority: 10
    THREAD: Clock; Priority: 12 [Daemon] [Alive]
    THREAD: Idle thread; Priority: 0 [Daemon] [Alive]
    THREAD: Async Garbage Collector; Priority: 1 [Daemon] [Alive]
    THREAD: Reference handler; Priority: 10 [Daemon] [Alive]
    THREAD: Finalizer; Priority: 8 [Daemon] [Alive]
    THREAD: SoftReference sweeper; Priority: 9 [Daemon] [Alive]
    THREAD GROUP: main; Max Priority: 10
        THREAD: main; Priority: 5 [Alive] <== current
        THREAD: PrTestThread#0; Priority: 1 [Alive]
        THREAD: PrTestThread#1; Priority: 2 [Alive]
        THREAD: PrTestThread#0; Priority: 4 [Alive]
        THREAD: PrTestThread#1; Priority: 4 [Alive]

Step 0: COUNTERS: 0 0 103563 101999
Step 1: COUNTERS: 0 0 206999 208476
Step 2: COUNTERS: 0 0 314999 312189
Step 3: COUNTERS: 0 0 419999 416889
Step 4: COUNTERS: 0 0 527999 520335
Step 5: COUNTERS: 0 67070 600000 600000
Step 6: COUNTERS: 0 295645 600000 600000
Step 7: COUNTERS: 0 521522 600000 600000
Step 8: COUNTERS: 145375 600000 600000 600000
Step 9: COUNTERS: 374097 600000 600000 600000
Step 10: COUNTERS: 515023 600000 600000 600000
Step 11: COUNTERS: 600000 600000 600000 600000
```

From the output, it is obvious that lower-priority threads do not have any chance to run until all the higher-priority threads finish their execution.

You'll have to play with the maximum value setting for the counters to get reasonable results for your machine. Do not use a value so low that everything is done in two or three steps. However, anything taking over 20 steps may be a little much.

Here is the output when the same program is run on a time-sliced system with no yielding:

```
C:\MasteringJava\Ch08>java PriorityTest 0
Using yield()? NO
THREAD GROUP: system; Max Priority: 10
     THREAD: Signal dispatcher; Priority: 10 [Daemon] [Alive]
     THREAD: Reference handler; Priority: 10 [Daemon] [Alive]
     THREAD: Finalizer; Priority: 8 [Daemon] [Alive]
     THREAD GROUP: main; Max Priority: 10
          THREAD: main; Priority: 5 [Alive] <== current
          THREAD: PrTestThread#0; Priority: 1 [Alive]
          THREAD: PrTestThread#1; Priority: 2 [Alive]
          THREAD: PrTestThread#0; Priority: 4 [Alive]
          THREAD: PrTestThread#1; Priority: 4 [Alive]

Step 0: COUNTERS: 60965 61129 546422 441717
Step 1: COUNTERS: 126821 123038 1052759 951456
Step 2: COUNTERS: 188446 182858 1555466 1484050
Step 3: COUNTERS: 252345 246123 2000000 2000000
Step 4: COUNTERS: 764587 861142 2000000 2000000
Step 5: COUNTERS: 1302086 1435581 2000000 2000000
Step 6: COUNTERS: 1900295 1977578 2000000 2000000
Step 7: COUNTERS: 2000000 2000000 2000000 2000000
```

Running the program on a different operating system may generate a different pattern of output. You are at the mercy of the scheduling algorithm of either the operating system and/or the particular port of the JDK.

Interestingly, the lower-priority threads get more chances to run than in the previous run with yielding. This is probably because yielding disturbs the scheduler's original plan to execute lower-priority threads by forcing the scheduler to look for threads with equal priority first. With no yielding, all the schedules for lower-priority threads can be smoothly exercised.

Finally, the program is run with no yielding on an implementation with no time-slicing:

```
harpoon:/users/me/java/examples/ch8> java PriorityTest 0
Using yield()? NO
THREAD GROUP: system; Max Priority: 10
    THREAD: Clock; Priority: 12 [Daemon] [Alive]
    THREAD: Idle thread; Priority: 0 [Daemon] [Alive]
    THREAD: Async Garbage Collector; Priority: 1 [Daemon] [Alive]
    THREAD: Reference handler; Priority: 10 [Daemon] [Alive]
    THREAD: Finalizer; Priority: 8 [Daemon] [Alive]
    THREAD: SoftReference sweeper; Priority: 9 [Daemon] [Alive]
     THREAD GROUP: main; Max Priority: 10
        THREAD: main; Priority: 5 [Alive] <== current
        THREAD: PrTestThread#0; Priority: 1 [Alive]
        THREAD: PrTestThread#1; Priority: 2 [Alive]
        THREAD: PrTestThread#2; Priority: 4 [Alive]
        THREAD: PrTestThread#3; Priority: 4 [Alive]

Step 0:  COUNTERS: 0 0 203552 0
Step 1:  COUNTERS: 0 0 203552 210978
Step 2:  COUNTERS: 0 0 413376 210978
Step 3:  COUNTERS: 0 0 413376 422790
Step 4:  COUNTERS: 0 0 600000 444539
Step 5:  COUNTERS: 0 57353 600000 600000
Step 6:  COUNTERS: 0 272848 600000 600000
Step 7:  COUNTERS: 0 488745 600000 600000
Step 8:  COUNTERS: 100596 600000 600000 600000
Step 9:  COUNTERS: 314749 600000 600000 600000
Step 10: COUNTERS: 587513 600000 600000 600000
Step 11: COUNTERS: 600000 600000 600000 600000
```

The lower-priority threads have no chance to run until all the higher-priority threads finish. Even threads with equal priority values do not have the chance to run until the main thread preempts the running thread. When a thread is preempted, it will be put to the end of the waiting queue. When the main thread relinquishes program control after printing the counter values, the previously waiting thread that is ahead in the queue will get the chance to run. You can see proof of this in the output listing: only one of the highest-priority threads advances its counter between each printing.

Thread Local Variables

Introduced into the Core API in Java 1.2, the concept of thread local variables is actually not new to Java. A similar class existed within the internal `sun.server.util` package of the Java Web Server product. Apparently, there was enough demand to make the design pattern a standard part of Java, so the concept has moved into the `java.lang.ThreadLocal` and `java.lang.InheritableThreadLocal` classes. So, what exactly are they? Well, thread local variables permit individual thread instances to have independent copies of variables.

Normally you will rarely need to use `ThreadLocal` variables, although `InheritableThreadLocal` is more likely. They become important when you need static variables to store an identifier, probably for database access or a session identifier. Then, you share the variable only within a particular running thread or a thread and all its descendants.

> **NOTE**   A `ThreadLocal` variable is initialized via its protected `initialValue()` method. The default initial value of a `ThreadLocal` variable is `null`. So, to provide a different initial value, you must subclass `ThreadLocal` and override the method. You can also change the value at a later time with the `set()` method.

The following example demonstrates the differences between class variables and `ThreadLocal` variables. Using multithreading, the program creates several instances of a class and counts the number created in the `counter` class variable. For each thread, the static `threadLocal` variable is also available. The value of `threadLocal` is used as the amount of time to sleep. The inner class, `MyThreadLocal`, offers up to 1,000 milliseconds for the thread to sleep via its `initialValue()` method. Notice that both variables are `static`, meaning one would expect there to be one copy of each variable for all instances of the class.

```
public class LocalThreadVars implements Runnable {
  static private class MyThreadLocal extends ThreadLocal {
    protected Object initialValue() {
      return new Double (Math.random() * 1000.0);
    }
  }
  static ThreadLocal threadLocal = new MyThreadLocal();
  static int counter = 0;
  private LocalThreadVars() {
```

```
        counter++;
      }
      public void run() {
        LocalThreadVars myLTV = new LocalThreadVars();
        displayValues();
        try {
          Thread.currentThread().sleep (
            ((Double)threadLocal.get()).longValue());
          myLTV.displayValues();
        } catch (InterruptedException e) {
          e.printStackTrace();
        }
      }
      private void displayValues() {
        System.out.println (threadLocal.get() + "\t" + counter +
          "\t" + Thread.currentThread().getName());
      }
      public static void main (String args[]) {
        LocalThreadVars ltv = new LocalThreadVars();
        ltv.displayValues();
        for (int i=0;i<5;i++) {
          Thread t = new Thread (ltv);
          t.start();
        }
      }
    }
```

After running the program, you'll think otherwise. Here is an example of the output the program produces. As the program utilizes random numbers, your output will most likely differ.

```
353.6782033483381        1        main
607.6189861951625        2        Thread-0
204.82242103443437       3        Thread-1
216.68547449023978       4        Thread-2
960.1210961092618        5        Thread-3
221.4544981562063        6        Thread-4
204.82242103443437       6        Thread-1
216.68547449023978       6        Thread-2
221.4544981562063        6        Thread-4
607.6189861951625        6        Thread-0
960.1210961092618        6        Thread-3
```

Notice how the `counter` variable is shared across threads, but the `threadLocal` variable isn't. If the `ThreadLocal` static variable was shared across threads, you would see the same value repeated for all values, instead of just for multiple classes within the same thread.

You'll appreciate the `ThreadLocal` class more once you are doing network programming. For now, just be aware of its existence and keep it in the back of your mind for when you need it.

Daemon Threads

Daemon threads are service threads. They exist to provide services to other threads. They normally enter an endless loop waiting for clients requesting services. When all the active threads remaining are daemon threads, the Java virtual machine will exit.

For example, a timer thread that wakes up in regular intervals is a good candidate for daemon threads. This timer thread can notify other threads regularly about the timeouts. When no other thread is running, there is no need for the timer thread's existence.

To create a daemon thread, call the `setDaemon()` method immediately after the thread's creation and before the execution is started. The constructor of the thread is a good candidate for making this method call. By default, all the threads created by a daemon thread are also daemon threads. The synopsis of the `setDaemon()` method is:

```
setDaemon (boolean isDaemon)
```

When *isDaemon* is `true`, the thread is marked as a daemon thread; otherwise, it is marked as a non-daemon thread.

Summary

A thread is a single line of execution within a program. Multiple threads can run concurrently in a single program. A thread is created by either subclassing the `Thread` class or implementing the `Runnable` interface. In either case, a public `run()` method is defined as the thread body to be run in the newly created execution context when the thread's `start()` method is called. In addition to the `start()`

method, there are join(), yield(), and sleep() methods defined in the Thread class to control the execution of a thread. The stop(), suspend(), and resume() methods exist but have become deprecated with Java 1.2 and should be avoided.

Any thread that has not been destroyed yet is always in one of four states: newly created, runnable, blocked, or dead. When the state of a thread is changed into the blocked state by I/O blocking or a call to the suspend(), wait(), or sleep() method, a counter-event of the event putting the thread into the blocked state will move the thread back to the runnable state. These counter-events are I/O being finished for I/O blocking, the resume() method being called for a suspend() method call, the notify() or notifyAll() method being called for the wait() method call, and a time-out occurring for the sleep() method call. Also, at any time a thread can be interrupt()ed, causing an InterruptedException to be thrown.

Every thread is the member of exactly one thread group, which can be nested. All the threads and thread groups in a program form a tree with the system thread group as the root. The deprecated stop(), suspend(), and resume() methods are defined in class ThreadGroup to allow for manipulating all the threads inside a thread group by a single method call. Abundant methods are defined in the Thread and ThreadGroup classes to get the information about a thread or a thread group.

Synchronization is a way of avoiding data corruption caused by simultaneous access to the same data. In Java, the monitor model implements synchronization. A monitor is a guarded place for methods and blocks of statements. Only one thread is allowed in a monitor at a time. Every object can become a monitor if there are synchronized instance methods defined in the class the object is instantiated from, or synchronized blocks of statements that refer to the object. The wait() method is used inside a monitor for a thread to wait for another thread to call the called object's notify() or notifyAll() method.

Every thread has a priority value associated with it. In case multiple threads are competing for execution, the thread with the highest priority is preferred. Java's scheduling is preemptive; that is, a higher-priority thread will preempt the lower-priority running thread and be executed immediately.

When you need class variables that are unique for each thread, you need to use the ThreadLocal class. For a hierarchy of threads, InheritableThreadLocal allows you to share a variable. These allow you to create things like identifiers that exist purely for the life of the running thread. Then, when the thread finishes running, the local thread variables no longer exist.

A daemon thread is a service thread. When all the active threads remaining are daemon threads, the Java virtual machine will exit. A thread is marked as a daemon thread by calling the `setDaemon()` method.

Multithreading allows for multiple lines of execution at the same time. Multiple threads running concurrently cannot only improve the utilization of resources, but they can also open the door for easier and creative programming of multimedia or animation effects. Having the threading capability defined in the language will definitely encourage the creation of multithreaded programs. You can expect to see more and more multithreaded applets on the Web, enriching your Web-surfing experiences.

PART II

Applying Standard
Java Classes

CHAPTER
NINE

9

Standard Java Packages

- Package `java.lang`

- Package `java.util`

- Package `java.io`

- Package `java.awt`

- Package `javax.swing`

- Package `java.net`

- Package `java.applet`

- Advanced programming packages

This chapter introduces the Java packages, focusing on seven of the most commonly used ones. But before learning about the individual packages, you will see how these packages relate to Java's class hierarchy.

Java Packages and the Class Hierarchy

Java has been object-oriented from day one. And as befits real object-oriented languages, Java comes with a standard set of support classes, versus hybrids like C++, which are only now getting standardized support libraries. Java's classes are very different from the familiar libraries that accompany procedural languages like C or Pascal. Because these support classes exploit the full potential of object-oriented languages, they transcend simple libraries. Class inheritance is by far the most common and most powerful feature used. (See Chapters 3 and 5 for more information about class inheritance.)

The entire Java hierarchy can be viewed from two organizational angles: as an object-oriented inheritance hierarchy and as groups of classes in packages. The inheritance hierarchy groups classes that share common implementation aspects (that is, code or variables). Java packages simply collect classes on a more pragmatic basis: Classes with related functionality are bundled together in the same package, whether they share code, data, or neither. In addition to their obvious structuring benefits, packages use namespace partitioning, which means that every class contained in a package has a unique name that cannot conflict (collide) with class names defined elsewhere. For example, two companies could safely sell code for classes with identical names. A bubble-sorting class from Mango Macrosystems might be called `mango.utilities.Bubble`, while a similar product from Sun-So-Soft Inc. might be called `sosoft.utils.Bubble`. The class names are the same, but Java uses the package names and subpackage names to distinguish one class from another.

The language's strict single inheritance scheme determines the way Java's standard classes relate to one another in terms of object-oriented inheritance. The resulting inheritance tree is, therefore, a pure tree, and not a graph, as is the case with multiple inheritance, object-oriented hierarchies. Multiple inheritance, of sorts, is employed within the Java classes by using the language's powerful interface mechanism (discussed in Chapter 5).

Multiple Inheritance versus Single Inheritance

Multiple inheritance is a mechanism that allows one class to inherit from more than one superclass. This produces the net effect of mixing characteristics of multiple classes into a new class.

Multiple inheritance was introduced to solve single inheritance's straightjacket effect. For example, say that you have a single inheritance hierarchy branching into two fundamental subtrees, `Living` and `InAnimate`. From `Living` grows the successive subclass branch `Plant–FruitTree–Banana`. The `InAnimate` branch could have a `Valuable–Food` sub-branch. Now, `Food` might quite understandably want to have `Banana` as its subclass as well. Single inheritance does not let you have both. Class `Banana` is either a `FruitTree` or a `Food`; it can inherit from only one superclass hierarchy, not two (or more). The single inheritance tree shown here illustrates the limitations of pure single inheritance.

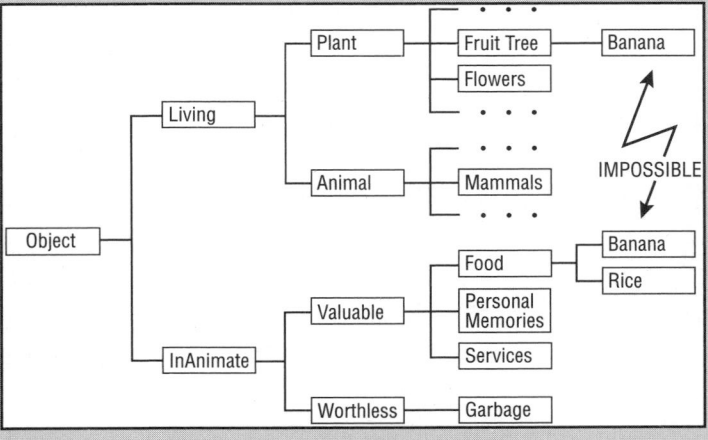

Since packages give you an easy handle on the entire hierarchy, they will now be your guides as you explore the Java class hierarchy. The Java 1.2 release has about 60 `java.*` packages. This chapter examines the seven most commonly used packages:

- Package `java.lang` contains the main language support classes. These deal with object wrappers, strings, multithreading, and related areas.

- Package `java.util` contains language support classes of a more utilitarian nature. These include collection and calendar classes, as well as some useful abstract designs codified by the interfaces `Comparator, Iterator,` and `Observer`.

- Package `java.io` provides device-independent file and stream I/O services.

- Package `java.awt` hides the bulk of all graphical classes. Because it contains Java's Abstract Window Toolkit (AWT), contained in `java.awt` and twelve subpackages, the package should really be considered as the heart of the entire hierarchy.

- Package `javax.swing` offers classes for components, higher-level controls, and pluggable look-and-feel.

- Package `java.net` combines the classes supporting low-level Internet programming plus World Wide Web and HTML support.

- Package `java.applet` contains a single class with support for HTML embedded Java applets.

Package *java.lang*—Main Language Support

The `java.lang` package collection of classes is flat and shallow. The majority of `java.lang` classes extend class `Object` directly, which is the root for the entire Java class hierarchy, not just the root for `java.lang`.

The `Number` subhierarchy is a good example of how object-oriented inheritance works and when to apply it. Classes `Byte, Short, Integer, Long, Float,` and `Double` have things in common, so a superclass was created to hold (*encapsulate*) these shared traits. Note that class `Number` is also declared `abstract`. You cannot make (*instantiate*) objects directly from an abstract class—you can do this from only concrete classes. Although having an abstract parent class (*superclass*) is common, it is by no means necessary. Concrete classes can be the local roots of entire subhierarchies (class `Object` is a prime example).

Of all the packages, package `java.lang` is exceptional, because it is the only package you never need to explicitly import in your programs. The compiler does so by implicitly adding the following line at the top of all your source files:

```
import java.lang.*;
```

The asterisk in this line means that all of the package's classes are imported. This does not import classes in subpackages.

Package `java.lang` gets special treatment because some of its classes are so low-level that they are considered part of the Java language proper. The dividing line between language and external libraries might be important to language designers, but to application programmers the difference is mostly academic. BASIC, for example, has its string-manipulation commands defined as part of the language definition. C, on the other hand, relies on an external (and internationally recognized) standard library of functions to accomplish those tasks. Since Java adheres more to the C philosophy of keeping a language core as simple as possible, it too relies on an external collection of methods for anything beyond the simplest data processing or algorithmic control.

The following types of classes are contained in package `java.lang`:

- Type wrapper classes
- String support classes
- A math library class
- Multithreading support classes
- Low-level system-access classes
- Error and exception classes

The following sections look at these classes in more detail.

The Type Wrapper Classes

Java deals with two different types of entities: primitive types and true objects. Numbers, booleans, and characters behave very much like the familiar equivalents of procedural languages such as Pascal, C, or even C++. Other object-oriented languages, like Smalltalk, do not handle these primitive types in the same way. Smalltalk, for example, uses objects for everything—numbers are objects, booleans are objects, characters are objects, and so on.

NOTE   Although the Smalltalk language originated in an era when the punched card ruled the world (1972), it still manages to be the reference by which new object-oriented languages are judged. Every object-oriented language since has tried to improve on Smalltalk, but most barely manage to equal it. Viewed purely as an object-oriented language, Java comes very close indeed.

Although Java is truly object-oriented, it does not use objects for the most primitive types for the usual reason: performance. Manipulating primitive types without any object-oriented overhead is quite a bit more efficient. However, a uniform and consistent playing field, made up of only objects, is simpler and can be significantly more powerful.

Java contains many subsystems that can work only with objects. With many of these subsystems, the need frequently arises to have the system handle numbers, flags (booleans), or characters. How does Java get around this dilemma? By wrapping the primitive types up in some object sugar coating. You can easily create a class, for example, whose sole purpose is encapsulating a single integer. The net effect would be to obtain an integer object, giving you the universality and power that comes with dealing with only objects (at the cost of some performance degradation).

Package `java.lang` contains such "type wrapper" classes for every Java primitive type:

- Class `Integer` for primitive type `int`
- Class `Long` for primitive type `long`
- Class `Byte` for primitive type `byte`
- Class `Short` for primitive type `short`
- Class `Float` for primitive type `float`
- Class `Double` for primitive type `double`
- Class `Character` for primitive type `char`
- Class `Boolean` for primitive type `boolean`
- Class `Void` for primitive type `void`

Among the numeric types, classes Integer, Long, Byte, Short, Float, and Double are so similar that they all descend from an abstract superclass called Number. Essentially, every one of these classes allows you to create an object from the equivalent primitive type, and vice versa.

The String Classes

Two string-support classes exist in java.lang: String and StringBuffer. Class String supports "read-only" strings; class StringBuffer supports modifiable strings. Although both classes obviously have a few things in common, they are unrelated in that neither inherits from a common "string" superclass.

Class String contains the following core functionality:

- String length function
- Substring extraction
- Substring finding and matching
- String comparison, using the Comparable interface, among many other means
- Uppercase and lowercase conversion
- Leading and trailing whitespace elimination
- Conversion to and from char arrays
- Conversion from primitive types to String type
- Appending strings (converted from any type, including objects)
- Inserting strings (again converted from any type)

The conversion and whitespace-stripping methods might seem contradictory in view of the read-only nature of String strings. This is true, but class String does not break its own rules. During these operations, String creates new read-only strings from the old ones, which it unceremoniously discards in the process. Class StringBuffer, conversely, concentrates on operations that typically modify the string or change its length.

The *Math* Library Class

Class Math groups together a typical and quite conservative collection of mathematical functions. The functions provided can be classified as follows:

- Absolute value, ceiling, floor, min, and max functions. These are suitably overloaded so that you can pass in any numeric type without having your arguments automatically cast to different types, thereby possibly losing accuracy.

- Square root, power, logarithm, and exponential functions. All of these take and return double values only (double, not float, is the default floating-point accuracy used by Java). You do not need to use casts when passing other numeric types, like int or float, because Java's compiler will automatically convert (compatible) argument types for you. A constant for the natural logarithm base is defined as a double precision value in the constant Math.E.

- Trigonometric functions (sin, cos, tan, asin, acos, atan). All of these functions work with angles expressed in radians instead of degrees. A full circle in radians is 2*PI radians (as opposed to 360 degrees). Pi is conveniently defined to double precision as the Math class constant Math.PI.

- A pseudo-random number generator function. One method, random(), is provided as a basis for randomness in applications. Random numbers are very important in simulations, statistical analysis, and, of course, games.

The Multithreading Support Classes

Two classes, Thread and ThreadGroup, and one interface, Runnable, are the gateways to adding multithreaded behavior in your applications or applets. Multithreading amounts to having a multitasking operating system within your own application. Several program threads can execute in parallel and at the same time.

Similar to the way that a multitasking operating system is more powerful and flexible than a single-tasking operating system, users greatly benefit from multithreaded applications. For example, a printing command can be handled in the background, repaginating a long document can be done while the user carries on editing that same document, and so on. Java is one of the rarer languages that provides multithreading from within the language itself (Ada is another example; C, C++, LISP, Pascal, and BASIC all lack built-in multithreading support).

The `java.lang` class `Thread` is the more important class of the two. It provides a collection of methods that allows you to perform the following tasks:

- Create new threads. This lets your applications spread independent jobs over several internal "subprograms." Overall application performance increases when several of these threads need to do I/O operations.

- Start threads. When a thread is initially created, it does not start running immediately. You need to start it explicitly with a `start()` command. To stop a thread, it should periodically check a status variable and return in an orderly fashion. This ensures all resources used are released properly.

- Put threads to sleep for a given amount of time, or yield execution. When a thread has no more work to do while sitting in a loop, the thread should put itself to sleep to let other threads use more of the processor's resources. Also, CPU-intensive threads should periodically pause to permit other threads to execute.

- Change thread priority, name, or daemon status. Threads have several attributes that can be dynamically altered as the thread runs. The priority attribute in particular will affect the proportion of processing resources the thread receives from the processor. Threads can also be flagged as being daemon threads.

- Query thread attributes. Any thread can find out what its priority, name, or daemon status is. This is useful when you launch several thread clones (differentiated only by name, for example) who nevertheless need to act as individuals (like twins in real life).

- Use the `Runnable` interface to tell the thread what to do.

- Use `ThreadLocal` and `InheritableThreadLocal` class instances to provide thread-level, private, static variables.

Class `ThreadGroup` encapsulates methods similar to those listed for `Thread`, except that a thread group is just that—a scope for related threads to operate in. They allow a number of related threads to share attributes and be affected in bulk by thread group changes. See Chapter 8 for more information about threads and multithreading.

The Low-Level System-Access Classes

A handful of classes offer access to system information and resources: System, Runtime, and Process.

Class System encapsulates the classic file handles stdin (as System.in), stdout (as System.out), and stderr (as System.err). These allow you to write output to or get input from the console in the usual way. In addition to these class variables, the following method types are contained in System:

- Platform-optimized array copying

- Catastrophic exit (terminates application and the Java interpreter subsystem!)

- System properties querying

- Security policy related methods

Class Runtime offers specific runtime-environment access via the following method types:

- Available system memory and memory usage advice

- Platform-specific program launching, with the help of the Process class

Class Process provides access to stdin, stdout, and stderr for the executing program's process, as well as the return value of the program.

The Error and Exception Classes

The difference between errors and exceptions is that errors signify trouble in the Java VM (Virtual Machine), and exceptions signify trouble in an executing program. There are about 20 error classes and more than 25 exception classes in JDK 1.2.

Throwable is the root class of all the exception classes; it is an immediate subclass of the Object class. The methods in class Throwable retrieve error messages associated with exceptions and note where exceptions occur.

The immediate subclasses of class Throwable are class Error and class Exception. The subclasses of Error are basically used for signaling abnormal system conditions, such as when the Java VM runs out of memory or when there is a stack overflow in the interpreter. In general, these error conditions are unrecoverable and should not be handled.

On the other hand, the subclasses of class `Exception` represent conditions that are potentially recoverable. For example, an `Exception` subclass signals the end of file input; a program that encounters this condition should not crash—it should simply cease reading from the file.

See Chapter 7 for more information about Java exceptions and exception handling.

Package *java.util*—Utilitarian Language Support

Package `java.util` contains more abstract datatype (ADT) classes plus 13 interfaces, most of which are being introduced in Java 1.2 to support the Collection Framework, described in Chapter 17. Package `java.util` uses inheritance more than package `java.lang`. For example, the `Properties` class is an extension (subclass) of class `Hashtable`, which itself is an extension of `Dictionary`. As we discuss more packages later, you will see that the hierarchies gradually become deeper and more complex.

> **NOTE**
>
> Notice how `Stack` is implemented as a subclass of a `Vector`. One class you would expect to see alongside `Stack` is some form of the `Queue` class. However, queue support (first-in, first-out or FIFO) is provided via the `LinkedList` class.

The following are the main classes contained in package `java.util`:

- Core collection interfaces: `Collection`, `Set`, `SortedSet`, `List`, `Map`, and `SortedMap`

- Concrete implementations: `ArrayList`, `HashMap`, `HashSet`, `Hashtable`, `LinkedList`, `Properties`, `Stack`, `TreeMap`, `TreeSet`, `Vector`, and `WeakHashMap`

- Abstract implementations: `AbstractCollection`, `AbstractList`, `Abstract-Map`, `AbstractSequentialList`, `AbstractSet`, and `Dictionary`

- Infrastructure interfaces: `Iterator`, `ListIterator`, `Comparable` (from `java.lang`), and `Comparator`

- Infrastructure classes: `Collections` and `Arrays`

- `Date` and its supporting calendar and time classes

- `Locale` and its supporting resource bundle classes

- `BitSet`

This package also includes three other interfaces:

- `Enumeration`

- `Observer` (and class `Observable`)

- `EventListener`

The following sections look at these classes and interfaces in more detail.

The Core Collection Interfaces

The interfaces `Collection`, `Set`, `SortedSet`, `List`, `Map`, and `SortedMap` offer the basis for the Collection Framework. They provide unordered groups via `Collection`, collections without duplicates via `Set`, ordered groups via `List`, and key-value pair collections via `Map`, as well as sorted groups with `SortedSet` and `SortedMap`. The methods of these interfaces are used for the following tasks:

- Adding elements

- Finding elements

- Accessing elements

- Removing elements

- Listing elements

- Getting size information

TIP   You may notice that several interfaces and classes in the `java.util` package provide duplicate functionality. Prior to Java 1.2, the `Enumeration` interface with the `Vector`, `Hashtable`, and `Dictionary` classes were the basis for collection-oriented support. The Collections Framework introduced in Java 1.2 provides a more complete basis for working with groups of objects. New programs should use the newer classes, instead of older ones.

The Concrete Collection Implementation Classes

The `ArrayList, HashMap, HashSet, Hashtable, LinkedList, Properties, Stack, TreeMap, TreeSet, Vector`, and `WeakHashMap` classes are what you will most frequently use from `java.util`. They represent the actual implementations of the core collection interfaces:

- `ArrayList` is a resizable array that implements the `List` interface. The `Vector` class acts like an `ArrayList`, while `Stack` offers a last-in, first-out vector of objects.

- `HashMap` and `HashSet` offer hash table backed collections that implement the `Map` and `Set` interfaces, respectively. `Hashtable` functions similarly to a `HashMap`, while `Properties` is a specific `String` hash table that can be easily saved and restored. `WeakHashMap` offers a hash table of weak references.

- `LinkedList` is a doubly linked list and implements the `List` interface. It can be used for queues and stacks.

- `TreeMap` and `TreeSet` are balanced binary tree implementations that implement the `Map` and `Set` interfaces, respectively.

`Vector` and `Hashtable` provide synchronized access to their elements, while the remaining new classes offer unsynchronized access. For the new classes, access can be synchronized externally with synchronizing wrappers provided for you. See Chapter 8 for additional information on thread synchronization and communications between threads.

The Abstract Collection Implementations

The AbstractCollection, AbstractList, AbstractMap, AbstractSequential-List, and AbstractSet classes offer skeleton implementations of the collections. When creating your own collections, you will almost definitely subclass one of these, instead of implementing the repeatable, basic operations of the interfaces yourself. For instance, for the AbstractCollection interface, only iterator() and size() have to be written. Operations like add and remove are common for all implementations.

Also, while Dictionary falls into this category, the Map interface and AbstractMap class supercede its usage in the 1.2 JDK.

The Infrastructure Interfaces and Classes

There are three infrastructure interfaces in java.util: Iterator, ListIterator, and Comparator. With the addition of the Comparable interface in java.lang, these interfaces offer the framework for iterating through the list and ordering the elements.

NOTE   The Iterator interface is meant to eventually replace Enumeration. New code should try to avoid the Enumeration interface in favor of Iterator.

When it is necessary to examine all the elements of a collection, you will use Iterator and ListIterator. Interface Iterator provides an impressive example of Java's powerful interface feature. It defines the behavior (in terms of methods to be supported) of being able to enumerate every component, element, object, or entry—in short, everything contained by any class having some "container" quality. ListIterator extends Iterator to permit changing of the underlying collection and bi-directional walkthroughs. The Iterator interface forces any class to implement three methods: hasNext(), next(), and an optional remove(). The key two methods mean any object that supports enumerating its components via this standard (method) interface can be explored using the following standard Java while loop:

```
iter = someCollection.iterator();
while (iter.hasNext()) {
    containedObj = iter.next();
    // process this object
}
```

The Comparable and Comparator interfaces provide sort order control. Many classes, like String, Date, and URL, already implement the Comparable interface, so sorting internal Java classes is relatively easy. When it comes time to order your own classes, you will use these interfaces.

The infrastructure classes, Collections and Arrays, use the infrastructure interfaces to sort and search the collections. The simplicity of the interfaces permits amazing results, all depending on the collection used:

- Sorting using a tuned quick-sort algorithm
- Searching using a binary search algorithm
- Finding the minimum or maximum element of a collection
- Sorting and searching using a provided Comparator

The Date and Support Classes

Class Date encapsulates the representation of an instant of time, with millisecond precision. The date support classes are TimeZone, SimpleTimeZone, Calendar, and GregorianCalendar. These provide the following types of methods for interpreting and modifying date information:

- Altering year, month, day, hour, minute, and second components
- Querying year, month, day, hour, minute, and second components
- Converting to and from strings and long integers
- Comparing date and time values (including calendar arithmetic)
- Time-zone support

The Locale and Supporting Classes

Class Locale provides the basis for internationalization of Java programs. The locale support classes are ResourceBundle, ListResourceBundle, and PropertyResourceBundle. Through these classes, you can provide runtime customization of text messages for different languages and localities.

The `java.text` package also contains many classes for internationalization support: for instance, `DateFormat`, `MessageFormat`, and `NumberFormat`. These classes permit formatting of text to be in the local customs with respect to month, day, and year ordering, and monetary symbols, among many other things.

The *BitSet* Class

Class `BitSet` implements a set of bits. Unlike many other bit set classes or language features in other languages, this bit set has no limits. You can therefore go way beyond the typical 32- or 256-bit limits imposed by other implementations. `BitSet` operations include the following:

- Setting, clearing, and getting single bits

- Anding, oring, and xoring bit sets together

- Comparing bit sets

The *Observer* Interface and *Observable* Class

Interface `Observer` and class `Observable` together exemplify the way Java's designers have tried to avoid reinventing the wheel, an all too common occurrence in software development. The `Observer-Observable` metaphor addresses a design obstacle slightly more abstract than the enumeration problem solved by the `Iterator` interface.

Sometimes, within an application, it is necessary for a change in an object to trigger changes in other objects; these changes may, in turn, trigger changes in yet other objects. In short, you have a number of objects that are in some way dependent on other objects; this is called a *dependency network*. Java's class hierarchy designers developed the `Observer-Observable` duo to solve this design obstacle.

The mechanism enforced by this duo is quite simple: Any root object that needs to send some kind of notification to other objects should be subclassed from class `Observable`, and any objects that need to receive such notifications should implement interface `Observer`. The following is the sole method interface `Observer` requires:

```
public void update(Observable o, Object arg)
```

To establish the dependency, any observer objects (that is, any objects implementing interface `Observer`) are added to the observable object (that is, the object subclassed from class `Observable`). Whenever this observable object changes, it can then call its `Observable` method `notifyObservers( )`.

Package *java.io*—File and Stream I/O Services

Package `java.io` contains a whole arsenal of I/O-related classes. A top-level classification organizes them as follows:

- Byte input and output streams

- Character readers and writers

- Stream, reader, and writer filtering

- Stream tokenization

- Class `RandomAccessFile`

As you can see from the inheritance tree, the I/O stream branches form the bulk of the tree. A *stream* is an abstract concept used frequently in the context of I/O programming. It represents a linear, sequential flow of bytes of input or output data. Streams can be "flowing toward you," in which case you have an *input stream*, or they can "flow away from you," in which case you refer to an *output stream*. You read from input streams (that is, you read the data a stream delivers to you), and you write to output streams (that is, you transfer data to a stream).

The key point about streams is that they shield you from the input or output devices to which you are ultimately talking. If your code deals with these abstract objects (streams) instead, you can easily switch to different physical I/O devices without changing any of the I/O processing code in your application. This is the main raison d'être of streams.

Readers and writers are similar to input and output streams, but their basic unit of data is a Unicode character.

The stream, reader, and writer classes in package `java.io` can be classified into two types according to their main concern:

- Classes linking a stream, reader, or writer to a concrete I/O data source or destination

- Classes enhancing stream, reader, or writer functionality

The `java.io` package and its classes are discussed in detail in Chapter 19. The following sections provide an overview of the functionality of this package.

The *InputStream* Class

Class `InputStream` is an abstract class from which the entire input stream sub-hierarchy inherits. Essentially, any input stream can simply read one or more bytes (and only bytes) of data from whatever data source it supports (the mark/reset-related functionality is not supported by default). Five subclasses deal with specific data sources for the input stream:

- An array of bytes

- An external file

- Piped stream (of type `PipedInputStream`)

- Two or more other input streams concatenated together

- A `String` (and not a `StringBuffer` as you could be forgiven for thinking) passed as the constructor's argument

---

WARNING   `LineNumberInputStream` and `StringBufferInputStream` are not recommended. Their usage is functionally replaced with `LineNumberReader` and, the more appropriately named, `StringReader`.

Figure 9.1 will help you visualize the relationship between an input stream and its data source. The figure depicts class `ByteArrayInputStream`, an input stream that lets you read from the stream, as usual, a single byte or a block of bytes at a time (as defined by class `InputStream`). In the case of class `ByteArrayInputStream`, the bytes read in this way originated from an array of bytes. Other classes will have other data sources; for example, class `FileInputStream` will take its data from a file.

FIGURE 9.1:

Data source and input stream

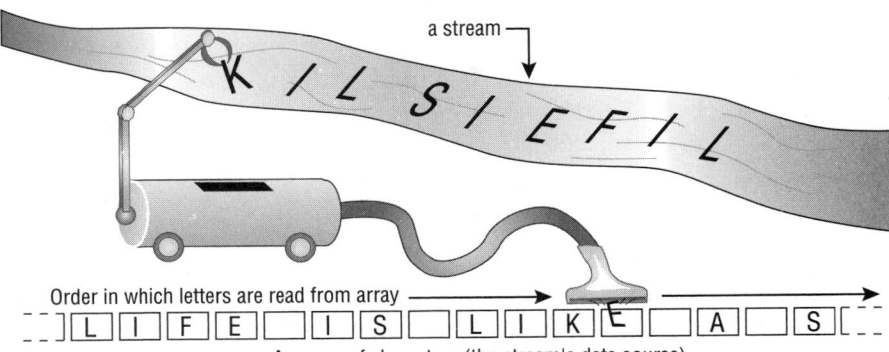

The input streams you have seen so far read bytes from various sources of data; you might think of them as low-level input streams. The remaining input streams in the java.io package read bytes from low-level streams and organize the input into higher-level information. The abstract class FilterInputStream is the root for the subtree grouping together most of these extra classes, which perform the following functions:

- Insert a performance-enhancing input buffering mechanism between the InputStream class's standard reading functionality and your application

- Add support for reading all of Java's primitive types previously saved to a stream

- Add the option of undoing the last single-byte read operation

- Read objects from a low-level stream

TIP

The FilterInputStream subclasses can be powerfully combined with other InputStream classes. For example, you could create a ByteArrayDataInput-Stream or a FilePushbackInputStream. To do this, you would pass an instance of a data source-type InputStream (Byte, File, Pipe, Sequence, or String) object as argument to the constructor of the filter-type InputStream (Buffered, Data-Input, LineNumber, or Pushback). Because these FilterInputStream subclasses are themselves InputStreams, you could even combine several filtering types. You could therefore conceivably create a BufferingPushbackLineNumberingString-InputStream (although by then you would be breaking every readability rule in the book). This same technique is possible with OutputStreams.

The *OutputStream* Class

Class OutputStream is an abstract class from which the entire output stream sub-hierarchy inherits. An output stream's sole requirement is to be able to write a single byte or write an array of bytes. (Flushing and closing the stream are peripheral to what an output stream is all about.) As is the case with input streams, output streams cannot exist on their own; they need to be connected to a data destination before becoming useful.

OutputStream's subclasses can be similarly classified according to their main concern: choice of data destination (called *sink*) or choice of enhanced stream writing behavior. Figure 9.2 will help you visualize the relationship between an output stream and its data sink. The figure depicts the scenario for class File-OutputStream. All the bytes that were written to the stream end up stored in an external file; you specify the file when you create the output stream.

FIGURE 9.2:

An output stream and a data sink

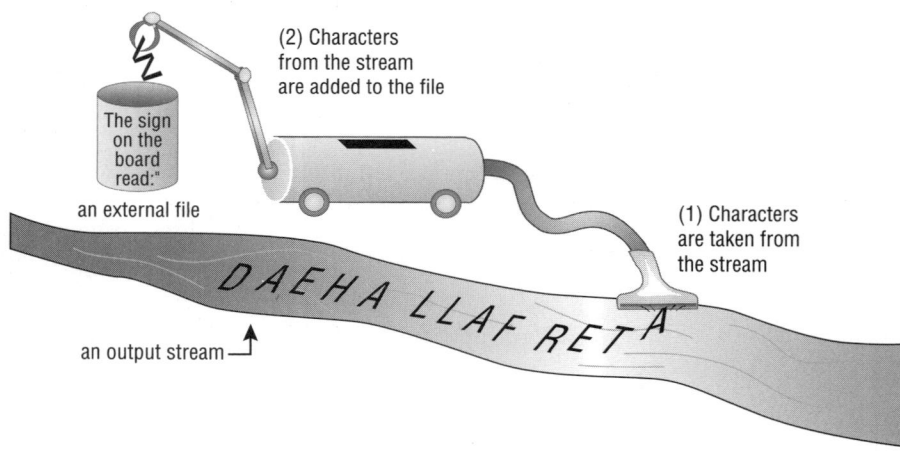

The output stream classes that enhance output stream behavior almost all descend from the output equivalent of FilterInputStream (described in the previous section): FilterOutputStream.

The *Reader* and *Writer* Classes

Class Reader is the abstract character-oriented counterpart of InputStream. Reader has nine subclasses. Like input streams, these classes fall into two categories: low-level readers that take raw character input from various sources and high-level filtering readers that organize the data delivered by low-level readers.

Class `Writer` is the abstract character-oriented counterpart of `OutputStream`. `Writer` has eight subclasses, which also fall into the low-level and high-level categories. Low-level writers deliver character output to various destinations. High-level filtering writers convert organized input to characters that are delivered to other writers.

The *RandomAccessFile* Class

Class `RandomAccessFile` encapsulates full byte-level read and write access to files. This class is rather odd when compared to the other classes in the I/O hierarchy. You would expect the class to be derived from both an abstract input class and an abstract output class (plus some seeking functionality), but since `Random-AccessFile` descends directly from `Object`, a rather conventional (that is, not object-oriented) design approach was used instead.

The methods implemented by `RandomAccessFile` can be summarized into the following groups:

- Reading of primitive types and byte arrays (in binary form)
- Writing of primitive types and byte arrays (in binary form)
- Positioning of the file pointer (seeking)

The *StreamTokenizer* Class

Class `StreamTokenizer` extracts identifiable substrings and punctuation from an input stream according to user-defined rules. This process is called *tokenizing* because the stream is reduced to tokens. Tokens typically represent keywords, variable names, numerical constants, string literals, and syntactic punctuation (like brackets, equal signs, and so on). `StreamTokenizer` includes various methods that affect the rules for parsing the input stream into tokens. It also contains the `nextToken()` method to extract the next token from the input stream.

Text tokenizing is a common technique used to reduce the complexity of textual input. The archetypal application that uses text tokenizing is the programming-language compiler. Compilers do not analyze your source file as is, because that would lead to an onslaught of independent characters. Instead, compilers analyze a stream of tokens representing and extracted from your source file. Keywords, identifiers, punctuation, comments, strings, and so on are first compressed into easy-to-manipulate tokens. Only after this lexical-analysis stage does a compiler start to check the complex grammar of any programming (or other) language. The Java compiler (`javac`) uses the `StreamTokenizer` class for this purpose.

NOTE   The `java.util.zip` and `java.util.jar` packages contain classes that support the reading and writing of compressed .GZ, .ZIP and .JAR files.

Package *java.awt*—Heart of the Hierarchy

The package `java.awt` is organized into the following main groups.

- Two GUI component branches
  - The `Component` subtree, with another important subtree, the `Container` subtree buried slightly deeper within it
  - The `MenuComponent` subtree
- Layout manager classes
  - `FlowLayout`
  - `BorderLayout`
  - `CardLayout`
  - `GridLayout`
  - `GridBagLayout` and `GridBagConstraints`
  - `Insets`
- Graphics classes
  - `Graphics`, `Graphics2D`, and `PrintGraphics`
  - `Image`
  - `Color` and `SystemColor`

- Font
- FontMetrics
- AlphaComposite and Composite
- BasicStroke and Stroke
- GraphicsConfigTemplate, GraphicsConfiguration, Graphics-Device, and GraphicsEnvironment
- GradientPaint and TexturePaint
- RenderingHints
- Geometry classes
  - Point
  - Polygon
  - Dimension
  - Rectangle
  - Shape
- Event classes
  - Event
  - AWTEvent
  - AWEventMulticaster
  - EventQueue
  - ActiveEvent
- Miscellaneous classes
  - MediaTracker
  - Toolkit
  - PrintJob
  - Cursor
  - ComponentOrientation

Java's AWT package is the largest and most important package of the entire hierarchy. This is what you would expect in an age when the design and implementation of application GUIs can easily consume more than one-third of software-development resources. The AWT aims to significantly reduce this proportion by allowing GUIs to be platform independent in a hassle-free way—a revolutionary step. The whole hierarchy is there to make the lives of application developers easier, but in particular it was meant to make GUI development quick and painless.

All the classes outlined next are 100 percent hardware and software independent. This means your Java GUI-based applications will run on every Java-capable platform.

GUI Classes

The bulk of the classes within the package `java.awt` relates to GUI creation and management. The classes can be classified into the following groups:

- Widget classes
- Container classes
- Widget layout classes
- Menu classes

Widget Classes

The fundamental building blocks of GUI designs are called *widgets*, *gadgets*, or *buttons*, depending on the GUI school of thought that invented them. The most common term, and the one used in this book, is widgets (for window gadgets). Java implements a nice variety of them, all of which are easily deployed in your GUI designs, as you will see in later chapters.

- Class `Button` implements that bread-and-butter widget: the button. The simplest and by far most common incarnation is the labeled variety. You can also have buttons with iconic identification (not supported by class `Button`, but provided by the `javax.swing.JButton` class, described later).

- A `Canvas` component provides a drawable area. As such, it is invisible (it has no graphical representation) but can detect mouse click and move events, which can then be used by the application.

- Classes `Checkbox` and `CheckboxGroup` implement checkable items. The latter class forces the former into a mutually exclusive grouping, commonly known as *radio buttons*.

- Class `Choice` implements a multiple-choice component, typically with only a few choices (use `List` for more items). The graphical implementation for a `Choice` usually looks like a pop-up menu.

- The `Component` class is an abstract superclass for widgets.

- A `Label` is used to give GUI zones a title or to label other widgets. It just encapsulates a single line of read-only text.

- A `List` is a heavy-duty list display and item selection widget. It comes with a vertical scrollbar and allows selection of multiple items at the same time.

- A `Scrollbar` component is the Java slider control, which can be either horizontal or vertical. If a `List` object does not provide enough listing functionality, you could design your own custom lister by incorporating a vertical `Scrollbar` object, in a `Panel` subclass, for example. This widget represents a continuous range of values that can be "sampled" at any time by the application. Clicks on the scrollbar's arrow icons are treated as "line-increment" commands that move the scrollbar cursor according to a defined line increment. Similarly, clicks above or below the cursor are interpreted as "page-increment" commands with analogous results.

- The text-entry components start with `TextComponent`, which is the abstract superclass of `TextField` and `TextArea`. The `TextField` widget is the pillar of GUI form screens. It allows you to enter any text within a short, single-line input window. `TextArea` is a variant of the `TextField` widget. It allows multiple lines of text, such as for free-form "memo" type fields. Both `TextField` and `TextArea` allow unconstrained data entry, which often isn't what an application needs. To implement entry fields that accept only strict types of data (text only, numbers only, dates only, and so on), you need to subclass either `TextField` or `TextArea` (depending on your requirements) and enhance their behavior by validating the user's input to the type of data allowed.

While some of these components are used in various examples, the Swing component set is what is described in more detail in Chapter 13. Newly created programs should use those components instead.

Container Classes

An application's window typically is not just an unstructured heap of clickable or selectable components. Well-designed GUIs are highly structured to aid you in navigating the interface. This structuring can be in part achieved by using component containers. A window can be subdivided into areas or zones, each containing related buttons, choices, lists, and so on. When you use containers to implement these visual and logical areas, you mirror the hierarchy in your code. This is just another example of the key object-oriented principle of projecting the vocabulary and structures of the problem domain into your code. The container classes in Java's AWT are also the entities on which the layout manager classes work (see the following section).

WARNING Do not confuse the term *container*, as used by Java's AWT, with the more general term *container class*, as used by other object-oriented frameworks. AWT containers are GUI component containers. Generic container classes, on the other hand, are abstract datatype classes that can contain other objects (for example, linked lists, stacks, bags, and vectors).

The AWT containers include the following:

- A class, `Container`, which is the generic widget container on which layout managers act. All the other container classes are derived from this superclass.

- The `Panel` class is a concrete incarnation of class `Container`. It does not have a graphic representation—not even a simple outline. You typically subclass a `Panel`, or `Container`, to define and control a logical grouping of widgets.

- Class `Frame` is the building block class for producing full-fledged windows. (There is also a `Window` class, which produces "windows" without any borders or a menu bar.) Frames have titles, background colors, optional menu bars, and layout managers.

- Class `Dialog` is used for implementing direct application-to-user feedback or questions. Typical uses include pop-up warning dialog windows, quit confirmation dialog boxes, and so on. The `Dialog` class is not a self-contained component like, for example, `Frame`. In fact, it relies on class `Frame` to provide it with a display medium in which to display itself.

- Class FileDialog implements the indispensable file Open/Save/Save As dialog window, complete with filename filtering capability, plus any transparent extras provided by the native operating system. On Windows 95, for example, the Java FileDialog widget allows the user to create new directories on the fly, before saving a file.

- The ScrollPane class implements a container with scrollbars so that a large component can be viewed through a small viewport.

Widget Layout Classes

One of Java's innovations in the field of GUI programming is its GUI component-placement strategy. With other GUI frameworks, you usually need to specify pixel coordinates for all of your components. Even with GUI building tools, you need to position your components absolutely. Java was designed to be platform independent, but since AWT still relies on the host's native windowing system to provide it with its window and button building blocks, it is not possible to specify component dimensions and placement with absolute precision. The AWT uses an automatic layout system based on layout managers instead:

- With the FlowLayout class, every component is positioned and sized in the same way flowing text is in a WYSIWYG word processor: from left to right, and then overflowing to the next line when the first line is filled, and so on.

- The BorderLayout class positions and scales components according to the conventional distribution of components around a generic window. It allows components to be laid out along the top, bottom, left, or right edges of a window and leaves one large central area for the remainder of the components. The other areas will recover any unassigned areas.

- The GridLayout class, as the name suggests, enforces a simple grid layout. But unlike what you would expect from a grid layout, you cannot specify the positions of your components using two-dimensional coordinates; you must use a one-dimensional index. (You can use GridBagLayout to avoid this annoying situation.)

- The GridBagLayout class extends the approach taken by class GridLayout. It basically allows any one component to use up more than one grid cell, in either a horizontal or vertical direction. Extra control over the precise layout process is provided by instances of a helper class: class `GridBagConstraints`. This is the most powerful layout manager of all the standard offerings.

- Class `CardLayout` embodies the concept of a number of cards that can be flipped through, with only one card visible at any one time. This layout management style is most commonly used to implement multiple "pages" (or cards) that the user can view by selecting their "tabs." Since class `CardLayout` does not go beyond laying out the components, the trendy rendering of the card tabs themselves should be handled by another class. The standard component to do this is `JTabbedPane`, found in the `javax.swing` package.

- The `Insets` class encapsulates information about how close to a container's edge a component may be placed.

The layout managers are discussed in detail in Chapter 12.

Menu Classes

Drop-down or pop-up menus associated with windows are part of any modern application. Java's AWT supports complete menu functionality (submenus and checkable menu items are included) using a small and surprisingly easy-to-use set of menu classes:

- Class `MenuBar` acts as the anchor for the entire collection of menus connected to an application, or to be more precise, connected to a `Frame`. Every Java `Frame` can have its own menu bar with menu items responding to selections private to its context.

- The `Menu` class is the logical building block for any menu system. Menus hold logically related menu items and/or submenus. A menu is identified primarily by a simple menu title.

- The `PopupMenu` class implements a menu that can be popped up at any point of a GUI.

- The `MenuComponent` class is the abstract superclass of `MenuItem` and `CheckboxMenuItem`, which represent the menu items that a user selects on a menu.

- The `MenuShortcut` class encapsulates a keyboard shortcut for a menu item.

> **NOTE**   Don't let the class hierarchy confuse you. A `MenuItem` (or `CheckboxMenuItem`) is *logically* the leaf component in a final, concrete menu system. But as far as the object-oriented hierarchy is concerned, a `MenuItem` must be a `Menu` object's parent. This is totally counterintuitive, but can be understood as follows: Wherever you have a menu item, you can in fact substitute an entire submenu for it. So, class `Menu` must be a subclass of `MenuItem`. In any case, this admittedly chicken-and-egg type situation does not in any way complicate AWT menu programming. The fact is that adding menus to applications is probably the easiest thing you can do within AWT.

You'll find more information about Java's menu-related support in Swing in Chapter 13.

The Graphics Classes

For animation or special effects, you need something very different from standard GUI classes. You need to be able to control colors and imagery without any of the window-metaphor constraints imposed by a set of GUI classes. Java provides both elementary rendering classes and more sophisticated rendering; `Graphics` is the core class in the elementary area, while `Graphics2D` is for the more sophisticated variety. The `Graphics` classes are discussed in detail in Chapter 10, which discusses animation and images. The `Graphics2D`-related classes are explored in Chapter 11, which examines the Java-2D framework, introduced with Java 1.2. The following sections provide an overview of the functionality of these classes.

The *Graphics* and *Graphics2D* Classes and *PrintGraphics* Interface

`Graphics` is an abstract class that supports a simple 2D painting model with the usual rendering primitives. Specifically, the following classes of methods are provided:

- Text rendering

- Rectangular area copying (also called blitting)

- Filled and outlined rectangles, ovals, polygons, and arcs

- Lines
- Coordinate system translation
- Clipping rectangle support
- Changing current drawing color
- Various graphics state querying functions

`PrintGraphics` is an interface that closely resembles `Graphics` but renders to a printer.

`Graphics2D` is an extension of `Graphics` that supports a more complex 2D painting model. The class supports the following capabilities:

- Drawing images while performing transformations
- Drawing shapes with support for various rendering qualities like antialiasing, rendering for speed versus quality, wide lines, gradient file, among many others
- Text rendering with support for things like clipping the draw region
- Coordinate system translation
- Various graphics state querying functions

The *Image* Class

Class `Image` encapsulates a platform-independent image data structure. This approach shields you from the profusion of hardware- or software-dependent bitmap "standards" (bitplane, chunky, interleaved, and so on). The methods provided by class `Image` allow you to perform the following tasks:

- Query the image's dimensions
- Query the image's properties (for example, source image format, copyright information, and so on)
- Create a graphics context for the image so you can use the `Graphics` rendering methods on this image

The *Color* and *SystemColor* Classes

Class Color encapsulates a platform-independent color data structure. As with bitmapped images, a color can be implemented in a variety of ways. The Color class shields you from these platform dependencies. The provided methods support the following:

- Conversion between RGB (Red, Green, Blue) and HSB (Hue, Saturation, Brightness) color models
- Accessing the red, green, and blue color components
- Increasing or decreasing the brightness of a color

The SystemColor class is a subclass of Color. It provides access to prevailing Desktop colors.

The *Font* and *FontMetrics* Classes

The Font and FontMetrics classes give you a platform-independent way of accessing and querying the platform local fonts. The methods let you do the following:

- Specify a font family, style, and point size
- Query font attributes and metrics (family name, style, point size, character and string widths, ascender and descender lengths)

The *AlphaComposite* Class and *Composite* Interface

The Composite interface describes how to blend images to implement effects like transparency. AlphaComposite is a specific effect for the blending to produce transparency, while other effects are possible by implementing the interface on your own.

The *BasicStroke* Class and *Stroke* Interface

The Stroke interface provides the means to describe the logical pen to use for drawing operations. While the Graphics primitives only support drawing single pixel-wide colored lines, Graphics2D operations support a more rules-based approach. BasicStroke is a specific implementation that supports pen width, dash attributes, end caps, and line join decorations.

The *GraphicsConfigTemplate, GraphicsConfiguration, GraphicsDevice*, and *GraphicsEnvironment* Classes

These four classes describe the makeup of the Graphics2D operation destinations, whether they are a printer, monitor, or other display type. Each graphics environment may consist of a number of graphic devices. Then, each graphics device has one or more graphics configuration.

The *GradientPaint* and *TexturePaint* Classes

Along with the Color class, the GradientPaint and TexturePaint classes provide the pattern for Graphics2D operations. GradientPaint provides a linear color gradient, while TexturePaint offers an image to use as the fill pattern. Color is used for the simple, solid, case.

The *RenderingHints* Class

You use the RenderingHints class to enable optional drawing attributes, like antialiasing, for the Graphics2D object.

Geometry Classes

Package java.awt contains four geometry classes. These encapsulate the mathematical concepts point, polygon, rectangle, and dimension:

- The Point class represents a simple (x, y) data structure along with two methods: setLocation() and translate(). As with all geometry classes, integers are used instead of floating-point numbers. This reflects the main use of these classes as helper classes for GUI programming (and not pure math, which assumes numbers and shapes to have infinite precision).

NOTE   There is a floating-point version of setLocation() for Point. However, it only rounds the floating-point number to the nearest integer.

- The Polygon class represents an ordered collection of points treated as the definition of a polygon. Three methods enhance the data structure: addPoint() modifies the polygon to include the new point, getBounds() calculates the smallest rectangle enclosing all points of the polygon, and contains() tests whether a given point lies inside or outside the polygon.

- The Dimension class is a pure data structure holding a width and height variable. No methods enhance the raw data structure (in other words, this is really equivalent to a C structure or a Pascal record).

- The Rectangle class represents a rectangle at a certain (x,y) position. The class adds several methods to manipulate rectangles (move, shrink, grow, calculate intersection with other rectangles, and test whether a point is inside a rectangle).

- The Shape interface implemented by Polygon, Rectangle, and several classes in the java.awt.geom package describes the path that forms a geometric shape. The shape can then be drawn with the draw(Shape) method of Graphics2D.

Although these classes have nothing to do with rendering or with GUI programming per se, they are used by those higher-level classes to improve code reuse, robustness, and readability. Since GUI programming constantly involves dealing with positions and rectangular component dimensions or outlines, it makes sense to localize (abstract) some representation and a set of common operations for those positions and dimensions. This way, you avoid scattering your code with bits of identical functionality with slightly differing implementations.

WARNING   If you are familiar with the geometry classes prior to Java 1.2, you might want to look at them again. Their inheritance hierarchy, and capabilities, changed significantly between Java 1.1 and Java 1.2. Also, you may want to look into the subpackage java.awt.geom for additional geometry support classes.

Miscellaneous AWT Classes

The following java.awt classes do not fall neatly into any category:

- The classes that support event handling are AWTEvent, AWTMulticaster-Event, and EventQueue. The Event class supports the earlier (before version 1.1) Java event model, which is incompatible with the more modern 1.1 model. Event handling is discussed in detail in Chapter 14.

- The Cursor class allows you to specify an appearance for the mouse cursor.

- The MediaTracker class keeps track of images loaded from a server.

- The PrintJob class mediates between a Java program and a printer.

- The Toolkit class allows you to access specific resources of the underlying window system, which includes binding to AWT components, as well as querying for system font names or for the best size for a cursor image.

- The ComponentOrientation class helps you position components in a language sensitive manner. While Western European alphabets are left to right, others are right to left or top to bottom.

Package *javax.swing*

Introduced in the 1.2 Java Development Kit, the java.swing packages comprise the second generation of Java graphical widgets.

> **NOTE**
>
> While most things like AWT are acronyms, Swing is not. Supposedly, it involves a loose association of the Java character "Duke," to Duke Ellington and his saying "It don't mean a thing if it ain't got that swing." Also, a Sun engineer commented about swing music being the "in" sound now.

The comp.sun.java.swing classes can be grouped into the following responsibility areas:

- The JComponent branch for widgets

- Layout manager classes

  - BoxLayout

  - OverlayLayout

  - ScrollPaneLayout

  - ViewportLayout

  - SizeRequirements

- The Model classes and interfaces

- The Manager classes
  - DesktopManager and DefaultDesktopManager
  - FocusManager and DefaultFocusManager
  - MenuSelectionManager
  - RepaintManager
  - ToolTipManager
  - UIManager
- The AbstractAction and KeyStroke classes and Action interface
- Miscellaneous classes
  - BorderFactory
  - ImageIcon and Icon interface
  - LookAndFeel
  - ProgressMonitor and ProgressMonitorInputStream
  - SwingUtilities
  - GrayFilter
  - Timer

In addition to the above core javax.swing package, many subpackages provide additional support:

javax.swing.border	Defines various border rendering styles
javax.swing.colorchooser	Support classes for color choosing component
javax.swing.event	Swing-specific event classes
javax.swing.filechooser	Support classes for choosing files
javax.swing.plaf.*	Pluggable Look-and-Feel support classes
javax.swing.table	Table usage support classes

`javax.swing.text.*`	Text component support classes, including HTML and Rich Text Format (RTF)
`javax.swing.tree`	Tree component support classes
`javax.swing.undo`	Undo/redo implementation support classes

All of the Swing components and architecture will be described more fully in Chapters 13 and 15, which describe the Swing architecture in more detail. Chapter 14 describes event handling and is also important. While these chapters describe the common pieces shared with the AWT widgets, like `Component`, `Container`, the layout managers, and the events, using the AWT widgets is not described and is discouraged.

> **NOTE**   The `com.sun.*` APIs represent interfaces that Sun has fully committed to supporting and whose stability you can rely on. They just may not be available from all Java runtimes. If you happen to be using a Java 1.1+ runtime without support for the Swing packages, you can download them from Sun at `http://java.sun.com/products/jfc/`. Besides `com.sun.*` packages, you may run across some `sun.*` packages. These packages are completed unsupported packages, primarily used for Java internals.

JComponent Classes

Like `java.awt`, the majority of classes within package `com.sun.java.swing` are related to GUI creation.

- **JButton and JLabel**   The Swing button and label widgets, providing support for a single line of text, an image, and pop-up tool tips.

- **JPanel and Box**   The container widgets, providing support for buffering of painting operations, user-defined borders, and much more.

- **JMenu, JMenuItem, JSeparator, JCheckBoxMenuItem, JRadioButtonMenuItem, JMenuBar, and JPopupMenu**   The menu widgets: a menu, menu item, menu separator, toggleable menu items, menu bar, and pop-up menu. Each can have a single line of text, an image, and popup tool tips.

- **JToggleButton, JRadioButton, JCheckBox,** and **ButtonGroup**   The toggle-able widgets: alone, in a group, or out. The last class is for grouping support.

- **JColorChooser**   A pop-up widget for the selection of color values.

- **JComboBox** and **JList**   The widgets offering a group of choices, no longer limited to just text. Also, the JComboBox provides support for entering a choice when the desired choice is not offered.

- **JFileChooser**   Widget for directory and file selection.

- **JInternalFrame, JDesktopPane,** and **JDesktopIcon**   Widgets that provide a desktop to work with, which support opening, closing, and resizing internal frame, like a desktop manager.

- **JLayeredPane** and **JRootPane**   Widgets that offer a layering effect when displaying components on top of components on top of components.

- **JOptionPane**   For creating and displaying standard dialog boxes with icons signifying type of message shown.

- **JProgressBar**   Widgets for showing progress of a multi-step operation.

- **JSlider** and **JScrollBar**   Widgets for selecting a range of values, with and without labels to show available range.

- **JScrollPane** and **JViewPort**   Widgets to display a single large component within a smaller area. JScrollPane offers scrollbars, while JViewPort doesn't.

- **JSplitPane**   A widget that holds two widgets. Once created, the user can resize each.

- **JTabbedPane**   A tabbed widget that offers access to multiple panels.

- **JTable**   A widget for the display of multi-columnar data.

- **JTextComponent, JTextField, JPasswordField, JTextArea, JTextPane,** and **JEditorPane**   The widgets for text input and display. JTextComponent is the parent of all, while the rest offer single or multiline text support. The most sophisticated are JTextPane for the display of formatted text and images and JEditorPane for a lightweight HTML renderer.

- **JToolBar** and **JToolTip**   Widgets to create tool bars and help text in the form of pop-up tool tips.

- **JTree**   A widget to display hierarchical data.

- **JApplet** The Swing applet widget, this adds support for displaying menus within applets.

- **JWindow, JDialog, and JFrame** The Swing window, dialog box, and frame widgets, extending upon the base AWT widgets.

Layout Manager Classes

In addition to the half dozen or so layout manager classes in AWT, there are more available in `javax.swing`. These offer the same benefits available with the `java.awt` layout managers, which are basically platform-independent applications:

- With the `BoxLayout` class, components are laid out either vertically or horizontally in a single column or row. Each component does not have to be the same size and there is support for providing spacers between components.

- The `OverlayLayout` class offers support for arranging components one on top of another.

- Class `ScrollPaneLayout` provides the layout manager used by the `JScrollPane` with areas for your own scrollbars, headers, and corner images. Usually, you will never use this outside of the one created for you when you use `JScrollPane`.

- The `ViewportLayout` class is similar to `ScrollPaneLayout` in that it exists for the `JViewport` class' benefit. It offers sizing and alignment support for when objects in viewport are larger than space permits.

- Class `SizeRequirements` is a support class for the layout managers, to help calculate component sizes and positions.

Model Classes and Interfaces

The Swing widgets offer two means of operations. You can store their data internally and let them act accordingly, or you can store the data externally. When the data is truly stored outside the widget, the means used is the model classes provided within the `javax.swing` package. By storing the data externally, you can change the widget used and the view of the data, without worrying about losing anything. While working in this manner creates more robust and maintainable programs, its takes longer to set up initially. The way that Swing uses these

model classes is discussed in the "Model/View/Controller Architecture" section
of Chapter 15.

Manager Classes

Like just about everything in Swing, you can customize the behavior of almost
everything. The various manager classes in javax.swing offer help in allowing
you to customize the user's experiences with your programs. For instance, if you
don't like the way those little tool tip messages are displayed when you rest
your mouse over a widget, you can use the ToolTipManager to adjust behavior
like the delay time. Each of the Manager classes is responsible for its own area of
the Swing experience.

AbstractAction and *KeyStroke* Classes and *Action* Interface

The AbstractAction, KeyStroke, and Action classes (and interface) provide an
alternative to the simple-minded approach of handling events within the AWT
widgets. Normally, developers would program responses to specific user behavior during the course of an application. This is fine for things that live in isolated
worlds. However, by declaring a well-defined services protocol, developers can
define services related to objects, register them with the objects, and then let others use the services when they need them. For instance, if you define how to save
a JTextArea, a multiline-input field, you would normally associate that behavior
with the File ➤ Save menu. However, if you were to register the "save" Action with
the JTextArea, when you want to save the text somewhere else, you would just
ask the JTextArea how to do it. The JTextArea knows what Action operations
it supports. You would find your AbstractAction implementation supporting
"save" present and associate it to some other interface. The KeyStroke class is
also available, to support keyboard-oriented events.

Miscellaneous Swing Classes

The following javax.swing classes do not fall neatly into any category:

- The BorderFactory class works with the border subpackage. Using the
  Abstract Factory creation pattern, the BorderFactory class creates Border

objects without your specifying the actual concrete class that implements the `Border` interface.

- The `ImageIcon` class provides an implementation of the `Icon` interface for `Image` objects. You use icons for displaying images with labels, buttons, and menus, among many other places.

- Along with several `.plaf` subpackages, the `LookAndFeel` class provides the basis for Swing's pluggable look-and-feel support.

- The `ProgressMonitor` and `ProgressMonitorInputStream` pair provides a pre-built generic pop-up window to permit users to interrupt the loading of files.

- The `SwingUtilities` class provides a set of convenience routines for common operations. Among many others, methods exist for finding a component's top-level window and checking which mouse button a mouse event is for.

- The `GrayFilter` represents an image-related support class used by Swing that the development team thought other developers would welcome. `GrayFilter` turns any image into a "grayscale" image.

- The `Timer` class provides the means to signal periodic operations.

Package *java.net*—Internet, Web, and HTML Support

The `java.net` package is one of the other main features of the Core Java API. It provides very high-level interfaces to the rather less sophisticated set of data-communication protocols (and their associated APIs) called TCP/IP and UDP/IP. The `java.net` classes hide many of the technical quagmires inherent to low-level Internet programming.

The `java.net` classes can be grouped according to the following responsibilities:

- Internet addressing (classes `InetAddress` and `URL`)
- TCP/IP connection-oriented classes (various `Socket` classes)
- UDP/IP connectionless classes (`DatagramPacket`, `DatagramSocket`, and `MulticastSocket`)

- URL Authentication classes (`Authenticator`, `PasswordAuthentication`, `URLDecoder`, and `URLEncoder`)

- MIME content type handlers (`ContentHandler` and `URLStreamHandler`)

- Web-related classes (various `URLConnection` classes)

NOTE   In terms of complexity—and, therefore, ease of use—the UDP protocol lies between the Transmission Control Protocol (TCP) protocol (the low-level protocol) and the Internet Protocol (IP) protocol (the high-level protocol). UDP is a datagram-oriented protocol, which means data packets travel individually (like letters in the postal system), without any guarantees of delivery. This is because—unlike TCP—UDP does not attempt to detect or correct loss of packets. This lack of protocol overhead is what makes UDP interesting for certain types of applications, such as broadcasting currency exchange rates, to gain speed at the cost of an occasional lost update. However, most Internet applications do not use the UDP protocol to achieve their functionality, but instead use the TCP protocol, which supports a guaranteed delivery end-to-end link.

The following is a brief overview of the commonly used `java.net` classes. Many of these are discussed in greater detail in Chapter 20, which covers network programming:

- The `InetAddress` class deals with Internet addresses in their mnemonic (*host.domain*) form and their 32-bit numeric form (*byte.byte.byte.byte*).

- The URL class encapsulates a Uniform Resource Locator (URL) specification plus associated methods, including opening a connection to the URL resource (a Web page, a file, or telnet port), retrieving the URL resource, and querying URL fields (protocol, host, filenames, and port number).

- The `ServerSocket` and `Socket` classes together provide complete TCP/IP connectivity support. Each class supports one side of the client/server application model. Class `Socket` is used to implement a client; class `ServerSocket` is used to implement a server. Class `Socket` provides methods to connect any stream (as input or output) to a socket to communicate through. This way, you can essentially separate internetworking technicalities (and pitfalls!) from your application by working at the abstract stream level instead.

NOTE

Sockets are the software interfaces that connect an application to the network beyond. On the Internet, each machine has 65,536 (64K) addressable sockets it can use. All standard Internet services (like e-mail, FTP, and so on) use agreed-upon socket numbers, colloquially termed "well-known port numbers." Server programs listen to these sockets for any incoming service request. A client program needs to open a socket of its own before it can connect to a server socket at the other end.

- The `DatagramPacket` and `DatagramSocket` together provide User Datagram Protocol (UDP) Internet services. Through class `DatagramPacket`, you can specify a packet's Internet host destination (using an `InetAddress` instance), the port (or socket) to connect to on that host, and the binary contents of the packet. You can then send or receive datagrams via an instance of class `DatagramSocket`.

- The `Authenticator` class provides access to password-protected URLs. By providing `PasswordAuthentication`, you can easily read from destinations requiring challenge-confirm access.

Package *java.applet*—HTML Embedded Applets

A big reason for Java's runaway success is that it's a highly efficient and easy-to-learn language for distributed software components. Java applets are nothing more or less than distributed software components. Even so, the standard class framework contains little that explicitly deals with those instrumental applets.

The `java.applet` package looks very barren compared to the other packages. Its sole contents are one class and three interfaces. Class `java.applet.Applet` is the main repository for methods supporting applet functionality.

The methods it makes available can be grouped into the following categories:

- Applet initialization, restarting, and freezing
- Embedded HTML applet parameter support
- High-level image loading

- High-level audio loading and playing for applets and applications
- Origins querying (getDocumentBase() and getCodeBase())
- Simple status displaying (showStatus(String))

Miscellaneous Java Packages

Other Java packages support more advanced or less commonly used features. Here is a brief summary of their functionality:

javax.swing.accessibility   This package provides developers easy access to assistive technologies like screen readers and Braille terminals.

java.awt.color, java.awt.font, and java.awt.geom   These packages support the Java 2D framework. They will be covered in Chapter 11.

java.awt.datatransfer   The classes in this package support clipboard data-transfer models.

java.awt.dnd   Drag-and-drop functionality is now provided in version 1.2. Using a series of drag sources and drop targets, Java programs can interact with Java and native applications. Both the data transfer model and drag-and-drop functionality are discussed in Chapter 16.

java.awt.event   This extensive package supports event delegation. Event delegation is covered in Chapter 14.

java.awt.im   This small package adds support for native input methods of Asian languages.

java.awt.image   The classes in this package are related to image processing. Some of the capabilities are described in Chapters 10 and 11.

java.awt.peer   This package contains classes that "glue" AWT components to the underlying window system. If you are writing Java programs, you will never need to use these interfaces.

java.awt.print   The classes in this package extend the printing capabilities introduced in Java 1.1 to include support for printing pages and books.

java.beans   This package supports development of components, called "Beans," that are so reusable that they can interact with non-Java systems such as ActiveX and LiveConnect. JavaBeans are covered in Chapter 22.

java.beans.beancontext   The classes here represent the JavaBeans Runtime Containment and Services Protocol for the discovery of services available from the surrounding environment.

java.lang.ref   This package describes a set of classes that offer weak references, or caching. Use with the reference objects does not count as usage when it comes time for garbage collection.

java.lang.reflect   The classes in this package support *object reflection*. This is a feature whereby it is possible to inspect the makeup of the class of an arbitrary object.

java.math   This package is very different from the more commonly used `java.lang.Math` class, which provides standard mathematical functions in the form of static methods. The `java.math` package contains two rarely used classes that represent decimal and integer numbers of arbitrarily high precision.

java.rmi, java.rmi.activation, java.rmi.dgc, java.rmi.registry, and **java.rmi.server**   These packages support Remote Method Invocation (RMI), which permits an object to make a method call on an object running on a different machine. RMI is covered in Chapter 25.

java.security, java.security.acl, java.security.cert, java.security.interfaces, and **java.security.spec**   The classes in these packages support secure data communication. This functionality is discussed in Chapter 24.

javax.servlet   This package provides the means to embed Java servlet programs within Web servers, to replace CGI (Common Gateway Interface) scripts. Chapter 23 provides in-depth coverage of the functionality.

java.sql   This package provides classes and interfaces that support Java Database Connectivity (JDBC), which is discussed in Chapter 21.

java.text   This package provides classes that format internationalized text.

java.util.mime   This package provides support for describing Multipurpose Internet Mail Extension (MIME) types.

Summary

Java's standard class hierarchy contains a wide variety of classes that, given some time and effort to learn, should allow you to write applications within realistic time frames. The collection of classes spans a wide spectrum, with no significant gaps to obstruct real-life software development. As Java has matured, the breadth of packages available has grown quite a bit, leaving few rough edges. Sun is working hard to fill in the missing holes, making sure that Java is enveloped by a world-class collection of supporting classes.

Animation and Images

- Basics of rendering images

- Graphics state information

- Techniques for animation

- Processing images

Of all our senses, vision is the most high-performance, high-bandwidth input device nature has given us. No wonder there has been a serious demand, ever since their earliest use in the 1950s, for computer systems to evolve into systems that interact through text and pictures instead of through switches and indicator lights. No other requirement shaped the evolution of computers so dramatically as that of the need for the (bitmapped) GUI.

Graphical programming, animation, and image manipulation have become necessary skills for any modern application developer. This chapter introduces you to some of the basic techniques, set in the context of Java and its standard classes. More advanced concepts are left to the next chapter.

Java's Basic Drawing Tools

Class `Graphics` in the `java.awt` package encapsulates a small collection of rendering (that is, drawing) primitives that you can use to dynamically generate images at runtime. Here is its definition:

```
public class Graphics extends Object {
  protected Graphics();
  public abstract void clearRect (int x, int y, int width, int height);
  public abstract void clipRect (int x, int y, int width, int height);
  public abstract void copyArea (int x, int y, int width, int height,
    int dx, int dy);
  public abstract Graphics create();
  public Graphics create (int x, int y, int width, int height);
  public abstract void dispose();
  public void draw3DRect (int x, int y, int width, int height, boolean raised);
  public abstract void drawArc (int x, int y, int width, int height,
    int startAngle, int arcAngle);
  public void drawBytes (byte data[], int offset, int length, int x, int y);
  public void drawChars (char data[], int offset, int length, int x, int y);
  public abstract boolean drawImage (Image img, int x, int y,
    ImageObserver observer);
  public abstract boolean drawImage (Image img, int x, int y,
    int width, int height, ImageObserver observer);
  public abstract boolean drawImage (Image img, int x, int y,
    Color bgcolor, ImageObserver observer);
  public abstract boolean drawImage (Image img, int x, int y,
```

```
        int width, int height, Color bgcolor,  ImageObserver observer);
public abstract boolean drawImage (Image img, int dx1, int dy1,
    int dx2, int dy2, int sx1, int sy1, int sx2, int sy2,
    ImageObserver observer);
public abstract boolean drawImage (Image img, int dx1, int dy1,
    int dx2, int dy2, int sx1, int sy1, int sx2, int sy2,
    Color bgcolor, ImageObserver observer);
public abstract void drawLine (int x1, int y1, int x2, int y2);
public abstract void drawOval (int x, int y, int width, int height);
public abstract void drawPolygon (int xPoints[], int yPoints[],
    int nPoints);
public void drawPolygon (Polygon p);
public abstract void drawPolyline (int xs[], int ys[], int nPoints);
public void drawRect (int x, int y, int width, int height);
public abstract void drawRoundRect (int x, int y, int width, int height,
    int arcWidth, int arcHeight);
public abstract void drawString (String str, int x, int y);
public abstract void drawString(AttributedCharacterIterator iterator, int x,
    int y);
public void fill3DRect (int x, int y, int width, int height, boolean raised);
public abstract void fillArc (int x, int y, int width, int height,
    int startAngle, int arcAngle);
public abstract void fillOval (int x, int y, int width, int height);
public abstract void fillPolygon (int xPoints[], int yPoints[],
    int nPoints);
public void fillPolygon (Polygon p);
public abstract void fillRect (int x, int y, int width, int height);
public abstract void fillRoundRect (int x, int y, int width, int height,
    int arcWidth, int arcHeight);
public void finalize();
public abstract Shape getClip();
public abstract Rectangle getClipBounds();
public Rectangle getClipBounds(Rectangle rect);
public abstract Color getColor();
public abstract Font getFont();
public FontMetrics getFontMetrics();
public abstract FontMetrics getFontMetrics (Font f);
public boolean hitClip(int x, int y, int width, int height);
public abstract void setClip (int x, int y, int width, int height);
public abstract void setClip (Shape clip);
public abstract void setColor (Color c);
public abstract void setFont (Font font);
```

```
public abstract void setPaintMode();
public abstract void setXORMode (Color c1);
public String toString();
public abstract void translate (int x, int y);
}
```

Each platform that supports Java has its own (subclassed) implementation of Graphics. Class Graphics itself is abstract and cannot be instantiated. Whenever you obtain a Graphics object (called a *graphics context* or *graphics handle*), you are actually using some platform-specific subclass of Graphics.

NOTE   If you look at the declaration of the Graphics class constructor, you will see that it declared **protected**. Only subclasses can use the Graphics constructor.

If you browse the methods defined by Graphics, you will quickly get a feel for what it is all about: plain 2-D rendering. (More advanced 2-D rendering is covered in the next chapter.) The Graphics class is nothing fancy and most definitely does not support 3-D. (For 3-D graphics, Sun has the standard Java 3D API.) The methods can be classified broadly into the categories listed in Table 10.1.

TABLE 10.1: Graphics Methods by Category

Category	Methods
Drawing lines	**drawLine()**
Drawing filled and outlined shapes:	
Rectangles	**drawRect(), clearRect(), fillRect(), drawRoundRect(), fillRoundRect(), draw3DRect(), fill3DRect()**
Polygons	**drawPolygon(), fillPolygon(), drawPolyline()**
Ovals	**drawOval(), fillOval()**
Arcs	**drawArc(), fillArc()**
Text rendering	**drawString(), drawChars(), drawBytes()**
Copying rectangular areas	**copyArea()**
Changing current graphics state	**setColor(), setPaintMode(), setXORMode(), setFont()**

Continued on next page

TABLE 10.1 CONTINUED: Graphics Methods by Category

Category	Methods
Querying graphics state	**getColor(), getFont(), getFontMetrics(), getClipBounds(), getClip()**
Translating the coordinate system	**translate()**
Clipping rectangle support	**clipRect(), setClip()**
Collision detection support	**hitClip()**
Image rendering	**drawImage()**
Image creation	**create()**

NOTE   One notable omission from the list in Table 10.1 is pixel plotting. Although the need for plotting individual pixels arises less frequently than the need for using higher primitives, not having any pixel routines is annoying. The main workaround for drawing single pixels in the AWT is to either call `fillRect()` or `drawLine()`, using parameters that define 1 × 1 pixel rectangles or lines, respectively. Another (not obvious) approach to plotting single pixels is to use the `MemoryImageSource` class. See the Mandelbrot program at the end of the chapter for an example.

The following sections discuss most of the methods listed in Table 10.1. These are the basic tools that you will use for animation and enhancing your GUIs.

Drawing Lines and Rectangles

The following methods support basic rendering of lines and rectangles:

```
public void drawLine (int x1, int y1, int x2, int y2);
public void fillRect (int x, int y, int width, int height);
public void drawRect (int x, int y, int width, int height);
public void clearRect (int x, int y, int width, int height);
```

The artistic applet shown in Figure 10.1 demonstrates these methods for drawing lines and rectangles. Here is the code behind the output of Figure 10.1:

```
import java.awt.*;
public class Picasso extends java.applet.Applet {
```

```
public void paint (Graphics g) {
    g.fillRect (30, 10, 200, 100);
    g.clearRect (50, 30, 70, 50);
    g.drawRect (60, 50, 40, 20);
    g.drawLine (10, 55, 250, 55);
}
}
```

FIGURE 10.1:

Picasso applet

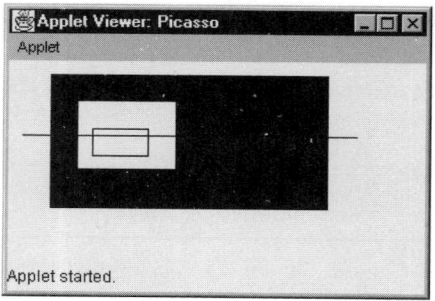

All rectangle-rendering methods take the same parameters: the coordinates of the upper-left corner of the rectangle plus the width and height of the rectangle. With the addition of the `java.awt.Stroke` interface of the Java2D API, you can now configure pen width and decorations. The use of `Stroke` is described in Chapter 11.

Rounded-Corner and 3-D Effect Rectangles

Slightly more complex than the methods above are the following rectangle-drawing methods, which support rounded corners or a 3-D lighting effect:

```
public void drawRoundRect (int x, int y, int width, int height,
    int arcWidth, int arcHeight);
public void fillRoundRect (int x, int y, int width, int height,
    int arcWidth, int arcHeight);
public void draw3DRect (int x, int y, int width, int height, boolean raised);
public void fill3DRect (int x, int y, int width, int height, boolean raised);
```

For the rounded-corner variants, in addition to the normal rectangle-defining arguments—*x, y, width*, and *height*—you need to specify the dimensions of an imaginary rectangle acting as a bounding box for the corner. The following program illustrates the control this invisible box has by varying its size for different instances of an identical base rectangle:

```java
import java.awt.*;

public class Corner extends java.applet.Applet {
  static final int RWIDTH = 40;
  static final int RHEIGHT = 30;
  public void paint (Graphics g) {
    for (int i=0; i< 7; i++) {
      int cornerBoxSize = (i+1)*4;
      if (i%2 == 0) {
        g.fillRoundRect(10 + i*(RWIDTH+10), 40, RWIDTH, RHEIGHT, cornerBoxSize,
          cornerBoxSize);
      } else {
        g.drawRoundRect(10 + i*(RWIDTH+10), 40, RWIDTH, RHEIGHT, cornerBoxSize,
          cornerBoxSize);
        g.drawRect(10+ i*(RWIDTH+10)+RWIDTH-cornerBoxSize, 40, cornerBoxSize,
          cornerBoxSize);
      }
    }
  }
}
```

When run, the applet produces the output shown in Figure 10.2.

FIGURE 10.2:

Rounded rectangles with varying rounding degrees

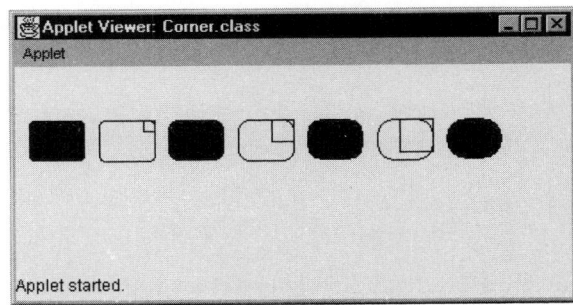

Note how the code alternates between filled and outlined rounded rectangles: It uses a modulo two (%2) function to determine if the loop's index i is odd or not. Adding 10 to the x-coordinates of all boxes drawn is done simply to move the string of boxes to the right a bit, away from the left edge of the applet's window.

Drawing Polygons

Class `Graphics` supports outlined or filled polygons, and there are no limitations on their concavity or self-intersection. (Many other toolkits cannot handle self-intersecting or concave polygons.) In addition to polygons, the class also supports polylines. A *polyline* is a connected series of lines. Polylines are generally not closed; the only way to close a polyline is to specify a final point that is identical to the initial point.

TIP

A concave polygon—as opposed to a convex one—is one whose outline has one or more indentations. (Or, put mathematically, a concave polygon has one or more negative angles between successive line segments.) An easy mnemonic aid for remembering the difference between concave and convex is to associate the word *cave* with concave.

The following `Graphics` methods deal with polygon rendering:

```
public void drawPolygon(int xPoints[], int yPoints[], int nPoints);
public void drawPolygon(Polygon p);
public void fillPolygon(int xPoints[], int yPoints[], int nPoints);
public void fillPolygon(Polygon p);
public void drawPolyline(int xPoints[], int yPoints[], int nPoints);
```

Notice that `drawPolyline()` does not take a `Polygon` as an argument, but rather two arrays of coordinates. There is no `fillPolyline()` method, since that would be functionally equivalent to `fillPolygon()`. Except for `drawPolyline()`, both the outline and filled versions come in two flavors:

- They can take a low-level (and error-prone) collection of arguments defining a polygon.

- They can take an instance of class `Polygon`, another AWT class that is useful when working with graphical polygons.

The following listing uses the latter, more readable option to demonstrate some of the polygons that you can produce. Figure 10.3 shows the output of the listing.

```
import java.awt.*;

public class Polys extends java.applet.Applet {
  public void paint (Graphics g) {
    Polygon convex, concave, selfintersecting;
```

```
convex = new Polygon();
convex.addPoint(20,20);
convex.addPoint(60,24);
convex.addPoint(50,50);
convex.addPoint(21,75);
convex.addPoint(10,30);

concave = new Polygon();
concave.addPoint(100+ 20,20);
concave.addPoint(100+ 60,24);
concave.addPoint(100+ 25,50);
concave.addPoint(100+ 21,75);
concave.addPoint(100+ 10,30);
concave.addPoint(100+ 20,20);

selfintersecting = new Polygon();
for(int i=0; i< 10; i++) {
  selfintersecting.addPoint(200+ (int)(Math.random()*80),
                            20 + (int)(Math.random()*80));
}
g.fillPolygon(convex);
g.drawPolygon(concave);
g.fillPolygon(selfintersecting);
  }
}
```

FIGURE 10.3:

Filled convex, outlined
concave, and filled self-
intersecting polygons

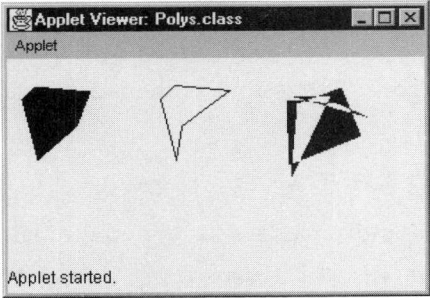

The position of the polygon is implicitly defined by the list of the polygon's vertices. The polygon-rendering methods cannot position the polygon (for example, by taking x, y coordinates as extra arguments), as the drawLine() and drawRect()

methods do for lines and rectangles, respectively. See the discussion of `translate()` later in the chapter to learn how to tackle this problem.

The Polygon Class

The definition of class `Polygon` is simple:

```
public class Polygon extends Object implements Serializable, Shape {
    public int npoints;
    public int xpoints[];
    public int ypoints[];
    public Polygon();
    public Polygon(int xpoints[], int ypoints[], int npoints);
    public void addPoint(int x, int y);
    public boolean contains(double x, double y);
    public boolean contains(double x, double y, double w, double h);
    public boolean contains(int x, int y);
    public boolean contains(Point p);
    public boolean contains(Point2D p);
    public boolean contains(Rectangle2D r);
    public Rectangle getBounds();
    public Rectangle2D getBounds2D();
    public PathIterator getPathIterator(AffineTransform at);
    public PathIterator getPathIterator(AffineTransform at, double flatness);
    public boolean intersects(double x, double y, double w, double h);
    public boolean intersects(Rectangle2D rect);
    public void translate(int deltaX, int deltaY);
}
```

This class cannot draw polygons itself; it is used only to define the outline of polygons. This is done with method `addPoint()`, as in the sample program.

Drawing Ovals

Ovals and circles are supported through the following two methods:

```
public void drawOval(int x, int y, int width, int height);
public void fillOval(int x, int y, int width, int height);
```

The difference between an oval and the more frequently supported ellipse shape is that the major and minor diameters of ovals are always parallel to the x- and y-axes. Ellipses usually can be rotated at will. Nevertheless, an oval is needed most of the time. Figure 10.4 shows a colorful effect obtained by drawing ever-shrinking, filled ovals. (The same result could be obtained by using outlined ovals, but using the filled variety is far more impressive at run time.)

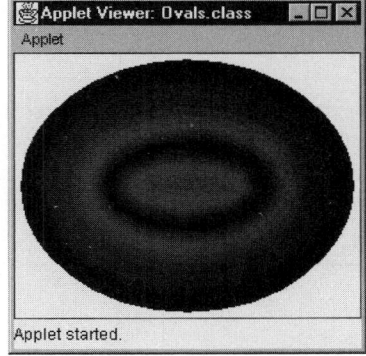

The code that generated Figure 10.4 is listed here.

```
import java.awt.*;

public class Ovals extends java.applet.Applet {

    float hue = 0.0f;
    float saturation = 1.0f;
    float brightness = 1.0f;

    public void paint(Graphics g) {
        int w,h;
        float zeroToOne;

        w = getBounds().width; h = getBounds().height;
        g.setColor(Color.darkGray);
        g.draw3DRect(0, 0, w-1, h-1, false);

        g.translate(5,5);
        w -= 10; h -= 10;

        int squareSide = Math.min(w, h);
        for (int i=0, half=squareSide/2; i < half; i++) {
            zeroToOne = ((float) i) / (squareSide/2.0f);
```

```
                hue= zeroToOne;
                brightness = zeroToOne;
                g.setColor(Color.getHSBColor(hue, saturation, brightness));
                g.fillOval(i, i, w - 2*i, h - 2*i);
              }
            }
          }
```

> **NOTE**   Since the oval-rendering methods take an enclosing bounding box specification, rather than center coordinates and radii (as is common in other graphics tool-boxes), you "slide" a shrinking bounding box from the top-left corner toward the center of the eye to achieve your result. Using other ellipse APIs, you would normally keep the center fixed and decrease the radii.

Drawing Arcs

Arcs are elliptical segments (or, more frequently, just circular segments). Two Graphics methods let you render arcs:

```
public void drawArc(int x, int y, int width, int height, int startAngle,
  int arcAngle);
public void fillArc(int x, int y, int width, int height, int startAngle,
  int arcAngle);
```

Filled arcs look like pieces of pie. The arc and the two radii that join the endpoints of the arc to the center of the circle bound the filled region. The JDK contains an interactive ArcTest program to demonstrate the arc-rendering methods. Unfortunately, this program uses text fields to input starting angles and arc size (again in degrees). The following modified version of this program uses more user-friendly scrollbars. (You'll learn more about the event handling code used in the program in Chapter 14.)

```
/*
 * @(#)ArcTest.java 1.4 97/02/05
 *
 * Copyright (c) 1997 Sun Microsystems, Inc. All Rights Reserved.
 * Copyright (c) 1998 John Zukowski
 *
 * Sun grants you ("Licensee") a non-exclusive, royalty free, license to use,
 * modify and redistribute this software in source and binary code form,
 * provided that i) this copyright notice and license appear on all copies of
```

```
 * the software; and ii) Licensee does not utilize the software in a manner
 * which is disparaging to Sun.
 *
 * This software is provided "AS IS," without a warranty of any kind. ALL
 * EXPRESS OR IMPLIED CONDITIONS, REPRESENTATIONS AND WARRANTIES, INCLUDING ANY
 * IMPLIED WARRANTY OF MERCHANTABILITY, FITNESS FOR A PARTICULAR PURPOSE OR
 * NON-INFRINGEMENT, ARE HEREBY EXCLUDED. SUN AND ITS LICENSORS SHALL NOT BE
 * LIABLE FOR ANY DAMAGES SUFFERED BY LICENSEE AS A RESULT OF USING, MODIFYING
 * OR DISTRIBUTING THE SOFTWARE OR ITS DERIVATIVES. IN NO EVENT WILL SUN OR ITS
 * LICENSORS BE LIABLE FOR ANY LOST REVENUE, PROFIT OR DATA, OR FOR DIRECT,
 * INDIRECT, SPECIAL, CONSEQUENTIAL, INCIDENTAL OR PUNITIVE DAMAGES, HOWEVER
 * CAUSED AND REGARDLESS OF THE THEORY OF LIABILITY, ARISING OUT OF THE USE OF
 * OR INABILITY TO USE SOFTWARE, EVEN IF SUN HAS BEEN ADVISED OF THE
 * POSSIBILITY OF SUCH DAMAGES.
 *
 * This software is not designed or intended for use in on-line control of
 * aircraft, air traffic, aircraft navigation or aircraft communications; or in
 * the design, construction, operation or maintenance of any nuclear
 * facility. Licensee represents and warrants that it will not use or
 * redistribute the Software for such purposes.
 */

import java.awt.*;
import java.awt.event.*;
import java.applet.*;

/**
 * An interactive test of the Graphics.drawArc and Graphics.fillArc
 * routines. Can be run either as a standalone application by
 * typing "java ArcTest" or as an applet in the AppletViewer.
 */
public class ArcTest extends Applet {
  ArcControls controls;    // The controls for marking and filling arcs
  ArcCanvas canvas;        // The drawing area to display arcs

  public void init() {
    setLayout(new BorderLayout());
    canvas = new ArcCanvas();
    add("Center", canvas);
    add("South", controls = new ArcControls(canvas));
  }
```

```java
      public void destroy() {
        remove(controls);
        remove(canvas);
      }

      public void start() {
        controls.setEnabled(true);
      }

      public void stop() {
        controls.setEnabled(false);
      }

      public void processEvent(AWTEvent e) {
        if (e.getID() == Event.WINDOW_DESTROY) {
          System.exit(0);
        }
      }

      public static void main(String args[]) {
        Frame f = new Frame("ArcTest");
        ArcTest arcTest = new ArcTest();

        arcTest.init();
        arcTest.start();

        f.add("Center", arcTest);
        f.setSize(300, 300);
        f.show();
      }

    }

class ArcCanvas extends Canvas {
  int startAngle = 0;
  int endAngle = 45;
  boolean filled = false;
  Font font;

  public void paint(Graphics g) {
    Rectangle r = getBounds();
    int hlines = r.height / 10;
```

```
    int vlines = r.width / 10;

    g.setColor(Color.pink);
    for (int i = 1; i <= hlines; i++) {
      g.drawLine(0, i * 10, r.width, i * 10);
    }
    for (int i = 1; i <= vlines; i++) {
      g.drawLine(i * 10, 0, i * 10, r.height);
    }

    g.setColor(Color.red);
    if (filled) {
      g.fillArc(0, 0, r.width - 1, r.height - 1, startAngle, endAngle);
    } else {
      g.drawArc(0, 0, r.width - 1, r.height - 1, startAngle, endAngle);
    }

    g.setColor(Color.black);
    g.setFont(font);
    g.drawLine(0, r.height / 2, r.width, r.height / 2);
    g.drawLine(r.width / 2, 0, r.width / 2, r.height);
    g.drawLine(0, 0, r.width, r.height);
    g.drawLine(r.width, 0, 0, r.height);
    int sx = 10;
    int sy = r.height - 28;
    g.drawString("S = " + startAngle, sx, sy);
    g.drawString("E = " + endAngle, sx, sy + 14);
  }

  public void redraw(boolean filled, int start, int end) {
    this.filled = filled;
    this.startAngle = start;
    this.endAngle = end;
    repaint();
  }
}

class ArcControls extends Panel implements ActionListener {
  Scrollbar s;
  Scrollbar e;
  ArcCanvas canvas;
```

```
public ArcControls(ArcCanvas canvas) {
  Button b = null;

  this.canvas = canvas;
  setLayout (new GridLayout(3, 1));
  add(s = new Scrollbar(Scrollbar.HORIZONTAL, 0,  1, 0, 360));
  add(e = new Scrollbar(Scrollbar.HORIZONTAL, 45, 1, 0, 360));
  Panel subPanel = new Panel();
  b = new Button("Fill");
  b.addActionListener(this);
  subPanel.add(b);
  b = new Button("Draw");
  b.addActionListener(this);
  subPanel.add(b);
  add (subPanel);
}

public void actionPerformed(ActionEvent ev) {
  String label = ev.getActionCommand();
  canvas.redraw(label.equals("Fill"), s.getValue(), e.getValue());
}
}
```

Figure 10.5 shows an example of the output from the improved ArcTest program.

TIP

The starting and ending angle positions to the **drawArc** and **fillArc** routines start with 0 degrees at the three o'clock position and work their way counterclockwise to 90 degrees at twelve o'clock, 180 degrees at nine o'clock, 270 degrees at six o'clock, and back to 360 degrees at three o'clock.

This program consists of three classes reflecting the three main components of the applet:

- The applet itself
- The canvas area to draw the arcs (and the grid backdrop)
- The control panel at the bottom of the window

The heart of the program is the `paint()` method of `ArcCanvas`, which invokes either the `drawArc()` or `fillArc()` method using the user-selectable starting and ending arc angles. The exact method is determined by the current drawing mode

FIGURE 10.5:

JDK ArcTest program with
an improved user interface

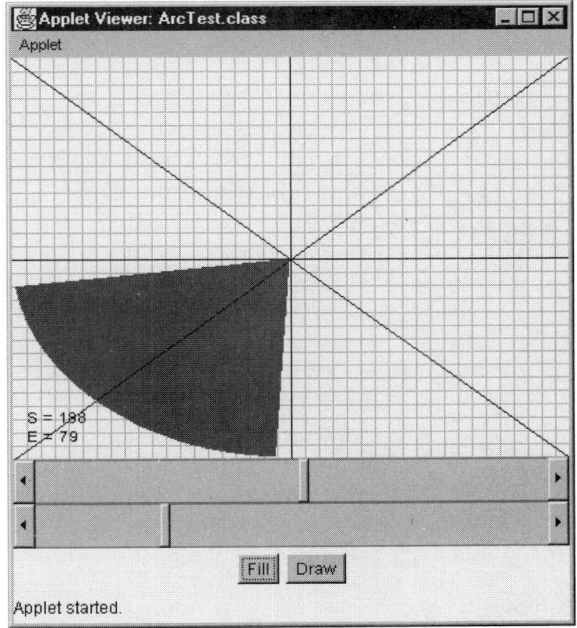

(fill or outline) used by the program. The angles that both arc methods take need to be in degrees and not radians (with 0 coding for three o'clock). The remainder of the program consists mainly of GUI code (as is so often the case with "real" applications), which applies the GUI techniques described in previous chapters.

Rendering Text

The Graphics class supports only simple left-to-right, horizontal text rendering. Rotated text is not supported. Four methods support text rendering:

```
public void drawString(String str, int x, int y);
public abstract void drawString(AttributedCharacterIterator iterator, int x,
   int y);
public void drawChars(char data[], int offset, int length, int x, int y);
public void drawBytes(byte data[], int offset, int length, int x, int y);
```

Method drawString() is the usual method for drawing text strings. It takes a string and the starting (rendering) position for the first letter of your string. The rendering position for text is always the left-most point on the text's baseline. The two other text-rendering methods use arrays of `byte` or `char` as their text source but allow a substring to be rendered. Here is a demonstration program using the latter.

```
import java.awt.*;

public class Text extends java.applet.Applet {
  public void paint (Graphics g) {
    String subject = "ZigZagging Text";
    char text[] = subject.toCharArray();
    g.setFont(new Font("Serif", Font.PLAIN, 16));
    for (int i=0, len=text.length; i <= len-3; i+=2) {
      if (i==0) {
        g.drawChars(text, 0, len, 20, 20);
      } else if (i == len-3) {
        g.drawChars(text, 0, len, 20, 20 + (i/2)*17);
      } else {
        g.drawChars(text, (len-3-i), 4, 20+ (len-3-i)*7, 20+ (i/2)*17);
      }
    }
  }
}
```

The output of this example is shown in Figure 10.6.

FIGURE 10.6:

Zigzag text using
drawChars()

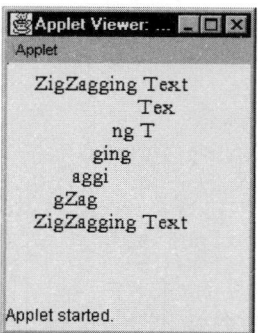

The program uses the `setFont()` method to change the currently used rendering font. Method `setFont()` takes a `Font` object that can be constructed on the fly using a new `Font("<fontFamilyName>", <fontStyle>, pointSize)`. See the discussion of `setFont()` later in the chapter for details.

Moving Rectangular Areas

The copyArea() method is the only method for moving a graphics area available within Graphics. The Graphics2D class, described fully in Chapter 11, contains support for higher-level graphics transformation:

```
public void copyArea(int x, int y, int width, int height, int dx, int dy)
```

Since it does not allow any type of masking, copyArea() is most useful for scrolling areas vertically or horizontally. The x, y, width, and height arguments specify the area to move, and the dx and dy arguments specify by how many pixels and in which direction. As you can see from the method's signature, only screen-to-screen copies are supported. You cannot grab a screen area and store it for future use—for example, to copy it back to the screen at a later date.

Figure 10.7 shows one of those executive toy-type applets that relies on moving rectangular puzzle pieces horizontally and vertically. The program that follows produced the (animated) output of Figure 10.7.

FIGURE 10.7:

Puzzle applet

> **NOTE**
> You can move an image from an off-screen buffer into the screen using the draw-Image() method; this is discussed in the "Animation Basics" section later in this chapter.

```java
import java.awt.*;

public class Puzzle extends java.applet.Applet {

    Graphics g;
    Color bg;
```

```
    int pieceWidth, pieceHeight;

    static final int PUZ_WIDTH  = 5;
    static final int PUZ_HEIGHT = 5;

    static final int MOVE_UP = 0;// these values are designed so that negating
    static final int MOVE_DOWN= 3; // one produces the opposite direction, e.g.,
    static final int MOVE_RIGHT = 1; // ~MOVE_UP = MOVE_DOWN(when ANDed with 3)
    static final int MOVE_LEFT= 2;

    int holeX = 0;// starting spot for the puzzle's "hole"
    int holeY = 0;

    int xDirs[] = {0,1,-1,0}; // dxs and dys indexable by one of the MOVE_s
    int yDirs[] = {-1,0,0,1};
    int xDir, yDir;
    int x,y; // pixel coordinates of a puzzle piece

/**************************************************************************
 * Work out the size of the puzzle pieces from the available applet area.
 **************************************************************************/
    public void init() {
      pieceWidth= (getBounds().width-20) /PUZ_WIDTH;
      pieceHeight = (getBounds().height-20)/PUZ_HEIGHT;
    }
/**************************************************************************
 * Draw a nice background for the puzzle. Draw the pieces and start
 * animating the lot.
 **************************************************************************/
    public void paint (Graphics g) {
      this.g = g;
      g.translate(10,10);
      bg = getBackground();
      g.setFont(new Font("Serif", Font.BOLD, 85));
      g.drawString("Hey!",10,70);
      g.setColor(Color.gray);
      g.drawString("Hey!",12,72);
      drawPieces();
      while(true) {
        occupyHole();// animate the puzzle by moving pieces
      }
    }
```

```
/*********************************************************************
 * At init time, draw the piece outlines over the backdrop picture.
 *********************************************************************/
  private void drawPieces() {
    for (int row=0; row < PUZ_HEIGHT; row++) {
      for (int col=0; col < PUZ_WIDTH; col++) {
        drawPieceAt(row,col);
      }
    }
  }
/*********************************************************************
 * Pick a valid, random neighbor around the hole, then move
 * that neighbor into the hole's spot. The old neighbor's
 * cell becomes the new hole.
 *********************************************************************/
  private void occupyHole() {
    int neighborDir; // randomly chosen neighbor cell direction
    int moveDir;     // opposite direction (to move into hole cell)
    int neighborX;
    int neighborY;
    // choose a random neighboring direction 0..3
    do {
      neighborDir = (int) (Math.random()*4);
    } while (cellIsIllegal(neighborDir)); // but avoid going off grid
    neighborX = holeX + xDirs[neighborDir];
    neighborY = holeY + yDirs[neighborDir];
//  System.out.println("Hole: " + holeX + "," + holeY);
//  System.out.println("Nbor: " + neighborX + "," + neighborY);
    moveDir = (~neighborDir)&3; // opposite dir UP<->DOWN, RIGHT<->LEFT
    movePiece (neighborX, neighborY, moveDir);
    holeX = neighborX;
    holeY = neighborY;
    delay(0.5);
  }
/*********************************************************************
 * Check that a tentative neighbor cell is within the puzzle.
 *********************************************************************/
  private boolean cellIsIllegal(int direction) {
    xDir = xDirs[direction];
    yDir = yDirs[direction];
    int withinX = holeX + xDir;
    int withinY = holeY + yDir;
```

```
      if ((withinX < 0) || (withinX >= PUZ_WIDTH))
        return true;
      else if ((withinY < 0) || (withinY >= PUZ_HEIGHT))
        return true;
      else
        return false;
    }
/*************************************************************************
 * Graphically move a piece in one of the four directions.
 *************************************************************************/
    private void movePiece(int row, int col, int direction) {
      xDir = xDirs[direction];
      yDir = yDirs[direction];
      x = row * pieceWidth;
      y = col * pieceHeight;
      if (xDir != 0) {
        for (int i=0; i < pieceWidth; i++) {
          g.copyArea(x+(i * xDir),y, pieceWidth, pieceHeight, xDir, 0);
          delay(0.004);
        }
      } else {
        for (int i=0; i < pieceHeight; i++) {
          g.copyArea(x,y+(i * yDir), pieceWidth, pieceHeight, 0, yDir);
          delay(0.004);
        }
      }
    }
/*************************************************************************
 * At initialization time, cut up the background into puzzle pieces.
 * Each piece has an outline that is slightly inset to avoid
 * smearing when copyArea() slides pieces around.
 *************************************************************************/
    private void drawPieceAt(int row, int col) {
      x = row * pieceWidth;
      y = col * pieceHeight;
      g.setColor(bg);
      g.drawRect(x,y, pieceWidth, pieceHeight);
      g.drawRect(x+1,y+1, pieceWidth-2, pieceHeight-2);
      g.setColor(Color.gray);
      g.drawRect(x+1,y+1, pieceWidth-3, pieceHeight-3);
    }
```

```
/********************************************************************/
   private void delay(double seconds) {
     try {Thread.sleep((int) (seconds*1000));
     } catch (Exception ignored) {
     }
   }
 }
```

NOTE When you run this applet, you will see that the program does not contain any of the game's logic. Adding this is left as an exercise for the reader. Also, the `paint()` method never returns. Proper multithreaded animation techniques are described in the "Multithreaded Applets" section of Chapter 18.

The core of the program is the `movePiece()` method. It takes the puzzle piece coordinates of the square to move, as well as a direction in which to move the piece. The pieces are moved smoothly, one pixel at a time, using repeated calls to `copyArea()`. Note that `copyArea()` does not alter the source area at all. Therefore, when sliding a rectangular image one pixel at a time in a given direction, a graphical trace may be left behind, depending on the pixel contents of the trailing edge. To avoid this, the program draws the "outlines" for the pieces a couple of pixels on the inside of the piece, surrounded by an invisible outline of background color. This way, pieces can slide around without leaving any traces.

Managing the Graphics State

Beyond being a collection of rendering primitives, what other function does a `Graphics` object have? Its crucial function is to allow a multitude of different graphic contexts to coexist. When the `paint()` method hands you a `Graphics` object, that object holds all graphical attributes or state for your applet's drawing area. Your applet's drawing origin (coordinates 0,0), for example, is situated in the top-left corner of the applet's drawing area and not in the top-left corner of the browser's window or the top-left corner of the screen. A `Graphics`-controlled drawing area has several more such attributes besides the customized coordinate origin. `Graphics` objects also keep track of the following:

- The current clipping area
- The current drawing color

- The current drawing mode
- The current font to use for any text rendering

These attributes can be altered and/or queried by the `Graphics` methods discussed in the following sections.

Translating the Coordinate System

If you look back at the source code of the polygon-drawing example, you will see that the polygons were "manually" spaced apart by adding 100 to the x-coordinates of the second polygon and 200 to the x-coordinates of the third polygon. This can be avoided by using the `translate()` method:

```
public void translate(int x, int y)
```

Using this method makes the source code much more readable. Here is how the code body could be improved with `translate()`, achieving the same result as in Figure 10.3 (shown earlier):

```
concave = new Polygon();
concave.addPoint( 20,20);
concave.addPoint( 60,24);
concave.addPoint( 25,50);
concave.addPoint( 21,75);
concave.addPoint( 10,30);
concave.addPoint( 20,20);

selfintersecting = new Polygon();
for(int i=0; i< 10; i++) {
  selfintersecting.addPoint( (int) (Math.random()*80),
    (int) (Math.random()*80));
}
g.fillPolygon(convex);

g.translate(100,0);
g.drawPolygon(concave);

g.translate(100,20);
g.fillPolygon(selfintersecting);
```

Note that translations are cumulative. Each invocation of `translate()` translates the current coordinate system, which might already have been translated. To "undo" the last translation, you must remember the amount of the previous translation and then apply the inverse translation. This is done by translating with the previous translation values negated:

```
translate(tx,ty);
// paint stuff
translate(-tx,-ty);
// back to where we were before
```

Specifying a Clipping Area

When you specify drawing coordinates that lie outside your applet's drawing area, none of the graphics primitives complain. Instead, they simply restrict whatever they draw to be within the applet's bounds() and clip any rendering that would draw outside this area. This clipping rectangle can be changed to any other rectangular area located within the original applet drawing area using the clipRect() method. You can discover what the current clipping rectangle is set to by calling getClipBounds(), which returns a Rectangle instance. Here are the signatures for these two methods:

```
public void clipRect(int x, int y, int width, int height)
public Rectangle getClipBounds()
```

The following applet's paint() method proves that the initial clipping rectangle for an applet is identical to the applet's bounds():

```
public void paint (Graphics g) {
  System.out.println(g.getClipBounds());
  System.out.println(getBounds());
}
```

If you ran this code within a minimal applet class, it would produce the following output (or similar output with different width and height values but identical between the lines):

```
java.awt.Rectangle[x=0,y=0,width=200,height=150]
java.awt.Rectangle[x=0,y=0,width=200,height=150]
```

Current Drawing Color

Every Graphics context has a current (foreground) drawing color. Surprisingly enough, there is no associated current background drawing color. Java does have a concept of background color, but only in the context of GUI components (via the setBackground() and getBackground() methods in class Component). You alter the rendering color used by calls to setColor(). Finding out which color is being used for all current rendering is done via calls to getColor():

```
public void setColor(Color c)
public Color getColor()
```

The type of objects handled by both calls are instances of class Color. Here is its definition:

```
public class  Color extends Object implements Paint, Serializable {
  public static final Color black;
  public static final Color blue;
  public static final Color cyan;
  public static final Color darkGray;
  public static final Color gray;
  public static final Color green;
  public static final Color lightGray;
  public static final Color magenta;
  public static final Color orange;
  public static final Color pink;
  public static final Color red;
  public static final Color white;
  public static final Color yellow;
  public Color(float r, float g, float b);
  public Color(float r, float g, float b, float a);
  public Color(int rgb);
  public Color(int rgba, boolean hasAlpha);
  public Color(int r, int g, int b);
  public Color(int r, int g, int b, int a);
  public Color(ColorSpace cspace, float compArray[], float alpha);
  public static int HSBtoRGB(float hue, float saturation, float brightness);
  public static float[] RGBtoHSB(int r, int g, int b, float hsbvals []);
  public static Color decode(String num) throws NumberFormatException;
  public static Color getColor(String name);
  public static Color getColor(String name, int defaultValue);
  public static Color getColor(String name, Color defaultValue);
  public static Color getHSBColor(float h, float s, float b);
  public Color brighter();
  public synchronized PaintContext createContext(ColorModel cm, Rectangle r,
    Rectangle2D r2d, AffineTransform xform, RenderingHints hints);
  public Color darker();
  public boolean equals(Object obj);
  public int getAlpha();
```

```
public int getBlue();
public float[] getColorComponents(float compArray[]);
public float[] getColorComponents(ColorSpace cspace, float compArray[]);
public ColorSpace getColorSpace();
public float[] getComponents(float compArray[]);
public float[] getComponents(ColorSpace cspace, float compArray[]);
public int getGreen();
public int getRGB();
public float[] getRGBColorComponents(float compArray[]);
public float[] getRGBComponents(float compArray[]);
public int getRed();
public int getTransparency();
public int hashCode();
public String toString();
}
```

The Color constructors should be your main focus. You can construct a new color by specifying one of the following sets:

- Red, green, and blue primary components in the integer range 0–255

- Red, green, and blue primary components in the float range 0.0F–1.0F

- A single integer encoding red, green, and blue in the standard 8-bits-per-primary format

- Hue, saturation, and brightness values in the float range 0.0F–1.0F (this is via the getHSBColor() static method and not via a constructor)

If your color requirements can be satisfied by the basic palette, the Color class defines some class constants of type Color (itself): white, gray, lightGray, dark-Gray, black, red, pink, orange, yellow, green, magenta, cyan, and blue. As with all class constants, you need to prepend the name of the class to use these—for example, Color.blue.

Current Drawing Mode

All rendering can be executed in one of two modes, paint or XOR mode, using these two methods:

```
public void setPaintMode()
public void setXORMode(Color c1)
```

Paint mode simply overwrites any pixels already there, in the current drawing color. XOR mode applies a color-swapping function (reminiscent of, but not equal to, bitwise exclusive oring). The swapped colors are the color being passed as the argument to `setXORMode()`, the current drawing color, and the current background color. The following applet demonstrates the effect:

```java
import java.awt.*;
public class XOR extends java.applet.Applet {

  public void paint (Graphics g) {
    g.setFont(new Font("Serif", Font.BOLD, 32) );
    g.drawString("Java", 10, 30);
    g.drawString("Sumatra", 10, 60);

    // draw both strings on top of another in both paint and XOR mode

    g.setPaintMode();
    g.drawString("Java", 10, 100);
    g.drawString("Sumatra (Paint)", 10, 100);

    g.setXORMode(Color.gray);
    g.drawString("Java", 10, 130);
    g.drawString("Sumatra (XOR)", 10, 130);
  }
}
```

Figure 10.8 shows paint and XOR drawing modes. Additionally, combining of colors is described in the "Compositing" section of Chapter 11.

FIGURE 10.8:

Paint and XOR drawing modes

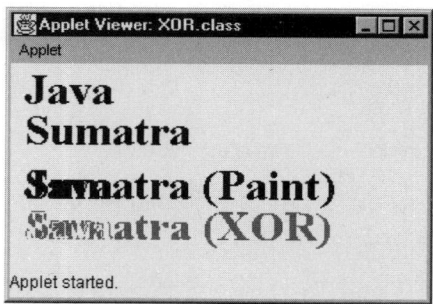

Current Font

Two methods are provided to handle font aspects:

```
public void setFont(Font font)
public Font getFont()
```

You specify the current font using the `setFont()` method. The argument it takes is a `Font` object, which is usually constructed in place, within the argument brackets of `setFont()`. The `Font` constructor has the following signature:

```
public Font(String name, int style, int size)
```

The `name` argument denotes the font family and typically can be `Monospaced`, `Dialog`, `DialogInput`, `SansSerif`, or `Serif` (on Windows and Solaris platforms). The style argument can be `Font.PLAIN`, `Font.BOLD`, or `Font.ITALIC`. These can be specified either alone or in combination (by oring them together).

NOTE   If you do not use one of the standard font names listed above, the Java program will try to use a locally installed Java font. Prior versions of Java supported font names of `Helvetica`, `TimesRoman`, `Courier`, and `ZapfDingbats`. So, if you are upgrading a program and want to use a standard Java font name, perform the following changes: `Helvetica` is now known as `SansSerif`, `TimesRoman` as `Serif`, and `Courier` as `Monospaced`. `ZapfDingbats` has a place in the Unicode character set, so you would specify a character in the range of \u2700-\u27BF to represent the dingbat symbol.

The *size* argument is the fontscaling in pixels. The following demo program combines `Font` and `FontMetrics` (which are explained in the next section). It determines the list of all available fonts (available to Java, that is) and renders samples of each with expanding point sizes. This example obtains the fonts at run time on any platform.

```
import java.awt.*;
public class FontList extends java.applet.Applet {

   GraphicsEnvironment ge = GraphicsEnvironment.getLocalGraphicsEnvironment();
   String fontList[] = ge.getAvailableFontFamilyNames();
   Font fonts[] = ge.getAllFonts();

   public void paint(Graphics g) {
      Font theFont;
      FontMetrics fm;
      int fontHeight = 0;
```

```
        for (int i = 0, n=fontList.length; i < n; i+=2) {
          System.out.println(fontList[i]);
          theFont = new Font(fontList[i], Font.PLAIN, 11);
          g.setFont(theFont);
      g.drawString(fontList[i] + " " + " 11 point", 10, fontHeight);
          System.out.println(fontList[i+1]);
          theFont = new Font(fontList[i+1], Font.PLAIN, 11);
          g.setFont(theFont);
          fm = getFontMetrics(theFont);
          fontHeight += fm.getHeight();
          g.drawString(fontList[i+1] + " " + "11 point", 200, fontHeight);
        }
      }
    }
    ...
```

Figure 10.9 shows the output of the program.

FIGURE 10.9:

Java AWT fonts

You obtain a list of available font names by using the `GraphicsEnvironment` class's `getAvailableFontFamilyNames()` method. For an array of fonts (1 point in size), you would use the `getAllFonts()` method. You get a `GraphicsEnvironment` object in the first instance (to invoke `getAvailableFontFamilyNames()` on) by using the `GraphicsEnvironment` class method `getLocalGraphicsEnvironment()`.

NOTE   The `GraphicsEnvironment` class will be revisited in Chapter 11.

Accessing the Current Font's FontMetrics

Two more font-related methods are provided to access a font's set of metrics:

```
public FontMetrics getFontMetrics()
public FontMetrics getFontMetrics(Font f)
```

Whenever you render anything around rendered text, you need to know the precise dimensions of the various fonts. If you do not know these dimensions, your output will not be symmetrical or centered correctly, or worse, subsequent rendering might "collide" with parts of the text. All modern computer fonts come with a set of *metrics* that define various heights and widths for the font. Consult the JDK online documentation on class `FontMetrics` to learn about these font metrics. The following program demonstrates how to get a font's `FontMetrics` object and use it, in this case, to highlight the metrics graphically as shown in Figure 10.10.

FIGURE 10.10:

Font metrics for font Serif

In addition to producing the graphical output shown in Figure 10.10, the program also dumps the following metrics to the console (for a "`Serif`" font requested to be 100 points):

```
ascent 101
descent 22
```

```
height 128
leading 5
maxAdv 145
maxAsc 101
maxDes 22
```

The metrics listed were obtained on a Windows NT host machine. Because font metrics vary across platforms, the program might print different values on your machine. Here is the program behind the console output and Figure 10.10:

```java
import java.awt.*;
public class FMetrics extends java.applet.Applet {

  Font theFont = new Font("Serif", Font.PLAIN, 100);;

  public void paint(Graphics g) {
    int baseline = 100;
    String testStr= "WIactiyg";

    g.setFont(theFont);
    FontMetrics fm = g.getFontMetrics();

    int ascent  = fm.getAscent();
    System.out.println("ascent " + ascent);
    int descent = fm.getDescent();
    System.out.println("descent " + descent );
    int height  = fm.getHeight();
    System.out.println("height " + height);
    int leading = fm.getLeading();
    System.out.println("leading " + leading );
    int maxAdv  = fm.getMaxAdvance();
    System.out.println("maxAdv " + maxAdv);
    int maxAsc  = fm.getMaxAscent();
    System.out.println("maxAsc " + maxAsc);
    int maxDes  = fm.getMaxDescent();
    System.out.println("maxDes " + maxDes);

    g.drawString(testStr, 10, baseline);

    drawHLine(baseline);
    drawHLine(baseline-ascent);
    drawHLine(baseline-maxAsc);
    drawHLine(baseline+descent);
    drawHLine(baseline+maxDes);
```

```
      drawHLine(baseline+maxDes+leading);

      int charX = 10;
      for (int i=0; i< testStr.length(); i++) {
        drawVLine(charX);
        charX += fm.charWidth(testStr.charAt(i));
      }
    }
    void drawHLine(int y) {
     getGraphics().drawLine(10,y,500,y);
    }
    void drawVLine(int x) {
     getGraphics().drawLine(x,10,x,200);
    }
  }
```

Note that the FontMetrics object is not obtained from the font it relates to. The Graphics object is the entity that gives you a FontMetrics object for the currently selected rendering font. Note also that you can improve readability and keep the code short by writing two simple little utility-rendering functions: drawHLine() and drawVLine(). Simple methods that are only a couple of lines long can greatly improve the readability of your programs.

Animation Basics

The essence of all animation is moving pictures—a sequence of still images displayed at a fast enough rate to fool the brain into thinking the animation is continuous. Once the animation rate (the frame rate) is fast enough, the discrete, static pictures merge into a constant flow of movement.

Movies use a frame rate of 24 frames per second (fps). In other words, the images are renewed at 24 hertz (Hz, or cycles per second). Normal televisions use 60Hz (for the United States NTSC broadcasting standard) or 50Hz (for the European PAL standard), although recently, newer (digital) models using 100Hz have invaded the marketplace. Multisync computer monitors can display their frames from "slow" television rates to approximately 120Hz. Faster update rates mean less image flicker and consequently more solid or realistic-looking animations.

Redrawing an entire screen or even just a sizable window in 1/24 of a second is no mean feat—especially if its content is complex and needs many computations to redraw it. Fortunately, animation effects can be achieved without having to redraw the entire drawing canvas each time. Modifying only those areas that contain the changing parts can be just as effective.

The following applet demonstrates this technique. It draws only one new straight line for each new "frame," but the way in which it does this is fascinating to watch. Figure 10.11 shows a snapshot of the Qix applet in action.

```java
import java.awt.* ;
import java.util.Random ;

public class Qix extends java.applet.Applet {

  private Random rnd = new Random();

  private Rectangle bounceRect;
  private Rectangle colorBounce;
  private BouncyPoint endPoint1,endPoint2;
  private BouncyPoint R_Bouncer, G_Bouncer, B_Bouncer;
  private int startx1, startx2, starty1, starty2;

  public void paint (Graphics g) {

    bounceRect = getBounds(); // applet's bbox
    bounceRect.x = 0;
    bounceRect.y = 0;

    startx1 = 4 + ((rnd.nextInt()&1023) % (bounceRect.width - 8));
    startx2 = 4 + ((rnd.nextInt()&1023) % (bounceRect.width - 8));
    starty1 = 4 + ((rnd.nextInt()&1023) % (bounceRect.height -8));
    starty2 = 4 + ((rnd.nextInt()&1023) % (bounceRect.height -8));

    endPoint1 = new BouncyPoint(bounceRect, startx1, starty1,-1.0, 1.5);
    endPoint2 = new BouncyPoint(bounceRect, startx2, starty2, 1.0,-2.5);

    colorBounce = new Rectangle(0,0, 255,255);
    R_Bouncer = new BouncyPoint(colorBounce, 200,0, 1.0, 0.0);
    G_Bouncer = new BouncyPoint(colorBounce, 200,0, -1.0, 0.0);
    B_Bouncer = new BouncyPoint(colorBounce, 200,0, -2.0, 0.0);

    while (true) {
      endPoint1.carryOnBouncing(); // bounce the two line endpoints around
```

```
          endPoint2.carryOnBouncing();
          R_Bouncer.carryOnBouncing(); // bounce the colors around too
          G_Bouncer.carryOnBouncing();
          B_Bouncer.carryOnBouncing();

          g.setColor(new Color(R_Bouncer.x, G_Bouncer.x, B_Bouncer.x));
          g.drawLine(endPoint1.x, endPoint1.y, endPoint2.x, endPoint2.y);

          try { Thread.sleep(10); } catch (Exception ignored) {}
      }
  }

/*****************************************************************************
 * This implements a (commonly employed) bouncing "endpoint,"
 * i.e., you could use 2 instances of this to animate a bouncing line
 * or use 4 of these to animate a Bezier curve or a stretchy, bouncy rectangle
 *****************************************************************************/

  class BouncyPoint extends Point {

    private Rectangle boundingBox;
    private double x_direction;
    private double y_direction;

    BouncyPoint (Rectangle limits, int startx, int starty, double dx, double dy) {

        super(startx, starty);
        boundingBox = limits;
        x_direction = dx;
        y_direction = dy;
    }

    public boolean carryOnBouncing () {

        boolean boing=false;

        // add velocity to current position
        // if resulting position outside box, undo move and reverse speed

        x += (int) x_direction;
        if (! boundingBox.contains(x,y)) {
          x -= (int) x_direction;
```

```
      x_direction = - x_direction;
      boing = true;
    }

    y += (int) y_direction;
    if (! boundingBox.contains(x,y)) {
      y -= (int) y_direction;
      y_direction = - y_direction;
      boing = true;
    }
    return boing;
  }

  public String toString() {
    return super.toString() + "-Speed dx=" + x_direction +
      " dy=" + y_direction;
  }
 }
}
```

FIGURE 10.11:

Qix animation applet

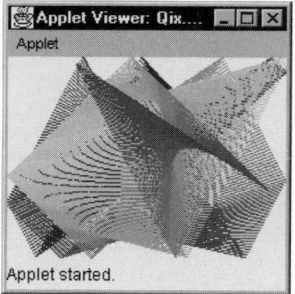

NOTE   Qix was one of the classic arcade games of the early 1980s. The object of the game was to gradually restrict the movements of the "Qix"—some sort of energy field—by building a fence around it. If the Qix touched you while you were in the middle of building a fence, you died.

The applet relies on a perfectly reusable class whose sole purpose is to "bounce around" a 2-D point within a rectangular box. The BouncyPoint class extends the `java.awt.Point` class (which consists mainly of an *x, y* coordinate). Two Bouncy-Point instances are used to hold the moving endpoints of the animated line. The gradual color animation is also handled by more `BouncyPoint` instances. The program uses the numeric ping-pong functionality of a `BouncyPoint` to modify the red, green, and blue color components independently. Since each color primary is just a one-dimensional scalar, only the *x* part of a `BouncyPoint` is used for the colors.

| **WARNING** | This Qix applet has a serious shortcoming: It never returns from its `paint()` method. A `while(true)` loop was used to implement an infinite loop that controls the (infinite) animation. Applets that do this are useless in real-life Web pages, because they soak up CPU resources that should normally be shared among all applets. To keep the topic focused on graphics, this flaw is ignored throughout this chapter's applets; the issue is addressed in detail in Chapter 18. |

Working with Java Images

Animating a straight line—or any other graphics primitive—is fine for screen-saver programs or to relax a stressed-out manager, but sooner or later you will want to animate predrawn cartoons or even a large sequence of (digital) video frames. For this purpose, Java supports an `Image` class, along with other related classes.

Techniques for Image Manipulation

The Java API is rather confusing with regard to image manipulations. Several packages, classes, and methods deal with images in one way or another:

- The `java.awt.Image` class is abstract, so you cannot create `Image` instances from it. (This is a bit like having a succulent apple pie behind bulletproof glass.)

- The `java.awt.image` package is entirely devoted to image processing.

- In package `java.applet`, two `getImage()` methods are tucked away in class `Applet`.

- Class `Component` defines two `createImage()` methods.

- Class `Graphics` contains several `drawImage()` methods.

Here is a sample program that draws an image inside an applet:

```java
import java.awt.*;

public class GetImage extends java.applet.Applet {

  Image myimg;

  public void init() {
    myimg = getImage(getDocumentBase(), "image.gif");
  }

  public void paint(Graphics g) {
    if (myimg != null)
      g.drawImage(myimg, 0, 0, this);
  }
}
```

This applet produces a window like that shown in Figure 10.12.

FIGURE 10.12:

A GIF image displayed by
an applet

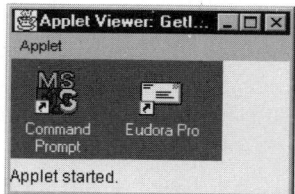

The applet's core consists of two statements: `getImage()` and `drawImage()`. This, fortunately (or unfortunately, depending on your viewpoint), is the simplest aspect of using Java images; the remainder of the material is uphill all the way.

Class `Image` is abstract and therefore cannot be the source for `Image` instances itself. Other classes must create instances of `Image` for you. Methods that construct and return objects are sometimes called *factory methods*. In this example, the applet method `getImage()` is a factory method for `Image` objects. This method not only creates brand new `Image` objects, it also performs the handy function of loading an external image file and turning it into a runtime usable `Image` object, ready to be rendered. The image formats that are supported are mainly XBM, GIF, and JPEG; GIF and JPEG are the de facto Internet image file formats.

The signature of the `getImage()` method used in the example is:

```
public Image getImage(URL url, String name)
```

The URL parameter allows this method to grab image files from any willing Internet site in the world! Another `Applet` method, `getDocumentBase()`, specifies the URL origin (directory) of the picture as whatever site the applet's HTML document came from. If you run the applet on your own machine, this document base URL will have the form of a file URL, such as `file:/C:/JAVA/MASTERING/../../page.html`. If you run the applet from a Web server, the document base URL will have the form of an HTTP URL, such as `http://www.sybex.com/Java/Mastering/../page.html`. The name parameter is the image file's filename in the specified directory, whether local or halfway around the world.

To actually show the image on screen, you use the `drawImage()` method from class `Graphics`. Throughout Java's scattered image-support classes and methods, you can count on one thing: You always use `drawImage()` to render the image. The parameters it takes are the x, y coordinates for the top-left corner where the image is to be drawn and a `this` parameter:

```
g.drawImage(image, x, y, this);
```

And what about the `this` parameter? Your first clue is embedded in the online documentation description for `getImage()`: "This method returns immediately, even if the image does not exist. The actual image data is loaded when it is first needed." This means the `getImage()` statement does not actually get the image after all. The reason is the Internet: The entire image-processing and image-handling support that Java gives us takes the Internet's daily reality into account. In particular, the design reflects the unpredictable delays that occur when accessing remote Internet files and the length of time it takes to download any sizable files (image files often range between 1KB and 100KB, depending on complexity, color depth , and so on).

The `Image` subsystem deals with these issues by separating the loading of images from their actual use. The example code says "load that image and draw it," not knowing or caring about Internet response times or transfer rates, so the two (loading and using images) are completely separated. Another way of saying this is that the image loading is asynchronous, meaning that the main program does not wait for the load to finish (if it did wait, that would be a synchronous approach). What really goes on behind the scenes is not this simple, but it's all to make Java applet development easier and improve performance for the user.

The exact details of the mechanisms used to fetch the image all the way from a remote site and into the `Image` object are platform dependent. In general, the `get-Image()` method creates an `Image` object that, when asked to draw itself, will start the download process and render the image bit by bit, as the image data is received. This is the function of the `this` parameter in the `drawImage()` call.

Here is the method's signature:

```
public boolean drawImage(Image img, int x, int y, ImageObserver observer)
```

You can see that the last parameter must be of type `ImageObserver`. Image observers are explained in the next section.

The ImageObserver Interface

To understand why `drawImage()` needs an `ImageObserver`, you must first understand what an `ImageObserver` is. `ImageObserver` is an interface and not a class. Its definition is very short (although that doesn't make its purpose any easier to understand):

```
public interface ImageObserver {
  public static final int ABORT;
  public static final int ALLBITS;
  public static final int ERROR;
  public static final int FRAMEBITS;
  public static final int HEIGHT;
  public static final int PROPERTIES;
  public static final int SOMEBITS;
  public static final int WIDTH;
  public abstract boolean imageUpdate(Image image, int infoflags, int x, int y,
    int width, int height);
}
```

Apart from the collection of constants, it defines a single method to be implemented by an `ImageObserver`: `imageUpdate()`.

The Image-Loading Chain of Events

Here is how all of the various pieces fall into place: `getImage()` does not actually load the image; `drawImage()` does. But since loading images from the Internet can be a lengthy process (or even worse, the loading process can fail), even it returns immediately. Method `drawImage()` kicks off the asynchronous loading of the image it wants to render and returns immediately. Another invisible Java subsystem that runs in a different thread actually does all the hard work of transferring the image over the network. Each time this image-loading system has a reasonable chunk of new image data, it tells the ImageObserver for the image that some extra data is available. It does this through an invocation of the image-Update() method.

Again, the ImageObserver in this case is the applet. To understand its response to an imageUpdate(), you will want to sneak a peek at the API source itself. The default imageUpdate() method is found in class Component:

```
/**
 * Repaints the component when the image has changed.
 * …
 * @return true if image has changed; false otherwise.
 */
public boolean imageUpdate(Image img, int flags, int x, int y, int w, int h) {
  int rate = -1;
  if ((flags & (FRAMEBITS|ALLBITS)) != 0) {
    rate = 0;
  } else if ((flags & SOMEBITS) != 0) {
    if (isInc) {
      try {
        rate = incRate;
        if (rate < 0)
          rate = 0;
      } catch (Exception e) {
        rate = 100;
      }
    }
  }
  if (rate >= 0) {
    repaint(rate, 0, 0, width, height);
  }
  return (flags & (ALLBITS|ABORT)) == 0;
}
```

What you are looking for is that last if statement: if… repaint(). Most of the time, a call to imageUpdate() will trigger a repaint() of the applet, which, in turn, means the applet's familiar paint() method will be called. And what does the applet's paint() method do? drawImage()! And then you are back to where you started. Only this time, your drawImage() will have a chunk of its image to render, which it does before terminating again. In the meantime, the background image-loading thread continues loading data, which it will again pass on as a stream of image chunks. This cycle continues until the entire image is loaded and displayed.

Although this long chain of cause and effect is admittedly arduous, it is a small price to pay for the advantages you gain:

- The logic of your applets does not need to be concerned with multithreaded, asynchronous loading of image data. Everything is taken care of behind the scenes (by daemon Java threads).

- The images are rendered on the screen as the data comes in. This is a handy form of user feedback, because, at any point, the user can ascertain the progress of the images being loaded.

- Multiple images can be loaded in parallel by using multiple TCP connections to exploit the bandwidth wasted by and inherent in any burst-pause-burst-pause communication link.

This last point is at least as important as the first. If image loading were left up to the thousands of applet programmers out there to program, chances are that the vast majority of applets would use very inefficient (that is, slow) "brute force" algorithms to load images. Instead, the API designers implemented a complex but high-performance system to be used by all developers.

Some aspects of this implementation are not completely hidden from the application developer. The component `repaint()` methods are a case in point. Two of the overloaded variants take a repaint timeout value. To understand what a timeout parameter has to do with refreshing a graphical display, add a simple `System.out.println()` to your applet and observe the applet's `paint()` dynamics carefully. Add the following line after the `drawImage()` statement in the `paint()` method:

```
System.out.prinln("Had to paint!");
```

If you now rerun the applet, the console should print a number of "Had to paint!" lines:

```
Had to paint!
Had to paint!
Had to paint!
Had to paint!
```

paint() is called several times like this because each time a new image chunk becomes available, the imageUpdate() method causes the applet to repaint itself. In fact, things are even more subtle than that. Suppose you have an applet with a dozen images, all loaded and displayed using the simple getImage()/drawImage() duo. Since many of the images will be loaded in parallel, new image data will become available in a fairly continuous flow, leading to an onslaught of image-Update() events. It is clear that calling the applet's (re)paint() method each time any of the images has more data available would be inefficient overkill. And that's where the timeout comes in: The AWT defines an incremental draw rate property that determines how long the system can buffer image data before actually updating it on the screen.

If you look back at the default implementation for imageUpdate(), this is what all the rate (redraw rate) code is about before the if... repaint() at the end. In effect, the imageUpdate() method is saying, "Okay, image loader, thanks very much for the new data, but let me see if the user really needs to see this data displayed right now." The method determines the refresh rate to be used and passes this on to repaint(). Internally, repaint() determines if this refresh timeout has expired or not. If not, it delays the full repaint, thereby avoiding a potentially expensive call to paint().

As you have seen, a minuscule applet can be a deceptively simple facade hiding some seriously nontrivial software activity. Fortunately, you can rely on this complex machinery to do the hard work for you, all by using two simple methods: getImage() and drawImage().

Animation's Worst Enemy: Flicker

What if you do not need to load already stored images? Instead, you want to use the Graphics class rendering methods to construct an image from scratch and then render that image. This is possible, but you will not be able to use the applet method getImage(); images obtained via getImage() cannot be drawn into with the Graphics drawing primitives. Your Image object will need to come from the BufferedImage class.

NOTE   Prior to Java 1.2, the Image object would have come from another factory method in another class: createImage() in class Component.

Here is an example of an applet that creates an image of a ball and bounces it around the applet over a simple background:

```java
import java.awt.*;
import java.awt.image.BufferedImage;

public class Ball extends java.applet.Applet {

  final static int BALL_RADIUS = 70;

  Image ball = null;

  public void init() {
    ball = new BufferedImage (BALL_RADIUS, BALL_RADIUS,
      BufferedImage.TYPE_INT_RGB);
    Graphics ballG = ball.getGraphics();

    for (int i=0; i<60; i++) {
      ballG.setColor(new Color((float)Math.random(),
       (float)Math.random(),
       (float)Math.random() ) );
      int x1 = (int)(Math.random()*BALL_RADIUS);
      int y1 = (int)(Math.random()*BALL_RADIUS);
      int x2 = (int)(Math.random()*BALL_RADIUS);
      int y2 = (int)(Math.random()*BALL_RADIUS);
      ballG.drawLine(x1,y1, x2,y2);
    }

    ballG.setColor(Color.white);
    for (int i=-20; i<=0; i++) {
      ballG.drawOval(i,i, BALL_RADIUS + ((-i)*2), BALL_RADIUS + ((-i)*2));
    }
  }
  public void paint(Graphics g) {

    for (int x = 0; x <400; x++) {
      double angle = ((double)x) / 20;
      int y = (int) (Math.abs( Math.sin(angle) )*80);
      g.setColor (Color.white);
      g.fillRect(0,0, getBounds().width, getBounds().height);
      g.setColor (Color.black);
      drawBackground(g);
```

```
      g.drawImage(ball, x, 80-y, this);
      delay(25);
    }
    System.out.println("paint() done!!");
  }
  private void drawBackground(Graphics g) {
    for (int i= 0; i<10; i++) {
      g.drawLine(0, i*10, 400, i*10);
    }
  }
  private void delay (int millis) {
    try { Thread.sleep(millis); } catch (Exception ignored) {}
  }
}
```

Figure 10.13 shows a snapshot frame of the animation.

FIGURE 10.13:

Bouncing ball animation

TIP

You don't need to be a latter-day Newton to breathe some gravity-like controlled motion into an object. The motion of the ball in this applet follows a sine curve whose negative lobes have been folded up using the `Math.abs()` method. It might not be an accurate modeling of physical reality, but it looks good. And that is what animation is primarily about.

This applet's `init()` method starts by creating a blank ball image, which is accomplished by creating a `BufferedImage` object. The class is a little more complicated than is appropriate here, so we'll save a more detailed discussion of the class for Chapter 11. The only thing you really need to know about now is that the constructor takes three parameters: width, height, and type of image created.

There are several class constants of the `BufferedImage` class to describe the types. For most cases, `TYPE_INT_RGB`, which states that each pixel is represented internally by an integer in Red-Green-Blue (RGB) format, is sufficient.

To start drawing into your off-screen image, you need to obtain the `Graphics` handle associated with this image. This is done with a call to `getGraphics()`, which returns a `Graphics` object. Once you have such an object in your possession, you can use all of the graphics-rendering methods as usual. The applet draws a ball-like object consisting of random lines of random colors. The `paint()` method then proceeds by repeatedly erasing the entire applet, redrawing the background for the animation, and drawing the ball in its next position.

You probably have noticed the problem with this animation already: It flickers like mad. And Walt Disney's animations do not flicker at all, do they? Time for bouncing ball, take two.

Smooth Animation Using Double Buffering

Animation flicker occurs when animation contains sharp and repetitive discontinuities in movement and/or colors within successive frames. In the bouncing ball applet's case, the problem is the on-screen wiping of the applet area. This causes a repeated and massive color discontinuity that spoils the animation. You need to wipe the whole frame; otherwise, the bouncing ball will leave behind a trace of itself. You can see this by commenting out the `g.fillRect()` statement. After several frames, the applet looks like the one depicted in Figure 10.14.

FIGURE 10.14:

Bouncing ball animation with wipe step removed

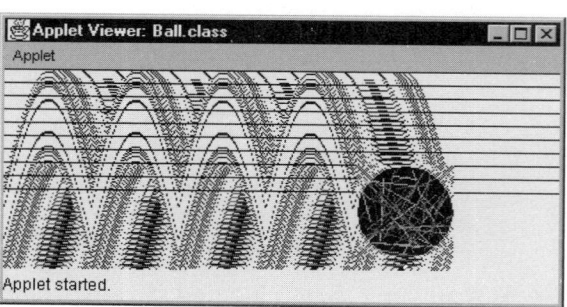

If you could only treat the entire applet drawing area as the same type of off-screen image as the ball itself, then maybe you could do all of the animation steps off-screen and display the finished frames in the applet on-screen. The following program is an enhanced version of Ball.java that does exactly that:

```java
import java.awt.*;
import java.awt.image.BufferedImage;

public class Ball2 extends java.applet.Applet {

  final static int BALL_RADIUS = 70;

  Image ball = null;
  Image applet = null;

  Graphics appG, ballG;

  public void paint(Graphics g) {

    if (ball == null) {
      applet = new BufferedImage (getBounds().width, getBounds().height,
BufferedImage.TYPE_INT_RGB);
      ball = new BufferedImage (BALL_RADIUS, BALL_RADIUS,
BufferedImage.TYPE_INT_RGB);
      appG = applet.getGraphics();
      ballG = ball.getGraphics();
      for (int i=0; i<60; i++) {
        ballG.setColor(new Color((float)Math.random(),
         (float)Math.random(), (float)Math.random()));
        int x1 = (int)(Math.random()*BALL_RADIUS);
        int y1 = (int)(Math.random()*BALL_RADIUS);
        int x2 = (int)(Math.random()*BALL_RADIUS);
        int y2 = (int)(Math.random()*BALL_RADIUS);
        ballG.drawLine(x1,y1, x2,y2);
      }
      ballG.setColor(Color.white);
      for (int i=-20; i<=0; i++) {
        ballG.drawOval(i,i, BALL_RADIUS + ((-i)*2), BALL_RADIUS + ((-i)*2));
      }
    }
    for (int x = 0; x <400; x++) {
      double angle = ((double)x) / 20;
      int y = (int) (Math.abs(Math.sin(angle))*80);
      appG.setColor (Color.white);
```

```
        appG.fillRect(0,0, getBounds().width, getBounds().height);
        appG.setColor (Color.gray);
        drawBackground(appG);
        appG.drawImage(ball, x, 80-y, this);
        g.drawImage(applet, 0,0, this);
        delay(25);
      }
    }
    private void drawBackground(Graphics g) {
      for (int i= 0; i<10; i++) {
        g.drawLine(0, i*10, 400, i*10);
      }
    }
    private void delay (int millis) {
      try {Thread.sleep(millis);
      } catch (Exception ignored) {}
    }
}
```

In this newer incarnation of the bouncing ball applet, a second BufferedImage was created to obtain a second off-screen image buffer of exactly the same dimensions as the applet. This image is used to draw everything previously drawn directly into the applet. Therefore, an extra Graphics context appG is needed to provide drawing access to this new image. The rest of the code is identical, except for the use of appG instead of the usual g. Finally, you still need to use the Graphics object for the on-screen applet (g) when you draw the completed frame, in the blink of an eye, into the applet using g.drawImage().

When you run this new applet, you will see that all of the flicker has magically disappeared. This technique is called *double buffering,* and it is one of the most basic computer graphics techniques for smooth animation. The technique can be summarized as follows:

1. Do all your drawing off-screen.

2. Copy the finished product (a single animation frame) to the screen.

3. Repeat the previous two steps as quickly as possible.

Since the frames displayed on-screen never differ beyond the changes intended by the animation itself, flicker is completely eliminated.

Avoiding Jerkiness in Animation

If your animation rate drops below, say, 20 fps, your animation will suffer from *jerkiness*. Home computer flight simulators are often a prime example of jerky animations. The scenery frames take so much time to generate (because of the complexity of the scenes and the expensive calculations) that the program simply can't produce a new frame every 1/50 of a second.

Once your animations become complex, they might also suffer from dropping frame rates. It will then be a question of optimizing the animation for speed—a subject that could fill an entire volume. Here are some pointers with which you can start:

- Draw as little as possible.
- Reduce the complexity of your animation.
- Use faster rendering algorithms.
- Reduce the dimensions of the animation (shrink the viewport).
- Use tricks like color cycling to animate parts cheaply.
- Use textures to cheaply introduce detail (or complexity).
- Use fixed-point integer math for 3-D calculations.
- Use lookup tables with precalculated results where complex math is involved.

NOTE   If these applets used Swing's `JApplet`, to be described in Chapter 13, the class would do the double buffering for you. While this is nice, it doesn't optimize anything and double buffers the entire applet's area. If you are only performing an animation in a small area of the applet, the remaining area would also be double buffered. Sometimes, it is best to do the double buffering yourself.

Image Processing

Image processing is a broad term for a large collection of diverse computer graphics applications. The following list is just a sampling of what image processing is used for:

- Optical character recognition (OCR)

- Image compression and decompression

- Movie special effects

- Image interpretation (for factory robots, automated car control, surveillance, and so on)

- Image cleanup (digitally cleaning up old movie classics)

These applications all have something in common: Any real-time aspect of the application is secondary to achieving the primary goal, which is usually very expensive in terms of CPU resources. Modern full-color images easily need over 1MB of storage alone. (An 800 × 600, 24-bit-per-pixel picture requires nearly 1.4MB.) Any algorithm that needs to analyze or process such a picture will almost necessarily fall short of having real-time response characteristics. But this does not mean image processing is used any less for that reason.

Java supports image processing in various ways, all of them having one feature in common: platform independence. You can manipulate colors and bitmaps extensively in hardware-independent ways, using an image pipeline metaphor, before they are output to the screen. The pipeline metaphor is analogous to the streams I/O model provided by the `java.io` package (discussed in Chapter 19). Before exploring the pipeline model, as embodied by the `ImageProducer` and `ImageConsumer` interfaces, you need to understand how color itself can be represented and manipulated.

Color Models

Color emanating from a radiating source can be decomposed into the three primary additive colors: red, green, and blue (RGB). All colors used by computers are mixtures of these three colors. The spectrum of a computer's palette will be determined by the number of different red, green, and blue shades that are available. This is, in turn, determined by the number of bits the hardware uses to encode the red, green, and blue primaries. The number of bits used has evolved historically from 1 bit each to the current norm of 8 bits each. The first systems, which used 1 bit per primary, could display eight different colors. Those eight colors are listed in Table 10.2.

Modern systems use 8 bits per primary, so they can display 16.7 million colors. In between, there are numerous asymmetrical bit-assignment combinations that invariably favor green; allocating, for example, 5 bits for red and blue and 6 bits for green. (This is because the human eye is more discerning when it comes to shades of green.)

TABLE 10.2: Minimal Eight-Color Palette

Color	Red Bit	Green Bit	Blue Bit
Black	0	0	0
Red	1	0	0
Green	0	1	0
Blue	0	0	1
Yellow	1	1	0
Cyan	0	1	1
Magenta	1	0	1
White	1	1	1

The end result is that there are a large number of incompatible color representations out there. Instead of choosing one (the most popular one, for example) and enforcing its use by all Java programmers, Java defines a software layer that shields you from these platform dependencies. The abstract class ColorModel is the key to this buffer layer:

```
public abstract class ColorModel extends Object implements Transparency {
  protected int pixel_bits;
  protected int transferType;
  public ColorModel(int bits);
  protected ColorModel(int pixel_bits, int bits[], ColorSpace cspace,
    boolean hasAlpha, boolean isAlphaPremultiplied, int transparency,
    int transferType);
  public static ColorModel getRGBdefault();
  public ColorModel coerceData(WritableRaster raster,
    boolean isAlphaPremultiplied);
  public SampleModel createCompatibleSampleModel(int w, int h);
  public WritableRaster createCompatibleWritableRaster(int w, int h);
  public boolean equals(Object obj);
  public void finalize();
  public abstract int getAlpha(int pixel);
  public int getAlpha(Object inData);
  public WritableRaster getAlphaRaster(WritableRaster raster);
  public abstract int getBlue(int pixel);
  public int getBlue(Object inData);
  public final ColorSpace getColorSpace();
```

```
    public int[] getComponentSize();
    public int getComponentSize(int componentIdx);
    public int[] getComponents(int pixel, int components[], int offset);
    public int[] getComponents(Object obj, int components[], int offset);
    public int getDataElement(int components[], int offset);
    public Object getDataElements(int rgb, Object pixel);
    public abstract int getGreen(int pixel);
    public int getGreen(Object inData);
    public float[] getNormalizedComponents(int components[], int offset,
       float normComponents[], int normOffset);
    public int getNumColorComponents();
    public int getNumComponents();
    public int getPixelSize();
    public int getRGB(int pixel);
    public int getRGB(Object inData);
    public abstract int getRed(int pixel);
    public int getRed(Object inData);
    public int getTransparency();
    public int[] getUnnormalizedComponents(float normComponents[], int normOffset,
       int components[], int offset);
    public final boolean hasAlpha();
    public final boolean isAlphaPremultiplied();
    public boolean isCompatibleRaster(Raster raster);
    public boolean isCompatibleSampleModel(SampleModel sm);
    public Object setDataElements(int components[], int offset, Object obj);
    public String toString();
}
```

The main feature of any ColorModel is that it allows you to use pixels that are encoded using almost any hardware-encoding scheme (the notable exception is bitplane-based architectures). A customized ColorModel should allow you to extract the universal red, green, and blue (and alpha transparency) components from any pixel encoded using any color-coding scheme. Although Java's image-processing classes support this flexible color model independence, they still define a default preferred color architecture: the popular 32-bit alpha/red/green/blue pixel format that uses the following bit assignments:

bits 0–7	blue
bits 8–15	green
bits 16–23	red
bits 24–31	alpha transparency

The `java.awt.image` package has three concrete incarnations of this abstract `ColorModel` class: classes `DirectColorModel`, `IndexColorModel`, and `Component-ColorModel`.

Class `DirectColorModel` encapsulates a `ColorModel` reflecting a True Color–style color architecture. In such a system, pixels hold the color value they represent themselves. This is in contrast to indexed architectures, in which pixels hold an index value used to index a table holding the final color values. And this is what class `IndexColorModel` models: a `ColorModel` using a color lookup table (CLUT) color architecture. `ComponentColorModel` reflects an architecture that can handle more arbitrary color spaces, like representing colors by their hue, saturation, and brightness values.

This color model independence means your applications have almost limitless flexibility in the way they encode pictures "behind the scenes."

Algorithmic Image Generation

Images are usually external files containing photographs, diagrams, or other art that was produced sometime in the past. There is one other fascinating source for images: the computer itself, or rather algorithms that generate pictures dynamically, using numerical methods. Class `MemoryImageSource` exists just for those types of applications needing per-pixel control over their images. Its constructor takes an array of `int` (or `byte`) representing a two-dimensional pixel map. Therefore, with this class, you can implement rendering algorithms of arbitrary complexity, since you have full and efficient access to every pixel of an image. (Remember that the `Graphics` class does not have a single-pixel-plotting method.) The program below demonstrates this by generating the classic fractal: the Mandelbrot set.

```java
import java.awt.*;
import java.awt.image.*;

public class Mandelbrot {

  public static void main(String[] args) {
    new MandelWindow();
  }

  static class MandelWindow extends Frame {

    Image img;
```

```java
int w = 256;
int h = 256;
int pix[] = new int[w * h];

MandelWindow() {

  int index = 0;
  int iter;
  double p,q, psq, qsq, pnew, qnew;
  double a,b;// real and imaginary axis

  setSize(260,300);
  setVisible(true);
  Graphics g = getGraphics();

  double WIDTH_STEP = 4.0/w;
  double HEIGHT_STEP = 4.0/h;

  for (int y=0; y < h; y++) {
    b = ((double)(y-128))/64;
    for (int x=0; x < w; x++) {
      a = ((double)(x-128))/64;
      p=q=0;
      iter = 0;
      while (iter < 32) {
        // see if point a,b is in the set
        psq = p*p; qsq = q*q;
        if (psq+qsq >= 4.0) break;
        pnew = psq - qsq + a;
        qnew = 2 * p*q + b;
        p = pnew;
        q = qnew;
        iter++;
      }
      if (iter == 32) {
        pix[index] = 255<<24 | 255;
      }
      index++;
    }
  }
}
```

```
    for (float i=0.0F; i< 1.0F; i+=0.01F) {// draw a pretty background
      g.setColor(new Color(i,0,0));
      g.drawLine(0,0,(int)(300*Math.cos(i*1.5)),(int)(300*Math.sin(i*1.5)) );
    }

    img = createImage(new MemoryImageSource(w, h, pix, 0, w));
    g.drawImage(img, 0,0, null);
  }
 }
}
```

Figure 10.15 shows the applet's output (which on a 180MHz Pentium PC, using the standard Sun JDK, is generated in a very respectable time of less than three seconds).

FIGURE 10.15:

Mandelbrot set generated via a MemoryImageSource

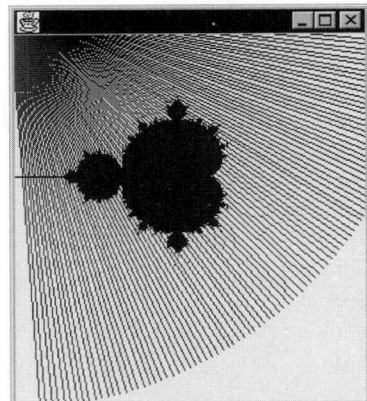

The code clearly shows the power of class MemoryImageSource: You simply declare any old array of int values (pix in this example) to hold the pixels you will "plot" yourself, and then generate the image using any rendering algorithm of your choice.

Now you are just a createImage() and drawImage() away from seeing the result displayed by your Java program. Plotting pixels in such arrays can be done extremely efficiently (more efficiently even than plotting individual pixels directly to the screen using some kind of plotPixel(x,y,color) method). The sample program does not even address the array two dimensionally (although, logically, it is a 2-D array w pixels wide and h pixels high). Instead, it uses a most efficient linear (one-dimensional) sequential addressing (pix[index]). The actual plotting of a pixel is done by storing 255<<24 | 255 as its value. This, under the default RGB color model, means alpha equals 255 (completely opaque, bits 24–31) and blue equals 255; in other words, an everyday "pure blue" pixel. Since you are not plotting pixels for the points outside the Mandelbrot set, the set is surrounded by fully transparent (alpha equals 0) pixels, thus letting the background show through in those areas. (You are relying on newly allocated int arrays containing only zeros, which is guaranteed by the language itself.)

TIP   The mathematics behind the Mandelbrot set involves complex numbers and requires some understanding of nonlinear equations. Consult any good book on fractals if you want to know the ins and outs of the Mandelbrot (and other) fractals. A good reference is *The Beauty of Fractals,* by Peitgen and Richter (published by Springer-Verlag).

If you look at the definition of class MemoryImageSource, you will notice that most of its constructors allow you to specify a ColorModel to be used with the memory image:

```
public class MemoryImageSource extends Object implements ImageProducer {
  public MemoryImageSource(int w, int h, int pix[], int off, int scan);
  public MemoryImageSource(int w, int h, int pix[], int off, int scan,
    Hashtable props);
  public MemoryImageSource(int w, int h, ColorModel cm, byte pix[], int off,
    int scan);
  public MemoryImageSource(int w, int h, ColorModel cm, byte pix[], int off,
    int scan, Hashtable props);
  public MemoryImageSource(int w, int h, ColorModel cm, int pix[], int off,
    int scan);
  public MemoryImageSource(int w, int h, ColorModel cm, int pix[], int off,
    int scan, Hashtable props);
  public synchronized void addConsumer(ImageConsumer ic);
  public synchronized boolean isConsumer(ImageConsumer ic);
  public void newPixels();
  public synchronized void newPixels(byte newpix[], ColorModel cm, int offset,
    int scansize);
  public synchronized void newPixels(int x, int y, int w, int h);
  public synchronized void newPixels(int x, int y, int w, int h,
```

```
    boolean framenotify);
  public synchronized void newPixels(int newpix[], ColorModel cm, int offset,
    int scansize);
  public synchronized void removeConsumer(ImageConsumer ic);
  public void requestTopDownLeftRightResend(ImageConsumer ic);
  public synchronized void setAnimated(boolean animated);
  public synchronized void setFullBufferUpdates(boolean fullBuffers);
  public void startProduction(ImageConsumer ic);
}
```

In this example, the Mandelbrot class uses the simplest constructor that conveniently avoids ColorModel issues. This means that your memory image actually uses the AWT preferred color model: the default 32-bit ARGB format (defined in the section on color models). But the image-processing flexibility of the java.awt.image package does not force you to use this. Therefore, you could ignore what Java prefers and impose a 4-bit VGA color-encoding scheme. (This is used purely for illustrative purposes and in no way suggests that VGA schemes—that is, limitations—still have a place in modern graphics applications.) The following code implements the new Mandelbrot class using a VGA color model.

```
import java.awt.*;
import java.awt.image.*;

public class MandelIndex {

  public static void main(String[] args) {
    new MandelWindow();
  }

  static class MandelWindow extends Frame {
    final static byte[] vGAreds = {-128, -1, 0, 0, 0, 0, -128, -1,
      0, 0, -128, -1, 0, -128, -64, -1};
    final static byte[] vGAgreens = {0, 0, -128, -1, 0, 0,-128, -1,
      -128, -1, 0, 0, 0, -128, -64, -1};
    final static byte[] vGAblues= {0, 0, 0, 0,-128,-1, 0, 0,-
      128,-1, -128, -1,0,-128,-64, -1};
    Image img;
    int w = 512;
    int h = 512;
    byte pix[] = new byte[w * h];

    MandelWindow() {
```

```
int index = 0;
int iter;
double p,q, psq, qsq, pnew, qnew;
double a,b;// real and imaginary axis
setSize(512,400);
setVisible(true);
Graphics g = getGraphics();
double WIDTH_STEP = 4.0/w;
double HEIGHT_STEP = 4.0/h;
for (int y=0; y < h; y++) {
  b = ((double)(y-256))/128;
  for (int x=0; x < w; x++) {
    a = ((double)(x-256))/128;
    p=q=0;
    iter = 0;
    while (iter < 32) { // see if point a,b is in the set
      psq = p*p; qsq = q*q;
      if (psq+qsq >= 4.0) break;
      pnew = psq - qsq + a;
      qnew = 2 * p*q + b;
      p = pnew;
      q = qnew;
      iter++;
    }
    if (iter == 32) {
      pix[index] = 15;// VGA color 15
    } else {
      pix[index] = 4; // VGA color 4
    }
    index++;
  }
}
img = createImage(new MemoryImageSource(w, h, new IndexColorModel(8, 16,
  vGAreds, vGAgreens, vGAblues), pix, 0, w));
g.drawImage(img, 0,0, null);
    }
  }
}
```

To modify the Mandelbrot class to plot VGA-style pixels instead of expensive 32-bit pixels, start by declaring an array of bytes instead of ints, and then change the actual plotting. It is now much simpler to do this, of course: You store color index numbers instead of specifying the color value itself. The `if` statement colors a pixel white (VGA color 15) if it is inside the set and colors all other pixels blue (VGA color 4) for all points outside the `Mandelbrot` set. Then, to convince `drawImage()` to use the VGA-style coloring scheme, you use an explicitly defined color model that allows Java to map your VGA pixels to its own preferred 32-bit style. (`drawImage()` doesn't know anything about VGA.) Since VGA uses a color lookup table mechanism, you create an instance of an `IndexColorModel` that defines this mapping and tell it that your pixels are only 8 bits wide and that the lookup table holds only 16 color entries. The lookup table itself is passed as three separate byte lookup arrays, one for each primary color:

```
new IndexColorModel(8, 16, vGAreds, vGAgreens, vGAblues)
```

TIP

Note that the color byte arrays are filled with some bytes in the range 128–255 using negative values. The Java range for bytes is –128 through +127, because bytes are always signed numbers (like all other numerical types in Java). Literally specifying the unsigned byte value 255, for example, is not possible without using casts. And since using a cast for each item in the arrays would seriously degrade readability, we chose to go negative, using the two's complement scheme. The signed byte –128 is equivalent to the unsigned byte 128. Likewise, –1 is equivalent to 255, and so on.

Since `createImage()` binds this custom color model to the image you are creating, any subsequent `drawImage()` calls will use this color model to translate the custom pixel encoding to whatever the native image subsystem implementation uses (one safe bet is that it will not be using VGA).

If you wanted to eliminate the use of the verbose `IndexColorModel` constructor by subclassing `IndexColorModel` into a `VGAColorModel` class (say, to enhance readability) and using the constructor for the new class instead, something interesting happens to the program. Here is the readability enhancing `VGAColorModel` class:

```
import java.awt.image.IndexColorModel;
public class VGAColorModel extends IndexColorModel {

  final static byte[] vGAreds = {-128, -1, 0, 0, 0, 0, -128, -1, 0,
      0, -128, -1,0,-128,-64, -1};
    final static byte[] vGAgreens = {0, 0, -128, -1, 0, 0, -128, -1, -128,
      -1, 0, 0, 0, -128, -64, -1};
```

```
final static byte[] vGAblues= {0, 0, 0, 0, -128, -1, 0, 0,-128, -1, -128,
    -1,0,-128,-64, -1};

public VGAColorModel() {
    super(8, 16, vGAreds, vGAgreens, vGAblues);
  }
}
```

With this new class, you can now call:

```
new MemoryImageSource(w, h, new VGAColorModel(), pix, 0, w)
```

The unexpected result comes when you run the program again using the new class: It is much slower. The drop in performance cannot have anything to do with the Mandelbrot calculations (since nothing changed here), so the slowdown must be attributed to the drawImage() method. Without the subclass, our VGA Mandelbrot appears on-screen in less than 1 second. Using the subclass, it takes 7.5 seconds!

Why the discrepancy in time? To begin, the core method of class ColorModel is getRGB(). This method is used by the image subsystem to construct in-core images in optimized formats that are native to the platform running your Java programs—for example, BMP format on Windows machines or X-Bitmaps on X-Windows machines. So, for every pixel in your images, whatever their encoding is, the image subsystem needs to invoke the getRGB() method on the associated color model being used for this image. If you could subclass IndexColorModel without overriding this getRGB() method (which you cannot do anyway, because it is declared final in IndexColorModel), Java's dynamic lookup mechanism will fail to find this method in the VGAColorModel class. Undeterred (this is why it is called dynamic), it will then follow the inheritance chain up to the superclass to see if the method is available there, which, sure enough, it is.

Did one paltry extra level of inheritance cause such a huge performance hit? (If it had, Java would be unusable.) The real cause lies in the declaration of the original getRGB() method. It was declared final; that is, you could not override it in subclasses. And final methods are very quick to call (there is no dynamic lookup whatsoever). Your first version did not subclass IndexColorModel, so the getRGB() method was called statically (that is, quickly). Then, you forced this method to be accessed via a dynamic method lookup, clearly showing the difference in the performance of static versus dynamic method binding. And that is the cause for the performance hit. Had the original method not been declared final, the difference would have been far less striking.

The Producer-Consumer Design Pattern

A *design pattern* is a design solution that has been proven to work time and time again. As such, you can use off-the-shelf design patterns in your software (or in construction, electronics, or architecture) with a better than even chance that the design pattern will be a solid foundation for solving the problem at hand (if you pick the right pattern for the type of problem you're dealing with). There are many kinds of design patterns out there, most of which have not yet been identified as such. The realization that the field of software also has its own design patterns is a rather recent development in computer science.

The following are some patterns that have already been identified and are used by the Java API:

Iterator   Embodied by the `Iterator` interface in package `java.util`.

Observer   Embodied by the `Observer` interface and the `Observable` class in package `java.util`.

Composite   Embodied by the AWT classes `Component` and `Container`.

The Iterator and Observer patterns are made available by Java in their most powerful forms: as interfaces. An `Enumeration` does not care what you are enumerating through it, and the `Observer`/`Observable` duo does not care what is being observed or who is doing the observing. Unfortunately, this generality has not been applied within the AWT. Classes `Component` and `Container` are an implementation of the Composite design pattern (which allows a system to handle individual objects or collections of those objects in the same way), but the design pattern itself is not made available to application programmers. It is used within the AWT, but not "exported," as are the `java.util` design patterns.

Package `java.awt.image` also relies on a common design pattern (again without making available the guts of the abstraction): the Producer-Consumer design pattern. As with so many of these patterns, the focus lies on decoupling systems. Decoupling is a powerful technique used to introduce more flexibility into a system.

NOTE   You saw a strong example of decoupling in this chapter with the `draw-Image()`method of `Graphics`. It decouples (internally) the drawing of an image from the image's data source.

The image Producer-Consumer design pattern is enforced using two interfaces: `ImageProducer` and `ImageConsumer`. Concrete classes that implement these interfaces are symbiotically linked together to form an image-generation pipeline. An `ImageProducer` is nothing without an `ImageConsumer`, and vice versa. This bidirectional dependence is defined by the methods each calls on the other.

Here are the definitions for both interfaces, since neither can be explained in isolation:

```
public interface ImageProducer {
  public abstract void addConsumer(ImageConsumer ic);
  public abstract boolean isConsumer(ImageConsumer ic);
  public abstract void removeConsumer(ImageConsumer ic);
  public abstract void requestTopDownLeftRightResend(ImageConsumer ic);
  public abstract void startProduction(ImageConsumer ic);
}
public interface ImageConsumer {
  public static final int COMPLETESCANLINES;
  public static final int IMAGEABORTED;
  public static final int IMAGEERROR;
  public static final int RANDOMPIXELORDER;
  public static final int SINGLEFRAME;
  public static final int SINGLEFRAMEDONE;
  public static final int SINGLEPASS;
  public static final int STATICIMAGEDONE;
  public static final int TOPDOWNLEFTRIGHT;
  public abstract void imageComplete(int status);
  public abstract void setColorModel(ColorModel model);
  public abstract void setDimensions(int width, int height);
  public abstract void setHints(int hintflags);
  public abstract void setPixels(int x, int y, int w, int h, ColorModel model,
    byte pixels[], int off, int scansize);
  public abstract void setPixels(int x, int y, int w, int h, ColorModel model,
    int pixels[], int off, int scansize);
  public abstract void setProperties(Hashtable props);
}
```

If you recall the Observable-Observer design pattern explained in Chapter 9, then you should have no problem understanding this pair; there is a strong similarity between the two design patterns. While the loose coupling of the Observable-Observer duo consists of a simple notification implemented by an invocation of the `update()` observer method, with image Producer-Consumer pairs there is actual (and substantial) data transfer of image data. This is achieved in much the same way as with the Observable-Observer pair: the `ImageProducer` calls methods on the `ImageConsumer` to transfer image data and other information. The main method is `setPixels()`. Here is this method's signature (the types of all the `int` arguments have been stripped out to fit the whole signature on one line):

```
void setPixels(x,y, w,h, ColorModel model, byte pixels[], off, scansize)
```

When an `ImageProducer` wants to transfer some image data it has produced to an `ImageConsumer`, it invokes the `setPixels()` method on that consumer. The arguments tell the consumer which subrectangle is being transferred (the *x,y* and *w,h* arguments) and what that rectangle contains as pixels. In practice, these subrectangles will almost always be complete, consecutive strips of the picture. An `ImageProducer` that produced its data as a patchwork collage of rectangles would be rather strange. (There is, however, nothing to stop a producer from having such image-production dynamics, and it would not be an error.)

This image data is specified as a one-dimensional array of pixels (`byte` or `int`), an offset into that array, and the size of a horizontal (scan) line of the image. The consumer requires the `scansize` argument in cases when the rectangle being transferred is narrower than the width of the picture. To extract the individual lines from the subrectangle correctly, the consumer must skip bytes in the array to go to the next line of the subrectangle. The amount to skip is calculated as `scansize-w`.

How does an `ImageProducer` know which `ImageConsumer` it should hand image data to and when? Here, the responsibility lies with the consumer. It creates the producer-consumer connection by announcing itself to an `ImageProducer` as being interested in receiving image data, by calling the `addConsumer()` method on the producer. The consumer also starts the image factory rolling by calling the `startProduction()` `ImageProducer` method.

As you can guess from the other methods in both interfaces, there is quite a bit more to the protocol between these two partners. But here is a concrete example. You have already manipulated an `ImageProducer` in one of the examples earlier in this chapter. Class `MemoryImageSource`, which was used to generate the Mandelbrot image, is an `ImageProducer`, because it implements the `ImageProducer` interface. If you look back at its definition, you will see that it has the five required interface methods. So, somewhere in the Mandelbrot program, you should have its inseparable `ImageConsumer`, too. While it is not stated explicitly anywhere, the image created with the `createImage()` method internally uses an `ImageConsumer` for the image data it represents. This hidden consumer will activate the producer-consumer protocol at some later point, when a `drawImage()` is done on an `Image`.

There are several benefits to having this decoupling between image data and the entities that actually use this data:

- The path between image data and image user (consumer) can be of arbitrary complexity and therefore very flexible. If `createImage()` took a pointer to a pixel bitmap in memory, your options would be rather limited. But since it takes a reference to an `ImageProducer` instead, the data can come from anywhere.

- The image transfer from producer to consumer can be asynchronous. Although the consumer starts the image-production process, it does not control the sequence of image subrectangles produced or their timing. This is the producer's province.

- You can create image-processing pipelines. This is achieved by having classes that are both producer and consumer—consumer of some previous stage's output and producer of the next stage's input. A possible pipeline is depicted in Figure 10.16.

FIGURE 10.16:

An image-processing pipeline

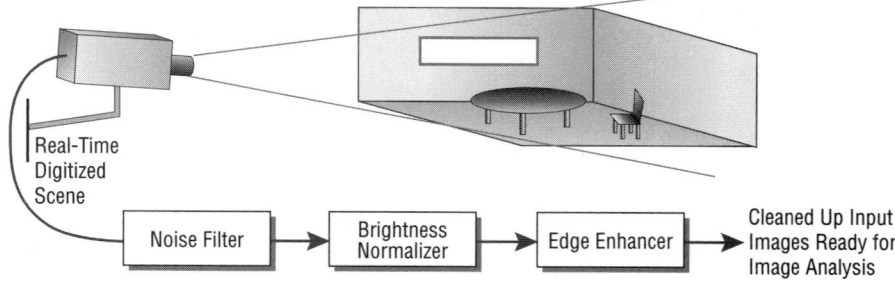

Each stage in an image-processing pipeline is usually called a filter. Java's `java.awt.image` package includes explicit support for such filters. The next section explores the classes that deal with image filtering.

TIP

The Producer-Consumer design pattern is just one of many patterns described in the excellent reference book *Design Patterns,* by Gamma, Helm, Johnson, and Vlissides (published by Addison-Wesley).

Image Filtering

The generic term image *filtering* is almost synonymous with image processing. One of the core image-processing techniques is filtering (that is, altering) an image pixel by pixel, although the term is used in the wider sense of image manipulation as well. Pixel-by-pixel processing of images is supported by several classes in java.awt.image.

First of all, there is class FilteredImageSource, which like MemoryImageSource is an ImageProducer:

```
public class FilteredImageSource extends Object implements ImageProducer {
    public FilteredImageSource(ImageProducer orig, ImageFilter imgf);
    public synchronized void addConsumer(ImageConsumer ic);
    public synchronized boolean isConsumer(ImageConsumer ic);
    public synchronized void removeConsumer(ImageConsumer ic);
    public void requestTopDownLeftRightResend(ImageConsumer ic);
    public void startProduction(ImageConsumer ic);
}
```

The key to understanding this class is its constructor: Instead of taking an array of pixels (as with MemoryImageSource), this class takes another ImageProducer plus a filter object to combine the two into a new, filtered image. The filter object must be of type ImageFilter, of which five concrete subclasses are provided in the java.awt.image package: CropImageFilter, RGBImageFilter, Replicate-ScaleFilter, AreaAveragingScaleFilter, and BufferedImageFilter. There is a sixth filter, GrayFilter, in the com.sun.java.swing package.

Using the CropImageFilter subclass, you can create sub-images of a bigger image. With RGBImageFilter, you can filter the colors of an image either pixel by pixel or—if the image uses a CLUT color model—in bulk by simply modifying the image's palette. (GrayFilter is a specialized RGBImageFilter.) With Replicate-ScaleFilter and AreaAveragingScaleFilter, you can rescale an image. (Area-AveragingScaleFilter is a subclass of ReplicateScaleFilter that uses a faster algorithm.) BufferedImageFilter permits single-input/single-output operations where the output is the BufferedImage input. More on BufferedImage-Filter in Chapter 11.

The following program demonstrates the use of the RGBImageFilter and Crop-ImageFilter filters on a color image file. The RGBImageFilter is used to implement a color-to-gray filter, and the CropImageFilter is used to cut a 40 × 40-pixel sub-image from the original, which is then pasted back onto the original, magnified to three times its original size. The magnification is achieved simply by specifying a final image size of 120 × 120 pixels. Figure 10.17 shows the resulting output window.

```java
import java.awt.*;
import java.awt.image.*;

public class Filters extends java.applet.Applet {
  Image oldImage, newImage, subImage;
  ImageProducer filtered, cropped;
  public void init() {
    oldImage = getImage(getDocumentBase(), "market.gif");
    filtered = new FilteredImageSource(oldImage.getSource(),
      new GrayFilter());
    cropped= new FilteredImageSource(oldImage.getSource(),
      new CropImageFilter (300,70,40,40));

    newImage = createImage(filtered);
    subImage = createImage(cropped);
  }
  public void paint(Graphics g) {
    if (newImage != null)
      g.drawImage(newImage, 0, 0, this);
    g.clearRect(20,20,140,140);
    if (subImage != null)
      g.drawImage(subImage, 30, 30, 120, 120, this);

    System.out.println(".");
  }
  static class GrayFilter extends RGBImageFilter {
    public GrayFilter() {
      canFilterIndexColorModel = true;
    }
    public int filterRGB(int x, int y, int rgb) {
      int alpha,r,g,b;
      int gray;
      alpha = rgb & (0xFF << 24);
      r = (rgb >> 16) & 0xFF;
      g = (rgb >>8) & 0xFF;
      b = (rgb >>0) & 0xFF;
      gray= (r+g+b)/3;
      return alpha | gray<<16 | gray<<8 | gray;
    }
  }
}
```

FIGURE 10.17:

Use of ImageFilters on an orginal color picture

This program loads the image file using a getImage() call and then creates two new images based on the original. Both derived images are obtained using the FilteredImageSource class to combine the picture with a filter. For the grayscale version of the picture, an instance of the GrayFilter that was subclassed from RGB-ImageFilter is used. For the sub-image, an instance of a CropImageFilter is used (there is no need to subclass it). The two new FilteredImageSource objects are not yet images that can be passed to drawImage(). Since FilteredImageSource objects are only ImageProducers, you need to turn them into images with the two calls to createImage(). All of these steps should be done only once, so they are located in the applet's init() method. The actual drawing of the applet is done in the paint() method, where both processed images are drawn using drawImage() invocations.

The GrayFilter color filter has two aspects to it: the overridden filterRGB() method and the constructor. Method filterRGB() is called with individual pixels to be processed. The x and y parameters received by the filterRGB()method are the coordinates of the pixel to be processed. Because you do not need to use these coordinates (the color filter is pixel position-independent), you signal the outside world that this RGBImageFilter can short-circuit the bulk filtering of an image's pixels by simply filtering its palette only. This is much faster than processing every single pixel of an Image, which makes the simple canFilterIndex-ColorModel = true; assignment well worth the effort of creating the custom constructor.

Although the filtering architecture supported by the classes you have seen so far can be used for many filtering tasks, some image-filtering algorithms need to access arbitrary source-image pixels to determine the output value of any given pixel. For this type of filter, you'll examine the BufferedImageOp interface in Chapter 11 to perform operations like convolution of an Image, allowing neighboring pixels to affect the filtering operation. While this type of filter is available directly with ImageFilter, the ImageFilter class cannot handle this easily.

Summary

This chapter dealt with a lot of graphics-related material, beginning with the basics: graphics-rendering primitives and how to manipulate Graphics contexts. Then you had a look at animation and the key requirements for any good animation: absence of flicker and high frame rates. You learned how double buffering can eliminate all flicker, which led to an exploration of the complex Image AWT subsystem. Although easily accessible to application programmers, asynchronous background loading of images is not entirely transparent to the application level and might require the use of MediaTracker and other safeguards for robust implementations. You also explored the image-processing aspects of the java.awt.image package through the core metaphor of image producer-consumer pairs and the classes—MemoryImageSource, FilteredImageSource, PixelGrabber—that, in one way or other, implement the metaphor.

2D Graphics and Imaging

- Graphics processing

- Text processing

- Image handling

- Graphics device hookups

- Color management

The Java 2D API, introduced with JDK 1.2, greatly expands on the graphical capabilities available with Java. While earlier versions of Java allowed you to do things like draw lines, you were forced to draw single color lines that were one pixel wide. If you wanted anything more, you had to do it yourself. Now, with the 2D API, many advanced graphics and imaging capabilities exist for doing two-dimensional graphics that should keep almost everyone happy.

The Java 2D API is part of the Java Media APIs of Java. It is the only API that comes standard with the JDK. The remaining Java Media APIs are currently either still under development or not a core API and available separately as a standard extension. In addition to Java 2D, Java Media currently consists of the Java 3D, Java Advanced Imaging, Java Media Framework, Java Sound, Java Speech, and Java Telephony APIs.

There are five areas where the Java 2D API enhances Java's graphical and imaging capabilities. These include graphics processing, where you can now control things like the fill pattern or line style; text processing, where you have advanced text layout control; image handling, where filtering and formatting capabilities are enhanced; support for graphics device hookups, with additional printing capabilities available; and color management where support for arbitrary color spaces exists. The support for all these capabilities can be found in bits and pieces of the following packages: `java.awt`, `java.awt.color`, `java.awt.font`, `java.awt.geom`, `java.awt.image`, and `java.awt.image.renderable`.

Graphics Processing

The Java 2D API extends Java's support for basic drawing operations. While you could draw arcs, ovals, rectangles, and polygons before, with the basic `Graphics` class, the only options were the colors to use for the outline and fill. You could not draw anything transparently, nor could you do much else, without resorting to plotting points. Here, we'll take a look at how the `Graphics2D` class now enables enhanced graphics processing.

Moving to Graphics2D

Drawing in Java involves a basic three-step approach:

- Specify the drawing attributes with methods like setColor(), setFont(), setPaintMode(), and setXORMode()

- Identify the shape to draw

- Draw it

In the Graphics world, without the Java 2D API, the identification and drawing parts are somewhat interconnected. The drawing process involves identifying the bounding rectangle of the shape to draw while calling a specific method for each shape to draw (possibly with some shape-specific attributes like arc angles).

Drawing with Graphics2D involves the same three-step approach. However, the identification and drawing of the shape are somewhat different. In the general case, you specify a shape to draw by creating an object that implements the Shape interface. If you wanted to live in a world where everything was specified like a Polygon, you would identify individual coordinates of the shape with a GeneralPath. To draw the more common shapes there are several classes available that implement Shape. For instance, the Arc2D class would be used to draw an arc. Other 2D classes that implement Shape are Line2D, Rectangle2D, RoundRectangle2D, Ellipse2D, QuadCurve2D, and CubicCurve2D. The Shape interface has been around since Java 1.1, however its definition changed with Java 1.2. The current definition is shown below.

```
public interface Shape {
  public abstract boolean contains(double x, double y);
  public abstract boolean contains(double x, double y, double w, double h);
  public abstract boolean contains(Point2D p);
  public abstract boolean contains(Rectangle2D r);
  public abstract Rectangle getBounds();
  public abstract Rectangle2D getBounds2D();
  public abstract PathIterator getPathIterator(AffineTransform at);
  public abstract PathIterator getPathIterator(AffineTransform at,
    double flatness);
  public abstract boolean intersects(double x, double y, double w,
    double h);
  public abstract boolean intersects(Rectangle2D r);
}
```

Once you've identified the shape to draw, it is then time to draw it. This is done with one of three Graphics2D methods: clip(), draw(), or fill(); each taking a Shape object as its parameter. The clip() method would be used to shrink the drawing area down to the intersection of the specified shape with the current clipping area, affecting future drawing operations. The draw() method uses the current Stroke to draw the outline of the Shape. And the fill() method uses the current Paint pattern to fill in the Shape. All of these permit the drawing operations to go through an AffineTransform to map the current 2D coordinate space to a new one. This permits operations like drawing a rotating rectangle to be done fairly easily. You can also specify a Composite interface implementer to define how existing pixels are combined with the drawing color during the various operations.

NOTE   In addition to drawing geometric shapes, you can treat drawn text as a Shape, too, through TextLayout. We'll look at TextLayout later.

Before creating a program to demonstrate these capabilities, let's take a look at the Graphics2D class definition:

```
public abstract class Graphics2D extends Graphics {
  protected Graphics2D();
  public abstract void clip(Shape s);
  public abstract void draw(Shape s);
  public abstract void drawGlyphVector(GlyphVector, float, float);
  public abstract boolean drawImage(Image img, AffineTransform xform,
    ImageObserver obs);
  public abstract void drawImage(BufferedImage img, BufferedImageOp op,
    int x, int y);
  public abstract void drawRenderableImage(RenderableImage img,
    AffineTransform xform);
  public abstract void drawRenderedImage(RenderedImage img,
    AffineTransform xform);
  public abstract void drawString(String str, float x, float y);
  public abstract void drawString(String str, int x, int y);
  public abstract void drawString(AttributedCharacterIterator iterator,
    float x, float y);
  public abstract void drawString(AttributedCharacterIterator iterator,
    int x, int y);
  public abstract void fill(Shape s);
  public abstract Color getBackground();
```

```
    public abstract Composite getComposite();
    public abstract GraphicsConfiguration getDeviceConfiguration();
    public abstract FontRenderContext getFontRenderContext();
    public abstract Paint getPaint();
    public abstract Object getRenderingHint(String hintKey);
    public abstract RenderingHints getRenderingHints();
    public abstract Stroke getStroke();
    public abstract AffineTransform getTransform();
    public abstract boolean hit(Rectangle rect, Shape s, boolean onStroke);
    public abstract void rotate(double theta);
    public abstract void rotate(double theta, double x, double y);
    public abstract void scale(double sx, double sy);
    public abstract void setBackground(Color c);
    public abstract void setComposite(Composite comp);
    public abstract void setPaint(Paint paint);
    public abstract void setRenderingHint(String hintKey, Object hintValue);
    public abstract void setRenderingHints(RenderingHints hints);
    public abstract void setStroke(Stroke stroke);
    public abstract void setTransform(AffineTransform xform);
    public abstract void shear(double shx, double shy);
    public abstract void transform(AffineTransform xform);
    public abstract void translate(double tx, double ty);
    public abstract void translate(int tx, int ty);
}
```

While some methods may look similar to the plain Graphics class—since it does subclass Graphics this shouldn't seem strange—most of the operations are new and different. We'll now create a program to show the simplest case of using Graphics2D to draw a rectangle from a GeneralPath and an arc through Arc2D. As we progress through the remaining capabilities of Graphics2D, we'll enhance the output shown in Figure 11.1 somewhat.

FIGURE 11.1:

Rectangle and Arc through Graphics2D

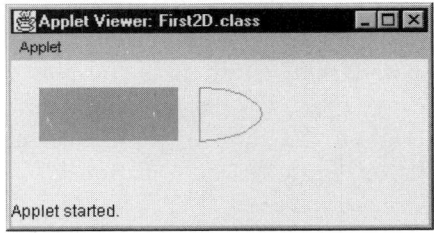

The program behind Figure 11.1 is shown next.

```java
import java.awt.*;
import java.awt.geom.*;

public class First2D extends java.applet.Applet {
  public void paint (Graphics g) {
    Graphics2D g2d = (Graphics2D)g;

    // Set Attributes
    g2d.setColor (Color.cyan);

    // Define each shape
    GeneralPath rectangle = new GeneralPath (GeneralPath.WIND_EVEN_ODD);
    rectangle.moveTo (20f, 20f);
    rectangle.lineTo (120f, 20f);
    rectangle.lineTo (120f, 60f);
    rectangle.lineTo (20f, 60f);
    rectangle.closePath();

    Arc2D arc = new Arc2D.Double (90, 20, 90, 40, 270, 180, Arc2D.CHORD);

    // Draw shape
    g2d.fill (rectangle);
    g2d.draw (arc);
  }
}
```

Two things you may be wondering about here are the parameter to the General-Path constructor and the last parameter to the Arc2D.Double constructor. With regard to GeneralPath, the parameter defines the rule used to determine when a point is within the shape. The two options are WIND_EVEN_ODD and WIND_NON_ZERO. The even/odd winding rule says a point is within a shape if there are an odd number of intersections between itself and the outer limits of the shape. If even, it is outside. The non-zero winding rule draws a ray from the point to check and traverses the shape's path, counting the number of times the ray is passed along the way. If the ray is passed the same number of times from left to right along the path as from right to left, then the point is outside the shape. The rules exhibit different results, as Figure 11.2 demonstrates.

FIGURE 11.2:

Comparing even/odd with
non-zero winding rules

As far as Arc2D goes, there are three types of arcs you can create: CHORD, OPEN, and PIE. As shown, CHORD draws an arc and connects the endpoints with a straight line. OPEN leaves the endpoints unconnected, while PIE connects the endpoints like a pie chart through the center point.

Configurable Stroking Parameters

If you associate a Stroke to the Graphics2D object, with setStroke(), you can change the pattern used to draw the outside border of the shape. Stroke itself is a simple interface, shown next.

```java
public interface Stroke {
    public abstract Shape createStrokedShape(Shape s);
}
```

And, the BasicStroke class implements the interface for you, making changing the associated Stroke rather easy. Through the various constructors, you can change the default one-pixel-width line connected by square end caps to be practically any single color line with a variety of different end caps.

```java
public class BasicStroke extends Object implements Stroke {
    public static final int CAP_BUTT;
    public static final int CAP_ROUND;
    public static final int CAP_SQUARE;
    public static final int JOIN_BEVEL;
    public static final int JOIN_MITER;
    public static final int JOIN_ROUND;
    public BasicStroke();
    public BasicStroke(float width);
    public BasicStroke(float width, int cap, int join);
    public BasicStroke(float width, int cap, int join, float miterLimit);
```

```
    public BasicStroke(float width, int cap, int join, float miterLimit,
        float dash[], float dashPhase);
    public Shape createStrokedShape(Shape s);
    public boolean equals(Object obj);
    public float[] getDashArray();
    public float getDashPhase();
    public int getEndCap();
    public int getLineJoin();
    public float getLineWidth();
    public float getMiterLimit();
}
```

To demonstrate BasicStroke, we'll add a solid blue stroke around the rectangle from Figure 11.1 and place a dashed stroke around the arc. To stroke the outline of the rectangle, we fill it, then draw it, changing the stroke in between. Notice we've also changed the program to use the easier Rectangle2D class. To place a dashed stroke around the arc, you need to specify how you want the dash ends to appear and join, as well as the dash separation and dash size. This is shown in Figure 11.3 below.

FIGURE 11.3:

Changing the stroke pattern

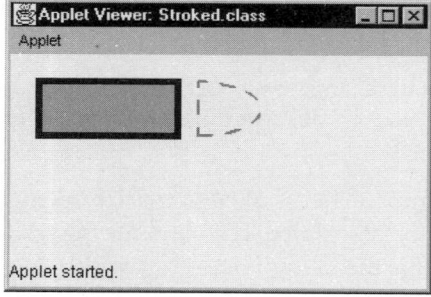

The following shows the source code used to generate Figure 11.3.

```
import java.awt.*;
import java.awt.geom.*;

public class Stroked extends java.applet.Applet {
    public void paint (Graphics g) {
        Graphics2D g2d = (Graphics2D)g;

        // Rectangle
        Rectangle2D rectangle = new Rectangle2D.Double (20, 20, 100, 40);
```

```
   g2d.setColor (Color.cyan);
   g2d.fill (rectangle);
   g2d.setColor (Color.blue);
   g2d.setStroke(new BasicStroke(5f));
   g2d.draw (rectangle);

   // Arc
   g2d.setColor (Color.green);
   g2d.setStroke (new BasicStroke(2f, BasicStroke.CAP_ROUND,
     BasicStroke.JOIN_ROUND, 3f, new float[] {10f}, 0f));
   Arc2D arc = new Arc2D.Double (90, 20, 90, 40, 270, 180, Arc2D.CHORD);
   g2d.draw (arc);
   }
}
```

Since we haven't shown how clip() works yet, let's move the arc over the rectangle, so that the only part drawn is the intersection of the two. This would involve clipping with the arc first, to define the drawing area to be used when drawing the rectangle. Notice that neither the color nor the stroke defined when the arc is clipped has any bearing on the drawn rectangle. These are drawing attributes, not part of the shape definition. Since the arc is never drawn (with draw() or fill()), these settings are ignored. Figure 11.4 shows the result of this concoction.

FIGURE 11.4:

Clipping what is drawn

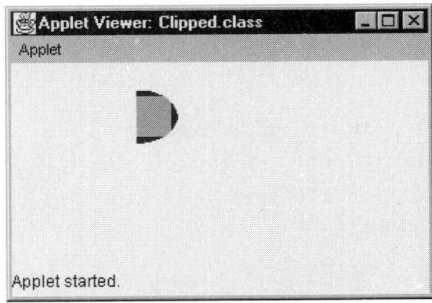

The program that generated Figure 11.4 follows:

```
import java.awt.*;
import java.awt.geom.*;

public class Clipped extends java.applet.Applet {
  public void paint (Graphics g) {
```

```
Graphics2D g2d = (Graphics2D)g;

// Arc
g2d.setColor (Color.green);
g2d.setStroke (new BasicStroke(2f, BasicStroke.CAP_ROUND,
  BasicStroke.JOIN_ROUND, 3f, new float[] {10f}, 0f));
Arc2D arc = new Arc2D.Double (60, 20, 60, 40, 270, 180, Arc2D.CHORD);
g2d.clip (arc);

// Rectangle
Rectangle2D rectangle = new Rectangle2D.Double (20, 20, 100, 40);
g2d.setColor (Color.cyan);
g2d.fill (rectangle);
g2d.setColor (Color.blue);
g2d.setStroke(new BasicStroke(10f));
g2d.draw (rectangle);

  }
}
```

Arbitrary Fill Styles

Now that we've changed the stroking pattern of the drawing outline, let's see how we can also change the fill pattern. The Java 2D API supports both cyclic and acyclic gradient fills as well as matting of images and retains the ability to fill with solid colors. Java defines the Paint interface to deal with fill styles, and Color, GradientPaint, and TexturePaint are the implementers.

For painting with a solid color, you can still use the setColor() method inherited from Graphics. For consistency with the other two painting mechanisms you'll soon learn about, when working with Graphics2D, you should use the new setPaint() method. For instance, to paint in blue you would call set-Paint (Color.blue).

Gradient painting involves gradually changing one color to another. Through the GradientPaint class, you no longer have to do the conversion yourself. All you have to do is tell the class the starting and ending point and colors. Then, when you call the fill() method of Graphics2D, it gradually changes the color at the starting point to the color at the ending point. If the area asked to fill goes beyond the rectangle formed by the starting and ending points, there is an optional boolean parameter. When this parameter is specified, a true value means the gradient should cycle. If the value is false, then the colors are solid in the two directions that go away from the bounded area—the default behavior. Figure 11.5 demonstrates the three possible outcomes: no optional parameter, `true` optional parameter, and `false` optional parameter. You can specify the endpoints by either using two sets of floating point numbers for endpoints or using two `Point2D` objects. To help show where the actual points are in the different areas drawn, a black line is drawn to connect them.

FIGURE 11.5:

The three gradient fill options

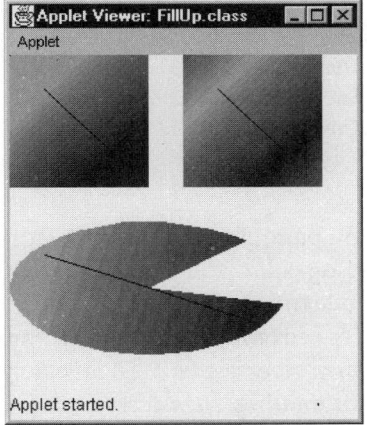

The following program generated the three possible gradients shown in Figure 11.5. Notice that the first and third fill options are really the same.

```java
import java.awt.*;
import java.awt.geom.*;

public class FillUp extends java.applet.Applet {
  public void paint (Graphics g) {
    Graphics2D g2d = (Graphics2D)g;

    GradientPaint gp = new GradientPaint (25, 25, Color.cyan, 75, 75,
Color.blue);
    g2d.setPaint (gp);
    Rectangle2D rectangle = new Rectangle2D.Double (0, 0, 100, 100);
    g2d.fill (rectangle);

    gp = new GradientPaint (150, 25, Color.cyan, 200, 75, Color.blue, true);
    g2d.setPaint (gp);
    rectangle = new Rectangle2D.Double (125, 0, 100, 100);
```

```
        g2d.fill (rectangle);

        Point2D p2d1 = new Point2D.Float (25, 150);
        Point2D p2d2 = new Point2D.Float (175, 200);
        gp = new GradientPaint (p2d1, Color.cyan, p2d2, Color.blue, false);
        g2d.setPaint (gp);
        Arc2D arc = new Arc2D.Double (0, 125, 200, 100, 45, 300, Arc2D.PIE);
        g2d.fill (arc);

        g.setColor (Color.black);
        g.drawLine (25, 25, 75, 75);
        g.drawLine (150, 25, 200, 75);
        g.drawLine (25, 150, 175, 200);
    }
}
```

Texture painting is similar to gradient painting. However, instead of a starting and ending color, you provide a `BufferedImage` and area to use as the texture: `TexturePaint(BufferedImage texture, Rectangle2D rect)`. Since the texture is a `BufferedImage`, you can draw anything you want onto it, from text to image files to any other content. The rectangle specifies the piece of the `BufferedImage` to use for matting, so you could draw a large figure and crop a small piece out of it. Figure 11.6 demonstrates an image as the texture to use when filling a shape. Since the texture doesn't change between calls to `paint()`, it is best created outside of `paint()` so the image file is only fetched once.

FIGURE 11.6:

Filling shapes with an image texture

The program that generated Figure 11.6 follows. The image file used for the texture can be found on the CD-ROM, or you can use your own image file.

```java
import java.awt.*;
import java.awt.geom.*;
import java.awt.image.*;
import java.net.URL;

public class TextureIt extends java.applet.Applet {

  TexturePaint tp = getImageTexture ("sybex.gif");

  public TexturePaint getImageTexture(String imageFile) {
    URL url = getClass().getResource("sybex.gif");
    Image img = getToolkit().getImage(url);
    try {
      MediaTracker tracker = new MediaTracker(this);
      tracker.addImage(img, 0);
      tracker.waitForID(0);
    } catch (Exception e) {
    }
    int width = img.getWidth(this);
    int height = img.getHeight(this);
    BufferedImage buffImg =
      new BufferedImage(width, height, BufferedImage.TYPE_INT_ARGB);
    Graphics g = buffImg.getGraphics();
    g.drawImage(img, 0, 0, this);
    Rectangle2D rect = new Rectangle(0, 0, width, height);
    return new TexturePaint(buffImg, rect);
  }

  public void paint (Graphics g) {
    Graphics2D g2d = (Graphics2D)g;

    g2d.setPaint (tp);
    Rectangle2D rectangle = new Rectangle2D.Double (0, 0, 200, 100);
    g2d.fill (rectangle);

    Arc2D arc = new Arc2D.Double (0, 125, 200, 100, 45, 300, Arc2D.PIE);
    g2d.fill (arc);
  }
}
```

Antialiased Rendering

Antialiasing is a way to get rid of the jagged edges that happen when you draw pixels within a raster grid. If you try to scale something from a small finely drawn image to one much larger, you'll notice a staircase effect with any horizontal lines. Even without scaling, you may notice the jaggies.

When you draw something antialiased, there is a performance cost. It is also possible that the display device won't support antialiasing. Because of these two characteristics, enabling antialiasing is done through a rendering hint, which could be ignored by the display device. You use the `RenderingHints` class, shown here, to specify rendering hints.

```
public class RenderingHints extends Object implements Cloneable {
    public static final String KEY_ALPHA_INTERPOLATION;
    public static final String KEY_ANTIALIASING;
    public static final String KEY_COLOR_RENDERING;
    public static final String KEY_DITHERING;
    public static final String KEY_FRACTIONALMETRICS;
    public static final String KEY_INTERPOLATION;
    public static final String KEY_RENDERING;
    public static final String KEY_TEXT_ANTIALIASING;
    public static final String VALUE_ALPHA_INTERPOLATION_DEFAULT;
    public static final String VALUE_ALPHA_INTERPOLATION_QUALITY;
    public static final String VALUE_ALPHA_INTERPOLATION_SPEED;
    public static final String VALUE_ANTIALIAS_DEFAULT;
    public static final String VALUE_ANTIALIAS_OFF;
    public static final String VALUE_ANTIALIAS_ON;
    public static final String VALUE_COLOR_RENDER_DEFAULT;
    public static final String VALUE_COLOR_RENDER_QUALITY;
    public static final String VALUE_COLOR_RENDER_SPEED;
    public static final String VALUE_DITHER_DEFAULT;
    public static final String VALUE_DITHER_DISABLE;
    public static final String VALUE_DITHER_ENABLE;
    public static final String VALUE_FRACTIONALMETRICS_DEFAULT;
    public static final String VALUE_FRACTIONALMETRICS_OFF;
    public static final String VALUE_FRACTIONALMETRICS_ON;
    public static final String VALUE_INTERPOLATION_BICUBIC;
    public static final String VALUE_INTERPOLATION_BILINEAR;
    public static final String VALUE_INTERPOLATION_NEAREST_NEIGHBOR;
    public static final String VALUE_RENDER_DEFAULT;
    public static final String VALUE_RENDER_QUALITY;
    public static final String VALUE_RENDER_SPEED;
    public static final String VALUE_TEXT_ANTIALIAS_DEFAULT;
    public static final String VALUE_TEXT_ANTIALIAS_OFF;
```

```
        public static final String VALUE_TEXT_ANTIALIAS_ON;
        public RenderingHints(String key, Object value);
        public synchronized Object clone();
        public Object get(String key);
        public synchronized Enumeration keys();
        public Object put(String key, Object value);
        public synchronized Object remove(String key);
        public synchronized String toString();
    }
```

All the methods of the RenderingHints class can, for the most part, be ignored. You just tell the Graphics2D instance to setRenderingHint(), where the first parameter is a key and the second parameter is the appropriate setting. In the case of antialiasing, KEY_ANTIALIASING would be the key and the setting would be one of VALUE_ANTIALIAS_OFF or VALUE_ANTIALIAS_ON (or VALUE_ANTIALIAS_DEFAULT, which is a platform-specific default, usually off). All of the hints follow this naming convention, so it is easy to see which keys and values go together.

Figure 11.7 demonstrates the use of setting rendering hints, specifically antialiasing. Notice that both the shape and text drawn is antialiased.

FIGURE 11.7:

Antialiasing: left is disabled, right is enabled

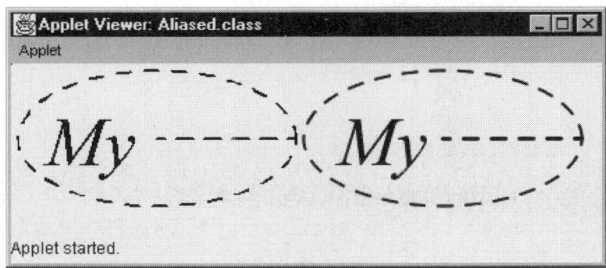

The following program generated the two ovals and text drawn in Figure 11.7.

```java
import java.awt.*;
import java.awt.geom.*;

public class Aliased extends java.applet.Applet {
    public void paint (Graphics g) {
        Graphics2D g2d = (Graphics2D)g;

        g2d.setColor (Color.black);
        g2d.setStroke (new BasicStroke(2f, BasicStroke.CAP_ROUND,
            BasicStroke.JOIN_ROUND, 3f, new float[] {10f}, 0f));
        Arc2D arc = new Arc2D.Double (5, 5, 200, 100, 0, 360, Arc2D.PIE);
```

```
        g2d.draw (arc);
        g2d.setFont (new Font ("Serif", Font.ITALIC, 50));
        g2d.drawString ("My", 25, 75);
        g2d.setRenderingHint(RenderingHints.KEY_ANTIALIASING,
          RenderingHints.VALUE_ANTIALIAS_ON);
        arc = new Arc2D.Double (210, 5, 200, 100, 0, 360, Arc2D.PIE);
        g2d.draw (arc);
        g2d.drawString ("My", 235, 75);
    }
  }
```

If you wanted only the text to be drawn antialiased, you would change the setRenderingHint() line to the following:

```
g2d.setRenderingHint(RenderingHints.KEY_TEXT_ANTIALIASING,
  RenderingHints.VALUE_TEXT_ANTIALIAS_ON);
```

Drawing Curves

While you've previously seen how to draw an arc with the Arc2D class, there are several other means of drawing curved shapes within the Java 2D API. These involve the Ellipse2D, QuadCurve2D, and CubicCurve2D classes, as well as the quadTo() and curveTo() methods of the GeneralPath class. Technically speaking, you can also use the lineTo() method of GeneralPath. However, this would require you to calculate each point manually or have a very straight curve.

Curve Classes

Using the four curve classes allows you to create most of the necessary general curve shapes. The Arc2D and Ellipse2D work like the similar functions in the regular Graphics object. You still work from the bounding rectangle, but instead of using the drawArc(), fillArc(), drawOval(), and fillOval() methods, you create either an Arc2D or Ellipse2D shape and tell the Graphics2D object to draw() or fill() it. Creating an instance is done through one of two subclasses of each. Creating an Arc2D is done with either an Arc2D.Float or Arc2D.Double. Ellipse2D has two similarly named subclasses in Ellipse2D.Float and Ellipse2D.Double. The Float subclasses store the defining values with the precision of a float, while the Double subclasses use double precision.

The Arc2D or Ellipse2D classes (as well as Rectangle2D and RoundRectangle2D) are all subclasses of the abstract RectangularShape class, shown here.

```
public abstract class RectangularShape extends Object
    implements Shape, Cloneable {
```

```
public Object clone();
public boolean contains(Point2D p2d);
public boolean contains(Rectangle2D r2d);
public Rectangle getBounds();
public double getCenterX();
public double getCenterY();
public Rectangle2D getFrame();
public abstract double getHeight();
public double getMaxX();
public double getMaxY();
public double getMinX();
public double getMinY();
public PathIterator getPathIterator(AffineTransform at, double flatness);
public abstract double getWidth();
public abstract double getX();
public abstract double getY();
public boolean intersects(Rectangle2D r2d);
public abstract boolean isEmpty();
public abstract void setFrame(double x, double y, double w, double h);
public void setFrame(Point2D loc, Dimension2D size);
public void setFrame(Rectangle2D r2d);
public void setFrameFromCenter(double centerX, double centerY,
    double cornerX, double cornerY);
public void setFrameFromCenter(Point2D center, Point2D corner);
public void setFrameFromDiagonal(double x1, double y1, double x2,
    double y2);
public void setFrameFromDiagonal(Point2D p1, Point2D p2);
}
```

While there are many things inherited by all the subclasses, the important things to point out are the many setFrameXXX methods. These provide different ways to change the bounding rectangle; the setFrameFromCenter() methods are especially interesting as they allow you to actually work from a center point (and a corner, but not a radius).

NOTE   Rectangle2D or RoundRectangle2D have not been explained specifically, but their usage is practically identical to the Graphics usage with drawRect(), fillRect(), drawRoundRect(), and fillRoundRect(). With the RoundRectangle2D, you just have to remember to pass in the horizontal and vertical diameters of the arc of the four corners.

The QuadCurve2D and CubicCurve2D classes are different from the other curve classes in that they do not describe closed shapes, but instead describe a curved line. The QuadCurve2D class creates second-order curves using a quadratic formula, while the CubicCurve2D class creates third-order cubic curves. The cubic curve class uses a concept called Bezier curves to define the actual points on the curved line. After creating the curved line, you would then either draw() or fill() it. In the fill() case, you can think of the starting and ending point as connected to give you a closed region.

TIP

Bezier curves are continuous curves that have great mathematical properties, which go well beyond the scope of this book. If interested in learning more about Bezier curves, consider reading *Computer Graphics for Java Programmers* by Ammeraal from Wiley & Sons or *Introduction to Computer Graphics* by Foley from Addison Wesley.

When creating a QuadCurve2D, you specify the starting and ending point, as well as a control point. The Shape created will be the continuous curved path from starting point to ending point, where the rest of the curve is pulled toward the control point. Figure 11.8 demonstrates drawing ellipses and quadratic curves. To better illustrate the points on the quadratic curve, the individual points are plotted, too.

FIGURE 11.8:

Drawing ellipses and quadratic curves

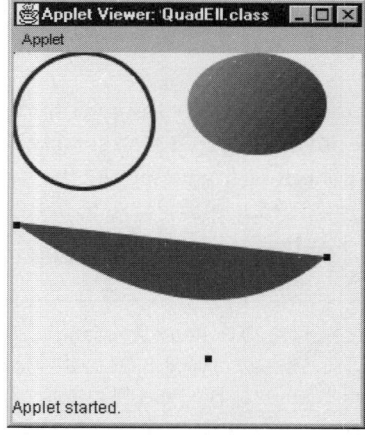

The source code used to generate Figure 11.8 follows.

```
import java.awt.*;
import java.awt.geom.*;
public class QuadEll extends java.applet.Applet {
  public void paint (Graphics g) {
    Graphics2D g2d = (Graphics2D)g;
    g2d.setRenderingHint(RenderingHints.KEY_ANTIALIASING,
      RenderingHints.VALUE_ANTIALIAS_ON);
    g2d.setPaint (Color.blue);
    g2d.setStroke(new BasicStroke(3));
    // Circle
    Ellipse2D ellipse = new Ellipse2D.Float (0, 0, 100, 100);
    g2d.draw (ellipse);
    GradientPaint gp = new GradientPaint (125, 0, Color.cyan, 225, 75,
      Color.blue);
    g2d.setPaint (gp);
    // Oval
    ellipse = new Ellipse2D.Float (125, 0, 100, 75);
    g2d.fill (ellipse);
    // Quad Curve
    QuadCurve2D quad = new QuadCurve2D.Float (0, 125, 140, 225, 225, 150);
    g2d.setPaint (Color.red);
    g2d.fill (quad);
    // Quad Curve Points
    g.setColor (Color.black);
    g.fillRect (0, 125, 5, 5);
    g.fillRect (138, 223, 5, 5);
    g.fillRect (223, 148, 5, 5);
  }
}
```

If you want to create a CubicCurve2D instead, you still specify a starting and ending point. However, instead of one control point, you specify two. Unless the curve is linear, the curve will not go through either control point. Instead, the points on the curves are calculated by weighted interpolation of the endpoints with the control points, pulling the curved path towards the control points between the two endpoints. Figure 11.9 shows several cubic curves, this time with just the control points drawn.

FIGURE 11.9:

Drawing cubic Bezier curves

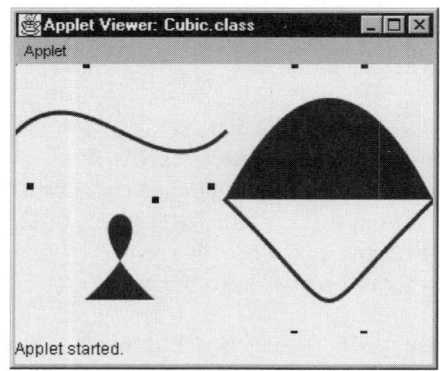

```
import java.awt.*;
import java.awt.geom.*;
public class Cubic extends java.applet.Applet {
  public void paint (Graphics g) {
    Graphics2D g2d = (Graphics2D)g;
    g2d.setRenderingHint(RenderingHints.KEY_ANTIALIASING,
      RenderingHints.VALUE_ANTIALIAS_ON);
    g2d.setPaint (Color.blue);
    g2d.setStroke(new BasicStroke(3));
    CubicCurve2D cubic = new CubicCurve2D.Float (0, 50, 50, 0, 100, 100,
      150, 50);
    g2d.draw (cubic);
    cubic = new CubicCurve2D.Float (50, 175, 140, 90, 10, 90, 100, 175);
    g2d.fill (cubic);
    cubic = new CubicCurve2D.Float (150, 100, 200, 0, 250, 0, 300, 100);
    g2d.fill (cubic);
    cubic = new CubicCurve2D.Float (150, 100, 250, 200, 200, 200, 300, 100);
    g2d.draw (cubic);
    // Curve Points
    g.setColor (Color.black);
    g.fillRect (48, -2, 5, 5);    g.fillRect (98, 98, 5, 5);
    g.fillRect (138, 88, 5, 5);   g.fillRect (8, 88, 5, 5);
    g.fillRect (198, -2, 5, 5);   g.fillRect (248, -2, 5, 5);
    g.fillRect (248, 198, 5, 5);  g.fillRect (198, 198, 5, 5);
  }
}
```

GeneralPath Curves

The quadTo() and curveTo() methods of the GeneralPath class allow you to use quadratic curves and cubic curves as segments of a GeneralPath. Instead of providing a starting point to the QuadCurve2D and CubicCurve2D classes, the quadTo() and curveTo() methods use the current position as the starting point. You then only need to provide the control point(s) and endpoint.

```
public synchronized void quadTo(float controlX, float controlY,
  float endX, float endY);
public synchronized void curveTo(float controlX1, float controlY1,
  float controlX2, float controlY2, float endX, float endY);
```

To demonstrate the quadTo() and curveTo() methods, the following program connects curves similar to those shown in Figures 11.8 and 11.9.

```java
import java.awt.*;
import java.awt.geom.*;
public class PathCurves extends java.applet.Applet {
  public void paint (Graphics g) {
    Graphics2D g2d = (Graphics2D)g;
    g2d.setRenderingHint(RenderingHints.KEY_ANTIALIASING,
      RenderingHints.VALUE_ANTIALIAS_ON);
    g2d.setPaint (Color.blue);
    g2d.setStroke(new BasicStroke(3));

    GeneralPath shape = new GeneralPath (GeneralPath.WIND_EVEN_ODD);
    shape.moveTo (20, 20);
    shape.quadTo (160, 120, 245, 45);
    shape.curveTo (195, 95, 295, 145, 245, 195);
    shape.curveTo (-80, 110, 345, 110, 20, 195);
    shape.curveTo (400, 250, 200, 250, 20, 20);
    g2d.fill (shape);
  }
}
```

Figure 11.10 shows what the connected figure looks like. You may wish to change the fill() line to draw() to better visualize.

FIGURE 11.10:

Drawing curves on a
`GeneralPath`

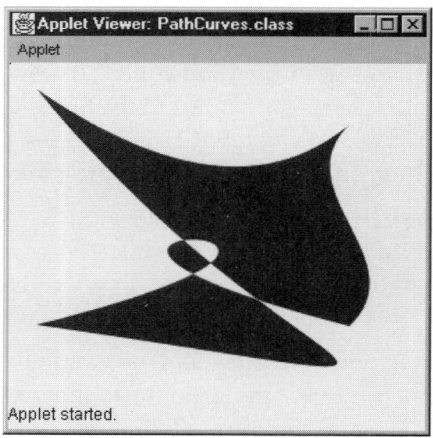

Transforms

The Java2D API supports transforming drawing coordinates. These transformations allow you to rotate, scale, flip, shear, or just plain change the locations of drawing operations. For math-oriented people, the coordinate transforming involves multiplying a 3×3 matrix with the original x and y coordinates (using 1 for the z-space). The content of the matrix defines the actual transformation.

While the `AffineTransform` class is responsible for the transformations, you seldom need to look beyond the static methods of the class to perform the transformations:

```
public static AffineTransform getRotateInstance(double theta);
public static AffineTransform getRotateInstance(double theta, double x,
    double y);
public static AffineTransform getScaleInstance(double scaleX,
    double scaleY);
public static AffineTransform getShearInstance(double shiftX,
    double shiftY);
public static AffineTransform getTranslateInstance(double translateX,
    double translateY);
```

Once you understand the different transformations you can perform, just create an `AffineTransform` for that specific transformation. And, similar to chaining multiple `ImageFilter` objects together, you can chain multiple `AffineTranform` instances together to perform higher order transformations with `concatenate()`.

The simplest of the transformations is the translation one, from `getTranslate-Instance()`. This acts identically to the `translate()` method of `Graphics`. All drawing operations are translated by the coordinates provided.

Scaling is next up on the complexity scale. The `getScaleInstance()` method replaces the `AreaAveragingScaleFilter` and `ReplicateScaleFilter` filters if you are using the image producer-consumer model explained in Chapter 10. The `getScaleInstance()` parameters define the scaling factor along the x and y axis. These could make your images smaller or larger in both directions, or just one.

If you wish to perform a rotation transformation, you need to use one of the `get-RotateInstance()` methods. They require an angle in radians to determine how far to rotate. To go from degrees to radians, the calculation is radians = degrees * π/180. Rotating in a positive direction is clockwise; negative is counterclockwise. When you rotate, you either rotate around the origin (0, 0) or from some other point.

Shearing is the most complicated to explain. Basically, it is a translation operation making the x and y axes nonperpendicular. The actual translation involves multiplying each position by the shearing factors you provide, in both the x and y directions. This factoring allows parallel lines to stay parallel but any perpendicular lines to diverge.

Figure 11.11 should help you visualize shearing as well as the other transformations. For each of the transformations besides shearing, a solid rectangle is drawn in the original position.

FIGURE 11.11:

Transforming draw operations

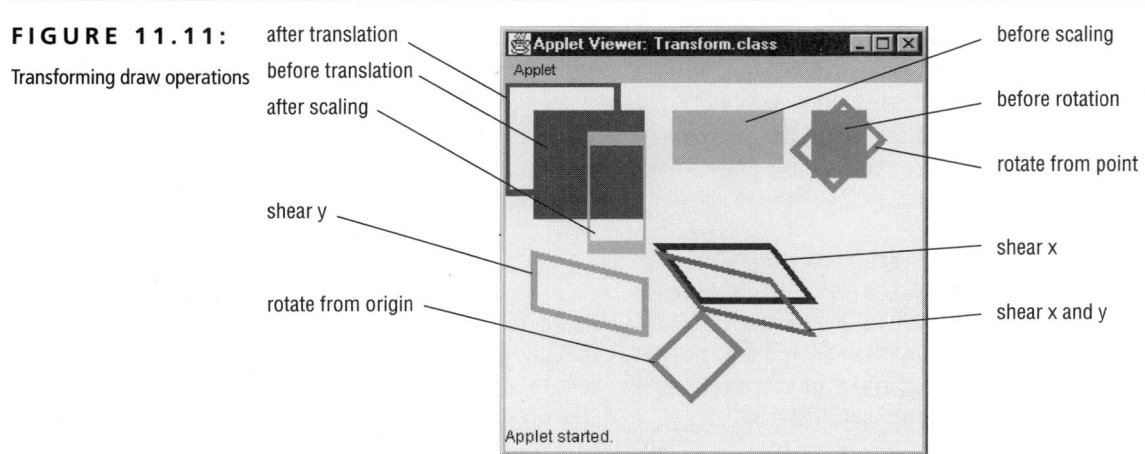

The source involved in creating the different transformations in Figure 11.11 is shown below. They all involve transforming plain rectangles to help you visualize the complexity of the operations.

```java
import java.awt.*;
import java.awt.geom.*;

public class Transform extends java.applet.Applet {

  public void paint (Graphics g) {
    Graphics2D g2d = (Graphics2D)g;

    g2d.setStroke(new BasicStroke(5f));

    // Translated Rectangle
    g2d.setColor (Color.red);
    Rectangle2D rectangle = new Rectangle2D.Double (20, 20, 80, 80);
    AffineTransform at = AffineTransform.getTranslateInstance(-20, -20);
    g2d.setTransform (at);
    g2d.draw (rectangle);
    // reset transformations
    g2d.setTransform (new AffineTransform());
    g2d.fill (rectangle);

    // Scaled Rectangle
    g2d.setColor (Color.orange);
    rectangle = new Rectangle2D.Double (120, 20, 80, 40);
    at = AffineTransform.getScaleInstance(.5, 2);
    g2d.setTransform (at);
    g2d.draw (rectangle);
    // reset transformations
    g2d.setTransform (new AffineTransform());
    g2d.fill (rectangle);

    // Rotated Rectangle
    g2d.setColor (Color.green);
    rectangle = new Rectangle2D.Double (220, 20, 40, 50);
    at = AffineTransform.getRotateInstance((45*java.lang.Math.PI)/180,
      rectangle.getCenterX(), rectangle.getCenterY());
    g2d.setTransform (at);
```

```
    g2d.draw (rectangle);
    // Rotate from origin
    at = AffineTransform.getRotateInstance((45*java.lang.Math.PI)/180);
    g2d.setTransform (at);
    g2d.draw (rectangle);
    // reset transformations
    g2d.setTransform (new AffineTransform());
    g2d.fill (rectangle);

    // Sheared Rectangle
    g2d.setColor (Color.blue);
    rectangle = new Rectangle2D.Double (20, 120, 80, 40);
    at = AffineTransform.getShearInstance(.75, 0);
    g2d.setTransform (at);
    g2d.draw (rectangle);
    g2d.setColor (Color.cyan);
    at = AffineTransform.getShearInstance(0, .25);
    g2d.setTransform (at);
    g2d.draw (rectangle);
    g2d.setColor (Color.magenta);
    at = AffineTransform.getShearInstance(.75, .25);
    g2d.setTransform (at);
    g2d.draw (rectangle);
  }
}
```

Compositing

Before the Java 2D API, whenever you drew a line in a solid color there were two options for painting that color. Either it was completely opaque, obscuring what was previously drawn there; or it was drawn in XOR mode, combining the current color with the drawing color to form a third, such that if the same drawing operation happened again, the original color would return. With the help of the AlphaComposite class, you can now blend colors when you draw an image. This allows you to draw a red box over a blue box and get a purple box.

The AlphaComposite class has eight constants that define the blending rules. How each affects the blending is described in Table 11.1. Keep in mind that this affects the drawing of rectangular image areas.

TABLE 11.1: The AlphaComposite blending constants

Mode	Blending Effect
CLEAR	Clears color and alpha of destination
DST_IN	Of source and destination shapes, only draws part of destination that overlaps with source
DST_OUT	Of source and destination shapes, only draws part of destination that doesn't overlap with source
DST_OVER	Destination is combined over source
SRC	Source color and alpha is drawn
SRC_IN	Of source and destination shapes, only draws part of source that overlaps with destination
SRC_OUT	Of source and destination shapes, only draws part of source that doesn't overlap with destination
SRC_OVER	Source is combined over destination

When you get an AlphaComposite object, you specify the alpha value of the color to draw, in addition to the rule. This will be in the range of 0.0 to 1.0 and can be thought of as the percentage of the background that the color lets bleed through. The way to get an instance of the class is through the static getInstance() method. If you do not specify a percentage, then 1.0 is used. Also, a public class variable exists for each rule of type AlphaComposite, where the alpha value is 1.0. These are named as follows: Clear, DstIn, DstOut, DstOver, Src, SrcIn, SrcOut, and SrcOver.

This particular example is the hardest to demonstrate on paper. To help you understand the rules, Figure 11.12 shows each of the eight rules drawn with an alpha value of .33, .67, and 1.0, from top to bottom. The source figure is a green triangle on the left of the rectangle. The destination figure, or first one drawn, is a magenta triangle that takes up the top right of the rectangle. This provides both shapes with an overlapping and non-overlapping area. Notice that the shapes are drawn into separate buffered images before combining. This allows you to better specify the initial composite setting for each.

FIGURE 11.12:

Drawing with alpha composites

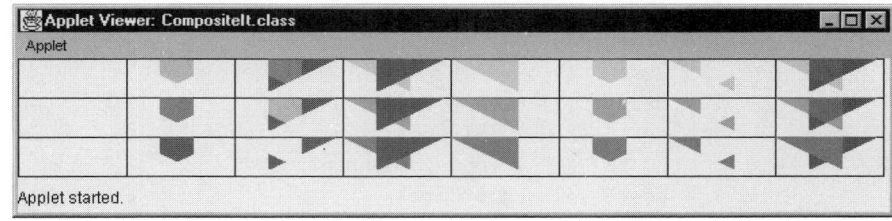

The source used to generate Figure 11.2 follows.

```java
import java.awt.*;
import java.awt.image.*;
import java.awt.geom.*;
public class CompositeIt extends java.applet.Applet {
  int rules[] = {
    AlphaComposite.CLEAR, AlphaComposite.DST_IN, AlphaComposite.DST_OUT,
    AlphaComposite.DST_OVER, AlphaComposite.SRC, AlphaComposite.SRC_IN,
    AlphaComposite.SRC_OUT, AlphaComposite.SRC_OVER};
  float percents[] = {.33f, .67f, 1.0f};
  BufferedImage source, dest;
  GeneralPath sourcePath, destPath;
  public void init() {
    sourcePath = new GeneralPath();
    sourcePath.moveTo (0,   0);   sourcePath.lineTo (50, 0);
    sourcePath.lineTo (50, 25);   sourcePath.closePath();
    source = new BufferedImage(80, 30, BufferedImage.TYPE_INT_ARGB);
    destPath = new GeneralPath();
    destPath.moveTo (25,  0);    destPath.lineTo (75, 0);
    destPath.lineTo (25, 25);    destPath.closePath();
    dest = new BufferedImage(80, 30, BufferedImage.TYPE_INT_ARGB);
  }
  public void paint (Graphics g) {
    Graphics2D g2d = (Graphics2D)g;
    Graphics2D sourceG = source.createGraphics();
    Graphics2D destG = dest.createGraphics();

    AffineTransform at = new AffineTransform();
    Composite originalComposite = g2d.getComposite();
    for (int i=0; i<3; i++) {
      for (int j=0, n=rules.length; j<n; j++) {
```

```
        at = AffineTransform.getTranslateInstance (j*80, i*30);
        g2d.setTransform (at);
        g.drawRect (0, 0, 80, 30);
        destG.setComposite(AlphaComposite.Clear);
        destG.fillRect(0, 0, 80, 30);
        destG.setComposite(AlphaComposite.Src);
        destG.setPaint (Color.magenta);
        destG.fill (destPath);
        sourceG.setComposite(AlphaComposite.Clear);
        sourceG.fillRect(0, 0, 80, 30);
        sourceG.setComposite(AlphaComposite.getInstance (AlphaComposite.SRC,
          percents[i]));
        sourceG.setPaint(Color.green);
// Above two setComposite/setPaint lines same as:
//        sourceG.setComposite(AlphaComposite.Src);
//        sourceG.setPaint(new Color (0.0f, 1.0f, 0.0f, percents[i]));
        sourceG.fill(sourcePath);
        destG.setComposite(AlphaComposite.getInstance (rules[j]));
        destG.drawImage(source, 0, 0, null);
        g2d.drawImage(dest, 0, 0, this);
      }
    }
  }
}
```

Notice in the source comment that you can set the alpha percentage in either the setComposite() method, or in the constructor for Color. Which method you use depends on your preference.

Text Processing

The Java 2D API provides many text processing capabilities not previously available in Java. For instance, Chapter 10 showed you how to access all the platform-specific fonts. In addition, you can use text as a clipping or drawing shape.

Extended Font Support

As shown in the "Current Font" section of Chapter 10, you can access any of the platform-specific fonts available on the user's Java runtime environment. While you can access any of the fonts, it is wise not to directly specify their names in your source code. Otherwise, you could specify a font that a particular user may not have available on their platform, resulting in the system guessing at which font to use. What is best is to either use the Java standard font names, like Serif, SansSerif, and Monospaced, or to provide the user with a pop-up in which to choose a font. As long as you populate the pop-up font list at run time, you'll never run into the problem of hard-coding an unavailable font name into your source. The other option is a Swing component that allows a user to interactively select a font to use. This latter option is shown in Chapter 15.

Getting the font list is done in one of two ways. Both are done through the GraphicsEnvironment class, from which you get a GraphicsEnvironment instance through its getLocalGraphicsEnvironment() method. Once you have a GraphicsEnvironment, you can ask getAllFonts(), which returns an array of Font objects, one for each font available in the system. Each font represents the one-point version of the font. In other words, you wouldn't directly use it to draw strings with. You would need to use deriveFont() to create a new Font with the appropriate size and style characteristics.

```
Font fonts[] =
  GraphicsEnvironment.getLocalGraphicsEnvironment().getAllFonts();
Font f = fonts[2].deriveFont(Font.BOLD, 24);
```

The second means of getting the font list is with getAvailableFontFamily-Names(). This returns an array of String objects, each containing the name of a specific font available on the user's runtime platform. Once you have a specific font family name to use, you would create a Font object from it of the desired size and characteristics.

```
GraphicsEnvironment ge =
  GraphicsEnvironment.getLocalGraphicsEnvironment();
String fontList[] = ge.getAvailableFontFamilyNames();
Font theFont = new Font(fontList[2], Font.PLAIN, 10);
```

NOTE   The JAVA_FONTS environment variable (or java.awt.fonts System property) can be set to change the default font directory. This allows you to create a directory with a subset of all your system's available fonts, enabling Java to respond more quickly because it won't need to generate metrics for all fonts when first accessing the GraphicsEnvironment.

Advanced Text Layout

Instead of just drawing a string with the drawString() method of Graphics, the TextLayout class allows you to do many new and interesting things. For instance, you can ask for the outline of text string in a certain font, then use that outline as the clipping region when drawing an image. Figure 11.13 shows off these capabilities as well as drawing the image unclipped. You just need to create a TextLayout, based on a String, Font, and FontRenderContext. Then you can get its Shape from getOutline(), which allows you to perform an AffineTransform to transform the shape, as well as specify the coordinates for an origin.

FIGURE 11.13:

Using text outline for clipping

The following source performed the clipping operation in Figure 11.13.

```
import java.awt.*;
import java.awt.font.*;
public class ClipImage extends java.applet.Applet {
  Image img;
  public void init() {
    img = getImage(getClass().getResource("jaeger.jpg"));
    try {
      MediaTracker tracker = new MediaTracker(this);
      tracker.addImage(img, 0);
      tracker.waitForID(0);
    } catch (Exception e) {
    }
  }
  public void paint (Graphics g) {
    Graphics2D g2d = (Graphics2D)g;
```

```
        FontRenderContext frc = g2d.getFontRenderContext();
        Font f = new Font ("Serif", Font.ITALIC | Font.BOLD, getWidth()/4);
        TextLayout tl = new TextLayout("Jaeger", f, frc);
        float width = (float) tl.getBounds().getWidth();
        Shape sha = tl.getOutline(null, (getWidth()-width)/2, getHeight()/3);
        g2d.drawImage(img, 0, getHeight()/3, this);
        g2d.clip(sha);
        g2d.drawImage(img, 0, 0, this);
    }
}
```

The TextLayout class provides many more capabilities, similar to working with FontMetrics and Graphics. The class definition of TextLayout follows to help you see some of these additional capabilities.

```
public final class TextLayout extends Object implements Cloneable {
    public static final TextLayout.CaretPolicy DEFAULT_CARET_POLICY;
    public TextLayout(String string, Font font, FontRenderContext frc);
    public TextLayout(String string, Map map, FontRenderContext frc);
    public TextLayout(AttributedCharacterIterator aci, FontRenderContext frc);
    public void draw(Graphics2D g2d, float x, float y);
    public boolean equals(TextLayout tl);
    public boolean equals(Object obj);
    public float getAdvance();
    public float getAscent();
    public byte getBaseline();
    public float[] getBaselineOffsets();
    public Shape getBlackBoxBounds(int firstEndpt, int secondEndpt);
    public Rectangle2D getBounds();
    public float[] getCaretInfo(TextHitInfo hit);
    public float[] getCaretInfo(TextHitInfo hit, Rectangle2D bounds);
    public Shape getCaretShape(TextHitInfo hit);
    public Shape getCaretShape(TextHitInfo hit, Rectangle2D bounds);
    public Shape[] getCaretShapes(int offset);
    public Shape[] getCaretShapes(int offset, Rectangle2D bounds);
    public Shape[] getCaretShapes(int offset, Rectangle2D bounds,
      TextLayout.CaretPolicy policy);
    public int getCharacterCount();
    public byte getCharacterLevel(int index);
    public float getDescent();
    public TextLayout getJustifiedLayout(float width);
    public float getLeading();
    public Shape getLogicalHighlightShape(int firstEndpt, int secondEndpt);
```

```
    public Shape getLogicalHighlightShape(int firstEndpt, int secondEndpt,
      Rectangle2D bounds);
    public int[] getLogicalRangesForVisualSelection(TextHitInfo firstEndpt,
      TextHitInfo secondEndpt);
    public TextHitInfo getNextLeftHit(int offset);
    public TextHitInfo getNextLeftHit(int offset,
      TextLayout.CaretPolicy policy);
    public TextHitInfo getNextLeftHit(TextHitInfo hit);
    public TextHitInfo getNextRightHit(int offset);
    public TextHitInfo getNextRightHit(int offset,
      TextLayout.CaretPolicy policy);
    public TextHitInfo getNextRightHit(TextHitInfo hit);
    public Shape getOutline(AffineTransform trans, float x, float y);
    public float getVisibleAdvance();
    public Shape getVisualHighlightShape(TextHitInfo firstEndpt,
      TextHitInfo secondEndpt);
    public Shape getVisualHighlightShape(TextHitInfo firstEndpt,
      TextHitInfo secondEndpt, Rectangle2D bounds);
    public TextHitInfo getVisualOtherHit(TextHitInfo hit);
    public int hashCode();
    public TextHitInfo hitTestChar(float x, float y);
    public TextHitInfo hitTestChar(float x, float y, Rectangle2D bounds);
    public boolean isLeftToRight();
    public boolean isVertical();
    public String toString();
  }
```

Image Handling

The Java 2D API includes many enhanced image-handling capabilities added to the java.awt.image package. These include the previously demonstrated ability to create in-memory images with BufferedImage as well as more advanced filtering operations. Plus, outside the 2D API, you can now directly access the image data as the JPEG format, for saving and later reloading.

Flexible Image Formatting

Whenever you wish to create images in memory so you can perform such operations as double buffering, you use the BufferedImage class. A BufferedImage is a type of Image that you can draw behind the scenes and then eventually draw to the screen. That is, in fact, how double buffering works.

When you first create the buffered area, you specify the size and specify how it maintains the buffered data internally. These are specified by the TYPE_* class constants defined in BufferedImage, listed here:

```
public static final int TYPE_3BYTE_BGR;
public static final int TYPE_4BYTE_ABGR;
public static final int TYPE_4BYTE_ABGR_PRE;
public static final int TYPE_BYTE_BINARY;
public static final int TYPE_BYTE_GRAY;
public static final int TYPE_BYTE_INDEXED;
public static final int TYPE_CUSTOM;
public static final int TYPE_INT_ARGB;
public static final int TYPE_INT_ARGB_PRE;
public static final int TYPE_INT_BGR;
public static final int TYPE_INT_RGB;
public static final int TYPE_USHORT_555_RGB;
public static final int TYPE_USHORT_565_RGB;
public static final int TYPE_USHORT_GRAY;
```

Each of these allows you to specify how data is stored internally. It is actually stored within a DataBuffer within a Raster, associated to the BufferedImage. Examining a Raster allows you to set/get specific pixel values of the image. Instead of getting the whole Raster with getRaster(), you can get a Raster tile. Working with tiles allows you to associate a TileObserver that will be notified when the tile data changes.

WARNING   There is no Tile class. A tile just represents a potentially writable area of the image with which you can work.

The most common forms of BufferedImage created are TYPE_INT_RGB, which represents a regular DirectColorModel without an alpha value; TYPE_INT_ARGB, which represents a regular DirectColorModel with an alpha value; and TYPE_BYTE_INDEXED for IndexColorModel. While the other types are all valid, they tend to be used for more specialized circumstances.

Creating a BufferedImage is a simple process. Just call the constructor with the width, height, and type:

```
BufferedImage bi = new BufferedImage (400, 200, BufferedImage.TYPE_INT_RGB);
```

Once you have your `BufferedImage` instance, you can draw to either a `Graphics` object, received from `getGraphics()`, or a `Graphics2D` object, by creating one with the `createGraphics()` method of `BufferedImage`.

```
Graphics g = bi.getGraphics();
Graphics2D g2d = bi.createGraphics();
```

If you wish to create a `BufferedImage` that is optimized for a graphics device, you would ask the `GraphicsConfiguration`. This would allow the device to draw it quickly. Assuming you're in the `paint()` method and g is the `Graphics` parameter to `paint()`, the following would create the optimal `BufferedImage`:

```
Graphics2D g2d = (Graphics2D)g;
GraphicsConfiguration gc = g2d.getDeviceConfiguration();
BufferedImaged bi = gc.createCompatibleImage(width, height);
```

Extended Imaging Operations

While you could always create image filters that examined neighboring pixels when filtering an image, doing this with `ImageFilter` is very awkward and tedious. The Java 2D API adds a `BufferedImageFilter`, which requires a `BufferedImageOp` to define the operation, that permits `BufferedImage` objects to be filtered. Filtering a `BufferedImage` with `BufferedImageFilter` is done in-place, so the original image is no longer available after the operation. If you don't want to have the original image replaced, you would use the `filter()` method of `BufferedImageOp`, which allows you to specify a source and destination `BufferedImage`. However, some filters may not support this.

There are several different operations available to filter buffered images. Most are just re-implementations of specific `ImageFilter` subclasses for easier use in the `Graphics2D` world. A list of the specific `BufferedImageOp` interface implementers follows:

AffineTransformOp   For performing affine transformations, like the `AffineTransform` class

ColorConvertOp   For performing color mappings, like the `RGBImageFilter`

ConvolveOp   For performing weighted convolutions of pixels, based on neighboring pixel values

LookupOp   For performing non-uniform modifications to the original image via a mapping operation

RescaleOp   For scaling images, like the `ReplicateScaleFilter` and `AreaAveragingScaleFilter` classes

All of the above filtering operations work on `Raster` objects, as well as `BufferedImages`. In addition, one other works only on `Raster` objects. This implements the `RasterOp` interface and is listed below:

BandCombineOp   Combines bands within a `Raster`

The most interesting of the filtering operations is the `ConvolveOp` for convolution. When you convolute an image, you calculate a weighted sum of neighboring pixels. A `Kernel` specifies the weighting with `ConvolveOp`. Creating a `Kernel` allows you to specify how neighborly the weighting will be. For instance, if you wanted a convolution that blurs the image somewhat, your kernel might be created like so:

```
public static final float[] LOW_PASS =
    { 0.1f, 0.1f, 0.1f,
      0.1f, 0.2f, 0.1f,
      0.1f, 0.1f, 0.1f};
Kernel kernel = new Kernel(3, 3, LOW_PASS);
```

Notice that the sum of the values in the filtering matrix is one; this is done on purpose. Convoluting involves summing the product of the neighboring pixels to create a new pixel value. This is why it should be one.

Once you have a Kernel, you would then create a `ConvolveOp` and filter a `BufferedImage`. The additional parameters to the constructor describe the edge conditions and rendering hints. EDGE_NO_OP means do a direct copy of the original pixel without modifications. The default operation is EDGE_ZERO_FILL, which clears out the edge pixels.

```
ConvolveOp cop = new ConvolveOp(kernel, ConvolveOp.EDGE_NO_OP, null);
cop.filter(biSrc, biDst);
g.drawImage (bi, x, y, this);
```

If the specific `BufferedImageOp` implementer supports in-place filtering, you can also just place the operation in the `drawImage()`.

```
g2d.drawImage (bi, cop, x, y);
```

If you look closely at Figure 11.14, you'll notice a blurring effect on the image shown earlier in Figure 11.13. This is the result of the filtering.

FIGURE 11.14:

Convoluting an image with a low pass filter

The following source puts all the pieces together to create the example shown in Figure 11.14.

```java
import java.awt.*;
import java.awt.geom.*;
import java.awt.image.*;
public class ConvolveIt extends java.applet.Applet {

  private static final float[] LOW_PASS =
  { 0.1f, 0.1f, 0.1f,
    0.1f, 0.2f, 0.1f,
    0.1f, 0.1f, 0.1f};
  BufferedImage bi;
  ConvolveOp cop;
  public void init() {
    Image img = getImage(getClass().getResource("jaeger.jpg"));
    try {
      MediaTracker tracker = new MediaTracker(this);
      tracker.addImage(img, 0);
      tracker.waitForID(0);
    } catch (Exception e) {
    }
    bi = new BufferedImage (img.getWidth(this), img.getHeight(this),
      BufferedImage.TYPE_INT_RGB);
    Graphics2D big = bi.createGraphics();
    AffineTransform at = new AffineTransform();
    big.drawImage(img, at, this);
```

```
      Kernel kernel = new Kernel(3, 3, LOW_PASS);
      cop = new ConvolveOp(kernel, ConvolveOp.EDGE_NO_OP, null);
   }
   public void paint (Graphics g) {
     Graphics2D g2d = (Graphics2D)g;
     if (bi != null) {
       g2d.drawImage(bi, cop, 10, 10);
     }
   }
}
```

JPEG Encoding

While not part of the 2D API, Java includes support for reading and writing JPEG files with the JPEGImageDecoder and JPEGImageEncoder classes found in the com.sun.image.codec.jpeg package. Using these classes requires you to understand how to do I/O operations. So, if you are not familiar with working with I/O in Java, you may want to skip ahead to Chapter 19 and come back to this section.

Reading JPEG files can still be done with getImage() to get back an Image object. Instead of reading the file back as an Image object, though, you can now read it in as a BufferedImage or a Raster. These allow you to more directly use the JPEG image as a buffer that you can directly modify. If you want to use the Image as a buffer, you have to create the buffer, then draw the Image onto it. However, with JPEGImageDecoder, you can decodeAsBufferedImage() and get a BufferedImage directly.

The process of reading an image with JPEGImageDecoder is a two-step operation. You have to ask a JPEGCodec to create a JPEG decoder for you with createJPEGDecoder(), which requires an InputStream parameter (quite possibly the file from which you are reading). Then you read it with decodeAsBufferedImage().

```
FileInputStream in = new FileInputStream(filename);
JPEGImageDecoder decoder = JPEGCodec.createJPEGDecoder(in);
BufferedImage bi = decoder.decodeAsBufferedImage();
```

The process of writing the JPEG image data is newly available; there is no equivalent way that comes with Sun's JDK that preserves the JPEG image compression format. In writing, you have to ask the JPEGCodec to create a JPEG encoder with createJPEGEncoder(). The actual writing operation is done with the encode() method of JPEGImageEncoder. One additional operation you might do when you write the JPEG image is set the various encoding parameters, as settable from the JPEGEncodeParam whose definition is shown here.

```
public interface JPEGEncodeParam extends Cloneable, JPEGDecodeParam {
    public abstract void addMarkerData(int marker, byte data[]);
    public abstract Object clone();
    public abstract void setACHuffmanComponentMapping(int component, int table);
    public abstract void setACHuffmanTable(int tableNum, JPEGHuffmanTable
        huffTable);
    public abstract void setDCHuffmanComponentMapping(int component, int table);
    public abstract void setDCHuffmanTable(int tableNum, JPEGHuffmanTable
        huffTable);
    public abstract void setDensityUnit(int unit);
    public abstract void setHorizontalSubsampling(int component, int subsample);
    public abstract void setImageInfoValid(boolean flag);
    public abstract void setMarkerData(int marker, byte data[][]);
    public abstract void setQTable(int tableNum, JPEGQTable qTable);
    public abstract void setQTableComponentMapping(int component, int table);
    public abstract void setQuality(float quality, boolean forceBaseline);
    public abstract void setRestartInterval(int restartInterval);
    public abstract void setTableInfoValid(boolean flag);
    public abstract void setVerticalSubsampling(int component, int subsample);
    public abstract void setXDensity(int xDensity);
    public abstract void setYDensity(int yDensity);
}
```

So, if you wanted to set the image quality to 100%, you would first get the default parameters from the JPEG encoder, with getDefaultJPEGEncodeParam(bi), and then set the quality with setQuality(). The whole writing process is shown here and you can access this image file as a JPEG file from outside of Java:

```
FileOutputStream out = new FileOutputStream(filename);
JPEGImageEncoder encoder = JPEGCodec.createJPEGEncoder(out);
JPEGEncodeParam param = encoder.getDefaultJPEGEncodeParam(bi);
param.setQuality(1.0f, false);
encoder.setJPEGEncodeParam(param);
encoder.encode(bi);
```

WARNING   While the com.sun.image.codec.jpeg classes come standard with Sun's development and runtime environments, the classes may not be available from other vendors.

Graphics Device Hookups

The Java 2D API encapsulates the configuration of the output device so that you can query it at run time. This allows you to create programs that can query this configuration and optimize themselves based on such configuration. This involves both screen devices and printing devices.

Graphics Configuration

The description of the current output device is encapsulated in a `GraphicsDevice` class. From the graphics device, you can get its `GraphicsConfiguration` to determine the `ColorModel` used by the graphics device. This would allow you to configure operations based on the color model in use. Most frequently, you get this `GraphicsDevice` from the `Graphics2D` object you are using to draw. This could be the `Graphics2D` passed to `paint()` acquired from a `BufferedImage` or created from the `GraphicsEnvironment`. The `printModelType()` method of the following program shows just how you might determine the optimization technique based on the color model. Besides the color model of the system used, different color models are used from `BufferedImage` objects.

```java
import java.awt.*;
import java.awt.event.*;
import java.awt.image.*;

public class GraphicsInfo extends Frame {
  public GraphicsInfo() {
    super ("Graphics Info");
  }
  public void printModelType (ColorModel cm) {
    if (cm instanceof DirectColorModel) {
      System.out.println ("DirectColorModel");
    } else if (cm instanceof IndexColorModel) {
      System.out.println ("IndexColorModel");
    } else {
      System.out.println ("Unknown ColorModel");
    }
  }
  public void paint (Graphics g) {
    Graphics2D g2d = (Graphics2D)g;
    GraphicsConfiguration gc = g2d.getDeviceConfiguration();
    printModelType (gc.getColorModel());
```

```
      BufferedImage bi = new BufferedImage (20, 20,
        BufferedImage.TYPE_BYTE_INDEXED);
      Graphics2D g2d2 = bi.createGraphics();
      GraphicsConfiguration gc2 = g2d2.getDeviceConfiguration();
      printModelType (gc2.getColorModel());
      bi = new BufferedImage (20, 20, BufferedImage.TYPE_INT_ARGB);
      g2d2 = bi.createGraphics();
      gc2 = g2d2.getDeviceConfiguration();
      printModelType (gc2.getColorModel());
      bi = new BufferedImage (20, 20, BufferedImage.TYPE_USHORT_565_RGB);
      g2d2 = bi.createGraphics();
      gc2 = g2d2.getDeviceConfiguration();
      printModelType (gc2.getColorModel());
    }
    public static void main (String args[]) {
      Frame f = new GraphicsInfo();
      f.addWindowListener (new WindowAdapter() {
        public void windowClosing(WindowEvent e) {
          System.exit(0);
        }
      });
      f.setSize(300, 300);
      f.setVisible(true);
    }
  }
```

In addition to encapsulating the device information, the local Graphics-Environment allows you to determine the locally installed fonts, among other things, as shown by its class definition.

```
public abstract class GraphicsEnvironment extends Object {
  protected GraphicsEnvironment();
  public static GraphicsEnvironment getLocalGraphicsEnvironment();
  public abstract Graphics2D createGraphics(BufferedImage bi);
  public abstract Font[] getAllFonts();
  public abstract String[] getAvailableFontFamilyNames();
  public abstract String[] getAvailableFontFamilyNames(Locale l);
  public abstract GraphicsDevice getDefaultScreenDevice();
  public abstract Font[] getFonts(Map m);
  public abstract GraphicsDevice[] getScreenDevices();
  public abstract boolean registerFont(byte fontData[]);
}
```

Examining the font information was shown earlier in the "Extended Font Support" section.

Printing

Printing with Java isn't part of the Java 2D API, but its description seems to fit in best here. It is described in the `java.awt.print` package and primarily involves four classes and two interfaces.

PrinterJob   Used to initiate a printing operation. Can display an optional system-specific print dialog, which allows the user to configure the printing properties.

PageFormat   Describes the printable area, with support from the Paper class.

```
public class PageFormat extends Object implements Cloneable {
  public static final int LANDSCAPE;
  public static final int PORTRAIT;
  public static final int REVERSE_LANDSCAPE;
  public PageFormat();
  public Object clone();
  public double getHeight();
  public double getImageableHeight();
  public double getImageableWidth();
  public double getImageableX();
  public double getImageableY();
  public double[] getMatrix();
  public int getOrientation();
  public Paper getPaper();
  public double getWidth();
  public void setOrientation(int v) throws IllegalArgumentException;
  public void setPaper(Paper paper);
}
```

Printable   The interface that needs to be implemented to describe what to print. Its `print()` method will be repeatedly called until `NO_SUCH_PAGE` is returned.

```
public interface Printable {
  public static final int NO_SUCH_PAGE;
  public static final int PAGE_EXISTS;
  public abstract int print(Graphics g, PageFormat pf, int pageIndex)
    throws PrinterException;
}
```

Book   When printing multi-page documents, it manages pagination with the help of the `Pageable` interface. This management of multiple pages is automatically done for you.

The basic process of printing is a three-step operation, four if you display a print dialog, and more if you want to print a multi-page document:

1. Create a `PrinterJob`

2. Set its printable area

3. Display print dialog (optional)

4. Print area

The following source demonstrates these capabilities. The printing operation is initiated every time the screen needs to be repainted. Normally, you would associate this behavior with selecting a button. However, event handling isn't described until Chapter 14. In the case of a screen dump, the `print()` method would normally just call the `paint()` method to draw the screen.

```java
import java.awt.*;
import java.awt.event.*;
import java.awt.geom.*;
import java.awt.image.*;
import java.awt.print.*;

public class PrintIt extends Frame implements Printable {
  public PrintIt() {
    super ("Printing is Fun");
  }
  public void paint (Graphics g) {
    PrinterJob printJob = PrinterJob.getPrinterJob();
    printJob.setPrintable(this);
    if (printJob.printDialog()) {
      try {
        printJob.print();
      } catch (PrinterException e) {
        e.printStackTrace();
      }
    }
  }
  public int print(Graphics g, PageFormat pf, int pageIndex)
      throws PrinterException {
    // Stop after first page (index 0)
    if (pageIndex >= 1) {
      return Printable.NO_SUCH_PAGE;
    }
```

```
    // Translate coordiantes to drawable area
    g.translate((int) pf.getImageableX(), (int) pf.getImageableY());
    Graphics2D g2d = (Graphics2D)g;
    g2d.setStroke(new BasicStroke(4f));
    g2d.drawLine (20, 20, 20, 120);
    g2d.drawLine (40, 20, 40, 120);
    g2d.drawLine (20, 70, 40, 70);
    g2d.drawLine (60, 70, 60, 120);
    g2d.drawLine (60, 40, 60, 45);
    return Printable.PAGE_EXISTS;
  }
  public static void main (String args[]) {
    Frame f = new PrintIt();
    f.addWindowListener (new WindowAdapter() {
      public void windowClosing(WindowEvent e) {
        System.exit(0);
      }
    });
    f.setSize(300, 300);
    f.setVisible(true);
  }
}
```

NOTE   Printing from applets is restricted for security reasons. Untrusted applets cannot initiate a print job. Keep in mind that the browser could initiate the printing, though.

Color Management

While you've been using some of the color support classes already, Color and
ColorModel to name two, these are just a small part of the big color management
picture with the Java 2D API. The primary purpose of all this color support is to
manage output to different color spaces.

ICC Profile Support

The ICC Profile Format Specification, Version 3.4, August 15, 1997, from the International Color Consortium (ICC—http://www.color.org) defines a way to map

the device-dependent color space of a particular device to a device-independent mapping. This is called the device's profile and is represented by the `ICC_Profile` class. This profiling technique allows you to do all your work on screen with RGB values yet still be able to print to a grayscale or color printer. The reason this works is that each is able to understand the device-independent mapping and can transform that into the specific color space it uses.

The `ICC_ProfileGray` and `ICC_ProfileRGB` classes represent two specific profiles available in the `java.awt.color` package. Under normal circumstances, the profile does all its work behind the scenes.

Color Conversion and Spaces

The most common color space for device-independent representation is a three-component XYZ color space developed by the International Commission on Illumination (CIE). If you are familiar with this CIEXYZ specification, you can specify all your colors in a device-independent manner. Fortunately (or unfortunately), you don't have to worry about CIEXYZ unless you are creating a new output device type. The default `ColorSpace` of Java programs is `CS_sRGB`, as defined by `http://www.w3.org/pub/WWW/Graphics/Color/sRGB.html`. The conversion to CIEXYZ is already configured so you do not have to worry about conversion of the color space to a device-independent representation.

In addition to the `CS_sRGB` color space, there are several others available, as defined in the `ColorSpace` class and available from its `getInstance()` method. They are `CS_GRAY` for a gray scale space, `CS_LINEAR_RGB` for a linear RGB space, `CS_PYCC` for Photo YCC conversion, and the previously mentioned `CS_CIEXYZ` space.

If you are interested in determining what `ColorSpace` is being used, you can find out by asking the `Color` or `ColorModel`, both of which contain `getColorSpace()` methods.

Summary

This chapter showed how Java has moved beyond the simple graphics drawing world available before the Java 2D API. Now, there are many more sophisticated graphics capabilities available with the `Graphics2D` class. You learned how to draw, fill, and clip with different Shape objects, as well as how to Stroke or Paint areas with something other than a solid color. You learned how to draw smooth lines and how to draw quadratic and cubic curves. The AffineTransform class then showed you how to rotate, translate, and shear your drawings; and Alpha-Composite showed you how to blend multiple images together. After that, you learned how to use the path of text as a Shape to use for drawing, filling, or clipping. You also explored how to create an in-memory image with BufferedImage and how to filter it with BufferedImageOp subclasses. Two non-Java 2D capabilities were also explored: JPEG encoding and printing. Lastly, the way in which Java maintains device-specific information was also explored, by using graphic devices and in maintaining their color profile.

CHAPTER

TWELVE

12

GUI Layout Management

- The AWT environments: applets and applications

- How the layout manager classes interact with their client classes

- The primary six layout managers and related containers

- How layout managers are implemented

Java's big trump card is its Abstract Window Toolkit (AWT). It is an object-oriented graphical user interface (GUI) framework that allows you to design modern, accessible, graphical application interfaces—which isn't a revolutionary step in and of itself. But Java's AWT lets you design and implement GUIs that run unmodified (unported, even) on PCs running Windows 95, Windows 98, Windows NT, or OS/2; Macs running MacOS; or even Unix machines running X-Windows, the windowing environment on Unix platforms. And that is revolutionary.

This chapter begins with a discussion of Java's approach to GUI design and then explains the differences in the applet and application environments in which AWT can be used. The remainder of the chapter describes Java's layout managers in detail, since these are fundamental to any Java GUI implementation and, even more relevant, GUI design. Without layout managers, Java's cross-platform GUI architecture would be virtually crippled.

Java's GUI Approach

Ever since Xerox's pioneer work in the 1970s and Apple's subsequent mass-market introduction of mouse- and icon-driven user interfaces, developers have needed to pick competing GUI "standards" and stick to them religiously. Mastering any given GUI standard is not a trivial exercise, so it is not surprising that developers do not switch GUI APIs at the drop of a hat. Like computer languages themselves, GUIs have been thoroughly mutually incompatible. This, and the associated lack of a standard terminology, greatly segregated the various GUI schools, a wasteful and divisive state of affairs. Java's GUI approach could abolish the GUI wars by supporting a functionally equivalent set of most modern GUI components and presenting them through a new platform-independent API.

> **NOTE**   The jargon wars will rage for a while longer. Java's AWT introduces new terms and concepts and uses some existing terms in incompatible ways (sigh). In Java land, when we talk about a component, we mean a GUI element, a widget, a gadget, a control, or a button (depending on the GUI background you have).

At this point, you might ask yourself whether AWT also imposes a new look and feel on our brave new (Java) world. If you are used to, for example, the Macintosh user interface, it is annoying to suddenly have an application that stubbornly thrusts upon you a Windows95-style interface instead. Modern machines have personalities that they impose on us through their native and often proprietary GUI. AWT respects these personalities by employing the underlying machine's native GUI API to construct its own universal components or manage its behavior itself. Java applications built around AWT reassuringly retain the Mac look and feel on Macs and the Windows look and feel on PCs. Or, if you prefer, you can easily use an interface that appears the same on all platforms. AWT is that flexible.

Since AWT consequently does not specify the exact look and feel—and therefore the dimensions and exact pixel rendering—of your GUI elements, how do you ensure your GUIs will look great on every platform? The AWT answer is layout managers. These fundamental AWT classes are responsible for laying out all the visual components in aesthetically acceptable ways without requiring you to specify absolute positions. Unfortunately, this process is not yet fully automatic. Java's AWT does not have artificial intelligence or graphic design experts embedded in its layout managers. Instead, your applications give these layout managers hints as to component placement and preferred sizes. These hints vary from quite vague ("north," "center," or "third" placements) to quite specific (grid coordinates).

AWT Environments: Applets and Applications

Before embarking on your exploration of Java's novel layout system and the components it affects so thoroughly, you need to understand the two quite different contexts in which a Java GUI can be embedded. Java's AWT can be used in the following two environments:

- Java applets (mini-Web applications)
- Stand-alone applications

Both have different frameworks to respect. The AWT itself is not aware of the context you choose to deploy it in, but the chosen context means different coding techniques, possibilities, and limitations for your Java programs. The easiest context to start using is Java applets.

The Code Framework for Applets

As you've learned, an applet is a small program that runs embedded in a Web browser's HTML page. As such, any applet has a drawing or work area equal to an imaginary picture situated in the same spot, as illustrated in Figure 12.1.

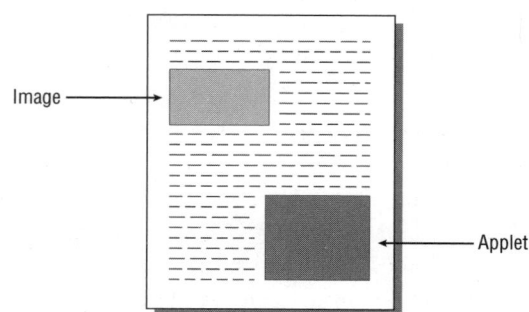

Image

Applet

When applet code starts running, it can immediately use its applet area without any further initializations or checks. For example, the first statement in an applet could be to draw a diagonal line across its surface. The ease with which you can have an applet up and running is what makes applets easier to write than applications (although it gets more complex for nontrivial applets). It is quite possible to write simple little applets without knowing much about the underlying AWT mechanisms.

Here is an example that draws the diagonal line:

```
import java.awt.Graphics;
public class Appletlet extends java.applet.Applet {
  public void paint (Graphics g) {
    g.drawLine (0,0, 100,100);
  }
}
```

As you can see, the applet has no lengthy initializations whatsoever before it starts using AWT classes. Here you use the Graphics class to draw a line with its drawLine() method (Chapter 10 discussed Java's drawing primitives and the Graphics class). To write an applet, you begin by extending (or *subclassing*) class Applet. That's because the browser needs your applets to be instances of the Applet class. Any old Java program will not do. The paint() method used in this example is an Applet method that you override.

WARNING   Make sure you understand the difference between overriding a method and simply inventing a new one. *Overriding* a method means you cannot change the name or syntax of the method to anything else but the original method signature defined in the superclass you are extending—in our example, `public void paint(Graphics g)`. If the signature differs in any way, you are creating a new method, not overriding an existing one. Sometimes, subtle bugs can slip through when you meant to override a method but instead failed to use the same signature. The compiler won't generate an error, and your code will invoke the wrong method at run time (the superclass' method).

Applet Methods

Whenever the browser needs to draw the page containing this applet, it tells the applet to draw itself by calling the `paint()` method. For simplistic applets, this calling protocol between the browser and your applet might be all that you need, but for more complex applets (for example, those using animation), this approach is too limited. In fact, the browser calls many more `Applet` methods that were not overridden here, so only a small subset of the full browser-applet protocol was used.

For starters, the browser calls the `init()` method to initialize an applet. There was not an `init()` method in the simple example because nothing needed to be initialized. But if your applet has any initialization to do (namely, code it needs to execute only once, at the start of its execution), it should put all this code in an overridden `init()` method. Here is an example that overrides the `init()` method:

```
import java.awt.Graphics;
import java.util.Date;
public class Applet2 extends java.applet.Applet {
  String message;
  public void init () {
    Date date = new Date (System.currentTimeMillis());
    message = "I was born at: " + date.toString();
  }
  public void paint (Graphics g) {
    g.drawString (message, 10, 20);
  }
}
```

In addition to the paint() method responsible for the redrawing of the applet, you now have a customized init() method. This method will be called once by the browser before the applet is displayed. In this example, the init() method records the date and time at the moment the applet is initialized and converts this to a string that the paint() method will use to draw this frozen time when the applet needs to be redrawn.

Graphically printing a string is done with the Graphics drawString() method. It takes a string and the coordinates for the string's position.

The browser invokes three more methods on an applet during an applet's life cycle:

start()   When the applet's HTML page comes into view or the browser is deiconified

stop()   When the applet's HTML page is left or the browser is iconified

destroy()   When the browser's garbage collector determines the applet is no longer necessary to keep in memory

To see the full browser-applet protocol in action, type in the following program, compile it, and tell your favorite Web browser to load a Web page with the applet embedded in it. Make sure your browser shows "Java console output." On Netscape's Navigator browser, you enable this by selecting Show Java Console in the program's Options menu. For Internet Explorer, it actually logs output to disk instead of sending it to the console. Here's the code:

```java
import java.awt.Graphics;
public class AppletLife extends java.applet.Applet {
  public void init () {
    System.out.println("Browser wants me to: initialize myself");
  }
  public void start () {
    System.out.println("Browser wants me to: start running");
  }
  public void stop () {
    System.out.println("Browser wants me to: stop running");
  }
  public void paint (Graphics g) {
    System.out.println("Browser wants me to: redraw myself");
  }
```

```
public void destroy () {
    System.out.println("Browser wants me to: clean up before being removed.");
}
}
```

The first time you load the HTML page, you should see the following output printed to the Java console:

```
Browser wants me to: initialize myself
Browser wants me to: start running
Browser wants me to: redraw myself
```

This means the `init()`, `start()`, and `paint()` Applet methods are always called when an applet is first loaded and run. The sequence can differ from what is listed here; due to asynchronous aspects of the protocol, the `paint()` method can legally be called before the `start()` method. The `init()` method, however, is guaranteed to be called before all others.

Now, whenever the browser window needs to repaint itself—for example, after having been obscured by another window overlapping it—you should see an additional:

```
Browser wants me to: redraw myself
```

This is because the browser needed to completely redraw itself to undo the graphically inconsistent picture it was showing.

Remember that the entire GUI desktop metaphor your machine maintains is just a clever, graphical illusion. Any computer has a flat, uniform screen bitmap that doesn't enforce or care about these "overlapping" and clipping rectangular areas called "windows." The "natural behavior" of a computer screen is much more like that of a painting canvas in a painting program: The canvas has no restrictions whatsoever. In a GUI environment, then, when windows are depth-arranged in this plain bitmap environment, it means some windows will be partially or entirely overwritten, while others will need to redraw themselves. Since your applet is part of a window, it too must play along to maintain the illusion. If not, your applet will soon become graphically corrupted, or more likely, erased completely. This is why it is important to have an applet repaint itself using the `paint()` method whenever the browser commands it to (and as quickly as possible, as always).

If you load a different Web page in your browser or just iconify it, you should see your applet print the following line:

```
Browser wants me to: stop running
```

You will probably wonder what this means since your applet was not executing any code at the time anyway. Think about the kind of applications applets can be used for—animation, real-time updating of information fetched from an Internet server, general entertainment, and so on. All these types of applets are real-world applets, and they are very different from what has been demonstrated so far in this book. Real-world applets usually run constantly.

To illustrate, imagine that the `start()` method in your last applet never ended because it had to animate something all the time. Such an applet would be very wasteful of processor resources if it kept on animating even after the user switched to a different page. Yet that is exactly what it would do if you didn't take any steps to avoid this problem; the way to avoid the problem is by using threads.

In Chapter 8, you saw how threads allow you to do several things at the same time. Imagine all of an applet's core processing and functionality (the animating, for example) being run in a separate thread. This way, whenever the applet's page is displaced by a new page, you can simply freeze the thread, and when the applet's page is reloaded, you can let the thread run again; this is the real purpose of the `start()` and `stop()` methods of `Applet`. They assume that all your applets are written with multithreading in the first place. In later chapters, you will learn how to actually write applets built around a thread, but for now, just keep in mind that `start()` and `stop()` are really meant to control applet threads so that they do not consume processor resources while they are not in view.

WARNING You can also control sounds produced by your applet with the `start()` and `stop()` methods. Most sounds keep playing forever because they just loop around. To have a sound stop playing when the user leaves your applet's page, you need to explicitly stop that sound.

If you now click on your browser's Back button to revisit the page with our applet, or deiconify the browser, you will see the console print:

```
Browser wants me to: start running
Browser wants me to: redraw myself
```

Because the browser assumed your applet thread had been put to sleep when you switched pages, it now asks your applet to wake up the thread again, immediately followed by an urgent request to repaint the applet. This is because the applet's facade was overwritten a long time ago by the previous page and any of its applets.

The final method (literally) that a browser can invoke on applets is the `destroy()` method. Just quit your browser altogether and carefully watch the console window again. What you should have seen just before the console vanished was:

```
Browser wants me to: stop running
Browser wants me to: clean up before being removed
```

The final call to `destroy()` gives your applet an opportunity to release any persistent and/or expensive resources it had locked while in existence. Files, I/O streams, network connections, unwritten buffers, and similar resources might need some extra closing bookkeeping operations before the applet is discarded.

WARNING Java's garbage-collection feature means that ex-Pascal/C/C++ programmers can suddenly ignore cleanup issues with a vengeance. While the language feature itself is to be applauded (buggy cleanup code has been the cause of innumerable problems in the past), developers should not be lulled into a false sense of comfort. Java's garbage collection works only on objects that have no more parts of your application referencing them. Open files, output buffers, and network connections, for example, are more than just simple objects. You should therefore remain conscious of the (old) issues of correct code termination (the opposite of code initialization). Files should still be closed, output buffers flushed, and network connections disconnected properly.

Automating the Applet Tag Process

You may find the process of modifying the <APPLET CODE= ...> HTML tag repetitive and a waste of time. You can make your life easier by automating the process. The following is a shell utility written in Java that takes your applet's class name (without the .HTML extension) and generates a minimal HTML file with the <APPLET> tag pointing correctly to your applet. The program uses file and stream I/O, so you may wish to ignore its internals until you are ready for the chapter dealing exclusively with the `java.io` package (Chapter 19).

```
/****************************************************************************
 * GenAppletHTML utility
 *--------------------------------------------------------------------------
 * Usage: java GenAppletHTML <AppletName>
 *
 * This Java application generates an HTML file named after the class file,
 * which can be passed to the JDK appletviewer utility to test applets.
 ****************************************************************************/
```

```java
import java.io.*;
public class GenAppletHTML {
  public static void main (String args[]) throws IOException {
    FileWriter fw;
    PrintWriter html;
    // we need the name of an applet as argument
    if (args.length == 0) {
      System.out.println("Please specify the name of the applet to view.");
      System.exit(10);
    }
    // give usage summary if user asks for it
    if (args[0].indexOf("?") != -1 || args[0].equals("-h")) {
      System.out.println("Usage: java GenAppletHTML <AppletName>");
      System.exit(0);
    }
    // guard against illegal class names being passed (GIGO)
    if (!(Character.isLowerCase (args[0].charAt(0)) ||
          Character.isUpperCase (args[0].charAt(0)))) {
      System.out.println("'" + args[0] + "' is not a legal class name.");
      System.exit(11);
    }
    // enforce convention of class names starting with a capital letter
    if (Character.isLowerCase (args[0].charAt(0))) {
      System.out.println(
        "Class names should (by convention) start with a capital letter.");
      System.out.println(args[0]);
      System.out.println('^');
      System.out.println("is lower case.");
      System.exit(12);
    }
    // open file (combining FileOutputWriter and PrintWriter)

    fw = new FileWriter (args[0] + ".html");
    html = new PrintWriter (fw);

    /* Generate an HTML file with the following structure:
       <HTML>
       <HEAD></HEAD>
       <BODY>
       <HR>
       <APPLET CODE= ........ WIDTH=400 HEIGHT=300>
       <PARAM NAME=arg1 VALUE="val1">
```

```
     <PARAM NAME=arg2 VALUE="val2">
     </APPLET>
     <HR>
     </BODY>
     </HTML>
  */
  html.print("<HTML><HEAD></HEAD><BODY><HR><APPLET CODE=");
  html.print(args[0] + ".class ");
  html.println("WIDTH=400 HEIGHT=300>");
  html.println("<PARAM NAME=arg1 VALUE=\"val1\" >");   // note backslash esc
  html.println("<PARAM NAME=arg2 VALUE=\"val2\" >");
  html.println("</APPLET><HR></BODY></HTML>");
  html.close();
  }
}
```

To run the program, you invoke it as a stand-alone application; that is, from the command line:

```
C:\> java GenAppletHTML MyApplet
```

This would generate the file MyApplet.html. The GenAppletHTML utility is useful mainly on non-Unix machines that lack powerful batch-processing command languages. It also nicely illustrates how Java can be used as a powerful and universal batch-programming language.

You should now have a clear overview of applet internals. As you can see, the difficulties lie not in any special precautions you need to take when using AWT classes in applets. The precautions to be taken are imposed on you by the browser-applet calling protocol.

The Code Framework for Applications

Since stand-alone applications are by definition responsible for every aspect of themselves, such Java programs are free from any browser protocol and do not inherit a window or drawing area to use "straight away."

Because they do not rely on a browser protocol, anything goes for applications: They do not need to be subclasses of class Applet and do not consequently need any overridden init(), paint(), start(), or stop() methods. An application can be any class, as long as it has the obligatory static main() method as a starting point for the code.

The absence of an inherited window or drawing area is the main difference when you are writing applications instead of applets (if you are used to writing applets). Applications do not have a convenient window in which to draw or add GUI components. All this needs to be somehow acquired by the application itself, and this is how a minimal application does it:

```java
import java.awt.Frame;
import java.awt.Color;
import java.awt.event.WindowEvent;
import java.awt.event.WindowAdapter;
public class Application {
  public static void main (String args[]) {
    Frame myWindow = new Frame("Window !");
    myWindow.setBackground(Color.blue);
    myWindow.setSize(300,300);
    myWindow.setVisible(true);
    myWindow.addWindowListener (new WindowAdapter() {
      public void windowClosing (WindowEvent e) {
        System.exit(0);
      }
    });
  }
}
```

The program first creates a window (which initially is not visible) by constructing a new `Frame` object.

WARNING   Java *frames* are other people's normal *windows*. This unfortunate class nomenclature is only made worse by another AWT class called `Window`. A Java `Window` is a featureless rectangular pane (no title bar, menu bar, Close button, or Resize button) from which you can construct windows that ignore any and all local GUI style conventions. As such, class `Window` is used far less than class `Frame`.

The `Frame` constructor takes a string that will be the window's title. After construction, the frame's background color is set to blue. Next, the program specifies a size for this window using the `setSize()` method (the window still is not visible). And finally, it commands the window to pop open and display itself by invoking the `setVisible()` method. For simple applications of the same (trivial) complexity as the first applet example presented in this chapter, this is all that is required to set up a window in which you can then draw and/or build a GUI.

The final part of the program uses Java's event-handling capabilities. This will be more fully described in Chapter 14. For now, just understand that this allows the program to stop when the user asks the frame to close, by selecting its Close button.

Now that we've looked at the fundamental difference between the code frameworks required for applets and applications, it is time to attack this chapter's main topic: designing GUIs using the AWT layout manager classes.

Designing Java GUIs with Layout Managers

Layout managers are so important to Java GUI programming that a discussion of them should precede talk of Java buttons, menus, sliders, and text fields. To explain how layout managers work, concrete AWT components will be used as the passive subjects of the layout process; in this case, simple buttons that will not respond to any clicks will do the trick. Please indulge this approach and ignore the nagging questions relating to these buttons you will see being manipulated on your screen. You will learn about buttons (and every other component) in Chapter 11, after you have seen how layout managers manipulate components in general. Also, note the examples use the AWT `Button` class instead of the Swing `JButton` class. Please save questions related to this, too, until the next chapter.

Before exploring the different preprogrammed layout styles, you need to understand how the layout manager classes interact with their client classes: classes `Container` and `Component`.

Containers, Components, and Layout Managers

You will kick off your exploration of layout management with another simple applet. Type in (or copy from the accompanying CD-ROM) the following program:

```
import java.awt.*;
public class FlowLayoutTest extends java.applet.Applet {
  public void init() {

    setLayout(new FlowLayout());   // default for applets
    add(new Button("First"));
```

```
        add(new Button("Second"));
        add(new Button("Third"));
        add(new Button("Fourth"));
        add(new Button("Fifth"));
    }
}
```

This class implements a simple applet with five buttons laid out according to the style enforced by the FlowLayout layout manager. Figure 12.2 shows an example of an applet using this layout.

FIGURE 12.2:

An applet using its default layout: FlowLayout

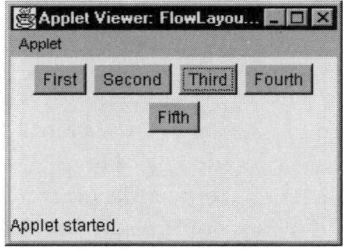

You will by now recognize the familiar hallmarks of applet code. For applets, you need the following:

- A class that extends class java.applet.Applet (or simply Applet if you explicitly import java.applet.Applet at the beginning of your source files)

- An init() method that contains all of the code for a minimalist applet (or init(), paint(), start(), and stop() methods for real-life applets)

NOTE   The example does not include any paint() method this time because it doesn't need one. AWT GUI elements are repainted automatically by the applet.

The *setLayout* Method

With the first line of method init(), the applet invokes the setLayout() method. This lets the applet pick one of the available layout styles for the GUI components it will use—in this case, the five buttons added immediately after the setLayout()

statement. Because you are extending class `Applet`, it would seem this `setLayout()` method comes from class `Applet`. But check out this class definition:

```
public class Applet extends Panel {
  public Applet();
  public void destroy();
  public AppletContext getAppletContext();
  public String getAppletInfo();
  public AudioClip getAudioClip(URL url);
  public AudioClip getAudioClip(URL baseUrl, String name);
  public URL getCodeBase();
  public URL getDocumentBase();
  public Image getImage(URL url);
  public Image getImage(URL baseUrl, String name);
  public Locale getLocale();
  public String getParameter(String name);
  public String[][] getParameterInfo();
  public void init();
  public boolean isActive();
  public static final AudioClip newAudioClip(URL url);
  public void play(URL url);
  public void play(URL baseUrl, String name);
  public void resize(int width, int height);
  public void resize(Dimension dim);
  public final void setStub(AppletStub stub);
  public void showStatus(String msg);
  public void start();
  public void stop();
}
```

You can see the `init()` method that is overridden in most applet programs in this chapter. But it appears that `setLayout()` is not a method belonging to `Applet`.

You might want to see if `setLayout()` is defined in `Panel` since `Applet` is itself a subclass of class `Panel`:

```
public class Panel extends Container {
  public Panel();
  public Panel(LayoutManager layout);
  public void addNotify();
}
```

No luck again. (This class looks very anemic indeed—just a constructor and a mysterious `addNotify()` instance method.) Yet method `setLayout()` must be defined somewhere! Consider further class `Panel`. It is a subclass of a yet higher-level class, class `Container`. Here is what a `Container` is all about:

```java
public class Container extends Component {
    public Container();
    public Component add(Component comp);
    public Component add(Component comp, int index);
    public void add(Component comp, Object constraints);
    public void add(Component comp, Object constraints, int index);
    public Component add(String name, Component comp);
    public synchronized void addContainerListener(ContainerListener l);
    protected void addImpl(Component comp, Object constraints, int index);
    public void addNotify();
    public void doLayout();
    public Component findComponentAt(int x, int y);
    public Component findComponentAt(Point p);
    public float getAlignmentX();
    public float getAlignmentY();
    public Component getComponent(int n);
    public Component getComponentAt(int x, int y);
    public Component getComponentAt(Point p);
    public int getComponentCount();
    public Component[] getComponents();
    public Insets getInsets();
    public LayoutManager getLayout();
    public Dimension getMaximumSize();
    public Dimension getMinimumSize();
    public Dimension getPreferredSize();
    public void invalidate();
    public boolean isAncestorOf(Component c);
    public void list(PrintStream out, int indent);
    public void list(PrintWriter out, int indent);
    public void paint(Graphics g);
    public void paintComponents(Graphics g);
    public void print(Graphics g);
    public void printComponents(Graphics g);
    protected void processContainerEvent(ContainerEvent e);
    protected void processEvent(AWTEvent e);
    public void remove(Component comp);
    public void remove(int index);
    public void removeAll();
    public void removeContainerListener(ContainerListener l);
    public void removeNotify();
    public void setLayout(LayoutManager mgr);
```

```
    public void update(Graphics g);
    public void validate();
    protected void validateTree();
}
```

Finally, there is the setLayout() method, fourth from the bottom of the alphabetical list. So, in your program you can simply call setLayout() without any further qualifiers because the Applet you extend is in fact also a Container (and a Panel, too, in the same way that a dog can be a mammal and an animal at the same time). Normally, invoking a method is always done "on an object": object.someMethod(). But the unqualified use of a method implicitly means "on myself": this.someMethod(). The Applet subclass therefore invokes setLayout() on itself, thus selecting some layout style for itself. The argument for the method is any LayoutManager object.

The *add* Method

Having identified the origins of the setLayout() method and part of the meaning of the statement it is used in, your next question should be: Why is this method defined in class Container? The answer is quite simple and brings you back to this chapter's main topic, layout managers. Associated with every container is its own, private layout manager. This is because layout managers lay out components contained by a container. Class Container is there to allow you to group related GUI elements. So now you can readily understand what the second core method is for any Container: method add() (the same add() used in the sample program to add the five buttons to the applet).

These points are summarized here; they are key to the understanding of this and virtually all other AWT programs:

- Every container has its own layout manager (that is, layout style).

- Individual components are grouped together in containers.

- Every applet is a container.

When applet code invokes an add() method on itself, it does so in its role as a container.

NOTE   In the case of applications, the window (that is, Java frame) used by the application acts as the container. It can therefore use exactly the same add() and setLayout() methods to construct GUIs.

If you now look back at some of the methods class `Container` defines, they will make a lot more sense:

```
public Component add(Component comp)
public Component add(Component comp, int index)
public void add(Component comp, Object constraints)
public void add(Component comp, Object constraints, int index)
public void add(String constraints, Component comp)
```

These overloaded methods all add a new GUI element to the container (the applet or the application's window). The `Component` type specified in all these methods is the root class for the entire GUI elements branch of the `java.awt` package hierarchy (refer back to Figure 9.6 and 9.8 in Chapter 9).

When an AWT method requires a `Component` type parameter, what it really means is that it requires any subclass of class `Component`: a `JButton`, a `JPanel`, a `JComponent`, a `JTextField`, a `JScrollBar`, and so on. This is analogous to the numerous Java methods that specify argument type `Object`, when, in fact, they mean "any object type." In both cases, these methods rely on the fact that subclasses of a particular superclass are considered compatible with that superclass. A `JButton`, for example, essentially is a `Component`. Similarly, a `String` is an `Object`.

> **TIP**
>
> Whenever you see type **Component** specified in an AWT method's signature, mentally substitute this type with any of the many Swing JComponents.

Class `Container` is hiding silently in the list of `Component` subclasses, which means a container can `add()` one or more subcontainers to itself since `Container` is a subclass of `Component`! It is important you understand this nesting capability because it is used frequently and allows your GUI designs to be more modular and therefore more flexible (in exactly the same way as black-box nesting applied to code makes your programs more modular and flexible). Having nested containers, each with their own layout style, gives you a powerful and flexible way to organize your GUI logically and make it aesthetically pleasing.

> **TIP**
>
> When you explore layout managers later, bear in mind that rarely is one layout manager alone used to manage the layout for an entire GUI. Layout managers are almost always used in combination.

Now, take a look back at the five add( ) method variants. Your program used the first one to add some buttons to the applet. The other variants allow you to put components in specific spots by passing a position argument. To this end, the second add( ) needs a numerical position argument, the next add( ) uses an Object as its positional constraints, the fourth requires numerical and Object arguments, and the last add( ) takes the position as a string label.

To demonstrate the add(comp, pos) method, modify your simple applet so that it reads:

```
add(new Button("First"));
add(new Button("Second"));
add(new Button("Third"));
add(new Button("Fourth"));
add(new Button("Fifth"), 2);   // << change here
```

If you run the applet, you will see the order of the buttons has been changed to first, second, fifth, third, fourth. The extra 2 argument in the last add( ) inserted the fifth button in between the second and third buttons already added to the container.

Now that you understand the hows and whys of your applet's init() method, you can focus your attention on the six primary component layout styles AWT provides: FlowLayout, BorderLayout, CardLayout, GridLayout, BoxLayout, and GridBagLayout.

NOTE   ScrollPaneLayout, ViewportLayout, and OverlayLayout are available in the javax.swing package. However, developers hardly ever use them directly. Various AWT components utilize them internally.

The *FlowLayout* Manager

The FlowLayout layout manager is the simplest layout manager in the AWT. As the name suggests, it lays out your GUI elements in a flowing, writing-like fashion, similar to how a word processor arranges words in a paragraph. The exact behavior can be understood more intuitively by running the following program:

```
import java.awt.*;
import java.awt.event.*;
public class FlowingButtons {
  public static void main (String args[]) {
    Frame win = new Frame();
```

```
win.setLayout (new FlowLayout());
win.setSize(120,180);
win.setVisible(true);
win.addWindowListener (new WindowAdapter() {
  public void windowClosing (WindowEvent e) {
    System.exit(0);
  }
});
for (int i = 0; i < 15; i++) {
  win.add (new Button (Integer.toString(i)));
  win.validate();
  try {
    Thread.sleep(1500);
  } catch (Exception e) {
  }
  System.out.println(i);
}
}
}
```

Figure 12.3 shows the program's window when it is two-thirds of the way through its loop.

FIGURE 12.3:

A centering FlowLayout

The program successively adds one button at a time and forces a redisplay of all the buttons so far. This way, you can see exactly what effect the layout manager has on the size and location of the buttons.

This program is not an applet this time. It lacks the code hallmarks of an applet, so it must be an application (you can run it without using your Web browser or the appletviewer utility). Like all applications, the program starts executing with its static main() method. Here, you create a new window with the Frame() constructor. Then, you select the FlowLayout layout manager for this window, size the window to some initial dimensions, and order it to display itself.

The setLayout() method should not confuse you now: It is the same Container.setLayout() method you saw earlier. And a Frame (like an Applet) is a subclass of Container, so it is perfectly entitled to invoke the method on itself, too. But since your sample class does not subclass Frame (it explicitly creates a Frame instance), you have to invoke setLayout() on your window using the fully qualified object.method() notation.

Once the window is visible, the program enters a short loop that adds and displays increasing numbers of buttons. The validate() method indirectly notifies the layout manager for the window (that is, the Container for the buttons) and redisplays the result.

The program uses the simplest FlowLayout object constructor possible: the one taking no arguments. But FlowLayout can be customized somewhat by specifying an optional alignment style and the minimum gaps to use between the components.

```
public FlowLayout(int align)
public FlowLayout(int align, int hgap, int vgap)
```

The alignment parameter should be one of these five FlowLayout class constants:

```
public final static int LEFT
public final static int CENTER
public final static int RIGHT
public final static int LEADING
public final static int TRAILING
```

The default constructor used so far is actually shorthand for:

```
new FlowLayout(FlowLayout.CENTER)
```

This is why the sample program centered all the buttons on each line. You can familiarize yourself with the predictable results of the four other alignment styles by substituting the line:

```
win.setLayout (new FlowLayout());
```

with:

```
win.setLayout (new FlowLayout (FlowLayout.RIGHT));
```

and again with FlowLayout.LEFT, FlowLayout.LEADING, and FlowLayout .TRAILING.

The third FlowLayout constructor lets you specify a pixel component spacing in both the horizontal and vertical directions.

WARNING Be careful with any AWT features that let you specify component positions, dimensions, or spacing in absolute terms. As explained earlier, AWT's way of positioning components is platform independent. Using only relative positional and dimensional specifications for components and containers allows layout managers to produce acceptable GUI layouts on all platforms. From the moment that you start "descending" into absolutes, you might be improving the look of the GUI on your machine, but it will degrade or even corrupt the layout of the same GUI running on a different platform.

Unlike most classes you will use when writing Java programs, most layout manager classes are not called directly at all (apart from their various constructors). This makes them very simple to use. Using the `setLayout()` method, you just pick one of the existing managers, and from then on the container will be managed by that layout manager. If you are curious about the internal workings of layout managers or think you need to write one yourself to use in your software productions, look at the "Layout Managers Internals: Interface *LayoutManager*" section later in the chapter.

NOTE The `LEADING` and `TRAILING` constants were introduced in Java 1.2 to better handle language-sensitive component orientations other than left-to-right. If the orientation of the container is not `ComponentOrientation.LEFT_TO_RIGHT`, the default, then the `LEFT` and `RIGHT` constants have reversed behavior, while `LEADING` and `TRAILING` force components to the leading or trailing edge, no matter which orientation.

Container Insets

One layout feature that is not a layout manager and yet affects all layout styles is called *insets*. Every container can define a border to be left clear of any components. This border is called the container's insets. If you look back at the definition for class `Container`, you'll see a method with the following signature:

```
public Insets getInsets()
```

The method is there to be overridden by your classes and must return an instance of an `Insets` object. Class `Insets` is simple; here is its definition:

```
public class Insets extends Object implements Cloneable {
    public int bottom;
    public int left;
    public int right;
    public int top;
```

```
    public Insets(int top, int left, int bottom, int right);
    public Object clone();
    public boolean equals (Object obj);
    public String toString();
}
```

Since it does not have any instance methods to speak of, it is not much of a class; it is more of a pure data structure. The constructor for the Insets class takes four parameters that together specify the border to be left clear of components. This is illustrated in the following example of how insets affect the final layout of a container. The following is a Java application program that creates a window laid out using the FlowLayout style and using custom insets. Four different getInsets() methods are listed disabled. You should enable them one at a time (by taking away the double-slash comments), compile, and run each version. Each getInsets() method accentuates insetting one edge at a time. Figure 12.4 shows the results.

```
import java.awt.*;
import java.awt.event.*;
//-------------------------------------------------------------------
public class InsetTest {
  public static void main (String args[]) {
    MyFrame win = new MyFrame();
    win.setLayout (new FlowLayout());
    win.add (new Button("One"));
    win.add (new Button("Two"));
    win.add (new Button("Three"));
    win.add (new Button("Four"));
    win.pack();
    win.setVisible(true);
    win.addWindowListener (new WindowAdapter() {
      public void windowClosing (WindowEvent e) {
        System.exit(0);
      }
    });
    System.out.println (win.getInsets());
  }
  //---------------------------------------------------------------
  static class MyFrame extends Frame {
    // public Insets getInsets() {return new Insets(100, 2, 2, 2);}
    // public Insets getInsets() {return new Insets(25, 100, 2, 2);}
    // public Insets getInsets() {return new Insets(25, 2, 100, 2);}
    public Insets getInsets() {return new Insets(25, 2, 2, 100);}
  } // End of class
  //---------------------------------------------------------------
} // End of main class
```

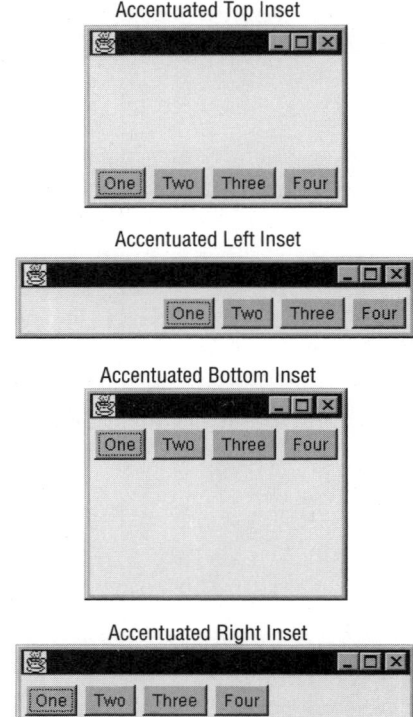

FIGURE 12.4:

Using custom insets

The *BorderLayout* Manager

The second layout manager is not quite as simple as FlowLayout. Class Border-Layout enforces a five-zone layout, as depicted in Figure 12.5. The BorderLayout manager is the default layout manager for Frame and JApplet (the Applet subclass when using the Swing components). The zones reflect the typical distribution of components in and around a window.

The five zones in Figure 12.5 are, in fact, filled by exactly the same type of buttons as those used by the FlowLayout example.

BorderLayout, as you can see, sizes its components so that they expand to fill the space available to them. Here is the program that created the output of Figure 12.5:

```
import java.awt.*;
public class BorderLayoutTest extends java.applet.Applet {
```

```
public void init() {
  setLayout(new BorderLayout());
  add(new Button("North"), BorderLayout.NORTH);
  add(new Button("South"), BorderLayout.SOUTH);
  add(new Button("West"), BorderLayout.WEST);
  add(new Button("East"), BorderLayout.EAST);
  add(new Button("Center"), BorderLayout.CENTER);
}
}
```

FIGURE 12.5:

A BorderLayout

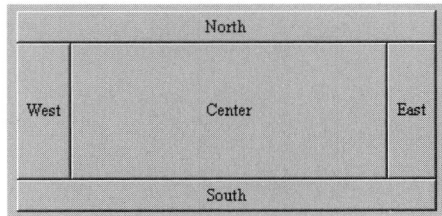

NOTE   Like FlowLayout, BorderLayout had additional constants introduced in Java 1.2 to better handle language-sensitive component orientations. The equivalent of NORTH and SOUTH are BEFORE_FIRST_LINE and AFTER_LAST_LINE, respectively. Replacing EAST and WEST is BEFORE_LINE_BEGINS and AFTER_LINE_ENDS. These replace EAST and WEST respectively if the ComponentOrientation of the container is LEFT_TO_RIGHT and get reversed if the orientation is RIGHT_TO_LEFT.

The coding differences with the FlowLayout example lie, for one, with the selection of a BorderLayout layout by passing an instance of the BorderLayout class to setLayout(). Second, the add() method used when adding components to a container with a BorderLayout is not the simple add(Component) one. You need to use the labeled add(Component comp, Object constraints) overloaded variant. As you can see from the code, the position is indicated by name instead of by number. This makes the code much more readable.

A BorderLayout can deal with only five components to be laid out: four components located flush against the four edges of a container and one component located centrally and occupying the bulk of the container's surface area. When using a BorderLayout manager, you are not obliged to specify all five components. Figure 12.6 shows what BorderLayout does when the "Center" component is left out.

FIGURE 12.6:

A BorderLayout with its "Center" component missing

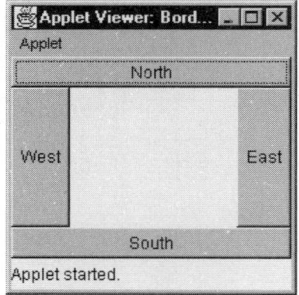

As you can see, the four edge components do not grow to fill the void created by the missing center component. Only when one or more of the edge components is left out will the space vacated by those be used by other components. Although there are 32 (2^5) different BorderLayout component combinations, the subset shown in Figure 12.7 should suffice to give you an accurate feel for how BorderLayout manipulates components when not all five are specified. Basically, when enough space is available, the north and south quadrants are the width of the area and the height of the component; the east and west quadrants are the remaining height of the area and the width of the component. Center is everything else.

WARNING   Besides class constants, you can use position strings with BorderLayout. These position strings are case-sensitive and are "North", "South", "East", "West", "Center", "First", "Last", "Before", and "After". For example, passing "NORTH" or "north" instead of "North" will not work. Moreover, the compiler has no way of enforcing this, so your code will compile without error if you do make case mistakes. Using a badly cased position string will result in the runtime exception IllegalArgumentException being thrown. It is safer to use the class constants, especially if you have a tendency to spell *center* as *centre*.

As with the FlowLayout layout manager, a variant of the BorderLayout constructor allows you to specify additional horizontal and/or vertical spacing when the border layout is applied. Replace the setLayout() line with the following line to see which effects you can obtain:

```
setLayout(new BorderLayout(10,50));
```

FIGURE 12.7:

A subset of Border-
Layout component
combinations

"North" Component Missing

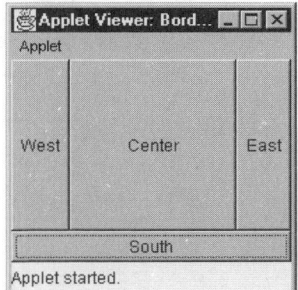

"North" and "West" Components Missing

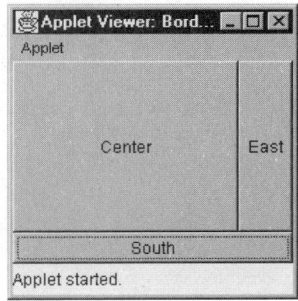

"East" Component Missing

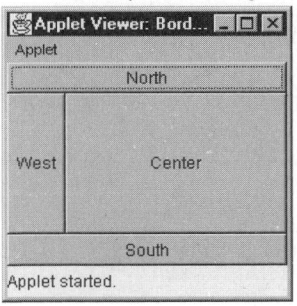

"North", "South", "East", and
"West" Components Missing

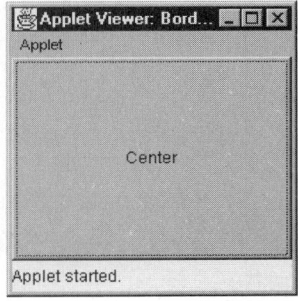

"Center", "East", and "West"
Components Missing

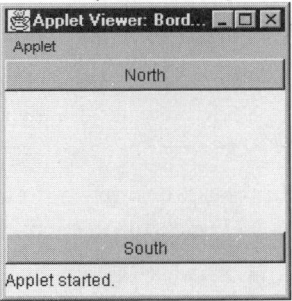

Figure 12.8 shows the unattractive layout that results from this change. A
10-pixel spacing was inserted between horizontally separated components, and
a 50-pixel spacing was used to space the components vertically. See the (clearly
justified) warning regarding the use of such absolute values in the section about
FlowLayout, earlier in the chapter.

FIGURE 12.8:

An ugly BorderLayout obtained by specifying excessive gaps

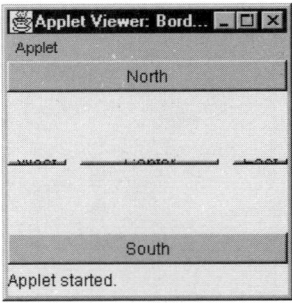

TIP

You can avoid problematic layouts like the one in Figure 12.8 by not relying on absolute distances or dimensions within your GUI designs. For GUIs that use a Frame as container, you normally call **pack()** just before displaying the window. This **pack()** method (defined in class **Window**) does a full layout of the **Frame**, using the components' preferred sizes as guidelines for the layout process.

The *CardLayout* Manager and *JTabbedPane*

The CardLayout layout manager is not really a layout manager as such. What it does is let you define any number of "cards" containing, typically, a logically related collection of components. Figure 12.9 shows a typical card-based configuration window (which wasn't implemented using Java but could easily be).

NOTE

Other GUI frameworks use the term *page* or *sheet* instead of *card*.

The following program demonstrates the use of CardLayout with five cards containing a single button each:

```
import java.awt.*;
import java.awt.event.*;
public class Cards extends Frame
    implements ActionListener {
  CardLayout layout;
  public Cards() {
    super ("CardLayout Tester");
    layout = new CardLayout();
```

```
      setLayout(layout);
      for (int i=0; i<5; i++) {
        Button b = new Button("Card " + i + " Button");
        add (b, "Btn"+i);
        b.addActionListener(this);
      }
    }
    public void actionPerformed(ActionEvent e) {
      layout.next(this);
    }
    public static void main (String args[]) {
      Frame f = new Cards();
      f.setSize (200, 150);
      f.setVisible(true);
      f.addWindowListener (new WindowAdapter() {
        public void windowClosing (WindowEvent e) {
          System.exit(0);
        }
      });
    }
  }
```

FIGURE 12.9:

A typical card-based GUI

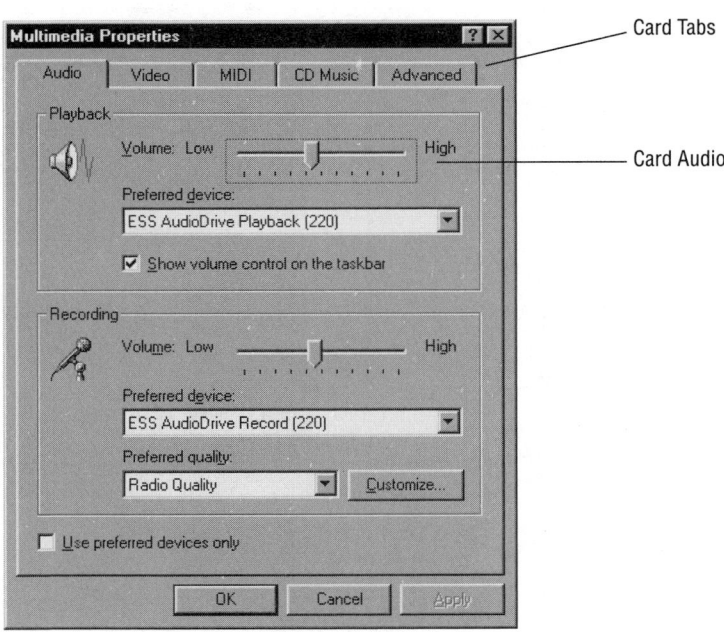

Card Tabs

Card Audio

Notice the add() method used to add cards to a CardLayout. As with border layouts, you need to use the constraints variety to pass a card name (in addition to the card itself) to the layout manager. Later, you can refer to your cards by name, instead of indexed by number, for example. Also note that a CardLayout variable was created. In the previous layout manager examples, you simply had a new *SomeLayoutManager*() within the brackets of the setLayout() call. But in this example, you actually need to refer to your CardLayout object after you have created it—this is why you need the variable to keep a reference to it.

To demonstrate the ability to cycle through the cards, this applet was made to listen for action from any of the buttons; the next card is displayed whenever you click on one of the buttons. The next() method tells the application to show the next card under its control. When it reaches the last card and you ask it to show the next() card again, it simply cycles back to the beginning.

NOTE   The sample application uses the addActionListener() and actionPerformed() methods for handling events. Event handling is discussed in detail in Chapter 14.

Figure 12.10 shows the frame produced by the program.

FIGURE 12.10:

CardLayout's default layout

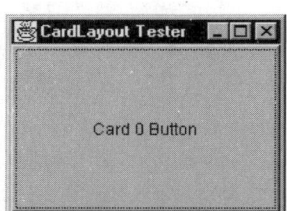

You probably expected to see a full-fledged rendering of our five different cards (as in Figure 12.9), including the clickable tabs to select any one of the cards. Unfortunately, CardLayout does not do this for you. You must either implement the tabs and the card outlines yourself or use the JTabbedPane container. The following program expands on the previous example to demonstrate the usage of JTabbedPane:

```
import java.awt.*;
import java.awt.event.*;
import javax.swing.*;
public class Cards2 extends Frame {
```

```
        public Cards2() {
          super ("JTabbedPane Tester");
          JTabbedPane jtp = new JTabbedPane();
          for (int i=0; i<5; i++) {
            Button b = new Button("Card " + i + " Button");
            jtp.addTab ("Btn"+i, b);
          }
          add (jtp, BorderLayout.CENTER);
        }
        public static void main (String args[]) {
          Frame f = new Cards2();
          f.setSize (250, 150);
          f.setVisible(true);
          f.addWindowListener (new WindowAdapter() {
            public void windowClosing (WindowEvent e) {
              System.exit(0);
            }
          });
        }
      }
```

Each card is added with the addTab( ) method, instead of the plain add( ) method. Also, notice the event-handling code to move between cards is automatically performed by the JTabbedPane. Because of this added value of JTabbedPane, you'll find yourself almost never using CardLayout. Figure 12.11 shows the output of the new and improved version of the program.

FIGURE 12.11:

Using JTabbedPane, instead of CardLayout

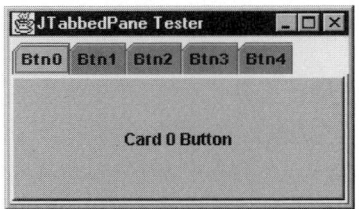

JTabbedPane also supports the display of images on the tabs and tool tips when the mouse is rested over a tab with **addTab** (String title, Icon icon, Component component) and **addTab** (String title, Icon icon, Component component, String tip). You'll learn more about icons and tool tips in the next chapter.

JSplitPane

The JSplitPane isn't exactly a layout manager. However, its behavior seems to fit in best during the discussion of them. The JSplitPane is similar to the JTabbed-Pane in that it is a self-contained container that provides additional functionality, above and beyond a regular container. In the case of the JTabbedPane, the added functionality is a list of tabs and associated pages. For the JSplitPane, you get a container that can be split vertically or horizontally, where the user, or programmer, can resize each area by moving a splitter bar.

To use a JSplitPane, you create it with the appropriate orientation and the components to scroll, although any of these can be changed at run time. For a vertical pane, where the components are on the top and bottom, you would specify an orientation of JSplitPane.VERTICAL_SPLIT:

```
new JSplitPane (JSplitPane.VERTICAL_SPLIT, topComponent, bottomComponent);
```

For the horizontal variety, creating is similar, but with JSplitPane.HORIZONTAL _SPLIT:

```
new JSplitPane (JSplitPane.HORIZONTAL_SPLIT, leftComponent, rightComponent);
```

There is another constructor variety that adds a boolean second parameter that specifies whether the components are continuously redrawn when the divider is moved:

```
new JSplitPane (orientation, boolean isContinuousLayout, component1, component2);
```

The two other capabilities you'll probably want to do with a JSplitPane is move the divider:

```
JSplitPane.setDividerLocation (int position)
```

or

```
JSplitPane.setDividerLocation (float percentage)
```

And enable what is dubbed "one-touch expandable." When enabled, additional arrows are provided on the divider to more easily collapse one part of the split pane or expand it back to its original size.

```
JSplitPane.setOneTouchExpandable (boolean expandable)
```

Figure 12.12 shows an example of the screen, after moving the dividers around a little. Notice that one of the panes has one-touch expandable enabled. There is no visual distinction to tell if continuous layout is enabled.

FIGURE 12.12:

A JSplitPane

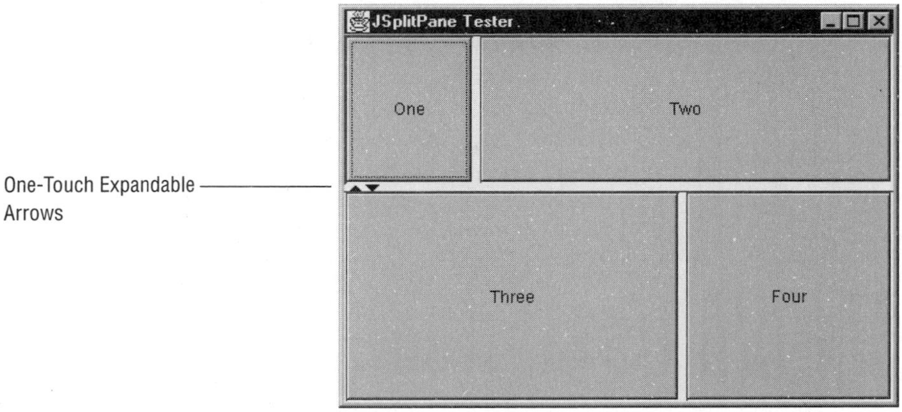

One-Touch Expandable
Arrows

The following program created Figure 12.12 and demonstrates the use of JSplit-Pane. To split more than two components, you need to specify a JSplitPane as one of the two components inside a JSplitPane.

```java
import java.awt.*;
import java.awt.event.*;
import javax.swing.*;
public class Split extends Frame {
  JSplitPane jsp1, jsp2, jsp3;
  public Split() {
    super ("JSplitPane Tester");
    Button one = new Button ("One");
    Button two = new Button ("Two");
    jsp1 = new JSplitPane(
      JSplitPane.HORIZONTAL_SPLIT,
      true, one, two);
    one = new Button ("Three");
    two = new Button ("Four");
    jsp2 = new JSplitPane(
      JSplitPane.HORIZONTAL_SPLIT,
      false, one, two);
    jsp3 = new JSplitPane(
      JSplitPane.VERTICAL_SPLIT,
      true, jsp1, jsp2);
    jsp3.setOneTouchExpandable (true);
    add (jsp3, BorderLayout.CENTER);
  }
```

```
public static void main (String args[]) {
  Frame f = new Split();
  f.setSize (400, 300);
  f.setVisible(true);
  f.addWindowListener (new WindowAdapter() {
    public void windowClosing (WindowEvent e) {
      System.exit(0);
    }
  });
}
}
```

The *GridLayout* Manager

The GridLayout layout manager enforces a grid-based layout on components.
Figure 12.13 shows an example of this type of layout.

FIGURE 12.13:

A GridLayout

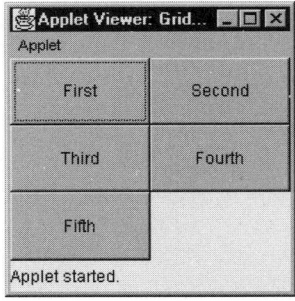

Here is the program that produced the applet in Figure 12.13:

```
import java.awt.*;
public class GridLayoutTest extends java.applet.Applet {
  public void init() {
    setLayout(new GridLayout(3,2));
    add(new Button("First"));
    add(new Button("Second"));
    add(new Button("Third"));
    add(new Button("Fourth"));
    add(new Button("Fifth"));
  }
}
```

When Implementation Interferes with Interface

Unfortunately, the decoupling of the adding order and positioning of components in the layout cannot be taken to its logical extreme by, for example, coding a button layout using a jumbled up sequence like this:

```
add(new Button("Fifth"), 4);
add(new Button("Second"), 1);
add(new Button("Third"), 2);
add(new Button("Fourth"), 3);
add(new Button("First"), 0);
```

The first **add()** will throw an **IllegalArgumentException** ("illegal component position") exception. This is because the semantics of the **add()** method insert a component at the given position. Internally, class **Container** uses an array, and as you know, you cannot index array elements beyond the end of the array. So in trying to avoid an **ArrayIndexOutOf-Bounds** exception, the **Container** code checks to see whether the component can be safely inserted at the given position specified. It would have been much more intuitive for this method to have the semantics of simply placing a component at a given position (namely, overwriting the array element) and expanding the array automatically if positions are specified beyond the end of the array.

When implementation details like these affect the use of a class in such a counterproductive way, this is a sure sign of poor design and should prompt a reworking of the semantics. The design of the component management inside class Container should allow a jumbled up sequence of **add()** methods to add its components without making a fuss at all.

You specify the number of grid rows and columns to the constructor for class `GridLayout`. In this example, three rows and two columns were used. Again, five test buttons were added using the default `add(Component)` method. Notice the order in which the buttons end up: The linear adding sequence is used to fill the rows top to bottom. If this implicit ordering is not suitable for your program, you can use the second `Container add()` method, which takes an additional single numerical position argument, as follows:

```
add(new Button("First"), 0);
add(new Button("Second"), 1);
add(new Button("Third"), 2);
add(new Button("Fourth"), 3);
add(new Button("Fifth"), 4);
```

The resulting layout is exactly the same as in Figure 12.13. In other words, you have simply separated the adding order from the positioning.

WARNING   If the requested number of cells is significantly different from the actual number of cells, the actual number of rows and columns may not be what you expect. For instance, if you request a 3 × 3 grid, but only add four components, you'll get a 2 × 2 grid, not three buttons in the first row and one in the second. When going over the requested total, this favors keeping the number of rows requested. Also, you can specify 0 as the requested number of rows or columns for that dimension to grow without bounds.

Because grid cells are usually specified using two-dimensional grid coordinates instead of one linear, one-dimensional coordinate, you are probably wondering why you have not seen an add(Component, x, y) method. The answer is rather subtle: All these add() methods are not methods belonging to any layout managers but instead are defined in class Container. This is because the add() methods primarily add components to a container. The laying-out process is not yet relevant at this stage of adding components—it usually happens much later, right before the GUI is displayed, as a result of a display command.

The GridLayout manager was no doubt added to AWT quite a bit later than the class Container was designed and specified. So it was not anticipated that some future layout manager would like to have a two-dimensional add() method. This oversight can be understood if you consider that class Container uses a one-dimensional array to hold all the components it manages. In that light, it would indeed have been uncommon for a programmer to think ahead and imagine a future requirement for an add() with two-dimensional position coordinates. To overcome these limitations, you can use the GridBagLayout manager, explained in a later section, which is more flexible (and more difficult) than the GridLayout manager.

The *BoxLayout* Manager and *Box*

One of the new layout managers introduced in Java 1.2 is the BoxLayout. The BoxLayout is similar to both FlowLayout and GridLayout. BoxLayout is like FlowLayout in that it tries to size components based on their preferred size. However, BoxLayout is unlike FlowLayout in that a row of added components will not wrap when it reaches the end of a row (or column). With regards to GridLayout, BoxLayout acts like a GridLayout with a single row or column. The difference between the two is that components in a BoxLayout can each have their own size.

So, how do you use BoxLayout? Normally you don't. You actually use the **Box** container instead. In turn, it uses the BoxLayout internally. First, you create a box, specifying the direction via one of two BoxLayout constants (X_AXIS or Y_AXIS):

```
Box box1 = new Box (BoxLayout.X_AXIS); // horizontal
Box box2 = new Box (BoxLayout.Y_AXIS); // vertical
```

then, you just add components like you normally do:

```
box1.add (new Button ("Left");
box1.add (new Button ("Center");
box1.add (new Button ("Right");
box2.add (new Button ("Top");
box2.add (new Button ("Center");
box2.add (new Button ("Bottom");
```

If you don't want to bother with the BoxLayout constants, you can ask a box for a box in the appropriate direction via createHorizontalBox() or create-VerticalBox().

Box even lets you create fixed-size filler areas:

```
public static Component createRigidArea (Dimension dim);
public static Component createHorizontalStrut (int width);
public static Component createVerticalStrut (int height);
```

or expandable areas with the following set of methods:

```
public static Component createGlue();
public static Component createHorizontalGlue();
public static Component createVerticalGlue();
```

For the createRigidArea(), createHorizontalStrut(), and createVertical-Strut() methods, you create a fixed-sized component, then add() it between two other components to ensure a fixed distance between the components. Figure 12.14 shows an example of this type of layout.

FIGURE 12.14:

A vertical Box with fixed distances, or struts, between components, before and after resizing

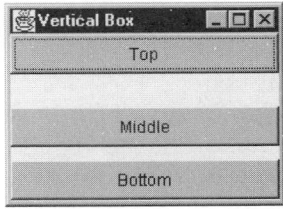
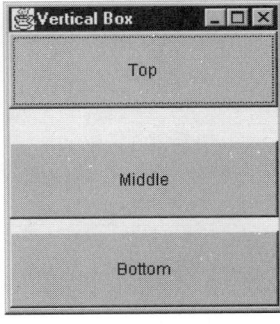

Here is the program that produced the frames in Figure 12.14. Notice that the width of the rigid area created is ignored:

```
import java.awt.*;
import java.awt.event.*;
import javax.swing.*;
public class VerticalBox {
  public static void main (String args[]) {
    Frame f = new Frame("Vertical Box");
    Box box = Box.createVerticalBox();
    box.add (new Button ("Top"));
    box.add (Box.createVerticalStrut (25));
    box.add (new Button ("Middle"));
    box.add (Box.createRigidArea (new Dimension (5000000, 10)));
    box.add (new Button ("Bottom"));
    f.add (box, BorderLayout.CENTER);
    f.setSize (200, 150);
    f.setVisible (true);
    f.addWindowListener (new WindowAdapter() {
      public void windowClosing (WindowEvent e) {
        System.exit(0);
      }
    });
  }
}
```

For the createGlue(), createHorizontalGlue(), and createVerticalGlue() methods, what you create is a growable component that, once added, will consume any extra space when a screen is sized to an area larger than the other components. Figure 12.15 demonstrates this type of filled growth.

Here is the program that produced the frames in Figure 12.15. Notice that where the glue is added determines where the extra space goes:

```
import java.awt.*;
import java.awt.event.*;
import javax.swing.*;
public class HorizontalBox {
  public static void main (String args[]) {
    Frame f = new Frame("Horizontal Boxes");
    Box box = Box.createHorizontalBox();
    box.add (Box.createHorizontalGlue());
    box.add (new Button ("Left"));
    box.add (new Button ("Right"));
    f.add (box, BorderLayout.NORTH);
```

```
box = Box.createHorizontalBox();
box.add (new Button ("Left"));
box.add (Box.createHorizontalGlue());
box.add (new Button ("Right"));
f.add (box, BorderLayout.CENTER);
box = Box.createHorizontalBox();
box.add (new Button ("Left"));
box.add (new Button ("Right"));
box.add (Box.createHorizontalGlue());
f.add (box, BorderLayout.SOUTH);
f.setSize (200, 150);
f.setVisible (true);
f.addWindowListener (new WindowAdapter() {
  public void windowClosing (WindowEvent e) {
    System.exit(0);
  }
});
}
}
```

FIGURE 12.15:

A horizontal Box before
and after a resizing

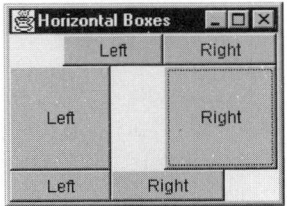

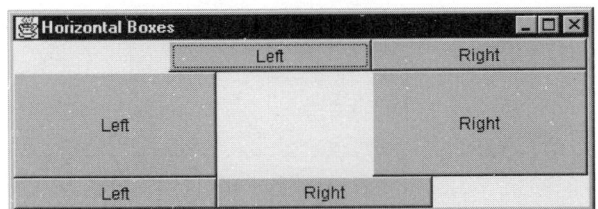

The *GridBagLayout* Manager and *GridBagConstraints*

All of the examples used to demonstrate the different layout managers so far simply use buttons that have not been asked to appear drawn to any set size. Before inspecting the last and most complex standard layout manager, class GridBagLayout, you first should learn a bit about component sizes.

Component Dimensions

Every Component can give hints to layout managers as to how big or small it would like to appear in the GUI. Three sizes can be explicitly specified: a preferred, a minimum, and a maximum size. To specify these for your AWT components, you need to create a subclass of the generic component class (Button, List, TextField, and so on) and override the following three Component methods:

```
public class Component extends Object implements ImageObserver {
    :
    :
  public Dimension getPreferredSize();
  public Dimension getMaximumSize();
  public Dimension getMinimumSize();
    :
    :
}
```

Because there is no way to specify these size hints for non-subclassed components, these methods are not used in the previous examples. (Using them would have required creating Button subclasses in all of the layout manager examples, and that would have detracted your attention from the core layout manager issues.) In real-life applets and applications, however, windows and their contents can be resized (unless you take explicit steps to force a window to be of fixed size). But when a user shrinks your window, it can reach a point where simply linearly scaling every component accordingly will result in either an ugly or a plainly nonfunctional GUI. Similarly, when a user stretches your window, a point may be reached where your components scaled up proportionally will look ridiculous. Methods getPreferredSize(), getMinimumSize(), and getMaximumSize() help layout managers size your components so that the result of any window resizing operation remains acceptable.

> **NOTE** The Swing components that you'll learn about in the next chapter have methods setMaximumSize(Dimension), setMinimumSize(Dimension), and setPreferredSize(Dimension) that allow you to change component sizes without subclassing.

If you rerun the GridLayout demos using the JDK tool appletviewer and play around with the applet window size, you will see that the five buttons can be stretched or shrunk to very extreme sizes. You can counter this flexibility overkill by creating Button subclasses that specify some reasonable sizes using getPreferredSize() and getMinimumSize(), and using a layout manager that honors these hints, like GridBagLayout (GridLayout does not). The way this is done is by overriding the methods. For example:

```
public Dimension getPreferredSize() {
  return new Dimension(200,150);
}
```

If this overridden method was included in any Component subclass you created, it would tell any layout manager that this component's preferred dimensions are 200×150 pixels.

NOTE   Most layout managers provided within Java's AWT ignore any requested maximum size. While the default value returned by getMaximumSize() is new Dimension (Short.MAX_VALUE, Short.MAX_VALUE), the layout manager may ignore any overriding of this setting. In certain cases, like with BoxLayout, a layout manager will honor the requested maximum.

An Introduction to *GridBagLayout*

GridBagLayout is special among the standard layout managers in that it uses a helper class (GridBagConstraints) to specify a whole host of layout parameters, normally one class instance per component. The GridBagLayout manager's main (but by no means only) advantage over GridLayout is that it allows a component to use up more than one grid cell.

A component's size can be specified as the number of horizontal and/or vertical grid cells the component should occupy on the grid. The helper GridBag-Constraints class, which is defined as follows, controls these parameters:

```
public class GridBagConstraints extends Object implements
            Cloneable, java.io.Serializable {
  public static final int BOTH;
  public static final int CENTER;
  public static final int EAST;
  public static final int HORIZONTAL;
  public static final int NONE;
  public static final int NORTH ;
  public static final int NORTHEAST;
  public static final int NORTHWEST;
  public static final int RELATIVE;
  public static final int REMAINDER;
  public static final int SOUTH;
  public static final int SOUTHEAST;
```

```
    public static final int SOUTHWEST;
    public static final int VERTICAL;
    public static final int WEST;
    public int anchor, fill;
    public int gridx, gridy;
    public int gridwidth, gridheight;
    public Insets insets;
    public int ipadx, ipady;
    public double weightx, weighty;
    public GridBagConstraints();
    public Object clone();
}
```

This class consists essentially of instance variables and a collection of class constants (it also has a constructor and an overridden implementation of the `Object clone()` method, discussed later in the chapter).

NOTE   If you look at the list of `GridBagConstraints` class constants, you can really appreciate the problem of Java's unfortunate and remarkable lack of enumerated type support. Every constant is typed as a thoroughly nondescriptive `int`, whereas a Pascal type declaration for the same would be infinitely more readable:

```
TYPE
    FillBehavior = {NONE, HORIZONTAL, VERTICAL, BOTH};
    AnchorType = {CENTER, NORTH, NORTHEAST, EAST,
                  SOUTHEAST, SOUTH, SOUTH WEST, WEST,
                  NORTHWEST}
VAR
    fill : FillBehavior;
    anchor : AnchorType;
```

The most important `GridBagConstraints` fields are `gridx`, `gridy`, `gridwidth`, and `gridheight`. These fields control a component's placement and size in the grid. Unlike with the one-dimensional placement limitations of the `add()` method for components added to a `GridLayout`, the `gridx` and `gridy` fields allow you to specify `GridBagLayout` components in any order and in two dimensions. With a `GridBagLayout`, you use a special version of `add()` that takes the `GridBagConstraints` as its second parameter.

Figure 12.16 shows a sample `GridBagLayout` that clearly demonstrates the additional possibilities the class provides over classes `FlowLayout` and `GridLayout`.

FIGURE 12.16:

A GridBagLayout

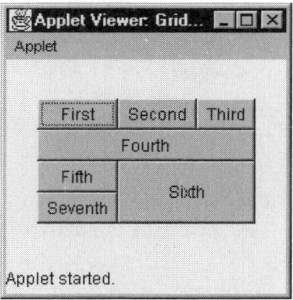

Here is the program that produced the GUI layout in Figure 12.16:

```java
import java.awt.*;
public class Gridbag extends java.applet.Applet {
  public void init() {
    GridBagLayout gb = new GridBagLayout();
    GridBagConstraints gbc = new GridBagConstraints();
    Button b;
    setLayout(gb);
    gbc.gridwidth  = 1;
    gbc.gridheight = 1;
    gbc.gridx = 0;
    gbc.gridy = 0;
    gbc.fill = GridBagConstraints.BOTH;
    b = new Button("First");
    add(b, gbc);
    b = new Button("Second");
    gbc.gridx = 1;
    gbc.gridwidth = 2;
    add(b, gbc);
    b = new Button("Third");
    gbc.gridx = 3;
    gbc.gridwidth = 1;
    add(b, gbc);
    b = new Button("Fourth");
    gbc.gridx = 0;
    gbc.gridy++;
    gbc.gridwidth = 4;
    add(b, gbc);
    b = new Button("Fifth");
```

```
        gbc.gridy++;
        gbc.gridwidth = 1;
        add(b, gbc);
        b = new Button("Sixth");
        gbc.gridx = 1;
        gbc.gridwidth = 3;
        gbc.gridheight = 2;
        add(b, gbc);
        b = new Button("Seventh");
        gbc.gridx = 0;
        gbc.gridy++;
        gbc.gridwidth = 1;
        gbc.gridheight = 1;
        add(b, gbc);
    }
}
```

This applet's init() method begins by creating one new GridBagLayout object and one helper GridBagConstraints object. After setting the current layout to GridBagLayout, the code initializes "constraint" parameters for the first object to be added. Filling in GridBagConstraints fields does this. You set the width and height to 1 cell and start adding components in the top-left corner of the grid (grid coordinates 0,0).

The next line sets the fill style for the components. This determines how a component will fill the available space if that space allows it to stretch beyond its preferred size. The legal values for the fill variable are NONE, HORIZONTAL, VERTICAL, and BOTH. You then associate these layout parameters with your component by calling the add() method, passing the GridBagConstraints as a second argument.

To summarize, adding a component to a GridBagLayout-style container consists of these two steps:

1. Set any desired GridBagConstraints parameters.

2. Invoke the two-parameter version of the add() method to add the component to the container.

Regarding the first step, there is an interesting subplot going on in the sample code. First, you initialize some of the GridBagConstraints object's fields, and then you add the button to its container. This lets the GridBagLayout manager bind the first button with the GridBagConstraints object as defined at that point. You then proceed to modify some of the GridBagConstraints values and call add() again to bind the second button with your same but modified Grid-BagConstraints object (you have only one instance for the entire program). You just changed its gridx and gridwidth instance variables, but left the gridy and gridheight variables alone. This means you have just clobbered half of the GridBagConstraints parameters for button one.

Remember that Java objects are passed by reference and not by value (that is, objects are not copied). Shouldn't you therefore have needed to create a new GridBagConstraints object for each button? Normally, yes, but in this exceptional case, no. The reason lies hidden inside the GridBagLayout class itself. Method setConstraints() uses the clone() method to make a copy of the GridBagConstraints objects given to it. And this is why you can safely use a single GridBagConstraints object instance for any number of components.

The clone() method is available only on classes that implement the Cloneable interface. If you check back at the definition of GridBagConstraints, you will see that this class does just that. Since very few classes do implement this interface, this type of object "pass-by-value" feature is rare in Java. The norm is that method arguments let your objects have full (shared) access to the passed object, and thus the programming technique used in our example would be quite incorrect. In this instance, however, it has become a Java idiom, so you can improve readability of code sections dealing with GridBagLayout managers by exploiting the object-cloning behavior.

There is one more GridBagConstraints parameter to be introduced. To see its effect, recompile and run the applet with the following line removed:

```
gbc.fill = GridBagConstraints.BOTH;
```

Figure 12.17 shows an example of the resulting GridBagLayout.

FIGURE 12.17:

A GridBagLayout with fill set to NONE

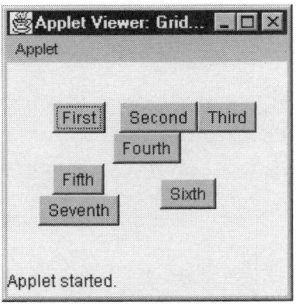

Applet started.

The layout suddenly looks very un-gridlike (if you look closely, the Second and Sixth buttons are not aligned to any grid). This is because of the other `GridBag-Constraints` parameter: `anchor`. Without an explicit value for the `fill` parameter, you simply get its default: NONE. This means that any components will be sized to their preferred size (if possible). The odd-looking placement of buttons Second and Six is the result of the default `anchor` style. This default style centers components within the grid space they allocated, using `gridwidth` and `gridheight`. If you now add the following line (where you removed the fill style line), you should obtain the result shown in Figure 12.18.

```
gbc.anchor = GridBagConstraints.NORTHWEST;
```

FIGURE 12.18:

A `GridBagLayout` with fill set to NONE and anchor set to NORTHWEST

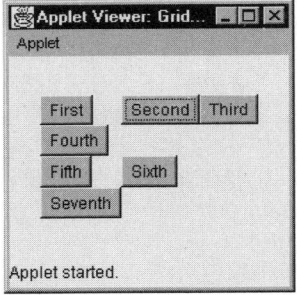

The valid values for the `anchor` parameter are CENTER, NORTH, EAST, NORTHEAST, SOUTHEAST, SOUTH, SOUTHWEST, WEST, and NORTHWEST.

NOTE

`GridBagLayout` is extremely flexible, and this discussion has given only an overview of the functionality of the class. For more information, refer to the online documentation and experiment on your own. Also, the *Java Developers Handbook* (published by Sybex) contains an in-depth discussion on this and many other more advanced Java programming topics.

Now that you have been introduced to the standard AWT layout managers, you will next explore the innards of layout managers. The following section explains what all layout managers have in common.

Layout Manager Internals: Interface *LayoutManager*

Layout managers are powerful black boxes to help you design GUIs rapidly. But what if you want to write your own GUI? If you look up the (online) class definition for `FlowLayout`, `BorderLayout`, `CardLayout`, `GridLayout`, or `GridBagLayout`, you will see that these classes all implement the same interface: `LayoutManager` (or the subinterface `LayoutManager2`). The `LayoutManager` interface is the key to understanding layout manager internals. Here is its definition:

```
public interface LayoutManager {
    public abstract void addLayoutComponent(String name, Component comp);
    public abstract void layoutContainer(Container parent);
    public abstract Dimension minimumLayoutSize(Container parent);
    public abstract Dimension preferredLayoutSize(Container parent);
    public abstract void removeLayoutComponent(Component comp);
}
```

The methods the interface asks you to implement can be grouped as follows:

- Adding/removing components to a container
- Calculating preferred and minimum container sizes
- Actually doing the layout operation

You might think the `addLayoutComponent()` method is a direct analog of the `add()` container methods. However, this is only partially correct. A layout manager's `addLayoutComponent()` method is called only by a container's `add(String, Component)` method and not by the simpler `add(Component)` method. Layout managers `FlowLayout` and `GridLayout` implement their `addLayoutComponent()` methods as follows:

```
public void addLayoutComponent(String name, Component comp) {
}
```

That's right—a void body. These managers don't manage the growing collection of components added to their associated container, because they don't need to. The container object keeps track of all the components it contains (that is its primary function, after all). And when `layoutContainer()` is called, the layout manager receives a handle to the container it should lay out. Via this handle, the layout manager can access all of the container's components, in sequence, with the `Container` methods `getComponentCount()` and `getComponent()`. This is how some layout managers can afford to have empty `addLayoutComponent()` and `removeLayoutComponent()` methods. But this is not universal.

Besides implementing the `LayoutManager` interface, a layout manager can implement the subinterface `LayoutManager2`. Here is its definition:

```
public interface LayoutManager2
    extends java.awt.LayoutManager {
  public abstract void addLayoutComponent(Component comp, Object
constraints);
  public abstract float getLayoutAlignmentX(Container parent);
  public abstract float getLayoutAlignmentY(Container parent);
  public abstract void invalidateLayout(Container parent);
  public abstract Dimension maximumLayoutSize(Container parent);
}
```

Layout managers `BorderLayout`, `BoxLayout`, `CardLayout`, and `GridBagLayout` have non-empty bodies for these methods because they require `add (Component, Object)` to access the `LayoutManager2` `addLayoutComponent (Component comp, Object constraints)` method. While the unlabeled `add()` essentially just adds a component to the container's internal list, the constrained `add()` also tells the container's layout manager about the component.

Method `layoutContainer()` is the heart of any layout manager—it is where all the laying out finally takes place. Here the layout manager will use the container's insets and all the components' sizes to determine exactly how to size and position each component.

As an example, this is the `BorderLayout` manager's `layoutContainer()`:

```
public void layoutContainer(Container target) {
  Insets insets = target.getInsets();
  int top = insets.top;
  int bottom = target.height - insets.bottom;
  int left = insets.left;
  int right = target.width - insets.right;

  boolean ltr = target.getComponentOrientation().isLeftToRight();
  Component c = null;

  if ((c=getChild(NORTH,ltr)) != null) {
    c.setSize(right - left, c.height);
```

```
        Dimension d = c.getPreferredSize();
        c.setBounds(left, top, right - left, d.height);
        top += d.height + vgap;
    }
    if ((c=getChild(SOUTH,ltr)) != null) {
        c.setSize(right - left, c.height);
        Dimension d = c.getPreferredSize();
        c.setBounds(left, bottom - d.height, right - left, d.height);
        bottom -= d.height + vgap;
    }
    if ((c=getChild(EAST,ltr)) != null) {
        c.setSize(c.width, bottom - top);
        Dimension d = c.getPreferredSize();
        c.setBounds(right - d.width, top, d.width, bottom - top);
        right -= d.width + hgap;
    }
    if ((c=getChild(WEST,ltr)) != null) {
        c.setSize(c.width, bottom - top);
        Dimension d = c.getPreferredSize();
        c.setBounds(left, top, d.width, bottom - top);
        left += d.width + hgap;
    }
    if ((c=getChild(CENTER,ltr)) != null) {
        c.setBounds(left, top, right - left, bottom - top);
    }
}
```

BorderLayout starts by determining the available working area by subtracting the insets from the container's dimensions. It then proceeds to lay out its five possible components, north, south, east, west, and center, in that sequence. Remember that BorderLayout components must be added using the labeled **add** or the constrained add, add(Component, Object). BorderLayout therefore manages its "list" of components by storing each component directly into private variables. The getChild() method is then asked to fetch the appropriate componet from these variables according to the container's orientation. (This is done by its addLayoutComponent() method.) The actual layout logic is, of course, totally manager dependent. What all managers need to have in common, however, is the use of the preferred, minimum, and maximum sizes of components to make their layout decisions. Components are eventually positioned and sized using their setBounds() method.

These are the other two `LayoutManager` methods:

```
public abstract Dimension preferredLayoutSize(Container parent)
public abstract Dimension minimumLayoutSize(Container parent)
```

and one for LayoutManager2:

```
public abstract Dimension maximumLayoutSize(Container parent)
```

These three are in fact very similar to `layoutContainer()`, except they do not actually lay out the components. Their goal is to work out what the size of the container could be set to if a layout were done honoring all components' preferred, minimum, or maximum sizes. The logic for these three methods is virtually identical to that of `layoutContainer()`, barring the `setSize()` and `setBounds()` calls. Additionally, method `minimumLayoutSize()` calls the `getMinimumSize()` method on components instead of calculating a size for them, while `maximumLayoutSize()` calls `getMaximumSize()`.

Summary

This chapter taught you the absolute basics of how to use Java's AWT. You saw the two fundamentally different contexts in which AWT can be used: applets and applications. Applets are bound to the applet-browser protocol; applications need to build their GUIs from scratch, starting with a window to hold the GUI. You then studied Java's solution to platform-independent GUI designing: layout managers.

Layout managers are responsible for laying out your GUI's graphical elements in such a way that the resulting windows or screens look acceptable on all Java platforms. Layout managers interact closely with container classes (which are all descendants of class `Container`), for which they perform the layout function; and with component classes (all descendants of class `Component`), which are the objects being laid out. AWT currently provides nine preprogrammed layout styles that, when used in concert, offer enough layout flexibility to create modern, functional, and platform-independent GUIs. The six primary preprogrammed layout managers are, in increasing order of complexity, `FlowLayout`, `GridLayout`, `BorderLayout`, `BoxLayout`, `CardLayout`, and `GridBagLayout`, which relies on a helper class called `GridBagConstraints`. The `OverlayLayout`, `ScrollPaneLayout`, and `Viewport-Layout` managers are available but are rarely used outside of their components. Also, the layout-oriented special Java containers `JTabbedPane`, `JSplitPane`, and

Box were discussed, providing layout management capabilities, directly within these Java containers.

For those rare occasions when the standard AWT layout managers are not sufficient for your purposes, you looked at how layout managers themselves are implemented, with a view on designing your own. Essentially, and regardless of layout approach, the sole requirement for any layout manager class is that it implements the LayoutManager interface or its subinterface LayoutManager2.

C H A P T E R

T H I R T E E N

13

Swing GUI Components

■ The AWT GUI superclass and its methods

■ Buttons, checkboxes, lists, tables, and other GUI components

■ Menu support components

Modern GUIs are rich in graphical elements employed to make the human-computer interface (HCI) as productive as possible. Buttons and menus are still the ubiquitous and original classics, but nowadays a whole collection of descendants has evolved. The spectrum of popular buttons and menus ranges from radio buttons, pop-up menus, and slider controls to the more complex components, such as list and tree views, toolbars, and progress status windows.

Java's AWT contains two set of components. The first set is a healthy mix of the simpler components, which JDK 1.0 and JDK 1.1 provided. More recently, Sun introduced the Swing component set, which is part of the Java Foundation Classes (JFC) that comes with JDK 1.2. This set replaces all the AWT components with its own simple components and provides additional complex components. If you are creating real-world applications for desktop computing, you should avoid the original AWT components completely and stick with the Swing component set.

> **NOTE**   Although the Java Foundation Classes are part of JDK 1.2, the Swing component set is usable with either JDK 1.1 or 1.2. To get the latest development package for Java 1.1 usage, got the The Swing Connection at `http://java.sun.com/products/jfc/tsc/`. While externally, the Java 1.1 and 1.2 versions may appear the same from an API perspective, internally the classes may be different.

The Swing components examined in this chapter include buttons, labels, toggle buttons, combo boxes, list boxes, scrollbars, sliders, text, scrollpanes, tables, and toolbars. Common functionality shared across these components and others—like borders, tool tips, and icons—is also described. Finally, the Swing menu-related components are described.

You can access and use all of these components via their corresponding Swing classes. Before systematically exploring the individual components, you will want to take a close look at the granddad of all components: class Component itself.

The Superclass of the AWT GUI Classes: *Component*

GUI elements have many things in common. And when classes have things in common, you immediately think "abstraction." Object-oriented methodology demands there be a superclass to any group of classes with identifiable, shared characteristics.

A superclass localizes code and/or data structures that would otherwise be duplicated and scattered around your systems (negatively affecting code robustness and flexibility). The AWT GUI classes have one such superclass, class Component, and the Swing GUI classes have one such superclass, class JComponent. The JComponent is in turn a subclass of Container, which was described in Chapter 12, and is a subclass of Component. We'll look at JComponent after Component.

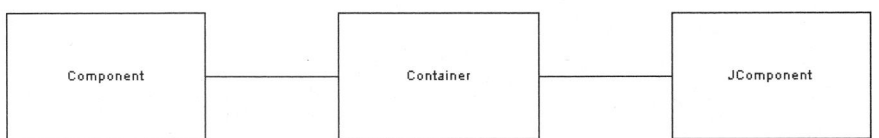

Here is what every component has in common with every other AWT component; in other words, class Component:

```
public class Component extends Object
    implements ImageObserver, MenuContainer, Serializable {
  public static final float BOTTOM_ALIGNMENT;
  public static final float CENTER_ALIGNMENT;
  public static final float LEFT_ALIGNMENT;
  public static final float RIGHT_ALIGNMENT;
  public static final float TOP_ALIGNMENT;
  public synchronized void add(PopupMenu popup);
  public synchronized void addComponentListener(ComponentListener l);
  public synchronized void addFocusListener(FocusListener l);
  public synchronized void addInputMethodListener(InputMethodListener l);
  public synchronized void addKeyListener(KeyListener l);
  public synchronized void addMouseListener(MouseListener l);
  public synchronized void addMouseMotionListener(MouseMotionListener l);
  public void addNotify();
  public synchronized void addPropertyChangeListener(PropertyChangeListener l);
  public synchronized void addPropertyChangeListener(String propertyName,
    PropertyChangeListener l);
  public int checkImage(Image image, int width, int height,
    ImageObserver observer);
  public int checkImage(Image image, ImageObserver observer);
  protected AWTEvent coalesceEvents(AWTEvent existingEvent, AWTEvent newEvent);
  public boolean contains(int x, int y);
  public boolean contains(Point p);
  public Image createImage(int width, int height);
  public Image createImage(ImageProducer producer);
  protected final void disableEvents(long eventsToDisable);
```

```
public final void dispatchEvent(AWTEvent e);
public void doLayout();
protected final void enableEvents(long eventsToEnable);
public void enableInputMethods(boolean b);
protected void firePropertyChange(String propertyName, Object oldValue,
    Object newValue);
public float getAlignmentX();
public float getAlignmentY();
public Color getBackground();
public Rectangle getBounds();
public Rectangle getBounds(Rectangle returnValue);
public ColorModel getColorModel();
public Component getComponentAt(int x, int y);
public Component getComponentAt(Point p);
public ComponentOrientation getComponentOrientation();
public Cursor getCursor();
public synchronized DropTarget getDropTarget();
public Font getFont();
public FontMetrics getFontMetrics(Font font);
public Color getForeground();
public Graphics getGraphics();
public int getHeight();
public InputContext getInputContext();
public InputMethodRequests getInputMethodRequests();
public Locale getLocale();
public Point getLocation();
public Point getLocation(Point returnValue);
public Point getLocationOnScreen();
public Dimension getMaximumSize();
public Dimension getMinimumSize();
public String getName();
public Container getParent();
public Dimension getPreferredSize();
public Dimension getSize();
public Dimension getSize(Dimension returnValue);
public Toolkit getToolkit();
public final Object getTreeLock();
public int getWidth();
public int getX();
public int getY();
public boolean hasFocus();
public boolean imageUpdate(Image img, int flags,
```

```
    int x, int y, int w, int h);
public void invalidate();
public boolean isDisplayable();
public boolean isDoubleBuffered();
public boolean isEnabled();
public boolean isFocusTraversable();
public boolean isLightweight();
public boolean isOpaque();
public boolean isShowing();
public boolean isValid();
public boolean isVisible();
public void list();
public void list(PrintStream out);
public void list(PrintStream out, int indent);
public void list(PrintWriter out);
public void list(PrintWriter out, int indent);
public void paint(Graphics g);
public void paintAll(Graphics g);
protected String paramString();
public boolean prepareImage(Image image, int width, int height,
    ImageObserver observer);
public boolean prepareImage(Image image, ImageObserver observer);
public void print(Graphics g);
public void printAll(Graphics g);
protected void processComponentEvent(ComponentEvent e);
protected void processEvent(AWTEvent e);
protected void processFocusEvent(FocusEvent e);
protected void processInputMethodEvent(InputMethodEvent e);
protected void processKeyEvent(KeyEvent e);
protected void processMouseEvent(MouseEvent e);
protected void processMouseMotionEvent(MouseEvent e);
public synchronized void remove(MenuComponent popup);
public synchronized void removeComponentListener(ComponentListener l);
public synchronized void removeFocusListener(FocusListener l);
public synchronized void removeInputMethodListener(InputMethodListener l);
public synchronized void removeKeyListener(KeyListener l);
public synchronized void removeMouseListener(MouseListener l);
public synchronized void removeMouseMotionListener(MouseMotionListener l);
public void removeNotify();
public synchronized void removePropertyChangeListener(
    PropertyChangeListener l );
public synchronized void removePropertyChangeListener(String propertyName,
```

```
        PropertyChangeListener l);
    public void repaint();
    public void repaint(int x, int y, int width, int height);
    public void repaint(long tm);
    public void repaint(long tm, int x, int y, int width, int height);
    public void requestFocus();
    public void setBackground(Color c);
    public void setBounds(int x, int y, int width, int height);
    public void setBounds(Rectangle r);
    public void setComponentOrientation(ComponentOrientation orientation);
    public synchronized void setCursor(Cursor cursor);
    public synchronized void setDropTarget(DropTarget dt);
    public void setEnabled(boolean b);
    public synchronized void setFont(Font f);
    public void setForeground(Color c);
    public void setLocale(Locale l);
    public void setLocation(int x, int y);
    public void setLocation(Point p);
    public void setName(String name);
    public void setSize(int width, int height);
    public void setSize(Dimension d);
    public void setVisible(boolean b);
    public String toString();
    public void transferFocus();
    public void update(Graphics g);
    public void validate();
}
```

Rather a long and intimidating collection of methods, isn't it? This is because the behavior of Swing components can be complex and multifaceted.

Although class **Component** is huge, very few of its methods are actually used frequently by the vast majority of programs. Even so, class **Component** is so fundamental to Java AWT and Swing programming that a study of its method groups is in order. The following sections discuss each of this class's method groups. Keep in mind that every component (that is, all of the descendant classes of **Component** and **JComponent**) supports all of these methods.

NOTE   Class **Component** implements the interface **ImageObserver**, which specifies only a single method, **imageUpdate()**, to be implemented. Chapter 10 described the function of this method and the relevance of all components being **ImageObservers**.

Event-Handling Methods

The most important group of Component methods is those relating to event handling. With event-driven Java programs, or for any language, the event handling mechanisms is the most important:

```
public synchronized void addComponentListener(ComponentListener l);
public synchronized void addFocusListener(FocusListener l);
public synchronized void addInputMethodListener(InputMethodListener l);
public synchronized void addKeyListener(KeyListener l);
public synchronized void addMouseListener(MouseListener l);
public synchronized void addMouseMotionListener(MouseMotionListener l);
public synchronized void removeComponentListener(ComponentListener l);
public synchronized void removeFocusListener(FocusListener l);
public synchronized void removeInputMethodListener(InputMethodListener l);
public synchronized void removeKeyListener(KeyListener l);
public synchronized void removeMouseListener(MouseListener l);
public synchronized void removeMouseMotionListener(MouseMotionListener l);
protected void processComponentEvent(ComponentEvent e);
protected void processEvent(AWTEvent e);
protected void processFocusEvent(FocusEvent e);
protected void processInputMethodEvent(InputMethodEvent e);
protected void processKeyEvent(KeyEvent e);
protected void processMouseEvent(MouseEvent e);
protected void processMouseMotionEvent(MouseEvent e);
protected AWTEvent coalesceEvents(AWTEvent existingEvent, AWTEvent newEvent);
public final void dispatchEvent(AWTEvent e);
protected final void disableEvents(long eventsToDisable);
protected final void enableEvents(long eventsToEnable);
```

These methods deal with event listeners, or more specifically, listeners deal with an event when it happens. Event listeners are part of Java's event-delegation model. This model is discussed in detail in Chapter 14. The property change listener methods look like event-handling methods:

```
public synchronized void addPropertyChangeListener(PropertyChangeListener l);
public synchronized void addPropertyChangeListener(String propertyName,
    PropertyChangeListener l);
protected void firePropertyChange(String propertyName, Object oldValue,
    Object newValue);
public synchronized void removePropertyChangeListener(
    PropertyChangeListener l );
public synchronized void removePropertyChangeListener(String propertyName,
    PropertyChangeListener l);
```

However, they are related more closely to JavaBeans and are discussed in Chapter 22.

Component Moving and Resizing Methods

The following Component methods are related to moving and resizing GUI elements:

```
public void setLocation(int x, int y);
public void setLocation(Point p);
public void setSize(int width, int height);
public void setSize(Dimension d);
public void setBounds(int x, int y, int width, int height);
public void setBounds(Rectangle r);
```

As you learned in Chapter 12, AWT is novel in its way of positioning and sizing an application's GUI elements. With Java, you always rely on a layout manager (class) to give your components their final, absolute positions and dimensions. The methods listed here are for the layout managers to use, and not for you to call. This is the general rule, although you can use these methods on class Window and its children. Layout managers have no say on where you put windows or how big or small you make them (their jurisdiction is the contents of windows, not the windows themselves). The way you position or size your application windows on a given desktop is your business.

Position and Geometry Querying Methods

The following methods of Component are related to querying the position and geometry of GUI components:

```
public Point getLocation();
public Point getLocationOnScreen();
public Rectangle getBounds(Rectangle returnValue);
public Dimension getSize();
public Point getLocation(Point returnValue);
public Rectangle getBounds();
public Dimension getSize(Dimension returnValue);
public int getHeight();
public int getWidth();
public int getX();
public int getY();
public boolean contains(int x, int y);
public boolean contains(Point p);
```

Since layout managers have so much control over the final placement and size of your components, these methods allow you to find out what the layout managers finally decided upon in terms of position and size, once the layout is done.

The three get*XXX* methods that have a parameter store their return value in the preallocated object passed in as the parameter, instead of allocating new objects on the heap. This can result in a substantial performance improvement when frequently called.

Graphics and Rendering Methods

The following methods of Component are related to graphics and graphical components:

```
public Graphics getGraphics();
public ColorModel getColorModel();
public Font getFont();
public FontMetrics getFontMetrics(Font font);
public Color getForeground();
public Color getBackground();
public synchronized void setFont(Font f);
public synchronized void setForeground(Color c);
public synchronized void setBackground(Color c);
public Toolkit getToolkit();
```

The most important of these methods is getGraphics(). When working with entire windows (class JPanel or JFrame), you can draw inside them using any of the rendering methods of class Graphics, but only after you have obtained the graphics context for your drawing medium (see Chapter 10 for details of the Graphics class). You use getGraphics() to obtain a component's associated graphics context.

The other methods let you query or set some graphical Component attributes, such as the font used for any text rendering and the foreground and background colors for the component.

Layout Manager Methods

Several Component methods are for layout managers:

```
public Dimension getPreferredSize();
public Dimension getMinimumSize();
```

```
public Dimension getMaximumSize();
public void doLayout();
public float getAlignmentX();
public float getAlignmentY();
public ComponentOrientation getComponentOrientation();
public void setComponentOrientation(ComponentOrientation orientation);
```

Methods getPreferredSize() and getMinimumSize() have already been discussed in our study of layout managers. To briefly reiterate, these methods need to be overridden by your Component subclasses (MyButton, ZIPCodeTextField, and so on) to let the layout managers know how to size them under various packing conditions.

The doLayout() method forces an immediate layout for the component. You should never call this method yourself; it is called by the validate() method.

The getAlignmentX() and getAlignmentY() methods are used by some layout managers to position components relative to other components within the same area.

The getComponentOrientation() and setComponentOrientation() are used for language-sensitive orientation and have an effect on the laying out of components by a layout manager.

Self-Painting Methods

The following are the Component class self-painting methods:

```
public void paint(Graphics g);
public void update(Graphics g);
public void paintAll(Graphics g);
public void repaint();
public void repaint(int x, int y, int width, int height);
public void repaint(long tm);
public void repaint(long tm, int x, int y, int width, int height);
public void print(Graphics g);
public void printAll(Graphics g);
```

Here, paint(), update(), and repaint() are the important methods. You have already seen paint() in action: You need to override it to refresh your applet. That's right—the paint() method is not an Applet method at all; it is a Component method. All Swing components redraw themselves via an overridden paint() method in JComponent.

You might have wondered why we never suggested you clear your applet window by filling it to a background color, before starting to redraw it. This is because the paint() method starts with a clean slate each time, courtesy of method update(). The update() method does three things:

- Clears the component's visible area, using the component's background color

- Sets the Graphics object's color to the component's foreground color

- Calls paint(), passing in the Graphics object

If you want to avoid this window-cleaning action, you can override the update() method instead of overriding paint(). You saw how this technique was used in Chapter 10.

The repaint() methods are usually called by external entities (the browser, for example) to request a Component redraw. The repaint() variant with the empty argument list is a possible exception. You can call it to force an update()—and, therefore, a paint(), too—to happen as soon as possible. See Chapter 10 for information about delayed repainting.

Parent/Subcomponent Methods

Three Component methods deal with parents and subcomponents:

```
public Container getParent();
public Component getComponentAt(int x, int y);
public Component getComponentAt(Point p);
```

In practice, a Component is almost always part of a nested GUI hierarchy of parent containers, containers, and subcontainers. Any Component can discover whether it is part of a container by using the getParent() method (a null return value means that the Component is the topmost container).

If a Component is a Container itself, it can find out which component is located at its relative coordinates (x,y) by calling getComponentAt() on itself.

State Changing and Querying Methods

The following are the Component methods for changing and querying a component's state:

```
public void setEnabled(boolean cond);
```

```
public void setVisible(boolean cond);
public void validate();
public void invalidate();
public boolean isValid();
public boolean isVisible();
public boolean isShowing();
public boolean isEnabled();
public boolean isDisplayable();
public boolean isDoubleBuffered();
public boolean isLightweight();
public boolean isOpaque();
```

Any Component can find itself in one of three boolean states: enabled/disabled, showing/hiding, or valid/invalid.

You disable components to make them unresponsive to user selections; this is sometimes called *graying out* or *ghosting*. Or you can hide a component if it is to be unavailable for prolonged periods. (Disabling a component means it is only temporarily unavailable.)

You can also invalidate components after you have modified them by adding (with the add() method) or removing (with the remove() method) components. This forces the layout manager of the component's container to re-layout the container's components. You need to call validate() to revalidate their state and have the screen updated accordingly. A component is displayable when it is in a visible window.

All Swing components are lightweight; they aren't AWT components that represent real widgets on the user's platform. Also, all Swing components use double buffering for drawing, while AWT components do not.

An opaque component is one that is not see-through. When a component is opaque, whatever is behind the component is hidden. If a component is not opaque, the background shows through the areas of the component that are not drawn onto.

Image-Related Methods

The following are the image-related methods in the Component class:

```
public Image createImage(ImageProducer producer);
public Image createImage(int width, int height);
```

```
public boolean imageUpdate(Image img, int flags, int x, int y, int w, int h);
public boolean prepareImage(Image image, int width, int height,
  ImageObserver observer);
public boolean prepareImage(Image image, ImageObserver observer);
public int checkImage(Image image, int width, int height,
  ImageObserver observer);
public int checkImage(Image image, ImageObserver observer);
```

Components like JApplet and JFrame can be used to draw images in. These are some of the methods you need to create and load images. Image creation and manipulation were covered in Chapter 10. With most Swing components, you display an image on each component with the help of the Icon interface and ImageIcon class (both described later), not these methods.

Input Method Methods

The following are the input method–related methods in the Component class:

```
public InputContext getInputContext();
public InputMethodRequests getInputMethodRequests();
public void enableInputMethods(boolean b);
```

The input context and methods describe the communication mechanism with text components. These are most frequently necessary when working with languages where there isn't a direct mapping of keyboard buttons to alphabetic characters.

Component Peer Methods

The Component class has two methods for peer communications:

```
public void addNotify();
public void removeNotify();
```

Every component has some methods to let it communicate with its peer. Earlier you learned that the AWT components rely on native components to retain the native platform's look and feel for GUIs. The Swing components do not rely on peers. However, the outermost container of the components, like JFrame or JWindow, still rely on the native platform's control.

> **WARNING** Keeping two different but equivalent systems in sync is always a tricky and fragile balancing act. If the entities lose their synchronization for any reason (like a bug), the whole system breaks down. Primarily because of compatibility problems caused by poor implementations of AWT peers, Swing was introduced. Because most Swing components do not rely on AWT peers, the problem with earlier incompatible Java systems is no longer an issue.

The methods addNotify() and removeNotify() are used to force the creation and destruction, respectively, of the peer. Application programmers should rarely call the peer-related methods. These are low-level methods used purely by the components themselves to communicate with their peers. In particular, calling addNotify() or removeNotify() could disrupt the abstract-component/concrete-component protocol, resulting in serious out-of-sync inconsistency problems.

The Swing Superclass of GUI Classes

While Component is the superclass of all AWT components, including the Swing component set, the JComponent class is of more interest when working with the Swing component set. Here, even more commonality is defined:

```
public abstract class JComponent extends Container implements Serializable {
  public static final String TOOL_TIP_TEXT_KEY;
  public static final int UNDEFINED_CONDITION;
  public static final int WHEN_ANCESTOR_OF_FOCUSED_COMPONENT;
  public static final int WHEN_FOCUSED;
  public static final int WHEN_IN_FOCUSED_WINDOW;
  protected AccessibleContext accessibleContext;
  protected EventListenerList listenerList;
  protected transient ComponentUI ui;
  public JComponent();
  public void addAncestorListener(AncestorListener);
  public void addNotify();
  public synchronized void addPropertyChangeListener(PropertyChangeListener l);
  public synchronized void addVetoableChangeListener(VetoableChangeListener l);
  public void computeVisibleRect(Rectangle r);
  public boolean contains(int x, int y);
  public JToolTip createToolTip();
```

```
public void firePropertyChange(String propertyName, boolean oldValue, boolean newValue);
public void firePropertyChange(String propertyName, byte oldValue, byte newValue);
public void firePropertyChange(String propertyName, char oldValue, char newValue);
public void firePropertyChange(String propertyName, double oldValue, double newValue);
public void firePropertyChange(String propertyName, float oldValue, float newValue);
public void firePropertyChange(String propertyName, int oldValue, int newValue);
protected void firePropertyChange(String propertyName, Object oldValue, Object newValue);
public void firePropertyChange(String propertyName, long oldValue, long newValue);
public void firePropertyChange(String propertyName, short oldValue, short newValue);
protected void fireVetoableChange(String propertyName, Object oldValue, Object newValue)
➥ throws PropertyVetoException;
public AccessibleContext getAccessibleContext();
public ActionListener getActionForKeyStroke(KeyStroke ks);
public float getAlignmentX();
public float getAlignmentY();
public boolean getAutoscrolls();
public Border getBorder();
public Rectangle getBounds(Rectangle r);
public final Object getClientProperty(Object key);
protected Graphics getComponentGraphics(Graphics g);
public int getConditionForKeyStroke(KeyStroke ks);
public int getDebugGraphicsOptions();
public Graphics getGraphics();
public int getHeight();
public Insets getInsets();
public Insets getInsets(Insets returnValue);
public Point getLocation(Point p);
public Dimension getMaximumSize();
public Dimension getMinimumSize();
public Component getNextFocusableComponent();
public Dimension getPreferredSize();
public KeyStroke[] getRegisteredKeyStrokes();
public JRootPane getRootPane();
public Dimension getSize(Dimension d);
public Point getToolTipLocation(MouseEvent e);
public String getToolTipText();
public String getToolTipText(MouseEvent e);
public Container getTopLevelAncestor();
public String getUIClassID();
public Rectangle getVisibleRect();
public int getWidth();
public int getX();
```

```java
public int getY();
public void grabFocus();
public boolean hasFocus();
public boolean isDoubleBuffered();
public boolean isFocusCycleRoot();
public boolean isFocusTraversable();
public boolean isManagingFocus();
public static boolean isLightweightComponent(Component c);
public boolean isOpaque();
public boolean isOptimizedDrawingEnabled();
public boolean isPaintingTile();
public boolean isRequestFocusEnabled();
public boolean isValidateRoot();
public void paint(Graphics g);
protected void paintBorder(Graphics g);
protected void paintChildren(Graphics g);
protected void paintComponent(Graphics g);
public void paintImmediately(int x, int y, int w, int h);
public void paintImmediately(Rectangle r);
protected void processComponentKeyEvent(KeyEvent e);
protected void processFocusEvent(FocusEvent e);
protected void processKeyEvent(KeyEvent e);
protected void processMouseMotionEvent(MouseEvent e);
public final void putClientProperty(Object key, Object value);
public void registerKeyboardAction(ActionListener l, KeyStroke ks, int condition);
public void registerKeyboardAction(ActionListener l, String command, KeyStroke ks, int
➥ condition);
public void removeAncestorListener(AncestorListener l);
public void removeNotify();
public synchronized void removePropertyChangeListener(PropertyChangeListener l);
public synchronized void removeVetoableChangeListener(VetoableChangeListener l);
public void repaint(Rectangle r);
public void repaint(long tm, int x, int y, int w, int h);
public boolean requestDefaultFocus();
public void requestFocus();
public void resetKeyboardActions();
public void reshape(int x, int y, int w, int h);
public void revalidate();
public void setAlignmentX(float f);
public void setAlignmentY(float f);
public void setAutoscrolls(boolean b);
```

```
  public void setBorder(Border b);
  public void setDebugGraphicsOptions(int opt);
  public void setDoubleBuffered(boolean b);
  public void setMaximumSize(Dimension d);
  public void setMinimumSize(Dimension d);
  public void setNextFocusableComponent(Component c);
  public void setOpaque(boolean b);
  public void setPreferredSize(Dimension d);
  public void setRequestFocusEnabled(boolean b);
  public void setToolTipText(String text);
  protected void setUI(ComponentUI c);
  public void setVisible(boolean b);
  public void unregisterKeyboardAction(KeyStroke ks);
  public void update(Graphics g);
  public void updateUI();
}
```

Several of these methods should look familiar, as JComponent takes advantage of Java's ability to override existing methods to provide more customized behavior. Additionally, JComponent adds the ability of every Swing component to specify its own border, tool tip text, and user interface. Specifying a component's user interface is part of Swing's advanced capabilities and is described in Chapter 15, "Model/View/Controller Architecture." The remaining changes will be discussed after describing an actual component.

Adding Components to Your GUI

The following sections describe some of the Swing components you can add to your Java applets and applications:

JButton	JScrollBar
JPanel	JSlider
JLabel	JTextField
JToggleButon	JPasswordField
JCheckbox	JTextArea
JRadioButton	JToolBar

JComboBox	JInternalFrame
JScrollPane	JTable
JList	

Additionally, the JApplet, Icon, ImageIcon, AbstractButton, Border, BorderFactory, JToolTip, ToolTipManager, and ButtonGroup classes and interfaces are described.

How to programmatically interact with the Swing components for event handling is covered in Chapter 14, "Event Handling." Advanced components and capabilities of Swing are covered in Chapter 15.

Adding Buttons

Launch any application on any modern desktop computer, and you will see buttons all over the place. Several types of buttons are generally used to manipulate windows on every platform:

- A resizing button

- Minimize (or iconify) and maximize buttons

- A close button

Buttons are contained within many other elements. Toolbars are collections of buttons. Scrollbars consist of at least three buttons: two for the up and down arrows (or left and right) and one stretched-out button for the scroll area. Status bars can also contain buttons camouflaged as simple labels. Whatever its exact appearance, a button always boils down to a frequently rectangular window area that has associated with it a unique behavior. From this definition, it is just a small step to graphically highlight this rectangular area by drawing its outline and adding a descriptive label or icon to identify it.

Java's idea of a button is just that: a border, a label, an icon, and some methods for handling events. Here is its class definition:

```
public class JButton extends AbstractButton
    implements Accessible {
  public JButton();
  public JButton(Icon icon);
  public JButton(String label);
  public JButton(String label, Icon icon);
```

```
    public AccessibleContext getAccessibleContext();
    public String getUIClassID();
    public boolean isDefaultButton();
    public boolean isDefaultCapable();
    public void setDefaultCapable(boolean b);
    public void updateUI();
}
```

Most of the details of JButton are inherited from the AbstractButton class. Before we look at that, let's see how to use JButton. All you need to understand is how to use the constructors. The most commonly used constructor for a JButton takes a String, which will be depicted on the button as its label. Figure 13.1 shows an example of a Java JButton component.

FIGURE 13.1:

A JButton component

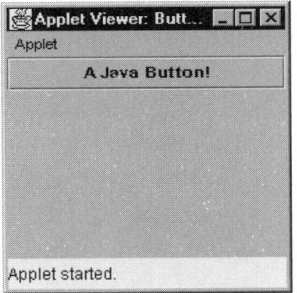

Adding buttons to Java applets or applications is easy, as you can see in the following program, which created the button shown in Figure 13.1:

```
import java.awt.*;
import javax.swing.*;
public class ButtonTest extends JApplet {
  public void init() {
    JButton b;
    b = new JButton("A Java Button!");
    getContentPane().add(b, BorderLayout.NORTH);
  }
}
```

This applet simply declares a variable b of type JButton, creates a new JButton object for it, and adds (with the add() method) this button to the applet's content pane. The button label, "A Java Button!" was specified as the string argument to the `Button` constructor. As you can see in Figure 13.1, the button is placed in the top area of the screen. This is because the default layout manager for Swing applets is `BorderLayout` and the north area was provided as the parameter to `add()`. The `ButtonTest` class subclasses `JApplet`.

JApplet vs. Applet

Swing applets must subclass `JApplet`, instead of the `java.applet.Applet` class for non-Swing applets. There are three major differences between `JApplet` and `Applet`:

- The default layout manager for `JApplet` is `BorderLayout`; for `Applet` it is `FlowLayout`.

- Adding components to a `JApplet` is done with `getContentPane().add()` instead of the `add()` method of `Applet`.

- Swing applets add support for pull-down menus. This is not an option with `Applet`.

The first `import` statement makes all `java.awt` classes available to the compilation unit (the source file). In this instance, you could have simply used the following line instead since this is the only AWT class used in the program:

```
import java.awt.BorderLayout;
```

NOTE   Contrary to popular Java beliefs, importing whole packages does not increase the size of your executables. The `import` statements only make class definitions visible to other classes at compilation time. The actual linking is done at run time, not compile time. This explains why the executables do not swell up by importing external classes, as they do with most other compiled languages.

The second `import` statement makes all the `javax.swing` classes available. Here the program uses the `JApplet` and `JButton` classes from this package. As with `BorderLayout`, these could be specifically imported:

```
import javax.swing.JButton;
import javax.swing.JApplet;
```

You can change the label of a `JButton` at any time using the `setText()` method (inherited from `AbstractButton`). Similarly, you can find out which `JButton` you are manipulating by asking the button what its label is with `getText()`.

Displaying Images on Buttons

To use two of the JButton constructors, (public JButton(Icon icon) and public JButton(String label, Icon icon), you need to examine the Icon interface, specified here:

```
public interface Icon {
  public abstract int getIconHeight();
  public abstract int getIconWidth();
  public abstract void paintIcon(Component c, Graphics g, int x, int y);
}
```

To have an image on a button, you have to provide a class that implements the Icon interface. As an example, Figure 13.2 displays a pie-chart piece in a button, with and without a label:

FIGURE 13.2:

Two JButton components with icons

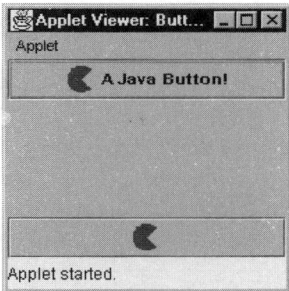

Here is the demonstration program behind Figure 13.2:

```
import java.awt.*;
import javax.swing.*;
public class ButtonIconTest extends JApplet {
  static class PieIcon implements Icon {
    Color color;
    public PieIcon (Color c) {
      color = c;
    }
    public int getIconWidth() {
      return 20;
    }
    public int getIconHeight() {
      return 20;
    }
```

```
    public void paintIcon(Component c, Graphics g, int x, int y) {
      g.setColor (color);
      g.fillArc (x, y, getIconWidth(), getIconHeight(), 45, 270);
    }
  }
  public void init() {
    JButton b;
    Icon icon = new PieIcon(Color.red);
    b = new JButton("A Java Button!", icon);
    getContentPane().add(b, BorderLayout.NORTH);
    b = new JButton(icon);
    getContentPane().add(b, BorderLayout.SOUTH);
  }
}
```

In this program, the inner class PieIcon implements the Icon interface. The icon is 20 pixels wide (the getIconWidth() method) and 20 pixels high (the getIconHeight() method). Then, the paintIcon() method describes how to draw the icon, in this case just drawing a filled arc of the appropriate color.

TIP

The first parameter of paintIcon(), the Component, is usually ignored. The component provides the means for an icon to inquire about the characteristics of its enclosing component, such as for its drawing color.

If you notice from the way Icon is defined, there is no mention of images. Anything that you can describe how to draw can be displayed as an Icon for a Swing component. If you happen to want to provide an Image as the Icon for a component, the ImageIcon class is available. With ImageIcon, you only really need to know how to create one, and nine constructors help here:

```
public ImageIcon();
public ImageIcon(byte[] data);
public ImageIcon(byte[] data, String description);
public ImageIcon(Image image);
public ImageIcon(Image image, String description);
public ImageIcon(String filename);
public ImageIcon(String filename, String description);
public ImageIcon(URL location);
public ImageIcon(URL location, String description);
```

NOTE You can specify a description for an **ImageIcon** for use with assistive technologies, like a screen reader for a sight-impaired person. These textual descriptions should be short and to the point. Long descriptions take more time to read, while the descriptions are supposed to help a person, not slow them down.

You could use the following code to create the icon:

```
Icon icon = new ImageIcon ("games.gif", "Sybex Game Books");
```

Once you have the **Icon** object, you can then associate it to the component to display an image as an icon within a Swing component. Figure 13.3 displays a file as an icon in a button, with and without a label:

FIGURE 13.3:

A JButton component with an image as its icon

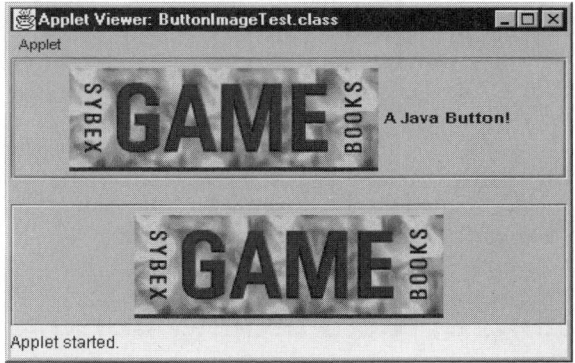

Here is the demonstration program behind Figure 13.3:

```java
import java.awt.*;
import javax.swing.*;
public class ButtonImageTest extends JApplet {
  public void init() {
    JButton b;
    Icon icon = new ImageIcon("games.gif");
    b = new JButton("A Java Button!", icon);
    getContentPane().add(b, BorderLayout.NORTH);
    b = new JButton(icon);
    getContentPane().add(b, BorderLayout.SOUTH);
  }
}
```

TIP When using `ImageIcon`, you don't have to worry about the normal asynchronous loading behavior of `Image`. An image to be displayed in an `ImageIcon` is loaded synchronously—meaning you will never see a partial image loaded.

If the image you wish to display as an icon is an animated GIF, you need to specify an image observer, described in Chapter 10. The following demonstrates the necessary changes, with the new or changed lines in bold:

```
import java.awt.*;
import javax.swing.*;
public class ButtonImageTest2 extends JApplet {
  public void init() {
    JButton b;
    ImageIcon icon = new ImageIcon("nxSeriesGif.gif");
    b = new JButton(icon);
    icon.setImageObserver (b);
    getContentPane().add(b, BorderLayout.NORTH);
  }
}
```

As printed media doesn't demonstrate animation well, you'll have to run the `ButtonImageTest2` applet from the CD files to see the animated GIF file at work.

Defining Borders around Buttons

Like you'll soon discover with everything else in Swing, if you don't like how something looks, you can change it. For instance, you can redefine the type of border to appear around a button or any `JComponent` subclass. With the exception of the `BorderFactory` class found in `javax.swing`, all the dealings with borders are found in the `javax.swing.border` package. Figure 13.4 illustrates the class hierarchy of the border classes.

The basis of all the borders is the `Border` interface:

```
public interface Border {
  public abstract Insets getBorderInsets(Component c);
  public abstract boolean isBorderOpaque();
  public abstract void paintBorder(Component c, Graphics g, int x, int y,
    int w, int h);
}
```

FIGURE 13.4:

Package com.sun
.java.swing.border
inheritance tree

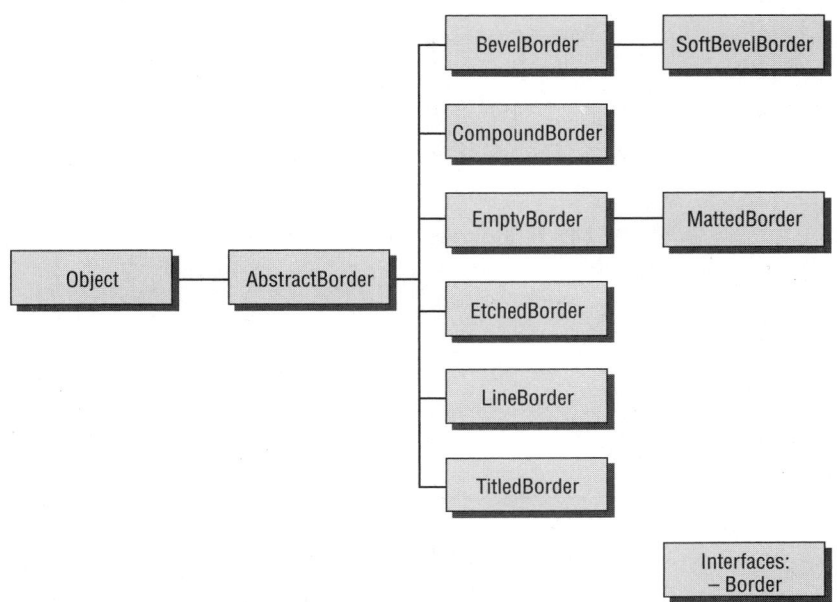

Like the Icon interface, the Border interface describes how to draw something—in this case, a border around a component. While the last chapter described Insets as the area where a layout manager doesn't place components; with respect to borders, the getBorderInsets() return value describes exactly where to draw the border. The isBorderOpaque() method states whether a border completely covers its background or is transparent. Finally, the paintBorder() method is the worker of the interface, describing how to actually draw the border.

In most cases it isn't necessary to implement the border yourself. You just use one of the existing Border implementers:

BevelBorder   Provides a simple 3-D appearance by drawing different colored lines to show depth.

CompoundBorder   Allows you to combine any two borders to create a richer border.

EmptyBorder   A border that only occupies space.

EtchedBorder   Provides an etched border to show depth.

LineBorder   Allows you to specify any color or thickness to create a border.

MatteBorder   A border that allows tiling of any color or icon. With a solid color, this differs from LineBorder in that you can have different sizes for each side of the border.

SoftBevelBorder   Provides a 3-D beveled border where the default colors used are not as sharply contrasting as BevelBorder.

TitledBorder   Allows you to place a text string on the border.

Also, when working with borders you never need to know the specific border class with which you are working. All you need to do is ask the BorderFactory to create the appropriate border:

```
Border b = BorderFactory.createRaisedBevelBorder());
aJComponent.setBorder (b);
```

TIP

By using the border factory, instead of the border classes directly, if the same border is requested multiple times, the factory creates the border only once. The second requester is passed a reference to the first border.

To demonstrate borders, Figure 13.5 displays an icon within a MatteBorder of a button with a label. The ImageIcon used is the same one shown in Figure 13.3.

FIGURE 13.5:

A JButton component surrounded by a MatteBorder

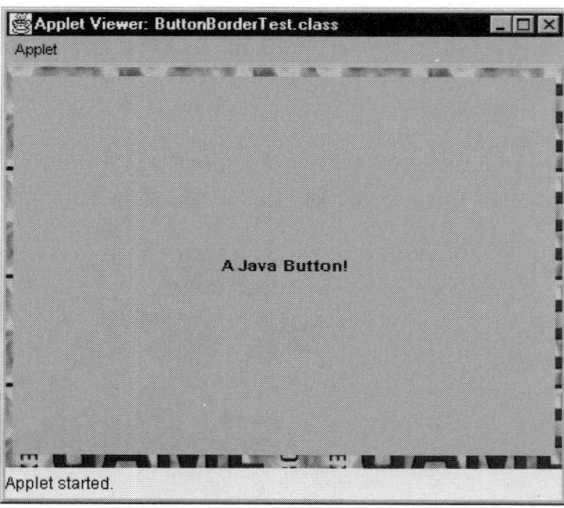

The following is the source of the demonstration program behind Figure 13.5:

```
import java.awt.*;
import javax.swing.*;
import javax.swing.border.*;
public class ButtonBorderTest extends JApplet {
  public void init() {
    JButton b;
    Icon icon = new ImageIcon("games.gif");
    b = new JButton("A Java Button!");
    Border bored = BorderFactory.createMatteBorder(10, 5, 10, 5, icon);
    b.setBorder (bored);
    getContentPane().add(b, BorderLayout.CENTER);
  }
}
```

When you run the program, you quickly learn that the program doesn't necessarily do what you may expect. You now have the same border appear when the button is selected or not. For most of the JComponent widgets, this isn't a problem. The same border should always appear around it. However, in the JButton case, you may wish to implement the Border interface yourself and offer two borders—one for when the button is pressed and one for when it isn't. We'll examine this again in Chapter 15 where we provide a fix. For now, let's look at AbstractButton, the superclass of JButton.

Sharing *AbstractButton*

The parent class of JButton is AbstractButton. The AbstractButton class is also the superclass of JMenuItem and its child classes the menu components, as well as JToggleButton and its child classes JCheckBox and JRadioButton. Basically, in order to understand any of these classes completely, you need to understand the shared behavior inherited from AbstractButton. The class definition is specified here:

```
public abstract class AbstractButton extends JComponent
    implements ItemSelectable, SwingConstants {
    public static final String BORDER_PAINTED_CHANGED_PROPERTY;
    public static final String CONTENT_AREA_FILLED_CHANGED_PROPERTY;
    public static final String DISABLED_ICON_CHANGED_PROPERTY;
    public static final String DISABLED_SELECTED_ICON_CHANGED_PROPERTY;
    public static final String FOCUS_PAINTED_CHANGED_PROPERTY;
    public static final String HORIZONTAL_ALIGNMENT_CHANGED_PROPERTY;
    public static final String HORIZONTAL_TEXT_POSITION_CHANGED_PROPERTY;
```

```
public static final String ICON_CHANGED_PROPERTY;
public static final String MARGIN_CHANGED_PROPERTY;
public static final String MNEMONIC_CHANGED_PROPERTY;
public static final String MODEL_CHANGED_PROPERTY;
public static final String PRESSED_ICON_CHANGED_PROPERTY;
public static final String ROLLOVER_ENABLED_CHANGED_PROPERTY;
public static final String ROLLOVER_ICON_CHANGED_PROPERTY;
public static final String ROLLOVER_SELECTED_ICON_CHANGED_PROPERTY;
public static final String SELECTED_ICON_CHANGED_PROPERTY;
public static final String TEXT_CHANGED_PROPERTY;
public static final String VERTICAL_ALIGNMENT_CHANGED_PROPERTY;
public static final String VERTICAL_TEXT_POSITION_CHANGED_PROPERTY;
protected ActionListener actionListener;
protected transient ChangeEvent changeEvent;
protected ChangeListener changeListener;
protected ItemListener itemListener;
protected ButtonModel model;
public AbstractButton();
public void addActionListener(ActionListener l);
public void addChangeListener(ChangeListener l);
public void addItemListener(ItemListener l);
protected int checkHorizontalKey(int key, String exception);
protected int checkVerticalKey(int key, String exception);
protected ActionListener createActionListener();
protected ChangeListener createChangeListener();
protected ItemListener createItemListener();
public void doClick();
public void doClick(int pressTime);
protected void fireActionPerformed(ActionEvent e);
protected void fireItemStateChanged(ItemEvent e);
protected void fireStateChanged();
public String getActionCommand();
public Icon getDisabledIcon();
public Icon getDisabledSelectedIcon();
public int getHorizontalAlignment();
public int getHorizontalTextPosition();
public Icon getIcon();
public Insets getMargin();
public int getMnemonic();
public ButtonModel getModel();
public Icon getPressedIcon();
public Icon getRolloverIcon();
```

```
        public Icon getRolloverSelectedIcon();
        public Icon getSelectedIcon();
        public Object[] getSelectedObjects();
        public String getText();
        public ButtonUI getUI();
        public int getVerticalAlignment();
        public int getVerticalTextPosition();
        protected void init(String text, Icon icon);
        public boolean isBorderPainted();
        public boolean isContentAreaFilled();
        public boolean isFocusPainted();
        public boolean isRolloverEnabled();
        public boolean isSelected();
        protected void paintBorder(Graphics g);
        public void removeActionListener(ActionListener l);
        public void removeChangeListener(ChangeListener l);
        public void removeItemListener(ItemListener l);
        public void setActionCommand(String com);
        public void setBorderPainted(boolean b);
        public void setContentAreaFilled(boolean b);
        public void setDisabledIcon(Icon icon);
        public void setDisabledSelectedIcon(Icon icon);
        public void setEnabled(boolean b);
        public void setFocusPainted(boolean b);
        public void setHorizontalAlignment(int alignment);
        public void setHorizontalTextPosition(int textPosition);
        public void setIcon(Icon icon);
        public void setMargin(Insets insets);
        public void setMnemonic(char mnemonic);
        public void setMnemonic(int mnemonic);
        public void setModel(ButtonModel bm);
        public void setPressedIcon(Icon icon);
        public void setRolloverEnabled(boolean b);
        public void setRolloverIcon(Icon icon);
        public void setRolloverSelectedIcon(Icon icon);
        public void setSelected(boolean b);
        public void setSelectedIcon(Icon icon);
        public void setText(String s);
        public void setUI(ButtonUI ui);
        public void setVerticalAlignment(int alignment);
        public void setVerticalTextPosition(int textPosition);
        public void updateUI();
}
```

While several of these methods are related to event handling, which is described in the next chapter, three sets of methods are worth highlighting:

Icons `setDisabledIcon()`, `setDisabledSelectedIcon()`, `setIcon()`, `setPressedIcon()`, `setRolloverIcon()`, `setRolloverSelectedIcon()`, and `setSelectedIcon()`

Positioning You can position the text and icon anywhere within the button: `setHorizontalAlignment(int alignment)`, `setHorizontal-TextPosition(int textPosition)`, `setVerticalAlignment(int alignment)`, and `setVerticalTextPosition(int textPosition)`.

Mnemonics You can associate a convenience keyboard character for a button.

Changing Button Icons

When working with any of the `AbstractButton` children, you can specify a different icon for every state of an abstract button. Which states are actually used depends on the particular subclass. For instance, with a `JButton`, the default icon displayed is configured with `setIcon()`. This is the icon for when the button is just sitting there doing nothing and the user is off working on another part of the application. On the other hand, if you would like a different icon to appear when the button is pressed, you would change this icon by associating a different icon via `setPressedIcon()`. You can even display a different icon when the mouse moves over a button with `setRolloverIcon()`. This behavior also needs to be enabled with `setRolloverEnabled()` because of the overhead required to check mouse locations whenever the mouse moved. The other icon methods work in the same manner but just respond to different behaviors.

To demonstrate the changing of icons for a `JButton`, Figure 13.6 shows three different states of a program. Instead of showing different colors or images for the different states, different shapes are drawn. The normal icon has the base of a triangle shown on the bottom of the button. The pressed icon has the base shown on the top of the button. For the rollover icon, the base is on a side.

Here is the demonstration program behind Figure 13.6:

```
import java.awt.*;
import javax.swing.*;
public class ChangingButtonIconTest extends JApplet {
  static class TriangleIcon implements Icon {
    static class State {
      public static final State NORMAL  = new State();
```

FIGURE 13.6:

A JButton with alternate icons

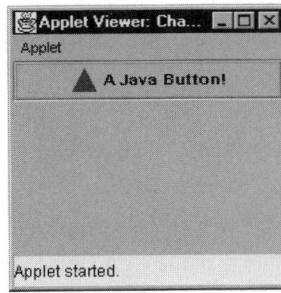 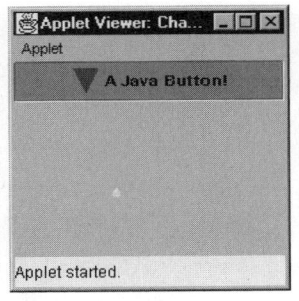 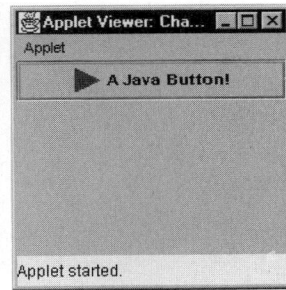

Normal   Pressed   Rollover

```
      public static final State PRESSED  = new State();
      public static final State ROLLOVER = new State();
      private State() {}
    }
    State state;
    Color color;
    public TriangleIcon (Color c, State state) {
      color = c;
      this.state = state;
    }
    public int getIconWidth() {
      return 20;
    }
    public int getIconHeight() {
      return 20;
    }
    public void paintIcon(Component c, Graphics g, int x, int y) {
      g.setColor (color);
      Polygon p = new Polygon();
      if (state == State.NORMAL) {
        p.addPoint (x+(getIconWidth() / 2), y);
        p.addPoint (x, y+getIconHeight()-1);
        p.addPoint (x+getIconWidth()-1, y+getIconHeight()-1);
      } else if (state == State.PRESSED) {
        p.addPoint (x, y);
        p.addPoint (x+getIconWidth()-1, y);
        p.addPoint (x+(getIconWidth() / 2), y+getIconHeight()-1);
      } else {
        p.addPoint (x, y);
```

```
            p.addPoint (x, y+getIconHeight()-1);
            p.addPoint (x+getIconWidth()-1, y+(getIconHeight() / 2));
        }
      g.fillPolygon (p);
    }
}
public void init() {
  JButton b;
  Icon normalIcon = new TriangleIcon(Color.red, TriangleIcon.State.NORMAL);
  Icon pressedIcon = new TriangleIcon(Color.red, TriangleIcon.State.PRESSED);
  Icon rolloverIcon = new TriangleIcon(Color.red,
    TriangleIcon.State.ROLLOVER);
  b = new JButton("A Java Button!", normalIcon);
  // or b = new JButton("A Java Button!");
  //    b.setIcon (normalIcon);
  b.setPressedIcon (pressedIcon);
  b.setRolloverIcon (rolloverIcon);
  b.setRolloverEnabled (true);
  getContentPane().add(b, BorderLayout.NORTH);
  }
}
```

Positioning Text and Icons

The SwingConstants interface holds the key for positioning text and icons within an AbstractButton. Since AbstractButton implements the interface, the constants are available as constants of AbstractButton, so you never really need to know about the SwingConstants class.

The different positioning methods have their biggest effect when both a text label and icon are present with the button. By default, the text label is placed to the right of the icon and both are centered vertically. By modifying this default behavior, both can be displayed on top of one another, or more likely, you can move the text label around the icon.

For positioning of the text and icon, the setVerticalTextPosition() method accepts parameters of CENTER, TOP, and BOTTOM. The initial setting is CENTER. The setHorizontalTextPosition() method accepts value of CENTER, RIGHT, and LEFT. The initial setting here is RIGHT. So, with values of TOP and RIGHT, the text would be aligned to the top of the icon and on its right, and TOP and CENTER would place the text above the icon.

The alignment methods of setVerticalAlignment(int alignment) and set-HorizontalAlignment(int alignment) specify where to place the text label or icon when the button has extra space available. By default these values are both CENTER. However, vertical alignment can also be TOP or BOTTOM, while horizontal can be RIGHT or LEFT. Figure 13.7 shows the PieIcon from an earlier section in different areas of a JButton.

FIGURE 13.7:

A JButton with roving icons

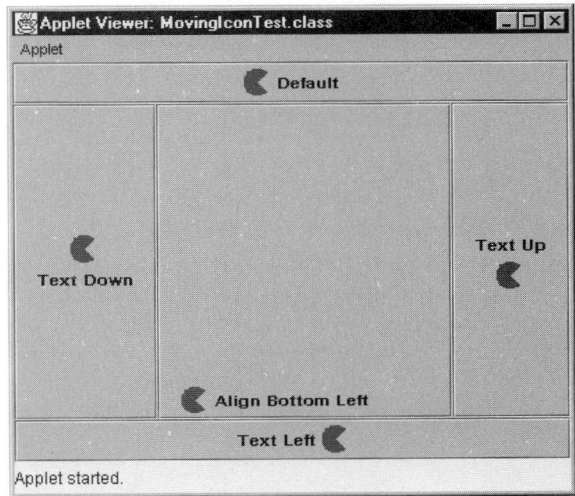

Here is the demonstration program behind Figure 13.7:

```
import java.awt.*;
import javax.swing.*;
public class MovingIconTest extends JApplet {
  static class PieIcon implements Icon {
    Color color;
    public PieIcon (Color c) {
      color = c;
    }
    public int getIconWidth() {
      return 20;
    }
    public int getIconHeight() {
      return 20;
    }
    public void paintIcon(Component c, Graphics g, int x, int y) {
      g.setColor (color);
      g.fillArc (x, y, getIconWidth(), getIconHeight(), 45, 270);
    }
```

```
    }
    public void init() {
      JButton b;
      Icon icon = new PieIcon(Color.red);
      b = new JButton("Default", icon);
      getContentPane().add(b, BorderLayout.NORTH);
      b = new JButton("Text Left", icon);
      b.setHorizontalTextPosition (JButton.LEFT);
      getContentPane().add(b, BorderLayout.SOUTH);
      b = new JButton("Text Up", icon);
      b.setHorizontalTextPosition (JButton.CENTER);
      b.setVerticalTextPosition (JButton.TOP);
      getContentPane().add(b, BorderLayout.EAST);
      b = new JButton("Text Down", icon);
      b.setHorizontalTextPosition (JButton.CENTER);
      b.setVerticalTextPosition (JButton.BOTTOM);
      getContentPane().add(b, BorderLayout.WEST);
      b = new JButton("Align Bottom Left", icon);
      b.setHorizontalAlignment (JButton.LEFT);
      b.setVerticalAlignment (JButton.BOTTOM);
      getContentPane().add(b, BorderLayout.CENTER);
    }
  }
```

Setting Button Mnemonics

When creating buttons or menu items, some people like having keyboard mnemonics associated with each so screen navigation can be done without moving one's hands from the keyboard. These are not keyboard accelerators like Ctrl+P usually meaning Print in most Microsoft Windows applications. A keyboard mnemonic provides the ability to select Alt+F to open the File menu. When a button has a mnemonic associated with it, the appropriate keyboard key is shown underlined within its text label.

TIP

If a button doesn't have a text label and a mnemonic is associated to the button, the mnemonic still works. If the character in the mnemonic is not part of the text label, the mnemonic still works. In both cases, while the mnemonic works, the user has no way to know what it is.

Figure 13.8 shows a button with a valid mnemonic character, an invalid mnemonic character with a text label, and a mnemonic character but no label. Notice the underlined *J* in the top button.

FIGURE 13.8:

JButtons with keyboard
mnemonics set

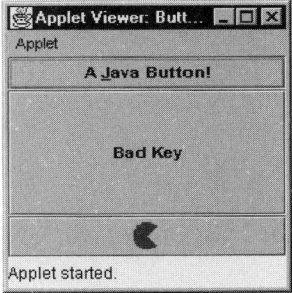

The following is the source code for the previous program:

```java
import java.awt.*;
import javax.swing.*;
public class ButtonMnemonicTest extends JApplet {
  static class PieIcon implements Icon {
    Color color;
    public PieIcon (Color c) {
      color = c;
    }
    public int getIconWidth() {
      return 20;
    }
    public int getIconHeight() {
      return 20;
    }
    public void paintIcon(Component c, Graphics g, int x, int y) {
      g.setColor (color);
      g.fillArc (x, y, getIconWidth(), getIconHeight(), 45, 270);
    }
  }
  public void init() {
    JButton b;
    Icon icon = new PieIcon(Color.red);
    b = new JButton("A Java Button!");
    b.setMnemonic ('J');
    getContentPane().add(b, BorderLayout.NORTH);
    b = new JButton(icon);
    b.setMnemonic ('B');
    getContentPane().add(b, BorderLayout.SOUTH);
```

```
        b = new JButton("Bad Key");
        b.setMnemonic ('I');
        getContentPane().add(b, BorderLayout.CENTER);
    }
}
```

Working with Tool Tips

Before moving on to the other Swing JComponent classes, one thing shared by all is tool tips. You can specify text to display when the user rests the mouse over a particular component. While the class to support this is JToolTip, it isn't necessary to even know about the existence of the class. Setting the tool tip for a component only requires you to call the setToolTipText(String tip) method of JComponent. Once the text is set, just rest the mouse over the appropriate component. Figure 13.9 demonstrates the appearance of tool tip text for a JButton.

FIGURE 13.9:

A JButton with tool tip text showing

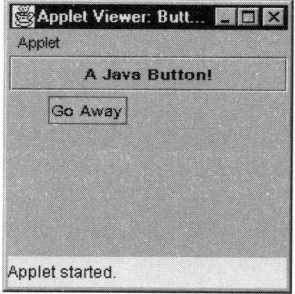

The following is the source code for the program from Figure 13.9:

```
import java.awt.*;
import javax.swing.*;
public class ButtonTipTest extends JApplet {
  public void init() {
    JButton b;
    b = new JButton("A Java Button!");
    b.setToolTipText ("Go Away");
    getContentPane().add(b, BorderLayout.NORTH);
  }
}
```

Configuring the Tool Tip Manager

While setting and using tool tips is easy, sometimes you may not like how quickly, or slowly, the tips appear or disappear. Or you may just want to disable them altogether, at the program level. For these settings, you need the help of the Tool-TipManager class. To get the program's tool tip manager, you ask the ToolTip-Manager for its sharedInstance(), a static method. Once you have the manager, you can inquire about settings with one set of methods:

```
public int getDismissDelay(); // initially 4 seconds
public int getInitialDelay(); // initially _ second
public int getReshowDelay();  // initially _ second
public boolean isEnabled();   // initially true
```

Or change settings with another. All the times work in milliseconds:

```
public void setDismissDelay(int delay);
public void setEnabled(boolean b);
public void setInitialDelay(int delay);
public void setReshowDelay(int delay);
```

So, to disable tool tips for a program, you would just add ToolTipManager .sharedInstance().setEnabled (false); to your program.

Grouping with *JPanel*

The JPanel class offers a generic lightweight container class. You can either use JPanel or Container to group your components together when laying out a screen. The advantage of using JPanel over Container is the components within the JPanel will be drawn in a double-buffered fashion, and you can place a Border around a JPanel. Figure 13.10 demonstrates bordered JPanel components. If neither of these capabilities is desired, you can stick to Container. The four constructors are really the only necessary pieces of the class definition to understand:

```
public JPanel();
public JPanel(boolean isDoubleBuffered);
public JPanel(LayoutManager layout);
public JPanel(LayoutManager layout, boolean isDoubleBuffered);
```

Here is the demonstration program behind Figure 13.10:

```
import java.awt.*;
import javax.swing.*;
import javax.swing.border.*;
public class PanelTest extends JApplet {
```

```
private void fill (Container c) {
  for (int i=0;i<3;i++) {
    c.add (new JButton ("" + i));
  }
}
public void init() {
  JPanel jp = new JPanel (new FlowLayout());
  fill (jp);
  Border bored = BorderFactory.createTitledBorder ("Hello");
  jp.setBorder (bored);
  getContentPane().add(jp, BorderLayout.NORTH);
  jp = new JPanel (new GridLayout(3, 1));
  fill (jp);
  bored = BorderFactory.createBevelBorder (BevelBorder.RAISED, Color.red,
    Color.blue);
  jp.setBorder (bored);
  getContentPane().add(jp, BorderLayout.CENTER);
  jp = new JPanel (new GridLayout(1, 3));
  fill (jp);
  bored = BorderFactory.createLineBorder (Color.green);
  jp.setBorder (bored);
  getContentPane().add(jp, BorderLayout.EAST);
}
}
```

FIGURE 13.10:

Three JPanel components
with borders and different
layout managers

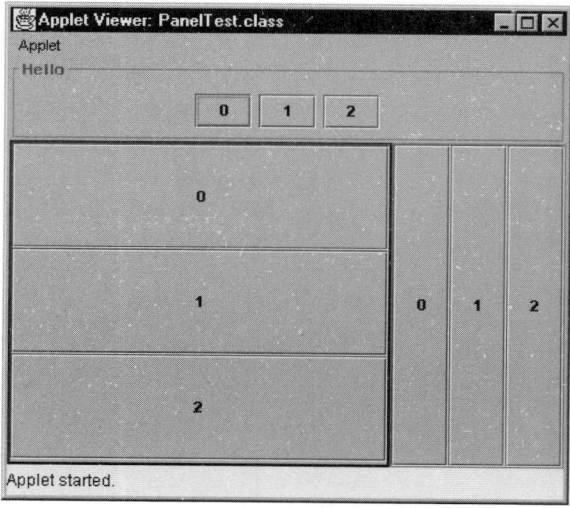

Adding Labels to Items

A JLabel component is simply a passive (that is, completely non-interactive) and unassuming single line of text with an icon. Here is its class definition:

```
public class JLabel extends JComponent implements SwingConstants, Accessible {
  protected Component labelFor;
  public JLabel();
  public JLabel(Icon icon);
  public JLabel(Icon icon, int horizontalAlignment);
  public JLabel(String text);
  public JLabel(String text, int horizontalAlignment);
  public JLabel(String text, Icon icon, int horizontalAlignment);
  protected int checkHorizontalKey(int key, String message);
  protected int checkVerticalKey(int key, String message);
  public AccessibleContext getAccessibleContext();
  public Icon getDisabledIcon();
  public int getDisplayedMnemonic();
  public int getHorizontalAlignment();
  public int getHorizontalTextPosition();
  public Icon getIcon();
  public int getIconTextGap();
  public Component getLabelFor();
  public String getText();
  public LabelUI getUI();
  public String getUIClassID();
  public int getVerticalAlignment();
  public int getVerticalTextPosition();
  public void setDisabledIcon(Icon icon);
  public void setDisplayedMnemonic(char c);
  public void setDisplayedMnemonic(int i);
  public void setFont(Font font);
  public void setHorizontalAlignment(int horizontalAlignment);
  public void setHorizontalTextPosition(int textPosition);
  public void setIcon(Icon icon);
  public void setIconTextGap(int gap);
  public void setLabelFor(Component c);
  public void setText(String test);
  public void setUI(LabelUI ui);
  public void setVerticalAlignment(int verticalAlignment);
  public void setVerticalTextPosition(int textPosition);
  public void updateUI();
}
```

Most of the definition should look familiar from `AbstractButton`. Because a `JLabel` isn't a selectable button, `JLabel` couldn't subclass `AbstractButton`. Behavior-wise, most methods are identical. The most noticeable exception is the existence of keyboard mnemonics for labels. When you specify the mnemonic with `setDisplayedMnemonic()` you also need to associate the label to a component via `setLabelFor()`. Then, when a user presses the mnemonic, the input focus is moved to the associated component. This works best when the component is a text component, which cannot have its own mnemonic.

You might use `JLabel` components, for example, to label areas of your GUI that are grouped together in a `JPanel`. Figure 13.11 illustrates three `JLabel` components.

FIGURE 13.11:

Three JLabel components

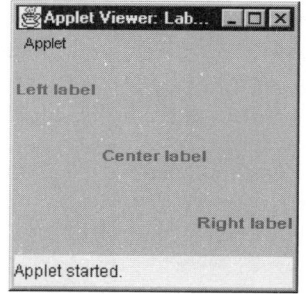

Here is the demonstration program behind Figure 13.11:

```
import java.awt.*;
import javax.swing.*;
public class LabelTest extends JApplet {
  public void init() {
    Container c = getContentPane();
    c.setLayout(new GridLayout(3,1));
    c.add(new JLabel("Left label")); // default left justify
    c.add(new JLabel("Center label", JLabel.CENTER)); // center
    c.add(new JLabel("Right label", JLabel.RIGHT)); // right justify
  }
}
```

For its horizontal alignment, you can choose between LEFT, CENTER, or RIGHT. The label's text and alignment properties can be queried with the methods `public int getHorizontalAlignment()`, `public int getHorizontal-TextPosition()`, `public int getVerticalAlignment()`, `public int` getVerticalTextPosition(), and public String getText() or changed with matching setXXX() methods.

The alignment of a label will have a visual effect only if the layout manager that controls the JLabel component allows components to appear sized to dimensions other than their getMinimumSize(). Changing the alignment of labels within a FlowLayout, for example, has no effect because FlowLayout always sizes components to their most compact dimensions.

In addition to text and alignment, a JLabel can also have an icon. Usage is identical to JButton. Configure the icon in the constructor, change it with setIcon(Icon icon) or setDisabledIcon(Icon icon), query for it with getIcon() and getDisabledIcon(), and even configure the gaps between the text and icon with setIconTextGap(int gap).

Adding Toggle Buttons

A JToggleButton component is a two-state button typically used on toolbars to indicate the state of a toggleable option, like bold, italics, or underline font enabled when using a word processor. Here are the constructors:

```
public JToggleButton();
public JToggleButton(Icon icon);
public JToggleButton(Icon icon, boolean selected);
public JToggleButton(String text);
public JToggleButton(String text, boolean selected);
public JToggleButton(String text, Icon icon);
public JToggleButton(String text, Icon icon, boolean selected);
```

Figure 13.12 shows an example of JToggleButton components.

FIGURE 13.12:

JToggleButton components

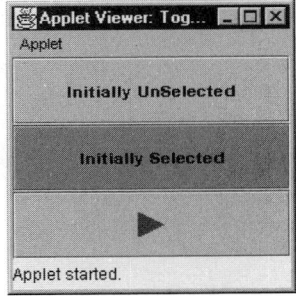

Here is the program behind Figure 13.12:

```java
import java.awt.*;
import javax.swing.*;
public class ToggleTest extends JApplet {
  static class TriangleIcon implements Icon {
    static class State {
      public static final State NORMAL   = new State();
      public static final State PRESSED = new State();
      public static final State SELECTED = new State();
      public static final State ROLLOVER = new State();
      private State() {}
    }
    State state;
    Color color;
    public TriangleIcon (Color c, State state) {
      color = c;
      this.state = state;
    }
    public int getIconWidth() {
      return 20;
    }
    public int getIconHeight() {
      return 20;
    }
    public void paintIcon(Component c, Graphics g, int x, int y) {
      g.setColor (color);
      Polygon p = new Polygon();
      if (state == State.NORMAL) {
        p.addPoint (x+(getIconWidth() / 2), y);
        p.addPoint (x, y+getIconHeight()-1);
        p.addPoint (x+getIconWidth()-1, y+getIconHeight()-1);
      } else if (state == State.PRESSED) {
        p.addPoint (x, y);
        p.addPoint (x+getIconWidth()-1, y);
        p.addPoint (x+(getIconWidth() / 2), y+getIconHeight()-1);
      } else if (state == State.SELECTED) {
        p.addPoint (x+getIconWidth()-1, y);
        p.addPoint (x+getIconWidth()-1, y+getIconHeight()-1);
        p.addPoint (x, y+(getIconHeight() / 2));
      } else {
        p.addPoint (x, y);
```

```
            p.addPoint (x, y+getIconHeight()-1);
            p.addPoint (x+getIconWidth()-1, y+(getIconHeight() / 2));
        }
        g.fillPolygon (p);
    }
}
public void init() {
    Icon normalIcon = new TriangleIcon(Color.red, TriangleIcon.State.NORMAL);
    Icon pressedIcon = new TriangleIcon(Color.red, TriangleIcon.State.PRESSED);
    Icon selectedIcon = new TriangleIcon(Color.red, TriangleIcon.State.SELECTED);
    Icon rolloverIcon = new TriangleIcon(Color.red, TriangleIcon.State.ROLLOVER);
    Container c = getContentPane();
    c.setLayout (new GridLayout (0, 1));
    JToggleButton b = new JToggleButton ("Initially UnSelected");
    c.add (b);
    b = new JToggleButton ("Initially Selected", true);
    c.add (b);
    b = new JToggleButton (normalIcon);
    b.setPressedIcon (pressedIcon);
    b.setSelectedIcon (selectedIcon);
    b.setRolloverIcon (rolloverIcon);
    b.setRolloverEnabled (true);
    c.add (b);
    }
}
```

NOTE   Notice that the toggle button also supports a selected icon. Since the toggle button has a notion of being selected, in addition to being pressed, you can provide yet another icon.

Adding Checkboxes

A Checkbox component is a two-state button typically used in GUIs containing selectable items (such as in voting forms or option preference pages). Here are its constructors:

```
public JCheckBox();
public JCheckBox(Icon icon);
public JCheckBox(Icon icon, boolean selected);
public JCheckBox(String text);
```

```
public JCheckBox(String text, boolean selected);
public JCheckBox(String text, Icon icon);
public JCheckBox(String text, Icon icon, boolean selected);
```

Usage of JCheckBox is identical to ToggleButton. The only difference is the physical appearance. Instead of the whole button being selected, only the icon associated with the JCheckBox appears selected. If no icon is specified, a default one appears. Figure 13.13 shows an example of a JCheckbox component.

FIGURE 13.13:

A JCheckBox component

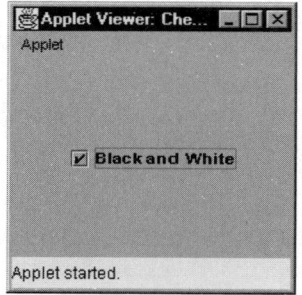

Here is the demonstration program behind Figure 13.13:

```
import java.awt.*;
import javax.swing.*;
public class CheckBoxTest extends JApplet {
  public void init() {
    JCheckBox cb = new JCheckBox("Black and White");
    cb.setHorizontalAlignment (JCheckBox.CENTER);
    getContentPane().add(cb, BorderLayout.CENTER);
  }
}
```

The program declares and constructs a JCheckBox object that is labeled with the string passed as argument to the JCheckBox constructor. Next, for appearance sake, the JCheckBox is centered in the screen. The JCheckBox component is then added, as usual, with the add() method of getContentPane(). By default, a checkbox's state is initially false. You can create a checkbox with a specified initial state by calling an alternate version of the constructor: JCheckbox (String, boolean). The boolean parameter provides the checkbox's initial state. There are additional constructors to specify the icon to use for the JCheckBox, too.

Adding Radio Buttons into Button Groups

To define a group of checkboxes to be mutually exclusive you use the JRadio-Button class, instead of JCheckBox. It has a similar set of seven constructors as JToggleButton and JCheckBox:

```
public JRadioButton();
public JRadioButton(Icon icon);
public JRadioButton(Icon icon, boolean selected);
public JRadioButton(String text);
public JRadioButton(String text, boolean selected);
public JRadioButton(String text, Icon icon);
public JRadioButton(String text, Icon icon, boolean selected);
```

You also need one extra helper class: ButtonGroup. Here is its definition:

```
public class ButtonGroup extends Object implements Serializable {
  protected Vector buttons;
  public ButtonGroup();
  public void add(AbstractButton ab);
  public Enumeration getElements();
  public ButtonModel getSelection();
  public boolean isSelected(ButtonModel bm);
  public void remove(AbstractButton ab);
  public void setSelected(ButtonModel bm, boolean b);
}
```

The purpose of ButtonGroup is to provide the scope for the mutually exclusive group and to manage the group's state.

TIP

Notice that ButtonGroup works with a group of AbstractButton components, not specifically JRadioButton. You'll use ButtonGroup with JRadioButton-MenuItem also. Technically speaking, you can also put things like JToggleButton in a button group, if that is the behavior you desire.

Here is a demonstration program that uses a ButtonGroup instance to define a mutually exclusive collection of radio buttons:

```
import java.awt.*;
import javax.swing.*;
public class RadioTest extends JApplet {
  public void init() {
    Container c = getContentPane();
```

```
      c.setLayout (new GridLayout (0, 1));
      ButtonGroup group = new ButtonGroup();
      JRadioButton option = new JRadioButton ("Black and White", true);
      group.add (option);
      c.add (option);
      option = new JRadioButton ("256 Greyscale", false);
      group.add (option);
      c.add (option);
      option = new JRadioButton ("True Color", false);
      group.add (option);
      c.add (option);
   }
}
```

As you can see, you need to add each radio button to the group separately. You cannot specify the group at creation time. The second constructor argument is the initial state for the checkbox: `false` for deselected and `true` for selected. Within any group of radio buttons, you can make only one selected. Figure 13.14 shows the result of the above program.

FIGURE 13.14:

Mutually exclusive radio buttons

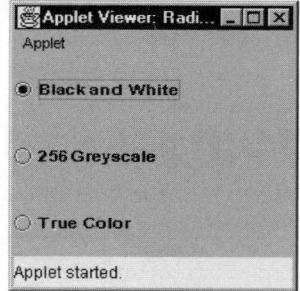

Note the layout of the buttons in Figure 13.14. This format is the result of changing the layout to `GridLayout`, instead of the default `BorderLayout` used by Swing applets. Also, as with `JCheckBox` and `JToggleButton`, you can specify your own icons.

To change the state of any `JRadioButton` that is part of a button group, you need to use the `ButtonGroup` method `setSelected(ButtonModel bm, boolean selected)` to ensure that the mutual exclusiveness is maintained (you should not use the `AbstractButton` method `setSelected()`). To get the `ButtonModel` for a `JRadioButton`, ask for it with `getModel()`.

Adding Combo Box (Pull-Down) Lists

The JComboBox class encapsulates a pull-down choice list component. It has the following definition:

```
public class JComboBox extends JComponent
    implements ActionListener, ItemSelectable, ListDataListener, Accessible {
  protected String actionCommand;
  protected ComboBoxModel dataModel;
  protected ComboBoxEditor editor;
  protected boolean isEditable;
  protected KeySelectionManager keySelectionManager;
  protected boolean lightWeightPopupEnabled;
  protected int maximumRowCount;
  protected ListCellRenderer renderer;
  protected Object selectedItemReminder;
  public JComboBox();
  public JComboBox(ComboBoxModel m);
  public JComboBox(Object obj[]);
  public JComboBox(Vector v);
  public void actionPerformed(ActionEvent e);
  public void addActionListener(ActionListener l);
  public void addItem(Object obj);
  public void addItemListener(ItemListener l);
  public void configureEditor(ComboBoxEditor e, Object o);
  public void contentsChanged(ListDataEvent e);
  protected KeySelectionManager createDefaultKeySelectionManager();
  protected void fireActionEvent();
  protected void fireItemStateChanged(ItemEvent e);
  public AccessibleContext getAccessibleContext();
  public String getActionCommand();
  public ComboBoxEditor getEditor();
  public Object getItemAt(int pos);
  public int getItemCount();
  public KeySelectionManager getKeySelectionManager();
  public int getMaximumRowCount();
  public ComboBoxModel getModel();
  public ListCellRenderer getRenderer();
  public int getSelectedIndex();
  public Object getSelectedItem();
  public Object[] getSelectedObjects();
  public ComboBoxUI getUI();
  public String getUIClassID();
```

```
public void hidePopup();
public void insertItemAt(Object obj, int pos);
public void intervalAdded(ListDataEvent e);
public void intervalRemoved(ListDataEvent e);
public boolean isEditable();
public boolean isFocusTraversable();
public boolean isLightWeightPopupEnabled();
public boolean isPopupVisible();
public void processKeyEvent(KeyEvent e);
public void removeActionListener(ActionListener e);
public void removeAllItems();
public void removeItem(Object obj);
public void removeItemAt(int pos);
public void removeItemListener(ItemListener l);
public boolean selectWithKeyChar(char c);
protected void installAncestorListener();
protected void selectedItemChanged();
public void setActionCommand(String command);
public void setEditable(boolean b);
public void setEditor(ComboBoxEditor e);
public void setEnabled(boolean b);
public void setKeySelectionManager(KeySelectionManager ksm);
public void setLightWeightPopupEnabled(boolean b);
public void setMaximumRowCount(int count);
public void setModel(ComboBoxModel m);
public void setPopupVisible(boolean b);
public void setRenderer(ListCellRenderer r);
public void setSelectedIndex(int pos);
public void setSelectedItem(Object obj);
public void setUI(ComboBoxUI ui);
public void showPopup();
public void updateUI();
}
```

As with past components, advanced capabilities are described in later chapters. For now, we'll just look at how to create a JComboBox, add options, and support editability when available options aren't sufficient.

The JComboBox component allows a user to select one of several options or items in one space-saving place. When GUI real estate becomes crowded, you can substitute a collection of mutually exclusive radio buttons with a single, compact JComboBox component. Figure 13.15 shows an example of a pull-down list created with this component.

FIGURE 13.15:

A JComboBox component

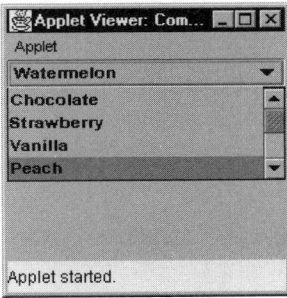

Here is the demonstration program behind Figure 13.15:

```java
import java.awt.*;
import javax.swing.*;
public class ComboTest extends JApplet {
  public void init() {
    String flavors[] = {"Chocolate", "Strawberry", "Vanilla", "Peach",
      "Butter Pecan", "Watermelon", "Blueberry", "Double Fudge"};
    JComboBox jc = new JComboBox (flavors);
    jc.setMaximumRowCount (4);
    getContentPane().add(jc, BorderLayout.NORTH);
  }
}
```

This applet initializes the entire list of choices of the JComboBox from a String array. If you need to add entries one at a time, you would use the addItem() method. Once the choice list is specified, the maximum row count setting is configured to four. This says that when the pull-down list is shown, show four choices at most. Finally, the combo box is added to the applet's content pane, with add().

Class JComboBox provides methods that allow you to access and/or set the currently selected item in the list:

getSelectedItem()   Returns the object of the item itself

getSelectedIndex()   Returns the index position of the item

getSelectedObjects()   Returns an array that contains the item

setSelectedIndex(int pos)   Selects an item by index position

setSelectedItem(Object anObject)   Selects an item by name (if parameter not a String, using toString method of Object to make it one)

JComboBox components are ideal for reasonably small lists of selectable items (say, from 3 to 20 items). But if you have only two choices, it might be better to use radio buttons instead (unless the list of choices is dynamic and is expected to grow beyond two). If, on the other hand, your list of choices becomes large, you should consider using a JList.

In the event you do not know all available choices to add to the JComboBox, you can allow the user the option of entering an additional choice. This does not add a choice to the list but lets the user type in a new one. When setEditable() is called, with a value of true, you can think of it as an "Other" choice always available, where the user specifies exactly what "Other" means.

Adding Scroll Panes

The JScrollPane component is an interesting component. It acts as a container for one component, providing scrolling support for that component, if it is larger than the space available within the JScrollPane. Here are its constructors:

```
public JScrollPane();
public JScrollPane (int vsbPolicy, int hsbPolicy);
public JScrollPane (Component view);
public JScrollPane (Component view, int vsbPolicy, int hsbPolicy);
```

The vertical scrollbar policy and horizontal scrollbar policy values are available from the ScrollPaneConstants interface that JScrollPane implements. They are VERTICAL_SCROLLBAR_ALWAYS, VERTICAL_SCROLLBAR_AS_NEEDED, VERTICAL_SCROLLBAR_NEVER for the vertical policy, and HORIZONTAL_SCROLLBAR_ALWAYS, HORIZONTAL_SCROLLBAR_AS_NEEDED, and HORIZONTAL_SCROLLBAR_NEVER for the horizontal one.

The following example scrolls a JLabel with large ImageIcon placed within it. The JLabel is larger than the ScrollPane that contains it, so scrollbars appear automatically.

```
import java.awt.*;
import javax.swing.*;
public class ScrollPaneTest extends JApplet {
  public void init() {
    Icon icon = new ImageIcon ("jbcover.jpg");
    JLabel lab = new JLabel (icon);
    JScrollPane pane = new JScrollPane(lab);
    getContentPane().add(pane, BorderLayout.CENTER);
  }
}
```

Figure 13.16 shows the applet produced by this demonstration program.

FIGURE 13.16:

A JScrollPane holding
a JLabel

Adding Lists

Consider a JList component as a heavyweight analog of a JComboBox component. Here is its class definition:

```
public class JList extends JComponent implements Scrollable, Accessible {
  public JList();
  public JList(ListModel lm);
  public JList(Object obj[]);
  public JList(Vector v);
  public void addListSelectionListener(ListSelectionListener l);
  public void addSelectionInterval(int anchor, int lead);
  public void clearSelection();
  protected ListSelectionModel createSelectionModel();
  public void ensureIndexIsVisible(int pos);
  protected void fireSelectionValueChanged(int first, int last, boolean adj);
  public AccessibleContext getAccessibleContext();
  public int getAnchorSelectionIndex();
  public Rectangle getCellBounds(int start, int end);
  public ListCellRenderer getCellRenderer();
  public int getFirstVisibleIndex();
  public int getFixedCellHeight();
  public int getFixedCellWidth();
  public int getLastVisibleIndex();
  public int getLeadSelectionIndex();
  public int getMaxSelectionIndex();
  public int getMinSelectionIndex();
  public ListModel getModel();
  public Dimension getPreferredScrollableViewportSize();
```

```
        public Object getPrototypeCellValue();
        public int getScrollableBlockIncrement(Rectangle r, int orient, int dir);
        public boolean getScrollableTracksViewportHeight();
        public boolean getScrollableTracksViewportWidth();
        public int getScrollableUnitIncrement(Rectangle r, int orient, int dir);
        public int getSelectedIndex();
        public int[] getSelectedIndices();
        public Object getSelectedValue();
        public Object[] getSelectedValues();
        public Color getSelectionBackground();
        public Color getSelectionForeground();
        public int getSelectionMode();
        public ListSelectionModel getSelectionModel();
        public ListUI getUI();
        public String getUIClassID();
        public boolean getValueIsAdjusting();
        public int getVisibleRowCount();
        public Point indexToLocation(int index);
        public boolean isSelectedIndex(int index);
        public boolean isSelectionEmpty();
        public int locationToIndex(Point p);
        public void removeListSelectionListener(ListSelectionListener l);
        public void removeSelectionInterval(int start, int end);
        public void setCellRenderer(ListCellRenderer r);
        public void setFixedCellHeight(int h);
        public void setFixedCellWidth(int w);
        public void setListData(Object obj[]);
        public void setListData(Vector v);
        public void setModel(ListModel lm);
        public void setPrototypeCellValue(Object obj);
        public void setSelectedIndex(int index);
        public void setSelectedIndices(int index[]);
        public void setSelectedValue(Object obj, boolean b);
        public void setSelectionBackground(Color c);
        public void setSelectionForeground(Color c);
        public void setSelectionInterval(int start, int end);
        public void setSelectionMode(int mode);
        public void setSelectionModel(ListSelectionModel lm);
        public void setUI(ListUI ui);
        public void setValueIsAdjusting(boolean b);
        public void setVisibleRowCount(int count);
        public void updateUI();
    }
```

The following are the main differences between the JList and JComboBox components:

- Lists are used for much longer lists of items.

- Lists are used when multiple selections are needed.

- Lists typically use up a large proportion of a GUI's real estate.

- Class JList contains many more methods supporting its functionality.

- Class JComboBox supports selecting choices not specified.

Figure 13.17 shows an example of a JList component.

FIGURE 13.17:

A JList component

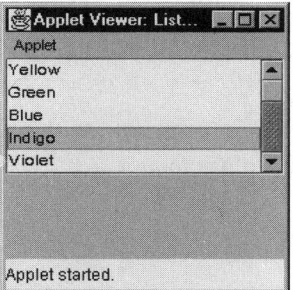

Here is the demonstration program behind Figure 13.17:

```
import java.awt.*;
import javax.swing.*;
public class ListTest extends JApplet {
  public void init() {
    String[] colors = {"Red", "Orange", "Yellow",
      "Green", "Blue", "Indigo", "Violet"};
    JList colorList = new JList(colors);
    colorList.setVisibleRowCount (5);
    JScrollPane pane = new JScrollPane (colorList);
    getContentPane().add(pane, BorderLayout.NORTH);
  }
}
```

The first thing you learn when using the JList class is you must provide the scrolling support. This seems rather odd. However, you must place the JList within a JScrollPane when you want to offer the ability to scroll through a list of choices. Otherwise, whatever doesn't fit on the screen won't be shown.

JList components come in three interactive varieties: one that allows multiple selections (the default mode), one that permits a single interval of selections, and another that behaves like a JComboBox or JRadioButton component in that it accepts only single (mutually exclusive) selections. To configure and process multiple selections, the following methods are available:

> **void setSelectionMode(int mode)**   Lets you change the multiple-selection behavior of a JList. Available modes are: SINGLE_SELECTION, SINGLE_ INTERVAL_SELECTION, and MULTIPLE_INTERVAL_SELECTION

> **int[] getSelectedIndices()**   Returns an array of indices specifying the multiple selection

> **Object[] getSelectedValues()**   Similar to getSelectedIndexes(), except that it returns an array of selected objects

> **int getSelectionMode()**   Tells you whether a JList currently accepts multiple selections

---

WARNING   You should not use setSelectionMode() to change list behavior after the JList component becomes active; after that point, changing a list's response to multiple selections will surely confuse the user!

Providing Sliders

When you want your GUI users to enter numerical values that can range contiguously from a minimum value to a maximum value, you should provide them with slider controls to achieve this efficiently. Java's support for slider controls comes in the form of class JSlider, which is defined as follows:

```
public class JSlider extends JComponent implements SwingConstants, Accessible {
    protected transient ChangeEvent changeEvent;
    protected ChangeListener changeListener;
    protected int majorTickSpacing;
    protected int minorTickSpacing;
    protected int orientation;
    protected BoundedRangeModel sliderModel;
    protected boolean snapToTicks;
```

```
public JSlider();
public JSlider(BoundedRangeModel brm);
public JSlider(int orient);
public JSlider(int min, int max);
public JSlider(int min, int max, int value);
public JSlider(int orient, int min, int max, int value);
public void addChangeListener(ChangeListener l);
protected ChangeListener createChangeListener();
public Hashtable createStandardLabels(int increment);
public Hashtable createStandardLabels(int increment, int start);
protected void fireStateChanged();
public AccessibleContext getAccessibleContext();
public int getExtent();
public boolean getInverted();
public Dictionary getLabelTable();
public int getMajorTickSpacing();
public int getMaximum();
public int getMinimum();
public int getMinorTickSpacing();
public BoundedRangeModel getModel();
public int getOrientation();
public boolean getPaintLabels();
public boolean getPaintTicks();
public boolean getPaintTrack();
public boolean getSnapToTicks();
public SliderUI getUI();
public String getUIClassID();
public int getValue();
public boolean getValueIsAdjusting();
public void removeChangeListener(ChangeListener l);
public void setExtent(int extent);
public void setInverted(boolean b);
public void setLabelTable(Dictionary d);
public void setMajorTickSpacing(int n);
public void setMaximum(int max);
public void setMinimum(int min);
public void setMinorTickSpacing(int n);
public void setModel(BoundedRangeModel m);
public void setOrientation(int orient);
public void setPaintLabels(boolean b);
public void setPaintTicks(boolean b);
public void setPaintTrack(boolean b);
```

```
public void setSnapToTicks(boolean b);
public void setUI(SliderUI ui);
public void setValue(int value);
public void setValueIsAdjusting(boolean b);
public String toString();
protected void updateLabelUIs();
public void updateUI();
}
```

To better support the entering of a value within a range, a JSlider can display tick marks to help the user position the slider as they select a value. A JSlider can also place labels along with the tick marks. Both of these options, plus the ability to enable only stopping the slider at an actual result, make the JSlider component very user friendly. Figure 13.18 shows both a vertical and horizontal JSlider, without any configuration options set.

FIGURE 13.18:

Plain vertical and horizontal JSlider

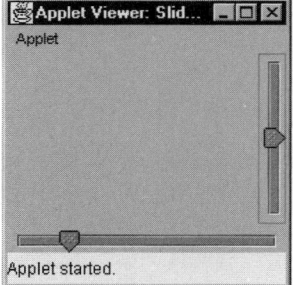

Here is the demonstration program behind Figure 13.18:

```
import java.awt.*;
import com.sun.java.swing.*;
public class SliderTest extends JApplet {
  public void init() {
    JSlider upDown, leftRight;
    upDown = new JSlider(JSlider.VERTICAL, 0, 100, 50);
    leftRight = new JSlider(JSlider.HORIZONTAL, 0, 10, 2);
    getContentPane().add(upDown, BorderLayout.EAST);
    getContentPane().add(leftRight, BorderLayout.SOUTH);
  }
}
```

This applet creates two JSlider objects: one vertical (by specifying JSlider class constant JSlider.VERTICAL), the other horizontal (using JSlider.HORIZONTAL). The extra numeric arguments passed to the Scrollbar constructor are as follows:

minimum and maximum   The minimum and maximum values this scrollbar can represent; for example, 0–100 (for percentages), 6–120 (for ages), 1–31 (for dates)

value   The starting position for the slider knob (some value within the range minimum…maximum)

While the previous applet works fine, a user cannot naturally see where the different values are. With a little work, you can add tick marks and labels to make the slider more friendly to the user. Figure 13.19 shows the updated program, with various options set.

FIGURE 13.19:

Configured vertical and horizontal JSlider

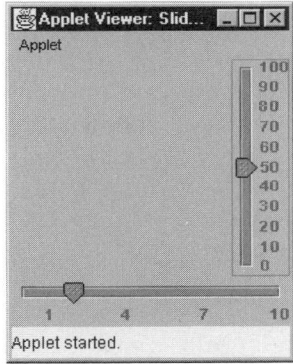

The following highlights the changes made to the source of the demonstration program behind Figure 13.19:

```
import java.awt.*;
import javax.swing.*;
import java.util.*;
public class SliderTest2 extends JApplet {
  public void init() {
    JSlider upDown, leftRight;
    upDown = new JSlider(JSlider.VERTICAL, 0, 100, 50);
    upDown.setMajorTickSpacing (10);
    upDown.setPaintLabels (true);
    leftRight = new JSlider(JSlider.HORIZONTAL, 0, 10, 2);
```

```
        Hashtable h = new Hashtable();
        h.put (new Integer (1), new JLabel("1"));
        h.put (new Integer (4), new JLabel("4"));
        h.put (new Integer (7), new JLabel("7"));
        h.put (new Integer (10), new JLabel("10"));
        leftRight.setLabelTable (h);
        leftRight.setPaintLabels (true);
        getContentPane().add(upDown, BorderLayout.EAST);
        getContentPane().add(leftRight, BorderLayout.SOUTH);
    }
}
```

NOTE   Chapter 14 explains how to respond to slider movements and how to retrieve the value a JSlider is indicating. If you aren't familiar with hashtables, they are covered in Chapter 17.

Besides JSlider, the Swing component set also offers a JScrollBar. The JScrollBar is primarily of use when you are defining your own scrolling region. Due to the infrequency of its use because of the availability of JScrollPane, it will not be described. It functions similarly to a JSlider.

Adding Text Fields

A JTextField implements that old favorite: a single-line text input box. Here is its class definition:

```
public class JTextField extends JTextComponent implements SwingConstants {
    public static final String notifyAction;
    public JTextField();
    public JTextField(int columns);
    public JTextField(Document doc, String text, int columns);
    public JTextField(String text);
    public JTextField(String text, int columns);
    public synchronized void addActionListener(ActionListener l);
    protected Document createDefaultModel();
    protected void fireActionPerformed();
    public AccessibleContext getAccessibleContext();
    public Action[] getActions();
    protected int getColumnWidth();
    public boolean isValidateRoot();
    public int getColumns();
    public int getHorizontalAlignment();
```

```
    public BoundedRangeModel getHorizontalVisibility();
    public Dimension getMinimumSize();
    public Dimension getPreferredSize();
    public int getScrollOffset();
    public String getUIClassID();
    protected String paramString();
    public void postActionEvent();
    public synchronized void removeActionListener(ActionListener l);
    public void scrollRectToVisible(Rectangle r);
    public void setActionCommand(String command);
    public void setColumns(int columns);
    public void setFont(Font font);
    public void setHorizontalAlignment(int align);
    public void setScrollOffset(int offset);
}
```

Text fields share behavior with a related class called JTextArea (discussed next). Both inherit from an intermediate superclass called JTextComponent. Here is the definition of the JTextComponent class:

```
public abstract class JTextComponent extends JComponent
    implements Scrollable, Accessible {
  public static final String DEFAULT_KEYMAP;
  public static final String FOCUS_ACCELERATOR_KEY;
  public JTextComponent();
  public void addCaretListener(CaretListener l);
  public static Keymap addKeymap(String name, Keymap parent);
  public void copy();
  public void cut();
  protected void fireCaretUpdate(CaretEvent e);
  public AccessibleContext getAccessibleContext();
  public Action[] getActions();
  public Caret getCaret();
  public Color getCaretColor();
  public int getCaretPosition();
  public Color getDisabledTextColor();
  public Document getDocument();
  public char getFocusAccelerator();
  public Highlighter getHighlighter();
  public Keymap getKeymap();
  public static Keymap getKeymap(String name);
  public Insets getMargin();
  public Dimension getPreferredScrollableViewportSize();
  public int getScrollableBlockIncrement(Rectangle r, int orient, int dir);
```

```
public boolean getScrollableTracksViewportHeight();
public boolean getScrollableTracksViewportWidth();
public int getScrollableUnitIncrement(Rectangle rec, int orient, int dir);
public String getSelectedText();
public Color getSelectedTextColor();
public Color getSelectionColor();
public int getSelectionEnd();
public int getSelectionStart();
public String getText();
public String getText(int offset, int len) throws BadLocationException;
public TextUI getUI();
public boolean isEditable();
public boolean isFocusTraversable();
public boolean isOpaque();
public static void loadKeymap(Keymap map, KeyBinding bind[], Action act[]);
public Rectangle modelToView(int pos) throws BadLocationException;
public void moveCaretPosition(int pos);
public void paste();
protected void processComponentKeyEvent(KeyEvent e);
public void read(Reader r, Object desc) throws IOException;
public void removeCaretListener(CaretListener l);
public static Keymap removeKeymap(String name);
public void replaceSelection(String content);
public void select(int begin, int end);
public void selectAll();
public void setCaret(Caret c);
public void setCaretColor(Color c);
public void setCaretPosition(int pos);
public void setDisabledTextColor(Color c);
public void setDocument(Document doc);
public void setEditable(boolean b);
public void setEnabled(boolean b);
public void setFocusAccelerator(char c);
public void setHighlighter(Highlighter high);
public void setKeymap(Keymap map);
public void setMargin(Insets in);
public void setOpaque(boolean b);
public void setSelectedTextColor(Color c);
public void setSelectionColor(Color c);
public void setSelectionEnd(int pos);
public void setSelectionStart(int pos);
public void setText(String text);
public void setUI(TextUI ui);
```

```
   public void updateUI();
   public int viewToModel(Point p);
   public void write(Writer w) throws IOException;
}
```

Any text component contains some text to manage and render. The user may be allowed to edit this text, and the user can always select some part of it by click-dragging the mouse pointer over the required text. This selection ability is used in part to support the general clipboard cut/copy/paste mechanism of the host operating system. The majority of the methods defined by class JTextComponent relate to these text component issues shared by the JTextField and JTextArea components. Figure 13.20 shows a simple JTextField component embedded in an applet along with a right-justified JTextField, possibly for numeric input.

FIGURE 13.20:

A JTextField component with selected text and a right-justified JTextField

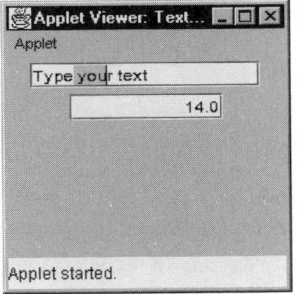

Here is the demonstration program behind Figure 13.20:

```java
import java.awt.*;
import javax.swing.*;
public class TextFieldTest extends JApplet {
  public void init() {
    Container c = getContentPane();
    c.setLayout (new FlowLayout());
    JTextField text = new JTextField("Type your text", 15);
    c.add(text);
    text = new JTextField("14.0", 10);
    text.setHorizontalAlignment (JTextField.RIGHT);
    c.add(text);
  }
}
```

Adding a JTextField component is similar to adding the other simple Swing components: You call its constructor and use the add() method to place the resulting object in your container. In this example, the first JTextField sets its initial value to the string "Type your text" with a column width of 15. This second parameter does not limit the input to fifteen, only the display to approximately 15 characters.

JTextField components have one interesting feature that might come in handy: You can have either left-, right-, or center-justified text. This can come in handy for numerical applications.

Hiding Password Fields

The JTextField class has a subclass JPasswordField that accepts text that is masked on the screen to prevent bystanders from reading the text. Here is the definition of the JPasswordField class:

```
public class JPasswordField extends JTextField {
    public JPasswordField();
    public JPasswordField(int columns);
    public JPasswordField(Document doc, String text, int columns);
    public JPasswordField(String text);
    public JPasswordField(String text, int columns);
    public void copy();
    public void cut();
    public boolean echoCharIsSet();
    public AccessibleContext getAccessibleContext();
    public char getEchoChar();
    public char[] getPassword();
    public String getUIClassID();
    public void setEchoChar(char c);
}
```

The main application of this feature is for password entry, as shown in Figure 13.21.

FIGURE 13.21:

A JPasswordField or two

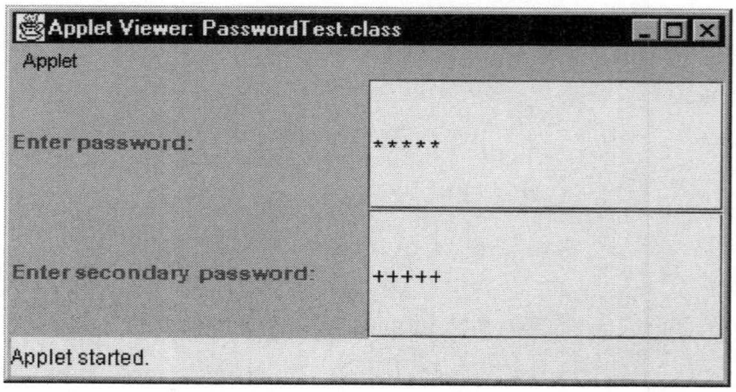

Here is the program that produced the applet shown in Figure 13.21:

```java
import java.awt.*;
import javax.swing.*;
public class PasswordTest extends JApplet {
  public void init() {
    Container c = getContentPane();
    c.setLayout (new GridLayout(2, 2));
    c.add(new JLabel("Enter password:") );
    JPasswordField passwordField = new JPasswordField(10);
    c.add(passwordField);
    c.add(new JLabel("Enter secondary password:") );
    passwordField = new JPasswordField(10);
    passwordField.setEchoChar ('+');
    c.add(passwordField);
  }
}
```

The "echo" character is used to mask the real characters on the screen. A conservative asterisk (*) is the default character used for that purpose. The second password field has a mask of a plus sign (+).

Placing Text Areas

The JTextArea component, as its name suggests, is used when larger amounts of text need to be input or, more often, just displayed. Here is its class definition:

```java
public class JTextArea extends JTextComponent {
  public JTextArea();
  public JTextArea(int rows, int cols);
  public JTextArea(Document doc);
  public JTextArea(Document doc, String text, int rows, int cols);
  public JTextArea(String text);
  public JTextArea(String text, int rows, int cols);
  public void append(String str);
  protected Document createDefaultModel();
  public AccessibleContext getAccessibleContext();
  protected int getColumnWidth();
  public int getColumns();
  public int getLineCount();
  public int getLineEndOffset(int offset) throws BadLocationException;
```

```
    public int getLineOfOffset(int offset) throws BadLocationException;
    public int getLineStartOffset(int offset) throws BadLocationException;
    public boolean getLineWrap();
    public Dimension getMinimumSize();
    public Dimension getPreferredScrollableViewportSize();
    public Dimension getPreferredSize();
    protected int getRowHeight();
    public int getRows();
    public boolean getScrollableTracksViewportWidth();
    public int getScrollableUnitIncrement(Rectangle r, int orient, int dir);
    public int getTabSize();
    public String getUIClassID();
    public boolean getWrapStyleWord();
    public void insert(String str, int pos);
    public boolean isManagingFocus();
    protected String paramString();
    public void replaceRange(String str, int start, int end);
    public void setColumns(int cols);
    public void setFont(Font f);
    public void setLineWrap(boolean b);
    public void setRows(int rows);
    public void setTabSize(int size);
    public void setWrapStyleWord(boolean b);
}
```

Figure 13.22 shows a typical JTextArea component.

FIGURE 13.22:

A JTextArea component

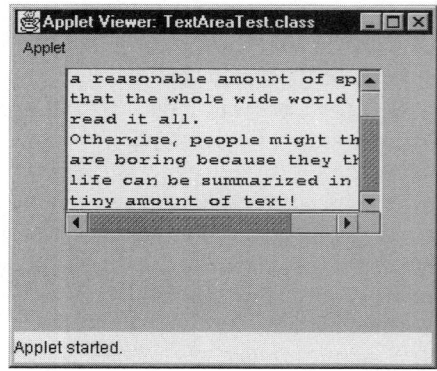

Here is the demonstration program behind Figure 13.22. Like a JList component, a JTextArea must be placed within a JScrollPane.

```
import java.awt.*;
import javax.swing.*;
public class TextAreaTest extends JApplet {
   JTextArea disp;
   String multiLineText =
      "If you want to tell the story\n"
    + "of your life, you better set aside\n"
    + "a reasonable amount of space so\n"
    + "that the whole wide world can \n"
    + "read it all.\n"
    + "Otherwise, people might think you\n"
    + "are boring because they think your \n"
    + "life can be summarized in such a \n"
    + "tiny amount of text!";
  public void init() {
    Container c = getContentPane();
    c.setLayout (new FlowLayout());
    disp = new JTextArea(multiLineText, 7, 30);
    JScrollPane pane = new JScrollPane (disp);
    c.add(pane);
  }
}
```

The JTextArea constructor used in the program lets you specify the initial block of text and the dimensions of the JTextArea box (in character rows and columns). Note how a single String composed of multiple lines is created. This is achieved by embedding new line characters in a String directly, using the standard control character escape sequence \n. For scrollbars you must remember to add the JTextArea to a JScrollPane if the size of the text exceeds the component's visible area.

Dragging Toolbars

The JToolBar component offers a potentially draggable container to place a component in. Here is its class definition:

```
public class JToolBar extends JComponent implements SwingConstants, Accessible {
  public JToolBar();
  public JToolbar(int orientation);
  public JButton add(Action act);
  protected void addImpl(Component comp, Object constraints, int index);
```

```
    public void addSeparator();
    protected PropertyChangeListener createActionChangeListener(JButton jb);
    public AccessibleContext getAccessibleContext();
    public Component getComponentAtIndex(int index);
    public int getOriented();
    public int getComponentIndex(Component c);
    public int getOrientation();
    public Insets getMargin();
    public ToolBarUI getUI();
    public String getUIClassID();
    public boolean isBorderPainted();
    public boolean isFloatable();
    protected void paintBorder(Graphics g);
    public void addSeparator(Dimension dim);
    public void setBorderPainted(boolean b);
    public void setFloatable(boolean b);
    public void setMargin(Insets in);
    public void setOrientation(int orientation);
    public void setUI(ToolBarUI ui);
    public void updateUI();
}
```

Figure 13.23 shows a typical JToolBar usage: placing a set of commonly sized components onto the toolbar, with a separator between two of them.

FIGURE 13.23:

A JToolBar example

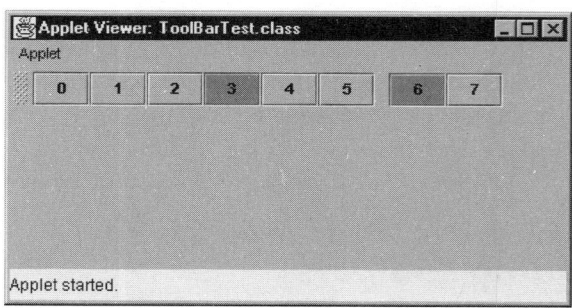

Here is the demonstration program behind Figure 13.23.

```
import java.awt.*;
import javax.swing.*;
public class ToolBarTest extends JApplet {
  public void init() {
    JToolBar bar;
```

```
Container c = getContentPane();
bar = new JToolBar();
JToggleButton jb;
for (int i=0; i < 8; i++) {
  jb = new JToggleButton ("" + i);
  bar.add (jb);
  if (i == 5) {
    bar.addSeparator();
  }
}
c.add(bar, BorderLayout.NORTH);
}
}
```

When running the program be sure to drag the toolbar around and move it outside the applet.

NOTE   Any component can be placed on a JToolBar.

Working with Internal Frames

A JInternalFrame is a component that offers resizable, iconified, draggable windows within the confines of an outer container. The windows can't be moved outside the outer container. This outer container tends to be a JDesktopPane, which is a subclass of JLayeredPane, but can be anything. The class definition of JInternalFrame follows:

```
public class JInternalFrame extends JComponent implements Accessible,
    WindowConstants, RootPaneContainer {
public static final String CONTENT_PANE_PROPERTY;
public static final String FRAME_ICON_PROPERTY;
public static final String GLASS_PANE_PROPERTY;
public static final String IS_CLOSED_PROPERTY;
public static final String IS_ICON_PROPERTY;
public static final String IS_MAXIMUM_PROPERTY;
public static final String IS_SELECTED_PROPERTY;
public static final String LAYERED_PANE_PROPERTY;
public static final String MENU_BAR_PROPERTY;
public static final String ROOT_PANE_PROPERTY;
public static final String TITLE_PROPERTY;
 protected boolean closable;
```

```
protected JDesktopIcon desktopIcon;
protected Icon frameIcon;
protected boolean iconable;
protected boolean isClosed;
protected boolean isIcon;
protected boolean isMaximum;
protected boolean isSelected;
protected boolean maximizable;
protected boolean resizable;
protected JRootPane rootPane;
protected boolean rootPaneCheckingEnabled;
protected String title;
public JInternalFrame();
public JInternalFrame(String title);
public JInternalFrame(String title, boolean resizable);
public JInternalFrame(String title, boolean resizable, boolean closable);
public JInternalFrame(String title, boolean resizable, boolean closable,
    boolean maximizable);
public JInternalFrame(String title, boolean resizable, boolean closable,
    boolean maximizable, boolean iconifiable);
protected void addImpl(Component comp, Object constraints, int index);
public void addInternalFrameListener(InternalFrameListener l);
protected JRootPane createRootPane();
public void dispose();
protected void fireInternalFrameEvent(int id);
public AccessibleContext getAccessibleContext();
public Color getBackground();
public Container getContentPane();
public int getDefaultCloseOperation();
public JInternalFrame.JDesktopIcon getDesktopIcon();
public JDesktopPane getDesktopPane();
public Color getForeground();
public Icon getFrameIcon();
public Component getGlassPane();
public int getLayer();
public JLayeredPane getLayeredPane();
public JMenuBar getJMenuBar();
public JRootPane getRootPane();
public String getTitle();
public InternalFrameUI getUI();
public String getUIClassID();
public final String getWarningString();
```

```
public boolean isClosable();
public boolean isClosed();
public boolean isIcon();
public boolean isIconifiable();
public boolean isMaximizable();
public boolean isMaximum();
public boolean isResizable();
protected void setRootPane(JRootPane pane);
protected void setRootPaneCheckingEnabled(boolean b);
protected boolean isRootPaneCheckingEnabled();
public boolean isSelected();
public void moveToBack();
public void moveToFront();
public void pack();
public void removeInternalFrameListener(InternalFrameListener l);
public void reshape(int x, int y, int width, int height);
public void setBackground(Color c);
public void setClosable(boolean b);
public void setClosed(boolean b) throws PropertyVetoException;
public void setContentPane(Container c);
public void setDefaultCloseOperation(int operation);
public void setDesktopIcon(JInternalFrame.JDesktopIcon d);
public void setForeground(Color c);
public void setFrameIcon(Icon icon);
public void setGlassPane(Component glass);
public void setIcon(boolean b) throws PropertyVetoException;
public void setIconifiable(boolean b);
public void setJMenuBar(JMenuBar menu);
public void setLayer(Integer layer);
public void setLayeredPane(JLayeredPane layered);
public void setLayout(LayoutManager manager);
public void setMaximizable(boolean b);
public void setMaximum(boolean b) throws PropertyVetoException;
public void setResizable(boolean b);
public void setSelected(boolean selected) throws PropertyVetoException;
public void setTitle(String title);
public void setUI(InternalFrameUI ui);
public void setVisible(boolean b);
public void show();
public void toBack();
public void toFront();
public void updateUI();
}
```

Figure 13.24 shows a demonstration of a `JInternalFrame`. Three `JInternal-Frame` components are placed inside a `JDesktopPane`.

FIGURE 13.24:

A JDesktopPane with three JInternalFrames

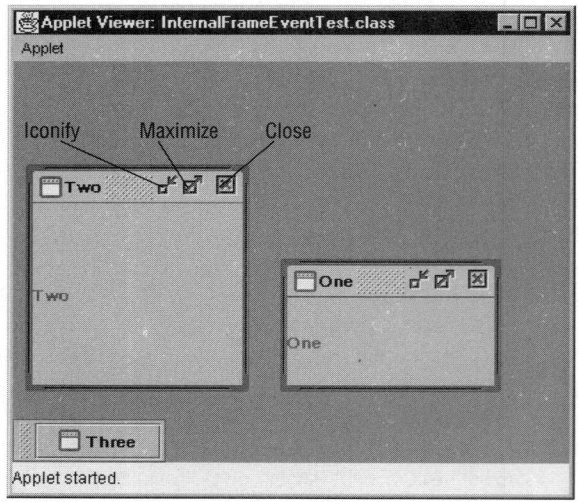

The demonstration program behind Figure 13.24 follows.

```java
import java.awt.*;
import javax.swing.*;
import java.awt.event.*;
public class InternalFrameEventTest extends JApplet {
  public void init() {
    Container c = getContentPane();
    JLayeredPane desktop = new JDesktopPane();
    desktop.setOpaque(false);
    c.add(desktop, BorderLayout.CENTER);
    desktop.add (createLayer ("One"), JLayeredPane.POPUP_LAYER);
    desktop.add (createLayer ("Two"), JLayeredPane.DEFAULT_LAYER);
    desktop.add (createLayer ("Three"), JLayeredPane.PALETTE_LAYER);
  }
  public JInternalFrame createLayer (String label) {
    return new SelfInternalFrame(label);
  }
  class SelfInternalFrame extends JInternalFrame {
    public SelfInternalFrame(String s) {
```

```
        getContentPane().add (new JLabel (s), BorderLayout.CENTER);
        setBounds (50, 50, 100, 100);
        setResizable (true);
        setClosable (true);
        setMaximizable (true);
        setIconifiable (true);
        setTitle (s);
      }
    }
  }
```

Setting Tables

The JTable component is one of the more complex widgets within the Swing component set. In fact, it has a whole package, java.awt.swing.table, all to itself. However, there is a simple way of creating a JTable that we'll discuss here. The rest of JTable's usage will be left to Chapter 15.

The JTable class allows you to display columnar data. JTable has a constructor that takes two parameters: public JTable(Object data[][], Object columnHeaders[]). The two-dimensional data parameter is the actual data to display in the table. The one-dimensional columnHeaders parameter is for the text of each column header. By having both parameters be String arrays, you can easily create a JTable object without dealing with anything going on behind the scenes.

Figure 13.25 shows the demonstration of this simplified approach to JTable.

FIGURE 13.25:

A JTable example

Applet started.

Here is the program behind Figure 13.25.

```
import java.awt.*;
import javax.swing.*;
public class TableTest extends JApplet {
  String data[][]  = {
    {"John", "Jones", "Admiral"},
    {"George", "Washington", "General"},
    {"Max", "Klinger", "Corporal"},
    {"Frank", "Burns", "Major"},
    {"Doug", "MacArthur", "General"},
    {"Roberta", "Lee", "Private"},
    {"Georgette", "Grant", "Captain"},
    {"Harry", "Junior", "Sergeant"}
  };
  String columns [] = {"First Name", "Last Name", "Rank"};
  public void init() {
    JTable jt = new JTable (data, columns);
    JScrollPane pane = new JScrollPane (jt);
    getContentPane().add(pane, BorderLayout.CENTER);
  }
}
```

As with JList and JTextArea, the JTable requires you to create a JScroll-Pane to place the table in.

There is much more to do when working with JTable. Skip ahead to Chapter 15 if you can't wait.

Using Menu System Components

The Swing menu components are no different from any of the other components. In fact, they descend from AbstractButton components like JButton and JToggle-Button. The superclass of all the menu components is JMenuItem. Its subclasses are JMenu, JCheckBoxMenuItem, and JRadioButtonMenuItem. Besides being able to add any of these components anywhere that you can add every other Swing component, you can also place them on a JMenuBar and then place the JMenuBar on a JApplet or JFrame.

The remaining menuing component is a JPopupMenu. We'll briefly discuss it here. However, we'll describe how it works in Chapter 14 because it requires you to understand event handling beforehand.

Adding Menu Bars

The main purpose of the JMenuBar class is to group together a collection of JMenu instances. In this respect, its add() method is its core method (analogous to the add() methods of class Container). The JMenuBar class has the following definition:

```java
public class JMenuBar extends JComponent implements Accessible, MenuElement {
    public JMenuBar();
    public JMenu add(JMenu menu);
    public AccessibleContext getAccessibleContext();
    public Component getComponent();
    public Component getComponentAtIndex(int index);
    public int getComponentIndex(Component c);
    public JMenu getHelpMenu();
    public Insets getMargin();
    public JMenu getMenu(int);
    public int getMenuCount();
    public SingleSelectionModel getSelectionModel();
    public MenuElement[] getSubElements();
    public MenuBarUI getUI();
    public String getUIClassID();
    public boolean isBorderPainted();
    public boolean isManagingFocus();
    public boolean isSelected();
    public void menuSelectionChanged(boolean b);
    protected void paintBorder(Graphics g);
    public void processKeyEvent(KeyEvent e, MenuElement path[],
      MenuSelectionManager mgr);
    public void processMouseEvent(MouseEvent e, MenuElement path[],
      MenuSelectionManager mgr);
    public void setBorderPainted(boolean b);
    public void setHelpMenu(JMenu menu);
    public void setMargin(Insets in);
    public void setSelected(Component c);
    public void setSelectionModel(SingleSelectionModel m);
    public void setUI(MenuBarUI ui);
    public void updateUI();
}
```

The MenuBar class also supports the concept of a "Help" menu. A single menu on the menu bar can be designated as being the Help menu. Its behavior, position, and rendering can then reflect this special status (this is done in platform-specific ways).

Adding Menus

The main purpose of the JMenu class is to group together a collection of JMenu-Items and other submenus. The core JMenu method is the add() method, which is used to incrementally specify the list of menu items (or menus) contained by the menu. Here is the definition of the JMenu class:

```
public class JMenu extends JMenuItem implements Accessible, MenuElement {
    protected JMenu.WinListener popupListener;
    public JMenu();
    public JMenu(String label);
    public JMenu(String label, boolean tearOff);
    public Component add(Component c);
    public JMenuItem add(Action act);
    public JMenuItem add(JMenuItem item);
    public void add(String label);
    public void addMenuListener(MenuListener l);
    public void addSeparator();
    protected PropertyChangeListener createActionChangeListener(JMenuItem item);
    protected JMenu.WinListener createWinListener(JPopupMenu popup);
    public void doClick(int pressTime);
    protected void fireMenuCancelled();
    protected void fireMenuDeselected();
    protected void fireMenuSelected();
    public AccessibleContext getAccessibleContext();
    public Component getComponent();
    public int getDelay();
    public JMenuItem getItem(int pos);
    public int getItemCount();
    public Component getMenuComponent(int pos);
    public int getMenuComponentCount();
    public Component[] getMenuComponents();
    public JPopupMenu getPopupMenu();
    public MenuElement[] getSubElements();
    public String getUIClassID();
```

```
    public JMenuItem insert(Action a, int pos);
    public JMenuItem insert(JMenuItem item, int pos);
    public void doClick(int pressTime);
    public void insert(String label, int pos);
    public void insertSeparator(int pos);
    public boolean isMenuComponent(Component c);
    public boolean isPopupMenuVisible();
    public boolean isSelected();
    public boolean isTearOff();
    public boolean isTopLevelMenu();
    public void menuSelectionChanged(boolean b);
    public String paramString();
    protected void processKeyEvent(KeyEvent e);
    public void remove(int pos);
    public void remove(JMenuItem item);
    public void removeAll();
    public void removeMenuListener(MenuListener l);
    public void setAccelerator(KeyStroke stroke);
    public void setDelay(int delay);
    public void setMenuLocation(int x, int y);
    public void setModel(ButtonModel bm);
    public void setPopupMenuVisible(boolean b);
    public void setSelected(boolean b);
    public void updateUI();
}
```

The JMenu class also implements a feature not universally supported on all platforms: tear-off menus. With a tear-off menu, a menu can be made to stay open, making items easily selectable. Marking a JMenu as being a tear-off menu may have no effect if a machine's look and feel does not support such a feature.

You can also add a separator to a menu at any point in the list using a call to addSeparator(). This is handy when your menus become rather long. Adding separators between groups of related items structures the menu and prevents it from becoming a messy, endless list of choices.

NOTE When you add a separator with addSeparator(), you are actually adding another JComponent to the menu. In this case, the component is a JSeparator. Rarely do you use the class directly. However, it does exist and is available for creating vertical lines on screen.

Adding Menu Items

The JMenuItem class (and its close relatives, JCheckboxMenuItem and JRadioButton-MenuItem) embodies the final, user-selectable menu item. Here is its definition:

```
public class JMenuItem extends AbstractButton
    implements Accessible, MenuElement {
  public JMenuItem();
  public JMenuItem(Icon icon);
  public JMenuItem(String label);
  public JMenuItem(String label, int mnemonic);
  public JMenuItem(String label, Icon icon);
  public void addMenuDragMouseListener(MenuDragMouseListener l);
  public void addMenuKeyListener(MenuKeyListener l);
  protected void fireMenuDragMouseDragged(MenuDragMouseEvent e);
  protected void fireMenuDragMouseEntered(MenuDragMouseEvent e);
  protected void fireMenuDragMouseExited(MenuDragMouseEvent e);
  protected void fireMenuDragMouseReleased(MenuDragMouseEvent e);
  protected void fireMenuKeyPressed(MenuKeyEvent e);
  protected void fireMenuKeyReleased(MenuKeyEvent e);
  protected void fireMenuKeyTyped(MenuKeyEvent e);
  public KeyStroke getAccelerator();
  public AccessibleContext getAccessibleContext();
  public Component getComponent();
  public MenuElement[] getSubElements();
  public String getUIClassID();
  protected void init(String label, Icon icon);
  public boolean isArmed();
  public void menuSelectionChanged(boolean b);
  public void processKeyEvent(KeyEvent e, MenuElement path[],
    MenuSelectionManager mgr);
  public void processMenuDragMouseEvent(MenuDragMouseEvent e);
  public void processMenuKeyEvent(MenuKeyEvent e);
  public void processMouseEvent(MouseEvent e, MenuElement path[],
    MenuSelectionManager mgr);
  public void removeMenuDragMouseListener(MenuDragMouseListener);
  public void removeMenuKeyListener(MenuKeyListener);
  public void setAccelerator(KeyStroke stroke);
  public void setArmed(boolean b);
  public void setEnabled(boolean v);
  public void setUI(MenuItemUI ui);
  public void updateUI();
}
```

Menu items can be dynamically enabled or disabled to reflect the state of the application. For example, an Edit menu usually grays out (disables) the Cut and Copy menu items when there is no currently selected aspect of the project (text, picture, waveform, and so on). As soon as the user selects all or part of the project, the menu items become available by enabling them.

Adding Checkbox Menu Items

The JCheckBoxMenuItem class incorporates an on/off state, which is depicted graphically in a menu using a check mark or other glyph to that effect. Here is its definition:

```
public class JCheckBoxMenuItem extends JMenuItem
    implements SwingConstants, Accessible {
  public JCheckBoxMenuItem();
  public JCheckBoxMenuItem(Icon icon);
  public JCheckBoxMenuItem(String label);
  public JCheckBoxMenuItem(String label, boolean selected);
  public JCheckBoxMenuItem(String label, Icon icon);
  public JCheckBoxMenuItem(String label, Icon icon, boolean selected);
  public AccessibleContext getAccessibleContext();
  public synchronized Object[] getSelectedObjects();
  public boolean getState();
  public String getUIClassID();
  protected void init(String label, Icon icon);
  public void requestFocus();
  public synchronized void setState(boolean b);
  public void updateUI();
}
```

Adding Radio Button Menu Items

The JRadioButtonMenuitem class is like a JRadioButton, but on a menu. It incorporates an on/off state, but it is placed in a group so only one in the group is set.

Here is its definition:

```
public class JRadioButtonMenuItem extends JMenuItem
```

```
      implements Accessible {
   public JRadioButtonMenuItem();
   public JRadioButtonMenuItem(Icon icon);
   public JRadioButtonMenuItem(String label);
   public JRadioButtonMenuItem(String label, Icon icon);
   public AccessibleContext getAccessibleContext();
   public String getUIClassID();
   protected void init(String label, Icon icon);
   public void requestFocus();
   public void updateUI();
}
```

Adding Pop-Up Menus

The JPopupMenu class is a subclass of JComponent. You construct and populate a pop-up menu just as you would a regular menu. The difference between regular menus and pop-up menus is that you do not attach a pop-up menu to a menu bar. Instead, you temporarily display a pop-up menu above some other component. This component is called the invoker and is set with setInvoker(). When the user makes a selection, the pop-up menu goes away.

To display a pop-up menu, you use this method:

```
show(Component source, int x, int y)
```

The Component parameter is the component above which the pop-up menu will be displayed. The two int parameters are the x- and y-coordinates where the pop-up menu will appear, with respect to the coordinate system of the component.

A Program to Construct a Menu Bar

The following application program uses menu classes to construct a menu bar attached to a simple window. Because all the menuing classes are so intertwined, there is just one example demonstrating all:

```
import java.awt.*;
import javax.swing.*;
public class MenuTest {
  public static void main (String args[]) {
    JFrame f = new MainWindow();
    f.setSize(400, 300);
    f.setVisible(true);
```

```
      }
    static class MainWindow extends JFrame {
      public MainWindow() {
        super("MenuTest Window");
        FileMenu fileMenu = new FileMenu();
        HelpMenu helpMenu = new HelpMenu();
        JMenuBar mb = new JMenuBar();
        mb.add(fileMenu);
        mb.add(helpMenu);
// Not yet implemented
//      mb.setHelpMenu(helpMenu);
        setJMenuBar(mb);
      }
    }
    static class FileMenu extends JMenu {
      public FileMenu() {
        super("File", true);   // tear-off menu
        add(new JMenuItem("Open"));
        add(new JMenuItem("Close"));
        add(new JMenuItem("Exit"));
      }
    }
    static class HelpMenu extends JMenu {
      public HelpMenu() {
        super("Help");
        add(new JMenuItem("About MenuTest"));
        add(new JMenuItem("Class Hierarchy"));
        addSeparator();
        add(new JCheckBoxMenuItem("Balloon Help"));
        JMenu subMenu = new JMenu("Categories");
        JRadioButtonMenuItem rb;
        ButtonGroup group = new ButtonGroup();
        subMenu.add(rb = new JRadioButtonMenuItem("A Little Help"));
        group.add (rb);
        subMenu.add(rb = new JRadioButtonMenuItem("A Lot of Help"));
        group.add (rb);
        add(subMenu);
      }
    }
  }
```

Note how cleanly the program is structured to follow the main objects of its particular problem domain; the startup class MenuTest relies on a MainWindow class to create its application window. The MainWindow class in turn relies on two inner classes to implement one menu each: menus FileMenu and HelpMenu. The two menu classes construct themselves privately, without encumbering the rest of the program with details of their menus' composition. This nesting of abstraction levels is an application of the information-hiding principle made possible by object-oriented design and implementation. (The MenuTest class does not care about the structure of the menus attached to the window; it just wants to pop up the window—with or without menus.)

In class MainWindow, the menu bar is constructed by creating a new JMenuBar object and then using the add() method to link the two menus to it. To attach it to the window, you call the JFrame setJMenuBar() method, passing in the JMenuBar instance. In class HelpMenu, you build this menu by first defining its title (by calling the standard JMenu constructor and passing the menu title label as a String). Then several calls to add() create the list of menu items that the menu should contain. An addSeparator() invocation separates the normal items from the two special menu items at the end of this menu. The first special menu item is the "Balloon Help" JCheckboxMenuItem, which can be toggled on or off. The second special item is an entire submenu containing two JRadioButtonMenuItems. Figure 13.26 shows the menu bar in action.

FIGURE 13.26:

JMenuBar with JMenus and JMenuItems (and submenu)

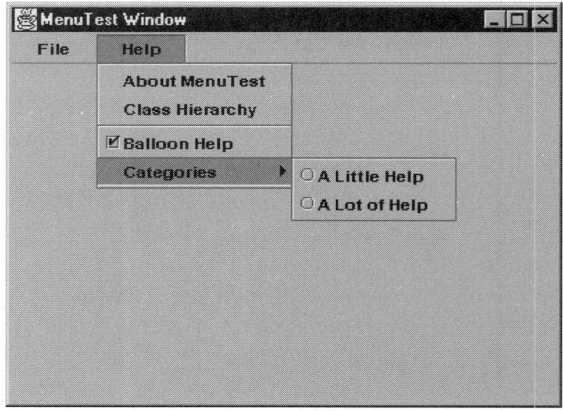

Summary

The Swing hierarchy provides one concrete GUI component branch: the `Component` branch that leads to the `JComponent` branch. All the Swing widgets are subclasses of the large, but abstract, superclass `Component`.

In this chapter, you explored how to use the `JButton`, `JPanel`, `JLabel`, `JToggleButton`, `JCheckBox`, `JRadioButton`, `JComboBox`, `JScrollPane`, `JList`, `JSlider`, `JTextField`, `JPasswordField`, `JTextArea`, `JToolBar`, `JInternalFrame`, and `JTable` components. Also, you looked at the supporting cast of `JApplet`, `AbstractButton`, `Icon`, `ImageIcon`, `Border`, `BorderFactory`, `JToolTip`, `ToolTipManager`, and `ButtonGroup`. You rounded out your tour of the Swing component set by looking at how menu systems are constructed and attached to an application window, a `JFrame`. In combination, all these elements can be used to construct clear, functional, and—last but not least—portable GUIs.

CHAPTER
FOURTEEN

Event Handling

- Event-driven applications

- Event delegation

- Java's event-class hierarchy

- Event types in the `java.awt.event` package

- Event types in the `javax.swing.event` package

14

An *event* is an unexpected external happening that imposes itself on you. If a firefighter shouts "Fire! Everyone out of the building!" while demolishing your front door, that is an event. If you are asleep early in the morning and your alarm clock goes off, that is another event (less traumatic maybe, but equally annoying). In software systems, events have similar attributes, but programs are less flexible than humans in dealing with the unexpected. Code must be in place to recognize and handle every possible event or else your program will be oblivious to unexpected events (and may even crash).

In the context of hardware and systems programming, events are called *interrupts*. When you press a key, the electronics inside your keyboard interrupt your desktop system to send it the keycode of the key you pressed. Your machine responds by immediately halting whatever it was doing, receiving the key's identifying code, acknowledging the interrupt, and resuming whatever it was doing before the interrupt occurred. Within the field of GUI design and programming, user events (like a mouse click) have much the same urgency as their lower-level interrupt counterparts. Responsiveness is one of the most important attributes a GUI should have.

This chapter explains event-driven programming, your choices for handling events in your Java programs, and Java's event types.

Event-Driven Programming

Event handling lies at the very heart of GUI programming. Unlike first-generation applications, in which programs imposed a rigid sequence of program–user interaction, modern applications put the user in charge. The user controls the sequence of operations that the application executes via a GUI, which waits for the user to activate a button or slider or menu. This approach is called *event-driven programming*.

An event-driven application typically constructs a GUI at initialization time, displays the GUI, and then enters a tight loop waiting for user events to request an operation: the application's main event loop. When such an event (or *trigger*) occurs, a large `switch` statement determines the generated event type and invokes a corresponding action, as shown in the following pseudo-code:

```
while not quitting
|    wait for a GUI event
|    grab event
|    switch depending on event type
```

```
|    |    button click       : handle button clicks
|    |    textfield entry    : handle textfield entries
|    |    slider movement    : handle slider movements
|    |    choice selection   : handle choice selections
|    |    eventtype x         : handle events of type x
|    |    eventtype y         : handle events of type y
|    |    eventtype z         : handle events of type z
|    |    default             : beep (error)
```

In a realistic event-processing situation, the `switch` statement typically would be quite a bit longer. This central switchboard is a common scenario when the implementation language is of the older procedural kind, such as Pascal or C. In object-oriented languages, the script has been modified slightly.

Java's Event-Delegation Model

In Java, events are objects. The `java.awt.event` package defines a rich hierarchy of event types, described later in this chapter. Through this package, instances of the various event classes are constructed when users use GUI components. It is up to the programmer to decide how to handle the generated event. For example, when a user clicks on a button, the system constructs an instance of class `Action-Event`, in which it stores details about the event (when, where, and so on). At this point, the programmer has three options:

- Ignore the event.

- Have the event handled by the component (in this case, a button) where the event originated.

- Delegate event handling to some other object, possibly yourself, or objects called *listeners*.

The following sections examine each of these options.

Ignoring the Event

In the absence of any explicit event-handling code, events will be ignored. You already saw this in Chapter 13, where a sample applet was presented for each type of component. You could activate all the components (that is, you could move the slider, push the button, select from the list, and so on), and the components would respond visually, but the test programs do not do anything about your input.

NOTE

Components like `JScrollPane` are the exception in this area. When you move its scrollbars, the enclosed component moves accordingly. Some components like this one provide built-in event handling that you don't have to worry about.

Just because it is possible to respond to input from a component, it is not necessary to do so. Consider a hypothetical Java-based mail tool, with a text area for composing messages, a text field for entering a recipient, and a Send button. While composing a mail message, a user types and clicks with the mouse, creating a large number of events in the text area and the text field. This hypothetical program could provide event-handling code to deal with these events, but what would that code do? The only time the program cares about the state of the text area and the text field is when the user clicks the Send button. A clean implementation of this program would handle events from only the Send button; the event would read the contents of the other two components and build an appropriate mail message. This example shows there are times when the best response to an event is none at all.

Handling the Event in the Originating Component

A *self-contained* component is one that handles the events that it generates. None of the Swing or AWT components are self-contained; if you want a component to handle its own events, you need to create a subclass. The subclass must do two things:

- Enable receipt of events by calling `enableEvents()` with the necessary event mask setting

- Provide a `processActionEvent()` method, which will be called when the component is activated

The following code implements a simple self-contained button:

```
import java.awt.*;
import java.awt.event.*;
public class SelfButton extends Button {
  public SelfButton (String label) {
```

```
      super(label);
      enableEvents(AWTEvent.ACTION_EVENT_MASK);
   }
   public void processActionEvent (ActionEvent e) {
      super.processActionEvent (e);
      System.out.println("Action!");
   }
}
```

The constructor calls enableEvents(), passing in AWTEvent.ACTION_EVENT_ MASK, which tells the button component that it is interested in action events.

When a user clicks on a SelfButton, the system generates an action event and then checks whether the SelfButton has enabled action events. Since action events are enabled, the system calls the processActionEvent() method. In the example, this method does its default behavior and then just prints a brief message.

By passing in different event masks to enableEvents(), you can sensitize a component to catch many different kinds of events; all of the event handlers have names of the format processXXXEvent(), where XXX stands for the event type. (The various event types are discussed later in "Java's Event Types.")

You use a self-contained component just like any other component: construct one, and then add it to a container. The following code produces a simple applet that demonstrates the use of SelfButton:

```
import java.applet.*;
public class SelfButtonTest extends Applet {
   public void init() {
      add (new SelfButton("Push Me"));
   }
}
```

Figure 14.1 shows the SelfButtonTest applet. The button looks like an ordinary button. This is not surprising—SelfButton doesn't *look* any different from a button; it just *behaves* differently when activated.

FIGURE 14.1:

A self-contained button

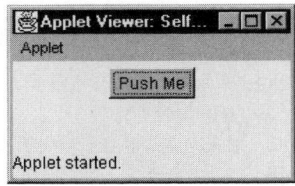

Most of the Swing components do not support the self-containing event-handling concept described here. See "Delegating the Event to Yourself" later in this chapter for how to create self-contained components with both the newer Swing component set and the original AWT component sets.

Delegating the Event

One of the fundamental principles of object-oriented design is that the object best suited to the task should perform the task. There will be times when self-contained components are not the way to go because the component may not be the object best suited to handling its own events.

The process of assigning an object to handle a component's events is called *delegation*. The event-handling objects are called *listeners*. To tell a button that it should delegate handling of action events to some listener, you call the button's `addActionListener()` method, passing in a reference to the desired listener. Every component class in AWT has one `addXXXListener()` method for each event type that the component generates.

A component may have multiple listeners for an event type. If, for example, a button has five action listeners, each of the listeners will be notified when the button is activated. This is sometimes useful, but it has two drawbacks. First, there is no guarantee about the order in which listeners will be notified. Second, spreading event-handling responsibility among several objects can quickly lead to code that is difficult to maintain. However, multiple listeners ensure that the object most interested in the event knows about it.

When a button with an action listener is clicked, the listener receives an `action-Performed()` call. The listener class should implement this method however it is supposed to respond. The following example has a button in an applet. The button delegates action handling to a third object, which is an instance of class `TestListener`:

```
import  java.awt.*;
import  java.awt.event.*;
public class ButtonDelegateTest extends java.applet.Applet {
  public void init() {
    Button b = new Button("I have a listener!");
    add(b);
    ActionListener listener = new TestListener();
```

```
      b.addActionListener(listener);
   }
 class TestListener implements ActionListener {
   public void actionPerformed (ActionEvent e) {
     System.out.println ("Listener here: the button was clicked.");
   }
 }
}
```

You should notice several things about this program:

- The button is a plain `Button`, not a subclass. When you use event delegation, your design takes on some complexity, but you are spared the necessity of subclassing.

- There is the call to `addActionListener()`. This is called on the button, passing in the test listener. This means that before `addActionListener()` can be called, the listener must be constructed.

- The declaration line for `TestListener` says that the class implements the `ActionListener` interface.

`ActionListener` is a simple interface with only one method:

```
public interface ActionListener extends EventListener {
   public abstract void actionPerformed(ActionEvent e);
}
```

The declaration for method `addActionListener()` requires that the listener parameter implement this interface:

```
public void addActionListener(ActionListener listener);
```

Since the listener is required to implement the interface, you know that when an action event occurs, the system can safely make an `actionPerformed()` call on the listener, because the listener definitely has an `actionPerformed()` method.

Figure 14.2 shows the `ButtonDelegateTest` applet.

FIGURE 14.2:

A button with an action listener

Delegating the Event to Yourself

As the "Handling the Event in the Originating Component" section shows, you can easily handle events yourself by enabling an event mask and overriding an event-processing method. While there is nothing wrong with the way this works, it is much easier to just add yourself as the event listener. The SelfButton from above can be changed to the following (the two changes made are bold):

```
import java.awt.*;
import java.awt.event.*;
public class SelfButton2 extends Button implements ActionListener {
  public SelfButton2 (String label) {
    super(label);
    addActionListener (this);
  }
  public void actionPerformed (ActionEvent e) {
    System.out.println("Action!");
  }
}
```

The self-contained class implements the listener for the event, and the constructor adds itself as a listener. It's that easy. Functionally, the two programs are identical.

Java's Event Types

So far, you have looked at one type of event: the action event. There are actually 16 concrete event types, which are contained in the java.awt.event and com .sun.java.swing.event packages. (There is also an intermediate superclass, InputEvent, which is the parent of KeyEvent and MouseEvent.) All of the event classes, except two, MenuEvent and PopupMenuEvent, extend from two abstract superclasses: java.util.EventObject and java.awt.AWTEvent. The event-inheritance hierarchy is shown in Figure 14.3.

The ancestor of the hierarchy is java.util.EventObject, which provides a method called getSource(). This method returns the component in which the event took place. One level below java.util.EventObject is java.awt.AWTEvent, which provides a method called getID(). This method returns an int that describes the nature of the event. For example, calling getID() on an instance of Mouse-Event results in an int whose value might be MouseEvent.MOUSE_PRESSED, MouseEvent.MOUSE_DRAGGED, or one of several other possible values, depending on which specific mouse activity triggered the event.

FIGURE 14.3:

The Java AWT event-class hierarchy

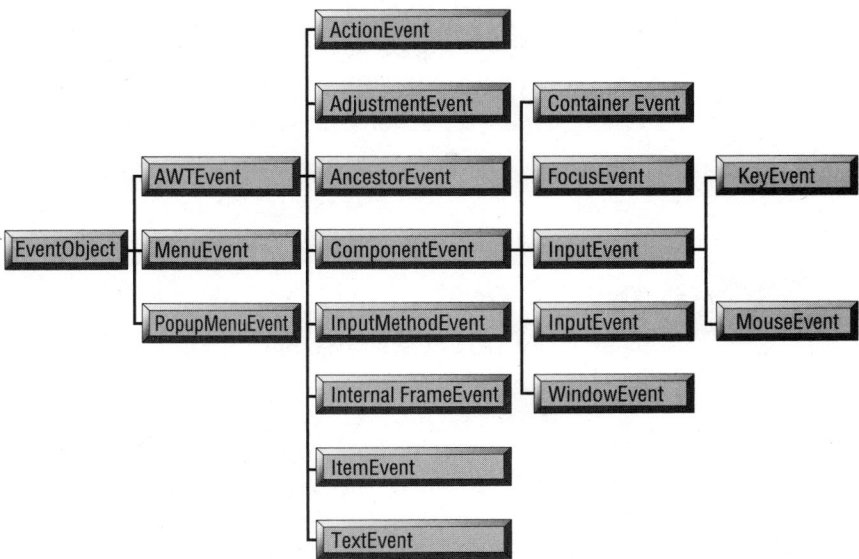

As explained earlier in the chapter, events may be delegated to a listener or they may be handled by the originating component. If you will be delegating component event handling to listeners, you will need to know the answers to these questions:

- For each event type, which component types can generate the event?

- For each event type, what interface should the listener implement?

- For each event type, which method in the listener is called?

If your components handle their own events, they will have to provide their own listener or you will need to know the answers to the following questions:

- For each event type, which component types can generate the event?

- For each event type, what value should a component pass to `enableEvents()` to receive notification when the event happens?

- For each event type, which method is called in the component when the event occurs?

For all of the components that handle their own events in the following sections, they will provide a self-listener. This is done primarily because it is less error prone. In the first `SelfButton` example in this chapter, if the `processActionEvent()` method didn't have the call to super's `processActionEvent()` and something else was listening for action events, this other listener would never be notified.

Besides `ActionEvent`, which has already been discussed, there are 17 non-superclass event types. These event types are explained in the following sections.

Adjustment Events

Adjustment events are sent by scrollbars. Here is the definition of the `Adjustment-Event` class:

```
public class AdjustmentEvent extends AWTEvent {
    public static final int ADJUSTMENT_FIRST;
    public static final int ADJUSTMENT_LAST;
    public static final int ADJUSTMENT_VALUE_CHANGED;
    public static final int BLOCK_DECREMENT;
    public static final int BLOCK_INCREMENT;
    public static final int TRACK;
    public static final int UNIT_DECREMENT;
    public static final int UNIT_INCREMENT;
    public AdjustmentEvent(Adjustable source, int id, int type, int value);
    public Adjustable getAdjustable();
    public int getAdjustmentType();
    public int getValue();
    public String paramString();
}
```

TIP   Some of the event classes define constants for the range of values for the IDs of the different subtypes of the event. These are defined by constants with names ending in _FIRST and _LAST. Their purpose is such that if you subclass the event class and define your own subtype, you can specify an ID outside the used range. They do not define different subtypes of events.

If a component delegates its adjustment events, the delegate must implement the `AdjustmentListener` interface. The following is the definition of this interface:

```
public interface AdjustmentListener extends EventListener {
    public abstract void adjustmentValueChanged(AdjustmentEvent e);
}
```

The applet code listed next constructs two scrollbars. The first is an ordinary (that is, not subclassed) scrollbar that delegates adjustment events to the applet; when the scrollbar moves, the applet writes a message to the console. The second scrollbar is a subclass called `SelfScrollbar`. This subclass handles its own adjustment events; when the `SelfScrollbar` moves, the scrollbar itself writes a message to the console.

```java
import java.awt.*;
import javax.swing.*;
import java.awt.event.*;
public class AdjustmentEventTest extends JApplet  {
  public void init() {
    Container c = getContentPane();
    // A plain scrollbar that delegates to the applet
    JScrollBar sbar1 = new JScrollBar();
    sbar1.addAdjustmentListener(new AdjustmentListener() {
      public void adjustmentValueChanged(AdjustmentEvent e)  {
        System.out.println("Scrollbar #1: " + e.getValue());
      }
    });
    c.add(sbar1, BorderLayout.WEST);
    // A subclass that handles its own adjustment events
    SelfScrollbar sbar2 = new SelfScrollbar();
    c.add(sbar2, BorderLayout.EAST);
  }
  class SelfScrollbar extends JScrollBar implements AdjustmentListener {
    public SelfScrollbar() {
      addAdjustmentListener (this);
    }
    public void adjustmentValueChanged(AdjustmentEvent e)  {
      System.out.println("Scrollbar #2: " + e.getValue());
    }
  }
}
```

The first scrollbar delegates adjustment events to the new anonymous adjustment listener created. The second (subclassed) scrollbar handles its own adjustment events by implementing the `AdjustmentListener` interface.

Ancestor Events

Ancestor events are sent by JComponents when an ancestor of the component is added, moved, or removed from the component hierarchy. Here is the definition of the AncestorEvent class:

```
public class AncestorEvent extends AWTEvent {
  public static final int ANCESTOR_ADDED;
  public static final int ANCESTOR_MOVED;
  public static final int ANCESTOR_REMOVED;
  public AncestorEvent(JComponent source, int id, Container ancestor,
    Container ancestorParent);
  public Container getAncestor();
  public Container getAncestorParent();
  public JComponent getComponent();
}
```

If a component delegates its ancestor events, the delegate must implement the AncestorListener interface. The following is the definition of this interface:

```
public interface AncestorListener extends EventListener {
  public abstract void ancestorAdded(AncestorEvent e);
  public abstract void ancestorMoved(AncestorEvent e);
  public abstract void ancestorRemoved(AncestorEvent e);
}
```

The following applet code creates a button and associates an ancestor listener to it. When the button is added to the applet's content area, the listener is notified via ancestorAdded(). If you move the browser or appletviewer, the listener is notified via ancestorMoved(). When the applet is shut down, the listener is notified via ancestorRemoved().

```
import java.awt.*;
import javax.swing.*;
import java.awt.event.*;
import javax.swing.event.*;
public class AncestorEventTest extends JApplet {
  public void init() {
    Container c = getContentPane();
    JButton jb = new JButton();
    jb.addAncestorListener(new AncestorListener() {
      public void ancestorAdded(AncestorEvent e) {
```

```
      System.out.println ("Added");
    }
    public void ancestorMoved(AncestorEvent e) {
      System.out.println ("Moved");
    }
    public void ancestorRemoved(AncestorEvent e) {
      System.out.println ("Removed");
    }
  });
  c.add (jb, BorderLayout.CENTER);
}
}
```

TIP   A future version of Java will move this event to `Component` or `Container`, instead of being specific to the Swing component set.

Component Events

The component events occur when a component is hidden, moved, resized, or shown. While the layout manager of the container of the component automatically handles the screen updates related to the changes, other parties may be interested when the event happens. Here is the definition of the `ComponentEvent` class:

```
public class ComponentEvent extends AWTEvent {
  public static final int COMPONENT_FIRST;
  public static final int COMPONENT_HIDDEN;
  public static final int COMPONENT_LAST;
  public static final int COMPONENT_MOVED;
  public static final int COMPONENT_RESIZED;
  public static final int COMPONENT_SHOWN;
  public ComponentEvent(Component comp, int id);
  public Component getComponent();
  public String paramString();
}
```

A component can delegate the handling of component events to any implementer of the `ComponentListener` interface:

```
public interface ComponentListener extends EventListener {
  public abstract void componentHidden(ComponentEvent e);
```

```
    public abstract void componentMoved(ComponentEvent e);
    public abstract void componentResized(ComponentEvent e);
    public abstract void componentShown(ComponentEvent e);
  }
```

Every component can have a component listener. The following program demonstrates component listening. Two buttons are added to a JSplitPane. The button labeled *Special* reports component events.

```
import java.awt.*;
import javax.swing.*;
import java.awt.event.*;
public class ComponentEventTest extends JApplet  {
  public void init() {
    Container c = getContentPane();
    JButton jb = new JButton("Special");
    jb.addComponentListener(new ComponentListener() {
      public void componentHidden(ComponentEvent e) {
        System.out.println ("Hidden");
      }
      public void componentMoved(ComponentEvent e) {
        System.out.println ("Moved");
      }
      public void componentResized(ComponentEvent e) {
        System.out.println ("Resized");
      }
      public void componentShown(ComponentEvent e) {
        System.out.println ("Shown");
      }
    });
    jb.addActionListener(new ActionListener() {
      public void actionPerformed (ActionEvent e) {
        Component comp = (Component)e.getSource();
        comp.setVisible(false);
      }
    });
    JButton jb2 = new JButton ("Other");
    JSplitPane pane = new JSplitPane (JSplitPane.VERTICAL_SPLIT, true, jb2, jb);
    c.add (pane, BorderLayout.CENTER);
  }
}
```

Container Events

Container events occur when a component is added to or removed from a container. A container event is an ancestor event, without the ability to be told when the container moves. Here is the definition of the `ContainerEvent` class:

```
public class ContainerEvent extends ComponentEvent {
    public static final int COMPONENT_ADDED;
    public static final int COMPONENT_REMOVED;
    public static final int CONTAINER_FIRST;
    public static final int CONTAINER_LAST;
    public ContainerEvent(Component source, int id, Component child);
    public Component getChild();
    public Container getContainer();
    public String paramString();
}
```

A container can process its own events by calling `enableEvents(AWTEvent.CONTAINER_EVENT_MASK)` and providing a `processContainerEvent()` method. Alternatively, a container can delegate container events to a listener that implements the `ContainerListener` interface:

```
public interface ContainerListener extends EventListener {
    public abstract void componentAdded(ContainerEvent e);
    public abstract void componentRemoved(ContainerEvent e);
}
```

Typically, most programs that use the Swing component set will not need to do anything about container events. Instead, they will use ancestor events.

Focus Events

Focus events are sent when a component gains or loses keyboard input focus. The following is the definition of the `FocusEvent` class:

```
public class FocusEvent extends ComponentEvent {
    public static final int FOCUS_FIRST;
    public static final int FOCUS_GAINED;
    public static final int FOCUS_LAST;
    public static final int FOCUS_LOST;
    public FocusEvent(Component source, int id);
    public FocusEvent(Component source, int id, boolean temporary);
    public boolean isTemporary();
    public String paramString();
}
```

A component can process its own focus events by calling enableEvents(AWTEvent .FOCUS_EVENT_MASK) and providing a processFocusEvent() method. Alternatively, you can delegate focus events to a listener that implements the Focus-Listener interface:

```
public interface FocusListener extends EventListener {
  public abstract void focusGained(FocusEvent e);
  public abstract void focusLost(FocusEvent e);
}
```

The following applet uses a BorderLayout manager to put a text field at NORTH and a text area at CENTER. The text field delegates its focus events to the applet, which prints a line of output when focus is gained or lost. The text area is a subclass that handles its own focus events; it too prints a line of output when focus is gained or lost.

```
import java.awt.*;
import javax.swing.*;
import java.awt.event.*;
public class FocusEventTest extends JApplet implements FocusListener {
  public void init() {
    Container c = getContentPane();
    // A text field that delegates to the applet
    JTextField tf = new JTextField();
    tf.addFocusListener(this);
    c.add (tf, BorderLayout.NORTH);
    // A subclass that handles its own focus events
    SelfTextArea sta = new SelfTextArea();
    c.add(sta, BorderLayout.CENTER);
  }
  public void focusGained(FocusEvent e) {
    System.out.println("Text Field gained focus");
  }
  public void focusLost(FocusEvent e) {
    System.out.println("Text Field lost focus");
  }
  class SelfTextArea extends JTextArea {
    public SelfTextArea() {
      addFocusListener (new FocusListener() {
        public void focusGained(FocusEvent e) {
          System.out.println("Text Area gained focus");
        }
        public void focusLost(FocusEvent e) {
```

```
                System.out.println("Text Area lost focus");
            }
        });
    }
    }
}
```

The text field delegates its focus events to the applet, so the applet must implement the FocusListener interface. The text area handles its own focus events by creating an anonymous focus listener.

Input Method Events

Components generate input method events when creating characters that require multiple keystrokes. This is usually used when working with Asian character sets for Japanese, Chinese, or Korean text. The following is the InputMethodEvent definition:

```
public class InputMethodEvent extends AWTEvent {
    public static final int CARET_POSITION_CHANGED;
    public static final int INPUT_METHOD_FIRST;
    public static final int INPUT_METHOD_LAST;
    public static final int INPUT_METHOD_TEXT_CHANGED;
    public InputMethodEvent(Component source, int id, TextHitInfo caret,
        TextHitInfo visiblePosition);
    public InputMethodEvent(Component source, int id,
        AttributedCharacterIterator text, int committedCharacterCount,
        TextHitInfo caret, TextHitInfo visiblePosition);
    public void consume();
    public TextHitInfo getCaret();
    public int getCommittedCharacterCount();
    public AttributedCharacterIterator getText();
    public TextHitInfo getVisiblePosition();
    public boolean isConsumed();
    public String paramString();
}
```

A component can delegate the handling of input method events to any implementer of the InputMethodListener interface:

```
public interface InputMethodListener extends EventListener {
    public abstract void caretPositionChanged(InputMethodEvent e);
    public abstract void inputMethodTextChanged(InputMethodEvent e);
}
```

Due to the highly targeted audience of these capabilities, a usage example is left as an exercise for the interested reader.

TIP   Additional information on the Input Method Framework is described in the specification, available from `http://java.sun.com/products/jdk/1.2/docs/guide/intl/spec.html`.

Internal Frame Events

The `JInternalFrame` class is the only generator of internal frame events. Internal frame events are generated when a `JInternalFrame` is opened, closed, closing, iconified, deiconified, activated, or deactivated. The following is the `InternalFrameEvent` definition, which is generated when these events happen:

```
public class InternalFrameEvent extends AWTEvent {
    public static final int INTERNAL_FRAME_ACTIVATED;
    public static final int INTERNAL_FRAME_CLOSED;
    public static final int INTERNAL_FRAME_CLOSING;
    public static final int INTERNAL_FRAME_DEACTIVATED;
    public static final int INTERNAL_FRAME_DEICONIFIED;
    public static final int INTERNAL_FRAME_FIRST;
    public static final int INTERNAL_FRAME_ICONIFIED;
    public static final int INTERNAL_FRAME_LAST;
    public static final int INTERNAL_FRAME_OPENED;
    public InternalFrameEvent(JInternalFrame source, int id);
    public String paramString();
}
```

A component can delegate the handling of internal frame events to any implementer of the `InternalFrameListener` interface:

```
public interface InternalFrameListener extends EventListener {
    public abstract void internalFrameActivated(InternalFrameEvent e);
    public abstract void internalFrameClosed(InternalFrameEvent e);
    public abstract void internalFrameClosing(InternalFrameEvent e);
    public abstract void internalFrameDeactivated(InternalFrameEvent e);
    public abstract void internalFrameDeiconified(InternalFrameEvent e);
    public abstract void internalFrameIconified(InternalFrameEvent e);
    public abstract void internalFrameOpened(InternalFrameEvent e);
}
```

The following program extends Chapter 13's JInternalFrame demonstration to include the InternalFrameEvent. When something is done to one of the layered panes, an event is generated and an appropriate message is displayed on the console.

```java
import java.awt.*;
import javax.swing.*;
import java.awt.event.*;
import javax.swing.event.*;
public class InternalFrameEventTest extends JApplet {
  public void init() {
    Container c = getContentPane();
    JLayeredPane desktop = new JDesktopPane();
    desktop.setOpaque(false);
    c.add(desktop, BorderLayout.CENTER);
    desktop.add (createLayer ("One"), JLayeredPane.POPUP_LAYER);
    desktop.add (createLayer ("Two"), JLayeredPane.DEFAULT_LAYER);
    desktop.add (createLayer ("Three"), JLayeredPane.PALETTE_LAYER);
  }
  public JInternalFrame createLayer (String label) {
    return new SelfInternalFrame(label);
  }
  class SelfInternalFrame extends JInternalFrame {
    public SelfInternalFrame(String s) {
      getContentPane().add (new JLabel (s), BorderLayout.CENTER);
      addInternalFrameListener(new InternalFrameListener() {
        public void internalFrameActivated(InternalFrameEvent e) {
          System.out.println ("Activated" + e.getSource());
        }
        public void internalFrameClosed(InternalFrameEvent e) {
          System.out.println ("Closed");
        }
        public void internalFrameClosing(InternalFrameEvent e) {
          System.out.println ("Closing");
        }
        public void internalFrameDeactivated(InternalFrameEvent e) {
          System.out.println ("Deactivated");
        }
        public void internalFrameDeiconified(InternalFrameEvent e) {
          System.out.println ("Deiconified");
        }
        public void internalFrameIconified(InternalFrameEvent e) {
```

```
            System.out.println ("Iconified");
         }
         public void internalFrameOpened(InternalFrameEvent e) {
            System.out.println ("Opened");
         }
      });
      setBounds (50, 50, 100, 100);
      setResizable (true);
      setClosable (true);
      setMaximizable (true);
      setIconifiable (true);
      setTitle (s);
   }
  }
 }
```

Initially the three layered panes appear on top of each other. You can then drag them all over the desktop. There is an ordering of the layers because of the layer specified when the layered pane is added to the desktop pane.

Item Events

Item events are generated by components that present users with items from which to choose. The components that generate these events are Checkbox, Checkbox-MenuItem, Choice, List, AbstractButton, and JComboBox. While item event generation is available at the AbstractButton level, only the JToggleButton, JCheckBox, JRadioButton, JCheckBoxMenuItem, and JRadioButtonMenuItem actually generate the events. The capabilities are defined at the AbstractButton level to ease subclassing and reusability. The following is the definition of the ItemEvent class:

```
public class ItemEvent extends AWTEvent {
  public static final int DESELECTED;
  public static final int ITEM_FIRST;
  public static final int ITEM_LAST;
  public static final int ITEM_STATE_CHANGED;
  public static final int SELECTED;
  public ItemEvent(ItemSelectable source, int id, Object item, int stateChange);
  public Object getItem();
  public ItemSelectable getItemSelectable();
  public int getStateChange();
  public String paramString();
}
```

A component can delegate item events to a listener that implements the Item-Listener interface:

```
public interface ItemListener extends EventListener {
  public abstract void itemStateChanged(ItemEvent e);
}
```

The applet listed below contains two JComboBox components. The first component delegates its item events to the applet. The SelfCombo is a subclass that handles its own item events. Both event handlers print a message to the console:

```
import java.awt.*;
import javax.swing.*;
import java.awt.event.*;
public class ItemEventTest extends JApplet implements ItemListener {
  public void init() {
    Container c = getContentPane();
    JComboBox jc = new JComboBox (new String[] {"Ice Cream", "Frozen Yogurt",
      "Sorbet"});
    jc.addItemListener(this);
    c.add(jc, BorderLayout.NORTH);
    JComboBox sc = new SelfCombo(new String[] {"Chocolate", "Vanilla",
      "Strawberry", "Mocha", "Peppermint Swirl", "Blackberry Ripple",
      "Butterscotch", "Spumoni"});
    c.add(sc, BorderLayout.SOUTH);
  }
  public void itemStateChanged(ItemEvent e)  {
    if (e.getStateChange() == ItemEvent.SELECTED)
      System.out.println ("New item from combo1: " +
        e.getItemSelectable().getSelectedObjects()[0]);
  }
  class SelfCombo extends JComboBox {
    public SelfCombo (String elements[]) {
      super (elements);
      setMaximumRowCount (4);
      setSelectedIndex (0);
      addItemListener (new ItemListener() {
        public void itemStateChanged(ItemEvent e)  {
          if (e.getStateChange() == ItemEvent.SELECTED)
            System.out.println ("New item from combo2: " +
              e.getItemSelectable().getSelectedObjects()[0]);
        }
      });
    }
  }
}
```

When listening for item events, it's good practice to check the state changes, too. You are also notified for deselection.

Key Events

Key events are generated when the user presses or releases a key on the keyboard. The definition of the KeyEvent class is shown below. It is extensive because there are a large number of constants. The KEY_*XXX* constants appear in the event's id field and describe the key event: KEY_PRESSED indicates a key was pushed down, KEY_RELEASED indicates a key was released, and KEY_TYPED denotes a key press followed by a key release. For example, pressing SHIFT+A to get a capitalized *A* would generate two key-press events (one for each key), one key-typed event, and two key-released events when the keys are released. The CHAR_UNDEFINED constant is for when there isn't a valid key character for a key press (or release).

The remaining constants all have names that begin with VK, which stands for Virtual Key. The VK constants are values that are returned by the getKeyCode() method; they represent keys on the keyboard. Thus, there is a VK_SLASH, but no value representing a question mark, because question marks are typed by shifting the slash key.

Here's the KeyEvent class definition:

```
public class KeyEvent extends InputEvent {
   public static final char CHAR_UNDEFINED;
   public static final int KEY_FIRST;
   public static final int KEY_LAST;
   public static final int KEY_PRESSED;
   public static final int KEY_RELEASED;
   public static final int KEY_TYPED;
   public static final int VK_0;
   public static final int VK_1;
   public static final int VK_2;
   ...
// There are 188 constants in KeyEvent that define specific key codes as
// returned by getKeyCode( ). These all begin with "VK_" and can be
// found by looking in the online documentation.
   ...
   public static final int VK_X;
   public static final int VK_Y;
   public static final int VK_Z;
```

```
    public KeyEvent(Component source, int id, long when, int modifiers,
      int keyCode);
    public KeyEvent(Component source, int id, long when, int modifiers,
      int keyCode, char keyChar);
    public char getKeyChar();
    public int getKeyCode();
    public boolean isActionKey();
    public String paramString();
    public void setKeyChar(char keyChar);
    public void setKeyCode(int keyCode);
    public void setModifiers(int modifiers);
  }
```

A component can process its own key events by calling enableEvents(AWTEvent
.KEY_EVENT_MASK) and providing a processKeyEvent() method. Alternatively, a
component can delegate key events to a listener that implements the KeyListener
interface:

```
public interface KeyListener extends EventListener {
    public abstract void keyPressed(KeyEvent e);
    public abstract void keyReleased(KeyEvent e);
    public abstract void keyTyped(KeyEvent e);
}
```

The following applet puts a text field in the north BorderLayout area and a text
area in the center of screen. The text field delegates its key events to the applet, whose
event handler generates a line of output. The text area is a subclass that handles its
own key events; its key event handler also generates one line of output:

```
import java.awt.*;
import java.awt.event.*;
import javax.swing.*;
public class KeyEventTest extends JApplet implements KeyListener {
  public void init() {
    Container c = getContentPane();
    // A text field that delegates to the applet
    JTextField tf = new JTextField();
    tf.addKeyListener(this);
    c.add(tf, BorderLayout.NORTH);
    // A text area subclass that handles its own item events
    SelfKeyTextArea sta = new SelfKeyTextArea();
    c.add(sta, BorderLayout.CENTER);
  }
  public void keyTyped(KeyEvent e) {
```

```
      System.out.println("Key typed in text field: " + e.getKeyChar());
   }
   public void keyPressed(KeyEvent e)  { }
   public void keyReleased(KeyEvent e) { }

   class SelfKeyTextArea extends JTextArea {
      public SelfKeyTextArea() {
        enableEvents(AWTEvent.KEY_EVENT_MASK);
      }
      public void processKeyEvent(KeyEvent e) {
        super.processKeyEvent(e);
        if (e.getID() == KeyEvent.KEY_TYPED)
          System.out.println("Key typed in text area: " + e.getKeyChar());
      }
   }
}
```

This program has a few features that have not been present in this chapter's previous examples. First, observe the applet's two empty methods, keyPressed() and keyReleased(). These methods seem to contribute absolutely nothing to the program. They handle events that are not of interest, and the event handlers do nothing. The reason they appear is to appease the compiler. To be a key listener, the applet subclass must declare that it implements the KeyListener interface. This interface is listed at the beginning of this section; it contains three methods: key-Typed(), keyPressed(), and keyReleased(). Unless all three methods appear in the definition of the applet subclass, the compiler will not be satisfied.

Understanding Event Adapters

The java.awt.event package offers a number of "adapter" classes; there is one adapter for each listener interface that has multiple methods. (The events found in com.sun .java.swing.event do not always have these adapter classes when its listener interface contains multiple methods.) These adapter classes implement the corresponding interfaces, with all methods consisting of empty curly brackets. To create a listener class that cares only about a subset of an interface's methods, you can subclass the appropriate adapter and not worry about the undesired methods; you will inherit the empty stubs for them. Unfortunately, this scheme works only if your listener does not need to be a subclass of something other than the adapter. Such is the case with the example in this section, which cannot subclass KeyAdapter because it already subclasses Applet.

The second thing to notice about the example is that the `processKeyEvent()` method in class `SelfTextArea` needs to inspect the key-event object to determine what type of key event has taken place. This was accomplished by calling the key event's `getID()` method.

Menu Events

Menu events are generated when the user opens or closes a `JMenu`. The `MenuEvent` is a direct subclass of `EventObject`, not an `AWTEvent` subclass. This means there isn't an *id* for the different sub-event types, as with most of the other events. Here is the definition for the `MenuEvent` class:

```
public class MenuEvent extends EventObject {
   public MenuEvent(Object source);
}
```

A component cannot process its own menu events by calling `enableEvents()`. This option is only available for `AWTEvent` subclasses. The component must delegate menu events to a listener that implements the `MenuListener` interface:

```
public interface MenuListener extends EventListener {
   public abstract void menuCanceled(MenuEvent e);
   public abstract void menuDeselected(MenuEvent e);
   public abstract void menuSelected(MenuEvent e);
}
```

You can use menu events to customize the contents of a `JMenu` when the user selects it. This allows you to enable or disable individual menu items based upon the current state of the system. While this customization works fine, you'll learn about a better way in the next chapter with the help of the `Action` interface. The following program uses a subset of last chapter's example menuing program to demonstrate the use of menu events.

```
import java.awt.*;
import javax.swing.*;
import javax.swing.event.*;
public class MenuTest {
   public static void main (String args[]) {
      JFrame f = new MainWindow();
      f.setSize(400, 300);
      f.setVisible(true);
   }
```

```
static class MyMenuListener implements MenuListener {
  public void menuCanceled(MenuEvent e) {
    JMenu m = (JMenu)e.getSource();
    System.out.println ("Canceled: " + m.getText());
  }
  public void menuDeselected(MenuEvent e) {
    JMenu m = (JMenu)e.getSource();
    System.out.println ("Deselected: " + m.getText());
  }
  public void menuSelected(MenuEvent e) {
    JMenu m = (JMenu)e.getSource();
    System.out.println ("Selected: " + m.getText());
  }
}
static class MainWindow extends JFrame {
  public MainWindow() {
    super("MenuTest Window");
    JMenu fileMenu = new FileMenu();
    JMenu helpMenu = new HelpMenu();
    MenuListener theML = new MyMenuListener();
    fileMenu.addMenuListener (theML);
    helpMenu.addMenuListener (theML);
    JMenuBar mb = new JMenuBar();
    mb.add(fileMenu);
    mb.add(helpMenu);
    setJMenuBar(mb);
  }
}
static class FileMenu extends JMenu {
  public FileMenu() {
    super("File", true);   // tear-off menu
    add(new JMenuItem("Open"));
    add(new JMenuItem("Close"));
    add(new JMenuItem("Exit"));
  }
}
static class HelpMenu extends JMenu {
  public HelpMenu() {
    super("Help");
    add(new JMenuItem("About MenuTest"));
    add(new JMenuItem("Class Hierarchy"));
    addSeparator();
```

```
        add(new JCheckBoxMenuItem("Balloon Help"));
      }
    }
  }
```

In the MenuListener methods, the (JMenu)e.getSource() casting operation can be done without checking if the event source is an instance of JMenu because the only type of object that can generate a MenuEvent is a JMenu.

Mouse Events

Mouse events are generated when the user clicks a mouse button or moves the mouse. There are seven mouse event types, represented by the constants in the MouseEvent class. These constants are the possible values for a mouse event's id field. Here is the definition for the MouseEvent class:

```
public class MouseEvent extends InputEvent {
    public static final int MOUSE_CLICKED;
    public static final int MOUSE_DRAGGED;
    public static final int MOUSE_ENTERED;
    public static final int MOUSE_EXITED;
    public static final int MOUSE_FIRST;
    public static final int MOUSE_LAST;
    public static final int MOUSE_MOVED;
    public static final int MOUSE_PRESSED;
    public static final int MOUSE_RELEASED;
    public MouseEvent(Component source, int id, long when, int modifiers,
        int x, int y, int clickCount, boolean popupTrigger);
    public int getClickCount();
    public Point getPoint();
    public int getX();
    public int getY();
    public boolean isPopupTrigger();
    public String paramString();
    public synchronized void translatePoint(int x, int y);
}
```

Generally speaking, programs treat mouse-moved and mouse-dragged events very differently from the way they treat the other five event types. Java provides two mouse-event listener types and two mouse-event masks so programs can deal separately with ordinary mouse events (pressed, released, clicked, entered, and exited) and mouse-motion events (moved and dragged).

A component can process its own ordinary mouse events by calling `enable-Events(AWTEvent.MOUSE_EVENT_MASK)` and providing a `processMouseEvent()` method. Alternatively, a component can delegate ordinary mouse events to a listener that implements the `MouseListener` interface:

```
public interface MouseListener extends EventListener {
    public abstract void mouseClicked(MouseEvent e);
    public abstract void mouseEntered(MouseEvent e);
    public abstract void mouseExited(MouseEvent e);
    public abstract void mousePressed(MouseEvent e);
    public abstract void mouseReleased(MouseEvent e);
}
```

A component can process its own mouse-motion events by calling `enable-Events(AWTEvent.MOUSE_MOTION_EVENT_MASK)` and providing a `processMouseMotionEvent()` method. Alternatively, a component can delegate mouse-motion events to a listener that implements the `MouseMotionListener` interface:

```
public interface MouseMotionListener extends EventListener {
    public abstract void mouseDragged(MouseEvent e);
    public abstract void mouseMoved(MouseEvent e);
}
```

TIP
When dealing with Swing components, every `JComponent` can process mouse motion events. However, only the menuing components can process the non-motion mouse events. Because of this, when you need to handle mouse events directly by the component that generates them, it is best to just add yourself as a mouse or mouse motion listener.

The following applet creates two components. The first is a label and displays a `JPopupMenu` when the appropriate mouse event is generated. The way to tell if the event is "appropriate" is by asking it with `isPopupTrigger()`. The reason you have to ask is that the event is different, based upon the user's platform. For instance, on Windows platforms, if you right-click on something when you release the mouse button, a customized menu will appear based upon where the click happened. On UNIX workstations running Motif, this customized menu appears when the mouse button is pressed, not released. The mouse button used may also differ.

The second component is a bordered double-buffered panel and handles all event listening itself. It draws a line when the user drags the mouse. The mouse press event defines the starting point. While dragging the mouse, the line is drawn in red to the current position. When the mouse is released the line color changes to black. A history of past lines drawn is not maintained. The other mouse event types are ignored.

```java
import java.awt.*;
import java.awt.event.*;
import javax.swing.*;

public class MouseEventTest extends JApplet {
  public void init() {
    Container c = getContentPane();
    c.setLayout(new GridLayout(2, 1));
    JLabel lab = new JLabel ("Popup Available");
    final JPopupMenu pop = new JPopupMenu ();
    JMenuItem item;
    pop.add (item = new JMenuItem ("Cut"));
    pop.add (item = new JMenuItem ("Copy"));
    pop.add (item = new JMenuItem ("Paste"));
    pop.addSeparator();
    pop.add (item = new JMenuItem ("Select All"));
    pop.setInvoker (lab);
    lab.addMouseListener (new MouseAdapter() {
      public void showPopup (MouseEvent e) {
        pop.show (e.getComponent(), e.getX(), e.getY());
      }
      public void mousePressed (MouseEvent e) {
        if (e.isPopupTrigger()) {
          showPopup (e);
        }
      }
      public void mouseReleased (MouseEvent e) {
        if (e.isPopupTrigger()) {
          showPopup (e);
        }
      }
    });
    c.add (lab);
    c.add (new SelfMousePanel());
  }
```

```
    class SelfMousePanel extends JPanel implements MouseListener,
MouseMotionListener {
    private int startX, startY, endX, endY;
    Color color = Color.black;
    public SelfMousePanel() {
        super (true); // double buffer
        setOpaque (false);
        setBorder (BorderFactory.createLoweredBevelBorder());
        addMouseListener (this);
        addMouseMotionListener (this);
    }
    public void paint (Graphics g) {
        g.setColor (color);
        g.drawLine (startX, startY, endX, endY);
    }
    public void mousePressed(MouseEvent e) {
        color = Color.red;
        startX = endX = e.getX();
        startY = endY = e.getY();
        repaint();
    }
    public void mouseReleased(MouseEvent e) {
        color = Color.black;
        repaint();
    }
    public void mouseDragged(MouseEvent e) {
        endX = e.getX();
        endY = e.getY();
        repaint();
    }
    public void mouseMoved(MouseEvent e) {}
    public void mouseClicked(MouseEvent e) {}
    public void mouseEntered(MouseEvent e) {}
    public void mouseExited(MouseEvent e) {}
    }
}
```

Notice that the panel subclass declares that it implements not one but *two* interfaces. There is nothing wrong with this—Java's single inheritance concerns extending classes and has nothing to do with implementing interfaces.

TIP

Instead of implementing both interfaces, you could create an inner class that sub-classes `MouseInputAdapter`. This provides stubs for methods of both motion and non-motion mouse events. The set of all mouse handling events is included in the `MouseInputListener` interface, which basically just defines an interface that implements both `MouseListener` and `MouseMotionListener`.

Paint Events

A paint event is sent to a component when the component updates or paints itself. Here is the definition of the `PaintEvent` class:

```
public class PaintEvent extends ComponentEvent {
   public static final int PAINT;
   public static final int PAINT_FIRST;
   public static final int PAINT_LAST;
   public static final int UPDATE;
   public PaintEvent(Component source, int id, Rectangle updateRect);
   public Rectangle getUpdateRect();
   public String paramString();
   public void setUpdateRect(Rectangle r);
}
```

Java programs deal with paint events by overriding the `paint()` and `update()` methods. There is no `PaintListener` interface.

Pop-Up Menu Events

A pop-up menu event is similar to the menu event, except that it works with a JPopupMenu, instead of a JMenu. Like MenuEvent, PopupEvent subclasses Event-Object, not AWTEvent. The event happens prior to the display of a pop-up menu, when the menu is canceled, and prior to the pop-up menu going away. Here is the definition of the PopupMenuEvent class:

```
public class PopupMenuEvent extends EventObject {
   public PopupMenuEvent(Object);
}
```

Because PopupMenuEvent is not an AWTEvent subclass, the pop-up menu can-not process its own pop-up menu events by calling `enableEvents()`. The menu must delegate pop-up menu events to a listener that implements the Popup-MenuListener interface:

```
public interface PopupMenuListener extends EventListener {
   public abstract void popupMenuCanceled(PopupMenuEvent e);
   public abstract void popupMenuWillBecomeInvisible(PopupMenuEvent e);
   public abstract void popupMenuWillBecomeVisible(PopupMenuEvent e);
}
```

Running the following program demonstrates when the different subtypes of the event are generated, calling the appropriate interface method. By using the event, you can customize the pop-up menu when it is time to display it:

```
import java.awt.*;
import java.awt.event.*;
import javax.swing.*;
import javax.swing.event.*;
public class PopupEventTest extends JApplet {
   public void init() {
      Container c = getContentPane();
      JLabel lab = new JLabel ("Popup Available");
      final JPopupMenu pop = new JPopupMenu ();
      JMenuItem item;
      pop.add (item = new JMenuItem ("Cut"));
      pop.add (item = new JMenuItem ("Copy"));
      pop.add (item = new JMenuItem ("Paste"));
      pop.addSeparator();
      pop.add (item = new JMenuItem ("Select All"));
      pop.setInvoker (lab);
      pop.addPopupMenuListener (new PopupMenuListener() {
         public void popupMenuCanceled(PopupMenuEvent e) {
            System.out.println ("Canceled");
         }
         public void popupMenuWillBecomeInvisible(PopupMenuEvent e) {
            System.out.println ("Becoming Invisible");
         }
         public void popupMenuWillBecomeVisible(PopupMenuEvent e) {
            System.out.println ("Becoming Visible");
         }
      });
      lab.addMouseListener (new MouseAdapter() {
         public void showPopup (MouseEvent e) {
            pop.show (e.getComponent(), e.getX(), e.getY());
         }
```

```
    public void mousePressed (MouseEvent e) {
      if (e.isPopupTrigger()) {
        showPopup (e);
      }
    }
    public void mouseReleased (MouseEvent e) {
      if (e.isPopupTrigger()) {
        showPopup (e);
      }
    }
  });
  c.add (lab, BorderLayout.CENTER);
  }
}
```

As a reminder, you still need to associate an `ActionListener` to each `JMenu-Item` on the pop-up menu if you want to respond to its selection.

Text Events

Text events are sent to text components (AWT text fields and text areas, not the Swing text field and text area components) when a change occurs to the text they contain. This happens when the user types or when the program executes a method such as `setText()`. The following is the definition of the `TextEvent` class:

```
public class TextEvent extends AWTEvent {
  public static final int TEXT_FIRST;
  public static final int TEXT_LAST;
  public static final int TEXT_VALUE_CHANGED;
  public TextEvent(Object source, int id);
  public String paramString();
}
```

A text component can process its own text events by calling `enableEvents-(AWTEvent.TEXT_EVENT_MASK)` and providing a `processTEXTEvent()` method. Alternatively, a text component can delegate text events to a listener that implements the `TextListener` interface:

```
public interface TextListener extends EventListener {
  public abstract void textValueChanged(TextEvent e);
}
```

The following applet contains two text areas: the upper one delegates text events to that applet, and the lower one handles its own text events. Both event handlers just print a message to the console:

```java
import java.awt.*;
import java.awt.event.*;

public class TextEventTest extends java.applet.Applet
    implements TextListener {
  public void init() {
    setLayout(new GridLayout(2, 1));
    // A text area that delegates to the applet
    TextArea ta1 = new TextArea();
    ta1.addTextListener(this);
    add(ta1);
    // A text area subclass that handles its own item events
    SelfTextTA ta2 = new SelfTextTA();
    add(ta2);
  }
  public void textValueChanged(TextEvent e) {
    System.out.println("UPPER get text event: " + e);
  }
}

class SelfTextTA extends TextArea {
  public SelfTextTA() {
    enableEvents(AWTEvent.TEXT_EVENT_MASK);
  }
  public void processTextEvent(TextEvent e) {
    System.out.println("LOWER get text event: " + e);
  }
}
```

The Swing text components deal with an enhanced `DocumentEvent` when their contents are altered. This is covered in the next chapter, as it requires understanding the underlying architecture of the Swing component model.

Window Events

Window events are sent when a change happens to a window. Here is the definition of the `WindowEvent` class:

```
public class WindowEvent extends ComponentEvent {
  public static final int WINDOW_ACTIVATED;
  public static final int WINDOW_CLOSED;
  public static final int WINDOW_CLOSING;
  public static final int WINDOW_DEACTIVATED;
  public static final int WINDOW_DEICONIFIED;
  public static final int WINDOW_FIRST;
  public static final int WINDOW_ICONIFIED;
  public static final int WINDOW_LAST;
  public static final int WINDOW_OPENED;
  public WindowEvent(Window source, int id);
  public Window getWindow();
  public String paramString();
}
```

Applets rarely need to be concerned with window events. Applications with GUIs are more often concerned with window events.

The most common use for window events has to do with a strange feature of Java's Frame. The frame's window decoration is drawn and maintained by the underlying window system, not by Java. No matter what the underlying system may be, there is always a mechanism provided for destroying a frame. For example, in Windows 95, you can click on the little X icon in the upper-right corner. This window-destruction mechanism is not very destructive to a Java frame. All that happens is a window event is sent to the frame. The frame must explicitly respond to this event; the default behavior, if no event handler is set, is the same as the default behavior for any other Java event: The event is ignored.

Java's JFrame is a little bit different. By default a JFrame will hide itself if you try to destroy it. Other available operations are nothing or destruction. These are set by calling setDefaultCloseOperation() with a parameter of a JFrame class constant: DO_NOTHING_ON_CLOSE, HIDE_ON_CLOSE (the default), or DISPOSE_ON_CLOSE.

Since users expect to be able to close a window (frame) from the window decoration, it is a good idea to equip all frames with a window event handler that destroys the frame on detection of a window-closing event. If the frame is the basis of an application, you can also exit the application here. The code below does just that. Since there is only one frame, the event handler not only destroys the frame, it also exits the application.

```
import java.awt.*;
import javax.swing.*;
import java.awt.event.*;
public class KillableFrame extends JFrame {
```

```
public static void main(String args[]) {
  KillableFrame frame = new KillableFrame();
  frame.setVisible(true);
}
public KillableFrame() {
  setSize(250, 250);
  setDefaultCloseOperation(DISPOSE_ON_CLOSE);
  addWindowListener (new WindowAdapter() {
    public void windowClosing (WindowEvent e) {
      System.exit(0);
    }
  });
}
public void paint(Graphics g) {
  g.drawString("Use window decoration to exit.", 20, 100);
}
}
```

Without the window listener exiting the application, the frame will disappear and the program will continue. In this case, if main() did anything else besides just show a JFrame, it would continue.

Summary

This chapter began with a look at the concept of event-driven programming. You then saw the details of Java's fairly complicated event-handling infrastructure.

The most important thing to remember is you have three choices: You can ignore an event, you can have a component handle its own event, or you can delegate an event to another object. It goes without saying that the choice you make can have a profound effect on the quality of your program. Maintenance could be a breeze or a nightmare. When choosing an event-handling strategy, the most important consideration should be the long-term robustness of the program. All other issues, including momentary convenience, are secondary.

CHAPTER
FIFTEEN

15

Advanced Swing Capabilities

- Advanced Swing event handling

- User dialogs

- Model/View/Controller architecture

- Pluggable Look and Feel

- Complex Swing components

In the past two chapters, we looked at the simpler form-oriented components and how to respond to the user's interactions with the Java 1.1 event-handling mechanism. In this chapter, we'll explore additional event-handling capabilities introduced by the Swing component set. We'll also explore some common dialog boxes available for displaying messages or prompting for user input. Then we'll take a second look at some of the earlier components and use them in a new way. Also, we'll examine several controls for the first time, describing capabilities that required purchasing or building with earlier Java releases.

In examining the new components, we'll examine a concept called Model/View/Controller (or MVC), first introduced in the 1970s by another object-oriented language, Smalltalk. We'll look at how to use the Swing components in an MVC manner and see how MVC allows Swing to offer a Pluggable Look and Feel, allowing you to change the visual representation of components without changing how you programmatically use the components.

Advanced Swing Event Handling

In addition to working with events using the 1.1 event-handling mechanisms, there are several options incorporated within Swing that either enhance existing capabilities or offer alternatives. These include a support class for managing your custom listener lists through simplifying component creation by just providing the event handler and a special event handling process for keyboard events. Also, we explain special considerations for using Swing components in multithreaded applications.

Managing Listener Lists

When creating components, you need to provide support for managing lists of event listeners within your newly defined components. For instance, if you are defining a calendar component, you may want to have the calendar generate an `ActionEvent` whenever the user double-clicks on today's date. This can be done very easily, in a thread-safe manner, with the help of the `AWTEventMulticaster` support class of the `java.awt` package. You use `AWTEventMulticaster` to add and remove listeners, just like for other components, and provide a method to loop through the list of listeners when the specific event happens.

```
ActionListener actionListener = null;
public void addActionListener (ActionListener l) {
```

```
    actionListener = AWTEventMulticaster.add (actionListener, l);
}
public void removeActionListener (ActionListener l) {
    actionListener = AWTEventMulticaster.remove (actionListener, l);
}
public void fireListener (ActionEvent e) {
    if (actionListener != null) {
        actionListener.actionPerformed (e);
    }
}
```

NOTE   The naming of some of these methods will be described in more detail when JavaBeans are discussed further in Chapter 22.

The AWTEventMulticaster class is handy when you are managing a list of specific AWT event listeners. However, if you create your own event and listener type, AWTEventMulticaster is not able to support the event directly. It must be subclassed and customized, or you must use an alternative way to manage the list.

Since the functionality is widely necessary and has a high potential for code that is not thread-safe, Sun decided to add a support class that can be used for any list of listeners, as long as the listener extends from the EventListener interface. The class is called EventListenerList, from the javax.swing.event package, and the equivalent code for the previous operation follows:

```
EventListenerList listenerList = new EventListenerList();
public void addActionListener(ActionListener l) {
    listenerList.add (ActionListener.class, l);
}
public void removeActionListener (ActionListener l) {
    listenerList.remove (ActionListener.class, l);
}
protected void fireListener(ActionEvent e) {
    Object listeners[] = listenerList.getListenerList();
    for (int i = listeners.length-2; i>=0; i-=2) {
        if (listeners[i] == ActionListener.class) {
            ((ActionListener)listeners[i+1]).actionPerformed(e);
        }
    }
}
```

The nice part about using `EventListenerList` is it works with all event listener types, not just the AWT or Swing ones. The only real difference between the two is the `fireListener()` method. While both notify each and every listener, with the new way you have to manually check the list for specific listener types. This reasoning is twofold: because you can share the list with multiple listener types and it doesn't know which method of the listener to call. It is because of this generality of functionality that the class works with every event listener list thrown at it.

Abstracting Action Listening

The `Action` interface of the `javax.swing` package offers a specialized `Action-Listener` with a default implementation in the `AbstractAction` class. With `AbstractAction`, you create the listener and can associate it with many components. If you wish to disable the specific event, you disable the `AbstractAction` and it notifies the components that are listening. What follows is the `Action` interface and `AbstractAction` class definition that describes these capabilities:

```
public interface Action extends ActionListener {
  public static final String DEFAULT;
  public static final String LONG_DESCRIPTION;
  public static final String NAME;
  public static final String SHORT_DESCRIPTION;
  public static final String SMALL_ICON;
  public abstract void addPropertyChangeListener (PropertyChangeListener l);
  public abstract Object getValue(String key);
  public abstract boolean isEnabled();
  public abstract void putValue(String key, Object value);
  public abstract void removePropertyChangeListener (PropertyChangeListener
    l);
  public abstract void setEnabled(boolean b);
}
```

and

```
public abstract class AbstractAction extends Object implements Action,
    Cloneable, Serializable {
  public AbstractAction();
  public AbstractAction(String name);
  public AbstractAction(String name, Icon icon);
```

```
    public synchronized void addPropertyChangeListener
(PropertyChangeListener
      l);
    public Object getValue(String key);
    public boolean isEnabled();
    public synchronized void putValue(String key, Object value);
    public synchronized void removePropertyChangeListener
      (PropertyChangeListener l);
    public synchronized void setEnabled(boolean value);
}
```

The first thing you may notice is that although AbstractAction implements ActionListener, via implementing Action, there is no actionPerformed() method. That is why the class is abstract. When you create AbstractAction objects, you define what action to perform.

Besides the missing routine, you may have noticed five constants in the Action interface, as well as getValue() and putValue() methods in the AbstractAction class. The constants of Action are the keys used by the getValue() / putValue() methods. Once you've put a value for an Action, when you associate that Action with an appropriate JComponent, it will inquire about the value of these settings and use them to create a label, icon, or possibly even tooltip text.

The Swing components that support actions are JMenu, JPopupMenu, and JTool-Bar. So, if you need the same functionality on two of those controls, describing the ActionListener as an AbstractAction permits greater control and flexibility.

To demonstrate the capabilities, Figure 15.1 shows a sample of the same action shown on multiple toolbars. More frequently, you will use the same action on a toolbar and a menu. The center button toggles the state of the action when selected, which in turn toggles the components on the toolbars associated with the action.

FIGURE 15.1:

Simplified action example

```java
import java.awt.*;
import java.awt.event.*;
import javax.swing.*;

public class ActionTester {

  static class MyAction extends AbstractAction {
    public MyAction (String name, Icon icon) {
      super (name, icon);
    }
    public void actionPerformed (ActionEvent e) {
      System.out.println ("Selected: " + getValue (Action.NAME));
    }
  }
  public static void main (String args[]) {
    Frame f = new Frame ("Hello World");
    f.addWindowListener (new WindowAdapter() {
      public void windowClosing (WindowEvent e) {
        System.exit(0);
      }
    });
    Icon icon = new RedOvalIcon();
    final Action action = new MyAction("Hello", icon);
    JToolBar jt1 = new JToolBar();
    jt1.add (action);
    f.add (jt1, BorderLayout.NORTH);
    JToolBar jt2 = new JToolBar();
    jt2.add (action);
    f.add (jt2, BorderLayout.SOUTH);
    JButton jb = new JButton ("Toggle Action");
    jb.addActionListener (new ActionListener () {
      public void actionPerformed (ActionEvent e) {
        action.setEnabled(!action.isEnabled());
      }
    });
    f.add (jb, BorderLayout.CENTER);
    f.setSize (200, 200);
    f.setVisible(true);
  }

  static class RedOvalIcon implements Icon {
```

```
        public void paintIcon (Component c, Graphics g, int x, int y) {
          g.setColor(Color.red);
          g.fillOval (x, y, getIconWidth(), getIconHeight());
        }
        public int getIconWidth() {
          return 10;
        }
        public int getIconHeight() {
          return 20;
        }
      }
    }
```

NOTE   There are special `AbstractAction` classes for dealing with text actions. They are described with the rest of the text capabilities in the "Advanced Text Support" section later in this chapter.

Registering Keyboard Events

There are two ways to handle any keyboard actions for components. You can add a `KeyListener`, then watch every key that is pressed for your specific key of interest. While this works perfectly fine, the means for watching for specific key events can be done much more easily with the help of the `KeyStroke` class described below.

```
public class KeyStroke extends Object implements Serializable {
  public static KeyStroke getKeyStroke(char keyChar);
  public static KeyStroke getKeyStroke(char keyChar, boolean onKeyRelease);
  public static KeyStroke getKeyStroke(int keyCode, int modifiers);
  public static KeyStroke getKeyStroke(int keyCode, int modifiers,
    boolean onKeyRelease);
  public static KeyStroke getKeyStroke(String representation);
  public static KeyStroke getKeyStrokeForEvent(KeyEvent event);
  public boolean equals(Object obj);
  public char getKeyChar();
  public int getKeyCode();
  public int getModifiers();
  public int hashCode();
  public boolean isOnKeyRelease();
  public String toString();
}
```

There are close to 200 VK_ constants in the KeyEvent class to help you create a keystroke with a keyCode. Once you've created the keystroke, you register it with a JComponent via registerKeyboardAction(), specifying an ActionListener to notify when the keystroke is activated. The onKeyRelease parameter specifies whether the event happens when the key is first pressed, the default behavior when not specified, or when it is released. As a demonstration, the following program associates different action listeners for ALT-B, CTRL-C, and SHIFT-D to different buttons within a JFrame.

```java
import java.awt.*;
import java.awt.event.*;
import javax.swing.*;

public class KeyTester {
  static class MyActionListener implements ActionListener {
    String msg;
    MyActionListener (String s) {
      msg = s;
    }
    public void actionPerformed (ActionEvent e) {
      System.out.println (msg);
    }
  }
  public static void main (String args[]) {
    JFrame f = new JFrame ("Hello World");
    f.addWindowListener (new WindowAdapter() {
      public void windowClosing (WindowEvent e) {
        System.exit(0);
      }
    });
    JButton jb1 = new JButton ("Hello");
    JButton jb2 = new JButton ("Strange");
    JButton jb3 = new JButton ("World");
    f.getContentPane().add (jb1, BorderLayout.NORTH);
    f.getContentPane().add (jb2, BorderLayout.CENTER);
    f.getContentPane().add (jb3, BorderLayout.SOUTH);

    KeyStroke stroke1 = KeyStroke.getKeyStroke (KeyEvent.VK_B,
      ActionEvent.ALT_MASK, true);
    jb1.registerKeyboardAction (new MyActionListener("Action Happened"),
      stroke1, JComponent.WHEN_FOCUSED);
```

```
    KeyStroke stroke2 = KeyStroke.getKeyStroke (KeyEvent.VK_C,
      ActionEvent.CTRL_MASK, false);
    jb2.registerKeyboardAction (new MyActionListener(
      "Action Didn't  Happen"), stroke2, JComponent.WHEN_IN_FOCUSED_WINDOW);
    KeyStroke stroke3 = KeyStroke.getKeyStroke (KeyEvent.VK_D,
      ActionEvent.SHIFT_MASK, false);
    jb3.registerKeyboardAction (new MyActionListener("What Happened?"),
      stroke3, JComponent.WHEN_ANCESTOR_OF_FOCUSED_COMPONENT);
    f.setSize (200, 200);
    f.show();
  }
}
```

TIP   The last parameter of `registerKeyboardAction()` specifies additional conditions about when the keystroke will be activated. Available options are `WHEN_FOCUSED`, `WHEN_IN_FOCUSED_WINDOW`, and `WHEN_ANCESTOR_OF_FOCUSED_COMPONENT`. These describe, respectively, when the specific component has the focus, when anything within the window that contains the component has focus, or when anything in the ancestry hierarchy (not siblings) has focus.

Working with Multiple Threads

By design, access to the Swing component properties should be limited to the event dispatching thread. This means that while you can ask a JTextField for its contents in another thread with getText(), the value you get back may not be the correct current value. Normally, this isn't a problem, as most component access is already done from this thread. For instance, if you wish to print the contents of the text field when the user selects a button, you are already in the event dispatching thread to respond to the button selection.

When does this become a problem? Any time a program is responding to non-AWT generated events or if you wish to spawn off a separate thread to do a lengthy operation so the interface remains responsive. Both of these issues require some extra work to perform properly if you need to access the Swing components from the other thread.

How do you solve the problem? The SwingUtilities class provides two methods to help: invokeLater() and invokeAndWait(). Both require a Runnable object, which will then run in the event dispatching thread. All you need to do is define a class that implements Runnable, usually as an anonymous inner class, and pass it off to one of the two methods. The invokeLater() method returns immediately, allowing the current thread to continue. With invokeAndWait(), the original thread blocks until the Runnable object completes its operation. So, if you wanted to just print the contents of a JTextField, this could be done within the invokeLater() call. However, if you need to process the results, you would call invokeAndWait(), where you get the current setting within the call. Both of these examples are shown below.

```
final JTextField jt …;
// process running in non-event thread
SwingUtilities.invokeLater(new Runnable() {
  public void run() {
    System.out.println (jt.getText());
  }
});

final String[] curValue = {""};
try {
  SwingUtilities.invokeAndWait(new Runnable() {
    public void run() {
      curValue[0] = jt.getText();
    }
  });
} catch (InvocationTargetException e) {
} catch (InterruptedException e) {
}
processString (curValue[0]);
```

One thing worth noting, the repaint(), revalidate(), and invalidate() methods can be called from any thread as they do not directly access the components.

NOTE   The Swing Connection at Sun's Web site offers an excellent article, titled "Using a Swing Worker Thread," which describes these issues. You can find it located at `http://java.sun.com/products/jfc/tsc/swingdoc-current/swing_worker.html`. The article includes a helper class SwingWorker that simplifies the process of creating background threads to perform lengthy operations.

User Dialogs

Swing provides a common way of displaying message pop-up dialogs and prompting for user input from *modal* dialog boxes. The six primary components for this purpose are JOptionPane, JColorChooser, DateChooser, JFileChooser, FontChooser, and MoneyChooser for the input of general user input or confirmation, or more specifically general messages, colors, dates, filenames, fonts, and monetary values, respectively.

> **NOTE**   When a modal dialog box is displayed within a method, the method does not continue until the user dismisses the dialog box.

Message Dialogs

The JOptionPane is the primary component for informing users of information and prompting for user input. The class definition, shown here, provides numerous class constants and methods.

```
public class JOptionPane extends JComponent {
    public static final int CANCEL_OPTION;
    public static final int CLOSED_OPTION;
    public static final int DEFAULT_OPTION;
    public static final int ERROR_MESSAGE;
    public static final String ICON_PROPERTY;
    public static final int INFORMATION_MESSAGE;
    public static final String INITIAL_SELECTION_VALUE_PROPERTY;
    public static final String INITIAL_VALUE_PROPERTY;
    public static final String INPUT_VALUE_PROPERTY;
    public static final String MESSAGE_PROPERTY;
    public static final String MESSAGE_TYPE_PROPERTY;
    public static final int NO_OPTION;
    public static final int OK_CANCEL_OPTION;
    public static final int OK_OPTION;
    public static final String OPTIONS_PROPERTY;
    public static final String OPTION_TYPE_PROPERTY;
    public static final int PLAIN_MESSAGE;
```

```
public static final int QUESTION_MESSAGE;
public static final String SELECTION_VALUES_PROPERTY;
public static final Object UNINITIALIZED_VALUE;
public static final String VALUE_PROPERTY;
public static final String WANTS_INPUT_PROPERTY;
public static final int WARNING_MESSAGE;
public static final int YES_NO_CANCEL_OPTION;
public static final int YES_NO_OPTION;
public static final int YES_OPTION;
public JOptionPane();
public JOptionPane(Object msg);
public JOptionPane(Object msg, int msgType);
public JOptionPane(Object msg, int msgType, int optType);
public JOptionPane(Object msg, int msgType, int optType, Icon icon);
public JOptionPane(Object msg, int msgType, int optType, Icon icon,
  Object options[]);
public JOptionPane(Object msg, int msgType, int optType, Icon icon,
  Object options[], Object initialValue);
public static JDesktopPane getDesktopPaneForComponent(Component parent);
public static Frame getFrameForComponent(Component parent);
public static Frame getRootFrame();
public static void setRootFrame(Frame newRoot);
public static int showConfirmDialog(Component parent, Object msg);
public static int showConfirmDialog(Component parent, Object msg,
  String title, int optType);
public static int showConfirmDialog(Component parent, Object msg,
  String title, int optType, int msgType);
public static int showConfirmDialog(Component parent, Object msg,
  String title, int optType, int msgType, Icon icon);
public static String showInputDialog(Component parent, Object msg);
public static String showInputDialog(Component parent, Object msg,
  String title, int msgType);
public static Object showInputDialog(Component parent, Object msg,
  String title, int msgType, Icon icon, Object options[],
  Object initialValue);
public static String showInputDialog(Object msg);
public static int showInternalConfirmDialog(Component parent, Object msg);
public static int showInternalConfirmDialog(Component parent, Object msg,
  String title, int optType);
public static int showInternalConfirmDialog(Component parent, Object msg,
```

```
     String title, int optType, int msgType);
public static int showInternalConfirmDialog(Component parent, Object msg,
     String title, int optType, int msgType, Icon icon);
public static String showInternalInputDialog(Component parent,
     Object msg);
public static String showInternalInputDialog(Component parent, Object msg,
     String title, int msgType);
public static Object showInternalInputDialog(Component parent, Object msg,
     String title, int msgType, Icon icon, Object selections[],
     Object initialValue);
public static void showInternalMessageDialog(Component parent,
     Object msg);
public static void showInternalMessageDialog(Component parent, Object msg,
     String title, int msgType);
public static void showInternalMessageDialog(Component parent, Object msg,
     String title, int msgType, Icon icon);
public static int showInternalOptionDialog(Component parent, Object msg,
     String title, int optType, int msgType, Icon icon, Object options[],
     Object initialValue);
public static void showMessageDialog(Component parent, Object msg);
public static void showMessageDialog(Component parent, Object msg,
     String title, int msgType);
public static void showMessageDialog(Component parent, Object msg,
     String title, int msgType, Icon icon);
public static int showOptionDialog(Component parent, Object msg,
     String title, int optType, int msgType, Icon icon, Object options[],
     Object initialValue);
public JDialog createDialog(Component parent, String title);
public JInternalFrame createInternalFrame(Component parent, String title);
public AccessibleContext getAccessibleContext();
public Icon getIcon();
public Object getInitialSelectionValue();
public Object getInitialValue();
public Object getInputValue();
public int getMaxCharactersPerLineCount();
public Object getMessage();
public int getMessageType();
public int getOptionType();
public Object[] getOptions();
public Object[] getSelectionValues();
```

```
    public OptionPaneUI getUI();
    public String getUIClassID();
    public Object getValue();
    public boolean getWantsInput();
    public void selectInitialValue();
    public void setIcon(Icon icon);
    public void setInitialSelectionValue(Object newValue);
    public void setInitialValue(Object newValue);
    public void setInputValue(Object newValue);
    public void setMessage(Object newMessage);
    public void setMessageType(int newType);
    public void setOptionType(int newType);
    public void setOptions(Object newOptions[]);
    public void setSelectionValues(Object newValues[]);
    public void setUI(OptionPaneUI newUI);
    public void setValue(Object newValue);
    public void setWantsInput(boolean newValue);
    public void updateUI();
}
```

Working with JOptionPane has two modes. You can create a JOptionPane by using the various constructors and other nonstatic, public methods, but this mode is rather unnecessary. The easier way of working with JOptionPane is using the various factory methods, creating specific types with show*XXX*Dialog. These methods allow you to configure all the options and show the dialog in one easy step, returning the user's selection when appropriate.

NOTE   Factory methods are ways of creating an object without using the constructor for its class. First demonstrated in Chapter 13, with BorderFactory, factory methods allow implementation details to be hidden, possibly in subclasses, by well-defined interfaces, hopefully simplifying their usage in the process.

There are four forms of dialogs: message, confirmation, input, and option. Each provides slightly different behavior, but each follows the same general pattern. As Figure 15.2 shows, there are four areas of each display, one each for an icon, message, input, and options. The form of dialog used determines what goes into each quadrant. And you can specify if the created option dialog is an internal dialog (JInternalFrame) or external dialog (JDialog). Which you use depends upon the behavior you desire.

FIGURE 15.2:

General option dialog appearance

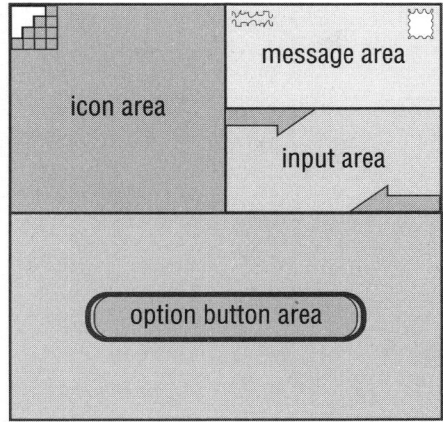

Message Dialogs

Message dialogs are for the general display of informational messages. By default, they provide an icon specific to the type of message (informational, error, warning, or plain—question, too, but not an appropriate option here), an area for the message, and an "OK" button. The showMessageDialog(Component parent, Object msg, String title, int msgType) method provides the single method most frequently used to create message dialogs. The parameters act as follows:

parent   The parent component for the dialog. This is used for positioning the dialog. If passed as null, the dialog would be centered for the screen. Otherwise, the dialog is centered based on the parent.

Msg   The message to display. This is an Object, not a String. If the parameter is not a String, its toString() method would be called to get a String.

Title   The window title for the dialog box.

MsgType   The type of message. Used to determine which icon to display. Value values are ERROR_MESSAGE, INFORMATION_MESSAGE, WARNING_ MESSAGE, QUESTION_MESSAGE, and PLAIN_MESSAGE. For message dialogs, QUESTION_MESSAGE is not really an appropriate option, as the user can only select OK, and not Yes/No.

Leaving off the window title and message type parameters provides a "Confirm" title and an informational type. Figure 15.3 demonstrates the appearance of an informational message dialog:

FIGURE 15.3:

An Informational message dialog

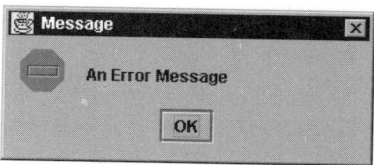

The different ways to display the message dialog are shown here. The first way is clearly the better, and easier, way of working with dialogs. The other examples are shown only in this way.

```
JOptionPane.showMessageDialog (f, "Show me the money", "Window Title",
    JOptionPane.INFORMATION_MESSAGE);
```
or

```
JOptionPane pane = new JOptionPane ();
pane.setMessage ("Show me the money");
pane.setMessageType (JOptionPane.INFORMATION_MESSAGE);
JDialog dialog = pane.createDialog (f, "Window Title");
dialog.show();
```

Figure 15.4 shows the same dialog with the other message types.

FIGURE 15.4:

Informational message dialogs

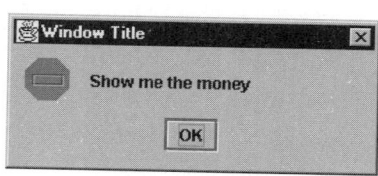

ERROR_MESSAGE

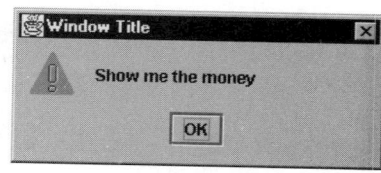

WARNING_MESSAGE

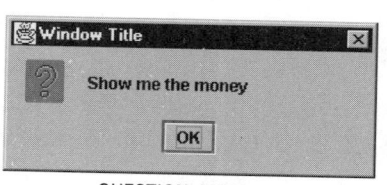

QUESTION_MESSAGE

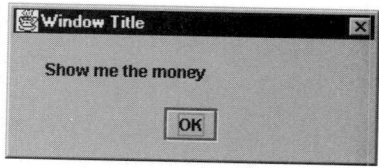

PLAIN_MESSAGE

Confirmation Dialogs

As the name implies, confirmation dialogs are for accepting or rejecting a given action. For confirmation dialogs, the primary way to create them is with show-ConfirmDialog(Component parent, Object msg, String title, int opt-Type). The optType passed in determines what options the user gets to select from:

YES_NO_CANCEL_OPTION   User picks from "Yes," "No," and "Cancel" buttons

YES_NO_OPTION   User picks from "Yes" and "No" buttons

OK_CANCEL_OPTION   User picks from "OK" and "Cancel" buttons

You can also pass in a message type with showConfirmDialog(Component parent, Object msg, String title, int optType, int msgType), where the types are the same as for message dialogs. Without the msgType parameter, the setting is for QUESTION_MESSAGE.

Since confirmation dialogs require user response, the showConfirmDialog() methods return what the user selected in the form of one of the following: YES_OPTION, NO_OPTION, OK_OPTION, CANCEL_OPTION, and CLOSED_OPTION. Other than CLOSED_OPTION, each corresponds to its respectively named button. With CLOSED_OPTION, it means the user opted to close the window without selecting anything and should probably be treated like cancel, if that is an option, or no if it is not. Figure 15.5 shows one possible confirmation dialog.

FIGURE 15.5:

A confirmation dialog

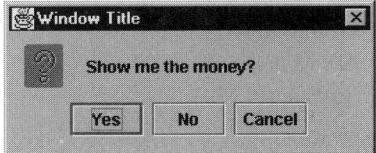

The code used to create Figure 15.5 and handle the response follows.

```
int returnValue = JOptionPane.CANCEL_OPTION;
while (returnValue != JOptionPane.YES_OPTION) {
  returnValue = JOptionPane.showConfirmDialog (f, "Show me the money?",
    "Maguire", JOptionPane.YES_NO_CANCEL_OPTION);
  if (returnValue == JOptionPane.YES_OPTION) {
    System.out.println ("Congratulations for saying yes");
  } else if (returnValue == JOptionPane.NO_OPTION) {
    System.out.println ("How dare you say no");
```

```
      } else { // Closed / Cancel
        System.out.println ("Get real");
      }
    }
```

Input Dialogs

Input dialogs are for accepting user input from either a text field or a list of options (combo-box). If you wish to prompt for input from a text field, you would most likely use showInputDialog(Component parent, Object msg, String title, int msgType), where msgType would most likely be QUESTION_MESSAGE. If you wish to provide a list of options for the user to pick from, you would use show-InputDialog(Component parent, Object msg, String title, int msgType, Icon icon, Object options[], Object initialValue). To use the default icon for a message type, just pass null as the icon parameter. Both forms display OK and Cancel buttons for the user to pick from and return the entered/selected value. If the user selects Cancel or closes the dialog, the returned value is null. Figure 15.6 shows the two types of input dialogs.

FIGURE 15.6:

Text and selection input dialogs

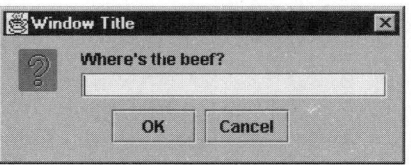
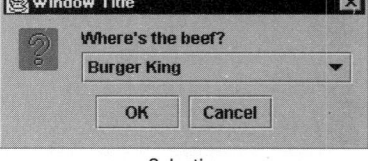

Text   Selection

The source used to generate and handle both of the dialogs in Figure 15.6 is below.

```
String input = null;
while ((input == null)) {
  input = JOptionPane.showInputDialog (f, "Where's the beef?", "Hungry?",
    JOptionPane.QUESTION_MESSAGE);
  if ((input != null) && (input.length() == 0))
    input = null;
}
System.out.println ("Entered: " + input);
// Second
input = null;
while (input == null) {
  String options[] = {"Burger King", "McDonalds", "Roy Rogers", "Wendy's"};
```

```
    input = (String)JOptionPane.showInputDialog (f, "Where's the beef?",
      "Hungry?", JOptionPane.QUESTION_MESSAGE, null, options, options[0]);
}
System.out.println ("Entered: " + input);
```

Option Dialogs

Option dialogs are of the catchall variety, not for any specific purpose and configurable to do just about anything. In fact, all the other dialogs are just specialized option dialogs. You have complete control of everything through a single method: `int showOptionDialog(Component parentComponent, Object message, String title, int optionType, int messageType, Icon icon, Object[] options, Object initialValue)`.

There are two keys to remember when using option dialogs directly. First, the `options` list is converted to buttons for the user to select from. The return value is the position of the object selected. Secondly, and somewhat more difficult to grasp, is the `message` parameter. In the basic case of a `Component`, `Icon`, or non-array object, the `message` parameter object is just placed within the pane. For an `Icon`, it is put in a `JLabel`. For an object, like a `String`, it too is wrapped into a `JLabel`, with the help of `toString()`. If, however, the parameter is an array the elements are treated as a series of messages and arranged into a vertical box, one on top of each other. For instance, to display a text area with a String for the user to accept a licensing agreement, you manual configure the components of the option pane. This is shown in Figure 15.7 below.

FIGURE 15.7:

A Generic option pane with message and text area

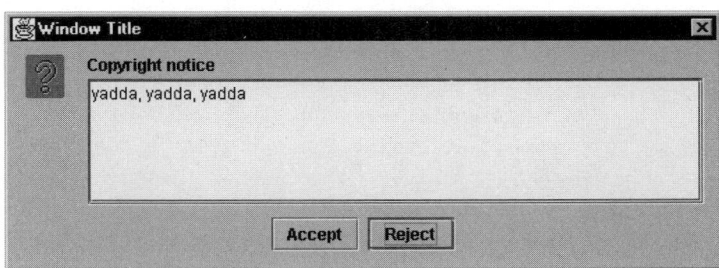

The following source can be used to ensure a user accepts the licensing agreement shown in Figure 15.7.

```
String choices[] = new String [] {"Accept", "Reject"};
String licenseLabel = "Copyright notice";
```

```
String license = "yadda, yadda, yadda";
JScrollPane sp = new JScrollPane (new JTextArea (license, 6, 40));
Object msgs[] = new Object [] {licenseLabel, sp};
int returnValue2 = JOptionPane.CLOSED_OPTION; // -1
while (returnValue2 != 0) {
  returnValue2 = JOptionPane.showOptionDialog(f, msgs, "User Agreement",
    JOptionPane.OK_CANCEL_OPTION, JOptionPane.QUESTION_MESSAGE, null,
    choices, choices[1]);
}
```

Color Choosers

Where JOptionPane is available for the display of informational messages and the acquisition of general user input, the JColorChooser component is a specialized input mechanism for users to select a color. While most frequently you will just create and display the chooser in one step with showDialog(Component parent, String total, Color initialValue), the following class definition shows that you can manipulate the chooser directly, just like the various option panes. While you can access all these capabilities, you don't need to.

```
public class JColorChooser extends JComponent implements Serializable {
    public static final String CHOOSER_PANELS_PROPERTY;
    public static final String PREVIEW_PANEL_PROPERTY;
    public static final String SELECTION_MODEL_PROPERTY;
    public JColorChooser(); // Defaults to white
    public JColorChooser(Color intialValue);
    public JColorChooser(ColorSelectionModel colorSelectionModel);
    public void addChooserPanel(AbstractColorChooserPanel panel);
    public static JDialog createDialog(Component parent, String title,
        boolean modal, JColorChooser chooser, ActionListener okAction,
        ActionListener cancelAction);
    public AccessibleContext getAccessibleContext();
    public AbstractColorChooserPanel[] getChooserPanels();
    public Color getColor();
    public JComponent getPreviewPanel();
    public ColorSelectionModel getSelectionModel();
    public ColorChooserUI getUI();
    public String getUIClassID();
    public AbstractColorChooserPanel removeChooserPanel
        (AbstractColorChooserPanel panel);
    public void setChooserPanels(AbstractColorChooserPanel panels[])
```

```
    public void setColor(Color value);
    public void setColor(int redValue, int greenValue, int blueValue);
    public void setColor(int rgbValue);
    public void setPreviewPanel(JComponent preview);
    public void setSelectionModel(ColorSelectionModel model);
    public void setUI(ColorChooserUI chooserUI);
    public static Color showDialog(Component parent, String total,
      Color initialValue);
    public void updateUI();
}
```

FIGURE 15.8:

The two input mechanisms of a JColorChooser

Swatches

RGB

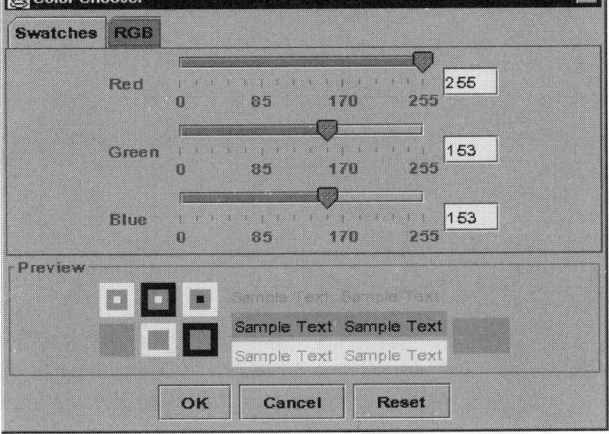

To demonstrate the JColorChooser, the following program places a button with a frame. When the button is selected, a JColorChooser is displayed to change the background color of the button.

```
import java.awt.*;
import java.awt.event.*;
import javax.swing.*;

public class ColorTester {
  public static void main (String args[]) {
    final JFrame f = new JFrame("Color Tester");
    f.addWindowListener (new WindowAdapter() {
      public void windowClosing (WindowEvent e) {
        System.exit(0);
      }
    });
    final JButton b = new JButton ("Change Button Background");
    f.getContentPane().add (b, BorderLayout.CENTER);
    b.addActionListener (new ActionListener() {
      public void actionPerformed(ActionEvent e) {
        Color color = JColorChooser.showDialog(f, "Color Chooser",
          b.getBackground());
        b.setBackground(color);
        b.repaint();
      }
    });
    f.setSize (300, 100);
    f.show();
  }
}
```

NOTE   There are several support classes for the JColorChooser in the com.sun .java.swing.colorchooser package.

Date Choosers

The user dialog for the selection of dates is called DateChooser. It allows a user to pick a date, a time, or both. You then use that information to update another object. The class allows you to customize it for time zones and locales. By setting a Locale, you change the means of entering time values to the appropriate customs and change the names shown to the appropriate language. Once the user enters a date, time, or both, depending on the configuration, you get the value back from the getDate() method. In addition to the basic functions of a DateChooser, the DateChooser.MiniCal offers a minimal calendar class for selecting dates.

> **NOTE**
>
> A specific Locale represents a language dialect or geographical area. Certain operations can be customized based on locales, to present an internationalized version of a program, where users would see monetary values as well as dates in the proper format. For instance, in certain countries, 01/02/1998 is February 1st, 1998. However, if the locale were Locale.US, this would be accepted as January 2nd, 1998. Configuring the locale to the proper region of a user allows that user to be most comfortable and productive.

> **NOTE**
>
> In the 1.2beta4 JDK, the DateChooser was only available in a preview fashion. Hence, this description is incomplete. A fuller description will be placed at the book's Web site once the capabilities are finalized.

File Choosers

The dialog for the selection of filenames is called JFileChooser. It allows a user to choose the name of a file for opening or saving. Then you, the programmer, take the information selected and use it to open or save a file. The class definition, shown here, indicates just how customizable the file chooser is.

```
public class JFileChooser extends JComponent implements Accessible {
    public static final String ACCESSORY_CHANGED_PROPERTY;
    public static final String APPROVE_BUTTON_MNEMONIC_CHANGED_PROPERTY;
    public static final String APPROVE_BUTTON_TEXT_CHANGED_PROPERTY;
    public static final String
      APPROVE_BUTTON_TOOL_TIP_TEXT_CHANGED_PROPERTY;
    public static final int APPROVE_OPTION;
    public static final String APPROVE_SELECTION;
    public static final int CANCEL_OPTION;
    public static final String CANCEL_SELECTION;
    public static final String CHOOSABLE_FILE_FILTER_CHANGED_PROPERTY;
    public static final int CUSTOM_DIALOG;
```

```java
public static final String DIALOG_TYPE_CHANGED_PROPERTY;
public static final int DIRECTORIES_ONLY;
public static final String DIRECTORY_CHANGED_PROPERTY;
public static final int ERROR_OPTION;
public static final int FILES_AND_DIRECTORIES;
public static final int FILES_ONLY;
public static final String FILE_FILTER_CHANGED_PROPERTY;
public static final String FILE_HIDING_CHANGED_PROPERTY;
public static final String FILE_SELECTION_MODE_CHANGED_PROPERTY;
public static final String FILE_SYSTEM_VIEW_CHANGED_PROPERTY;
public static final String FILE_VIEW_CHANGED_PROPERTY;
public static final String MULTI_SELECTION_ENABLED_CHANGED_PROPERTY;
public static final int OPEN_DIALOG;
public static final int SAVE_DIALOG;
public static final String SELECTED_FILE_CHANGED_PROPERTY;
public JFileChooser();
public JFileChooser(FileSystemView fileSystem);
public JFileChooser(File currentDirectory);
public JFileChooser(File currentDirectory, FileSystemView fileSystem);
public JFileChooser(String path);
public JFileChooser(String path, FileSystemView fileSystem);
public boolean accept(File f);
public void addActionListener(ActionListener l);
public void addChoosableFileFilter(FileFilter filter);
public void approveSelection();
public void cancelSelection();
public void changeToParentDirectory();
public void ensureFileIsVisible(File f);
public FileFilter getAcceptAllFileFilter();
public AccessibleContext getAccessibleContext();
public JComponent getAccessory();
public int getApproveButtonMnemonic();
public String getApproveButtonText();
public String getApproveButtonToolTipText();
public FileFilter[] getChoosableFileFilters();
public File getCurrentDirectory();
public String getDescription(File f);
public String getDialogTitle();
public int getDialogType();
public FileFilter getFileFilter();
public int getFileSelectionMode();
public FileSystemView getFileSystemView();
```

```
public FileView getFileView();
public Icon getIcon(File f);
public String getName(File f);
public File getSelectedFile();
public File[] getSelectedFiles();
public String getTypeDescription(File f);
public FileChooserUI getUI();
public String getUIClassID();
public boolean isDirectorySelectionEnabled();
public boolean isFileHidingEnabled();
public boolean isFileSelectionEnabled();
public boolean isMultiSelectionEnabled();
public boolean isTraversable(File f);
public void removeActionListener(ActionListener l);
public boolean removeChoosableFileFilter(FileFilter filter);
public void rescanCurrentDirectory();
public void resetChoosableFileFilters();
public void setAccessory(JComponent);
public void setApproveButtonMnemonic(char mnemonic);
public void setApproveButtonMnemonic(int mnemonic);
public void setApproveButtonText(String text);
public void setApproveButtonToolTipText(String text);
public void setCurrentDirectory(File f);
public void setDialogTitle(String title);
public void setDialogType(int type);
public void setFileFilter(FileFilter filter);
public void setFileHidingEnabled(boolean b);
public void setFileSelectionMode(int mode);
public void setFileSystemView(FileSystemView fileSystem);
public void setFileView(FileView view);
public void setMultiSelectionEnabled(boolean b);
public void setSelectedFile(File f);
public void setSelectedFiles(File f[]);
public int showDialog(Component parent, String approveButtonText);
public int showOpenDialog(Component parent);
public int showSaveDialog(Component parent);
public void updateUI();
}
```

Do not be overwhelmed with the lengthy definition. In its simplest form, you just create the JFileChooser and show it. Then, the return status reports if the user selected Cancel or not. If they didn't, you open or save to the selected file.

```
JFileChooser chooser = new JFileChooser();
```

```
int status = chooser.showOpenDialog (aFrame);
// or int status = chooser.showSaveDialog (aFrame);
if (status == JFileChooser.APPROVE_OPTION) {
  File f = chooser.getSelectedFile();
  processFile (f);
}
```

When the file chooser is shown, the window in Figure 15.9 appears, most likely starting in a different directory.

FIGURE 15.9:

The basic JFileChooser

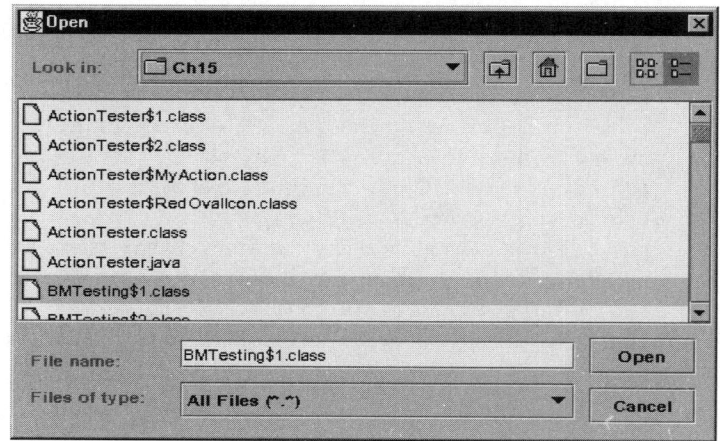

Like all Swing components, each component can have multiple visual appearances. For instance, if your appearance is set to Windows, you will see the standard Window file dialog when showing a JFileChooser.

As you'll soon see with other Swing components, you can customize practically everything with the JFileChooser. Want to have selectable file filters so users can choose just image files, Java source files, or HTML files? Associate a FileFilter with addChoosableFileFilter() that just displays GIF and JPEG files. Want to have different icons next to different file extensions? Create a FileView and connect it with setFileView(). Figure 15.10 shows just how this might appear.

FIGURE 15.10:

An enhanced JFileChooser

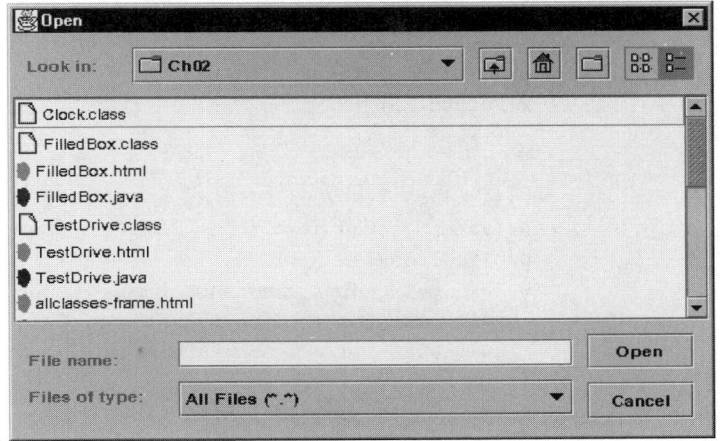

The program used to customize the JFileChooser for Figure 15.10 follows. The customized FileView object is called IconView and displays different color AnOval-Icon instances based upon the file extension. The ExtensionFilter class allows you to specify what filename extensions are selectable for a FileFilter.

```java
import java.awt.*;
import java.io.File;
import java.util.HashMap;
import java.awt.event.*;
import javax.swing.*;
import javax.swing.filechooser.*;
import javax.swing.event.*;

public class EnhancedFileTester extends JPanel {
  class AnOvalIcon implements Icon {
    Color color;
    public AnOvalIcon (Color c) {
      color = c;
    }
    public void paintIcon (Component c, Graphics g,
        int x, int y) {
      g.setColor(color);
      g.fillOval (x, y, getIconWidth(), getIconHeight());
    }
```

```
      public int getIconWidth() {
        return 10;
      }
      public int getIconHeight() {
        return 15;
      }
    }
    public class IconView extends FileView {
      private HashMap hash = new HashMap();
      public IconView () {
        hash.put ("htm", new AnOvalIcon (Color.red));
        hash.put ("html", new AnOvalIcon (Color.green));
        hash.put ("java", new AnOvalIcon (Color.blue));
      }
      public String getName (File f) {
        String s = f.getName();
        if (s.length() == 0) {
          s = f.getAbsolutePath();
        }
        return s;
      }
      public String getDescription (File f) {
        return f.getName();
      }
      public String getTypeDescription (File f) {
        return f.getAbsolutePath();
      }
      public Icon getIcon (File f) {
        String path = f.getAbsolutePath();
        int pos = path.lastIndexOf( '.' );
        if ((pos >= 0) && (pos < (path.length() - 1)) ) {
          String ext = path.substring (pos + 1).toLowerCase();
          return (Icon)hash.get (ext);
        }
        return null;
      }
      public Boolean isTraversable (File file) {
        return (new Boolean (file.isDirectory()));
      }
    }
    public class ExtensionFilter extends FileFilter {
```

```java
        private String extensions[];
        private String description;
        public ExtensionFilter (String description, String extension) {
          this (description, new String[] {extension});
        }
        public ExtensionFilter (String description, String extensions[]) {
          this.description = description;
          this.extensions = (String[])extensions.clone();
        }
        public boolean accept (File file) {
          if (file.isDirectory()) {
            return true;
          }
          int count = extensions.length;
          String path = file.getAbsolutePath();
          for (int i =0;i < count;i++) {
            String ext = extensions[i];
            if (path.endsWith(ext) &&
                (path.charAt(path.length()-ext.length()) == '.')) {
              return true;
            }
          }
          return false;
        }
        public String getDescription() {
          return (description == null ? extensions[0] : description);
        }
      }
      public EnhancedFileTester() {
        JButton jb = new JButton("Open File Viewer");
        add (jb);
        jb.addActionListener(new ActionListener() {
          public void actionPerformed (ActionEvent e) {
            JFileChooser chooser = new JFileChooser();
            FileFilter type1 = new ExtensionFilter (
              "Java source", ".java");
            FileFilter type2 = new ExtensionFilter (
              "Image files", new String[] {".jpg", ".gif", "jpeg", "xbm"});
            FileFilter type3 = new ExtensionFilter (
              "HTML files", new String[] {".htm", ".html"});
            chooser.addChoosableFileFilter (type1);
```

```
        chooser.addChoosableFileFilter (type2);
        chooser.addChoosableFileFilter (type3);
        chooser.setFileFilter (type2); // Initial filter setting
        FileView view = new IconView();
        chooser.setFileView (view);
        int status = chooser.showOpenDialog (EnhancedFileTester.this);
        if (status == JFileChooser.APPROVE_OPTION) {
          File f = chooser.getSelectedFile();
          System.out.println (f);
        }
      }
    });
  }
  public static void main (String args[]) {
    JFrame f = new JFrame ("Table Example");
    JPanel j = new EnhancedFileTester();
    f.addWindowListener(new WindowAdapter() {
      public void windowClosing(WindowEvent e) {
        System.exit(0);
      }
    });
    f.getContentPane().add (j, BorderLayout.CENTER);
    f.setSize (300, 200);
    f.show();
  }
}
```

TIP   Be careful you do not confuse the `FileFilter` classes in the `java.io` and `javax.swing.filechooser` packages.

One thing not demonstrated here that you might wish to add is an accessory (like a file previewer) via `setAccessory(JComponent accessory)`. This would be displayed to the right of the file list. In order for the accessory to work, you register the accessory component as a `PropertyChangeListener` with the `JFileChooser`:

```
chooser.addPropertyChangeListener(theAccessory)
```

And listen for the `JFileChooser.SELECTED_FILE_CHANGED_PROPERTY` Property-ChangeEvent. Property change events work similarly to AWT events but happen when a property changes for an object, usually via a set*XXX*() method. This concept will be explained further in the JavaBeans chapter, Chapter 22.

```
public void propertyChange(PropertyChangeEvent e) {
  String prop = e.getPropertyName();
  if (prop == JFileChooser.SELECTED_FILE_CHANGED_PROPERTY) {
    f = (File) e.getNewValue();
    if (isShowing()) {
      // change display settings for new image
      changeStuff(f);
      repaint();
    }
  }
}
```

NOTE In addition to `FileView`, which controls the display of the filenames, there is also `FileSystemView`. Most of what `FileSystemView` does is part of the `File` class of Java 1.2. However, prior to Java 1.2 there was no standard interface to access such information as root partitions, file types, and hidden files. With the abstract `FileSystemView` and the concrete `WindowsFileSystemView`, `UnixFileSystemView`, and `GenericFileSystemView` classes, this is now possible. It is highly probable that Java vendors for other operating systems will provide additional concrete implementations of `FileSystemView` for platforms like Macintosh. Most developers will not need to access the classes directly though.

Font Choosers

The user dialog for the selection of fonts is called `FontChooser`. It allows a user to choose the family, style, and size for a font. Then you, the programmer, take the font selected and use it to change some text style. The class definition shows how you can configure the font chooser. Normally, however, you would just use the `ask()` method, as it will display the chooser in a dialog box.

To display a `FontChooser`, you just `ask()` for one, then use the `Font` value returned. This value would be `null` if the user selected the Cancel button. The `ChangeListener` parameter to `ask()` allows a listener to be notified if the user selects OK or Apply. This allows you to dynamically update the font of something visible on the screen. When a listener is present (not null), the displayed dialog is not modal. If the listener is null, then the dialog is modal.

```
JTextArea jt = …;
Font initialFont = new Font ("Serif", Font.PLAIN, 24));
```

```
Font f = FontChooser.ask(jt, "Change Font", initialFont, null);
if (f != null)
    jt.setFont (f);
```

The initial text shown with the initial font specified is "Toy box". You could change this with the `setPreviewString()` method. However, you would then not be able to use the `ask()` method.

NOTE

In the 1.2beta4 JDK, the `FontChooser` was only available in a preview fashion. Hence, a screen shot is not shown. A fuller example will be placed at the book's Web site once the capabilities are finalized.

In addition to the `FontChooser` class for choosing fonts, there is a `FontChooser.Patch` class. The patch is a component that you would display somewhere on the screen. Displayed on the component are the current font name, size, and style. When selected by clicking on it with the mouse, a `FontChooser` appears, allowing the user to change the current font of the patch. Setting the initial font of the patch is either done in the constructor, `Patch (Font initialFont)`, or by the `setSelectedFont(Font newFont)` method. To retrieve the selected font, use the `getSelectedFont()` method.

Money Choosers

To enter monetary values, you can present the user with a `MoneyChooser`. It allows users to enter monetary values in the custom of the current `Locale`, including monetary symbol, as well as comma and period placement. Once the user enters a setting, you get the value back as a `double` with the `getValue()` method.

If showing a calculator is enabled with `setCalculatorEnable(true)`, then a mini calculator icon is shown. When selected, this would bring up an instance of a `Calculator` class, that the user can use to help with the math and pass the value back to the `MoneyChooser`.

NOTE

In the 1.2beta4 JDK, the `MoneyChooser` was only available in a preview fashion. Hence, this description is incomplete. A fuller description will be placed at the book's Web site once the capabilities are finalized.

Model/View/Controller Architecture

The Model/View/Controller (MVC) architecture is a second way that you can use the Swing components. As the name implies, the architecture is made up of three parts: a Model, a View, and a Controller.

The Model defines the state of a system: what the underlying logical representation is.

The View defines how the user sees the Model: what the visual representation is.

The Controller defines how the user interacts with the Model.

To help you understand the concepts, think of a grid of numbers. The numbers that make up the grid, and their row/column position, define a Model. At position (4, 2) the value may be –24.5. The View defines how a user sees the data. So, for an accounts payable system, a negative number might be shown in red or surrounded by parenthesis (). Or, you may just want to show the negative number in a different font. The Model itself does NOT change, the value is always –24.5. Only the user's View of the Model changes. Quite possibly, that Model can become a chart. Again, the grid of numbers does not change. How the user sees that grid does. If the value of a number in the grid changes, changing the Model, each View of that Model will automatically be updated. For instance, if –24.5 became 3.14, then it would no longer be shown in red and the chart View will automatically be updated.

The third part the Controller defines how the user interacts with the Model. This is tightly coupled with the View. If a View is a bar chart, and the user drags a bar down, this could decrease the associated number in the grid. Because of the tight coupling of Controller and View, these two concepts are combined into one object, frequently called a *delegate*. In Swing, they are also referred to as UI objects, or UI delegates.

You've already seen MVC at work somewhat. When we described the JFile-Chooser, we installed a new FileView. The list of filenames never changed. The only thing that changed was the icon. You can also play with the displayed name by modifying the getName() method. While this would change the displayed name of the file, the getSelectedFile() method would still return the real name, not the displayed name. That is MVC at work.

NOTE   While MVC is frequently thought of with visual components, it is not restricted to that environment.

With every Swing component, there is a Model and quite possibly two. The second Model comes into play when there is a special selection mechanism. For instance, a `ListModel` describes the data behind a `JList` component. The `ListModel` will say what elements to display in a `JList`. The second Model associated with a `JList` is its list selection mechanism. Is it in single or multi-selection mode? This too is a Model and is represented by `ListSelectionModel`. Selection Models tend to be related to the graphical representation or interaction with a component.

Using Button Model

To help you understand the concept further, let's look at the simplest component of all: the `JButton`. If you remember from Chapter 13, the `JButton` component can have quite a few different icons. Each of these icons represents a different button state. These states are described in the button's Model, not the icons. Since the text label is only a visual part of the button, this is not part of the Model. You'll see that here in the `ButtonModel` class definition:

```
public interface ButtonModel extends ItemSelectable {
    public abstract void addActionListener(ActionListener l);
    public abstract void addChangeListener(ChangeListener l);
    public abstract void addItemListener(ItemListener l);
    public abstract String getActionCommand();
    public abstract int getMnemonic();
    public abstract boolean isArmed();
    public abstract boolean isEnabled();
    public abstract boolean isPressed();
    public abstract boolean isRollover();
    public abstract boolean isSelected();
    public abstract void removeActionListener(ActionListener l);
    public abstract void removeChangeListener(ChangeListener l);
    public abstract void removeItemListener(ItemListener l);
    public abstract void setActionCommand(String command);
    public abstract void setArmed(boolean b);
    public abstract void setEnabled(boolean b);
    public abstract void setGroup(ButtonGroup group);
    public abstract void setMnemonic(int key);
    public abstract void setPressed(boolean b);
```

```
public abstract void setRollover(boolean b);
public abstract void setSelected(boolean b);
}
```

The `DefaultButtonModel` is the specific Model that is used by default. It is basically in charge of notifying any Views when the state of the Model changes. To demonstrate the connection of Models and buttons, the following creates two `JButton` objects, or Views, that share the same Model. Because they share the same Model, when one is selected so is the other, notifying both sets of `ActionListeners`.

```java
import javax.swing.*;
import java.awt.*;
import java.awt.event.*;

public class BMTesting {
  public static void main (String args[]) {
    JFrame f = new JFrame ("Button Model Tester");
    JButton jb1 = new JButton ("Hello");
    ButtonModel bm = jb1.getModel();
    JButton jb2 = new JButton ("World");
    jb2.setModel (bm);
    Container c = f.getContentPane();
    c.add (jb1, BorderLayout.NORTH);
    c.add (jb2, BorderLayout.SOUTH);
    jb1.addActionListener (new ActionListener () {
      public void actionPerformed (ActionEvent e) {
        System.out.println ("Selected One");
      }
    });
    jb2.addActionListener (new ActionListener () {
      public void actionPerformed (ActionEvent e) {
        System.out.println ("Selected Two");
      }
    });
    f.addWindowListener (new WindowAdapter() {
      public void windowClosing (WindowEvent e) {
        System.exit(0);
      }
    });
    f.pack();
    f.show();
  }
}
```

Understanding Button Delegates

The UI delegate for a JButton is called ButtonUI or, more specifically, Basic-ButtonUI. This describes things like color, size, and how to draw the borders, icon, and text. Also, margins are defined to describe the selectable area. When the delegate detects an action within its borders, it notifies the Model. In turn, the Model checks to see if it needs to change. If it does, then the UI object may change as a result. All this happens primarily behind the scenes. The UI object does not store things like the current text of the label. It does however describe how to draw that text. You can change the physical appearance of the JButton by changing its look and feel. This leads us to the Pluggable Look and Feel part of Swing.

Pluggable Look and Feel

Because of MVC's separation of Model and View, it is very easy to change how an object appears to the user without changing the state of that object. In fact, Swing comes with Look and Feels for Windows, Motif, Macintosh, and Metal.

What this means is you can change from one appearance to another with a few simple method calls. By default, Metal is the appearance users experience when running Java applications. However, if you wish them to see their local look and feel, you can modify it to show this instead. The remaining parts of your program are not modified, as the only thing that changed is the appearance or View of each object. We are not talking about any specific program here, just the general sense of any program that uses Swing components.

Figure 15.11 shows how multiple look and feels would appear in one application. Normally, you would not mix these.

FIGURE 15.11:

Changing Look and Feels

The source for the program that generated Figure 15.11 follows.

```
import javax.swing.*;
import java.awt.*;
import java.awt.event.*;
```

```
public class LocalLF {
  public static void main (String args[]) {
    JFrame f = new JFrame ("Look and Feel");
    JButton jb1 = new JButton ("Hello");
    try {

UIManager.setLookAndFeel(UIManager.getSystemLookAndFeelClassName());
    } catch (Exception ex) {
      System.err.println ("Could not swap LookAndFeel");
    }
    JButton jb2 = new JButton ("World");
    Container c = f.getContentPane();
    c.add (jb1, BorderLayout.NORTH);
    c.add (jb2, BorderLayout.SOUTH);
    f.addWindowListener (new WindowAdapter() {
      public void windowClosing (WindowEvent e) {
        System.exit(0);
      }
    });
    f.setSize(150, 100);
    f.show();
  }
}
```

NOTE   The Windows Look and Feel is only available on the Windows platform.

Complex Swing Components

Prior chapters only demonstrated how to interact with components using the event-dispatching mechanism introduced by Java 1.1. Because of MVC, each of the components supports a secondary mechanism. While this secondary means may appear more difficult to configure and use, as programs get more complex, you'll notice how much easier it is to maintain MVC-oriented applications.

Lists and Combo Boxes

Whenever you work with JList and JComboBox objects, you will need to provide a set of elements to display. Each of these objects manages their element set internally as a ListModel or ComboBoxModel respectively. ComboBoxModel is just a specialized ListModel with a selected element, while JList handles selection with ListSelectionModel. A ListCellRenderer displays each element of a JList or JComboBox.

Now you'll put all the pieces together to create a JList and JComboBox that shares a data Model. The data will consist of a series of parts, along with a quantity on hand and price. You'll also provide an easy way to increase your merchandise list to show that as this grows so does the JList and JComboBox.

ListModel/ComboBoxModel

The ListModel consists of four methods:

```
public interface ListModel {
    public abstract void addListDataListener(ListDataListener l);
    public abstract Object getElementAt(int index);
    public abstract int getSize();
    public abstract void removeListDataListener(ListDataListener l);
}
```

and ComboBoxModel adds two more:

```
public interface ComboBoxModel extends ListModel {
    public abstract Object getSelectedItem();
    public abstract void setSelectedItem(Object item);
}
```

To create our own data Model, we could create a class that implements Combo-BoxModel to satisfy both needs. However, the behavior for managing the listener list would be common for all data Models, and there is a class AbstractListModel that handles this for us:

```
public abstract class AbstractListModel implements ListModel, Serializable {
    protected EventListenerList listenerList;
    public AbstractListModel();
    public void addListDataListener(ListDataListener l);
    protected void fireContentsChanged(Object source, int ind0, int ind1);
    protected void fireIntervalAdded(Object source, int ind0, int ind1);
    protected void fireIntervalRemoved(Object source, int ind0, int ind1);
    public void removeListDataListener(ListDataListener l);
}
```

Since managing the list of objects in the data Model would practically always be the same, there is even a support class for that: DefaultListModel.

```
public class DefaultListModel extends AbstractListModel {
```

```
    public DefaultListModel();
    public void add(int, Object);
    public void addElement(Object obj);
    public int capacity();
    public void clear();
    public boolean contains(Object elem);
    public void copyInto(Object anArray[]);
    public Object elementAt(int index);
    public Enumeration elements();
    public void ensureCapacity(int minCapacity);
    public Object firstElement();
    public Object get(int index);
    public Object getElementAt(int index);
    public int getSize();
    public int indexOf(Object elem);
    public int indexOf(Object elem, int index);
    public void insertElementAt(Object, int index);
    public boolean isEmpty();
    public Object lastElement();
    public int lastIndexOf(Object elem);
    public int lastIndexOf(Object elem, int index);
    public Object remove(int index);
    public void removeAllElements();
    public boolean removeElement(Object elem);
    public void removeElementAt(int index);
    public void removeRange(int fromIndex, int toIndex);
    public Object set(int index, Object element);
    public void setElementAt(Object obj, int index);
    public void setSize(int newSize);
    public int size();
    public Object[] toArray();
    public String toString();
    public void trimToSize();
  }
```

So, to create a data Model to use with both JList and JComboBox, extend DefaultListModel and add in the ComboBoxModel methods. The key method to use in DefaultListModel is addElement(), which is used to add each element into the Model. For the ComboBoxModel part, you just need to store the value somewhere and notify everyone via fireContentsChanged() when the value changes.

```
// Our data
final String partsList[][] = {
```

```
      {"Eye of Newt", "10", "99¢"},
      {"Toe of Frog", "12", "$18.99"},
      {"Wool of Bat", "1", "$10.00"},
      {"Tongue of Dog", "25", "$1.25"},
      {"Wolf Nipple Chips", "15", "$12.95"},
      {"Spleen of Ocelot", "18", "$2.50"},
      {"Black Acorn", "150", "75¢"},
      {"Pinch of Salt", "5000", "15¢"},
      {"Sphere of Power", "2", "$50.00"}
   };

   class PartsListModel extends DefaultListModel implements ComboBoxModel {
      Object currentValue;
      public PartsListModel() {
         for (int i=0, n=partsList.length;i<n;i++) {
            addElement(partsList[i]);
         }
      }
      // ComboBoxModel methods
      public Object getSelectedItem() {
         return currentValue;
      }
      public void setSelectedItem(Object anObject) {
         currentValue = anObject;
         fireContentsChanged(this, -1, -1);
      }
   }
```

To listen for changes to the list or combo box Model, you would register a
ListDataListener. Then, when the event happens, you would be notified with
a ListDataEvent.

```
   public interface ListDataListener extends EventListener {
      public abstract void contentsChanged(ListDataEvent e);
      public abstract void intervalAdded(ListDataEvent e);
      public abstract void intervalRemoved(ListDataEvent e);
   }

   public class ListDataEvent extends EventObject {
      public static final int CONTENTS_CHANGED;
      public static final int INTERVAL_ADDED;
      public static final int INTERVAL_REMOVED;
```

```
    public ListDataEvent(Object source, int type, int index0, int index1);
    public int getIndex0();
    public int getIndex1();
    public int getType();
}
```

ListCellRenderer

If you were to use this Model in the program now, the JList or JComboBox would display each element in an illegible way, like [Ljava.lang.String;@704ad524. Basically, this says that each element is a String array, which is absolutely correct. To correct this situation, all you have to do is define your own ListCellRenderer.

```
public interface ListCellRenderer {
    public abstract Component getListCellRendererComponent(JList list,
       Object value, int index, boolean isSelected, boolean cellHasFocus);
}
```

What is frequently done for a renderer is to subclass JLabel, as it tends to serve as a good renderer. Then the value parameter to getListCellRendererComponent() is converted into something displayable. For instance, if the value were a filename, you could see different Views as text or an image. In this particular case, the value, added by addElement() above, is a String array, so it just needs to be converted into something displayable. The component also needs to be made opaque so the background doesn't bleed through.

```
class MyLabelRenderer extends JLabel implements ListCellRenderer {
    public MyLabelRenderer() {
      setOpaque(true);
    }
    public Component getListCellRendererComponent(JList list,
        Object value, int index, boolean isSelected, boolean cellHasFocus) {
      if (value != null) {
        String values[] = (String[])value;
        String setting = values[0] + " / " + values[1] + " / " + values[2];
        setText(setting);
      }
      setBackground(isSelected ? Color.blue : Color.white);
      setForeground(isSelected ? Color.white : Color.blue);
      return this;
    }
}
```

ListSelectionModel

The selection Model of the list is one of three constants of ListSelectionModel: SINGLE_SELECTION, SINGLE_INTERVAL_SELECTION, or MULTIPLE_INTERVAL_SELECTION. The last is the default. While DefaultListSelectionModel is the default implementation of ListSelectionModel used, neither class definition is really necessary. All you need to know are the three constants to change the selection Model. To place a list into single selection mode, you would perform the following steps.

```
ListSelectionModel lsm = jl.getSelectionModel();
lsm.setSelectionMode(ListSelectionModel.SINGLE_SELECTION);
```

If you were interested in when a range was selected, you would add a List-SelectionListener to the ListSelectionModel or JList. This does not tell you directly which element is selected, though. You have to use an index provided by its ListSelectEvent to get at the position in the Model. What follows is the class definition for the ListSelectionListener and ListSelectionEvent.

```
public interface ListSelectionListener extends EventListener {
  public abstract void valueChanged(ListSelectionEvent e);
}

public class ListSelectionEvent extends EventObject {
  public ListSelectionEvent(Object source, int begin, int end, boolean adj);
  public int getFirstIndex();
  public int getLastIndex();
  public boolean getValueIsAdjusting();
  public String toString();
}

JList jl = …;
jl.addListSelectionListener (new ListSelectionListener() {
  public void valueChanged (ListSelectionEvent e) {
    if (!e.getValueIsAdjusting()) {
      String element[] = (String[])pcm.getElementAt(e.getFirstIndex());
      System.out.println (element[0] + " : " + element[1] + " : " +
        element[2]);
    }
  }
});
```

Figure 15.12 shows what everything put together would look like.

FIGURE 15.12:

A JList and JComboBox
sharing the same Model

FIGURE 15.12:

A JList and JComboBox
sharing the same Model

The source for the complete example follows. While this does duplicate some of
the code from above, having everything together should help you try out the
example and see where everything fits together.

```java
import javax.swing.*;
import javax.swing.event.*;
import java.awt.*;
import java.awt.event.*;

public class ListIt {

  final String partsList[][] = {
    {"Eye of Newt", "10", "99¢"},
    {"Toe of Frog", "12", "$18.99"},
    {"Wool of Bat", "1", "$10.00"},
    {"Tongue of Dog", "25", "$1.25"},
    {"Wolf Nipple Chips", "15", "$12.95"},
    {"Spleen of Ocelot", "18", "$2.50"},
    {"Black Acorn", "150", "75¢"},
    {"Pinch of Salt", "5000", "15¢"},
    {"Sphere of Power", "2", "$50.00"}
  };

  class PartsListModel extends DefaultListModel
      implements ComboBoxModel {
    Object currentValue;
    public PartsListModel() {
      for (int i=0, n=partsList.length;i<n;i++) {
```

```
        addElement(partsList[i]);
      }
    }
    // ComboBoxModel methods
    public Object getSelectedItem() {
      return currentValue;
    }
    public void setSelectedItem(Object anObject) {
      currentValue = anObject;
      fireContentsChanged(this, -1, -1);
    }
  }
  class MyLabelRenderer extends JLabel implements ListCellRenderer {
    public MyLabelRenderer() {
      setOpaque(true);
    }
    public Component getListCellRendererComponent(JList list,
        Object value, int index, boolean isSelected, boolean cellHasFocus) {
      if (value != null) {
        String values[] = (String[])value;
        String setting = values[0] + " / " + values[1] + " / " + values[2];
        setText(setting);
      }
      setBackground(isSelected ? Color.blue : Color.white);
      setForeground(isSelected ? Color.white : Color.blue);
      return this;
    }
  }
  public ListIt() {
    JFrame f = new JFrame ("List Models");
    final PartsListModel pcm = new PartsListModel();
    ListCellRenderer lcr = new MyLabelRenderer();
    JList jl = new JList (pcm);
    jl.setCellRenderer (lcr);
    ListSelectionModel lsm = jl.getSelectionModel();
    lsm.setSelectionMode(ListSelectionModel.SINGLE_SELECTION);
    jl.addListSelectionListener (new ListSelectionListener() {
      public void valueChanged (ListSelectionEvent e) {
        if (!e.getValueIsAdjusting()) {
          String element[] = (String[])pcm.getElementAt(e.getFirstIndex());
          System.out.println (element[0] + " : " + element[1] + " : " +
```

```
            element[2]);
      }
    }
  });
  JScrollPane jsp = new JScrollPane (jl);
  JComboBox jc = new JComboBox(pcm);
  jc.setRenderer (lcr);
  JButton jb = new JButton ("Add Merchandise");
  jb.addActionListener (new ActionListener() {
    public void actionPerformed (ActionEvent e) {
      pcm.addElement (partsList[(int)(Math.random()*partsList.length)]);
    }
  });
  Container c = f.getContentPane();
  c.add (jsp, BorderLayout.NORTH);
  c.add (jc, BorderLayout.CENTER);
  c.add (jb, BorderLayout.SOUTH);
  f.addWindowListener (new WindowAdapter() {
    public void windowClosing (WindowEvent e) {
      System.exit(0);
    }
  });
  f.setSize(250, 250);
  f.show();
}

public static void main (String args[]) {
  new ListIt();
}
```

Tables

In Chapter 13, you saw how easy it is to create a JTable from a two-dimensional array of elements. Here, we'll look at all the underlying structures involved and how you can customize practically everything. The data Model for a table is TableModel. The table is then made up of multiple columns from this data Model, and Table-ColumnModel controls the visually oriented column Model for the table. The now familiar ListSelectionModel controls the selection of cells, rows, and columns, with help from several JTable methods. TableCellRenderer defines how each cell of the table is displayed, and TableCellEditor describes the mechanism to edit cells. All these support classes of `JTable` are found in the `javax.swing.table` package. The `JTable` class itself is found in `javax.swing`. Its definition is shown below.

```
public class JTable extends JComponent implements TableModelListener,
    Scrollable, TableColumnModelListener, ListSelectionListener,
    CellEditorListener, Accessible {
  public static final int AUTO_RESIZE_ALL_COLUMNS;
  public static final int AUTO_RESIZE_LAST_COLUMN;
  public static final int AUTO_RESIZE_OFF;
  public JTable();
  public JTable(TableModel tm);
  public JTable(TableModel tm, TableColumnModel tcm);
  public JTable(TableModel tm, TableColumnModel tcm, ListSelectionModel lm);
  public JTable(int rows, int columns);
  public JTable(Object rowData[][], Object colData[]);
  public JTable(Vector rowData, Vector colData);
  public void addColumn(TableColumn column);
  public void addColumnSelectionInterval(int index0, int index1);
  public void addNotify();
  public void addRowSelectionInterval(int index0, int index1);
  public void clearSelection();
  public void columnAdded(TableColumnModelEvent e);
  public int columnAtPoint(Point p);
  public void columnMarginChanged(ChangeEvent e);
  public void columnMoved(TableColumnModelEvent e);
  public void columnRemoved(TableColumnModelEvent e);
  public void columnSelectionChanged(ListSelectionEvent e);
  public int convertColumnIndexToModel(int column);
  public int convertColumnIndexToView(int column);
  public void createDefaultColumnsFromModel();
  public boolean editCellAt(int row, int column);
  public boolean editCellAt(int row, int column, EventObject e);
  public void editingCanceled(ChangeEvent e);
  public void editingStopped(ChangeEvent e);
  public AccessibleContext getAccessibleContext();
  public boolean getAutoCreateColumnsFromModel();
  public int getAutoResizeMode();
  public TableCellEditor getCellEditor();
  public Rectangle getCellRect(int row, int column, boolean includeSpacing);
  public boolean getCellSelectionEnabled();
  public TableColumn getColumn(Object obj);
```

```
public Class getColumnClass(int column);
public int getColumnCount();
public TableColumnModel getColumnModel();
public String getColumnName(int column);
public boolean getColumnSelectionAllowed();
public TableCellEditor getDefaultEditor(Class c);
public TableCellRenderer getDefaultRenderer(Class c);
public int getEditingColumn();
public int getEditingRow();
public Component getEditorComponent();
public Color getGridColor();
public Dimension getIntercellSpacing();
public TableModel getModel();
public Dimension getPreferredScrollableViewportSize();
public int getRowCount();
public int getRowHeight();
public boolean getRowSelectionAllowed();
public int getScrollableBlockIncrement(Rectangle r, int orient, int dir);
public boolean getScrollableTracksViewportHeight();
public boolean getScrollableTracksViewportWidth();
public int getScrollableUnitIncrement(Rectangle r, int orient, int dir);
public int getSelectedColumn();
public int getSelectedColumnCount();
public int[] getSelectedColumns();
public int getSelectedRow();
public int getSelectedRowCount();
public int[] getSelectedRows();
public Color getSelectionBackground();
public Color getSelectionForeground();
public ListSelectionModel getSelectionModel();
public boolean getShowHorizontalLines();
public boolean getShowVerticalLines();
public JTableHeader getTableHeader();
public String getToolTipText(MouseEvent e);
public TableUI getUI();
public String getUIClassID();
public Object getValueAt(int row, int column);
public boolean isCellEditable(int row, int column);
public boolean isCellSelected(int row, int column);
public boolean isColumnSelected(int column);
public boolean isEditing();
public boolean isOpaque();
```

```
        public boolean isRowSelected(int row);
        public void moveColumn(int fromColumn, int toColumn);
        public Component prepareEditor(TableCellEditor e, int row, int column);
        public void removeColumn(TableColumn column);
        public void removeColumnSelectionInterval(int index0, int index1);
        public void removeEditor();
        public void removeRowSelectionInterval(int index0, int index1);
        public int rowAtPoint(Point p);
        public void selectAll();
        public void setAutoCreateColumnsFromModel(boolean b);
        public void setAutoResizeMode(int mode);
        public void setCellEditor(TableCellEditor e);
        public void setCellSelectionEnabled(boolean b);
        public void setColumnModel(TableColumnModel tcm);
        public void setColumnSelectionAllowed(boolean b);
        public void setColumnSelectionInterval(int index0, int index1);
        public void setDefaultEditor(Class c, TableCellEditor e);
        public void setDefaultRenderer(Class c, TableCellRenderer r);
        public void setEditingColumn(int column);
        public void setEditingRow(int row);
        public void setGridColor(Color color);
        public void setIntercellSpacing(Dimension dim);
        public void setModel(TableModel tm);
        public void setPreferredScrollableViewportSize(Dimension dim);
        public void setRowHeight(int height);
        public void setRowSelectionAllowed(boolean b);
        public void setRowSelectionInterval(int index0, int index1);
        public void setSelectionBackground(Color color);
        public void setSelectionForeground(Color color);
        public void setSelectionMode(int mode);
        public void setSelectionModel(ListSelectionModel lsm);
        public void setShowGrid(boolean b);
        public void setShowHorizontalLines(boolean b);
        public void setShowVerticalLines(boolean b);
        public void setTableHeader(JTableHeader header);
        public void setUI(TableUI ui);
        public void setValueAt(Object obj, int row, int column);
        public void sizeColumnsToFit(boolean b);
        public void tableChanged(TableModelEvent e);
        public void updateUI();
        public void valueChanged(ListSelectionEvent e);
    }
```

For `JTable`, you'll create a custom Model, cell renderer, and cell editor. You'll also be able to set several options by visual controls.

> **NOTE**
>
> The designers of `JTable` did not intend for it to be used as a spreadsheet. The underlying data Model of a table tends to be heavyweight (full), where a spreadsheet's Model tends to be sparsely populated.

TableModel

The `TableModel` interface defines the underlying data structure of a `JTable`.

```
public interface TableModel {
   public abstract void addTableModelListener(TableModelListener l);
   public abstract Class getColumnClass(int column);
   public abstract int getColumnCount();
   public abstract String getColumnName(int column);
   public abstract int getRowCount();
   public abstract Object getValueAt(int row, int column);
   public abstract boolean isCellEditable(int row, int column);
   public abstract void removeTableModelListener(TableModelListener l);
   public abstract void setValueAt(Object obj, int row, int column);
}
```

To create your own data Model, you could implement all the methods to satisfy your needs. However, like `ListModel` and `AbstractListModel`, the behavior for managing the listener list would be common for all data Models. There is a class, like `AbstractListModel`, called `AbstractTableModel` that handles this for us:

```
public abstract class AbstractTableModel implements TableModel,
      Serializable {
   protected EventListenerList listenerList;
   public AbstractTableModel();
   public void addTableModelListener(TableModelListener l);
   public int findColumn(String columnName);
   protected void fireTableCellUpdated(int row, int column);
   protected void fireTableChanged(TableModelEvent e);
   protected void fireTableDataChanged();
   protected void fireTableRowsDeleted(int firstRow, int lastRow);
   protected void fireTableRowsInserted(int firstRow, int lastRow);
   protected void fireTableRowsUpdated(int firstRow, int lastRow);
   protected void fireTableStructureChanged();
```

```
    public Class getColumnClass(int column);
    public String getColumnName(int column);
    public boolean isCellEditable(int row, int column);
    public void removeTableModelListener(TableModelListener l);
    public void setValueAt(Object obj, int row, int column);
}
```

If you compare TableModel and AbstractTableModel, you'll notice that some methods are missing: getColumnCount(), getRowCount(), and getValueAt(). These are the methods that a specific table Model would need to implement. For an editable Model, you would also need to implement setValueAt(). There is a support class for managing the data structure, too: DefaultTableModel.

```
public class DefaultTableModel extends AbstractTableModel
    implements Serializable {
  public DefaultTableModel();
  public DefaultTableModel(int, int);
  public DefaultTableModel(Object[], int);
  public DefaultTableModel(Object[][], Object[]);
  public DefaultTableModel(Vector, int);
  public DefaultTableModel(Vector, Vector);
  public void addColumn(Object);
  public void addColumn(Object, Object[]);
  public void addColumn(Object, Vector);
  public void addRow(Object[]);
  public void addRow(Vector);
  public int getColumnCount();
  public String getColumnName(int);
  public Vector getDataVector();
  public int getRowCount();
  public Object getValueAt(int, int);
  public void insertRow(int, Object[]);
  public void insertRow(int, Vector);
  public boolean isCellEditable(int, int);
  public void moveRow(int, int, int);
  public void newDataAvailable(TableModelEvent);
  public void newRowsAdded(TableModelEvent);
  public void removeRow(int);
  public void rowsRemoved(TableModelEvent);
  public void setColumnIdentifiers(Object[]);
  public void setColumnIdentifiers(Vector);
  public void setDataVector(Object[][], Object[]);
```

```
  public void setDataVector(Vector, Vector);
  public void setNumRows(int);
  public void setValueAt(Object, int, int);
}
```

To demonstrate working with your own table Model, you'll create a Model with three columns, a non-editable identifier, a name, and a favorite color. If you were to use this Model, the last column would display a less than desirable result. When `TableCellRenderer` is discussed later, you'll see a better rendering for color displayed.

```
class MyTableModel extends DefaultTableModel {
  Object data[][] = {
    {"Willie", Color.red},
    {"Ned", Color.orange},
    {"Homer", Color.yellow},
    {"Barney", Color.green},
    {"Marge", Color.blue},
    {"Bart", Color.magenta},
    {"Lisa", Color.cyan},
    {"Maggie", Color.pink},
    {"Troy", Color.black},
    {"Moe", Color.gray}
  };
  MyTableModel() {
    setColumnIdentifiers (new String[] {"ID", "Name", "Color"});
    for (int i=0,n=data.length;i<n;i++)
      addRow (new Object[] {new Integer (i+1), data[i][0], data[i][1]});
  }
  public boolean isCellEditable (int row, int column) {
    return (column != 0);
  }
}
```

To listen for changes to the table Model, you would register a `TableModel-Listener`. Then when the Model changes, you would be notified with a `TableModelEvent`.

```
public interface TableModelListener extends EventListener {
  public abstract void tableChanged(TableModelEvent e);
}

public class TableModelEvent extends EventObject {
```

```
    public static final int ALL_COLUMNS;
    public static final int DELETE;
    public static final int HEADER_ROW;
    public static final int INSERT;
    public static final int UPDATE;
    public TableModelEvent(TableModel model);
    public TableModelEvent(TableModel model, int row);
    public TableModelEvent(TableModel model, int firstRow, int lastRow);
    public TableModelEvent(TableModel model, int firstRow, int lastRow,
      int column);
    public TableModelEvent(TableModel model, int firstRow, int lastRow,
      int column, int type);
    public int getColumn();
    public int getFirstRow();
    public int getLastRow();
    public int getType();
}
```

TableColumnModel

The Model for each column with a table is described by the TableColumnModel interface.

```
    public interface TableColumnModel {
      public abstract void addColumn(TableColumn column);
      public abstract void addColumnModelListener(TableColumnModelListener l
      public abstract TableColumn getColumn(int col);
      public abstract int getColumnCount();
      public abstract int getColumnIndex(Object obj);
      public abstract int getColumnIndexAtX(int xPos);
      public abstract int getColumnMargin();
      public abstract boolean getColumnSelectionAllowed();
      public abstract Enumeration getColumns();
      public abstract int getSelectedColumnCount();
      public abstract int[] getSelectedColumns();
      public abstract ListSelectionModel getSelectionModel();
      public abstract int getTotalColumnWidth();
      public abstract void moveColumn(int fromColumn, int toColumn);
      public abstract void removeColumn(TableColumn column);
      public abstract void removeColumnModelListener(
        TableColumnModelListener l);
      public abstract void setColumnMargin(int margin);
```

```
    public abstract void setColumnSelectionAllowed(boolean b);
    public abstract void setSelectionModel(ListSelectionModel model);
  }
```

In most cases, the `DefaultTableColumnModel` implementation is sufficient. It adds support for managing the list of `TableColumnModelListeners`, among other things.

```
  public class DefaultTableColumnModel implements TableColumnModel,
      PropertyChangeListener, ListSelectionListener, Serializable {
    protected transient ChangeEvent changeEvent;
    protected int columnMargin;
    protected boolean columnSelectionAllowed;
    protected EventListenerList listenerList;
    protected ListSelectionModel selectionModel;
    protected Vector tableColumns;
    protected int totalColumnWidth;
    public DefaultTableColumnModel();
    public void addColumn(TableColumn column);
    public void addColumnModelListener(TableColumnModelListener l);
    protected ListSelectionModel createSelectionModel();
    protected void fireColumnAdded(TableColumnModelEvent e);
    protected void fireColumnMarginChanged();
    protected void fireColumnMoved(TableColumnModelEvent e);
    protected void fireColumnRemoved(TableColumnModelEvent e);
    protected void fireColumnSelectionChanged(ListSelectionEvent e);
    public TableColumn getColumn(int column);
    public int getColumnCount();
    public int getColumnIndex(Object obj);
    public int getColumnIndexAtX(int xPos);
    public int getColumnMargin();
    public boolean getColumnSelectionAllowed();
    public Enumeration getColumns();
    public int getSelectedColumnCount();
    public int[] getSelectedColumns();
    public ListSelectionModel getSelectionModel();
    public int getTotalColumnWidth();
    public void moveColumn(int fromColumn, int toColumn);
    public void propertyChange(PropertyChangeEvent e);
    protected void recalcWidthCache();
    public void removeColumn(TableColumn column);
    public void removeColumnModelListener(TableColumnModelListener l);
    public void setColumnMargin(int margin);
    public void setColumnSelectionAllowed(boolean b);
```

```
        public void setSelectionModel(ListSelectionModel model);
        public void valueChanged(ListSelectionEvent e);
    }
```

The TableColumnModelListener interface describes the events that can happen to alter the TableColumnModel. You would either receive a TableColumnModel-Event, ListSelectionEvent (described earlier), or ChangeEvent, depending upon the actual event that happens.

```
    public interface TableColumnModelListener extends EventListener {
        public abstract void columnAdded(TableColumnModelEvent e);
        public abstract void columnMarginChanged(ChangeEvent e);
        public abstract void columnMoved(TableColumnModelEvent e);
        public abstract void columnRemoved(TableColumnModelEvent e);
        public abstract void columnSelectionChanged(ListSelectionEvent e);
    }

    public class TableColumnModelEvent extends EventObject {
        public TableColumnModelEvent(TableColumnModel source, int from, int to);
        public int getFromIndex();
        public int getToIndex();
    }

    public class ChangeEvent extends EventObject {
        public ChangeEvent(Object source);
    }
```

ListSelectionModel Revisited

The ListSelectionModel defines the selection capabilities. What is selectable depends on what is enabled: for column selection, the View (JTable) controls this with the setColumnSelectionAllowed(boolean) method; for row selection, the method is setRowSelectionAllowed(boolean); and, to get at cell-level selection, the method is setCellSelectionEnabled(boolean). When cell-level selection is enabled, the state of the other two are not changed, they are just overridden. Again, the three constants of ListSelectionModel are important: SINGLE_SELECTION, SINGLE_INTERVAL_SELECTION, or MULTIPLE_INTERVAL_SELECTION.

To demonstrate the effects of different Models, the following methods will scroll through the different modes and selection Models.

```
    JButton selectionType = new JButton ("Next Type");
    selectionType.addActionListener (new ActionListener() {
```

```
    public void actionPerformed (ActionEvent e) {
      boolean rowSet = jt.getRowSelectionAllowed();
      boolean colSet = jt.getColumnSelectionAllowed();
      boolean cellSet = jt.getCellSelectionEnabled();
      // think binary arithmetic
      boolean setRow = !rowSet;
      boolean setCol = rowSet ^ colSet;
      boolean setCell = rowSet & colSet; // only toggled on
      jt.setRowSelectionAllowed(setRow);
      jt.setColumnSelectionAllowed(setCol);
      jt.setCellSelectionEnabled(setCell);
      System.out.println ("Row Selection Allowed? " + setRow);
      System.out.println ("Column Selection Allowed? " + setCol);
      System.out.println ("Cell Selection Enabled? " + setCell);
      jt.repaint();
    }
});
JButton selectionMode = new JButton ("Next Mode");
selectionMode.addActionListener (new ActionListener() {
  public void actionPerformed (ActionEvent e) {
    ListSelectionModel lsm = jt.getSelectionModel();
    int mode = lsm.getSelectionMode();
    int nextMode;
    String nextModeString;
    if (mode == ListSelectionModel.SINGLE_SELECTION) {
      nextMode = ListSelectionModel.SINGLE_INTERVAL_SELECTION;
      nextModeString = "Single Interval Selection";
    } else if (mode == ListSelectionModel.SINGLE_INTERVAL_SELECTION) {
      nextMode = ListSelectionModel.MULTIPLE_INTERVAL_SELECTION;
      nextModeString = "Multiple Interval Selection";
    } else {
      nextMode = ListSelectionModel.SINGLE_SELECTION;
      nextModeString = "Single Selection";
    }
    lsm.setSelectionMode(nextMode);
    System.out.println ("Selection Mode: " + nextModeString);
    jt.repaint();
  }
});
```

TableCellRenderer

The TableCellRenderer interface describes how to customize the display of a particular cell.

```
public interface TableCellRenderer {
  public abstract Component getTableCellRendererComponent(JTable table,
    Object value, boolean isSelected, boolean hasFocus, int row, int col);
}
```

The tree cell rendering works similarly to the ListCellRenderer. Whatever object was passed in for a particular column of the data Model will be passed in to the value parameter of the getTableCellRendererComponent() method. Keep in mind that the Model has no concept of where the column will physically be displayed in the View. What is column 1 in the Model could be column 3 in the View.

For your renderer here, you're going to create a custom renderer for the third column, the color object in the Model. You'll make the whole cell the color value, and change the border when selected.

```
class MyTableCellRenderer extends JLabel implements TableCellRenderer {
  final Border blueBorder = BorderFactory.createLineBorder(Color.blue);
  MyTableCellRenderer () {
    setOpaque (true);
  }
  public Component getTableCellRendererComponent(JTable table,
    Object value, boolean isSelected, boolean hasFocus, int row, int col)
  {
    setBackground((Color)value);
    if (isSelected)
      setBorder (blueBorder);
    else
      setBorder (BorderFactory.createEmptyBorder());
    return this;
  }
}
```

When you install a table cell renderer, you specify the specific column you want the renderer to be used for with the following:

```
TableColumnModel tcm = jt.getColumnModel();
TableColumn column = tcm.getColumn (tcm.getColumnCount()-1);
TableCellRenderer renderer = new MyTableCellRenderer();
column.setCellRenderer (renderer);
```

Figure 15.13 shows what everything so far put together would look like.

And, here is the complete source for the program.

```java
import javax.swing.*;
import javax.swing.border.*;
import javax.swing.event.*;
import javax.swing.table.*;
import java.awt.*;
import java.awt.event.*;
import java.util.*;

public class TableIt {

  class MyTableCellRenderer extends JLabel implements TableCellRenderer {
    final Border blueBorder = BorderFactory.createLineBorder(Color.blue);
    MyTableCellRenderer () {
      setOpaque (true);
    }
    public Component getTableCellRendererComponent(JTable table, Object
        value, boolean isSelected, boolean hasFocus, int row, int col) {
      setBackground((Color)value);
      if (isSelected)
        setBorder (blueBorder);
      else
        setBorder (BorderFactory.createEmptyBorder());
      return this;
    }
  }
}
```

```
class MyTableModel extends DefaultTableModel {
  Object data[][] = {
    {"Willie", Color.red},
    {"Ned", Color.orange},
    {"Homer", Color.yellow},
    {"Barney", Color.green},
    {"Marge", Color.blue},
    {"Bart", Color.magenta},
    {"Lisa", Color.cyan},
    {"Maggie", Color.pink},
    {"Troy", Color.black},
    {"Moe", Color.gray}
  };
  MyTableModel() {
    setColumnIdentifiers (new String[] {"ID", "Name", "Color"});
    for (int i=0,n=data.length;i<n;i++)
      addRow (new Object[] {new Integer (i+1), data[i][0], data[i][1]});
  }
  public boolean isCellEditable (int row, int column) {
    return (column != 0);
  }
}

public TableIt() {
  JFrame f = new JFrame ("Tables");
  TableModel tm = new MyTableModel ();
  final JTable jt = new JTable (tm);

  TableColumnModel tcm = jt.getColumnModel();
  TableColumn column = tcm.getColumn (tcm.getColumnCount()-1);
  TableCellRenderer renderer = new MyTableCellRenderer();
  column.setCellRenderer (renderer);

  JButton selectionType = new JButton ("Next Type");
  selectionType.addActionListener (new ActionListener() {
    public void actionPerformed (ActionEvent e) {
      boolean rowSet = jt.getRowSelectionAllowed();
      boolean colSet = jt.getColumnSelectionAllowed();
      boolean cellSet = jt.getCellSelectionEnabled();
      // think binary arithmetic
      boolean setRow = !rowSet;
```

```
          boolean setCol = rowSet ^ colSet;
          boolean setCell = rowSet & colSet;
          jt.setRowSelectionAllowed(setRow);
          jt.setColumnSelectionAllowed(setCol);
          jt.setCellSelectionEnabled(setCell);
          System.out.println ("Row Selection Allowed? " + setRow);
          System.out.println ("Column Selection Allowed? " + setCol);
          System.out.println ("Cell Selection Enabled? " + setCell);
          jt.repaint();
      }
    });
    JButton selectionMode = new JButton ("Next Mode");
    selectionMode.addActionListener (new ActionListener() {
      public void actionPerformed (ActionEvent e) {
        ListSelectionModel lsm = jt.getSelectionModel();
        int mode = lsm.getSelectionMode();
        int nextMode;
        String nextModeString;
        if (mode == ListSelectionModel.SINGLE_SELECTION) {
          nextMode = ListSelectionModel.SINGLE_INTERVAL_SELECTION;
          nextModeString = "Single Interval Selection";
        } else if (mode == ListSelectionModel.SINGLE_INTERVAL_SELECTION) {
          nextMode = ListSelectionModel.MULTIPLE_INTERVAL_SELECTION;
          nextModeString = "Multiple Interval Selection";
        } else {
          nextMode = ListSelectionModel.SINGLE_SELECTION;
          nextModeString = "Single Selection";
        }
        lsm.setSelectionMode(nextMode);
        System.out.println ("Selection Mode: " + nextModeString);
        jt.repaint();
      }
    });
    JPanel jp = new JPanel();
    jp.add (selectionType);
    jp.add (selectionMode);
    JScrollPane jsp = new JScrollPane (jt);
    Container c = f.getContentPane();
    c.add (jsp, BorderLayout.CENTER);
    c.add (jp, BorderLayout.SOUTH);
    f.addWindowListener (new WindowAdapter() {
```

```
          public void windowClosing (WindowEvent e) {
             System.exit(0);
          }
      });
      f.setSize(300, 250);
      f.show();
   }

   public static void main (String args[]) {
      new TableIt();
   }
}
```

TableCellEditor

If you run the program and double-click on a cell that isn't in the first column, you will be able to edit the contents of the cell. This works fine for the name column. However, for the color column, this fails miserably. You need to install a custom TableCellEditor.

```
public interface TableCellEditor extends CellEditor {
   public abstract Component getTableCellEditorComponent(JTable table,
      Object value, boolean isSelected, int row, int column);
}
```

The table cell editor works similarly to table cell renderer, except it is used for editing the contents. Most of the work of cell editing is defined by the CellEditor interface.

```
public interface CellEditor {
   public abstract void addCellEditorListener(CellEditorListener l);
   public abstract void cancelCellEditing();
   public abstract Object getCellEditorValue();
   public abstract boolean isCellEditable(EventObject e);
   public abstract void removeCellEditorListener(CellEditorListener l);
   public abstract boolean shouldSelectCell(EventObject e);
   public abstract boolean stopCellEditing();
}
```

By default, the editor for everything in a table is DefaultCellEditor, a text field, which in the case of a color is not appropriate, since it can't convert the text string displayed into a Color object.

```
public class DefaultCellEditor implements TableCellEditor, TreeCellEditor,
   java.io.Serializable {
```

```
      protected transient ChangeEvent changeEvent;
      protected int clickCountToStart;
      protected DefaultCellEditor.EditorDelegate delegate;
      protected JComponent editorComponent;
      protected EventListenerList listenerList;
      public DefaultCellEditor(JCheckBox jc);
      public DefaultCellEditor(JComboBox jc);
      public DefaultCellEditor(JTextField jt);
      public void addCellEditorListener(CellEditorListener l);
      public void cancelCellEditing();
      protected void fireEditingCanceled();
      protected void fireEditingStopped();
      public Object getCellEditorValue();
      public int getClickCountToStart();
      public Component getComponent();
      public Component getTableCellEditorComponent(JTable table, Object value,
        boolean isSelected, int row, int column);
      public Component getTreeCellEditorComponent(JTree tree, Object value,
        boolean isSelected, boolean isExpanded, boolean isLeaf, int row);
      public boolean isCellEditable(EventObject e);
      public void removeCellEditorListener(CellEditorListener l);
      public void setClickCountToStart(int count);
      public boolean shouldSelectCell(EventObject e);
      public boolean stopCellEditing();
    }
```

By defining our own TableCellEditor, we can make a JColorChooser work as our color editor. Most of the work is in implementing the CellEditor interface. Since the actual table cell is changed to a JButton, the JColorChooser is made to appear outside the table.

```
class MyColorChooser extends JButton implements TableCellEditor {
    final int CLICK_COUNT_TO_START = 2;
    protected EventListenerList listenerList = new EventListenerList();
    transient protected ChangeEvent changeEvent = null;

    public void addCellEditorListener(CellEditorListener l) {
      listenerList.add(CellEditorListener.class, l);
    }
    public void removeCellEditorListener(CellEditorListener l) {
      listenerList.remove(CellEditorListener.class, l);
    }
```

```java
public void cancelCellEditing() {
  Object[] listeners = listenerList.getListenerList();
  for (int i=listeners.length-2; i>=0; i-=2) {
    if (listeners[i]==CellEditorListener.class) {
      if (changeEvent == null)
        changeEvent = new ChangeEvent(this);
      ((CellEditorListener)listeners[i+1]).editingCanceled(changeEvent);
    }
  }
}
public Object getCellEditorValue() {
  return getBackground();
}
public boolean isCellEditable(EventObject e) {
  boolean retValue = false;
  if (e instanceof MouseEvent) {
    if (((MouseEvent)e).getClickCount() >= CLICK_COUNT_TO_START) {
      requestFocus();
      retValue = true;
    }
  }
  return retValue;
}
public boolean shouldSelectCell(EventObject e) {
  boolean retValue = false;
  if (isCellEditable(e)) {
    if (e == null || ((MouseEvent)e).getClickCount() >=
        CLICK_COUNT_TO_START) {
      requestFocus();
      retValue = true;
    }
  }
  return retValue;
}
public boolean stopCellEditing() {
  Object[] listeners = listenerList.getListenerList();
  for (int i=listeners.length-2; i>=0; i-=2) {
    if (listeners[i]==CellEditorListener.class) {
      if (changeEvent == null)
        changeEvent = new ChangeEvent(this);
      ((CellEditorListener)listeners[i+1]).editingStopped(changeEvent);
    }
  }
```

```
      return true;
    }
    private void changeColor(Color c) {
      if (c != null)
        setBackground (c);
      setForeground ((c == Color.black) ? Color.white : Color.black);
    }
    public Component getTableCellEditorComponent (JTable table,
        Object value, boolean isSelected, int row, int column) {
      changeColor((Color)value);
      addActionListener(new ActionListener() {
        public void actionPerformed (ActionEvent e) {
          Color color = JColorChooser.showDialog(MyColorChooser.this,
            "Color Chooser", MyColorChooser.this.getBackground());
          MyColorChooser.this.changeColor(color);
        }
      });
      return this;
    }
  }
```

Installation of a `TableCellEditor` is similar to a `TabelCellRenderer`.

```
TableCellEditor editor = new MyColorChooser();
column.setCellEditor (editor);
```

Once installed, activating the editor would bring up a `JColorChooser`, like in Figure 15.8, for the user to change the colors.

Advanced Text Support

When using all the different `JTextComponent` subclasses, you are always using the MVC architecture. Thankfully, this is mostly hidden from you, and you don't have to deal with MVC if you don't want to. The data Model for all the text components is `Document`. A `Document` is made of various `Element` objects to describe the structure of the document. An `AttributeSet` describes the contents of each `Element`. The actual View of the document is `View`. All the text support classes are found in the `javax.swing.text` package and subpackages.

As the different components are described, you'll build a text field that only accepts floating-point numeric input. It could easily be modified, though, to only accept ranges or integer input instead.

Document

The Document interface describes a structure for holding the content of a text component. Technically speaking, the structure can hold content that isn't text. It would then be up to the control to determine how to display something like an image file.

```java
public interface Document {
    public static final String StreamDescriptionProperty;
    public static final String TitleProperty;
    public abstract void addDocumentListener(DocumentListener l);
    public abstract void addUndoableEditListener(UndoableEditListener l);
    public abstract Position createPosition(int offset)
        throws BadLocationException;
    public abstract Element getDefaultRootElement();
    public abstract Position getEndPosition();
    public abstract int getLength();
    public abstract Object getProperty(Object key);
    public abstract Element[] getRootElements();
    public abstract Position getStartPosition();
    public abstract String getText(int offset, int length)
        throws BadLocationException;
    public abstract void getText(int offset, int length, Segment segment)
        throws BadLocationException;
    public abstract void insertString(int offset, String str, AttributeSet as)
        throws BadLocationException;
    public abstract void putProperty(Object key, Object value);
    public abstract void remove(int offset, int length)
        throws BadLocationException;
    public abstract void removeDocumentListener(DocumentListener l);
    public abstract void removeUndoableEditListener(UndoableEditListener l);
    public abstract void render(Runnable r);
}
```

The AbstractDocument is a specific Document implementation that serves as the basis for all the text components, since things like managing listener lists are common to all Document implementers. In addition to managing listener lists, AbstractDocument serves as a gatekeeper for content modifications.

```java
public abstract class AbstractDocument implements Document, Serializable {
    protected static final String BAD_LOCATION;
    public static final String ContentElementName;
```

```
public static final String ElementNameAttribute;
public static final String ParagraphElementName;
public static final String SectionElementName;
protected EventListenerList listenerList;
protected AbstractDocument(AbstractDocument.Content data);
protected AbstractDocument(AbstractDocument.Content data,
  AbstractDocument.AttributeContext context);
public void addDocumentListener(DocumentListener l);
public void addUndoableEditListener(UndoableEditListener l);
protected Element createBranchElement(Element parent, AttributeSet set);
protected Element createLeafElement(Element parent, AttributeSet set,
  int pos0, int pos1);
public synchronized Position createPosition(int offset)
  throws BadLocationException;
public void dump(PrintStream stream);
protected void fireChangedUpdate(DocumentEvent e);
protected void fireInsertUpdate(DocumentEvent e);
protected void fireRemoveUpdate(DocumentEvent e);
protected void fireUndoableEditUpdate(UndoableEditEvent e);
protected final AbstractDocument.AttributeContext getAttributeContext();
protected final AbstractDocument.Content getContent();
protected final synchronized Thread getCurrentWriter();
public abstract Element getDefaultRootElement();
public Dictionary getDocumentProperties();
public final Position getEndPosition();
public int getLength();
public final Object getProperty(Object key);
public Element[] getRootElements();
public final Position getStartPosition();
public String getText(int offset, int length) throws BadLocationException;
public void getText(int offset, int length, Segment segment)
  throws BadLocationException;
public void insertString(int offset, String str, AttributeSet as)
  throws BadLocationException;
protected void insertUpdate(AbstractDocument.DefaultDocumentEvent e,
AttributeSet set);
public final void putProperty(Object key, Object value);
protected final synchronized void readLock();
protected final synchronized void readUnlock();
public void remove(int offset, int length) throws BadLocationException;
public void removeDocumentListener(DocumentListener l);
public void removeUndoableEditListener(UndoableEditListener l);
```

```
    protected void removeUpdate(AbstractDocument.DefaultDocumentEvent e);
    public void render(Runnable r);
    public void setDocumentProperties(Dictionary d);
    protected final synchronized void writeLock();
    protected final synchronized void writeUnlock();
}
```

The two concrete implementations are PlainDocument and DefaultStyled-Document. PlainDocument offers a document for a single font and color style. You'll create a subclass of this for our NumericInputField.

```
public class PlainDocument extends AbstractDocument {
    public static final String lineLimitAttribute;
    public static final String tabSizeAttribute;
    public PlainDocument();
    protected PlainDocument(AbstractDocument.Content content);
    protected AbstractDocument.AbstractElement createDefaultRoot();
    public Element getDefaultRootElement();
    protected void insertUpdate(AbstractDocument.DefaultDocumentEvent e,
        AttributeSet set);
    protected void removeUpdate(AbstractDocument.DefaultDocumentEvent e);
}
```

For a document to accept floating point input, or any customized input, you only have to override two methods: insertString() and remove(), both from AbstractDocument. Here is the definition of our FloatingPointNumberDocument class.

```
import javax.swing.text.*;

public class FloatingPointNumberDocument extends PlainDocument {
    private float currentValue;

    public FloatingPointNumberDocument(float initialValue) {
        currentValue = initialValue;
    }
    public float getValue() {
        return currentValue;
    }
    public void insertString(int offset, String str, AttributeSet attr)
        throws BadLocationException {
        if (str!=null) {
            String newValue = null;
```

```java
      if (getLength() == 0) { // Nothing there yet
        newValue = str;
      } else {
        String currentContent = getText(0, getLength());
        StringBuffer sb = new StringBuffer (currentContent);
        sb.insert (offset, str);
        newValue = sb.toString();
      }
      boolean valid = false;
      try {
        Float f = Float.valueOf (newValue);
        float ff = f.floatValue();
        if (currentValue == ff) return;
        currentValue = ff;
        valid = true; // No exception thrown
      } catch (NumberFormatException e) {
      }
      if (valid) {
        super.insertString (offset, str, attr);
      } else {
        java.awt.Toolkit.getDefaultToolkit().beep();
      }
    }
  }
  public void remove(int offset, int length) throws
BadLocationException {
    if (length == getLength()) {
      currentValue = 0.0f;
      super.remove (offset, length);
    } else {
      String newValue = null;
      if ((offset + length) == getLength()) {
        // delete from end
        newValue = getText(0, offset);
      } else {
        // delete from middle
        String currentContent = getText(0, getLength());
        newValue = currentContent.substring (0, offset) +
          currentContent.substring (offset+1, currentContent.length());
      }
      boolean valid = false;
      try {
```

```
            Float f = Float.valueOf (newValue);
            float ff = f.floatValue();
            if (currentValue == ff) return;
            currentValue = ff;
            valid = true; // No exception thrown
          } catch (NumberFormatException e) {
          }
          if (valid) {
            super.remove (offset, length);
          } else {
            java.awt.Toolkit.getDefaultToolkit().beep();
          }
        }
      }
    }
```

NOTE

Because the input must always be a valid floating-point number, there are some awkward characteristics. To enter a negative number, you must enter a digit first, prior to entering the negative sign before it. To enter a decimal point, you must first enter a digit after the decimal point, then go back and put in the decimal point.

To demonstrate the new Document, the following FloatingTextField class can be used as an input field that only accepts floating-point numbers. There is a test program in main() to demonstrate.

```
import java.awt.*;
import java.awt.event.*;
import javax.swing.*;

public class FloatTextField extends JTextField {
  public FloatTextField () {
    this (0.0f);
  }
  public FloatTextField (float f) {
    this (f, 10);
  }
  public FloatTextField (float f, int columns) {
    super (new FloatingPointNumberDocument(f), String.valueOf (f),
columns);
  }
  public float getValue () {
```

```
          return ((FloatingPointNumberDocument)getDocument()).getValue();
        }
        public static void main (String args[]) {
          JFrame f = new JFrame ("Tables");
          FloatTextField ftf1 = new FloatTextField ();
          ftf1.setText ("4.5"); // invalid value would fail
          FloatTextField ftf2 = new FloatTextField ((float)Math.PI, 20);
          Container c = f.getContentPane();
          c.add (ftf1, BorderLayout.NORTH);
          c.add (ftf2, BorderLayout.SOUTH);
          f.addWindowListener (new WindowAdapter() {
            public void windowClosing (WindowEvent e) {
              System.exit(0);
            }
          });
          f.setSize(300, 250);
          f.show();
        }
      }
```

`DefaultStyledDocument` is for highly formatted content, like HTML.

```
public class DefaultStyledDocument extends AbstractDocument
    implements StyledDocument {
  public static final int BUFFER_SIZE_DEFAULT;
  public DefaultStyledDocument();
  public DefaultStyledDocument(AbstractDocument.Content c, StyleContext s);
  public DefaultStyledDocument(StyleContext s);
  public Style addStyle(String name, Style parent);
  protected AbstractDocument.AbstractElement createDefaultRoot();
  public Color getBackground(AttributeSet set);
  public Element getCharacterElement(int pos);
  public Element getDefaultRootElement();
  public Font getFont(AttributeSet attr);
  public Color getForeground(AttributeSet attr);
  public Style getLogicalStyle(int position);
  public Element getParagraphElement(int position);
  public Style getStyle(String name);
  protected void insert(int offset, DefaultStyledDocument.ElementSpec
    data[]) throws BadLocationException;
  protected void insertUpdate(AbstractDocument.DefaultDocumentEvent e,
    AttributeSet attr);
  public void removeStyle(String name);
```

```
    protected void removeUpdate(AbstractDocument.DefaultDocumentEvent e);
    public void setCharacterAttributes(int offset, int length,
      AttributeSet attr, boolean replace);
    public void setLogicalStyle(int position, Style style);
    public void setParagraphAttributes(int offset, int length,
      AttributeSet attr, boolean replace);
}
```

First you'll see how to specify the text attributes for different elements of the document, then `DefaultStyledDocument` will be described.

If you are interested in when the underlying Model of a text component changes, you can register a `DocumentListener`. This allows you to get `DocumentEvent` objects when the contents change. If you are trying to limit what goes into the Model, create a new `Document` type, do not wait for the Model to change, and then check if the value is changed.

```
public interface DocumentListener extends EventListener {
    public abstract void changedUpdate(DocumentEvent e);
    public abstract void insertUpdate(DocumentEvent e);
    public abstract void removeUpdate(DocumentEvent e);
}

public interface DocumentEvent {
    public abstract DocumentEvent.ElementChange getChange(Element element);
    public abstract Document getDocument();
    public abstract int getLength();
    public abstract int getOffset();
    public abstract DocumentEvent.EventType getType();
}
```

Element

Each of the pieces of a document that are manipulated is an `Element`. For instance, if you tell a paragraph to be right justified, the paragraph is the element.

```
public interface Element {
    public abstract AttributeSet getAttributes();
    public abstract Document getDocument();
    public abstract Element getElement(int);
    public abstract int getElementCount();
    public abstract int getElementIndex(int);
    public abstract int getEndOffset();
```

```
    public abstract String getName();
    public abstract Element getParentElement();
    public abstract int getStartOffset();
    public abstract boolean isLeaf();
}
```

Various public inner classes of `AbstractDocument` describe specific implementations. In general, you insert or modify text to have a specific attribute set, described next. The elements are then created to maintain the set of attributes.

AttributeSet and *JTextPane*

To configure the attributes of an element, you get to work with many different classes. The basic interface is `AttributeSet`. It describes a read-only collection of attributes. When setting attributes, you need to be able to add to the collection. This involves the `MutableAttributeSet` interface. The `SimpleAttributeSet` is the concrete implementation you use to set attributes up. One set of attributes could be 36-point bold text. Another set could be right-justified blue text. To add attributes to a set, you pass off the set to an object. So, the specific methods of the classes are irrelevant.

You modify the attribute set with `StyleContext`, through a series of methods, like `setFontSize()`, `setLineSpacing()`, and even `setComponent()`.

```
    public class StyleConstants {
      public static final int ALIGN_CENTER;
      public static final int ALIGN_JUSTIFIED;
      public static final int ALIGN_LEFT;
      public static final int ALIGN_RIGHT;
      public static final Object Alignment;
      public static final Object Background;
      public static final Object Bold;
      public static final Object ComponentAttribute;
      public static final String ComponentElementName;
      public static final Object FirstLineIndent;
      public static final Object FontFamily;
      public static final Object FontSize;
      public static final Object Foreground;
      public static final Object IconAttribute;
      public static final String IconElementName;
      public static final Object Italic;
      public static final Object LeftIndent;
```

```
        public static final Object LineSpacing;
        public static final Object NameAttribute;
        public static final Object ResolveAttribute;
        public static final Object RightIndent;
        public static final Object SpaceAbove;
        public static final Object SpaceBelow;
        public static final Object TabSet;
        public static final Object Underline;
        public static int getAlignment(AttributeSet set);
        public static Component getComponent(AttributeSet set);
        public static float getFirstLineIndent(AttributeSet set);
        public static String getFontFamily(AttributeSet set);
        public static int getFontSize(AttributeSet set);
        public static Color getForeground(AttributeSet set);
        public static Icon getIcon(AttributeSet set);
        public static float getLeftIndent(AttributeSet set);
        public static float getLineSpacing(AttributeSet set);
        public static float getRightIndent(AttributeSet set);
        public static float getSpaceAbove(AttributeSet set);
        public static float getSpaceBelow(AttributeSet set);
        public static TabSet getTabSet(AttributeSet set);
        public static boolean isBold(AttributeSet set);
        public static boolean isItalic(AttributeSet set);
        public static boolean isUnderline(AttributeSet set);
        public static void setAlignment(MutableAttributeSet set, int i);
        public static void setBold(MutableAttributeSet set, boolean b);
        public static void setComponent(MutableAttributeSet set, Component c);
        public static void setFirstLineIndent(MutableAttributeSet set, float f);
        public static void setFontFamily(MutableAttributeSet set, String s);
        public static void setFontSize(MutableAttributeSet set, int i);
        public static void setForeground(MutableAttributeSet set, Color c);
        public static void setIcon(MutableAttributeSet set, Icon i);
        public static void setItalic(MutableAttributeSet set, boolean b);
        public static void setLeftIndent(MutableAttributeSet set, float f);
        public static void setLineSpacing(MutableAttributeSet set, float f);
        public static void setRightIndent(MutableAttributeSet set, float f);
        public static void setSpaceAbove(MutableAttributeSet set, float f);
        public static void setSpaceBelow(MutableAttributeSet set, float f);
        public static void setTabSet(MutableAttributeSet set, TabSet t);
        public static void setUnderline(MutableAttributeSet set, boolean b);
        public String toString();
    }
```

So, to create a 36-point bold font, you would do the following:

```
SimpleAttributeSet bold36 = new SimpleAttributeSet();
StyleConstants.setFontSize(bold36, 36);
StyleConstants.setBold(bold36, true);
```

Once you have an `AttributeSet`, what do you do with it? Well, the `JTextPane` uses `DefaultStyledDocument` to support multi-format content. You can select content and change its attributes or add text with attributes.

```
public class JTextPane extends JEditorPane {
    public JTextPane();
    public JTextPane(StyledDocument doc);
    public Style addStyle(String name, Style parent);
    protected EditorKit createDefaultEditorKit();
    public AttributeSet getCharacterAttributes();
    public MutableAttributeSet getInputAttributes();
    public Style getLogicalStyle();
    public AttributeSet getParagraphAttributes();
    public boolean getScrollableTracksViewportWidth();
    public Style getStyle(String name);
    public StyledDocument getStyledDocument();
    protected final StyledEditorKit getStyledEditorKit();
    public String getUIClassID();
    public void insertComponent(Component comp);
    public void insertIcon(Icon icon);
    public void removeStyle(String name);
    public void replaceSelection(String content);
    public void setCharacterAttributes(AttributeSet set, boolean replace);
    public void setDocument(Document doc);
    public final void setEditorKit(EditorKit kit);
    public void setLogicalStyle(Style style);
    public void setParagraphAttributes(AttributeSet set, boolean replace);
    public void setStyledDocument(StyledDocument doc);
}
```

To add text with the `bold36` attribute from above, you would do the following:

```
JTextPane jtp = new JTextPane();
Document doc = jtp.getDocument();
try {
    doc.insertString(doc.getLength(), "Mastering Java", bold36);
} catch (BadLocationException e) {
    // Handle Exception
}
```

Figure 15.14 shows how this would appear. Normally, you would do this type of behavior from menu items against the highlighted text.

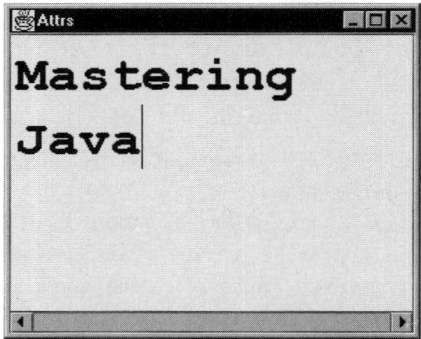

View

The View class primarily serves to paint() the Element objects that make up a Document. View objects are acquired from the UI delegates.

Editor Kits and Text Actions

Each text component uses an EditorKit to define the set of actions that can be done for the component. By default, the kit used is DefaultEditorKit, which defines behaviors for cut, copy, and paste support, as well as cursor movement. In addition, the specialized kit for HTML is HTMLEditorKit, and the custom kit for RTF is RTFEditorKit, both of which are based on StyledEditorKit. The StyledEditorKit defines behavior for changing font characteristics like size, type, and style.

Behavior like cut, copy, and paste are special Action objects called TextAction. They work by automatically finding the last focused text component performing the designated action against them.

```
public abstract class TextAction extends AbstractAction {
    public TextAction(String name);
    public static final Action[] augmentList(Action list1[], Action list2[]);
    protected final JTextComponent getFocusedComponent();
    protected final JTextComponent getTextComponent(ActionEvent e);
}
```

To use the actions associated with a text component, you get the list of actions and find the specific one you are looking for based on keys provided by the editor kits. This gives you an `ActionListener` that you can associate with a button, toolbar, menu item, or some other component. When the component is activated, the processing is automatically done against the last focused text component.

```
// get command table
Hashtable commands = new Hashtable();
Action actions[] = jt.getActions();
for (int i = 0,n=actions.length; i < n; i++) {
  Action a = actions[i];
  commands.put(a.getValue(Action.NAME), a);
}
// Find a specific command
Action cutAction = (Action)commands.get (DefaultEditorKit.cutAction);
```

The `DefaultEditorKit` class definition below shows the names of some actions you can find. Others are available through `StyledEditorKit` and `JTextField` even has one (`notifyAction`).

```
public class DefaultEditorKit extends EditorKit {
   public static final String backwardAction;
   public static final String beepAction;
   public static final String beginAction;
   public static final String beginLineAction;
   public static final String beginParagraphAction;
   public static final String beginWordAction;
   public static final String copyAction;
   public static final String cutAction;
   public static final String defaultKeyTypedAction;
   public static final String deleteNextCharAction;
   public static final String deletePrevCharAction;
   public static final String downAction;
   public static final String endAction;
   public static final String endLineAction;
   public static final String endParagraphAction;
   public static final String endWordAction;
   public static final String forwardAction;
   public static final String insertBreakAction;
   public static final String insertContentAction;
   public static final String insertTabAction;
   public static final String nextWordAction;
```

```java
    public static final String pageDownAction;
    public static final String pageUpAction;
    public static final String pasteAction;
    public static final String previousWordAction;
    public static final String readOnlyAction;
    public static final String selectAllAction;
    public static final String selectLineAction;
    public static final String selectParagraphAction;
    public static final String selectWordAction;
    public static final String selectionBackwardAction;
    public static final String selectionBeginAction;
    public static final String selectionBeginLineAction;
    public static final String selectionBeginParagraphAction;
    public static final String selectionBeginWordAction;
    public static final String selectionDownAction;
    public static final String selectionEndAction;
    public static final String selectionEndLineAction;
    public static final String selectionEndParagraphAction;
    public static final String selectionEndWordAction;
    public static final String selectionForwardAction;
    public static final String selectionNextWordAction;
    public static final String selectionPreviousWordAction;
    public static final String selectionUpAction;
    public static final String upAction;
    public static final String writableAction;
    public DefaultEditorKit();
    public Object clone();
    public Caret createCaret();
    public Document createDefaultDocument();
    public Action[] getActions();
    public String getContentType();
    public ViewFactory getViewFactory();
    public void read(InputStream stream, Document doc, int pos)
      throws IOException, BadLocationException;
    public void read(Reader reader, Document doc, int pos)
      throws IOException, BadLocationException;
    public void write(OutputStream stream, Document doc, int pos, int len)
      throws IOException, BadLocationException;
    public void write(Writer writer, Document doc, int pos, int len)
      throws IOException, BadLocationException;
}
```

HTML Viewer

The JEditorPane is used to display and edit specialized formatted text, like HTML or Rich-Text-Format (RTF).

```
public class JEditorPane extends JTextComponent {
  public JEditorPane();
  public JEditorPane(String urlString) throws IOException;
  public JEditorPane(URL initialPage) throws IOException;
  public static EditorKit createEditorKitForContentType(String type);
  public static void registerEditorKitForContentType(String type,
    String className);
  public synchronized void addHyperlinkListener(HyperlinkListener l);
  public void fireHyperlinkUpdate(HyperlinkEvent e);
  public AccessibleContext getAccessibleContext();
  public final String getContentType();
  public final EditorKit getEditorKit();
  public EditorKit getEditorKitForContentType(String type);
  public URL getPage();
  public boolean getScrollableTracksViewportWidth();
  public String getUIClassID();
  public boolean isManagingFocus();
  public synchronized void removeHyperlinkListener(HyperlinkListener l);
  public final void setContentType(String type);
  public void setEditorKit(EditorKit kit);
  public void setEditorKitForContentType(String type, EditorKit kit);
  public void setPage(String urlString) throws IOException;
  public void setPage(URL url) throws IOException;
}
```

The JEditorPane uses an EditorKit object to determine how to format content. Specialized kits are provided for HTML and RTF in subpackages of com.sun.java.swing.text. For HTML, it is not a full-fledged HTML Viewer, but is more for limited usage. For instance, it supports tables but not forms or frames.

NOTE   Two more complete HTML renderers are Sun's own HotJava Bean (http://java.sun.com/products/hotjava/bean/) and ICEsoft's ICE Browser (http://www.icesoft.no/ICEBrowser/).

The `JEditorPane` supports the concept of hyperlinks within the document. You register a `HyperlinkListener` to get a type of `HyperlinkEvent`. The `HyperlinkEvent.EventType` class identifies types.

```java
public interface HyperlinkListener extends EventListener {
    public abstract void hyperlinkUpdate(HyperlinkEvent e);
}

public class HyperlinkEvent extends EventObject {
    public HyperlinkEvent(Object source, HyperlinkEvent.EventType e, URL url);
    public HyperlinkEvent.EventType getEventType();
    public URL getURL();
}

public static final class HyperlinkEvent.EventType {
    public static final HyperlinkEvent.EventType ACTIVATED;
    public static final HyperlinkEvent.EventType ENTERED;
    public static final HyperlinkEvent.EventType EXITED;
    public String toString();
}
```

Figure 15.15 shows off using `JEditorPane` as a simple HTML displayer.

FIGURE 15.15:

A `JEditorPane` viewing an HTML file

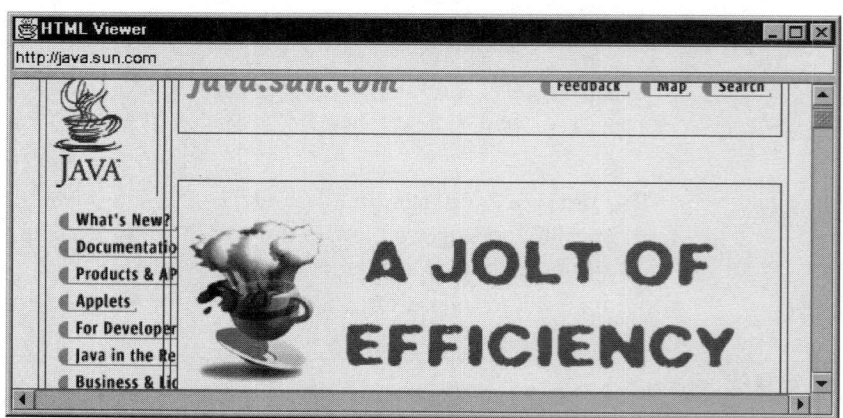

The program behind Figure 15.15 follows:

```java
import java.awt.*;
import java.awt.event.*;
import java.io.*;
import java.net.*;
```

```java
import java.util.*;
import javax.swing.*;
import javax.swing.text.*;
import javax.swing.event.*;

public class HTMLIt extends JPanel {
  HTMLIt() {
    setLayout (new BorderLayout (5, 5));
    final JEditorPane jt = new JEditorPane();
    final JTextField input =
      new JTextField("http://java.sun.com");
    input.addActionListener (new ActionListener() {
      public void actionPerformed (ActionEvent e) {
        try {
          jt.setPage (input.getText());
        } catch (IOException ex) {
          JOptionPane.showMessageDialog (
            HTMLIt.this, "Invalid URL",
            "Invalid Input",
            JOptionPane.ERROR_MESSAGE);
        }
      }
    });
    add (input, BorderLayout.NORTH);
    // make read-only
    jt.setEditable(false);
    // follow links
    jt.addHyperlinkListener(new HyperlinkListener () {
      public void hyperlinkUpdate(final HyperlinkEvent e) {
        if (e.getEventType() ==
            HyperlinkEvent.EventType.ACTIVATED) {
          SwingUtilities.invokeLater(new Runnable() {
            public void run() {
              // Save original
              Document doc = jt.getDocument();
              try {
                URL url = e.getURL();
                jt.setPage(url);
                input.setText (url.toString());
              } catch (IOException io) {
                JOptionPane.showMessageDialog (
                  HTMLIt.this, "Can't follow link",
                  "Invalid Input",
```

```
                       JOptionPane.ERROR_MESSAGE);
                    jt.setDocument (doc);
                  }
               }
             });
           }
         }
       });
       JScrollPane pane = new JScrollPane();
       pane.getViewport().add(jt);
       add(pane, BorderLayout.CENTER);
     }
     public static void main (String args[]) {
       JFrame f = new JFrame ("HTML Viewer");
       JPanel j = new HTMLIt();
       f.addWindowListener(new WindowAdapter() {
         public void windowClosing(WindowEvent e) {
           System.exit(0);
         }
       });
       f.getContentPane().add (j, BorderLayout.CENTER);
       f.setSize (400, 300);
       f.show();
     }
   }
```

Trees

Swing provides a hierarchical display component with JTree. The data Model for a tree is TreeModel and is made up of many TreeNode objects. The means of selecting nodes within the tree is defined by the TreeSelectionModel; you select a TreePath. TreeCellRenderer defines how each element of the tree is displayed. All the support classes of JTree are found in the javax.swing.tree package.

TreeModel

The TreeModel interface defines the underlying data structure of a JTree.

```
public interface TreeModel {
  public abstract void addTreeModelListener(TreeModelListener l);
  public abstract Object getChild(Object parent, int index);
  public abstract int getChildCount(Object parent);
```

```
   public abstract int getIndexOfChild(Object parent, Object child);
   public abstract Object getRoot();
   public abstract boolean isLeaf(Object node);
   public abstract void removeTreeModelListener(TreeModelListener l);
   public abstract void valueForPathChanged(TreePath path, Object newValue);
}
```

As with most of the other components, there is a default implementation. In this case it is `DefaultTreeModel`. It manages the notification of listeners when the data Model changes.

```
   public class DefaultTreeModel implements Serializable, TreeModel {
     public DefaultTreeModel(TreeNode root);
     public DefaultTreeModel(TreeNode root, boolean allowsChildren);
     public void addTreeModelListener(TreeModelListener l);
     public boolean asksAllowsChildren();
     public Object getChild(Object parent, int index);
     public int getChildCount(Object index);
     public int getIndexOfChild(Object parent, Object child);
     public TreeNode[] getPathToRoot(TreeNode node);
     protected TreeNode[] getPathToRoot(TreeNode node, int depth);
     public Object getRoot();
     public void insertNodeInto(MutableTreeNode newChild,
       MutableTreeNode parent, int index);
     public boolean isLeaf(Object node);
     public void nodeChanged(TreeNode node);
     public void nodeStructureChanged(TreeNode node);
     public void nodesChanged(TreeNode node, int childIndices []);
     public void nodesWereInserted(TreeNode node, int childIndices[]);
     public void nodesWereRemoved(TreeNode node, int childIndices[],
       Object removedChildren[]);
     public void reload();
     public void reload(TreeNode node);
     public void removeNodeFromParent(MutableTreeNode node);
     public void removeTreeModelListener(TreeModelListener l);
     public void setAsksAllowsChildren(boolean allowsChildren);
     public void valueForPathChanged(TreePath path, Object newValue);
   }
```

To find out when the Model of a tree changes, you would register a `TreeModel-Listener`. This allows you to get `TreeModelEvent` objects when the tree structure changes.

```
public interface TreeModelListener extends EventListener {
  public abstract void treeNodesChanged(TreeModelEvent e);
```

```
   public abstract void treeNodesInserted(TreeModelEvent e);
   public abstract void treeNodesRemoved(TreeModelEvent e);
   public abstract void treeStructureChanged(TreeModelEvent e);
}

public class TreeModelEvent extends EventObject {
   public TreeModelEvent(Object source, TreePath path);
   public TreeModelEvent(Object source, TreePath path, int childIndices[],
     Object children[]);
   public TreeModelEvent(Object source, Object path[]);
   public TreeModelEvent(Object source, Object path[], int childIndices[],
Object[]);
   public int[] getChildIndices();
   public Object[] getChildren();
   public Object[] getPath();
   public TreePath getTreePath();
   public String toString();
}
```

TreeNode

The most frequently used classes when working with JTree are the nodes. Due
to the tree's hierarchical nature, you have to manually create nodes and connect
them together before you have your whole tree together. The basis of the node is
the TreeNode interface.

```
public interface TreeNode {
   public abstract Enumeration children();
   public abstract boolean getAllowsChildren();
   public abstract TreeNode getChildAt(int childIndex);
   public abstract int getChildCount();
   public abstract int getIndex(TreeNode node);
   public abstract TreeNode getParent();
   public abstract boolean isLeaf();
}
```

You can think of a specific TreeNode as a read-only tree. You cannot modify the
node using just the methods of this interface. In order to enable a tree node to have
children, or to disown children, you must move to MutableTreeNode. This interface
includes support for adding and removing children, as well as changing the parent.

```
public interface MutableTreeNode extends TreeNode {
   public abstract void insert(MutableTreeNode child, int index);
   public abstract void remove(MutableTreeNode node);
```

```
      public abstract void remove(int index);
      public abstract void removeFromParent();
      public abstract void setParent(MutableTreeNode node);
      public abstract void setUserObject(Object obj);
   }
```

Since both of these are interfaces, you would expect there to be a concrete implementation of them. That class is `DefaultMutableTreeNode`, which comes with a hefty set of methods, primarily for tree traversal.

```
public class DefaultMutableTreeNode implements Cloneable, MutableTreeNode,
   Serializable {
   public static final Enumeration EMPTY_ENUMERATION;
   public DefaultMutableTreeNode();
   public DefaultMutableTreeNode(Object userObject);
   public DefaultMutableTreeNode(Object userObject, boolean allowsChildren);
   public void add(MutableTreeNode newChild);
   public Enumeration breadthFirstEnumeration();
   public Enumeration children();
   public Object clone();
   public Enumeration depthFirstEnumeration();
   public boolean getAllowsChildren();
   public TreeNode getChildAfter(TreeNode aChild);
   public TreeNode getChildAt(int index);
   public TreeNode getChildBefore(TreeNode aChild);
   public int getChildCount();
   public int getDepth();
   public TreeNode getFirstChild();
   public DefaultMutableTreeNode getFirstLeaf();
   public int getIndex(TreeNode aChild);
   public TreeNode getLastChild();
   public DefaultMutableTreeNode getLastLeaf();
   public int getLeafCount();
   public int getLevel();
   public DefaultMutableTreeNode getNextLeaf();
   public DefaultMutableTreeNode getNextNode();
   public DefaultMutableTreeNode getNextSibling();
   public TreeNode getParent();
   public TreeNode[] getPath();
   public DefaultMutableTreeNode getPreviousLeaf();
   public DefaultMutableTreeNode getPreviousNode();
   public DefaultMutableTreeNode getPreviousSibling();
   public TreeNode getRoot();
```

```
    public TreeNode getSharedAncestor(DefaultMutableTreeNode aNode);
    public int getSiblingCount();
    public Object getUserObject();
    public Object[] getUserObjectPath();
    public void insert(MutableTreeNode newChild, int childIndex);
    public boolean isLeaf();
    public boolean isNodeAncestor(TreeNode anotherNode);
    public boolean isNodeChild(TreeNode anotherNode);
    public boolean isNodeDescendant(DefaultMutableTreeNode anotherNode);
    public boolean isNodeRelated(DefaultMutableTreeNode anotherNode);
    public boolean isNodeSibling(TreeNode anotherNode);
    public boolean isRoot();
    public Enumeration pathFromAncestorEnumeration(TreeNode aNode);
    public Enumeration postorderEnumeration();
    public Enumeration preorderEnumeration();
    public void remove(MutableTreeNode aChild);
    public void remove(int childIndex);
    public void removeAllChildren();
    public void removeFromParent();
    public void setAllowsChildren(boolean allowsChildren);
    public void setParent(MutableTreeNode newParent);
    public void setUserObject(Object userObject);
    public String toString();
}
```

You build your tree by creating multiple `DefaultMutableTreeNode` instances. To build up a calendar-type tree, with children of weekdays and months, where each of those has their expected children, you would have to go through a process like the following one. It is a very tedious part of working with `JTree`. However, once the tree is built there is much that can be done.

```
DefaultMutableTreeNode root =
  new DefaultMutableTreeNode("Calendar");
DefaultMutableTreeNode months =
  new DefaultMutableTreeNode("Months");
root.add(months);
String monthLabels[] = {"January", "February", "March", "April", "May",
  "June", "July", "August", "September", "October", "November", "December"};
for (int i=0,n=monthLabels.length;i<n;i++)
  months.add (new DefaultMutableTreeNode(monthLabels[i]));
DefaultMutableTreeNode weeks =
  new DefaultMutableTreeNode("Weeks");
root.add(weeks);
```

```
String weekLabels[] = {"Monday", "Tuesday", "Wednesday", "Thursday",
  "Friday", "Saturday", "Sunday"};
for (int i=0,n=weekLabels.length;i<n;i++)
  weeks.add (new DefaultMutableTreeNode(weekLabels[i]));
JTree jt = new JTree (root);
JScrollPane jsp = new JScrollPane (jt);
```

TreeSelectionModel

The tree selection Model of the list is one of three constants of `TreeSelectionModel`: CONTIGUOUS_TREE_SELECTION, SINGLE_TREE_SELECTION, and DISCONTIGUOUS_TREE_SELECTION. The last is the default. The default implementation of `TreeSelectionModel` is `DefaultTreeSelectionModel`.

The `TreeSelectionModel` allows you to track when the selected nodes of a tree change. You register a `TreeSelectionListener` and get `TreeSelectionEvents`.

```
public interface TreeSelectionListener extends EventListener {
  public abstract void valueChanged(TreeSelectionEvent e);
}
```

```
public class TreeSelectionEvent extends EventObject {
  public TreeSelectionEvent(Object source, TreePath path, boolean isNew,
    TreePath oldLeadSelectionPath, TreePath newLeadSelectionPath);
  public TreeSelectionEvent(Object, TreePath[], boolean areNew[],
    TreePath oldLeadSelectionPath, TreePath newLeadSelectionPath);
  public Object cloneWithSource(Object newSource);
  public TreePath getNewLeadSelectionPath();
  public TreePath getOldLeadSelectionPath();
  public TreePath getPath();
  public TreePath[] getPaths();
  public boolean isAddedPath();
  public boolean isAddedPath(TreePath path);
}
```

Before you register a tree selection listener, you need to describe the object you get back from tree selection events: `TreePath`.

TreePath

As the name implies, a `TreePath` represents a path between nodes. In the case of a `TreeSelectionEvent`, it is from the tree's root to the selected node.

```
public class TreePath implements Serializable {
  public TreePath(Object singlePath);
```

```
    public TreePath(Object path[]);
    public boolean equals(Object obj);
    public Object getLastPathComponent();
    public Object[] getPath();
    public Object getPathComponent(int element);
    public int getPathCount();
    public int hashCode();
    public boolean isDescendant(TreePath path);
    public String toString();
}
```

The following TreeSelectionListener will print the path from root to selected node:

```
jt.addTreeSelectionListener (new TreeSelectionListener() {
  public void valueChanged (TreeSelectionEvent e) {
    TreePath path = e.getPath();
    System.out.println ("Picked: " + path.getLastPathComponent());
    Object elements[] = path.getPath();
    for (int i=0, n=elements.length; i<n; i++) {
      System.out.print ("->" + elements[i]);
    }
    System.out.println ();
  }
});
```

If you selected Tuesday in the previously created tree, the output would be as follows:

```
Picked: Tuesday
->Calendar->Weeks->Tuesday
```

TreeCellRenderer

A TreeCellRenderer is used to display each cell of the tree. When customizing the display, usually you would use a JLabel and configure the icon and text based upon the value of the node of the tree and the current settings.

```
public interface TreeCellRenderer {
  public abstract Component getTreeCellRendererComponent(JTree tree,
    Object value, boolean selected, boolean expanded, boolean leaf,
    int row, boolean hasFocus);
}
```

Figure 15.16 demonstrates a custom tree cell renderer.

FIGURE 15.16:

JTree with Custom Tree-
CellRenderer

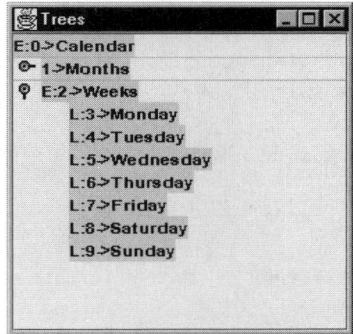

The source for the custom renderer follows.

```
class MyCellRenderer extends JLabel implements TreeCellRenderer {
  MyCellRenderer () {
    setOpaque (true);
  }
  public Component getTreeCellRendererComponent(JTree tree,
      Object value, boolean selected, boolean expanded,
      boolean leaf, int row, boolean hasFocus) {
    StringBuffer text = new StringBuffer();
    if (expanded)
      text.append("E:");
    if (leaf)
      text.append("L:");
    if (hasFocus)
      text.append("H:");
    text.append (row + "->");
    text.append (value.toString());
    setBackground(selected ? Color.blue : Color.yellow);
    setForeground(selected ? Color.yellow : Color.blue);
    setText(text.toString());
    return this;
  }
}
```

To install the renderer, you simply tell the JTree. It is the one renderer for the entire tree. Any customizations would have to be done to the TreeCellRenderer implementer.

```
jt.setCellRenderer(new MyCellRenderer());
```

The source for the complete JTree example follows.

```java
import javax.swing.*;
import javax.swing.event.*;
import javax.swing.tree.*;
import java.awt.*;
import java.awt.event.*;

public class TreeIt {

  class MyCellRenderer extends JLabel implements TreeCellRenderer {
    MyCellRenderer () {
      setOpaque (true);
    }
    public Component getTreeCellRendererComponent(JTree tree,
        Object value, boolean selected, boolean expanded,
        boolean leaf, int row, boolean hasFocus) {
      StringBuffer text = new StringBuffer();
      if (expanded)
        text.append("E:");
      if (leaf)
        text.append("L:");
      if (hasFocus)
        text.append("H:");
      text.append (row + "->");
      text.append (value.toString());

      setBackground(selected ? Color.blue : Color.yellow);
      setForeground(selected ? Color.yellow : Color.blue);

      setText(text.toString());
      return this;
    }
  }

  public TreeIt() {
    JFrame f = new JFrame ("Trees");
    DefaultMutableTreeNode root =
      new DefaultMutableTreeNode("Calendar");
    DefaultMutableTreeNode months =
      new DefaultMutableTreeNode("Months");
    root.add(months);
```

```
       String monthLabels[] = {"January", "February", "March", "April", "May",
         "June", "July", "August", "September", "October", "November",
         "December"};
       for (int i=0,n=monthLabels.length;i<n;i++)
         months.add (new DefaultMutableTreeNode(monthLabels[i]));
       DefaultMutableTreeNode weeks =
         new DefaultMutableTreeNode("Weeks");
       root.add(weeks);
       String weekLabels[] = {"Monday", "Tuesday", "Wednesday", "Thursday",
         "Friday", "Saturday", "Sunday"};
       for (int i=0,n=weekLabels.length;i<n;i++)
         weeks.add (new DefaultMutableTreeNode(weekLabels[i]));
       JTree jt = new JTree (root);
       jt.addTreeSelectionListener (new TreeSelectionListener() {
         public void valueChanged (TreeSelectionEvent e) {
           TreePath path = e.getPath();
           System.out.println ("Picked: " + path.getLastPathComponent());
           Object elements[] = path.getPath();
           for (int i=0, n=elements.length; i<n; i++) {
             System.out.print ("->" + elements[i]);
           }
           System.out.println ();
         }
       });
       jt.setCellRenderer(new MyCellRenderer());

       JScrollPane jsp = new JScrollPane (jt);
       Container c = f.getContentPane();
       c.add (jsp, BorderLayout.CENTER);
       f.addWindowListener (new WindowAdapter() {
         public void windowClosing (WindowEvent e) {
           System.exit(0);
         }
       });
       f.setSize(250, 250);
       f.show();
     }

     public static void main (String args[]) {
       new TreeIt();
     }
   }
```

Client Properties

The Swing User Interface manager maintains a list of properties for all the different components. This allows you to alter the appearance of components, like changing the display font for tool tips or displaying lines connecting nodes in trees, without subclassing components. To get the list of properties, just ask the UIManager:

```java
import java.util.*;
import javax.swing.*;
public class ListProps {
  public static void main (String args[]) {
    Hashtable defaultProps = UIManager.getDefaults();
    Enumeration enum = defaultProps.keys();
    while (enum.hasMoreElements()) {
      Object key = enum.nextElement();
      System.out.println("Property: " + key);
      System.out.println("Value: " + defaultProps.get(key) + '\n');
    }
  }
}
```

This will print a rather lengthy list that you can examine when you run the program. To change a specific property, you would call the putClientProperty() method of a specific JComponent. For instance, to change the line style of a JTree to angled, you would call:

```java
jt.putClientProperty("JTree.lineStyle", "Angled");
```

This change results in Figure 15.16 transforming into Figure 15.17.

FIGURE 15.17:

JTree with modified line style

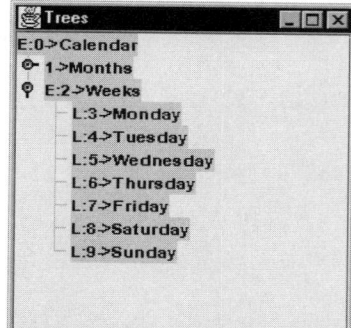

Practically everything is settable with client properties, if you can figure out which property to change. Unfortunately, you cannot ask a component what its client properties are.

Summary

This chapter dealt with many parts of Swing you do not *have* to use. If you wish to use the Swing components strictly as simple graphical components, you are free to do that. However, there are many better and smarter ways to use the Swing components to make your programs more maintainable. Event handling can be better delegated to `Actions`, and keyboard events can be dealt with by `KeyStrokes`, without having to manually monitor user input. Instead of manually creating user dialogs, Swing provides many common dialogs for messages and general input, as well as specific input of colors, dates, files, and fonts.

Also, the Model/View/Controller architecture offers a common way of separating data from display, enabling better-designed enterprise applications. With MVC, you can plug in any available look and feel, since the appearance and data Model are completely separate. In addition, familiar components have new capabilities and several more complex components become available. With these components, you can build richer applications enhancing user experiences.

CHAPTER
SIXTEEN

Transferring Data

- Using transferable objects

- Working with the clipboard

- Dragging and dropping

16

The java.awt.datatransfer and java.awt.dnd packages encompass two very different, yet similar capabilities. These data transfer capabilities available within Java are to transfer data to a clipboard as well as to drag and drop within an application or between applications. The means that both packages use to transfer data is the same, so it will be explained first.

Transferable Objects

Objects that are transferable to/from an application's clipboard or for drag and drop must implement the Transferable interface, shown here.

```
public interface Transferable {
  public abstract Object getTransferData(DataFlavor flavor)
    throws UnsupportedFlavorException, IOException;
  public abstract DataFlavor[] getTransferDataFlavors();
  public abstract boolean isDataFlavorSupported(DataFlavor flavor);
}
```

NOTE A clipboard is an area within memory for storing temporary information in support of cut, copy, and paste tasks. There tends to be two types of clipboards: a "System" clipboard to share data between applications and private clipboards for sharing data within a single application.

When looking at the interface definition, the first thing that you may ask is "What's a DataFlavor?" A flavor is a way to represent data when it is being transferred. This allows the receiving class to ask for a flavor it understands. As the following class definition shows, there is much that needs to be done to describe how the data is represented.

```
public class DataFlavor implements Externalizable, Cloneable {
  public static final DataFlavor javaFileListFlavor;
  public static final String javaJVMLocalObjectMimeType;
  public static final String javaRemoteObjectMimeType;
  public static String javaSerializedObjectMimeType;
  public static final DataFlavor plainTextFlavor;
  public static final DataFlavor stringFlavor;
  public DataFlavor();
  public DataFlavor(Class representationClass, String humanPresentableName);
  public DataFlavor(String mimeType) throws MimeTypeParseException,
```

```
      ClassNotFoundException;
   public DataFlavor(String mimeType, String humanPresentableName);
   public DataFlavor(String primaryType, String subType,
      MimeTypeParameterList params, Class representationClass,
      String humanPresentableName);
   public Object clone() throws CloneNotSupportedException;
   public boolean equals(DataFlavor dataFlavor);
   public boolean equals(Object obj);
   public boolean equals(String s);
   public boolean equals(MimeType mt);
   public String getHumanPresentableName();
   public String getMimeType();
   public String getParameter(String paramName);
   public String getPrimaryType();
   public Class getRepresentationClass();
   public String getSubType();
   public boolean isFlavorJavaFileListType();
   public boolean isFlavorRemoteObjectType();
   public boolean isFlavorSerializedObjectType();
   public final boolean isMimeTypeEqual(DataFlavor dataFlavor);
   public boolean isMimeTypeEqual(String mimeType);
   public boolean isMimeTypeEqual(MimeType mimeType);
   public boolean isMimeTypeSerializedObject();
   public boolean isRepresentationClassInputStream();
   public boolean isRepresentationClassRemote();
   public boolean isRepresentationClassSerializable();
   protected String normalizeMimeType(String mimeType);
   protected String normalizeMimeTypeParameter(String name, String value);
   public synchronized void readExternal(ObjectInput oi) throws IOException,
      ClassNotFoundException;
   public void setHumanPresentableName(String humanPresentableName);
   public synchronized void writeExternal(ObjectOutput oo)
      throws IOException;
}
```

Thankfully, the class defines several constants for frequently used flavors: java-FileListFlavor, javaJVMLocalObjectMimeType, javaRemoteObjectMimeType, javaSerializedObjectMimeType, plainTextFlavor, and stringFlavor. When you decide you want some information to be Transferable, you decide in which flavors you are going to make the data available. These flavors are dealt with internally as the familiar Internet standard of MIME types, and there is a MimeType class to help. However, it is rarely necessary to think in terms of MIME types. It is just the naming scheme Java reuses to identify flavors. You may display the

DataFlavor as the presentable name with `getHumanPresentableName()`, but that would be the only time you would see something like `application/x-java-serialized-object`, which happens to be the presentable name for `javaSerializedObjectMimeType`.

NOTE   If you are not familiar with MIME types, they are defined by RFC 2045 and 2046. MIME stands for Multipurpose Internet Mail Extension.

This is the way flavors work. When you have some information to transfer, you identify the formats so that the target object can receive the data. For instance, if the source of a transfer is the contents of a `JTextPane`, which supports multi-attributed text, you might support three flavors:

- A flavor based on `javaSerializedObjectMimeType` to preserve the attributes, so it can be pasted into another `JTextPane`

- A `stringFlavor`, so anyone who understands UNICODE strings can receive it, but will lose formatting information

- A `plainTextFlavor`, where each character is represented by only 8 bits, losing data from any non-ASCII characters

This allows the target of the data transfer to ask the `Transferable` object if it supports a `DataFlavor` it understands, via either `getTransferDataFlavors()` to get a list of all flavors or `isDataFlavorSupported(DataFlavor)` to inquire about a specific one. The target would start with the richest form it understands, hoping to retain as much information as possible. If the target object was a `JTextArea`, which doesn't support multi-attributed text, the best flavor it could ask for is `stringFlavor`.

As the concept of transferring Java `String` objects is fairly common, Java provides the `StringSelection` support class to help. It provides a `Transferable` object that can provide the target with its data as one of two flavors: `stringFlavor` or `plainTextFlavor`.

```
public class StringSelection implements Transferable, ClipboardOwner {
    public StringSelection(String string);
    public synchronized Object getTransferData(DataFlavor flavor)
        throws UnsupportedFlavorException, IOException;
    public synchronized DataFlavor[] getTransferDataFlavors();
    public boolean isDataFlavorSupported(DataFlavor flavor);
    public void lostOwnership(Clipboard clip, Transferable t);
}
```

Clipboard

As previously stated, the clipboard is an area within memory for storing temporary information in support of cut, copy, and paste tasks. Asking the Toolkit object, with getSystemClipboard(), provides access to the system clipboard. You can also create private clipboards, inaccessible beyond the scope of the program. The Clipboard class is rather simple and defines the scope of its capabilities:

```
public class Clipboard {
  public Clipboard(String name);
  public synchronized Transferable getContents(Object obj);
  public String getName();
  public synchronized void setContents(Transferable t, ClipboardOwner own);
}
```

WARNING   By default, access to the system clipboard is protected by the security manager and not permitted from applets.

Basically, you can name the clipboard (from the constructor) as well as set or get its contents. When you place something on the clipboard, it actually isn't *copied* until someone tries to get it, so the source must be sure the object is available while it remains on the clipboard. To find out when an object placed on the clipboard has been replaced is done with the help of the ClipboardOwner interface.

```
public interface ClipboardOwner {
  public abstract void lostOwnership(Clipboard clip, Transferable t);
}
```

The previously mentioned StringSelection class handles this for you if you are transferring String objects. It just retains a reference to the String to transfer. For other types of transferable objects, you would have to do the same. If the originally copied data were no longer available, it would be necessary to throw an IOException.

As the "Editor Kits and Text Actions" section of Chapter 15 showed, when working with the Swing text components, the cut, copy, and paste operations are automatically handled for you with the help of the installed EditorKit. So, you normally do not have to worry about creating code to access the clipboard. However, to demonstrate the capabilities, we'll create a program that manually does copy and paste with a JTextArea. Figure 16.1 shows the sample program screen.

FIGURE 16.1:

Clipboard accessing program

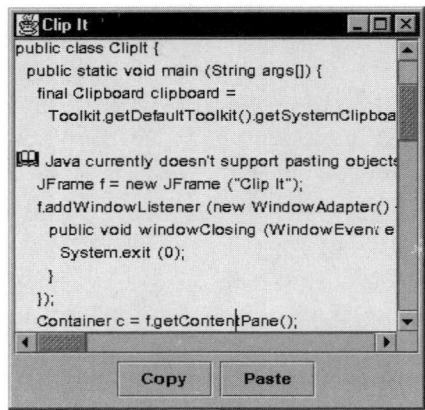

The program behind the application shown in Figure 16.1 follows. Be sure to try pasting from external applications, not just from what was copied with the program.

```java
import java.awt.*;
import java.awt.event.*;
import javax.swing.*;
import java.awt.datatransfer.*;
import java.io.IOException;
public class ClipIt {
  public static void main (String args[]) {
    final Clipboard clipboard =
      Toolkit.getDefaultToolkit().getSystemClipboard();
    JFrame f = new JFrame ("Clip It");
    f.addWindowListener (new WindowAdapter() {
      public void windowClosing (WindowEvent e) {
        System.exit (0);
      }
    });
    Container c = f.getContentPane();
    final JTextArea jt = new JTextArea();
    JScrollPane pane = new JScrollPane (jt);
    c.add (pane, BorderLayout.CENTER);
    JButton copy = new JButton ("Copy");
    copy.addActionListener (new ActionListener() {
      public void actionPerformed (ActionEvent e) {
        String selection = jt.getSelectedText();
        StringSelection data = new StringSelection (selection);
        clipboard.setContents (data, data);
      }
```

```
    });
    JButton paste = new JButton ("Paste");
    paste.addActionListener (new ActionListener() {
      public void actionPerformed (ActionEvent e) {
        Transferable clipData = clipboard.getContents(clipboard);
        if (clipData != null) {
          try {
            String s = (String)(clipData.getTransferData(
              DataFlavor.stringFlavor));
            jt.replaceSelection (s);
          } catch (UnsupportedFlavorException ee) {
            System.err.println ("Unsupported flavor: " + ee);
          } catch (IOException ee) {
            System.err.println ("Unable to get data: " + ee);
          }
        }
      }
    });
    JPanel p = new JPanel();
    p.add (copy);
    p.add (paste);
    c.add (p, BorderLayout.SOUTH);
    f.setSize (300, 300);
    f.setVisible (true);
  }
}
```

> **NOTE**   Java does not currently support pasting objects like images from external applications. You could copy an **ImageIcon** and treat it as a **javaSerializedObject-MimeType**. However, it would then only be pasteable into another Java program, or a program that understands Java's serialization mechanism, which will be described in the "Object Persistence and Serialization" section of Chapter 19.

Drag and Drop

Drag and drop within Java is similar to accessing the clipboard, except the process of moving the data is a little more complicated. The data that you wish to transfer still needs to implement the Transferable interface. Besides the data to transfer, there is a source and a destination. The source of the dragging implements the `DragSourceListener` interface:

```
public interface DragSourceListener extends EventListener {
    public abstract void dragDropEnd(DragSourceDropEvent e);
    public abstract void dragEnter(DragSourceDragEvent e);
    public abstract void dragExit(DragSourceEvent e);
    public abstract void dragOver(DragSourceDragEvent e);
    public abstract void dropActionChanged(DragSourceDragEvent e);
}
```

While the target implements `DropTargetListener`:

```
public interface DropTargetListener extends EventListener {
    public abstract void dragEnter(DropTargetDragEvent e);
    public abstract void dragExit(DropTargetEvent e);
    public abstract void dragOver(DropTargetDragEvent e);
    public abstract void drop(DropTargetDropEvent e);
    public abstract void dropActionChanged(DropTargetDragEvent e);
}
```

One thing should be pointed out. There are three different event types for each set of five methods: `DragSourceEvent`, `DragSourceDragEvent`, and `DragSource-DropEvent` for dragging; and `DropTargetEvent`, `DropTargetDropEvent`, and `DropTargetDragEvent` for dropping. This requires a little extra care when implementing each interface.

The source of a dragging is a `DragSource`. The draggable object would create an instance of `DragSource` within its constructor.

```
public class DragSource extends Object {
    public static final Cursor DefaultCopyDrop;
    public static final Cursor DefaultCopyNoDrop;
    public static final Cursor DefaultLinkDrop;
    public static final Cursor DefaultLinkNoDrop;
    public static final Cursor DefaultMoveDrop;
    public static final Cursor DefaultMoveNoDrop;
    public DragSource();
    public static DragSource getDefaultDragSource();
    public static boolean isDragImageSupported();
    public DragGestureRecognizer createDefaultDragGestureRecognizer(
        Component target, int actions, DragGestureListener l);
    public DragGestureRecognizer createDragGestureRecognizer(
        Class recognizerAbstractClass, Component target, int actions,
        DragGestureListener l);
    protected DragSourceContext createDragSourceContext(DragSourceContextPeer
```

```
dscp, DragGestureEvent dgl,
  Cursor dragCursor,  Image dragImage,  Point imageOffset,  Transferable t,
 DragSourceListener l) ;
public FlavorMap getFlavorMap();
public void startDrag(DragGestureEvent trigger, Cursor dragCursor, Image
dragImage, Point dragOffset,
  Transferable t, DragSourceListener l)  throws InvalidDnDOperationException
public void startDrag(DragGestureEvent trigger, Cursor dragCursor, Image
dragImage, Point imageOffset,
  Transferable t, DragSourceListener l, FlavorMap map)  throws
InvalidDnDOperationException;
public void startDrag(DragGestureEvent trigger, Cursor dragCursor,
Transferable t, DragSourceListener l)
   throws InvalidDnDOperationException;
public void startDrag(DragGestureEvent trigger, Cursor dragCursor,
Transferable t, DragSourceListener l,  FlavorMap map)
   throws InvalidDnDOperationException;
```

The other thing you must do in the constructor is create a `DragGestureRecognizer`. Since detecting when the dragging has started is platform specific, this is available from the `Toolkit` via `createDragGestureRecognizer()`. Instead of asking the Toolkit for the recognizer, there is a convenience method `createDefaultDragGestureRecognizer()` available from `DragSource` that both creates the recognizer and registers a `DragGestureListener`.

```
public interface DragGestureListener extends EventListener {
   public abstract void dragGestureRecognized(DragGestureEvent e);
}
```

It is within this `dragGestureRecognized()` method that you notify the `DragSource` the dragging has started and call its `startDrag()` method.

To put all this together, create a draggable `JLabel` object. This involves subclassing `JLabel` and implementing `DragSourceListener` and `DragGestureListener`. The actual `DragSourceListener` methods do nothing, as all the work will be in the `dragGestureRecognized()` method.

```
import java.awt.*;
import java.awt.dnd.*;
import java.awt.datatransfer.*;
import javax.swing.*;
import javax.swing.event.*;

public class DraggableLabel extends JLabel implements DragSourceListener,
    DragGestureListener {
```

```
DragSource dragSource;

public DraggableLabel(String s) {
  super (s);
  dragSource = new DragSource();
  dragSource.createDefaultDragGestureRecognizer(this,
    DnDConstants.ACTION_COPY, this);
}

public void dragGestureRecognized(DragGestureEvent e) {
   StringSelection text = new StringSelection (getText());
   dragSource.startDrag (e, DragSource.DefaultCopyDrop, text, this);
}

public void dragDropEnd (DragSourceDropEvent e) {
}

public void dragEnter (DragSourceDragEvent e) {
}

public void dragExit (DragSourceEvent e) {
}

public void dragOver (DragSourceDragEvent e) {
}

public void dropActionChanged (DragSourceDragEvent e) {
}
}
```

The only part not explained yet is the DnDConstants. The different actions of the events are defined within the DnDConstants class.

```
public final class DnDConstants {
  public static final int ACTION_COPY;
  public static final int ACTION_COPY_OR_MOVE;
  public static final int ACTION_LINK;
  public static final int ACTION_MOVE;
  public static final int ACTION_NONE;
  public static final int ACTION_REFERENCE;
  public DnDConstants();
}
```

NOTE

In JDK 1.2beta4, this is an abstract class. However, it should be changed to an interface by the time 1.2 is released.

The component you'll drop the draggable label into is a `JList`. This involves subclassing and implementing the `DropTargetListener`. There are two methods of the interface that we need to implement: `dragEnter()` and `drop()`. In `dragEnter()` you need to tell the component what type of drag events you accept. Then in `drop()` you accept the drop, process the dragged data, and tell the event you're done with it. As with clipboard operations, the dragged data is dealt with via flavors.

```java
import java.awt.*;
import java.awt.dnd.*;
import javax.swing.*;
import java.awt.datatransfer.*;
import java.io.IOException;
import java.util.Vector;

public class DroppableList extends JList implements DropTargetListener {

  DropTarget dropTarget;
  Vector v = new Vector();

  public DroppableList() {
    dropTarget = new DropTarget (this, this);
  }

  public void dragEnter (DropTargetDragEvent e) {
    e.acceptDrag (DnDConstants.ACTION_COPY);
  }

  public void dragExit (DropTargetEvent e) {
  }

  public void dragOver (DropTargetDragEvent e) {
  }

  public void drop (DropTargetDropEvent e) {
    try {
      Transferable tr = e.getTransferable();
      if (tr.isDataFlavorSupported (
          DataFlavor.stringFlavor)) {
```

```
            e.acceptDrop (DnDConstants.ACTION_COPY_OR_MOVE);
            String s = (String)tr.getTransferData (
              DataFlavor.stringFlavor);
            v.add (s);
            setListData (v);
            paintImmediately(getVisibleRect());
            e.getDropTargetContext().dropComplete(true);
          } else {
            System.err.println ("Rejected");
            e.rejectDrop();
          }
        } catch (IOException io) {
          io.printStackTrace();
          e.rejectDrop();
        } catch (UnsupportedFlavorException ufe) {
          ufe.printStackTrace();
          e.rejectDrop();
        }
      }

      public void dropActionChanged (DropTargetDragEvent e) {
      }
    }
```

To demonstrate the droppable list and draggable label, Figure 16.2 shows a program with four labels around the list after several drag operations.

FIGURE 16.2:

Drag and Drop
demonstration program

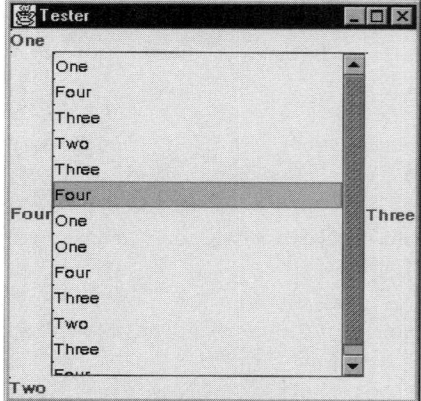

The test program behind Figure 16.2 is below:

```
import java.awt.*;
import java.awt.event.*;
import javax.swing.*;
import javax.swing.event.*;

public class Tester {
  public static void main (String args[]) {
    Frame f = new Frame("Tester");
    DraggableLabel north = new DraggableLabel ("One");
    DraggableLabel south = new DraggableLabel ("Two");
    DraggableLabel east  = new DraggableLabel ("Three");
    DraggableLabel west  = new DraggableLabel ("Four");
    DroppableList  list  = new DroppableList();
    JScrollPane pane = new JScrollPane (list);
    f.add (north, BorderLayout.NORTH);
    f.add (south, BorderLayout.SOUTH);
    f.add (east,  BorderLayout.EAST);
    f.add (west,  BorderLayout.WEST);
    f.add (pane,  BorderLayout.CENTER);
    f.setSize (300, 300);
    f.addWindowListener (new WindowAdapter() {
      public void windowClosing(WindowEvent e) {
        System.exit(0);
      }
    });
    f.setVisible (true);
  }
}
```

Summary

This chapter described how you deal with transferring data, both with clipboards and with drag and drop operations. While the tasks are definitely different, they share several common characteristics. By understanding the Transferable interface, as well as the DataFlavor way of dealing with the data, you should have no problem with either operation.

CHAPTER

SEVENTEEN

17

Java Collections

- Reviewing arrays

- Vector, Enumeration, Dictionary, Hashtable, and BitSet

- Collection, Set, List, and Map

- Synchronization and readability

- Algorithms and sorting

Developing in Java frequently requires you to work with unknown quantities of objects. Even when working with fixed amounts of objects, sequential access (arrays) is not always the best access method. To support working with groups of objects, Java provides a whole slew of classes. In fact, the concept is so important that how Java handles collections of objects changed dramatically in Java 1.2. An entirely new set of around 25 classes was added to the `java.util` package to describe the Java Collections API framework.

This chapter reviews data structures. Starting off with the familiar array object, we look at how Java handles a single object representing a group of objects. Next, we go through the various pre-Collections API containers. Although new programs should avoid the historic collection classes, existing programs still use them. Understanding how they work, and their limitations, will help you understand why the new collection classes were added. Finally, the chapter explores the Collections framework introduced in Java 1.2.

NOTE   If you like the Java 1.2 Collections framework, you can use a subset in Java 1.1. Download the libraries from `http://java.sun.com/beans/infobus/#collections` and read the informational file at `http://java.sun.com/beans/infobus/collectionsreadme.html` for usage instructions.

Arrays Review

Chapter 6 provided an overview of Java arrays. Basically, an array is a fixed-size collection of objects of the same type. Besides storing objects, arrays can also store primitive datatypes. When you create an array, you specify the type of object (or *primitive*) to store in the array and the number of elements you wish to store. This allows array usage to be type-safe and very efficient. Since you can only store one type of data in an array, you can only get that same type back. Also, since you've allocated all the space for the array at declaration time, placing an element into an array is very fast. But therein lies the potential problem with arrays. You must allocate all their space at once, and they cannot get bigger than you anticipated— at least not without an expensive array copy operation. If you know the datatype beforehand and you know what the final size should be, you're OK with arrays. Otherwise, you need to look at one of Java's other collection classes.

Working with an array is just like working with any other object. You can access its single instance variable `length` to discover the array's size or you can get the element at a certain location by passing an `int` to the brackets (`[]`) of an array reference variable. Array access also always performs bounds checking and throws an `ArrayIndexOutOfBoundsException` if you attempt to access a nonexistent element.

WARNING   The index into an array cannot be a `long` variable. This is a compile-time error, instead of a runtime exception.

The following program demonstrates array usage by performing runtime type checking to determine the array datatype. When the array is an array of integers, the square root of each element is printed. When the array is an array of doubles, the trigonometric sine function is performed:

```java
public class MyArrays {
  public static void printValues (Object array) {
    if (array instanceof int[]) {
      // Cast to int array
      int intArray[] = (int[])array;
      int len = intArray.length;
      for (int i=0;i<len;i++) {
        System.out.print (Math.sqrt (intArray[i]) + " ");
      }
    } else if (array instanceof double[]) {
      // cast to double array
      double doubleArray[] = (double[])array;
      int len = doubleArray.length;
      for (int i=0;i<len;i++) {
        System.out.print (Math.sin (doubleArray[i]) + " ");
      }
    }
    System.out.println ();
  }
  public static void main (String args[]) {
    int ints[] = {1, 4, 9, 16, 25, 36};
    double doubles[] = {0.0, Math.PI / 6.0,
        Math.PI / 2.0, 3.0 * Math.PI / 2.0};
    printValues (ints);
    printValues (doubles);
```

```
    try {
      ints[90] = 27;
    } catch (ArrayIndexOutOfBoundsException e) {
      System.err.println ("Invalid array access: " + e.getMessage());
    }
  }
}
```

The output from running the program follows:

```
1.0 2.0 3.0 4.0 5.0 6.0
0.0 0.49999999999999994 1.0 -1.0
Invalid array access: 90
```

NOTE The second value on the second line is really 0.5 when rounded off. The `print` method does not provide the means to format output and ½ cannot be specifically stored internally in binary.

Vectors, Stacks, and Enumeration

The historic collection classes have existed since the beginning of Java's time. While there is nothing technically wrong with them, their usage should be limited to the maintenance of Java 1.0 and 1.1 programs. The primary, historic collection classes that provide ordered access are `Vector` and `Stack`. The interface `Enumeration` offers the means to step through the contents.

Working with Vectors

While arrays are required to be of fixed size and have a homogenous datatype, class `Vector` encapsulates a heterogeneous linked-list and array hybrid:

- Vectors are heterogeneous because they do not insist on each element being of a certain type—many object types can be mixed within one vector.

- Vectors are an array hybrid because they can grow dynamically when elements are added.

Here is the definition of Vector:

```
public class Vector extends AbstractList
    implements List, Cloneable, Serializable {
  protected int capacityIncrement;
  protected int elementCount;
  protected Object elementData[];
  public Vector();
  public Vector(int initialCapacity);
  public Vector(int initialCapacity, int capacityIncrement);
  public Vector(Collection c);
  public void add(int index, Object obj);
  public synchronized boolean add(Object obj);
  public synchronized boolean addAll(int index, Collection c);
  public synchronized boolean addAll(Collection c);
  public synchronized void addElement(Object obj);
  public int capacity();
  public void clear();
  public synchronized Object clone();
  public boolean contains(Object obj);
  public synchronized boolean containsAll(Collection c);
  public synchronized void copyInto(Object anArray[]);
  public synchronized Object elementAt(int index);
  public Enumeration elements();
  public synchronized void ensureCapacity(int minCapacity);
  public synchronized boolean equals(Object obj);
  public synchronized Object firstElement();
  public synchronized Object get(int index);
  public synchronized int hashCode();
  public int indexOf(Object obj);
  public synchronized int indexOf(Object obj, int startIndex);
  public synchronized void insertElementAt(Object obj, int index);
  public boolean isEmpty();
  public synchronized Object lastElement();
  public int lastIndexOf(Object obj);
  public synchronized int lastIndexOf(Object obj, int startIndex);
  public synchronized Object remove(int index);
  public boolean remove (Object obj);
  public synchronized removeAll (Collection c);
  public synchronized void removeAllElements();
  public synchronized boolean removeElement(Object obj);
  public synchronized void removeElementAt(int index);
  public synchronized boolean retainAll (Collection c);
```

```
    public synchronized Object set(int index, Object obj);
    public synchronized void setElementAt(Object obj, int index);
    public synchronized void setSize(int newSize);
    public int size();
    public synchronized Object[] toArray();
    public synchronized Object[] toArray(Object aType[]);
    public synchronized String toString();
    public synchronized void trimToSize();
}
```

NOTE   If you've used the historical collection classes prior to Java 1.2, you may notice that some of these have been retrofitted into the Collections API added with Java 1.2.

Since vectors can store any datatype, all vector operations work with the `Object` class. This means you lose the type safety provided by an array. And, whenever you access anything acquired from a vector, you have to cast it back to its original type. This, and the cost associated with dynamic growth, are the penalties associated with using `Vector`.

While working with arrays, you access the size with the `length` instance variable and set elements with an assignment (=) operation. For a vector, the length is acquired with the `size()` method and assignment is via the `set(int position, Object obj)` or `setElementAt(Object obj, int position)` method. Neither `set()` nor `setElementAt()` support dynamic growth. For a vector to grow without bounds, you would use either `add(Object obj)` or `addElement(Object obj)`, which both add the object at the end. Retrieval of elements is via either the `get(int position)` or the `getElement(int position)` method.

TIP   If you need to store a primitive datatype within a vector, or any other collection besides an array, you need to use the wrapper classes found in the `java.lang` package. For instance, to store an `int`, you wrap it into an `Integer`: `Integer in = new Integer (5)`. Then, you can add the `Integer` object `in` to the collection.

To demonstrate the vector class, the following program works with some of its basic operations. It stores planets in a vector and then prints out each planet object, using the implicit call to `Object.toString()` made by `println()`.

```
import java.util.*;
public class ThePlanets {
  static class Planet {
```

```
      private String name;
      Planet (String s) {
        name = s;
      }
      public String toString() {
        return getClass().getName() + "[" + name + "]";
      }
    }
    public static void main (String args[]) {
      String names[] = {"Mercury", "Venus", "Earth",
        "Mars", " Jupiter", "Saturn", "Uranus",
        "Neptune", "Pluto"};
      int namesLen = names.length;
      Vector planets = new Vector (namesLen);
      for (int i=0; i < namesLen; i++) {
        planets.addElement (new Planet (names[i]));
      }
      int planetsLen = planets.size();
      for (int i=0; i < planetsLen; i++) {
        System.out.println (planets.elementAt (i));
      }
    }
  }
```

While this shows the basic vector operations, you will frequently need to do something more with each element retrieved from the vector than an operation inherited from `Object`. The following example extends the first by adding the number of moons to each planet definition. Instead of using the `toString()` method to print the planet data, specific methods of `Planet` are used to get information about the vector elements:

```
import java.util.*;
public class ThePlanetsAndMoons {
  static class Planet {
    private String name;
    private int moonCount;
    Planet (String s, int moons) {
      name = s;
      moonCount = moons;
    }
    public String toString() {
      return getClass().getName() + "[" + name + "-" + moonCount + "]";
    }
```

```
        public final String getName() {
          return name;
        }
        public final int getMoonCount () {
          return moonCount;
        }
      }
      public static void main (String args[]) {
        String names[] = {"Mercury", "Venus", "Earth",
          "Mars", "Jupiter", "Saturn", "Uranus",
          "Neptune", "Pluto"};
        int moons[] = {0, 0, 1, 2, 16, 18, 17, 8, 1};

        int namesLen = names.length;
        Vector planets = new Vector (namesLen);
        for (int i=0; i < namesLen; i++) {
          planets.addElement (new Planet (names[i], moons[i]));
        }
        Planet p;
        int planetsLen = planets.size();
        for (int i=0; i < planetsLen; i++) {
          p = (Planet)(planets.elementAt (i));
          System.out.println (p.getName() + " : " + p.getMoonCount());
        }
      }
    }
```

To demonstrate the potential for problems, the following defines a new class
Comet and adds one to the planets vector used previously. Since Vector allows
you to add anything to the vector, addElement() doesn't cause any problems.
However, when you cast the value retrieved with elementAt() to a Planet,
you'll get a ClassCastException thrown:

```
    static class Comet {
      private String name;
      Comet (String s) {
        name = s;
      }
      public String toString() {
        return getClass().getName() + "[" + name + "]";
      }
      public final String getName() {
```

```
        return name;
    }
}
...
planets.addElement (new Comet ("Hale-Bopp"));
...
    // Exception thrown here for Comet
    p = (Planet)(planets.elementAt (i));
```

This just goes to show that you should always know what you are getting out of a collection when you use any of them.

NOTE

For an online multimedia tour of the solar system, stop by `http://seds.lpl` `.arizona.edu/nineplanets/nineplanets/nineplanets.html`.

TIP

In C++, the ability to specify the use of a specific datatype for something at compile-time is supported directly in the language by templates. The concept itself is called *parameterized types*. Java provides support for neither parameterized types nor collections of a specific datatype.

Pushing Stacks

Class `Stack` implements that old faithful data structure: a simple last-in-first-out (LIFO) stack. In Java, the `Stack` class is actually a subclass of `Vector`. So, in addition to all the vector operations, you can also push objects onto the stack, pop objects off the stack, peek at the object on the top of the stack, check whether the stack is empty, and search for an object on the stack. The definition of class `Stack` shows off this functionality:

```
public class Stack extends Vector {
    public Stack();
    public boolean empty();
    public synchronized Object peek();
    public synchronized Object pop();
    public Object push (Object obj);
    public synchronized int search (Object obj);
}
```

The following provides a simple demonstration of the Stack class. Notice that the Vector methods are available since Stack is a subclass; however, they should be avoided for clarity sake:

```
import java.util.Stack;
public class JupiterMoons {
  public static void main (String args[]) {
    String names[] = {"Metis", "Adrastea", "Amalthea", "Thebe",
      "Io", "Europa", "Ganymede", "Callisto", "Leda", "Himalia",
      "Lysithea", "Elara", "Ananke", "Carme", "Pasiphae", "Sinope"
    };
    int namesLen = names.length;
    Stack moons = new Stack ();
    for (int i=0; i < namesLen-1; i++) {
      moons.push (names[i]);
    }
    // Vector methods still work
    moons.addElement (names[namesLen-1]);
    while (!moons.empty()) {
      System.out.print (moons.pop() + " ");
    }
    System.out.println();
  }
}
```

Running the program generates the following output:

```
Sinope Pasiphae Carme Ananke Elara Lysithea Himalia Leda Callisto
➡ Ganymede Europa Io Thebe Amalthea Adrastea Metis
```

Stepping through Enumerations

While the Vector and Stack classes have natural orderings, there are times when you don't really care about the actual order a collection is traversed, only that every node is visited. Or, you may only care that you have a collection of objects, not what the underlying data structure is. This allows you to think at a higher level during your application's design. For instance, there may come a time when a vector is inefficient because you need frequent additions in the middle of a collection. If that time comes, you shouldn't need to change everything just because you want to use a LinkedList (found in Java 1.2) instead of a Vector. The appropriate Java 1.1 interface that offers that level of abstraction is Enumeration, defined here:

```
public interface Enumeration {
  public abstract boolean hasMoreElements();
  public abstract Object nextElement();
}
```

NOTE   The Gamma, et al., *Design Patterns* book (Addison Wesley, ISBN 0-201-63361-2) describes this pattern as an `Iterator`. In Java 1.2, *Iterator* is the actual interface name used to represent the behavior.

The `Enumeration` interface requires any collection-oriented class to implement two methods: `hasMoreElements()` and `nextElement()`. These two methods mean that any object that supports enumerating its components can be explored using the following `while` loop:

```
Enumeration enum = someContainer.methodReturningEnumeration();
while (enum.hasMoreElements()) {
  Object obj = enum.nextElement();
  // process this object
}
```

When working with `Vector`, you get the set of elements with the `elements()` method. Since `Stack` is a subclass of `Vector`, you use `elements()` there, too. Now, instead of the following block of code from the earlier example:

```
Planet p;
for (int i=0, n=planets.size(); i < n; i++) {
  p = (Planet)(planets.elementAt (i));
  System.out.println (p.getName() + " : " + p.getMoonCount());
}
```

you would walk through the `planets` enumeration with this code:

```
Enumeration enum = planets.elements();
Planet p;
while (enum.hasMoreElements()) {
  p = (Planet)(enum.nextElement());
  System.out.println (p.getName() + " : " + p.getMoonCount());
}
```

When creating your own types of collections, you need to implement the two methods of `Enumeration` interface. The following program demonstrates this by converting any array into an `Enumeration`; just pass your array to `ArrayEnumerationFactory.makeEnumeration()` and you're all set.

```
import java.lang.reflect.Array;
import java.util.Enumeration;
final public class ArrayEnumerationFactory {
  static public Enumeration makeEnumeration (final Object obj) {
    Class type = obj.getClass();
```

```java
      if (!type.isArray()) {
        throw new IllegalArgumentException (obj.getClass().toString());
      } else {
        return (new Enumeration() {
          int size = Array.getLength(obj);
          int cursor;
          public boolean hasMoreElements() {
            return (cursor<size);
          }
          public Object nextElement() {
            return Array.get (obj, cursor++);
          }
        });
      }
    }
    public static void main (String args[]) {
      Enumeration enum = makeEnumeration (args);
      while (enum.hasMoreElements()) {
        System.out.println (enum.nextElement());
      }
      enum = makeEnumeration (new int[] {1, 3, 4, 5});
      while (enum.hasMoreElements()) {
        System.out.println (enum.nextElement());
      }
      try {
        enum = makeEnumeration (new Double(Math.PI));
      } catch (IllegalArgumentException e) {
        System.err.println ("Can't enumerate that: " + e.getMessage());
      }
    }
  }
```

The class includes a sample test run in the `main()` method. Running the program with the following input:

```
java ArrayEnumerationFactory one two three
```

produces the following output:

```
one
two
three
1
3
4
5
Can't enumerate that: class java.lang.Double
```

Dictionaries, Hashtables, and Properties

While arrays, vectors, and stacks provide ordered access to your collections' contents, maintaining that order can be costly. To provide an alternative collection methodology where order or sequential access isn't necessary, Java provides support for key-value pair collections. Instead of looking up elements by an integer position, you provide a key for every value you would like to place in your collection, like a lookup map. Figure 17.1 shows an example of this lookup scheme.

The abstract class to support this concept in the historical collections group is `Dictionary`. `Hashtable` and `Properties` provide two specific implementations of these capabilities.

FIGURE 17.1:

Dictionary lookup example

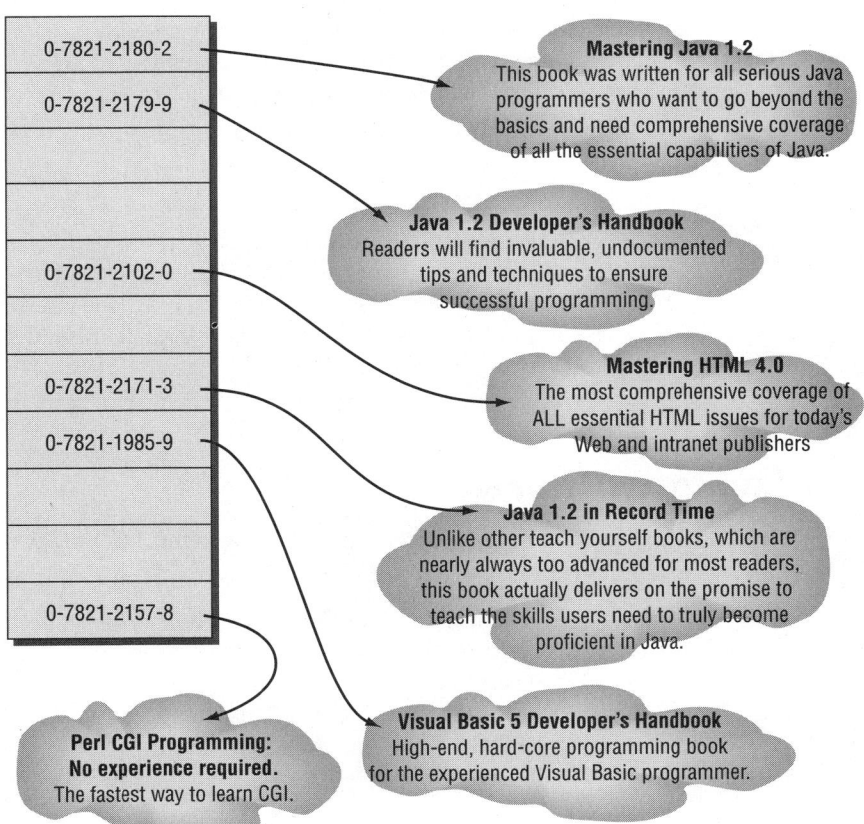

Thumbing through Dictionaries

The abstract `Dictionary` class describes the interface for working with key-value maps. The way a dictionary works is if you provide an object as a key, it will return at most one object as its value from the collection. If the key isn't in the map, you get nothing back, or `null` in Java terms. The same object can be the value for multiple keys. However, the key can only be the handle for one value term. How the actual key-value pairs are stored is dependent on the specific implementation. The abstract `Dictionary` definition follows:

```
public abstract class Dictionary {
   public Dictionary();
   public abstract Enumeration elements();
   public abstract Object get(Object);
   public abstract boolean isEmpty();
   public abstract Enumeration keys();
   public abstract Object put(Object, Object);
   public abstract Object remove(Object);
   public abstract int size();
}
```

NOTE Technically speaking, `Dictionary` should be an interface as all the methods are abstract. Apparently, `Dictionary` predates the concept of interfaces within Java, so it is just an abstract class. Since `Dictionary` is one of those historical collection classes, you should really use the **Map** interface, introduced in Java 1.2, when working with key-value collections.

Living with Hashtables

The `Hashtable` class represents a concrete implementation of the `Dictionary` architecture, shown here:

```
public class Hashtable extends Dictionary
      implements Map, Cloneable, Serializable {
   public Hashtable();
   public Hashtable(int initialCapacity);
   public Hashtable(int initialCapacity, float loadFactor);
   public Hashtable(Map m);
```

```
    public synchronized void clear();
    public synchronized Object clone();
    public synchronized boolean contains(Object value);
    public synchronized boolean containsKey(Object key);
    public boolean containsValue(Object value);
    public synchronized Enumeration elements();
    public Set entrySet();
    public synchronized boolean equals(Object obj);
    public synchronized Object get(Object key);
    public synchronized int hashCode();
    public boolean isEmpty();
    public Set keySet();
    public synchronized Enumeration keys();
    public synchronized Object put(Object key, Object value);
    public synchronized void putAll(Map m);
    protected void rehash();
    public synchronized Object remove(Object key);
    public int size();
    public synchronized String toString();
    public Collection values();
}
```

The class name is so called because of the means of storing the keys. When you provide the key for a value to the hashtable, the data structure generates a hash code and uses that as the means to look up the value when it is necessary to retrieve it. As long as the algorithm for generating the hash codes always generates the same value for the same key (two keys are equivalent if `equals()` says so) and distributes the codes as evenly as possible, the hashtable represents an efficient means of storing key-value pairs. The means of generating a key's hash code is by the `hashCode()` method, either the one from `Object`, or an overridden version from a subclass.

NOTE   Two entries are not necessarily equal if `hashCode()` returns the same value. In fact, if many entries result in the same hash code value, this is usually the result of a poor hashing algorithm. If you've overridden the `hashCode()` method, you should redesign how you generate hash codes for instances of your class. For instance, the length of a `String` is a bad hashing algorithm, as many unequal strings would have the same code.

The operations you can do with a `Hashtable` are mostly inherited from `Dictionary` (or part of the new `Map` interface).

- Adding a key-value pair is done with `put (Object key, Object value)`
- Getting a value for a key is done with `get (Object key)`
- Removing an element is done with `remove (Object key)`
- Checking the size is done with `size()`
- Checking if the size is 0 is done with `empty()`
- Getting the set of all keys or values is done with `keys()` or `elements()`, which both return an `Enumeration`
- Getting the set of all keys or values for use with the newer Collections API is done with `keySet()` or `entrySet()`, which both return a `Set`

Additionally, `Hashtable` allows you to empty out the collection with `clear()`, check if a specific key is present with `containsKey (Object key)`, or even check if a value is present with `containsValue (Object value)`. The last operation, while possible, is very expensive since a hashtable is being used backwards.

Using the planet names as the keys and the planet diameter (in kilometers) as the values, the following demonstrates the use of `Hashtable`:

```
import java.util.Enumeration;
import java.util.Hashtable;
public class PlanetDiameters {
  public static void main (String args[]) {
    String names[] = {"Mercury", "Venus", "Earth",
      "Mars", "Jupiter", "Saturn", "Uranus",
      "Neptune", "Pluto"};
    float diameters[] = {4800f, 12103.6f, 12756.3f,
      6794f, 142984f, 120536f, 51118f, 49532f, 2274f};
    Hashtable hash = new Hashtable();
    for (int i=0, n=names.length; i < n; i++) {
      hash.put (names[i], new Float (diameters[i]));
    }
    Enumeration enum = hash.keys();
    Object obj;
    while (enum.hasMoreElements()) {
      obj = enum.nextElement();
```

```
      System.out.println (obj + ": " + hash.get(obj));
    }
  }
}
```

Running the program produces the following results:

```
Earth: 12756.3
Mercury: 4800.0
Uranus: 51118.0
Pluto: 2274.0
Saturn: 120536.0
Jupiter: 142984.0
Neptune: 49532.0
Venus: 12103.6
Mars: 6794.0
```

Notice that the resulting order has absolutely no correlation to the order the elements were added. Also, like with `Vector`, the `get()` routine returns an `Object`. If you need to call a method of the specific class that was added into the table, you have to cast the value returned to the appropriate class.

Examining Properties

When the objects to store in your hashtable are strings, you should consider using the `Properties` class. Instead of having to cast return values to the `String` class, the `Properties` class does this for you with its supporting methods:

```
public class Properties extends Hashtable {
  protected Properties defaults;
  public Properties();
  public Properties(Properties defaults);
  public String getProperty(String key);
  public String getProperty(String key, String defaultValue);
  public void list(PrintStream out);
  public void list(PrintWriter out);
  public synchronized void load(InputStream in) throws IOException;
  public Enumeration propertyNames();
  public synchronized Object put(Object key, Object value);
  public synchronized Object setProperty(String key, String value);
  public synchronized void store(OutputStream out, String header)
    throws IOExcepition
}
```

Since `Properties` is a `Dictionary` subclass, you can continue to add entries with `put()` and retrieve entries with `get()`. However, these methods work with `Object` values. The more natural way to work with the `Properties` class is with the following methods:

- Adding a key-value String pair is done with `setProperty (String key, String value)`.

- Getting a value for a key is done with `getProperty (String key)` or `getProperty (String key, String defaultValue)`, for when `key` is not set.

- Getting the set of all keys is done with `propertyNames()` instead of `keys()`. `Properties` can have default values. Using `propertyNames()` creates an `Enumeration` that is the union of the `keys()` and the default values.

Besides the convenience methods, you can also load properties from an input stream, like a file, or save them, with `load()` and `store()` respectively. (The `save()` method was deprecated because it didn't throw an `IOException` when there were problems saving.) The way property settings are specified in a text file is separated by an equal sign (=).

If the file `planet.properties` contained the following values:

```
Mercury=god of commerce, travel and thievery
Venus=goddess of love and beauty
Earth=not derived from Greek/Roman mythology
Mars=god of War
Jupiter=King of the Gods
Saturn=god of agriculture
Uranus=deity of the Heavens
Neptune=god of the Sea
Pluto=god of the underworld
```

you would have nine properties, one for each planet name. The following program would then load the file, add a new property for a fictitious 10th planet, save the properties to a new file, list all properties and values to standard output, and finally locate a specific one:

```
import java.io.*;
import java.util.Properties;
public class PlanetProperties {
  public static void main (String args[]) throws IOException {
    String header = "A header";
    Properties props = new Properties();
```

```
    props.load (new FileInputStream ("planets.properties"));
    props.setProperty ("Planet X", "god of dreams");
    props.store (new FileOutputStream ("save.the.planets"), header);
    props.list (System.out);
    System.out.println (props.getProperty ("Pluto"));
  }
}
```

The most common use of Properties is with a list of system properties. If you ask the System class for its list of properties (getProperties()), you can find out information like the version of Java the person running the program is using, the URL of where to send bug reports for that specific version of Java, and even what directory to store temporary files in. Just add System.getProperties().list (System.out); to the previous program to see.

Bit Sets

Class BitSet implements a set of bits or a vector of boolean values. Unlike many of the other bit set classes or language features in other languages, this bit set has no limits. You can therefore go way beyond the typical 32- or 256-bit limits imposed by other implementations. First, let's look at the class definition:

```
public class BitSet implements Cloneable, Serializable {
  public BitSet();
  public BitSet(int nbits);
  public void and(BitSet set);
  public void andNot(BitSet set);
  public void clear(int bitIndex);
  public Object clone();
  public boolean equals(Object obj);
  public boolean get(int bitIndex);
  public int hashCode();
  public int length();
  public void or(BitSet set);
  public void set(int bitIndex);
  public int size();
  public String toString();
  public void xor(BitSet set);
}
```

BitSet operations include the following:

- Setting, clearing, and getting single bits
- Anding, and notting, oring, and xoring bit sets together
- Comparing bit sets

The following program demonstrates their usage, by placing in a BitSet whether or not a planet has an even number of moons. Normally, you would store much larger groups of bits in a BitSet to truly save space:

```java
import java.util.*;
public class TwoBitPlanets {
  public static void main (String args[]) {
    String names[] = {"Mercury", "Venus", "Earth",
      "Mars", "Jupiter", "Saturn", "Uranus",
      "Neptune", "Pluto"};
    int moons[] = {0, 0, 1, 2, 16, 18, 17, 8, 1};

    int namesLen = names.length;
    BitSet bits = new BitSet(namesLen);
    for (int i=0; i < namesLen; i++) {
      if ((moons[i] % 2) == 0) {
        bits.set (i);
      }
    }
    for (int i=0; i < namesLen; i++) {
      System.out.println (names[i] + " Even # Moons? " + bits.get(i));
    }
  }
}
```

NOTE   Although BitSet is part of the historical collection classes, the new Collections framework has no replacement. Also, the size() method of BitSet returns the size of the internal structure used, not necessarily the maximum bit number utilized. Since the bit values are stored with the help of a double, size() jumps up by 64 when necessary. More frequently you want the length() method, which returns the highest set bit position.

Collections and Iterators

The world of Java collection classes was overturned in Java 1.2. A set of about 25 classes was added to the `java.util` package to define the Java Collections API. Figure 17.2 shows the class hierarchy diagram showing the makeup of this framework.

FIGURE 17.2:

FIGURE 17.2:

The Collections Framework Class Hierarchy diagram

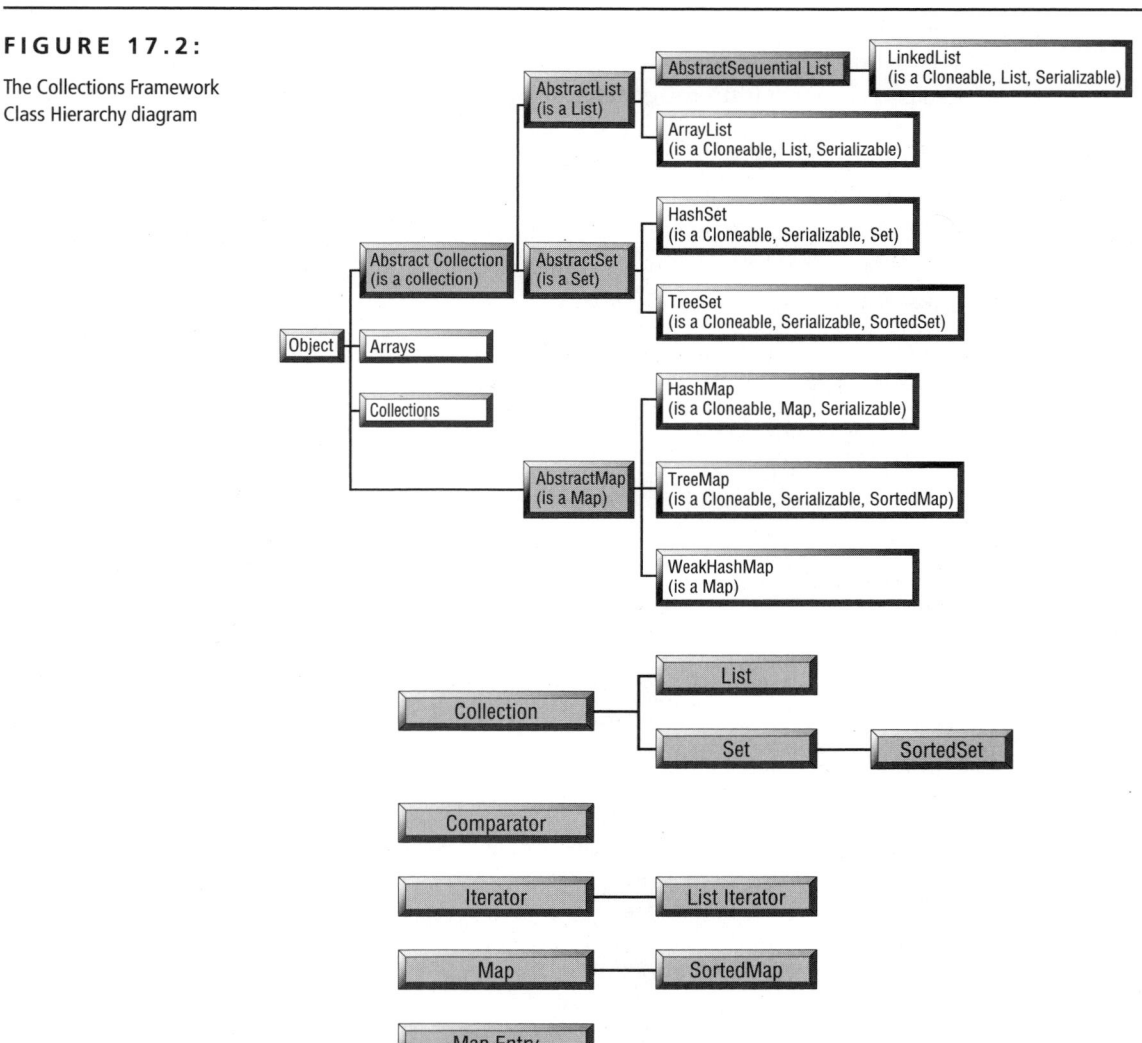

As the diagram shows, the four interfaces, `Collection`, `List`, `Map`, and `Set`, describe the different types of collections. For each type of collection, there are specific implementations, depending upon the type of data structure used to store the collection. These are the classes like `ArrayList`, `TreeSet`, and `HashMap`. The remaining classes in the hierarchy are support related. For instance, the `Iterator` interface replaces the `Enumeration` interface from the historical collection classes.

When working with the various framework classes, you always have to create specific implementations of the data structures, as the system needs to know how to store objects within the collection. However, when you access the actual collection, you should use the interface methods. This allows you to change data structures, for instance, from an array-backed collection to a hashtable-backed one, if the circumstances require it. Then, since the collection class still implements the same collection interface, no other code will need to change. For instance, the following shows how you would create a `HashMap`:

```
Map phoneBook = new HashMap();
```

If later you decide to maintain a sorted phone book, you can change the data structure from a `HashMap` to a `TreeMap`:

```
Map phoneBook = new TreeMap ();
```

Since you only accessed the `phoneBook` variable through the `Map` interface, the rest of your code would stay the same, and your phone list will always be sorted.

Of the four primary interfaces, `Collection` and `Map` are the basic two. A `Collection` is any group of objects, while `Map` is like `Dictionary` and works with key-value pairs. Two interfaces extend `Collection`: `Set` and `List`. A `Set` behaves like its mathematical definition: no duplicates; while `List` preserves a sequence or ordering, similar to `Vector`'s behavior. The `SortedMap` and `SortedSet` interfaces offer sorted traversal through the elements of `Map` and `Set` respectively

To get started with the new API, let's look at the `Collection` interface definition:

```
public interface Collection {
  public abstract boolean add(Object obj);
  public abstract boolean addAll(Collection c);
  public abstract void clear();
  public abstract boolean contains(Object obj);
  public abstract boolean containsAll(Collection c);
  public abstract boolean equals(Object obj);
  public abstract int hashCode();
  public abstract boolean isEmpty();
  public abstract Iterator iterator();
```

```
    public abstract boolean remove(Object obj);
    public abstract boolean removeAll(Collection c);
    public abstract boolean retainAll(Collection c);
    public abstract int size();
    public abstract Object[] toArray();
    public abstract Object[] toArray(Object obj[]);
}
```

Collection operations include the following:

- Adding elements

- Removing elements

- Checking the contents

- Working with the elements

Most of the operations are self-explanatory. However, a couple deserve a little explanation. The retainAll() method combines two collections by performing the set theory intersection operation. The original collection is modified to include any elements in the Collection parameter that are not already members of the collection. The toArray() method allows you to convert a Collection into an array. This may be necessary for historical purposes, where you need to send a set of data to another program that doesn't work with the collection classes yet. The following program demonstrates the capabilities of the Collection interface, using the soon-to-be-described ArrayList class as the data structure:

```
import java.util.*;
public class PlanetSet {
  public static void main (String args[]) {
    String names[] = {"Mercury", "Venus", "Earth",
      "Mars", "Jupiter", "Saturn", "Uranus",
      "Neptune", "Pluto"};
    int namesLen = names.length;
    Collection planets = new ArrayList();
    for (int i=0; i < namesLen; i++) {
      planets.add (names[i]);
    }
    Object s[] = planets.toArray();
    String s[] = (String[])planets.toArray(new String[0]);
    for (int i=0, n=s.length; i < n; i++) {
      System.out.println (s[i]);
    }
```

```
        planets.remove (names[3]);
        System.out.println (names[1] + " " + planets.contains (names[1]));
        System.out.println (names[3] + " " + planets.contains (names[3]));
    }
}
```

In order to access each element of the collection, the `toArray()` method was used. While this works perfectly well, the more appropriate way to do this is with the `Iterator` interface. This interface, defined here, replaces the `Enumeration` interface from the historical collection classes:

```
public interface Iterator {
    public abstract boolean hasNext();
    public abstract Object next();
    public abstract void remove();
}
```

As with `Enumeration`, you can have a similar `while` loop to get through all the elements. Thankfully, the method names are a little nicer and a `remove()` method has been added. The new `remove()` method is actually an optional interface method, though. Yes, this sounds contradictory—an optional interface method— but it actually is the truth. When a collection doesn't support removing entries during iteration, or ever, the method will throw the new exception `Unsupported-OperationException`.

WARNING This is not the only place you will see `UnsupportedOperationException` possibly thrown. Various modification methods of the collection classes are considered optional and will throw this exception. While this is a `RuntimeException`, programmatically trying to perform an unsupported operation is a programming error that should be encountered, and corrected, before a program reaches real users.

In the previous example, you can print the contents of every element of the collection with the following code:

```
Iterator it = planets.iterator();
while (it.hasNext()) {
    System.out.println (it.next());
}
```

Now that we've described the top-level collection framework, let's take a look at some of the concrete implementations.

The Generic Collection Library

ObjectSpace offers a Java package called the Generic Collection Library for Java (JGL). (The acronym comes from a prior name that infringed on Sun's Java trademark.)

For any developer transitioning from C++, JGL offers a set of collection classes that is consistent with the C++ Standard Template Library (STL). Prior to the 1.2 JDK, it was probably the best collections-oriented package available, and many IDE vendors licensed it for inclusion with their tools.

However, although similarities to the STL were JGL's strong selling points, it required a large framework for support. The Java Collections API introduced in the 1.2 JDK is much smaller in size and appears, conceptually, to be easier to understand.

For more information on the JGL package, stop by its Web site at http://www.objectspace .com/jgl/.

Sets

As previously mentioned, a *set* is a collection with no duplicates. Since this doesn't add any new behavior, only adding stipulations to existing behavior, the Set interface is identical to the Collection interface. To avoid duplication, adding elements to a set relies on the equals() method of the element being added to establish the uniqueness of the object.

There are two specific types of sets with which you can work. The recommended general-purpose Set data structure is HashSet. A HashSet is a Set collection backed by a hashtable. Like the Hashtable class, elements added to the hashtable need to implement the hashCode() method.

The other set structure is good under specific circumstances. The TreeSet is the other available Set implementation. As the name implies, it is backed by a (balanced) tree data structure. If ordering is important, then TreeSet is the set collection of choice. The TreeSet class relies on the methods in the SortedSet interface, shown here, when examining the tree in an ordered fashion:

```
public interface SortedSet extends Set {
  public abstract Comparator comparator();
```

```
   public abstract Object first();
   public abstract SortedSet headSet(Object toElement);
   public abstract Object last();
   public abstract SortedSet subSet(Object fromElement, Object toElement);
   public abstract SortedSet tailSet(Object fromElement);
}
```

The following program demonstrates using the Set interface. The primary goal here is to show that duplicates are not added to the set:

```java
import java.util.*;
public class MoonSet {
  public static void main (String args[]) {
    String names[] = {"Metis", "Adrastea", "Amalthea", "Thebe",
      "Io", "Europa", "Ganymede", "Callisto", "Leda", "Himalia",
      "Lysithea", "Elara", "Ananke", "Carme", "Pasiphae", "Sinope"
    };
    Set moons = new HashSet ();
    int namesLen = names.length;
    int index;
    for (int i=0; i < 100; i++) {
      index = (int)(Math.random()*namesLen);
      moons.add (names[index]);
    }
    Iterator it = moons.iterator();
    while (it.hasNext()) {
      System.out.println (it.next());
    }
  }
}
```

Lists and *ListIterator*

The List interface is your basic positional collection. When you add elements to a list, you can add each at a specific position or at the end. The following shows the interface's definition:

```java
public interface List extends Collection {
  public abstract void add(int index, Object element);
  public abstract boolean add(Object obj);
  public abstract boolean addAll(int index, Collection c);
```

```
   public abstract boolean addAll(Collection c);
   public abstract void clear();
   public abstract boolean contains(Object obj);
   public abstract boolean containsAll(Collection c);
   public abstract boolean equals(Object obj);
   public abstract Object get(int index);
   public abstract int hashCode();
   public abstract int indexOf(Object obj);
   public abstract boolean isEmpty();
   public abstract Iterator iterator();
   public abstract int lastIndexOf(Object obj);
   public abstract ListIterator listIterator();
   public abstract ListIterator listIterator(int startPosition);
   public abstract Object remove(int);
   public abstract boolean remove(Object obj);
   public abstract boolean removeAll(Collection c);
   public abstract boolean retainAll(Collection c);
   public abstract Object set(int index, Object element);
   public abstract int size();
   public abstract subList(int fromIndex, int toIndex);
   public abstract Object[] toArray();
}
```

There are two specific implementations of List in the Collections framework: ArrayList and LinkedList. An ArrayList is similar in functionality to a Vector—both maintain the collection within a resizable array. When maintaining List-type collections, you will probably maintain them in an ArrayList. The downfall of ArrayList is if you must do frequent inserts and removals in the middle of the list, which is where LinkedList shines. LinkedList is a doubly linked list, with references to the previous and next elements at each node. Because of this linkage, sequential access is satisfactory, but random access is slow, relative to an ArrayList.

Class ArrayList provides two methods and three constructors, in addition to the List interface methods. In addition, ArrayList implements the Cloneable interface:

```
   public ArrayList();
   public ArrayList(int initialCapacity);
   public ArrayList(Collection c);
   public Object clone();
   public void ensureCapacity(int minCapacity);
   public void trimToSize();
```

The `LinkedList` class has its own set of constructors and methods to add, as well as also implementing `Cloneable`:

```
public LinkedList();
public LinkedList(Collection c);
public void addFirst(Object obj);
public void addLast(Object obj);
public Object clone();
public Object getFirst();
public Object getLast();
public Object removeFirst();
public Object removeLast();
```

If you desire a stack data structure, you can use `LinkedList` and add elements with `addFirst()` and remove them with `removeFirst()`. For a first-in-first-out (FIFO) queue, you would add with `addLast()` and remove with `removeFirst()`; the reverse is also possible, `addFirst()`/`removeLast()`; however, it seems more natural to add to the end and remove from the beginning.

The following example revisits the planets and moon count example from the previous `Vector` example, listing the planets in reverse order:

```
import java.util.*;
public class PlanetsAndMoonsList {
  static class Planet {
    private String name;
    private int moonCount;
    Planet (String s, int moons) {
      name = s;
      moonCount = moons;
    }
    public String toString() {
      return getClass().getName() + "[" + name + "-" + moonCount + "]";
    }
    public final String getName() {
      return name;
    }
    public final int getMoonCount () {
      return moonCount;
    }
  }
  public static void main (String args[]) {
    String names[] = {"Mercury", "Venus", "Earth",
```

```
      "Mars", "Jupiter", "Saturn", "Uranus",
      "Neptune", "Pluto"};
    int moons[] = {0, 0, 1, 2, 16, 18, 17, 8, 1};

    int namesLen = names.length;
    List planets = new ArrayList (namesLen);
    for (int i=0; i < namesLen; i++) {
      planets.add (new Planet (names[i], moons[i]));
    }
    for (int i=planets.size()-1; i >= 0; --i) {
      Planet p = (Planet)(planets.get (i));
      System.out.println (p.getName() + " : " + p.getMoonCount());
    }
  }
}
```

Working with *ListIterator*

While the Iterator interface is available for every Collection, those collections that also implement the List interface have the ListIterator interface available to them, as well. Instead of just providing uni-directional traversal of a collection, with possible removal of elements, ListIterator is bi-directional, with possible removal, replacement, and addition of elements. Here is its definition:

```
public interface ListIterator Iterator {
  public abstract void add(Object obj);
  public abstract boolean hasNext();
  public abstract boolean hasPrevious();
  public abstract Object next();
  public abstract int nextIndex();
  public abstract Object previous();
  public abstract int previousIndex();
  public abstract void remove();
  public abstract void set(Object obj);
}
```

The following program demonstrates the interface by rearranging the solar system:

```
import java.util.*;
public class MovingPlanets {
  public static void main (String args[]) {
    String names[] = {"Mercury", "Venus", "Earth",
```

```
                          "Mars", "Jupiter", "Saturn", "Uranus",
                          "Neptune", "Pluto"};
              int namesLen = names.length;
              List planets = new ArrayList();
              for (int i=0; i < namesLen; i++) {
                planets.add (names[i]);
              }
              ListIterator lit = planets.listIterator();
              String s;
              lit.next();
              lit.next();
              s = (String)lit.next();
              lit.remove();
              lit.next();
              lit.next();
              lit.next();
              lit.add(s);
              lit.next(); // Gets back just added
              lit.previous();
              lit.previous();
              s = (String)lit.previous();
              lit.remove();
              lit.next();
              lit.next();
              lit.add(s);

              Iterator it = planets.iterator();
              while (it.hasNext()) {
                System.out.println (it.next());
              }
          }
      }
```

The output from running this program follows:

```
Mercury
Venus
Mars
Saturn
Earth
Jupiter
Uranus
Neptune
Pluto
```

TIP

> If `next()` or `previous()` went past an end of the `List`, `NoSuchElementException` would be thrown.

Maps

Like a `Dictionary` or phone book, a `Map` is used to maintain key-value pair collections. Every entry in the collection is added by providing a value and the key to look it up. If someone asks you for Joe's phone number, and you don't know his number, you look it up in a phone book. The key here is "Joe," and the value is his phone number. The actual definition of the `Map` interface follows:

```
public interface Map {
    public abstract void clear();
    public abstract boolean containsKey(Object key);
    public abstract boolean containsValue(Object value);
    public abstract Set entrySet();
    public abstract boolean equals(Object obj);
    public abstract Object get(Object key);
    public abstract int hashCode();
    public abstract boolean isEmpty();
    public abstract Set keySet();
    public abstract Object put(Object key, Object value);
    public abstract void putAll(Map m);
    public abstract Object remove(Object key);
    public abstract int size();
    public abstract Collection values();
}
```

Besides adding entries and looking up values, you can work with three collections of the `Map`: the set of keys (`keySet()`), the collection of values (`values()`), and a set of both (`entrySet()`). If you ask for both, each element of the collection is an instance of the `Map.Entry` inner-interface, defined here:

```
public static interface Map.Entry {
    public abstract boolean equals(Object obj);
    public abstract Object getKey();
    public abstract Object getValue();
    public abstract int hashCode();
    public abstract Object setValue(Object value);
}
```

Three concrete implementations of Map are provided with the collection classes: HashMap, WeakHashMap, and TreeMap. HashMap serves as your general-purpose map, backed by a hashtable. WeakHashMap is your map backed by a hashtable with weak references; if you do not retain a reference to a key outside the map, the garbage collector can free it.

NOTE   Examine the `java.lang.ref.WeakReference` class and `http://java.sun .com/products/jdk/1.2/docs/guide/refobs/` for more information about weak references.

TreeMap is your map backed by a balanced tree. When looking at its keys or values, these collections will be sorted. If sorting is a must, but you don't want the cost associated with adding a node, you can sort a HashMap after all the nodes have been added, when you truly need to get the results sorted:

```
Map map = new HashMap()
// add entries
map = new TreeMap (map);
```

The following example converts the earlier planet-diameter example to use a TreeMap:

```
import java.util.*;
public class DiameterMap {
  public static void main (String args[]) {
    String names[] = {"Mercury", "Venus", "Earth",
      "Mars", "Jupiter", "Saturn", "Uranus",
      "Neptune", "Pluto"};
    float diameters[] = {4800f, 12103.6f, 12756.3f,
      6794f, 142984f, 120536f, 51118f, 49532f, 2274f};
    Map map = new TreeMap();
    for (int i=0, n=names.length; i < n; i++) {
      map.put (names[i], new Float (diameters[i]));
    }
    Iterator it = map.keySet().iterator();
    Object obj;
    while (it.hasNext()) {
      obj = it.next();
      System.out.println (obj + ": " + map.get(obj));
    }
  }
}
```

Now, the output will appear in sorted planet name (key) order:

```
Earth: 12756.3
Jupiter: 142984.0
Mars: 6794.0
Mercury: 4800.0
Neptune: 49532.0
Pluto: 2274.0
Saturn: 120536.0
Uranus: 51118.0
Venus: 12103.6
```

TreeMap is the only map that allows you to get a submap: headMap(Object toKey) returns a map of everything less than key, tailMap(Object fromKey) returns a map of everything greater than key, while subMap(Object fromKey, Object toKey) returns a map within a certain range. These are all part of the SortedMap interface, described here:

```
public interface SortedMap extends Map {
   public abstract Comparator comparator();
   public abstract Object firstKey();
   public abstract SortedMap headMap(Object toKey);
   public abstract Object lastKey();
   public abstract SortedMap subMap(Object fromKey, Object toKey);
   public abstract SortedMap tailMap(Object toKey);
}
```

Synchronization and Readability

If you've used the historical collection classes of Java, you know that one of their biggest problems is performance. It's not that they were designed to be slow; they were designed to *always* be thread-safe. That means if you have multiple running threads accessing a single data structure, all access to the data structure is safe and synchronized appropriately. This is great when you have multiple running threads accessing a single data structure. However, when you do not require the synchronized behavior, there is no way to turn it off. All usage of classes like Hashtable and Vector are synchronized.

The collection classes added with Java 1.2 take another route. Instead of synchronizing everything, they synchronize nothing. If you need the synchronized behavior, after you have a collection to work with, you ask the Collections class to make it synchronized. Defined here, the Collections class provides this and other behavior to be described shortly. Since all the methods of `Collections` are static, and the constructor is private, you do not need to, nor can you, create any instances of the class:

```
public class Collections {
    public static final List EMPTY_LIST;
    public static final Set EMPTY_SET;
    public static int binarySearch(List list, Object key);
    public static int binarySearch(List list, Object key, Comparator comp);
    public static void copy(List to, List from);
    public static Enumeration enumeration(Collection coll);
    public static void fill(List list, Object o);
    public static Object max(Collection coll);
    public static Object max(Collection coll, Comparator comp);
    public static Object min(Collection coll);
    public static Object min(Collection coll, Comparator comp);
    public static List nCopies(int count, Object obj);
    public static void reverse(List list);
    public static Comparator reverseOrder();
    public static void shuffle(List list);
    public static void shuffle(List list, Random r);
    public static Set singleton(Object o);
    public static void sort(List list);
    public static void sort(List list, Comparator comp);
    public static Collection synchronizedCollection(Collection coll);
    public static List synchronizedList(List list);
    public static Map synchronizedMap(Map map);
    public static Set synchronizedSet(Set set);
    public static SortedMap synchronizedSortedMap(SortedMap map);
    public static SortedSet synchronizedSortedSet(SortedSet set);
    public static Collection unmodifiableCollection(Collection coll);
    public static List unmodifiableList(List list);
    public static Map unmodifiableMap(Map map);
    public static Set unmodifiableSet(Set set);
    public static SortedMap unmodifiableSortedMap(SortedMap);
    public static SortedSet unmodifiableSortedSet(SortedSet);
}
```

For instance, to synchronize access to a `Map`, you would do the following:

```
Map map = new HashMap()
map = Collections.synchronizedMap (map);
// access map from multiple threads
```

TIP When you synchronize a collection, it is good practice to not store the new collection in a new variable. If you do, it is possible you could still access the collection unsynchronized from the old one.

Besides synchronization, the Collections class also offers the ability to convert a specific collection to read-only mode. What this does is cause any method that would alter the collection to throw an UnsupportedOperationException. So, to make a collection read-only, you create it, fill it up, and then make it unmodifiable. If you make it unmodifiable before filling it up, you get an UnsupportedOperation-Exception thrown:

```
Map map = new HashMap()
// add entries
map = Collections.unmodifiableMap (map);
```

Algorithms and Sorting

The Java Collections API includes many algorithmic capabilities behind the scenes. For instance, up to this point, when various balanced tree-oriented collections were mentioned, how the tree was sorted was not. The time has come to describe this behavior and other similar capabilities. For random sorting or reordering of a List, just use Collections.shuffle().

Comparable and Comparator

Two interfaces are available to support sorting. The Comparable interface is for when a class has a natural ordering. Given many objects of the same type, the interface allows one to order all of them. The interface definition for Comparable is:

```
public interface Comparable {
    public abstract int compareTo(Object obj);
}
```

A negative return value signals the instance of the interface implementer comes before the parameter, zero signifies both are equal, and a positive value means the parameter comes first. When a class implements the Comparable interface, objects of the class can be used as the key for a tree-oriented collection. If an object doesn't implement `Comparable`, but you still wish it to be a key, you can implement the `Comparator` interface and have it do the comparisons for you:

```
public interface Comparator {
    public abstract int compare (Object obj1, Object obj2);
}
```

NOTE   The Java 1.2 classes that implement the `Comparable` interface are: `BigDecimal`, `BigInteger`, `Byte`, `Character`, `CollationKey`, `Date`, `Double`, `File`, `Float`, `Integer`, `Long`, `ObjectStreamField`, `Short`, `String`, and `URL`.

To demonstrate, let's compare the results of sorting with the default `String` comparison and a comparator that doesn't distinguish between uppercase and lowercase characters. To help, we need the `Arrays` class, shown here:

```
public class Arrays {
    public static List asList(Object array[]);
    public static int binarySearch(byte a[], byte key);
    public static int binarySearch(char a[], char key);
    public static int binarySearch(double a[], double key);
    public static int binarySearch(float a[], float key);
    public static int binarySearch(int a[], int key);
    public static int binarySearch(Object a[], Object key);
    public static int binarySearch(Object a[], Object key, Comparator comp);
    public static int binarySearch(long a[], long key);
    public static int binarySearch(short a[], short key);
    public static boolean equals(boolean[], boolean a2[]);
    public static boolean equals(byte a1[], byte a2[]);
    public static boolean equals(char a1[], char a2[]);
    public static boolean equals(double a1[], double a2[]);
    public static boolean equals(float a1[], float a2[]);
    public static boolean equals(int a1[], int a2[]);
    public static boolean equals(Object a1[], Object a2[]);
    public static boolean equals(long a1[], long a2[]);
    public static boolean equals(short a1[], short a2[]);
    public static void fill(boolean a[], boolean val);
    public static void fill(boolean a[], int from, int to, boolean val);
    public static void fill(byte a[], byte val);
    public static void fill(byte a[], int from, int to, byte val);
    public static void fill(char a[], char val);
    public static void fill(char a[], int from, int to, char val);
    public static void fill(double a[], double val);
```

```
   public static void fill(double a[], int from, int to, double val);
   public static void fill(float a[], float val);
   public static void fill(float a[], int from, int to, float val);
   public static void fill(int a[], int val);
   public static void fill(int a[], int from, int to, int val);
   public static void fill(Object a[], int from, int to, Object val);
   public static void fill(Object a[], Object val);
   public static void fill(long a[], int from, int to, long val);
   public static void fill(long a[], long val);
   public static void fill(short a[], int from, int to, short val);
   public static void fill(short a[], short val);
   public static void sort(byte a[]);
   public static void sort(char a[]);
   public static void sort(double a[]);
   public static void sort(float a[]);
   public static void sort(int a[]);
   public static void sort(Object a[]);
   public static void sort(Object a[], Comparator comp);
   public static void sort(long a[]);
   public static void sort(short a[]);
}
```

The Arrays class is like Collections, all static methods and no constructor, just a collection of utilities for working with arrays.

The Arrays class provides a sort() method for sorting any array. Once an array is sorted, you could also perform a quick binary search to find an element in the array. For the following example, the program sorts a list of names with the default String Comparable interface, then sorts with the case-insensitive Comparator one:

```
import java.util.*;
public class SortingPlanets {
  static class InsensitiveComp implements Comparator {
    public int compare (Object a1, Object a2) {
      String s1 = a1.toString().toLowerCase();
      String s2 = a2.toString().toLowerCase();
      return s1.compareTo (s2);
    }
  }
  public static void main (String args[]) {
    String names[] = {"Mercury", "Venus", "Earth",
      "Mars", "Jupiter", "Saturn", "Uranus",
      "Neptune", "Pluto",
```

```
            "mercury", "venus", "earth",
            "mars", "jupiter", "saturn", "uranus",
            "neptune", "pluto"
        };
        Arrays.sort(names);
        int namesLen = names.length;
        for (int i=0; i<namesLen; i++) {
          System.out.print (names[i] + " ");
        }
        System.out.println ();
        Arrays.sort(names, new InsensitiveComp());
        for (int i=0; i<namesLen; i++) {
          System.out.print (names[i] + " ");
        }
        System.out.println ();
    }
}
```

Running the program produces the following output. Notice how the second run through ignores case:

```
Earth Jupiter Mars Mercury Neptune Pluto Saturn Uranus Venus earth
➥ jupiter mars mercury neptune pluto saturn uranus venus
Earth earth Jupiter jupiter Mars mars Mercury mercury neptune Neptune
➥ pluto Pluto Saturn saturn Uranus uranus Venus venus
```

WARNING   If you perform a `binarySearch()` on an array, remember to `sort()` first. If you don't, undefined behavior occurs, including the possibility of an infinite loop.

TIP   To sort an object array in reverse order, use `Arrays.sort(anObjectArray, Collections.reverseOrder())`.

Miscellaneous Utilities

Besides sorting and searching with `Arrays` and `Collections`, you can use `Collections` to find the minimum and maximum values of your `Collection`. Unlike when you use `binarySearch()`, you do not have to `sort()` your collection beforehand. Just use the `min()` and `max()` methods of `Collections`, which take an optional `Comparator`.

Going between old and new style collections is relatively easy, too. To create an `Enumeration` from any `Collection`, just use `Collections.enumeration()`. To go from an array to a `List`, use `Arrays.asList()`.

Summary

Working with data structures in Java has many options, all depending upon your specific needs. While Java 1.2 introduces the Java Collections API, the historical collection classes are still available and readily used with all the code out there. Knowing about arrays, `Vector`, `Dictionary`, `Hashtable`, `Properties`, and `BitSet` will help you with Java 1.0 and 1.1 code. Understanding `Collection`, `Set`, `List`, and `Map`, along with all their implementations, will put you well on your way to success with the new Collections framework of 1.2. Where possible, using only the 1.2 collection classes (and arrays) is the way to go.

CHAPTER

EIGHTEEN

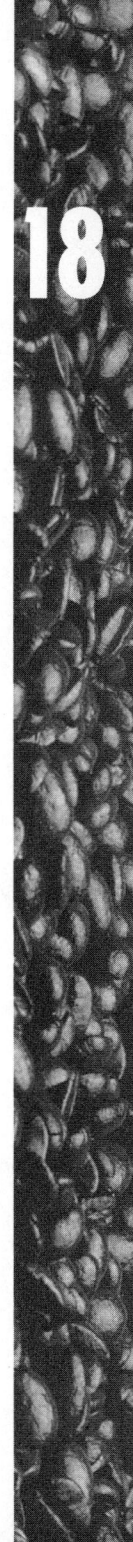

18

Advanced Applet Programming

- Simple, GUI-driven applets

- Applet pitfalls

- Well-behaved, multithreaded applets

- Tips on minimizing applet loading time

So far, the applets you have seen in this book have all been quick demonstrations of some Java class or Java method. Real-life applets, however, are usually seriously cool, functional, and/or perfectly compatible with all Java browsers.

It is a fact of life that the Web is a strange chimera of endless entertainment and serious information broadcasting. On one hand, you have an exploding population of people who use the Web as a vehicle to project their personality (through Web home pages that ooze unrestrained individuality); on the other hand, you have the world's businesses frantically trying to capture cyberspace market segments, by any means. Both groups are turning to Java to gain an edge over the competition, whether that competition is a multinational Wall Street–listed arch rival or the guy halfway across the globe whose Web page is nearly as cool as yours. Whichever category you find yourself in, writing real-life applets will test your creative and programming skills to the fullest. But before you start dreaming of having your applet listed in the JARS (Java Applet Rating Service, `http://www.jars.com`) Top 1% charts, you will want to work a little bit more on the basics.

This chapter begins with simple, GUI-driven applets and progresses to real-life, functional, multithreaded applets that will please your users.

Purely GUI-Driven Applets

Using the techniques presented so far, you can write some fairly functional applets. As long as you rely purely on a GUI to control your applet's functionality, you already have sufficient knowledge to design and implement programs like simple editors (paint programs, text editors, and so on) or even small games. To demonstrate what can be achieved with just a few buttons and a display area, you will develop a calculator. How about a scientific calculator that allows you to calculate the cosine of the logarithm of your next telephone bill?

Example: A Stack-Based Calculator

Start with some analysis first. What is the most elementary structure of any calculator? Answer: a large number of buttons and a display. These two aspects can form your top-level division of concern for the applet you are going to write. Although modern calculator displays can plot graphics and even print text, this example is restricted to supporting simple numbers in scientific notation.

As you know, scientific notation uses a compact notation for huge and very small numbers by expressing numbers as a base number (the mantissa) raised to some power of ten. Since your calculator will have this scientific bias, you might as well design it as a stack calculator. The choice of architecture is appropriate because of its simplicity compared with normal calculators. Moreover, stacks happen to be very relevant to Java: The Java VM (Virtual Machine) is a stack-based architecture with more than a passing resemblance to the calculator presented here.

The second feature of the calculator applet you will write is its display, or rather the digits it displays. Java has a number of fonts that provide a couple of digit styles, but none look like real calculator digits. Real calculators have relied (until recently) on seven-segment display elements to construct digits and numbers (first using LEDs, light-emitting diodes, then switching to LCD, liquid crystal display, technology). To give your calculator an authentic feel, you will design your own scalable, seven-segment digit character set from scratch (quite literally). Figure 18.1 shows the applet's convincing calculator appearance.

FIGURE 18.1:

A scientific calculator

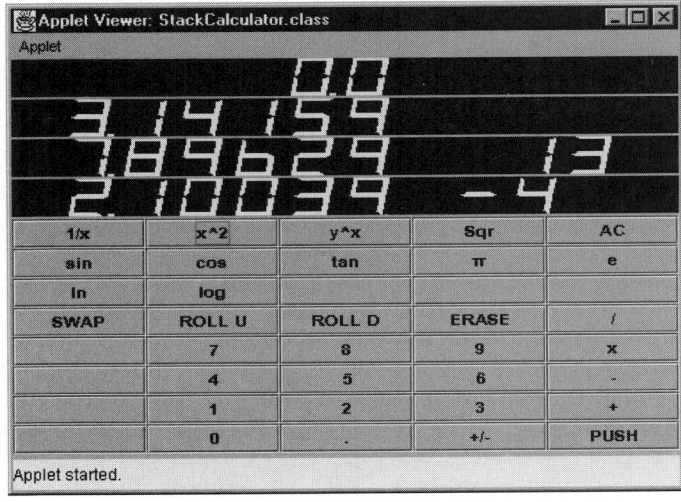

What Is a Stack Calculator?

Another name for stack calculators is *Reverse Polish Notation* (RPN) calculators. These types of calculators were used on the Apollo missions to the moon because the RPN system allows faster entry of complex calculations.

On a conventional calculator, you would add 10 and 20 by entering 10, then hitting the plus key, entering 20, and then hitting the equal key to calculate and display the result. With an RPN calculator, you would do this same addition by entering 10, then pressing the Enter key, entering 20, and finally hitting the plus key. When you press the plus key, the result is displayed; there is no need for you to press an equal key. In fact, there is no equal key on an RPN calculator (which may confuse and frustrate people not accustomed to using them).

The advantage of stack calculators becomes clear when working with complex expressions that involve prioritizing subcalculations using brackets. On RPN calculators (which do not have brackets either), the stack of the machine automatically provides for a prioritizing and remembering mechanism. It is this simple time-saving device (not having to type brackets) that prompted NASA to pick RPN calculators over the conventional type.

The applet's GUI design naturally reflects the functional and structural division of any calculator: There is a display area and a buttons panel. The StackCalculator applet program is subdivided into the following five classes:

- **StackCalculator**   The applet framework
- **KeyPanel**   The customized component holding all the calculator keys and their associated functions
- **LCDDigitDisplay**   The customized component dealing with the numeric display
- **CalcStack**   A class encapsulating the calculator's stack architecture
- **SevenSegmentDigits**   A class encapsulating a scalable character set of calculator-style digits

This is simply an application of the divide-and-conquer principle. These five classes cleanly subdivide the program, thus simplifying the overall problem of designing and writing a stack-based calculator applet. Although this applet can still be considered fairly trivial in terms of programming difficulty or complexity, it is already much too big to implement as one monolithic chunk of code (that is, in one class). As you have learned, breaking up problems into smaller subproblems that you solve individually, by implementing a class for each one, is good practice as well as a good way to prevent things from going wrong.

Now take a look at each of the calculator software blocks in turn, in top-down order:

```
import java.awt.*;
import javax.swing.*;

public class StackCalculator extends JApplet {
   static final int STACK_DEPTH = 4;        // an N-entry stack calculator

   public void init() {
     LCDDigitDisplay lCDDisplay = new LCDDigitDisplay (STACK_DEPTH);
     KeyPanel calculatorKeys = new KeyPanel (8, 5, lCDDisplay);
     Container c = getContentPane();
     c.add(lCDDisplay, BorderLayout.NORTH);
     c.add(calculatorKeys, BorderLayout.CENTER);
   }
   public String getAppletInfo() {
     StringBuffer s = new StringBuffer();
     s.append("Stack Calculator\n");
     s.append((char) 169);                  // Copyright symbol
     s.append("1996-8 Sybex, Inc., All Rights Reserved\n");
     return s.toString();
   }
   public String[][] getParameterInfo() {
     String[][] result = {
         {"NONE", "NONE", "This applet takes no HTML parameters"},
     };
     return result;
   }
}
```

Top-level applet code does not come much cleaner than this. It is devoid of almost any application-relevant code and concentrates on its proper, prime concern: being an applet. As such, it overrides only three JApplet methods, inherited from Applet: init(), getAppletInfo(), and getParameterInfo().

Methods getAppletInfo() and getParameterInfo() are optional but add a touch of polish to the applet. They are there for browsers to call when users pick the browser's About Applet or Applet Info menu options (the exact menu titles differ from browser to browser). The getAppletInfo() method usually returns a string containing information such as author, version, and copyright (plus anything else you care to add to it). The getParameterInfo() method returns an array of String triplets describing all the parameters your applet accepts via the <PARAM NAME="parameterName" VALUE="parameterValue"> HTML parameters. Each triplet consists of the parameter's name, its type, and a short description explaining the parameter's function.

The heart of this applet is its init() method. It constructs two custom components: one for the calculator display (lCDDisplay) and one for the calculator keys panel (calculatorKeys). These two components are then positioned in the applet as in any real calculator, with keys below the display.

And that is it. The applet has no more concerns. It does not deal with any of the calculator logic, the display refreshing, or the button presses. This means, quite patently, that the objects the applet creates manage themselves.

The Calculator Keys Panel

The KeyPanel class is the real processing heart of the calculator. Here is how it works:

```java
import java.awt.*;
import java.awt.event.*;
import javax.swing.*;


/***********************************************************************
 * The KeyPanel class encapsulates the entire calculator
 * buttons "panel" and all the mathematical
 * (and other) operations the buttons perform.
 ***********************************************************************/
class KeyPanel extends JPanel implements ActionListener {

    int rowSize;
    LCDDigitDisplay display;          // the stack display
    CalcStack       stack;            // the stack within the display

    // The calculator buttons are arranged as an array of 8 rows of 5 buttons

    private String[] keyLabels = {
        "1/x",   "x^2",   "y^x",    "Sqr",    "AC",     // row 0
```

```
      "sin",    "cos",    "tan",    "\u03c0", "e",      // row 1
      "ln",     "log",    "   ",    "   ",    "   ",    // row 2
      "SWAP",   "ROLL U", "ROLL D", "ERASE",  "/",      // row 3
      "   ",    "7",      "8",      "9",      "x",      // row 4
      "   ",    "4",      "5",      "6",      "-",      // row 5
      "   ",    "1",      "2",      "3",      "+",      // row 6
      "   ",    "0",      ".",      "+/-",    "PUSH"    // row 7
   };

   public KeyPanel (int rows, int columns, LCDDigitDisplay lcd) {
     rowSize = columns;
     display = lcd;
     stack = display.getStack();
     setLayout(new GridLayout(rows, columns));
     JButton b[] = new JButton [rows*columns];
     for (int i=0, n=keyLabels.length; i < n; i++) {
        b[i] = new JButton (keyLabels[i]);
        b[i].addActionListener(this);
        add (b[i]);
     }
   }

   public void actionPerformed(ActionEvent e) {
     // if any of the 0..9 digit keys is pressed
     String label = e.getActionCommand();

     if (label.equals(keyLabel(4,1)) ||
         label.equals(keyLabel(4,2)) ||
         label.equals(keyLabel(4,3)) ||
         label.equals(keyLabel(5,1)) ||
         label.equals(keyLabel(5,2)) ||
         label.equals(keyLabel(5,3)) ||
         label.equals(keyLabel(6,1)) ||
         label.equals(keyLabel(6,2)) ||
         label.equals(keyLabel(6,3)) ||
         label.equals(keyLabel(7,1))) {
       enterDigit(Integer.valueOf((String)label).intValue());
     } else if (label.equals(keyLabel(0,0))) {
       inverse();
     } else if (label.equals(keyLabel(0,1))) {
       square();
     } else if (label.equals(keyLabel(0,2))) {
```

```
    power();
  } else if (label.equals(keyLabel(0,3))) {
    squareRoot();
  } else if (label.equals(keyLabel(0,4))) {
    allClear();
  } else if (label.equals(keyLabel(1,0))) {
    sine();
  } else if (label.equals(keyLabel(1,1))) {
    cosine();
  } else if (label.equals(keyLabel(1,2))) {
    tan();
  } else if (label.equals(keyLabel(1,3))) {
    constantPI();
  } else if (label.equals(keyLabel(1,4))) {
    constantE();
  } else if (label.equals(keyLabel(2,0))) {
    ln();
  } else if (label.equals(keyLabel(2,1))) {
    log();
  } else if (label.equals(keyLabel(2,2))) {
  } else if (label.equals(keyLabel(2,3))) {
  } else if (label.equals(keyLabel(2,4))) {
  } else if (label.equals(keyLabel(3,0))) {
    swap();
  } else if (label.equals(keyLabel(3,1))) {
    rollUp();
  } else if (label.equals(keyLabel(3,2))) {
    rollDown();
  } else if (label.equals(keyLabel(3,3))) {
    delDigit();
  } else if (label.equals(keyLabel(3,4))) {
    divide();
  } else if (label.equals(keyLabel(4,4))) {
    times();
  } else if (label.equals(keyLabel(5,4))) {
    subtract();
  } else if (label.equals(keyLabel(6,4))) {
    add();
  } else if (label.equals(keyLabel(7,2))) {
    decimal();
  } else if (label.equals(keyLabel(7,3))) {
    changeSign();
```

```
    } else if (label.equals(keyLabel(7,4))) {
      enter();
    }
    System.out.println("Pressed the " + label + " key");
}

  private void enterDigit(int digit) {
    display.addDigit(digit);
  }

  private void delDigit() {
    display.removeDigit();
  }

  private void enter() {
    stack.pushValue(0);
    display.redrawStack(false);
  }

  private void changeSign() {
    stack.setAccumulator(-stack.getAccumulator());
    display.redrawStack(false);
  }

  private void squareRoot() {
    if (stack.getAccumulator() >= 0.0) {
      stack.setAccumulator(Math.sqrt(stack.getAccumulator()));
      display.redrawStack(true);
    }
  }

  private void square() {
    stack.setAccumulator(Math.pow(stack.getAccumulator(), 2));
    display.redrawStack(true);
  }

// Sine, cosine and tangents all take an angle in RADIANS
  private void sine() {
    stack.setAccumulator(Math.sin(stack.getAccumulator()));
    display.redrawStack(true);
  }
  private void cosine() {
```

```
      stack.setAccumulator(Math.cos(stack.getAccumulator()));
      display.redrawStack(true);
    }
    private void tan() {
      stack.setAccumulator(Math.tan(stack.getAccumulator()));
      display.redrawStack(true);
    }

    private void log() {
      if (stack.getAccumulator() > 1.0) {
        stack.setAccumulator(Math.log(stack.getAccumulator()) / Math.log(10.0));
        display.redrawStack(true);
      }
    }
    private void ln() {
      if (stack.getAccumulator() > 1.0) {
        stack.setAccumulator(Math.log(stack.getAccumulator()));
        display.redrawStack(true);
      }
    }

    // Raise next-on-stack (NOS) element to the power of top-of-stack (TOS)
    private void power() {
      double pow = Math.pow (stack.getStackElement(1), stack.getAccumulator());
      stack.drop();
      stack.setAccumulator (pow);
      display.redrawStack(true);
    }
    private void constantE() {
      stack.setAccumulator(Math.E);
      display.redrawStack(true);
    }
    private void constantPI() {
      stack.setAccumulator(Math.PI);
      display.redrawStack(true);
    }
    private void inverse() {
      if (stack.getAccumulator() != 0.0) {
        stack.setAccumulator(1.0/ stack.getAccumulator());
        display.redrawStack(true);
      }
    }
```

```java
    private void decimal() {
      display.decimal();
    }
    private void rollUp() {
      stack.rollUp(1);
      display.redrawStack(true);
    }
    private void rollDown() {
      stack.rollDown(1);
      display.redrawStack(true);
    }
// Swap TOS and NOS
    private void swap() {
      stack.swap();
      display.redrawStack(true);
    }
    private void allClear() {
      stack.clearStack();
      display.redrawStack(true);
    }
    private void add() {
      double sum = stack.getAccumulator() + stack.getStackElement(1);
      stack.drop();
      stack.setAccumulator (sum);
      display.redrawStack(true);
    }
    private void times() {
      double prod = stack.getAccumulator() * stack.getStackElement(1);
      stack.drop();
      stack.setAccumulator (prod);
      display.redrawStack(true);
    }
    private void subtract() {
      double diff = stack.getStackElement(1) - stack.getAccumulator();
      stack.drop();
      stack.setAccumulator (diff);
      display.redrawStack(true);
    }
    private void divide() {
      double div = stack.getStackElement(1) / stack.getAccumulator();
      stack.drop();
      stack.setAccumulator (div);
```

```
        display.redrawStack(true);
      }
      public String keyLabel (int row, int column) {
        return keyLabels[row*rowSize + column];
      }
      public Dimension getPreferredSize() {
        return new Dimension(300,200);
      }
      public Dimension getMinimumSize() {
        return getPreferredSize();
      }
    }
```

Before you focus on the application side of this class, you should see what class KeyPanel does on the Java and AWT level. To begin, KeyPanel is subclassed from JPanel. This is because you need your calculator buttons laid out using a different layout manager than the one the applet itself uses. And to specify a different layout for an area, you first need to create a new Container: the keys JPanel. Since calculator keys are universally laid out in rows and columns, a natural choice for a layout manager is GridLayout. The constructor for the KeyPanel class takes a reference (read: link) to the numeric display component that the applet created. Class KeyPanel needs to have this link so that it can call on the display to perform various functions. The design of your calculator means that the key panel is the active, controlling entity among the five classes.

The first thing the KeyPanel class does with the reference to the display object is to ask the display to hand it a reference to the numerical calculation stack embedded in the display object. As you will see, the very heart of the calculating machine (the stack) actually "belongs" to the display. This design decision is fairly arbitrary; the core calculator stack could have been created by the key panel object itself, or even by the applet. Whatever approach is taken, the key panel, the display, and the stack objects need to communicate with each other one way or another. The KeyPanel constructor then performs its main function, which is to create the panel of calculator buttons from a constant lookup array of button labels.

The next method is the event-processing heart of the applet: the actionPerformed() method of the KeyPanel. Every button has the KeyPanel registered as an action listener. This means that when any button is clicked, the same actionPerformed() method is called. This method consists of a large selection of if constructs that try to determine the origin of the button press event. The keyLabel() method is used to enhance program readability. This method takes two-dimensional (row, column) coordinates and returns the label for the button located at that position. This is much more readable than addressing the one-dimensional `String keyLabels` array directly.

If the `actionPerformed()` method traps a button press on one of the digit keys (0 to 9), it converts the digit `String` label into an equivalent integer and tells the display to deal with it via the `enterDigit()` method. (The key panel does not concern itself with the technicalities of data entry and editing; it is completely stateless.) Likewise, it matches up each of the remaining buttons with a method that incarnates its function. For example, when the button at position row=0, column=4 is pressed, the AC (All Clear) function is executed.

If you now take a look at some of the methods called to respond to button presses—for example, the `cosine()` method—you will see that you have reached the inner sanctum of your calculator. These methods are where the calculator's main functions are executed.

The `cosine()` example shows you the general approach for all these methods: Perform the calculator operation and then refresh the numeric display to show the result. The math functions that the calculator provides are implemented on top of class `Math` methods. The exact implementation of the calculation stack itself is hidden from `KeyPanel` by a class that encapsulates all details: `CalcStack`. The cosine function shows how this separation of function and use is nevertheless reunited; the stack object provides the `getAccumulator()` and `setAccumulator()` methods to retrieve and set the current value for the TOS element. Using these two methods, it then becomes trivial to take the cosine of the TOS element and store the result back in the stack. You can now easily figure out how all the other functions are (equally trivially) implemented.

NOTE   If you look at the label for the pi key, it is specified as \u03c0. This is the Unicode character for the Greek symbol for the pi character.

The Calculator Display

The next calculator element to examine is `LCDDigitDisplay`. Here is how it works:

```
import java.awt.*;
import java.util.*;
import javax.swing.*;
```

```
class LCDDigitDisplay extends JComponent {

  CalcStack    stack;             // the stack of numbers
  int          stackDepth;        // how many items stack holds
  Dimension    displaySize,oldSize; // canvas drawing area dimension
  Dimension    digitSize;
  SevenSegmentDigits lcd = null;  // ref to LCD-style 7-segment digits
  boolean freshNumber = true;
  int     decimalPosition = 0;
  Stack   undoStack;              // undo system for ERASEing digits
  private static final int LINE_GAP = 2;

  public LCDDigitDisplay(int depth) {
    stackDepth = depth;
    stack = new CalcStack(stackDepth);
    newNumber(); // reset all entry modes
  }

/** Reset all number constructing/editing state */
  private void newNumber() {
    freshNumber = true;
    decimalPosition = 0;
    undoStack = new Stack();
  }

/** An extra digit is being entered. Depending on which
 *  mode we're in, this digit should be added before or
 *  after the decimal point. */
  public void addDigit (int digit) {
    int changed = 1; // how many lines in stack need to be redrawn
    rememberUndo();  // remember current value for possible digit erase
    if (freshNumber) {              // brand new number ?
      stack.rollUp(1);
      stack.setAccumulator(0.0);  // clear A
      freshNumber = false;        // accumulate digits from now on
      changed = stackDepth;       // entire stack needs redrawing
    }
    // if we're not entering decimals yet, we can simply shift
    // the number up a digit by x10 and adding the digit in.
    double acu = stack.getAccumulator();
    if (decimalPosition == 0) {
      stack.setAccumulator(acu * 10.0 + digit);
```

```
    } else {
      // if we should add a decimal, we've got to add a fraction
      // scaled to the decimal place we've reached so far
      stack.setAccumulator(acu + ((float)digit)/decimalPosition);
      decimalPosition *= 10;
    }
    redrawStack(false);
  }

  public void removeDigit () {
    undo();                     // restore number and state to previous
    redrawStack(false);
  }

/***********************************************************
 * We're using a stack holding previous values and editing
 * state so that we can cheaply revert back to a
 * previous number if user erases a digit.
 ***********************************************************/

  public void rememberUndo() {
    undoStack.push(new Double( stack.getAccumulator() ) );
    undoStack.push(new Boolean( freshNumber )          );
    undoStack.push(new Integer( decimalPosition )      );
  }

  public void undo() {
    if (!undoStack.empty()) {
      decimalPosition = ((Integer) undoStack.pop()).intValue();
      freshNumber     = ((Boolean) undoStack.pop()).booleanValue();
      stack.setAccumulator(((Double) undoStack.pop()).doubleValue());
    } else {
      newNumber();
      stack.setAccumulator(0.0);
    }
  }

  /** User pressed '.'. From now on, we have to add decimals */
  public void decimal() {
    if (decimalPosition == 0) {
      decimalPosition = 10;   // tenths, hundredths, etc.
    }
  }
```

```
public CalcStack getStack() {
  return stack;
}
public void redrawStack(boolean newNumber) {
  if (newNumber)
    newNumber();
  repaint();
}
public void paint(Graphics g) {
  displaySize = getSize();

  // If we haven't initialized the LCD digits class, or if
  // the size of our drawing Canvas has changed,
  // initialize LCD digits

  if ((lcd == null) || (displaySize.width != oldSize.width) ||
      (displaySize.height != oldSize.height)) {

    oldSize = displaySize;       // remember new size
    digitSize = new Dimension(displaySize.width/12,
                        (displaySize.height/stackDepth) - LINE_GAP);
    // create scaled LCD digit "character set"
    lcd = new SevenSegmentDigits(digitSize);
  }
  for(int i=0, y; i<stackDepth; i++) {
    y = (stackDepth-i-1) * (digitSize.height + LINE_GAP);
    g.fillRect(0,y,displaySize.width, digitSize.height);
    lcd.drawNumber(stack.getStackElement(i), g, 0, y);
  }
}
public Dimension getMinimumSize() {
  return getPreferredSize();
}
public Dimension getPreferredSize() {
  return new Dimension(100, 120);
}
}
```

Class LCDDigitDisplay is responsible for the appearance of your calculator's numeric display. It is also a subclass of JComponent, so you can draw inside its area to your heart's content. Start with its constructor; all it does is create the numeric stack and reset the data-entry mode variables. The constructor is obviously not where all the action is hidden, in this case. The action is spread over two parts of the class: in the `addDigit()` and `removeDigit()` methods, and the `redrawStack()` and related display redrawing methods (including the overridden `Component` `paint()` method).

If you think about how a humble calculator works, you should first realize that there is more to pressing a digit key and seeing the digit appear in the display than meets the eye. If you use an accumulator to hold the current value being composed, then how do sequentially entered digits translate into a number being formed? Say the display already holds 12, and you enter an additional 7. The display then holds 127. The numbers 12 and 7 were transformed into a new number, 127, by multiplying by ten and adding the new digit. But what if the display holds 3.14 and you enter an additional 1? The number 3.14 multiplied by 10 is 31.4, plus 1 equals 32.4. Oops—you need to tune your algorithm a bit here.

When the decimal-point key is pressed, the data-entry algorithm should enter a new mode: decimal-entry mode. Any digits entered should first be divided by some power of ten, and then the result should be added to the current accumulator, without multiplying it beforehand by ten. The power of ten is determined by the position of the next decimal. This algorithm is implemented by the `addDigit()` method. (The test for `freshNumber` is not part of this algorithm; it is used to start with 0.0 whenever a first digit is being entered.)

Real calculators not only let you input numbers as just explained, but they are also forgiving when it comes to little errors; they have an erase key to erase the last digits entered. The stack calculator applet also has a key for this purpose. One possible way to have implemented this would have been to undo the last digit added by somehow reversing the step using the same input data as the `addDigit()` method: the accumulator's value and the decimal-entry mode variable (`decimalPos`). But while this is possible, it is overly complex and unnecessary. Instead, you can cheat by remembering the value of the accumulator (and its associated decimal-entry state) before you change it, so that you can restore it to its original state if an "erase digit" request arrives. This remember-and-undo mechanism relies on another stack—a `java.util.Stack` this time—to store each undoable step. Check out `rememberUndo()` and `undo()` for the details.

Both `addDigit()` and `removeDigit()` need to update the display to reflect the change in value of the number being constructed or edited. For this, they rely on `refreshStack()`, which tells `paint()` to update the display.

If you ignore the first `if` statement of `paint()` for a moment, you will see that the method consists of a loop that simply redraws the numbers held by the stack. To render the digits of the values, you could have used `drawString()` and some standard Java `Font`. Instead, your initial project requirement was that you would use dynamically rendered LCD-style seven-segment digit characters. So the expected `drawString()` has been replaced by `lcd.drawNumber()`. Object `lcd` is an instance of class `SevenSegmentDigits`. This class has the nontrivial responsibility of generating (at run time) a character set of seven-segment style digits. Since it would be highly inefficient to generate these digit images on the fly (that is, as `drawNumber()` required them), the `lcd` object creates and caches (stores) them for later use, as part of its own initialization. And that is why the construction of the `lcd` object is conditional in `refreshStack()`. The `if` statement tests whether the `lcd` object has been created yet or if the `JComponent` area has changed dimensions. In both cases, the digit character set needs to be (re)generated—scaled to fit the dimensions of the `JComponent`.

Later, you will see what goes on when the `lcd` object's constructor is invoked. But first, you should return to code aspects more fundamental to the operation of the calculator.

The Calculator Stack

Class `CalcStack` is used as a front end for the calculator's numeric stack data structure. Here is the source code for it:

```
/***********************************************************************
 * The CalcStack class encapsulates the numeric stack and all its
 * nonmathematical manipulations (i.e., stack manipulations only)
 *
 * Neither java.util.Stack nor LinkedList was used because the stack
 * we need can't have an infinite capacity and because we only need
 * doubles on our stack, not full-blown objects.
 ***********************************************************************/
public class CalcStack {

  double stack[];        // the stack at the heart of the machine
  int    stackDepth;

// Constructor: build a stack of given capacity
  public CalcStack(int depth) {
    stackDepth = depth;
    stack = new double[stackDepth];
    clearStack();
  }
```

```
public void pushValue(double x) {
  rollUp(1);
  setAccumulator(x);
}
public void rollUp(int times) {
  double lastVal;
  for (int r=0; r < times; r++) {
    lastVal = stack[stackDepth-1];
    for (int i = stackDepth-2; i >= 0; i-) {
      stack[i+1] = stack[i];
    }
    stack[0] = lastVal;
  }
}
public void rollDown(int times) {
  rollUp(stackDepth-times);
}
public void swap() {
  double temp;
  temp = stack[0];
  stack[0] = stack[1];
  stack[1] = temp;
}
public void clearStack() {
  for (int i=0; i < stackDepth; i++) {
    stack[i] = 0.0;
  }
}
public void drop() {
  rollDown(1);
  stack[stackDepth-1] = stack[stackDepth-2];
}
public void setAccumulator(double x) {
  stack[0] = x;
}
public double getAccumulator() {
  return stack[0];
}
public double getStackElement(int n) {
  return stack[n];
}
}
```

The unassuming statement `double stack[];` in the instance variables section at the top of class `CalcStack` is the core data structure for the entire program. The stack calculator applet relies on this array of `double` values to build all of its functionality around. Or rather, it relies on it indirectly, since class `CalcStack` mediates all access to this stack structure. This mediation is done through the methods provided by the class:

```
class CalcStack {
    public CalcStack(int stackDepth)
    public void clearStack()
    public void drop()
    public double getAccumulator()
    public double getStackElement(int n)
    public void pushValue(double x)
    public void rollDown(int times)
    public void rollUp(int times)
    public void setAccumulator(double x)
    public void swap()
}
```

It is clear, from the absence of a `pop()` method, that this stack has some very unstacklike properties. This is because the characteristics of a stack have been somewhat modified to be more productive for a calculator application:

- A `CalcStack` has a fixed size. It has *N* slots that are always filled with numbers. Real stacks, on the other hand, can be empty, half-empty (or half-full), or full.

NOTE   This example uses four number slots, but you can change the size by changing the STACK_DEPTH constant in the applet class and recompiling.

- A `CalcStack` can "roll" its contents "up" or "down." The best way for you to see what this means is to enter a number in the calculator applet and press the ROLL U and ROLL D buttons.

- When you remove the top-of-stack value (via a `getAccumulator()` and a `drop()`), the last slot keeps its original value (it is not cleared to 0.0).

Why not provide a `pop()`, which combines a `getAccumulator()` and `drop()`? You could, but the current design is more efficient. For example, to add two numbers together, the brute force solution would be to use the following algorithm (in pseudo-code):

```
a = pop()
b = pop()
sum = a + b
push(sum)
```

This code requires three full stack shuffles—two for the pop() methods and one for the push() method—but your code requires only a single stack shuffle. While this is not critical with small stacks of 4 elements, it could make a huge difference if you had a stack with 20 or 50 elements.

The Seven-Segment Digits Subsystem

The only remaining class to be dissected is SevenSegmentDigits:

```
/********************************************************************
 * Class SevenSegmentDigits encapsulates scalable 7-segment digits,
 * which can be rendered individually or as full double values
 ********************************************************************/
import java.awt.*;
import java.awt.image.*;
import java.util.StringTokenizer;

public class SevenSegmentDigits {

  protected Image[] digits;      // holds the computed images for digits 0..9
  protected Dimension scale;     // the scale user wanted the digits in

  static final int NUM_DIGITS = 10 + 1;  // one extra for minus symbol
  static final int ox   = 207;
  static final int oy   =  53;
  static final int segW = 230;
  static final int segH = 227;

  int originalWidth;
  static final double italicPercent = 0.15; // width to use for italicizing
  int italicRange;
  int decimalW, decimalH, decimalXoff, decimalYoff;

   // the vertices making up a 7-seg display cell
```

```
static final int[] points  = {207,53, 385,53, 207,280, 385,280, 240,75,
  360,75, 240,258, 360,258, 207,159,385,159,240,144, 360,144,
  240,176, 360,176};

  // each segment is a polygon composed of vertices

static final int[][] segDefs  = {{0,1,5,4}, {0,4,10,8}, {1,5,11,9},
  {8,10,11,9,13,12}, {8,12,6,2}, {9,13,7,3}, {6,7,3,2}};

// each digit is a collection of "ON" segments

// minus sign is "digit 10"
  static final String[] digitDefs= {"ABCEFG", "CF", "ACDEG", "ACDFG", "BCDF",
    "ABDFG", "BDEFG", "ACF", "ABCDEFG", "ABCDF", "D"};

/***********************************************************************
 * Constructor: note the size we've got the scale the digits
 * to and dynamically render them (a la PostScript)
 ***********************************************************************/
  public SevenSegmentDigits (Dimension size) {

    scale      = size;

    originalWidth  = scale.width;
    scale.width = (int) (scale.width * (1.0 - italicPercent));
    italicRange = originalWidth - scale.width;

    digits = new Image[NUM_DIGITS];

    for(int digit=0; digit < NUM_DIGITS; digit++) {
      digits[digit] = renderDigit(digit);
    }

    // decimal point image is calculated from digit size only

    decimalW = scale.width/6;
    decimalH = scale.height/10;
    decimalXoff = scale.width - decimalW;
    decimalYoff = scale.height - decimalH;
  }
```

```
/*********************************************************************
 * Render a 7-segment digit from its segment list definition.
 * Return as an Image to be stored.
 *********************************************************************/
  protected Image renderDigit(int number) {

    Image digitImage;
    Graphics g;
    String segments;

    digitImage = new BufferedImage (originalWidth, scale.height,
      BufferedImage.TYPE_INT_RGB);
    g = digitImage.getGraphics();

    segments = digitDefs[number];

    for(int seg=0; seg < segments.length(); seg++) {
      int segIndex = segments.charAt(seg)-'A';
      renderSegment(g, segIndex);
    }
    return digitImage;
  }
/*********************************************************************
 * Render a segment polygon in the given Graphics context.
 * This is where all the "clever" stuff happens:
 * we normalize coordinates of the segment to 0.0 .. 1.0 range
 * we scale them to the sizes required
 * we render the segment as a polygon
 *********************************************************************/
  protected void renderSegment (Graphics g, int segment) {

    int segDef[] = segDefs[segment];
    Polygon p = new Polygon();

    for(int vertex=0; vertex < segDef.length; vertex++) {

      int v = segDef[vertex];
      int x = points[v * 2 + 0] - ox;       // translate to origin
      int y = points[v * 2 + 1] - oy;
```

```
          double normX = ((double)x) / segW;    // normalize to 0.0..1.0
          double normY = ((double)y) / segH;

          int polyX = (int) (normX * scale.width); // scale to requested size
          int polyY = (int) (normY * scale.height);

          polyX += (1.0 - normY) * italicRange;    // italicize digits

          p.addPoint(polyX, polyY);
        }
        g.fillPolygon(p);
    }
/*************************************************************************
 * digitImage() gives clients access to the rendered digits
 *************************************************************************/
  public Image digitImage(int digit) {
    return digits[digit];
  }
/*************************************************************************
 * drawNumber() renders a double value in the given
 * gfx context at (x,y)
 *************************************************************************/
  public void drawNumber (double number, Graphics g, int x, int y) {

      String doubleStr = clean(Double.toString(number), 5);
      boolean isNegative = (doubleStr.charAt(0) == '-');
      int exponentPos = doubleStr.indexOf('E');
      int decimalPos = doubleStr.indexOf('.');
      int significantDigits = 6;  // we need toString() to gen 6 signif. digits
      int digitIndex = 0;
      int digitSlot;
      int digit;
      int digitX = 0 ;

      Color savedColor = g.getColor();
      g.setColor (Color.white);
      significantDigits = doubleStr.length();

      // if number is negative, render a minus in left-most slot
      if (isNegative) {
        g.drawImage(digitImage(10), x, y, null);   // draw minus
        significantDigits-;
```

```
      digitIndex = 1;
    }
    if (exponentPos != -1) {
      significantDigits -= (doubleStr.length() - exponentPos);
      // exponent positions, e.g., "E99"
    }
    if (decimalPos != -1) {
      significantDigits--;  // a decimal point isn't a digit either
    }

    // calculate the starting digit slot to align all numbers neatly
    digitSlot = 7 - significantDigits;  // slot 1 for max signif. digits

/* SOME DEBUGGING CODE HERE. YOU CAN ENABLE THIS IF YOU ENHANCE THIS CODE

    System.out.println("significantDigits " + significantDigits);
    System.out.println("digitIndex " + digitIndex);
    System.out.println("digitSlot " + digitSlot);
    System.out.println("isNeg " + isNegative);
    System.out.println("Exp " + exponentPos);
*/

    // now the mantissa rendering loop: render all signficant digits
    while (significantDigits != 0) {
      if ((digit = doubleStr.charAt(digitIndex++)) != '.') {
        digit -= '0';
        digitX = x + digitSlot*originalWidth;
        g.drawImage(digitImage(digit), digitX, y, null);
        significantDigits--;
        digitSlot++;
      } else {  // render decimal point in same slot as last digit
        g.fillRect(digitX + decimalXoff, y + decimalYoff, decimalW, decimalH);
      }
    }
    // if number contains an exponent, render that too
    if (exponentPos != -1) {
      if (doubleStr.charAt(exponentPos + 1) == '-') {  // draw minus
        g.drawImage(digitImage(10), x + 8*originalWidth, y, null);
        exponentPos++; // skip minus
      }
      digitIndex = exponentPos + 1;      // skip 'E' or 'E'
      digitSlot = 9;
```

```
        while (digitIndex < doubleStr.length()) { // render 'ENN'
          digit = doubleStr.charAt(digitIndex++) - '0';
          digitX = x + digitSlot*originalWidth;
          g.drawImage(digitImage(digit), digitX, y, null);
          digitSlot++;
        }
      }
      g.setColor (savedColor);
  }


  /***********************************************************************
   * Strip extraneous decimal chars from a numeric string.
   ***********************************************************************/
    private String clean(String src, int nDecimals) {
      String clean = "";
      StringTokenizer st = new StringTokenizer(src, "E.", true);
      boolean atDecimal = false;
      while (st.hasMoreTokens()) {
        String token = st.nextToken();
        if (atDecimal) {
          if (token.length() > 5  && Character.isDigit(token.charAt(0))) {
            token = token.substring(0, 5);
          }
          atDecimal = false;
        } else if (token.equals(".")) {
          atDecimal = true;
        }
        clean += token;
        // debug line System.out.println(clean);
      }
      return clean;
    }
}
```

Although this class only provides a more realistic-looking alternative to numbers rendered using a standard AWT font and drawString(), class SevenSegment-Digits packs a lot of interesting code.

Since your goal for this subsystem is to obtain scalable digits (so the display can be sized according to the applet's dimensions), you need to reject the easy approach of storing every digit as an external GIF (or other) image file. Such inflexible bitmap fonts are not easily scalable and, even when forced, the scaled results are of poor quality. Instead, you use vector definitions for your characters. Scalable fonts can be defined in a very compact space by storing some mathematical (vector) definition of their outline. A magnifying glass held up to any real calculator shows you how digits are usually constructed in the LCD. Figure 18.2 shows the structure of the seven-segment display building block used in every calculator.

FIGURE 18.2:

Seven-segment display and a configuration for digit 3

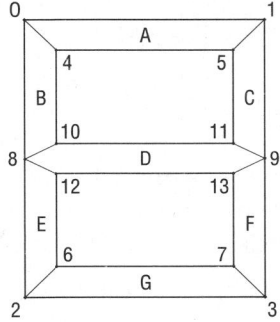
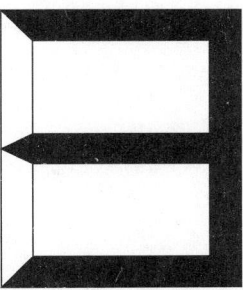

Digit '3' = "ACDFG"

If you now describe every digit as the collection of "on" segments (that is, lit segments) needed to represent it and every segment as the list of vertices forming a polygon outline for the segment, you would have a flexible, compact definition for the entire digit character set. The `points[]`, `segDefs[]`, and `digitDefs[]` arrays together define the calculator's character set in this way.

The `points` array holds the (x, y) pairs of the nodes (or vertices) from which a seven-segment display is constructed. The exact values of these coordinates were obtained using a simple painting program, and as you will see later, these values are mostly irrelevant to the rest of the code. The `segDefs` array defines each segment as a list of vertices (a vertex is encoded as an index into the `points[]` array). Similarly, the `digitDefs[]` array defines digits themselves as a list of segments. Although, for readability, letters were used instead of segment array indices. (Later, the code simply translates the letters to numeric indices, anyway.) The 3 digit, for example, is encoded as the segment list A-C-D-F-G.

NOTE   One thing to note at this stage is that the definitions of the digits are in regular (roman) typeface and not italicized. If you ran the StackCalculator applet, you noticed that the digits were actually in italics. This is achieved algorithmically at the rendering stage. You will see how a bit later.

If you now have a look at the constructor for the `SevenSegmentDigits` class, you will see that it takes one argument: a `Dimension`. The `Dimension` argument will be used to scale the digits to the requested size. The caching mechanism you will use is to render each digit into a separate, off-screen `Image` object. It is these `Image` objects that will simply be stored by the class, so that the `drawNumber()` method can recall them and blast them onto the screen without any further overhead. (This, by the way, is exactly the same technique used by all modern font-rendering subsystems, in laser printers and computer operating systems.)

As you learned in Chapter 10, to create an off-screen image, you create a `BufferedImage` instance. If you happen to have a `Component` handy, you could use its `createImage()` method. However, since class `SevenSegmentDigits` is not a `Component` itself (you are not extending any class, except `Object`, implicitly), you cannot just say "`createImage()`" on its own. Instead, you'll use the `BufferedImage` class to create a usable `Image` structure.

> **NOTE**   Creating off-screen images for double buffering is automatically done for you when using the Swing containers: `JPanel`, `JApplet`, and so on. So, if that were the case, if you do nothing, you still get the double-buffered effect.

Once the constructor has taken note of the arguments it received (by making local copies), it performs a one-off calculation, which adjusts the digit dimensions to be used for the remainder of the code. The calculation has to do with the algorithmic italicizing of the digits. Figure 18.3 shows why an adjustment is required.

FIGURE 18.3:

Character width adjustment necessary for italicizing digits

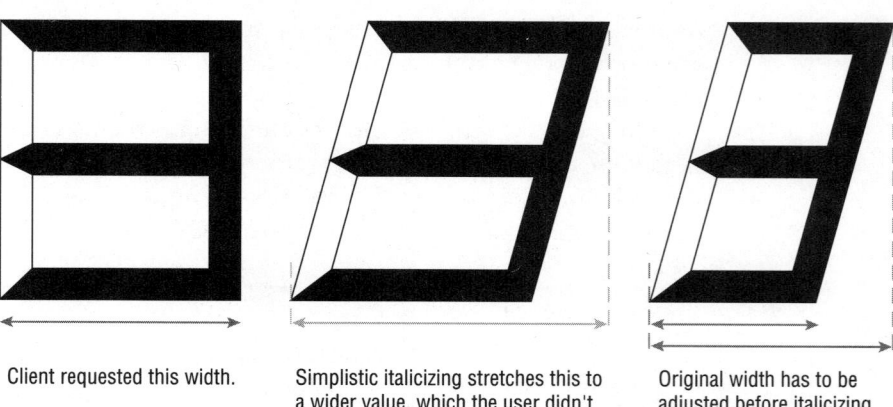

Client requested this width.   Simplistic italicizing stretches this to a wider value, which the user didn't ask for.   Original width has to be adjusted before italicizing takes place.

The constructor adjusts the requested width by -15 percent to make room for the later skewing of the digits, which must remain entirely within the bounding box dimensions requested. The difference in width between the original digits and the new digits will be the possible skewing range you will vary as a function of the character's height.

Once this initialization step has been taken, the `SevenSegmentDigits` object is ready to render every digit and cache them into an array of `Image` objects, called `digits` in the sample program. Note that the `for` loop actually renders 11 "digits." The minus sign (segment D on its own) is rendered, too, as the eleventh digit.

A different approach is required for the decimal point. Since the decimal point never occupies a digit slot in the display, but instead is positioned inside the slot of the units digit, you actually render a decimal point using a simple `fillRect()` when needed. The alternative—overstriking the previous digit with a decimal-point image and relying on transparency—would be considerably more complicated (although, to be honest, the `fillRect()` solution is a bit of a kludge, too).

The `renderDigit()` method called by the constructor is straightforward. It creates a new `Image` object in which to draw the digit, gets the `Graphics` context from the `Image`, and draws every segment of the requested digit. The `renderSegment()` method, on which `renderDigit()` relies, is the method that contains all the interesting code.

Method `renderSegment()` essentially constructs a polygon, which it then renders using `fillPolygon()`. The calculation of the polygon coordinates is the heart of the vector digit scaling and italicizing algorithm. First, the original vertex coordinates have to be normalized to fit an imaginary bounding box 1.0 units wide by 1.0 units tall. This step makes it easier to scale the digits to any final user-requested dimensions; you just multiply by those dimensions. The `ox`, `oy`, `segW`, and `segH` variables used in this process are defined as constants at the start of our class. Their values are obtained empirically by looking at the arbitrary coordinate system you use to define the digit vertices.

NOTE There is absolutely no significance in the fact that point 0 is located at (207,53). What is important is that this point acts as the origin for all other points and that you need to translate all points by those coordinates before you can apply the scaling.

The `polyX += (1.0 - normY) * italicRange;` statement is where the italic "style" is applied. It skews the points horizontally (by affecting their x-coordinates) as a function of the digit's height. Once all calculated coordinates have been added to the `Polygon` object used to hold them, the `renderDigit()` method uses `fill-Polygon()` to draw the scaled and italicized segment.

Finally, the `drawNumber()` method draws the various digits to represent a `double` passed to it as an argument. Its internal workings are left to you to discover.

As you can see, you can write a lot of applet code while relying purely on the GUI of your applet to activate various parts of your program. Sooner or later, however, you will write an applet that deviates from this approach, and this will be the source of a lot of problems. You will need to experiment to get things right. The following section will short-circuit this (painful) learning experience by highlighting the problem and giving you the solution to the problem without further delay.

Selfish Applets

The StackCalculator applet does not have a main loop that needs to "do" something all the time. It can afford to be fully functional by simply relying on the user to activate various elements of its user interface and on related short bursts of processing or graphical activity. But many programs are not so lucky; for example, consider an animation applet. It has a main loop that keeps on updating the animation frames. To illustrate the pitfall awaiting writers of this type of applet, Figure 18.4 shows a screen saver–like StarField applet that goes for the "cool" attribute but fails miserably in the compatibility department.

FIGURE 18.4:

StarField animation applet

Example: Animating a Star Field

Before the simple mistake committed by this applet is explained, take a look at the things it does right. Animating a star field and creating the illusion of flying through space can be achieved in a variety of ways. This applet actually models real 3-D objects (points, actually) flying toward the observer.

The main instance variable of the `StarField` class is an array holding a large number of `Star` objects. A `Star` object has two attributes: its (x, y ,z) position in 3-D space and its star temperature (which, as in reality, determines its color). A `Star` has one main instance method, `draw()`, which draws the star in a window viewport. Class `Star` also has a class method `setViewPort()` that allows a client to tell class `Star` the dimensions of the viewport in which to render the stars.

The core of the program is very simple:

- Move stars toward observer (by adding a dz, for delta z, speed to their z coordinate)

- Project stars from 3-D to 2-D (using a perspective projection formula)

- Render depth-cued stars in 2-D viewport

All of these steps are executed sequentially for each star in `Star` method `draw()`. If you refer to the listing, you will see that the code first checks whether the star has moved past (behind) the observer. If so, the star has become invisible, so it needs to be eliminated from the model. This is done by simply recycling that `Star` object by rerandomizing its 3-D position (in exactly the same way as during `Star` constructor time).

The perspective projection is achieved using these standard formulas:

$$\text{screen } x = (D * x)/z$$

$$\text{screen } y = (D * y)/z$$

The division by z is the key to understanding these equations. Objects located farther away from us appear smaller; mathematically, if an object's z-coordinate is bigger, its size will correspondingly shrink. Figure 18.5 illustrates this relationship graphically.

FIGURE 18.5:

Perspective projection

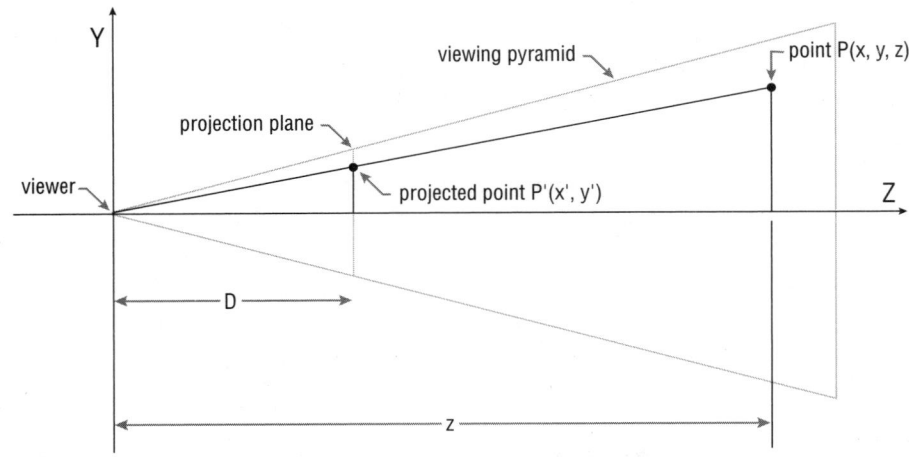

The 3-D to 2-D Perspective Projection

The z-coordinate of the stars can also be used for a simple and highly effective 3-D graphics effect: depth cueing. This is based on the physical reality that less and less light will reach an observer the farther an object is located from the observer. In other words, the object becomes less bright. With modern 256-color (or more) bitmapped displays, you can easily modulate the brightness of anything you draw by multiplying each red, green, and blue primary color component by the same scaling factor.

The applet uses one final technique to improve the realism of the effect: It physically scales the infinitely small star point (in this model) depending on its distance from the viewer. To reduce flicker, a simpler technique than double buffering is used: Erase only what changes. Whenever a star draws itself, it first erases its previous position. This way, you avoid having to wipe the whole viewport window for every star field redraw. The following code reveals the remaining nitty-gritty details of the implementation:

```java
import java.awt.*;

public class StarField extends java.applet.Applet {

    // Instance variables
    private final int NUM_STARS = 70; // the more stars, the slower the
                                      // animation
```

```java
    private Star[] stars = new Star[NUM_STARS]; // this array holds the
                                                // StarField
    private final int lensFactor = 200;

/***********************************************************************
 * Create a cloud of random stars. Cloud is housed in an array of Star.
 ***********************************************************************/
  public void init() {

    for(int i=0; i< stars.length; i++) {
      stars[i] = new Star(7500);            // argument is depth Z range
    }
    System.out.println("Stars initialized!");
  }


/***********************************************************************
 * First time only: wipe background to deep space black.
 * Forever:
 *    draw starfield
 ***********************************************************************/
  public void paint(Graphics g) {

    g.setColor(Color.black);
    Dimension size = getSize();
    Star.setViewPort(size);        // class method !
    g.fillRect(0, 0, size.width, size.height);

    while(true) {
      for(int i=0, n=stars.length; i < n; i++) {
        stars[i].draw(g, lensFactor);
      }
    }
  }


/***********************************************************************
 * Class Star
 * This class encapsulates the attributes and self-drawing
 * method of a star.
 ***********************************************************************/
  static class Star {
```

```
    private static int maxDepth;
    private static Dimension viewport; // applet window dimensions

    private int x,y,z;    // star position
    private int dz;       // star speed (parallel to z axis)

    private int sx,sy;    // projected screen x,y
    private int osx,osy;  // old screen x,y

    private int starTemperature;  // 0..100

/*************************************************************************
 * Randomly position a star in space by generating random (x,y,z)
 * coordinates.
 * Assign the star a random Z speed towards the viewer.
 * Assign the star a random star color (determined by its temperature).
 *************************************************************************/
    Star (int depth) {

      maxDepth = depth;   // note the maximum z distance allowed
      randomizeStar();
    }


/*************************************************************************
 * Give current star a random position and a random speed
 *************************************************************************/
    private final void randomizeStar() {

      x = (int) ((Math.random()-0.5) * 10000);
      y = (int) ((Math.random()-0.5) * 10000);
      z = (int) (Math.random() * maxDepth);    // spread throughout volume
      dz = 70 + (int)(Math.random() * 130);    // at random speeds
      starTemperature = (int)(100*Math.random());
    }
/*************************************************************************
 * This method projects and clips a star from 3-D to 2-D and renders
 * the depth-cued star in the viewport. To eliminate flicker, the stars
 * erase their own old positions before drawing their new position.
 * This eliminates the need for a global fillRect() to clear the whole
 * viewport, which would create a lot of flicker.
 *************************************************************************/
    final void draw (Graphics g, int lensFactor) {
```

```
float brightness;      //   0.0    ..   1.0
int starSize;          //   1      ..   5

z -= dz;                   // move stars toward us

// recycle stars which have gone past viewer (viewer has z=0)
if (z <= 0) {
  newStar(g);
}

sx = (int) (lensFactor*x/z);    // project (x,y,z) to screen (x',y')
sy = (int) (lensFactor*y/z);

sx += viewport.width/2;    // center starfield in viewport
sy += viewport.height/2;

// clip stars which moved outside of our viewing pyramid
if ((sx < 0) || (sx > viewport.width) || (sy < 0) ||
    (sy > viewport.height)) {
  newStar(g);
}
brightness = (float) (maxDepth - z) / maxDepth;
starSize = (int) (brightness * 5);

g.setColor(Color.black);
g.fillRect(osx, osy, starSize, starSize);

// sprinkle sky with small amounts of colored stars
// 85% are gray-white (equal amounts of R,G,B)
// 10% are yellow (equal amounts of R and G only)
// 3% are red (only R)
if (starTemperature > 15) {
  g.setColor(new Color(brightness, brightness, brightness));
} else if (starTemperature > 5) {
  g.setColor(new Color(brightness, brightness, 0.0F));
} else if (starTemperature > 2) {
  g.setColor(new Color(brightness, 0.0F, 0.0F));
} else {             // remaining 2% are blue
  g.setColor(new Color(0.0F, 0.0F, brightness));
}
// draw star
g.fillRect(sx, sy, starSize, starSize);
```

```
      osx = sx;    // remember star's position to erase it next time
      osy = sy;
    }
/**********************************************************************
 * When a star goes past viewer or moves out of view (above, below, left
 * or right), that star should be eliminated and reused to make
 * room for a new star, which is "born in the depths of space."
 **********************************************************************/
    private void newStar(Graphics g) {
      randomizeStar();
      z = maxDepth;      // but start them all the way at "the far end"
      g.setColor(Color.black);    // erase old star's twinkle
      g.fillRect(osx, osy, 5,5);
    }

    static void setViewPort(Dimension d) {
      viewport = d;
    }


/**********************************************************************
 * provide a toString()that summarizes a Star's state. This was
 * used only during development.
 **********************************************************************/
    public String toString() {
      return "("+ x +","+ y +","+ z +") sx=" + sx +" sy=" + sy;
    }
  }
}
```

If you run this applet embedded within any HTML page containing other applets, you will immediately see the problem: This applet uses up all the available CPU resources and consequently prevents other applets from running.

Look at the applet's `paint()` method. It never returns! An infinite loop was used in a method that is called (indirectly) by the browser. Method `paint()` is not meant to hold an applet's main body of code (which can legally contain infinite loops). If you run the applet using the appletviewer tool, you will notice that appletviewer itself ceases to function completely, because it relies on the `paint()` method to return before it can continue dealing with other things (like responding to menu selections). Obviously, an applet's body code needs to go somewhere else. In fact, you need a different approach altogether to get out of this situation. The next section offers the solution.

Multithreaded Applets

To allow the StarField applet to function in a well-behaved way among other applets located on the same page, you need to refer back to Chapter 12, where the start() and stop() applet methods were explained. Remember that applets have a "life cycle" that consists of the following main events:

- Applet initialization (the init() method of Applet is called).

- Applet gets browser's go-ahead to run (the start() method of Applet is called).

- Applet gets browser order to stop (the stop() method of Applet is called).

- Applet is told to clean up before being killed (the destroy() method of Applet is called).

The browser framework in which an applet runs imposes all of these methods. And all of them assume one important technical detail: that your applet is using a thread other than the painting thread for all its main logic. So far, these applets have not spawned any threads for their functionality to be sidetracked into. However, for the majority of applets, this is a necessary implementation evil.

Chapter 8 explained how to create new threads and how to control these independent program flows. Here is a summary of the basics of threads:

- Any thread must be a subclass of Thread or must implement the Runnable interface.

- A newly created thread must be started by invoking its start() method.

- A thread should stop when some conditional variable is set.

- A thread's code starts running with its run() method.

So far, all the applet examples have used the init() or paint() methods to hold the applet's main code. Neither is the correct location for the main code of the current example. The correct place to put the main applet logic is in a thread's run() method. This way, any endless loops (like the StarField applet's while(true) endless loop) will be controllable by whomever controls the thread. And the applet is the logical choice for the controlling entity. Figure 18.6 illustrates the relationship between the browser, the applet, and its thread.

FIGURE 18.6:

Time sequences between the browser, applet, and applet thread

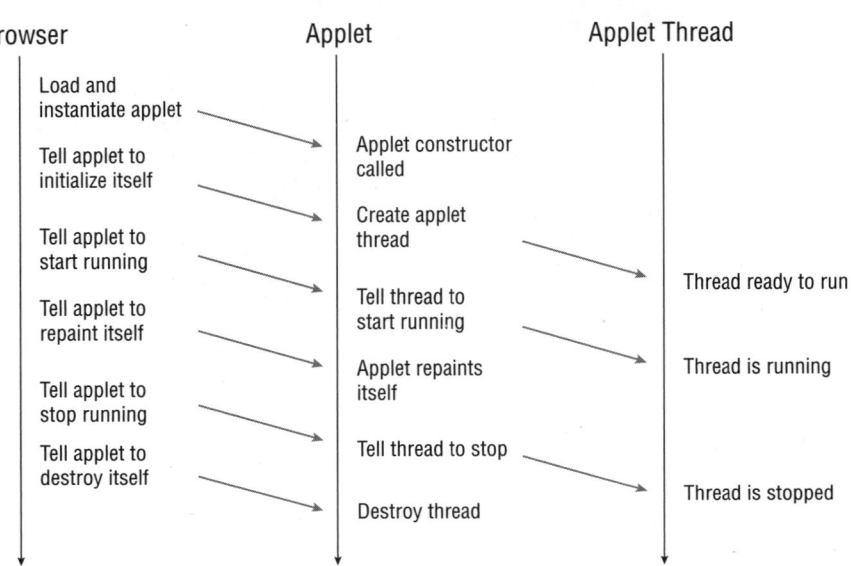

Browser	Applet	Applet Thread
Load and instantiate applet	Applet constructor called	
Tell applet to initialize itself	Create applet thread	
Tell applet to start running	Tell thread to start running	Thread ready to run
Tell applet to repaint itself	Applet repaints itself	Thread is running
Tell applet to stop running	Tell thread to stop	
Tell applet to destroy itself	Destroy thread	Thread is stopped

Since this browser/applet/applet thread model is the one assumed by all browsers, it is surprising that the basic `java.applet.Applet` class does not reflect this assumption. Fortunately, object-oriented subclassing allows you to remedy the situation by enhancing the `Applet` class to mirror the model. Once you have this new, improved applet class, you can use it instead of the vanilla `Applet` class at very little extra cost, giving you vastly enhanced functionality.

Extending the Applet Base Class to Support Multithreading

To extend class `Applet` to support having the applet logic execute in a thread, you simply need to add the thread creation, starting, and stopping operations in the appropriate places. The `AppletTemplate` class does exactly that:

```
import java.awt.*;
import java.applet.*;


/**
 *   Template for all good multi-threaded applets
 *   @author Tim Rohaly
 */
```

```java
public class AppletTemplate extends Applet implements Runnable {

  protected Thread theThread;

  /**
   * Provides a way for author to associate information with
   * an applet. Can be used for copyright, contact information, etc.
   * @return credits
   */
  public String getAppletInfo() {
    StringBuffer s = new StringBuffer();

    s.append("Applet Template\n");
    s.append((char)   169);             // Copyright symbol
//  s.append((char)0x2122);             // Trademark symbol
    s.append("1996-8 ORC Incorported, All Rights Reserved\n");

    return s.toString();
  }

  /**
   * Called once to initialize the Applet.
   * Create Components, lay them out, and perform any
   * initializations here.
   */
  public void init() {
    super.init();
  }

  /**
   * Called to start the Applet initially, and whenever Applet
   * is restarted (revisiting a page, for instance).
   * Start up threads here.
   */
  public void start() {
    super.start();
    if (theThread == null) {
      theThread = new Thread(this);
      theThread.start();
    }
  }
```

```
/**
 * Stop the thread whenever the Applet is iconified or the
 * user leaves the page. Guaranteed to be called before destroy().
 * Stop threads here.
 */
public void stop() {
  theThread = null;
}

/**
 * Used to clean up system resources.
 */
public void destroy() {
  super.destroy();
}

/**
 * Used to do any drawing to screen.
 * @param g Graphic to use
 */
public void paint(Graphics g) {
  super.paint (g);
}

 /**
  * All work should be done here.
  */
public void run() {
  Thread currentThread = Thread.currentThread();
  // By default, update display ever half second
  while (currentThread == theThread) {
    repaint();
    try {
      currentThread.sleep(500);
    } catch (InterruptedException e) {
    }
  }
}
}
```

The main additions to java.applet.Applet are the start() and stop() methods. Method start() now turns any AppletTemplate subclass (that is, your applets) into a thread and starts it.

Your applets can be transformed into threads because class `AppletTemplate` implements the `Runnable` interface. Or to be more accurate, you will implement that interface by putting all applet main logic in an overridden `run()` method. When the browser moves to a different page, the `stop()` method will automatically kill the applet thread. This means you need to be very careful that your `run()` method does not contain any initialization code; otherwise, this code will be re-executed each time your applet reappears. The proper place for true initialization code is the applet's usual `init()` method.

The `run()` method of the `AppletTemplate` subclass class must follow the pattern used by `AppletTemplate`. This primarily involves ensuring that the variable `theThread` has not been set to null to signify it is time to stop the thread. The inner part of the `while` loop would be the applet-specific logic.

```
public void run() {
  Thread currentThread = Thread.currentThread();
  // By default, update display ever half second
  while (currentThread == theThread) {
    repaint();
    try {
      currentThread.sleep(500);
    } catch (InterruptedException e) {
    }
  }
}
```

The `AppletTemplate` could be modified slightly so that the specifics of `run()` stayed within `AppletTemplate` and the subclass just provided a different method to run repeatedly with a delay time. This is left as an exercise for the reader, though.

NOTE   If you are using the Swing component set within your applet, you would need to modify this to subclass JApplet instead of Applet.

Using the AppletTemplate Class

Now that you have written the `AppletTemplate` class, you can forget almost everything about needing a thread in which to run your applets. The class takes care of almost everything for you. You keep using `init()`, `paint()`, and `update()` as usual, and you put your applet's main code inside the run() method. The following example does this, and as you'll see, it does not concern itself further with any thread issues whatsoever (information hiding and code reuse at its best!).

To demonstrate how easy it is to work with the new AppletTemplate class, here is a very short applet that contains a main loop (the analogue of the StarField applet's problematic infinite animation loop). This applet behaves properly, respecting the browser-applet protocol in every respect:

```
import java.awt.*;

public class Counter extends AppletTemplate {

  int counter;
  public void run() {
    Thread currentThread = Thread.currentThread();
    while (currentThread == theThread) {
      try {
        currentThread.sleep(100);
      } catch (InterruptedException e) {
      }
      counter++;
      repaint();
    }
  }

  public void paint(Graphics g) {
    g.drawString(String.valueOf(counter), 10,20);
  }
}
```

By building on the AppletTemplate class, this Counter applet uses multithreading and obeys the start() and stop() orders of the browser, and yet none of these technical details encumber its implementation. Since these technicalities serve only to obstruct your main goal of writing an applet with some required functionality, this is just as well.

NOTE The Counter applet has no purpose other than to demonstrate that an applet with a main loop can be made to coexist with browsers and other applets.

Example: An Analog Clock

As an example of a much more functional, well-behaved applet that uses the AppletTemplate class, you will design an analog clock applet. Digital clocks, in this digital age, are not a challenge to design, because their core can simply consist of the trivial one-liner that generates a string based on the current time. Analog clocks are a bit harder, because you need to render the time by drawing a clock face and its hour, minute, and second hands. Figure 18.7 shows what you are trying to achieve.

FIGURE 18.7:

GrandmotherClock applet

First, you should analyze the challenge. You can access the system's local time by constructing a java.util.Date object without any arguments. You must somehow convert this time into the graphical representation of Figure 18.7. The first step is to extract hour, minute, and second information from the Date object; this is done with another class: GregorianCalendar.

Designing with Radius and Angle Values

The first observation is that an analog clock can be viewed as a full 360-degree circle and that the hands can be thought of as indicating angles. Although it is 15:19:38 on this example's clock, you should think of it as though the hour hand is indicating (roughly) -12 degrees, the minute hand -24, and the second hand -138 degrees. Shifting your view of analog clocks from indicating times to indicating angles greatly simplifies the design of your program. This is because you can calculate pixel positions within circles easily if you have two values: a radius and an angle. This conversion from (radius, angle) to (x, y) coordinates is called conversion from polar coordinates to Cartesian (grid) coordinates. The formulas rely on sine and cosine for the transformation:

x = radius * cos(angle)

y = radius * sin(angle)

This set of equations produces (x, y) points located on the circle centered around the origin and having a *radius*. Since the clock circle is not located in the origin $(0,0)$, you need to translate all the coordinates by adding the coordinate of the new circle origin (ox, oy):

$x = ox$ + radius * cos(angle)

$y = oy$ + radius * sin(angle)

This is all the math you will need to write any analog clock program. The angle arguments are in radians, but you will convert your degree angles into radians only at the last minute, just before plugging them into the formulas.

This clock uses several decreasing radii for the following things:

- The clock face (this is the main radius from which all others are derived)
- The second hand
- The minute hand
- The smallest hand: the hour hand

The main clock face radius is calculated from the width and height the applet was given by the <APPLET> "WIDTH=.." and "HEIGHT=.." HTML tag parameters.

The core of the program consists of the calculations transforming the current time in the three clock-hand angles. This is done in the draw() method of class AnalogClock by transforming the 0–59 or 0–23 ranges into the 0–359 range of a full circle. Since zero seconds, minutes, or hours equals +90 degrees on a circle, you simply rotate the derived angles to compensate for this.

Once the angles are obtained, all that remains is to draw the hands. Here, an effort was made to eliminate flicker as much as possible, while at the same time trying to keep the updating algorithm as simple as possible. This is done by observing that for most of the time (59 seconds out of every minute), the only movement on the clock is the second hand indicating the passage of seconds. To animate the seconds, you should not, therefore, erase the whole clock and redraw it every new second. A simple (and frequently employed) technique is to remember the second hand's last position and erase only the second hand next time round, before redrawing it in its new position. This is the same technique employed to control flicker in the StarField applet: Remember old positions and erase old graphics before drawing new graphics. Only when the seconds tick over from 59 seconds to 00 seconds does the minute hand (and maybe the hour hand as well) need updating. This is when all clock hands are erased before they are repainted in their new positions.

This is the core of the program described. Peripheral to this is the main class structure for the program: The `AppletTemplate` class is being extended to hold all the applet-related aspects of the clock applet. All the analog clock aspects are encapsulated (and ready to be reused) in a separate class called `AnalogClock`.

Code Structured for Readability

When you look at the source code, note the following aspects of the code:

- Every method has a very well-defined function.

- None of the methods are too long.

- The code displays several levels of abstraction.

- The code is well commented.

- The variable identifiers were made as readable as possible.

- Similar code lines were formatted to align features vertically, clearly highlighting their similarities.

Here is the listing for the GrandmotherClock applet:

```
/***************************************************************************
 * GrandmotherClock Applet                                    (C) Sybex
 *-------------------------------------------------------------------------
 * An analog clock with hour, minute and second hands.
 * Uses APPLET PARAMETERS
 *  - Timezone : Time zone from which this clock came
 *  - Title    : The clock's title string beneath the clock face
 *
 ***************************************************************************/

import java.awt.*;          // mainly for Graphics
```

```java
import java.util.*;          // mainly for date support

public class GrandmotherClock extends AppletTemplate {

  // GrandmotherClock instance variables. All private

  private AnalogClock clock;  // the underlying clock we build on
  private Date theTime;

  private Font theFont = new Font("TimesRoman",Font.BOLD,16);
  private int width;
  private int height;
  private int radius;

  private String title;       // the text printed below the clock
  private int strx = -1;
  private int stry = -1;

  private double hourOffset;  // the time offset for this time zone
  private final long hourMillis = 1000*60*60; // no. of milliseconds in 1 hour

/*************************************************************************
 * Work out clock size from applet dims, grab applet params, calc title
 * string y coordinate (x coordinate calc needs FontMetrics which we can
 * not access yet from init()).
 *************************************************************************/
  public void init() {

    // set clock dimensions
    Dimension size = getSize();
    width  = size.width;
    height = size.height-20;      // leave room for clock title
    radius = Math.min(width, height)/2;

    // grab applet parameters
    // Timezone can be -12..0..12
    // Title is any reasonable string
    String timezone = getParameter("Timezone");
    if (timezone == null) {
      timezone = "0";
    }
    hourOffset = Double.valueOf(timezone).doubleValue();
```

```java
      title = getParameter("Title");
      if (title == null) {
        title = "Local time";
      }
      stry = size.height-5;
  }
/************************************************************************
 * Forever:
 *    get local system time, adjust TZ
 *    redraw clock
 *    wait a second
 ************************************************************************/
  public void run() {

    Thread currentThread = Thread.currentThread();
    while (currentThread == theThread) {
      theTime = new Date();
      if (hourOffset != 0.0) {
         theTime.setTime(theTime.getTime() + (long)(hourOffset*hourMillis));
      }
      repaint();
      try {
        currentThread.sleep(1000);
      } catch (InterruptedException e) {
      }
    }
  }
/************************************************************************
 * Applet clock time updating (called indirectly by repaint())
 *
 * If clock has never been drawn yet, create clock, redraw clock face
 * (the circular hour and minute marks).
 * Draw the clock hands to reflect the time.
 ************************************************************************/
  public void update(Graphics g) {
    if (clock == null) {
      clock = new AnalogClock(0,0, radius, Color.black, getBackground());
      paint(g);
    }
    clock.draw(g, theTime);
  }
```

```
/************************************************************************
 * Applet full clock repaint
 *
 * If clock already exists (paint() can be called before first update()),
 *   order clock to redraw itself.
 *   If title string x coordinate hasn't been calculated yet,
 *   calc strx to center the title beneath the clock face.
 *   Draw clock title.
 ************************************************************************/
  public void paint(Graphics g) {
    if (clock != null) {
      clock.drawFace(g);
      if (strx == -1) {
        strx = radius - g.getFontMetrics().stringWidth(title)/2;
      }
      g.drawString(title, strx, stry);
    }
  }
/************************************************************************
 * getAppletInfo() is called by some browsers when the user requests
 * the browser's "About.." or "Applet info" menu options.
 * This method should always return some basic information on the
 * applet.
 ************************************************************************/
  public String getAppletInfo() {
    return
      "Author: John Doe\n"
    + "Title : GrandmotherClock v1.0\n"
    + "Copyright 1996 LVA";
  }
/************************************************************************
 * getParameterInfo() is also called by some browsers when the user
 * requests the browser's "About.." or "Applet info" menu options.
 * This method should return an array of String triplets containing
 * parameter name/type/description
 ************************************************************************/
  public String[][] getParameterInfo() {
    String[][] paramDescriptions = {
      {"Timezone", "double", "Which Time Zone this clock comes from."},
      {"Title"   , "String", "Simply the title to use for this clock."}};
    return paramDescriptions;
  }
}
```

The heart of this applet is its `run()` method. Since the clock needs to run permanently, the method contains a `while` loop that continues to run until the Web page changes. The loop queries the local system time, orders a repainting of the clock (just the hands!), and then goes to sleep for a second.

The `repaint()` call will eventually lead to the `update()` method being called, which is overridden to ask the underlying `clock` object to update its graphically depicted time. The `update()` method is also responsible for the creation of the `AnalogClock` instance. The `if` statement uses whether or not the `clock` object has already been constructed as its cue to trigger the first full redraw of the clock (the clock face), via a call to `paint()`. The clock face is drawn only when the applet needs to be repainted in full or at initialization time. The clock's entire rendering is the responsibility of class `AnalogClock`, listed here:

```java
import java.awt.*;
import java.util.*;

/**************************************************************************
 * Class AnalogClock
 * This is where all analog clock matters are encapsulated, as
 * opposed to applet related things, in particular, time to hand
 * angles calculations and clock face and hands rendering.
 **************************************************************************/
class AnalogClock {

  private int radius;          // clock radius
  private int ox,oy;           // clock center
  private Color fg,bg;         // foreground and background colors

  private int secondsAngle,secondsAngleOld;    // all angles in degrees
  private int minutesAngle,minutesAngleOld;
  private int hoursAngle;

  private int secondsLength;
  private int minutesLength,minutesLength2;
  private int hoursLength,hoursLength2;

  // to convert degrees to radians
  private static final double toRadians = Math.PI/180.0;
```

```
/**************************************************************************
 * CONSTRUCTOR
 *  Work out hand lengths as proportions of the given radius.
 **************************************************************************/
  AnalogClock(int x, int y, int radius, Color fg, Color bg) {

    this.ox     = x + radius;
    this.oy     = y + radius;
    this.radius = radius;
    this.fg     = fg;
    this.bg     = bg;

    // the lengths of the hands are controlled by the percentages here
    secondsLength = (int) (0.88*radius);     // 88% of available radius
    minutesLength = (int) (0.85*radius);
    hoursLength   = (int) (0.75*radius);

    // these secondary lengths determine the diamond shape of
    // the hour and minute hands
    minutesLength2 = (int) (0.80*minutesLength);
    hoursLength2   = (int) (0.70*hoursLength);
  }
/**************************************************************************
 * Draw the circular marks around the clock's edge indicating
 * mins and hours every five minutes, Render a bigger mark.
 **************************************************************************/
  void drawFace(Graphics g) {

    for (int angle=0; angle < 360; angle+= 6) {          // 6  = 1 minute
      if ((angle % 30) == 0) {                           // 30 = 5 minutes
        drawRadialLine(g, angle-1, radius-6, radius-2);
        drawRadialLine(g, angle  , radius-8, radius);
        drawRadialLine(g, angle+1, radius-6, radius-2);
      } else {
        drawRadialLine(g, angle, radius-4, radius);
      }
    }
  }
/**************************************************************************
 * Redraw the clock's hands to reflect the time.
 * This is done in an intelligent way to avoid flicker:
 *   1) calculate angles of all hands
```

```
*    2) if minutes haven't changed, erase previous second hand cheaply
*       else erase all hands
*    3) draw all hands
*    4) remember position of minute and second hands for next time
*************************************************************************/
  void draw(Graphics g, Date time) {
    GregorianCalendar calendar = new GregorianCalendar();
    calendar.setTime(time);
    int secs = calendar.get(Calendar.SECOND);
    int mins = calendar.get(Calendar.MINUTE);
    int hrs = calendar.get(Calendar.HOUR);
    secondsAngle = -90 + secs*6 ;    // 0..59 -> 0..360
    minutesAngle = -90 + mins*6 ;    // 0..59 -> 0..360
    hoursAngle   = -90 +  hrs*30;    // 0..11 -> 0..360

    // let hour hand track minutes in hour smoothly !
    hoursAngle   += (mins*6)/12;

    g.setColor(bg);
    if (minutesAngle != minutesAngleOld) {
      // erase all hands by wiping clock interior (leaving time marks)
      g.fillOval(ox-secondsLength, oy-secondsLength,
               2*secondsLength, 2*secondsLength);
    } else {
      drawSeconds(g, secondsAngleOld);
    }

    g.setColor(fg);
    drawSeconds(g, secondsAngle);
    drawMinutes(g, minutesAngle);
    drawHours  (g, hoursAngle);

    secondsAngleOld = secondsAngle;
    minutesAngleOld = minutesAngle;
  }
/*************************************************************************
 * All hand drawing routines rely on lower-level methods.
 *************************************************************************/
  void drawSeconds(Graphics g, int angle) {
    drawRadialLine(g, angle, 0, secondsLength);
  }
  void drawMinutes(Graphics g, int angle) {
```

```
        drawHand(g, angle, 3, minutesLength, minutesLength2);
    }
    void drawHours(Graphics g, int angle) {
        drawHand(g, angle, 6, hoursLength, hoursLength2);
    }
/*************************************************************************
 * drawRadialLine is used to draw the second hand and the time
 * marks around the edge of the clock face.
 *************************************************************************/

    void drawRadialLine(Graphics g, int angle, int innerR, int outerR) {
        int x1,y1, x2,y2;
        x1 = ox + (int) (innerR*Math.cos(angle*toRadians) );
        y1 = oy + (int) (innerR*Math.sin(angle*toRadians) );
        x2 = ox + (int) (outerR*Math.cos(angle*toRadians) );
        y2 = oy + (int) (outerR*Math.sin(angle*toRadians) );
        g.drawLine(x1,y1, x2,y2);
    }
/*************************************************************************
 * drawHand builds a 4-point polygon to represent a clock hand
 * and draws the polygon on the clock face.
 *************************************************************************/
    void drawHand(Graphics g, int angle, int handThickness,
                  int totalLength, int intermediateLength) {
        Polygon hand;
        int x,y;

        hand = new Polygon();
        hand.addPoint(ox,oy);

        x = ox + (int) (intermediateLength*Math.cos((angle-handThickness)
                        *toRadians) );
        y = oy + (int) (intermediateLength*Math.sin((angle-handThickness)
                        *toRadians) );
        hand.addPoint(x,y);

        x = ox + (int) (totalLength*Math.cos(angle*toRadians) );
        y = oy + (int) (totalLength*Math.sin(angle*toRadians) );
        hand.addPoint(x,y);

        x = ox + (int)
            (intermediateLength*Math.cos((angle+handThickness)*toRadians) );
```

```
   y = oy + (int)
       (intermediateLength*Math.sin((angle+handThickness)*toRadians) );
   hand.addPoint(x,y);

   g.fillPolygon(hand);         // renders the hand on the clock
 }
}
```

Class AnalogClock relies heavily on the elementary trigonometry explained earlier. Read through the code, which is well commented, to see the details of how this class works.

Minimizing Applet Loading Times

As you can see, real and functional applets are not small. This means that the more functionality you add, the longer your applet will take to load over the Internet. As applets become more popular, more and more Internet bandwidth is used up to transfer these competing applets from their server machines to your client machine running your favorite Web browser. This can mean only one thing: more bandwidth pressure on the Internet and a resulting (further) slowing of response times. Therefore, in this climate of scarce bandwidth, it is important to minimize not only the amount of Internet resources your applet uses but also the response times to maintain a swift, interactive feel. You can achieve these goals in three ways:

- Minimize the size of the applet's executable.
- Minimize the number of classes used.
- Use Java Archive (JAR) files.
- Minimize the applet's initialization time.

Keeping Executables Small

Large files take longer to travel over the Internet than shorter files, and applets do not get any special treatment. If you have already looked at the size of the *.class files your Java compiler generates, you should be extremely impressed by their compactness. Compared to compiled C or C++ code, these Java executables are positively minute. There are two reasons for this:

- Java machine code is very compact.

- Every standard class imported by a Java program is not a physical part of the program.

Nevertheless, being able to shave off a number of bytes can mean the difference between a ten-second load and a twelve-second load (and to a user, waiting always feels like an eternity). This wide discrepancy is a result of packet segmentation, a property of Internet file transfers. You must have noticed the phenomenon when surfing the Web: The progress indicator fills up burst by burst, and just before completing the load, it indicates that it is stuck waiting for just a few dozen more bytes to finish. It is at this stage that you wish your applet was a couple of dozen bytes shorter.

The explanation for this frequent delay right at the end of a load has to do with the segmentation of a transmitted file. Although the Internet (the TCP protocol, to be correct) accepts data streams of arbitrary length, the networking devices (routers, in particular) responsible for getting this data from point A to point B usually have strict upper limits on the size of packets that they can deal with. This limit is frequently 256, 512, 1,024, or 2,048 bytes. Therefore, when an applet is transmitted over the network, it is segmented into N-1 packets of some fixed size plus one last tail packet containing the remaining few bytes. All of these packets travel independently and must be reassembled into the original applet executable byte stream at the client's end. When the last packet is unfortunate enough to be delayed, you can wait seconds for just a few bytes more to complete the load. And that's annoying at best.

So what can you do? Try to round down the size of your applet's classes to multiples of, say, 512 bytes? Unfortunately, it isn't that simple. The Internet is comprised of an incredibly diverse collection of networking hardware, which means that the resulting maximum transmission unit (MTU) used for any end-to-end communication can be almost anything. (The MTU is the largest packet fragment size used by the route chosen by your packets.) The best approach is to try to keep your class files as small as possible in the hope that, most of the time, those last few bytes will not need to be part of that awkward final fragmented packet. (Having said that, aiming for multiples of 256 bytes might work out well in practice.)

What techniques are available to shrink class sizes without having to waste too much time in the process? Here are some possibilities:

- Remove debugging code.

- Shrink string literals (by editing them to be a bit shorter, reducing verbosity).

- Compile with the javac -O (optimize) option enabled.

- Remove methods and variables that are never used.

Minimizing the Number of Classes

Few applets consist of only one class that relies exclusively on the standard Java classes for all its building blocks. Rather, the norm is that your applets will rely on classes you wrote yourself. All of these classes will need to be loaded separately by the Java VM, and here lies another inefficiency waiting to be optimized.

The problem is that, for example, loading 20 small blocks of data separately takes longer than loading one equivalent chunk 20 times the size of the small blocks. This is a result of the overhead incurred by creating network connections for each block (read: class) to be fetched. This means that you should keep a close watch on the number of extra classes your applets rely on.

One area where your project can generate lots of classes is with GUI code. As you learned in Chapter 14, you can approach the event-processing aspect of your GUI by creating anonymous inner classes or implementing interfaces yourself. The more anonymous inner classes you use, the more class files you will create. It pays to design your GUI with this issue in mind. This does not mean you should try to pack everything in one monstrous class; that would be ignoring every software engineering principle in the book. A compromise solution is always available.

Java Archive (JAR) Files

The 1.1 release of the JDK introduces JAR files. JAR files are like tar or zip files; they are aggregates of files. You create JAR files using the `jar` command.

If you aggregate all of the `.class` files of an applet into a single archive, a browser can read that archive from a server in a single operation. This greatly reduces the overhead of a multiple-file applet. The 1.1 class loader knows how to automatically extract classes from archives, so this technique involves no extra development on the client side. On the server side, you need to expand the `<applet>` line in your HTML file. For example, if your JAR file is called `myClasses.jar`, you will need to add the following to your `applet` tag:

```
<applet code=… archive = "myClasses.jar">
```

If you wish to list multiple `.jar` files, you will have to separate each with a comma. And keep in mind that you do not have to place all the files from an applet within the JAR file. You can include only the 80% or so most frequently used. Then, the remaining classes will be loaded only when needed.

Being Quick on Your Feet

People hate waiting. But once the waiting is over, they need time to process the change that has finally occurred. This means your applets should start doing something as soon as possible: Say "Hello" to the user, ask the user's name, show a progress indicator—in other words, keep the user busy. In the meantime, the applet can frantically continue to initialize itself, in the background. This necessitates the use of extra threads to interact with the user while the time-consuming initializations continue as the main thread. In this way, you can turn an annoyingly slow applet into a lightning quick applet that entertains its viewers to boot!

Remember: "Time flies when you're having fun." The rate at which time flows can indeed vary tremendously depending on your own perception of it. You can alter your users' perception of your applets' load times by cunningly exploiting this phenomenon. The way you do this can only enhance the applet.

TIP

Disney is a master of this concept. People are always waiting at Disney's various entertainment facilities, yet they rarely get upset during the process because Disney tries to hide the fact that you are waiting. They also tell you in advance approximately how long you have to wait. If you can do the same with your applets, your users should be much happier. (And, when in Walt Disney World, get in the line to the left, as most people automatically get in the one to the right.)

Summary

Applets that rely on a passive GUI to activate aspects of their functionality are the simplest types to implement. The stack calculator applet presented in this chapter is an example of this simpler type. However, the majority of real-life applets need to use multithreading. There is no way you can write a well-behaved (that is, usable) applet that contains an infinite loop (such as an animation loop) without relying on at least one dynamically created thread.

This chapter demonstrated how to add this inevitable thread and how to control it the way the browser protocol meant it to be controlled. Since the majority of applets cannot do without this thread for their main code, you learned how to extend the base `Applet` class into an `AppletTemplate` class. This gives you all the thread functionality you need, once and for all, in an easy-to-use, almost transparent way. A small, real-life clock applet was then presented to illustrate how all of the issues discussed in previous chapters come together, including the use of the new `AppletTemplate` class. Finally, you saw some techniques to make your applets load quickly and seem fast.

CHAPTER

NINETEEN

Streams and Input/Output Programming

- ■ Java's platform-independent methods for file manipulation

- ■ Simple file I/O

- ■ Stream input and output classes for byte manipulation

- ■ Stream readers and writers for character manipulation

- ■ Object streams for serialization

A computer's simplest model consists of a three-stage pipeline: input, processing, and output. Input and output (I/O) are therefore a fundamental aspect of computing. A computer wouldn't be much good without being able to accept data from the outside world and, as soon after as possible, present its computed results.

For this reason, computers are always accompanied by built-in or peripheral I/O interfaces (called *ports*), such as a serial port, parallel port, keyboard port, audio port, video port, SCSI port, and so on. With these ports, you can hook up actual I/O devices, such as modems, laser printers, keyboards, hi-fi systems, monitors, and hard disks, respectively.

This chapter describes how Java, through its `java.io` package, provides device- and platform-independent classes for file and stream manipulation.

I/O Software Layers

Because I/O devices are constantly being improved (and will eventually become obsolete), their programming necessitates constant code changes to keep track of the products' evolving features. This is obviously an unmanageable situation, which is why device drivers were introduced.

A *device driver* shields the application (to a certain extent) from the ever-changing programming model of a given I/O device. Nevertheless, device drivers aren't immutable over time. At some point, the physical I/O device will have been perfected with such radically new features—or simply have evolved so much—that the driver, too, will need to change its application interface. To address this problem, an extra layer of software is needed to protect the application from this slower, but equally inevitable, evolution in device drivers. This extra device-independent I/O layer is provided by the operating system. It is device independent because the services it presents are uniform for all the different I/O devices. Figure 19.1 illustrates these software layers. A layering (or buffering) approach such as this allows a slowly evolving (or frozen, in the case of existing legacy) application to remain compatible with the very latest hardware, which evolves almost on a monthly basis.

Taking the discussion one step further, you can view different operating systems as entities that exhibit too many I/O-related differences for any one application to deal with. And that, finally, is why programming languages wrap yet another layer of I/O software around the two layers depicted in Figure 19.1. Java provides this final layer in the form of an entire hierarchy of classes in package java.io. The classes it contains shield any application from operating-system–dependent (but nevertheless generic) I/O handling.

At the heart of this java.io package lies the concepts of streams and files. Because few applications can do without creating, processing, or managing files, we'll discuss the file classes first, and then move on to the bulk of the package: the stream classes.

FIGURE 19.1:

Software layers that deal with different levels of evolution rate

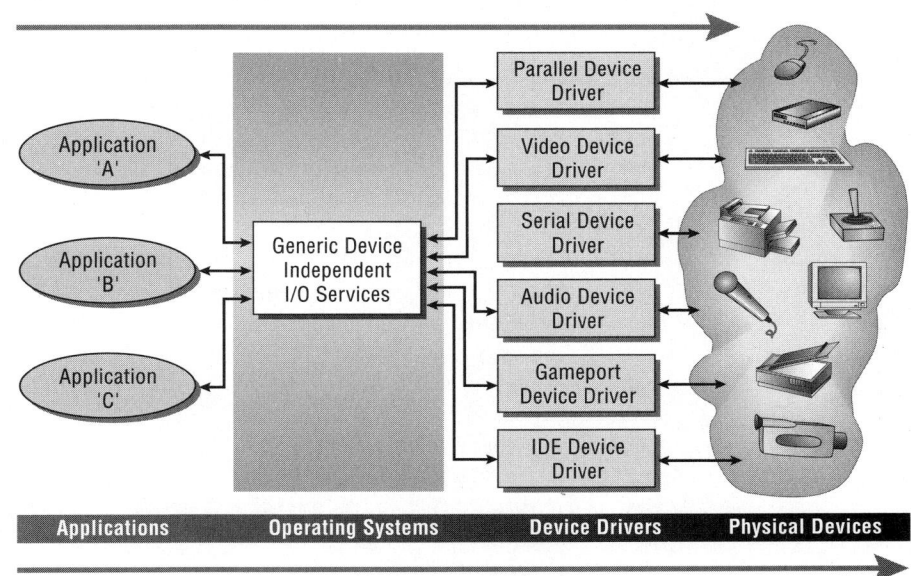

Java's File-Management Methods

An operating system's filing system is one of the most basic services provided to applications. Historically, it was one of the very first services to be developed. During the 1950s, the ability of a computer to automatically locate and load a program into its memory was not something computer programmers could take for granted.

Today, all filing systems allow a hierarchical directory structure of arbitrary complexity to organize files of almost equally arbitrary length (4GB is a common limit per file). Filenames identify files and are usually limited in length to 32–256 characters. Although all filing systems are essentially identical in terms of these basic services, their exact implementations make them (as usual) mutually incompatible.

Java's *File* Class

To shield Java applications from this incompatibility obstacle, class `File` defines platform-independent methods for manipulating a file maintained by a native filing system. Here is the definition of class `File`:

```java
public class File extends Object implements Serializable, Comparable {
    public static final String pathSeparator;
    public static final char pathSeparatorChar;
    public static final String separator;
    public static final char separatorChar;

    public File(String path);
    public File(String path, String name);
    public File(File dir, String name);
    public boolean canRead();
    public boolean canWrite();
    public int compareTo(File anotherFile);
    public int compareTo(Object o);
    public boolean createNewFile();
    public static File createTempFile (String prefix) throws IOException;
    public static File createTempFile (String pattern, File dir)
        throws IOException;
    public boolean delete();
    public void deleteOnExit();
    public boolean equals(Object obj);
    public boolean exists();
    public File getAbsoluteFile();
    public String getAbsolutePath();
    public File getCanonicalFile() throws IOException;
    public String getCanonicalPath() throws IOException;
    public String getName();
    public String getParent();
    public File getParentFile();
    public String getPath();
```

```
    public int hashCode();
    public boolean isAbsolute();
    public boolean isDirectory();
    public boolean isFile();
    public boolean isHidden();
    public long lastModified();
    public long length();
    public String[] list();
    public String[] list(FilenameFilter filter);
    public File[] listFiles();
    public File[] listFiles(FileFilter filter);
    public File[] listFiles(FilenameFilter filter);
    public static File[] listRoots();
    public boolean mkdir();
    public boolean mkdirs();
    public boolean renameTo(File dest);
    public boolean setLastModified(long when);
    public boolean setReadOnly();
    public String toString();
    public URL toURL() throws MalformedURLException;
}
```

As you can see from the list of supported methods, class File does not allow you to access the contents of the file. No read() or write() methods of File let you do this. Class File primarily names files, queries file attributes, and manipulates directories or temporary files, all in a system-independent way. The following is a description of what you can do with files without opening them.

Naming Files

Files are named in two manners. You can either provide both a directory and a file within the directory, or you can provide both, combined into one value. Either way, you are providing the full name of a file you wish to potentially access. The benefit of providing a directory and file name separately is that you don't have to worry about how to combine the two. For instance, on Microsoft Windows–based platforms, the separator character is the forward slash character ('\'). On UNIX platforms, it is the backward slash character ('/'). While you can ask the File class what the separator character is via the separator class variable, why bother combining the two terms yourself if you can let the constructor of the File class do it for you?

To demonstrate, the following code fragment attempts to create three `File` objects. Each line does succeed in creating a `File` object. However, if you try to use the `File` object, only the second or third attempts will succeed on all platforms, as they do not have a file separator value hard-coded into the source code.

```
File f1 = new File ("tmp/foo");
File f2 = new File ("tmp", "foo");
File f3 = new File (new File ("tmp"), "foo");
```

Querying File Attributes

Class `File` provides a handful of methods for querying a minimal set of file attributes:

- Whether the file exists

- Whether the file is read protected

- Whether the file is write protected

- Whether the file is, in fact, a directory

- Whether the file is hidden

Discovering other common file attributes, such as whether a file is a system or an archived file, is not supported. As with Java's AWT classes, the designers of these classes have taken the least common denominator of all filing systems for their model. If Java included features (like an archived attribute) that aren't supported by some systems, its universal compatibility across platforms would be jeopardized.

The following program shows how to use a `File` instance to query the attributes of a file. The file is specified as a command-line parameter:

```
import java.io.*;
public class Attr {

    public static void main (String args[]) {

        File    path;

        path = new File(args[0]);   // grab command-line argument
```

```
        String exists    = path.exists()       ? "Yes" : "No";
        String canRead   = path.canRead()      ? "Yes" : "No";
        String canWrite  = path.canWrite()     ? "Yes" : "No";
        String isFile    = path.isFile()       ? "Yes" : "No";
        String isHid     = path.isHidden()     ? "Yes" : "No";
        String isDir     = path.isDirectory()  ? "Yes" : "No";
        String isAbs     = path.isAbsolute()   ? "Yes" : "No";

        System.out.println ("File attributes for '" + args[0] + "'");

        System.out.println ("Exists         : " + exists);
        if (path.exists()) {
          System.out.println ("Readable       : " + canRead);
          System.out.println ("Writable       : " + canWrite);
          System.out.println ("Is directory   : " + isDir);
          System.out.println ("Is file        : " + isFile);
          System.out.println ("Is hidden      : " + isHid);
          System.out.println ("Absolute path  : " + isAbs);
        }
      }
    }
```

You can experiment with this program by passing it various filenames and directory names, either relative or absolute.

NOTE   Note the use of the ternary operator (?:) to select either a "Yes" or "No" string for variables. This approach is more compact than the logical equivalent of using if–else statements.

Manipulating Directories

A handier program would be one that could list the contents of a directory, like the dir or ls commands in most operating systems. Fortunately, class File supports directory-list generation via its list() and listFiles() methods. Here's another program that recursively (that is, calling upon itself) lists directories and their contents:

```
import java.io.*;
import java.util.*;
public class Dir {
```

```
      static int indentLevel = -1;

    Dir (String path) {
      listPath (new File (path));
    }

    void listPath (File path) {
      File files[];  // list of files in a directory

      indentLevel++;                    // going down...

      // create list of files in this dir
      files = path.listFiles();

// Sort with help of Collections API
    Arrays.sort (files);
      for (int i=0, n=files.length; i < n; i++) {
        for (int indent=0; indent < indentLevel; indent++) {
          System.out.print("    ");
        }

        System.out.println(files[i].toString());

        if (files[i].isDirectory()) {
          // recursively descend dir tree
          listPath(files[i]);
        }
      }
      indentLevel--;                    // and going up
    }

    public static void main (String args[]) {
      new Dir(args[0]);
    }
  }
```

The program relies on a couple of interesting concepts. First of all, it calls itself recursively in the statement listPath(files[i]). This repeated invocation of the listPath() method restarts listPath() with a new path, initialized to contain the deeper directory to list.

The directory listing is sorted, using the `Arrays` class of the `Collections` API, described in Chapter 17.

To highlight the current directory level, the contents of a directory are indented according to its nesting level in the filing hierarchy. The depth of the recursion level, tracked in the class variable `indentLevel`, determines this nesting level. When a method exits, class variables are not destroyed as are simple method variables. The program relies on this behavior to track the recursion level across multiple invocations of `listPath()`.

Static variables have one more interesting attribute: They are not allocated anew each time a new instance of a class is made. Therefore, they are also called class variables. (This aspect of variable `indentLevel` is not relevant in the program because it does not explicitly create multiple instances of class `Dir`, although `Dir` is instantiated once when the example program is loaded.)

Manipulating Temporary Files

One nice feature of the `File` class, added with Java 1.2, is support for temporary files. Prior to Java 1.2, if your program needed to use a temporary file, you had to manage the file location and name all by yourself. Now, thanks to the static `createTempFile()` methods and the `java.io.tmpdir` system property, you can guarantee that the `File` object created by the method did not previously exist. Also, by calling `deleteOnExit()`, you can ensure the file will be deleted if the Java environment ends naturally.

NOTE   The system property `java.io.tmpdir` contains the system-dependent temporary file location. This would typically be `C:\TEMP` for Microsoft Windows platforms and `/tmp` for UNIX systems.

Java's *RandomAccessFile* Class

Class `File` doesn't let you read or write files, but other classes provide this functionality. To read or write files, you can use one of two approaches. You can use the extremely powerful stream classes (which are discussed later in this chapter), or you can use class `RandomAccessFile`. The latter option is easy to use but has severe limitations if you want to start writing flexible or more complex applications. Class `RandomAccessFile` does I/O only on files, whereas the stream I/O classes can do I/O on almost anything, including files. So, bear in mind that there is a much more powerful way to do the same procedures (see "Java's I/O Stream-Manipulation Methods" later in this chapter for more information).

The definition of class `RandomAccessFile` neatly sums up its functionality:

```
public class RandomAccessFile extends Object implements DataInput, DataOutput {
    public RandomAccessFile(File file, String mode) throws IOException;
    public RandomAccessFile(String name, String mode) throws IOException;

    public native void close() throws IOException;
    public final FileDescriptor getFD() throws IOException;
    public native long getFilePointer() throws IOException;
    public native long length() throws IOException;
    public native int read() throws IOException;
    public int read(byte b[]) throws IOException;
    public int read(byte b[], int off, int len) throws IOException;
    public final boolean readBoolean() throws IOException;
    public final byte readByte() throws IOException;
    public final char readChar() throws IOException;
    public final double readDouble() throws IOException;
    public final float readFloat() throws IOException;
    public final void readFully(byte b[]) throws IOException;
    public final void readFully(byte b[], int off, int len) throws IOException;
    public final int readInt() throws IOException;
    public final String readLine() throws IOException;
    public final long readLong() throws IOException;
    public final short readShort() throws IOException;
    public final int readUnsignedByte() throws IOException;
    public final int readUnsignedShort() throws IOException;
    public final String readUTF() throws IOException;
    public native void seek(long pos) throws IOException;
    public native void setLength(long newLength) throws IOException;
    public int skipBytes(int n) throws IOException;
    public void write(byte b[]) throws IOException;
    public void write(byte b[], int off, int len) throws IOException;
    public native void write(int b) throws IOException;
    public final void writeBoolean(boolean v) throws IOException;
    public final void writeByte(int v) throws IOException;
    public final void writeBytes(String s) throws IOException;
    public final void writeChar(int v) throws IOException;
```

```
    public final void writeChars(String s) throws IOException;
    public final void writeDouble(double v) throws IOException;
    public final void writeFloat(float v) throws IOException;
    public final void writeInt(int v) throws IOException;
    public final void writeLong(long v) throws IOException;
    public final void writeShort(int v) throws IOException;
    public final void writeUTF(String str) throws IOException;
}
```

In terms of organization, the class can be viewed simply as implementing the two interfaces `DataInput` and `DataOutput`. Class `RandomAccessFile` does not add much functionality beyond the methods defined in these two interfaces. Here is the definition for interface `DataOutput`:

```
public interface DataOutput extends Object {
    public abstract void write(byte b[]) throws IOException;
    public abstract void write(byte b[], int off, int len) throws IOException;
    public abstract void write(int b) throws IOException;
    public abstract void writeBoolean(boolean v) throws IOException;
    public abstract void writeByte(int v) throws IOException;
    public abstract void writeBytes(String s) throws IOException;
    public abstract void writeChar(int v) throws IOException;
    public abstract void writeChars(String s) throws IOException;
    public abstract void writeDouble(double v) throws IOException;
    public abstract void writeFloat(float v) throws IOException;
    public abstract void writeInt(int v) throws IOException;
    public abstract void writeLong(long v) throws IOException;
    public abstract void writeShort(int v) throws IOException;
    public abstract void writeUTF(String str) throws IOException;
}
```

The `DataOutput` interface specifies a list of output (writing) methods that allow you to write any kind of simple Java type. It also requires all implementing classes to be able to write bytes or blocks of bytes. Outputting objects, beyond `String`, is supported by the more advanced `ObjectOutput` interface, discussed later in this chapter. The exact bitstream produced by these methods should not concern you because a symmetrical interface (`DataInput`) specifies the equivalent reading methods that allow you to read back any data written out.

Here is the definition for the companion `DataInput` interface:

```
public interface DataInput extends Object {
    public abstract boolean readBoolean() throws IOException;
```

```
public abstract byte readByte() throws IOException;
public abstract char readChar() throws IOException;
public abstract double readDouble() throws IOException;
public abstract float readFloat() throws IOException;
public abstract void readFully(byte b[]) throws IOException;
public abstract void readFully(byte b[], int off, int len) throws IOException;
public abstract int readInt() throws IOException;
public abstract String readLine() throws IOException;
public abstract long readLong() throws IOException;
public abstract short readShort() throws IOException;
public abstract int readUnsignedByte() throws IOException;
public abstract int readUnsignedShort() throws IOException;
public abstract String readUTF() throws IOException;
public abstract int skipBytes(int n) throws IOException;
}
```

Some of the asymmetrical differences of the two interfaces are the `skipBytes()` method, the unsigned number reading methods, and the `readLine()` method instead of the `writeBytes()`/`Chars()` methods. In actuality, the two interfaces really are each other's opposites. Class `RandomAccessFile`, then, if you look back at its definition, is mainly the implementation of these two interfaces. The following are the main additional methods in `RandomAccessFile`:

```
void seek(long pos) throws IOException
long getFilePointer() throws IOException
long length() throws IOException
void close() throws IOException
void setLength(long newLength) throws IOException;
```

There is no `open()` method because constructing a `RandomAccessFile` object opens the file for you. The `seek()` method is the method that reflects the class's random-access reading and writing capability. Using `seek()`, you can position the file pointer to any position within the file to read or write in any place. You are not limited to sequential reads or writes (although that is what the reading and writing methods default to). Method `getFilePointer()` lets you find out where the next read or write will occur. For a newly opened file, it is always position 0; in other words, the beginning of the file. The `setLength()` method is good for truncating a file, when `newLength` < `length()`. If `newLength` > `length()`, the new contents are undefined.

By now, you have noticed the universal exception type used by class Random-AccessFile (and the DataInput and DataOutput interfaces), which signals a failure within any of its methods: exception IOException. The explicit throws clause at the end of every method's signature means you are required to either:

- Add explicit error-handling code to methods that use RandomAccessFile by enclosing uses within a try-catch pair.

- Let the exception bubble up to the caller of your method by declaring your methods to throw IOException in turn.

As an example of using this class, including the explicit handling of possible exceptions, the following program uses two RandomAccessFile objects to compare two files:

```java
import java.io.*;
public class Diff {

//----------------------------------------------------------------
// program main()
//
// check command-line argument (filename)
// open & load files
// process files
// close files
//----------------------------------------------------------------

  public static void main (String args[]) {

    RandomAccessFile fh1 = null;
    RandomAccessFile fh2 = null;

    int  bufsize;          // size of smallest file
    long filesize1 = -1;
    long filesize2 = -1;
    byte buffer1[];        // the two file caches
    byte buffer2[];

    // check what you get as command-line arguments

    if (args.length == 0 || args[0].equals("?") ) {
      System.err.println ("File Diff v1.2 (c) 06/98 L. Vanhelsuwe");
      System.err.println ("-----");
      System.err.println ("USAGE: java Diff <file1> <file2> | ?");
```

```
    System.err.println ();
    System.exit(0);
  }

  // open file ONE for reading

  try {
    fh1 = new RandomAccessFile (args[0], "r");
    filesize1 = fh1.length();
  } catch (IOException ioErr) {
    System.err.println ("Could not find " + args[0]);
    System.err.println (ioErr);
    System.exit(100);
  }

  // open file TWO for reading

  try {
    fh2 = new RandomAccessFile (args[1], "r");
    filesize2 = fh2.length();
  } catch (IOException ioErr) {
    System.err.println ("Could not find " + args[1]);
    System.err.println (ioErr);
    System.exit(100);
  }

  if (filesize1 != filesize2) {
    System.out.println ("Files differ in size !");
    System.out.println ("'" + args[0] + "' is " + filesize1 + " bytes");
    System.out.println ("'" + args[1] + "' is " + filesize2 + " bytes");
  }

  // allocate two buffers large enough to hold entire files

  bufsize = (int) Math.min(filesize1, filesize2);
  buffer1 = new byte [bufsize];
  buffer2 = new byte [bufsize];

  try {
    fh1.readFully (buffer1, 0, bufsize);
    fh2.readFully (buffer2, 0, bufsize);

    // now the HEART of the program...
```

```
      for (int i = 0; i < bufsize; i++) {
        if (buffer1[i] != buffer2[i]) {
          System.out.println ("Files differ at offset " + i);
          break;
        }
      }
   } catch (IOException ioErr) {
     System.err.println ("ERROR: An exception occurred while processing the
     ➡ files");
     System.err.println (ioErr.toString());
   } finally {
     try {
       fh1.close();
       fh2.close();
     } catch (IOException ignored) {}
   }
  }
}
```

The program uses a performance-enhancing trick that is often useful when processing files. It buffers the entire files in memory by reading them, in one swoop, using readFully(). This technique can be much quicker than reading a file bit by bit in a loop. Once the two files are cached in memory, they can be compared very quickly using simple array accesses (the nearest Java gets to the even more efficient pointer addressing of C and C++).

Remember the I/O method invocations need to be surrounded by try-catch statements. Because Java (quite rightly) insists that programs catch potential exceptional circumstances or events, you must explicitly add error-handling code for those occasions. The alternative would be to declare the main() method as being able to throw an IOException itself. While this strategy would have made the example easier to read, it would not be good programming practice. The main() method is the topmost method, and any exceptions it throws will be thrown straight into the user's face. This is not acceptable, so you should opt to catch the errors explicitly and translate them into more user-friendly error messages (instead of erroneous behavior!).

Because exceptions can seriously disturb an algorithm's programmed flow of control (exceptions are essentially goto statements), you need to ensure both files are closed under all circumstances. You do this in the finally statement at the end of the main() method. Regardless of whether any exceptions occurred, the code within the finally statement will always execute so that statement is the perfect place to put your file close() calls.

Java's I/O Stream-Manipulation Methods

The invention of streams is surprisingly recent, dating back to 1984 when Dennis Ritchie (who co-designed the C language with Brian Kernighan) implemented the first stream I/O system for AT&T's Unix operating system. Software streams are linear flows of data. As with real rivers of water, users can come up to a stream and sequentially fish out (in other words, read) items floating toward them, or they can throw items into the stream (that is, write) in the secure knowledge that the items will be carried to a known destination at the end of a stream.

Every stream has either a data source (like a spring), in the case of input streams, or a destination (called a *sink*, like a river's delta), in the case of output streams. Both input and output streams, therefore, have the need to be connected to something before they will do any useful work. Input streams should be connected to some device producing data, and output streams should be connected to some device that can accept data (see Chapter 9).

The package java.io consists mostly of stream, reader, and writer I/O classes. Stream input and output classes manipulate bytes; readers and writers manipulate characters (recall that in Java, unlike C, a character is two bytes). The package defines four root classes from which most of the package's stream subclasses are derived. Not surprisingly, they are InputStream, OutputStream, Reader, and Writer. Study these abstract classes before tackling any of the concrete stream classes; all stream classes rely on the fundamental functionality of the superclasses.

Input Streams and Readers

All input streams can read bytes of data from some kind of data source. Their core functionality is reading data in the form of bytes (and only bytes). This reading can be done on a byte-by-byte basis or in blocks of arbitrary length. All other functionality encapsulated in InputStream is peripheral to this elementary reading functionality. Here is the full definition of class InputStream:

```
public abstract class InputStream extends Object {
    public InputStream();
    public int available() throws IOException;
    public void close() throws IOException;
    public synchronized void mark(int readlimit);
    public boolean markSupported();
    public abstract int read() throws IOException;
```

```
    public int read(byte b[]) throws IOException;
    public int read(byte b[], int off, int len) throws IOException;
    public synchronized void reset() throws IOException;
    public long skip(long n) throws IOException;
}
```

The three mark-related methods—mark(), reset(), and markSupported()—deal with an optional input stream support for undoing read() methods. All input streams should implement markSupported() but are free to return either true or false. Most return false, meaning that mark() and reset() don't do anything (or throw exceptions). Abstract class InputStream itself implements markSupported() to return false, so all classes that inherit from InputStream without overriding this method do not support marks.

When the mark feature is supported, the system works as follows: You can mark any position (in an input stream) to come back to later if you want to undo the reading of data that has been read since the mark was placed. The readlimit argument to the mark() method determines how far you can read ahead while still legally being able to reset() the reading position to the marked position. The readlimit is expressed in bytes. It is used to internally allocate a buffer for all the data that potentially needs to be unread. If you read past the readlimit and still do a reset(), the results are undefined.

A whole collection of concrete classes descends from class InputStream:

- FileInputStream
- ByteArrayInputStream
- StringBufferInputStream
- SequenceInputStream
- PipedInputStream
- ObjectInputStream
- FilterInputStream
  - BufferedInputStream
  - DataInputStream
  - LineNumberInputStream
  - PushbackInputStream

All of these classes have one thing in common (apart from being subclasses of InputStream): All of their constructors let you specify a data source in one way or another. In the case of the FileInputStream, ByteArrayInputStream, String-BufferInputStream, SequenceInputStream, ObjectInputStream, and Piped-InputStream classes, this data source is the attribute that differentiates that class from the others in the list. A FileInputStream, for example, is just that because the data stream that flows from it is sourced from a file that is part of your machine's filing system. In the same way, a PipedInputStream is just that because the stream that flows from it is sourced from a pipe (a *pipe* is a mechanism that allows two different processes to communicate). And so on...

All the FilterInputStream descendants have a very different purpose. Their constructors also allow you to specify a data source, but this is in the form of another input stream as the source for the stream. However, if that were all FilterInput-Streams could do, there would be little point in them; they would simply pass on the data unmodified. However, the purpose of FilterInputStreams is not to connect to any specific data source (like the previous classes) but to enhance streams. Streams can be enhanced either by altering the stream's data itself (for example, by compressing it) or by adding handy features to the minimal functionality enshrined in class InputStream.

The abstract Reader class is very similar to InputStream. Here is its definition:

```
public abstract class Reader extends Object  {
  public abstract void close() throws IOException;
  public void mark(int readAheadLimit) throws IOException;
  public boolean markSupported();
  public int read() throws IOException;
  public int read(char cbuf[]) throws IOException;
  public abstract int read(char cbuf[], int off, int len) throws IOException;
  public boolean ready() throws IOException;
  public void reset() throws IOException;
  public long skip(long n) throws IOException;
}
```

The difference between readers and input streams is that readers manage characters while input streams manage bytes. Reader has the following subclasses:

- FileReader

- CharArrayReader

- StringReader

- PipedReader
- InputStreamReader
- FilterReader
  - BufferedReader
  - LineNumberReader
  - PushbackReader

Readers, like input streams, have various possible data sources, such as files and strings. The filter subclasses take other readers as their data sources and modify the source's characters. Most (but not all) of the input stream classes have corresponding reader classes.

FileInputStream and *FileReader*

Class `FileInputStream` is an input stream whose data is sourced from an everyday file. As such, you could consider it as (nearly) half of class `RandomAccessFile`, which allows you to read and write files. You could use two `FileInputStream` objects to implement the featured file difference program with equal ease. The constructors for class `FileInputStream` are what the class really adds to the abstract class `InputStream`:

```
public FileInputStream(File file) throws FileNotFoundException
public FileInputStream(FileDescriptor fd) throws FileNotFoundException
public FileInputStream(String name) throws FileNotFoundException
```

These constructors create a new `FileInputStream` object and, at the same time, open the file, ready for reading. The first constructor takes a filename as a `String`, but you should avoid doing this if the filename has any platform-dependent characters in it. For example, a filename of abc\def would work fine on a Windows platform but would fail on a Unix machine.

The second constructor is the one more commonly employed. It takes a platform-independent `File` object describing which file needs to be accessed.

The constructors for `FileReader` are identical to those for `FileInputStream`:

```
public FileReader(File file) throws FileNotFoundException
public FileReader(FileDescriptor fd) throws FileNotFoundException
public FileReader(String name) throws FileNotFoundException
```

File input streams should be used only for reading byte-oriented data. For text files, file readers are preferred because reader classes support full 16-bit characters.

Here is a program that uses the `FileReader` class to read a text file and calculate its word frequencies:

```java
import java.io.*;
import java.util.TreeMap;
import java.util.Iterator;

public class WC {

  public static void main (String args[]) throws IOException {

    WordFrequencyCounter wfr;
    FileReader          longText;
    StreamTokenizer     wordStream;
    String              word;
    int                 tok;

    if (args.length != 1) {
      System.err.println( "Usage: java WC <textfile>" );
      System.exit(10);
    }

    wfr        = new WordFrequencyCounter();
    longText   = new FileReader (args[0]);
    wordStream = new StreamTokenizer (longText);

    // treat any punctuation as word delimiters

    wordStream.whitespaceChars ('!','@');

    while ((tok = wordStream.nextToken()) != StreamTokenizer.TT_EOF) {
      if (tok == StreamTokenizer.TT_WORD) {
        word = wordStream.sval;
        wfr.count (word);
      }
    }

    Iterator it = wfr.keySet().iterator();
    while (it.hasNext()) {
      word = (String) it.next();
      System.out.println (wfr.frequency(word) + " " + word);
    }
  }
}
```

```
//-------------------------------------------------------------------
class WordFrequencyCounter extends TreeMap {

// no constructor needed; this class is just a fancy sorted tree

//-------------------------------------------------------------------
// first see if this word has already been encountered;
// if not, then create a fresh counter for it;
// otherwise, increment its counter
//-------------------------------------------------------------------

  public synchronized int count (String word) {

    Integer counter;

    counter = (Integer) get(word);
    if (counter == null) {
      counter = new Integer(1);
    } else {
      counter = new Integer (counter.intValue() + 1);
    }
    put(word, counter);
    return counter.intValue();
  }

//-------------------------------------------------------------------
// find out how many times this word has been encountered
//-------------------------------------------------------------------

  public synchronized int frequency (String word) {

    Integer counter;

    counter = (Integer) get(word);
    if (counter == null) {
      return 0;
    } else {
      return counter.intValue();
    }
  }
} // End of class WordFrequencyCounter
```

The program consists of two classes: the main driver class WC (which stands for Word Counter, in case you were wondering) and a thoroughly reusable WordFrequencyCounter class. The main class (WC) opens the file specified as a command-line argument by creating a FileReader object. It then passes that object straight to another java.io class: StreamTokenizer.

Class StreamTokenizer takes a reader as an argument to its constructor and then allows you to have the stream tokenized. In this case, *tokenized* simply means chopped up into its constituent words. The StreamTokenizer method nextToken() divides the file stream up into words and makes the stream of words available via the StreamTokenizer instance variable sval (String value). The StreamTokenizer class is discussed in more detail later in the chapter.

The individual words thus extracted from the stream are then passed on to the WordFrequencyCounter object, whose duty it is to keep track of which words have already been encountered and, if so, how many times. It keeps track by relying heavily on the functionality provided by class TreeMap, part of package java.util.

A Java TreeMap implements a sorted map, or dictionary, data structure. Dictionaries consist of paired entries: the first half called the *key* and the second half called the *value*. The program uses a dictionary to track the number of occurrences of each word because dictionary keys cannot occur more than once. Therefore, the word itself is the key to the dictionary entry, with the count being the value of the entry. Although the word count need only be a humble integer, a Java TreeMap requires objects for both keys and values. Primitive datatypes (like boolean, char, and int) are not supported. That's why you should use a heavyweight Integer object instead, to hold the counter. The main TreeMap methods are put(key, value) and get(key). Because the WordFrequencyCounter class extends TreeMap, it is able to use these methods unqualified, in other words acting on itself (the this object reference is implied).

There's another interesting aspect to this program: To actually list every encountered word, along with its associated frequency, the program uses the iteration and sorting capability of TreeMap.

ByteArrayInputStream and *StringBufferInputStream*

The ByteArrayInputStream and StringBufferInputStream classes are virtually identical. They both create input streams from strings of bytes. ByteArrayInputStream does this literally, from an array of bytes. StringBufferInputStream uses a String (and not a StringBuffer) as its array of bytes.

Because Java `Strings` are essentially arrays of Java `chars` (in other words, 16-bit wide Unicode characters), you might wonder how the resulting byte (input) stream is structured: low byte first or high byte first? Well, neither. `StringBufferInput-Stream` discards the high byte of the Unicode characters. Although this is fine for Java characters in the range 0 to 255, all other characters that make use of Unicode's vastly expanded encoding space will lose information or be corrupted in the string-to-stream transformation.

The following are the main constructors for the two classes:

```
public ByteArrayInputStream (byte buf[])
public StringBufferInputStream (String s)
```

The two classes have one major but subtle difference. Neither class copies its respective input data into internal buffers. Therefore, in the case of `ByteArrayInput-Stream`, the source array might be modified by the client application at any time while the stream is being used. This type of conflict can be the source of bugs that are very hard to find. This problem cannot occur for `StringBufferInputStreams`, because the source `String` can never be modified "under the stream's nose." For this reason alone, it is safer to always convert a byte array that will be used as a stream into a string by using the `String` constructor `String(byte array[])` or `String (byte array[], String encoding)`.

CharArrayReader and *StringReader*

The `CharArrayReader` and `StringReader` classes are the character-oriented counterparts of byte array input streams and string buffer input streams. The main constructors for these classes are:

```
public CharArrayReader (char chars[])
public StringReader (String s)
```

As with the corresponding streams, there is a possible data-integrity problem. If a `char` array reader's array is modified, the reader's behavior could be unpredictable. This is not an issue with a string reader because the data source is an unchangeable string.

SequenceInputStream

Class `SequenceInputStream` allows you to seamlessly glue together two or more input streams to create one long, concatenated stream. (There is no corresponding reader class.) Whenever you read from such a "super" stream and an EOF (end of file) is encountered by one of the building block streams, class `SequenceInput-Stream` proceeds to the next stream in the list (without letting the EOF reach you). Only when the last input stream is exhausted do you get an EOF (a -1 returned by `read()`). The constructors give you two ways of specifying the sequence of streams:

```
public SequenceInputStream(InputStream s1, InputStream s2)
public SequenceInputStream(Enumeration e)
```

The first form is convenient when you only need to glue two input streams together. The second form is more general in its ability to take an open-ended list of input streams. The required argument type is rather surprising, though. You would expect a type-safe array of `InputStream` (for example, an `Input-Stream[]` list) to be the ideal way to specify an ordered list of `InputStreams`. Instead, a much fuzzier `Enumeration` object is expected. Since any `Enumeration` object must implement the `hasMoreElements()` and `nextElement()` methods, you might think you need to create a brand-new class that implements interface `Enumeration` simply to specify a list of input streams to this constructor. However, there's an easier workaround: Declare a simple `Vector` in which you `add-Element()` the sequence of `InputStreams`, and then use the `Vector` method `elements()` to get an `Enumeration` object that will do the trick.

PipedInputStream and *PipedReader*

Pipes are another Unix invention. In fact, the concept is close to the stream concept, except that the application of pipes is less generic. Pipes are typically used when two different processes (or tasks or threads) need to communicate large(ish) amounts of data in a synchronized fashion.

Remember from Chapter 8 that one of the most difficult aspects of using multiple threads is their synchronization. Few multithreaded systems can avoid the need, at one time or another, to have some threads rendezvous for whatever purpose. If that purpose is the exchange of data, pipes can cleanly solve the problem. A less technical example is the use of the vertical-bar character | (pipe) to chain together programs at the Unix or DOS command prompts. For example:

```
C:\> DIR | SORT | MORE
```

creates two pipes, the first connecting the output of the DIR command to the input of the SORT command. The second pipe would similarly connect the output of

SORT to the input of MORE. The result would be a directory listing that is sorted by the SORT utility before being displayed page by page.

Class `PipedInputStream` requires you to connect it with another pipe, an instance of `PipedOutputStream`. The two classes can only be used with each other and are useless without one another. Their respective constructors are as follows:

```
public PipedInputStream(PipedOutputStream src) throws IOException
public PipedOutputStream(PipedInputStream snk) throws IOException
```

The reader/writer constructors are:

```
public PipedReader(PipedWriter src) throws IOException
public PipedWriter(PipedReader snk) throws IOException
```

Perfect symmetry! (Don't you just love it when software is this beautiful?) If you analyze these constructors long enough, you will notice that something is in fact missing: How do you create a connection between two pipes if you need to pass the (already constructed) instance of the other type as an argument to the constructor? It's a catch-22 situation that you need to bypass using one of the other types of constructors:

```
public PipedInputStream()
public PipedReader()
public PipedOutputStream()
public PipedWriter()
```

These four constructors allow you to create a pipe object that is not connected yet. To complete the actual connection, you call the respective `connect()` method.

The following program demonstrates the use of the piped stream classes in their useful context: interthread communication. The program has a distinct oil industry flavor to it—or should that be smell? It uses the image of a crude oil tanker that finds an oil refinery, connects itself to the refinery using pipes (the subject of this section), and transfers its crude to the refinery to be processed. The refinery returns the crude back onboard as an unspecified refined substance. Here's the program bringing this image to life:

```
import java.io.*;

public class PipeTest {
  public static void main (String args[]) {
    new OilRefinery();
    try { // delay arrival
```

```
      Thread.currentThread().sleep(500);
    } catch (InterruptedException e) {
    }
    new SuperTanker();
  }

  // This class consists of a Thread that can accept "pipline" hook-ups
  // via the "clickClunk" method. Clients have to find us though from
  // our Thread name "ThePipeTerminal"
  static class OilRefinery extends Thread {
    static final int EOF = -1;
    boolean alone = true;
    // Can't connect piped until "clickClunk"
    PipedReader inPipe;
    PipedWriter outPipe;

    public OilRefinery() {
      start(); // Start the thread
    }

    public synchronized void run() {
      int ch;
      // Open for business
      setName ("ThePipeTerminal");
      System.out.println ("Processing plant operational and on-line");
      while (alone) {
        try {
          wait(); // Non-busy wait for connection
        } catch (InterruptedException ohLeaveMeAlone) {
        }
      }
      System.out.println ("Client arrived");
      // At this point, a client has connected up to the pipes
      // so process the flow of oil
      try {
        while ((ch = inPipe.read()) != EOF) {
          // add some value to raw input...
          outPipe.write (Character.toUpperCase((char)ch));
        }
      } catch (IOException pipeMalfunction) {
      }
```

```java
    try {
      outPipe.close();  // signal client "The show's over!"
    } catch (IOException ignored) {
    }
    alone = true;
    System.out.println ("Processing plant shutting down.");
  }
  // This is the method clients have to call to connect up to
  // the processing plant
  public synchronized boolean clickClunk (PipedWriter clientOutputPipe,
                                          PipedReader clientInputPipe) {
    System.out.println ("Client arrives to hook-up its pipes");
    try {
      inPipe = new PipedReader (clientOutputPipe);
      outPipe = new PipedWriter (clientInputPipe);
    } catch (IOException connectionFailed) {
      System.err.println ("Hook up failed");
      return false;
    }
    System.out.println ("Hook-up successful");
    alone = false;
    notify();
    return true;
  }
} // End of class OilRefinery

// This class implements a processing plant client, say a
// supertanker that arrives at the plant to unload its
// crude oil and load up with refined oil
static class SuperTanker {
  OilRefinery pipeTerminal = null;
  PipedReader returnPipe = new PipedReader();
  PipedWriter crudePipe = new PipedWriter();

  public SuperTanker() {
    pipeTerminal = (OilRefinery) findThread ("ThePipeTerminal");
    if (pipeTerminal == null) {
      System.err.println ("Snow blizzards prevent rendezvous");
      System.exit (100);
    } else {
      if (pipeTerminal.clickClunk (crudePipe, returnPipe)) {
```

```
          haveOilProcessed();
      } else {
        System.err.println ("Failed to connect to processing plant");
      }
      try {
        crudePipe.close();
      } catch (IOException brokenValves) {
        System.err.println ("Couldn't close valves!");
      }
    }
  }

  // Send data (oil) to processing plant, which refines data and
  // sends it back via second pipe stream
  public void haveOilProcessed() {
    String oilToBeRefined = "Crude Oil";

    try {
      crudePipe.write (oilToBeRefined);
      crudePipe.close();

      // Get back refined oil
      int ch;
      while ((ch = returnPipe.read()) != -1) {
        System.out.print ((char)ch);
      }
      System.out.println();
    } catch (IOException oilFlowFailure) {
      System.err.println ("Pipe malfunction");
    }
  }

  // This generic method locates the refinery thread
  // Note that threads may start/end while checking
  public Thread findThread (String target) {
    int SAFETY_MARGIN = 10;
    // Find master ThreadGroup which all others descend
    ThreadGroup rootGroup = Thread.currentThread().getThreadGroup();
    while (rootGroup.getParent() != null) {
      rootGroup = rootGroup.getParent();
    }
```

```
        Thread threadList[] =
          new Thread [rootGroup.activeGroupCount() + SAFETY_MARGIN];
        int count = rootGroup.enumerate (threadList);
        Thread aThread;
        for (int i=0;i<count;i++) {
          aThread = threadList[i];
          if (aThread == null)
            continue;
          if (aThread.getName().equals (target)) {
            return aThread;
          }
        }
        return null;
      }
    } // End of class SuperTanker

  } // End of class PipeTest
```

The program is interesting for more than just its use of `PipedReader` and `PipedWriter`. Have a close look at what goes on in this tongue-in-cheek simulation. First of all, the main program just creates two instances of the main classes of the program—`OilRefinery` and `SuperTanker`. As the `main()` method clearly shows, neither object knows about the other. So initially both objects are completely independent.

If you look at what the `OilRefinery` object does when constructed, it just starts itself up as an independent thread. (Class `OilRefinery` can do this because it is a subclass of `Thread`.) Starting up the thread means the constructor returns immediately and the `run()` method starts executing. The body of the `OilRefinery` thread explicitly labels itself so other entities in the same Java Virtual Machine can rendezvous with it. It then goes into a semi-sleep state that waits for a client (a SuperTanker ship) to arrive and request its service.

Now, switch perspectives and look at what the `SuperTanker` object has been up to until now. If you follow its constructor, you'll see it begins by finding the `OilRefinery` thread by scanning all threads in the root `ThreadGroup`. Once found, it hands the `OilRefinery` object two pipe objects: a `PipedWriter` for the crude and a `PipedReader` for the processed oil the `OilRefinery` returns to the supertanker. The `OilRefinery` takes those two pipes (via its `clickClunk()` method) and connects these pipes to its own pipes. Then a tanker output pipe is the plant's input pipe, and the plant's output pipe is the tanker's input pipe. See Figure 19.2 for a graphic representation of the connections.

FIGURE 19.2:

PipedReaders and PipedWriters in a realistic scenario

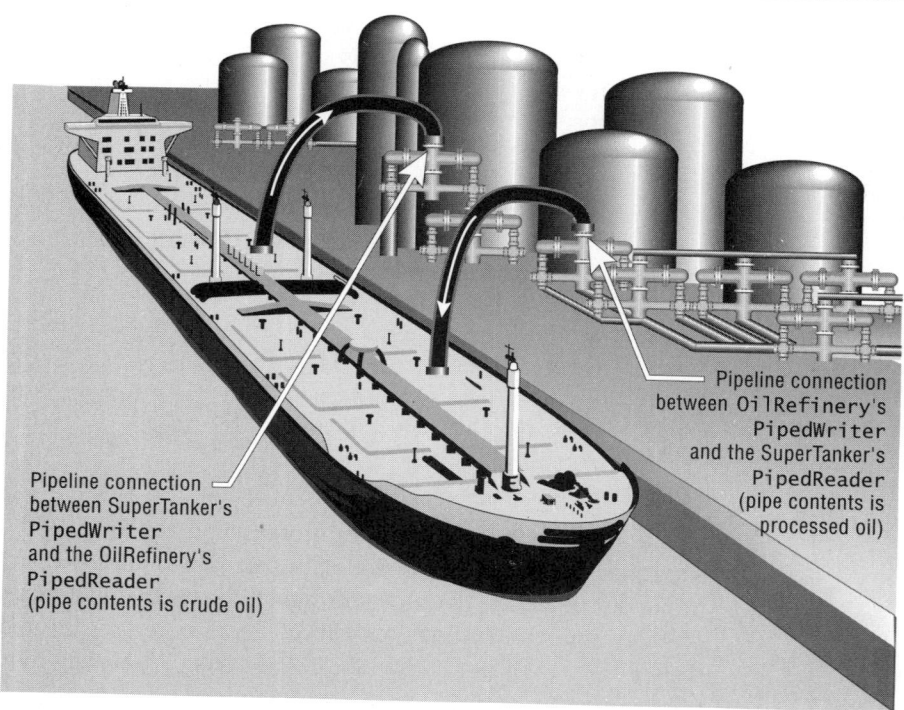

Pipeline connection between OilRefinery's PipedWriter and the SuperTanker's PipedReader (pipe contents is processed oil)

Pipeline connection between SuperTanker's PipedWriter and the OilRefinery's PipedReader (pipe contents is crude oil)

As part of the clickClunk() method, the OilRefinery wakes up its main thread by changing the state of a boolean and calling notify(). Meanwhile, the SuperTanker object starts its main transfer of crude in the haveOilProcessed() method. The key statement here is the write() invocation on the output Piped-Writer. This data eventually finds its way to the read() on the OilRefinery's PipedReader. To symbolize the oil refinery process, the received data (the string of chars reading *Crude Oil*) gets changed to all uppercase. These "processed" bytes are then sent out of the refinery. They return back to the ship via a write() to the OilRefinery's PipedWriter. The SuperTanker then receives these characters and prints them.

An important detail in this interaction is that any writing entity has to signal the other party that there is no more data by *closing* the output stream. The SuperTanker object does this straight after the write() to its PipedWriter and the OilRefinery similarly does a close() after it has detected the end of data on its input stream. This is the only way the receiving end can get an end-of-file indication that allows it to break out of its reading loop. It is possible to use other methods as end-of-message indicators; however, it is necessary to flush() the stream to ensure transit of previously written data.

Now that the two pipe stream classes have been explained, look at how the SuperTanker object managed to rendezvous with the OilRefinery thread. Any thread running within a Java Virtual Machine is part of a hierarchical collection of ThreadGroups. To find a given thread, you therefore have to first find the top of this ThreadGroup (tree) hierarchy so you can then traverse the entire tree in search of the thread you are after. This is what the findThread() method does in class SuperTanker. The method relies on two key methods: getParent() to (stepwise) find the top of the hierarchy and enumerate() to list all instances of Thread in the group. That's all there is to it.

ObjectInputStream

Object input and output streams support object *serialization*. With serialization, what you read or write is not a byte or an array of bytes, but an object and everything it references. This is certainly more complicated than writing any other kind of data. Many issues are involved, including security, data privacy, and class version management.

With serialization, an object can be stored outside the Java VM (Virtual Machine) that created it and restored later. For example, a painting program might represent its state as an object of a class (probably a quite complicated class) called Picture. When the user wants to save the painting, the program can open a file output stream and pass that stream to the constructor of an object output stream. Then, with a single method, the program can save the entire Picture, which can be written to the object output stream, through the file output stream and onto the disk. Later, perhaps in a different invocation of the painting program, an object input stream and a file input stream can restore the Picture object so that the user can continue working.

Serialization also plays an essential role in Remote Method Invocation (RMI), whereby a Java program can make a method call on an object running on a different machine. RMI must support passing method parameters to the remote object and returning return values to the caller. Parameters and return values might be objects; if this is the case, the RMI infrastructure uses object input streams and object output streams to serialize the data. All the serialization pieces are discussed together at the end of this chapter, while Chapter 25 discusses RMI in more detail.

> **NOTE**
>
> If the `ObjectInputStream` source is a `PipedInputStream`, then the corresponding `ObjectOutputStream` must be connected to the `PipedOutputStream` before its thread continues. Otherwise, the thread will be forever blocked at the point of creation.

InputStreamReader

The input stream reader was designed for converting byte-oriented situations to character-oriented situations. An input stream reader reads bytes from an input stream and converts them to characters, according to a mapping algorithm. The default mapping recognizes bytes as common ASCII characters and converts them to Java's Unicode characters.

The constructor for the `InputStreamReader` class takes an input stream as its data source:

```
public InputStreamReader(InputStream src)
```

FilterInputStream and FilterReader

Classes `FilterInputStream` and `FilterReader` are the superclasses for the `java.io` classes `BufferedInputStream`, `BufferedReader`, `DataInputStream`, `LineNumberInputStream`, `LineNumberReader`, `PushbackInputStream`, and `PushbackReader`. `FilterInputStream` is pseudo-abstract, and `FilterReader` is genuinely abstract. The important point is that they are both for subclassing, not for instantiating.

The `FilterInputStream` class looks like this:

```
public class FilterInputStream extends InputStream {

    protected InputStream in;
    protected FilterInputStream (InputStream in)
    public int available() throws IOException;
    public void close() throws IOException;
    public synchronized void mark(int readlimit);
    public boolean markSupported();
    public int read() throws IOException;
    public int read(byte b[]) throws IOException;
    public int read(byte b[], int off, int len) throws IOException;
```

```java
  public synchronized void reset() throws IOException;
  public long skip(long n) throws IOException;
}
```

Not surprisingly, class `FilterReader` is similar:

```java
public abstract Class FilterReader extends Reader {
  protected Reader in;
  protected FilterReader (Reader in);
  public void close() throws IOException;
  public void mark(int readAheadLimit) throws IOException;
  public boolean markSupported();
  public int read() throws IOException;
  public int read(char cbuf[], int off, int len) throws IOException;
  public boolean ready() throws IOException;
  public void reset() throws IOException;
  public long skip(long n) throws IOException;
}
```

BufferedInputStream and BufferedReader

Class `BufferedInputStream` enhances bare-bones `InputStream` by adding a buffer of bytes to `InputStream`, which usually improves reading performance significantly. `BufferedReader` adds a buffer of characters to `Reader`. To demonstrate the speed-up, here's a program that uses a vanilla `FileReader` to read in a whole file, byte by byte:

```java
import java.io.*;
import java.util.*;
public class Unbuffered {

  public static void main (String args[]) {
    Reader reader;
    int ch;

    System.out.println("Start! " + new Date());

    try {
      reader = new FileReader (args[0]);
      while ((ch=reader.read()) != -1) {
          // read entire file
      }
    } catch (IOException ioErr) {
      System.err.println (ioErr.toString());
```

```
        System.exit(100);
    }

    System.out.println ("Stop! " + new Date());
  }
}
```

When you run this program on a reasonably large file (for example, Windows 95's COMMAND.COM, which is 92,870 bytes), it takes 16 seconds to simply read in every byte. Now if you change the `Reader` assignment line into the following two lines:

```
FileReader fr = new FileReader (args[0]);
reader = new BufferedReader (fr);
```

the time has been reduced to less than three seconds! A five-fold improvement. Clearly, taking the trouble to "wrap" unbuffered input streams up in an instance of a `BufferedReader` pays off handsomely. The exact performance gain is determined by the size of the buffer used by the `BufferedReader` object. While the example uses the default constructor (resulting in a default, but undefined, buffer size being used), you can explicitly set the buffer size, at constructor time, by using constructors with the following, predictable signatures:

```
public BufferedInputStream (InputStream in, int size)
public BufferedReader (Reader in, int size)
```

Classes `BufferedInputStream` and `BufferedReader` are among the few standard `java.io` classes that implement the mark and reset mechanism.

DataInputStream

Remember the `DataInput` interface discussed earlier in the chapter as part of class `RandomAccessFile`? Well, here is the only other class that implements this interface: class `DataInputStream`. This `RandomAccessFile`/`DataInputStream` kinship also exists in the output branch of the `java.io` classes. Class `DataOutputStream` implements interface `DataOutput`, which was also implemented by `RandomAccessFile`. Therefore, there is data-format compatibility between data written by `Random-AccessFile` and data read back in by `DataInputStream`, or, conversely, data written by `DataOutputStream` can be read back via a `RandomAccessFile`. In practice, though, this cross-communication does not occur often because data will be written and read back using the naturally corresponding class, most often simply `DataOutputStream` and `DataInputStream`.

Here is the definition of class DataInputStream:

```
public class DataInputStream extends FilterInputStream implements DataInput {
    public DataInputStream(InputStream in);
    public final static String readUTF(DataInput in) throws IOException;
    public final int read(byte b[]) throws IOException;
    public final int read(byte b[], int off, int len) throws IOException;
    public final boolean readBoolean() throws IOException;
    public final byte readByte() throws IOException;
    public final char readChar() throws IOException;
    public final double readDouble() throws IOException;
    public final float readFloat() throws IOException;
    public final void readFully(byte b[]) throws IOException;
    public final void readFully(byte b[], int off, int len) throws IOException;
    public final int readInt() throws IOException;
    public final long readLong() throws IOException;
    public final short readShort() throws IOException;
    public final int readUnsignedByte() throws IOException;
    public final int readUnsignedShort() throws IOException;
    public final String readUTF() throws IOException;
    public final int skipBytes(int n) throws IOException;
}
```

The DataInput interface implicitly specifies that implementing classes should handle an EOF differently than by simply returning −1 (EOF is used to denote end of stream, not just files). Instead, methods should throw an EOFException object (class EOFException is a subclass of IOException; this is why the definition does not talk about EOFException). This means that a different coding template can be used to read streams via a DataInputStream. You can simply implement an endless loop that does not check for EOF, and rely on exception-catching code to correctly handle the EOF condition. The following program demonstrates this:

```
import java.io.*;
public class EOF {

    public static void main(String args[]) {

        DataInputStream is;
        byte ch;

        try {
```

```
        is = new DataInputStream(new FileInputStream("EOF.java"));

        while (true) {   // no need to check for EOF: exception deals with it

          ch = is.readByte();
          System.out.print ((char) ch);
          System.out.flush();
        }

      } catch (EOFException eof) {
        System.out.println (" >> Normal program termination.");
      } catch (FileNotFoundException noFile) {
        System.err.println("File not found! " + noFile);
      } catch (IOException io) {
        System.err.println("I/O error occurred: " + io);
      } catch (Throwable anything) {
        System.err.println("Abnormal exception caught !: " + anything);
      }
    }
  } // End of class EOF
```

LineNumberReader

Class LineNumberReader adds line-number tracking for text-input streams. The following two methods are provided to manage the line-number tracking feature:

```
public int getLineNumber()
public void setLineNumber(int lineNumber)
```

The following program uses the class to print any text file with line numbers starting each line:

```
import java.io.*;
public class Lineno {

  public static void main (String args[]) {

    FileReader        fileReader = null;
    BufferedReader    bufferedReader = null;
    LineNumberReader  lineNumberReader = null;
    String            line;
```

```
try {
  fileReader = new FileReader (args[0]);
  bufferedReader = new BufferedReader (fileReader);
  lineNumberReader = new LineNumberReader (bufferedReader);

  while ((line = lineNumberReader.readLine()) != null) {
    int lineNo = lineNumberReader.getLineNumber();
    System.out.println (lineNo + " " + line);
  }
} catch (IOException ioErr) {
  System.err.println (ioErr.toString());
  System.exit(100);
  }
 }
}
```

The program uses a three-stage input pipeline:

```
args[0] file -> fileReader -> bufferedReader -> lineNumberReader
```

The data read from lineNumberReader travels the length of the stream, originating in the file specified in the command line and passing through fileReader and bufferedReader. The bufferedReader was used to turbo-charge the whole program, and the LineNumberReader was used to provide the line numbers themselves.

Note that the order of the different stream types can be important. In this example, it wouldn't make any sense to, say, put the buffered reader object last in the chain. Buffered input streams and readers always need to be the second link in the chain so that all downstream stages can benefit from the buffering (equivalent BufferedOutputStream and BufferedWriter objects always need to be last-but-one in any output chain).

NOTE   In this case, you could have easily tracked the line number by trivially using an integer variable that is incremented for every loop iteration, but it would be reinventing the wheel, which is not what object-oriented programming is about. The Java API classes represent software reuse handed to us on a plate. If you want software reusability to mean something within your software-development cycle, you should make a valiant effort to become familiar with the valuable functionality provided by the different Java packages. This way, you can cut your program-development time by simply relying on prewritten (and debugged!) classes.

PushbackInputStream and *PushbackReader*

Classes `PushbackInputStream` and `PushbackReader` add a pushback (undo) capability to an input stream or reader. In both classes, the following methods deal with the new feature:

```
public void unread(int ch) throws IOException
public void unread(byte/char ch[]) throws IOException
public void unread(byte/char ch[], int offset, int len) throws IOException
```

Note that these methods allow you to do slightly more than simply undo the last read: They allow you to cheat and push back different characters than the ones originally read.

Tokenizing Input Streams

There's one `java.io` input class that does not descend from `InputStream` but really ought to: class `StreamTokenizer`. You already briefly encountered the class in the word-frequency program presented in the discussion of `FileInputStream`.

Tokenizing some input means reducing it to a simpler stream of tokens. These tokens represent recurring chunks of data in the stream. Any Java compiler, for example, would check for grammatical correctness of your programs by checking the sequence of tokens representing reserved word strings like `class`, `import`, `public`, `void`, and so on. By not requiring you to deal with the exact character sequences themselves, tokenizing as a technique has two main advantages:

- It reduces code complexity.

- It allows for flexible, quick changes in input syntax.

If, for instance, the Java designers had at some stage wanted to rename the reserved word `extends` to `subclasses`, they could have done so easily without impacting the compiler in any way. The tokenizing stage of the compiler would still deliver the same TOKEN_EXTENDS token to the grammar-checking stage, even though Java source codes would now contain the word `subclasses` everywhere.

StreamTokenizer

Class `StreamTokenizer` can be used to turn any input stream into a stream of tokens. The programming model for the class is that a stream can contain three types of entities:

- Words (that is, multicharacter tokens)

- Single-character tokens

- Whitespace (including C/C++/Java-style comments)

Before you start processing a stream into tokens, you must define which ASCII characters should be treated as one of the three possible input types, called *defining the syntax table* for the stream. Once the syntax table is defined, you can proceed by extracting actual tokens. Look at how it is done in practice by first checking out the structure and services of class StreamTokenizer:

```
public class StreamTokenizer extends Object {
    public static final int TT_EOF = -1;
    public static final int TT_EOL = '\n';
    public static final int TT_NUMBER = -2;
    public static final int TT_WORD = -3;
    public double nval;
    public String sval;
    public int ttype;

    public StreamTokenizer(Reader r);

    public void commentChar(int ch);
    public void eolIsSignificant(boolean flag);
    public int lineno();
    public void lowerCaseMode(boolean flag);
    public int nextToken() throws IOException;
    public void ordinaryChar(int ch);
    public void ordinaryChars(int low, int hi);
    public void parseNumbers();
    public void pushBack();
    public void quoteChar(int ch);
    public void resetSyntax();
    public void slashSlashComments(boolean flag);
    public void slashStarComments(boolean flag);
    public String toString();
    public void whitespaceChars(int low, int hi);
    public void wordChars(int low, int hi);
```

To begin with, this class has some public instance variables: ttype, sval, and nval. These stand for token type, string value, and number value, and, contrary to object-oriented rules, the class expects clients to actually access these fields. You need to do this after calling the core method for class StreamTokenizer: nextToken(). This method is the token-producing conveyor belt. Its return value tells you what type of token it produced. It can either be a multicharacter TT_WORD token or a single-character token, in which case the return value holds the ASCII code for that character. If the stream is exhausted, nextToken() returns TT_EOF. If you have enabled end-of-line checking by invoking eolIsSignificant(true), TT_EOL will be returned each time the end of a line is reached. If you have enabled number parsing by invoking parseNumbers(), TT_NUMBER will be returned each time numbers are encountered in the stream (possibly in scientific notation).

When nextToken() returns either a TT_WORD or TT_NUMBER token-type return value, you need to dig the actual string or numeric values out of the sval and nval instance variables, respectively. (This is very un–object-oriented; simple access methods could have been provided—like getWord() and getNumber()— to accomplish those same tasks.)

Before starting to call nextToken(), you should set up the syntax table for the input stream. This setup is done via a number of methods that assign different types of significance to different input characters. Method whitespaceChars() lets you define a character range with no significance whatsoever: Whitespace can be skipped altogether by the stream tokenizer. Method wordChars() lets you define another range of characters that should be treated as building-block characters for "words." In the Java compiler example, all characters that can legally be part of identifiers (like variable names or method names) should be defined as word characters. This definition lets the tokenizer treat identifiers, for example, as the atomic wholes they actually are.

An Example: Tokenizing HTML

The following sample program uses class StreamTokenizer to tokenize another structured language that is relevant to the Java developer: HTML. The program consists of a new subclass of StreamTokenizer called HTMLTokenizer (what else?), which can identify a common subset of HTML tags. The driver program (HTML-text) uses the new class to extract all text from a Web page. Here is the listing for the HTML text program:

```
import java.io.*;
public class HTMLtext {

  public static void main (String args[]) throws IOException {
    FileReader    htmlInput;
    HTMLTokenizer htmlTokens;
    int           tagType;
```

```java
    if (args.length != 1) {
      System.err.println("Usage: HTMLtext <file.html>");
      System.exit(10);
    }

    htmlInput = new FileReader (args[0]);
    htmlTokens= new HTMLTokenizer (htmlInput);

    while ((tagType = htmlTokens.nextHTML())
        != HTMLTokenizer.HTML_EOF) {

      if (tagType == HTMLTokenizer.HTML_TEXT) {
        System.out.println ("TEXT: " + htmlTokens.sval);
      } else if (tagType == HTMLTokenizer.HTML_UNKNOWN) {
         System.out.println ("UNKNOWN TAG: '" + htmlTokens.sval +"'");
      } else if (tagType == HTMLTokenizer.TAG_PRE) {
        if (htmlTokens.nextHTML() == HTMLTokenizer.HTML_TEXT) {
          System.out.println (htmlTokens.sval);
          htmlTokens.nextHTML();   // swallow </PRE>
        }
      }
    }
  }
}

//-----------------------------------------------------------------
// Class HTMLTokenizer is a form of StreamTokenizer that knows about
// HTML tags (but not HTML structure!).
//-----------------------------------------------------------------
class HTMLTokenizer extends StreamTokenizer {

  static int HTML_TEXT    = -1;
  static int HTML_UNKNOWN = -2;
  static int HTML_EOF     = -3;

// The following class constants are used to identify HTML tags.
// Note that each tag type has an odd- and even-numbered ID,
// depending on whether the tag is a start or end tag.
// These constants are returned by nextHTML().

  static int TAG_HTML       = 0,   TAG_html       = 1;
  static int TAG_HEAD       = 2,   TAG_head       = 3;
  static int TAG_BODY       = 4,   TAG_body       = 5;
```

```
static int TAG_H1           = 6,  TAG_h1          = 7;
static int TAG_H2           = 8,  TAG_h2          = 9;
static int TAG_H3           = 10, TAG_h3          = 11;
static int TAG_H4           = 12, TAG_h4          = 13;
static int TAG_H5           = 14, TAG_h5          = 15;
static int TAG_H6           = 16, TAG_h6          = 17;
static int TAG_H7           = 18, TAG_h7          = 19;
static int TAG_CENTER       = 20, TAG_center      = 21;
static int TAG_PRE          = 22, TAG_pre         = 23;
static int TAG_TITLE        = 24, TAG_title       = 25;
static int TAG_HORIZONTAL   = 26;
static int TAG_DT           = 28, TAG_dt          = 29;
static int TAG_DD           = 30, TAG_dd          = 31;
static int TAG_DL           = 32, TAG_dl          = 33;
static int TAG_IMAGE        = 34, TAG_image       = 35;
static int TAG_BOLD         = 36, TAG_bold        = 37;
static int TAG_APPLET       = 38, TAG_applet      = 39;
static int TAG_PARAM        = 40, TAG_param       = 41;
static int TAG_PARAGRAPH    = 42;
static int TAG_ADDRESS      = 44, TAG_address     = 45;
static int TAG_STRONG       = 46, TAG_strong      = 47;
static int TAG_LINK         = 48, TAG_link        = 49;
static int TAG_ORDERED_LIST = 50, TAG_ordered_list = 51;
static int TAG_LIST         = 52, TAG_list        = 53;
static int TAG_LIST_ITEM    = 54, TAG_list_item   = 55;
static int TAG_CODE         = 56, TAG_code        = 57;
static int TAG_EMPHASIZE    = 58, TAG_emphasize   = 59;

// When extending this list, make sure that substring collisions
// do not introduce bugs. For example: tag "A" has to come after
// "ADDRESS"; otherwise all "ADDRESS" tags will be seen as "A" tags.

String[] tags = {"HTML", "HEAD", "BODY",
                 "H1", "H2", "H3", "H4", "H5", "H6", "H7",
                 "CENTER", "PRE", "TITLE", "HR",
                 "DT", "DD", "DL", "IMG", "B",
                 "APPLET", "PARAM",
                 "P", "ADDRESS", "STRONG",
                 "A", "OL", "UL", "LI", "CODE", "EM"
                };

boolean outsideTag = true;
```

```
//----------------------------------------------------------------
// The HTMLTokenizer relies on a two-state state machine: the stream
// can be "inside" a tag (between < and >) or "outside" a tag
// (between > and <).
//----------------------------------------------------------------
  public HTMLTokenizer (Reader reader) {
    super(reader);

    resetSyntax();            // start with a blank character type table
    wordChars(0, 255);        // you want to stumble over < and > only,
    ordinaryChars('<','<');   // all the rest is considered "words"
    ordinaryChars('>','>');

    outsideTag = true;        // you start being outside any HTML tags
}
//----------------------------------------------------------------
// grab next HTML tag, text, or EOF
//----------------------------------------------------------------
  public int nextHTML() throws IOException {
    int tok;

    switch (tok = nextToken()) {
      case StreamTokenizer.TT_EOF:
        return HTML_EOF;

      case '<':
        outsideTag = false; // we're inside
        return nextHTML();  // decode type

      case '>':
        outsideTag = true;
        return nextHTML();

      case StreamTokenizer.TT_WORD:
        if (!outsideTag) {
          return tagType();     // decode tag type
        } else {
          if (onlyWhiteSpace(sval)) {
            return nextHTML();
          } else {
            return HTML_TEXT;
          }
        }
```

```
        default:
            System.out.println ("ERROR: unknown TT " + tok);
    }
    return HTML_UNKNOWN;
}
//------------------------------------------------------------------
// Inter-tag words that consist only of whitespace are swallowed
// (skipped); this method tests whether a string can be considered
// whitespace.or not.
//------------------------------------------------------------------
  protected boolean onlyWhiteSpace (String s) {

    char ch;

    for(int i=0; i < s.length(); i++) {
      ch = s.charAt(i);
      if (!(ch==' ' || ch=='\t' || ch=='\n' || ch=='\r')) {
        return false;
      }
    }
    return true;
  }
//------------------------------------------------------------------
// You've just hit a '<' tag start character; now identify the type
// of tag you're dealing with.
//------------------------------------------------------------------
  protected int tagType () {

    boolean endTag = false;
    String input;
    int start = 0;
    int tagID;

    input = sval;

    if (input.charAt(0) == '/') {    // is this an end tag (like
</HTML>)?
        start++;                 // skip slash
        endTag = true;
    }
    // go through the list of known tags, try to match one
    for (int tag=0; tag < tags.length; tag++) {
```

```
            if (input.regionMatches (true, start, tags[tag],
                                      0, tags[tag].length())) {
              tagID = tag*2 + (endTag ? 1 : 0);
              return tagID;
            }
          }
          return HTML_UNKNOWN;
        }
      } // End of class HTMLTokenizer
```

Because the HTMLTokenizer class extends StreamTokenizer, it is no surprise that the example followed the StreamTokenizer's programming model, even if it is less than perfect. The new class needs no syntax table initialization, though, nor does it provide any methods in this respect. Its key method is nextHTML(), which is modeled after nextToken(). Method nextHTML() returns token IDs of the form TAG_XXX where XXX is some HTML tag type. To help remember all the different HTML token constants, the convention of using a lowercased equivalent, TAG_xxx, is used to denote end tags. For example, if <HEAD> is a start tag, then </HEAD> is its corresponding end tag. Their respective token constants are TAG_HEAD and TAG_head.

The parsing approach embodied by HTMLTokenizer is to treat the opening and closing angle brackets (< and >) as the only special characters in the HTML input stream. All other characters are regarded as "word" characters, even whitespace. This unconventional syntax table approach greatly simplifies the remaining logic of the class and is implemented in the constructor for HTMLTokenizer. The next-HTML() method can rely on always being either inside or outside a tag. If it switches from out to in, it is a simple matter of identifying the tag while noting whether this is a start or an end tag (end tags have a slash character before the tag label).

Because inter-tag whitespace should not be taken into account when parsing HTML files, it is filtered out manually (StreamTokenizer's whitespace-filtering capability is not relied on). All other inter-tag data is the raw text for the Web page, stripped of any HTML markups.

TIP

Because this sample program does not implement support for HTML 4 tags, you may wish to enhance the program yourself. The program is very easily enhanced by adding new tag strings to the tags array and adding the corresponding TAG_xxx ID constant for the new tag. You may also wish to look at or use the classes of the com.sun.java.swing.text.html.parser package.

Output Streams and Writers

The second main hierarchy branch in package java.io consists of all stream and writer classes concerned with output. The roots for this branch are the classes OutputStream and Writer. Here is the full definition of class OutputStream:

```
public abstract class OutputStream extends Object {
  public OutputStream();
  public void close() throws IOException;
  public void flush() throws IOException;
  public abstract void write(int b) throws IOException;
  public void write(byte b[]) throws IOException;
  public void write(byte b[], int off, int len) throws IOException;
}
```

The definition for Writer is nearly identical:

```
public abstract class Writer extends Object {
  public Writer();
  public Writer(Object lock);
  public void close() throws IOException;
  public void flush() throws IOException;
  public abstract void write(int b) throws IOException;
  public void write(byte b[]) throws IOException;
  public void write(byte b[], int off, int len) throws IOException;
}
```

The second form of the constructor takes an object as an argument. When this form is used, the writer will synchronize its writing, flushing, and closing operations on the object's lock; this prevents competing threads from corrupting the writer's data. (See Chapter 8 for information about locks and synchronization.)

Output streams and writers are even simpler than input streams and readers in that they do not support the mark/reset mechanism (it simply does not make sense for output). The core functionality is to be able to write bytes or characters one at a time or in blocks. The destination for this written data can be anything, in theory; in practice, the concrete destinations of files, byte arrays, and network connections are supported (the latter via java.net classes, discussed in Chapter 20). Because there is very little difference between output and input (apart from the direction of information flow), what follows is a condensed overview of the output stream and writer classes.

ByteArrayOutputStream and CharArrayWriter

The ByteArrayOutputStream and CharArrayWriter classes are the exact opposites of ByteArrayInputStream and CharArrayReader. The classes provide for some extra methods above the minimal write() methods defined by OutputStream and Writer. Here is the full definition of ByteArrayOutputStream:

```
public class ByteArrayOutputStream extends OutputStream {
  protected byte buf[];
  protected int count;

  public ByteArrayOutputStream();
  public ByteArrayOutputStream(int size);
  public synchronized void reset();
  public int size();
  public synchronized byte toByteArray()[];
  public String toString();
  public String toString(int hibyte);
  public String toString(String enc) throws UnsupportedEncodingException;
  public synchronized void write(byte b[], int off, int len);
  public synchronized void write(int b);
  public synchronized void writeTo(OutputStream out) throws IOException;
}
```

The definition of CharArrayWriter is almost identical:

```
public Class CharArrayWriter extends Writer {
  public CharArrayWriter();
  public CharArrayWriter(int initialSize);
  public void close();
  public void flush();
  public void reset();
  public int size();
  public char toCharArray()[];
  public String toString();
  public void write(char c[], int off, int len);
  public void write(int c);
  public void write(String str, int off, int len);
  public void writeTo(Writer out) throws IOException;
}
```

After these classes have been written to, the data may be retrieved by calling toByteArray() (for a ByteArrayOutputStream) or toCharArray() (for a CharArrayWriter).

WARNING
Byte array output streams and character array writers write to memory. They should be used only when the amount of data to be written can safely be accommodated in memory. Writing a few bytes or a few thousand bytes is reasonable; writing a few megabytes will cause problems!

FilterOutputStream and *FilterWriter*

The `FilterOutputStream` and `FilterWriter` classes are the superclasses of the higher-level filtering output streams and writers. Like their input counterparts, they are supposed to be subclassed, not directly instantiated. The following is the definition of `FilterOutputStream`:

```
public class FilterOutputStream extends OutputStream {
    public FilterOutputStream(OutputStream out);
    public void close() throws IOException;
    public void flush() throws IOException;
    public void write(byte b[]) throws IOException;
    public void write(byte b[], int off, int len) throws IOException;
    public void write(int b) throws IOException;
}
```

And here is the definition of `FilterWriter`:

```
public abstract class FilterWriter extends Writer {
    public void close() throws IOException;
    public void flush() throws IOException;
    public void write(char cbuf[], int off, int len) throws IOException;
    public void write(int c) throws IOException;
    public void write(String str, int off, int len) throws IOException;
}
```

BufferedOutputStream and *BufferedWriter*

Buffering output can enhance writing performance in exactly the same way as buffering input enhances reading performance. The `BufferedOutputStream` and `BufferedWriter` classes are the same as `BufferedInputStream` and `Buffered-Reader`, except they work with output. The following program highlights the difference a write buffer makes by writing a file without buffering and then writing a file with buffering:

```
import java.io.*;
import java.util.*;
```

```java
public class BufferDiff {

  public static void main (String args[]) throws IOException {

    FileOutputStream     unbufStream;
    BufferedOutputStream bufStream;

    unbufStream = /* a raw file stream */
      new FileOutputStream("test.one");
    bufStream   = new BufferedOutputStream(
      new FileOutputStream("test.two"));

    System.out.println ("Write file unbuffered: " +
      time (unbufStream) + "ms");
    System.out.println ("Write file   buffered: " +
      time (bufStream  ) + "ms");
  }

  static int time (OutputStream os) throws IOException {

    Date then = new Date();

    for (int i=0; i<50000; i++) {
      os.write(1);
    }
    os.close();
    return (int)((new Date()).getTime() - then.getTime());
  }
}
```

When run, the program produced the following statistics on my machine:

```
Write file unbuffered: 8190ms
Write file   buffered: 1370ms
```

As you can see, the simple wrapping of a `BufferedOutputStream` object around the final destination stream (that is, the last stage in a chain of output streams) substantially improves write performance.

DataOutputStream

Class `DataOutputStream` implements the `DataOutput` interface, which was described earlier in the chapter in the discussion of class `RandomAccessFile`.

Basically, interface DataOutput specifies methods for saving (writing) every type of Java primitive type plus String. Although the exact representation of the types output this way is irrelevant, the reality is that DataOutputStream generates a binary stream; that is, output not interpretable by people.

When you need to keep external databases whose sizes are an issue, binary is usually the most efficient representation. Say your application manipulates large 3-D models. The definition for those models consists of large amounts of triplets (x,y,z), each of type double, plus extra data of various data types. Such models would probably best be saved in binary to conserve storage resources.

NOTE   There is no writer equivalent to DataOutputStream. This makes sense, because writers deal with characters, not with binary representations of other data types.

For smaller entities, say configuration files, binary is not your best choice. Representing data in readable ASCII format is much more attractive. Another output stream class, class PrintStream (discussed shortly), can be used instead to create a readable stream of data, but PrintStream is not as useful as it seems because of a major flaw in the java.io hierarchy: There is no corresponding input class to read the data back in. If you need to design a file format for a configuration file, a completely different class might be the best solution: class Properties from package java.util (also discussed in a bit).

The Endian Wars Are Over

Whenever binary files containing numbers are moved from one architecture to another, the issue of "endianness" crops up. Different CPUs order the bytes in a multibyte number (say a four-byte int) according to little-endian (least significant byte at lowest address) or big-endian (most significant byte at lowest address) schemes.

When a number is written to a file by a little-endian processor, and then subsequently read back by a big-endian processor (or vice versa), the number will have been corrupted (unless it is 0 or −1). Java's DataOutputStream and DataInputStream classes protect you from this pitfall because, although Java data files are exchanged between very different physical machines, the exchange actually takes place between two (identical) Java VMs (which, by the way, both use the big-endian scheme).

ObjectOutputStream

As explained in the discussion of ObjectInputStream, object input and output streams read and write entire objects. More precisely, they write the state of an object's instance variables. This is a more complicated operation than you might guess. Some instance variables are themselves references to other objects, and they also must be written to an object output stream or read from an object input stream.

The process of writing out an object's state is called *serialization*. Reading in an object's state is called *deserialization*. Serialization and deserialization are useful in their own right; they are also essential for RMI, which allows method calls to be made on objects running on external machines. For more information about serialization and deserialization, see the "Object Persistence and Serialization" section later in this chapter; for RMI see Chapter 25.

Properties

Although the Properties class is not part of the java.io package (it is part of java.util), it is so closely related to I/O issues that it is discussed here. This class has the following definition:

```
public class Properties extends Hashtable {
  public Properties();
  public Properties(Properties defaults);
  public String getProperty(String key);
  public String getProperty(String key, String defaultValue);
  public void list(PrintStream out);
  public void list(PrintWriter out);
  public synchronized void load(InputStream in) throws IOException;
  public Enumeration propertyNames();
  public synchronized Object put(Object key, Object value);
  public synchronized Object setProperty(String key, String value);
  public synchronized void store(OutputStream out, String header)
  ➡ throws IOException;
}
```

Class Properties is basically a Hashtable with load() and save() methods added. These take input and output streams, respectively, as arguments, so you can send or receive your Properties objects to or from more than just an external file. You can think of a configuration file as a kind of dictionary, pairing configuration variables with their values.

The following program demonstrates how a set of configuration variables can be saved as a Properties configuration file.

```java
import java.io.*;
import java.util.*;

public class Config {

  public static void main (String args[]) {

    Properties      config;
    FileOutputStream fos;

    // some dummy configuration variables to save in a config file

    Double proficiencyScore = new Double(Math.PI);
    Boolean hasCDROM = Boolean.FALSE;
    String userName = "Dudley";

    try {
      fos = new FileOutputStream ("myprogram.cfg");

      config = new Properties();

      config.put ("proficiency", proficiencyScore.toString());
      config.put ("hasCDROM"   , hasCDROM.toString());
      config.put ("name"       , userName.toString());

      config.store (fos, "My Program's very own config file");
    } catch (IOException io) {
      System.err.println ("Failed to save configuration... what now ?");
      System.err.println (io);
    }
  }
}
```

The imaginary configuration variables proficiencyScore, hasCDROM, and userName are saved in an ASCII file of the following format:

```
#My Program's very own config file
#Tue May 19 17:23:46 EDT 1998
hasCDROM=false
name=Dudley
proficiency=3.141592653589793
```

As you can see, the Properties class time-stamps and date-stamps these files internally and adds the String you passed to the save() method to the top of the file (as a comment). This allows you to store copyright or other information in the file.

Note that all configuration variables saved via a Properties object must be objects (primitive types are not supported) and also must be converted to String before being put into the Properties dictionary using the put() Hashtable method. To read back the configuration file and initialize your variables from it, you need to load() the Properties object back (via an input stream) and then extract and convert the variables stored as Strings. Here is the other half of the sample program:

```java
import java.io.*;
import java.util.*;

public class LoadConfig {

  public static void main (String args[]) {

    Properties config;
    FileInputStream fis;
    Double proficiencyScore;
    Boolean hasCDROM;
    String userName;

    try {
      fis = new FileInputStream ("myprogram.cfg");

      config = new Properties();
      config.load (fis);

      proficiencyScore =
Double.valueOf(config.getProperty("proficiency"));
      hasCDROM        =
Boolean.valueOf(config.getProperty("hasCDROM"));
      userName        = config.getProperty("name");

      System.out.println ("proficiency = " + proficiencyScore );
      System.out.println ("hasCDROM    = " + hasCDROM );
      System.out.println ("name        = " + userName );

    } catch (IOException io) {
      System.err.println ("Failed to load configuration... what now ?");
      System.err.println (io);
    }
  }
}
```

PrintStream and *PrintWriter*

Class `PrintStream` resembles class `DataOutputStream` because the methods it defines mirror the type of `write()` methods provided by `DataOutputStream`. The difference is that they come in two flavors: `print(..)` and `println(..)`. Here is the definition of class `PrintStream`:

```
public class PrintStream extends FilterOutputStream {
    public PrintStream (OutputStream out);
    public PrintStream(OutputStream out, boolean autoFlush);
    public boolean checkError();
    public void close();
    public void flush();
    public void print(boolean b);
    public void print(char c);
    public void print(char s[]);
    public void print(double d);
    public void print(float f);
    public void print(int i);
    public void print(long l);
    public void print(Object obj);
    public void print(String s);
    public void println();
    public void println(boolean x);
    public void println(char x);
    public void println(char x[]);
    public void println(double x);
    public void println(float x);
    public void println(int x);
    public void println(long x);
    public void println(Object x);
    public void println(String x);
    public void write(int b);
    public void write(byte buf[], int off, int len);
}
```

The `PrintWriter` class is similar. Here is its definition:

```
public class PrintWriter extends Writer {
    public PrintWriter(OutputStream out);
    public PrintWriter(OutputStream out, boolean autoFlush);
    public PrintWriter (Writer out);
    public PrintWriter(Writer out, boolean autoFlush);
    public boolean checkError();
```

```
    public void close();
    public void flush();
    public void print(boolean b);
    public void print(char c);
    public void print(char s[]);
    public void print(double d);
    public void print(float f);
    public void print(int i);
    public void print(long l);
    public void print(Object obj);
    public void print(String s);
    public void println();
    public void println(boolean x);
    public void println(char x);
    public void println(char x[]);
    public void println(double x);
    public void println(float x);
    public void println(int x);
    public void println(long x);
    public void println(Object x);
    public void println(String x);
    public void write(char buf[]);
    public void write(char buf[], int off, int len);
    public void write(int c);
    public void write(String s);
    public void write(String s, int off, int len);
}
```

The constructors to the PrintStream class are deprecated in JDK 1.2. The only PrintStream objects that should ever exist are System.out (standard output) and System.err (standard error). Use of PrintWriter is strongly encouraged.

There is a difference between these print() methods and the write() methods of DataOutputStream. PrintStream and PrintWriter convert all of their arguments to character representations. PrintStream converts to 8-bit ASCII representations; PrintWriter converts to 16-bit UNICODE representations.

You have actually been using a PrintStream object ever since your first encounter with Java:

```
System.out.println ("Hello World!");
```

Object out is a static PrintStream variable in class System. Various instances of the overloaded print() and println() methods have been used in most of the programs. The difference between the two is that print() does not force the immediate writing of the data (called *flushing*). It can remain buffered in the stream until a newline character is written or until an explicit flush() is done on the PrintStream.

Classes PrintStream and PrintWriter allow you to pass any object as an argument. The mechanism used to convert any object into a string representation is to call the object's toString() method. If you create a new class that doesn't override toString() of class Object, you will inherit its default implementation, which is to output the class name along with the object's hashcode, produced by the hashCode()method of Object. The following program demonstrates a println() on an instance of a brand new class:

```java
public class Print {

  public static void main (String args[]) {
    BrandNew anObject = new BrandNew();

    System.out.println (anObject);
  }
}

class BrandNew {

}
```

The new class BrandNew (which is empty and doesn't even have a custom constructor) is no problem for the println (Object obj) method because it can still invoke the parent Object toString() method, which, in this case, produces the following output for object anObject:

```
BrandNew@1ec614
```

The consistent overloading of both print() and println() methods means that you can literally throw any (single) argument at these methods, without needing to cast. They will perform what you intuitively would expect them to by converting the argument to a string representation and writing this string to the output stream.

Object Persistence and Serialization

Ordinarily, a Java object lasts no longer than the program that created it. An object may cease to exist during run time if it is reaped by the garbage collector. If it avoids that fate, it still dies when the user terminates the browser (for an applet) or the object's runtime environment (for an application).

In this context, *persistence* is the ability of an object to *record* its state so it can be reproduced in the future, perhaps in another environment. For example, a persistent object might store its state in a file. The file can then be used to *restore* the object in a different runtime environment. It is not really the object itself that persists, but rather the information necessary to construct a replica of the object.

An object records itself by writing out the values that describe its state. This process is known as *serialization* because the object is represented by an ordered series of bytes. Java provides classes that write objects to streams and restore objects from streams.

The main task of serialization is to write the values of an object's instance variables. If a variable is a reference to another object, the referenced object must also be serialized. This process is recursive; serialization may involve serializing a complex tree structure that consists of the original object, the object's objects, the object's object's objects, and so on. An object's ownership hierarchy is known as its *graph*.

Criteria for Serialization

Not all classes are capable of being serialized. Only classes that implement the `Serializable` or `Externalizable` interfaces may successfully be serialized. Both of these interfaces are in the `java.io` package. A serializable object can be serialized by an external object, which in practice is a type of output stream; an externalizable object must be capable of writing its own state, rather than letting the work be done by another object.

You can serialize any class as long as it meets the following criteria:

- The class, or one of its superclasses, must implement the `java.io.Serializable` interface.

- The class must participate with the `writeObject()` method to control data that is being saved and append new data to existing saved data.

- The class must participate with the `readObject()` method to read the data that was written by the corresponding `writeObject()` method.

If a serializable class has variables that should not be serialized, those variables must be marked with the `transient` keyword; then the serialization process will ignore them.

NOTE Implementing writeObject() and readObject() methods and throwing the Not-SerializableException will prevent serialization of an object. The ObjectOutput-Stream (or ObjectInputStream) will catch the exception and abort the process.

The Serializable Interface

The Serializable interface does not have any methods. When a class declares that it implements Serializable, it is declaring that it participates in the serializable protocol. When an object is serializable and the object's state is written to a stream, the stream must contain enough information to restore the object. This must hold true even if the class being restored has been updated to a more recent (but compatible) version.

The *Externalizable* Interface

The Externalizable interface identifies objects that can be saved to a stream but that are responsible for their own states. When an externalizable object is written to a stream, the stream is only responsible for storing the name of the object's class; the object must write its own data. The Externalizable interface is defined as:

```
public interface Externalizable extends Serializable {

    public void writeExternal (ObjectOutput out)
        throws IOException;

    public void readExternal (ObjectInput in)
        throws IOException, ClassNotFoundException;
}
```

An externalizable class must adhere to this interface by providing a writeExternal() method for storing its state during serialization and a readExternal() method for restoring its state during deserialization.

Creating Output Streams for Serialization

Objects that can serialize other objects implement the ObjectOutput interface from the java.io package. This interface is intended to be implemented by output stream classes. The interface's definition is:

```
public interface ObjectOutput extends DataOutput {
    public void writeObject(Object obj) throws IOException;
```

```
    public void write (int b) throws IOException;
    public void write(byte b[]) throws IOException;
    public void write(byte b[], int off, int len) throws IOException;
    public void flush() throws IOException;
    public void close() throws IOException;
}
```

The essential method of the interface is writeObject (Object obj), which writes obj to a stream. Static and transient data of obj is ignored; all other variables, including private ones, are written.

Exceptions can occur while accessing the object or its fields or while attempting to write to the storage stream. If these occur, the stream that the interface is built on will be left in an unknown and unusable state. If this happens, the external representation of the object is corrupt.

The ObjectOutput interface extends the DataOutput interface. DataOutput methods support writing of primitive datatypes. For example, the writeDouble() method writes data of type double, and writeBoolean() writes data of type boolean. These primitive-type writing methods are used for writing an object's primitive instance variables.

The primary class that implements the ObjectOutput interface is ObjectOutput-Stream. This class is similar to other output stream classes, discussed previously. Note that objects are represented as streams of bytes, rather than characters, so they are represented by streams rather than character-oriented writers.

When an object is to be serialized to a file, the first step is to create an output stream that talks to the file:

```
FileOutputStream fos = new FileOutputStream ("obj.ser");
```

The next step is to create an object output stream and chain it to the file output stream:

```
ObjectOutput objout = new ObjectOutputStream (fos);
```

The object output stream automatically writes a header into the stream; the header contains a magic number and a version. This data is written automatically with the writeStreamHeader() method when the object output stream is created. As explained later in this chapter, an object input stream reads this header and verifies the object before returning its state.

After writing the header, the object output stream can write the bit representation of an object to the output stream using the writeObject() method. For example, the following code constructs an instance of the Point class and serializes it:

```
objout.writeObject (new Point(15, 20));
objout.flush();
```

This example shows that serializing an object to a stream is not very different from writing primitive data to a stream. The next section investigates restoring serialized objects from input streams. The example writes objects to a file, but the output stream can just as easily be chained to a network connection stream.

WARNING   The serialization output format changed between Java 1.1 and Java 1.2. If you are trying to write streams in a Java 1.2 environment to be read by Java 1.1 systems, you should call ObjectOutputStream.useProtocolVersion (ObjectStream-Constants.PROTOCOL_VERSION_1). By default, in Java 1.2, the version is PROTO-COL_VERSION_2. Reading automatically detects and handles versioning issues.

Using Object Input Streams for Deserialization

The ObjectInputStream class deserializes a serialized stream. It is responsible for maintaining the state of the stream and all of the objects that have been serialized to that stream. By using the methods of this class, a program can restore a serialized object from a stream, as well as the entire tree of objects referred to by the primary object. Primitive data types may also be read from an object input stream.

Only one class constructor exists in the ObjectInputStream class:

```
public ObjectInputStream(InputStream in)
    throws IOException, StreamCorruptedException
```

The constructor calls the class's readStreamHeader() method to verify the header and the version that were written into the stream by the corresponding object output stream. If a problem is detected with the header or the version, a StreamCorruptedException is thrown.

The primary method of the ObjectInputStream class is readObject(), which deserializes an object from the data source stream. The deserialized object is returned as an Object; the caller is responsible for casting it to the correct type.

During deserialization, the system maintains a list of objects that have been restored from the stream. This list is called the *known objects table*.

If the data being maintained is of a primitive type, it is simply treated as a sequence of bytes and restored from the input stream. If the data being restored is a string, it is read using the string's UTF (Unicode Transfer Format) encoding; the string will be added to the known objects table. If the object being restored is an array, the type and length of the array are determined. Next, memory for the array is allocated, and each of the elements contained in the array is read using the appropriate method. Once the array is reconstructed, it is added to the known objects table; if it is an array of objects (as opposed to primitives), then each object is deserialized and added to the known objects table. When an ordinary object (that is, not a string or an array) is restored, it is added to the known objects table; then the objects to which the original object refers are restored recursively and added to the known objects table.

Once an object has been retrieved from a stream, it must be validated so it can become a full-fledged object and be used by the program that deserialized it. The `validateObject()` method is called when a complete graph of objects has been retrieved from a stream. If the primary object cannot be made valid, the validation process will stop and an exception will be thrown.

Security Considerations for Serialized Objects

Serialization can involve storing an object's data on a disk file or transmitting the data across a network. In both cases, there is a potential security problem because the data is located outside the Java runtime environment, beyond the reach of Java's security mechanisms.

The `writeExternal()` method is public, so any object can make an externalizable or serializable object write itself to a stream. Caution should be exercised when deciding whether `writeExternal()` should serialize sensitive private data. When an object is restored via an ordinary `readExternal()` call, its sensitive values are restored back into private variables and no harm is done. However, while the serialized data is outside the system, an attacker could access the data, decode its format, and obtain the sensitive values. A similar form of attack would involve modifying data values so, for example, a password is replaced or a bank balance is incremented. A less precise attack would simply corrupt the serialized data.

When an object is serialized, all the reachable objects of its ownership graph are potentially exposed. For example, a serialized object might have a reference to a reference to a reference to an instance to a class that maintains caching information. An attacker could reserialize the cache and gain access to the file system of the machine where the serialized object originated.

The best protection for an object with fields that should not be stored is to label those fields with the transient keyword. Transient fields, like static fields, are not serialized and are therefore not exposed.

If a class cannot be serialized in a manner that upholds the integrity of the system containing it, that class should not implement the Serializable interface. Moreover, it should not be referred to by any class that will be serialized.

Externalizable objects (that is, ones that take care of writing their own data) often use the technique of including invariant data among their instance variables. These invariants serve no useful purpose during normal operation of the class. They are inspected after deserialization; an unexpected value indicates that the external serialized representation has been corrupted.

Serialization Exceptions

Seven types of exceptions can be thrown during the serialization or deserialization of an object. All seven types are extensions of ObjectStreamException, which is an extension of IOException. The exceptions are described here:

InvalidClassException   Typically thrown when the class type cannot be determined by the reserializing stream or when the class that is being returned cannot be represented on the system retrieving the object. The exception is also thrown if the deserialized class is not declared public or if it does not have a public default (no-argument) constructor.

NotSerializableException   Typically thrown by externalizable objects (which are responsible for their own reserialization) on detection of a corrupted input stream. The corruption is generally indicated by an unexpected invariant value.

StreamCorruptedException   Thrown when a stored object's header or control data is invalid.

NotActiveException   Thrown if the registerValidation() method is called outside the readObject() method.

InvalidObjectException   Thrown when a restored object cannot be made valid after deserialization.

OptionalDataException   Thrown when a stream is supposed to contain an object in it, but it actually contains only primitive data.

WriteAbortedException   Thrown during reserialization (reading), when an input stream detects that its data is incomplete because of abnormal termination of the writing process.

Writing and Reading an Object Stream

Writing an object to a stream is a simple process, similar to writing any other kind of high-level structure. You must create a low-level output stream to provide access to the external medium (generally a file or network). Next, a high-level stream is chained to the low-level stream; for serialization, the high-level stream is an object output stream.

The following code fragment constructs an instance of `Point` and writes it to a file called `point.ser` on the local file system:

```
Point p = new Point(13, 10);
FileOutputStream f = new FileOutputStream ("Point.ser");
ObjectOutputStream s = new ObjectOutputStream (f);
try {
  s.writeObject (p);
  s.flush ();
} catch (IOException e) {
}
```

Restoring the object involves opening a file input stream on the file and chaining an object input stream to the file input stream. The `Point` object is read by calling `readObject()` from the object input stream; the return value is of type `Object` and must be cast by the caller. The following code fragment shows how all this is accomplished:

```
Point p = null;
FileInputStream f = new FileInputStream ("Point.ser");
ObjectInputStream s = new ObjectInputStream (f);
try {
  p = (Point)s.readObject ();
} catch (IOException e) {
}
```

The next section develops a simple sample program that saves and restores an object.

A Serialization Example

The example presented here is a simple painting program that can store its display list to a file. (A *display list* is a data structure that contains an abstract description of what should appear on the screen.) The program allows the user to draw rectangles with the mouse; pressing down on the mouse button defines one corner of a rectangle and releasing the button defines the opposite corner. The display list is a vector that contains two instances of the `Point` class for each rectangle. One point represents the mouse-down corner of the rectangle.

The PersisTest application is a subclass of `Frame`. A panel across the top of the frame contains four control buttons. The frame's `paint()` method clears the screen to white and then traverses the display list vector, drawing one black rectangle for each pair of points in the vector.

The four control buttons support clearing, saving, restoring, and quitting. The handler for the Save button uses the writing technique discussed in the previous section to store the display list vector in a file. The filename must be specified in the command-line argument. The handler for the Restore button deserializes a vector, replacing the old display list with the new vector.

To test the application, invoke it with a filename as a command-line argument:

```
java PersisTest filename
```

Then use the mouse to draw some rectangles. Next, click the Save button to write the display list to the file. Clear the screen or draw more rectangles. Finally, click the Restore button. The display will change back to the state it was in when you clicked the Save button. You can even terminate the application and restart it; it will still restore correctly from the external file.

This example could achieve the same result by opening a data output stream instead of an object output stream and writing four `int` values for each rectangle. The benefit to using serialization lies in the dramatic improvement in program maintainability. If you were to store and restore the display list by using data input and output streams, any change in the format of the display list would force a change in both the writing and the reading code. With serialization, the display list data format is irrelevant.

The following is the source code listing for the PersisTest program:

```
import java.awt.*;
import java.awt.event.*;
```

```java
import java.io.*;
import java.util.ArrayList;

public class PersisTest extends Frame
    implements MouseListener, ActionListener {
  ArrayList displayList;
  String pathname;
  Button clearBtn, saveBtn, restoreBtn, quitBtn;

  public static void main (String args[])    {
    if (args.length == 0) {
      System.err.println ("Usage: java PersisTest filename");
      System.exit (0);
    }

    PersisTest that = new PersisTest (args[0]);
    that.show();
  }

  public PersisTest (String pathname) {
    this.pathname = pathname;
    displayList = new ArrayList();

    // Handle our own mouse clicks.
    addMouseListener (this);

    // Build the GUI. Make this object a listener for all actions.
    setLayout (new BorderLayout());
    Panel pan = new Panel();
    clearBtn = new Button ("Clear");
    clearBtn.addActionListener (this);
    pan.add (clearBtn);
    saveBtn = new Button ("Save");
    saveBtn.addActionListener (this);
    pan.add (saveBtn);
    restoreBtn = new Button ("Restore");
    restoreBtn.addActionListener (this);
    pan.add (restoreBtn);
    quitBtn = new Button ("Quit");
    quitBtn.addActionListener (this);
    pan.add (quitBtn);
    add (pan, BorderLayout.NORTH);
```

```
      setSize (350, 200);
    }

    public void paint (Graphics g) {
      // Clear to white.
      g.setColor (Color.white);
      g.fillRect (0, 0, getSize().width, getSize().height);

      // Traverse display list, drawing 1 rect for each 2 points
      // in the array list.
      g.setColor (Color.black);
      int i = 0;
      while (i < displayList.size()) {
        Point p0 = (Point)(displayList.get (i++));
        Point p1 = (Point)(displayList.get (i++));
        int x = Math.min (p0.x, p1.x);
        int y = Math.min (p0.y, p1.y);
        int w = Math.abs (p0.x - p1.x);
        int h = Math.abs (p0.y - p1.y);
        g.drawRect (x, y, w, h);
      }
    }

    public void mousePressed (MouseEvent e) {
      // Store x and y in display list array list.
      Point p = new Point (e.getX(), e.getY());
      displayList.add (p);
    }

    public void mouseReleased (MouseEvent e) {
      // Store x and y in display list array list, and request repaint.
      Point p = new Point (e.getX(), e.getY());
      displayList.add (p);
      repaint();
    }

    // Unused methods of MouseListener interface.
    public void mouseClicked (MouseEvent e) { }
    public void mouseEntered (MouseEvent e) { }
    public void mouseExited  (MouseEvent e) { }
```

```java
public void actionPerformed (ActionEvent e) {
  if (e.getSource() == clearBtn) {
    // Repaint with an empty display list.
    displayList = new ArrayList();
    repaint();
  } else if (e.getSource() == saveBtn) {
    // Write display list array list to an object output stream.
    try {
      FileOutputStream fos = new FileOutputStream (pathname);
      ObjectOutputStream oos = new ObjectOutputStream (fos);
      oos.writeObject (displayList);
      oos.flush();
      oos.close();
      fos.close();
    } catch (IOException ex) {
      System.err.println ("Trouble writing display list array
list");
    }
  } else if (e.getSource() == restoreBtn) {
    // Read a new display list array list from an object input
stream.
    try {
      FileInputStream fis = new FileInputStream (pathname);
      ObjectInputStream ois = new ObjectInputStream (fis);
      displayList = (ArrayList)(ois.readObject());
      ois.close();
      fis.close();
      repaint();
    } catch (ClassNotFoundException ex) {
      System.err.println ("Trouble reading display list array
list");
    } catch (IOException ex) {
      System.err.println ("Trouble reading display list array
list");
    }
  } else if (e.getSource() == quitBtn) {
    setVisible (false);
    dispose();
    System.exit (0);
  }
}
}
```

Summary

Computers need to interact with the outside world to be useful. They need to input external information, process it, and output results. Almost every computer language includes a generic I/O support layer that shields applications, written in those languages, from the more turbulent world of rapidly changing and very different I/O devices "out there." Java's answer to (or rather, its arsenal to cope with) the I/O issue is the `java.io` package, which provides device- and platform-independent classes for file and stream manipulation.

The way that Java supports streams is especially powerful and flexible. The stream classes support an unlimited chaining mechanism that allows you to mix and match stream classes to achieve any desired I/O functionality. Creating your own enhanced stream classes, to be inserted anywhere along an input or output chain, is straightforward. The type of power and flexibility that the `java.io` hierarchy puts in the hands of developers is possible only because of the application of pure object-oriented techniques, and, it has to be said, clever design.

CHAPTER

TWENTY

Network Programming

- The TCP/IP protocol suite

- Internet addressing methods

- Low-level communication using UDP

- Connecting to servers using TCP

- Accessing password-protected resources

- Server system design

- The Factory design pattern

When Java was developed, GUIs had already become commonplace, so Java is accompanied by its AWT. Nevertheless, Java is also a child of the Internet era, and so it comes with an entire package of classes devoted to Internet and Web support.

In fact, Java is the first mainstream programming language to provide built-in support for high-level Internet programming. Using other languages, the only way to write applications for the Internet is to descend into the technical depths of operating system–dependent networking APIs. With Java, writing a program that accesses a computer on the other side of the planet is easier than ever, and there is no need to grind through your machine's reference volumes for operating system networking support.

This chapter briefly reviews the main networking protocols and then describes the classes in the `java.net` package. The examples presented here demonstrate how to connect to remote servers and fetch resources, as well as how to design a simple server system. You'll also learn about the Factory design pattern and the factory interfaces in `java.net`.

Java's Networking Protocols: TCP/IP

Java's view of networking means TCP/IP, and only TCP/IP. Novell, IBM, and DEC proprietary networking protocols do not make the grade—and quite rightly so, since TCP/IP is the only true "open" networking standard that links together the four corners of the globe, via the Internet.

TCP/IP stands for Transmission Control Protocol/Internet Protocol, the two data communication protocols on which the Internet relies for all its functionality. With the Internet, a whole collection of related protocols run on top of TCP/IP, using TCP/IP to communicate behind the scenes. SMTP (Simple Mail Transfer Protocol) and NNTP (Network News Transfer Protocol) are examples of two older (but still ubiquitous) protocols. The new kid on the block, HTTP (Hypertext Transfer Protocol), has become so much a part of the Internet, and therefore TCP/IP, that many people confuse the Web with the Internet.

IP: The Heart of Internet Data Communications

Whatever application protocol is used to implement an Internet service, IP lies at the heart of all Internet data communications. IP is a datagram protocol, which means transmitted packets of information (*packets*, for short) are not guaranteed to be delivered. IP packets also do not form part of a stream of related packets; IP is a *connectionless* protocol. Each IP packet travels on its own, like an individual letter in a postal network (or a guru looking for enlightenment). Figure 20.1 shows the structure of an IP packet.

FIGURE 20.1:

The IP datagram packet format

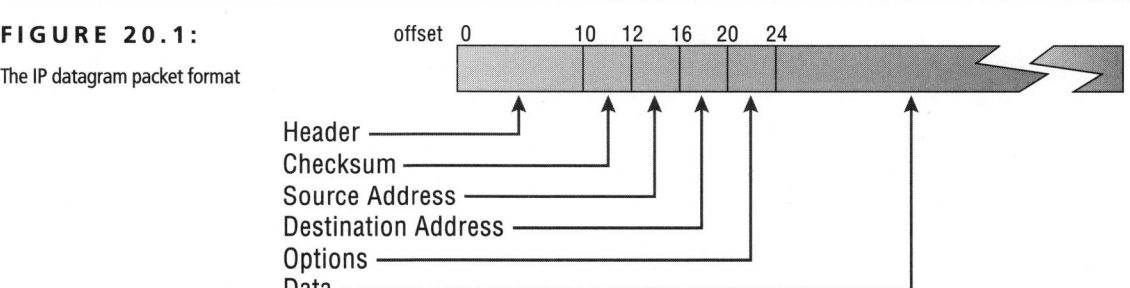

The various fields at the beginning of a packet (also called a *frame*) are collectively known as the *frame header*. The IP frame header determines the IP protocol's functionality and its limitations. Foremost in this respect is the addressing structure employed to encode the source (sender) and destination addresses. Thirty-two bits have been allocated for each of these address fields, which means the Internet can have a maximum of 2^{32} (4,294,967,296) different machines connected to its global network.

NOTE   The maximum number of machines may sound sufficient, but this address space is already close to exhausted. The Internet Architecture Board (IAB) is working hard to introduce a less restrictive upgrade to IP, called IP Next Generation (IPng).

Instead of writing down 32-digit long bitstrings, like 11001110110000110001011111010000, Internet addresses are almost always expressed in their human-readable, textual form (for example, www.sybex.com). On the rarer occasions when the address needs to be expressed numerically, these 32-bit IP addresses are written as four decimal bytes (for example, 192.31.32.255). The remainder of the header encodes a collection of fields, including the total packet length in bytes. Sixteen bits are allocated for this field, so an IP packet can be a maximum of 64KB long.

TCP: For Guaranteed Delivery

Since IP packets are never guaranteed to arrive at their destination, a higher-level protocol, TCP, provides a basic service that does guarantee delivery. TCP manages this by using IP as a building block. The structure of a TCP packet is shown in Figure 20.2.

FIGURE 20.2:

The TCP packet format

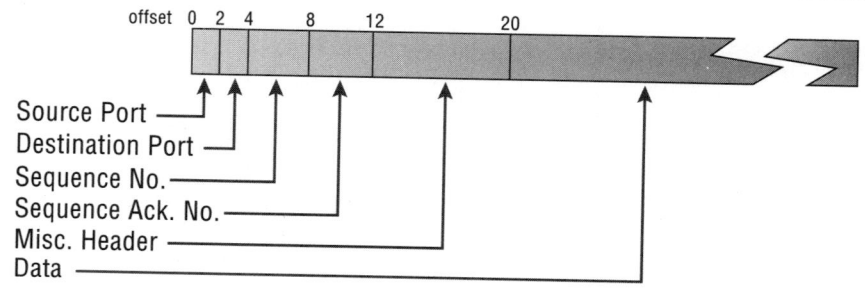

Source Port
Destination Port
Sequence No.
Sequence Ack. No.
Misc. Header
Data

Whereas IP is a connectionless datagram service, TCP presents a *connection-oriented* data stream service (like the telephone network). Before sending data via TCP, a computer needs to connect with the computer at the other end; only then can data be exchanged. Another difference is that the TCP protocol sends and receives arbitrary amounts of data as one big stream of byte data. IP, on the other hand, is theoretically limited to sending a 65,536-byte packet, which would be insufficient for sending many files or even many large GIF images embedded in Web pages. TCP solves this problem by breaking up the user's data stream into separate IP packets, numbering them, and then reassembling them on arrival. This is the function of the sequence number and sequence acknowledge number fields.

The most important TCP header fields, from a user's standpoint, are the source and destination port fields. While IP allows you to send an IP packet to an individual machine on the network, TCP forces you to refine this addressing by adding a destination port address. Every machine that talks TCP/IP has 65,536 different TCP ports (or *sockets*) it can talk through, as shown in Figure 20.3.

A large collection of standard port numbers has been defined. Table 20.1 shows some port addresses for familiar Internet services; for example, port 21 is universally used for file transfers using FTP (File Transfer Protocol), and port 80 is used for all communications with World Wide Web HTML servers. In later examples, you will talk to port 25 on your Internet provider's machine to send e-mail, and to port 80 of any Web server in the world to request a Web page to be transmitted to you.

FIGURE 20.3:

TCP ports and well-known
port numbers

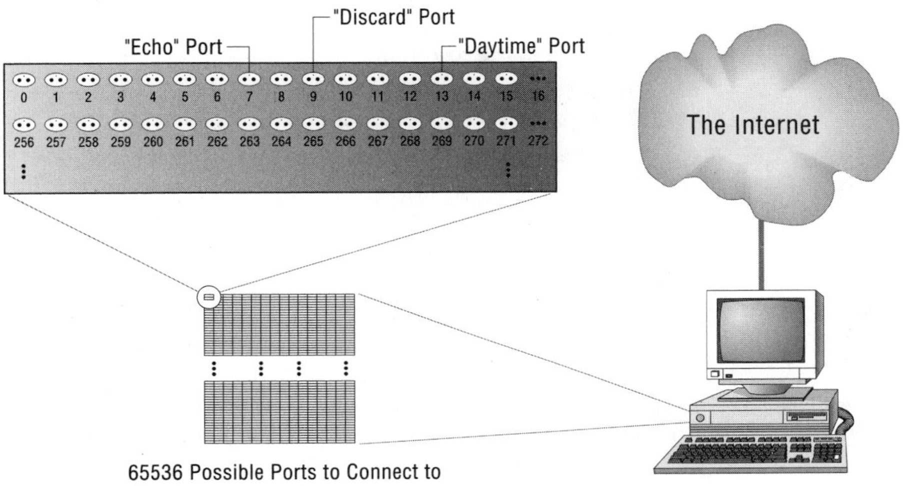

65536 Possible Ports to Connect to

TABLE 20.1: Standard TCP Port Numbers

Port Name	Port Number	Service Description
echo	7	Echoes whatever you send to it
discard	9	Discards whatever you send to it
daytime	13	Produces the destination machine's local time
qotd	17	Produces the "quote of the day" for that machine
charge	19	Produces a test stream of characters (character generator)
ftp-data	20	FTP data port
ftp	21	FTP control port
telnet	23	Telnet protocol port
smtp	25	SMTP port
finger	79	Finger protocol port
http	80	Web server port
pop3	110	POP version 3 port
nntp	119	NNTP port

The majority of application-level TCP/IP protocols (like SMTP for e-mail transfer) rely on TCP, not IP, to achieve their functionality. This is because they invariably need guaranteed or error-free transmission of unlimited amounts of data.

One more low-level IP protocol, besides TCP, builds on IP to achieve its functionality: UDP (User Datagram Protocol). UDP is a datagram protocol with the same 64KB packet-size limit of IP, but it also allows port addresses to be specified. In fact, every machine has two sets of 65,536 ports to communicate through: one for TCP and one for UDP. The TFTP (Trivial File Transfer Protocol) protocol does the equivalent of FTP, but over UDP communications. Instead of the TCP dealing with problems like dropped packets, TFTP does. The end result is still the transfer of a file.

Now that you have reviewed some TCP/IP basics, you are ready to explore the core `java.net` package classes.

Internet Addressing

One of the `java.net` classes allows you to manipulate a 32-bit IP address (that is, an Internet host address) in a more high-level fashion than by just using a single 32-bit integer. Class `InetAddress` essentially lets you convert a textual Internet address of the form *host.subdomain.domain* into an object representing that address.

Here is the definition for class `InetAddress`:

```
public final class InetAddress extends Object
    implements Serializable {
  public static InetAddress[] getAllByName (String host)
    throws UnknownHostException;
  public static InetAddress getByName (String host)
    throws UnknownHostException;
  public static synchronized InetAddress getLocalHost()
    throws UnknownHostException;
  public boolean equals (Object obj);
```

```
    public byte[] getAddress();
    public String getHostAddress();
    public String getHostName();
    public int hashCode();
    public boolean isMulticastAddress();
    public String toString();
}
```

The class deviates from the object-oriented norm by not providing a constructor and relying instead on static class methods, `getByName()` and `getAllByName()`, to create `InetAddress` instances. These methods take as their argument the textual address of any host on the Internet, in the form of a `String`. You can also turn the Internet address of your own machine (localhost) into an `InetAddress` by calling `InetAddress.getLocalHost()`.

To experiment with the `InetAddress` methods, and most other `java.net` methods and classes, you need to have your machine online. That is, you need to be connected to a live TCP/IP network, if not the Internet itself. One of the reasons for this is that the `java.net` classes need to be able to do full domain name lookups via the Domain Name System (DNS). You already learned that Internet addresses are encoded as 32-bit integers within the IP packets exchanged on the Internet. Mnemonic addresses like www.miningco.com or web.mit.edu are used only for your benefit, and they must be translated to 32-bit addresses for any real Internet communication to be initiated based on those addresses.

The Domain Name System

How does the translation from textual address to numeric address take place? Does your machine contain a huge file listing every Internet machine in the world, along with its numeric address? Not nowadays. This was the situation during the earlier years of the Internet when there were a couple of hundred machines worldwide. With the exponential growth in hosts connecting to the Internet, this approach became unsustainable (it did not scale well).

Today, every machine configured to talk TCP/IP needs to know at least one numeric address of another, very special machine it can talk to directly, without needing to translate any textual address to the real 32-bit address: the address of a DNS server. This DNS server is responsible for translating the cozy textual Internet addresses into hard (but efficient) numeric Internet addresses.

The Internet's DNS system is like a global (distributed) telephone book for all of the Internet's host machines; given a mnemonic address, the DNS system will return the IP address (the telephone number) of a host.

Looking Up a Textual Address

Method getByName() in class InetAddress is the transparent interface to the DNS service. When you invoke getByName(), your machine will contact the DNS server "directly" (using its numeric address) and ask to look up and return the numeric address for the textual address you passed to getByName(). If your machine is not online, this lookup mechanism will fail, and an UnknownHostException will be thrown (which is why you generally need to be online when working with java.net classes), unless you are looking up your own machine's IP address, passing your machine's name as a string.

The following program demonstrates the address lookup possibilities of class InetAddress:

```java
import java.net.*;
public class DNSLookup {

  public static void main (String args[]) throws UnknownHostException {
    InetAddress someHost;
    byte bytes[];
    int fourBytes[] = new int[4];

    if (args.length == 0) {
      someHost = InetAddress.getLocalHost();
    } else {
      someHost = InetAddress.getByName (args[0]);
    }

    System.out.print ("Host '"+ someHost.getHostName() +"' has address: ");

    bytes = someHost.getAddress();
    for (int i=0; i<4; i++) {
      fourBytes[i] = bytes[i] & 255;
    }

    System.out.println (fourBytes[0] + "." +
                        fourBytes[1] + "." +
                        fourBytes[2] + "." +
                        fourBytes[3]);
  }
}
```

The program takes a host name string as a command-line argument. If no host name is specified, the lookup will be performed for your own machine's address. Here is an example of the output when no command-line arguments are entered:

```
Host 'telework' has address: 194.222.15.21
```

Getting a Numeric Address

To get the numeric address, use `getAddress()`, which returns an array of four bytes. To print these bytes, interpreted as unsigned values, you cannot just cast to an `int` datatype; negative byte values will be sign-extended to equally negative `int` values. The bytes need to be copied into an array of integers while anding with 255 to undo the sign-extending.

Note that class `InetAddress` overrides `toString()` (like all good classes), which, in this context, outputs a `String` containing much the same information as we constructed manually. For example, this code:

```
System.out.println (InetAddress.getLocalHost());
```

produces this:

```
telework/194.222.15.21
```

Communicating with Remote Systems

Now that you know how to specify an Internet destination using instances of class `InetAddress`, how do you actually communicate with a remote system? Package `java.net` provides several ways.

Low-Level Communication Using UDP

The most basic method of communicating with a remote system is to use UDP datagrams. A UDP datagram is embodied in an instance of class `DatagramPacket`:

```
public final class DatagramPacket extends Object {
  public DatagramPacket (byte buf[], int length);
  public DatagramPacket(byte buf[], int offset, int length);
  public DatagramPacket (byte buf[], int length, InetAddress addr,
    int port);
```

```
   public DatagramPacket (byte buf[], int offset, int length,
     InetAddress addr, int port);
   public synchronized InetAddress getAddress();
   public synchronized byte[] getData();
   public synchronized int getLength();
   public synchronized int getOffset();
   public synchronized int getPort();
   public synchronized void setAddress (InetAddress addr);
   public synchronized void setData (byte buf[]);
   public synchronized void setData (byte buf[], int offset, int length);
   public synchronized void setLength (int length);
   public synchronized void setPort (int port);
}
```

Class `DatagramPacket` provides four constructors: two to receive datagrams and two to transmit datagrams. With both sets of constructors, you need to specify a byte buffer and its length (the `buf` array can be bigger than `length`, but not smaller). The transmitting constructors additionally need the destination machine and port number for the datagram (in each of these constructor's case, the byte buffer contains the message).

As you can see, the class does not actually give you the means for sending or receiving any datagrams. This functionality is the responsibility of a companion class, class `DatagramSocket`:

```
public final class DatagramSocket extends Object {
   public DatagramSocket() throws SocketException;
   public DatagramSocket (int port) throws SocketException;
   public DatagramSocket (int port, InetAddress laddr)
     throws SocketException;
   public void close();
   public InetAddress getLocalAddress();
   public int getLocalPort();
   public synchronized int getReceiveBufferSize() throws
SocketException;
   public synchronized int getSendBufferSize() throws SocketException;
   public synchronized int getSoTimeout() throws SocketException;
   public synchronized void receive (DatagramPacket p) throws
IOException;
   public void send (DatagramPacket p) throws IOException;
   public synchronized void setReceiveBufferSize(int size)
     throws SocketException;
   public synchronized void setSendBufferSize(int size)
```

```
      throws SocketException;
   public synchronized void setSoTimeout (int timeout)
      throws SocketException;
}
```

The methods of interest here are the send() and receive() methods. The send() method simply takes a DatagramPacket instance and sends the datagram's data to the previously defined host and port address. The receive() method also takes a DatagramPacket instance, but this time as a recipient for a datagram to be received. You can extract the data from a received datagram using the getData() method in class DatagramPacket. To demonstrate the transmit and receive capacities of both classes, here is a short example that addresses MIT's Web server and asks it what the local time is (at MIT, this is Eastern Standard Time).

```
import java.net.*;

public class GetDate {

  final static int PORT_DAYTIME = 13;   // well-known daytime port

  public static void main (String args[]) throws Exception {
    DatagramSocket  dgSocket;
    DatagramPacket  datagram;
    InetAddress     destination;
    byte msg[] = new byte[256];

    dgSocket    = new DatagramSocket();
    destination = InetAddress.getByName ("web.mit.edu");

    datagram    = new DatagramPacket (msg, msg.length, destination,
                                      PORT_DAYTIME);
    dgSocket.send(datagram);

    datagram = new DatagramPacket (msg, msg.length);
    dgSocket.receive(datagram);

    String received = new String (datagram.getData());
    System.out.println ("The time in beautiful Cambridge is now: " + received);

    dgSocket.close();

  }
} // end of class GetDate
```

The program first creates a datagram socket that it will use to both transmit and receive. It then proceeds by creating an instance of a transmit datagram packet to send to the daytime port service on MIT's server. The server's mechanical response is always to return a time-stamped datagram (in ASCII). This datagram must be caught in a brand new `DatagramPacket` instance. (The program does not reuse the transmit packet for receive purposes; the only reuse that occurs is that of the variable name datagram.) Once the response datagram is received, the time is extracted from the datagram as an ASCII byte array and converted to a `String` that is printed to the console.

The simplicity of this example hides a serious problem. Neither the sent nor the received datagrams are ever guaranteed to arrive at their destinations. This means that the server might never receive your initial datagram. Moreover, if it does, its response might never reach your machine. UDP is useful mainly whenever low-value information needs to be broadcast or when information needs to be transmitted on a frequent basis so that losing a communication now and then does not affect the service. For most communications, however, you need guaranteed delivery of your data—and that is TCP's domain.

Connecting to Servers Using TCP

The programming model for TCP communication is similar to that of UDP, except that it does not rely on a class to encapsulate TCP packets. This is to be expected, because TCP is a stream protocol. It allows you to send arbitrary amounts of data. The core class is simply called `Socket`:

```
public class Socket extends Object {
  public Socket (InetAddress address, int port) throws IOException;
  public Socket (InetAddress address, int port, InetAddress localAddr,
    int localPort) throws IOException;
  public Socket (String host, int port)
    throws UnknownHostException, IOException;
  public Socket (String host, int port, InetAddress localAddr,
    int localPort) throws IOException;
  public static synchronized void setSocketImplFactory (
    SocketImplFactory fac) throws IOException;
  public synchronized void close() throws IOException;
  public InetAddress getInetAddress();
  public InputStream getInputStream() throws IOException;
  public InetAddress getLocalAddress();
  public int getLocalPort();
  public OutputStream getOutputStream() throws IOException;
```

```
    public int getPort();
    public synchronized int getReceiveBufferSize() throws SocketException;
    public synchronized int getSendBufferSize() throws SocketException;
    public int getSoLinger() throws SocketException;
    public synchronized int getSoTimeout() throws SocketException;
    public boolean getTcpNoDelay() throws SocketException;
    public synchronized void setReceiveBufferSize(int size)
       throws SocketException;
    public synchronized void setSendBufferSize(int size)
       throws SocketException;
    public void setSoLinger (boolean on, int val)
       throws SocketException;
    public synchronized void setSoTimeout (int timeout)
       throws SocketException;
    public void setTcpNoDelay (boolean on) throws SocketException;
    public String toString();
}
```

To use the Socket class, you need to understand the Socket constructors and the two stream access methods. The constructors need to have an instance of an InetAddress object or a String to specify the destination machine to which you want to connect. If this were an IP support class, this would be all that is required. However, since this is a TCP support class, the constructors also need a port address for the remote machine. Using this class puts you in the role of a client (within the client/server application model), so you cannot specify any old number for this port address; you must stick to one of the well-known port numbers (see Table 20.1, earlier in the chapter).

All TCP connections actually involve two ports: a port on the remote machine and a port on the local machine, through which the client communicates. You do not need to specify the local port number because the TCP/IP software allocates these ephemeral ports dynamically. They are called *ephemeral* ports because, unlike server ports, they exist only for the duration of a volatile client/server transaction. Server ports remain in use as long as the server software (also called a *daemon*) is running.

NOTE   On Unix, the server programs that manage the different ports are all implemented as background daemon tasks. That is why their names all end with *d*, as in smtpd for the SMTP service, ftpd for the FTP service, telnetd for the Telnet service, and so on.

Now you will work through some examples that rely on the Socket class to reach out onto the Internet.

Getting Internet Protocol Specifications

You can obtain the full specifications for every Internet protocol (IP, UDP, TCP, SMTP, FTP, HTTP, and so on) by retrieving the standards documents themselves. These are called Request for Comments (RFCs). For example, RFCs 821 and 822 contain all the information about SMTP. RFCs are available by anonymous FTP from various sites, including `mit.edu`. An even more convenient way is to send an e-mail message to `rfc-info@isi.edu`, with a body containing two lines, such as:

Retrieve: RFC

Doc-ID: RFC0821

The server will send you the document (ASCII of course) by e-mail within the next 24 hours. What a service!

Of course you can simply go to `http://info.internet.isi.edu/1/in-notes/rfc` and retrieve the document directly.

Connecting to an SMTP Mail Server

If you want to deliver e-mail to a machine, you need to knock on that machine's port number 25. Once invited in, you also need to talk to the entity behind that port using a very strict, but simple, data communications protocol called SMTP. The following steps summarize the way this protocol works:

1. The SMTP server sends an initial identification string.

2. You reply by telling it which machine you are sending from.

3. If okay, the server replies with an acknowledge.

4. You reply by giving it the "From:" e-mail address (the sender's address).

5. If okay, the server replies with an acknowledge.

6. You reply by giving it the "To:" e-mail address (the address of the person you want the message to travel to).

7. If okay, the server replies with an acknowledge.

8. You send the entire e-mail message, line by line, and end the message with a single line containing a full stop ('.').

9. The server again acknowledges receipt of the message.

10. You sign off by sending QUIT.

The entire exchange is in readable ASCII—no binary flags or cryptic fields within this protocol. If you delve into the fascinating world of Internet protocols, you will see that they are in fact very common among Internet protocols. (Data communications protocols outside the Unix-derived sphere of the Internet usually rely on complex packet structures encoded in binary.) Few of the Internet's application protocols employ the much more complex (but more efficient) binary representation for their protocol data units (PDUs), which are the packet types used to manage a communications protocol between two peers).

NOTE   Sun provides a library of classes called JavaMail to more easily handle working with SMTP services. You can find out about the library from `http://java.sun.com/products/javamail/index.html`. Sun provides an implementation, without source, that developers may use and ship royalty-free.

An Example: Sending an E-Mail Message

The sample program presented here demonstrates how easy it is to talk TCP with any (willing) port on a remote machine. It actually allows you to send an e-mail message from the command line by specifying the filename of the message to send, the "From" and "To" e-mail addresses, and the address of a mail host that will accept (and possibly forward) the mail message. You should use your usual mail drop-off point. Here's the program:

```
import java.io.*;
import java.net.*;

public class SMTPDemo {

  public static void main (String args[])
      throws IOException, UnknownHostException {
    String msgFile;
    String from, to, mailHost;

    if (args.length != 4) {
      System.out.println ("Usage: java SMTPDemo msgFile from to mailHost");
      System.exit (10);
    }
```

```
    msgFile   = args[0];
    from      = args[1];
    to        = args[2];
    mailHost  = args[3];

    checkEmailAddress (from);
    checkEmailAddress (to);

    SMTP mail = new SMTP (mailHost);
    if (mail != null) {
      if (mail.send (new FileReader (msgFile), from, to) ) {
        System.out.println ("Mail sent.");
      } else {
        System.out.println ("Connect to SMTP server failed!");
      }
    }
    System.out.println ("Done.");
  }

  static void checkEmailAddress (String address) {
    if (address.indexOf('@') == -1) {
      System.out.println ("Invalid e-mail address '" + address + "'");
      System.exit (10);
    }
  }
}

//-----------------------------------------------------------------
class SMTP {

  public final static int SMTP_PORT = 25;

  InetAddress mailHost;
  InetAddress ourselves;
  BufferedReader in;
  PrintWriter out;

  public SMTP (String host) throws UnknownHostException {

    mailHost = InetAddress.getByName (host);
    ourselves= InetAddress.getLocalHost();
```

```
    System.out.println ("mailhost = " + mailHost);
    System.out.println ("localhost= " + ourselves);
    System.out.println ("SMTP constructor done\n");
}

public boolean send (FileReader msgg, String from, String to) throws IOException {
    Socket smtpPipe;
    InputStream inn;
    OutputStream outt;
    BufferedReader msg;

    msg = new BufferedReader (msgg);

    smtpPipe = new Socket (mailHost, SMTP_PORT);
    if (smtpPipe == null) {
        return false;
    }

    // get raw streams
    inn  = smtpPipe.getInputStream();
    outt = smtpPipe.getOutputStream();

    // turn into usable ones
    in  = new BufferedReader (new InputStreamReader (inn));
    out = new PrintWriter (new OutputStreamWriter (outt), true);

    if (inn==null || outt==null) {
        System.out.println ("Failed to open streams to socket.");
        return false;
    }

    String initialID = in.readLine();
    System.out.println (initialID);

    System.out.println ("HELO " + ourselves.getHostName());
            out.println ("HELO " + ourselves.getHostName());

    String welcome = in.readLine();
    System.out.println(welcome);

    System.out.println ("MAIL From:<" + from + ">");
            out.println ("MAIL From:<" + from + ">");
```

```
String senderOK = in.readLine();
System.out.println (senderOK);

System.out.println ("RCPT TO:<" + to + ">");
        out.println ("RCPT TO:<" + to + ">");

String recipientOK = in.readLine();
System.out.println(recipientOK);

System.out.println ("DATA");
        out.println ("DATA");

String line;
while ((line = msg.readLine()) != null) {
  out.println(line);
}
System.out.println (".");
        out.println (".");

String acceptedOK = in.readLine();
System.out.println (acceptedOK);

System.out.println ("QUIT");
        out.println ("QUIT");

    return true;
  }
}
```

The SMTP demonstration program defines a new class called SMTP that provides a single method, **send( )**. This method allows clients to send some e-mail message to an e-mail recipient. Note that this implementation of **send( )** simply swallows the responses from the server without checking for errors. This is not robust enough to be used in the real world (see RFC 821 for the error codes to check for in a secure implementation of the **send( )** method). However, the main program does do a simple check on the e-mail addresses to see if they at least contain the @ character, something all fully qualified addresses require.

Looking at the program's source code, you might wonder where all the low-level, technical data communications code is hiding. The bulk of the program simply uses stream input and output methods. That is exactly where the protocol logic is hiding: Class **Socket** lets clients communicate via everyday input and output streams that happen to connect all the way to the machine and its socket at the other end. These streams are obtained via the `getInputStream()` and `getOutputStream()` methods. It is therefore possible (and desirable, as was done in the `send()` method) to upgrade the raw `InputStream` and `OutputStream` streams by encapsulating them in more high-level streams like a `BufferedReader` to read and a `Print-Writer` to write. (See Chapter 19 for a details about the I/O stream classes.) Using these two stream enhancers, you can treat both incoming and outgoing data as lines of ASCII text, which, in the case of the SMTP, is most appropriate.

Connecting to an HTTP Web Server

Another protocol that operates in this transparent, ASCII line-based format is HTTP, on which the Web relies. The HTTP protocol is based on an exchange of multiline request and response headers. As is always the case in a client/server situation, it is the client (that is, the browser) that initiates the communication by sending the server a request header. The server then replies to this request by sending a response header, which usually includes any requested resources (Web page, image file, audio clip, and so on) as appended data.

The most common type of request header formats is appropriately called a "GET" request. The format of the GET header is as follows:

```
"GET" <URL> "HTTP/1.0"
```

This client request header has three components:

- The request method (GET)
- The resource URL
- The version of the HTTP protocol used for the exchange (HTTP/1.0)

If the request can be satisfied by the server, it replies with a response header. Here is an example of a server's response header:

```
HTTP/1.0 200 OK
Server:Apache/1.0.2
Content-type: text/html
Last-Modified: Fri, 04 Sep 1998 12:34:56 PST

<HTML><HEAD>..
..
..
```

The following are the important aspects to note about the HTTP response header:

- It starts with a status reply (the 200 OK).

- It contains the type of resource returned (in the Content-type field).

- It contains an empty line that separates the header from the actual data.

In the response header example, you can see the beginning of a requested HTML file stream in (right after the blank line). Other non-ASCII resources would similarly start just past the empty line. In the case of an audio clip, for example, this data might be encoded in nonreadable binary.

An Example: Downloading a Web Page

The following program allows you to grab any Web page off the Internet from the command line. Here is the program's source code:

```java
import java.io.*;
import java.net.*;

public class GetWebPage {

  public static void main (String args[])
      throws IOException, UnknownHostException {
    String resource, host, file;
    int slashPos;

    if (args.length != 1) {
      System.out.println ("Usage: java GetWebPage <URL>");
      System.exit (10);
    }

    if (!args[0].startsWith ("http://")) {
      System.out.println ("Please specify a legal http URL.");
      System.exit (10);
    }

    resource = args[0].substring (7);   // skip HTTP://

    slashPos = resource.indexOf('/');  // find host/file separator
    if (slashPos < 0) {
```

```
      resource = resource + "/index.html";
      slashPos = resource.indexOf ('/');
    }
    file = resource.substring (slashPos); // isolate host and file parts
    host = resource.substring (0,slashPos);

    System.out.println ("Host to contact: '" + host +"'");
    System.out.println ("File to fetch  : '" + file +"'");

    HTTP webConnection = new HTTP (host);
    if (webConnection != null) {
      BufferedReader in = webConnection.get (file);
      String line;
      while ((line = in.readLine()) != null) {  // read until EOF
        System.out.println( line );
      }
    }
    System.out.println ("\nDone.");
  }
}

//-------------------------------------------------------------------
class HTTP {

  public final static int HTTP_PORT = 80;

  InetAddress wwwHost;
  DataInputStream in;
  PrintStream out;

  public HTTP (String host) throws UnknownHostException {

    wwwHost = InetAddress.getByName (host);
    System.out.println ("WWW host = " + wwwHost);
  }

  public BufferedReader get (String file) throws IOException {
    Socket httpPipe;
    InputStream inn;
    OutputStream outt;
    BufferedReader ir;
    PrintWriter out;
```

```
httpPipe = new Socket (wwwHost, HTTP_PORT);
if (httpPipe == null) {
  return null;
}

// get raw streams
inn  = httpPipe.getInputStream();
outt = httpPipe.getOutputStream();

// turn into useful ones
ir   = new BufferedReader (new InputStreamReader (inn));
out  = new PrintWriter (new OutputStreamWriter (outt), true);

if (inn==null || outt==null || ir==null || out==null) {
  System.out.println ("Failed to open streams to socket.");
  return null;
}

// send GET request
System.out.println ("GET " + file + " HTTP/1.0\n");
      out.println ("GET " + file + " HTTP/1.0\n");

  // read response until blank separator line
String response;
while ((response = ir.readLine()).length() > 0) {
  System.out.println (response);
}

return ir;  // return BufferedReader to let client read resource
}
}
```

As with the SMTP demonstration program, a separate class, HTTP in this example, is created to encapsulate the details about the protocol. Instead of a send() method, the program implements a get() method. This method creates a new Socket in the same way the SMTP class did. It then proceeds to get the input and output streams associated with the socket, so it can send and receive data over the HTTP link. The heart of the get() method is the sending of the GET HTTP header followed by the "parsing" of the response header returned by the Web server.

The minimalistic implementation given here restricts itself to simply reading and echoing the response header lines until the separator line is encountered.

From that point on, all remaining data is part of the resource requested by the main program, so the input stream itself is returned to the caller, who can then proceed with reading the resource stream (oblivious of the fact that an ASCII header preceded it).

Here is a transcript of a sample session with the GetWebPage program:

```
C:\>java GetWebPage http://www.ping.be/~ping3100/index.html
Host to contact: 'www.ping.be'
File to fetch  : '/~ping3100/index.html'
WWW host = www.ping.be/193.74.114.17
GET /~ping3100/index.html HTTP/1.0

HTTP/1.0 200 OK
Server: Netscape-Communications/1.1
Date: Saturday, 06-Dec-97 18:55:39 GMT
Content-type: text/html

<HTML>
<HEAD>
<TITLE>
Home Page for Laurence Vanhelsuwe
</TITLE>
</HEAD>
---------------- Bulk of HTML file cut ------------
</HTML>

Done.
```

If you specified a nonexistent file on a Web server, you would get the familiar browser error "404: Not Found." Here is what the GetWebPage program prints when we ask it to get a nonexistent file:

```
HTTP/1.0 404 Not Found
Server: Netscape-Communications/1.1
Date: Saturday, 06-Dec-97 18:56:39 GMT
Content-type: text/html

<HEAD><TITLE>File Not Found</TITLE>
</HEAD>
<BODY> Error 404: Not Found <P> The file or resource you
       requested could not be found anywhere on this server.
</BODY>
```

Beyond the 404 error, the exact response depends on the Web server.

Fetching Other Web Resources

Note that the `content-type` field returned by all Web servers uses a standard format called the MIME (Multipurpose Internet Mail Extensions) type. Table 20.2 shows some common MIME types and their meanings.

TABLE 20.2:   Standard MIME Types

MIME Type	Origin
application/octet-stream	Generic binary byte stream emanating from unspecified application
application/pdf	Adobe Acrobat file
application/postscript	PostScript language file
application/rtf	Rich Text Format word-processor file
application/x-tex	TeX Typesetter file
audio/basic	.snd or .au sound clip file
audio/x-aiff	Audio IFF file
audio/x-wav	.wav file
image/gif	.gif image file
image/jpeg	.jpg image file
image/tiff	.tif image file
image/x-xbitmap	.xbm image file
text/html	.html or .htm file
text/plain	.txt, .c, .cpp, .h, .pl, .java files
video/mpeg	.mpg file
video/quicktime	.mov or .qt Apple QuickTime file
video/x-sgi-movie	.movie Silicon Graphics file

To fetch other Web resources, like images or audio files, you could use the same technique demonstrated in the `GetWebPage` program, except that you would need different methods or classes to deal with the different types of content returned by the server.

Before you start investing mammoth amounts of effort to deal with each of these content types, you should know that Java already has a general solution:

```
import java.net.*;
import java.io.*;

public class GetContent {

    public static void main (String args[])
        throws MalformedURLException, IOException {
      Object obj;

      obj = (new URL ("http://www.ping.be/~ping3100/gif/ball.gif"
        )).getContent();
      System.out.println (obj.getClass().getName());
    }
}
```

This two-line program (if you ignore the necessary skeleton code) essentially does the same as the 90-odd line `GetWebPage` program! The only difference is that the `GetContent` program retrieves an image file from a Web server instead of an HTML file. No more sockets, no more input or output streams, and no more protocol-specific concerns. So, how does it work? And does it work for all the MIME types listed in Table 20.2? The answer to these questions lies in a new class introduced in this program: class URL. This class is discussed next.

Performing Operations on URLs

Class URL defines a Web URL (Uniform Resource Locator) plus some operations you can perform on URLs. In its most primitive capacity, this class is similar to `InetAddress` in that it just lets you create an object that addresses, or points to, something. In the case of class `InetAddress`, its instances point to Internet hosts; in the case of class URL instances, these objects point to Web resources (Web pages, text files, image files, sound clips, and so on). Here is the definition of class URL:

```
public class URL extends Object implements Comparable, Serializable {
    public URL (String spec) throws MalformedURLException;
    public URL (String protocol, String host, int port, String file)
        throws MalformedURLException;
    public URL (String protocol, String host, String file)
        throws MalformedURLException;
    public URL (URL context, String spec) throws MalformedURLException;
```

```
    public static synchronized void setURLStreamHandlerFactory
      (URLStreamHandlerFactory fac);
    public int compareTo (Object obj);
    public boolean equals (Object obj);
    public final Object getContent() throws IOException;
    public String getFile();
    public String getHost();
    public int getPort();
    public String getProtocol();
    public String getRef();
    public int hashCode();
    public URLConnection openConnection() throws IOException;
    public final InputStream openStream() throws IOException;
    public boolean sameFile (URL other);
    public String toExternalForm();
    public String toString();
}
```

The arguments for the simplest constructor reflect the basic structure of all well-formed URL addresses:

```
<protocol> <host address> [<:port number>] <resource spec>
```

The fields hold the following information:

- The protocol field can be `http:`, `ftp:`, `gopher:`, `news:`, `telnet:`, `mailto:`, or any supported protocol.

- The host address is any legal host address, such as `www.apple.com`.

- The port number field is optional and denotes the port number to connect to, if the default port for this protocol is to be overridden.

- The resource specification field is usually the full path of a file on the remote machine's file system, although this can be anything the protocol requires—for example, the name of a newsgroup for the `news:` protocol.

Here are some legal URL examples:

```
http://www.who.org:8080/index.htm

http://java.sun.com/jdc/earlyAccess/index.html#jdkdocs

ftp://ftp.uni-paderborn.de/pub/Aminet/README

news:comp.lang.java.programmer
```

```
gopher:gopher.ucdavis.edu

mailto:president@whitehouse.gov

jdbc:odbc:mydatabase
```

Note the first URL, which overrides the standard Web server port (80) to a less common port 8080. Note also the second URL, which specifies a reference (that is, a location) within the index.html document by appending a #, followed by the name of the reference in the document.

The second URL object constructor mirrors these URL components in its list of arguments. The third constructor is similar, except that it omits the need to specify a port number explicitly; it uses the default for the given protocol (port 21 for FTP, port 80 for HTTP, and so on). The GetContent program in the previous section uses the first constructor (the most compact) to create a class URL instance. It just takes a URL string, as you would type it into any Web browser's URL text-entry field.

Controlling the HTTP Link

Once you have constructed a class URL instance, you can extract any of the URL component fields using the getPort(), getProtocol(), getHost(), getFile(), and getRef() methods. The core URL method, however, is getContent(), which is used in the demonstration program. You do not need to explicitly specify the type of resource addressed; the program will fetch the resource and return it in an appropriate form. For example, an Image object would be returned for a GIF or JPEG image resource. What class URL hides is that it relies heavily on a closely related class, class URLConnection, to do all its dirty work:

```
public abstract class URLConnection extends Object {
  public static boolean getDefaultAllowUserInteraction();
  public static synchronized URLConnection.Callback
getDefaultCallback();
  public static String getDefaultRequestProperty (String key);
  public static FileNameMap getFileNameMap();
  public static String guessContentTypeFromStream (InputStream is)
    throws IOException;
  public static synchronized void setContentHandlerFactory
    (ContentHandlerFactory fac);
  public static void setDefaultAllowUserInteraction (boolean
    defaultallowuserinteraction);
  public static synchronized void setDefaultCallback
```

```
    (URLConnection.Callback);
public static void setDefaultRequestProperty (String key, String
  value);
public static void setFileNameMap (FileNameMap map);
public abstract void connect() throws IOException;
public boolean getAllowUserInteraction();
public URLConnection.Callback getCallback();
public Object getContent() throws IOException;
public String getContentEncoding();
public int getContentLength();
public String getContentType();
public long getDate();
public boolean getDefaultUseCaches();
public boolean getDoInput();
public boolean getDoOutput();
public long getExpiration();
public String getHeaderField (int n);
public String getHeaderField (String name);
public long getHeaderFieldDate (String name, long Default);
public int getHeaderFieldInt (String name, int Default);
public String getHeaderFieldKey (int n);
public long getIfModifiedSince();
public InputStream getInputStream() throws IOException;
public long getLastModified();
public OutputStream getOutputStream() throws IOException;
public Permission getPermission() throws IOException;
public String getRequestProperty (String key);
public URL getURL();
public boolean getUseCaches();
public void setAllowUserInteraction (boolean allowuserinteraction);
public boolean setCallback(URLConnection.Callback);
public void setDefaultUseCaches (boolean defaultusecaches);
public void setDoInput (boolean doinput);
public void setDoOutput (boolean dooutput);
public void setIfModifiedSince (long ifmodifiedsince);
public void setRequestProperty (String key, String value);
public void setUseCaches (boolean usecaches);
public String toString();
}
```

As the size of class URLConnection suggests, it gives you much more control over the HTTP link created when activating (opening) a URL connection. For example, the following methods are all convenience methods that let you query the values of the HTTP response header fields the Web server sends back:

String getContentType()   Returns the MIME type of this resource

int getContentLength()   Returns the size in bytes of this resource

String getContentEncoding()   Returns the encoding used to transmit the resource

long getDate()   Gets the date and time stamp for this response header

long getExpiration()   Gets the date and time when this resource becomes stale (and should be reloaded to get an up-to-date version)

long getLastModified()   Gets the date and time stamp for the moment the resource was last altered

Only the content type field is mandatory, so all other methods can return nulls (for `String` return types) or 0 (for numeric return types), if the server does not volunteer the information.

NOTE

Content type and content encoding are two different things. Content encoding tells you in which encoding scheme the resource is returned. Common encodings are straight 8-bit binary, UUencoded, and base64 encodings. The last two are used when the entire HTTP response needs to be "seven-bit clean"—that is, the most significant bit of every byte needs to be zero.

Two `URLConnection` methods are similar to the two key `Socket` methods you saw earlier: `getInputStream()` and `getOutputStream()`. These methods are also important within the context of class `URLConnection`. Class URL also makes available an `openStream()` method (but no corresponding output stream method), by calling the underlying `URLConnection` class' `getInputStream()`.

Several methods within class `URLConnection` deal with resource-caching issues. It is common for Web browsers to cache in-line images, and even entire source code of Web pages, for future, accelerated loading and display. The downside of this caching is that the original Web pages or pictures may undergo important changes that would pass you by if the browser's caching kept all cached resources indefinitely.

The following methods deal with this resource caching:

void setDefaultUseCaches(boolean defaultusecaches) Sets the default caching behavior (on or off) for future instances of the class

boolean getDefaultUseCaches() Queries whether future instances will use caching

void setUseCaches(boolean usecaches) Allows you to change the caching behavior of a URLConnection object on the fly

boolean getUseCaches() Queries whether a URLConnection object caches resources

Finally, two utility functions are provided to guess the content:

protected static String guessContentTypeFromName (String fname) Guesses the content of a file, judging by its name alone

public static String guessContentTypeFromStream (InputStream is) Guesses the content of a stream by peeking at its actual content, relying on mark()/reset() to avoid consuming any data

Unfortunately, one of these methods is declared protected, so you can only guess the type from the contents, unless you subclass URLConnection.

NOTE Besides URLConnection, its two subclasses, HttpURLConnection and JarURL-Connection, offer specialized information about a URL connection.

Using Password Authentication

Java 1.2 introduces the ability to use authentication with your URL connections. If accessing a URL would normally prompt for a username and password if attempted from within a browser, you can pre-install an Authenticator for when the authentication is necessary. This will notify you when a username and password is needed, and you can act accordingly to get the information.

The Authenticator is an abstract class, so you need to create a subclass to actually use it. While technically no methods are abstract, in order for the authentication functionality to work, you need to override the getPasswordAuthentication()

method to return an instance of `PasswordAuthentication`, with the desired username and password. Here is the definition of class `Authenticator` and `PasswordAuthentication`:

```java
public abstract class Authenticator extends Object {
    public Authenticator();
    public static PasswordAuthentication requestPasswordAuthentication
        (InetAddress addr, int port, String protocol, String prompt,
        String scheme);
    public static void setDefault (Authenticator a);
    protected PasswordAuthentication getPasswordAuthentication();
    protected final int getRequestingPort();
    protected final String getRequestingPrompt();
    protected final String getRequestingProtocol();
    protected final String getRequestingScheme();
    protected final InetAddress getRequestingSite();
}

public final class PasswordAuthentication extends Object {
    public PasswordAuthentication (String userName, String password);
    public char[] getPassword();
    public String getUserName();
}
```

With the `Authenticator`, notice that everything except the constructor is either `static` or `protected`. The one `protected` method that isn't `final`, `getPasswordAuthentication()`, provides the clue as to what method to override, in case you forget. If you need to prompt for the username and password, you can show the `getRequestedPrompt()` text and ask for the input. Otherwise, you can just pass the necessary information to the subclass constructor, as done in the following example. Once you have the information, you create a `PasswordAuthentication` instance and return it. The following program offers a demonstration, getting the URL, username, and password from the command line. The `MyAuthenticator` class does the authentication and is installed with the `Authenticator.setDefault()` line. You are on your own to find a URL whose password and username you know.

```java
import java.io.*;
import java.net.*;

public class AuthDemo {

  public static void main (String args[])
```

```
        throws MalformedURLException, IOException {
    String urlString, username, password;

    if (args.length != 3) {
      System.out.println ("Usage: java AuthDemo URL username password");
      System.exit (10);
    }

    urlString = args[0];
    username  = args[1];
    password  = args[2];

    Authenticator.setDefault (new MyAuthenticator (username, password));

    URL url = new URL (urlString);
    InputStream content = (InputStream)url.getContent();
    BufferedReader in   = new BufferedReader (
      new InputStreamReader (content));
    String line;
    while ((line = in.readLine()) != null) {
      System.out.println (line);
    }

    System.out.println("Done.");
  }
}


//------------------------------------------------------------------
class MyAuthenticator extends Authenticator {
  private String username, password;
  public MyAuthenticator (String user, String pass) {
    username = user;
    password = pass;
  }
  protected PasswordAuthentication getPasswordAuthentication() {
    System.out.println ("Requesting Port    : " + getRequestingPort());
    System.out.println ("Requesting Prompt  : " + getRequestingPrompt());
    System.out.println ("Requesting Protocol: " + getRequestingProtocol());
    System.out.println ("Requesting Scheme  : " + getRequestingScheme());
    System.out.println ("Requesting Site    : " + getRequestingSite());
    return new PasswordAuthentication (username, password.toCharArray());
  }
}
```

NOTE   If you connect to a URL without installing an `Authenticator` and the URL requires authentication, there is no exception thrown. The Web server will probably just display a message saying you do not have access, which this program then reads. To demonstrate, either comment out the `Authenticator.setDefault()` line or provide an invalid username/password combination.

To uninstall an `Authenticator`, call `setDefault()` with a parameter of `null`.

Writing Server Systems

So far, this chapter has focused on the client aspect of client/server computing, since the majority of Java developers will view the world from that perspective. But if you are part of the minority that needs to write server (not client) software, this section is for you. The `java.net` package contains all you need to write any server system, using class `ServerSocket`:

```
public class ServerSocket extends Object {
   public ServerSocket (int port) throws IOException;
   public ServerSocket (int port, int backlog) throws IOException;
   public ServerSocket (int port, int backlog,
      InetAddress bindAddr) throws IOException;
   public static synchronized void setSocketFactory (
      SocketImplFactory fac) throws IOException;
   public Socket accept() throws IOException;
   public void close() throws IOException;
   public InetAddress getInetAddress();
   public int getLocalPort();
   public synchronized int getSoTimeout() throws IOException;
   public synchronized void setSoTimeout (int timeout)
      throws SocketException;
   public String toString();
}
```

The first constructor is all you need to get going; it creates a new listening socket on your machine that can accept incoming connections from clients across the network.

The port number argument specifies on which server port your server will be available to the world. If you want to write a standard server, such as an SMTP or

FTP server, you need to use its respective well-known port addresses (refer back to Table 20.1). On the other hand, if you want to create a brand new Internet service, you will need to use a port number that no one else is using. Since the full port number range is 0–65,535, there are plenty of choices, provided that you stay clear of certain ranges:

- The range 0–1023 is reserved for "standard" Internet protocols. These ranges are controlled by the IANA (Internet Assigned Numbers Authority).

- The region from 1024 onward is used for client ephemeral ports.

- Some systems use the range starting at 32,768 for ephemeral ports too, so it is best to avoid these numbers as well.

For testing purposes, port number 8001 is quite commonly used, although anything within the 8–16K or 48–64K ranges is fine.

Once you create a new `ServerSocket` object, it does not listen yet on its port for client requests to arrive. This only starts when you call the `accept()` method on the `ServerSocket` object. The `accept()` method will not return until a client connects to the server. If you like, you can call the `setSoTimeout()` method to assign a timeout to the server socket (this must be done before the `accept()` call). If no client connects to the server before the timeout expires, a `java.io.Interrupted-IOException` will be thrown.

As you can see from the list of methods `ServerSocket` provides, there are no reading or writing methods, nor does `ServerSocket` let you have the input and output streams to the socket. This is because a `ServerSocket` is not used for the actual communication. A `ServerSocket` produces a new `Socket` instance for the server software to talk to the connecting client. This `Socket` instance is created (and returned) when a connection is accepted by the `accept()` method. This means the server programming model is almost identical to that of the client programming model; you just use the input and output streams connected to a socket to implement the required protocol.

A Simple Server Program

The example presented here is a simplistic server that actually behaves like a real server. When a client connects to its port, the server sends an initial welcome identification string and then waits for a client command (the server protocol is modeled on the SMTP). The only commands the program implements are HELP and

QUIT—not very functional, but these two commands should be implemented by all line-based protocols (and SMTP, NNTP, and FTP support HELP and QUIT). Here is the server:

```
import java.util.*;
import java.io.*;
import java.net.*;

public class ServerTest {

  final static int SERVER_PORT = 8001;  // our server's own port

  public static void main (String args[]) {
    Server server;
    String clientRequest;
    BufferedReader reader;
    PrintWriter writer;

    server = new Server (SERVER_PORT);
    reader = new BufferedReader (new InputStreamReader (server.in));
    writer = new PrintWriter (new OutputStreamWriter (server.out),
true);

    // send initial string to client.
    writer.println ("Java Test server v0.03, " + new Date());

    while (true) {
      try {
        // what does client have to say to us ?
        clientRequest = reader.readLine();
        System.out.println ("Client says: " + clientRequest);
        if (clientRequest.startsWith ("HELP")) {
          writer.println ("Vocabulary: HELP QUIT");
        } else {
          if (clientRequest.startsWith ("QUIT")) {
            System.exit(0);
          } else {
            writer.println ("ERR: Command '" + clientRequest +
              "' not understood.");
          }
        }
```

```
          } catch (IOException e) {
            System.out.println ("IOEx in server " + e);
          }
        }
      }
    }
    //-------------------------------------------------------------------
    class Server {

      private ServerSocket server;
      private Socket socket;

      public InputStream in;
      public OutputStream  out;

      public Server (int port) {

        try {
          server = new ServerSocket (port);
          System.out.println ("ServerSocket before accept: " + server);
          System.out.println ("Java Test server v0.03, on-line!");

          // wait for a client to connect to our port
          socket = server.accept();
          System.out.println ("ServerSocket after  accept: " + server);

          in  = socket.getInputStream();
          out = socket.getOutputStream();

        } catch (IOException e) {
          System.out.println ("Server constructor IOEx: " + e);
        }
      }
    }
```

When you run this program, your console should print:

```
C:\> java ServerTest
ServerSocket before accept:
ServerSocket[addr=0.0.0.0/0.0.0.0,port=0,localport=8001]
Java Test server v0.03, on-line!
```

The Client for the Sample Server

The sample server seems to work; however, you do not have any client that knows about the protocol just invented, and the server expects clients to talk only to this protocol. You can quickly solve this problem by writing a client program customized to talk to your new server. Both the client and the server will be tested on the same machine, but it does not matter; the client program will simply connect to machine "localhost" at port 8001 (your server's port). Here is the client:

```java
import java.io.*;
import java.net.*;

public class ClientTest {

  public static void main (String args[]) {
    String welcome, response;
    Client client;
    BufferedReader reader;
    PrintWriter writer;

    client = new Client ("localhost", 8001);

    try {
      reader = new BufferedReader (new InputStreamReader (client.in));
      writer = new PrintWriter (new OutputStreamWriter (client.out), true);

      welcome = reader.readLine();
      System.out.println ("Server says: '"+ welcome +"'");

      System.out.println ("HELLO");
      writer.println("HELLO");
      response =  reader.readLine();
      System.out.println ("Server responds: '"+ response +"'");

      System.out.println ("HELP");
      writer.println ("HELP");
      response = reader.readLine();
      System.out.println ("Server responds: '"+ response +"'");

      System.out.println ("QUIT");
      writer.println("QUIT");
    } catch (IOException e) {
      System.out.println ("IOException in client.in.readln()");
```

```
        System.out.println(e);
      }
      try {
        Thread.sleep(2000);
      } catch (Exception ignored) {}
    }
  }
//---------------------------------------------------------------
class Client {

  // make input and output streams available to user classes
  public InputStream in;
  public OutputStream out;

  // the socket itself remains ours though...
  private Socket client;

  public Client (String host, int port) {
    try {
      client = new Socket (host, port);
      System.out.println ("Client socket: " + client);
      in = client.getInputStream();
      out= client.getOutputStream();
    } catch (IOException e) {
      System.out.println("IOExc : " + e);
    }
  }
}
```

If you run this client program in a new console window while the server is still online and waiting for client connections, you should see the client go through its paces as follows:

```
C:\> java ClientTest
Client socket:
Socket[addr=localhost/127.0.0.1,port=8001,localport=1034]
Server says: 'Java Test server v0.04, Fri Sep 04 10:12:37 EDT 1998'
HELLO
Server responds: 'ERR: Command 'HELLO' not understood.'
HELP
Server responds: 'Vocabulary: HELP QUIT'
QUIT

C:\>
```

While the client printed these lines, your server printed the following lines, reflecting its perspective on the exchanges:

```
ServerSocket after accept:
ServerSocket[addr=0.0.0.0/0.0.0.0,port=0,localport=8001]
Client says: HELLO
Client says: HELP
Client says: QUIT

C:\>
```

As you can see, both parties communicate together without a hitch. Of course, this is because the protocol used here is trivial—it is stateless to start with, which always keeps things very simple indeed—and no real network was involved. Although real TCP packets were created, they didn't travel far; they just looped back internally within the TCP/IP stack.

Real protocols usually rely heavily on a number of states the protocol can find itself in—for example, idle, connecting, connected, resyncing, disconnecting. These different states require you to implement state machines to manage the protocol. State machines that have more than just a few states and accept more than just a few possible events quickly become very complex, necessitating formal mathematical methods to prove their correctness.

Unfortunately, protocol state machines usually are nontrivial because real networks can be the cause of many different types of events and situations. Packets can become corrupted due to line noise, and they can fail to arrive altogether if networking equipment suddenly fails. Packets can even be delayed for so long that the receiver thinks the packet got lost and then suddenly—"pop!"—the original packet arrives, throwing the receiver out of synchronization with the sender. You need to take all these factors into account when designing a protocol, unless you build your application protocol on a protocol that already takes care of these issues, which is exactly the function of TCP, on which most (but not all) Internet protocols are based.

TIP Developing and debugging client/server protocols are much easier if you use a line-based ASCII protocol and use Telnet to exercise the server. You can even test the ServerTest program by using Telnet to connect to it instead of using the ClientTest program. Try it yourself with "telnet localhost 8001" after starting up the server again. You will also discover that writing your own Telnet utility (in Java) is very easy indeed.

Factories and the Factory Design Pattern

While browsing the classes in `java.net`, you might have noticed the term *factory* here and there. Package `java.net` contains three interfaces that all contain the word *factory* in their names. To understand how these interfaces work, you need to know what factory classes are in the context of object-oriented software.

Solving Problems with Factory Classes

You know what factories are in real life—organizations that produce a variety of related products. In object-oriented software, the factory metaphor applies to classes that can construct objects with diverging (but related) characteristics without invoking the constructors for the objects' concrete classes. The factory design pattern can be used whenever a class needs to instantiate objects from classes it doesn't yet know about.

As an example, consider how a Web browser might need the factory design pattern to solve a problem. Most Web resources are transferred by browsers using the HTTP protocol, but you might have noticed that this is not always the case. At some point, your browser's address input field might start with the characters *ftp://* instead of *http://*. What's going on? Your browser was instructed to fetch a resource using a different protocol than the usual HTTP. It switched to FTP to fetch a file or a directory, but without informing you of the quite dramatic change in internal operation. If a resource's URL specified a protocol other than one currently supported (HTTP, FTP, NNTP, and so on), your browser would have a problem: It would not know how to handle this foreign protocol.

An analogous obstacle can occur within Web pages themselves. Most browsers can deal with in-line images in GIF or JPEG format, but not some future popular image format. In the cases of new protocols and new image file formats, the browser software is stuck because of its lack of dynamic extensibility (addressed by plug-ins in Netscape's browser, as described in Chapter 1). If it could only load or call on classes that can deal with new protocols or new image or file formats, there would be no problem. And that is exactly what Sun's HotJava browser (which is written in Java, of course) can do, by relying on the factory design pattern to get around these problems transparently. Factory classes can construct new protocol or content handlers to allow a browser to support an emerging standard without changing the browser itself.

Factory classes obviously cannot suddenly manufacture new objects on the fly to deal with these new developments. (For this to be possible, a lot more effort on the part of our artificial intelligence colleagues would be needed.) The way the factory classes are able to produce the goods is by loading new protocol or file format handler classes off the Internet. They do this the first time the new protocol or format is encountered; subsequently, they just load the classes off the client's local disk, as with all other classes. The factory design pattern essentially decouples systems from each other, thereby adding a new level of flexibility.

Java's Factory Interfaces

Now that you have some insight into the factory design pattern, you can examine the three `java.net` factory interfaces:

`ContentHandlerFactory`   Builds ContentHandler objects

`SocketImplFactory`   Builds SocketImpl objects

`URLStreamHandlerFactory`   Builds URLStreamHandler objects

Notice that these are all interfaces rather than classes. None of the existing `java.net` classes implement any of these interfaces, but several `java.net` classes rely on external classes to be one or another of the above factory type. (These classes are external and unknown, by definition, because that is the mechanism that allows future browser extensions without needing to alter the browser any further.) Class URL, for example, requires a `URLStreamHandlerFactory` (-typed) object for its `setURLStreamHandlerFactory()` method. Similarly, class `URLConnection` requires a `ContentHandlerFactory` object for its `setContentHandlerFactory()` method. `Socket` and `ServerSocket` work similarly with interface `SocketImplFactory`. These lean heavily on their respective factories to off-load nitty-gritty functionality to objects created by those factories.

As an example, consider what goes on behind the scenes when you invoke `getContent()` on a plain URL instance (as in the example for the URL class, presented earlier in the chapter). First, a connection is created to the resource, giving you a URLConnection object. Then, `getContent()` is called on the new URLConnection object instead (`getContent()` is also a method for class URLConnection). The URLConnection object has associated with it a `ContentHandlerFactory` object that can produce appropriate content handlers via its sole `createContentHandler()` method. The argument that this factory method takes is a `String` specifying a MIME type. Now the HTTP protocol dictates that Web servers always respond to GET HTTP requests using an HTTP response header that specifies the type of data it replies, as in the following header for a GIF picture:

```
Server:Apache/1.0.2
Content-type: image/gif
```

```
Content-length: 23746
Last-Modified: Fri, 21 Sep 1997 12:34:51 PST
```

Without "touching" the resource itself (say, to read the first 10 bytes to figure out what type of resource it is), the URLConnection object can already determine the exact MIME type for the resource. Then, given the MIME type, the factory can produce a subclass of ContentHandler that can deal with this type of content.

If you look at the simple definition of the ContentHandler superclass, you will see a very relevant method waiting in hiding:

```
public abstract class ContentHandler extends Object {
    public ContentHandler();
    public abstract Object getContent (URLConnection urlc) throws IOException;
}
```

Yet another getContent()! This is the one (or, rather, the one implemented by the subclass produced by the factory method) that does the real content fetching and produces an object of the appropriate type for the resource. For example, if a GIF image was fetched, the getContent() method would return an Image, and not a (useless) simple Object, as hinted at by the method signature for get-Content(). Figure 20.4 illustrates how class URL relies on a factory to discover the resource content.

FIGURE 20.4:

How the URL class uses a factory class

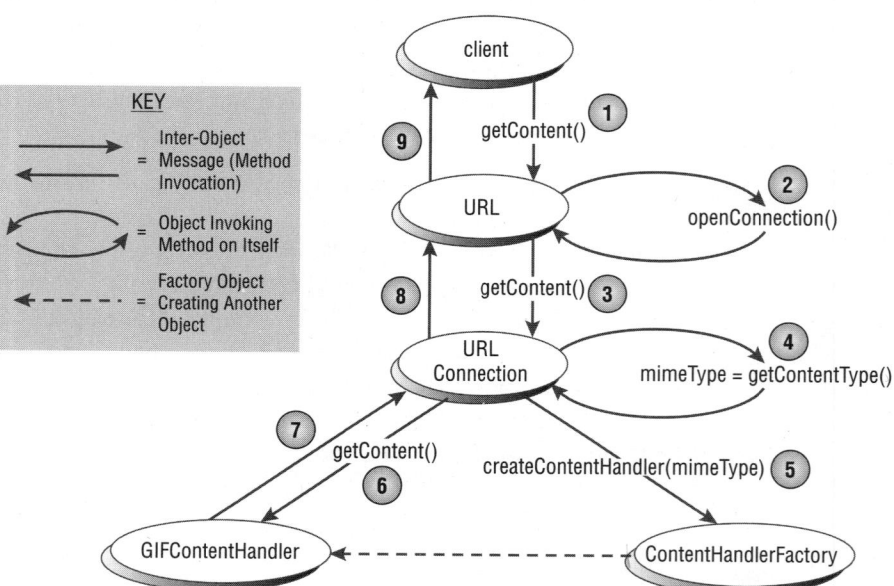

Here is a summary of the steps described here and depicted in the figure:

1. A client class wants to get the content for a resource defined by a URL.

2. The URL opens an HTTP connection to the Web server, creating a URL-Connection object.

3. The URL object calls getContent() on the URLConnection object.

4. The URLConnection determines which type of resource this is from the HTTP response header (the Content-type field).

5. The URLConnection calls its ContentHandlerFactory to provide it with an appropriate ContentHandler subclass.

6. Upon instantiation of this content handler, the URLConnection calls it to deal with the specific resource (a GIF image in this example).

7. The prefabricated content handler returns the resource in a form best suited to it (Image for GIF images, String for text files, and so on).

8. The URLConnection passes the resource object back to the URL.

9. The URL passes the resource object back to the client (who now is very happy).

NOTE

More steps are actually involved than those shown in Figure 20.4. The extra steps are an attempt to reduce the poor performance resulting from needing to create a new ContentHandler object for every client getContent() invocation. What class URLConnection adds to the picture is a caching step (involving a Hashtable, between steps 4 and 5), which often means that a suitable ContentHandler is already available without needing to be fabricated by the factory (at, more or less, great expense).

Summary

Java supports network programming through various classes dealing with the TCP/IP suite of data communication protocols. The core java.net class is class Socket that, together with class InetAddress to address hosts, allows you to write client software that connects itself to any server on the Internet. These connections are brought about via specific ports—called well-known ports on the server side and ephemeral ports on the client side.

You also learned how most of the Internet's application-level protocols (SMTP, FTP, HTTP, NNTP, and so on) are ASCII, line-based protocols. This greatly facilitates development, debugging, and day-to-day protocol problem-solving, because the communication link can be intercepted and deciphered easily by any person familiar with the protocol. For example, HTTP was shown to use a simple system of request and response headers that can be generated and viewed using a simple, standard tool like Telnet.

Finally, you learned about the nontrivial workings of the factory classes and their relationship to Java's key, dynamic extensibility in the field of yet-to-be-developed protocols and future Web resource types.

PART III

Advanced Topics

CHAPTER
TWENTY-ONE

21

Java Database Connectivity (JDBC)

- Java as a database front end

- Database client/server methodology

- Two- and three-tier database design

- The JDBC API

- A JDBC database example

- JDBC drivers

- JDBC-ODBC bridge

- Alternative connectivity strategies

In the current information age, a database is the tool used to collect and manipulate data. The database forms the foundation of the infrastructure of many companies. While the database system is well suited to the storage and retrieval of data, people need some sort of visual front-end application to see and use the data stored.

The problem is complicated by the existence of heterogeneous computers in most companies. The art and marketing departments may have Macintosh systems, the engineers could have high-end Unix workstations, while the sales force is probably using some variation of Microsoft Windows (Windows 95, Windows NT 4, Windows NT 3.51, or Windows 3.1) on PCs. To expose the data in a corporate database, developers must consider all of the various system permutations on which they wish to deploy.

This chapter will look at Java as the way to solve the database front-end Tower of Babel, by providing a single and consistent application programming interface: the Java Database Connectivity API.

Java as a Database Front End

Java offers several benefits to the developer creating a front-end application for a database server. Java is a "write once, run anywhere" language. This means that Java programs may be deployed without recompilation on any of the computer architectures and operating systems that possess a Java Virtual Machine. For large corporations, just having a common development platform is a big savings: no longer are programmers required to write to the many platforms a large corporation may have. Java is also attractive to third party developers—a single Java program can answer the needs of both small and large customers.

In addition, there is a cost associated with the deployment and maintenance of the hardware and software of any system (client) the corporation owns. Systems such as Windows PCs, Macintosh, and Unix desktop-centric clients (*fat clients*) can cost corporations between $10,000 and $15,000 per installation seat. Java technology now makes it possible for any company to use a smaller system footprint. These systems are based on a Java chip set and can run any and all Java programs from a built-in Java operating system.

Java-based clients (*thin clients*) that operate with a minimum of hardware resources, yet run the complete Java environment, are expected to cost around

$750 per seat. According to various studies, the savings for a corporation moving 10,000 fat client systems to thin client systems could be as much as $100 million annually. While Pentium systems are available for under $1,000 too, the cost to configure and maintain them, with their local storage, is where the cost savings primarily comes from.

It follows, then, that the incentive to create Java-based solutions for corporate systems is big. Corporations are extremely interested in shifting their applications from architecture- and operating-system–specific models to network-centric models. Java represents a long-term strategy in saving resource costs.

For the developer, Java represents a huge market opportunity. There are very few medium-to-large organizations that do not use databases for some portion of their business operation, while most use databases for *every* aspect of their business, from human resources to front-line customer sales.

This chapter examines Java Database Connectivity (JDBC), including how to use the current JDBC API to connect Java applications and applets to database servers.

NOTE   For JDBC access from server-side Java programs, see Chapter 23, "Java Servlets."

Database Client/Server Methodology

The evolution of relational data storage began in 1970 with the work of Dr. E. F. Codd, who proposed a set of 12 rules for identifying relationships between pieces of data. Codd's rules formed the basis for the development of systems to manage data. Today, Relational Database Management Systems (RDBMS) are the result of Codd's vision.

Data in an RDBMS are stored as rows of distinct information in tables. A structured language is used to query (retrieve), store, and change the data. The Structured Query Language (SQL) is an ANSI standard, and all major commercial RDBMS vendors provide mechanisms for issuing SQL commands.

The early development of RDBMS applications utilized an integrated model of user interface code, application code, and database libraries. This single binary model ran only on a local machine, typically a mainframe. The applications were simple but inefficient and did not work over LANs. The model did not scale, and the application and user interface code was tightly coupled to the database libraries. Figure 21.1 illustrates the monolithic single-tier database design.

FIGURE 21.1:

The monolithic single-tier database design

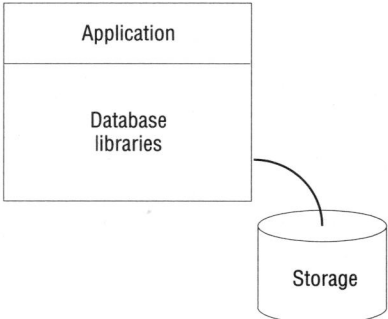

Further, the monolithic approach did not allow multiple instances of the application to communicate with *each other*. So there was often contention between instances of the application.

> **NOTE**
>
> It is typical for RDBMS and DBMS (Database Management System) to be used interchangeably because most major commercial databases are relational and support some form of SQL to allow the user to query the relations between data tables.

Two-Tier Database Design

Two-tier models appeared with the advent of server technology. Communication-protocol development and extensive use of local and wide area networks allowed the database developer to create an application front end that accessed data through a connection (*socket*) to the back-end server. Figure 21.2 illustrates a two-tier database design, where the client software is connected to the database through a socket connection.

Client programs (applying a user interface) send SQL requests to the database server. The server returns the appropriate results, and the client is responsible for the formatting and display of the data. Clients still use a vendor-provided library of functions that manage the communication between client and server. Most of these libraries are written in the C language.

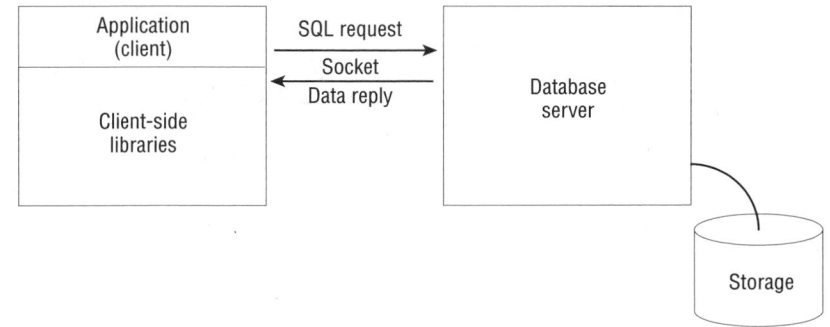

Commercial database vendors realized the potential for adding intelligence to the database server. They created proprietary techniques that allowed the database designer to develop macro programs for simple data manipulation. These macros, called *stored procedures*, can cause problems relating to version control and maintenance. Because a stored procedure is an executable program living on the database, it is possible for the stored procedure to attempt to access named columns of a database table after the table has been changed. For example, if a column with the name id is changed to cust_id, the meaning of the original stored procedure is lost. The advent of *triggers* can compound these difficulties when the data returned from a query are not expected. (Triggers are stored procedures executed automatically when some action, like insert, happens with a particular table or tables.) Again, this can be the result of the trigger reading a table column that has been altered.

Despite the success of client/server architectures, two-tier database models suffer a number of limitations:

- The vendor-provided library limits them. Switching from one database vendor to another requires a rewrite of a significant amount of code to the client application.

- Version control is an issue. When the vendor updates the client-side libraries, the applications that utilize the database must be recompiled and redistributed.

- Vendor libraries deal with low-level data manipulation. Typically the base library only deals with queries and updates of single rows or columns of data. This can be enhanced on the server-side by creating a stored procedure, but the complexity of the system then increases.

- All of the intelligence associated with using and manipulating the data is implemented in the client application, creating large client-side run times. This drives up the cost of each client set.

Three-Tier Database Design

Today there is a great deal of interest in multi-tier design. In a multi-tier design, the client communicates with an intermediate server that provides a layer of abstraction from the RDBMS. There does not have to be just three tiers, but conceptually this is the next step. Figure 21.3 illustrates a three-tier database design.

FIGURE 21.3:

A three-tier database design

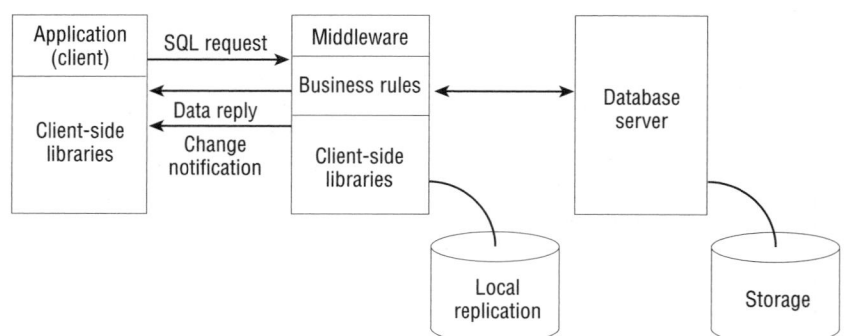

The intermediate layer is designed to handle multiple client requests and manage the connection to one or more database servers. The three-tier design gives the middle tier the following advantages over the two-tier design:

- It is multithreaded to manage multiple client connections simultaneously.

- It can accept connections from clients over a variety of vendor-neutral protocols (from HTTP to TCP/IP), then hand off the requests to the appropriate vendor-specific database servers, returning the replies to the appropriate clients.

- It can be programmed with a set of "business rules" that manage the manipulation of the data. Business rules could include anything from restricting access to certain portions of data to making sure that data is properly formatted before being inserted or updated.

- It prevents the client from becoming too heavy by centralizing process-intensive tasks and abstracting data representation to a higher level.

- It isolates the client application from the database system and frees a company to switch database systems without having to rework the business rules.

- It can asynchronously provide the client with the status of a current data table or row.

As an example of this last point, suppose that a client application had just completed a query of a particular table. If a subsequent action by another distinct client *changed* that data, the first client could receive notification from an intelligent middle-tier program.

The JDBC API

The JDBC API is designed to allow developers to create database front ends without having to continually rewrite their code. Despite standards set by the ANSI committee, each database system vendor has a unique way of connecting and, in some cases, communicating with their system.

The ability to create robust, platform-independent applications and Web-based applets prompted developers to consider using Java to develop front-end connectivity solutions. At the outset, third-party software developers met the need by providing proprietary solutions, using native methods to integrate client-side libraries or creating a third tier and a new protocol.

The Java Software Division, Sun Microsystems' division responsible for the development of Java products, worked in conjunction with database and database-tool vendors to create a DBMS-independent mechanism that would allow developers to write their client-side applications without concern for the particular database being used. The result is the JDBC API, which is part of the core JDK 1.2.

JDBC provides application developers with a *single* API that is uniform and database independent. The API provides a standard to write to and a standard that takes all of the various application designs into account. The secret is a set of Java interfaces that are implemented by a driver. The driver takes care of the translation of the standard JDBC calls into the specific calls required by the database it supports. In the following figure, the application is written once and moved to the various drivers. The application remains the same; the drivers change. Drivers may be used to develop the middle tier of a multi-tier database design, also known as *middleware*, as illustrated in Figure 21.4.

In addition to providing developers with a uniform and DBMS-independent framework, JDBC also provides a means of allowing developers to retain the specific functionality that their database vendor offers. JDBC drivers must support the ANSI SQL-2 Entry Level standard, but JDBC allows developers to pass query strings directly to the connected driver. These strings may or may not be ANSI

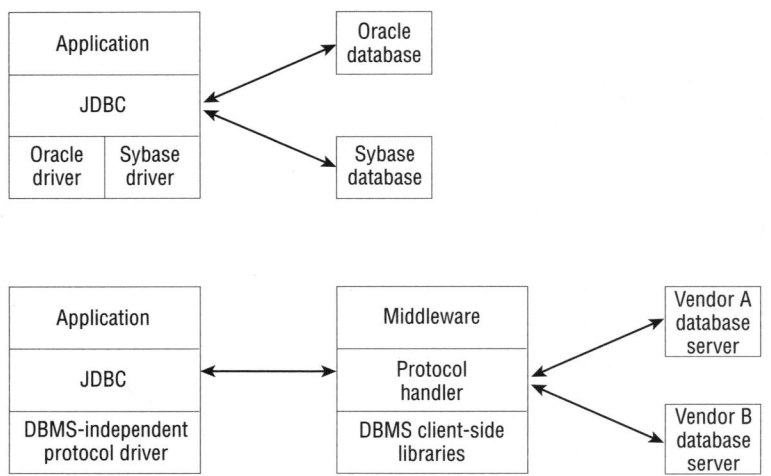

SQL, or even SQL at all. The use of these strings is up to the underlying driver. Of course use of this feature limits the freedom of the application developer to change database back ends.

> **NOTE**
>
> For additional information on SQL, you may want to get Martin Gruber's *SQL Instant Reference* book from Sybex or purchase the standards documents from ANSI at `http://www.ansi.org`. Also, Tina London offers an online SQL reference resource at `ftp://www.bf.rmit.edu.au/pub/Oracle/notes/TinaLondon.txt`.

JDBC is *not* a derivative of Microsoft's Open Database Connectivity specification (ODBC). JDBC is written entirely in Java and ODBC is a C interface. While ODBC is usable by non-C languages, like Visual Basic, it has the inherent development risks of C, like memory leaks. However, both JDBC and ODBC are based on the X/Open SQL Command Level Interface (CLI). Having the same conceptual base allowed work on the API to proceed quickly and makes acceptance and learning of the API easier. Sun provides a JDBC-ODBC bridge that translates JDBC to ODBC. This implementation, done with native methods, is very small and efficient.

> **NOTE**
>
> While still small and efficient, the 1.2 JDK includes a new version of the JDBC-ODBC bridge.

In general, there are two levels of interfaces in the JDBC API: the Application layer, where the developer uses the API to make calls to the database via SQL and retrieve the results, and the Driver layer, that handles all communication with a specific Driver implementation.

Every JDBC application (or applet) must have at least one JDBC driver, and each driver is specific to the type of DBMS used. A driver does not, however, need to be directly associated with a database.

The API Components

As mentioned earlier, there are two distinct layers within the JDBC API: the Application layer, which database-application developers use, and the Driver layer, which the driver vendors implement. It is important to understand the Driver layer, if only to realize that the driver creates some of the objects used at the Application layer. Figure 21.5 illustrates the connection between the Driver and Application layers.

FIGURE 21.5:

JDBC API components

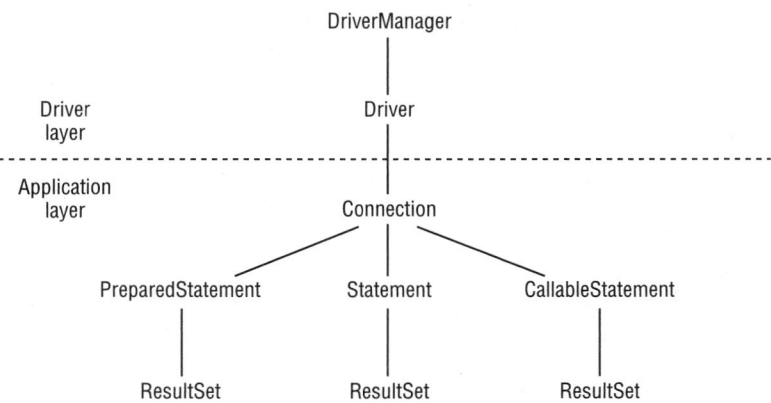

Fortunately, the application developer need only use the standard API interfaces in order to guarantee JDBC compliance. The Driver developer is responsible for developing code that interfaces to the database and supports the JDBC application level calls.

There are four main interfaces that every Driver layer must implement, and one class that bridges the Application and Driver layers. The four interfaces are the `Driver, Connection, Statement,` and `ResultSet`. The `Driver` interface implementation is where the connection to the database is made. In most applications, the `Driver` is accessed through the `DriverManager` class—providing one more layer of abstraction for the developer.

The `Connection`, `Statement`, and `ResultSet` interfaces are implemented by the driver vendor, but these interfaces represent the methods that the application developer will treat as real object classes and allow the developer to create statements and retrieve results. So the distinction in this section between Driver and Application layers is artificial—but it allows the developer to create database applications without having to think about where the objects are coming from or worry about what specific driver the application will use.

The Driver Layer

There is a one-to-one correspondence between the database and the JDBC Driver. This approach is common in multi-tier designs. The `Driver` class is an interface implemented by the driver vendor. The other important class is the `DriverManager` class, which sits above the Driver and Application layers. The `DriverManager` is responsible for loading and unloading drivers and making connections through drivers. The `DriverManager` also provides features for logging and database login timeouts.

NOTE   As shown in Figure 21.4, the driver does not have to connect directly to a database and can support a new protocol for a multi-tier database design.

The *Driver* Interface   Every JDBC program must have at least one JDBC driver implementation. The `Driver` interface allows the `DriverManager` and JDBC Application layers to exist independently of the particular database used. A JDBC driver is an implementation of the `Driver` interface class.

Drivers use a string to locate and access databases. The syntax of this string is very similar to a URL string. The purpose of a JDBC URL string is to separate the application developer from the driver developer. Sun defines the following goals for driver URLs:

- The name of the driver-access URL should define the type of database being used.

- The user (application developer) should be free from any of the administration of creating the database connection. Therefore, any database connection information (host, port, database name, user access, and passwords) should be encoded in the URL.

- A network naming system may be used in order to prevent the user from having to specifically encode the exact hostname and port number of the database.

The URL syntax used by the World Wide Web supports a standard syntax that satisfies these goals. A JDBC URL has the following syntax and structure:

```
jdbc:<subprotocol>:<subname>
```

where `<subprotocol>` defines the type of driver, and `<subname>` provides the network encoded name. For example:

```
jdbc:oracle:products
```

Here the database driver is an Oracle driver and the subname is a local database called `products`. This driver is designed to know how to use the subname when making the connection to the Oracle database.

A network naming service may also be specified as the subprotocol, rather than using a specific database driver name. In this case the subprotocol would define the naming service:

```
jdbc:localnaming:human-resources
```

Here the subprotocol defines a local service that can resolve the subname `human-resources` to a database server. This approach can be useful when the application developer wants to isolate the user from the actual location, name, database username, and database password. This URL specifies that a driver named `localnaming` be specified. This could be a Java program that contains a simple flat-file lookup, translates `human-resources` into `hrdatabase1.eng:888/personnel`, and knows to use the username `user` and password `matilda`. The details of the connection are kept hidden from the user.

Typically the application developer will know specifically where the database is located and may not wish to use redirection to locate the database. In this case, the URL may be expanded to include the location of the host and specific port and database information:

```
jdbc:msql://dbserver.eng:1112/bugreports
```

Here an `msql` database driver type is used to locate a server named `dbserver` in the `eng` domain and attempt to connect to a database server on port 1112 that contains a `bugreports` database, using the default username and password to connect.

More on DriverPropertyInfo

For each possible property, a *DriverPropertyInfo* instance is provided. There are five instance variables available to describe the property, enabling the automated creation of a graphical screen to prompt for information:

name	name of property
description	short description of property (may be null)
required	boolean value describing if property is required
value	current/default property value (may be null)
choices	array of possible values for property (may be null)

> **NOTE**
>
> It is possible for subprotocol names to overlap. To help prevent this, Sun informally maintains a registry of reserved names. For more information on registering a JDBC subprotocol name, consult the JDBC Specification.

The driver vendor implements the `Driver` interface by creating methods for each of the following interface methods:

Signature: `public interface Driver`

`public abstract Connection connect (String url, Properties info) throws SQLException` The driver implementation of this method should check the subprotocol name of the URL string passed for a match with this driver. If there is a match, the driver should then attempt to connect to the database using the information passed in the remainder of the URL. A successful database connection will return an instance of the driver's implementation of a `Connection` interface (object). The `SQLException` should be thrown only if the driver recognizes the URL subprotocol but cannot make the database connection. A `null` is returned if the URL does not match a URL the driver expected. The username and password are included in a container class called `Properties`.

`public abstract DriverPropertyInfo[] getPropertyInfo(String url, Properties info) throws SQLException` If you are not aware of which properties to use when calling `connect()`, you can ask the `Driver` if the supplied properties are sufficient to establish a connection. If they aren't, an array of necessary properties is provided with the help of the `Driver-PropertyInfo` class.

`public abstract boolean acceptsURL (String url) throws SQL-Exception` It is also possible to explicitly "ask" the driver if a URL is valid. But note that the implementation of this method (typically) only checks if the subprotocol specified in the URL is valid, not whether a connection can be made.

`public int getMajorVersion()` Returns the driver's major version number. If the driver's version was at 4.3, this would return the integer 4.

`public int getMinorVersion()` Returns the driver's minor version number. If the driver's version was at 4.3, this would return the integer 3.

`public boolean jdbcCompliant()` Returns whether or not the driver is a complete JDBC implementation. For legacy systems or lightweight solutions, it may not be possible, or necessary, for a complete implementation.

The `connect()` method of `Driver` is the most important method and is called by the `DriverManager` to obtain a `Connection` object. As Figure 21.5 previously showed, the `Connection` object is the starting point of the JDBC Application layer. The `Connection` object is used to create `Statement` objects that perform queries.

The `connect()` method typically performs the following steps:

- Checks to see if the URL string provided is valid
- Opens a TCP connection to the host and port number specified
- Attempts to access the named database table (if any)
- Returns an instance of a `Connection` object

NOTE `Connection` is a Java interface, so the object returned is actually a reference to the driver's implementation of the `Connection` interface.

The *DriverManager* Class The `DriverManager` class is really a utility class used to manage JDBC drivers. The class provides methods to obtain a connection through a driver, register and de-register drivers, set up logging, and set login timeouts for database access. All of the methods in the `DriverManager` class listed below are static and may be referenced through the following class name:

Signature: `public interface DriverManager`

> `public static synchronized Connection getConnection (String url, Properties info) throws SQLException` This method (and the other `getConnection()` methods) attempts to return a reference to an object implementing the `Connection` interface. The method sweeps through an internal collection of stored `Driver` classes, passing the URL string and `Properties` object `info` to each in turn. The first `Driver` class that returns a `Connection` is used. `info` is a reference to a `Properties` container object of tag/value pairs, typically username/password. This method allows several attempts to make an authorized connection for each driver in the collection.

> `public static synchronized Connection getConnection (String url) throws SQLException` This method calls `getConnection (url, info)` above with an empty `Properties` object (`info`).

> `public static synchronized Connection getConnection (String url, String user, String password) throws SQLException` This method creates a `Properties` object (`info`), stores the user and password strings in it, and then calls `getConnection (url, info)` above.

> `public static synchronized void registerDriver(java.sql.Driver driver) throws SQLException` This method stores the instance of the `Driver` interface implementation into a collection of drivers, along with the program's current security context to identify where the driver came from.

> `public static void setLogStream(java.io.PrintWriter out)` This method sets an internal `java.io.PrintWriter` reference to the `PrintWriter` object passed to the method.

> `public static void setLoginTimeout(int seconds)` This method sets the permissible delay a driver should wait when attempting a database login.

Drivers are registered with the `DriverManager` class either at initialization of the `DriverManager` class or when an instance of the driver is created.

When the `DriverManager` class is loaded, a section of static code (in the class) is run, and the class names of drivers listed in a Java property named `jdbc.drivers` are loaded. This property can be used to define a list of colon-separated driver class names, such as:

```
jdbc.drivers=imaginary.sql.Driver:oracle.sql.Driver:weblogic.sql.Driver
```

Each driver name is a class filename (including the package declaration) that the DriverManager will attempt to load through the current CLASSPATH. The Driver-Manager uses the following call to locate, load, and link the named class:

```
Class.forName(driver);
```

If the jdbc.drivers property is empty (unspecified), then the application programmer must create an instance of a driver class.

In both cases, the Driver class implementation must explicitly register itself with the DriverManager by calling:

```
DriverManager.registerDriver (this);
```

Here is a segment of code from the imaginary Driver (for the Mini-SQL database). The Driver registers itself whenever an instance of the imaginary driver is created:

```
...
public class iMsqlDriver implements java.sql.Driver
{
 static {
  try {
   new iMsqlDriver();
  }
  catch( SQLException e ) {
   e.printStackTrace();
  }
 }
 /**
  * Constructs a new driver and registers it with
  * java.sql.DriverManager.registerDriver() as specified by the
  * JDBC draft protocol.
  */
 public iMsqlDriver() throws SQLException {
  java.sql.DriverManager.registerDriver(this);
 }
 ...
```

The primary use of the `DriverManager` is to get a `Connection` object reference through the `getConnection` method:

```
Connection conn;
conn = DriverManager.getConnection (
  "jdbc:sybase://dbserver:8080/billing", dbuser, dbpasswd);
```

This method goes through the list of registered drivers and passes the URL string and parameters to each driver in turn through the driver's `connect()` method. If the driver supports the subprotocol and subname information, a `Connection` object reference is returned.

The `DriverManager` class is not required to create JDBC applications, as it is possible to get a `Connection` object directly from the `Driver`:

```
Connection conn;
Driver sybDriver = new SybaseDriver();
conn = sybDriver.connect("jdbc:sybase://dbserver:8080/billing", props);
```

This means of obtaining a connection is not as clean and leaves the application developer dependent on the `Driver` implementation class to provide security checks.

The Application Layer

The Application layer encompasses three interfaces that are implemented at the Driver layer but are used by the application developer. In Java, the interface provides a means of using a general name to indicate a specific object. The general name defines methods that *must* be implemented by the specific object classes. For the application developer, this means that the specific `Driver` class implementation is irrelevant. Just coding to the standard JDBC APIs will be sufficient. This is, of course, assuming that the driver is JDBC compliant. Recall that this means the database at least supports ANSI SQL-2 Entry Level.

The three main interfaces are `Connection`, `Statement`, and `ResultSet`. A `Connection` object is obtained from the driver implementation through the `DriverManager.getConnection()` method call. Once a `Connection` object is returned, the application developer may create a `Statement` object to issue against the database. The result of a `Statement` is a `ResultSet` object, which contains the results of the particular statement (if any).

Connection Basics   The `Connection` interface represents a session with the database connection provided by the `Driver`. Typical database connections include the ability to control changes made to the actual data stored through transactions. A *transaction* is a set of operations that are completed in order. A *commit* action makes the operations store (or change) data in the database. A *rollback* action undoes the previous transaction before it has been committed. On creation, JDBC Connections are in an *auto-commit* mode; there is no rollback possible. So after getting a Connection object from the driver, the developer should consider setting auto-commit to false with the setAutoCommit(boolean b) method.

When auto-commit is disabled, the Connection will support both Connection .commit() and Connection.rollback() method calls. The level of support for transaction isolation depends on the underlying support for transactions in the database.

A portion of the Connection interface definition follows:

Signature: public interface Connection

Statement createStatement () throws SQLException The Connection object implementation will return an instance of an implementation of a Statement object. The Statement object is then used to issue queries.

PreparedStatement prepareStatement (String sql) throws SQL-Exception The Connection object implementation will return an instance of a PreparedStatement object that is configured with the sql string passed. The driver may then send the statement to the database, if the database (driver) handles precompiled statements. Otherwise the driver may wait until the PreparedStatement is executed by an execute method. An exception may be thrown if the driver and database do not implement precompiled statements.

CallableStatement prepareCall (String sql) throws SQLException The Connection object implementation will return an instance of a CallableStatement. CallableStatements are optimized for handling stored procedures. The driver implementation may send the sql string immediately when prepareCall() is complete or may wait until an execute() method occurs.

void setAutoCommit (boolean autoCommit) throws SQLException Sets a flag in the driver implementation that enables commit/rollback (false) or makes all transactions commit immediately (true).

void commit () throws SQLException Makes all changes made since the beginning of the current transaction (either the opening of the Connection or since the last commit() or rollback()).

void rollback() throws SQLException Drops all changes made since the beginning of the current transaction.

The primary use of the `Connection` interface is to create a statement:

```
Connection msqlConn;
Statement stmt;

msqlConn = DriverManager.getConnection (url);
stmt = msqlConn.createStatement();
```

This statement may be used to send SQL statements that return a single result set in a `ResultSet` object reference or a count of the number of records affected by the statement. Statements that need be called a number of times with slight variations may be executed more efficiently using a `PreparedStatement`. The `Connection` interface is also used to create a `CallableStatement` whose primary purpose is to execute stored procedures.

TIP

The primary difference between `Statement`, `PreparedStatement`, and `Callable-Statement` is that `Statement` does not permit any parameters within the SQL statement to be executed. `PreparedStatement` permits `In` parameters, and `CallableStatement` permits `Inout` and `Out` parameters. `In` *parameters* are parameters that are passed into an operation. `Out` *parameters* are parameters passed by reference; they are expected to return a result of the reference type. `Inout` *parameters* are `Out` parameters that contain an initial value that may change as a result of the operation. JDBC supports all three parameter types.

Most of the time, the developer knows the database specifics beforehand and creates the application accordingly. However, JDBC provides an interface that may be used to dynamically determine database specific information. The `Connection` interface `getMetaData` method will return a `DatabaseMetaData` object. The instance of the class that implements the interface provides information about the database as a whole, including access information about tables and procedures, column names, data types, and so on. The implementation details of `Database-MetaData` are dependent upon the database vendor's ability to return this type of information.

Statement Basics   A *statement* is the vehicle for sending SQL queries to the database and retrieving a set of results. Statements can be SQL updates, inserts, deletes, or queries (via Select). The `Statement` interface provides a number of methods designed to make the job of writing queries to the database easier. There are other methods to perform other operations with a `Statement`.

Signature: `public interface Statement`

> **`ResultSet executeQuery(String sql) throws SQLException`**
> Executes a single SQL query and return the results in an object of type `ResultSet`.
>
> **`int executeUpdate(String sql) throws SQLException`** Executes a single SQL query that does not return a set of results, but a count of rows affected.
>
> **`boolean execute(String sql) throws SQLException`** A general SQL statement that may return multiple result sets and/or update counts. This method is most frequently used when you do not know what can be returned, probably because of a user entering the SQL statement directly. The `getResultSet()`, `getUpdateCount()`, and `getMoreResults()` methods are used to retrieve the data returned.
>
> **`ResultSet getResultSet () throws SQLException`** Returns the current data as the result of a statement execution as a `ResultSet` object. Note that if there are no results to be read or if the result is an update count, this method returns `null`. Also note that once read, the results are cleared.
>
> **`int getUpdateCount() throws SQLException`** Returns the status of an `Update`, `Insert`, or `Delete` query or a stored procedure. The value returned is the number of rows affected. A -1 is returned if there is either no update count or if the data returned is a result set. Once read, the update count is cleared.
>
> **`boolean getMoreResults() throws SQLException`** Moves to the next result in a set of multiple results/update counts. This method returns `true` if the next result is a `ResultSet` object. This method will also close any previous `ResultSet` read.

Statements may or may not return a `ResultSet` object, depending on the `Statement` method used. The `executeUpdate()` method, for example, is used to execute SQL statements that do not expect a result (except a row count status):

```
int rowCount;
rowCount = stmt.executeUpdate (
  "DELETE FROM customer WHERE CustomerID = 'McG10233'");
```

SQL statements that return a single set of results can use the **executeQuery()** method. This method returns a single **ResultSet** object. The object represents the row information returned as a result of the query:

```
ResultSet results;
results = stmt.executeQuery ("SELECT * FROM stock");
```

SQL statements that execute stored procedures (or trigger a stored procedure) may return more than one set of results. The **execute()** method is a general-purpose method that can return a single result set, a result count, or some combination thereof. The method returns a **boolean** flag that is used to determine whether there are more results. Because a result set could either contain data or the count of an operation that returns a row count, the **getResultSet()**, **getMoreResults()**, and **getUpdateCount()** methods are used.

For example:

```
// Assume SQLString returns multiple result sets
// true if a ResultSet is returned
boolean result = stmt.execute (SQLString);
int count = stmt.getUpdateCount();

// Now loop until there are no more results or update counts
while (result || (count != -1)) {
  // Is the result a ResultSet?
  if (result) {
    results = stmt.getResultSet();
    // Process result set
  } else if (count != -1) {
    // Do something with count
  }
  result = stmt.getMoreResults();
  count = stmt.getUpdateCount();
}
```

The **PreparedStatement** interface extends the **Statement** interface. When there is a SQL statement that requires repetition with minor variations, the **PreparedStatement** provides an efficient mechanism for passing a precompiled SQL statement that uses input parameters.

Signature: `public interface PreparedStatement extends Statement`

PreparedStatement parameters are used to pass data into a SQL statement, so they are considered In parameters and are filled in by using setType methods:

```
// Assume priceList is an array of prices that needs
// to be reduced for a 10% off sale, and reducedItems
// is an array of item IDs
int reduction = 10;
PreparedStatement ps = msqlConn.prepareStatment (
  "UPDATE Catalog SET Price = ? WHERE ItemID = ?");
// Do the updates in a loop
for (int i = 0; i < reducedItems.length(); i++) {
  // Note that the setType methods set the value of the
  // parameters noted in the SQL statement with question
  // marks (?). They are indexed, starting from 1 to n.
  ps.setFloat (1, (priceList[i]*((float)(100-reduction)/100)));
  ps.setString (2, reducedItems[i]);
  if (ps.executeUpdate() == 0) {
    throw new SQLException ("No Item ID: " + reducedItems[i]);
  }
}
```

NOTE   The setType methods fill the value of parameters (marked by question marks) in a PreparedStatement. These parameters are indexed from 1 to *n*.

Parameters hold their current values until either a new setType method is called or the method clearParameters() is called for the PreparedStatement object. In addition to the execute methods inherited from Statement, PrepareStatement declares the following setType methods. Each method takes two arguments: a parameter index and the primitive or class type, as illustrated in Table 21.1.

The CallableStatement interface is used to execute SQL stored procedures. CallableStatement inherits from the PreparedStatement interface, so all of the execute and setType methods are available. Stored procedures have a varying syntax among database vendors, so JDBC defines a standard way for all RDBMSs to call stored procedures.

Signature: public interface CallableStatement extends PreparedStatement

The JDBC uses an escape syntax that allows parameters to be passed as In parameters and Out parameters. The syntax also allows a result to be returned; and if this syntax is used, the parameter must be registered as an Out parameter.

Here is an example of a `CallableStatement` returning an `Out` parameter:

```
CallableStatement cs = conn.prepareCall ("{call getQuote (?, ?)}");
cs.setString (1, stockName);
// java.sql.Types defines SQL data types that are returned
// as Out parameters
cs.registerOutParameter (2, Types.FLOAT);
stmt.executeUpdate();
float quote = stmt.getFloat (2);
```

TABLE 21.1: set*Type* Methods

Method Signature	Java Type	SQL Type from the Database
void setByte (int index, byte b)	byte	TINYINT
void setShort (int index, short s)	short	SMALLINT
void setInt (int index, int i)	int	INTEGER
void setLong (int index, long l)	long	BIGINT
void setFloat (int index, float f)	float	FLOAT
void setDouble (int index, double d)	double	DOUBLE
void setBigDecimal (int index, BigDecimal bd)	java.math.BigDecimal	NUMERIC
void setString (int index, String s)	java.lang.String	VARCHAR
void setCharacterStream (int index, Reader r, int length)	java.io.Reader	LONGVAR CHAR
void setBytes (int index, byte b[])	byte array	VARBINARY
void setBinaryStream (int index, InputStream is, int length)	java.io.InputStream	LONGVAR BINARY
void setDate (int index, Date d)	java.sql.Date	DATE
void setTime (int index, Time t)	java.sql.Time	TIME
void setTimestamp (int index, Timestamp ts)	java.sql.Timestam	TIMESTAMP
void setNull (int index, int sqlType)	—	java.sql.Types lists SQL types by number, and NULL is integer 0 (zero)
void setBoolean (int index, boolean b)	boolean	BIT

CallableStatement defines a set of getType methods that convert the SQL types returned from the database to Java types as shown in Table 21.2. These methods match the setType methods declared by PreparedStatement.

The get*Type* Methods access data in each column as the result of a query. Each column can be accessed by either its position in the row; numbered from 1 to *n* columns; or by its name, like custID.

TABLE 21.2: get*Type* Methods

Method Signature	Java Type	SQL Type from the Database
boolean getBoolean (int index)	boolean	BIT
byte getByte (int index)	byte	TINYINT
short getShort (int index)	short	SMALLINT
int getInt (int index)	int	INTEGER
long getLong (int index)	long	BIGINT
float getFloat (int index)	float	FLOAT
double getDouble (int index)	double	DOUBLE
BigDecimal getBigDecimal (int index)	java.math.BigDecimal	NUMERIC
String getString (int index)	String	CHAR, VAR CHAR or LONGVAR CHAR
byte[] getBytes (int index)	byte array	BINARY or VARBINARY
Date getDate (int index)	java.sql.Date	DATE
Time getTime (int index)	java.sql.Time	TIME
Timestamp getTimestamp (int index)	java.sql.Timestamp	TIMESTAMP

Note that it is the responsibility of the JDBC driver to convert the data passed from the database as SQL data types into Java values.

ResultSet Basics The ResultSet interface defines methods for accessing tables of data generated as the result of executing a Statement. ResultSet column values may be accessed in any order; they are indexed and may be selected by either the name or the number (numbered from 1 to *n*) of the column. ResultSet maintains the position of the current row, starting with the first row of data returned. The next() method moves to the next row of data.

A partial look at the ResultSet interface follows:

Signature: public interface ResultSet

> **boolean next() throws SQLException** Positions the ResultSet to the next row; ResultSet row position is initially the first row of the result set.

> **ResultSetMetaData getMetaData() throws SQLException** Returns an object that contains a description of the current result set: the number of columns, the type of each column, and properties of the results.

> **void close() throws SQLException** Normally a ResultSet is closed when another Statement is executed, but it may be desirable to release the resources earlier.

As with the CallableStatement above, the resulting data can be read through getType methods. For example:

```
// Pass a query to the statement object
ResultSet rs = stmt.executeQuery("SELECT * FROM stock WHERE
➥ quantity = 0");

// Get the results as their Java types
// Note that columns are indexed by an integer starting with 1,
// or by the name of column, as in "ItemID"
System.out.println ("Stock replenishment list");
while (rs.next()) {

    System.out.println ("Item ID: " + rs.getString("ItemID"));
    System.out.println ("Next ship date: " + rs.getDate(2));
    System.out.println ("");
}
```

The 1.2 JDK introduces several methods with the JDBC 2.0 API. With JDBC 2.0, additional capabilities are available that permit non-sequential reading of rows, as well as updating of rows, while reading. A partial look at the JDBC 2.0 methods of `ResultSet` follows:

`int getType() throws SQLException`   Returns the type of result set, determining the manner in which you can read the results. Valid return values are TYPE_FORWARD_ONLY, TYPE_STATIC, TYPE_KEYSET, or TYPE_DYNAMIC. If TYPE_FORWARD_ONLY is returned, most of the remaining methods will throw a SQLException if they are attempted.

`boolean first() throws SQLException`   Positions the `ResultSet` at the first row. Returns `true` if on a valid row, `false` otherwise.

`boolean last() throws SQLException`   Positions the `ResultSet` at the last row. Returns `true` if on a valid row, `false` otherwise.

`boolean previous() throws SQLException`   Positions the `ResultSet` at the previous row. Returns `true` if on a valid row, `false` otherwise.

`boolean absolute(int row) throws SQLException`   Positions the `ResultSet` at the designated row. If `row` requested is negative, positions `ResultSet` at row relative to end of set.

`boolean relative(int row) throws SQLException`   Positions the `ResultSet` at the row relative to the current position.

NOTE   The JDBC 2.0 API also permits the updating of rows, as you read each row from the `ResultSet`. You can delete the current row with `deleteRow()` or update the columns of the current row with methods like `updateInt (int col, int value)` or `updateFloat (String columnName, float value)`. There are two methods for each datatype: one accessing columns by column number, the other by column name. Once you are done updating a row, you tell the system to update the actual database with `updateRow()`.

ResultSetMetaData   Besides being able to read data from a `ResultSet` object, JDBC provides an interface to allow the developer to determine what type of data was returned. The `ResultSetMetaData` interface is similar to the `DatabaseMetaData` interface in concept, but is specific to the current `ResultSet`. As with `DatabaseMetaData`, it is unlikely that many developers will use this interface as most applications are written with an understanding of the database schema and column names and values. However, `ResultSetMetaData` is useful in dynamically determining the meta-data of a `ResultSet` returned from a stored procedure or from a user-supplied SQL statement.

The following code demonstrates the displaying of results with the help of `ResultSetMetaData` when the contents are unknown:

```
ResultSet results = stmt.executeQuery (sqlString);
ResultSetMetaData meta = results.getMetaData();
int columns = 0;
boolean first = true;
while (results.next()) {
  if (first) {
    columns = meta.getColumnCount();
    for (int i=1; i<=columns; i++) {
      System.out.print (meta.getColumnName(i) + "\t");
    }
    System.out.println();
    first=false;
  }
  for (int i=1; i<=columns; i++) {
    System.out.print (results.getString (i) + "\t");
  }
  System.out.println();
}
```

Sending and Receiving Large Data Chunks   SQL LONGVARBINARY and LONGVARCHAR data types can be of arbitrary size. The `getBytes()` and `get-String()` methods can read these types up to the limits imposed by the driver. The limits can be read through the `Statement.getMaxFieldSize()` method. For larger blocks of data, the JDBC allows developers to use input streams to return the data in chunks.

TIP   Streams must be read immediately following the query execution. They are automatically closed at the next receipt of a `ResultSet`.

Sending large blocks of data is also possible using `java.io.OutputStream` as parameters. When a statement is executed, the JDBC driver makes repeated calls to read and transmit the data in the streams.

NOTE
> The JDBC 2.0 API also adds the ability to use locator type objects `Array`, `Blob`, `Clob`, and `Struct` for reading and storing large objects. These are part of the emerging SQL3 standard. For a more complete description of these JDBC 2 capabilities, visit `http://java.sun.com/products/jdbc/jdbcsw2.html`.

Limitations Using JDBC (Applications vs. Applets)

There are two types of programs in the Java world: applications and applets. Each program type provides benefits, and the use of each is generally determined by the way in which the developer wishes the user to access the program.

Applications

Applications are Java programs that are developed as stand-alone executables. The user is expected to have access to the program executable (`.class` file) and the Java interpreter locally. For an intranet-based database front end, this strategy offers the benefits of faster startup (class files are local) and local disk utilization.

In addition, Java applications are trusted and are allowed greater flexibility with socket connections, making it possible for the client program to access multiple database systems on remote servers.

Java applications are becoming more prevalent as tools become available for GUI development and speed improvements are made possible through Just-in-Time (JIT) compilers/interpreters. Applications can also reduce or eliminate issues with browser security models and their differing Java implementations.

Applets

Applets are mini Java programs that require a Java-enabled browser to run. The browser provides an environment in which the applet can run, including drawing and viewing resources directly on the browser page. When a user moves or "surfs" to a browser page that contains an applet, the applet is automatically executed.

The process involves downloading the necessary Java applet code, including JDBC drivers and application layer software, automatically checking security restrictions on the code, and if OK, running the applet.

Applets provide several key benefits over applications:

Version control   It is possible to modify an applet almost on the fly by replacing the class file in the HTML page references.

Easier execution model   It takes very little effort to learn to use even the most sophisticated browsers and to execute a front-end client. The user simply navigates to the page where the application is located.

Online help   Creating the running program on a browser HTML page makes it extremely easy to embed Help links that can be developed separately from the running program.

A typical use of applets might be for training within a large organization, where the data being delivered is not critical and access can be limited to a two-tier model. (Three-tier models are possible but involve more complex layering schemes.) Another use may be the simple presentation of data to the Internet community, again where the quantity of data is not great and security of the data message is not paramount.

Applets, however, are severely constrained by the browser environment in the following ways:

- They cannot access any local files. This limits the use of local caching and table manipulation and storage to in-memory during the life of the applet.

- They cannot connect to arbitrary hosts. Socket connections are only allowed between the applet and the host that the applet originated from.

- They cannot load or run drivers that contain native methods (C language calls).

Additionally there is a considerable performance hit involved in loading applet code across an Internet (wide area) network connection.

Some of these constraints may be lifted or reduced with the introduction of trusted applets and browsers that accept them. Trusted applets may be code signed with a cryptographic key or may be stored in a trusted location. If the browser environment believes that the applets' source is trusted, then for security purposes they may be treated like applications, although there may still be limits regarding the location of databases on an Internet that are not related to the Java security manager. Trusted applets are the subject of future consideration in the development of the Java security model.

The other alternative that is more tangible and available today is the use of a three-tier model. In this approach, the applet is loaded from a middleware tier that provides the HTML page and HTTP server, and a multithreaded application (Java, C, or C++) that supports socket connections for multiple clients and, in turn, contacts remote database systems.

Calls to the third tier can be managed by developing a custom (proprietary) protocol, by using Remote Method Invocation (RMI), or by using an Object Request Broker (ORB). See the "Alternative Connectivity Strategies" section later in this chapter.

Security Considerations

The JDBC API follows the standard Java security model. In short, applications are considered trusted code, and applets are considered untrusted. In general, the job of writing a secure JDBC driver is left to the driver vendor.

The Java Virtual Machine employs its own well-documented security checks for untrusted applets, including the aforementioned restrictions. However, if a JDBC driver vendor wants to extend the model by adding features to their driver—for example, allowing multiple applets to use the same TCP socket connection to talk to a database—then it becomes the responsibility of the vendor to check that each applet is allowed to use the connection.

In addition to maintaining the integrity of the Java security model, both the JDBC driver vendor and JDBC application developer need to keep in mind that the JDBC API defines a means of executing database calls and does not define a network security model. The data sent over the wire to the database and the resulting table information (for example, to request customer credit card information) are exposed and can be read by any terminal that is capable of snooping the network.

A JDBC Database Example

The following is an example that uses the concepts presented in this chapter. It is artificial and only meant to illustrate the use of `Statement`, `PreparedStatement`, and `CallableStatement`.

The simple database has a table called *Customers*, which has the schema shown in Table 21.3.

TABLE 21.3: Customer Data Table

CustomerID	VARCHAR
LastName	VARCHAR
FirstName	VARCHAR
Phonenumber	VARCHAR
StreetAddress	VARCHAR
Zipcode	VARCHAR

Table 21.3 is part of a larger database that stores information related to a large catalog ordering system. Here is the definition of a simple Customer object with two primary methods, `insertNewCustomer()` and `getCustomer()`:

Signature: `public class Customer`

> **`public Customer (Connection conn)`**   The constructor for the class. The `Customer` constructor receives a `Connection` object, which it uses to create `Statement` references. In addition, the constructor creates a `PreparedStatement` and three `CallableStatement` objects.

> **`public String insertNewCustomer (String lname, String fname, String pnum, String addr, String zip) throws insertFailedException, SQLException`**   Creates a new customer record, including a new ID. The ID is created through a stored procedure that reads the current list of customer IDs and creates a new reference. The method returns the new ID created or throws an exception if the insert failed.

> **`public CustomerInfo getCustomer (String custID) throws selectException, SQLException`**   Returns an object that contains the data in the Customer table. An exception is thrown if the customer ID passed does not exist or is not properly formatted, or if the SQL statement fails.

> **`public static synchronized boolean validateZip (String zip) throws SQLException`**   Is a utility method to validate the zip code. A `true` value is returned if the zip code exists in the ZipCode table in the database.

> **`public static synchronized boolean validateID (String id) throws SQLException`**   Is a utility method to validate a customer ID. If the ID exists, the method returns `true`.

The source is as follows:

```
// Customer record class
// This class is used to store and access customer data from the database
import java.sql.*;

public class Customer {

  private Connection conn;
  private PreparedStatement insertNewCustomer;
  private CallableStatement getNewID;
  public static CallableStatement checkZip;
  public static CallableStatement checkID;

  // Customer constructor: store a local copy of the
  // Connection object create statements for use later
  public Customer (Connection c) {
    conn = c;

    try {
      insertNewCustomer = conn.prepareStatement(
        "INSERT INTO customers VALUES (?, ?, ?, ?, ?, ?)");

      getNewID = conn.prepareCall ("{call getNewID (?)}");
      checkID = conn.prepareCall ("{call checkID (?,?)}");
      checkZip = conn.prepareCall ("{call checkZip (?, ?)}");
    } catch (SQLException e) {
      System.err.println ("Cannot create statements");
    }
  }

  // Method for creating a new customer record.
  // The customerID is generated by a stored procedure
  // call on the database
  public String insertNewCustomer (String lname, String fname,
      String pnum, String addr, String zip)
      throws InsertFailedException, SQLException {

    String newID;

    // Get a new customer ID through the stored procedure
    if ((newID = getNewID ()) == null) {
```

```java
      throw new InsertFailedException ("could not get new ID");
    }

    // Insert the new customer ID
    insertNewCustomer.setString (1, newID);
    insertNewCustomer.setString (2, lname);
    insertNewCustomer.setString (3, fname);
    insertNewCustomer.setString (4, pnum);
    insertNewCustomer.setString (5, addr);
    insertNewCustomer.setString (6, zip);

    // Execute the statement
    if (insertNewCustomer.executeUpdate() != 1) {
      throw new InsertFailedException ("could not execute insert");
    }
    return (newID);
  }

  // Get a single customer record with this ID
  // Note: this method maps the returned data onto a
  // CustomerInfo container object
  public CustomerInfo getCustomer (String custID)
      throws SelectException, SQLException {

    // Check the ID first
    if (!validateID (custID)) {
      throw new SelectException ("no customer with ID: " + custID);
    }

    // Create the select statement
    Statement stmt = conn.createStatement();

    // Get the results
    ResultSet rs = stmt.executeQuery (
      "SELECT *FROM Customer WHERE CustID = " + custID);

    // Create a CustomerInfo container object
    CustomerInfo info = new CustomerInfo ();

    // Populate the CustomerInfo object
    // Columns are indexed starting with 1
```

```
    info.CustomerID = rs.getString (1);
    info.LastName = rs.getString (2);
    info.FirstName = rs.getString (3);
    info.PhoneNumber = rs.getString (4);
    info.StreetAddress = rs.getString (5);
    info.Zip = rs.getString (6);

    return (info);
}

// Method for validation of a customer's zip code
// This method is public so that it can be called from a user interface
public static synchronized boolean validateZip (String zip)
    throws SQLException {

  // Make call to stored procedure to validate zip code
  checkZip.setString (1, zip);
  checkZip.registerOutParameter (2, Types.BIT);
  checkZip.executeUpdate();
  return (checkZip.getBoolean(2));

}

// Method for validating a customer ID
// This method is public so that it can be called from a user interface
public static synchronized boolean validateID (String id)
    throws SQLException {

  // Make call to stored procedure to validate customer id
  checkID.setString (1, id);
  checkID.registerOutParameter (2, Types.BIT);
  checkID.executeUpdate();
  return (checkID.getBoolean(2));
}

// Method for retrieving a new customer ID from the database
private String getNewID () throws SQLException {

  // Make call to stored procedure to get
  // customer ID from DB
  getNewID.registerOutParameter (1, Types.VARCHAR);
```

```
        getNewID.executeUpdate();
        return (getNewID.getString(1));
    }
}


// Exceptions

// InsertFailedException is a general exception for
// SQL insert problems
class InsertFailedException extends SQLException {
  public InsertFailedException () {
  }
  public InsertFailedException (String reason) {
    super (reason);
  }
}

// SelectException is a general exception for SQL select problems
class SelectException extends SQLException {

  public SelectException (String reason) {
    super (reason);
  }
  public SelectException () {
  }
}
```

The CustomerInfo class is a simple container object. Container classes make it easier to pass a complete customer record to and from any method that manipulates the Customer table in the database. Data can be stored in the container class and passed as a single object reference, rather than having to pass each element as a single reference. The code for the class follows:

```
// A container object for the Customer table
public class CustomerInfo {
  String CustomerID;
  String LastName;
  String FirstName;
  String PhoneNumber;
  String StreetAddress;
  String Zip;
}
```

Finally, to test the simple `Customer` class, here is a simple Java application that illustrates loading a Sybase driver, making a connection, and passing the `Connection` object returned to a new instance of a `Customer` object. The code for the example program follows:

```
// A simple Java application that illustrates the use of
// DriverManager, Driver, Connection, Statement and ResultSet

import java.sql.*;

public class Example {

  Connection sybaseConn;

  public static void main (String arg[]) {

    // Look for the url, username and password
    if (arg.length < 3) {
      System.err.println ("Example use:");
      System.err.println ("java Example <url> <username> <password>");
      System.exit (1);
    }

    // Create an instance of the class
    Example ex = new Example ();

    // Initialize the connection
    ex.initdb (arg[0], arg[1], arg[2]);

    // Test the connection—write a customer and
    // then read it back
    ex.testdb ();
  }

  // method to initialize the database connection
  // The Connection object reference is kept globally
  public void initdb (String url, String user, String passwd) {
    // Try to open the database and get the connection
    try {

      // Note that this example assumes that
```

```
        // Java property "jdbc.drivers"
        // that is loading the appropriate driver(s) for
        // the url passed in the getConnection call.
        // It is possible to explicitly create an
        // instance of a driver as well, for example:
        // new sybase.sql.driver ();

        // Create a connection
        sybaseConn = DriverManager.getConnection
          (url, user, passwd);

    } catch (SQLException e) {
      System.err.println ("Database connection failed:");
      System.err.println (e.getMessage());
      System.exit (2);
    }
  }

// Simple method to test the Customer class methods
public void testdb () {
  String custID = null;

  // Create the instance of the Customer class
  Customer cust = new Customer (sybaseConn);

  try {
    // Now insert a new Customer
    custID = cust.insertNewCustomer (
      "Jones", "Bill", "555-1234", "5 Main Street", "01234");

  } catch (SQLException e) {

    System.err.println ("Insert failed:");
    System.err.println (e.getMessage());
    System.exit (3);
  }

  try {
    // Read it back from the database
    CustomerInfo info = cust.getCustomer (custID);
```

```
        } catch (SQLException e) {

          System.err.println ("Read failed:");
          System.err.println (e.getMessage());
          System.exit (4);
        }
      }
    }
```

This example illustrates the use of the `CallableStatements` to issue stored procedure calls that validate the zip code and validate the customer ID, and the use of the `PreparedStatement` to issue an Insert SQL statement with parameters that will change with each insert.

This example also illustrates code that will run with any JDBC driver that will support the stored procedures used in the `Customer` class. The driver class names are loaded from the `jdbc.drivers` property, so code recompilation is not required.

JDBC Drivers

One of the real attractions of the JDBC API is the ability to develop applications with the knowledge that all of the major database vendors are working in parallel to create drivers. A number of drivers are available both from database vendors and from third-party developers. In most cases, it is wise to shop around for the best features, cost, and support.

Drivers come in a variety of flavors according to their construction and the type of database they are intended to support. Sun categorizes database drivers in four ways:

1. A JDBC-ODBC bridge driver, shown in Figure 21.6, implemented with ODBC binary code and, in some cases, a client library as well. The bridge driver is made up of three parts: a set of C libraries that connect the JDBC to the ODBC driver manager, the ODBC driver manager, and the ODBC driver.

NOTE   ODBC is a database access API introduced by Microsoft that is very common on PCs. ODBC drivers are available for most PC-based database systems, enabling migration to JDBC without waiting for the ODBC driver vendor to create a JDBC driver.

FIGURE 21.6:

JDBC-ODBC bridge driver

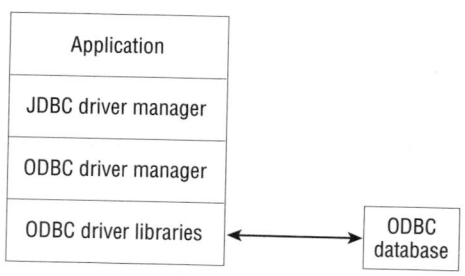

2. A native library-to-Java implementation, as shown in Figure 21.7. This driver uses native C language library calls to translate JDBC to the native client library. These drivers use C language libraries that provide vendor-specific functionality and tie these libraries (through native method calls) to the JDBC. These drivers were the first available for Oracle, Sybase, Informix, DB2, and other client-library–based RDBMSs.

FIGURE 21.7:

Native library-to-Java driver

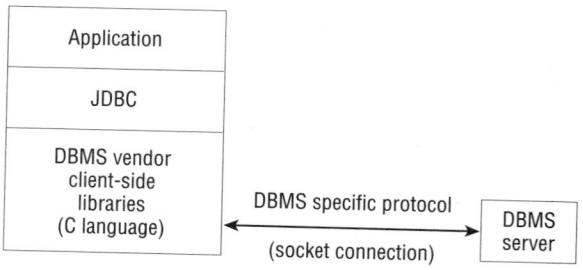

3. Figure 21.8 shows the structure of a network-protocol Java driver. JDBC calls are translated by this driver into a DBMS-independent protocol and sent to a middle-tier server over a socket. The middle-tier code can contact a variety of databases on behalf of the client. This approach is becoming the most popular and is by far the most flexible. It also deals specifically with issues relating to network security, including passing data through firewalls.

4. A native-protocol Java driver, shown in Figure 21.9. JDBC calls are converted directly to the network protocol used by the DBMS server. In this driver scenario, the database vendor supports a network socket, and the JDBC driver communicates over a socket connection directly to the database server. The client-side code can be written in Java. This solution has the benefit of being

one of the easiest to implement and is very practical for intranet use. However, because the network protocol is defined by the vendor and is typically proprietary, the driver usually comes only from the database vendor.

FIGURE 21.8:

DBMS-independent network protocol driver

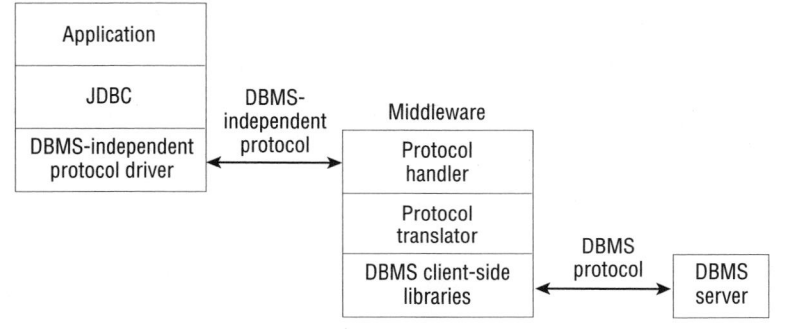

FIGURE 21.9:

DBMS-protocol all-Java driver

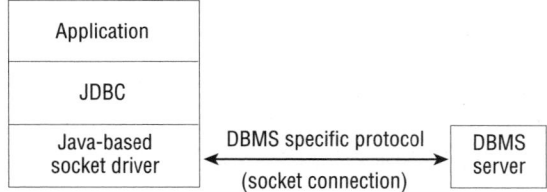

JDBC-ODBC Bridge

The JDBC-ODBC bridge is a JDBC driver that provides translation of JDBC calls to ODBC operations. There are a number of DBMS that support ODBC. When a company the size of Microsoft creates a standard for database access, there are sure to be vendors that follow. In fact there are more than 50 different ODBC drivers available.

As mentioned earlier, both JDBC and ODBC are based upon the X/Open CLI, so the translation between JDBC and ODBC is relatively straightforward. ODBC is a client-side set of libraries and a driver that is specific to the client's operating system and, in some cases, machine architecture.

From the developer's perspective, using a JDBC-ODBC bridge driver is an easy choice. Applications will still speak directly to the JDBC interface classes, so it is exactly the same as using any other JDBC driver. However, the implementation of a JDBC-ODBC bridge requires that the developer be aware of what is required to run the application. Because ODBC calls are made using binary C calls, the client must have a local copy of the ODBC driver, the ODBC driver manager, and the client-side libraries.

For these reasons, Sun makes the recommendation that the JDBC-ODBC bridge not be used for Web-based database access. For intranet access, the developer must distribute the Java program to the client machines as either a Java application or Java applet (which would run as a trusted source from the local client file system).

Current JDBC Drivers

JDBC drivers are being released from so many vendors that a definitive list is just not practical and would be obsolete by the time it was printed. For information on current driver vendors, their product names, and what databases they support, a good source is:

```
http://java.sun.com/products/jdbc/jdbc.drivers.html
```

Alternative Connectivity Strategies

JDBC represents a very easy way to save time and future investment when developing database applications. The API guarantees that a client program written to the JDBC standard will work with any JDBC-compliant driver and database combination. This next section discusses two alternative technologies coming from Sun that also provide a flexible way to preserve a development investment: Remote Method Invocation (RMI) and the Common Object Request Broker Architecture (CORBA).

Remote Method Invocation (RMI)

Both RMI and CORBA can also be used to connect client applications to databases, although there are some caveats to consider. RMI is analogous to Remote

Procedure Calls (RPC), the ability to call and run a procedure in another executing program. However, while RPC was not designed for distributed object systems, this is RMI's strength. RMI is designed to allow client applications to execute the methods of objects that exist on a remote server and execute these methods in such a way that it *appears* that the objects are local.

For database connectivity, this means that the developer can create an application that accesses database objects directly, even though these objects are actually implemented on the database server host. Because RMI provides mechanisms for allowing objects to be passed as serialized streams, it also supports protocols for passing these streams through firewalls.

Because RMI is a Java-to-Java solution, it is also possible to combine the best of JDBC and RMI for a multi-tier solution. For example, if the JDBC driver is written using RMI, then it becomes possible to write to a standard database interface definition *and* use object persistence and remote method calls via RMI, thereby extending the JDBC model.

For more information on RMI, see Chapter 25.

The Common Object Request Broker Architecture (CORBA)

The Common Object Request Broker Architecture (CORBA) is the result of years of work by the Object Management Group (OMG). The OMG is a consortium of more than 500 companies that have compiled a specification for a communications infrastructure that allows different computer languages on different computer architectures to access a distributed collection of objects.

For the database application developer, CORBA provides the ultimate flexibility in a heterogeneous development environment. The server could be developed in C or C++ and the client could be a Java applet. Currently Sun provides a Java Interface Definition Language (IDL) compiler that takes a CORBA 2.0 IDL file and creates the necessary support files, called stubs, for a client implementation.

CORBA is a standard (at version 2.0 as of this writing) that defines a definition language that is vendor- and language-neutral. The IDL is used to create a contract between a client and server implementation. IDL is not an implementation language itself; it merely describes object services and operations that may be performed on an implementation of those services.

At the core of CORBA is the Object Request Broker (ORB). The ORB is the principal component for the transmission of information (requests for operations and their results) between the client and server of a CORBA application. The ORB manages marshaling requests, establishes a connection to the server, sends the data, and executes the requests on the server side. The same process occurs when the server returns the results of the operation.

The CORBA 2.0 specification also defines an Internet interoperability protocol (IIOP) that defines the protocol of the connection between the client and server through the ORB. This allows developers to choose a client IDL compiler and server IDL compiler from two different vendors.

Besides Sun, there are several vendors that provide CORBA 2.0 compliance, including IIOP and Java IDL compilers.

For a closer look at CORBA, see Chapter 26. For a wealth of additional information on the OMG consortium, consult the `http://www.omg.org/` Web page.

Connectivity to Object Databases

Besides RMI and CORBA, another alternative is to use an object database, specifically one that supports Java's object model. There are several object database products for Java and, as a result of the Object Database Management Group (ODMG), a specification for storing Java objects in databases. The specification is called ODMG 2.0, Java object database vendors are shipping products that support it.

NOTE   To read about the ODMG 2.0 standard, consult the ODMG's Web site `http://www.odmg.org/` or *The Object Database Standard: ODMG 2.0* book (ISBN: 1-55860-463-4).

Connectivity with Web-Based Database Systems

While not specifically JDBC, and not always related to Java, there is another alternative to accessing databases from Web pages. It is possible to use HTML pages to send information to Common Gateway Interface (CGI) scripts. The CGI scripts then connect to the database and return results to the HTML page. Vendors in the Web-based database market have a variety of strategies for improving the performance of CGI with multithreaded applications written in C or C++ that handle the database connection and queries.

The 1.2 JDK provides a technology called *servlets* that replaces the need to use C, C++, or Perl for CGI scripts. The servlet can be instructed to open a database connection, retrieve a result, and return the data to the applet. For more information on servlet technology, proceed to Chapter 23.

Summary

The interest in Java has created a number of new strategies for moving data between the database system and the front-end user. In this chapter, the Java Database Connectivity API was presented as the primary technique for connecting Java applications to database systems. The JDBC solves the problem of connecting a single application to a multitude of database systems by isolating the interface that the developer uses and the driver that is used to connect to the database.

In addition, the chapter looked briefly at alternative connectivity strategies like Remote Method Invocation (RMI) and the Common Object Request Broker Architecture (CORBA).

CHAPTER
TWENTY-TWO

22

JavaBeans

- The JavaBean component model

- The Java "Bean"

- Bean introspection and customization

- Bean applications and the Beans Development Kit (BDK)

- Beans and other developing technologies

One of the real goals of software development is to recoup the investment in code by making it possible for the code to be reused in other development efforts, either in the same company or in other companies. In recent years, programmers have expended great energy on creating reusable software. The early efforts spent on OOP (object-oriented programming) are now coming full circle with the development of a programming language like Java, where the software will run on a variety of platforms without any additional work.

However, Java does not automatically allow software to be reusable. Java code may be well written, and thus allow another developer to make changes to the code easily, but the goal of reusable software is to allow developers to use the code *without* needing to recompile the code. Furthermore, true reuse implies that developers can integrate code pieces into their designs without needing to recompile *their* code either.

These are the goals of the JavaBeans API, which is the focus of this chapter.

The JavaBeans Component Model

JavaBeans are based on a software component model for Java. The model is specifically designed to allow third-party vendors to create and sell Java components that are integrated into other software products by other developers.

An application developer will purchase off-the-shelf components from a vendor, drag and drop them within a development tool, make any necessary modifications to each component, test them, and revise them as necessary without needing to write and compile code. Within the Java model, components may be modified or combined with other components to create new components or complete applications.

At run time, the end user may also modify components through properties that the component designer (or application developer) built in. These may be simple properties, like color or shape, or more sophisticated properties that affect the overall behavior of the component.

The component model specified by the JavaBeans 1.01 Specification defines five major services:

> **Introspection** A mechanism that allows components to publish the operations and properties they support and supports the discovery of such mechanisms in other components.

Communication   An event-handling mechanism for creating or "raising" an event to be received as a message by other components.

Persistence   A means of storing the state of a component.

Properties   A mechanism for control over the layout of a component. This includes the physical space that a component takes and the relationship of the component to other components when they are placed together on a container.

Customization   A mechanism for allowing developers control over changes that each component requires. Components should provide visibility for properties and operations (behavior) to a builder application. The application can then provide a developer with a means for modifying the component pieces in order to construct the appropriate application.

The component model allows software to be designed for modification. Each piece of software contains a set of properties, operations, and event handlers. Combining several components can create the specific runtime behavior a designer or developer wants. Components are held together in a container or toolkit, which provides the context for the application.

The Java Bean

A Java "Bean" is a single reusable software component. Beans are manipulated in a builder tool (container) to provide specific operational behavior. Beans are building blocks for creating applications. The most common Bean will most likely be a small-to-medium control program, but it is also possible to create a Bean that encompasses a complete application and to embed that Bean into a compound document. For example, Figure 22.1 illustrates a container panel that holds three components.

In general, Beans can be represented by simple GUIs; they can be button components, sliders, menu lists, and so on. These simple components provide a straightforward means of letting the user know what a Bean does. However, it is possible to create "invisible" Beans that are used to receive events and work behind the scenes. In any case, it is easiest to think of Beans as component building blocks designed to receive an event and process it so that some operation is carried out.

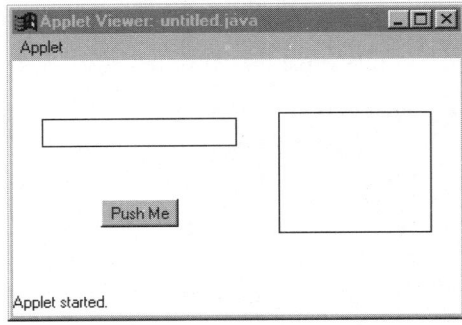

A Bean is neither a class library nor an API like JDBC. JDBC provides a means of querying databases; a Bean can connect the user to the JDBC queries (see Chapter 21 for information about JDBC). For example, a Bean may be used to provide a simple Select button in an application's user interface. This may, in turn, be a Bean that composes the appropriate database select statement and issues the request. Visually, the Bean used in this case would resemble a Java button, similar to the Bean shown here that looks like a Select button.

Bean Architecture

Beans are composed of three parts: properties, methods, and events. These parts are illustrated in Figure 22.2.

Bean properties describe the state of attributes of the Bean, including its physical representation. Bean properties are the primary mechanisms of change within a Bean, and they are set or retrieved through methods. In addition, methods are used to fire and receive events, the mechanism by which Beans communicate. Multiple Beans, connected by event methods, make up a complete system or application, as shown earlier in Figure 22.1.

JavaBean Event Model

Bean events are the mechanism for notification between Beans as well as between Beans and containers. A JavaBean uses an event to notify another JavaBean to take an action or to inform the Bean that a state change has occurred. An event is registered or published by the source and propagated (through a method call) to one or more target listeners.

A Bean event is passed as an object, an instance of a class that extends from `java.util.EventObject`. The event can be created directly from this class, as in the following example:

```
public class MyEvent extends java.util.EventObject {
  public MyEvent (Object source) {
    super (source);
  }
}
```

The JavaBeans model closely follows the JDK 1.1 AWT event model. This is helpful because many Bean components are visual GUI elements that are part of the AWT and Swing component hierarchies. At the lowest level, events are sent as the result of some change, input, or other occurrence on the visual component. The AWT defines the low-level hierarchy as follows:

```
java.util.EventObject
    java.awt.AWTEvent
        java.awt.event.ComponentEvent
            java.awt.event.ContainerEvent
            java.awt.event.FocusEvent
            java.awt.event.InputEvent
                java.awt.event.KeyEvent
                    com.sun.java.swing.event.MenuKeyEvent
                java.awt.event.MouseEvent
                    com.sun.java.swing.event.MenuDragMouseEvent
            java.awt.event.WindowEvent
        com.sun.java.swing.MenuEvent
        com.sun.java.swing.PopupMenuEvent
```

The AWT event hierarchy also defines a set of events that are used to provide events that occur at the higher level of the user interface. These higher-level events apply to multiple component types, as in the following:

```
java.util.EventObject
    java.awt.AWTEvent
        java.awt.event.ActionEvent
        java.awt.event.AdjustmentEvent
        java.awt.event.InputMethodEvent
        java.awt.event.InvocationEvent
        java.awt.event.ItemEvent
        java.awt.event.TextEvent
```

These lists are not meant to be all-inclusive lists of events previously defined within Java. However, they represent the ones that tend to be most frequently used. Also, you'll be using many throughout the examples in this chapter.

Beans send events as the single parameter to an event method of the target Bean. However, events encapsulate elements that may be used by the recipient of the event. For example:

```
public void fireAction (String command) {
    if (listener != null) {
        ActionEvent actionEvt = new ActionEvent(this, 0, command);
        listener.actionPerformed(actionEvt);
    }
}
```

Here, an event object with a `String` command is sent to the `listener` object, and the event method to be triggered is the `actionPerformed()` event.

Event Sources and Targets

The event model in JavaBeans is defined by event sources and event targets. The event source identifies itself as the initiator of an event by registering one or more event targets. Both the event source and the event target establish a set of methods that the event source will use to notify event listeners.

An event source attempts to send a desired event to an arbitrary collection of event targets. This mode is the default behavior of the event source and is called *multicast*. The event source keeps track of the event listeners for each kind of event it fires and notifies each target when an event is fired.

A multicast event allows a source object to notify several event listeners all at once, which is accomplished by keeping the state of every event listener registered:

```
private ActionListener listenerList = null;

public void addActionListener (ActionListener l) {
  listenerList = AWTEventMulticaster.add (listenerList, l);
}

public void removeActionListener (ActionListener l) {
  listenerList = AWTEventMulticaster.remove (listenerList, l);
}
```

NOTE   The `add/remove ActionListener` pair is typically synchronized to avoid multi-thread race conditions. (Race conditions occur when multiple processes try to do something with shared data and the outcome depends on the order of operations.) However, use of the `AWTEventMulticaster` and `EventListenerList` classes handle the synchronization issues for you.

Event sources may also be *unicast* sources, where the event source is required to keep track of a single target listener for each type of event it fires. A unicast event is sent to the specific single target listener.

The unicast event allows only one listener to be registered; otherwise, an exception, `java.util.TooManyListenersException`, is thrown. The unicast event listener stores just one instance of a listener:

```
private ActionListener l = null;

public synchronized void addActionListener (ActionListener l)
    throws java.util.TooManyListenersException {
  if (l == null) {
    this.l = l;
  } else {
    throw new java.util.TooManyListenersException ();
  }
}

public synchronized void removeActionListener (ActionListener l) {
  l = null;
}
```

The event target is an instance of a class that implements some (or all) of the EventListener interface—specifically, the event methods that class is interested in.

Each event type is tied to a single method, and event methods are typically grouped by their application. For example:

```
import java.awt.event.*;
public class MyActionEventListener implements ActionListener {

    // Provide an event method for the actionPerformed event
    public void actionPerformed (ActionEvent e) {

        // Pull the command out of the event
        String command = e.getActionCommand ();

        if (command.equals ("add")) {
            ...
        }
    }
}
```

Some people prefer to have a listener only listen for events for one event source. If that were the case, the if-block above would be unnecessary, as you would know for what source the event happened. This is how IDE tools tend to generate code.

The following is an example of the use of a multicast event source and event listener. This example illustrates how an event listener is registered with an event source and how the event source sends an event to each of the listeners registered.

```
import java.awt.*;
import java.awt.event.*;
public class MyApp {
  private ActionListener listenerList = null;

  public MyApp () {
    addActionListener (new MyActionEventListener ());
  }

  public void addActionListener (ActionListener l) {
    listenerList = AWTEventMulticaster.add (listenerList, l);
  }
```

```
public void removeActionListener (ActionListener l) {
  listenerList = AWTEventMulticaster.remove (listenerList, l);
}

public void fireAction (String command) {
  if (listenerList != null) {
    ActionEvent actionEvt = new ActionEvent(this, 0, command);
    listenerList.actionPerformed (actionEvt);
  }
}
...
}
```

In some cases, the event target cannot implement the interface directly, and an instance of an event-adapter class may be used to interpose between the source and one or more listeners. The `MouseInputAdapter` and `InternalFrameAdapter` classes are two such adapters found within the Swing event classes.

The event adapter implements one or more listener interfaces and allows a developer to use a single event to be sent to two different adapter classes that interpose between the source and listener. Besides allowing a developer to use a single event with multiple event sources to a single listener, adapters are useful for filtering events and implementing advanced features like event queues.

Bean Properties

The *properties* of a Bean describe attributes associated with the Bean, such as color, size, or the string to be used as a label. Properties may be used in a number of ways, depending on the environment in which the Bean is accessed. Properties can be changed at run time through their `get`/`set` methods, through a scripting environment, or in a property sheet that is part of a Bean builder/customization tool.

A property can be changed by the end user through a pair of `get`/`set` methods that is specific to the property. For example, there may be a color property for the Bean, and the end user can change the color of the Bean through a property dialog box provided with the Bean. The Bean provides two methods to allow the private color property to be accessed and changed:

```
public Color getFillColor (); // This Bean's object fill color
public void setFillColor (Color c);
```

Properties may be indexed to support a range of values, where the indexes are specified by `int` values. Indexed properties have four access methods, where the arrays of values may be accessed by either a single element or by the entire array:

```
void setLabel (int index, String label);
String getLabel (int index);
void setLabel (String [] labels);
String [] getLabel ();
```

The indexed methods should check array bounds and throw `java.lang.Array-IndexOutOfBoundsException` if the index is outside those bounds.

Other property types include bound properties and constrained properties. A bound property sends a notification of a change in value to other Beans when a property change occurs. A bound property raises an event when a change is made.

A bound property sends a notification that a change has been made. The notification process occurs by *binding* the property type to a `PropertyChangeListener` event listener. A Bean that wishes to notify itself, some other Bean, or the Bean container tool will include a pair of multicast event listener registration methods:

```
public void addPropertyChangeListener (PropertyChangeListener l);
public void removePropertyChangeListener (PropertyChangeListener l);
```

The `java.beans` package provides a class that supports bound properties. This class may be used to manage the listener list. For example:

```
private PropertyChangeSupport changes = new
PropertyChangeSupport(this);

public void setFillColor (Color newColor) {
  Color oldColor = currColor;
  currColor = newColor;
  changes.firePropertyChange ("color", oldColor, newColor);
  ...
}
```

The `firePropertyChange()` method will call the `propertyChange()` method on the object that implements the `PropertyChangeListener` interface. Listening for property change events allows multiple beans to maintain a common value, like their background color. When one changes, the change propagates to the others automatically, if each was registered as a `PropertyChangeListener`.

Constrained properties are validated by anyone interested when the property changes and rejected if the change is inappropriate. The user or developer is notified of a rejected property through an exception. For example:

```
public Dimension getSize () {
    return currSize;
}
public void setSize (Dimension d)
    throws SizeChangeRejectedException (){
    // Check the size and throw an exception
    // if it exceeds some preset value
    ...
}
```

Constrained properties use the `VetoableChangeListener` interface to validate changes. These are implemented in the Bean by including a pair of add/remove methods:

```
public void addVetoableChangeListener (VetoableChangeListener v);
public void removeVetoableChangeListener (VetoableChangeListener v);
```

Of course, the Bean property method should fire an event before the property is changed. For example:

```
private VetoableChangeSupport vetos = new VetoableChangeSupport(this);

public void setSize (Dimension newSize)
        throws PropertyVetoException {
    Dimension oldSize = currSize;
    vetos.fireVetoableChange ("size", oldSize, newSize);
    // No one vetoed, make the change
    currSize = newSize;
    changes.firePropertyChange ("size", oldSize, newSize);
    ...
}
```

NOTE   The `setSize()` method above shows size as both a constrained and bound property. Normally, constrained properties are bound. If they were not, someone who was listening with a `VetoableChangeListener` would not know if another listener vetoed the change. By listening for both, you can veto the change if the new value is inappropriate or act on the new value if nobody vetoed the change.

Bean Methods

Bean methods are the operations that are called from other components (that have an instance of the Bean), from the container, or from a scripting environment. Bean methods may be exported by making them public; this makes it possible to view the methods with a builder tool using Java introspection (more on this later).

Methods are used to set and get properties and fire and catch events. Bean methods may be either public or not. Methods that are private, protected, or friendly may not be visible from builder tools.

Bean Storage

Beans are stored in a JAR (Java Archive) format. Essentially, JAR files are Zip-formatted archive files with an optional component called a manifest file that can contain additional information about the contents of the JAR file.

Applications that use Beans are not required by the JavaBeans Specification to use JAR files or even to store beans as JAR files; however, the specification does propose that Beans should be shipped as JAR files initially.

> **TIP**
>
> For more information about Bean storage, see Chapter 11, "Packaging," of the Java-Beans Specification, version 1.01 and the JAR HTML file included in with the Beans Development Kit, under <installation directory>/doc/jar.html.

Inspecting and Customizing Beans

JavaBeans are received as pieces of software from vendors or developed internally within companies. A JavaBean is likely to be developed as a generic component; that is, designed to be customized by the developer at application creation time. This happens through two Java technologies that are maturing with the JavaBeans API:

- The Java Reflection API, a set of classes that is used to look into a class file and discover the properties (variables) and methods of the class

- The Java Serialization API, which is used to create a permanent storage of a class, including its current state

These two technologies are used to allow Beans to be investigated and discovered by a builder tool, then modified and stored for a particular application use.

The Bean Introspection Process

The JavaBean introspection process exposes the properties, methods, and events of a Bean. The introspection process is actually quite rote. Bean classes are assumed to have properties if there are methods that either set or get a property type:

```
public <PropertyType> get<PropertyName> ();
public void set<PropertyName> (<PropertyType p>);
```

If only one of the `get`/`set` methods is discovered, then `PropertyName` is determined to be read-only or write-only.

Properties that are boolean—that is, return a `boolean` type—may also have a `boolean` method:

```
public boolean is<PropertyName> ();
```

Indexed properties are also discovered when the method signatures include:

```
public <PropertyElement> get<PropertyName> (int a);
public <PropertyElement>[] get<PropertyName> ();
public void set<PropertyName> (int a, <PropertyElement> b);
public void set<PropertyName> (<PropertyElement> b[]);
```

Events are discovered by a pair of `add`/`remove` event methods. These are assumed to begin with `add` and `remove` and take an `<EventListenerType>` argument that extends the `java.util.EventListener` interface, where the type name ends with `Listener`. For example:

```
public void add<EventListenerType> (<EventListenerType> a);
public void remove<EventListenerType> (<EventListenerType> a);
```

Methods are discovered if the method access is public. This includes all of the property and event methods.

The *BeanInfo* Interface

The JavaBean API also provides an explicit interface to allow Bean designers to expose the properties, events, methods, and any global information about a Bean. A Bean vendor provides a `BeanInfo` interface by supplying a class that extends the `BeanInfo` interface and appends `BeanInfo` to the class name:

```
public class MyBeanBeanInfo implements java.util.BeanInfo {…
```

The `BeanInfo` interface provides a series of methods to access Bean information, but a Bean developer can also include private description files that the

`BeanInfo` class uses to define Bean information. By default, a `BeanInfo` object is created when introspection is run on the Bean.

The process follows these steps to discover the inner workings of a Bean:

- Walk the class and superclass chain of each target class.

- Look for a `BeanInfo` class name (the class name with `BeanInfo` appended to the end of the name).

- Use low-level reflection to study the class and create a `BeanInfo` object with the results.

TIP   Normally, you do not implement the `BeanInfo` interface directly; instead, you subclass `SimpleBeanInfo` and customize.

Bean Persistence

Java Beans are components that rely on state. When a Bean receives a state change, the Bean designer may desire to store, or *persist,* the changed state. State changes may occur as the result of some action, either during run time or development.

Beans may be stored in one of two ways: automatically through the Java Serialization mechanism; or through a custom externalization stream mechanism that will allow the Bean object complete control over the writing of its state, including the ability to mimic arbitrary existing data formats.

Normally, a Bean will store the parts of its internal state that would be used to define the Bean on re-creation. Typically, these are the Bean's look and feel and behavior. A Bean that references other Beans may wish to store these references, but this activity is inherently dangerous because it assumes the *referenced* Beans are also saved. Instead, references to other Beans should be rebuilt during the re-creation process. In this way, Beans may mark variables as `transient` to specify that the reference is volatile and will be rebuilt as necessary.

The Beans Development Kit (BDK)

The BDK is a pure Java application that allows Java developers to test reusable components that use the Bean event model. The BDK is dependent only on the 1.1

release of the JDK, and it is available for both Solaris Unix and Win32 platforms, as well as for a nonspecific platform version. The BDK is not intended as a commercial product; instead, the BDK provides a first look at Beans: how they are constructed and how they are applied through a simple and easy-to-use builder application.

Installing the BDK

The BDK is a complete system and contains source code for all of the applications, examples, and documentation. The BDK also contains a sample Bean builder and customizer application called BeanBox.

The month and year of release designate the BDK version. Currently, in the March '98 release, the BDK 1.0 is downloaded as either a Bourne shell executable (BDKMar98.bin) for Solaris Unix, a Win32 exe file (BDKMar98.exe) for Windows 95 and NT systems, or a ZIP file (BDKMar98.zip) for everything else. For Solaris Unix, the BDK is unpacked by running the shell executable:

```
% sh BDKMar98.bin
```

For Win32 systems the BDK is installed by copying the BDKMar98.exe file into a folder and double-clicking on it.

For other systems, it is a little more complicated. Just follow the directions provided when you download the BDK.

Both installations ask the user to agree to the terms of the distribution license agreement and then create a bdk directory that contains the following subdirectories:

Apis   Contains the source code for the Bean API

Beanbox   Contains the sample Bean builder tool, BeanBox

Demo   Stores the sample Beans in the BeanBox

Doc   Contains HTML files that describe the Bean API, the BeanBox, and examples

Jars   Holds the JAR files of the sample Beans that the BeanBox application will read and load

To use the BDK, the JDK 1.1 must also be loaded, and you run the run.bat or run.sh scripts from the beanbox directory. Under Windows 95 / NT, the BDK BeanBox is also available from the Start menu.

Using the BDK BeanBox

The BDK BeanBox application (located in the beanbox directory under the beans installation directory) is a simple test container that allows you to work with Bean components as follows:

- Drop Beans onto a composition window
- Resize and move Beans
- Alter Beans with property sheets
- Customize Beans with a customizer application
- Connect Beans together
- Save Beans through serialization
- Make Applets from current connections
- Restore Beans

You can also add new Beans to the BeanBox and then use existing components to create simple applications.

Figure 22.3 shows the BeanBox composition window (center), ToolBox palette (left), and PropertySheet window (right). The ToolBox palette displays the Beans that are available to be dropped onto the composition window. When a Bean is selected, the PropertySheet window displays the properties of the Bean that are available for editing.

To place a Bean in the composition window, select the Bean from the Bean's icon or name on the ToolBox palette, then click the mouse where the center of the Bean should go. The Bean is then drawn onto the composition window within a black-and-white–hashed boundary, as shown in Figure 22.4.

The File menu in the BeanBox composition window allows the current composition to be saved, cleared, or exited. The Load option on the File menu is used to restore the state of a saved composition. The LoadJar options allows you to extend the component palette. The MakeApplet option is for converting the current Bean-Box contents into an applet.

The Edit menu is used to change the currently selected Bean (or the composition window if no Bean is selected). The Edit menu includes Cut, Copy, and Paste options for selected Beans. Depending on the Bean selected, the Edit menu will also list the Events option, which allows you to "connect" Beans together.

FIGURE 22.3:

The BeanBox application

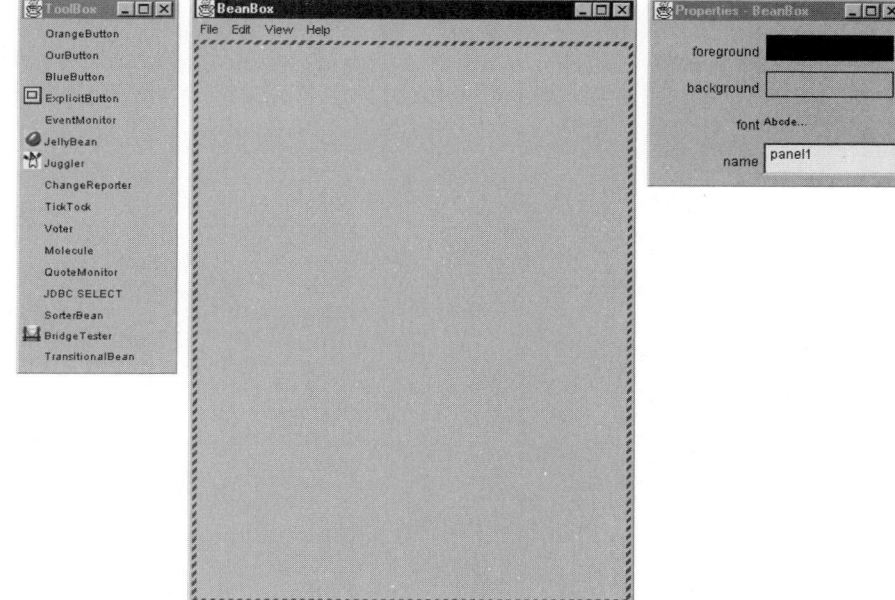

FIGURE 22.4:

A Bean in the BeanBox window

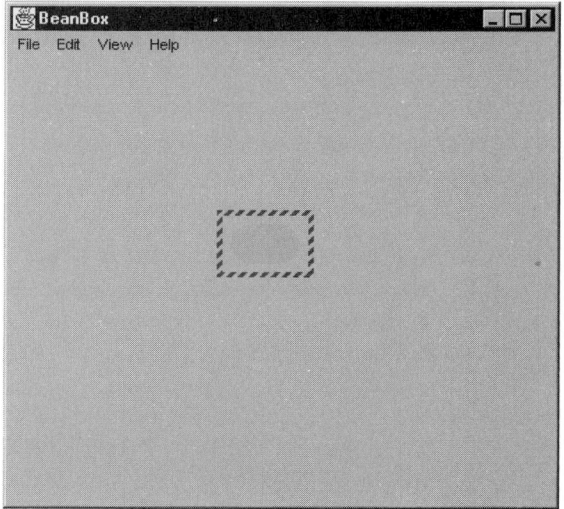

The Sample Beans

The BeanBox comes with a set of 16 sample Beans. Each of these has a different function and provides an example of various aspects of the JavaBeans API. The Beans provided with the BeanBox are listed in the ToolBox palette and described in Table 22.1.

T A B L E 2 2 . 1 : Sample Beans in the BeanBox

Bean	Description
OurButton	A subclass of a `java.awt.Canvas`. This Bean is the simplest button GUI component. When clicked, it will send a standard AWT `actionPerformed` method. OurButton exposes four properties (`label`, `fontSize`, `largeFont`, and `debug`) in addition to the standard `java.awt.Component` properties. These properties illustrate the use of getter/setter methods for `String`, `int`, Font class, and boolean parameter types.
ExplicitButton	A simple subclass of the OurButton Bean, which illustrates the effect that a `BeanInfo` class can have. The `ExplicitButtonBeanInfo` class includes a `PropertyDescriptor` method that defines default values for the `label`, `fontSize`, `largeFont`, and `debug` parameters. The `ExplicitButtonBean-Info` class also illustrates how to define icons that will appear to the left of the Bean name in the ToolBox palette and makes use of a simple `customizer` class, the `OurButtonCustomizer` class. This `customizer` appears in the Edit menu when this Bean is selected and allows the developer to edit the button label.
OrangeButton BlueButton	Specific instances of ExplicitButton with different background colors. These are NOT subclasses. These are saved (serialized) and restored from a `.ser` file with the background property set.
JellyBean	A simple visual component that draws a colored oval "jelly bean." This Bean illustrates the use of bound and constrained properties. The `color` property is a bound component and notifies the JellyBean when a change is made to the component. The `priceInCents` property is an example of a constrained property.
Juggler	Represents a threaded animation component that may be started and stopped by connecting a button-push event from an ExplicitButton or OurButton to the `start` and `stop` event methods supported by the Juggler Bean.
Voter	Designed to handle a `vetoableChange` event. By default, the Bean will reject all change requests (it is initially set to NO), but change requests will be accepted if the `vetoAll` property is set to `false`.

Continued on next page

TABLE 22.1 CONTINUED: Sample Beans in the BeanBox

Bean	Description
ChangeReporter	A `TextField` component that can be used to display `PropertyChange` events.
EventMonitor	A `TextArea` component that can be told to listen to all events of a particular bean. The component dynamically determines the events of a bean and generates code accordingly.
SorterBean	A serialized applet that accepts "BubbleSort", "QSort", or "BidirBubbleSort" as possible sorting algorithms.
Molecule	Similar to Juggler in concept. The Bean displays a 3-D representation of a molecule and accepts mouse input to rotate the molecule. It is also possible to rotate the molecule by attaching buttons to the `rotateX()` and `rotateY()` methods.
QuoteMonitor	Uses Remote Method Invocation (RMI) to contact a remote (or local) quote server and request a real or imaginary stock quote value. The RMI server is started by changing directories to the **demo** directory and executing **gnumake -f quote, gmk run &** on Solaris Unix or **start nmake -f quote,mk run** from a DOS prompt on a Win32 system.
JDBC Select	Uses the JDBC API to connect to a database at a specified URL and issue a select statement. It is complex and requires its own `customizer` to configure the JDBC URL string, database username, and password.
BridgeTester	Provides a set of property types and events that may be used to test other Bean components.
TransitionalBean	TransitionalBean uses the JDK 1.0.2 event model and will work with both JDK 1.1 and JDK 1.0.2.
TickTock	A nonvisual bean that sends PropertyChangeEvents at regular intervals.

Connecting Beans

You can connect Beans visually in the BeanBox tool. Figure 22.5 shows the Juggler Bean with two ExplicitButton Beans. The next step in making a simple animation application is to connect one of the buttons to the `start()` event method on the Juggler Bean and connect the other to a `stop()` event method.

After selecting one of the ExplicitButton Beans, you would choose Events from the Edit menu, then button push, then actionPerformed. This procedure is shown in Figure 22.6.

FIGURE 22.5:

The Juggler application

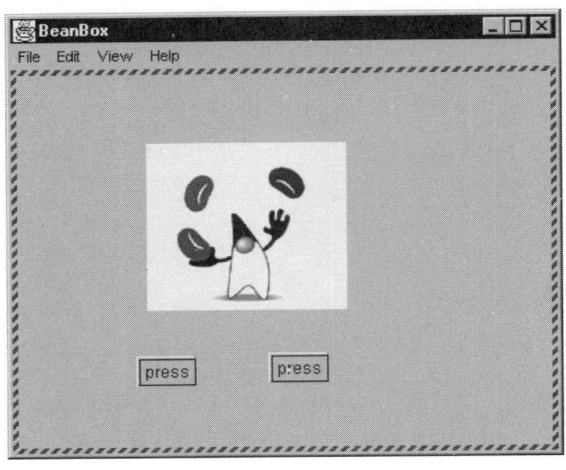

FIGURE 22.6:

Selecting the action-
Performed event

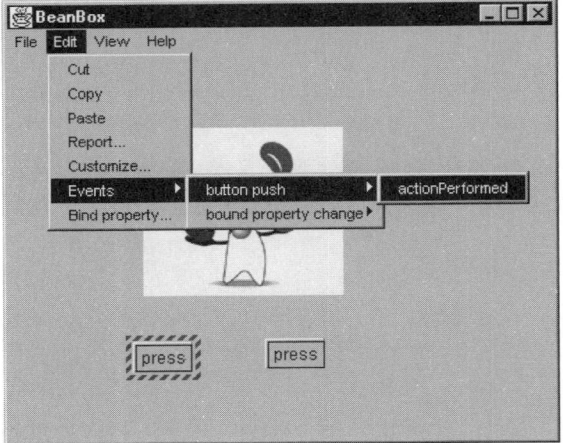

After this event is selected, the BeanBox will draw a rubber-banding line from the ExplicitButton Bean. This line illustrates the event source. The event target (listener) is selected by clicking on the Bean that the event source should go to. In this case, the Juggler Bean will receive an actionPerformed event. The Juggler Bean supports two methods that can receive an actionPerformed event (ActionEvent): startJuggling() and stopJuggling(). These appear in an EventTargetDialog pop-up window with other methods that accept no parameters, as shown in Figure 22.7.

FIGURE 22.7:

The EventTargetDialog
pop-up window for Juggler

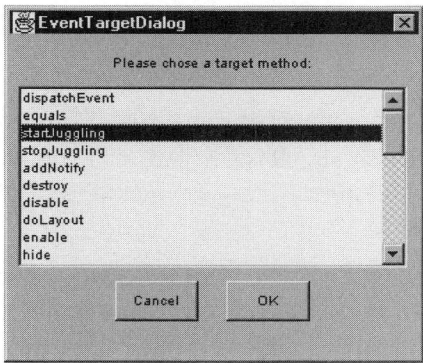

Selecting the startJuggling() method will connect the ExplicitButton's action-Performed event to the startJuggling() method of the Juggler Bean. The two Beans are now connected. Clicking the ExplicitButton with the mouse will send the event to the Juggler Bean, and the Bean will begin the animation (had it been stopped). To connect the other ExplicitButton to the Juggler stopJuggling() method, the steps above are repeated, and the stopJuggling() method is selected. The application is now completely functional after just a few mouse clicks. To complete the application, use the Property Sheet to label the two ExplicitButtons Start and Stop to indicate what actions they will have on the Juggler Bean.

Saving and Restoring Bean Applications

You can save Bean applications created in the BeanBox in their current state (including running or stopped, as in the case of the Juggler application) by selecting the Save option from the File menu. This opens a dialog box in which you can specify the name of the file to which the current set of Beans in the composition window is saved. To restore the application, use the File menu's Load option.

The BeanBox is not meant to be a production bean development tool for commercial use. It is just meant to provide a testing environment for your beans. For more serious JavaBeans development, look at Borland's JBuilder, IBM's VisualAge for Java, and Symantec's Visual Café for Java environments.

- The Clear and Load options on the File menu will clear the current set of Beans in the composition window without any warning, even if they are not already saved.

- The Save option on the File menu will not ask if you want to overwrite any current Bean application.

Creating a New Bean

The BDK also provides a means for adding new Beans to the BeanBox and testing them. The example presented here illustrates the process.

In the example, the new Bean will emulate the operation of a traffic signal light. The traffic signal is a rectangular component with three colored circles: red, yellow, and green. These are meant to emulate the functions of a real-life traffic signal: stop, slow, and go.

The traffic component will respond to a signal from a Walk button to cycle between its current state (either red or green; yellow is a transient state) to allow someone to cross the street. For simplicity, the component will be represented by a two-dimensional rectangle, as shown below.

This component is a visual component, so it will need to subclass from an AWT component. In addition to responding to a signal from the Walk button, the component should signal or support a second traffic light slave that would appear at a four-way intersection.

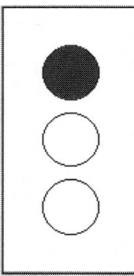

The TrafficLight Bean

The BDK provides a directory where it stores the example source code and a set of make files that are used to create the JAR files that the BeanBox requires. This directory is just below the installation directory of the BDK, in a directory named demo.

This directory contains the GNU make and Microsoft nmake for the sample Beans. For simplicity, the directory containing TrafficLight, called tlight, should be created in this location. Using this directory path and structure makes it possible to copy one of the existing make files in the BDK demo directory.

The TrafficLight Bean subclasses a java.awt.Canvas component. TrafficLight exposes two properties: defaultLight, which is a String representing the starting color of the light in its resting state; and a **boolean debug** property, which may be turned on or off through a property sheet in order to see the result of events as they are passed to and from the TrafficLight component.

Here is the source code for the TrafficLight component:

```
package sunw.demo.tlight;

import java.awt.*;
import java.awt.event.*;
import java.awt.image.*;
import java.beans.*;

// A Simple bean that represents a traffic light component

public class TrafficLight extends Canvas implements Runnable {

  private ActionListener l = null;

  private Thread me = null;

  private String defaultLight = "RED";
  private String currLight = defaultLight;

  private boolean debug = false;

  // Set the size of the Bean display
  public TrafficLight () {
    setSize (100, 200);
  }

  // Turn debugging on/off
  public void setDebugging (boolean state) {
    debug = state;
  }

  public boolean getDebugging () {
    return debug;
  }

  // Methods for get/set of the default light state
  public synchronized String getDefaultLightState () {
```

```
      return defaultLight;
}

public void setDefaultLightState (String state) {
  defaultLight = state;
  currLight = state;
  repaint();
}

// Display the current traffic light state
public void paint (Graphics g) {

  // Put a black border around it
  g.setColor (Color.black);
  g.drawRect (1, 1, 98, 198);

  // Paint the outline of the traffic light
  g.setColor (Color.white);
  g.fillRect (2, 2, 96, 196);

  // Paint the outline of the lights
  g.setColor (Color.black);
  g.drawOval (30, 30, 40, 40);
  g.drawOval (30, 80, 40, 40);
  g.drawOval (30, 130, 40, 40);

  // Debug
  if (debug) {
    System.out.println
        ("Current light state is: " + currLight);
  }

  // Which light is on?
  if (currLight.equals("RED")) {
    g.setColor (Color.red);
    g.fillOval (30, 30, 40, 40);
  } else {
    if (currLight.equals("YELLOW")) {
      g.setColor (Color.yellow);
      g.fillOval (30, 80, 40, 40);
    } else   {
```

```java
      if (currLight.equals("GREEN")) {
        g.setColor (Color.green);
        g.fillOval (30, 130, 40, 40);
      }
    }
  }
}

// Send a message to the light to start a cycle
public void start (ActionEvent x) {
  // Debug
  if (debug) {
    System.out.println ("Got a start Event!");
  }
  startCycle ();
}

// Start a light cycle
private synchronized void startCycle () {
  // Don't bother unless there is no cycle running already
  if (me == null) {
    me = new Thread (this);
    me.start ();
  }
}

// The run method
public void run () {
  // Debug
  if (debug) {
    System.out.println ("Started cycle");
  }

  while (me != null) {
    try {
      me.sleep (3000);
     } catch (InterruptedException e) {
    }

    // Get the current light state
    if (currLight.equals ("RED")) {
      // Cycle to green
```

```
          currLight = "GREEN";
          fireAction(currLight);
        } else {
          if (currLight.equals("GREEN")) {
            // Cycle through yellow to red
            currLight = "YELLOW";
          } else {
            // Otherwise, we are at YELLOW,
            // so cycle to RED
            currLight = "RED";
            fireAction(currLight);
          }
        }
        repaint ();
        // Break the cycle when the default state is reached
        if (currLight == defaultLight) {
          me = null;
        }
      }
    }
  }

  // Get an event that indicates a light
  // Change from another light
  // In which case, we will act as slave
  public void lightChange (ActionEvent x) {
    // Check the state of this event
    String command = x.getActionCommand();
    // Debug
    if (debug) {
      System.out.println ("Received event from traffic light: "
        + defaultLight + " command: go to " + command);
    }

    // If the other light went red, then check our default
    if (command.equals ("RED")) {
      if (currLight.equals ("GREEN")) {
        // ok, do nothing
      } else {
        // Cycle
        currLight = "GREEN";
        repaint ();
      }
```

```
      } else {
        if (command.equals ("GREEN")) {
          if (currLight.equals ("RED")) {
            // ok, do nothing
          } else {
            // Cycle
            currLight = "YELLOW";
            repaint ();
            try {
              Thread.sleep (3000);
            } catch (InterruptedException e) {
            }
            currLight = "RED";
            repaint ();
          }
        }
      }
    }

    // The fireAction method sends an event to the
    // slave TrafficLight to tell it we are changing
    // state
    public void fireAction (String s) {
      // Debug
      if (debug) {
        System.out.println ("Firing action event");
      }
      if (l != null) {
        ActionEvent actionEvt = new ActionEvent(this, 0, s);
        l.actionPerformed(actionEvt);
      }
    }

    // List ourselves as the source of an event
    // Just use Action for now...
    public void addActionListener (ActionListener l)
        throws java.util.TooManyListenersException {
      // Debug
      if (debug) {
        System.out.println ("Registering a listener");
      }
```

```
    // Is there an event listener already?
    if (this.l != null) {
      throw new java.util.TooManyListenersException ();
    }
    this.l = l;
  }

  public void removeActionListener (ActionListener l) {
    l = null;
  }
}
```

The TrafficLight component uses a pair of set/get methods to expose the Debugging and DefaultLightState properties. The paint() method for the component paints a white rectangle and three empty circles to indicate the red, yellow, and green lights for the TrafficLight Bean.

Public methods that take an ActionEvent argument may be connected to an actionPerformed event (like the Juggler Bean example discussed in the previous section). The TrafficLight Bean supports two such methods: a start() method that calls a private startCycle() method which, in turn, creates a thread and begins the cycle of changing the TrafficLight from its current state to its opposite state and back again. This method is intended to support the Walk button.

The lightChange() method is used to support a second traffic light slave. This method is used to connect two TrafficLight Beans. When one light is cycling, the other is notified through an event that the light should change. For example, if the first traffic light changes from green to red, then the second light (on the other intersection) will change from red to green.

The fireAction() method is used to notify another TrafficLight Bean that is registered as an ActionListener. Note that the TrafficLight Bean is an example of a unicast event source and therefore does not support more than a four-way intersection. The source code for the TrafficLight Bean is included on the CD-ROM accompanying this book.

The TrafficLight BeanInfo

To improve the bean user's experience with the TrafficLight Bean, we'll set up a specialized property editor for the color of the light. Since the light can only have three values (the strings RED, YELLOW, and GREEN), this simply involves creating an array of the possible string values and passing it back from the getTags()

method of a subclass of `PropertyEditorSupport`. What we are creating is what is called a property editor, as it allows you to specialize the editing of one of the bean's properties.

```
package sunw.demo.tlight;

import java.beans.*;
public class LightColorEditor extends PropertyEditorSupport {
  public String[] getTags() {
    String values[] = {
      "RED",
      "YELLOW",
      "GREEN" };
    return values;
  }
}
```

To use the property editor, you need to create a BeanInfo class for the Traffic-Light bean. This involves setting up the property descriptor for the `default-LightState` property of the bean.

```
package sunw.demo.tlight;

import java.beans.*;
public class TrafficLightBeanInfo extends SimpleBeanInfo {
  public PropertyDescriptor[] getPropertyDescriptors() {
    try {
      PropertyDescriptor pd =
        new PropertyDescriptor("defaultLightState", TrafficLight.class);
      pd.setPropertyEditorClass(LightColorEditor.class);
      PropertyDescriptor result[] = { pd };
      return result;
    } catch (Exception e) {
      System.err.println("Unexpected exception: " + e);
      return null;
    }
  }
}
```

Notice that with both a property editor and the BeanInfo, neither modifies the original TrafficLight bean. These classes are strictly necessary at design time, when someone is working with the bean in a builder tool. Once the final application has been created, these classes are unnecessary to ship to the end user.

Compiling the TrafficLight Bean and BeanInfo   The BDK provides a set of make files that make it easier to compile Bean components and place them in the appropriate classes directory, as well as putting them into JAR files that the BeanBox can read.

The following listing is an example of a GNU make file copied and modified from one of the existing make files in the demo directory below the installation directory of the BDK.

```
CLASSFILES= \
    sunw/demo/tlight/TrafficLight.class \
    sunw/demo/tlight/LightColorEditor.class \
    sunw/demo/tlight/TrafficLightBeanInfo.class

#GIFFILES= \
#   sunw/demo/tlight/TrafficLightIcon.gif

JARFILE= ../jars/tlight.jar

all: $(JARFILE)

# Create a JAR file with a suitable manifest.

$(JARFILE): $(CLASSFILES) $(GIFFILES)
    echo "Manifest-Version: 1.0" > manifest.tmp
    echo "" >> manifest.tmp
    echo "Name: sunw/demo/tlight/TrafficLight.class" >> manifest.tmp
    echo "Java-Bean: True" >> manifest.tmp
    jar cfm $(JARFILE) manifest.tmp sunw/demo/tlight/*.class $(GIFFILES)
        @/bin/rm manifest.tmp

%.class: %.java
    export CLASSPATH; CLASSPATH=../classes:.; \
    javac $<

clean:
    /bin/rm -f sunw/demo/tlight/*.class
    /bin/rm -f $(JARFILE)
```

NOTE   For a Win32 system, the make file for TrafficLight should be a copy of one of the .mk files, and the nmake utility is used to compile the make file.

To compile and create a JAR file (under Solaris Unix) the make file is compiled with gnumake, a GNU make utility:

```
% cd Beans/demo
% gnumake tlight.gmk
```

Once compiled correctly, the make file will create a manifest file for the Traffic-Light.class file and create an appropriate JAR file. The new JAR file is then copied into the jars directory, where the BeanBox can read it.

Inserting the New Bean into the BeanBox

When the BeanBox is started through its make file, the BeanBox application will load the JAR files that are located in the jars directory. To add the tlight JAR file created by the make file above, the BeanBox application is started through the make file:

```
%cd beans/beanbox
%gnumake run
```

> **NOTE**   For a Win32 system, the BeanBox will reload the JAR files with the command nmake run.

This forces the BeanBox to reload the JAR files in the jars directory and re-create the ToolBox palette with the TrafficLight component, as shown in Figure 22.8.

FIGURE 22.8:

The ToolBox with the TrafficLight Bean

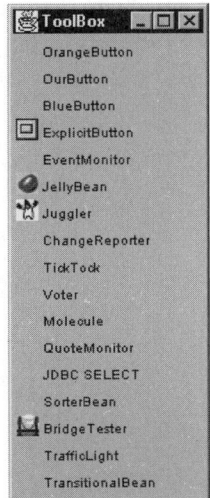

Testing the New Bean

To test the TrafficLight Bean, two instances of the new Bean and one instance of an ExplicitButton (for the Walk signal) are placed in the composition window, as shown in Figure 22.9.

FIGURE 22.9:

Two instances of the TrafficLight Bean and an ExplicitButton in the composition window

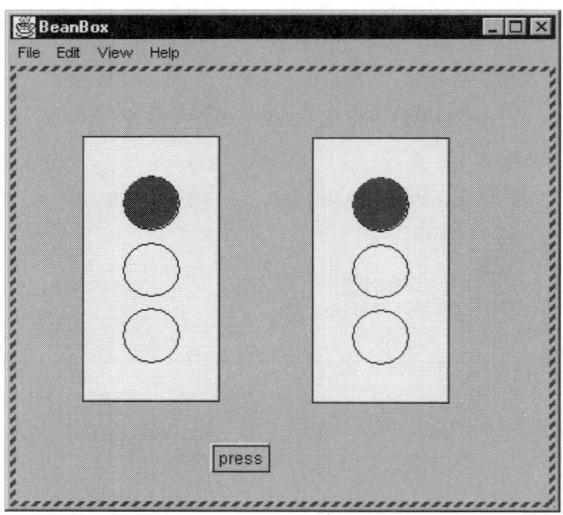

Using the Edit menu's Event item, the ExplicitButton `actionPerformed` event is connected to the `start()` event method of the first TrafficLight Bean. When the user presses the mouse button, the TrafficLight Bean will cycle to green, yellow, and then back to red (with a three-second delay between light changes).

Both TrafficLight Beans are in a RED state by default, so the second Bean's `defaultLightState` is changed to GREEN by selecting the **GREEN** value in the PropertySheet window for the second Bean.

FIGURE 22.10:

The traffic light property editor

Next, the first traffic light is connected to the second traffic light through an `actionPerformed` method to the second traffic light's `lightChange()` method.

This is done by repeating the steps for connecting the ExplicitButton. As a final step, the label of the ExplicitButton is changed from Press to Walk, as shown in Figure 22.11.

FIGURE 22.11:

The completed traffic light application

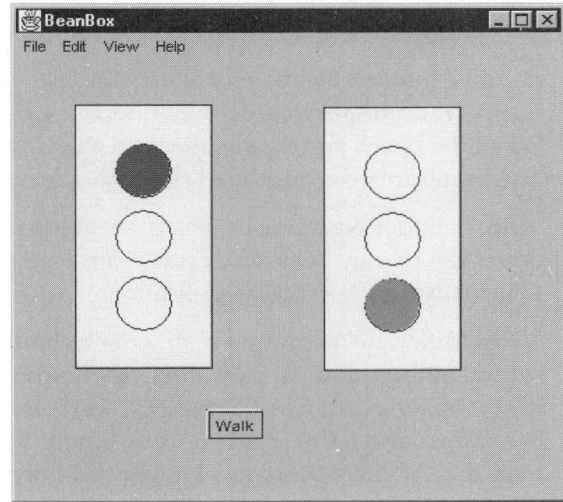

When the Walk button is clicked with the mouse, the first traffic light sends a signal to the second light to change and then begins its own change cycle. The second light changes from green to yellow to red, as the first traffic light changes from red to green, then to yellow, and finally to red.

NOTE   This section just scratches the surface of JavaBeans. For an even more in-depth look at JavaBeans, you may want to read Sybex's *Mastering JavaBeans*.

Integrating Beans in Other Technologies

Besides being reusable software components, Beans will also allow developers to integrate their code with other technologies, including access to Microsoft's ActiveX API, Lotus' InfoBus technology, and Netscape's JavaScript and Live-Connect technologies.

JavaBeans allow developers to create controls for ActiveX through COM events. The result is that the Bean will run in the ActiveX environment without any knowledge of the underlying environment and without needing to create any C++ code or tie the Bean development into any Microsoft tools. This requires the use of the JavaBeans Bridge for ActiveX available from `http://java.sun.com/beans/software/bridge/`.

Lotus' InfoBus technology allows the exchange of data between JavaBeans through additional well-defined interfaces, besides the Bean standard parts. When the Beans participate, they can share data easily without worry of protocol. The Beans are just considered producers or consumers of data on the InfoBus.

Beans under Netscape browsers are able to fire events to JavaScript, and JavaScript can change Bean properties. Netscape's Visual JavaScript tool allows you to visually build up these applications.

In addition to integration with other technologies, the JavaBean specification has several authors and partners from other industries, including Borland (JBuilder), IBM (VisualAge for Java), Sybase (PowerJ), Sun (Java Workshop and Java Studio), Symantec (Visual Café for Java), and others. These partners have created builder tools that facilitate Bean development and deployment.

Summary

The Java development environment continues to add more functionality and features. The Java language has gone from being an interesting departure from C++ to a serious multi-platform development language. The JavaBeans capabilities have moved Java into a next-generation tool, allowing developers to concentrate on writing code that is cross-platform and truly reusable.

CHAPTER

TWENTY-THREE

23

Java Servlets

- Advantages of servlets

- Servlet classes and methods

- Java Web Server configuration for servlets

- Server-side includes

- Communication between servlets

This chapter discusses the Servlet API and the origin of the servlet as an improved form of CGI (Common Gateway Interface) programming. The examples demonstrate the use of servlets in an HTTP environment and the key servlet mechanisms are introduced.

Available as part of the Servlet Development Kit, the Servlet API is considered a Standard Extension Package, not a Core API. Standard extensions are packages defined by Sun that are not part of the Core API. They belong to packages under the javax.* package hierarchy, instead of the java.* hierarchy. Any third-party provider can create the extension package for their system and programs will work everywhere the extension package is present.

Although, as programmers, you will be mainly concerned with the techniques for developing servlets, this chapter also covers some of the basic elements of the Java Web Server configuration. This knowledge will allow you to set up the server for servlet support and install and try out the examples. Servlets are to a Web server what applets are to the browser.

NOTE

> The Java Web Server is a commercial product. You can evaluate it for free for 30 days. After 30 days, it is free for non-commercial use, but commercial users will have to purchase it.

The Java Web Server, formerly known as Jeeves, is Sun's own Web server. The Java Web Server is just a part of a larger framework intended to provide you with a Web server and the tools to build customized network servers for any Internet or intranet client-server system.

NOTE

> Using servlets is not limited to the Java Web Server. All the major Web servers support servlets.

In addition to the fundamental facilities of servlets and the supporting Web server configuration, this chapter also discusses the server-side include (SSI) mechanism as it applies to servlets, as well as a number of techniques for arranging communication between servlets.

CGI Limitations

When HTML and the World Wide Web were first invented, the content of each displayed page was essentially static. Each URL referred directly to either a fixed page or a fixed element of a page. To allow for the possibility of more interaction, and for pages tailored to an individual request, the CGI mechanism was introduced.

CGI allows a URL to contain a basic reference, not to a page of HTML but to a program. In addition to that basic reference, parameters to control the execution can also be passed from the browser into the CGI program.

Although CGI is quite simple to use, both from the user's and the server administrator's point of view, it has a number of weaknesses:

Low performance   Most CGI programs are written using interpreted languages such as Unix shell scripts or PERL. This is not a requirement of the CGI specification, but appears to be the popular option. Using compiled languages improves speed but tends to raise platform-dependency issues.

Startup time   CGI programs run as separate processes, which generally involves significant startup time. This overhead occurs each time that the program is invoked. The startup time is compounded if you are using an interpreter.

Poor inter-CGI communication   Because each invocation of a CGI program starts a separate process, communicating between invocations must usually be done via files; hence, it can be quite slow. Communicating between different CGI programs on the same server is similarly cumbersome.

Security   Some variations of CGI have suffered from significant security weaknesses. Even when more recent standards and relatively safe languages like PERL are used, the system does not have a basic security framework, but relies instead on a collection of ad hoc rules.

A number of enhancements have been made to CGI to address these limitations. FastCGI avoids the process-startup overhead by using persistent processes, but using FastCGI's interprocess communication mechanism is still slow. Some C language APIs allow for programs to run inside the server, but these APIs are platform- or server-dependent and difficult to secure. They also tend to be rather complex.

Another choice that you have now is to use a servlet. Servlets can do the things that CGI is used for, and they have many advantages over CGI scripts.

Introducing Servlets and the Java Web Server

Since the arrival of Java, applets have provided a mechanism for Web pages to have not just tailored information, but actual interactive and dynamic content. As you've learned, with an applet, the process is run on the browser's own machine. In general, this configuration is an advantage because it improves response time and reduces network bandwidth requirements. But this configuration might present problems if your program has either of these requirements:

Privileged access to server facilities   An applet generally does not have any special access to services and information on a server. Even the server that supplied the applet cannot, in the absence of something like a digital signature, distinguish between a request from an applet that it might want to trust and any other request. Hence, an applet cannot be granted the right to read, say, a database on the server unless full access to that database is given to any HTTP request.

Protection of proprietary algorithms   In a number of ways, Java's byte-code is easier to reverse-engineer than other machine languages. This is partly because it is difficult to generate obfuscated bytecodes; the demands of the bytecode verifier will reject as illegal many forms of code that are not straightforward. Because of this fact, a proprietary algorithm of significant value should generally not be entrusted to an applet.

NOTE   One other reason to use a servlet is if you are concerned about browser incompatibility. If you do not know what version of a browser your end user is running, you may not be able to take advantage of some of the latest Java capabilities. Therefore, you may need to move the execution of part of your program to the Web server.

If any of these considerations apply, a servlet might be the better choice. With a servlet approach, the server can grant full access to local facilities, such as databases, and trust that the servlet itself will control the amount and precise nature of access that is effectively afforded to external users. So, for example, the rate at which requests can be made could be limited, and the origin of requests can be monitored and verified. If a proprietary algorithm is built into a servlet, the code never passes beyond the boundaries of the server; only the produced results do. If the code is not passed to the client, it cannot be saved and decompiled.

A servlet and applet can be used as a pair to gain the benefits of servlets and the interactive nature of applets. This paired approach can also be used to provide optimization of the data stream, possibly involving actual compression and, if desired, encryption. The data streams can be optimized in many cases simply by appropriate use of the methods of the `GZIPInputStream` and `GZIPOutputStream` classes in the `java.util` package, or by using object serialization, which was covered in Chapter 19. Encryption is typically handled by classes such as `SSLSocket`, which implements a Secure Sockets Layer for use in a Java program.

NOTE   The *SSLSocket* class is part of the SSL Standard Extension not the Servlet Standard Extension. The SSL Standard Extension also provides support for HTTPS, which provides an HTTP connection over an SSL secured transport mechanism.

To accompany the introduction of the servlet standard, a new Web server has been produced. The Java Web Server is Sun's Web server, written in Java, which supports the use of servlets. It is not part of the JDK distribution, but you can download it from the Sun site: `http://jserv.java.sun.com`. Because Java Web Server is written in Java, it can be used on any Java-capable platform. It also provides the security reassurances of Java in a networked environment. Many other servers already provide support for this mechanism. For an up-to-date list of third-party server implementations, see `http://jserv.java.sun.com/products/java-server/servlets/environments.html`. The Java Web Server does include SSL support.

NOTE   Running servlets requires a degree of administrative effort. Early versions of the Java Web Server had very few administrative support tools, requiring that all configuration be done with a text editor. More recently, interactive GUI-based administration tools have been added. Other Web servers have their own configuration mechanisms, which are likely to be similar to the ones in Sun's Web server. Configuration for the Java Web Server is discussed in this chapter. If you will be using another type of Web server with your Java servlets, see the documentation for your system for configuration information.

Servlet Development Setup

Before creating any servlets, you need to tell the compiler where to locate the servlet classes. The classes are delivered with the Java Servlet Development Kit (JSDK); the specific directory name you use will depend on where you installed it. If you installed the JSDK in C:\JSDK2.0, then you would find these classes in the `jsdk.jar` file in the lib subdirectory, under the JSDK installation directory. The JAR includes the `javax.servlet`, `javax.servlet.http`, and `sun.servlet` packages, which will be explained shortly. The `servletrunner` program, from the bin directory, provides additional support as an appletviewer-like tool to test servlets. Sample servlets, including a tutorial, are also available in the doc and examples subdirectory.

> **TIP**
>
> For more information about the Java Extensions Framework, see the "Support for Extensions and Applications in the Java 1.2 Platform" document at `http://java.sun.com/products/jdk/1.2/docs/guide/extensions/spec.html`.

In order for the compiler to find the servlet package, you need to copy the `jsdk.jar` file to the `ext` directory, under the Java Runtime Environment. By default, this would be `jre\lib\ext`, under your JDK installation directory. Once copied, it is not necessary to alter the CLASSPATH environment variable.

> **NOTE**
>
> There is nothing in the JSDK that is specific to Java 1.2. You can use it with Java 1.1 with no problems.

The Servlet API

At a superficial level, a servlet is much like an applet. It does not run as an application or start at a static `main()` method; rather, it is loaded and an instance is created. When the instance exists, it is given an environment from which it can determine details, such as the parameters with which it has been invoked.

In an Applet class, the behavior is largely determined by a few methods, which are called by the browser. These methods are init(), start(), stop(), destroy(), and paint(). In a class implementing the Servlet interface, the same basic concept is used, but the particular set of interesting methods is slightly different.

When a class implementing the Servlet interface is created, its init(Servlet-Config) method is called. This closely parallels the life cycle of an applet and is intended to allow the servlet to initialize itself. The ServletConfig parameter provides access to the initialization parameters of the servlet and the Servlet-Context, as the following interface definition shows:

```
public interface ServletConfig {
    abstract public String getInitParameter(String name);
    abstract public Enumeration getInitParameterNames();
    abstract public ServletContext getServletContext();
}
```

WARNING   Don't forget the ServletConfig parameter to the init() method or your method will never be called.

A servlet does not need to become active or inactive in the way that an applet does when it moves in and out of the current page. Also, a servlet does not have a GUI of its own. The Servlet interface, therefore, does not define the start(), stop(), or paint() methods. The main behavior of the servlet is required in response to a new connection at the server, and that connection results in a call to the service() method of the servlet.

The service() method takes two parameters. The interfaces ServletRequest and ServletResponse define these parameters. These interfaces provide accessor methods that allow the servlet to examine its environment, determine how it has been executed, and then decide what request it has received and how to provide a proper response. In particular, the input and output streams that are connected to the calling program, quite possibly a browser client, are accessible through these parameters.

The basic Servlet interface implementer, GenericServlet, is not protocol-specific. However, because a large proportion of servlets are likely to use HTTP as the basis of their communication, a subclass of the GenericServlet class, the HttpServlet class, is provided to give additional support methods that are useful when handling this protocol. Most of the examples in this chapter use the HttpServlet class.

Two additional support interfaces are defined for use with the HttpServlet class: the HttpServletRequest interface and the HttpServletResponse interface. These interfaces extend the ServletRequest and ServletResponse interfaces and provide additional accessor method definitions for handling HTTP-specific aspects of a servlet's environment, such as the header information that forms the initial part of an HTTP transaction.

The information that may be read from an HttpServletRequest includes the details of the request, such as the path and query string, along with authorization type and header fields. The HttpServletResponse class supports sending HTTP-specific errors and also redirects.

A Simple Servlet Example

The following example demonstrates the working environment of an Http-Servlet object, reporting the values of significant parameters as supplied by the call it receives.

```java
import java.io.*;
import java.util.*;
import javax.servlet.*;
import javax.servlet.http.*;
public class HelloServlet extends HttpServlet {
  public void init(ServletConfig config) {
    System.out.println("HelloServlet got an init()!");
    File f = new File (System.getProperty ("user.dir"));
    f = new File(f.getAbsolutePath());
    System.out.println("HelloServlet current directory is " + f);
  }
  public void service(HttpServletRequest req,
                      HttpServletResponse resp) {
    try {
      resp.setContentType("text/html");
      PrintWriter out = resp.getWriter();
      resp.setStatus(HttpServletResponse.SC_OK);
      out.println ("<html>");
      out.println ("<head><title>Hello World</title></head>");
      out.println ("<body>");
      out.println ("<H1>Hello World!</H1>");
      out.println ("<H2>This servlet was invoked with:</H2>");
      out.println ("<dl>");
      Enumeration e = req.getHeaderNames();
```

```
      while (e.hasMoreElements()) {
        String name = (String)e.nextElement();
        out.println ("<dt>" + name + "</dt><dd>" +
          req.getHeader(name) + "</dd>");
      }
      out.println ("<dt>Request method:</dt><dd>" +
        req.getMethod() + "</dd>");
      out.println ("<dt>Translated Request path info:</dt><dd>" +
        req.getPathTranslated() + "</dd>");
      out.println ("<dt>Request query string:</dt><dd>" +
        req.getQueryString() + "</dd>");
      out.println ("</dl>");
      out.println ("</body></head></html>");
    } catch (IOException e) {
      // Ignore it. Let the client worry...
    }
  }
}
```

Running the Servlet

To run servlets, you need a Web server that supports them. Later this chapter describes the use of Sun's Java Web Server, but any other servlet-capable server will work. To run a servlet, follow this sequence of actions:

1. Start your Web server, if it is not already running.

2. Configure the server to install the servlet (the servlet must be installed in the Web server).

3. Start your Web browser.

4. Direct the browser to the particular URL that refers to the new servlet.

> **NOTE**   Some servers might require that you restart them after installing a new servlet, but this is not the case with Sun's server when using the Web-based interactive administration tools. If you have a server that requires restarting after a servlet is installed, you should perform step 2 before step 1 in the above list.

Thankfully, testing servlets doesn't require all that work. The JSDK include a program called `servletrunner` that allows you to have a mini-Web server for testing servlets. You can use `servletrunner` to test out several of the examples in this chapter. To use `servletrunner` to test the `HelloServlet`, run `servletrunner` with the `-d` option, and specify the full current directory name as the parameter. For example, if your working directory was `C:\Mastering Java\Ch23`, then execute the following command:

```
servletrunner -d "C:\Mastering Java\Ch23"
```

You will find the source code and bytecode files for this servlet on the CD-ROM. If you are using Sun's server and are unfamiliar with its configuration for running servlets, see the "Servlet Configuration" section later in this chapter. Once a Web server is running and has the servlet installed, direct your browser to this URL:

```
http://localhost:8080/servlet/HelloServlet?Hello+World
```

Notice that this assumes you have configured your server to use port 8080. This is the default for Sun's Web server and `servletrunner`, and it is a sensible choice in any case because it allows the server to run on Unix systems without requiring root privilege.

When the browser has loaded, the page should show a heading and several entries in a list. Figure 23.1 shows an example of the kind of output you can expect to see.

Changing the Query String

You can experiment with modifications to the URL. The first part, which describes the protocol, host, port, and path, cannot be changed. The parts after the query character (?) form the *query string*.

The query string is qualifying information that may be changed within certain restrictions. You should not put spaces or non-alphanumeric characters in this string, except for the plus symbol (+), which signifies a space. If you need to represent any other characters, you should find the appropriate ASCII code for the character, in hexadecimal, and use that with a percent symbol (%) as a prefix. For example, the percent symbol itself is represented as %25.

When you change the query string, observe that all the output, except for the last line, remains the same. If you omit the query string entirely and simply use the following URL:

```
http://localhost:8080/servlet/HelloServlet
```

the output reports the request query string as null, which results from attempting to convert a null reference to a `String` object in the servlet itself.

FIGURE 23.1:

Typical output from
HelloServlet

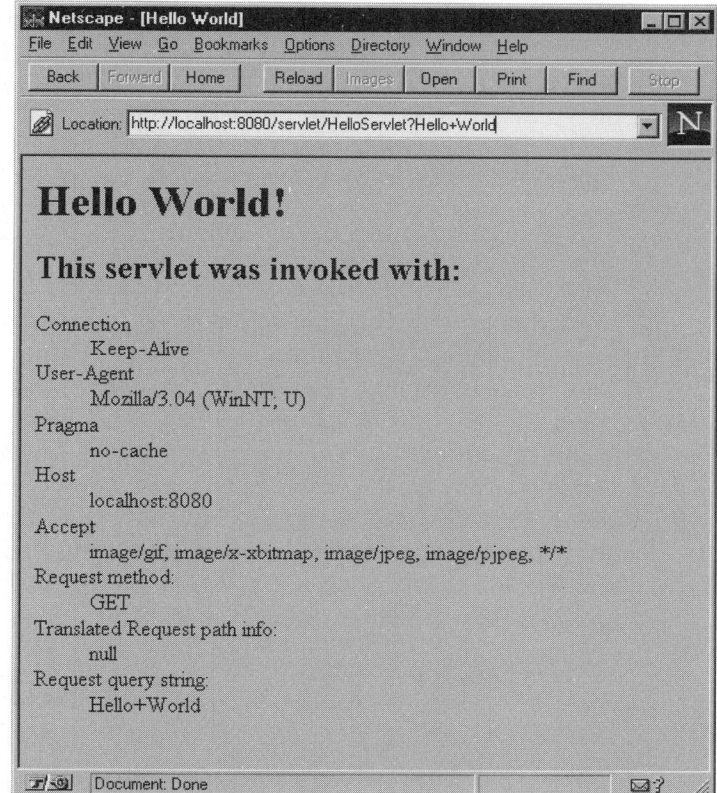

HelloServlet's Classes and Methods

The HelloServlet example simply extracts some of the available environment information, provided by the HttpServletRequest and HttpServletResponse objects, as the arguments to its service() method. HTML-formatted output is then returned to the caller via the output stream supplied by the server.

The HelloServlet class is a subclass of the HttpServlet class– rather than a direct subclass of the GenericServlet class–because a number of useful utility methods and definitions are provided by the HttpServlet class, and most servlets will use HTTP as their protocol. If you wish to write a servlet that uses some other—perhaps entirely proprietary—protocol, you should extend the GenericServlet class.

The Java Web Server is part of the much larger Server Toolkit. This kit allows you to build your own network server for arbitrary protocols, including ordinary client/server systems; it is not limited to HTTP and Web-related services. However, HTTP servlets provide good examples of the essence of any servlet and are the focus of this chapter. If you will be writing servlets for radically different services, see Chapter 20, which covers network programming. It describes other useful aspects of writing client/server systems with Java.

The GenericServlet class, or more precisely the Servlet interface, defines a method called service(), which takes two arguments that are objects that implement the ServletRequest and ServletResponse interfaces, respectively. The Http-Servlet class defines a new method called service() that takes different argument types. These two arguments are objects that implement the HttpServletRequest and HttpServletResponse interfaces, respectively. The new service() method therefore overloads the method name, rather than overriding it. Because the Web server thinks of the servlet simply as an object that implements the Servlet interface, and the Web server knows nothing about the HttpServlet class, it will call only the first service() method. In the HttpServlet class, this original service() servlet method is written to pass the call to the new service() method instead.

Inside a servlet, two streams are available for communication with the remote client. This example produces only a page of HTML; it does not read input from the client. Therefore, it requires only the output stream. In either a Servlet-Response object or—as is the case with an HttpServlet class like the Hello-Servlet example—an HttpServletResponse object, you can extract the output stream using either the getOutputStream() or getWriter() method. If you are implementing bi-directional communication, such as is required for the POST protocol, you will also need to use either the getInputStream() or getReader() method on the ServletRequest object.

The output from the servlet has two broad parts, which can be thought of as the status part and the content part. In the status part, this example specifies that the content type of its reply is text/html and the status is OK. Both of these operations use methods of the HttpServletResponse object. The first, setContentType(), takes an argument of the String class, which is used to specify the MIME-type string of the response to be sent. You must setContentType() before you get-Writer(), otherwise a runtime error will happen and garbage will be displayed. The status is specified using the setStatus() method; although for a reply of OK, this method is actually redundant. There are several SC_ constants within the

`HttpServletResponse` class for providing the appropriate status code as a response.

After setting up the status parts of the reply, `HelloServlet` then generates the HTML text, which is presented to the user in the client browser window. The output writer stream obtained from the `HttpServletResponse` object is an instance of the `PrintWriter` class. If you use `getOutputStream()`, it would return an instance of `javax.servlet.ServletOutputStream`, which defines `println()` methods with a variety of overloaded versions supporting different argument types. Think of it as a `PrintStream`.

The `getWriter()` method can throw an `IOException` if trouble occurs with the connection. Because of this exception, the bulk of the body of this `service()` method is wrapped in a `try` block. If the exception occurs in this example, it is simply ignored. In a servlet intended for production use rather than a simple example, the error would probably be logged. Later sections of this chapter examine the log mechanisms available to servlets.

Once the output writer has been obtained, the servlet must construct the page to provide to the client browser. Normally, this will involve some form of calculated or conditional response; otherwise, a simple HTML text file should define the page. The `HelloServlet` object will return an HTML page, which is a typical action, especially for servlets that are constructed based on the `HttpServlet` class. The HTML page is generated through a series of `println` statements.

After the initial page headings, a definition list is created. A *definition list* in HTML takes a series of entries, which are headings and body text pairs. The corresponding HTML tags used to define entries in such a list are <DT> and <DD>. The result has the general form of the latter part of this servlet's output, as shown earlier.

Construction of the list does not require any arguments, because the HTML definition list does not have a title of its own, only separate elements. After it has been constructed, lines like this one add the individual elements:

```
out.println ("<dt>Request method:</dt><dd>" +
    req.getMethod() + "</dd>");
```

Notice that two arguments are supplied. The first is the title part of the list element, and the second is the text that follows.

The information provided in this particular list is obtained from the request information carried by the first argument of the service() method. This argument is an instance of the HttpServletRequest class. In the HelloServlet example, several pieces of information are extracted and placed into the list; the first few pieces of information that are added are the header values.

An HTTP request has a number of attendant headers that define general aspects of the connection. The precise set of headers will depend on the browser being used to issue the request. You can see from the sample output of this servlet that information describing the actual browser forms one of the header fields. To obtain the headers, a servlet can use one of a number of getHeader() methods. This example, because it is simply going to output all the headers, uses the variation that fetches the enumeration of header names and loops until no more are found.

Normally, a particular header—such as the Accept list, which describes the preferred response types—would be required. For this purpose another overloaded getHeader() method is provided. This method accepts a String object as an argument and attempts to find the particular header specified by name in that argument. If any of these getHeader() methods cannot find the requested header, they simply return null.

In addition to accessing the headers, several other data items are available to the servlet. The HelloServlet example demonstrates three of them, which are obtained using the getMethod(), getPathTranslated(), and getQueryString() methods.

The getMethod() method returns the request type. This type is almost always one of the three strings GET, POST, or HEAD; although some other strings are permitted by the definition of HTTP. These strings name the type of request that the Web server received. The method used for general requests from a browser is GET. This type of request carries all the information from the browser to the server as part of the URL string. Requests from HTML forms commonly use the POST method, which sends the bulk of its data to the server as a stream rather than as part of the URL. In a servlet, this data stream is the input stream obtained from the ServletRequest object using the getInputStream() method. In the standard JDK HTTP protocol handler, opening the output stream from the client applet automatically turns the request into a POST type. The HEAD method constitutes a request for header information only, and it is typically used to determine if a cache entry can be reused or if it should be replaced with newer information.

Parsing Query Parameters

If your query string is of the standard form, where there are names and values separated by equal signs for the arguments (aKey=aValue&anotherKey=another+Value), then you can use the parseQueryString() method of HttpUtils to decode the URL-encoded string. The method places the parameters into a Hashtable, where you can then go fetch the values. The following code demonstrates how to examine the query parameters. Notice that each key can return multiple values so must be handled accordingly.

```
Hashtable hash = HttpUtils.parseQueryString
  (req.getQueryString());
Enumeration enum = hash.keys();
while (enum.hasMoreElements()) {
  String name = (String)enum.nextElement();
  out.println ("<dt>" + name + "</dt><dd>");
  String values[] = (String[])hash.get(name);
  for (int i=0,n=values.length;i<n; i++) {
    out.print (values[i]);
    if (i!=n-1) out.print ("/");
  }
  out.println ("</dd>");
}
```

For HTTP POST requests, you would use the parsePostData() method of HttpUtils.

The path information, returned from the getPathTranslated() method, describes the path on the server machine from which the servlet was loaded. As Figure 23.1 demonstrates, some servers may report this as null. This information might be very useful if a servlet needs to read from support files. However, you cannot rely on its availability.

NOTE   Also related to paths is the getPathInfo() method, which returns the path part of the original URL. In the conditions of this example, the getPathInfo() method returns /HelloServlet, treating the servlet part of the original URL as a server directive, not as part of the path itself. This treatment is entirely consistent because it is not actually a directory name. (For instance, in the Java Web Server, servlets are typically placed in a directory called servlets, and a translation takes place to convert the /servlet part of the URL.) In general, the getPathInfo() method is less useful because it does not relate directly to the local file system.

In many conventional requests to CGI services, the URL carries additional argument information that qualifies the particular request. The sample output shown earlier resulted from the full URL:

```
http://localhost:8080/servlet/HelloServlet?Hello+World
```

and, in this case, the query string was reported as `Hello+World`.

The `getQueryString()` method returns the full text of the query string from the invoking URL. Notice that the returned value is still in the URL-encoded format and might need to be converted before it is used.

Finally, after the definition list has been constructed, the closing HTML statements are added.

Other Important Servlet Methods

The preceding section described the basic use of the `HttpServlet` class and a number of supporting classes. A considerable number of additional methods are provided in the various classes that support servlets.

General Servlet Methods

When the server needs a servlet for the first time, it loads the class then creates an instance of it. The next step is to call the `init()` method, which can be used for general initialization of the servlet. You should ensure that only initialization is performed in the `init()` method, because it might be called to reset the servlet after it has already been used.

Web servers generally keep records about the accesses they receive, and servlets have the opportunity to do so, too. The `log()` method of the `ServletContext` interface takes a `String` argument with which it builds an entry that is written to the server's log file. Logs are generally written into a directory called logs under the server's home directory.

Information about the Request

Six more methods supply additional details about the request itself: `getContentLength()`, `getContentType()`, `getProtocol()`, and the trio `getParameter()`, `getParameterValues()`, and `getParameterNames()`. These are all member methods of the `ServletRequest` object.

The getContentLength() method returns the number of bytes of input that are to be supplied, or -1 in the event that this number is unknown. It is not good practice to allow a servlet to depend functionally on the content length that is reported, because the responsibility for providing this information rests with the client browser, and therefore the accuracy of the content length information is beyond your control. In general, input on an HTTP connection to a servlet will occur with a POST type request, so this value can be ignored for GET requests.

The getContentType() method returns a string that contains the MIME content type for the data that is to be sent to the servlet from the client browser. If no type has been specified by the client, or the connection is not issuing any data for use by the server, this method returns null. Some browsers specify content types of text/plain to indicate that the data is of no special type, some use content/unknown, and some use application/octet-stream. In general, it is likely that most servlets will expect a fairly specific type of data and may be written to handle just that. It also is likely that one particularly common input type will be argument values from a POST request. Form results in a POST request are normally reported using the MIME-type application/x-www-form-urlencoded.

The protocol used, which will typically be some version of HTTP, is reported by the getProtocol() method. This method returns a string of the form <Protocol>/<major_version>.<minor_version>. HTTP/1.0 is a typical return value from a Web browser client, although older browsers still exist that use HTTP/0.9. If the browser does not explicitly state the protocol type that it is using, the default (HTTP/0.9) is assumed and reported by the getProtocol() method. To get just the scheme of the URL, use getScheme(). This will return something like http or https.

CGI requests commonly include parameter information encoded onto the end of the URL itself in the form of name=value assignments. Multiple parameters should be separated using the ampersand character (&). Note that neither the equal symbol nor the ampersand should be converted to the external form using the percent (%) representation discussed earlier or they will lose their special meaning as separators and simply become part of the query string. Such information can be accessed by a servlet by using the getParameterNames(), getParameterValues(), and getParameter() methods. If a particular named parameter is expected and known to have only a single value, it is sufficient to use the getParameter() method, which takes a string argument specifying the name of the parameter to match and returns a string that represents the associated value. For example, given a URL like this:

```
http://localhost:8080/servlets/getparameter?quantity=maximum
```

the method call `getParameter("quantity")` would return the `String` value maximum. As with applets, all parameters are returned as `String` objects. If your servlet expects, say, an `int`, you must convert it. If a parameter could return multiple values (like `?quantity=maximum&quantity=minimum`), then you must use `getParameterValues()` to get all values back at once.

In some servlets, it might be inconvenient or impossible to predict the parameter names that are acceptable in advance of the call. In these circumstances, the `getParameterNames()` method is useful. This method returns an enumeration of the strings representing the names, but not the values, of the parameters that have been passed. For each of these names, the associated value can be obtained by calling either the `getParameter()` or `getParameterValues()` method.

Information about the Client

The request also carries information about the host of the client browser. The `getRemoteAddr()` method returns the IP address of the remote host, and the `getRemoteHost()` method returns its name.

WARNING   You should not attribute trust to any remote machine based solely on its name as extracted from either the `getRemoteAddr()` or `getRemoteHost()` method. Such a name will have been obtained from a reverse DNS lookup—a translation of the address into a name—and untrusted outsiders can subvert this process. If you need to allocate trust to particular hosts, either look up the name you trust and verify that the remote address you have matches one of those returned, or simply use addresses directly. Forward DNS lookups—that is, name-to-address translation—and actual IP addresses are much more difficult to subvert especially when the machines are in the same network. However, IP addresses can be falsified, too, so alternative security mechanisms should be examined. Some of these alternatives are explained in the following chapter on Java Security.

Length of Reply

In addition to the `getOutputStream()`, `getWriter()`, and `setContentType()` methods, the `ServletResponse` object also provides a method for specifying the length of content that is to be returned.

The `setContentLength()` method takes an integer argument that specifies the number of bytes of data that will be returned. Nothing in this method constrains the actual amount of data sent, so be careful to ensure that the value specified is correct. It is not necessary to use this method to set any value if it is difficult or inconvenient to calculate the correct value. However, if you choose not to use the `setContentLength()` method, the client browser will not be able to display a progress monitor.

Determining the size of a dynamically constructed page is easiest if the whole page is constructed in a buffer and then transmitted as a whole when complete. This strategy allows the size to be taken from the buffer size.

Accessing HTTP Header Information

A variety of headers are meaningful in the HTTP environment, and these can be accessed using methods in the `HttpServletRequest` and `HttpServletResponse` classes. Header values can be read using methods in the `HttpServletRequest` class. The `HelloServlet` example uses the `getHeaderNames()` method; this accesses the headers by their order. Another `getHeader()` method takes a `String` object as an argument and allows searching for specific headers.

Both the `getHeader()` method and `getHeaderNames()` return strings, or an enumeration of strings. Convenience methods are provided to translate these strings into either integer or date format.

When generating a reply, the headers may be set using a similar set of methods. In this case, the methods are members of the `HttpServletResponse` object. The basic `setHeader()` method takes two strings as arguments: the first names the header field, and the second specifies the value to be associated with the header. The `setIntHeader()` and `setDateHeader()` methods are convenience methods that take an `int` and a `long` representing a date, respectively. You can also redirect the client with `sendRedirect(String urlString)`.

Servlet Initialization Parameters

When a servlet is first loaded into a server, it can be configured via initialization parameters. These parameters are set by the administrator and are used for localization and installation of the servlet rather than configuration of a particular request. The initialization parameters are named, and the values associated with them can be read into the servlet from the `ServletContext` object—which is an interface to the server itself—by the method `getInitParameter()`. This method takes a string argument that should match the string name of the parameter in question. To obtain a list of all the parameters that have been configured, use the `getInitParameterNames()` method.

Servlet Configuration

This section briefly outlines how to configure Sun's Java Web Server to enable a servlet. The Java Web Server is supplied with a collection of servlets and an applet to support configuration from the browser interface. Two particular views within the administration applet are of interest for servlet configuration: the log-in view and the servlet-loading view. The main entry to the administration system is via the URL http://localhost:9090/ and is accessed via a Java-enabled browser (port 9090 is the administration port). The Java Web Server (httpd) must be started before you can access the administration system via this URL.

In the log-in view, two text fields and a Log In button are presented, as shown in Figure 23.2. The text fields prompt for a username and a password. By default, the administration login uses the username and password admin. Entering these into the text fields and selecting the Log In button changes the view to a supervisory control-panel view. This view has a list of the available services. Selecting the Web Service choice and clicking on the Manage button displays the administration functions window. (You can also just double-click on the Web Service choice.) Selecting the Servlets button changes the view in the window. Figure 23.3 shows this form.

FIGURE 23.2:

Logging in to the Java
Web Server

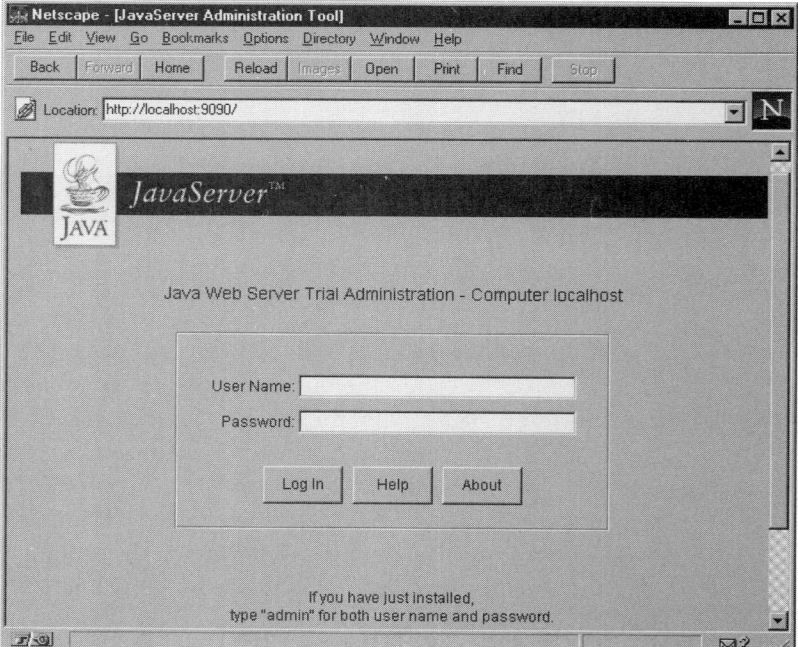

FIGURE 23.3:

The servlet form in the Java Web Server

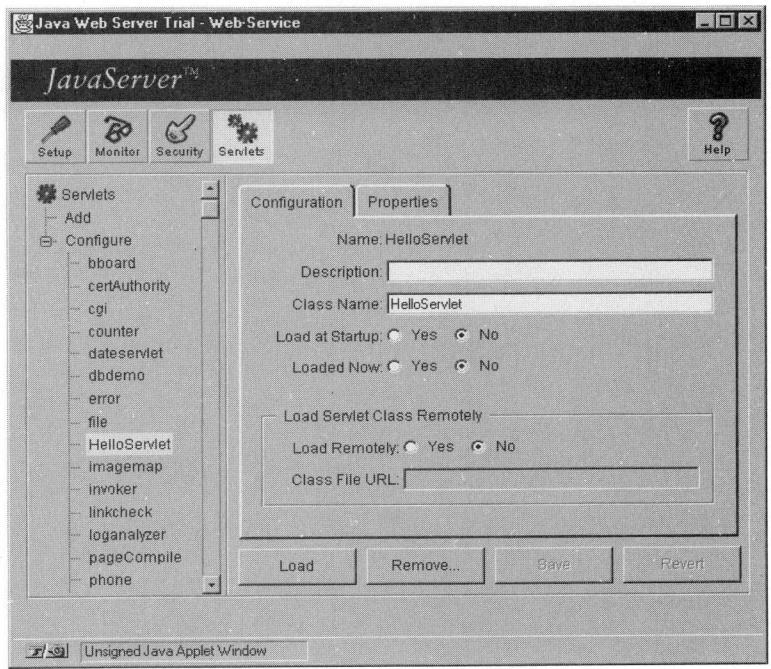

In the servlet-loading view, a list of currently known servlets is shown along with Add and Configure options. With the Add option, two text fields are provided for servlet name and class name, as well as enabling a servlet as a Bean servlet. After you add a servlet, you can configure it to have arguments and possibly remote loading. The name of a servlet can be a descriptive name and is not restricted to being the same as the class name. The class name entered should be the fully qualified class name, and the path should describe the base of any package hierarchy that should be searched.

If you want to formally add HelloServlet to the server, copy the Hello-Servlet.class file from your working directory to the servlets directory under the server installation directory. Next, select the Add option on the left of Figure 23.3 and just place **HelloServlet** in both fields, since the servlet is in the default package. Then select the Add button. The completed add screen is shown in Figure 23.4.

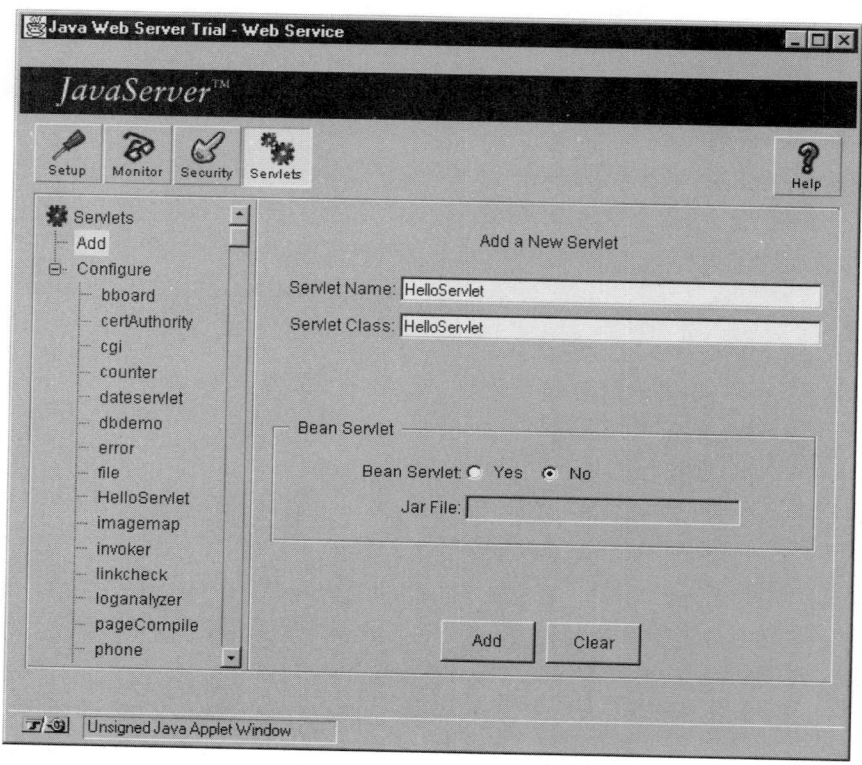

After adding a servlet, you can configure it by selecting the servlet name under the Configure option, which you can see in Figure 23.3. In configure mode, a pair of radio buttons allows you to indicate whether the servlet should be loaded automatically when the server starts. If "Load at Startup" is set to Yes, the servlet will be loaded in response to the first client request for its service. Once loaded, a servlet will remain resident in the server until it is shut down or you select No from the Loaded Now checkbox group. To minimize servlet startup time, most servlets should be loaded at Web server startup unless there is a real possibility that the servlet will not be invoked at all during a server session. There is also an option to load the server class from a remote URL, instead of from the Web server's file system. This option is not used by any of the examples in this chapter but is possible if you want to have a centralized servlet server.

The administration servlets actually act on underlying configuration files, which are maintained in the form of properties in a file called servlets.properties in the server installation's `properties\server\javawebserver\webpageservice` directory. A servlet is defined primarily by an entry of the form `servlet.`*`servlet-name`*`.code=classname`. For example, if a servlet referred to as `Useful` is defined in a class called `Use1`, the entry in the `servlets.properties` file would be `servlet.Useful.code=Use1`. Such an entry represents, in a single record, both the servlet name and the class that is to be loaded.

The code base for a servlet defaults to the `servlets` directory of the server installation but may be overridden by an entry of the form `servlet.`*`servlet-name`*`.codebase=`*`URL`*.

Arguments to the servlet are specified in the `servlets.properties` files by an entry of the form `servlet.`*`servletname`*`.initArgs=`*`comma_separated_list`*. For example, if two arguments called `one` and `two` are to be specified for a servlet called `Test`, and the arguments are to have the values `yes` and `maybe`, respectively, the `servlet.properties` file would contain the entry `servlet.Test.initArgs=one=yes,two=maybe`. Arguments are specified from the Properties tab when configuring the servlet.

While it wasn't required to add an entry for the `HelloServlet` to the Java Web Server, if you were to try to run the servlet at this point you would see output similar to Figure 23.1 again. One reason to add servlets to the server is to provide a name other than the class name. This allows you to have very descriptive class names, but to use shorter names when referring to the servlet at run time.

A Fuller Example of a Servlet

Now you are ready for a fuller servlet example. The following servlet combines a number of techniques to return an image representing the national flag of the country in which the host is apparently located. Of course, this idea is not entirely reliable, because many multinational and US-based companies use the `.com` top-level domain for all their offices, regardless of geographical location. Hence, a connection from a Sun Microsystems office in the United Kingdom would appear as if it were from `sun.com` and would be treated as if it were of US origin. However, despite this limitation, the example demonstrates a number of interesting and useful techniques.

```
import java.io.*;
import java.util.*;
```

```
import javax.servlet.*;
import javax.servlet.http.*;

public class NationalFlag extends HttpServlet {
  File flagDir;
  Hashtable flags = new Hashtable();

  private static final int SUFFIX      = 0;
  private static final int FILENAME    = 1;
  private static final int CONTENTTYPE = 2;

  private String defflagname[] = {
    "us",    "usa-flag.jpg", "image/jpeg"
  };

  private String flagnames[][] = {
    {"nl",   "nl-flag.jpg",   "image/jpeg"},
    {"fr",   "fr-flag.jpg",   "image/jpeg"},
    {"uk",   "uk-flag.jpg",   "image/jpeg"}
  };

  public void init(ServletConfig config) throws ServletException {
    super.init (config);
    String fileDir = getInitParameter("flagDirectory");
    if (fileDir == null) {
      fileDir = "servlets";
    }
    flagDir = new File(fileDir);
    if (!(flagDir.exists() && flagDir.isDirectory())) {
      log("Invalid flagDirectory value specified");
      throw new ServletException("Can't find flag Directory");
    } else {
      File f = new File(flagDir, defflagname[FILENAME]);
      if (!(f.exists() && f.canRead())) {
        log("can't find default flag ");
        throw new ServletException("Can't find default flag");
      }
    }
    for (int i = 0; i < flagnames.length; i++) {
      flags.put(flagnames[i][SUFFIX], flagnames[i]);
    }
  }
}
```

```
public void doGet (HttpServletRequest req, HttpServletResponse resp)
    throws ServletException, IOException {

  String country = null;
  if (req.getParameter("country") != null) {
    country = req.getParameter("country");
  } else {
    country = req.getRemoteHost();
    int i = country.lastIndexOf('.');
    if (i != -1) {
      country = country.substring(i + 1);
    }
  }
  String flagdef[] = (String [])(flags.get(country));
  if (flagdef == null) {
    flagdef = defflagname;
  }
  try {
    resp.setContentType(flagdef[CONTENTTYPE]);
    File f = new File(flagDir, flagdef[FILENAME]);
    int size = (int)f.length();
    resp.setContentLength(size);
    byte buffer[] = new byte[size];
    FileInputStream in = new FileInputStream(f);
    in.read(buffer);
    resp.getOutputStream().write(buffer);
  } catch (IOException e) {
    log("Trouble: " + e);
    throw e;
  } finally {
    resp.getOutputStream().close();
  }
}
}
```

Running the Servlet

To run this example, you need a running Web server that supports the servlet mechanism. Copy the class file from the CD-ROM into the appropriate directory in your server hierarchy. For the Java Web Server, this would be the servlets directory, under the installation directory.

This example requires the flag image files, too. Copy all the flag .jpg files from the CD-ROM into the servlet directory of your server.

In operation, this servlet must be able to locate the flag files. Although it uses the initialization parameter `flagDirectory` to allow these to be placed anywhere that is convenient, the servlet calculates a default directory if this parameter is not set. Provided your servlet directory is called `servlets` and is a subdirectory beneath the server's default directory, you will not need to set this parameter. (Note that this default directory could change in future releases.)

Once the files are in the correct places, configure the server to load this servlet if necessary, and then load the servlet from a browser. Typically, this would mean loading the URL:

```
http://localhost:8080/servlet/NationalFlag
```

If you have completed the installation according to the needs of your server, you should see the default flag, which is the Stars and Stripes. But since the local connection suggested here by `localhost` will probably not advertise your full domain name, even if you are in a non-US domain, you might see a representation of another national flag. The default flag is shown in Figure 23.5 below.

FIGURE 23.5:

The US flag, as shown from the NationalFlag servlet

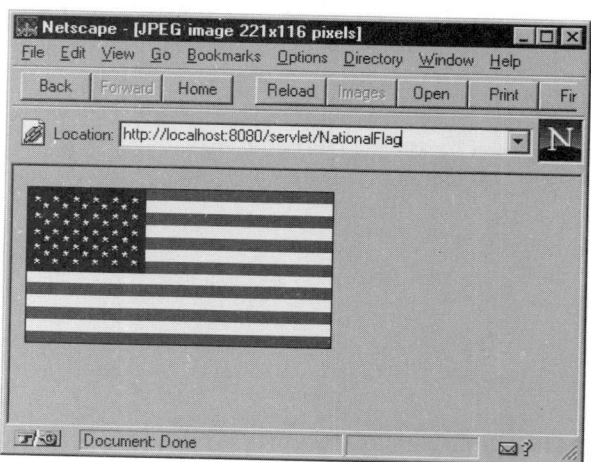

Because it is difficult in most cases to test this servlet from different geographical locations—or even to simulate the effect by modifying naming tables—and because the genuine local host name will be hidden in many installations, this example checks for a parameter that overrides the host name in controlling the choice of flag to return. The parameter is called country, and it may be set to any of the values us, uk, nl, or fr. These are the only countries that are supported by the image files on the CD-ROM. Test other countries by directing your browser to a URL of this form:

```
http://localhost:8080/servlet/NationalFlag?country=uk
```

You should find that the flag displayed changes to one appropriate to the country parameter value. In this particular case, you should see the Union Jack as shown in Figure 23.6.

FIGURE 23.6:

The UK flag, as shown from the NationalFlag servlet

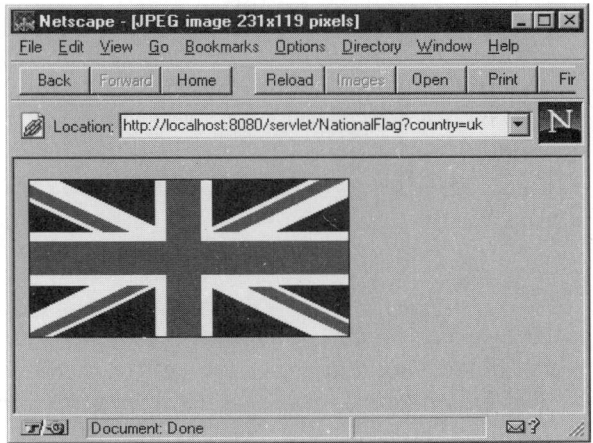

In normal use, this servlet would be embedded in a page using the IMG tag. A sample Web page is located on the CD-ROM in the file NatFlag.html. The key HTML entry is shown next:

```
<img src=/servlet/NationalFlag>
```

Copy this file into a suitable subdirectory in a public directory of your server and direct your browser to that URL. For the Java Web Server, this would be the public_html subdirectory. Provided you installed the NationalFlag servlet so that it is at the URL used above, you will see the Stars and Stripes embedded in a normal HTML page. If your servlet installation is different, you will need to edit the NatFlag.html file to reflect the particulars of your installation.

The NationalFlag Servlet's Classes and Methods

The first part of the NationalFlag servlet is its init() method. This method determines the directory from which image files are to be loaded and verifies that at least the default flag can be found in that directory. The init() method completes by building a hashtable containing the other flags that are available.

Each time the servlet is invoked, it tests to see whether the country parameter has been supplied. If it has, this value is used to determine which flag to return; if not, the host name of the client is used instead. Once the flag has been chosen, it is loaded into a buffer. The content type and length are set appropriately, and then the image data is sent to the client.

The servlet comprises two parts: the init() method and the doGet() method. The init() method performs the one-time initialization. First, it checks whether an initialization parameter called flagDirectory has been set. This parameter may be used to specify the directory in which the supporting flag image files are located. If no value is found for the flagDirectory variable, a default value is assumed, which is the subdirectory servlets beneath the server's default directory. For the Java Web Server, the current working directory of a running servlet is the base directory of the server; hence, it is the parent directory of the servlets directory.

Once a directory has been chosen as a string, a File object is constructed to represent it. Using that object, the init() method checks whether the file it describes is an existing directory. If it isn't, a log entry is made indicating the nature of the problem and a servlet exception is thrown.

Provided the directory chosen exists, the init() method proceeds by checking whether it contains a readable file for use as the default flag. The name for this file is taken from the defflagname array of strings. As before, if this is found not to be the case, a log entry is made and a servlet exception is thrown to indicate the problem.

If the init() method has found the default flag file, a Hashtable object is filled with descriptions of each known country, the associated flag filename, and the content type that describes the file. In this example, the Hashtable is filled from a predefined array, but in a production implementation, it could be filled using either properties or some other external file. Such an approach would allow greater flexibility and, hence, permit the addition of new flags without requiring recompilation.

The definitions of the init() method in the Servlet interface, the Generic-Servlet class, and the HttpServlet class allow the method to throw a Servlet-Exception object if required. This is important because it provides a means for the servlet to indicate to the server that the initialization has failed. If no exception is thrown, the init() method would be incorrectly deemed to have completed suc-·cessfully, and the servlet would be called whenever a request was received. This would then need to be rejected each time by the service() method.

Instead of the service() method, the NationalFlag servlet uses the doGet() method. Besides using the generic service() method, there are special methods for handling different HTTP services:

- doGet() for HTTP GET requests
- doPost() for HTTP POST requests
- doPut() for HTTP PUT requests
- doDelete() for HTTP DELETE requests
- doTrace() for HTTP TRACE requests
- doOptions() for HTTP OPTIONS requests

Here, the doGet() method must determine which flag image should be returned. If a country parameter is set for the request, the value of that parameter is used to determine the flag. However, if no country parameter is defined, the host name of the client is looked up, and the last part, following the last occurrence of a period, is used. The intention is that if a connection is received from a machine with, for example, the host name jaques.delores.fr, the fr part is extracted and taken to represent the connection's country of origin.

Once a country value has been determined, either from the end of the host name or from a parameter, it is used as the key to look up the corresponding flag in the hashtable of known flags. If no match is found in that table, the default flag is used. Note that in the NationalFlag example, the default flag is not actually entered in the Hashtable itself, which means that the handling of US connections is indistinguishable from the handling of undetermined connections. If you change this behavior under default conditions to return a special image indicating an unrecognized connection, all the various US suffixes (.com, .edu, and so forth) should be added to the Hashtable.

Each entry in the hashtable is an array of three strings. These describe the country identifier, the name of the flag file, and the MIME content type of the file. The country identifier is used as the key for the hashtable because this is the value that must be looked up to determine which flag is required. When a country has been identified, the MIME content type of the response is specified using the third of these strings from the hashtable entry. A `File` object is also created using the directory that was determined by the `init()` method and the individual filename from the second element of the hashtable entry. This `File` object is used to determine the actual size in bytes of the flag file, and this value is used to set the content length of the response. The length allows the client browser to indicate correctly the progress of the download.

A buffer is allocated using the indicated file size, and the whole file is read in via a `FileInputStream` object. Once this buffer has been filled, it is written to the output stream of the `HttpServletResponse` object, and thereby to the client.

During the execution of the `doGet()` method, a number of different methods are called that might cause an `IOException` object to be thrown. Any of these would be very difficult to recover from effectively, so in this servlet any such problem simply causes a log entry and is passed back to the server.

Regardless of any exceptions that might occur, the output channel is closed before the servlet returns. Any exception that occurs during this closure is simply passed to the server and otherwise ignored.

Server-Side Includes

The Java Web Server has the ability to perform a *server-side include* (SSI) using a servlet. With server-side inclusion, the server converts a placeholder in an HTML document into alternative dynamically calculated text each time the document is served to a client.

A server-side include is requested by two steps:

1. The document carries the extension `.shtml` rather than the normal `.html`.

2. The point at which the inclusion should be made is marked with a special tag.

Most servers, other than the Java Web Server, have adopted an HTML comment format to indicate the point of inclusion. In Sun's server, the SERVLET tag is used.

The format of the SERVLET tag is similar to the APPLET tag, and in its minimum form looks like this:

```
<servlet name=ServletName>
</servlet>
```

The servlet itself does not have a user interface at the client; therefore, a servlet tag—unlike an applet tag—does not require, and in fact cannot have, a width or height parameter. Furthermore, because the servlet is conventionally referenced by a name other than its class name, it is not necessary to specify a class name in this tag. If both a name and the class name are specified in the servlet tag, and the named servlet is already loaded in the server, that servlet will be invoked by its name. But if the servlet tag in an .shtml file has only the servlet name part, without a class name specified, the server checks all loaded servlets for the name given. If the servlet is not found preloaded, the tag is simply ignored.

However, with an appropriate servlet tag, it is not always necessary for a servlet to be preloaded. If the class name and servlet name are specified in the servlet tag, and the servlet is not found by name, it will be loaded using the specified class name and registered in the server for future use by the name given. If a class name part, but no servlet name part, is specified in the tag, the servlet will be reloaded every time the include is requested; this should be avoided.

The full format for specifying a server-side included servlet is:

```
<servlet name=ServletName code=ServletCode
      initParam1=initArg1 initParam2=initArg2 ...>
      <param name=param1 value=val1>
</servlet>
```

Notice that named parameters can be specified, using a format that exactly mimics the one used for applet parameters. Also, initialization parameters can be specified as part of the main part of the servlet tag.

Inter-Servlet Communication

One of the difficulties with standard CGI is that of communication. With traditional CGI mechanisms, communication between different CGI scripts tends to be rather slow because it involves either reading and writing files or using pipes to communicate between different processes.

Servlets are persistent in that once the server starts one, the servlet remains in existence to service all future requests; also, all servlets exist in the same Virtual Machine (VM) and, hence, in the same process space. These two considerations make it possible for different servlets to communicate conveniently and efficiently.

To effect communication between two servlets, the servlets must be able to obtain references to each other and must be designed to communicate. This section discusses these two aspects. Of course, the servlets must also have something useful to say to each other.

Finding a Servlet

When a servlet runs, it does so inside a Web server. The server provides a number of facilities to the servlets it runs, including the ability to locate other servlets on the same server. The Web server, from the API point of view, is encapsulated in the `ServletContext` interface, similar in principle to `AppletContext`. The servlet itself can obtain a reference to the Web server by issuing a call to the `getServletContext()` method. Note that this method is not defined in the `Servlet` interface, but in the `GenericServlet` class.

Once the servlet context has been obtained, two methods are available for locating servlets:

getServletNames()   Returns an enumeration of all the names of servlets in the server. Inside a servlet, this method cannot return an empty enumeration, because the servlet itself must be included in the list.

getServlet()   Takes a string argument and returns a reference to the servlet named by that string. This method will return null if the server does not know about the servlet that was requested.

Both the `getServletNames()` and `getServlet()` methods will return only those servlets that are currently loaded. Neither will cause the server to load any servlet, even if its name is known. For this reason, if servlets are to communicate, it is usually required that they be marked as loaded at startup in the administration system.

Communicating between Servlets

You can implement communication between servlets in several different ways. These are methods that allow programs of various types to communicate and are not specific to servlets.

Calling Each Other's Methods

If the two servlets are written at the same time and know each other's public API when they are compiled, they can call each other's methods. This situation would allow, for example, each servlet to implement a `getInfo()` and `setState()` method—the actual names are unimportant—so that each can call the appropriate method to control the other.

Using Stream Classes

It might be appropriate to use the `PipedReader` and `PipedWriter` classes. These classes are discussed in Chapter 19 as one of the ways that different threads can communicate, and their use is equally appropriate for servlets. To set up such a communication, each servlet must be able to obtain a handle on the streams of the other. The following code fragments describe one possible approach:

```java
public class TalkerServlet extends GenericServlet {
    public final PipedWriter myOutput = new PipedWriter ();
// body of class...
}

public class ListenerServlet extends GenericServlet {
  private PipedReader myInput = null;
  public void service(ServletRequest req,
                      ServletResponse resp) throws ServletException {
    if (myInput == null) {
      ServletContext context = getServletContext();
      Servlet theTalker = context.getServlet("TalkerServlet");
      if ((theTalker == null) ||
          !(theTalker instanceof TalkerServlet)) {
        throw new ServletException("Cannot find Talker");
      }
      TalkerServlet ts = (TalkerServlet)theTalker;
      try {
        myInput = new PipedReader(ts.myOutput);
      } catch (IOException io) {
        myInput = null; // ?
      }
    }
  }
}
```

In this scheme, one end of the reader/writer stream pair must be created first—in this case, the output side has been chosen–and it is created at the moment the `TalkerServlet` object is instantiated. Some time later, the other end of the stream can be created. In this example, the other end of the stream is not created in an `init()` method because there would be a risk of the servlets being created in the wrong order. To avoid this problem, the other end of the stream is created during the first call to the `service()` method of the `ListenerServlet` object. Provided that both the talker and the listener are loaded at server startup, this approach will work safely.

This approach is equally applicable for bidirectional communication. Although this sample code shows only one stream being set up, it would be simple to add an instance of the `PipedReader` class to the `TalkerServlet` class and attach that to a writer in the listener in the same way.

Using Static Variables

It is possible to use static variables as the basis for communication between classes. For example, using reader and writer streams, the mechanism shown in the previous section could be modified to use a static variable to provide access to the writer stream. In this way, it would not be necessary to use the `ServletContext` object to obtain a handle on the other `Servlet` object. Consider the following code fragments:

```
public class TalkerServlet extends GenericServlet {
  public static final PipedWriter myOutput;

  static {
    try {
      myOutput = new PipedWriter();
    } catch (IOException e) {
    }
  }
  // body of class…
}

public class ListenerServlet extends GenericServlet {
  private PipedReader myInput;
  public ListenerServlet() throws IOException {
    myInput = new PipedReader(TalkerServlet.myOutput);
  }
  // main body of class
}
```

Usually, the fact that the value of a static variable is shared between all instances makes this type of variable subject to misuse and misunderstanding in a fashion similar to global variables in non–object-oriented languages. However, in this case, because only one instance of a servlet is ever created in a Web browser environment, these particular difficulties do not arise.

By using the static variable, observe that the `TalkerServlet` class can create and advertise its `PipedWriter` object at the moment the class is loaded, which ensures that the `ListenerServlet` object can refer to that writer stream immediately. The approach also avoids the earlier requirement of ensuring that the servlets be loaded by the server at startup, because the VM itself will resolve any dependencies between the classes, as the language clearly defines the proper behavior. So if the `ListenerServlet` class refers to the `TalkerServlet` class in this way, the system, rather than the browser, ensures that the `TalkerServlet` class will be loaded if it is not already loaded.

Using Singleton Objects

A variation on the static variable idea is the concept of a *singleton* object. The singleton object is an object that is created and advertised as a static variable but has some protection against corruption from outside the class. You can set up a singleton by adhering to the following guidelines:

- Declare at least one constructor and mark all constructors for the class as private.

- Declare a private static variable of the same type as the class itself.

- Declare a nonprivate synchronized static method, which returns an instance of the class.

- In the static method, if the private variable described above is non-null, simply return it. However if the variable is null, create an instance of the class (remember, the private constructors are accessible to this method) and put the reference to the new object into the variable. Now return the value of that variable.

A code fragment following these guidelines looks like this:

```
public class Singleton {
  private static Singleton myself;
  private Singleton() {
    // set me up
  }
```

```
    public static synchronized Singleton getInstance() {
      if (myself == null) {
        myself = new Singleton();
      }
      return myself;
    }
  }
```

Now if two servlets need to communicate, they can both have instances variables that are of this Singleton class. The variables themselves do not need to be static, and can be private, but they will both refer to the same object. The classes would look like this:

```
public class XXXXServlet extends HttpServlet {
    private Singleton mySingleton = Singleton.getInstance();
    // rest of class
}
```

This approach is effectively just syntactic sugar on the basic idea of a static variable in the classes, but has the—potentially great—advantage of loosening the coupling between the talker and listener classes. When you use static variables directly, one of these classes must know about, and use explicitly, the other class and the variable name within it. Such coupling reduces maintainability of the classes. With the singleton object approach, this coupling is significantly reduced. The talker class could change its name and function entirely, the variable in which it stores its reference to the shared object could be changed or even deleted entirely, and the listener class would be unaffected.

Multithreading Servlets

When developing a servlet, you have to consider what happens when simultaneous requests to run the servlet occur. The simplest solution is to just have your servlet implement the SingleThreadModel interface. The SingleThreadModel interface is an empty interface that serves as a marker to the Web server. The interface indicates to the server that only one thread may call the service() method at a time (or the other servicing methods, like doGet() or doPut()). If the servlet does not implement the interface, you will have to deal with synchronization issues yourself to ensure that the servlet is thread safe.

Summary

This chapter started by explaining the limitations of using CGI, an earlier mechanism for dynamically calculated content. Then it described the relative advantages of using servlets and a Java-capable Web server for providing these services.

You then learned how to use the Servlet API classes and methods for creating servlets, including the `service()` method and the `HttpServletRequest` and `HttpServletResponse` classes.

Then, you learned how to configure the Java Web Server, Sun's Web server, to support your servlets. Other Java-based Web servers are available, and it is likely that they will need similar configuration to support servlets.

Next, a number of possible mechanisms for implementing communication between servlets was described. These mechanisms are appropriate for a variety of purposes and can actually be used for communication between all sorts of classes, not just servlets.

Finally, the `SingleThreadModel` interface was described for creating thread safe servlets.

If you expect to be writing extensive network-based services, the Java Web Server and the Servlet API are likely to enrich your study. In addition, if those services will connect to corporate databases, you should ensure that you are familiar with the general techniques of one of the database interface mechanisms, such as JDBC (Java Database Connectivity), which is used for relational database interfacing. For more information about JDBC, see Chapter 21.

CHAPTER

TWENTY-FOUR

Security

- Security concepts

- Controlling program capabilities

- Authorization in JDK 1.2

- Authenticating users

- Cryptographic APIs

Java has been designed from the very beginning with security in mind. From the design of the source language, which seeks to reduce common programmer errors while remaining acceptable in the mainstream, to the fundamental design of the bytecode language and virtual machine, security elements are evident everywhere. JDK 1.1 added API functionality for user security features, such as signatures and signing of JAR archives.

With the advent of JDK 1.2, security has been opened up to the control of the user or system administrator; security policy can be changed or extended without changes to program sources, and the trust allocated to imported classes can be controlled in a fine grained, feature by feature fashion, dependent upon either the origin of the class file or the signatures it carries. Most importantly, the fine-grained mechanisms allow you to grant a single privilege; for example, to read and write a file `C:\Windows\Temp\scratch.dat` to imported code without allowing it access to any other file or other sensitive part of your system.

This chapter discusses all aspects of Java security, including the foundations of control applied by operating systems in general and the essential terminology that is used, specifically, Java's VM security mechanisms (sometimes called the three-pronged approach). The new security policy mechanisms, keys and certificates, signing archives, and the APIs such as `MessageDigest` and `Signature` are also discussed.

Security Concepts

The fundamental purpose of all computer security is to control access to resources. Resources being protected might be items of data, I/O devices such as printers, or access to the CPU itself.

Who Are You?

If you are to keep control of the resources of a machine or network, you must first have a clear plan that tells what resources are being protected and what access is legitimate to them. This is called your security *policy*. Any use of a computer resource is initiated by a human (or perhaps a category, or group, of humans); therefore, the first requirement when implementing computer security is the ability to determine with confidence the identity of that human. There are two aspects to this problem. First the human must have a unique identity in the computer system and must use that identity when gaining access to the system. This is called *identification*.

In an ideal world, no one would lie about their identity (or anything else), but unfortunately in the real world, and especially a real world connected by the Internet, such deception is practiced regularly. The next aspect of any computer security system is therefore *authentication*. This is the process of attempting to prove that the human is indeed who he claims to be. Conventionally, authentication is achieved by means of a password. But stronger mechanisms exist, and the strongest authentication mechanism you are most likely to come across is a *smart card*. A smart card is a card that contains an embedded microprocessor and memory. The microprocessor is programmable and the memory is non-volatile, or long term. Provided the card is physically protected, it is much harder for an impostor to pretend to be you.

Sometimes you need to associate your identity with a document or file (often in Java, this is a JAR file containing classes), even though you will not be physically present when the files are used. To achieve this, a mechanism called a digital signature is commonly used. A *digital signature*, or just signature if the context is clearly electronic, is a validation code that is associated with a file, such that anyone can check that the signature is correct, but only one person can generate it. In this way, it effectively proves that a specific individual placed the signature on the file. Digital signatures are discussed more fully later in this chapter.

In a system that provides identification, authentication, and digital signatures as a means of identifying an individual, actions that are performed can be associated with that individual. This can be essential in, for example, electronic commerce, where it can be used to prove to the reasonable satisfaction of a legal body that the individual did indeed knowingly take part in the transaction. Such a concept of proof-of-involvement is normally called *non-repudiation*.

What Do You Want?

Once an individual has been identified and authenticated, some degree of access can be granted to a system's facilities. Some sort of database records what rights of access an individual should be granted. The granting of certain permissions, or access to certain facilities, is known as *authorization*.

Clearly there is little point in identifying an individual and keeping a database of the facilities each should have access to unless there is some mechanism built into the system that prevents access to unauthorized resources. This is commonly referred to as *resource control*. This is the foundation of the rest of the system; without it, the data structures that are used for identification, authentication, authorization, and so forth could be modified freely, and the whole security system would fail.

Did Someone Touch This?

Two particular reasons for controlling the access of individuals to resources are to protect data from unauthorized tampering and to preserve the secrecy of private data. These functions are primarily the responsibility of the authorization and resource control aspects of the system, but additional mechanisms may be used to strengthen this.

There are ways to keep a code that is representative of the contents of a file but uses only a few bytes of storage. If the file contents are changed, the code value will no longer match. If the codes are stored separately from the files they describe, then you will be able to tell if a file has been altered. Some of the common codes are called checksums, cyclic redundancy checks, or message digests. They differ in the mathematics used for generation and the size of the resulting code. In terms of sensitivity and reliability, the checksum is the weakest and the message digest is the strongest. Mechanisms of this sort can be used to detect both accidental and deliberate damage to data in any form. For example, the data might be stored in a file or transmitted over a network. Checks of this kind collectively provide *data integrity*.

It's None of Your Business!

If you require the strongest protection of data against unauthorized knowledge, then some form of *encryption* should be used. Encryption involves hiding data using a mathematical alteration scheme that is easy for the intended reader to reverse, but very difficult for anyone else to reverse. Encryption, sometimes also called enciphering, is different from encoding, which, in computing, is the term usually applied to nonsecret ways to represent data. For example, the ASCII and Unicode standards for representing characters using numbers are referred to as forms of coding.

Encryption usually uses a publicly known algorithm for changing the plain-text (original data) into the cipher-text (secret form) and back again. The secrecy comes from the use of special numbers, called keys, that are used to modify the way the encryption process proceeds. If secrecy is to be maintained, then some degree of secrecy must be applied to the keys.

Encryption mechanisms generally fall into two categories. In one case a single key is used (or two keys that have a simple relationship that allows one to be derived easily from the other) so that essentially the same key is used for encryption and decryption. Therefore, anyone who is equipped to encrypt data is equally well equipped to decrypt it. Such a scheme is known either as a *secret-key* or a *symmetric* cipher. In symmetric cryptography, the hard part is that the key itself must be kept hidden from everyone except the two people who are authorized to take part in the conversation. Since one party will create the key, transmitting the key to the other party in a secure fashion is a vital, and nontrivial, operation.

In the other category of encryption, different keys are used to encrypt and decrypt the data. Of course there is a mathematical relationship between the two keys, but the computation required to derive one from the other is sufficiently difficult (would take so long) that it is considered impossible to perform. Now, one key can be made public, while the other is kept secret by the originator of the pair. If people want to send a message to the originator of the key pair, they can encipher using the key that was published. This well-known key is commonly called the *public-key*. The resulting message can only be decrypted using the other key, which was retained by the originator of the pair. This is known as the *private-key*. Such a scheme is known as either *public-key cryptography* or *asymmetric cryptography*.

NOTE If a message is enciphered using the private-key, then it can be deciphered by anyone (since the corresponding public-key is well known). This does not provide for secrecy of the data, but the successful deciphering effectively proves that the message was created using the corresponding private key. If you know that only a particular individual holds the private key, then you know a message originated from that particular person. This is the basis of digital signatures.

Who Did That?

Sometimes things might go wrong despite the best efforts to maintain the system security. In such circumstances, it is helpful if some log exists that describes the actions that have been performed on the system. Keeping such a log is called *auditing*. Auditing is often performed for accounting and billing purposes, but it can be of value in helping to clear up a security breach (whether malicious or accidental). Auditing has a couple of disadvantages. First, it can take up a lot of space. So it is generally impractical to keep hard copy logs instead of soft copy or data file logs. Even so, the disk requirements can become huge. When a data file is being used, it is often possible for a malicious attacker to delete or modify the files so as to hide their tracks. Despite these reservations, a security sensitive site should audit carefully and check the logs regularly. In his book *The Cuckoo's Egg*, Clifford Stoll describes, in the style of a great spy novel, the true story of an international malicious attacker who was caught because of a 75-cent discrepancy between two different auditing mechanisms on a $2,387 bill.

Now that the components that make up a securable system have been outlined, you will see how it is possible to build a system that controls access to its resources. This implements the resource control feature described above. Keep in mind the fundamental role this plays in the system security. If resource control fails, the databases that implement identification, authentication, and so forth can be compromised.

Controlling Program Capabilities

In a conventional machine language, the instruction set is sufficiently complete to provide direct access to any part of memory and any part of the I/O system. In multi-user systems, special hardware is provided that can restrict access to memory and I/O while the system is running. When the operating system switches between processes as part of its time sharing operations, it also reconfigures this special hardware to prevent one process from having any access to the memory of another process. This control mechanism is often referred to as the Memory Management Unit (MMU.) The MMU itself is part of the I/O system, and the entire I/O space is normally inaccessible to ordinary user processes. Access to I/O, and hence to the MMU itself, is usually only permitted by a special pseudo-identity that can be recognized automatically by the hardware. This pseudo-identity represents the O/S itself and is often called *kernel mode*. Kernel mode is typically entered when a software interrupt is executed. Because software interrupts normally jump to code via pointers in a special memory area, and memory can be protected against improper modification by the MMU, there exists a self-consistent security mechanism that protects the memory of one process from accidental or malicious access by another. This security mechanism has the potential to control all access to I/O devices, such as disks, terminals, modems, etc. Figure 24.1 shows how these rules form a defensive circle to protect the system against attack or program error.

FIGURE 24.1:

The defensive circle of Memory Management

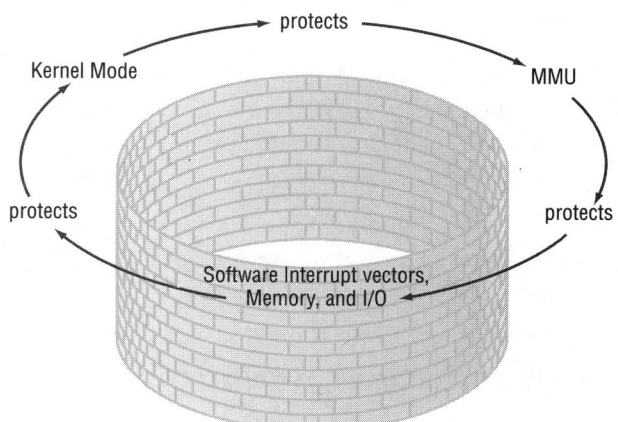

This approach has been a standard part of operating system design theory for at least twenty years, and most modern operating systems at least try to provide something along these lines. The scheme has two significant weaknesses in the context of Java programs. It doesn't even try to protect the memory of a process from misuse by that same process. Furthermore, the protection of both I/O devices and memory is wholly inadequate in the light of Java's ability to download executable code from untrusted, and potentially hostile, sources. Take a moment to consider what these two comments mean.

If a process has unrestricted access to its own memory space, then the contents of memory can be viewed in any way that suits the executing program. In many ways this is powerful, allowing compact use of memory and all manner of little tricks intended to enhance performance. Unfortunately it also means that programming mistakes can often go unnoticed until they have destroyed most of the program and its data and hidden their own tracks into the bargain. Such mistakes are usually called pointer errors and can be very difficult to track down. In a Java runtime system, the memory of a process is effectively inaccessible until specifically requested. When memory is requested, the process must state its purpose; for example, "I'd like space for an `int`," or "I'd like space for a `String`." After the memory has been requested, and its intended use has been stated, the system is able to ensure that all subsequent accesses to that memory are appropriate: that is, access to the `int` space is either a read or write of an `int` value and so forth. This "typesafe" operation has two major benefits. First, it protects the programmer against a great many bugs (and therefore a great deal of embarrassment) that often arise in conventional systems. Second, as the next section describes, it is a fundamental part of Java's security mechanisms.

In any system that allows downloadable code, there is the possibility that code might be badly written or malicious. Java therefore takes steps to protect the memory and I/O of the system, not only based on the identity of the user who initiated the process, but also based on the origin of the code that the process is executing.

The next section describes how Java protects memory against pointer errors and the system as a whole against the actions of untrusted code. These mechanisms form the basis of all Java security.

Java's Security Foundations

The last section looked at traditional memory management and considered some ways that Java's downloadable content capability requires more powerful control if a system is to remain secure. The essential goal of Java system security is to be able to control the capabilities of individual sections of code as they execute. Commonly a piece of code will be denied certain privileges if that code originated from an untrusted source.

Convention has it that there are three parts to Java's defense mechanisms. These are the Bytecode Verifier, Class Loaders, and the Security Manager. These three terms succinctly describe the three key elements of Java's runtime defenses. But there is one static feature upon which the bytecode verifier in particular depends, and that is the design of the JVM instruction set itself. This section discusses what these four terms mean and how these components form a securable system.

The JVM Instruction Set

There is one major difference between Java, as a platform, and other execution platforms upon which the whole of the Java security story rests. This is the design of the JVM instruction set itself. The first difference is that unlike almost any other machine language, the JVM instruction set does not address memory directly and, regardless of the underlying machine architecture, has no I/O instructions. The second difference is that every instruction is strongly typed; that is, the number of arguments and the type of each is unambiguously defined. This applies even to method calls.

If the JVM instruction set does not address memory directly, then how does it access data? The answer is the JVM instructions refer to memory in a symbolic way. For example, suppose there exists a reference to an object. That reference might or might not be an actual memory address in the conventional sense; but it is not known if that is so, and even if it is known, the knowledge has no value. If you want to read an int field from an object, you execute a JVM instruction like this:

```
getfield #4 <Field int x>
```

which reads an int value from a field of the object referred to by the top stack entry. The field is described by entry number four in the symbol table. The fourth entry of the symbol table describes an int called x. Because of the symbolic nature of this instruction, it is possible to check if the described field actually is an int value. If it is not, then the instruction can be rejected.

This idea of strongly typed instructions is used to allow modeling of any Java code, so that a certain degree of correctness may be proved or disproved for that code. This is the job of the bytecode verifier, which is examined next.

The Bytecode Verifier

When a class is first loaded, it is subjected to a number of checks. The first of these validate the format of the class file and the symbol table that is contained within the class file. Provided these checks are successful, the bytecode verifier is invoked next.

The bytecode verifier checks the flow of each method, instruction by instruction, with a view to proving the type-correctness of the method. For each method, the verifier starts by assuming that the method is invoked with the correct arguments. It then checks that each instruction in turn starts with the correct data types at the top of the stack and ends by providing the correct stack frame for the next instruction. This check covers all instructions, including method calls. It is possible to check the method calls since the class file carries full type information for method arguments and return values. The checks must also verify that all branch instructions are executed at points where the stack is correct for the instruction at the target of the branch.

Sometimes an instruction might refer to a field in another class that is not yet loaded. Rather than compel the loading of the other class, the verifier typically defers the checking of such instructions to the point where the instruction is first executed. In this way, if the code is never executed, the other class might never need to be loaded, but the checks are still completed before the code can run.

In addition to checking that all instructions (including method calls) are executed with the correct argument types, the verifier also checks that the accesses themselves are legal, thus enforcing the access control mechanisms private, protected, and default (*friendly*) access.

This bytecode verification process depends upon the design of the bytecode itself. It is possible to check that every instruction is executed with the data of the correct type on the stack because every instruction is fully typed. Separate instructions are provided, for example, for reading `int`, `long`, `float`, and `double` values.

Given that the bytecode verification process, along with the design of the bytecode language, proves the type-correctness and access-correctness of each method, it is possible to enforce other higher level checks. The security manager conventionally enforces these checks; and, although in JDK 1.2 that single class has been replaced by a system of several classes, the term *Security Manager* adequately describes this system.

The Security Manager

The security manager system builds upon the foundation provided by bytecode verification. Given that all methods are known to be executed with the correct argument types, the security manager's role is to check that individual calls to use protected resources, such as files, are acceptable at run time. To make these decisions, the security manager has information about the calling stack frames, the actual arguments to the call, and the security policy that the user has configured.

The most fundamental job that the security manager must perform involves the loading of native libraries. We saw in the earlier section that the bytecode language cannot express direct memory or I/O operations. Such machine control is left to libraries written in the underlying machine's language: that is, libraries containing native methods. Before any method can execute a native method, the enclosing class must link that library. This is done using the call `System.loadLibrary()` or `System.load()`. Note that it is not sufficient for the library to be loaded into the JVM, it is also necessary for the symbol table of the calling class to be linked to the library. Both load calls invoke the security manager. If the security manager decides that the call is inappropriate, it throws an exception and the loading is not performed. Typically, the security manager will reject a call to load a library if the requesting class is not local to the system.

Given that direct access to native methods is protected, it is necessary to protect indirect access to those methods. This is also the responsibility of the security manager system. First, the library classes must be coded carefully to ensure that the security manager is always invoked before the native method can be called. This is done by the following approach:

- All native methods should be declared as `private`, so that access to them is restricted to other methods in the same class.

- A limited set of nonprivate entry points should be provided.

- The entry points should check the arguments for validity and check with the security manager for permission to execute the body of the functionality. If and only if these checks are successful, then the native method is invoked; otherwise an exception is thrown.

The security manager has access to the stack frames of the calling thread to help decide if a call should be permitted. The security manager can use this to determine the class involved in each method call all the way up to the starting method of the thread. From the class, it can determine the origin of the code. Typically local code is trusted more highly than code loaded from a remote site, and code signed by a trusted entity is trusted more highly than unsigned code.

For example, suppose a call is made to try to create a `FileOutputStream`. If a Security Manager is installed in the JVM, then the constructor for `FileOutput-Stream` calls the `checkWrite()` method of the `SecurityManager` object. This typically checks the call stack to find out if any nonlocal code is involved in the call hierarchy, and if not, allows the `FileOutputStream` to be created. If, on the other hand, nonlocal code is involved, then the `checkWrite()` method checks with some kind of policy database to determine if the particular file to be created is allowed. So, an attempt to write to a file in the temporary directory might be permitted even though an attempt to write to another file would have been rejected.

Class Loaders

The final part of Java's security foundation is the class loader. So far this section has described a system that uses the design of the bytecode language to produce a verifiably typesafe system. The fact that programs are typesafe has then been used to support a runtime checking mechanism that ensures that calls to potentially sensitive resources are made by properly authorized code with acceptable arguments. These mechanisms, verification and security management, both support and are supported by the class loader system.

The only way to load a class into the JVM is via the `defineClass()` final protected native methods, which are declared in the abstract base class `java.lang.Class-Loader`. This method ensures that the verification system is called properly and is part of the type safety mechanism. The class loader is also responsible for performing some other checks that form part of the system security. The verification mechanisms ensure that access to a protected method is restricted to members of the same package and to subclasses, so you can be confident that access to the `defineClass()` method is restricted. The security management system allows runtime control of the execution of sensitive methods. The construction of a class loader, access to certain special package hierarchies (such as `sun.*`), and the ability to define new package members in some package hierarchies (such as `java.*`) are restricted by the security manager provided the class loader makes the effort to check.

These are the responsibilities of the class loader that impact system security:

- Ensure a class is properly named. Multiple or leading dots (for example, `.myutils.Bezier` or `myutils..netscape.cache.Bezier`) must be rejected since they might force local loading of a class from a location other than the proper classpath.

- Ensure local classes are loaded in preference to remote ones. This might cause a name clash, but it ensures that foreign code cannot usurp local code.

- Ensure that classes, once loaded, are cached. If a loaded class is not cached, it might be loaded twice, which would result in duplication of the static variables and possibly make an instance of the class unable to access its own private variables.

- Maintain separate namespaces for classes loaded by different class loaders. A namespace is like a prefix to the package name and arranges for identically named classes loaded by different class loaders to be treated as different classes. This behavior is especially important for applets.

In JDK 1.0 and 1.1 systems, you had to create a class loader if you wanted special loading behavior, such as loading from a network. Further, the responsibilities listed previously were left to you to implement. With JDK 1.2, the framework has been improved dramatically. First, if you do choose to implement a new class loader, you only need to subclass the `java.security.SecureClassLoader` and implement a single method, `findLocalClass()`. This method, `findLocalClass()`, is not particularly security sensitive and only needs to perform the actual loading of the bytecode file. More importantly, it is now possible to provide virtually all the functionality you might require from a specialist class loader simply by implementing a special protocol handler. This can then be used by the existing `java.net.URLClassLoader`, and you no longer risk jeopardizing the security of your system.

NOTE Creating protocol handlers is discussed in Sybex's *Java 1.2 Developer's Handbook*.

Summary

This section has covered lots of ideas, so it's probably a good idea to collect the vital ones together for a quick recap.

- The foundation of Java's security is the design of the bytecode language. This allows the type correctness of a program to be proven before it can run.

- The bytecode verifier implements the type safety proofs described above.

- The bytecode verifier is run as part of the process of installing a new class into the JVM. The type safety mechanisms themselves are used to control access to the crucial (`ClassLoader`) code that performs this installation.

- Given that an executing program is type safe, arguments are always of the expected type, and improper memory or I/O access is impossible.

- Since bytecodes cannot perform direct memory or I/O accesses, native methods are the only access to system resources. Native methods should be constructed to be `private`. (This is a general requirement if security is to be maintained; the language itself permits nonprivate native methods.)

- Based on the accessibility modifiers, the type safety mechanisms control access to native methods. Because private native methods are the only access to system resources and can only be accessed by other methods in the same class, accessible gatekeeper methods can use the argument lists and calling stack frame of a request to decide whether or not to permit a requested access. This decision making forms the security manager feature of Java.

- The type safety system is able to prevent any class from loading classes unless that class is a subclass of `ClassLoader`, and the security manager can prevent any untrusted code from creating any instance of a subclass of `ClassLoader`.

- Since the `ClassLoader` that loads a class forms part of the namespace of the class, the type safety mechanism can always identify foreign code properly.

- The class loader mechanism uses the security manager system to protect particularly sensitive packages, such as `sun.*` and `java.*`, for additional safety.

- The security argument that is formed by the bytecode verifier, security manager, and class loaders is a self-consistent but circular one. If any one part of the system is breached, the whole system fails.

- The security mechanisms depend upon the integrity of the files in the original JVM distribution. Adding new classes to the CLASSPATH (or the `sun.boot.class.path` property), replacing any classes in the distribution, modifying native libraries, or changing any of the executable programs (most especially the JVM) involves a risk to the security of your system and your users. Java cannot protect you, or protect itself, against any of the other routes by which malicious damage can occur. These routes include, but are not limited to, FTPing malicious executables, floppy disks with viruses, word-processor files containing macros, other forms of active content, attacks against your browser, attacks against other Internet services such as e-mail, and so forth. Java security is not an island: If an attacker compromises your machine, they can destroy your Java security from underneath.

This section has described the basis of Java's security mechanisms. These features provide the enhanced program robustness and reliability that comes from being able to check that method arguments are in the proper range for a call and also form the foundation for all the remaining security APIs. JDK 1.2 introduces a much more flexible mechanism for controlling access to resources by remote code than was provided for in earlier releases. The next section discusses this new system.

Monitoring Security Accesses

If you are interested in monitoring what the Java security mechanisms are doing, you can turn on debug-type messages by setting the `java.security.debug` System property. To get a list of available options, set the property to `help`:

```
java -Djava.security.debug=help xxx
```

This will display the available monitoring options. For instance, the `all` option allows you to monitor everything, like jar file verifications and all `checkPermission` results. Separate options are available for monitoring different security checks.

Authorization in JDK 1.2

Java controls access to machine resources based less on an individual's identity and more on the source of a class file. Decisions about access to the machine resources are generally made from the starting premise that the human who is operating the machine is entitled to perform any action that the underlying O/S will permit; therefore Java doesn't need to worry about limiting the operations. Instead, the access control mechanisms are directed at limiting the capabilities of pieces of executable code that have come from remote sources. The fundamental issues still apply: The code must be identified, authenticated, and granted access to local resources accordingly.

NOTE

Java is quite capable of performing user identification and authentication and includes an API as a work-in-progress to provide the mechanism for controlling access to arbitrary users. However, this is not the familiar mode for Java operation. You would not expect to have to log into your browser—although you might have to log into a remote Web site—and you would similarly not expect to have to log into your own Java programs.

The Access Control List APIs, which provide a framework for resource control, are described later in this chapter.

Resource Control with JDK 1.0 and 1.1

With JDK 1.0 and JDK 1.1, the resource control mechanism was relatively simple. All remote code was identifiable and all requests for resource access were passed through a single instance of the `SecurityManager` class. These calls were either permitted or denied based on the origin of the code in the calling stack frame. Local code would be trusted, while remote code would generally be untrusted. Remote code could be identified by the fact that the class loader used to load it was non-null. You can identify the class loader used to load a class by issuing a statement like this:

```
ClassLoader loader = this.getClass().getClassLoader();
```

which determines the class loader used to load the class that defines the object `this`.

This mechanism was simple and easy to understand, but relatively hard to modify. To implement any change to the security policy, for example, to trust classes that originated from one particular server, you had to write and install a whole new `SecurityManager` class. This was not particularly difficult, but since it was security-critical code, you had to pay close attention to what you were doing. Further, many system features in Java make extensive use of system resources, and as such there were many calls to the `SecurityManager` that were too nontrivial to understand.

Another significant difficulty with the 1.0/1.1 `SecurityManager` approach was that it was difficult to extend. The `SecurityManager` object would be installed in the system by calling the method `System.setSecurityManager()`, and this could only be used once per application. If you tried to install two security managers, they didn't nest, or parallel up, but the second attempt caused a security exception. And with applets, you couldn't install any `SecurityManager` because the browser already did this once. Now, to understand the problem, consider this scenario. You and a colleague are creating new libraries that provide access to special resources (it might be special hardware such as scanners or modems and the like, or it might be a database that should be kept for trusted code only). To add security checks to protect your code, you both create a special subclass of `Security-Manager` that adds an extra check method to protect your facility. Now, if an end user wants to protect both your systems, they cannot install both security managers. Instead they have to take the source for these and merge them together to produce a single `SecurityManager` class that provides access for both new facilities.

The JDK 1.2 Approach

The JDK 1.2 security system is much more flexible. It is possible to reconfigure the security policy without writing any code; instead a configuration file is provided. The file contains text that can, if you choose, be edited by hand. Further, it is possible to define the control mechanisms for new resources in a way that can be fully integrated with the system. Multiple independent new resources do not interfere with each other, and you can even use the text file for configuration of new resources exactly as you did for the built-in ones.

NOTE

The new security policy does not prevent the use of custom `SecurityManager` objects if you already have them. If you install such an object, it will work just as it did in the older JDKs, because the new control mechanisms are implemented via a new `SecurityManger` object. This means that if you install your `SecurityManager`, you will lose most of the new functionality and some of the flexibility. In most cases, it is relatively easy to take the policy of a custom `SecurityManager` and re-implement it using the new mechanism.

Permissions

The fundamental unit of the new security system is a base class called `Permission` in the `java.security` package. Instances of specific subclasses of this class are used to represent permissions to perform particular operations. For example, the `java.io.FilePermission` class is used to describe permission to access a file or files. Typically a `Permission` instance is created with two textual arguments. The first is called the *name* and the second is called the *action*. In fact, the titles of these arguments are only suggestions, but in the particular case of a FilePermission, they are accurate descriptions. So, if a `FilePermission` is created like this:

```
FilePermission fp = new FilePermission("/etc/passwd", "read");
```

then it describes the permission to read file `/etc/passwd`.

TIP

For filenames on Windows systems, you must specify a double backslash for each single backslash in the path. For instance, the `C:\Windows\TEMP` directory would be specified with `C:\\Windows\\TEMP`.

Simply creating the permission object does not grant permission however. When a privileged operation is attempted, a database of permissions is checked against the origin of the requesting code; if a matching one can be found then the operation is permitted. You will look at this in more detail shortly.

Permissions can be wildcarded—that is you can create a `FilePermission` that describes all files in a particular directory or all files in a particular tree. Some permissions can have wildcards applied to their action parts. It is important to appreciate that this behavior, while conventional, is implemented by the individual `Permission` subclasses, so you must check the documentation to determine if it is available in any particular case. Similarly, if you create new `Permission` classes, you must code any wildcard behavior yourself. The "Example Using Permissions" section later in this chapter looks at creating `Permission` classes. As an example, if you wanted to describe permission to read any file in the /tmp hierarchy, you would create a permission like this:

```
FilePermission fp = new FilePermission("/tmp/-", "read");
```

NOTE

To find out the directory to store temporary files, use the value of the System property `java.io.tmpdir`.

The Policy File

As previously stated, the mere existence of a particular `Permission` does not grant that permission; for that to happen, the `Permission` must be in a particular database. As an application programmer, you do not normally write code to create or maintain this database of permissions, since there is code built into the runtime system that does this before any application is started. In fact the database that contains the `Permission` objects, which is known as the *policy*, is loaded from a text file. A file called `java.security`, located in the subdirectory `jre\lib\security` under the base of the Java installation, contains two entires that are normally:

```
policy.url.1=file:${java.home}/lib/security/java.policy
policy.url.2=file:${user.home}/.java.policy
```

This entry causes the security policy to be loaded from a file called `java.policy` in the same `jre\lib\security` directory. Additionally, permissions are loaded into the policy from a file called `.java.policy` stored in the individual user's home directory. Clearly this is only relevant on a multi-user system, but in a Windows 95/98 system this depends on if user profiles are shared or not. For Windows NT, a user's login directory is under `\WinNT\Profiles`. So, for user `javajane`, the personal security policy file would be `\WinNT\Profiles\javajane\.java.policy`.

> **TIP**
>
> If you are unsure where to look for the user's `.java.policy` file, look at the System property `user.home`. You can also specify a policy filename by setting the `java.security.policy` option to the `java` command: `java -Djava.security.policy=mypolicies AppClass`.

The policy file contains a series of grant statements. Each of these contains a list of permissions that should be granted to code in a particular *protection domain*. The concept of a protection domain describes all classes loaded from the same source and signed by the same signer. So a grant statement looks like this:

```
grant signedBy "myfriend",  codeBase "http://friendly.com/" {
  permission java.io.FilePermission "/tmp/*", "read";
};
```

This entry indicates that code signed by an entity known as "myfriend" and loaded from anywhere beneath the base URL `http://friendly.com/` is granted permission to read any file in the `/tmp` directory. Code from other locations or not signed by myfriend will not be granted this privilege unless some other grant block says so.

You can specify multiple signers by using a comma-separated list of entity names, but this requires that the code be signed by *all* the named entities, not just any one from the list. If you wish to express that the trust is to be granted if code is signed by any one of a list, then you must use multiple grant blocks with duplicated contents.

Multiple permission lines may be included in each grant block; in which case all the listed permissions will be granted to code satisfying the requirements of signature and origin.

You can grant trust to unsigned code from a particular location, signed code from any location, or even unsigned code from any location simply by leaving out either or both of the `signedBy` or `codebase` fields. Hence, the default entry that is present in the `java.policy` file as distributed simply says:

```
grant {
   ...
```

and contains entries that grant limited access to system properties, mimicking the restricted permissions of untrusted code in JDKs 1.0 and 1.1.

The *Policytool*

Although it is relatively easy to edit the policy file by hand, it is perhaps a little daunting for "ordinary users" who are familiar neither with system administration nor with programming. Because of this, a GUI based tool, called `policytool`, exists to assist in the editing of policy files.

Figure 24.2 shows the `policytool` main window after a particular policy file has been opened. Notice that for each grant statement, there is one entry in the list. To add a new grant statement, press the "Add Policy Entry" button, and a dialog pops up inviting you to enter the signers and codebase for the new grant statement. Given an existing grant entry on the main window, you can view the associated permissions by pressing the "Edit Policy Entry" button or double-clicking on the associated policy. This brings up the window shown in Figure 24.3, which is also the starting point for editing the permission list. To add a new permission, press the "Add" button. This brings up the dialog shown in Figure 24.4. This dialog has four fields. The first is for the class of the permission to be granted. The choice box lists the built-in ones for ease of operation. The second is for the name of the permission. Recall that in the case of a `FilePermission`, this describes the file or directory node to which access is to be granted. The third describes the action associated with the permission. For files this might be "read" or "read, write, delete, execute." The list of pre-entered targets and actions changes based upon the selected permission. The final field, labeled "Signed By" refers to a part of the policy file we have not yet described. This allows you to specify that the permission class itself (or rather the JAR it is loaded from) must be signed.

The idea of signing the permission class warrants a little discussion. `Permission` classes themselves take a part in the decision to grant or deny access to the resources they describe, so a deliberately corrupted `Permission` class could readily breach the security system. The `signedBy` entry in the permission record allows you to require that the validity of the permission class is checked too, and it is vital for

FIGURE 24.2:

The policytool main window

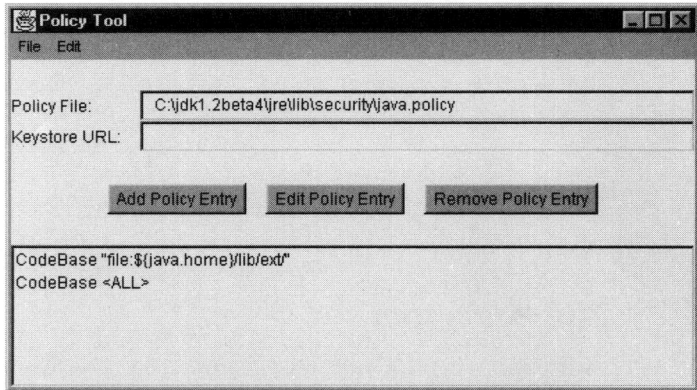

FIGURE 24.3:

The permission list for a grant statement

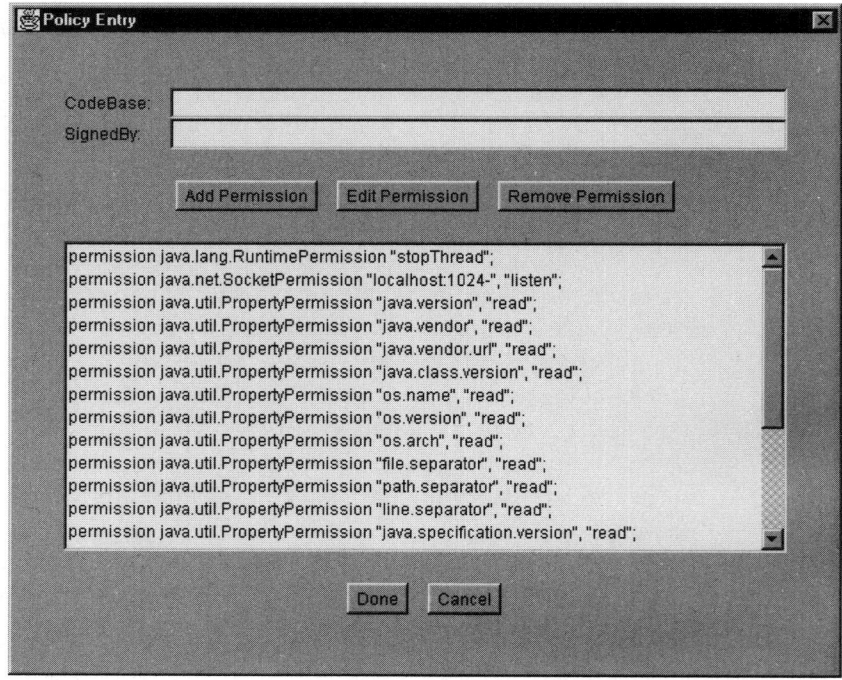

FIGURE 24.4:

Adding a permission to a grant statement

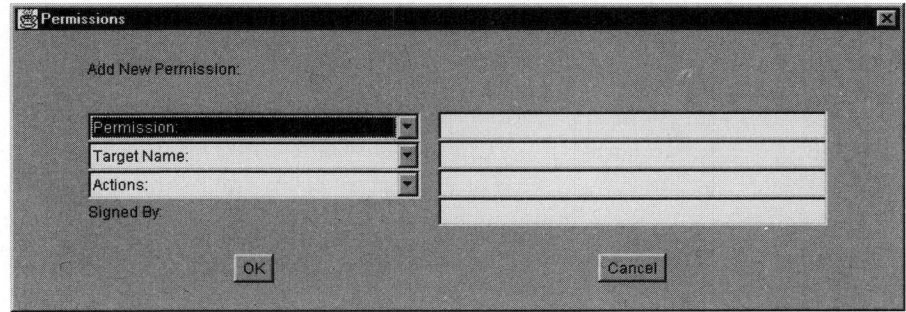

any permission classes that are loaded from an untrusted source. It is a wise precaution to add even your local permissions. However, remember that if you cannot protect your JVM distribution from hackers, then Java cannot protect you either. So do not allow signed local permissions to give you a false sense of security regarding ignoring the routine security administration of your machine.

The discussions of the way the policy file is used to describe permissions have made several references to entities that have signed code. So far you have not looked at how an identity is named, but this is addressed next.

Identifying the Code Source

The new security policy mechanisms used in JDK 1.2 revolve around the idea that code from a particular server, or that is identified by a particular digital signature, may be granted additional permissions. The signing entity is identified by an alias, such as "myfriend" in the earlier example. If you want to use a particular alias in the policy file, the alias name and associated public key must be installed in a local database. This database, like the policy database, is defined in the file `jre/lib/security/java.security`. The default entry is:

```
keystore.type=jks
```

which describes the implementation type for the public key database that is to be used by the system. This gets mapped to the `sun.security.provider.JavaKeyStore` class using the security provider mechanisms described later in the "Security Providers" section. This in turn uses a file called `.keystore` for permanent storage of keys. The file is kept in the user's home directory, or in the case of a Windows 95/98 system with shared user profiles, in the main Windows directory.

You will look at the use of the `keytool` in a moment, but there are two peripheral issues to discuss first. First, give some thought to the security of the keystore file itself. This file is used to store keys against the aliases to which they relate, and those aliases are used to grant permissions to imported code. Clearly this file must be protected carefully otherwise it might be possible for someone to install a modified key against an alias to which you have allocated a great deal of trust. If this happened, your trust would be misplaced. Of course, this is the same comment made before: you must protect your base JDK system, otherwise it cannot protect you. This is an important point and bears reiterating. Because of the need to protect the keystore file, it is encrypted; and each operation upon it requires the use of a password. Additionally, separate passwords can be applied to each key in the store if you wish.

What Is a Certificate?

Public key cryptography, and with it digital signature systems, depend upon one party creating a related pair of keys and keeping one secret, while the other is distributed freely to any interested recipient. From this starting point, one of two things can occur: the public key can be used to encrypt a message that can only be decrypted by the holder of the private key. Or the private key can be used to encrypt a message that can be decrypted by anyone who has the public key, but could only have been created by the holder of the private key that is paired with the public one. This latter scenario is how digital signatures work.

So, if you receive a message that decrypts successfully using a particular public key, what do you know about the origin of the message? Well, you know the holder of the private key that matches the public key you hold created the message. However, of itself, that does not tell you who the holder of the private key is. To verify the originator of the message, you need to have confidence about who holds the private key. For this to happen, you need to receive the public key in a way that makes you confident about its origin. This requirement might be satisfied if you meet the person face to face and they give you the public key. Similarly, perhaps with a different degree of certainty, the requirement might be satisfied if you receive notification via registered mail or courier, or perhaps if you telephone them and ask. In many cases, however, such mechanisms are unduly cumbersome for managing hundreds of keys. You need a better way.

Suppose you get a single public key from one person we will call Trent. You take all the precautions you think reasonably necessary to ensure its validity. This allows you to identify with confidence messages sent by Trent. Now, imagine that Trent sends you a message telling you about the public key of someone else; we'll call that person Alice. Trent assures us that he is certain the key is valid, and he tells us what he did to ensure this validity. Now, if (and only if) you trust Trent to be honest about what he tells you, and you also feel that the actions he took to ensure the key really belonged to the person called Alice were good enough, then you can trust the public key that Trent sent you. This level of trust can be assumed because Trent signed the message containing Alice's key. Messages that contain the public key of a third party and are signed by a trusted intermediary (Trent in our example) are called *certificates*. The trusted intermediary called a *certification authority*, and the *certification service practices* statement describes the process by which the certification authority decides if a key is genuinely the property of a particular third party. Each certification authority should issue such a statement, and you should consider if it is sufficient for your purposes before you trust certificates from a specific certification authority. Finally, the public key of a certification authority is generally distributed in the form of a certificate, signed by the certification authority itself, and called a *root certificate*. The signature attached to a root certificate serves only to maintain the format of the certificate; it does not attest to the validity of that root certificate. You must be sure that you obtain valid root certificates and take adequate steps to authenticate them. This has an important corollary: You must take care with the origin of your Web browser. It has become conventional for web browser software to come with root certificates for many authorities pre-installed. This is convenient if, and only if, you can still be sure about the authenticity of those certificates. Imagine you obtain your browser pre-installed from a hardware vendor or from an unfamiliar FTP site or on a floppy disk from someone at work. How sure can you be that the root certificates that are installed are all valid?

Using *keytool*

The keytool is a command line tool that manages keys using certificates. The keytool has two main jobs. The first is to create private and public key pairs for you to use. The second is to store certificates from other entities against an alias of your choosing.

Creating Your Own Keys   To create a pair of keys for your own use, use the -genkey option of keytool. You will be prompted for the keystore password and your personal details. The keystore password is used to protect the keystore as a whole, but you should bear in mind that you must still protect the keystore file, as the encryption used is relatively weak. This is necessary for it to be exportable from the U.S. The personal information covers your name, organization, and geographical location. You can leave any or all of this as "Unknown" if you wish while you are experimenting, but you will need to provide most of the information when creating a certificate for real use. A sample session follows, with responses in bold:

```
Enter keystore password:  mastering
What is your first and last name?
```

```
    [Unknown]:  John Zukowski
What is the name of your organizational unit?
    [Unknown]:  Publishing
What is the name of your organization?
    [Unknown]:  Sybex
What is the name of your City or Locality?
    [Unknown]:  San Francisco
What is the name of your State or Province?
    [Unknown]:  CA
What is the two-letter country code for this unit?
    [Unknown]:  US
Is <CN=John Zukowski, OU=Publishing, O=Sybex, L=San Francisco,
➥ ST=CA, C=US> correct?
    [no]:  yes
```

After you enter the requested information and confirm that it is correct, `key-store` pauses for a few moments. During this time, it is generating a public and private key pair for you and storing them in the form of a certificate. After generation, you are prompted for an alias specific password, which defaults to the same as the `keystore`:

```
Enter key password for <mykey>
        (RETURN if same as keystore password):
```

This certificate is signed, but because you signed it, the signature is not really useful. It simply indicates the certificate has not been accidentally corrupted and maintains the normal certificate format. If you want the certificate to be of general value, you must get it signed by one or more certification authorities; to do this, you must create a certificate-signing request.

By default, the `keytool` creates key pairs for use with DSA signatures. If you want keys for other algorithms, such as DES encryption, you use the `-keyalg` option to specify this. Be aware that key generation for encryption algorithms, like DES, is not available from Sun outside of the United States because of export restrictions.

NOTE   The Java Cryptography Extension 1.2 (JCE) is one library from Sun that includes support for DES encryption. However, it is restricted to U.S./Canada usage only. On the other hand, Baltimore Technologies offers the J/Crypto product, an enhanced Java security library. It *is* available outside North America since the company is based in Ireland, not Maryland, as the company name implies.

Importing a Certificate   If someone sends you a certificate of their own, you will need to install it into your `keystore` if you wish to use it later. This is done using the `-import` option. Each certificate is stored with an alias, which is the shorthand name by which you refer to the certificate, for example, in a policy file. If you do not specify an alias, then `keytool` always assumes you are referring to the default alias, which is "mykey." To import a new certificate, you must provide an alias that is different. The first certificate you should import is a certification authority certificate that will be referred to by other certificates.

Getting a Certificate C.A.-Signed   For your own certificate to be generally useful, you will probably want it to be signed by one of the well-known certification authorities. To achieve this, you must first generate a certificate-signing request that you will send to the C.A. The `keytool` generates a certificate-signing request with the option `-csr`. The resulting text output looks similar to this:

```
---BEGIN NEW CERTIFICATE REQUEST---
MIICfjCCAjsCAQAweTELMAkGA1UEBhMCR0IxEjAQBgNVBAgTCUJlcmtzaGlyZTESMBAGA1UEBxMJ
V29raW5naGFtMRgwFgYDVQQKEw9QdXJwbGUgQ3VwIEx0ZC4xEDAOBgNVBAsTB1Vua25vd24xFjAU
BgNVBAMTDVNpbW9uIFJvYmVydHMwggG3MIIBLAYHKoZIzjgEATCCAR8CgYEA/X9TgR11EilS3Oqc
Luzk5/YRt1I870QAwx4/gLZRJmlFXUAiUftZPY1Y+r/F9bow9subVWzXgTuAHTRv8mZgt2uZUKWk
n5/oBHsQIsJPu6nX/rfGG/g7V+fGqKYVDwT7g/bTxR7DAjVUE1oWkTL2dfOuK2HXKu/yIgMZndFI
AccCFQCXYFCPFSMLzLKSuYKi64QL8Fgc9QKBgQD34aCF1ps93su8q1w2uFe5eZSvu/o66oL5VOwL
PQeCZ1FZV4661FlP5nEHEIGAtEkWcSPoTCgWE7fPCTKMyKbhPBZ6i1R8jSjgo64eK7OmdZFuo38L
+iE1YvH7YnoBJDvMpPG+qFGQiaiD3+Fa5Z8GkotmXoB7VSVkAUw7/s9JKgOBhAACgYBYDZQZKLiM
/BpOao6FM6fVagcBaIW0fa8F5hyclfXe2TLVY2SYA8X2vsO3/CQYS/+zNbC913XBQbj2N3sXQWvh
v9p4/t5tz4EmLjLjDuugK8ri8UUTkOu8CdU+o5tBSENfdBVQ0r1tYx5gBVb41gHk+AYI1zTASOo3
X6WwM5opxqAAMAsGByqGSM44BAMFAAMwADAtAhQXNjE8Ryarg9iGnpwZvSCl2ze1BAIVAIRdyPH1
JzbzPy5UYRIoISIlhWHI
---END NEW CERTIFICATE REQUEST---
```

Although it looks strange, the certificate request contains only seven bit ASCII characters, so it can be sent by e-mail or any other convenient mechanism to the certification authority who then signs it. Well, to be more accurate, the certification authority will consider your request, take your money, go through their procedures for validating that you are who you claim to be and that the certificate signing request is truly yours, and then return a signed certificate to you. Since this is all rather tedious and expensive, you might prefer, while experimenting, to use a demonstration certificate. This is the same as an ordinary certificate but has a shorter expiration date and is signed by a different certification authority signature so that it will not be trusted by accident.

When you receive a certificate back from the C.A., you should install it over your original one. Use the -import option discussed above to do this. You must have installed the certification authorities' own certificate first. Save your new certificate in a file, for example, \temp\newcert, then issue the command:

```
keytool -import -file \temp\newcert
```

After this command, your alias will refer to the C.A.-signed certificate rather than the self-signed one.

> **NOTE**
>
> There is a difficulty in using most C.A.-signed certificates with the standard distribution of JDK 1.2. Almost all the certification authorities use the RSA/SHA standard for signing the certificates that they issue. The JDK as distributed only comes with the ability to handle DSA signatures. So, before you can install a signed certificate from any of the popular certification authorities, you must obtain a new security provider package that supports RSA signing. See the "Security Providers" section later for more on security providers.

Sending Your Certificate to Others Your certificate is not directly useful to you; rather it is of value when other people have copies of it. To obtain the distribution format of your certificate, you can use the -export option of keytool. With the additional -rfc option, using both -export and -rfc, this generates more seven-bit ASCII output in a style similar to that of the certificate-signing request shown previously. You send this output to your friends, colleagues, or anyone else, perhaps publishing it on your Web page. They can then install this in their own key databases and use it to validate your messages or send you encrypted messages, depending upon the key type that is embedded in the certificate.

Handling Multiple Certificates Sometimes you will want to have certificates of your own from more than one certification authority. To do this, you must have multiple copies of your own key information. The keytool actually keeps an alias name associated with every key certificate it stores; so far that alias has been the default, which is "mykey." If you want to store more than one certificate, and you will need to do so to store other people's certificates, then you must use different aliases for them. You can specify the alias to which any particular keytool operation relates by using the option -alias *alias* on the command line. All the commands we've looked at so far were effectively the same as if they had the additional text -alias mykey on the command line. To create a second copy of your own key information (both the public and private parts), use the -keyclone option.

For this, you should specify a new alias that will be used to refer to the newly created copy of your certificate. This is done using the -`dest` `newalias` arguments.

Signing JAR Files

Since JDK 1.1, JAR files can be signed. This is particularly important in JDK 1.2, since it forms one of the two bases for identifying the origin of a class and, hence, the allocation of trust. Signing a JAR and manual verification of the signatures on a JAR are both performed using the tool `jarsigner` in JDK 1.2. Previously JDK 1.1 overused the tool `javakey`.

Signing a JAR is quite simple, provided you have a private key in your `keystore` (achieved using the -`genkey` option for `keytool`, as described above). Simply issue a command of this form:

```
jarsigner archive.jar alias
```

substituting the name of your JAR archive for `archive.jar`, and your alias, for example `mykey`, in place of `alias`. When you issue this command, the `jarsigner` program will prompt you for the password that protects your `keystore` and, if appropriate, for the password that protects the alias entry, too. Be sure to specify an alias that has a private key associated with it, as you cannot sign with public keys.

Generally the signatures on a JAR archive are read and verified by a class loader when an application or applet uses the class. However, if you want to, you can validate signatures manually; this is also done using the `jarsigner` tool. Simply issue a command of this form:

```
jarsigner -verify -verbose archive.jar
```

and the output will list the files in the archive. Each file carries up to three informational letters at the left-hand column. One of these (a letter "m") indicates whether or not the file is listed in the manifest. Any file, except for files in the META-INF directory itself, will be in the manifest if it was added using the `jar` program, but it might not be if it was added with another program, such as a variant of ZIP. Perhaps more importantly, the letter "s" is used to indicate that a file is signed, while the letter "k" tells you that the signature matched a certificate in your `keystore`. It is important to appreciate that a signature can be verified (letter "s") without necessarily being a signature in which you have placed trust (letter "k").

The final output of the `jarsigner -verify -verbose archive.jar` command is usually the message "`jar verified`." This message indicates that the archive is intact and has not been corrupted.

If you omit the `-verbose` option from the `jarsigner -verify` command, you will only get the "jar verified" message, which tells you that signatures were found and intact but gives no indication about trust you have placed in them.

Provided you use the `-verbose` option, you can also add the `-ids` option. This causes the important details of each signature, such as the signer's name and the alias in your `keystore`, to be output with each file.

Sealing Packages in JAR Files

JAR files allow you to specify that a package they contain may not be extended by classes from other JARs. This is an important capability if you are delivering a potentially security-sensitive archive, and it should be combined with signing for the greatest protection.

The manifest file (`META-INF/MANIFEST.MF`) specifies sealing in one of two ways. You can indicate that all the packages in the JAR are sealed with this entry:

```
Archive-Sealed: true
```

or you can indicate that a seal applies to a specific package like this:

```
Name: mywork/utils/
Package-Sealed: true
```

This tag can also be used in reverse. If an entire archive is sealed with `Archive-Sealed: true`, then you can release the seal on one particular package by using this approach, but specifying `Package-Sealed: false` instead.

By default an archive is not sealed. This is compatible with the system before sealing JAR files was introduced.

To put entries into the manifest file, create a template manifest file that contains the entries you wish to specify, like this for file `manifest.tmp`:

```
Archive-Sealed: true

Name: mywork/utils/
Package-Sealed: false
```

Notice the blank line that separates entries in the file.

To use this as part of the manifest for a JAR archive you create, issue a `jar` command line of this form:

```
jar cmf manifest.tmp outfile.jar files_to_archive…
```

Notice that the m and f options indicate the use of an overriding manifest file and the explicit output file name and that the order of these options needs to match the order in which you provide the actual names of these files in the argument list.

Extending Browser Security

Internet Explorer and Netscape Communicator extend the security model for applets in a nonstandard way, different from both Java 1.1 and Java 1.2. The general concepts are similar to the Policy and Permission classes described above. However, neither is compatible with the other nor with the standard core Java security APIs. For instance, Microsoft supports signed CAB (cabinet) files, not JAR files, with their Permission Scoping API. While Netscape supports signed JAR files it does require the use of their Capabilities API. For information about either of these nonstandard facilities, visit the vendor's appropriate Java security Web pages:

Microsoft http://microsoft.com/java/security/default.htm

Netscape http://home.netscape.com/info/security-doc.html

Extending the Security System

The previous section discussed how the new 1.2 security model allows a great deal of flexibility over the security that applies to your own system. One of the most important features of this new security model, however, is its extensibility.

In the original security systems, a SecurityManager object represented the security policy, and the system prevented the installation of more than one of these. Although this was intended to ensure that security policy could not be inadvertently modified after it had been installed, there was a potentially serious inflexibility as a result. Imagine you have created a new native library that brings a particular facility into a Java system. Typically you are talking about accessing hardware devices, perhaps a serial port or a smart card reader. If you create such a library, you will also want to provide the means to control its security. To do this, you need to create a new SecurityManager with an additional check method. Unfortunately, of course, most browsers have their own SecurityManager, and you can't install both of them.

In the 1.2 security model, if you have a new library that needs to check for a particular permission, you can do this very easily. First, you create a new Permission class and document it. The end users of your library can now refer to this new permission in their policy files without having to alter the rest of the system. Second, when you write your library code, you make inquiries of the Access-Controller to determine if permission is granted for a particular operation.

When you implement a new Permission class, the bulk of the work goes into the implies() method. This is the method that the access control system queries when a decision must be made. The access control system maintains a database that is effectively an in-memory copy of the policy file. This database is a collection of Permission objects that represents what is allowed. When a library method is about to perform a sensitive operation, it creates a new instance of a Permission that represents what it wishes to do; this is called a request. This request is passed into the access controller, which then calls the implies() method of the Permission it has to see if the request should be granted. The idea is simple enough. If, for example, you have a FilePermission in your policy that indicates that read/write access is granted for files in the directory \temp and a request is issued to read the file \temp\ banana, the request should be granted. However, the Permission that describes the request ("\temp\banana", "read") does not exactly match the Permission that is in the policy ("\temp*", "read,write"), and it is the responsibility of the implies() method to ensure that this is correctly handled.

In fact, you often do not need to do any significant work when creating a new Permission class, since the supplied ones are often sufficient. The Basic-Permission class implements an implies() method that checks for wildcarding in both the name of the Permission and the action. All you need to do is create a new subclass and provide the appropriate constructors, since these are not inherited. You might think there isn't even any need to create a subclass. Couldn't you just use the BasicPermission class directly? Well, yes, you probably could. But by subclassing it, you reduce the chance of a naming conflict messing up your protection. Imagine two systems both wanting security from the BasicPermission class, but the names or action lists have similar contents. You could end up with Permission objects in the database that grant permission to both facilities by mistake. Furthermore, you should ensure that individual permission classes that are actually used are marked as final. It is important to ensure that the behavior of the implies() method cannot be usurped.

Example Using Permissions

It's time to take a look at a simple example of using the Permission classes to extend the security system. Since you may not have any special hardware or native libraries to protect, the example will be rather artificial; but it will demonstrate the point just the same.

You will pretend to have a smart card that provides the functionality discussed earlier; that is management of keys, certificates, and, for this example, medical records. SmartCard.java is the library class that represents the smart card's API.

```java
import java.io.*;
import java.security.*;
import java.util.*;
import smart.security.*;

public class SmartCard {
  private HashMap keypairs = new HashMap();
  private HashMap certificates = new HashMap();
  private String medicalNotes;
  private String emergencyInfo;

  public SmartCard() {
    keypairs.put("mine", "1234,5678");
    certificates.put("his", "2345");
    medicalNotes =
      "Checkup 3/1/95, all well. Shots up to date 4/1/97";
    emergencyInfo =
      "Likes Candy Corn in a crisis";
  }

  public Object getKeypair(String keyname) {
    SmartCardPermission p =
      new SmartCardPermission("key", "read");
    AccessController.checkPermission(p);
    // if checkPermission didn't thow an exception,
    // permission was granted, so if we got here,
    // we're ok to proceed
    return keypairs.get(keyname);
  }

  public void setKeypair(String keyname, Object key) {
    SmartCardPermission p =
      new SmartCardPermission("key", "write");
    AccessController.checkPermission(p);
    keypairs.put(keyname, key);
  }

  public Object getCertificate(String name) {
```

```
      SmartCardPermission p =
        new SmartCardPermission("certificate", "read");
      AccessController.checkPermission(p);
      return certificates.get(name);
    }

    public void setCertificate(String name,
      Object certificate) {
      SmartCardPermission p =
        new SmartCardPermission("certificate", "write");
      AccessController.checkPermission(p);
      keypairs.put(name, certificate);
    }

    public String getMedicalNotes() {
      SmartCardPermission p =
        new SmartCardPermission("medical.notes", "read");
      AccessController.checkPermission(p);
      return medicalNotes;
    }

    public String getEmergencyNotes() {
      SmartCardPermission p =
        new SmartCardPermission("medical.emergency", "read");
      AccessController.checkPermission(p);
      return emergencyInfo;
    }
  }
```

SmartCardPermission.java contains the Permission subclass that is used to control access to the SmartCard.

```
package smart.security;
import java.security.*;

public class SmartCardPermission extends BasicPermission {
  public SmartCardPermission(String name) {
    super(name);
  }
  public SmartCardPermission(String name, String action) {
    super(name, action);
  }
}
```

SmartUser.java is a simple test program that attempts to use the features of a SmartCard object.

```java
import java.security.*;

public class SmartUser {
  public static void main(String args[]) {
    SmartCard s = new SmartCard();
    try {
      System.out.println("keys are: " + s.getKeypair("mine"));
    }
    catch (SecurityException ex) {
      System.out.println("Permission to read keys refused");
    }
    try {
      s.setKeypair("another", "abcd,efgh");
      System.out.println("wrote a keypair");
    }
    catch (SecurityException ex) {
      System.out.println("Permission to write a key refused");
    }
    try {
      s.setCertificate("whose", "new123");
      System.out.println("wrote a certificate");
    }
    catch (SecurityException ex) {
      System.out.println(
        "Permission to write a certificate refused");
    }
    try {
      System.out.println(
        "got certificate: " + s.getCertificate("his"));
    }
    catch (SecurityException ex) {
      System.out.println(
        "Permission to read a certificate refused");
    }
    try {
      System.out.println(
        "Medical notes are: " + s.getMedicalNotes());
    }
    catch (SecurityException ex) {
```

```
          System.out.println(
            "Permission to read medical notes refused");
        }
        try {
          System.out.println(
            "Emergency notes are: " + s.getEmergencyNotes());
        }
        catch (SecurityException ex) {
          System.out.println(
            "Permission to read emergency notes refused");
        }
      }
    }
```

`TestSmart.java` is a loader program that serves to start the `SmartUser` object via a class loader, so that `SmartUser` is nonlocal code. This is so that `SmartUser` will need to be granted permissions explicitly in the policy file, rather than having all permissions by default.

```java
import java.net.*;
import java.lang.reflect.*;

public class TestSmart {
  public static void main(String args[]) throws Exception {
    URL source[] = {new File(args[0]).toURL()};
    URLClassLoader cl = new URLClassLoader(source);
    String emptyArgs[] = new String[0];
    try {
      Class c = cl.loadClass ("SmartUser");
      Method m = c.getMethod ("main",
        new Class[] {emptyArgs.getClass()});
      m.invoke (null, new Object[] {emptyArgs});
    }
    catch (InvocationTargetException ex) {
      ex.getTargetException().printStackTrace();
    }
  }
}
```

The class files for this example need to be in different places. All source files are located in the ch24 directory. However, the compiled `SmartUser.java` class file, `SmartUser.class`, needs to be in a different location, so at least on the CD, the `SmartUser.class` file is found in `Smart.jar`. This is because it must run as untrusted code and, hence, must not be found in the CLASSPATH. The last file, SmartCardPermission.java, is located in the subdirectory smart\security, which reflects its package naming. The remaining class files are alongside their source.

To create the appropriate files, execute the following commands:

```
javac -d . SmartCardPermission.java
[The SmartCardPermission.java file must be moved before compiling the
remaining source files.]
move SmartCardPermission.java smart\security\
javac SmartUser.java
jar cf Smart.jar SmartUser.class
del SmartUser.class
javac SmartCard.java
javac TestSmart.java
```

You will want to run the example several times, experimenting with different security policies. But first, run without granting any permission. Select the directory mastering\ch24 and issue a command of this form:

```
java TestSmart Smart.jar
```

This URL indicates that the contents of the JAR should be used, and the URL itself refers to the root of the JAR. It is important that the URL should end with a trailing exclamation point and slash ("!/") to indicate that it refers to the entire JAR rather than a single file or directory within the JAR. Change the path from the example shown to reflect the location of your CD-ROM drive, but stick with forward slashes as this is a URL rather than a file specification as such.

If the URL is correctly specified and all is well, you will see the following output:

```
Permission to read keys refused
Permission to write a key refused
Permission to write a certificate refused
Permission to read a certificate refused
Permission to read medical notes refused
Permission to read emergency notes refused
```

This indicates that the (untrusted) code in the class SmartUser was indeed denied any privileges over the SmartCard software.

Next, we need to grant some privileges. First, locate the file that contains your policy. On Windows, or any single user system, edit the file jre\lib\security\ java.policy located under the JDK installation directory. On a Unix, or other multi-user system, edit the `.java.policy` file in your home directory. Add a line like this to the block that starts `grant {`, that is, the block that grants permissions to unsigned foreign code:

```
permission smart.security.SmartCardPermission "*", "*";
```

Notice that this uses a wildcard for both the name and action part of the permission description. If you run the test again, you should see this output:

```
keys are: 1234,5678
wrote a keypair
wrote a certificate
got certificate: 2345
Medical notes are: Checkup 3/1/95, all well. Shots up to date 4/1/97
Emergency notes are: Likes Candy Corn in a crisis
```

which indicates that all the permissions were indeed granted. Now, although it is potentially useful to grant all permissions in this way, you will probably want to be a little more selective in most cases. Edit the policy file again and comment out the line you just added (do this with either `/* ... */` or `//` style comments). Next add the following line:

```
permission smart.security.SmartCardPermission "certificate", "read";
```

This time when you run the program, you should see that all the permissions are denied except for reading the certificate value.

A wildcard can be used in just one part of the permission arguments if you like. Put these entries, one at a time, into your policy file and determine what happens. Try this one first:

```
permission smart.security.SmartCardPermission "key", "*";
```

Then try this one:

```
permission smart.security.SmartCardPermission "medical.*", "read";
```

Granting Permission by Signing the JAR

The next demonstration is the allocation of trust to a signed jar file. The archive `Smart.jar` is unsigned, so you first need to copy it onto your hard disk where you will then sign it. It really doesn't matter where you put it, so if you're working with a Windows platform, use the directory `C:\Windows\Temp`; for Unix, `/tmp` will do. You can use any other directory that suits you, in which case simply change the commands shown here to suit the directory you choose.

First, make sure you have a public and private key pair. If you already have an appropriate entry in your `keystore`, then skip this step; otherwise issue this command:

```
keytool -genkey
```

and answer the questions about your personal details that follow. If you issue the command exactly as shown here, you will end up with a key pair associated with the alias "mykey," and the rest of these instructions assume that alias. If you have a different alias in your `keystore`, modify the commands you issue accordingly.

Once you have a key pair in the `keystore` database, you can sign your copy of the jar file. Issue the following command:

```
jarsigner c:\windows\temp\Smart.jar mykey
```

Once you have a signed archive, you can investigate allocating trust to that signature. Before that, though, execute the `jarsigner -verify -verbose c:\windows\ temp\Smart.jar` command to verify and list the contents of the archive. Your output should look similar to the following:

```
        186 Mon Jul 27 23:24:58 EDT 1998 META-INF/MYKEY.SF
       1049 Mon Jul 27 23:24:58 EDT 1998 META-INF/MYKEY.DSA
          0 Mon Jul 27 23:20:26 EDT 1998 META-INF/
smk    1815 Mon Jul 27 23:18:52 EDT 1998 SmartUser.class

  s = signature was verified
  m = entry is listed in manifest
  k = at least one certificate was found in keystore
  i = at least one certificate was found in identity scope

jar verified.
```

After verifying the signing of the archive, bring up the policy file in an editor again. Delete any entries still there that refer to the `smart.security.Smart-CardPermission` so you are starting fresh. Now add to the end of the file a single entry like this:

```
grant signedBy "mykey" {
  permission smart.security.SmartCardPermission "*", "*";
};
```

Save the file and issue these two commands in sequence:

```
java TestSmart Smart.jar
java TestSmart c:\windows\temp\Smart.jar
```

This time, you should see that the first command, which refers to the unsigned archive on the CD-ROM, gets no permissions granted. The second, which refers to the signed archive on your hard disk, is granted all permissions. This is because it was signed and the signature matched the public key in your keystore against the alias "mykey."

The most important class to understand in this experiment is SmartCardPermission.java. This is also the simplest. All it does is subclass BasicPermission, changing its name and restoring the two variations of constructor that are defined for the parent class. The idea is to demonstrate that the BasicPermission class defines a permission that is entirely useable for many circumstances, including those that need a rudimentary wildcard handling mechanism.

So that the SmartCardPermission class can be exercised, the file SmartCard.java contains a trivial database that simulates some of the features of a real smartcard. Each of the methods that are defined in the SmartCard class check if they should proceed by first constructing a new instance of SmartCardPermission that describes the operation that is being requested and then calling the AccessController .checkPermission() method. If the checkPermission() method simply returns, then permission is granted and the requested operation (read keys, or whatever) is completed. However, sometimes the checkPermission() method throws an exception. This behavior indicates that the permission is denied. If an exception is thrown by checkPermission(), then the requesting method in the SmartCard class simply abandons the effort by allowing the exception to propagate to its caller in turn.

If the permission mechanism is to be exercised, you need to load a class using a ClassLoader other than the system one. This means you need a class that uses a SmartCard class that is not located on the CLASSPATH. This class is defined in the source file SmartUser.java. The SmartUser class has a main() method that simply creates an instance of the SmartCard class and then tries to use its various methods. Because the methods might throw exceptions during the experiments, the SmartUser class catches these and outputs a message. If this were not done, you would only be able to verify one permission at a time, since the first denial would abandon the whole test. You do not normally need to catch security exceptions, although doing so allows you to output a more helpful description of the problem than an exception stack trace.

Since the SmartUser class must run as untrusted code, you need a startup program to invoke it. This program must create a ClassLoader to load the Smart-User class and then invoke the SmartUser.main() method. Fortunately for us, there is a classloader defined as java.net.URLClassLoader defined in JDK 1.2.

This classloader has one hugely useful feature. It makes it very easy to create an instance of a `ClassLoader` that loads from specified URLs. The invoking of the `main()` method must be manually done with Java's reflection API. This functionality is coded up in the `TestSmart` class.

Avoiding Checks on Callers

The general rule is that the least trusted class in the call hierarchy determines the trust placed on a method call. Sometimes a trusted class needs to perform a restricted operation (such as reading a file containing font information) as a legitimate part of performing a nonrestricted operation (such as drawing text) on behalf of untrusted callers. In the normal course of events, such a scenario would be rejected, as the aggregate trust level of the call stack would be inadequate for reading files. However, it is reasonable that the trusted class might do this, provided of course that it is coded carefully so that only the proper files can be read and that the information in them cannot be leaked in any potentially dangerous way to the caller.

If you are writing a trusted class that provides an unrestricted facility but uses restricted facilities to achieve its goal, you can achieve this using a pair of static method calls in the `AccessController` class. These are `AccessController.begin-Privileged()` and `AccessController.endPrivileged()`. When you write code using these methods, you should be careful to ensure that the privileged services you use are protected from the calling classes and that any potentially sensitive information your class obtains in this way cannot be leaked out.

Using the methods is relatively easy. You just issue the `beginPrivileged()` call immediately before requesting a restricted service and the `endPrivileged()` call immediately afterwards. Because the normal security controls are effectively switched off between these calls, it is very important that you keep the number of operations between the two calls to an absolute minimum. Usually you will only need to make a single method call between `begin/endPrivileged()` pairs. Further, to be absolutely certain that the `endPrivileged()` call is executed, it is normal to use a `try/finally` construction like this:

```
try {
  AccessController.beginPrivileged();
  // sensitive operation
}
finally {
  AccessController.endPrivileged();
}
```

Calling `beginPrivileged()` does not entirely shut off the security checks. What it actually does is simply stop the tests from considering the privilege of any callers above the current method in the stack. This does not grant any privilege to the class that calls the `beginPrivileged()` method. Neither does it allow the privilege of that method to be passed down into other method calls in other classes. All it does is to prevent the checks from going up the stack to the callers of this method.

Authenticating Users

The mechanisms provided by the `SecurityManager` system, mainly through the `AccessController`, are aimed at controlling the resource access of classes, based upon their origin. Of course, in many real programs it is the identity of the user that determines if a particular operation is permitted or not. In many cases, a user's access to resources can be handled by the underlying operating system. For example, on a multi-user system, Java might be willing to permit code to create a `FileInputStream` object, but the underlying O/S might reject the request on the basis that the user does not have read permission for that file. Sometimes, however, a Java program needs to make decisions of this sort. This is particularly true of servers that make a facility available over the network. This is because, in such a case, the process owner, who is the basis on which the O/S will permit or reject a resource access, does not reflect the identity of the requesting person.

To provide a solution in this scenario, you need the following elements:

- Identification of the user
- Authentication of the identity
- Resource containment

Now, Java's APIs do not directly provide for the first two of these, but there is an API that provides a framework for the implementation of resource containment. This is the Access Control List API.

Access Control Lists

The Access Control List, or ACL, API provides a basic framework for a system that determines if a resource access should be granted to a requester or not. The elements of the ACL API defined in the core Java packages are only interface specification; no implementation is available. However, there is a default implementation provided within Sun's JDK 1.2, implemented by classes in the `sun.*` package hierarchy. Because it is located in the `sun.*` package hierarchy, you cannot rely on it being present in any particular distribution. Despite this, the `sun.*` ACL implementation allows you to investigate the behavior of a typical ACL implementation in practice.

These are the interfaces that are defined in the `java.security.acl` package.

- `Acl`
- `AclEntry`
- `Group`
- `Owner`
- `Permission`

One additional interface, `Principal`, is used by the ACL API and is found in the `java.security` package. Concrete classes implementing these interfaces are used at runtime to build a data structure that describes a security policy.

For each resource you wish to control, you need a separate `Acl` object. An `Acl` object has a list of `AclEntry` objects, each of which has a polarity and is associated with a `Principal`. The polarity indicates if this `AclEntry` is granting or denying permissions. The `Principal` describes who or what the permissions relate to, typically either a single person or a group.

Broadly, the idea is this: For each resource that is to be controlled, you create an `Acl` object. For each distinct `Principal`, you can add an `AclEntry` listing permissions to be granted and an `AclEntry` listing permissions to be denied. Each `Permission` represents an action that might be performed upon the resource. This structure is shown in Figure 24.5.

For each `Principal`, there can be zero or one negative `AclEntry` denying permissions, and zero or one positive `AclEntry` granting permissions. A permission is not granted unless there is a positive entry, so at this point it might seem odd that the `AclEntry` can be negative. The reason is that a `Principal` might represent a group, where a group is itself a collection of `Principal` objects. Under such conditions, it is possible for several `AclEntry` objects to relate to the same single `Principal` object if that single `Principal` is a member of several groups.

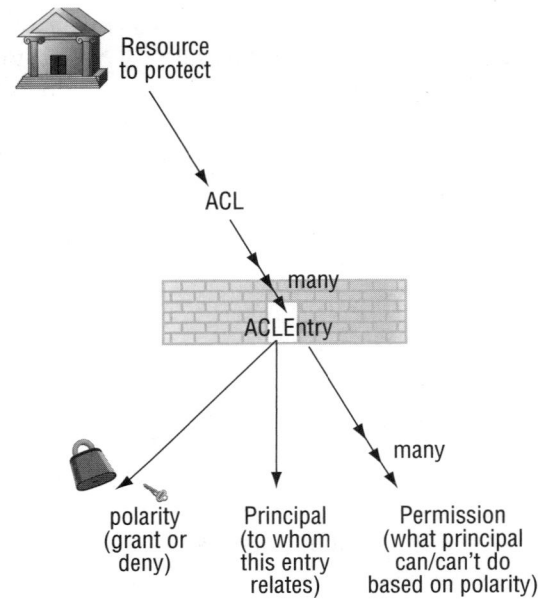

Now you have the possibility of both granting and denying entries for the same permission for the same target principal. So how does this conflict get resolved? Well, the rules are:

1. Individually specified permissions override group specified ones.
2. If individual permissions both grant and deny, then they are scrapped.
3. If group permissions both grant and deny, then they are scrapped.

So to determine if permission should be granted, these are the steps taken by the system:

1. Find the individual `Permission` objects for a specific `Principal`.
2. If a positive entry exists but a negative entry does not, then grant the permission.
3. Otherwise, if a negative entry exists but a positive entry does not, then deny the permission.
4. Otherwise, locate all the `Permission` objects in `AclEntry` objects that relate to groups of which the `Principal` is a member.

5. If there are positive entries but not negative ones, then grant the permission.

6. Otherwise, deny the permission.

Notice that conflicting, or absent, individual entries pass the argument to the group, while group permissions can only grant a permission if only positive entries exist. If negative group entries cancel positive group entries, the fallback position is that the permission is denied.

Clearly, conflicting individual entries should be regarded as an administrative error; however, it is quite reasonable to expect such conflicts in group entries since an individual can properly belong to more than one group.

Ownership

The calls that add entries to an `Acl` require two parameters. The second of these is the `AclEntry` that is to be added, but the first is a `Principal` referred to as an owner. An owner is specified when the `Acl` is first created, and more owners can be added later if required. The methods `addOwner()` and `deleteOwner()` take two arguments. The first is a reference to an existing owner, and the second is a reference to another owner to be added or removed. These methods are defined by the `Owner` interface, which is extended by the `Acl` interface.

The Acl Implementation Classes

Since the `java.security.acl` package contains only interfaces and not concrete classes, you must look elsewhere for implementations of this strategy. It turns out that there are implementations delivered with Sun's JDKs since version 1.1. However, these implementations are in the `sun.security.acl`; therefore it is not possible to use them in a program that seeks to be certified as 100% Java. Despite this, they are very easy to use and a short example is warranted.

The source for this example is listed below. Just compile and run the program to test it:

```
javac TryAcl.java
java TryAcl
```

This will result in the following output:

```
C:> java TryAcl
With empty entries: Read permission is not granted.
With group grant: Read permission is granted.
With individual deny: Read permission is not granted.
With individual grant: Read permission is granted.
With group deny: Read permission is not granted.
```

Notice how the permissions for group and individual entries merge. Satisfy yourself that you understand how the conflicting entries are handled.

In the first case, no permissions have been added, so the effect is that the permission is denied. When a group grant entry is added, and in the absence of any overriding individual entry or conflicting group entry, then permission is granted. Immediately an individual denial is added. This overrides the group permission, however, and permission is revoked. After adding a conflicting individual grant entry, the individual entries are ignored and the group grant entry becomes effective again, so the permission is granted. Finally, adding a group deny entry after the individual entries have canceled each other out results in the group entries canceling too; and the permission is again revoked.

```java
import java.util.*;
import java.security.*;
import java.security.acl.*;
import sun.security.acl.*;

public class TryAcl {

  public static void main(String args[]) {
    Principal principal = new PrincipalImpl("Individual");
    Principal owner = new PrincipalImpl("Owner");

    Group group = new GroupImpl("Group");
    group.addMember(principal);

    java.security.acl.Permission read =
      new PermissionImpl("Read");
    java.security.acl.Permission write =
      new PermissionImpl("Write");

    Acl acl = new AclImpl(owner, "acl");

    AclEntry principalGrantEntry =
      new AclEntryImpl(principal);
    AclEntry principalDenyEntry = new AclEntryImpl(principal);
    principalDenyEntry.setNegativePermissions();
    AclEntry groupGrantEntry = new AclEntryImpl(group);
    AclEntry groupDenyEntry = new AclEntryImpl(group);
    groupDenyEntry.setNegativePermissions();

    try {
      acl.addEntry(owner, principalGrantEntry);
```

```
      acl.addEntry(owner, principalDenyEntry);
      acl.addEntry(owner, groupGrantEntry);
      acl.addEntry(owner, groupDenyEntry);
    }
    catch (NotOwnerException ex) {
      System.out.println("owner isn't an owner of this ACL");
      System.exit(1);
    }

    System.out.print("With empty entries: ");
    System.out.print("Read permission is ");
    if (!acl.checkPermission(principal, read)) {
      System.out.print("not ");
    }
    System.out.println("granted.");

    groupGrantEntry.addPermission(read);
    System.out.print("With group grant: ");
    System.out.print("Read permission is ");
    if (!acl.checkPermission(principal, read)) {
      System.out.print("not ");
    }
    System.out.println("granted.");

    principalDenyEntry.addPermission(read);
    System.out.print("With individual deny: ");
    System.out.print("Read permission is ");
    if (!acl.checkPermission(principal, read)) {
      System.out.print("not ");
    }
    System.out.println("granted.");

    principalGrantEntry.addPermission(read);
    System.out.print("With individual grant: ");
    System.out.print("Read permission is ");
    if (!acl.checkPermission(principal, read)) {
      System.out.print("not ");
    }
    System.out.println("granted.");

    groupDenyEntry.addPermission(read);
    System.out.print("With group deny: ");
    System.out.print("Read permission is ");
    if (!acl.checkPermission(principal, read)) {
```

```
      System.out.print("not ");
    }
    System.out.println("granted.");
  }
}
```

The bulk of the code relates to building the data structures with which the `Acl` object works. The various constructors of the `*Impl` objects actually build the `Acl`, `AclEntry`, `Principal`, `Group`, and `Permission` objects. As each `Permission` is added to an `AclEntry`, a message is printed that includes the result of the test `acl.checkPermission(principal, read)`. The two arguments to this call are the `Principal` object for which the permission is being checked and the `Permission` object that describes what action the `Principal` wishes to take.

A number of significant implementation details are raised by this example. Notice that the `Permission` objects in use here are `java.security.acl.Permission`, not `java.security.Permission`. Because the same name, `Permission`, occurs in both the `java.security.acl` and `java.security` packages, and you need both packages since `Principal` is defined in `java.security`, you must either import the one you need explicitly, using the line:

```
import java.security.acl.Permission;
```

rather than:

```
import java.security.acl.*;
```

or you can take the approach used in this example and qualify the name `Permission` whenever it arises. Which one you adopt is a matter of stylistic preference.

Another point to emphasize is that the objects here are being created from classes in the `sun.security.acl` package, so the program is not 100% Pure Java. Since there are no implementations of the `java.security.acl` interfaces in the core packages, this is a difficult problem to resolve. Probably the best approach is to create a utility class that has static factory methods that create the various implementation objects. That way, changes in the implementation can be accommodated relatively easily. A second enhancement would be to use properties to define the implementation classes or package that should be used by the factory. Since you will need to invoke constructors that take arguments, you will need to use the reflection facilities to construct the instances.

It is clearly inappropriate for a real program to define the permissions and principals in code. Instead, some sort of file based mechanism should be used. Ideally, the mechanism should refer to the identity databases of the underlying machine, but that risks becoming platform dependent and needs careful encapsulation into implementation classes if portability is to be maintained.

It is crucial to appreciate that the `Acl` structures are not able to enforce access control by themselves. Their effectiveness depends upon a number of support features that you must provide in your program. Most importantly you must ensure that all access to the resource to be protected is granted only after the `Acl` object has been checked. This is easiest to implement if the resource is accessed through a single method that includes the `checkPermission()` method call.

The `Acl` facilities only relate to the decision making part of access control, they are not involved in identifying or authenticating the principals upon which their decisions are based. This is important; you cannot have a meaningful access control list implementation unless you first find a sensible way to identify the individuals and groups that will be controlled.

Cryptographic APIs

In JDK 1.1 and onward, there is a framework that provides an interface to cryptographic functionality. Due to US export controls, this framework is split into two separate parts, one part being in the core Java APIs and the other part not. The exportable, core, part is called the Java Cryptography Architecture or JCA, while the restricted part is called the Java Cryptography Extension, or JCE. The framework provided by these is extensible. As with so many other parts of the Java system, they use factory methods and interfaces (and abstract classes) to allow new implementations to be plugged into the system without requiring changes to client source code. The JCA provides for digital signatures, message digests, and key pair generators, while encrypted streams are provided by the JCE, that is, by the export restricted extension.

NOTE   There are implementations of encryption algorithms that have either been created outside the US or that have been granted export licenses from the US Further, it is a reasonable assumption that efforts are being made to obtain an export license for at least some part of the JCE: implementing "weak" algorithms or, more precisely, using weak keys. This section will only consider the facilities of the Sun-originated frameworks and will not discuss the nonstandard facilities.

First this section looks at the use of the cryptographic APIs and then it looks at how the framework can be extended to allow you to write new algorithm implementations and incorporate them into the Java runtime system.

Signatures

Digital signatures use asymmetric encryption to allow a degree of confidence that someone originated a message. The idea works like this: Alice generates a pair of keys for asymmetric encryption. One of these is passed to Bob by some means (the means is important; we'll come back to it). Next, Alice has a message she wants to send to Bob, and she wants Bob to know that she originated it. She could encrypt the message with the private key that only she knows and then sends the message to Bob. Bob would find that the message was successfully decrypted using the other, public, key that Alice had given him. This would show that the key that is a pair with this one encrypted the message and that Alice did the encryption.

Actually, what normally happens is slightly different from this, but the principle is the same. In most signature systems, Alice does not encrypt the message, but instead generates a Message Digest (which is like a checksum, but cryptographically difficult to forge) and then encrypts that digest value. The resulting, smaller data block is appended to the end of the message. Validation then consists of Bob calculating the digest value of the message body and decrypting the signature block; if the two values match, the message was properly signed.

Well, the mathematics are probably sound enough, but it is crucial to appreciate that all the mathematics demonstrate is that the message was encrypted with the other key of the pair. Bob needs to be certain the public key he received was part of the key pair originated by Alice, and not some other public key substituted by a third party. He also needs to be sure that Alice has kept her private key private. As described earlier, the key distribution problem is generally solved using certificates. However, this does not help in a situation where Alice might have given away her private key, for convenience (such as lending it to a friend while she was on holiday) or by accident (perhaps the key was stored on her computer, which was inadequately protected against malicious attack). It is, therefore, possible that some hacker could literally have stolen her key.

Calculating a Signature Value

Ignoring the social issues that are inextricably tied into this system, consider how you can write code that creates signatures. First, you will assume that your code already has a private key to use for the signing operation and an array of bytes that contain the data to be signed. This code fragment considers the variable `privateKey` to contain the reference to the signing key and the variable `data` to be a reference to an array of bytes that contain the message data:

```
1. Signature s = Signature.getInstance("SHA");
2. s.initSign(privateKey);
3. s.update(data);
4. byte signatureValue[] = s.sign();
```

Simple really, isn't it?

- Line 1 uses the factory method `getInstance()` to obtain a `Signature` object that will calculate SHA signatures. SHA is an algorithm that generates a 20-byte message digest from NIST FIPS 180-1. MD5 is another such algorithm that generates a 16-byte digest.

NOTE   Factory methods are ways of creating instances of a class without using a constructor.

- Line 2 initializes that `Signature` object using the private key.

- Line 3 uses the `update()` method to run the data block through the signature calculations. You can call the update method as many times as you need so that all the data to be signed are passed through the calculations. In fact there are three variations of `update()` methods: one takes a single byte, one takes a whole array of bytes, and the third takes an array of bytes along with a starting offset and length. These three `update()` methods are closely comparable with the `read()` methods of an `InputStream`.

- The final operation, after all the data have been processed, is to calculate the signature value itself. This occurs in line 4 where the `sign()` method is called. The `sign()` method returns an array of bytes that is the signature value. You need to then append this binary value to the message so the recipient can validate the signature. The `sign()` method returns an X.509 coded signature block. If you want to have a printable ASCII stream, you would have to convert the signature contents to Base 64 or some other notation.

Validating a Signature Value

When a message is received with a signature block, you will want to validate that signature. Where the public key is referred to via the variable `publicKey`, the message data are in an array referred to by the variable data, and the signature is in an array referred to by the variable signature. Validation is done like this:

```
1. Signature s = Signature.getInstance("SHA");
2. s.initVerify(publicKey);
3. s.update(data);
4. try {
5.    if (!s.verify(signature)) {
6.       System.out.println("Signature did not verify!");
7.    }
8.    else {
9.       System.out.println("Signature verified OK");
10.   }
11. }
12. catch (SignatureException se) {
13.    System.out.println("Signature format trouble -" +
14.       " signature not verified");
15. }
```

You probably notice a correspondence with the code used to create the signature. First, you obtain a Signature object exactly as before. In line 2 you initialize it; this time for verification rather than for signing. This involves providing the public key rather than the private one. The update() method, with all its variations, is the same at line 3. Finally, the verification is done by the method verify(), which returns true if the verification is successful, false if not, or throws a SignatureException in case of other problems. Causes of the SignatureException include trying to call verify() on a Signature object that was initialized using initSign() instead of initVerify() or if the signature is of the wrong format.

Although the handling of signature calculations is really quite simple, the examples just examined have ignored the problem of obtaining keys to use for the signing and verification operations. The next section addresses these questions.

Keys

JDK 1.2 provides an abstract base class called java.security.KeyStore that provides method definitions for all the methods needed to access an arbitrary key storage mechanism. Actually, it represents a certificate store, and certificates are used to represent keys, but the effect is the same.

In the file lib/security/java.security under the Java installation directory, there is an entry:

```
keystore.type=jks
```

This defines the implementation class to be used for the key storage facilities. That is, you ask KeyStore for what provider implements the keystore.type. This returns a sun.security.provider.JavaKeyStore, but that information isn't necessary. The JavaKeyStore provides the default implementation for key storage.The idea is that there is a factory method in the base class that allows a program to use the keystore mechanism locally installed without having to reconfigure the program code. You might want to use a different key storage mechanism if you have a means of storing keys on a smart card or in a database, for example.

Take a look at the code you need to load a private and public key pair for use with signing and verifying operations. In this code fragment, the following variables are assumed to be declared and initialized elsewhere:

Variable Name	Type	Purpose
storePass	String	The password for the keystore
keyPass	String	The individual password for the private key
me	String	The alias name of the key pair to be recovered

```
1. KeyStore ks = KeyStore.getInstance(KeyStore.getDefault+Type());
2. String ksfName = System.getProperty("keystore");
3. File ksFile = null;
4. if (ksfName == null) {
5.    ksfName = System.getProperty("user.home");
6.    if (ksfName == null) {
7.       ksfName = System.getProperty("user.dir");
8.    }
9.    ksFile = new File(ksfName, ".keystore");
10. } else {
11.    ksFile = new File(ksfName);
12. }
13. FileInputStream in = new FileInputStream(ksFile);
14. ks.load(in, storePass);
15. PrivateKey pk = ks.getPrivateKey(me, keyPass);
16. PublicKey pk = ks.getCertificate(me).getPublicKey();
```

In this code, line 1 uses the KeyStore.getInstance() factory method to create an instance of the keystore implementation that is specified in the file jre/lib/security/java.security. Lines 2 to 12 determine what file contains the keystore itself. Normally this should be in a file called .keystore located in the user's home directory. This code allows the use of a property to override the location. Also if no property is specified and the user's home directory returns `null`, then the code falls back to looking for the `.keystore` file in the current directory. When the filename has been determined, the file is opened as an input stream at line 13 and the contents of the file are read into the keystore at line 14. Notice that the `ks.load()` method on line 14 takes the keystore password as its second argument. Finally the keys themselves are loaded. Line 15 loads the private key and must provide, as the second argument to the `getPrivateKey()` method call, the password that protects that key. If no particular password was provided when the key was generated using `keytool`, then by default, `keytool` will use the same password as protects the entire `keystore`. At line 16, the public key is loaded. Notice that the public key is loaded from the certificate, while the private key is loaded directly from the keystore. Certificates exist to distribute public keys, not private ones. So the keystore keeps the private key, and the certificate keeps the public key, which is in turn kept by the keystore.

A Full Example Using *KeyStore* and *Signature*

The code fragments shown previously to exemplify the use of the `KeyStore` and `Signature` objects do not form complete examples that you can run. So, next is a working program that collects keys from the keystore and can sign or verify a file using those keys.

The source of the example follows:

```java
import java.security.*;
import java.io.*;

public class Signer {
  KeyStore ks;
  Signature sig;

  public static void main(String args[]) throws Exception {
    if ((args.length == 0) || (args[0].startsWith("-h"))) {
      System.out.println(
        "Usage: java Signer <textfile> <sigfile>" +
        " <alias> <storepass> [<keypass>]\n" +
        "Properties signature.algorithm, signer.verifyonly" +
        " and keystore recognized");
      System.exit(0);
    }
```

```java
      FileInputStream toSign = new FileInputStream(args[0]);
      File sigFile = new File(args[1]);
      String myAlias = args[2];
      char storePassword[] = args[3].toCharArray();
      char keyPassword[] = (args.length > 4) ?
        args[4].toCharArray() : storePassword;
      String algorithm =
        System.getProperty("signature.algorithm", "DSA");
      Signer that = new Signer(algorithm, storePassword);
      if (!Boolean.getBoolean("signer.verifyonly")) {
        that.sign(toSign, sigFile, keyPassword, myAlias);
      }
      toSign = new FileInputStream(args[0]);
      System.out.println("The signature does " +
        (that.verify(toSign, sigFile, myAlias) ? "" : "not ") +
        "verify correctly.");
    }

  public Signer(String algorithm, char storePass[])
      throws GeneralSecurityException, IOException {
    ks = KeyStore.getInstance(KeyStore.getDefaultType());
    String ksfName = System.getProperty("keystore");
    File ksFile = null;
    if (ksfName == null) {
      ksfName = System.getProperty("user.home");
      if (ksfName == null) {
        ksfName = System.getProperty("user.dir");
      }
      ksFile = new File(ksfName, ".keystore");
    } else {
      ksFile = new File(ksfName);
    }
    FileInputStream in = new FileInputStream(ksFile);
    ks.load(in, storePass);

    sig = Signature.getInstance(algorithm);
  }

  public void sign(InputStream source, File sigfile,
      char keyPass[], String me)
      throws GeneralSecurityException, IOException{
```

```
      PrivateKey pk = (PrivateKey)ks.getKey(me, keyPass);
      sig.initSign(pk);

      byte buffer[] = new byte[source.available() + 100];
      int count = 0;
      while ((count = source.read(buffer)) > 0) {
        sig.update(buffer, 0, count);
      }
      source.close();

      byte signatureBlock[] = sig.sign();
      FileOutputStream out = new FileOutputStream(sigfile);
      out.write(signatureBlock);
      out.close();
    }

  public boolean verify(InputStream signed,
      File sigfile, String me)
      throws GeneralSecurityException, IOException{

    PublicKey pk = ks.getCertificate(me).getPublicKey();
    sig.initVerify(pk);

    byte buffer[] = new byte[signed.available() + 100];
    int count = 0;
    while ((count = signed.read(buffer)) > 0) {
      sig.update(buffer, 0, count);
    }
    signed.close();

    FileInputStream sigin = new FileInputStream(sigfile);
    byte signatureBlock[] = new byte[sigin.available()];
    sigin.read(signatureBlock);
    sigin.close();

    return sig.verify(signatureBlock);
  }
}
```

To run the program you need to compile the source file and create a private and public key pair in your system's keystore. The keys should be of an algorithm type that supports signing, typically this would be DSA, which happens to be the default for the `keytool` program. To compile and create your keys, issue the following commands:

```
javac Signer.java
keytool -genkey -alias myself -keyalg DSA
```

This will prompt you to enter the keystore password and the personal details that identify the alias "myself." Answer the prompts accordingly, as demonstrated in the earlier "Creating Your Own Keys" section.

After this has been done, you have a public and private key pair in your keystore and can generate a signature for a file. Obtain a test file, any file will do, and issue a command of this form:

```
java Signer inputfile sigfile alias storepass
```

The program reads the .keystore database using the password provided as *storepass*. It extracts the key pair for the *alias* given and uses the private key to generate a signature block for the contents of *inputfile*. That signature is written out to the file *sigfile*.

If you modify the command line to look like this:

```
java -Dsigner.verifyonly=true Signer inputfile sigfile
    alias storepass
```

and the file *sigfile* already exists, then the program skips the signature generation phase and simply attempts to verify the signature that is already provided. If you modify either the *inputfile* or the *sigfile* with an editor or delete your key pair using the `-delete` option to the `keytool` command, you will find that the signature block no longer verifies.

You might recognize the significant parts of the program from the earlier discussions on signing and key handling. There are three key parts: loading the keys from the keystore, calculating the signature, and verifying the signature.

The constructor for the `Signer` class obtains a `KeyStore` object and loads it from the file. The code for this is almost exactly the same as was shown in the fragment describing loading a key store. In addition, the constructor creates a `Signature` object. The `KeyStore` and `Signature` objects are held in the `ks` and `sig` variables.

The `sign()` method uses the provided `KeyStore` and `Signature` objects to obtain the private key, then reads and generates a signature for the specified file. There are two slight differences between this code and the sample fragments

listed earlier. First, this code is organized differently. Here you do not create a
Signature object because that has already been done; similarly you simply extract
a private key since the keystore has already been set up. The second difference
is the update() method of the Signature object is called in a loop. This ensures
that the whole file is read even if more than one chunk is necessary. (Normally, this
would only happen, given the use of the available() method, if the input file was
a stream of some kind, such as the keyboard.) Finally, the sign() method writes the
resulting signature to a file.

The verify() method is similar in organization to the sign() method. It starts
by extracting the appropriate public key from the certificate for the alias requested,
then reads the input file, possibly in multiple chunks. Finally it reads the signature
file and verifies that the signature is correct using the sig.verify() method.

Message Digests

Message digests are similar to checksums or cyclic redundancy checks in that
they represent the contents of a message in a relatively short number of characters. The idea is that if two people calculate the digest value of the same message,
they will get the same result. And if the message is changed, even slightly, on its
way from one to the other, then the digest values calculated on the two versions
will be radically different. Another important property of a message digest is that
it is impractical to take a message and, by means of making changes to that message, deliberately arrange for the message to have a particular digest value.

So what does this mean? Well, suppose someone sends you a message, and
with it they send you the digest value of that message. When you receive the
message, you calculate the digest and find that the value matches the one you
received with the message. This tells you that the message is the same message
for which the digest was calculated. Does this tell you that the message has not
been tampered with? Well, no. It tells you that the message did not suffer any
accidental damage. However, if the message and the digest arrive by the same
route, then any malicious modification cannot be detected since all the attacker
has to do is calculate the digest that is appropriate to the altered message and
substitute that in the same way that the message was changed.

This might make it appear that a message digest is a relatively useless concept
in cryptography. That would not be true. What is important to realize is that the
digest itself doesn't tell you anything unless you are confident that the digest is
uncorrupted. You can gain confidence about this in several ways. For example, if

multiple copies of the digest are sent to you by independent means (such as by courier, telephone, FAX, e-mail, on a Web site, and by phone), the chances of a malicious interceptor being able to change all those versions are very slight. Further, if the digests that you receive by these means all match each other and match the digest you calculate for your message, then you can be confident that the message is unchanged.

Such a complex mechanism for distributing a digest is generally impractical and fortunately unnecessary. The normal way that a digest is used is as part of a digital signature. Since public key cryptography is computationally intensive, and slow, it is usual to sign a document by encrypting the message digest rather than the document itself. Since the digest is smaller, typically 512 to 1024 bits in length, the encryption is much faster than it would be for an entire message. However, since it is impractical to find a substitute message that generates the same digest as the original, the signature is still acceptably safe.

Now that you've seen the nature of message digests, take a look at how you can use the APIs provided in the `java.security` package to calculate message digest values for data. Consider the following `Digester` program that demonstrates this.

The program starts by opening the input file for which a digest needs to be calculated. It proceeds to choose the digest algorithm to use by checking if a property is defined that overrides the default. Next an output channel is selected; this can either be system output or a file specified on the command line. Either way, the output destination is encapsulated in a `PrintWriter` to allow the use of the `println()` method.

Once the channels are opened, a `MessageDigest` object of the correct algorithm is obtained using the factory method `MessageDigest.getInstance()`. Calculation of the digest is performed simply by calling the `update()` method as many times as necessary to ensure that all the data bytes have been processed. Finally, the `digest()` method is called to complete the calculation and return the result as an array of bytes. The entire calculation could have been performed using the `digest(byte[])` method if you could be sure that the data would arrive in a single block.

The digest value is output in signed hexadecimal simply by creating a `java.math.BigInteger` object from the byte array and using the `toString(int)` method to request output in hexadecimal. The source for this example follows:

```
import java.io.*;
import java.security.*;
import java.math.*;
```

```
public class Digester {
  public static void main(String args[]) throws Exception {
    FileInputStream in = new FileInputStream(args[0]);
    String algorithm = System.getProperty(
      "digester.algorithm", "SHA");
    OutputStream os = System.out;
    if (args.length == 2) {
      os = new FileOutputStream(args[1]);
    }
    PrintWriter out = new PrintWriter(os);

    MessageDigest md = MessageDigest.getInstance(algorithm);
    byte buffer[] = new byte[in.available() + 100];
    int count = 0;
    while ((count = in.read(buffer)) > 0) {
      md.update(buffer, 0, count);
    }
    byte digest[] = md.digest();

    BigInteger bi = new BigInteger(digest);
    out.println(bi.toString(16));
    out.close();
  }
}
```

To run the program, compile the source and issue a command of this form:

```
javac Digester.java
java Digester message
```

substituting the path and filename of a sample message file for *message*. Running **Digester** on itself produces the following output:

```
520b35b9cbee050a39b4b60d9793a55452d72722
```

The program calculates the SHA-1 digest value of the input file and prints the result as a hexadecimal number to its output. If you run the program several times, or run it on unaltered copies of the same file, you should always get the same digest value. However, if you change the file even by a single bit, you should see that the resulting digest value is radically changed.

Although the program calculates SHA-1 digest values by default, you can ask for other algorithms if they are installed in your system. JDK 1.1 and 1.2 are distributed with the MD5 algorithm installed, so you can try this if you wish. To invoke a different algorithm, set the value of the property "digester.algorithm" to the required text when running the program, like this:

```
java -Ddigester.algorithm=MD5 Digester Digester.java
```

One important point about the output is the value from this program is written in signed hexadecimal, while most systems that present digest values to users, such as e-mail, generally do so using the Base 64 notation. Therefore, if you calculate the digest value of an e-mail message, you will not see the same characters as the e-mail itself reports. In the case of e-mail there are two further complications: First you would need to be careful to select the correct boundaries for the message upon which you calculate the digest. E-mail headers are excluded from the digest calculation. The other complication is that e-mail digests are calculated on what is called the canonical form of the message. The canonical form refers to a particular way of representing the message that does not vary between platforms. In particular, line endings are represented by carriage-return, line-feed pairs.

Security Providers

You have seen that the use of the cryptographic APIs is fairly simple, and in part this is due to the architecture of the cryptographic framework. This architecture allows alternative implementations of the individual cryptographic functions to be installed easily by the user or system administrator and makes it possible for programs that use cryptographic functions to make use of these new facilities transparently.

The basis of this extensibility is encapsulated in a simple class called `java.security.Provider`. The `Provider` class is really just a lookup mechanism that provides information about the classes that provide the implementations of individual cryptographic functions. As a whole, the providing class has a name, version number, and description, which are also handled by the `Provider` object.

Consider the specific example of adding a new message digest algorithm. To avoid cluttering up the demonstration of creating and installing a new provider, and to avoid export control issues for this book, you'll implement a trivial algorithm: the checksum. You need to appreciate that a checksum is not a cryptographic algorithm in any sense, but it serves to calculate a repeatable value on a block of data. As such, it holds a place in the framework of code that we will produce.

Engine Classes

Although the `Provider` object is the central point of the implementation of a suite of cryptographic algorithms, none of the algorithm code is located there. Rather, each algorithm is implemented in what is called an engine class or Service Provider Interface (SPI) class. The engine classes, in JDK 1.2, are abstract superclasses of the individual cryptographic classes. So there is a `MessageDigestSpi` class that you need to subclass to produce a new provider package.

In the case of the message digest system, the `MessageDigestSpi` class definition follows:

```
public abstract class  MessageDigestSpi extends Object {
  public MessageDigestSpi();
  public Object clone() throws CloneNotSupportedException;
  protected abstract byte[] engineDigest();
  protected int engineDigest(byte buffer[],
    int offset, int length) throws DigestException;
  protected int engineGetDigestLength();
  protected abstract void engineReset();
  protected abstract void engineUpdate(byte input);
  protected abstract void engineUpdate(byte input[],
    int offset, int length);
}
```

There are really five distinct functions here: update, digest, reset, get length, and clone. The `engineUpdate()` methods are where the actual algorithm must be provided. The `engineDigest()` methods are called to complete the calculation and return the result. The `engineReset()` method should reset the calculation to the start, as if no input had been provided. The `engineGetDigestLength()` method is used to return the number of bytes in the byte array that is returned by the `engineDigest()` methods. Finally, you should implement the `clone()` method in an engine class if you want to be able to duplicate a particular digest part way through. If you implement the `clone()` method, you should also mark your engine class with the flag interface `implements Cloneable`.

For most engines, the method `engineGetDigestLength()` will return a constant value, or a value that is determined when the individual instance is created. This would be the case if the digest algorithm allowed for variable length results. The `engineReset()` method is usually just a case of setting to zero, or whatever their starting value should be, the variables that hold the state of the calculation. These methods are relatively obvious; the update and digest methods might warrant a closer look, however.

There are two `engineUpdate()` methods. One simply takes a byte and should update the current digest calculation using that value. The second takes an array of bytes along with an offset and length that indicate what part of the array should be used. It is possible to implement either of these methods in terms of the other, but a well-founded principle demands that all data transfer operations should be done in the largest block possible if efficiency is not to be thrown away. Because of this, you should generally implement the array-handling version first, and then implement the single-byte handling version either independently or as a call to the array handling version, like this:

```
// array handling method has the algorithm code in it
public void engineUpdate (byte buf[], int off, int len) {
  // calculate updates for sub-array
}

// byte handling method calls array handling method
public void engineUpdate(byte b) {
  // create an array with b as the only element
  byte [] buf = { b };
  engineUpdate(buf, 0, 1);
}
```

Adopting this approach has the benefit that large updates will be done relatively efficiently by a single call to the array-handling method and without multiple calls to the byte-handling method. This avoids the duplication of code, and resulting maintenance nightmare, that would occur if the byte-handling method also had all the code to implement the algorithm in question.

The `MessageDigestSpi` class also has two `engineDigest()` methods. One of these takes no arguments, while the other takes an array of bytes and two `int` values. The primary purpose of both is to complete the digest calculation and return the result. The version that takes no arguments creates an array of bytes and returns this as the result. The other takes an array of bytes as an argument along with an offset and byte count limit. Provided that it fits in the byte count limit, the result is placed in the caller-supplied array at the offset specified. Be careful to recognize that the array in this case is for output data, not input. This version of the `engineDigest()` method returns the number of bytes written into the array as an `int`. Again, it is possible to implement either of these methods in terms of each other. If you wish to implement the zero-argument version in terms of the three-argument version, you can do so like this:

```
public byte [] engineDigest() {
  byte rv[] = new byte[engineGetDigestLength()];
```

```
    engineDigest(rv, 0, rv.length);
    return rv;
}
```

Alternatively you can implement the three-argument version in terms of the zero argument version like this:

```
public int engineDigest(byte buffer[], int off, int len) {
    int realLength = engineGetDigestLength();
    if (len < realLength) {
        throw new RuntimeException(
            "Insufficient space provided for digest");
    }
    System.arraycopy(
        engineDigest(), 0, buffer, off, realLength);
    return realLength;
}
```

It is up to you which way you approach this question, whether to implement the three-argument version and call that from the zero-argument version or the other way around. There are two points to consider, however. First, if you implement both individually, you will have the usual maintenance nightmares when you want to fix a bug or extend the algorithm. You will also end up with twice as much code. The other point is that commonly you will be working with instances of java.math.BigInteger when performing these calculations, and although that class can easily provide you with the bytes they contain, they only do so directly by returning an array to you. This behavior is most readily compatible with implementing the zero argument engineDigest() method directly and implementing the three-argument version by calling the zero-argument one.

The *Provider* Class

Now that you have considered the requirements of the MessageDigestSpi class, take a look at the use of the provider class before going on to fully implement the checksum algorithm in a provider of your own. The opening of this section stated that the Provider class is not involved in implementing the cryptographic algorithm but is simply concerned with making the algorithm implementation classes available.

In fact, the Provider class extends java.util.Properties, which in turn extends the java.util.Hashtable class. Hashtable and Properties classes are used to store key-value pairs; in a sense they are container objects that are good at doing lookup operations on one of the two fields they contain. The Provider class uses this lookup capability to associate an algorithm name with an implementation class name. For example, you will implement a message digest algorithm, called "SUM", using an engine class `master.SumEngine`. To make this information available to the security class management system, you create a `Provider` object that contains "MessageDigest.SUM" and "master.SumEngine" as a key and value pair. If your provider offers other capabilities, such as algorithms for signatures or other digest algorithms, then another key-value pair will represent each capability.

Although the value part of the key-value pair in a provider is simply a fully qualified class name, the key part warrants an additional comment. The key is made up of two parts: first there is the category of algorithm that is being implemented—"MessageDigest" or "Signature" for example. Immediately following the algorithm category there should be a period "." and immediately after that there should be an algorithm name. Algorithm names need to be standardized, and in an attempt to ensure this, Sun has documented the names of all common algorithms and specified a (slightly empirical) mechanism for determining names for new algorithms. These names and mechanisms are detailed in appendix A of the document "Java Cryptography Architecture, API Specification & Reference," which is normally distributed as part of the JDK 1.2 documentation set in a file called `docs/guide/security/CryptoSpec.html`. The document is also available from the Sun Web site.

The `Provider` class, in addition to documenting the association between algorithms and implementation classes, also documents the entire provider. When you define a `Provider`, you specify the name, version number, and a description of the package as a whole.

Installing a Security Provider

Given a new security provider package, you need to be able to install it into your system before it can be used. There are two ways to achieve this: a dynamic way that makes the provider available to individual applications or a static way that makes the provider transparently available to any application.

To install a provider for use with a particular application, you add code of this form to the startup of that program:

```
java.security.Security.addProvider(new MyProvider());
```

or

```
java.security.Security.insertProviderAt(new MyProvider(), 1);
```

Both of these methods are checked by the security management system, and any untrusted code by default will be unable to install a provider. The first installs the provider at the bottom of the priority table, while the second form allows you to install the provider at a specified place in the priority table; in this case the top.

The priority table warrants a word of explanation: Because multiple providers can be installed simultaneously, and they might provide some of the same algorithms, there needs to be a mechanism to determine which provider to use in preference to others that can offer the requested algorithm. Associating a priority order with the providers does this, so requests for an algorithm are normally fulfilled using the highest priority, lowest number, provider possible.

NOTE It is possible to request a specific provider when making a `getInstance()` request by using an overloaded `getInstance()` method that takes two `String` objects as its arguments. These arguments represent first the algorithm name and second the requested provider name. If you use this, you should consider making a second request that doesn't specify a provider if the first fails. This approach avoids the risk of making the program dependent upon the installation of a specific provider. Better still, try to arrange for this kind of configuration to be tunable using properties, so that system administrators can update the program without your having to recompile any code.

Static installation of a provider is also quite easy. Under your Java installation directory there is a directory called `jre`. In that directory, there is another subdirectory `lib`. In that directory there is another subdirectory called `security`. And in that directory there is a file called `java.security`. With Sun's JDK, the `java.security` file contains a line like this:

```
security.provider.1=sun.security.provider.Sun
```

This line indicates that the highest priority (indeed only) security provider class in Sun's JDK distribution is supplied in the class `sun.security.provider.Sun`.

To add another provider to your system, simply edit this file and insert a new line that indicates the classname and priority of your provider. For example:

```
security.provider.2=master.SecurityProvider
```

Now that you know how to install security providers, the following example shows how to actually use your own provider.

A Full Provider Example

A security provider requires a minimum of two classes. You need to implement an algorithm as a subclass of one of the Service Provider Interface (Spi) classes, and you need a `Provider` class to describe the implementation class. This example actually uses three separate classes since the main program used to test the provider suite is located in a class by itself.

The first part of this set is the engine class itself. In this example, the provider only provides a single algorithm, so there is only a single engine class. In a commercial provider, you would commonly find more than one algorithm, so there would be multiple engine classes and multiple `put()` method calls in the `Provider` class described next.

Because this is an engine for a message digest algorithm, the class must subclass the `MessageDigestSpi` abstract base class. This requires you to implement the abstract methods in the `MessageDigestSpi` class definition that follows:

```
public abstract class  MessageDigestSpi extends Object {
  public MessageDigestSpi();
  public Object clone() throws CloneNotSupportedException;
  protected abstract byte[] engineDigest();
  protected int engineDigest(byte buf[], int off, int len)
    throws DigestException;
  protected int engineGetDigestLength();
  protected abstract void engineReset();
  protected abstract void engineUpdate(byte b);
  protected abstract void engineUpdate(byte data[],
    int off, int len);
}
```

as discussed in the earlier section "Engine Classes." These methods are quite simple because the checksum algorithm is simple. An ongoing value of checksum is maintained in the variable `val`, and this is updated by the `engineUpdate()` methods. The `engineDigest()` methods simply use the `BigInteger` class to convert the checksum in the variable `val` into an array of bytes. This is neither the fastest nor most memory-efficient way to achieve this conversion, but it is simple to read and hard to program incorrectly. The supporting methods `engineGetDigestLength()` and `engineReset()` simply return a constant value (four) and set the current sum value to zero respectively.

The last observation to be made about this particular engine class is that it declares `implements Cloneable`. This gives permission for the object to be cloned. If the clone() method is called on a SumEngine object, the Object.clone() method will be used and a simple bit for bit copy results. Such a copy is entirely appropriate in this example, as there is only one instance data field and that is of a primitive type. If you create more complex engine classes, you will probably need to give a little more thought before implementing the Cloneable interface. In particular, you will probably need to provide a clone() method of your own, and call super.clone() to perform a basic bit copy before performing some additional modifications to the resulting copied object.

First is source code for the SumEngine custom message digest provider.

```java
package master;
import java.math.*;
import java.security.*;

public class SumEngine extends MessageDigestSpi
    implements Cloneable {
  private int val;
  private static final int BYTE_COUNT = 4;

  public byte [] engineDigest() {
    BigInteger b = BigInteger.valueOf((long)val);
    return b.toByteArray();
  }

  public int engineDigest(byte buf[], int off, int len) {
    if (len < BYTE_COUNT) {
      throw new RuntimeException(
        "Insufficient space provided for digest");
    }
    System.arraycopy(
      engineDigest(), 0, buf, off, BYTE_COUNT);
    return BYTE_COUNT;
  }

  public int engineGetDigestLength() {
    return BYTE_COUNT;
  }

  public void engineReset() {
    val = 0;
  }
```

```
public void engineUpdate(byte data[], int off, int len) {
  int end = off + len;
  for (int i=off; i < end; i++) {
    val += data[i];
  }
}

public void engineUpdate(byte b) {
  // create an array with b as the only element
  byte buf[] = {b};
  engineUpdate(buf, 0, 1);
}
}
```

The `master.SecurityProvider` class itself is very simple. It has three essential features. First, it is a subclass of `java.security.Provider`. This is necessary if the security system is to recognize it as a valid provider. Second, the constructor calls the superclass constructor and passes three arguments to it. These are the provider name, the version number, and a comment field. A client program can extract this information if desired and perhaps display it to a user for acceptance before using the provider. Or the version number could be checked to ensure a certain minimum revision level.

The final feature of the provider is that it stores into its own `Hashtable` key-value pairs that describe the algorithms it implements and the classes that implement the engines for those algorithms. So, in this case the `put()` method adds the key "MessageDigest.SUM" and "master.SumEngine" for the value.

The `SecurityProvider` source follows:

```
package master;
import java.security.*;

public class SecurityProvider extends Provider {
  public SecurityProvider() {
    super("MasteringJava", 1.2,
      "Checksum example of a provider." +
      " Not cryptographicaly useful");
    put("MessageDigest.SUM", "master.SumEngine");
    // more algorithms simply need more put() calls
  }
}
```

Running the test program first checks if the property `install` is defined as true. If it is, then it calls the method `Security.addProvider()` to install the provider on a per-JVM runtime basis. Next a `FileInputStream` is opened using the first argument of the program as the file name. This entire file is read into a byte array in one go. Note that the approach of using the `available()` method is not suited to reading from standard input or other streams not connected to files where you do not know the size beforehand.

Once the data bytes are read, you call the `MessageDigest.getInstance()` method to request a checksum digest, then call the `update()` and `digest()` methods to obtain the checksum. If the provider is installed, this should work.

Finally the checksum value is output in hexadecimal using a `java.math.Big-Integer` to perform the conversion.

Below is the source for the testing program, `TestSum`:

```
import java.io.*;
import java.math.*;
import java.security.*;

public class TestSum {
  public static void main(String args[]) throws Exception {
    if (Boolean.getBoolean("install")) {
      System.out.println("Installing the provider");
      Security.addProvider(new master.SecurityProvider());
    }
    FileInputStream in = new FileInputStream(args[0]);
    byte data[] = new byte[in.available()];
    in.read(data);
    in.close();

    MessageDigest d = MessageDigest.getInstance("SUM");
    d.update(data);
    byte sum[] = d.digest();

    BigInteger bi = new BigInteger(sum);
    System.out.println("Checksum is: " + bi.toString(16));
  }
}
import java.security.*;
import java.io.*;
import java.math.*;
```

```
public class TestSum {
  public static void main(String args[]) throws Throwable {
    if (Boolean.getBoolean("install")) {
      System.out.println("Installing the provider");
      Security.addProvider(new purplecup.SecurityProvider());
    }
    FileInputStream in = new FileInputStream(args[0]);
    byte [] data = new byte[in.available()];
    in.read(data);
    in.close();

    MessageDigest d = MessageDigest.getInstance("SUM");
    d.update(data);
    byte [] sum = d.digest();

    BigInteger bi = new BigInteger(sum);
    System.out.println("Checksum is: " + bi.toString(16));
  }
}
```

Testing the Custom Security Provider

First, create the sources files and compile each of the files:

```
javac -d . SumEngine.java
javac -d . SecurityProvider.java
javac TestSum.java
```

Once compiled, you will run the test program three ways. First, without installing the provider at all, you'll prove that the SUM algorithm is not recognized. Next you will use two techniques to install the provider and show it in operation.

To show that the provider isn't installed, issue a command of the form:

```
java TestSum messagefile
```

This should fail and give you a message like this (the first line is the input):

```
%java TestSum TestSum.java
java.security.NoSuchAlgorithmException: algorithm SUM not available.
        at java.security.Security.getEngineClassName(Security.java:306)
        at java.security.Security.getEngineClassName(Security.java:327)
        at java.security.Security.getImpl(Security.java:515)
        at java.security.MessageDigest.getInstance(MessageDigest.java:129)
        at TestSum.main(TestSum.java:16)
```

Next run the program so that it installs the provider for you on a temporary basis. You can do this by issuing a modified startup command like this:

```
java -Dinstall=true TestSum messagefile
```

Notice the addition of "-Dinstall=true" to this command. Setting the property install to true causes the program to install the provider into the current JVM instance, allowing the rest of the program and the checksum calculation to proceed. You should see two output messages like this:

```
Installing the provider
Checksum is: d45d
```

The actual checksum you get will depend upon the message file you supply.

Finally, install the provider as part of your system. To do this, edit the file jre\lib\security\java.security located under your main Java installation directory. Find the line:

```
security.provider.1=sun.security.provider.Sun
```

which is about 40-50 lines from the top and, just below it, add this line:

```
security.provider.2=master.SecurityProvider
```

This line causes the security system to try to load a provider from the class master .SecurityProvider. To load the provider class successfully, the master subdirectory that contains the SecurityProvider.class file must be on the CLASSPATH. In your case, provided you have the current directory on your CLASSPATH and are running from the directory you compiled the source code, then this will be the case.

WARNING   Although this provider is harmless, and doesn't even try to provide any algorithms that you might want to use in security sensitive operations, you must remember to remove this configuration line from your system when you have completed this investigation. As a matter of principle, you should keep all security-related files as tidy as possible.

Once you have made the changes to the java.security file, run the program again. This time leave out the -Dinstall=true setting, like this:

```
java TestSum messagefile
```

You should find this time that the output consists of only one line that indicates the checksum value. The first line output when you used the -Dinstall=true setting, a line that said "Installing the provider," has not been issued. This demonstrates that the provider was picked up as part of the default system security configuration.

Remember to remove the provider by undoing the changes you made to your `java.security` file.

Summary

This chapter has covered a great deal of material. The following list will remind you of the key points covered.

- Terminology: identification, authentication, digital signature, non-repudiation, authorization, resource control, data integrity, encryption (symmetric and asymmetric), and auditing.

- There is a plan for Java security from the very foundations of the Virtual Machine. This plan is currently being subjected to formal verification and has already been subjected to enormous public scrutiny.

- The three features of bytecode language design along with the verifier, the `ClassLoader`, and the `SecurityManager` form a defensive circle wherein each part helps protect the others.

- The authorization mechanisms in JDK 1.2 offer a configurable policy file with the ability to set permissions, keys, and certificates, as well as sign JAR archives.

- The access control APIs in JDK 1.2, all hinging around the `AccessController` `.checkPermission()` method, but including the `beginPrivileged()` and `endPrivileged()` methods.

- The ACL APIs and the implementation of these provided in the `sun.security` `.acl` non-core package.

- Cryptographic APIs, handling the keystore, as well as writing and installing a cryptography provider.

If this chapter has done its job, you will now understand the security facilities of Java, appreciate at least some part of why Java is a platform and not just a language, and can compare Java's security facilities with other systems. Perhaps more importantly, you will be able to write security sensitive code with competence and use the cryptographic APIs to implement complex cryptographic facilities like digital signatures.

CHAPTER
TWENTY-FIVE

Remote Method Invocation

■ RMI overview

■ The RMI architecture

■ Advanced RMI

Java's *Remote Method Invocation* (*RMI*) feature enables a program in one Java Virtual Machine (JVM) to make method calls on an object located on a remote server machine within another JVM. In this chapter we discuss RMI, beginning with a look at the relationship between object persistence (from Chapter 19) and RMI.

RMI Overview

The Remote Method Invocation feature gives Java programmers the ability to distribute computing across a networked environment. Object-oriented design requires every task to be executed by the object most appropriate for that task. RMI takes this concept one step further by allowing a task to be performed on the *machine* most appropriate for the task.

RMI defines a `Remote` interface that can be used to create remote objects. A client can invoke the methods of a remote object with the same syntax that it uses to invoke methods on a local object. The RMI API provides classes and methods that handle all of the underlying communication and parameter referencing requirements for accessing remote methods. RMI also handles the serialization of objects that are passed as arguments to methods of remote objects.

The `java.rmi` and the `java.rmi.server` packages contain the interfaces and classes that define building blocks for creating server-side objects and client-side object stubs. A stub is a local representation of a remote object. The client makes calls to the stub, which automatically communicates with the server.

Object Persistence and Remote Method Invocation

When a Java program makes a remote method invocation, method parameters must be transmitted to the server and a return value must be sent back to the client. Primitive values can simply be sent byte by byte. However, passing objects, either as parameters or return values, requires a more sophisticated solution.

The remote object instance needs access to the entire graph of objects referenced by a parameter, passed to the object's method. The remote method might construct and return a complicated object that holds references to other objects. If this is the case, the entire graph must be returned; so any object passed to or returned from a remote method must implement either the `Serializable` or the `Externalizable` interface. Return to the "Object Persistence and Serialization" section of Chapter 19 for additional information on the usage of these two interfaces.

NOTE Remote method invocation is similar to the Remote Procedure Call (RPC) feature that Sun introduced in 1985. RPC also required a way to serialize parameter and return value data, although the situation was simpler because of the absence of objects. Sun developed a system called External Data Representation (XDR) to support data serialization. One significant difference between RPC and RMI is that RPC uses the fast but less-than-reliable UDP protocol; by default, RMI uses the slower but more reliable TCP/IP protocol. However, with `java.rmi.server.RMISocketFactory` class, the developer may choose to run RMI over other socket protocols.

The RMI Architecture

The RMI consists of three layers: the stubs/skeleton layer, the remote reference layer, and the transport layer. The relationships among these layers are shown in Figure 25.1.

FIGURE 25.1:

Architecture overview

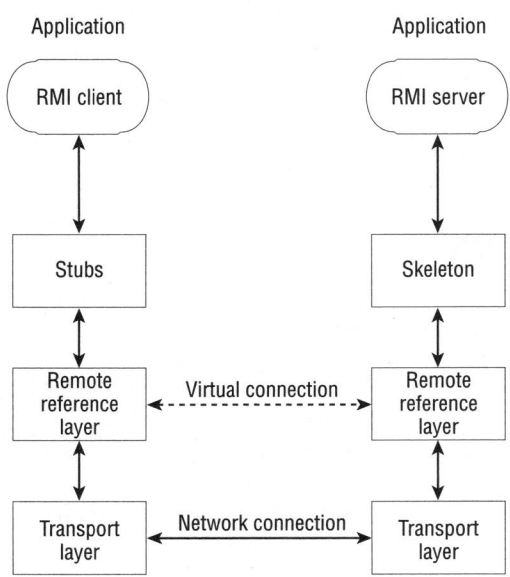

When a client invokes a remote method, the request starts at the top with the stub on the client side. The client references the stub as a proxy for the object on the remote machine; all the underlying functionality shown in Figure 25.1 is invisible to the client. The stub code is generated with the `rmic` compiler and uses the Remote Reference Layer (RRL) to pass method invocation requests to the server object.

Stubs

The *stub* is the client-side proxy representing the remote object. Stubs define all of the interfaces that the remote object implementation supports. The stub is referenced as any other local object by a program running on the client machine. It is a local object on the client side; it also maintains a connection to the server-side object. The Remote Reference Layer on the client side returns a marshal stream to the stub. The marshal stream is used by the RRL to communicate to the RRL on the server side. The stub serializes parameter data, passing the serialized data into the marshal stream.

After the remote method has been executed, the RRL passes any serialized return values back to the stub, which is responsible for deserializing.

The Skeleton

The *skeleton* is the server-side construct that interfaces with the server-side RRL. The skeleton receives method invocation requests from the client-side RRL. The server-side RRL must unmarshal any arguments that are sent to a remote method. The skeleton then makes a call to the actual object implementation on the server side. The skeleton is also responsible for receiving any return values from the remote object and marshaling them into the marshal stream.

Remote Reference Layer

The *Remote Reference Layer* (RRL) is responsible for maintaining an independent reference protocol that is not specific to any stub or skeleton model. This flexibility allows you to change the RRL if desired without affecting the other two layers. The RRL deals with the lower-level transport interface and is responsible for providing a stream to the stubs and skeleton layers.

The RRL uses a server-side and a client-side component to communicate via the transport layer. The client-side component contains information specific to the remote server. This information is passed to the server-side component and therefore is dependent only on the server-side RRL. The RRL on the server side is responsible for the reference semantics and deals with those semantics before delivering the remote method invocation to the skeleton. The transport layer handles the communication between client- and server-side components.

The Transport Layer

The transport layer is responsible for creating and maintaining connections between the client and server. The transport layer consists of four abstractions:

- An endpoint is used to reference the address space that contains a Java Virtual Machine (JVM). An *endpoint* is a reference to a specific transport instance.

- A *channel* is the pathway between two address spaces. This channel is responsible for managing any connections from the client to the server and vice versa.

- A *connection* is an abstraction for transferring data (arguments and return values) between client and server.

- The *transport* abstraction is responsible for setting up a channel between a local address space and a remote endpoint. The transport abstraction is also responsible for accepting incoming connections to the address space containing the abstraction.

The transport layer sets up connections, manages existing connections, and handles remote objects residing in its address space.

When the transport layer receives a request from the client-side RRL, it establishes a socket connection to the server. Next, the transport layer passes the established connection to the client-side RRL and adds a reference to the remote object to an internal table. At this point, the client is connected to the server.

The transport layer monitors the "liveness" of the connection. If a significant amount of time passes with no activity on the connection, the transport layer is responsible for shutting the connection down. The timeout period is 10 minutes.

RMI Example

This section takes you through the making, compiling, and running of an RMI application. To create an application that is accessible to remote clients, there are a number of steps that you must follow:

1. Define interfaces for the remote classes.

2. Create and compile implementation classes for the remote classes.

3. Create stub and skeleton classes using the `rmic` command.

4. Create and compile a server application.

5. Start the RMI Registry and the server application.

6. Create and compile a client program to access the remote objects.

7. Test the client.

In this chapter we develop a detailed example, using the steps listed here as a framework. The example will model a very simple credit card system. The server will support creating a new account, as well as performing transactions against an existing account. Because the intention of the example program is to show you how to use RMI, there will not be a client-side user interface; the client will simply make a few hard-coded invocations.

Step 1: Define Interfaces for Remote Classes

The program will use two remote classes. The `CreditCardImpl` class will maintain the user name, balance, available credit, and personal ID signature number for a single credit card account. The `CreditManager` will maintain a list of `Account` objects and create new ones when necessary. The server-side application will construct a single instance of `CreditManagerImpl` and make it available to remote clients.

Each of these classes must be described by an interface (`CreditCard` and `Credit-Manager`). The client-side stubs will implement these interfaces. The stub classes will be created in a later step by the `rmic` utility. Note that `rmic` requires that the interfaces must be public and extend the `Remote` interface, that each method must throw `RemoteException`, and that the stub and implementation code must reside in a package.

The definition of CreditCard is:

```
package credit;
import java.rmi.*;

public interface CreditCard extends Remote {

  /** This method returns a credit card's credit line. */
  public float getCreditLine() throws RemoteException;

  /** This method allows a card holder to pay all or some
      of a balance. Throws InvalidMoneyException if the
      money param is invalid. */
  public void payTowardsBalance(float money) throws
    RemoteException, InvalidMoneyException;

  /** This method allows the cardholder to make purchases
      against the line of credit. Throws
      CreditLineExceededException
      if the purchase exceeds available credit. */
  public void makePurchase(float amount, int signature) throws
    RemoteException, InvalidSignatureException,
    CreditLineExceededException;

  /** This method sest the card's personal i.d. signature. */
  public void setSignature(int pin) throws RemoteException;
}
```

The structure of CreditManager is similar, though it only defines two methods:

```
package credit;
import java.rmi.*;

public interface CreditManager extends Remote {

  /** This method finds an existing credit card for a given customer
      name. If the customer does not have an account, a new card will
      be "issued" with a random personal i.d. signature and a $5000
      starting credit line. */
  public CreditCard findCreditAccount(String Customer) throws
    DuplicateAccountException, RemoteException;

  /** This method creates a new Cedit Account with a random
```

```
          personal i.d. signature and a $5000 starting credit line. */
       public CreditCard newCreditAccount(String newCustomer) throws
          RemoteException;
    }
```

There are four trivial exception classes used here: CreditLineExceededException, DuplicateAccountException, InvalidMoneyException, and InvalidSignature-Exception. They extend Exception without adding new data or methods.

```
package credit;

public class CreditLineExceededException extends Exception {
}

package credit;

public class DuplicateAccountException extends Exception {
}

package credit;

public class InvalidMoneyException extends Exception {
}

package credit;

public class InvalidSignatureException extends Exception {
}
```

Step 2: Create and Compile Implementation Classes

The implementation classes are server-side classes that implement the interfaces listed previously.

The CreditCardImpl class implements the CreditCard interface that was defined earlier. This class must implement all of the methods in the CreditCard interface, and it must extend UnicastRemoteObject. To date there is no built-in support for multicast objects.

All four interfaces and classes declare that they belong to the credit package. Each of the source files should be compiled with the -d <directoryname> option to specify a destination directory for the resulting .class files. Within the destination directory, the compiler will automatically create a subdirectory called credit (if one does not already exist); the class files will be created in the `credit` subdirectory. The destination directory supplied to the -d option should be in the classpath. An easy way to compile the interfaces and classes is to specify the current working directory as the destination directory, as follows:

```
javac -d . CreditLineExceededException.java
javac -d . DuplicateAccountException.java
javac -d . InvalidMoneyException.java
javac -d . InvalidSignatureException.java
javac -d . CreditCard.java
javac -d . CreditCardImpl.java
javac -d . CreditManager.java
javac -d . CreditManagerImpl.java
```

The source code for the `CreditCardImpl` class follows.

```
package credit;

import java.rmi.*;
import java.rmi.server.*;
import java.io.Serializable;

/** This class is the remote object that will referenced by the skeleton
    on the server side and the stub on the client side. */

public class CreditCardImpl extends UnicastRemoteObject
    implements CreditCard, Serializable {

  private float currentBalance = 0;
  private float creditLine = 5000f;
  private int signature = 0;        // Like a p.i.n. number
  private String accountName;       // Name of owner

  /** Class constructor generates an initial pin.*/
  public CreditCardImpl (String customer) throws
      RemoteException, DuplicateAccountException {
    accountName = customer;
    signature = (int)(Math.random() * 10000);
  }

  /** Returns credit line. */
  public float getCreditLine() throws RemoteException {
```

```
    return creditLine;
  }

  /** Pays off some debt. */
  public void payTowardsBalance(float money) throws
      RemoteException, InvalidMoneyException {
    if (money <= 0) {
      throw new InvalidMoneyException ();
    } else {
      currentBalance -= money;
    }
  }

  /** Changes signature. */
  public void setSignature(int pin) throws RemoteException {
    signature = pin;
  }

  /** Makes a purchase. Makes sure enough credit is available,
      then increments balance and decrements available credit. */
  public void makePurchase (float amount, int signature) throws
      RemoteException, InvalidSignatureException,
      CreditLineExceededException {
    if (signature != this.signature) {
      throw new InvalidSignatureException();
    }
    if (currentBalance+amount > creditLine) {
      throw new CreditLineExceededException();
    } else {
      currentBalance += amount;
      creditLine -= amount;
    }
  }
}
```

The `CreditManagerImpl` class is responsible for creating and storing new accounts (as `CreditImpl` objects). This class stores the account objects within a HashMap, keyed by owner name.

```
package credit;

import java.rmi.*;
```

```java
import java.rmi.server.*;
import java.util.HashMap;

public class CreditManagerImpl extends UnicastRemoteObject
    implements CreditManager {
  private static transient HashMap accounts = new HashMap();

  /** This is the default class constructor that does nothing
      but implicitly call super(). */
  public CreditManagerImpl() throws RemoteException {
  }

  /** Creates a new account. Puts the customer name and the customer's
      credit card in the hashtable. */
  public CreditCard newCreditAccount(String customerName)
      throws RemoteException {
    CreditCardImpl newCard = null;
    try {
      newCard = new CreditCardImpl(customerName);
    } catch (DuplicateAccountException e) {
      return null;
    }
    accounts.put(customerName, newCard);
    return newCard;
  }

  /** Searches the hashtable for an existing account. If no account
      for customer name, one is created and added to hashtable.
      Returns the account. */
  public CreditCard findCreditAccount(String customer)
      throws DuplicateAccountException, RemoteException {
    CreditCardImpl account = (CreditCardImpl)accounts.get(customer);
    if (account != null) {
      return account;
    }
    // Create new account. Add credit card to hashtable.
    account = new CreditCardImpl(customer);
    accounts.put(customer, account);
    return account;
  }
}
```

Step 3: Create Stub and Skeleton Classes

Once the implementation classes are compiled, the next step is to create the stub and skeleton class files that are used to access the implementation classes. The stub classes are used by client code to communicate with the server skeleton code.

The `rmic` command automatically creates stub and skeleton code from the class definitions for the interface and implementation. The syntax of the command is:

```
rmic [options] package.interfaceImpl ...
```

For our example, the following command would create the stubs and skeletons for the `CreditCard` and `CreditManager` remote classes:

```
rmic -d . credit.CreditCardImpl credit.CreditManagerImpl
```

Note that the command requires specification of the package in which the class files reside; this is why all the source modules listed previously under Step 2 declared that they belonged to the `credit` package.

The `rmic` command creates four class files in the `credit` package directory:

- `CreditCardImpl_Skel.class`

- `CreditCardImpl_Stub.class`

- `CreditManagerImpl_Skel.class`

- `CreditManagerImpl_Stub.class`

Now that the stubs and skeletons have been created, the next step is to create a server-side application that makes these classes available to clients for remote invocation.

Step 4: Create and Compile the Server Application

Everything is now in place to create the server-side application. It will be an application class called `CardBank`, whose main job is to construct an instance of `CreditManager`. Except for the line that calls the `CreditManager` constructor, all the rest of the `CardBank` code involves making the credit manager object available to remote clients. The details of this process are explained after the following code listing.

```
package credit;
import java.rmi.*;
import java.rmi.registry.LocateRegistry;

public class CardBank {
```

```java
public static void main (String args[]) {
  if (args.length != 2) {
    System.err.println("Usage:");
    System.err.println("java credit.CardBank <server> <port>");
    System.exit (1);
  }

  String server = args[0];
  int port = Integer.parseInt (args[1]);

  // Create and install a security manager.
  System.setSecurityManager(new RMISecurityManager());

  try {
    // Specify registry location
    LocateRegistry.createRegistry (port);
    System.out.println
      ("Card Bank: defined registry port");

    // Create an instance of our Credit Manager.
    System.out.println
      ("CreditManagerImpl: create a CreditManager");
    CreditManagerImpl cmi = new CreditManagerImpl();

    // Bind the object instance to the remote registry. Use the
    // static rebind() method to avoid conflicts.
    System.out.println("CreditManagerImpl: bind it to a name");
    String urlString = "//" + server + ":" + port + "/" + "cardManager";

    Naming.rebind(urlString, cmi);

    System.out.println("CreditManager is now ready");

  } catch (Exception e) {
    System.out.println("An error occured");
    e.printStackTrace();
    System.out.println(e.getMessage());
  }
}
}
```

Applications, by default, run without security managers. In the main method, shown previously, the System.setSecurityManager() call installs an RMI security manager.

Trusting Local Code with an Installed Security Manager

As soon as you install a security manager, all code not loaded from the class path found in the System property `sun.boot.class.path` is untrusted. To trust the RMI example so it can work, you need to add the appropriate directory to your `java.policy` file to make sure it is within the boot class path. The appropriate entry to add to the `java.policy` file follows. (Your entry may differ, if you are working in a different directory.)

```
grant codeBase "file:/MasteringJava/ch25/" {permission
    java.security.AllPermission;
};
```

You may choose to be more restrictive with your permissions.

The RMI Registry listens on a particular port for registration information and requests for services. You specify this port with a simple `LocateRegistry.create-Registry (port)` call.

The server "publishes" an object instance by binding a specified name to the instance and registering that name with the RMI Registry. There are two methods that allow an instance to be bound and registered:

- `public static void bind(String name, Remote obj) throws AlreadyBoundException, MalformedUrlException, UnknownHostException, RemoteException`

- `public static void rebind(String name, Remote obj) throws MalformedUrlException, UnknownHostException, RemoteException`

Notice that both methods are static and ask for a name to reference the object, as well as the remote object instance that is bound to the name. In the current example, the object name is `cardManager`. Any reachable machine on the network can refer to this object by specifying the Registry host machine, port, and object name.

The `name` argument required by both `bind()` and `rebind()` is a URL-like string. This string can be in the format `protocol://host:port/bindingName`. Here `protocol` is `rmi`, `host` is the name of the RMI server, `port` is the port number on which the server should listen for requests, and `bindingName` is the exact name that should be used by a client when requesting access to the object. If just a name is given in the string, then default values are used. The defaults are `rmi` for the protocol, `localhost` for the server name, and 1099 for the port number.

Both `bind()` and `rebind()` associate a name with an object. They differ in their behavior when the name being bound has already been bound to an object. In this case, `bind()` will throw `AlreadyBoundException`, and `rebind()` will discard the old binding and use the new one.

Step 5: Start the RMI Registry and the Server Application

The RMI Registry is an application that provides a simple naming lookup service. When the `CardBank` calls `rebind()`, it is the Registry that maintains the binding. The Registry is an independent program, and it must be running before the server-side application is invoked. The program resides in the `java\bin` directory. It can be invoked by simply typing **rmiregistry** at the command line.

The following two command lines invoke the Registry and start up the card bank server. If you have multiple networked machines available, you can run `CardBank` on another machine and use that machine name instead of `localhost`.

```
start rmiregistry
java credit.CardBank localhost 12345
```

The card bank application prints several status lines as it starts up the service. If there are no errors, you should see the following output:

```
CardBank: defined registry port
CreditManagerImpl: create a CreditManager
CreditManagerImpl: bind it to a name
CreditManager is now ready
```

Once an object has been passed to the Registry, a client may request that the RMI Registry provide a reference to the remote object. The next section shows how this is done.

Step 6: Create and Compile the Client Program

The `Shopper` application needs to find a credit manager object on the remote server. The program assumes that the server name has been entered as the first command-line argument with the port as the second. This name is used to create a URL-like string of the format `rmi://<hostname>:<port>/cardManager`. The string is passed to the static `lookup()` method of the `Naming` class. The `lookup()` call communicates with the server and returns a handle to the remote object that was constructed and registered in Step 5 above. More accurately, what is returned is a handle to a stub that communicates with the remote object.

The return type from `lookup()` is `Remote`, which is the parent of all stub interfaces. When the return value is cast to type `CreditManager`, the methods of `CreditManager` can be invoked on it. The following code for the `Shopper` class shows how this is done.

The client expects three command-line arguments. The first argument specifies the server; use the same name specified when you started `CardBank`. (For testing on a single machine, specify `localhost` for the server name.) The second argument specifies a port; use the port number specified when you started `CardBank`. The third argument is a string that provides an account name. The client program asks the server-side credit manager object for a handle to the credit card object that represents this customer's account. (If the customer has no account yet, one will be created.) The initial random pin number is modified to something a user will find easier to remember. The client program then makes several purchases and one payment, reporting the available credit after each transaction. The client code is as follows:

```java
package credit;
import java.rmi.*;

public class Shopper {
  public static void main (String args[]) {
    CreditManager cm = null;
    CreditCard account = null;

    // Check the command line.
    if (args.length != 3) {
      System.err.println("Usage:");
      System.err.println(
        "java credit.Shopper <server> <port> <account name>");
      System.exit (1);
    }

    String server = args[0];
    int port = Integer.parseInt (args[1]);
    String name = args[2];

    // Create and install a security manager.
    System.setSecurityManager(new RMISecurityManager());
```

```
// Obtain reference to card manager.
try {
  String url = new String ("//" + server + ":" +
    port + "/cardManager");
  System.out.println ("Shopper: lookup cardManager, url = "
    + url);
  cm = (CreditManager)Naming.lookup(url);
} catch (Exception e) {
  System.err.println("Error in getting card manager" + e);
}

// Get user's account.
try {
  account = cm.findCreditAccount(name);
  System.out.println ("Found account for " + name);
} catch (Exception e) {
  System.err.println("Error in getting account for " + name);
}

// Do some transactions.
try {
  System.out.println("Available credit is: "
    + account.getCreditLine());
  System.out.println("Changing pin number for account");
  account.setSignature(1234);
  System.out.println("Buying a new watch for $100");
  account.makePurchase(100.00f, 1234);
  System.out.println("Available credit is now: " +
    account.getCreditLine());
  System.out.println("Buying a new pair of shoes for $160");
  account.makePurchase(160.00f, 1234);
  System.out.println("CardHolder: Paying off $136 of balance");
  account.payTowardsBalance(136.00f);
  System.out.println("Available credit is now: "+
    account.getCreditLine());
} catch (Exception e) {
  System.err.println("Transaction error for " + name);
}
  }
}
```

Step 7: Test *Shopper*

The final step, of course, is to execute the client code. It can be run from any computer that has access to the server and to the supporting classes. Here is a sample session output on a Unix machine, with the remote service running on a host named `sunbert` (the first line is the invocation; the rest is output):

```
% java credit.Shopper sunbert 12345 pogo
Shopper: lookup cardManager, url = //sunbert:12345/cardManager
Found account for pogo
Available credit is: 5000.0
Changing pin number for account
Buying a new watch for $100
Available credit is now: 4900.0
Buying a new pair of shoes for $160
CardHolder: Paying off $136 of balance
Available credit is now: 4740.0
```

After the client program has finished running, the remote objects are still alive. The execution shown above created a new account for the customer. A second invocation of the client will work with that account. The available credit numbers in the listing below reflect the current state of the account:

```
% java credit.Shopper sunbert 12345 pogo
Shopper: lookup cardManager, url = //sunbert:12345/cardManager
Found account for pogo
Available credit is: 4740.0
Changing pin number for account
Buying a new watch for $100
Available credit is now: 4640.0
Buying a new pair of shoes for $160
CardHolder: Paying off $136 of balance
Available credit is now: 4480.0
```

Advanced RMI

In the rest of this chapter, the Remote Method Invocation system will be explored in greater detail and new enhancements available in JDK 1.2 will be illustrated. So far, the examples shown in this chapter have just scratched the surface of what this powerful technology has to offer. While the RMI system released in JDK 1.1 demonstrated that it was a strong candidate for distributed Java systems, RMI in JDK 1.2 proves that Sun is not willing to let RMI be a flash in the pan.

New features in RMI include object activation and the ability to define and use a custom socket protocol. Object activation allows a client to request a reference to a remote object that is not currently active in a Java Virtual Machine. The `RMISocketFactory` allows developers to create their own wire protocols, change the wire protocol on a per-object basis, or make use of secure wire protocols like the Secure Socket Layer (SSL).

TIP

For more information on creating your own socket factories in RMI, see the tutorial at: `http://java.sun.com/products/jdk/1.2/docs/guide/rmi/rmisocket-factory.doc.html`.

In this chapter, other, less-documented features, such as the ability to perform callbacks in RMI, dynamic class loading in RMI, and object activation, are highlighted.

Performing Callback Operations

In the example shown previously in "RMI Example," a typical client-server application was demonstrated. The `CardBank` server created an instance of a `CardManager` object and served the instance of the object to the `Shopper` client using RMI. That example illustrated some of the underlying communications that RMI handles on the developer's behalf, such as the creation and use of network sockets.

However, what that example did not show was that RMI is capable of providing two-way communication between objects. For an object's reference to be sent from one place to another, the object's class only needs to implement a `Remote` interface and be "exported" to receive remote method calls. (By extending `UnicastRemote-Object`, an object is automatically exported.)

Once these two requirements have been met, it is possible in RMI to send a remote object from a "client" to a "server" so that the "server" is actually calling the remote methods of the "client" object. This is the nature of truly distributed applications: There is no distinction between "client" and "server." Each application provides or utilizes the services of another.

To demonstrate this concept with a practical example, the `CardBank` application illustrated previously will be extended. In that example, the customer received a credit line by simply passing their name to the `CreditManager`. In this example, the customer will fill out `CreditApplication` and send that application to the `CreditManager`.

The `CreditManager` instance will use methods provided by a `CreditApplication` to fill in data that the "customer" can then validate for the final credit application.

The way this works is that the client creates a local instance of a `CreditApplication` object and passes a reference to that instance to the server through the `Credit-Manager`, obtained through the Registry.

The server executes methods on the `CreditApplication` reference using the same mechanism the client uses: The server holds a reference to a stub instance that forwards requests to the client's local object.

Following the same steps as earlier is still appropriate. However, some are already completed.

Step 1: Define Interfaces for Remote Classes

The `CreditApplication` object is created the same way as any other RMI remote object. The object's remote methods are defined in an interface class that extends `java.rmi.Remote`.

```java
package credit;
import java.rmi.*;

public interface CreditApplication extends Remote {

    public String getCustName()
        throws RemoteException;

    public float getCreditLine ()
        throws RemoteException;

    public void setCreditLine (float amount)
        throws RemoteException;

    public String getCreditCardNumber()
        throws RemoteException;

    public void setCreditCardNumber (String cardNumber)
        throws RemoteException;
}
```

The `CreditManager` interface is modified so that the `CreditApplication` object can be sent to the credit manager. If the customer's application is accepted, the customer will then be issued a valid `CreditCard`.

```java
package credit;
import java.rmi.*;
```

```
public interface CreditManager extends Remote {

  /** This method finds an existing credit card for a
      given customer credit number. If the customer
      does not have an account, an InvalidAccountException
      is thrown. */
  public CreditCard findCreditAccount(String customer)
      throws InvalidAccountException, RemoteException;

  /** This method receives an CreditApplication object from
      the customer. On the customer's behalf the server will
      fill in the missing account number, initial credit line
      and rate. */
  public void applyForCard (CreditApplication app)
      throws DuplicateAccountException,
      AccountRejectedException, RemoteException;
}
```

The updated CreditManager requires two new exception classes: Invalid-AccountException and AccountRejectedException.

```
package credit;

public class InvalidAccountException extends Exception {
}
package credit;

public class AccountRejectedException extends Exception {
}
```

Step 2: Create and Compile Implementation Classes

The CreditApplicationImpl object creates an implementation of CreditApplication that provides behavior for each of the methods defined in the interface. In addition, CreditApplicationImpl defines the data that a credit application is expected to store. This class extends UnicastRemoteObject so that it may be automatically exported upon creation; it also implements a remote interface, Credit-Application, so that it may be passed *by reference* to the server. For cases where a class cannot extend UnicastRemoteObject, the developer can explicitly export an object through the static method, UnicastRemoteObject.exportObject().

```
package credit;
import java.rmi.*;
import java.rmi.server.*;
```

```
public class CreditApplicationImpl extends UnicastRemoteObject
    implements CreditApplication {

  private float creditLine;
  private float creditRate;
  private String creditCardNumber;
  private String custName;
  private String ssn;

  public CreditApplicationImpl (String name, String soc)
      throws RemoteException {
    custName = name;
    ssn = soc;
  }
  public String getCustName () {
    return custName;
  }
  public void setCreditLine (float amount) {
    creditLine = amount;
  }
  public float getCreditLine () {
    return creditLine;
  }
  public void setCreditCardNumber (String cardNumber) {
    creditCardNumber = new String (cardNumber);
  }
  public String getCreditCardNumber () {
    return creditCardNumber;
  }
}
```

The implementation of a `CreditManager` object is changed to reflect the new design. The `CreditManagerImpl` now uses a private method to create a credit account, which is only called if the customer's credit application is approved.

```
package credit;
import java.rmi.*;
import java.rmi.server.*;
import java.util.HashMap;

public class CreditManagerImpl extends UnicastRemoteObject
    implements CreditManager {
  private static transient HashMap accounts = new HashMap();
```

```
/** This is the default class constructor that does nothing
    but implicitly call super(). */
public CreditManagerImpl() throws RemoteException {
}

/** Creates a new account. Puts the customer name and the
    customer's credit card in the hashtable. */
private void newCreditAccount (String name, String cardNumber,
    float creditLine)
    throws DuplicateAccountException, RemoteException {
  CreditCardImpl newCard =
    new CreditCardImpl(name, cardNumber, creditLine);
  accounts.put(cardNumber, newCard);
}

/** Searches the hashtable for an existing account. If no
    account for customer name, one is created and added to
    hashtable. Returns the account. */
public CreditCard findCreditAccount(String cardNumber)
    throws InvalidAccountException, RemoteException {
  CreditCardImpl account =
    (CreditCardImpl)accounts.get(cardNumber);
  if (account != null) {
    return account;
  } else {
    throw new InvalidAccountException ();
  }
}

/** The Account Manager will determine (based upon the
    customer name and social security number) the credit line
    and credit rate. */

public void applyForCard (CreditApplication app)
    throws DuplicateAccountException,
    AccountRejectedException, RemoteException {

  // Check for duplicate
  if (accounts.get(app.getCreditCardNumber()) != null) {
    throw new DuplicateAccountException();
  }

  // Here, some other process would determine the
```

```
            // customer's credit rating...
            // For now, we'll hard code that number to 5000.
            float initialLine = 5000.0f;
            app.setCreditLine (initialLine);

            // Generate a credit card number the user can use
            String cardNumber = app.getCustName() +
              (int)(Math.random() * 20000);
            app.setCreditCardNumber (cardNumber);

            // Generate the customer credit card
            newCreditAccount (app.getCustName(),
              cardNumber, initialLine);
        }
      }
```

There is a slightly modified `CreditCardImpl` class, providing a modified constructor:

```
package credit;
import java.rmi.*;
import java.rmi.server.*;
import java.io.Serializable;

/** This class is the remote object that will referenced by the skeleton
    on the server side and the stub on the client side. */

public class CreditCardImpl extends UnicastRemoteObject
    implements CreditCard, Serializable {

  private float currentBalance = 0;
  private float creditLine = 0;
  private int signature = 0;        // Like a p.i.n. number
  private String accountName;       // Name of owner
  private String cardNumber;        // Card ID

  /** Class constructor generates an initial pin.*/
  public CreditCardImpl (String customer, String accountNum, float line) throws
      RemoteException, DuplicateAccountException {
    accountName = customer;
    cardNumber = accountNum;
    creditLine = line;
    signature = (int)(Math.random() * 10000);
  }
```

```java
/** Returns credit line. */
public float getCreditLine() throws RemoteException {
  return creditLine;
}

/** Pays off some debt. */
public void payTowardsBalance(float money) throws
    RemoteException, InvalidMoneyException {
  if (money <= 0) {
    throw new InvalidMoneyException ();
  } else {
    currentBalance -= money;
  }
}

/** Changes signature. */
public void setSignature(int pin) throws RemoteException {
  signature = pin;
}

/** Makes a purchase. Makes sure enough credit is available,
    then increments balance and decrements available credit. */
public void makePurchase (float amount, int signature) throws
    RemoteException, InvalidSignatureException,
    CreditLineExceededException {
  if (signature != this.signature) {
    throw new InvalidSignatureException();
  }
  if (currentBalance+amount > creditLine) {
    throw new CreditLineExceededException();
  } else {
    currentBalance += amount;
    creditLine -= amount;
  }
}
}
}
```

Once you've created all your new updated source files, you need to compile each of them:

```
javac -d . CreditApplication.java
javac -d . InvalidAccountException.java
javac -d . AccountRejectedException.java
```

```
javac -d . CreditManager.java
javac -d . CreditCardImpl.java
javac -d . CreditApplicationImpl.java
javac -d . CreditManagerImpl.java
```

Step 3: Create Stub and Skeleton Classes

```
rmic -d . credit.CreditCardImpl
rmic -d . credit.CreditApplicationImpl
rmic -d . credit.CreditManagerImpl
```

Step 4: Create and Compile the Server Application

The CardBank server does not change at all.

Step 5: Start the RMI Registry and the Server Application

Starting the server is the same as well:

```
start rmiregistry
java credit.CardBank localhost 12345
```

Step 6: Create and Compile the Client Program

The client application, now named Shopper2, is modified only slightly to include the step of applying for credit through a CreditApplication object.

```
package credit;
import java.rmi.*;

public class Shopper2 {
  public static void main(String args[]) {

    CreditManager cm = null;
    CreditApplicationImpl cardApp = null;
    CreditCard account = null;

    // Check the command line.
    if (args.length != 4) {
      System.err.println("Usage:");
      System.err.println("java credit.Shopper2 <server> " +
        "<port> <account name> <social security number>");
      System.exit (1);
    }
```

```java
// name parameters
String server = args[0];
int port = Integer.parseInt (args[1]);
String name = args[2];
String ssn = args[3];

// Create and install a security manager.
System.setSecurityManager(new RMISecurityManager());

// Obtain reference to card manager.
try {
  String url = new String ("//" + server + ":" + port +
    "/cardManager");
  System.out.println ("Shopper2: lookup cardManager, url = " + url);
  cm = (CreditManager)Naming.lookup(url);
} catch (Exception e) {
  System.out.println("Error in getting card manager" + e);
}


// Apply for a credit card
// Create an instance of a credit card application
// Send the credit application to the Credit Manager
try {
  cardApp = new CreditApplicationImpl(name, ssn);
  cm.applyForCard (cardApp);
} catch (DuplicateAccountException e) {
  System.out.println ("Duplicate Exception applying for credit");
  System.exit (1);
} catch (AccountRejectedException e) {
  System.out.println ("Reject Exception applying for credit");
  System.exit (1);
} catch (RemoteException e) {
  System.out.println ("Remote Exception applying for credit " + e);
  System.exit (1);
}

// The application was accepted, let's use the new card!
try {
  System.out.println ("New credit card number is: " +
    cardApp.getCreditCardNumber() + " with a credit line of: " +
    cardApp.getCreditLine());
  account =  cm.findCreditAccount(cardApp.getCreditCardNumber());
```

```
      System.out.println ("Found account: " +
        cardApp.getCreditCardNumber());
    } catch (Exception e) {
      System.out.println("Error in getting account for " + name);
    }

    // Do some transactions.
    try {
      System.out.println("Available credit is: "
        + account.getCreditLine());
      System.out.println("Changing pin number for account");
      account.setSignature(1234);
      System.out.println("Buying a new watch for $100");
      account.makePurchase(100.00f, 1234);
      System.out.println("Available credit is now: " +
        account.getCreditLine());
      System.out.println("Buying a new pair of shoes for $160");
      account.makePurchase(160.00f, 1234);
      System.out.println("CardHolder: Paying off $136 of balance");
      account.payTowardsBalance(136.00f);
      System.out.println("Available credit is now: "+
        account.getCreditLine());
    } catch (Exception e) {
      System.out.println("Transaction error for " + name);
    }
    System.exit(0);
  }
}
```

Remember to compile the new client application:

```
javac -d . Shopper2.java
```

Step 7: Test *Shopper2*

Once you've compiled everything, you can test out the updated application as before. Here is a sample session output on a Unix machine with the remote service running on the local machine (the first line is the invocation; the rest is output):

```
%java credit.Shopper2 localhost 12345 bobo 555-XX-1212
Shopper2: lookup cardManager, url = //localhost:12345/cardManager
New credit card number is: bobo10723 with a credit line of: 5000.0
Found account: bobo10723
Available credit is: 5000.0
```

```
Changing pin number for account
Buying a new watch for $100
Available credit is now: 4900.0
Buying a new pair of shoes for $160
CardHolder: Paying off $136 of balance
Available credit is now: 4740.0
```

Dynamic Class Loading

One of the primary features of RMI is that it has been designed from the ground up as a Java-to-Java distributed object system. RMI is distinct from other systems such as CORBA in that it is possible to send a complete object from one remote address space to another.

This feature makes it possible to pass not only data on the wire, but also behavior. Complete class definitions can be passed using the magic of serialization and the RMIClassLoader. RMI makes it very easy to send a full object graph by passing an object as the argument to a method call. The only requirement for passing an object is that the object be Serializable.

How is this useful? Passing an object to another address space makes it possible to use the resources of that address space: CPU cycles, files, access to a database, and so on. If the type of computation required by the object is complex, there is an advantage to the overall system to send it from a slower machine to a faster machine despite the overhead of transferring the object across the network.

> **NOTE** Both the callback mechanism and the dynamic class loading mechanism are triggered by passing objects as arguments to remote methods. The key difference between passing a remote reference (aka a stub instance) used in a callback versus the serialized instance of an object is determined by whether or not the object being passed implements the java.rmi.Remote interface. If an object implements the Remote interface, then its stub is serialized, rather than the object instance.

Here is the abstract LoanType class:

```
package bank.loan;
import java.io.Serializable;

public abstract class LoanType implements Serializable {
```

```
    private float monthlyPayment,interestRate;
    private int loanAmount, loanDuration;

    // This method is executed by the server on behalf of
    // the client.
    public abstract void calculatePayment();

    public LoanType(int amount, float rate, int term) {
      loanAmount=amount;
      interestRate=rate;
      loanDuration=term;
    }
    public void setMonthlyPayment(float payment) {
      monthlyPayment = payment;
    }
    public float getMonthlyPayment() {
      return monthlyPayment;
    }
    public int getLoanAmount() {
      return loanAmount;
    }
    public float getInterestRate() {
      return interestRate;
    }
    public int getLoanDuration() {
      return loanDuration;
    }
  }
```

The client defines an instance of a LoanType object by extending the abstract class and providing a method body for calculatePayment(). This class, Conventional-Loan, calculates the monthly payment for conventional mortgages:

```
  package bank.loan;

  public class ConventionalLoan extends LoanType {

    public ConventionalLoan(int amount, float rate, int term) {
      super(amount, rate, term);
    }
    public void calculatePayment() {
      // convert the interest rate to decimal percentage
      float interestRate = getInterestRate()/100;
```

```
      // calculate the monthly interest rate
      float monthlyInterestRate = interestRate/12;

      // convert the duration of the loan from years in to
      // months
      int numberOfMonths = getLoanDuration() * 12;

      float pmt = (float)(getLoanAmount()*(monthlyInterestRate /
        (1 - Math.pow((1 + monthlyInterestRate), -numberOfMonths)))));
      setMonthlyPayment(pmt);
   }
}
```

The client requests a reference to a LoanOfficer instance from the server application. The LoanOfficer interface defines the processLoan() method, which takes a single LoanType argument and returns a LoanType object, from which the client may extract the monthly payment amount. The implementation of the LoanOfficer interface provides a method body for processLoan() that executes the calculatePayment() method of the object passed.

```
package bank.loan;
import java.rmi.*;

public interface LoanOfficer extends Remote {
  public LoanType processLoan(LoanType loan)
    throws RemoteException;
}
```

The implementation of this object is named LoanOfficerImpl:

```
package bank.loan;
import java.rmi.*;
import java.rmi.server.*;

public class LoanOfficerImpl extends UnicastRemoteObject
    implements LoanOfficer {

  public LoanOfficerImpl() throws RemoteException {
  }

  public LoanType processLoan (LoanType loan)
      throws RemoteException  {
    loan.calculatePayment();
    return loan;
  }
}
```

Finally, the server application, `Lender`, creates an instance of a `LoanOfficerImpl` object and registers the implementation with the `rmiregistry`.

```java
package bank.loan;
import java.rmi.*;
import java.rmi.registry.LocateRegistry;

public class Lender {
  public static void main (String args[]) {
    if (args.length != 2) {
      System.err.println("Usage:");
      System.err.println("java bank.loan.Lender <server> <port>");
      System.exit (1);
    }

    String server = args[0];
    int port = Integer.parseInt (args[1]);

    // Create and install a security manager.
    System.setSecurityManager(new RMISecurityManager());


    try {
      // Specify registry location
      LocateRegistry.createRegistry (port);
      System.out.println
        ("CardBank: defined registry port");

      // Create an instance of our loan officer.
      System.out.println("Lender: create a LoanOfficer");
      LoanOfficerImpl loi = new LoanOfficerImpl();

      // Bind the object instance to the remote registry.
      // Use the static rebind() method to avoid conflicts.
      System.out.println("Lender: bind the LoanOfficer to a name");
      String urlString = "//" + server + ":" + port + "/" + "loanOfficer";
      Naming.rebind(urlString, loi);

      System.out.println("The LoanOfficer is ready to process requests");

    } catch (Exception e) {
      e.printStackTrace();
```

```
        System.out.println(e.getMessage());
      }
    }
  }
}
```

The client application creates an instance of a `ConventionalLoan`, then obtains a remote reference to a `LoanOfficer` object and passes the instance of the `ConventionalLoan` to `LoanOfficer` through the `processLoan()` method. First, the `LoanOfficerImpl` will look in its CLASSPATH for the class file. When the class is not found, it will use the URL supplied in the object's serialized form. This URL was set from the client's command-line via the `java.rmi.server.codebase` property. If the server cannot load the `ConventionalLoan` class from the client-supplied URL, it will fail with a `ClassNotFoundException`.

The client application takes five arguments: the hostname of the server, the server's port, the amount of the loan, the annual percentage rate (as a float), and the number of years for the life of the loan.

```
package bank.loan;
import java.rmi.*;

public class ConventionalLoanClient {

  public static void main (String args[]) throws Exception {

    LoanOfficer officer;
    ConventionalLoan conv;

    // Check the command line.
    if (args.length != 5) {
      System.err.println("Usage:");
      System.err.println(
        "java ConventionalLoanClient <server> <port> " +
        "<mortgage amount> <interest rate> <number of years>");
      System.exit (1);
    }

    String server = args[0];
    int port = Integer.parseInt (args[1]);
    int amount = Integer.parseInt(args[2]);
    float rate = (new Float(args[3])).floatValue();
    int length = Integer.parseInt(args[4]);
```

```
     // Create an new loan instance
     conv = new ConventionalLoan(amount, rate, length);

     // Create and install a security manager.
     System.setSecurityManager(new RMISecurityManager());

     // Obtain reference to loan officer.
     try {
       String url = new String ("//" + server + ":" + port + "/loanOfficer");
       System.out.println ("Conventional Client: lookup loanOfficer, " +
         "url = " + url);
       officer = (LoanOfficer)Naming.lookup(url);
     } catch (Exception e) {
       System.err.println("Error in getting loan officer " + e);
      throw e;
     }

     // Get the monthly payment
     try {
       // Use the existing reference to get back
       // the changed instance information
       conv = (ConventionalLoan)officer.processLoan(conv);
       System.out.println("Your monthly payment will be " +
         conv.getMonthlyPayment());
     } catch (Exception e1) {
       System.err.println("Error in processing loan " + e1);
       throw e1;
     }
   }
 }
}
```

Running the Example

So far, the examples illustrated in this chapter have made use of two Java virtual machines (three, if you count the rmiregistry) running on the same host with the same CLASSPATH variable set. For this example, in order to illustrate that classes are actually not loaded locally, the rmiregistry, server, and client will be isolated from each other through three steps.

First, the server classes (including the stub classes created by rmic) will not be physically located in the same directory as the client application. Second, the client class to be uploaded to the server (ConventionalLoan) will not be in the same directory as the server. And third, the Registry will be completely isolated from both client and server.

The following steps will compile everything and place the server files in C:\loan\ server and the client files in C:\loan\client. If you wish to use different directories, you will have to make the necessary changes yourself.

```
javac -d . LoanType.java
javac -d . ConventionalLoan.java
javac -d . LoanOfficer.java
javac -d . LoanOfficerImpl.java
rmic -d . bank.loan.LoanOfficerImpl
javac -d . Lender.java
javac -d . ConventionalLoanClient.java
mkdir \loan
mkdir \loan\server
mkdir \loan\server\bank
mkdir \loan\server\bank\loan
mkdir \loan\client
mkdir \loan\client\bank
mkdir \loan\client\bank\loan
copy bank\loan\Lender.class \loan\server\bank\loan
copy bank\loan\LoanOfficer.class \loan\server\bank\loan
copy bank\loan\LoanOfficerImpl.class \loan\server\bank\loan
copy bank\loan\LoanOfficerImpl_Skel.class \loan\server\bank\loan
copy bank\loan\LoanType.class \loan\server\bank\loan
copy bank\loan\ConventionalLoan.class \loan\client\bank\loan
copy bank\loan\ConventionalLoanClient.class \loan\client\bank\loan
copy bank\loan\LoanOfficer.class \loan\client\bank\loan
copy bank\loan\LoanOfficerImpl_Stub.class \loan\client\bank\loan
copy bank\loan\LoanType.class \loan\client\bank\loan
```

NOTE   You'll find the file setupLoan.bat on the CD to help you configure the client and server.

In order to load classes dynamically, the client and server applications must create and install an instance of a RMISecurityManager. Further, the client and server must declare the URL path to the classes that they are "serving" so that applications running in other JVMs can find these classes. The server will be "serving" the stub class for the LoanOfficerImpl, and the client will be "serving" the ConventionalLoan class definition.

To prove that the client's ConventionalLoan class and the server's stub classes are actually transferred between Java virtual machines, the CLASSPATH variable is not set and the rmiregistry is started in a directory isolated from the client and server:

```
C:\> start rmiregistry
```

The server application is started from the server directory, again, with the CLASSPATH variable not set. The server must let the Registry and the client know where to load classes that are being made available by the server, so the java.rmi.server.codebase property is set:

```
C:\loan\server>java -Djava.rmi.server.codebase=file:/loan/server
    bank.loan.Lender localhost 12345
```

TIP   The codebase property requires forward slashes to separate the directory names (of the path), and there must be a trailing slash on the last directory.

The output from the server looks like this:

```
Lender: defined registry port
Lender: create a LoanOfficer
Lender: bind the LoanOfficer to a name
The LoanOfficer is ready to process requests
```

The client application is started from the client directory, and, again, the CLASSPATH variable is not set. The client must let the server know where the ConventionalLoan class is located, so the client application also sets its codebase property:

```
C:\loan\client>java -Djava.rmi.server.codebase=file:/loan/client/
➥ bank.loan.ConventionalLoanClient localhost 12345 250000 7.5 30
```

This example shows a $250,000 mortgage at an annual percentage rate of $7\frac{1}{2}\%$ for 30 years on a server named "localhost" at port 12345. It reports a payment of:

```
Your monthly payment will be 1748.0345
```

NOTE   Don't forget to grant the appropriate directories permissions in java.policy.

Object Activation

In previous versions of RMI, in order to obtain a reference to a remote object, the server that generated the instance of the object had to be running (live) in a Java Virtual Machine. This simple mechanism is sufficient for most applications. However, for large systems that create a number of objects that are not used at the same time (or some objects that are not used at all), it is useful to have a mechanism to suspend those objects until they are needed.

The activation mechanism in JDK 1.2 provides this facility. Activation allows a Java object to be bound (named by the Registry) and then "activated" at some later date simply by referencing the object through the Registry. One of the primary benefits of this approach is that the application that creates the instance of the remote object can terminate or exit normally before the object is ever used. The ability to activate remote objects on request allows RMI system designers much greater flexibility in designing smaller "servers." In order to make activation work, the RMI team created another daemon process, the Java RMI Activation System Daemon (rmid).

The process of finding an object reference is illustrated in Figure 25.2.

FIGURE 25.2:

Object activation in RMI

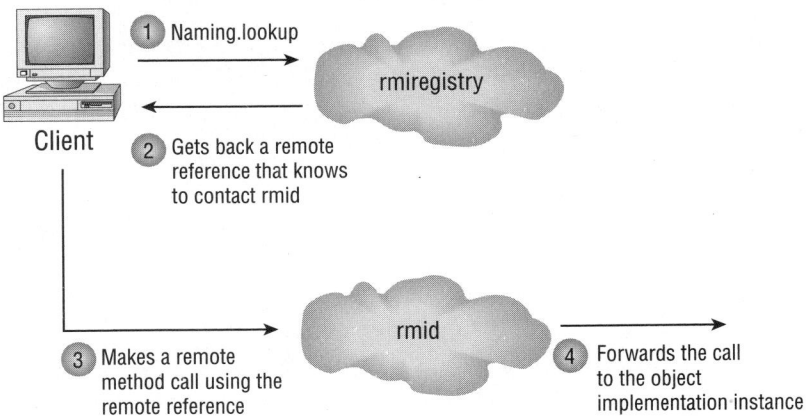

The rmid process must be run first through the command line:

```
C:\> start rmid
```

By default `rmid` will start on port number 1098 (`rmiregistry` is on port 1099 by default), but an alternate port may be specified:

```
C:\> start rmid -port 2002
```

To demonstrate the object activation feature, we will extend the loan-processing example presented in the previous section by activating `LoanOfficer` to approve the mortgage loan application.

Making an Object Activatable

To simplify the example and focus on the elements that make an object activatable, the `LoanOfficer` interface now defines a single method `isApproved()` that takes a single argument, a `LoanApplication` object, and returns a `boolean` result.

```
package bank.loan;
import java.rmi.*;

public interface LoanOfficer extends Remote {
  public boolean isApproved (LoanApplication app)
    throws RemoteException;
}
```

The `LoanOfficerImpl` class implements the `LoanOfficer` interface and extends the `Activatable` class instead of `UnicastRemoteObject`. Note that there is an additional constructor that could be defined for an activatable class, but this one constructor is all that is necessary for this example.

Like the `UnicastRemoteObject` examples seen earlier, an `Activatable` class needs only to implement a remote interface and to be "exported" to accept incoming method requests. By extending `java.rmi.activation.Activatable`, the `LoanOfficerImpl` class is exported automatically upon construction; but any class (except those that extend `UnicastRemoteObject` or `Activatable`) may be exported, using the static method, `Activatable.exportObject()`, as long as it directly or indirectly implements `java.rmi.Remote`.

```
package bank.loan;
import java.rmi.*;
import java.rmi.activation.*;

public class LoanOfficerImpl extends Activatable
    implements LoanOfficer {
```

```
public LoanOfficerImpl (ActivationID id, MarshalledObject data)
   throws RemoteException {

  // Register the LoanOfficerImpl with the activation
  // daemon and "export" it on an anonymous port
  super(id, 0);
}

public boolean isApproved(LoanApplication app)
   throws RemoteException {
  // Here, some other process would determine whether the customer
  // was approved for the loan.
  // For now, we'll let everyone be approved!
  return true;
}
}
```

The Activation Setup Class

The client side of this example is just like any other RMI client class, since the client requests a remote reference and has no idea that the object is activatable or running as a standard UnicastRemoteObject. The "server" side however is very different, since the "server" must register the activatable object with the activation system before it terminates.

NOTE   Since the "server" is not run again when the object is activated, the term "server" does not really apply. So the RMI team came up with the term "setup," which better defines what the activation application does before it exits.

The setup class, a modified Lender class, is a bit more complex than the server class for a UnicastRemoteObject. However, it is likely that this mechanism will be simplified in future releases.

The Lender works with the text representation of the URL that represents the location of the activatable class, LoanOfficerImpl. An ActivationGroupID is passed to the ActivationDesc object, which gets registered with rmid. Each new JVM that is started by rmid will only activate objects for a single ActivationGroupID. If a JVM that is associated with this class' ActivationGroupID is already running, then this object will be created in that JVM, rather than starting a new JVM. The `Activation-GroupID` gives fine-grained control over which JVM the activated object runs in.

Next, the static method `Activatable.register()` passes the `ActivationDesc` up to `rmid`. The activation group descriptor is all the information that `rmid` will need to create an instance of the activatable class. The `Activatable.register()` method returns a remote reference that is then used to register the activatable class with the `rmiregistry`.

Note that the setup class, `Lender`, then explicitly exits with `System.exit()`.

```java
package bank.loan;

import java.net.*;
import java.rmi.*;
import java.rmi.activation.*;
import java.security.*;
import java.util.*;

public class Lender {
  public static void main (String args[]) {
    if (args.length != 3) {
      System.out.println ("Usage: java bank.loan.Lender <server> " +
        "<port> <absolute path to class files>");
      System.exit (1);
    }

    String server = args[0];
    int port = Integer.parseInt (args[1]);
    String filePlace = args[2];

    //  Create and install a security manager.
    System.setSecurityManager(new RMISecurityManager());

    try {
      // Create an instance of our loan officer.
      System.out.println("Lender: create a LoanOfficer");

      Properties env = (Properties)System.getProperties().clone();
      ActivationGroupID groupID =
        ActivationGroup.getSystem().registerGroup(
        new ActivationGroupDesc(env, null));
```

```
    // Marshalled object is typically used to tell the activated
    // object where to find its persistent data.
    // Right here it is unused, but required for the ActivationDesc
    MarshalledObject commandLineInfo = null;
    ActivationDesc ad =
      new ActivationDesc(groupID, "bank.loan.LoanOfficerImpl",
      filePlace, commandLineInfo);

    // Register the activatable class with rmid
    LoanOfficer lo = (LoanOfficer)Activatable.register(ad);
    System.out.println("Registered with rmid");

    // Bind the object instance to the remote registry. Use the
    // static rebind() method to avoid conflicts.
    System.out.println("Lender: bind the LoanOfficer to a name");
    String urlString = "//" + server + ":" + port + "/" + "loanOfficer";
    Naming.rebind(urlString, lo);

    System.out.println("The LoanOfficer is ready to process requests");

  } catch (Exception e) {
    e.printStackTrace();
    System.out.println(e.getMessage());
  }

  // The work is done, now exit the program
  System.exit(0);
  }
}
```

On the client-side, the LoanApplication object is passed to the LoanOfficer object. The LoanApplication is a simple class that is constructed with the customer's social security number and the loan amount.

```
package bank.loan;
import java.io.Serializable;

public class LoanApplication implements Serializable {

  private String ssn;
  private int loanAmount;

  public LoanApplication (String loanInfo, int amount) {
```

```
      ssn = loanInfo;
      loanAmount = amount;
    }
    public String getApplicant() {
      return ssn;
    }
    public int getRequestedAmount() {
      return loanAmount;
    }
  }
```

The client, `LoanClient`, creates an instance of a `LoanApplication` and requests a `LoanOfficer` reference from the Registry.

```
package bank.loan;
import java.rmi.*;

public class LoanClient {

  public static void main (String args[]) throws Exception {

    LoanOfficer officer;
    LoanApplication app;

    // Check the command line.
    if (args.length != 4) {
      System.err.println("Usage:");
      System.err.println("java LoanClient <server> <port> " +
        "<social security number> <mortgage amount>");
      System.exit (1);
    }
    String server = args[0];
    int port = Integer.parseInt (args[1]);
    String applicant = args[2];
    int loanAmount = Integer.parseInt(args[3]);

    // Create the LoanApplication instance
    app = new LoanApplication(applicant, loanAmount);

    // Create and install a security manager.
    System.setSecurityManager(new RMISecurityManager());

    // Obtain reference to loan officer.
```

```
    try {
      String url = new String ("rmi://" + server + ":" + port +
        "/loanOfficer");
      System.out.println ("LoanClient: lookup loanOfficer, " +
        "url = " + url);
      officer = (LoanOfficer)Naming.lookup(url);
    } catch (Exception e) {
      System.err.println("Error in getting loan officer " + e);
      throw e;
    }

    // Get the loan approval
    try {
      boolean approved = officer.isApproved(app);
      System.out.print("Your request for " + loanAmount + " was ");
      if (!approved) {
        System.out.print("not ");
      }
      System.out.println("approved!");
    } catch (Exception e) {
      System.err.println("Error in processing loan " + e);
      throw e;
    }
    System.exit(0);
  }
}
```

The Registry looks up the LoanOfficer object that was registered by the setup application and returns to the client a remote reference, which contacts rmid, to create an instance of the class.

Without moving everything around, the following compiles and runs the server:

```
javac -d . Lender.java
javac -d . LoanApplication.java
javac -d . LoanOfficer.java
javac -d . LoanClient.java
javac -d . LoanOfficerImpl.java
rmic -d . bank.loan.LoanOfficerImpl
start rmiregistry
start rmid
java bank.loan.Lender localhost 12345 file:/MasteringJava/Ch25/
```

Then, in another window, start the client:

```
java bank.loan.LoanClient localhost 12345 XXXX 500000
```

Future Directions in RMI

By default, the Remote Method Invocation system communicates between remote address spaces using a custom protocol (the Java Remote Method Protocol) over a standard TCP/IP protocol. In November 1997, Sun announced its intention to provide an implementation of the Internet-Inter ORB Protocol (IIOP) for RMI. The schedule of this new protocol is not yet announced as of this writing, and its implementation may actually be preceded by changes to the Object Management Group's (CORBA) specification for passing objects by reference.

Summary

Sun introduced Remote Procedure Call support in 1985. To this day, RPC is an essential building block of many distributed applications. It seems likely that RMI will play a vital role in distributed Java applications where the distributed code will benefit from platform independence.

Java's persistent object support provides a very useful facility for storing and reconstituting objects. This feature is valuable in its own right; moreover, it plays an essential role in remote object invocation by providing a Java-standard protocol for reading and writing object data to and from I/O streams. While successful RMI programming involves a number of steps, the individual steps are not difficult. The example code listed in this chapter and provided on the CD-ROM provides a template for most development needs.

While RMI is constantly compared to CORBA as a distributed object technology, it is important to bear in mind that RMI is capable of sending a full object data graph from one remote Java Virtual Machine to another. This is a feature that is not available in standard CORBA implementations. Further RMI systems are becoming more widely integrated as customers find that RMI is easier to develop and understand than CORBA. With the addition of activation and the future integration of the IIOP protocol, RMI is well positioned to continue as an inexpensive and powerful tool for creating object frameworks.

CHAPTER
TWENTY-SIX

26

Java and CORBA

- Introduction to CORBA

- How CORBA works

- The basics of Java Language Mapping

- The future of CORBA

CORBA (Common Object Request Broker Architecture) is a distributed framework designed for support of heterogeneous architectures. While Java's RMI provides support for homogeneous architectures, where Java is at both ends and a wire is in the middle, CORBA allows you to connect two different systems. These systems may differ not only by the hardware (CPU and memory) they use, but also by their operating system and programming language. Java IDL provides an implementation of the CORBA 2.0 specification.

CORBA was created to solve a problem most large companies have: a variety of different system resources at work within the company. For example, the graphics department has Macintoshes running MacOS, the engineering department has Sun workstations running Solaris, management has PCs running either Windows 95 or NT, and central to the operation of the company is a large mainframe that runs a proprietary operating system.

Traditionally, computer manufacturers have attempted to solve the compatibility problem of a heterogeneous environment by creating a line of products that reach into all areas of a company's business. For example, a single vendor may offer a low-end system, a graphics system, and a high-end server system in order to move their customers from a heterogeneous environment to a homogenous one. This can sometimes solve the problem of compatibility, but it is costly and leads to vendor dependence by making a commitment to spend more money on a single vendor's solution.

Heterogeneous Systems Just Happen

In order to understand why companies frequently have heterogeneous environments, consider the following fictional case of a book publishing company, Sullivan Publishing.

Since the early 1900s, Sullivan Publishing has printed and bound books, all by hand. The initial "plant" was little more than a small warehouse with several bulky manual printing presses and a leather-cutting table for the book covers.

Over the next 70 years the business grew, so Sullivan Publishing moved into larger quarters and bought automatic printing presses and binding machines. As the company grew, so did the quantity of data associated with keeping track of inventories and costs related to production and marketing. In order to remain competitive, the company needed an information system that would support their manufacturing and inventory goals.

To meet their information needs during the 1970s and 1980s, the company purchased a large mainframe computer and hired a group of programmers to write and maintain programs to translate their business process into computer applications. These applications were designed to produce reports that management could use to evaluate the information compiled by the computer and to make decisions based upon that information.

The production group used programs to help them track the cost of raw goods and buy quality products from paper and ink dealers in volume at the appropriate time, so inventory did not sit idle on a shelf for too long. The marketing group used programs to generate readership trend analyses, to ensure that specific target markets were not missed. Finally, the graphics department created programs that helped them standardize logos and product branding and used other programs to produce books' cover artwork.

It is important to note that the *purpose* of the mainframe computer was to provide the decision makers in the company with tools to maintain and expand the business. The computer, the operating system, and the programming language(s) used to develop the programs were irrelevant to the real purpose of the system, which was to make more money for Sullivan Publishing.

As time went on, two events in the evolution of computer technology brought changes to the computer system. The first event was the evolution of the PC as an inexpensive business computer. The PC made it possible for a single department within the company to make relatively small purchases of computer equipment (compared to the mainframe) that would have no impact on the mainframe environment. The local PC resources provided an attractive alternative to the terminals attached to the mainframe: more programs, better performance, local storage, and better games!

The second evolution was the network, which allowed companies to tie their different computer resources together and to share files and data. The network was technically capable of connecting disparate systems because the protocols for the network were designed as standards, independent of a computer's hardware or operating system. This is important because without the network there is no concept of a distributed software architecture.

Unfortunately, the dream of sharing information between different systems proved difficult and expensive to implement. Programs could only share data if it was properly formatted to the computing environment that used it. Computer companies were not interested in the data needs of a printing company and therefore developed standards for the format of their data suited for their hardware and operating systems. Thus, data and files from the mainframe word processor were incompatible with the word processing programs on the PCs. Figure 26.1 shows just how this might look.

FIGURE 26.1:   **Sullivan Publishing**

Figure of the company described

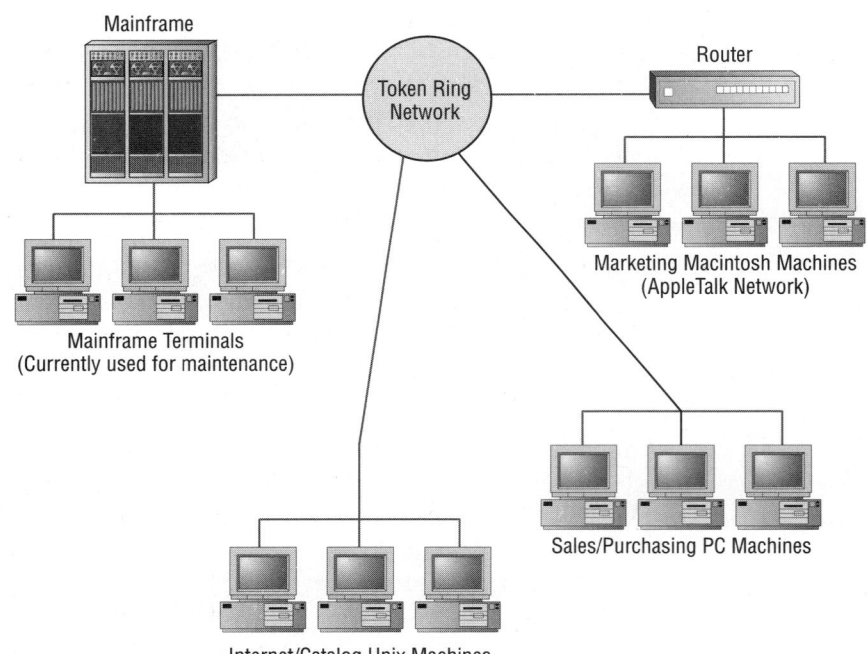

So now we come to the challenges of the late 1990s: First, the company would like all of their computers to seamlessly be able to share information; and second, they would like to offer an online buying service. Sullivan Publishing has evaluated several alternative proposals from a variety of computer vendors, each of which is promising to integrate the company's business onto a single platform that would make their computers work together as a system again. However, each vendor's proposal involves a significant amount of rewrite to the existing code base in addition to purchasing new hardware.

This situation is very common in most companies, although perhaps not as severe as in the example above. The short-term costs are lower than the initial mainframe costs but lead toward incompatibilities between systems because they are heterogeneous in nature.

What the MIS director of Sullivan Publishing would really like to do is invest in a new software framework that will allow the business to leave the existing hardware intact. This would entail migrating the existing software toward a network-centric model, where each computer system is part of the overall business system that Sullivan Publishing originally envisioned the mainframe would be. The MIS director would like to be able to move applications and systems toward a central model that emphasizes a common look at systems, regardless of their operating system and programming language requirements.

Further, the MIS director would like to be able to use the current "legacy" code in its current state, until all of the code can be understood, documented, and rewritten for more modern hardware.

Introducing CORBA

Several years ago, a group of engineers facing the same dilemma decided to form a consortium of their respective companies and design a reusable "system" that would enable multiple programming and operating system environments to work together; these engineers formed the Object Management Group (OMG). Working together, the OMG members have developed several hundred pages of specifications that define a framework of reusable components. The specification covers the architectural elements that are required to allow one hardware and software system to communicate to another. The OMG is now a consortium of over 700 companies, and the Common Object Request Broker Architecture (CORBA) is the framework that is the result of their work.

NOTE   All the documentation on CORBA is available from the technical library at OMG's Web site: `http://www.omg.org`.

The definition of a framework is a reusable collection of code that is almost "ready-to-use" and can be applied to problems with some customization. The CORBA framework is designed to make communication between remote address spaces easier to implement. The primary goal of CORBA is to provide software developers with a means for developing systems that are not reliant on a single operating system and/or programming language.

CORBA by itself is not a product that you can go to a store and buy. The CORBA standard defines how companies can create implementations of the standard. It is the implementations that you can purchase from companies like Iona Technologies, Visigenic (now part of Inprise, which was previously known as Borland), and others, including Sun Microsystems' soon to be phased out NEO.

CORBA Components

A CORBA implementation is composed of several pieces, depending upon the vendor's individual application of each standard. A typical CORBA vendor will supply:

- An Object Request Broker (ORB) implementation
- An Interface Definition Language (IDL) compiler
- One or more implementations of Common Object Services (COS), also known as CORBAServices
- Common Frameworks, also known as CORBAFacilities

Additionally, the CORBA 2.0 specification introduced the Internet Inter-ORB Protocol (IIOP) standard that specifies how ORBs communicate over networks.

Object Request Broker

The primary mechanism for connecting objects between remote address spaces is a function of the Object Request Broker (ORB). Consider the ORB to be an object bus or object pathway. When two CORBA systems wish to communicate between remote address spaces, the ORB makes sure that regardless of the hardware, operating system, and software development language used, the remote object invocations will succeed. This is shown in Figure 26.2.

Vendors typically implement an ORB in one of two ways: as a "library" of objects that form an extension of the CORBA run time or as a daemon process. In either case, the ORB is responsible for establishing communication with the remote system, marshaling parameters to make remote calls, and managing concurrency of simultaneous requests from multiple clients.

FIGURE 26.2:

Generic picture of ORB
communication

Generic Picture of ORB Communication

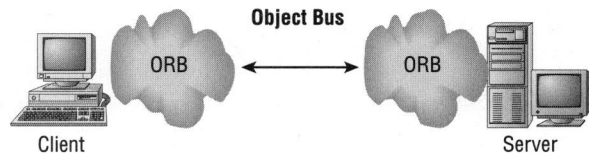

TIP   Marshaling is the technique used to bundle parameters, return values, and exceptions between systems for remote method calls. It basically involves converting data from the source platform's specific representation to a platform-neutral representation and finally to the destination platform's specific representation.

Common Object Services

The ORB does not make up the entire CORBA implementation. Services are required to assist the ORB, such as:

- **Naming Service**   The Naming Service provides a way for CORBA clients (and servers) to find objects on the network. An implementation server registers an object with a Naming Service using a hierarchical representation similar to a path used by a file name. Clients can request a reference to the object by name, using the Naming Service.

- **Event Service**   The Event Service allows a client or server to send a message in the form of an event object to one or more receivers. Objects can request to listen to a specific event channel and the Event Service notifies them of an event on that channel. The Event Service will store events before delivering them, so there is no requirement that the clients and servers are connected.

- **Security Service**   The Security Service provides a means to authenticate messages, authorize access to objects, and provide secure communications. This service in particular is now receiving a lot of attention.

- **Transaction Service**   The Transaction Service defines a means to control an action against a database or other subsystem. The Transaction Service allows clients and servers to commit or roll back a transaction, even when the transaction affects multiple databases.

There are a total of 15 services currently available, including Persistent Object Service, Concurrency Control Service, Life Cycle Service, Relationship Service, Externalization Service, Query Service, Licensing Service, Property Service, Time Service, Object Trader Service, and Object Collections Service.

In addition to the Common Object Services, there are Common Frameworks. The Common Frameworks define application-level services, typically for vertical markets, such as Oil and Gas, Transportation, and Document Preparation. The majority of the specifications for these frameworks are in review, but there are few vendors that support these specifications.

Interface Definition Language

The Object Request Broker, the Common Object Services, and the Common Frameworks would be difficult for any one vendor to implement if there were not some standard way to define the interfaces that each of these elements requires. The definitions of the interfaces in CORBA are created through a set of language constructs that are specified by the Interface Definition Language (IDL).

IDL provides a programming language neutral way to define how a service is implemented. The constructs that make up IDL are syntactically similar to C and C++ (and even Java), but cannot be compiled into a binary program directly. Instead, IDL is intended to be an intermediary language that defines the interfaces that a client will use and a server will implement. IDL is best thought of as a "contract" between the system that makes use of an object and a system that implements an object.

A developer, creating a CORBA system, models the system using IDL to define the interface that the system will support. This model is an abstract representation of the actual system. For example, the following is a simple IDL file:

```
module Calculator {
  interface Functions {
    float square_root ( in float number );
    float power (in float base, in float exponent );
  };
};
```

The syntax of IDL is familiar to the reader who has Java, C, or C++ experience, and, in fact, many IDL constructs were designed to be easily understood by these programmers.

This IDL file describes two function keys on a calculator, a square root function and a power function (a number raised to a power). The definition of these functions is abstract: There is no code describing the implementation of these functions, nor is there any definition of the language to be used to implement the functions.

This IDL specification is "compiled" using a tool that creates code for the specific operating system and programming language the developer needs. Currently, CORBA vendors support C, C++, Java, SmallTalk, and Ada. Some companies have their own implementations of other languages such as COBOL. Later in this chapter the Java mapping of the most useful IDL constructs will be covered in more detail.

NOTE   IDL files are "compiled," but this is really a misnomer and illustrates the limited nature of computer terms. An IDL file is actually *translated* from the general constructs that make up IDL to specific programming language constructs (like C, C++, or Java). However, the files generated by the translation process are not complete; they require the implementation details that the developer must fill in.

Internet Inter-ORB Protocol

The Internet Inter-ORB Protocol is a TCP/IP implementation of the General Inter-ORB Protocol (GIOP). The GIOP specification defines how ORBs communicate, including how messages are sent, how byte ordering is done for integers and floating point numbers, and how parameters are marshaled for remote object invocations.

With CORBA it is possible to build a client application using one vendor's ORB and IDL compiler, build a server or object implementation with a second vendor's ORB and IDL compiler, and create a set of common services for both client and server with yet a third vendor's ORB and IDL compiler. IIOP allows each of the three different vendors' products to communicate with each other using a standard set of protocol semantics.

And, when you consider that all three of these ORBs could be using a different programming language and running on a different hardware and operating system platform, you get the idea that CORBA is pretty cool!

NOTE   While not a CORBA component, per se, IIOP compatibility is required of CORBA vendors that wish to advertise that they are 2.0 compliant. The IIOP specification has probably done more to further the cause of CORBA then any other specification.

How CORBA Works

Now that the components that make up a CORBA system have been described, it should be helpful to see how each of these is used to develop a working CORBA system. The landscape of CORBA is ever changing. The description below applies in particular to Java IDL in the JDK 1.2, but the process will be similar in most other CORBA implementations.

The process of creating a CORBA system starts with the development of a design: the outline of what functionality the system is to provide. From there the design is translated into objects that provide the functionality required by the design. These objects are expressed in terms of IDL interfaces and collected into related modules. The IDL file(s) is then compiled to generate stub and skeleton code. Stubs become the interfaces that client applications will use, and skeletons provide interfaces to object implementations that servers will provide. This is similar to how Java and RMI work.

Once the IDL file is compiled, object implementations are created from the interface definition files that are generated, and a server application is created to provide a means for publishing the object references by name through the Naming Service. The client application requests a reference to an object by name through the Naming Service and a reference to a generic CORBA object is returned. This object reference is narrowed (like Java casting) to a reference that is actually the stub representation of the remote CORBA object.

Defining CORBA Objects

CORBA objects are first described abstractly in an IDL file. Actually, a CORBA application could be developed without using IDL at all, and in fact there are CORBA products that allow the developer to create Java and C++ code from a visual development tool, skipping over the creation of IDL files. However, the purpose of the IDL file is to provide a road map for the development of a sound CORBA system and requires that the developer think through the problem before generating any executable code. The IDL file also provides written documentation of the creation process and preserves the software design investment. An IDL file from 1998 will still continue to provide insight into the design of a system long after CORBA is transformed into a new software paradigm.

A CORBA object is also known as a "service." CORBA services provide operations that may or may not return any results. Note that in an IDL definition there is no concept of data. IDL interface definitions of services are true object-oriented descriptions; the data is not shown because it is always private and accessed only by an operation, which is public.

For example, in the IDL shown here:

```
module Calculator {
  interface Functions {
    float square_root ( in float number );
    float power ( in float base, in float exponent );
  };
};
```

Functions is a CORBA service (encapsulated in a package or library called Calculator) that describes two operations, square_root and power. An IDL compiler will generate language-specific files, depending upon the purpose of the compiler. For example, the IDL compiler for Java IDL will generate Java files.

Stubs and Skeletons

The names of the files generated by the IDL compiler depend upon the contents of the IDL file and the IDL compiler used. In the above IDL file, a package directory Calculator is generated and a Java interface file named Functions.java is generated in the Calculator directory. Functions.java contains abstract method declarations for the two operations.

Other generated files include stub and skeleton files. Stub files are used by client code to resolve references to remote CORBA objects. Skeleton files are used by server code (object implementation) to allow remote references to make upcalls to object implementations. Both stub and skeleton classes extend a common ORB class that allows these two objects to communicate. Both client and server applications utilize the Naming Service (tnameserv) to provide information about the remote object that is requested and served respectively.

Figure 26.3 on the following page illustrates how stubs and skeletons are used in a CORBA application. When the server is started, it creates, or is passed, an object that is to be referenced. This object implements the operations defined in the IDL file. In other words, it provides method bodies for the square_root and power methods. The Java class that provides the implementation of the operations defined in the IDL interface Functions also extends a generated class that defines skeleton methods. The server registers the reference to this object with the Naming Service.

FIGURE 26.3: **Stubs and Skeletons**

CORBA Stubs and Skeletons

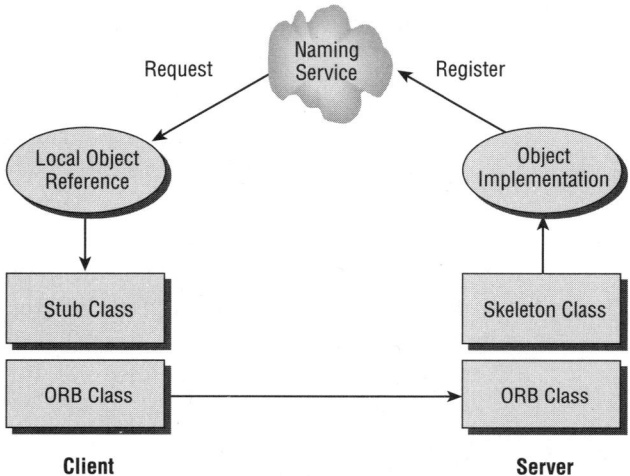

The client requests a reference to a remote object through the Naming Service. The reference that is returned is passed to a stub object. The client then invokes methods through the stub reference as if the object was local to the client. The stub in turn passes requests to the skeleton reference obtained through the Naming Service.

CORBA Servers

The Naming Service provides a reference to a CORBA object provided by a server. There are two types of CORBA objects: transient and persistent. Transient objects have the same lifetime as the server that created them: as long as the server is running the object is available. Persistent objects do not require a running server. If a request is made of an object that does not exist, an ORB daemon will start the appropriate server to create an object and return its reference. As of this writing, Java IDL provides only transient servers, but Java IDL clients can access persistent servers provided by other CORBA vendors.

CORBA servers can refer to an object's implementation in one of two ways: statically or dynamically. In both cases, client requests are not sent directly to the object implementation, but instead pass through a skeleton. The skeleton provides methods for handling the order of arguments passed to the method invocation on the object it represents and provides methods for marshaling results to be passed back to the stub.

Static skeletons are generated directly from the IDL interface declarations. These are the easiest to create because the order of the arguments and their type is known in advance (at compile time). Dynamic skeletons are more flexible, allowing method invocations on an object to be handled dynamically at run time. By default, the Java IDL compiler generates skeletons that use Java IDL's Dynamic Skeleton Interface.

There are two methods that Java IDL provides to connect the skeleton interfaces with the actual object implementation. One way is to inherit skeleton methods directly, by sub-classing the skeleton class generated by the IDL compiler. This approach is straightforward: Each IDL interface method has a direct correlation to a skeleton method.

However, there are times when it is desirable to reserve the superclass slot for another class, particularly in instances when the classes that are being wrapped by the CORBA skeleton classes already exist. In this case, another class may be used in between the skeleton and the implementation that delegates the method calls to the appropriate implementation class. These delegation-based skeletons are referred to as Ties. Java IDL provides a mechanism for creating a Tie implementation by simply specifying a flag to the `idltojava` application on the command line.

CORBA Clients

A client application invokes methods on CORBA objects. In order to invoke a method on a CORBA object, the client must know what methods are available and what arguments each method takes. A client can be written with static or dynamic method invocations.

Static method invocations are the easiest to write because they are generated and type-checked at compile time. Static invocations use the methods declared by the Java interfaces generated from IDL interface definitions.

Dynamic method invocations are more flexible; the client discovers the object definitions at run time. But dynamic method invocations do not type-check arguments, and it is the responsibility of the client to make sure that arguments are valid. Dynamic invocation also requires that the server supports an Interface Repository. The Interface Repository is used to provide the client with method names, types, and argument lists.

Object Adapter

Some CORBA implementations support the concept of an Object Adapter. The Object Adapter is responsible for creating server objects and returning the object reference (object ID). The Object Adapter is only used on the server side. CORBA specifies that at least one Basic Object Adapter (BOA) is supported. However, the current specification for the BOA is quite vague, and the result is that from vendor to vendor there are different semantics for the implementation of the BOA. These differences have made it difficult to port server-side code from one vendor's implementation to another.

The OMG has now released a new specification, deprecating the BOA and replacing it with the Portable Object Adapter (POA). This new specification carefully defines the requirements for a POA, making it possible to move server-side code from one vendor's implementation to another. The POA is described in IDL and will be instantiated as a CORBA object.

At this writing, the POA is still in the specification phase and not yet implemented. Java IDL currently only supports transient object servers, and therefore does not implement a BOA; instead a simplified object adapter for transient objects is built into the Java ORB class.

Java IDL Availability

The current release of the Java Development Kit (JDK) version 1.2 includes a 100% Pure Java ORB and a Naming Service (`tnameserv`) that follows the COS Naming Service specification. The Java IDL compiler (`idltojava`) is available separately at `http://java.sun.com/products/jdk/idl/`, and it creates the Java language mappings for IDL. Java IDL is CORBA 2.0 compliant, so it also communicates with any other IIOP (version 1.0) ORB.

Writing a Simple CORBA Service

As described earlier, CORBA services are expressed in terms of IDL interfaces. The Naming Service is actually an IDL file that describes the interfaces required to provide this "service." To introduce how Java IDL is used, a short example may be helpful.

Earlier the following IDL code was presented:

```
module Calculator {
  interface Functions {
```

```
    float square_root ( in float number );
    float power (in float base, in float exponent );
  };
};
```

This IDL file represents an example description of a CORBA service. An IDL interface named `Functions` is enclosed in the naming scope of a module named `Calculator`. The IDL interface `Functions` describes a single service that contains two operations: `square_root` and `power`. The `square_root` operation takes a single floating point argument, passed by value to the operation, and returns a single float result. The operation `power` takes two float arguments passed by value and returns a single float result. The `Calculator` naming scope encloses the service `Functions`.

Later in this chapter the semantics of IDL are described in greater detail. In this section, the following example will be used to introduce the mechanics of developing CORBA applications with Java IDL.

The basic steps are:

1. Create an IDL file that represents the interfaces desired.

2. Compile the IDL file using `idltojava`.

3. Compile the generated classes using `javac`.

4. Create an implementation class.

5. Create the implementation server.

6. Create the client application (or applet).

7. Compile the implementation, server, and client code.

8. Start the Naming Service application, `tnameserv`.

9. Start the server (which registers with the Naming Service).

10. Start the client.

The most important of these steps is the first, but many developers spend too little time in design. One of the drawbacks to a flexible framework is that the design of the framework is what drives the implementation. Changes that are made to the implementation are not reflected in the IDL file automatically, and most CORBA vendors do not provide tools that take an implementation back to IDL.

Compiling IDL files

For this example, assume that the IDL file shown before is in a file named
`calc.idl`. To compile the IDL file, use the `idltojava` compiler:

```
idltojava -fno-cpp calc.idl
```

TIP
The **-fno-cpp** option is used to turn off C/C++ pre-processing. Other options are described in the `jidlCompiler.html` document, shipped with the `idltojava` compiler.

The Java IDL compiler generates several files, shown in the following hierarchy in Figure 26.4:

FIGURE 26.4:

Generated IDL files

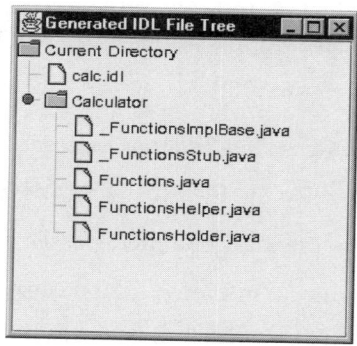

The IDL compiler looks at the IDL file and uses the constructs specified to generate specific Java files and directories. The module construct is used as a package specification, and the interface construct is used as a Java interface definition. In the example shown, the package name is `Calculator`, and the Java interface file generated is `Functions.java`.

Compile the Generated Classes

The `idltojava` IDL compiler only generates Java source code, so the generated classes must be compiled. The nice thing about this step is that none of the generated classes will throw compilation exceptions! To compile the generated classes, use the following compiler command:

```
javac Calculator\*.java
```

Creating the Implementation Class

The next step is to provide a Java class that implements the Java interface generated by the IDL compiler. It is recommended that the physical location of the classes you create remain separate from the generated classes. The generated classes are in the `Calculator` subdirectory already, so the created classes can be created one directory level above them.

Java IDL provides a file that makes this effort easy. The `_FunctionsImplBase` `.java` file is an abstract class file that extends `org.omg.CORBA.portable.Object‐ Impl`, and implements `Calculator.Functions` and `org.omg.CORBA.portable` `.Skeleton`. Extending this class provides the appropriate skeleton methods required to perform the up-calls from the ORB to the implementation methods.

The implementation class must provide method bodies for the interface methods described by the Functions interface (generated from the IDL file calc.idl):

```
/*
 * File: ./Calculator/Functions.java
 * From: calc.idl
 * Date: Tue Jun 16 10:59:20 1998
 *    By: idltojava Java IDL 1.2 Nov 10 1997 13:52:11 */

package Calculator;
public interface Functions
    extends org.omg.CORBA.Object {
    float square_root(float number);
    float power(float base, float exponent);
}
```

> **NOTE** As of JDK 1.1, all methods defined in an interface are implicitly public.

Therefore, the implementation class must provide methods for the **square_root** and **power** methods. By convention, the implementation class adds an "Impl" suffix to the interface name. The implementation class created is shown below:

```
// Implementation file for the Functions interface
//
import Calculator.*;
// First, extend the Implementation Base class
public class FunctionsImpl extends _FunctionsImplBase {
```

```
    // A constructor is not required, but is recommended
    public FunctionsImpl () {
    }
    // Implement the two special methods
    public float square_root (float number) {
      return (float)Math.sqrt ((double)number);
    }
    public float power (float base, float exponent) {
      return (float)Math.pow ((double)base, (double)exponent);
    }
  }
```

This simple implementation returns a square root using the `sqrt()` method and a power using the `pow()` method of the `java.lang.Math` class. Note that these methods take double type arguments and return a double as a result, so the arguments and the results of the methods must be cast to a float.

Creating the Implementation Server

The next step is to create a server class that will register the implementation object with the ORB and Naming Service and provide the connection to the implementation class. Like the implementation class, this Java class is not generated by the `idltojava` compiler.

```
  // The Calculator Server class
  import Calculator.*;
  import org.omg.CosNaming.*;
  import org.omg.CosNaming.NamingContextPackage.*;
  import org.omg.CORBA.*;

  public class CalculatorServer {
    public static void main(String args[]) {
      try{
        // create and initialize an instance of a server-sideORB
        ORB orb = ORB.init(args, null);

        // create implementation object and register it with the ORB
        FunctionsImpl fRef = new FunctionsImpl();
        orb.connect(fRef);

        // get a handle to the name server
        org.omg.CORBA.Object objRef =
```

```
          orb.resolve_initial_references("NameService");
      NamingContext ncRef = NamingContextHelper.narrow(objRef);

      // bind the Object Reference in Naming
      NameComponent nc = new NameComponent("Calc", "");
      NameComponent path[] = {nc};
      ncRef.rebind(path, fRef);

      // wait for invocations from clients
      java.lang.Object sync = new java.lang.Object();
      synchronized (sync) {
        sync.wait();
      }
    } catch (Exception e) {
      System.err.println("ERROR: " + e);
      e.printStackTrace();
    }
  }
}
```

The server code creates and initializes an ORB object, then creates a reference to the object implementation FunctionsImpl. The server must publish the object reference to the Naming Service in order for the object to be located. The name of the object reference is arbitrary and formed by creating a naming scope, similar to a file name and path. In the example above, the FunctionsImpl reference is named "Calc" and is a top-level name. Finally, the server waits (indefinitely) for an object request (through the newly created ORB reference). This server is an example of a transient object server: The object reference and the ORB require that the server application remain running.

Creating the Client Application

The client application will locate a reference to the Functions object using the Naming Service. The object reference returned is a CORBA object reference that must be cast or narrowed to the appropriate reference type. The server published the name of the reference as "Calc," so this is the object reference that the client will request of the Naming Service.

```
// Calculator Client
import Calculator.*;
import org.omg.CosNaming.*;
import org.omg.CORBA.*;
```

```
public class CalculatorClient {
  public static void main(String args[]) {
    try{
      // create and initialize an instance of a client-side ORB
      ORB orb = ORB.init(args, null);

      // get a handle to the name server
      org.omg.CORBA.Object objRef =
        orb.resolve_initial_references("NameService");
      NamingContext ncRef = NamingContextHelper.narrow(objRef);

      // look up the object bound to the name "Calc"
      NameComponent nc = new NameComponent("Calc", "");
      NameComponent path[] = {nc};

      // Use the Helper class to "cast" the generic CORBA object
      // reference to a Functions implementation. The object returned
      // by the narrow method is actually a _FunctionsStub object
      // that implements the methods in the Functions interface
      Functions fRef = FunctionsHelper.narrow(ncRef.resolve(path));

      // Use the reference to execute the interface methods
      float sqrt = fRef.square_root (10f);
      float pow = fRef.power (2f, 8f);

      System.out.println ("The square root of 10 is: " + sqrt);
      System.out.println ("2 to the 8th power is: " + pow);

    } catch (Exception e) {
      System.out.println("ERROR : " + e) ;
      e.printStackTrace();
    }
  }
}
```

The client program also creates an instance of an ORB, then requests a reference to an object that matches the naming scope created through the NamingContext reference. The object reference that the Naming Service returns is a general CORBA reference and must be cast before the object methods can be called. In addition, the client application will invoke methods on a stub that will represent the object reference. The Helper class, generated by idltojava, makes this easy by providing a method called narrow() that returns a reference to a Functions stub. With this reference, the square_root() and power() methods can be called.

Compile the Implementation, Client, and Server Code

The newly created implementation, server, and client Java class files are compiled next with the following command line:

```
javac -d . FunctionsImpl.java CalculatorServer.java
➥ CalculatorClient.java
```

Start the Naming Service Application

The Naming Service application, `tnameserv`, is provided with the JDK 1.2 release. It will listen on a port, number 900 by default, for name resolution and binding requests. Specifying an argument to `tnameserv` may change the default port number. For example, here the port number is changed to 1050:

```
tnameserv -ORBInitialPort 1050
```

The Naming Service application responds with the following output:

```
Initial Naming Context:
IOR:000000000000002849444c3a6f6d672e6f72672f436f734e616d696e672f4e616d6
➥96e67436f6e746578743a312e300000000001000000000000003400010000000000086
➥4656661756c7400040300000000001cafabcafe0000000234ba207b000000000000000
➥80000000000000000
TransientNameServer: setting port for initial object references to: 1050
```

Stringified Object References

The `tnameserv` output lists the Naming Service's Interoperable Object Reference (IOR) and the current port number that the Naming Service is listing on. The IOR string is another mechanism for locating a CORBA object reference. The IOR contains information about the location of the object, including hostname and IP address, as well as what services the object provides. The IOR is most useful for passing an object reference between two ORB implementations without the need for a Naming Service to locate an object reference.

This works as follows: The server publishes a "stringified" object reference (the string representation of the CORBA object reference) by converting the object reference to a string. For example, in the `CalculatorServer` source above:

```
try{
    // create and initialize the ORB
    ORB orb = ORB.init(args, null);
```

Continued on next page

```
        // create implementation object and register it with the ORB
        FunctionsImpl fRef = new FunctionsImpl();
        orb.connect(fRef);
        System.out.println (orb.object_to_string (fRef));
    }
```

The server will then report the IOR for the `FunctionsImpl` object. The `Calculator-Client` is passed the entire string output as an argument on the command line and converts the IOR string to an object reference:

```
    try{
        // create and initialize the ORB
        ORB orb = ORB.init(args, null);

        // Get a reference to an object from third argument
        // on the command line
        org.omg.CORBA.Object objRef = orb.string_to_object (args[2]);

        // Use the interface Functions to resolve the actual
        // object reference
        Functions fRef = FunctionsHelper.narrow(objRef);
    }
```

This approach to publishing and getting an object reference allows Java IDL (or any other CORBA client or server) to receive object references from other ORBs.

Start the Server

The server is started next, to register the implementation object with the Naming Service. The server must locate the Naming Service using the same port number, or it must locate the Naming Service using the IOR that the Naming Service published upon starting up. In this example the port number is used:

```
    java CalculatorServer -ORBInitialPort 1050
```

The server will run until it is killed.

Start the Client

The client application can now be run. The client must also be able to locate the Naming Service in order to contact the appropriate server for a reference to the implementation object:

```
    java CalculatorClient -ORBInitialPort 1050
```

The client application produces the following output, indicating that it was successful in locating the server, receiving a reference to the `FunctionsImpl` object, and executing square_root and power operations:

```
The square root of 10 is: 3.1622777
2 to the 8th power is: 256.0
```

Java Language Mapping Basics

This section briefly covers the IDL to Java language mapping. The complete mapping is beyond the scope of this chapter but available from `http://www.omg .org/library/schedule/Technology_Adoption.htm`. Chapters 5 through 8 of the Java mapping specification are provided as part of the Java IDL documentation (shipped with JDK 1.2). These chapters are available through `docs/guide/ idl/mapping/jidlMapping.html` under your JDK 1.2 installation directory, if you have Sun's JDK.

Overview

Programming conventions for Java and IDL differ slightly. IDL convention does not require capitalization for the names of modules, interfaces, or operations. In addition, IDL convention uses underscores instead of mixed case for long names. Some of the conventions adopted for IDL are the result of OMG adopting a definition language that crosses several programming languages and attempting to create a standard that satisfies the capabilities of each.

Here are some general guidelines to follow when developing IDL files:

- An IDL file is composed of several elements that together create a naming scope.

- Identifiers in IDL are case insensitive and may be used only once in the naming scope.

- IDL does not support the overloading and overriding of operations, although inheritance (single and multiple) is supported.

The next section will cover the most commonly used IDL constructs.

IDL Module

The IDL construct module is used to define the enclosing scope of a group of IDL interfaces. A module can contain one or more interfaces and can nest other module constructs. Each module construct compiles to a Java package name. For example:

```
//IDL
module BookStore {
  interface Account {
    ...
  };
};
```

The Java code generated by idltojava would include the following package declaration:

```
// Java code
package BookStore;
...
```

IDL Interface

The IDL interface construct maps to a Java interface class. The idltojava compiler generates the following Java files from a single IDL interface construct:

- A Java interface class with the same name as the interface identifier

- A generated implementation base class that contains the skeleton code required for the server side application

- A stub class

- A Helper class that is used to narrow the object reference returned from a Naming Service to the stub object required by the client

- A Holder class that is used to contain a reference to the IDL interface object if the interface is passed as an argument

Given the previous example, the following files are generated (under the Calculator package directory) using idltojava:

```
Functions.java            FunctionsHolder.java        _FunctionsStub.java
FunctionsHelper.java      _FunctionsImplBase.java
```

IDL interfaces can contain attributes, exceptions, and operations. An attribute defines a CORBA variable type that may be accessed by predefined methods. CORBA types can either be standard IDL types (listed in the following table) or another IDL interface.

TABLE 26.1: IDL to Java Type Mappings

IDL	Java
float	float
double	double
long, unsigned long	int
long long, unsigned long long	long
short, unsigned short	short
unsigned long	int
unsigned short	int
char, wchar	char
boolean	boolean
octet	byte
string, wstring	java.lang.String
enum, struct, union	class

An attribute will generate an accessor and mutator method for the type declared:

```
//IDL
attribute float price;
```

will generate the following Java methods:

```
// Generated Java methods
    float price();
    void price(float arg);
```

The attribute may also be declared `readonly`, in which case only an accessor method is declared. Note that the IDL compiler does not generate a `price` variable, just the methods to access the variable.

IDL operations get compiled to Java methods. Each operation must declare a return type and may have zero or more arguments. Arguments to operations declare the call semantics of the argument. These may be in, out, or inout. An in parameter is call-by-value and is mapped directly to the corresponding Java type (refer to the previous table). The out parameters use call-by-reference semantics. Java does not use call-by-reference, so out parameters are mapped onto a *Java-type*Holder class. This class encapsulates a data variable that contains the parameter, and the value of the class reference is passed. Finally, the inout parameter semantics are call-by-value/return-by-reference. This too is mapped onto a Java Holder class.

<table>
<tr><td>**TIP**</td><td>When to use the void return type: The use of void as the return type for an operation declared in and IDL is mainly a choice of style. But choosing to make an operation return a void allows for future modifications to the operation with less impact on the system as a whole. If an out parameter type is added to the IDL file, a new operation declaration is generated and may be implemented without removing the existing code.</td></tr>
</table>

Operations can declare that they raise an exception using the construct raises (*exception*). Exceptions in the raises clause must be declared before they can be used. For example:

```
// IDL
// ... code above not shown
interface account {
  void orderBooks (in BookList books, out string orderID)
    raises (StockException);
};
```

In the above operation, orderBooks declares an in parameter named books that is of type BookList, declares an out parameter that is a string, and raises an exception StockException.

A More Complete IDL Example

To continue the discussion of IDL constructs, a more complete example is useful. Here is the IDL that Sullivan Publishing could use for an online bookstore:

```
// Sample IDL
module BookStore {
```

```
exception StockException {
  string reason;
};

exception AccountException {
  string reason;
  float creditLine;
};

struct Book {
  string title;
  string author;
  string isbn_number;
  float price;
};

typedef sequence <Book> BookList;

interface BookOrder {
  readonly attribute BookList theOrder;
  void addBook (in Book theBook) raises (StockException);
  void removeBook (in Book theBook);
  void searchBook (in Book theBook, out Book result) raises (StockException);
};

interface BookOrderManager {
  BookOrder generateOrder ();
};

interface Account {
  readonly attribute string accountID;
  void getBookOrder (out BookOrder order);
  void orderBooks ( in BookOrder order ) raises (AccountException);
  void checkStatus ( in BookOrder order, out string status );
};

struct PayType {
  string cardType;
  string cardNumber;
  string expirationDate;
};
```

```
interface AccountManager {
  Account getAccount ( in string name, in PayType payment );
};
};
```

This IDL file defines four services, BookOrder, Account, AccountManager, and BookOrderManager. The AccountManager service will generate an Account for the customer and allow the customer to generate a book order. The Account service is used to generate a book order, order books, and check the status of a book order. The BookOrder service is used to add or remove books from an order, initiated through the BookOrderManager. A customer will open an account, generate a book order with one or more books that they add to the order, then place the order. Using their account ID, they can check the status of their order at any time.

If a book is not in stock, then a StockException is raised to let the customer know that the book is out of stock. An AccountException is raised if the credit card used to open the account is overdrawn or invalid.

Object Factories

This IDL also presents an example of an object factory. The factory concept is very important in the development of CORBA services. It is sometimes desirable to be able to create new objects on the fly at run time. This capability is important when the number of objects to be created is not known in advance. In the previous example, the number of accounts that Sullivan Publishing will have over the life of their company cannot be predetermined. It might be possible to create a number of objects in advance that can then be doled out, but how many is enough? 10? 100?

Rather than describe each service as a discrete object that exists on the server, an object factory allows the server to create an instance of an account object for each new customer request. The AccountManager service is responsible for receiving a request for a new account and then creating a new Account object for that request. Subsequent requests will always return the same object reference given that the account name is the same. Granted, using a single string to create a unique object is probably not enough, but the idea is that some given set of parameters defines what object reference to return. Figure 26.5 describes this object factory concept. Likewise, each Account may have one or more BookOrder objects, so again a factory is used to generate new BookOrder objects from the BookOrderManager object on request. The next section continues the discussion of IDL constructs.

FIGURE 26.5:   **Object Factory**

The object factory

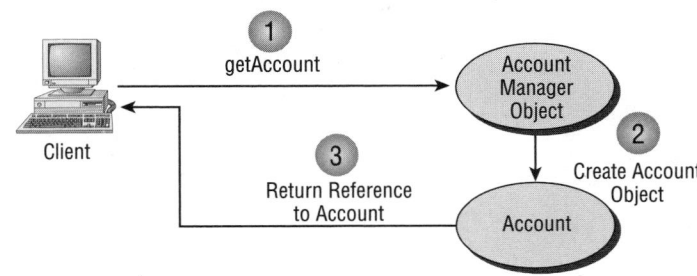

IDL Exception

IDL exceptions are passed as object references, as in Java, but do not map directly onto the Java Exception API. IDL Exceptions extend the `org.omg.CORBA.User-Exception` class. Exceptions may contain data that are accessed as public members of the named class and may be passed in the construction of the exception. For example, the following IDL:

```
exception AccountException {
    string reason;
    float creditLine;
};
```

gets compiled into a Java class definition (`AccountException.java`):

```
/*
 * File: ./BOOKSTORE/ACCOUNTEXCEPTION.JAVA
 * From: BOOKSTORE.IDL
 * Date: Tue Jun 16 12:30:30 1998
 *   By: idltojava Java IDL 1.2 Nov 10 1997 13:52:11
 */

package BookStore;
public final class AccountException
    extends org.omg.CORBA.UserException {
    // instance variables
    public String reason;
    public float creditLine;
    // constructors
    public AccountException() {
```

```
      super();
      }
      public AccountException(String __reason, float __creditLine) {
      super();
      reason = __reason;
      creditLine = __creditLine;
      }
   }
```

IDL struct

The IDL struct is a container class that may be used to pass a collection of data as a single object. An IDL struct maps to Java class with public data members. For example:

```
// IDL
   struct Book {
     string title;
     string author;
     string isbn_number;
     float price;
   };
```

This struct maps to a Java class that is final:

```
/*
 * File: ./BOOKSTORE/BOOK.JAVA
 * From: BOOKSTORE.IDL
 * Date: Tue Jun 16 12:30:30 1998
 *   By: idltojava Java IDL 1.2 Nov 10 1997 13:52:11
 */

package BookStore;
public final class Book {
    //     instance variables
    public String title;
    public String author;
    public String isbn_number;
    public float price;
    //     constructors
    public Book() { }
    public Book(String __title, String __author, String __isbn_number,
        float __price) {
    title = __title;
    author = __author;
```

```
        isbn_number = __isbn_number;
        price = __price;
        }
    }
```

IDL typedef

IDL provides a construct for naming new IDL types from existing types. The typedef construct does not directly map onto Java, so the IDL compiler will substitute and replace any instance of the typedef name for the actual type in the IDL before compiling it. The typedef construct makes it easier to write IDL files, particularly when sequences are required. Here are some example typedefs:

```
// IDL
typedef string CustomerName;
typedef long CustomerSalary;
typedef sequence <long> CustomerOrderID;
```

IDL sequence

IDL sequences are single dimension arrays that may be bounded or unbounded. A bounded sequence defines its maximum size in the declaration of the sequence. For example:

```
// IDL
typedef sequence <long, 10> openOrders;
```

Here a bounded sequence of 10 IDL long numbers is defined as the type openOrders. The bounds of a bounded sequence are checked as the argument is marshaled and sent. If the bounds of a bounded sequence are exceeded, a MARSHAL system exception is raised. Both bounded and unbounded sequences generate a Java Helper and Holder class for each sequence.

IDL Arrays

The IDL array construct is used to create a single-dimension, bounded array of IDL type. The array construct is mapped to Java the same way as the bounded sequence but uses different semantics. For example:

```
// IDL
const long length = 20;
typedef string custName[length];
```

IDL enum

The IDL enum construct is used to represent an enumerated list. For example:

```
enum CityList {Boston, NewYork, Philadelphia, Baltimore};
```

The enum construct maps to a Java final class with the same name:

```
/*
 * File: ./BOOKSTORE/CITYLIST.JAVA
 * From: BOOKSTORE.IDL
 * Date: Tue Jun 16 12:35:15 1998
 *   By: idltojava Java IDL 1.2 Nov 10 1997 13:52:11
 */

package BookStore;
public final class CityList {
    public static final int _Boston = 0,
                    _NewYork = 1,
                    _Philadelphia = 2,
                    _Baltimore = 3;
    public static final CityList Boston = new CityList(_Boston);
    public static final CityList NewYork = new CityList(_NewYork);
    public static final CityList Philadelphia = new CityList(_Philadelphia);
    public static final CityList Baltimore = new CityList(_Baltimore);
    public int value() {
        return _value;
    }
    public static final CityList from_int(int i)  throws
      org.omg.CORBA.BAD_PARAM {
          switch (i) {
            case _Boston:
                return Boston;
            case _NewYork:
                return NewYork;
            case _Philadelphia:
                return Philadelphia;
            case _Baltimore:
                return Baltimore;
            default:
                throw new org.omg.CORBA.BAD_PARAM();
        }
    }
}
```

```
    private CityList(int _value){
        this._value = _value;
    }
    private int _value;
}
```

Legacy Applications with CORBA

Sullivan Publishing, in one of its expansions, has purchased a book catalog service. Part of this purchase involved the acquisition of some C code used to validate searches for book records in a database. The current book catalog service is a phone-only service. Sullivan Publishing would like to use the Internet to allow customers to order books, but the company also wants to preserve the current code that exists for searching the book database and qualifying credit card numbers.

This is an excellent example for using CORBA. The legacy C code can be used as is, but it will be wrapped by an implementation that will expose the C code to the network.

Wrapping Legacy Code

When developing a new system, there may be previously written code that is not current or state-of-the-art but works perfectly well. It is also possible that engineers who have long since left the company could have written the code. This type of code is referred to as legacy code. One of the drawbacks to legacy code is that it is often deployed on a legacy hardware system as well. It is therefore desirable to be able to access this code on its existing hardware platform and expose its functionality to a network.

One of CORBAs primary benefits is that it allows developers to wrap legacy code with a CORBA object approach. An IDL description of the legacy interfaces is used to produce a set of CORBA objects. These objects can then make calls into the legacy code and expose the legacy system to a network. Figure 26.6 illustrates this approach.

Wrapping legacy code does require some understanding of the way the code works. The low-level implementation details are not important, but the way that the code is called or interfaced with other code modules is necessary to know. The interfaces and access methods become the foundation of an IDL interface, which is then used to create a CORBA system.

FIGURE 26.6:   **Legacy Code Wrapping**

Legacy code wrapping

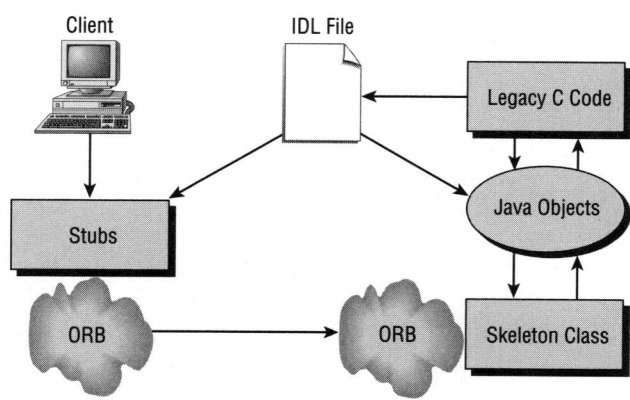

   In this example, Sullivan Publishing purchased inventory tracking software
designed to run on a Windows NT computer. The original code was not designed
to run on a network and the original source code is not available, so it is impractical to port the code directly to Java. However, the interface to the code is fairly
straightforward: The C code is compiled into a library. For example, calls to the
search routines are made as follows:

```
void search (Book *toFind, Book *result);
```

where the parameters are passed as a pointer to a struct that contains:

```
struct Book {
  char title [100];
  char author [100];
  char isbn[25];
  float price;
};
```

The developer defined the C function call and the C struct in IDL as follows:

```
// IDL
  struct Book {
    string title;
    string author;
    string isbn_number;
    float price;
  };
```

```
interface BookOrder {
  readonly attribute BookList theOrder;
  void addBook (in Book theBook) raises (StockException);
  void removeBook (in Book theBook);
  void searchBook (in Book theBook, out Book result) raises (StockException);
};
```

Since Sullivan Publishing would like to preserve the legacy C code for the search routine, the BookOrder object must be implemented on the Windows NT system. There are a couple ways to do this.

1. Use a CORBA vendor that supports a C language mapping and an NT ORB. Implement the BookOrder object in C, directly integrating the library call to the search function.

2. Write the implementation class for BookOrder in Java on the NT machine, and use a native method to call into the search function.

This is a book about Java, so the latter approach is shown here.

```java
// Implementation file for the BookOrder interface
//

import BookStore.*;
import java.util.Vector;

// First, extend the Implementation Base class
public class BookOrderImpl extends _BookOrderImplBase {

  // Keep a Vector of books to be ordered
  private Vector bookList;

  // Constructor
  public BookOrderImpl () {
    // initialize the Vector
    bookList = new Vector ();
  }

  // Implement the method to return the current list of books
  public Book[] theOrder() {
    Book [] bookOrder;
    // Turn the Vector into an array
    bookOrder = new Book [bookList.size()];
```

```
    for (int i = 0; i < bookList.size(); i++) {
      bookOrder[i] = (Book)bookList.elementAt (i);
    }
    return bookOrder;
  }

  public void addBook(Book theBook) throws StockException {
    // Add an element to the bookList Vector
    bookList.addElement (theBook);
  }

  public void removeBook(Book theBook) {
    // Remove an element from the bookList
    bookList.removeElement (theBook);
  }

  public void searchBook(Book theBook, BookHolder result)
      throws BookStore.StockException {
    // Call the native search function
    search (theBook, result);
    if (result == null) {
      throw new StockException ("No book found with ISBN number: "
        + theBook.isbn_number);
    }
  }

  // the native method for search
  private native void search (Book theBook, BookHolder result);

  // Load the native method from the specified library
  static {
    System.loadLibrary ("orderlib");
  }
}
```

Note that it is possible that the server application for the AccountManager object can reside on another machine, like a Sun workstation. The client application will request a reference to an AccountManager. Using this object reference, the client application will request an instance of an Account (by calling the getAccount() method). With this object reference, the client can generate a new BookOrder object by calling the getBookOrder() method. This method gets a reference to the Book-OrderManager on the Windows NT machine and returns a BookOrder object. To the client application, this all happens through local stub invocations!

CORBA in the Future

CORBA has received a great deal of attention lately with the addition of the Java language mapping and the introduction of the 2.0 specification for interoperability. Interestingly, the struggle within a lot of companies is about whether or not to rewrite all of their applications in Java. The Java language has alleviated a number of fears that companies have regarding obsolescence. The Java language is not platform specific, so choosing to rewrite or to restructure a company's applications based on Java is a wise choice. However, CORBA provides an intermediary solution to the problem of code rewrite. CORBA makes it possible to preserve a company's current investment in COBOL, C, C++, and Ada applications while making the transition to Java in the long-term.

CORBA's standards-based approach also frees company decision makers from having to make a single vendor choice. Systems that are developed using the CORBA framework and standards are easily adapted to other vendors' products with a minimum of code rewrite.

Java Enterprise Server API

Sun has announced that their flagship CORBA implementation, NEO, will no longer be supported after this year. This announcement came on the heels of Sun's announcement of the Java Enterprise Server APIs, also known as Enterprise Java-Beans (EJB). The EJB specification, available from `http://java.sun.com/products/ejb/docs.html`, outlines Sun's intent to continue to promote Java in the Enterprise and to create a cohesive strategy for bringing industry leaders into the party. The Enterprise Server API describes a collection of services and methodologies that allow for tremendous flexibility in the development of Enterprise level applications.

Several companies support the concepts outlined in the EJB white paper available from `http://java.sun.com/products/ejb/white_paper.html`, including WebLogic, BEA, GemStone, and Novera. For more information, look at the following Web pages:

- WebLogic: http://www.weblogic.com

- BEA Systems: http://www.beasys.com

- Novera: http://www.novera.com

- GemStone: http://www.gemstone.com

Summary

CORBA makes it possible to develop systems that are independent of a programming language and operating system. The introduction of Java to the programming world and the development of protocol standards have propelled CORBA into the current mainstream of computing. Once considered daunting to even technical engineers, CORBA is reaching more programmers, as the concepts of object design are now understood more easily with Java.

The future of distributed object programming will undoubtedly include CORBA, and it is likely that in a few years systems will be developed with visually driven tools, eliminating the need to develop IDL files altogether. Further, it is becoming increasingly apparent that software vendors have embraced the standards set forth by the OMG, and the future will include more interoperability across both software and hardware domains.

INDEX

Note to the Reader: Throughout this index **boldfaced** page numbers indicate primary discussions of a topic. *Italicized* page numbers indicate illustrations.

C

D

E

G

J

K

L

M

N

O

P

Q

S